U.S. ENVIRONMENTAL LAWS

1994 Edition

U.S. ENVIRONMENTAL LAWS

1994 Edition

Current through August 15, 1994

Edited by
Wallis E. McClain, Jr.

The Bureau of National Affairs Inc., Washington, D.C.

95 94 4 3 2 1

Published by BNA Books
1231 25th Street NW, Washington, DC 20037

International Standard Book Number: 0-87179-836-0
Printed in the United States of America

CONTENTS

FOREWORD

(from first edition)

The statutes collected in this volume, the environmental laws of the United States, are at the same time a monument to twenty years of work towards a cleaner and safer environment and a source of substantial contention and perplexity among both lawmakers and the general public. These statutes often appear to be working at cross-purposes to one another; there are even apparent conflicts of intent within the same statute. This suggests that our nation has not yet settled unequivocally on what we want our environmental protection effort to do. But I also believe that some of the confusion is rooted in the legal-philosophical parentage of the laws themselves.

Our environmental statutes arise from at least three separate legal traditions. The first of these is public health protection and it extends back to remote antiquity. There were Babylonian laws against the adulteration of bread and there were restrictions on the burning of coal in medieval England. Laws of quarantine and laws regarding the disposal of biological wastes are common in many societies. In America, until around 1970, this tradition was embodied in local ordinances regarding dumping, drinking water, open burning, and sewage treatment.

The second tradition derives from common law antecedents pertaining to property damage and personal injury. If you dump poison in a stream, and my cow drinks it and dies, I can bring suit against you for damages. Until recently, it had been very hard for private citizens to bring suit against firms for damages resulting from the normal operation of industrial plants.

But beginning in the 1950's, the number of such suits, and their success, began to increase, perhaps owing to greater public awareness of chemical hazards or to the apparently greater toxicity of the emissions of industry in the post-war period. We may, in fact, trace the tortuous history of the Clean Air Act back to a suit brought by the Martins family of Troutdale, Oregon, against the Reynolds Company. The Martins claimed that fluoride emissions from the Reynolds plant were poisoning their dairy cattle and injuring their own health. The major issue then (as it is now) was specifying the relation between the exposure and the health damage it may have caused. Responding to this issue, the state of Oregon set up a scientific panel to make such determinations and passed laws giving the state the right to sue in order to stop air pollution where it was deemed injurious to its citizens.

Other states felt obliged to do the same, including Washington, some of whose residents were suing the same plant. Much of the impetus for establishing national rules about what was safe in the air thus may have come from the prospect of the chaos that could have resulted from the nation's industrial plants' attempting to comply with dozens of different standards for the same pollutant, or worse, the prospect of industry shopping around for locations in states that were prepared to set the weakest standards.

The third tradition is a complex one and particularly American. It arises out of the conservation ethic, as exemplified early in this century by the preservation work of Roosevelt and Pinchot, and more recently by the new ecological consciousness. The older notion that America is a kind of earthly paradise being consumed by the base greed of its inhabitants was reinforced by the broader observation that the entire ecosphere is vulnerable to human activity.

The publication of *Silent Spring*, together with reports of oil spills, burning rivers, nuclear fallout, and so on, generated a crisis atmosphere, which, (also in the American tradition) produced a political movement demanding Federal government action. Obviously, the thinking went, the market economy cannot be trusted to control its own externalities of production. National planning was proposed and, to an extent, accepted as the solution.

These traditions, variously compounded, are expressed in the nine major environmental statutes, which are administered in whole or in part by a single organization, the Environmental Protection Agency. The fact that there are *nine* statutes, and that they derive from mixed legal traditions provides no little trouble to the Agency in their execution. Public health protection is rather a different business from preserving environmental values; establishing and administering a national plan (to clean the air, for example) is in some conflict with the need to establish an equitable solution for a particular area where, say, people are in danger of being hurt by emissions from an economically important industrial facility.

These conflicts tend to be exacerbated by the paradoxical nature of the American political consciousness. On the one hand, we want problems solved, and we have learned to look to government to solve them. On the other, we want it done with as little personal inconvenience or sacrifice as possible. For example, we are ideological "liberals" when we demand vigorous clean air programs, and operational "conservatives" when we resist inspection and maintenance programs for automobiles to achieve clean air. The execution of our environmental statutes over the past fifteen years reflects this paradox. If you read the environmental laws literally—especially the Clean Air and Clean Water Acts—you are reading a recipe for a quite radical reordering of American society. In fact, nothing of the sort has happened. To note one of many instances, our attempt to impose transportation plans on metropolitan areas to meet Clean Air Act standards failed in the mid-70s, as no doubt it would today. In real-world situations, Americans balance environmental values against other values, as does the Environmental Protection Agency, whether or not the law specifically allows it to so declare publicly.

Have these laws worked? Yes and no. The environment is certainly cleaner than it was, and *much* cleaner than it would have been had these laws not been passed. But the laws have not straightened out the conflicts inherent in their different philosophical antecedents. For example, the public health ethic demands that we take a protective stance in response to the *probability* that some exposure will result in an adverse health effect. This demand runs counter to the common law tradition that before we impose an economic penalty we establish the actuality of harm, or at least balance the equities in each particular case.

Most important, the laws do not recognize that the different compartments of the environment—air, water, and land—the interconnected Pollution moves easily among these compartments, either naturally or through the operation of pollution control apparatus. The ecological ethic built into these statutes mandates that each compartment be rendered pure, although in practical terms this can only be done at the expense of the other compartments. Pollution has to go somewhere, but the laws typically assume it away, or assume that, somehow, technologies can be developed that do not pollute at all.

This promise of an end to pollution is contained in each of our environmental laws. It is a noble goal, but it renders the laws less effective in fact than they could be, if a keener sense of the need to distinguish the important from the trivial were built into their basic structure.

Thus a gulf has developed between the expectations of environmental clean-up presented in much of the legislative language in this book and what we have been able to accomplish. This gulf can only contribute to the decline of faith in the ability of our democratic polity to solve its problems. One hopes, therefore, that the reader will regard these laws as works in progress. There will always be a tension between the economics of an industrial society and the health of its citizens and their environment. Oddly enough, as we become healthier and live longer, and thus as each life becomes more precious, we worry more about the imperfections of our protective machinery and any lapses noted from the illusion of perfect safety become more intolerable. This intolerance, however, interferes with the practical execution of environmental law. Of course we need goals, especially given the propensity of our civilization to live as if each generation were the last. But what we have yet to learn in environmental law is how to keep our eyes on the horizon without stumbling on the thickets around our feet.

William D. Ruckelshaus

March 1986

PREFACE

This is the fourth edition of *U.S. Environmental Laws* published by The Bureau of National Affairs, Inc. The environmental laws in this volume are current through at least August 15, 1994.

This new edition incorporates several important changes to the laws, including a new title to the Toxic Substances Control Act (TSCA) and new provisions to the Clean Water Act and the Comprehensive Environmental Response, Compensation, and Liability Act (CERCLA).

This volume contains the text of nine environmental statutes and summaries of an additional six important federal statutes. In all, five titles of the U.S. Code are represented: 7, 15, 16, 33, and 42. It should be remembered in using this volume, however, that there may be provisions of other laws that refer to or affect parts of these statutes without actually amending them. One example of this concerns a regulation issued by the Environmental Protection Agency in 1980 under the Resource Conservation and Recovery Act (RCRA). The rule dealt with when RCRA Subchapter III (Subtitle C) applies to a hazardous waste that is mixed with other, nonhazardous wastes and to waste that is derived from the treatment, storage, or disposal of a waste that is listed as hazardous under the statute. In 1991, the U.S. Court of Appeals for the District of Columbia Circuit vacated and remanded these so-called mixture and derived-from rules to EPA (*Shell Oil Co. v. EPA,* 950 F.2d 741, 34 ER Cases 1049). Then in October 1992, Congress included a provision in an appropriations bill (P.L. 102-389) mandating that the 1980 rules remain in place until they are revised by EPA. The provision also prohibited any revisions to those rules from taking place before October 1993.

While the Table of Contents simply lists the statutes covered, the more comprehensive Finding Lists—found after the introduction to each chapter—list the U.S. Code title and section numbers for each section of the statutes covered. Statutory section numbers refer to U.S. Code citation, with public law section numbers in brackets. References to section numbers within the text of the statutes are to public law section numbers.

The next major rewrites of federal environmental statutes will probably include the Clean Water Act and CERCLA. Although legislation was pending in the 103rd Congress to reauthorize CERCLA, the Clean Water Act, and the Safe Drinking Water Act, no action had been taken by the time Congress was planning its August 1994 recess.

While it seemed initially almost certain that Congress would pass superfund and Clean Water Act legislation in some form in 1994, the prospects for passage seemed much less secure in the waning months of the 103rd Congress. Rep. Norman Y. Mineta (D-Calif), one of the leading sponsors in the House of Representatives of Clean Water Act reform, declared in early summer that the legislation was dead, but later added that he planned to make one final effort to secure passage before adjournment. CERCLA reform gathered momentum following approval of Administration-backed legislation by most of the key congressional committees with jurisdiction, but many hurdles remained to be cleared.

The fate of other measures, including the Safe Drinking Water Act, is considerably less certain.

Attempts to elevate the Environmental Protection Agency to Cabinet status in the 102nd Congress went nowhere, despite general support for the action from the Bush Administration and from key leaders in Congress.Proponents cited the increased clout that a Cabinet department would have, in addition to the greater prestige such a department would enjoy in the international arena, where it appeared that the Clinton Administration would be playing a more active role than had the Bush or Reagan administrations.

Legislation (S 533) easily passed the Senate on a voice vote in October 1991, but a measure in the House of Representatives (HR 3121) stalled over a significant difference between the two versions. The Senate bill included a "takings" provision, calling for compensation of landowners who lose the use of their property because of environmental regulations, was added to the Senate version, but it was vigorously opposed by House leaders. Ultimately, the Cabinet measure died, largely as a result of the opposition to inclusion of such extraneous provisions to a "clean" bill, that is, one that would simply make EPA a Cabinet department.

The same problem plagued similar legislation in the first session of the 103rd Congress.

Again, the Senate approved a measure early on, handily passing S 171 by a vote of 79 to 15. Similar legislation was discussed in the House but not introduced until general agreement had been reached on the extent of its provisions. An early draft of the legislation was widely criticized for its inclusion of unpopular as well as non-germane items. Although the bill (HR 3425) cleared the House Government Operations Committee on a vote of 31 to 11, it was pulled from the floor to avoid a battle over a rule to limit amendments.

Included in the Senate bill was a provision to abolish the President's Council on Environmental Quality (CEQ), in accordance with President Clinton's recommendation in the fiscal 1994 budget proposal. CEQ's functions, including its important responsibilities regarding the National Environmental Policy Act (NEPA), would be transferred to a new White House office. The House Cabinet bill contained no such provision. Although considerable opposition to the plan emerged, largely out of fears that NEPA would not receive the attention it deserved, the House passed a separate measure (HR 3512) transferring CEQ's functions to a new White House Office of National Environmental Policy Act Compliance.

Opposition to the proposal to abolish CEQ has been considerable, both from environmental groups and congressional leaders. President Clinton established a new White House Office of Environmental Policy (OEP), and by summer of 1994, some support came for merging the new OEP into CEQ and adding enough staff for CEQ to fulfill its duties under NEPA. With other pressing issues facing the Administration and Congress, however, it appeared unlikely that any further substantive action would take place in the 103rd Congress.

It is still too early, perhaps, to assess the effectiveness of the Clinton Administration in building a new environmental partnership with Congress. Despite some successes, there are also signs of strain.

This is, after all, only the second time in the "environmental era," a period that we can roughly say started in 1970, that a Democratic president has worked with a Democratic Congress. But party affiliation notwithstanding, Congress and the executive branch remain separate institutions with different agendas. The Administration has already come under fire from Congress for not moving speedily enough in forwarding its recommendations on CERCLA and Clean Water Act reauthorization to Congress. Similarly, President Bill Clinton has been criticized for his tendency to deal with certain problems by issuing executive orders. Among those already issued are orders on federal procurement of recycled goods and on federal compliance with the Emergency Planning and Community Right-To-Know Act (EPCRA). In February 1994, President Clinton issued an executive order on "environmental justice," dealing with the effects of environmental pollution by federal agencies on low-income and minority communities.

During the Administration of President Reagan, who did not have a reputation as an environmental leader, Congress passed far-reaching environmental legislation. Many people saw in the Reagan years, in fact, a decline in the commitment made in the 1970s to clean up the mess caused by decades of neglect, inaction, and ignorance. Among the achievements of Congress during those years was passage of the 1984 amendments to the Resource Conservation and Recovery Act, which included a sweeping mandate to ban the disposal on land of untreated hazardous wastes. Congress also approved, largely in response to what it said was the inattention given by the Reagan Administration, the Superfund Amendments and Reauthorization Act (SARA) of 1986. Not only did SARA make major changes to the CERCLA, such as establishing a preference for permanent cleanups of waste sites, but Title III of the law, also known as EPCRA, requires businesses and industries across the nation to report to EPA their routine releases of hundreds of toxic substances. In addition, the 100th Congress, in a major assertion of its power and commitment to environmental protection, passed amendments to the Clean Water Act over the veto of President Reagan.

The election of President George Bush in 1988 caused many observers to predict that Congress and the Administration would renew their commitment to work in concert on protecting the environment. The Clean Air Act Amendments of 1990 was seen as real evidence of that renewal. However, congressional leaders complained bitterly during the four years under President Bush that EPA was not doing its job. Even after the bipartisan effort to amend the Clean Air Act was hailed as a major victory for the Administration, EPA was sued by Rep. Henry A. Waxman (D-Calif) and the Sierra Club for failing to meet the deadlines in the Act for issuing regulations that would implement the law.

Despite the stated intention of the Clinton Administration to seek unprecedented new protections for the environment, its accomplishments so far have been seen as relatively small ones. Despite supposedly common goals shared by Congress and the Administration, no major legislation has yet been passed. Indeed, some of the President's proposals, such as the plan to abolish CEQ, have been met with skepticism from some and outright hostility from others, including those who share his goals and agenda. On the other hand, considerable praise has been lavished on EPA for its emphasis on prevention of pollution rather than "end-of-the-pipe" solutions, for its attempt to seek innovative solutions to old problems (such as a "multimedia" proposal to regulate air and water emissions from the pulp and paper industry), and for its international initiatives.

Nonetheless, in his early months President Clinton was seen as inexperienced and ineffective in dealing with Congress. That assessment largely changed with his remarkable success in winning congressional approval for the North American Free Trade Agreement (NAFTA), which many observers saw as a looming and certain political defeat for the President almost up to the time of the vote. And the dramatic turnaround following an initial defeat suffered on a procedural vote on the omnibus crime bill in August 1994 seems to validate the earlier NAFTA success.

Whatever happens to CERCLA and the Clean Water Act, as well as the Safe Drinking Water Act, reauthorization of RCRA probably will not take place any earlier than the 104th Congress. Even then, issues will provedifficult, as they have in the past. Some issues, such as interstate transport of solid waste and "flow control," have proved divisive in the past and almost certainly will continue to be contentious in the future.

In some senses, environmental law is approaching "maturity." It is clear, however, that changing public perceptions about risks, growing scientific knowledge about the fate of pollutants in the environment, and political pressures will result in continuing evolution of these laws. This is what makes environmental law so challenging—and exciting.

I would like to thank the staff of BNA Books and the staffs of the many environmental publications of BNA's Environment and Safety Services Division for their help and advice in preparing this and earlier editions of *U.S. Environmental Laws.* Without their accumulated knowledge and experience, none of this would have been possible.

Wallis E. McClain Jr.
Managing Editor, *Environment Reporter*
Washington, DC

August 1994

1

Clean Air Act

INTRODUCTION

The original Clean Air Act was passed in 1955 (P.L. 84-159). In 1967 it was wholly replaced by the Air Quality Act of 1967 (P.L. 90-148), although the name Clean Air Act is still used. Amendments adopted in 1970 (P.L. 91-604) require the Environmental Protection Agency to set ambient air quality standards, to control emissions from stationary and mobile sources, to control emissions from new stationary sources, and to control hazardous air pollutants. The 1977 amendments (P.L. 95-95) adopted a standardized basis for rulemaking regarding criteria for national ambient air quality standards, new source performance standards, hazardous air pollution standards, motor vehicle standards, fuel and fuel additive provisions, and aircraft emission standards.

By the end of the 1980s, it had been recognized for years that the Act needed fixing. Attempts were made to tinker with the Act in the 1980s, but all had been thwarted by sharp political divisions, regional priorities, and by policies of the Reagan Administration not to back any proposal that would strengthen the law. Political paralysis had impeded every effort to amend the Act since the landmark 1977 action.

By the time the Senate in the 100th Congress dealt with the issue, there was a growing sense that some way around the intense political and philosophical differences among legislators would have to be found. Public concern about the effects of air pollution on health were growing, Canada was continuing to apply stiff pressure for controls on acid rain, and the world community was developing a united voice about the need to address global issues such as the "greenhouse effect" and depletion of the stratospheric ozone layer. It was also increasingly clear that a legislative solution would be needed to deal with the fact that more than 100 areas had failed to meet the 1977 Act's deadline of December 31, 1987, for coming into compliance with the ozone and carbon monoxide standards. Already by November 1987 EPA was making plans for dealing with non-attainment areas in the "post-attainment" period. The Air Act was silent on how violators should be treated. The agency proposed giving these areas a grace period before imposing sanctions such as construction bans. Congress extended the deadline until August 31, 1988, to give the legislators time to deal with comprehensive revision of the Air Act.

The major air bill in the 100th Congress was the Senate's S 1894. Even though the Senate Environment and Public Works Committee approved the measure in October 1987, opponents of bits and pieces of the legislation tried to stall its progress. Sen. Alan K. Simpson (RWyo), for example, tried to put together a bipartisan alliance to support a substitute measure on acid rain controls. Simpson had complained that the acid rain provisions of S 1894 would be too costly for Western states.

Despite the efforts of the bill's sponsor, Sen. George J. Mitchell (D-Maine), to reach acceptable compromises on the acid rain provisions, growing dissension eventually doomed the chances of S 1894 in the 100th Congress. Sen. Robert C. Byrd (D-WVa), the majority leader in the 100th Congress, had expressed concern that the acid rain provisions would mean a loss of coal-mining jobs in his state. He never scheduled the legislation for a floor vote. Finally, on October

4, 1988, Mitchell conceded defeat and said that it was impossible to get Clean Air Act amendments through before adjournment.

In the months preceding the 1988 national elections, however, things began to shift toward burgeoning environmentalism. After the dust from the presidential nominating conventions that summer had settled, it became clear that both candidates—George Bush and Michael Dukakis—were keenly aware that environmental protection had become a priority for a majority of the American voting public.

Shortly after the election, in a speech to the Republican Governors Association on November 22, 1988, Bush said the government should "begin work on an action program to reduce emissions that cause acid rain."

And then, on February 9, 1989, he stated his agenda more emphatically. In his first speech to Congress, he announced his intention to introduce legislation "for a new, more effective Clean Air Act. It will include a plan to reduce, by date certain, the emissions which cause acid rain, because the time for study alone has passed and the time for action is now."

Bush announced the Administration's proposals on June 12, 1989. The president said the proposal was founded on the five points of his environmental philosophy:

- Harness the power of the marketplace;
- Encourage local initiative;
- Emphasize prevention of pollution;
- Foster international cooperation; and
- Ensure strict enforcement and make polluters pay.

On July 27, Rep. John D. Dingell (D-Mich), along with Rep. Norman Lent (R-NY) as principal co-sponsor and 145 other representatives, introduced the president's proposal in the House of Representatives as HR 3030. On August 3, Sen. John H. Chafee (R-RI) introduced the measure in the Senate as S 1490. In the House, Lent on September 20 offered an Administration-backed substitute to the original bill. The substitute, according to House sources, simply refined and clarified the original HR 3030 and made technical corrections.

In the Senate, the Environment and Public Works Committee reached an early agreement on clean air legislation, passing a package (S 1630) by a vote of 15-1 on November 17,1989. But most of the really difficult issues were simply pushed aside for debate and action on the Senate floor.

Because of the deep division among the senators, some predicted a "donnybrook" when it was brought up for a vote by the full Senate. Sen. Steve Symms (R-Idaho), the lone dissenter in the committee vote, predicted that the 84 senators who did not serve on the Environment and Public Works Committee would take a dim view of some of the committee-passed provisions.

Although some 225 amendments were filed with the majority leader for floor consideration, the paralysis predicted by some never came. On April 4, 1990, the Senate voted 89-11 to pass S 1630. Only senators from Midwestern and Appalachian state opposed to the acid rain provisions and several conservative senators who opposed the entire package voted against it.

Only agreement in House-Senate conference on S 1630 remained. (The Senate bill number was used in conference.) By August 3, the conferees had agreed on provisions to phase out the use of ozone-depleting chemicals such as chlorofluorocarbons, halons, carbon tetrachloride, and methyl chloroform.

By September 10, the staff of the House and Senate conferees had drafted agreements on the permitting and urban air quality titles of the bill. On September 14, the conferees approved the staff agreements.

By early October, however, House and Senate staff had hammered out agreement on vehicle emissions and alternative fuels. Agreement on air toxics followed quickly, and following a lengthy, wearying session that ended at 5 a.m. on October 22, the conferees reached agreement on acid rain, enforcement, and miscellaneous provisions. Nine hours later, they met again to give their formal approval to the entire package.

On October 26, the House of Representatives voted 401-25 for the conference report. On October 27, the Senate followed suit, approving the report 89-10. Finally, more than 15 months after it began its work, the 101st Congress achieved what had eluded every Congress since the landmark 1977 amendments: it had agreed on a comprehensive rewrite of the Clean Air Act.

On November 15, 1990, President Bush signed S 1630 into law.

Title I of the new Clean Air Act Amendments of 1990 deals with urban air quality standards and significantly changed the procedures and schedules for urban areas to come into compliance with the ozone and carbon monoxide standards in the act. Revised state implementation plans are required, and all areas except those classified as marginal for non-attainment of the ozone standard of 0.12 parts per million, measured as a one-hour average, must reduce emissions of volatile organic compounds by 15 percent within six years. Measures specified in the amendments for control of VOCs include vapor recovery equipment on gasoline pumps, automobile inspection and maintenance (I/M) and enhanced I/M programs in areas classified as serious or severe for non-compliance with the ozone standard, and employee trip reduction programs.

Title II deals with mobile sources and generally requires tighter limits on exhaust emissions. A first tier of emission limits must be phased in between 1994 and 1998; a second tier would be even tighter and would go into effect in 2003 if EPA decided they were necessary. Reformulated gasoline is required in the nine areas of the United States with the worst ozone non-compliance records. Oxygenated gasoline is required in the areas of the United States that do not meet the federal standard for carbon monoxide. A pilot program in California requires the production and sale of 150,000 clean-fuel vehicles per year from 1995 through 1996 and 300,000 vehicles in 1999 and after. Other states could choose to join the California low-emission vehicle program.

Title III of the amendments law deals with toxic air pollutants and makes major changes to Section 112 of the act, adding a list of 189 specific toxic chemicals for which EPA must determine maximum achievable control technology (MACT). The section also deals with accidental chemical releases.

Title IV deals with acid rain and establishes a market-based system of buying and selling acid rain "allowances," which are equal to 1 ton of sulfur dioxide emissions and are allotted to existing sources of sulfur dioxide. Reductions are required in two phases, with the first phase directed at older, dirtier plants; in the second phase, all plants must meet more rigid standards.

Title V requires major sources emissions, emissions sources subject to acid rain controls, sources subject to new source performance standards, and sources of listed hazardous air pollutants to have permits. EPA must issue permit regulations, and states must adopt approved permit programs. The program is required to go into effect by Nov. 15, 1994, four years after passage of the amendments. Under a 'permit shield,' a plant is presumed to be in compliance with its Clean Air Act permit if it meets all the requirements of its permit.

Title VI requires that the production of the most destructive ozone-depleting chemicals (Class I ozone depleters) be phased out by 2000. The include chlorofluorocarbons, halons, and carbon tetrachloride. The production of methyl chloroform is to be banned by 2003. However, the Act permits the phase-out schedule to be accelerated. In fact, under the auspices of the Montreal Protocol on Substances that Deplete the Ozone Layer, the United States agreed to phase out these substances by the end of 1994 (halons) and 1995 (CFCs). Methyl chloroform is to be banned by 1996. Production of less destructive hydrofluorocarbons, listed as Class II ozone depleters, were required by the act to be frozen in 2015, but the parties to the Montreal Protocol agreed to phase them out between 1996 and 2030.

Title VII increases the enforcement authority of EPA and states. EPA officials have new authority to issue 'field citations' that need no formal review, much like a traffic ticket.

Title VIII deals with miscellaneous provisions, such as transferring authority to setting emission standards for outer continental shelf oil and gas rigs from the Secretary of the Interior to the EPA administrator, and sets requirements for a number of studies; Title IX of the amendments law provides for various research activities related to clean air.

The titles of the Clean Air Act Amendments of 1990 do not always correspond to the Clean Air Act title they amend. For example, Title III of the amendments deals with air toxics, which are in Section 112 of Title I of the Clean Air Act. Title III of the Clean Air Act is entitled 'General Provisions.' Similarly, section numbers of the amendments law do not correspond with section numbers in the Clean Air Act.

Since the passage of the amendments, the government's focus has shifted back to regulatory action and implementation of the Act.

Neither Congress nor environmental groups seemed particularly pleased with EPA's progress in issuing the regulations required by the act, however. In a settlement reached November 20, 1992, with the Sierra Club and Rep. Henry A. Waxman (D-Calif), both of whom had sued EPA for failure to issue regulations or reports by their statutory deadlines, the agency agreed to a schedule for issuing 19 separate actions.

However, the Sierra Club sued again, charging that the agency had missed a second round of deadlines. A settlement in that case, reached in the summer of 1993, set a schedule for issuance of 24 additional regulatory actions.

Meanwhile, attention centered on state efforts to meet the challenges of revising their state implementation plans. SIP revisions were due November 15, 1992, with details of how each state intended to bring its areas that had not yet met the ambient air quality standards of the Act into compliance. Other specific requirements included plans in all non-attainment areas except those classified as marginal to install vapor recovery equipment on gasoline pumps and plans in non-attainment areas classified as serious, sever, and extreme to require enhanced inspection and maintenance of motor vehicles and planes to reduce the number of vehicle miles traveled.

By November 15, 1993, another round of SIP revisions was due, including plans in all except marginal non-attainment areas to reduce emissions of volatile organic compounds by 15 percent over six years. In addition, states were required to revise their inspection and maintenance programs to bring them into conformity with EPA requirements.

Among the more important rules approved or proposed by the agency since the adoption of the 1990 amendments are the final core acid rain rules, final maximum achievable technology standards for dry cleaners and coke ovens, final transportation conformity rules (requiring federal transportation projects to conform to state plans to reduce emissions), the NESHAP (national emission standards for hazardous air pollutants) for almost 400 synthetic organic chemicals, rules for reformulated gasoline, and proposed rules for enhanced monitoring by owners and operators of major stationary sources of non-hazardous pollutants and sources subject to existing NESHAPs.

FINDING LIST

CLEAN AIR ACT

Enacted by Air Quality Act of 1967, Public Law 90–148, approved Nov. 21, 1967, 77 Stat. 392.

42 U.S.C. §§7401 et seq.

Amended by PL 91–604, Dec. 31, 1970; PL 92–157, Nov. 18, 1971; PL 93–15, April 9, 1973; PL 93–319, June 24, 1974; PL 95–95, Aug. 7, 1977; PL 95–190, Nov. 16, 1977; PL 95–623, Nov. 9, 1978; PL 96–209, March 14, 1980; PL 96–300, July 2, 1980; PL 97–23, July 17, 1981; PL 97–258, Sept. 13, 1982; PL 97–375, Dec. 21, 1982; PL 98–45, July 12, 1983; PL 98–213, Dec. 8, 1983; PL 100–418, Aug. 23, 1988; PL 101–549, Nov. 15, 1990; PL 102–187, Dec. 4, 1991.

TITLE I — AIR POLLUTION PREVENTION AND CONTROL

PART A — AIR QUALITY AND EMISSION LIMITATIONS

§7401. Findings and Purposes [Sec. 101]

(a) The Congress finds—

(1) that the predominant part of the Nation's population is located in its rapidly expanding metropolitan and other urban areas, which generally cross the boundary lines of local jurisdictions and often extend into two or more States;

(2) that the growth in the amount and complexity of air pollution brought about by urbanization, industrial development, and the increasing use of motor vehicles, has resulted in mounting dangers to the public health and welfare, including injury to agricultural crops and livestock, damage to and the deterioration of property, and hazards to air and ground transportation;

(3) that air pollution prevention (that is, the reduction or elimination, through any measures, of the amount of pollutants produced or created at the source) and air pollution control at its source is the primary responsibility of States and local governments; and

[§101(a)(3) amended by PL 101–549]

(4) that Federal financial assistance and leadership is essential for the development of cooperative Federal, State, regional, and local programs to prevent and control air pollution.

(b) The purposes of this title are—

(1) to protect and enhance the quality of the Nation's air resources so as to promote the public health and welfare and the productive capacity of its population;

(2) to initiate and accelerate a national research and development program to achieve the prevention and control of air pollution;

(3) to provide technical and financial assistance to State and local governments in connection with the development and execution of their air pollution prevention and control programs; and

(4) to encourage and assist the development and operation of regional air pollution prevention and control programs.

[§101(b)(4) amended by PL 101–549]

(c) Pollution Prevention. — A primary goal of this Act is to encourage or otherwise promote reasonable Federal, State, and local governmental actions, consistent with the provisions of this Act, for pollution prevention.

[§101(c) added by PL 101–549]

§7402. Cooperative Activities and Uniform Laws [Sec. 102]

(a) The Administrator shall encourage cooperative activities by the States and local governments for the prevention and control of air pollution; encourage the enactment of improved and, so far as practicable in the light of varying conditions and needs, uniform State and local laws relating to the prevention and control of air pollution; and encourage the making of agreements and compacts between States for the prevention and control of air pollution.

(b) The Administrator shall cooperate with and encourage cooperative activities by all Federal departments and agencies having functions relating to the prevention and control of air pollution, so as to assure the utilization in the Federal air pollution control program of all appropriate and available facilities and resources within the Federal Government.

(c) The consent of the Congress is hereby given to two or more States to negotiate and enter into agreements or compacts, not in conflict with any law or treaty of the United States, for (1) cooperative effort and mutual assistance for the prevention and control of air pollution and the enforcement of their respective laws relating thereto, and (2) the establishment of such agencies, joint or oth erwise, as they may deem desirable for making effective such agreements or compacts. No such agreement or compact shall be binding or obligatory upon any State a party thereto unless and until it has been approved by Congress. It is the intent of Congress that no agreement or compact entered into between States after the date of enactment of the Air

Quality Act of 1967, which relates to the control and abatement of air pollution in an air quality control region, shall provide for participation by a State which is not included (in whole or in part) in such air quality control region.

§7403. Research, Investigation, Training, and Other Activities [Sec. 103]

(a) The Administrator shall establish a national research and development program for the prevention and control of air pollution and as part of such program shall—

(1) conduct, and promote the coordination and acceleration of, research, investigations, experiments, demonstrations, surveys, and studies relating to the causes, effects (including health and welfare effects), extent, prevention, and control of air pollution;

[§103(a)(1) amended by PL 101–549]

(2) encourage, cooperate with, and render technical services and provide financial assistance to air pollution control agencies and other appropriate public or private agencies, institutions, and organizations, and individuals in the conduct of such activities;

(3) conduct investigations and research and make surveys concerning any specific problem of air pollution in cooperation with any air pollution control agency with a view to recommending a solution of such problem, if he is requested to do so by such agency or if, in his judgment, such problem may affect any community or communities in a State other than that in which the source of the matter causing or contributing to the pollution is located;

(4) establish technical advisory committees composed of recognized experts in various aspects of air pollution to assist in the examination and evaluation of research progress and proposals and to avoid duplication of research; and

(5) conduct and promote coordination and acceleration of training for individuals relating to the causes, effects, extent, prevention, and control of air pollution.

[§103(a)(5) added by PL 95–95]

(b) In carrying out the provisions of the preceding subsection the Administrator is authorized to—

(1) collect and make available, through publications and other appropriate means, the results of and other information, including appropriate recommendations by him in connection therewith, pertaining to such research and other activities;

(2) cooperate with other Federal departments and agencies, with air pollution control agencies, with other public and private agencies, institutions, and organizations, and with any industries involved, in the preparation and conduct of such research and other activities;

(3) make grants to air pollution control agencies, to other public or nonprofit private agencies, institutions, and organizations, and to individuals, for purposes stated in subsection (a)(1) of this section;

(4) contract with public or private agencies, institutions, and organizations, and with individuals, without regard to section 3324(a) and (b) of Title 31 and section 5 of title 41;

[§103(b)(4) amended by PL 97–258]

(5) establish and maintain research fellowships, in the Environmental Protection Agency and at public or nonprofit private educational institutions or research organizations;

[Former §103(b)(5) deleted and former (6) redesignated as (5) by PL 95–95]

(6) collect and disseminate, in cooperation with other Federal departments and agencies, and with other public or private agencies, institutions, and organizations having related responsibilities, basic data on chemical, physical, and biological effects of varying air quality and other information pertaining to air pollution and the prevention and control thereof;

[Former §103(b)(7) amended and redesignated as (6) by PL 101–549]

(7) develop effective and practical processes, methods, and prototype devices for the prevention or control of air pollution; and

[Former §103(b)(8) amended and redesignated as (7) by PL 101–549]

(8) construct facilities, provide equipment, and employ staff as necessary to carry out this Act.

[§103(b)(8) added by PL 101–549]

In carrying out the provisions of subsection (a), the Administrator shall provide training for, and make training grants to, personnel of air pollution control agencies and other persons with suitable qualifications and make grants to such agencies, to other public or nonprofit private agencies, institutions, and organizations for the purposes stated in subsection (a)(5). Reasonable fees may be charged for such training provided to persons other than personnel of air pollution control agencies but such training shall be provided to such personnel of air pollution control agencies without charge.

[§103(b) amended by PL 95–95]

(c) Air Pollutant Monitoring, Analysis, Modeling and Inventory Research. — In carrying out subsection (a), the Administrator shall conduct a program of research, testing, and development of methods for sampling, measurement, monitoring, analysis, and modeling of air pollutants. Such program shall include the following elements:

(1) Consideration of individual, as well as complex mixtures of, air pollutants and their chemical transformations in the atmosphere.

(2) Establishment of a national network to monitor, collect, and compile data with quantification of certainty in the status and trends of air emissions, deposition, air quality, surface water quality, forest condition, and visibility impairment, and to ensure the comparability of air quality data collected in different States and obtained from different nations.

(3) Development of improved methods and technologies for sampling, measurement, monitoring, analysis, and modeling to increase understanding of the sources of ozone percursors, ozone formation, ozone transport, regional influences on urban ozone, regional ozone trends, and interactions of ozone with other pollutants. Emphasis shall be placed on those techniques which—

(A) improve the ability to inventory emissions of volatile organic compounds and nitrogen oxides that contribute to urban air pollution, including anthropogenic and natural sources;

(B) improve the understanding of the mechanism through which anthropogenic and biogenic volatile organic compounds react to form ozone and other oxidants; and

(C) improve the ability to identify and evaluate region-specific prevention and control options for ozone pollution.

(4) Submission of periodic reports to the Congress, not less than once every 5 years, which evaluate and assess the effectiveness of air pollution control regulations and programs using monitoring and modeling data obtained pursuant to this subsection.

[§103(c) revised by PL 101–549]

(d) Environmental Health Effects Research. —

(1) The Administrator, in consultation with the Secretary of Health and Human Services, shall conduct a research program on the short term and long-term effects of air pollutants, including wood smoke, on human health. In conducting such research program the Administrator—

(A) shall conduct studies, including epidemiological, clinical, and laboratory and field studies, as necessary to identify and evaluate exposure to and effects of air pollutants on human health;

(B) may utilize, on a reimbursable basis, the facilities of existing Federal scientific laboratories and research centers; and

(C) shall consult with other Federal agencies to ensure that similar research being conducted in other agencies is coordinated to avoid duplication.

(2) In conducting the research program under this subsection, the Administrator shall develop methods and techniques necessary to identify and assess the risks to human health from both routine and accidental exposures to individual air pollutants and combinations thereof. Such research program shall include the following elements:

(A) The creation of an Interagency Task Force to coordinate such program. The Task Force shall include representatives of the National Institute for Environmental Health Sciences, the Environmental Protection Agency, the Agency for Toxic Substances and Disease Registry, the National Toxicology Program, the National Institute of Standards and Technology, the National Science Foundation, the Surgeon General, and the Department of Energy. This Interagency Task Force shall be chaired by a representative of the Environmental Protection Agency and shall convene its first meeting within 60 days after the date of enactment of this subparagraph.

(B) An evaluation, within 12 months after the date of enactment of this paragraph, of each of the hazardous air pollutants listed under section 112(b) of this Act, to decide, on the basis of available information, their relative priority for preparation of environmental health assessments pursuant to subparagraph (C). The evaluation shall be based on reasonably anticipated toxicity to humans and exposure factors such as frequency of occurrence as an air pollutant and volume of emissions in populated areas. Such evaluation shall be reviewed by the Interagency Task Force established pursuant to subparagraph (A).

(C) Preparation of environmental health assessments for each of the hazardous air pollutants referred to in subparagraph (B), beginning 6 months after the first meeting of the Interagency Task Force and to be completed within 96 months thereafter. No fewer than 24 assessments shall be completed and published annually. The assessments shall be prepared in accordance with guidelines developed by the Administrator in consultation with the Interagency Task Force and the Science Advisory Board of the Environmental Protection Agency. Each such assessment shall include—

(i) an examination, summary, and evaluation of available toxicological and epidemiological information for the pollutant to ascertain the levels of human exposure which pose a significant threat to human health and the associated acute, subacute, and chronic adverse health effects;

(ii) a determination of gaps in available information related to human health effects and exposure levels; and

(iii) where appropriate, an identification of additional activities, including toxicological and inhalation testing, needed to identify the types or levels of exposure which may present significant risk of averse health effects in humans.

[§103(d) revised by PL 101–549]

(e) Ecosystem Research. — In carrying out subsection (a), the Administrator, in cooperation, where appropriate, with the Under Secretary of Commerce for Oceans and Atmosphere, the Director of the Fish and Wildlife Service, and the Secretary of Agriculture, shall conduct a research program to improve understanding of the short-term and long-term causes, effects, and trends of ecosystems damage from air pollutants on ecosystems. Such program shall include the following elements:

(1) Identification of regionally representative and critical ecosystems for research.

(2) Evaluation of risks to ecosystems exposed to air pollutants, including characterization of the causes and effects of chronic and episodic exposures to air pollutants and determination of the reversibility of those effects.

(3) Development of improved atmospheric dispersion models and monitoring systems and networks for evaluating and quantifying exposure to and effects of multiple environmental stresses associated with air pollution.

(4) Evaluation of the effects of air pollution on water quality, including assessments of the short-term and long-term ecological effects of acid deposition and other atmospherically derived pollutants on surface water (including wetlands and estuaries) and groundwater.

(5) Evaluation of the effects of air pollution on forests, materials, crops, biological diversity, soils, and other terrestrial and aquatic systems exposed to air pollutants.

(6) Estimation of the associated economic costs of ecological damage which have occurred as a result of exposure to air pollutants.

Consistent with the purpose of this program, the Administrator may use the estuarine research reserves established pursuant to section 315 of the Coastal Zone Management Act of 1972 (16 U.S.C. 1461) to carry out this research.

[§103(e) revised by PL 101–549]

(f) Liquefied Gaseous Fuels Spill Test Facility. —

(1) The Administrator, in consultation with the Secretary of Energy and the Federal Coordinating Council for Science, Engineering, and Technology, shall oversee an experimental and analytical research effort, with the experimental research to be carried out at the Liquefied Gaseous Fuels Spill Test Facility. In consultation with the Secretary of Energy, the Administrator shall develop a list of chemicals and a schedule for field testing at the Facility. Analysis of a minimum of 10 chemicals per year shall be carried out, with the selection of a minimum of 2 chemicals for field testing each year. Highest priority shall be given to those chemicals that would present the greatest potential risk to human health as a result of an accidental release—

(A) from a fixed site; or

(B) related to the transport of such chemicals.

(2) The purpose of such research shall be to—

(A) develop improved predictive models for atmospheric dispersion which at a minimum—

(i) describe dense gas releases in complex terrain including man-made structures or obstacles with variable winds;

(ii) improve understanding of the effects of turbulence on dispersion patterns; and

(iii) consider realistic behavior of aerosols by including physicochemical reactions with water vapor, ground deposition, and removal by water spray;

(B) evaluate existing and future atmospheric dispersion models by—

(i) the development of a rigorous, standardized methodology for dense gas models; and

(ii) the application of such methodology to current dense gas dispersion models using data generated from field experiments; and

(C) evaluate the effectiveness of hazard mitigation and emergency response technology for fixed site and transportation related accidental releases of toxic chemicals. Models pertaining to accidental release shall be evaluated and improved periodically for their utility in planning and implementing evacuation procedures and other mitigative strategies designed to minimize human exposure to hazardous air pollutants released accidentally.

(3) The Secretary of Energy shall make available to interested persons (including other Federal agencies and businesses) the use of the Liquefied Gaseous Fuels Spill Test Facility to conduct research and other activities in connection with the activities described in this subsection."

[§103(f) revised by PL 101–549]

(g) Pollution Prevention and Emissions Control. — In carrying out subsection (a), the Administrator shall conduct a basic engineering research and technology program to develop, evaluate, and demonstrate nonregulatory strategies and technologies for air pollution prevention. Such strategies and technologies shall be developed with priority on those pollutants which pose a significant risk to human health and the environment, and with opportunities for participation by industry, public interest groups, scientists, and other interested persons in the development of such strategies and technologies. Such program shall include the following elements:

(1) Improvements in nonregulatory strategies and technologies for preventing or reducing multiple air pollutants, including sulfur oxides, nitrogen oxides, heavy metals, PM–10 (particulate matter), carbon monoxide, and carbon dioxide, from stationary sources, including fossil fuel power plants. Such strategies and technologies shall include improvements in the relative cost effectiveness and long-range implications of various air pollutant reduction and nonregulatory control strategies such as energy conservation, including end-use efficiency, and fuel-switching to cleaner fuels. Such strategies and technologies shall be considered for existing and new facilities.

(2) Improvements in nonregulatory strategies and technologies for reducing air emissions from area sources.

(3) Improvements in nonregulatory strategies and technologies for preventing, detecting, and correcting accidental releases of hazardous air pollutants.

(4) Improvements in nonregulatory strategies and technologies that dispose of tires in ways that avoid adverse air quality impacts. Nothing in this subsection shall be construed to authorize the imposition on any person of air pollution control requirements. The Administrator shall consult with other appropriate Federal agencies to ensure coordination and to avoid duplication of activities authorized under this subsection.

[§103(g) added by PL 101–549]

(h) NIEHS Studies —

(1) The Director of the National Institute of Environmental Health Sciences may conduct a program of basic research to identify, characterize, and quantity risks to human health from air pollutants. Such research shall be conducted primarily through a combination of university and medical school-based grants, as well as through intramural studies and contracts.

(2) The Director of the National Institute of Environmental Health Sciences shall conduct a program for the education and training of physicians in environmental health.

(3) The Director shall assure that such programs shall not conflict with research undertaken by the Administrator.

(4) There are authorized to be appropriated to the National Institute of Environmental Health Sciences such sums as may be necessary to carry out the purposes of this subsection.

[§103(h) added by PL 101–549]

(i) Coordination of Research. — The Administrator shall develop and implement a plan for identifying areas in which activities authorized under this section can be carried out in conjunction with other Federal ecological and air pollution research efforts. The plan, which shall be submitted to Congress within 6 months after the date of enactment of this subsection, shall include—

(1) an assessment of ambient monitoring stations and networks to determine cost effective ways to expand monitoring capabilities in both urban and rural environments;

(2) a consideration of the extent of the feasibility and scientific value of conducting the research program under subsection (e) to

include consideration of the effects of atmospheric processes and air pollution effects; and

(3) a methodology for evaluating and ranking pollution prevention technologies, such as those developed under subsection (g), in terms of their ability to reduce cost effectively the emissions of air pollutants and other airborne chemicals of concern.

Not later than 2 years after the date of enactment of this subsection, and every 4 years thereafter, the Administrator shall report to Congress on the progress made in implementing the plan developed under this subsection, and shall include in such report any revisions of the plan.

[§103(i) added by PL 101–549]

(j) Continuation of the National Acid Precipitation Assessment Program. —

(1) The acid precipitation research program set forth in the Acid Precipitation Act of 1980 shall be continued with modifications pursuant to this subsection.

(2) The Acid Precipitation Task Force shall consist of the Administrator of the Environmental Protection Agency, the Secretary of Energy, the Secretary of the Interior, the Secretary of Agriculture, the Administrator of the National Oceanic and Atmospheric Administration, the Administrator of the National Aeronautics and Space Administration, and such additional members as the President may select. The President shall appoint a chairman for the Task Force from among its members within 30 days after the date of enactment of this subsection.

(3) The responsibilities of the Task Force shall include the following:

(A) Review of the status of research activities conducted to date under the comprehensive research plan developed pursuant to the Acid Precipitation Act of 1980, and development of a revised plan that identifies significant research gaps and establishes a coordinated program to address current and future research priorities. A draft of the revised plan shall be submitted by the Task Force to Congress within 6 months after the date of enactment of this subsection. The plan shall be available for public comment during the 60 day period after its submission, and a final plan shall be submitted by the President to the Congress within 45 days after the close of the comment period.

(B) Coordination with participating Federal agencies, augmenting the agencies' research and monitoring efforts and sponsoring additional research in the scientific community as necessary to ensure the availability and quality of data and methodologies needed to evaluate the status and effectiveness of the acid deposition control program. Such research and monitoring efforts shall include, but not be limited to—

(i) continuous monitoring of emissions of precursors of acid deposition;

(ii) maintenance, upgrading, and application of models, such as the Regional Acid Deposition Model, that describe the interactions of emissions with the atmosphere, and models that describe the response of ecosystems to acid deposition; and

(iii) analysis of the costs, benefits, and effectiveness of the acid deposition control program.

(C) Publication and maintenance of a National Acid Lakes Registry that tracks the condition and change over time of a statistically representative sample of lakes in regions that are known to be sensitive to surface water acidification.

(D) Submission every two years of a unified budget recommendation to the President for activities of the Federal Government in connection with the research program described in this subsection.

(E) Beginning in 1992 and biennially thereafter, submission of a report to Congress describing the results of its investigations and analyses. The reporting of technical information about acid deposition shall be provided in a format that facilitates communication with policymakers and the public. The report shall include—

(i) actual and projected emissions and acid deposition trends;

(ii) average ambient concentrations of acid deposition precursors and their transformation products;

(iii) the status of ecosystems (including forests and surface waters), materials, and visibility affected by acid deposition;

(iv) the causes and effects of such deposition, including changes in surface water quality and forest and soil conditions;

(v) the occurrence and effects of episodic acidification, particularly with respect to high elevation watersheds; and

(vi) the confidence level associated with each conclusion to aid policymakers in use of the information.

(F) Beginning in 1996, and every 4 years thereafter, the report under subparagraph (E) shall include—

(i) the reduction in deposition rates that must be achieved in order to prevent adverse ecological effects; and

(ii) the costs and benefits of the acid deposition control program created by title IV of this Act.

[§103(j) added by PL 101–549]

(k) Air Pollution Conferences. — If, in the judgment of the Administrator, an air pollution problem of substantial significance may result from discharge or discharges into the atmosphere, the Administrator may call a conference concerning this potential air pollution problem to be held in or near one or more of the places where such discharge or discharges are occurring or will occur. All interested persons shall be given an opportunity to be heard at such conference, either orally or in writing, and shall be permitted to appear in person or by representative in accordance with procedures prescribed by the Administrator. If the Administrator finds, on the basis of the evidence presented at such conference, that the discharge or discharges if permitted to take place or continue are likely to cause or contribute to air pollution subject to abatement under part A of title I, the Administrator shall send such findings, together with recommendations concerning the measures which the Administrator finds reasonable and suitable to prevent such pollution, to the person or persons whose actions will result in the discharge or discharges involved; to air pollution agencies of the State or States and of the municipality or municipalities where such discharge or discharges will originate; and to the interstate air pollution control agency, if any, in the jurisdictional area of which any such municipality is located. Such findings and recommendations shall be advisory only, but shall be admitted together with the record of the conference, as part of the proceedings under subsections (b), (c), (d), (e), and (f) of section 108 ."

[§103(k) added by PL 101–549]

[Editor's Note: Section 101(c) of PL 95–95 provides: (c) The Administrator of the Environmental Protection Agency shall consult with the House Committee on Science and Technology on the environmental and atmospheric research, development, and demonstration aspects of this Act. In addition, the reports and studies required by this Act that relate to research, development and demonstration issues shall be transmitted to the Committee on Science and Technology at the same time they are made available to other committees of the Congress.]

§7404. Research Relating to Fuels and Vehicles
[Sec. 104]

(a) The Administrator shall give special emphasis to research and development into new and improved methods, having industrywide application, for the prevention and control of air pollution resulting from the combustion of fuels. In furtherance of such research and development he shall

(1) conduct and accelerate research programs directed toward development of improved, cost-effective techniques for

(A) control of combustion byproducts of fuels,

(B) removal of potential air pollutants from fuels prior to combustion,

(C) control of emissions from the evaporation of fuels,

(D) improving efficiency of fuels combustion so as to decrease atmospheric emissions, and

(E) producing synthetic or new fuels which when used, result in decreased atmospheric emissions,

[§104(a)(1) amended by PL 101–549]

(2) provide for Federal grants to public or nonprofit agencies, institutions, and organizations and to individuals, and contracts with public or private agencies, institutions, or persons, for payment of

(A) part of the cost of acquiring, constructing, or otherwise securing for research and development purposes, new or improved devices or methods having industrywide application of preventing or controlling discharges into the air of various types of pollutants;

(B) part of the cost of programs to develop low emission alternatives to the present internal combustion engine;

(C) the cost to purchase vehicles and vehicle engines or portions thereof for research, development, and testing purposes; and

(D) carrying out the other provisions of this section, without regard to section 3324(a) and (b) of Title 31 and section 5 of Title 41:

*Provided,*That research or demonstration contracts awarded pursuant to this subsection (including contracts for construction) may be made in accordance with, and subject to the limitations provided with respect to research contracts of the military departments in, section 2353 of title 10, United States Code, except that the determination, approval, and certification required thereby shall be made by the Administrator:

*Provided further,*That no grant may be made under this paragraph in excess of $1,500,000;

[§104(a)(2)(D) amended by PL 97–258].

(3) determine, by laboratory and pilot plant testing, the results of air pollution research and studies in order to develop new or improved processes and plant designs to the point where they can be demonstrated on a large and practical scale;

(4) construct, operate, and maintain, or assist in meeting the cost of the construction, operation, and maintenance of new or improved demonstration plants or processes which have promise of accomplishing the purposes of this Act;

(5) study new or improved methods for the recovery and marketing or commercially valuable byproducts resulting from the removal of pollutants.

(b) In carrying out the provisions of the section, the Administrator may

(1) conduct and accelerate research and development of cost-effective instrumentation techniques to facilitate determination of quantity and quality of air pollutant emissions, including, but not limited to, automotive emissions;

[§104(b)(1) amended by PL 101–549]

(2) utilize on a reimbursable basis, the facilities of existing Federal scientific laboratories;

(3) establish and operate necessary facilities and test sites at which to carry on the research, testing, development, and programming necessary to effectuate the purposes of this section;

(4) acquire secret processes, technical data, inventions, patent applications, patents, licenses, and an interest in lands, plants, and facilities, and other property or rights by purchase, license, lease, or donation; and

(5) cause on-site inspections to be made of promising domestic and foreign projects, and cooperate and participate in their development in instances in which the purposes of the Act will be served thereby.

(c) Clean Alternative Fuels. — The Administrator shall conduct a research program to identify, characterize, and predict air emissions related to the production, distribution, storage, and use of clean alternative fuels to determine the risks and benefits to human health and the environment relative to those from using conventional gasoline and diesel fuels. The Administrator shall consult with other Federal agencies to ensure coordination and to avoid duplication of activities authorized under this subsection.

[§104(c) revised by PL 101–549]

[Editor's Note: Section 901(e)—(h) of PL 101–549 provides language on required studies and available funding. Those provisions follow.]

[Sec. 901]

(e) Assessment of International Air Pollution Control Technologies. — The Administrator of the Environmental Protection Agency shall conduct a study that compares international air pollution control technologies of selected industrialized countries to determine if there exist air pollution control technologies in countries outside the United States that may have beneficial applications to this Nation's air pollution control efforts. With respect to each country studied, the study shall include the topics of urban air quality, motor vehicle emissions, toxic air emissions, and acid deposition. The Administrator shall, within 2 years after the date of enactment of this Act, submit to the Congress a report detailing the results of such study.

(f) Adirondack Effects Assessment. — The Administrator of the Environmental Protection Agency shall establish a program to research the effects of acid deposition on waters where acid deposition has been most acute. The Administrator shall enter into a multi-year contract for such purposes with an independent university which has a year-round field analytical laboratory on a body of water of not less than 25,000 acres nor greater than 75,000 acres, which lies within a geographic region designated as a Biosphere Reserve by the Department of State. The facility must have demonstrated the capability to analyze relevant data on said body of water over a period of 20 years as well as extensive ecosystem modeling capabilities. There are authorized to be appropriated to carry out this subsection not less than $6,000,000.

(g) Western States Acid Deposition Research. —

(1) The Administrator of the Environmental Protection Agency shall sponsor monitoring and research and submit to Congress annual and periodic assessment reports on—

(A) the occurrence and effects of acid deposition on surface waters located in that part of the United States west of the Mississippi River;

(B) the occurrence and effects of acid deposition on high elevation ecosystems (including forests, and surface waters); and

(C) the occurrence and effects of episodic acidification, particularly with respect to high elevation watersheds.

(2) The Administrator of the Environmental Protection Agency shall analyze data generated from the studies conducted under paragraph (1), data from the Western Lakes Survey, and other appropriate research and utilize predictive modeling techniques that take into account the unique geographic, climatological, and atmospheric conditions which exist in the western United States to determine the potential occurrence and effects of acid deposition due to any projected increases in the emission of sulfur dioxide and nitrogen oxides in that part of the United States located west of the Mississippi River. The Administrator shall include the results of the project conducted under this paragraph in the reports issued to Congress under paragraph (1).

(h) (1) In carrying out the provisions of section 103(f) of the Clean Air Act, the Secretary of Energy is authorized to enter into contracts and cooperative agreements with, and make grants to, non-profit entities affiliated with the University of Nevada and the University of Wyoming.

(2) Agreements, contracts, and grants described in paragraph (1) shall provide that such nonprofit entities—

(A) may provide basic technical and management personnel; and

(B) shall make available permanent research support facilities owned by the nonprofit entities.

(3) The nonprofit entities described in paragraphs (1) and (2) shall be authorized to make grants, accept contributions, and enter into agreements with other entities to carry out the provisions of this subsection.

(4) There are authorized to be appropriated to the Department of Energy $3,000,000 for fiscal year 1991 and such sums as may be necessary for each fiscal year thereafter to carry out the provisions of paragraph (1). Such amounts shall remain available until expended.

§7405. Grants for Support of Air Pollution Planning and Control Programs [Sec. 105]

(a) (1) (A) The Administrator may make grants to air pollution control agencies, within the meaning of paragraph (1), (2), (3), (4), or (5) of section 302, in an amount up to three-fifths of the cost of implementing programs for the prevention and control of air pollution or implementation of national primary and secondary ambient air quality standards. For the purpose of this section, 'implementing' means any activity related to the planning, developing, establishing, carrying-out, improving, or maintaining of such programs.

[§105(a)(1)(A) amended by PL 101–549]

(B) Subject to subsections (b) and (c) of this section, an air pollution control agency which receives a grant under subparagraph (A) and which contributes less than the required two-fifths minimum shall have 3 years following the date of the enactment of the Clean Air Act Amendments of 1990 in which to contribute such amount. If such an agency fails to meet and maintain this required level, the Administrator shall reduce the amount of the Federal contribution accordingly.

[§105(a)(1)(B) amended by PL 101–549]

(C) With respect to any air quality control region or portion thereof for which there is an applicable implementation plan under section 110, grants under subparagraph (A) may be made only to air pollution control agencies which have substantial responsibilities for carrying out such applicable implementation plan.

[§105(a)(1)(C) amended by PL 101–549]

(2) Before approving any grant under this subsection to any air pollution control agency within the meaning of sections 302(b)(2) and 302(b)(4), the Administrator shall receive assurances that such agency provides for adequate representation of appropriate State, interstate, local, and (when appropriate) international, interests in the air quality control region.

(3) Before approving any planning grant under this subsection to any air pollution control agency within the meaning of sections 302(b)(2) and 302(b)(4) , the Administrator shall receive assurances that such agency has the capability of developing a comprehensive air quality plan for the air quality control region, which plan shall include (when appropriate) a recommended system of alerts to avert and reduce the risk of situations in which there may be imminent and serious danger to the public health or welfare from air pollutants and the various aspects relevant to the establishment of air quality standards for such air quality control region, including the concentration of industries, other commercial establishments, population and naturally occurring factors which shall affect such standards.

(b) (1) From the sums available for the purposes of subsection (a) of this section for any fiscal year, the Administrator shall from time to time make grants to air pollution control agencies upon such terms and conditions as the Administrator may find necessary to carry out the purpose of this section. In establishing regulations for the granting of such funds the

Administrator shall, so far as practicable, give due consideration to (A) the population, (B) the extent of the actual or potential air pollution problem, and (C) the financial need of the respective agencies.

[Former §105(b) revised and redesignated as (b)(1) by PL 101–549]

(2) Not more than 10 per centum of the total of funds appropriated or allocated for the purposes of subsection (a) of this section shall be granted for air pollution control programs in any one State. In the case of a grant for a program in an area crossing State boundaries, the Administrator shall determine the portion of such grant that is chargeable to the percentage limitation under this subsection for each State into which such area extends.

Subject to the provisions of paragraph (1) of this subsection, no State shall have made available to it for application less than one-half of 1 per centum of the annual appropriation for grants under this section for grants to agencies within such State.

[Former §105(c) amended and redesignated as (b)(2) by PL 101–549]

(c) Maintenance of Effort. —

(1) No agency shall receive any grant under this section during any fiscal year when its expenditures of non-Federal funds for recurrent expenditures for air pollution control programs will be less than its expenditures were for such programs during the preceding fiscal year. In order for the Administrator to award grants under this section in a timely manner each fiscal year, the Administrator shall compare an agency's prospective expenditure level to that of its second preceding fiscal year. The Administrator shall revise the current regulations which define applicable nonrecurrent and recurrent expenditures, and in so doing, give due consideration to exempting an agency from the limitations of this paragraph and subsection (a) due to periodic increases experienced by that agency from time to time in its annual expenditures for purposes acceptable to the Administrator for that fiscal year.

(2) The Administrator may still award a grant to an agency not meeting the requirements of paragraph (l) of this subsection if the Administrator, after notice and opportunity for public hearing, determines that a reduction in expenditures is attributable to a non-selective reduction in the expenditures in the programs of all Executive branch agencies of the applicable unit of Government. No agency shall receive any grant under this section with respect to the maintenance of a program for the prevention and control of air pollu tion unless the Administrator is satisfied that such a grant will be so used to supplement and, to the extent practicable, increase the level of State, local, or other non-Federal funds. No grants shall be made under this section until the Administrator has consulted with the appropriate official as designated by the Governor or Governors of the State or States affected.

[New §105(c) added by PL 101–549]

(d) The Administrator, with the concurrence of any recipient of a grant under this section, may reduce the payments to such recipient by the amount of the pay, allowances, traveling expenses, and any other costs in connection with the detail of any officer or employee to the recipient under section 301 of this Act, when such detail is for the convenience of, and at the request of, such recipient and for the purpose of carrying out the provisions of this Act. The amount by which such payments have reduced shall be available for payment of such costs by the Administrator, but shall, for the purpose of determining the amount of any grant to a recipient under subsection (a) of this section, be deemed to have been paid to such agency.

(e) No application by a State for a grant under this section may be disapproved by the Administrator without prior notice and opportunity for a public hearing in the affected State, and no commitment or obligation of any funds under any such grant may be revoked or reduced without prior notice and opportunity for a public hearing in the affected State (or in one of the affected States if more than one State is affected).

[§105(e) added by PL 95–95]

§7406. Interstate Air Quality Agencies or Commissions [Sec. 106]

For the purpose of developing implementation plans for any interstate air quality control region designated pursuant to section 107 or of implementing section 176A (relating to control of interstate air pollution) or section 184 (relating to control of interstate ozone pollution), the administrator is authorized to pay, for two years, up to 100 per centum of the air quality planning program costs of any commission established under section 176A (relating to control of interstate air pollution) or section 184 (relating to control of interstate ozone pollution) or any agency designated by the Governors of the affected States, which agency shall be capable of recommending to the Governors plans for implementation of national primary and secondary ambient air quality standards and shall include representation from the States and appropriate political subdivisions within the air quality control region. After the initial two-year period the Administrator is authorized to make grants to such agency in an amount up to three-fifths of the air quality implementation program costs of such agency or such commission or commission.

[§106 amended by PL 101–549]

§7407. Air Quality Control Regions [Sec. 107]

(a) Each State shall have the primary responsibility for assuring air quality within the entire geographic area comprising such State by submitting an implementation plan for such State which will specify the manner in which national primary and secondary ambient air quality standards will be achieved and maintained within each air quality control region in such State.

(b) For purposes of developing and carrying out implementation plans under section 110—

(1) an air quality control region designated under this section before the date of enactment of the Clean Air Amendments of 1970, or a region designated after such date under subsection (c), shall be an air quality control region; and

(2) the portion of such State which is not part of any such designated region shall be an air quality control region, but such portion may be subdivided by the State into two or more air quality control regions with the approval of the Administrator.

(c) The Administrator shall, within 90 days after the date of enactment of the Clean Air Amendments of 1970, after consultation with appropriate State and local authorities, designate as an air quality control region any interstate area or major intrastate area which he deems necessary or appropriate for the attainment and maintenance of ambient air quality standards. The Administrator shall immediately notify the governors of the affected States of any designation made under this subsection.

(d) Designations.

[§107(d) revised by PL 101–549]

(1) (A) Submission by Governors of Initial Designations Following Promulgation of New or Revised Standards. — By such date as the Administrator may reasonably require, but not later than 1 year after promulgation of a new or revised national ambient air quality standard for any pollutant under section 109, the Governor of each State shall (and at any other time the Governor of a State deems appropriate the Governor may) submit to the Administrator a list of all areas (or portions thereof) in the State, designating as—

(i) nonattainment, any area that does not meet (or that contributes to ambient air quality in a nearby area that does not meet) the national primary or secondary ambient air quality standard for the pollutant,

(ii) attainment, any area (other than an area identified in clause (i)) that meets the national primary or secondary ambient air quality standard for the pollutant, or

(iii) unclassifiable, any area that cannot be classified on the basis of available information as meeting or not meeting the national primary or secondary ambient air quality standard for the pollutant.

The Administrator may not require the Governor to submit the required list sooner than 120 days after promulgating a new or revised national ambient air quality standard.

(B) Promulgation by EPA of Designations. —

(i) Upon promulgation or revision of a national ambient air quality standard, the Administrator shall promulgate the designations of all areas (or portions thereof) submitted under subparagraph (A) as expeditiously as practicable, but in no case later than 2 years from the date of promulgation of the new or revised national ambient air quality standard. Such period may be extended for up to one year in the event the Administrator has insufficient information to promulgate the designations.

(ii) In making the promulgations required under clause (i), the Administrator may make such modifications as the Administrator deems necessary to the designations of the areas (or portions thereof) submitted under subparagraph (A) (including to the boundaries of such areas or portions thereof). Whenever the Administrator intends to make a modification, the Administrator shall notify the State and provide such State with an opportunity to demonstrate why any proposed modification is inappropriate. The Administrator shall give such notification no later than 120 days before the date the Administrator promulgates the designation, including any modification thereto. If the Governor fails to submit the list in whole or in part, as required under subparagraph (A), the Administrator shall promulgate the designation that the Administrator deems appropriate for any area (or portion thereof) not designated by the State.

(iii) If the Governor of any State, on the Governor's own motion, under subparagraph (A), submits a list of areas (or portions thereof) in the State designated as nonattainment, attainment, or unclassifiable, the Administrator shall act on such designations in accordance with the procedures under paragraph (3) (relating to redesignation).

(iv) A designation for an area (or portion thereof) made pursuant to this subsection shall remain in effect until the area (or portion thereof) is redesignated pursuant to paragraph (3) or (4).

(C) Designations by Operation of Law. —(i) Any area designated with respect to any air pollutant under the provisions of paragraph (1)(A), (B), or (C) of this subsection (as in effect immediately before the date of the enactment of the Clean Air Act Amendments of 1990) is designated, by operation of law, as a nonattainment area for such pollutant within the meaning of subparagraph (A)(i).

(ii) Any area designated with respect to any air pollutant under the provisions of paragraph (1)(E) (as in effect immediately before the date of the enactment of the Clean Air Act Amendments of 1990) is designated by operation of law, as an attainment area for such pollutant within the meaning of subparagraph (A)(ii).

(iii) Any area designated with respect to any air pollutant under the provisions of paragraph (1)(D) (as in effect immediately before the date of the enactment of the Clean Air Act Amendments of 1990) is designated, by operation of law, as an unclassifiable area for such pollutant within the meaning of subparagraph (A)(iii).

(2) Publication of Designations and Redesignations. —

(A) The Administrator shall publish a notice in the Federal Register promulgating any designation under paragraph (1) or (5), or announcing any designation under paragraph (4), or promulgating any redesignation under paragraph (3).

(B) Promulgation or announcement of a designation under paragraph (1), (4) or (5) shall not be subject to the provisions of sections 553 through 557 of title 5 of the United States Code (relating to notice and comment), except nothing herein shall be construed as precluding such public notice and comment whenever possible.

(3) Redesignation. —

(A) Subject to the requirements of subparagraph (E), and on the basis of air quality data, planning and control considerations, or any other air quality-related considerations the Administrator deems appropriate, the Administrator may at any time notify the Governor of any State that available information indicates that the designation of any area or portion of an area within the State or interstate area should be revised. In issuing such notification, which shall be public, to the Governor, the Administrator shall provide such information as the Administrator may have available explaining the basis for the notice.

(B) No later than 120 days after receiving a notification under subparagraph (A), the Governor shall submit to the Administrator such redesignation, if any, of the appropriate area (or areas) or portion thereof within the State or interstate area, as the Governor considers appropriate.

(C) No later than 120 days after the date described in subparagraph (B) (or paragraph (1)(B)(iii)), the Administrator shall promulgate the redesignation, if any, of the area or portion thereof, submitted by the Governor in accordance with subparagraph (B), making such modifications as the Administrator may deem necessary, in the same manner and under the same procedure as is applicable under clause (ii) of paragraph (1)(B), except that the phrase '60 days' shall be substituted for the phrase '120 days' in that clause. If the Governor does not submit, in accordance with subparagraph (B), a redesignation for an area (or portion thereof) identified by the Administrator under subparagraph (A), the Administrator shall promulgate such redesignation, if any, that the Administrator deems appropriate.

(D) The Governor of any State may, on the Governor's own motion, submit to the Administrator a revised designation of any area or portion thereof within the State. Within 18 months of receipt of a complete State redesignation submittal, the Administrator shall approve or deny such redesignation. The submission of a redesignation by a Governor shall not affect the effectiveness or enforceability of the applicable implementation plan for the State.

(E) The Administrator may not promulgate a redesignation of a nonattainment area (or portion thereof) to attainment unless—

(i) the Administrator determines that the area has attained the national ambient air quality standard;

(ii) the Administrator has fully approved the applicable implementation plan for the area under section 110(k) ;

(iii) the Administrator determines that the improvement in air quality is due to permanent and enforceable reductions in emissions resulting from implementation of the applicable implementation plan and applicable Federal air pollutant control regulations and other permanent and enforceable reductions;

(iv) the Administrator has fully approved a maintenance plan for the area as meeting the requirements of section 175A ; and

(v) the State containing such area has met all requirements applicable to the area under section 110 and part D.

(F) The Administrator shall not promulgate any redesignation of any area (or portion thereof) from nonattainment to unclassifiable.

(4) Nonattainment Designations for Ozone, Carbon Monoxide and Particulate Matter (PM–10).—

(A) Ozone And Carbon Monoxide. —

(i) Within 120 days after the date of the enactment of the Clean Air Act Amendments of 1990, each Governor of each State shall submit to the Administrator a list that designates, affirms or reaffirms the designation of, or redesignates (as the case may be), all areas (or portions thereof) of the Governor's State as attainment, nonattainment, or unclassifiable with respect to the national ambient air quality standards for ozone and carbon monoxide.

(ii) No later than 120 days after the date the Governor is required to submit the list of areas (or portions thereof) required under clause (i) of this subparagraph, the Administrator shall promulgate such designations, making such modifications as the Administrator may deem necessary, in the same manner, and under the same procedure, as is applicable under clause (ii) of paragraph (1)(B), except that the phrase '60 days' shall be substituted for the phrase '120 days' in that clause. If the Governor does not submit, in accordance with clause (i) of this subparagraph, a designation for an area (or portion thereof), the Administrator shall promulgate the designation that the Administrator deems appropriate.

(iii) No nonattainment area may be redesignated as an attainment area under this subparagraph.

(iv) Notwithstanding paragraph (1)(C)(ii) of this subsection, if an ozone or carbon monoxide nonattainment area located within a metropolitan statistical area or consolidated metropolitan statistical area (as established by the Bureau of the Census) is classified under part D of this title as a Serious, Severe, or Extreme Area, the boundaries of such area are hereby revised (on the date 45 days after such classification) by operation of law to include the entire metropolitan statistical area or consolidated metropolitan statistical area, as the case may be, unless within such 45–day period the Governor (in consultation with State and local air pollution control agencies) notifies the Administrator that additional time is necessary to evaluate the application of clause (v). Whenever a Governor has submitted such a notice to the Administrator, such boundary revision shall occur on the later of the date 8 months after such classification or 14 months after the date of the enactment of the Clean Air Act Amendments of 1990 unless the Governor makes the finding referred to in clause (v), and the Administrator concurs in such finding, within such period. Except as otherwise provided in this paragraph, a boundary revision under this clause or clause (v) shall apply for purposes of any State implementation plan revision required to be submitted after the date of the enactment of the Clean Air Act Amendments of 1990.

(v) Whenever the Governor of a State has submitted a notice under clause (iv), the Governor, in consultation with State and local air pollution control agencies, shall undertake a study to evaluate whether the entire metropolitan statistical area or consolidated metropolitan statistical area should be included within the nonattainment area. Whenever a Governor finds and demonstrates to the satisfaction of the Administrator, and the Administrator concurs in such finding, that with respect to a portion of a metropolitan statistical area or consolidated metropolitan statistical area, sources in the portion do not contribute significantly to violation of the national ambient air quality standard, the Administrator shall approve the Governor's request to exclude such portion from the nonattainment area. In making such finding, the Governor and the Administrator shall consider factors such as population density, traffic congestion, commercial development, industrial development, meteorological conditions, and pollution transport.

(B) PM–10 designations. — By operation of law, until redesignation by the Administrator pursuant to paragraph (3)—

(i) each area identified in 52 Federal Register 29383 (Aug. 7, 1987) as a Group I area (except to the extent that such identification was modified by the Administrator before the date of the enactment of the Clean Air Act Amendments of 1990) is designated nonattainment for PM–10;

(ii) any area containing a site for which air quality monitoring data show a violation of the national ambient air quality standard for PM–10 before January 1, 1989 (as determined under part 50, appendix K of title 40 of the Code of Federal Regulations) is hereby designated nonattainment for PM–10; and

(iii) each area not described in clause (i) or (ii) is hereby designated unclassifiable for PM–10.

Any designation for particulate matter (measured in terms of total suspended particulates) that the Administrator promulgated pursuant to this subsection (as in effect immediately before the date of the enactment of the Clean Air Act Amendments of 1990) shall remain in effect for purposes of implementing the maximum allowable increases in concentrations of particulate matter (measured in terms of total suspended particulates) pursuant to section 163(b) , until the Administrator determines that such designation is no longer necessary for that purpose.

(5) Designations for Lead. — The Administrator may, in the Administrator's discretion at any time the Administrator deems appropriate, require a State to designate areas (or portions thereof) with respect to the national ambient air quality standard for lead in effect as of the date of the enactment of the Clean Air Act Amendments of 1990, in accordance with the procedures under subparagraphs (A) and (B) of paragraph (1), except that in applying subparagraph (B)(i) of paragraph (1) the phrase '2 years from the date of promulgation of the new or revised national ambient air quality standard' shall be replaced by the phrase '1 year from the date the Administrator notifies the State of the requirement to designate areas with respect to the standard for lead'.

(e) (1) Except as otherwise provided in paragraph (2), the Governor of each State is authorized, with the approval of the Administrator, to redesignate from time to time the air quality control regions within such State for purposes of efficient and effective air quality management. Upon such redesignation, the list under subsection (d) shall be modified accordingly.

(2) In the case of an air quality control region in a State, or part of such region, which the Administrator finds may significantly affect air pollution concentrations in another State, the Governor of the State in which such region, or part of a region, is located may redesignate from time to time the boundaries of so much air quality control region as is located within such State only with the approval of the Administrator and with the consent of all Governors of all States which the Administrator determines may be significantly affected.

(3) No compliance date extension granted under section 113(d) of the regional limitation provided in section 113(d)(5) if the violation of such limitation is due solely to a redesignation of a region under this subsection.

§7408. Air Quality Criteria and Control Techniques [Sec. 108]

(a) (1) For the purpose of establishing national primary and secondary ambient air quality standards, the Administrator shall within 30 days after the date of enactment of the Clean Air Amendments of 1970 publish, and shall from time to time thereafter revise, a list which includes each air pollutant—

(A) emissions of which, in his judgment, cause or contribute to air pollution which may reasonably be anticipated to endanger public health or welfare;

[§108(a)(1)(A) amended by PL 95–95]

(B) the presence of which in the ambient air results from numerous or diverse mobile or stationary sources; and

(C) for which air quality criteria had not been issued before the date of enactment of the Clean Air Amendments of 1970, but for which he plans to issue air quality criteria under this section.

(2) The Aministrator shall issue air quality criteria for an air pollutant within 12 months after

he has included such pollutant in a list under paragraph (1). Air quality criteria for an air pollutant shall accurately reflect the latest scientific knowledge useful in indicating the kind and extent of all identifiable effects on public health or welfare which may be expected from the presence of such pollutant in the ambient air, in varying quantities. The criteria for an air pollutant, to the extent practicable, shall include information on—

(A) those variable factors (including atmospheric conditions) which of themselves or in combination with other factors may alter the effects on public health or welfare of such air pollutant;

(B) the types of air pollutants which, when present in the atmosphere, may interact with such pollutant to produce an adverse effect on public health or welfare; and

(C) any known or anticipated adverse effects on welfare.

(b) (1) Simultaneously with the issuance of criteria under subsection (a), the Administrator shall, after consultation with appropriate advisory committees and Federal departments and agencies, issue to the States and appropriate air pollution control agencies information on air pollution control techniques, which information shall include data relating to the cost of installation and operation, energy requirements, emission reduction benefits, and environmental impact of the emission control technology. Such information shall include such data as are available on available technology and alternative methods of prevention and control of air pollution. Such information shall also include data on alternative fuels, processes, and operating methods which will result in elimination or significant reduction of emissions.

(2) In order to assist in the development of information on pollution control techniques, the Administrator may establish a standing consulting committee for each air pollutant include in a list published pursuant to subsection (a)(1), which shall be comprised of technically qualified individuals representative of State and local governments, industry, and the academic community. Each such committee shall submit as appropriate, to the Administrator information related to that required by paragraph (1).

(c) The Administrator shall from time to time review, and, as appropriate, modify, and reissue any criteria or information on control techniques issued pursuant to this section. Not later than six months after the date of the enactment of the Clean Air Act Amendments of 1977, the Administrator shall revise and reissue criteria relating the concentrations of NO_2over such period (not more than three hours) as he deems appropriate. Such criteria shall include a discussion of nitric and nitrous acids, nitrites, nitrates, nitrosamines, and other carcinogenic and potentially carcinogenic derivatives of oxides of nitrogen.

[§108(c) amended by PL 95–95]

(d) The issuance of air quality criteria and information on air pollution control techniques shall be announced in the Federal Register and copies shall be made available to the general public.

(e) The Administrator shall, after consultation with the Secretary of Transportation, and after providing public notice and opportunity for comment, and with State and local officials, within nine months after enactment of the Clean Air Act Amendments of 1989 and periodically thereafter as necessary to maintain a continuous transportation-air quality planning process, update the June 1978 Transportation-Air Quality Planning Guidelines and publish guidance on the development and implementation of transportation and other measures necessary to demonstrate and maintain attainment of national ambient air quality standards. Such guidelines shall include information on—

(1) methods to identify and evaluate alternative planning and control activities;

(2) methods of reviewing plans on a regular basis as conditions change or new information is presented;

(3) identification of funds and other resources necessary to implement the plan, including interagency agreements on providing such funds and resources;

(4) methods to assure participation by the public in all phases of the planning process; and

(5) such other methods as the Administrator determines necessary to carry out a continuous planning process.

[§108(e) added by PL 95–95;amended by PL 101–549]

(f) (1) The Administrator shall publish and make available to appropriate Federal, State, and local environmental and transportation agencies not later than one year after enactment of the Clean Air Act Amendments of 1990, and from time to time thereafter—

[§108(f) added by PL 95–95]

(A) information prepared, as appropriate, in consultation with the Secretary of Transportation, and after providing public notice and opportunity for comment, regarding the formulation and emission reduction potential of transportation control measures related to criteria pollutants and their precursors, including, but not limited to—

(i) programs for improved public transit;

(ii) restriction of certain roads or lanes to, or construction of such roads or lanes for use by, passenger buses or high occupancy vehicles;

(iii) employer-based transportation management plans, including incentives;

(iv) trip-reduction ordinances;

(v) traffic flow improvement programs that achieve emission reductions;

(vi) fringe and transportation corridor parking facilities serving multiple occupancy vehicle programs or transit service;

(vii) programs to limit or restrict vehicle use in downtown areas or other areas of emission concentration particularly during periods of peak use;

(viii) programs for the provision of all forms of high-occupancy, shared-ride services;

(ix) programs to limit portions of road surfaces or certain sections of the metropolitan area to the use of non-motorized vehicles or pedestrian use, both as to time and place;

(x) programs for secure bicycle storage facilities and other facilities, including bicycle lanes, for the convenience and protection of bicyclists, in both public and private areas;

(xi) programs to control extended idling of vehicles;

(xii) programs to reduce motor vehicle emissions, consistent with title II, which are caused by extreme cold start conditions;

(xiii) employer-sponsored programs to permit flexible work schedules;

(xiv) programs and ordinances to facilitate non-automobile travel, provision and utilization of mass transit, and to generally reduce the need for single-occupant vehicle travel, as part of transportation planning and development efforts of a locality, including programs and ordinances applicable to new shopping centers, special events, and other centers of vehicle activity;

(xv) programs for new construction and major reconstructions of paths, tracks or areas solely for the use by pedestrian or other non-motorized means of transportation when economically feasible and in the public interest. For purposes of this clause, the Administrator shall also consult with the Secretary of the Interior; and

(xvi) program to encourage the voluntary removal from use and the marketplace of pre-1980 model year light duty vehicles and pre-1980 model light duty trucks.

[§108(f)(1)(A) amended by PL 101–549]

(B) information on additional methods or strategies that will contribute to the reduction of mobile source related pollutants during periods in which any primary ambient air quality standard will be exceeded and during episodes for which an air pollution alert, warning or emergency has been declared;

(C) information on other measures which may be employed to reduce the impact on public health or protect the health of sensitive or susceptible individuals or groups; and

(D) information on the extent to which any process, procedure, or method to reduce or control such air pollutant may cause an increase in the emissions or formation of any other pollutant.

(2) In publishing such information the Administrator shall also include an assessment of—

(A) the relative effectiveness of such processes, procedures, and methods;

(B) the potential effect of such processes, procedures, and methods on transportation systems and the provision of transportation services; and

(C) the environmental, energy, and economic impact of such processes, procedures and methods.

(3) The Secretary of Transportation and the Administrator shall submit to Congress by January 1, 1993, and every 3 years thereafter a report that—

(A) reviews and analyzes existing State and local air quality-related transportation programs, including specifically any analyses of whether adequate funding is available to complete transportation projects identified in State implementation plans in the time required by applicable State implementation plans and any Federal efforts to promote those programs;

(B) evaluates the extent to which the Department of Transportation's existing air quality-related transportation programs and such Department's proposed budget will achieve the goals of and compliance with this Act; and

(C) recommends what, if any, changes to such existing programs and proposed budget as well as any statutory authority relating to air quality-related transportation programs that would improve the achievement of the goals of and compliance with the Clean Air Act.

[§108(f)(3) added by PL 101–549]

(4) In each report to Congress after the first report required under paragraph (3), the Secretary of Transportation shall include a description of the actions taken to implement the changes recommended in the preceding report.

[§108(f)(4) added by PL 101–549]

(g) Assessment of Risks to Ecosystems. —The Administrator may assess the risks to ecosystems from exposure to criteria air pollutants (as identified by the Administrator in the Administrator's sole discretion).

[§108(g) added by PL 101–549]

(h) RACT/BACT/LAER Clearinghouse. —The Administrator shall make information regarding emission control technology available to the States and to the general public through a central database. Such information shall include all control technology information received pursuant to State plan provisions requiring permits for sources, including operating permits for existing sources.

[§108(h) added by PL 101–549]

§7409. National Ambient Air Quality Standards [Sec. 109]

(a) (1) The Administrator—

(A) within 30 days after the date of enactment of the Clean Air Amendments of 1970, shall publish proposed regulations prescribing a national primary ambient air quality standard and a national secondary ambient air quality standard for each air pollutant for which air quality critera have been issued prior to such date of enactment; and

(B) after a reasonable time for interested persons to submit written comments thereon (but no later than 90 days after the initial publication of such proposed standards) shall by regulation promulgate such proposed national primary and secondary ambient air quality standards with such modifications as he deems appropriate.

(2) With respect to any air pollutant for which air quality criteria are issued after the date of enactment of the Clean Air Amendments of 1970, the Administrator shall publish, simultaneously with the issuance of such criteria and information, proposed national primary and secondary ambient air quality standards for any such pollutant. The procedure provided for in paragraph (1)(B) of this subsection shall apply to the promulgation of such standards.

(b) (1) National primary ambient air quality standards, prescribed under subsection (a) shall be ambient air quality standards the attainment and maintenance of which in the judgment of the Administrator, based on such criteria and allowing an adequate margin of safety, are requisite to protect the public health. Such primary standards may be revised in the same manner as promulgated.

(2) Any national secondary ambient air quality standard prescribed under subsection (a) shall specify a level of air quality the attainment and maintenance of which in the judgment of the Administrator, based on such criteria, is requisite to protect the public welfare from any known or anticipated adverse effects associated with the presence of such air pollutant in the ambient air. Such secondary stan dards may be revised in the same manner as promulgated.

(c) The Administrator shall, not later than one year after the date of the enactment of the Clean Air Act Amendments of 1977, promulgate a national primary ambient air quality standard for NO_2concentrations over a period of not more than 3 hours unless, based on the criteria issued under section 108(c) , he finds that there is no significant evidence that such a standard for such a period is requisite to protect public health.

[§109(c) added by PL 95–95]

(d) (1) Not later than December 31, 1980, and at five year intervals thereafter, the Administrator shall complete a thorough review of the criteria published under section 108 and the national ambient air quality standards promulgated under this section and shall make such revisions in such criteria and standards and promulgate such new standards as may be appropriate in accordance with section 108 and subsection (b) of this section. The Administrator may review and revise criteria or promulgate new standards earlier or more frequently than required under this paragraph.

(2) (A) The Administrator shall appoint an independent scientific review committee composed of seven members including at least one member of the National Academy of Sciences, one physician, and one person, representing State air pollution control agencies.

(B) Not later than January 1, 1980, and at five-year intervals thereafter, the committee referred to in subparagraph (A) shall complete a review of the criteria published under section 108 and the national primary and secondary ambient air quality standards promulgated under this section and shall recommend to the Administrator any new national ambient air quality-standards and revisions of existing criteria and standards as may be appropriate under section 108 and subsection (b) of this section.

(C) Such committee shall also

(i) advise the Administrator of areas in which additional knowledge is required to appraise the adequacy and basis of existing, new, or revised national ambient air quality standards,

(ii) describe the research efforts necessary to provide the required information,

(iii) advise the Administrator on the relative contribution to air pollution concentrations of natural as well as anthropogenic activity, and

(iv) advise the Administrator of any adverse public health, welfare, social, economic, or energy effects which may result from various strategies for attainment and maintenance of such national ambient air quality standards.

[§109(d) added by PL 95–95]

§7410. Implementation Plans [Sec. 110]

(a) (1) Each State shall, after reasonable notice and public hearings, adopt and submit to the Administrator, within 3 years (or such shorter period as the Administrator may prescribe) after the promulgation of a national primary ambient air quality standard (or any revision thereof) under section 109 for any air pollutant, a plan which provides for implementation, maintenance, and enforcement of such primary standard in each air quality control region (or portion thereof) within such State. In addition, such State shall adopt and submit to the Administrator (either as a part of a plan submitted under the preceding sentence or separately) within 3 years (or such shorter period as the Administrator may prescribe) after the promulgation of a national ambient air quality secondary standard (or revision thereof), a plan which provides for implementation, maintenance, and enforcement of such secondary standard in each air quality control region (or portion thereof) within such State. Unless a separate public hearing is provided, each State shall consider its plan implementing such secondary standard at the hearing required by the first sentence of this paragraph.

[§110(a)(1) amended by PL 101–549]

(2) Each implementation plan submitted by a State under this Act shall be adopted by the State after reasonable notice and public hearing. Each such plan shall—

(A) include enforceable emission limitations and other control measures, means, or techniques (including economic incentives such as fees, marketable permits, and auctions of emissions rights), as well as schedules and timetables for compliance, as may be necessary or appropriate to meet the applicable requirements of this Act;

(B) provide for establishment and operation of appropriate devices, methods, systems, and procedures necessary to—

(i) monitor, compile, and analyze data on ambient air quality, and

(ii) upon request, make such data available to the Administrator;

(C) include a program to provide for the enforcement of the measures described in subparagraph (A), and regulation of the modification and construction of any stationary source within the areas covered by the plan as necessary to assure that national ambient air quality standards are achieved, including a permit program as required in parts C and D;

(D) contain adequate provisions—

(i) prohibiting, consistent with the provisions of this title, any source or other type of emissions activity within the State from emitting any air pollutant in amounts which will—

(I) contribute significantly to nonattainment in, or interfere with maintenance by, any other State with respect to any such national primary or secondary ambient air quality standard, or

(II) interfere with measures required to be included in the applicable implementation plan for any other State under part C to prevent significant deterioration of air quality or to protect visibility,

(ii) insuring compliance with the applicable requirements of sections 126 and 115 (relating to interstate and international pollution abatement);

(E) provide (i) necessary assurances that the State (or, except where the Administrator deems inappropriate, the general purpose local government or governments, or a regional agency designated by the State or general purpose local governments for such purpose) will have adequate personnel, funding, and authority under State (and, as appropriate, local) law to carry out such implementation plan (and is not prohibited by any provision of Federal or State law from carrying out such implementation plan or portion thereof), (ii) requirements that the State comply with the requirements respecting State boards under section 128, and (iii) necessary assurances that, where the State has relied on a local or regional government, agency, or instrumentality for the implementation of any plan provision, the State has responsibility for ensuring adequate implementation of such plan provision;

(F) require, as may be prescribed by the Administrator—

(i) the installation, maintenance, and replacement of equipment, and the implementation of other necessary steps, by owners or operators of stationary sources to monitor emissions from such sources,

(ii) periodic reports on the nature and amounts of emissions and emissions-related data from such sources, and

(iii) correlation of such reports by the State agency with any emission limitations or standards established pursuant to this Act, which reports shall be available at reasonable times for public inspection;

(G) provide for authority comparable to that in section 303 and adequate contingency plans to implement such authority;

(H) provide for revision of such plan—

(i) from time to time as may be necessary to take account of revisions of such national primary or secondary ambient air quality standard or the availability of improved or more expeditious methods of attaining such standard, and

(ii) except as provided in paragraph (3)(C), whenever the Administrator finds on the basis of information available to the Administrator that the plan is substantially inadequate to attain the national ambient air quality standard which it implements or to otherwise comply with any additional requirements established under this Act;

(I) in the case of a plan or plan revision for an area designated as a nonattainment area, meet the applicable requirements of part D (relating to nonattainment areas);

(J) meet the applicable requirements of section 121 (relating to consultation), section 127 (relating to public notification), and part C (relating to prevention of significant deterioration of air quality and visibility protection);

(K) provide for—

(i) the performance of such air quality modeling as the Administrator may prescribe for the purpose of predicting the effect on ambient air quality of any emissions of any air pollutant for which the Administrator has established a national ambient air quality standard, and

(ii) the submission, upon request, of data related to such air quality modeling to the Administrator;

(L) require the owner or operator of each major stationary source to pay to the permitting authority, as a condition of any permit required under this Act, a fee sufficient to cover—

(i) the reasonable costs of reviewing and acting upon any application for such a permit, and

(ii) if the owner or operator receives a permit for such source, the reasonable costs of implementing and enforcing the terms and conditions of any such permit (not including any court costs or other costs associated with any enforcement action), until such fee requirement is superseded with respect to such sources by the Administrator's approval of a fee program under title V; and

(M) provide for consultation and participation by local political subdivisions affected by the plan.

[§110(a)(2) revised by PL 101–549]

(3) (A) [Deleted]

[§110(a)(3)(A) deleted by PL 101–549]

(B) As soon as practicable, the Administrator shall, consistent with the purposes of this Act and the Energy Supply and Environmental Coordination Act of 1974, review each State's applicable implementation plans and report to the State on whether such plans can be revised in relation to fuel burning stationary sources (or persons supply fuel to such sources) without interfering with the attainment and maintenance of any national ambient air quality standard within the period permitted in this section. If the Administrator determines that any such plan can be revised, he shall notify the State that a plan revision may be submitted by the State. Any plan revision which is submitted by the State shall, after public notice and opportunity for public hearing, be approved by the Administrator if the revision relates only to fuel burning stationary sources (or persons supplying fuel to such sources), and the plan as revised complies with paragraph (2) of this subsection. The Administrator shall approve or disapprove any revision no later than three months after its submission.

[§110(a)(3)(B) added by PL 93–319]

(C) Neither the State, in the case of a plan (or portion thereof) approved under this subsection, nor the Administrator, in the case of a plan (or portion thereof) promulgated under subsection (c), shall be required to revise an applicable implementation plan because one or more exemptions under section 118 (relating to Federal facilities), enforcement orders under section 113(d) , suspensions under section 110(f) or (g) (relating to temporary energy or economic authority), orders under section 119 (relating to primary nonferrous smelters), or extensions of compliance in decrees entered under section 113(e) (relating to iron- and steel-producing operations) have been granted, if such plan would have met the requirements of this section if no such exemptions, orders, or extensions had been granted.

[§110(a)(3)(C) added by PL 95–95; amended by PL 97–23]

(D) [Deleted]

[§110(a)(3)(D) deleted by PL 101–549]

(4) [Deleted]

[§110(a)(4) deleted by PL 101–549]

(5) (A) (i) Any State may include in a State implementation plan, but the Administrator may not require as a condition of approval of such plan under this section, any indirect source review program. The Administrator may approve and enforce, as part of an applicable implementation plan, an indirect source review program which the State chooses to adopt and submit as part of its plan.

(ii) Except as provided in subparagraph (B), no plan promulgated by the Administrator shall include any indirect source review program for any air quality control region, or portion thereof.

(iii) Any State may revise an applicable implementation plan approved under section 110(a) to suspend or revoke any such program included in such plan, provided that such plan meets the requirements of this section.

(B) The Administrator shall have the authority to promulgate, implement and enforce regulations under section 110(c) respecting indirect source review programs which apply only to federally assisted highways, airports, and other major federally assisted indirect sources and federally owned or operated indirect sources.

(C) For purposes of this paragraph, the term "indirect source" means a facility, building, structure, installation, real property, road, or highway which attracts, or may attract, mobile sources of pollution. Such term includes parking lots, parking garages, and other facilities subject to any measure for management of parking supply (within the meaning of section 110(c)(2)(D)(ii)), including regulation of existing off-street parking but such term does not include new or existing on-street parking. Direct emissions sources or facilities at, within, or associated with, any indirect source shall not be deemed indirect sources for the purpose of this paragraph.

(D) For purposes of this section the term "indirect source review program" means the facility-by-facility review of indirect sources of air pollution, including such measures as are necessary to assure, or assist in assuring, that a new or modified indirect source will not attract mobile sources of air pollution, the emissions from which would cause or contribute to air pollution concentrations—

(i) exceeding any national primary ambient air quality standard for a mobile source-related air pollutant after the primary standard attainment date, or

(ii) preventing maintenance of any such standard after such date.

(E) For purposes of this paragraph and paragraph (2)(B), the term "transportation control measure" does not include any measure which is an "indirect source review program".

[§110(a)(5) added by PL 95–95]

(6) No State plan shall be treated as meeting the requirements of this section unless such plan provides that in the case of any source which uses a supplemental, or intermittent control system for purposes of meeting the requirements of an order under section 113(d) or section 119 (relating to primary nonferrous smelter orders), the owner or operator of such source may not temporarily reduce the pay of any employee by reason of the use of such supplemental or intermittent or other dispersion dependent control system.

[§110(a)(6) added by PL 95–95]

(b) The Administrator may, wherever he determines necessary, extend the period for submission of any plan or portion thereof which implements a national secondary ambient air quality standard for a period not to exceed 18 months from the date otherwise required for submission of such plan.

(c) (1) The Administrator shall promulgate a Federal implementation plan at any time within 2 years after the Administrator—

[§110(c) revised by PL 93–319and further amended by PL 95–95; PL 101–549]

(A) finds that a State has failed to make a required submission or finds that the plan or plan revision submitted by the State does not satisfy the minimum criteriaestablished under section 110(k)(1)(A), or

(B) disapproves a State implementation plan submission in whole or in part, unless the State corrects the deficiency, and the Administrator approves the plan or plan revision, before the Administrator promulgates such Federal implementation plan.

(2) (A) [Deleted]

[§110(c)(2)(A) deleted by PL 101–549]

(B) No parking surcharge regulation may be required by the Administrator under paragraph (1) of this subsection as a part of an applicable implementation plan. All parking surcharge regulations previously required by the Administrator shall be void upon the date of enactment of this subparagraph. This subparagraph shall not prevent the Administrator from approving parking surcharges if they are adopted and submitted by a State as part of an applicable implementation plan. The Administrator may not condition approval of any implementation plan submitted by a State on such plan's including a parking surcharge regulation.

(C) [Deleted]

[§110(c)(2)(C) deleted by PL 101–549]

(D) For purposes of this paragraph—

(i) The term "parking surcharge regulation" means a regulation imposing or requiring the imposition of any tax, surchange, fee, or other charge on parking spaces, or any other area used for the temporary storage of motor vehicles.

(ii) The term "management of parking supply" shall include any requirement providing that any new facility containing a given number of parking spaces shall receive a permit or other prior approval, issuance of which is to be conditioned on air quality considerations.

(iii) The term "preferential bus/carpool lane" shall include any requirement for the setting aside of one or more lanes of a street or highway on a permanent or temporary basis for the exclusive use of buses or carpools, or both.

(E) No standard, plan, or requirement, relating to management of parking supply or preferential bus/carpool lanes shall be promulgated after the date of enactment to this paragraph by the Administrator pursuant to this section, unless such promulgation has been subjected to at least one public hearing which has been held in the area affected and for which reasonable notice has been given in such area. If substantial changes are made following public hearings, one or more additional hearings shall be held in such area after such notice.

(3) Upon application of the chief executive officer of any general purpose unit of local government, if the Administrator determines that such unit has adequate authority under State or local law, the Administrator may delegate to such unit the authority to implement and enforce within the jurisdiction of such unit any part of a plan promulgated under this subsection. Nothing in this paragraph shall prevent the Administrator from implementing or enforcing any applicable provision of a plan promulgated under this subsection.

[§110(c)(3) added by PL 95–95]

(4) [Deleted]

[§110(c)(4) deleted by PL 101–549]

(5) (A) Any measure in an applicable implementation plan which requires a toll or other charge for the use of a bridge located entirely within one city shall be eliminated from such plan by the Administrator upon application by the Governor of the State, which applica-

tion shall include a certification by the Governor that he will revise such plan in accordance with subparagraph (B).

(B) In the case of any applicable implementation plan with respect to which a measure has been eliminated under subparagraph (A), such plan shall, not later than one year after the date of the enactment of this subparagraph be revised to include comprehensive measures to:

[§110(c)(5)(B) amended by PL 101–549]

(i) establish, expand, or improve public transportation measures to meet basic transportation needs, as expeditiously as is practicable; and

(ii) implement transportation control measures necessary to attain and maintain national ambient air quality standards, and such revised plan shall, for the purpose of implementing such comprehensive public transportation measures, include requirements to use (insofar as is necessary) Federal grants, State or local funds, or any combination of such grants and funds as may be consistent with the terms of the legislation providing such grants and funds. Such measures shall, as a substitute for the tolls or charges eliminated under subparagraph (A), provide for emissions reductions equivalent to the reductions which may reasonably be expected to be achieved through the use of the tolls or charges eliminated.

(C) Any revision of an implementation plan for purposes of meeting the requirements of subparagraph (B) shall be submitted in coordination with any plan revision required under part D.

[§110(c)(5)(C) added by PL 95–95]

(d) [Deleted]

(e) [Deleted]

[§110(d) and (e) deleted by PL 101–549]

(f) (1) Upon application by the owner or operator of a fuel burning stationary source, and after notice and opportunity for public hearing, the Governor of the State in which such source is located may petition the President to determine that a national or regional energy emergency exists of such severity that—

(A) a temporary suspension of any part of the applicable implementation plan or any requirement under section 411 (concerning excess emissions penalties or offsets) of title IV of the Act may be necessary, and

(B) other means of responding to the energy emergency may be inadequate.

Such determination shall not be delegable by the President to any other person. If the President determines that a national or regional energy emergency of such severity exists, a temporary emergency suspension of any part of an applicable implementation plan adopted by the State may be issued by the Governor of any State covered by the President's determination under the conditions specified in paragraph (2) and may take effect immediately.

[§110(f)(1) amended by PL 101–549]

(2) A temporary emergency suspension under this subsection shall be issued to a source only if the Governor of such State finds that—

(A) there exists in the vicinity of such source a temporary energy emergency involving high levels of unemployment or loss of necessary energy supplies for residential dwellings; and

(B) such unemployment or loss can be totally or partially alleviated by such emergency suspension. Not more than one such suspension may be issued for any source on the basis of the same set of circumstances or on the basis of the same emergency.

(3) A temporary emergency suspension issued by a Governor under this subsection shall remain in effect for a maximum of four months or such lesser period as may be specified in a disapproval order of the Administrator, if any. The Administrator may disapprove such suspension if he determines that it does not meet the requirements of paragraph (2).

(4) This subsection shall not apply in the case of a plan provision or requirement promulgated by the Administrator under subsection (c) of this section, but in any such case the President may grant a temporary emergency suspension for a four month period of any such provision or requirement if he makes the determinations and findings specified in paragraphs (1) and (2).

(5) The Governor may include in any temporary emergency suspension issued under this subsection a provision delaying for a period identical to the period of such suspension any compliance schedule (or increment of progress) to which such source is subject under section 119 , as in effect before the date of the enactment of this paragraph or section 113(d) of this Act, upon a finding that such source is unable to comply with such schedule (or increment) solely because of the conditions on the

basis of which a suspension was issued under this subsection.

[§110(f) amended by PL 95–95]

(g) (1) In the case of any State which has adopted and submitted to the Administrator a proposed plan revision which the State determines—

(A) meets the requirements of this section, and

(B) is necessary (i) to prevent the closing for one year or more of any source of air pollution, and (ii) to prevent substantial increases in unemployment which would result from such closing, and which the Administrator has not approved or disapproved under this section within 12 months of submission of the proposed plan revision, the Governor may issue a temporary emergency suspension of the part of the applicable implementation plan for such State which is proposed to be revised with respect to such source. The determination under subparagraph (B) may not be made with respect to a source which would close without regard to whether or not the proposed plan revision is approved.

[§110(g)(1) amended by PL 101–549]

(2) A temporary emergency suspension issued by a Governor under this subsection shall remain in effect for a maximum of four months or such lesser period as may be specified in a disapproval order of the Administrator. The Administrator may disapprove such suspension if he determines that it does not meet the requirements of this subsection.

(3) The Governor may include in any temporary emergency suspension issued under this subsection a provision delaying for a period identical to the period of such suspension any compliance schedule (or increment of progress) to which such source is subject under section 119 as in effect before the date of the enactment of this paragraph or section 113(d) upon a finding that such source is unable to comply with such schedule (or increment) solely because of the conditions on the basis of which a suspension was issued under this subsection.

(h) (1) Not later than 5 years, after the date of the enactment of the Clean Air Act Amendments of 1990 and every three years thereafter, the Administrator shall assemble and publish a comprehensive document for each State setting forth all requirements of the applicable implementation plan for such State and shall publish notice in the Federal Register of the availability of such documents.

[§110(h)(1) amended by PL 101–549]

(2) The Administrator may promulgate such regul/ations as may be reasonably necessary to carry out the purpose of this subsection.

[Former §110(g) added by PL 95–95; redesignated as (h) by PL 95–190; amended by PL 101–549]

(i) Except for a primary nonferrous smelter order under section 119 , a suspension under section 110(f) or (g) (relating to emergency suspensions), an exemption under section 118 (relating to Federal facilities), an order under section 113(d) (relating to compliance orders), a plan promulgation under section 110(c), or a plan revision under section 110(a)(3) , no order, suspension, plan revision, or other action modifying any requirement of an applicable implementation plan may be taken with respect to any stationary source by the State or by the Administrator.

[Former §110(h) added by PL 95–95; redesignated as (i) by PL 95–190]

(j) As a condition for issuance of any permit required under this title, the owner or operator of each new or modified stationary source which is required to obtain such a permit must show to the satisfaction of the permitting authority that the technology system of continuous emission reduction which is to be used at will enable such source to comply with the standards of performance which are to apply to such source and that the construction or modification and operation of such source will be in compliance with all other requirements of this Act.

[Former §110(i) added by PL 95–95; redesignated as (j) by PL 95–190]

(k) Environmental Protection Agency Action on Plan Submissions —

(1) Completeness of Plan Submissions. —

(A) Completeness Criteria. — Within 9 months after the date of the enactment of the Clean Air Amendments of 1990, the Administrator shall promulgate minimum criteria that any plan submission must meet before the Administrator is required to act on such submission under this subsection. The criteria shall be limited to the information necessary to enable the Administrator to determine whether the plan submission complies with the provisions of this Act.

(B) Completeness Finding. — Within 60 days of the Administrator's receipt of a plan or plan revision, but no later than 6 months after the date, if any, by which a State is required to submit the plan or revision, the Administrator shall determine whether the minimum criteria established pursuant to subparagraph (A) have been met. Any plan or plan revision that a State submits to the Administrator, and that has not been determined by the Administrator (by the date 6 months after receipt of the submission) to have failed to meet the minimum criteria established pursuant to subparagraph (A), shall on that date be deemed by operation of law to meet such minimum criteria.

(C) Effect of Finding of Incompleteness. — Where the Administrator determines that a plan submission (or part thereof) does not meet the minimum criteria established pursuant to subparagraph (A), the State shall be treated as not having made the submission (or, in the Administrator's discretion, part thereof).

(2) Deadline for Action. — Within 12 months of a determination by the Administrator (or a determination deemed by operation of law) under paragraph (1) that a State has submitted a plan or plan revision (or, in the Administrator's discretion, part thereof) that meets the minimum criteria established pursuant to paragraph (1), if applicable (or, if those criteria are not applicable, within 12 months of submission of the plan or revision), the Administrator shall act on the submission in accordance with paragraph (3).

(3) Full and Partial Approval and Disapproval. — In the case of any submittal on which the Administrator is required to act under paragraph (2), the Administrator shall approve such submittal as a whole if it meets all of the applicable requirements of this Act. If a portion of the plan revision meets all the applicable requirements of this Act, the Administrator may approve the plan revision in part and disapprove the plan revision in part. The plan revision shall not be treated as meeting the requirements of this Act until the Administrator approves the entire plan revision as complying with the applicable requirements of this Act.

(4) Conditional Approval. — The Administrator may approve a plan revision based on a commitment of the State to adopt specific enforceable measures by a date certain, but not later than 1 year after the date of approval of the plan revision. Any such conditional approval shall be treated as a disapproval if the State fails to comply with such commitment.

(5) Calls for Plan Revisions. — Whenever the Administrator finds that the applicable implementation plan for any area is substantially inadequate to attain or maintain the relevant national ambient air quality standard, to mitigate adequately the interstate pollutant transport described in section 176A or section 184 , or to otherwise comply with any requirement of this Act, the Administrator shall require the State to revise the plan as necessary to correct such inadequacies. The Administrator shall notify the State of the inadequacies, and may establish reasonable deadlines (not to exceed 18 months after the date of such notice) for the submission of such plan revisions. Such findings and notice shall be public. Any finding under this paragraph shall, to the extent the Administrator deems appropriate, subject the State to the requirements of this Act to which the State was subject when it developed and submitted the plan for which such finding was made, except that the Administrator may adjust any dates applicable under such requirements as appropriate (except that the Administrator may not adjust any attainment date prescribed under part D, unless such date has elapsed).

(6) Corrections. — Whenever the Administrator determines that the Administrator's action approving, disapproving, or promulgating any plan or plan revision (or part thereof), area designation, redesignation, classification, or reclassification was in error, the Administrator may in the same manner as the approval, disapproval, or promulgation revise such action as appropriate without requiring any further submission from the State. Such determination and the basis thereof shall be provided to the State and public.

[§110(k) added by PL 101–549]

(l) Plan Revisions. — Each revision to an implementation plan submitted by a State under this Act shall be adopted by such State after reasonable notice and public hearing. The Administrator shall not approve a revision of a plan if the revision would interfere with any applicable requirement concerning attainment and reasonable further progress (as defined in section 171), or any other applicable requirement of this Act.

[§110(l) added by PL 101–549]

(m) Sanctions. — The Administrator may apply any of the sanctions listed in section 179(b) at any time (or at any time after) the Administrator makes a finding, disapproval, or determination under paragraphs (1) through (4), respectively, of section 179(a) in relation to any plan or plan item (as that term is defined by the Administrator) required under this Act, with respect to any portion of the State the Administrator determines reasonable and appropriate, for the purpose of ensuring that the requirements of this Act relating to such plan or plan item are met. The Administrator shall, by rule, establish criteria for exercising his authority under the previous sentence with respect to any deficiency referred to in section 179(a) to ensure that, during the 24–month period following the finding, disapproval, or determination referred to in section 179(a), such sanctions are not applied on a statewide basis where one or more political subdivisions covered by the applicable implementation plan are principally responsible for such deficiency.

[§110(m) added by PL 101–549]

(n) Savings Clauses. —

(1) Existing Plan Provisions. — Any provision of any applicable implementation plan that was approved or promulgated by the Administrator pursuant to this section as in effect before the date of the enactment of the Clean Air Act Amendments of 1990 shall remain in effect as part of such applicable implementation plan, except to the extent that a revision to such provision is approved or promulgated by the Administrator pursuant to this Act.

(2) Attainment Dates. — For any area not designated non-attainment, any plan or plan revision submitted or required to be submitted by a State—

(A) in response to the promulgation or revision of a national primary ambient air quality standard in effect on the date of the enactment of the Clean Air Act Amendments of 1990, or

(B) in response to a finding of substantial inadequacy under subsection (a)(2) (as in effect immediately before the date of the enactment of the Clean Air Act Amendments of 1990), shall provide for attainment of the national primary ambient air quality standards within 3 years of the date of the enactment of the Clean Air Act Amendments of 1990 or within 5 years of issuance of such finding of substantial inadequacy, whichever is later.

(3) Retention of Construction Moratorium in Certain Areas. — In the case of an area to which, immediately before the date of the enactment of the Clean Air Act Amendments of 1990, the prohibition on construction or modification of major stationary sources prescribed in subsection (a)(2)(I) (as in effect immediately before the date of the enactment of the Clean Air Act Amendments of 1990) applied by virtue of a finding of the Administrator that the State containing such area had not submitted an implementation plan meeting the requirements of section 172(b)(6) (relating to establishment of a permit program) (as in effect immediately before the date of enactment of the Clean Air Act Amendments of 1990) or 172(a)(1) (to the extent such requirements relate to provision for attainment of the primary national ambient air quality standard for sulfur oxides by December 31, 1982) as in effect immediately before the date of the enactment of the Clean Air Act Amendments of 1990, no major stationary source of the relevant air pollutant or pollutants shall be constructed or modified in such area until the Administrator finds that the plan for such area meets the applicable requirements of section 172(c)(5) (relating to permit programs) or subpart 5 of part D (relating to attainment of the primary national ambient air quality standard for sulfur dioxide), respectively.

[§110(n) added by PL 101–549]

(o) Indian Tribes. — If an Indian tribe submits an implementation plan to the Administrator pursuant to section 301(d) , the plan shall be reviewed in accordance with the provisions for review set forth in this section for State plans, except as otherwise provided by regulation promulgated pursuant to section 301(d)(2). When such plan becomes effective in accordance with the regulations promulgated under section 301(d), the plan shall become applicable to all areas (except as expressly provided otherwise in the plan) located within the exterior boundaries of the reservation, notwithstanding the issuance of any patent and including rights-of-way running through the reservation.

[§110(o) added by PL 101–549]

(p) Reports. — Any State shall submit, according to such schedule as the Administrator may prescribe, such reports as the Administrator may require relating to emission reductions, vehicle miles traveled, congestion levels, and any other information the Administrator may deem necessary to assess the development effectiveness, need for revision, or implementation of any plan or plan revision required under this Act.

[§110(p) added by PL 101–549]

§7411. Standards of Performance for New Stationary Sources [Sec. 111]

(a) For purposes of this section:

(1) The term 'standard of performance' means a standard for emissions of air pollutants which reflects the degree of emission limitation achievable through the application of the best system of emission reduction which (taking into account the cost of achieving such reduction and any nonair quality health and environmental impact and energy requirements) the Administrator determines has been adequately demonstrated.

(2) The term 'new source' means any stationary source, the construction or modification of which is commenced after the publication of regulations (or, if earlier, proposed regulations) prescribing a standard of performance under this section which will be applicable to such source.

(3) The term 'stationary source' means any building, structure, facility, or installation which emits or may emit any air pollutant. Nothing in Title II of this Act relating to nonroad engines shall be construed to apply to stationary internal combustion engines.

[§111(a)(3) amended by PL 101–549]

(4) The term 'modification' means any physical change in, or change in the method of operation of, a stationary source which increases the amount of any air pollutant emitted by such source or which results in the emission of any air pollutant not previously emitted.

(5) The term 'owner or operator' means any person who owns, leases, operates, controls, or supervises a stationary source.

(6) The term 'existing source' means any stationary source other than a new source.

(7) The term 'technological system of continuous emission reduction' means—

(A) a technological process for production or operation by any source which is inherently lowpolluting or nonpolluting, or

(B) a technological system for continuous reduction of the pollution generated by a source before such pollution is emitted into the ambient air, including precombustion cleaning or treatment of fuels.

[§111(a)(7) added by PL 95–95]

(8) A conversion to coal (A) by reason of an order under section 2(a) of the Energy Supply and Environmental Coordination Act of 1974 or any amendment thereto, or any subsequent enactment which supersedes such Act, or (B) which qualifies under section 113(d)(5)(A)(ii) of this Act, shall not be deemed to be a modification for purposes of paragraphs (2) and (4) of this subsection.

[PL 95–95added two subsections (a)(7). The second (a)(7) was redesignated as (8) by PL 95–190]

(b) (1) (A) The Administrator shall, within 90 days after the date of enactment of the Clean Air Amendments of 1970, publish (and from time to time thereafter shall revise) a list of categories of stationary sources. He shall include a category of sources in such list if in his judgment he determines it causes, or contributes significantly to air pollution which may reasonably be anticipated to endanger public health or welfare.

(B) Within one year after the inclusion of a category of stationary sources in a list under subparagraph (A), the Administrator shall publish proposed regulations, establishing Federal standards of performance for new sources within such category. The Administrator shall afford interested persons an opportunity for written comment on such proposed regulations. After considering such comments, he shall promulgate, within one year after such publication, such standards with such modifications as he deems appropriate. The Administrator shall, at least every 8 years, review and, if appropriate, revise such standards following the procedure required by this subsection for promulgation of such standards. Notwithstanding the requirements of the previous sentence, the Administrator need not review any such standard if the Administrator determines that such review is not appropriate in light of readily available information on the efficacy of such standard. Standards of performance on revisions thereof shall become effective upon promulgation. When implementation and enforcement of any requirement of this Act indicate that emission limitations and percent reductions beyond those required by the standards promulgated under this section are achieved in practice, the Administrator shall, when revising standards promulgated under this section, consider the emission limitations and percent reductions achieved in practice.

[§111(b)(1)(B) amended by PL 95–95; PL 101–549]

(2) The Administrator may distinguish among classes, types, and sizes within categories of new sources for the purposes of establishing such standards.

(3) The Administrator shall, from time to time, issue information on pollution control techniques for categories of new sources and air pollutants subject to the provisions of this section.

(4) The provisions of this section shall apply to any new sources owned or operated by the United States.

(5) Except as otherwise authorized under subsection (h), nothing in this section shall be construed to require, or to authorize the Administrator to require any new or modified source to install and operate any particular technological system of continuous emission reduction to comply with any new source standard of performance.

[§111(b)(5) added by PL 95–95]

(6) The revised standards of performance required by enactment of subsection (a)(1)(A)(i) and (ii) shall be promulgated not later than one year after enactment of this paragraph. Any new or modified fossil fuel fired stationary source which commences construction prior to the date of publication of the proposed revised standards shall not be required to comply with such revised standards.

[§111(b)(6) added by PL 95–95]

(c) (1) Each state may develop and submit to the Administrator a procedure for implementing and enforcing standards of performance for new sources located in such State. If the Administrator finds the State procedure is adequate, he shall delegate to such State any authority he has under this Act to implement and enforce such standards.

[§111(c)(1) amended by PL 95–95]

(2) Nothing in this subsection shall prohibit the Administrator from enforcing any applicable standard of performance under this section.

(d) (1) The Administrator shall prescribe regulations which shall establish a procedure similar to that provided by section 110 under which each State shall submit to the Administrator a plan which (A) establishes standards of performance for any existing source for any air pollutant (i) for which air quality criteria have not been issued or which is not included on a list published under section 108(a) or emitted from a source category which is regulated under section 112(b) but (ii) to which a standard of performance under this section would apply if such existing source were a new source, and (B) provides for the implementation and enforcement of such standards of performance. Regulations of the Administrator under this paragraph shall permit the State in applying a standard of performance to any particular source under a plan submitted under this paragraph to take into consideration, among other factors, the remaining useful life of the existing source to which such standard applies.

[§111(d)(1) amended by PL 95–95; PL 95–623; PL 101–549]

(2) The Administrator shall have the same authority—

(A) to prescribe a plan for a State in cases where the State fails to submit a satisfactory plan as he would have under section 110(c) in the case of failure to submit an implementation plan, and

(B) to enforce the provisions of such plan in cases where the State fails to enforce them as he would have under sections 113 and 114 with respect to an implementation plan.

In promulgating a standard of performance under a plan prescribed under this paragraph, the Administrator shall take into consideration, among other factors, remaining useful lives of the sources in the category of sources to which such standard applies.

(e) After the effective date of standards of performance promulgated under this section it shall be unlawful for any owner or operator of any new source to operate such source in violation of any standard of performance applicable to such source.

(f) (1) For those categories of major stationary sources that the Administrator listed under subsection (b)(1)(A) before the date of the enactment of the Clean Air Act Amendments of 1990 and for which regulations had not been proposed by the Administrator by such date, the Administrator shall—

(A) propose regulations establishing standards of performance for at least 25 percent of such categories of sources within 2 years after the date of the enactment of the Clean Air Act Amendments of 1990;

(B) propose regulations establishing standards of performance for at least 50 percent of such categories of sources within 4 years after the date of the enactment of the Clean Air Act Amendments of 1990; and

(C) propose regulations for the remaining categories of sources within 6 years after the date of the enactment of the Clean Air Act Amendments of 1990.

(2) In determining priorities for promulgating standards for categories of major stationary sources for the purpose of paragraph (1), the Administrator shall consider—

(A) the quality of air pollutant emissions which each such category will emit, or will be designed to emit;

(B) the extent to which such pollutant may reasonably be anticipated to endanger public health or welfare; and

(C) the mobility and competitive nature of each such category of sources and the consequent need for nationally applicable new source standards of performance.

(3) Before promulgating any regulations under this subsection or listing any category of major stationary sources as required under this subsection the Administrator shall consult with appropriate representatives of the Governors and of State air pollution control agencies.

[§111(f) added by PL 95–95; revised by PL 101–549]

(g) (1) Upon application by the Governor of a State showing that the Administrator has failed to specify in regulations under subsection (f)(1) any category of major stationary sources required to be specified under such regulations, the Administrator shall revise such regulations to specify any such category.

(2) Upon application of the Governor of a State, showing that any category of stationary sources which is not included in the list under subsection (b)(1)(A) contributes significantly to air pollution which may reasonably be anticipated to endanger public health or welfare (notwithstanding that such category is not a category of major stationary sources), the Administrator shall revise such regulations to specify such category of stationary sources.

(3) Upon application of the Governor of a State showing that the Administrator has failed to apply properly the criteria required to be considered under subsection (f)(2), the Administrator shall revise the list under subsection (b)(1)(A) to apply properly such criteria.

(4) Upon application of the Governor of a State showing that—

(A) a new, innovative, or improved technology or process which achieves greater continuous emission reduction has been adequately demonstrated for any category of stationary sources, and

(B) as a result of such technology or process, the new source standard of performance in effect under this section for such category no longer reflects the greatest degree of emission limitation achievable through application of the best technological system of continuous emission reduction which (taking into consideration the cost of achieving such emission reduction, and any non-air-quality health and environmental impact and energy requirements) has been adequately demonstrated, the Administrator shall revise such standard of performance for such category accordingly.

[Former §111(g)(5) and (6) removed and (7) and (8) redesignated as new (5) and (6) by PL 101–549]

(5) Unless later deadlines for action of the Administrator are otherwise prescribed under this section, the Administrator shall, not later than three months following the date of receipt of any application by a Governor of a State, either—

(A) find that such application does not contain the requisite showing and deny such application, or

(B) grant such application and take the action required under this subsection.

[§111(g)(5) amended by PL 101–549]

(6) Before taking any action required by subsection (f) or by this subsection, the Administrator shall provide notice and opportunity for public hearing.

[§111(g) added by PL 95–95]

(h) (1) For purposes of this section, if in the judgment of the Administrator, it is not feasible to prescribe or enforce a standard of performance, he may instead promulgate a design, equipment, work practice, or operational standard, or combination thereof, which reflects the best technological system of continuous emission reduction which (taking into consideration the cost of achieving such emission reduction, and any non-air quality health and environmental impact and energy requirements) the Administrator determines has been adequately demonstrated. In the event the Administrator promulgates a design or equipment standard under this subsection, he shall include as part of such standard such requirements as will assure the proper operation and maintenance of any such element of design or equipment.

(2) For the purpose of this subsection, the phrase 'not feasible to prescribe or enforce a standard of performance' means any situation in which the Administrator determines that

(A) a pollutant or pollutants cannot be emitted through a conveyance designed and constructed to emit or capture such pollutant, or that any requirement for, or use of, such conveyance would be inconsistent with any Federal, State, or local law, or (B) the application of measurement methodology to a particular class of sources is not practicable due to technological or economic limitations.

(3) If after notice and opportunity for public hearing, any person establishes to the satisfaction of the Administrator that an alternative means of emission limitation will achieve a reduction in emissions of any air pollutant at least equivalent to the reduction in emissions of such air pollutant achieved under the requirements of paragraph (1), the Administrator shall permit the use of such alternative by the source for purposes of compliance with this section with respect to such pollutant.

(4) Any standard promulgated under paragraph (1) shall be promulgated in terms of standard of performance whenever it becomes feasible to promulgate and enforce such standard in such terms.

(5) Any design, equipment, work practice, or operational standard, or any combination thereof, described in this subsection shall be treated as a standard of performance for purposes of the provisions of this Act (other than the provisions of subsection (a) and this subsection).

[§111(h) added by PL 95–95; 111(h)(5) added by PL 95–623]

(i) Any regulation promulgated by the Administrator under this section applicable to grain elevators shall not apply to country elevators (as defined by the Administrator) which have a storage capacity of less than two million five hundred thousand bushels.

[§111(i) added by PL 95–95]

(j) (1) (A) Any person proposing to own or operate a new source may request the Administrator for one or more waivers from the requirements of this section for such source or any portion thereof with respect to any air pollutant to encourage the use of an innovative technological system or systems of continuous emission reduction. The Administrator may, with the consent of the Governor of the State in which the source is to be located, grant a waiver under this paragraph, if the Administrator determines after notice and opportunity for public hearing, that—

(i) the proposed system or systems have not been adequately demonstrated,

(ii) the proposed system or systems will operate effectively and there is a substantial likelihood that such system or systems will achieve greater continuous emission reduction than that required to be achieved under the standards of performance which would otherwise apply, or achieve at least an equivalent reduction at lower cost in terms of energy, economic, or nonair quality environmental impact,

(iii) the owner or operator of the proposed source has demonstrated to the satisfaction of the Administrator that the proposed system will not cause or contribute to an unreasonable risk to public health, welfare, or safety in its operation, function, or malfunction, and

(iv) the granting of such waiver is consistent with the requirements of subparagraph (C). In making any determination under clause (ii), the Administrator shall take into account any previous failure of such system or systems to operate effectively or to meet any requirement of the new source performance standards. In determining whether an unreasonable risk exists under clause (iii), the Administrator shall consider, among other factors, whether and to what extent the use of the proposed technological system will cause, increase, reduce, or eliminate emissions of any unregulated pollutants; available methods for reducing or eliminating any risk to public health, welfare, or safety which may be associated with the use of such system; and the availability of other technological systems which may be used to conform to standards under this section without causing or contributing to such unreasonable risk. The Administrator may conduct such tests and may require the owner or operator of the proposed source to conduct such tests and provide such information as is necessary to carry out clause (iii) of this subparagraph. Such requirements shall include a requirement for prompt reporting of the emission of any unregulated pollutant from a system if such pollutant was not emitted, or was emitted in significantly lesser amounts a without use of such system.

(B) A waiver under this paragraph shall be granted on such terms and conditions as the Administrator determines to be necessary to assure—

(i) emissions from the source will not prevent attainment and maintenance of any national ambient air quality standards, and

(ii) proper functioning of the technological system or systems authorized.

Any such term or condition shall be treated as a standard of performance for the purposes of subsection (e) of this section and section 113 .

(C) The number of waivers granted under this paragraph with respect to a proposed technological system of continuous emission reduction shall not exceed such number as the Administrator finds necessary to ascertain whether or not such system will achieve the conditions specified in clauses (ii) and (iii) of subparagraph (A).

(D) A waiver under this paragraph shall extend to the sooner of—

(i) the date determined by the Administrator, after consultation with the owner or operator of the source, taking into consideration the design, installation, and capital cost of the technological system or systems being used, or

(ii) the date on which the Administrator determines that such system has failed to—

(I) achieve at least an equivalent continuous emission reduction to that required to be achieved under the standards of performance which would otherwise apply, or

(II) comply with the condition specified in paragraph (1)(A)(iii), and that such failure cannot be corrected.

(E) In carrying out subparagraph (D)(i), the Administrator shall not permit any waiver for a source or portion thereof to extend beyond the date—

(i) seven years after the date on which any waiver is granted to such source or portion thereof, or

(ii) four years after the date on which such source or portion thereof commences operation, whichever is earlier.

(F) No waiver under this subsection shall apply to any portion of a source other than the portion on which the innovative technological system or systems of continuous emission reduction is used.

(2) (A) If a waiver under paragraph (1) is terminated under clause (ii) of paragraph (1)(D), the Administrator shall grant an extension of the requirements of this section for such source for such minimum period as may be necessary to comply with the applicable standard of performance under this section. Such period shall not extend beyond the date three years from the time such waiver is terminated.

(B) An extension granted under this paragraph shall set forth emission limits and a compliance schedule containing increments of progress which require compliance with the applicable standards of performance as expeditiously as practicable and include such measures as are necessary and practicable in the interim to minimize emissions. Such schedule shall be treated as a standard of performance for purposes of subsection (e) of this section and section 113 .

[Former §111(j) and (k) added by PL 95–95; former (j) deleted and former (k) amended and redesignated as (j) by PL 95–190; amended by PL 95–623]

[Editor's Note: Sec. 403(b) and (c) of PL 101–549 provides language concerning new fossil fuel fired electric utility units. Those provisions follow.]

[Sec. 403]

(b) Revised Regulations. — Not later than three years after the date of enactment of the Clean Air Act Amendments of 1990, the Administrator shall promulgate revised regulations for standards of performance for new fossil fuel fired electric utility units commencing construction after the date on which such regulations are proposed that, at a minimum, require any source subject to such revised standards to emit sulfur dioxide at a rate not greater than would have resulted from compliance by such source with the applicable standards of performance under this section prior to such revision.

(c) Applicability. — The provisions of subsections (a) and (b) apply only so long as the provisions of section 403(e) of the Clean Air Act remain in effect.

§7412. National Emission Standards for Hazardous Air Pollutants [Sec. 112]

[§112 revised by PL 101–549]

(a) Definitions. — For purposes of this section, except subsection (r)—

(1) Major source. — The term 'major source' means any stationary source or group of stationary sources located within a contiguous area and under common control that emits or has the potential to emit considering controls, in the aggregate, 10 tons per year or more of any hazardous air pollutant or 25 tons per year or more of any combination of hazardous air pollutants. The Administrator may establish a lesser quantity, or in the case of radionuclides

different criteria, for a major source than that specified in the previous sentence, on the basis of the potency of the air pollutant, persistence, potential for bioaccumulation, other characteristics of the air pollutant, or other relevant factors.

(2) Area source. — The term 'area source' means any stationary source of hazardous air pollutants that is not a major source. For purposes of this section, the term 'area source' shall not include motor vehicles or nonroad vehicles subject to regulation under title II.

(3) Stationary source. — The term 'stationary source' shall have the same meaning as such term has under section 111(a) .

(4) New source. — The term 'new source' means a stationary source the construction or reconstruction of which is commenced after the Administrator first proposes regulations under this section establishing an emission standard applicable to such source.

(5) Modification. — The term 'modification' means any physical change in, or change in the method of operation of, a major source which increases the actual emissions of any hazardous air pollutant emitted by such source by more than a de minimis amount or which results in the emission of any hazardous air pollutant not previously emitted by more than a de minimis amount.

(6) Hazardous air pollutant. — The term 'hazardous air pollutant' means any air pollutant listed pursuant to subsection (b).

(7) Adverse environmental effect. — The term 'adverse environmental effect' means any significant and widespread adverse effect, which may reasonably be anticipated, to wildlife, aquatic life, or other natural resources, including adverse impacts on populations of endangered or threatened species or significant degradation of environmental quality over broad areas.

(8) Electric utility steam generating unit. — The term 'electric utility steam generating unit' means any fossil fuel fired combustion unit of more than 25 megawatts that serves a generator that produces electricity for sale. A unit that cogenerates steam and electricity and supplies more than one-third of its potential electric output capacity and more than 25 megawatts electrical output to any utility power distribution system for sale shall be considered an electric utility steam generating unit.

(9) Owner or operator. — The term 'owner or operator' means any person who owns, leases, operates, controls, or supervises a stationary source.

(10) Existing source. — The term 'existing source' means any stationary source other than a new source.

(11) Carcinogenic effect. — Unless revised, the term 'carcinogenic effect' shall have the meaning provided by the Administrator under Guidelines for Carcinogenic Risk Assessment as of the date of enactment. Any revisions in the existing Guidelines shall be subject to notice and opportunity for comment.

(b) List of Pollutants. — (1) Initial List. — The Congress establishes for purposes of this section a list of hazardous air pollutants as follows:

CAS number	Chemical name
75070	Acetaldehyde
60355	Acetamide
75058	Acetonitrile
98862	Acetophenone
53963	2-Acetylaminofluorene
107028	Acrolein
79061	Acrylamide
79107	Acrylic acid
107131	Acrylonitrile
107051	Allyl chloride
92671	4-Aminobiphenyl
62533	Aniline
90040	o-Anisidine
1332214	Asbestos
71432	Benzene (including benzene from gasoline)
92875	Benzidine
98077	Benzotrichloride
100447	Benzyl chloride
92524	Biphenyl
117817	Bis(2-ethylhexyl)phthalate (DEHP)
542881	Bis(chloromethyl)ether
75252	Bromoform
106990	1,3-Butadiene
156627	Calcium cyanamide
105602	Caprolactam
133062	Captan
63252	Carbaryl
75150	Carbon disulfide
56235	Carbon tetrachloride
463581	Carbonyl sulfide
120809	Catechol

CAS number	Chemical name
133904	Chloramben
57749	Chlordane
7782505	Chlorine
79118	Chloroacetic acid
532274	2-Chloroacetophenone
108907	Chlorobenzene
510156	Chlorobenzilate
67663	Chloroform
107302	Chloromethyl methyl ether
126998	Chloroprene
1319773	Cresols/Cresylic acid (isomers and mixture)
95487	o-Cresol
108394	m-Cresol
106445	p-Cresol
98828	Cumene
94757	2,4-D, salts and esters
3547044	DDE
334883	Diazomethane
132649	Dibenzofurans
96128	1,2-Dibromo-3-chloropropane
84742	Dibutylphthalate
106467	1,4-Dichlorobenzene(p)
91941	3,3-Dichlorobenzidene
111444	Dichloroethyl ether (Bis(2-chloroethyl)ether)
542756	1,3-Dichloropropene
62737	Dichlorvos
111422	Diethanolamine
121697	N,N-Diethyl aniline (N,N-Dimethylaniline)
64675	Diethyl sulfate
119904	3,3-Dimethoxybenzidine
60117	Dimethyl aminoazobenzene
119937	3,3[prime]-Dimethyl benzidine
79447	Dimethyl carbamoyl chloride
68122	Dimethyl formamide
57147	1,1-Dimethyl hydrazine
131113	Dimethyl phthalate
77781	Dimethyl sulfate
534521	4,6-Dinitro-o-cresol, and salts
51285	2,4-Dinitrophenol
121142	2,4-Dinitrotoluene
123911	1,4-Dioxane (1,4-Diethyleneoxide)
122667	1,2-Diphenylhydrazine
106898	Epichlorohydrin (1-Chloro-2,3-epoxypropane)
106887	1,2-Epoxybutane
140885	Ethyl acrylate
100414	Ethyl benzene
51796	Ethyl carbamate (Urethane)
75003	Ethyl chloride (Chloroethane)
106934	Ethylene dibromide (Dibromoethane)
107062	Ethylene dichloride (1,2-Dichloroethane)
107211	Ethylene glycol
151564	Ethylene imine (Aziridine)
75218	Ethylene oxide
96457	Ethylene thiourea
75343	Ethylidene dichloride (1,1-Dichloroethane)
50000	Formaldehyde
76448	Heptachlor
118741	Hexachlorobenzene
87683	Hexachlorobutadiene
77474	Hexachlorocyclopentadiene
67721	Hexachloroethane
822060	Hexamethylene-1,6-diisocyanate
680319	Hexamethylphosphoramide
110543	Hexane
302012	Hydrazine
7647010	Hydrochloric acid
7664393	Hydrogen fluoride (Hydrofluoric acid)
123319	Hydroquinone
78591	Isophorone
58899	Lindane (all isomers)
108316	Maleic anhydride
67561	Methanol
72435	Methoxychlor
74839	Methyl bromide (Bromomethane)
74873	Methyl chloride (Chloromethane)
71556	Methyl chloroform (1,1,1-Trichloroethane)
78933	Methyl ethyl ketone (2-Butanone)
60344	Methyl hydrazine
74884	Methyl iodide (Iodomethane)
108101	Methyl isobutyl ketone (Hexone)
624839	Methyl isocyanate
80626	Methyl methacrylate
1634044	Methyl tert butyl ether
101144	4,4-Methylene bis(2-chloroaniline)
75092	Methylene chloride (Dichloromethane)
101688	Methylene diphenyl diisocyanate (MDI)
101779	4,4[prime]-Methylenedianiline
91203	Naphthalene
98953	Nitrobenzene

CAS number	Chemical name
92933	4-Nitrobiphenyl
100027	4-Nitrophenol
79469	2-Nitropropane
684935	N-Nitroso-N-methylurea
62759	N-Nitrosodimethylamine
59892	N-Nitrosomorpholine
56382	Parathion
82688	Pentachloronitrobenzene (Quintobenzene)
87865	Pentachlorophenol
108952	Phenol
106503	p-Phenylenediamine
75445	Phosgene
7803512	Phosphine
7723140	Phosphorus
85449	Phthalic anhydride
1336363	Polychlorinated biphenyls (Arochlors)
1120714	1,3-Propane sultone
57578	beta-Propiolactone
123386	Propionaldehyde
114261	Propoxur (Baygon)
78875	Propylene dichloride (1,2-Dichloropropane)
75569	Propylene oxide
75558	1,2-Propylenimine (2-Methyl aziridine)
91225	Quinoline
106514	Quinone
100425	Styrene
96093	Styrene oxide
1746016	2,3,7,8-Tetrachlorodibenzo-p-dioxin
79345	1,1,2,2-Tetrachloroethane
127184	Tetrachloroethylene (Perchloroethylene)
7550450	Titanium tetrachloride
108883	Toluene
95807	2,4-Toluene diamine
584849	2,4-Toluene diisocyanate
95534	o-Toluidine
8001352	Toxaphene (chlorinated camphene)
120821	1,2,4-Trichlorobenzene
79005	1,1,2-Trichloroethane
79016	Trichloroethylene
95954	2,4,5-Trichlorophenol
88062	2,4,6-Trichlorophenol
121448	Triethylamine
1582098	Trifluralin

CAS number	Chemical name
540841	2,2,4-Trimethylpentane
108054	Vinyl acetate
593602	Vinyl bromide
75014	Vinyl chloride
75354	Vinylidene chloride (1,1-Dichloroethylene)
1330207	Xylenes (isomers and mixture)
95476	o-Xylenes
108383	m-Xylenes
106423	p-Xylenes
0	Antimony Compounds
0	Arsenic Compounds (inorganic including arsine)
0	Beryllium Compounds
0	Cadmium Compounds
0	Chromium Compounds
0	Cobalt Compounds
0	Coke Oven Emissions
0	Cyanide Compounds[1]
0	Glycol ethers[2]
0	Lead Compounds
0	Manganese Compounds
0	Mercury Compounds
0	Fine mineral fibers[3]
0	Nickel Compounds
0	Polycyclic Organic Matter[4]
0	Radionuclides (including radon)[5]
0	Selenium Compounds

NOTE: For all listings above which contain the word "compounds" and for glycol ethers, the following applies: Unless otherwise specified, these listings are defined as including any unique chemical substance that contains the named chemical (i.e., antimony, arsenic, etc.) as part of that chemical's infrastructure.

[1] X'CN where X = H' or any other group where a formal dissociation may occur. For example KCN or $Ca(CN)_2$

[2] Includes moni- and di- ethers of ethylene glycol, diethylene glycol, and triethylene glycol R - $(OCH2CH2)_n$ - OR' where

n = 1, 2, or 3

R = alkyl or aryl groups

R' = R, H, or groups which, when removed, yield glycol ethers with the structure: R - $(OCH2CH2)_n$ - OH. Polymers are excluded from the glycol category.

[3] Includes mineral fiber emissions from facilities manufacturing or processing glass, rock, or slag fibers (or other mineral derived fibers) of average diameter 1 micrometer or less.

[4] Includes organic compounds with more than one benzene ring, and which have a boiling point greater than or equal to 100°C.

[5] A type of atom which spontaneously undergoes radioactive decay.

[§112(b)(1) amended by PL 102–187]

(2) Revision of the List. — The Administrator shall periodically review the list established by this subsection and publish the results thereof and, where appropriate, revise such list by rule, adding pollutants which present, or may present, through inhalation or other routes of exposure, a threat of adverse human health effects (including, but not limited to, substances which are known to be, or may reasonably be anticipated to be, carcinogenic, mutagenic, teratogenic, neurotoxic, which cause reproductive dysfunction, or which are acutely or chronically toxic) or adverse environmental effects whether through ambient concentrations, bioaccumulation, deposition, or otherwise, but not including releases subject to regulation under subsection (r) as a result of emissions to the air. No air pollutant which is listed under section 108(a) may be added to the list under this section, except that the prohibition of this sentence shall not apply to any pollutant which independently meets the listing criteria of this paragraph and is a precursor to a pollutant which is listed under section 108(a) or to any pollutant which is in a class of pollutants listed under such section. No substance, practice, process or activity regulated under title VI of this Act shall be subject to regulation under this section solely due to its adverse effects on the environment.

(3) Petitions to Modify the List. —

(A) Beginning at any time after 6 months after the date of enactment of the Clean Air Act Amendments of 1990, any person may petition the Administrator to modify the list of hazardous air pollutants under this subsection by adding or deleting a substance or, in case of listed pollutants without CAS numbers (other than coke oven emissions, mineral fibers, or polycyclic organic matter) removing certain unique substances. Within 18 months after receipt of a petition, the Administrator shall either grant or deny the petition by publishing a written explanation of the reasons for the Administrator's decision. Any such petition shall include a showing by the petitioner that there is adequate data on the health or environmental defects of the pollutant or other evidence adequate to support the petition. The Administrator may not deny a petition solely on the basis of inadequate resources or time for review.

(B) The Administrator shall add a substance to the list upon a showing by the petitioner or on the Administrator's own determination that the substance is an air pollutant and that emissions, ambient concentrations, bioaccumulation or deposition of the substance are known to cause or may reasonably be anticipated to cause adverse effects to human health or adverse environmental effects.

(C) The Administrator shall delete a substance from the list upon a showing by the petitioner or on the Administrator's own determination that there is adequate data on the health and environmental effects of the substance to determine that emissions, ambient concentrations, bioaccumulation or deposition of the substance may not reasonably be anticipated to cause any adverse effects to the human health or adverse environmental effects.

(D) The Administrator shall delete one or more unique chemical substances that contain a listed hazardous air pollutant not having a CAS number (other than coke oven emissions, mineral fibers, or polycyclic organic matter) upon a showing by the petitioner or on the Administrator's own determination that such unique chemical substances that contain the named chemical of such listed hazardous air pollutant meet the deletion requirements of subparagraph (C). The Administrator must grant or deny a deletion petition prior to promulgating any emission standards pursuant to subsection (d) applicable to any source category or subcategory of a listed hazardous air pollutant without a CAS number listed under subsection (b) for which a deletion petition has been filed within 12 months of the date of enactment of the Clean Air Act Amendments of 1990.

(4) Further Information. — If the Administrator determines that information on the health or environmental effects of a substance is not sufficient to make a determination required by this subsection, the Administrator may use any authority available to the Administrator to acquire such information.

(5) Test Methods. — The Administrator may establish, by rule, test measures and other analytic procedures for monitoring and measuring emissions, ambient concentrations, deposition, and bioaccumulation of hazardous air pollutants.

(6) Prevention of Significant Deterioration. — The provisions of part C (prevention of significant deterioration) shall not apply to pollutants listed under this section.

(7) Lead. — The Administrator may not list elemental lead as a hazardous air pollutant under this subsection.

(c) List of Source Categories. —

(1) In General. — Not later than 12 months after the date of enactment of the Clean Air Act Amendments of 1990, the Administrator shall publish, and shall from time to time, but no less often than every 8 years, revise, if appropriate, in response to public comment or new information, a list of all categories and subcategories of major sources and area sources (listed under paragraph (3)) of the air pollutants listed pursuant to subsection (b). To the extent practicable, the categories and subcategories listed under this subsection shall be consistent with the list of source categories established pursuant to section 111 and part C. Nothing in the preceding sentence limits the Administrator's authority to establish subcategories under this section, as appropriate.

(2) Requirement for Emissions Standards. — For the categories and subcategories the Administrator lists, the Administrator shall establish emissions standards under subsection (d), according to the schedule in this subsection and subsection (e).

(3) Area Sources. — The Administrator shall list under this subsection each category or subcategory of area sources which the Administrator finds presents a threat of adverse effects to human health or the environment (by such sources individually or in the aggregate) warranting regulation under this section. The Administrator shall, not later than 5 years after the date of enactment of the Clean Air Act Amendments of 1990 and pursuant to subsection (k)(3)(B), list, based on actual or estimated aggregate emissions of a listed pollutant or pollutants, sufficient categories or subcategories of area sources to ensure that area sources representing 90 percent of the area source emissions of the 30 hazardous air pollutants that present the greatest threat to public health in the largest number of urban areas are subject to regulation under this section. Such regulations shall be promulgated not later than 10 years after such date of enactment.

(4) Previously Regulated Categories. —The Administrator may, in the Administrator's discretion, list any category or subcategory of sources previously regulated under this section as in effect before the date of enactment of the Clean Air Act Amendments of 1990.

(5) Additional Categories. — In addition to those categories and subcategories of sources listed for regulation pursuant to paragraphs (1) and (3), the Administrator may at any time list additional categories and subcategories of sources of hazardous air pollutants according to the same criteria for listing applicable under such paragraphs. In the case of source categories and subcategories listed after publication of the initial list required under paragraph (1) or (3), emission standards under subsection (d) for the category or subcategory shall be promulgated within 10 years after the date of enactment of the Clean Air Act Amendments of 1990, or within 2 years after the date on which such category or subcategory is listed, whichever is later.

(6) Specific Pollutants. — With respect to alkylated lead compounds, polycyclic organic matter, hexachlorobenzene, mercury, polychlorinated biphenyls, 2,3,7,8- tetrachlorodibenzofurans and 2,3,7,8-tetrachlorodibenzo-p-dioxin, the Administrator shall, not later than 5 years after the date of enactment of the Clean Air Act Amendments of 1990, list categories and subcategories of sources assuring that sources accounting for not less than 90 per centum of the aggregate emissions of each such pollutant are subject to standards under subsection (d)(2) or (d)(4). Such standards shall be promulgated not later than 10 years after such date of enactment. This paragraph shall not be construed to require the Administrator to promulgate standards for such pollutants emitted by electric utility steam generating units.

(7) Research Facilities. — The Administrator shall establish a separate category covering research or laboratory facilities, as necessary to assure the equitable treatment of such facilities. For purposes of this section, 'research or laboratory facility' means any stationary source whose primary purpose is to conduct research and development into new processes and products, where such source is operated under the close supervision of technically trained personnel and is not engaged in the manufacture of products for commercial sale in commerce, except in a de minimis manner.

(8) Boat Manufacturing. — When establishing emissions standards for styrene, the Administrator shall list boat manufacturing as a separate subcategory unless the Administrator finds that such listing would be inconsistent with the goals and requirements of this Act.

(9) Deletions from the List. —

(A) Where the sole reason for the inclusion of a source category on the list required under this subsection is the emission of a unique chemical substance, the Administrator shall delete the source category from the list if it is appropriate because of action taken under either subparagraphs (C) or (D) of subsection (b)(3).

(B) The Administrator may delete any source category from the list under this subsection, on petition of any person or on the Administrator's own motion, whenever the Administrator makes the following determination or determinations, as applicable:

(i) In the case of hazardous air pollutants emitted by sources in the category that may result in cancer in humans, a determination that no source in the category (or group of sources in the case of area sources) emits such hazardous air pollutants in quantities which may cause a lifetime risk of cancer greater than one in one million to the individual in the population who is most exposed to emissions of such pollutants from the source (or group of sources in the case of area sources).

(ii) In the case of hazardous air pollutants that may result in adverse health effects in humans other than cancer or adverse environmental effects, a determination that emissions from no source in the category or subcategory concerned (or group of sources in the case of area sources) exceed a level which is adequate to protect public health with an ample margin of safety and no adverse environmental effect will result from emissions from any source (or from a group of sources in the case of area sources).

The Administrator shall grant or deny a petition under this paragraph within 1 year after the petition is filed.

(d) Emission Standards. —

(1) In General. — The Administrator shall promulgate regulations establishing emission standards for each category or subcategory of major sources and area sources of hazardous air listed for regulation pursuant to subsection (c) in accordance with the schedules provided in subsections (c) and (e). The Administrator may distinguish among classes, types, and sizes of sources within a category or subcategory in establishing such standards except that, there shall be no delay in the compliance date for any standard applicable to any source under subsection (i) as the result of the authority provided by this sentence.

(2) Standards and Methods. — Emissions standards promulgated under this subsection and applicable to new or existing sources of hazardous air pollutants shall require the maximum degree of reduction in emissions of the hazardous air pollutants subject to this section (including a prohibition on such emissions, where achievable) that the Administrator, taking into consideration the cost of achieving such emission reduction, and any non- air quality health and environmental impacts and energy requirements, determines is achievable for new or existing sources in the category or subcategory to which such emission standard applies, through application of measures, processes, methods, systems or techniques including, but not limited to, measures which—

(A) reduce the volume of, or eliminate emissions of, such pollutants through process changes, substitution of materials or other modifications,

(B) enclose systems or processes to eliminate emissions,

(C) collect, capture or treat such pollutants when released from a process, stack, storage or fugitive emissions point,

(D) are design, equipment, work practice, or operational standards (including requirements for operator training or certification) as provided in subsection (h), or

(E) are a combination of the above. None of the measures described in subparagraph (A) through (D) shall, consistent with the provisions of section 114(c) , in any way comprise any United States patent or United States trademark right, or any confidential business information, or any trade secret or any other intellectual property right.

(3) New and Existing Sources. — The maximum degree of reduction in emissions that is deemed achievable for new sources in a category or subcategory shall not be less stringent than the emission control that is achieved in practice by the best controlled similar source, as determined by the Administrator. Emission standards promulgated under this subsection for existing sources in a category or subcategory may be less stringent than standards for new sources in the same category or subcategory but shall not be less stringent, and may be more stringent than—

(A) the average emission limitation achieved by the best performing 12 percent of the existing sources (for which the Administrator has emissions information), excluding those sources that have, within 18 months before the emission standard is proposed or within 30 months before such standard is promulgated, whichever is later, first achieved a level of emission rate or emission reduction which complies, or would comply if the source is not subject to such standard, with the low est achievable emission rate (as defined by section 171) applicable to the source category and prevailing at the time, in the category or subcategory for categories and subcategories with 30 or more sources, or

(B) the average emission limitation achieved by the best performing 5 sources (for which the Administrator has or could reasonably obtain emissions information) in the category or subcategory for categories or subcategories with fewer than 30 sources.

(4) Health Threshold. — With respect to pollutants for which a health threshold has been established, the Administrator may consider such threshold level, with an ample margin of safety, when establishing emission standards under this subsection.

(5) Alternative Standard for Area Sources. — With respect only to categories and subcategories of area sources listed pursuant to subsection (c), the Administrator may, in lieu of the authorities provided in paragraph (2) and subsection (f), elect to promulgate standards or requirements applicable to sources in such categories or subcategories which provide for the use of generally available control technologies or management practices by such sources to reduce emissions of hazardous air pollutants.

(6) Review and Revision. — The Administrator shall review, and revise as necessary (taking into account developments in practices, processes, and control technologies), emission standards promulgated under this section no less often than every 8 years.

(7) Other Requirements Preserved. — No emission standard or other requirement promulgated under this section shall be interpreted, construed or applied to diminish or replace the requirements of a more stringent emission limitation or other applicable requirement established pursuant to section 111, part C or D, or other authority of this Act or a standard issued under State authority.

(8) Coke Ovens —

(A) Not later than December 31, 1992, the Administrator shall promulgate regulations establishing emission standards under paragraphs (2) and (3) of this subsection for coke oven batteries. In establishing such standards, the Administrator shall evaluate—

(i) the use of sodium silicate (or equivalent) luting compounds to prevent door leaks, and other operating practices and technologies for their effectiveness in reducing coke oven emissions, and their suitability for use on new and existing coke oven batteries, taking into account costs and reasonable commercial door warranties; and

(ii) as a basis for emission standards under this subsection for new coke oven batteries that begin construction after the date of proposal of such standards, the Jewell design Thompson non-recovery coke oven batteries and other non-recovery coke oven technologies, and other appropriate emission control and coke production technologies, as to their effectiveness in reducing coke oven emissions and their capability for production of steel quality coke. Such regulations shall require at a minimum that coke oven batteries will not exceed 8 per centum leaking doors, 1 per centum leaking lids, 5 per centum leaking offtakes, and 16 seconds visible emissions per charge, with no exclusion for emissions during the period after the closing of self-sealing oven doors. Notwithstanding subsection (i), the compliance date for such emission standards for existing coke oven batteries shall be December 31, 1995.

(B) The Administrator shall promulgate work practice regulations under this subsection for coke oven batteries requiring, as appropriate—

(i) the use of sodium silicate (or equivalent) luting compounds, if the Administrator determines that use of sodium silicate is an effective means of emissions control and is achievable, taking into account costs and reasonable commercial warranties for doors and related equipment; and

(ii) door and jam cleaning practices. Notwithstanding subsection (i), the compliance date for such work practice regulations for coke oven batteries shall be not later than the date 3 years after the date of enactment of the Clean Air Act Amendments of 1990.

(C) For coke oven batteries electing to qualify for an extension of the compliance date for standards promulgated under subsection (f) in accordance with subsection (i)(8), the emission standards under this subsection for coke oven batteries shall require that coke oven batteries not exceed 8 per centum leaking doors, 1 per centum leaking lids, 5 per centum leaking offtakes, and 16 seconds visible emissions per charge, with no exclusion for emissions during the period after the closing of self-sealing doors. Notwithstanding subsection (i), the compliance date for such emission standards for existing coke oven batteries seeking an extension shall be not later than the date 3 years after the date of enactment of the Clean Air Act Amendments of 1990.

(9) Sources Licensed by the Nuclear Regulatory Commission. — No standard for radionuclide emissions from any category or subcategory of facilities licensed by the Nuclear Regulatory Commission (or an Agreement State) is required to be promulgated under this section if the Administrator determines, by rule, and after consultation with the Nuclear Regulatory Commission, that the regulatory program established by the Nuclear Regulatory Commission pursuant to the Atomic Energy Act for such category or subcategory provides an ample margin of safety to protect the public health. Nothing in this subsection shall preclude or deny the right of any State or political subdivision thereof to adopt or enforce any standard or limitation respecting emissions of radionuclides which is more stringent than the standard or limitation in effect under section 111 or this section.

(10) Effective Date. — Emission standards or other regulations promulgated under this subsection shall be effective upon promulgation.

(e) Schedule for Standards and Review. —

(1) In General. — The Administrator shall promulgate regulations establishing emission standards for categories and subcategories of sources initially listed for regulation pursuant to subsection (c)(1) as expeditiously as practicable, assuring that—

(A) emission standards for not less than 40 categories and subcategories (not counting coke oven batteries) shall be promulgated not later than 2 years after the date of enactment of the Clean Air Act Amendments of 1990;

(B) emission standards for coke oven batteries shall be promulgated not later than December 31, 1992;

(C) emission standards for 25 per centum of the listed categories and subcategories shall be promulgated not later than 4 years after the date of enactment of the Clean Air Act Amendments of 1990;

(D) emission standards for an additional 25 per centum of the listed categories and subcategories shall be promulgated not later than 7 years after the date of enactment of the Clean Air Act Amendments of 1990; and

(E) emission standards for all categories and subcategories shall be promulgated not later than 10 years after the date of enactment of the Clean Air Act Amendments of 1990.

(2) In determining priorities for promulgating standards under subsection (d), the Administrator shall consider—

(A) the known or anticipated adverse effects of such pollutants on public health and the environment;

(B) the quantity and location of emissions of reasonably anticipated emissions of hazardous air pollutants that each category or subcategory will emit; and

(C) the efficiency of grouping categories or subcategories according to the pollutants emitted, or the processes or technologies used.

(3) Published Schedule. — Not later than 24 months after the date of enactment of the Clean Air Act Amendments of 1990 and after opportunity for comment, the Administrator shall publish a schedule establishing a date for the promulgation of emission standards for each category and subcategory of sources listed pursuant to subsection (c)(1) and (3) which shall be consistent with the requirements of paragraphs (1) and (2). The determination of priorities for the promulgation of standards pursuant to this paragraph is not a rulemaking and shall not be subject to judicial review, except that, failure to promulgate any standard pursuant to the schedule established by this paragraph shall be subject to review under section 304 of this Act.

(4) Judicial Review. — Notwithstanding section 307 of this Act, no action of the Administrator adding a pollutant to the list under subsection (b) or listing a source category or subcategory under subsection (c) shall be a final agency action subject to judicial review, except that any such action may be reviewed under such section 307 when the Administrator issues emission standards for such pollutant or category.

(5) Publicly Owned Treatment Works. —The Administrator shall promulgate standards pursuant to subsection (d) applicable to publicly owned treatment works (as defined in title II of the Federal Water Pollution Control Act) not later than 5 years after the date of enactment of the Clean Air Act Amendments of 1990.

(f) Standard to Protect Health and the Environment. —

(1) Report. — Not later than 6 years after the date of enactment of the Clean Air Act Amendments of 1990 the Administration shall investigate and report, after consultation with the Surgeon General and after opportunity for public comment, to Congress on—

(A) methods of calculating the risk to public health remaining, or likely to remain, from sources subject to regulation under this section after the application of standards under subsection (d);

(B) the public health significance of such estimated remaining risk and the technologically and commercially available methods and costs of reducing such risks;

(C) the actual health effects with respect to persons living in the vicinity of sources, any available epidemiological or other health studies, risks presented by background concentrations of hazardous air pollutants, any uncertainties in risk assessment methodology or other health assessment technique, and any negative health or environmental consequences to the community of efforts to reduce such risks; and

(D) recommendations as to legislation regarding such remaining risk.

(2) Emission Standards. —

(A) If Congress does not act on any recommendation submitted under paragraph (1), the Administrator shall, within 8 years after promulgation of standards for each category or subcategory of sources pursuant to subsection (d), promulgate standards for such category or subcategory if promulgation of such standards is required in order to provide an ample margin of safety to protect public health in accordance with this section (as in effect before the date of enactment of the Clean Air Act Amendments of 1990) or to prevent, taking into consideration costs, energy, safety, and other relevant factors, an adverse environmental effect. Emission standards promulgated under this subsection shall provide an ample margin of safety to protect public health in accordance with this section (as in effect before the date of enactment of the Clean Air Act Amendments of 1990), unless the Administrator determines that a more stringent standard is necessary to prevent, taking into consideration costs, energy, safety, and other relevant factors, an adverse environmental effect. If standards promulgated pursuant to subsection (d) and applicable to a category or subcategory of sources emitting a pollutant (or pollutants) classified as a known, probable or possible human carcinogen do not reduce lifetime excess cancer risks to the individual most exposed to emissions from a source in the category or subcategory to less than one in one million, the Administrator shall promulgate standards under this subsection for such source category.

(B) Nothing in subparagraph (A) or in any other provision of this section shall be construed as affecting, of applying to the Administrator's interpretation of this section, as in effect before the date of enactment of the Clean Air Act Amendments of 1990 and set forth in the Federal Register of September 14, 1989 (54 Federal Resister 38044).

(C) The Administrator shall determine whether or not to promulgate such standards and, if the Administrator decides to promulgate such standards, shall promulgate the standards 8 years after promulgation of the standards under subsection (d) for each source category or subcategory concerned. In the case of categories or subcategories for which standards under subsection (d) are required to be promulgated within 2 years after the date of enactment of the Clean Air Act Amendments of 1990, the Administrator shall have 9 years after promulgation of the standards under subsection (d) to make the determination under the preceding sentence and, if required, to promulgate the standards under this paragraph.

(3) Effective date. — Any emission standard established pursuant to this subsection shall become effective upon promulgation.

(4) Prohibition. — No air pollutant to which a standard under this subsection applies may be emitted from any stationary source in violation of such standard, except that in the case of an existing source—

(A) such standard shall not apply until 90 days after its effective date, and

(B) the Administrator may grant a waiver permitting such source a period of up to 2 years after the effective date of a standard to comply with the standard if the Administrator finds that such period is necessary for the installation of controls and that steps will be taken during the period of the waiver to assure that the health of persons will be protected from imminent endangerment.

(5) Area sources. — The Administrator shall not be required to conduct any review under this subsection or promulgate emission limitations under this subsection for any category or

subcategory of area sources that is listed pursuant to subsection (c)(3) and for which an emission standard is promulgated pursuant to subsection (d)(5).

(6) Unique Chemical Substances. — In establishing standards for the control of unique chemical substances of listed pollutants without CAS numbers under this subsection, the Administrator shall establish such standards with respect to the health and environmental effects of the substances actually emitted by sources and direct transformation byproducts of such emissions in the categories and subcategories.

(g) Modifications. —

(1) Offsets. —

(A) A physical change in, or change in the method of operation of, a major source which results in a greater than de minimis increase in actual emissions of a hazardous air pollutant shall not be considered a modification, if such increase in the quantity of actual emissions of any hazardous air pollutant from such source will be offset by an equal or greater decrease in the quantity of emissions of another hazardous air pollutant (or pollutants) from such source which is deemed more hazardous, pursuant to guidance issued by the Administrator under subparagraph (B). The owner or operator of such source shall submit a showing to the Administrator (or the State) that such increase has been offset under the preceding sentence.

(B) The Administrator shall, after notice and opportunity for comment and not later than 18 months after the date of enactment of the Clean Air Act Amendments of 1990, publish guidance with respect to implementation of this subsection. Such guidance shall include an identification, to the extent practicable, of the relative hazard to human health resulting from emissions to the ambient air of each of the pollutants listed under subsection (b) sufficient to facilitate the offset showing authorized by subparagraph (A). Such guidance shall not authorize offsets between pollutants where the increased pollutant (or more than one pollutant in a stream of pollutants) causes adverse effects to human health for which no safety threshold for exposure can be determined unless there are corresponding decreases in such types of pollutant(s).

(2) Construction, Reconstruction and Modifications. —

(A) After the effective date of a permit program under title V in any State, no person may modify a major source of hazardous air pollutants in such State, unless the Administrator (or the State) determines that the maximum achievable control technology emission limitation under this section for existing sources will be met. Such determination shall be made on a case-by-case basis where no applicable emissions limitations have been established by the Administrator.

(B) After the effective date of a permit program under title V in any State, no person may construct or reconstruct any major source of hazardous air pollutants, unless the Administrator (or the State) determines that the maximum achievable control technology emission limitation under this section for new sources will be met. Such determination shall be made on a case-by-case basis where no applicable emission limitations have been established by the Administrator.

(3) Procedures for Modifications. — The Administrator (or the State) shall establish reasonable procedures for assuring that the requirements applying to modifications under this section are reflected in the permit.

(h) Work Practice Standards and Other Requirements. —

(1) In General. — For purposes of this section, if it is not feasible in the judgment of the Administrator to prescribe or enforce an emission standard for control of a hazardous air pollutant or pollutants, the Administrator may, in lieu thereof, promulgate a design, equipment, work practice, or operational standard, or combination thereof, which in the Administrator's judgment is consistent with the provisions of subsection (d) or (f). In the event the Administrator promulgates a design or equipment standard under this subsection, the Administrator shall include as part of such standard such requirements as will assure the proper operation and maintenance of any such element of design or equipment.

(2) Definition. — For the purpose of this subsection, the phrase 'not feasible to prescribe or enforce an emission standard' means any situation in which the Administrator determines that—

(A) a hazardous air pollutant or pollutants cannot be emitted through a conveyance designed and constructed to emit or capture such pollutant, or that any requirement for, or use of, such a conveyance would be inconsistent with any Federal, State or local law, or

(B) the application of measurement methodology to a particular class of sources is not practicable due to technological and economic limitations.

(3) Alternative Standard. — If after notice and opportunity for comment, the owner or operator of any source establishes to the satisfaction of the Administrator that an alternative means of emission limitation will achieve a reduction in emissions of any air pollutant at least equivalent to the reduction in emissions of such pollutant achieved under the requirements of paragraph (1), the Administrator shall permit the use of such alternative by the source for purposes of compliance with this section with respect to such pollutant.

(4) Numerical Standard Required. — Any standard promulgated under paragraph (1) shall be promulgated in terms of an emission standard whenever it is feasible to promulgate and enforce a standard in such terms.

(i) Schedule for Compliance. —

(1) Preconstruction and Operating Requirements. — After the effective date of any emission standard, limitation, or regulation under subsection (d), (f) or (h), no person may construct any new major source or reconstruct any existing major source subject to such emission standard, regulation or limitation unless the Administrator (or a State with a permit program approved under title V) determines that such source, if properly constructed, reconstructed and operated, will comply with the standard, regulation or limitation.

(2) Special Rule. — Notwithstanding the requirements of paragraph (1), a new source which commences construction or reconstruction after a standard, limitation or regulation applicable to such source is proposed and before such standard, limitation or regulation is promulgated shall not be required to comply with such promulgated standard until the date 3 years after the date of promulgation if—

(A) the promulgated standard, limitation or regulation is more stringent than the standard, limitation or regulation proposed; and

(B) the source complies with the standard, limitation, or regulation as proposed during the 3–year period immediately after promulgation.

(3) Compliance Schedule for Existing Sources. —

(A) After the effective date of any emissions standard, limitation or regulation promulgated under this section and applicable to a source, no person may operate such source in violation of such standard, limitation or regulation except, in the case of an existing source, the Administrator shall establish a compliance date or dates for each category or subcategory of existing sources, which shall provide for compliance as expeditiously as practicable, but in no event later than 3 years after the effective date of such standard, except as provided in subparagraph (B) and paragraphs (4) through (8).

(B) The Administrator (or a State with a program approved under title V) may issue a permit that grants an extension permitting an existing source up to 1 additional year to comply with standards under subsection (d) if such additional period is necessary for the installation of controls. An additional extension of up to 3 years may be added for mining waste operations, if the 4–year compliance time is insufficient to dry and cover mining waste in order to reduce emissions of any pollutant listed under subsection (b).

(4) Presidential Exemption. — The President may exempt any stationary source from compliance with any standard or limitation under this section for a period of not more than 2 years if the President determines that the technology to implement such standard is not available and that it is in the national security interests of the United States to do so. An exemption under this paragraph may be extended for 1 or more additional periods, each period not to exceed 2 years. The President shall report to Congress with respect to each exemption (or extension thereof) made under this paragraph.

(5) Early Reduction. —

(A) The Administrator (or a State acting pursuant to a permit program approved under title V) shall issue a permit allowing an existing source, for which the owner or operator demonstrates that the source has achieved a reduction of 90 per centum or more in emissions of hazardous air pollutants (95 per centum in the case of hazardous air pollutants which are particulates) from the source, to meet an alternative emission limitation reflecting such reduction in lieu of an emission limitation promulgated under subsection (d) for a period of 6 years from the compliance date for the otherwise applicable standard, provided that such reduction is achieved before the otherwise applicable standard under subsection (d) is first proposed Nothing in this paragraph shall preclude a State from requiring reductions in excess of those specified in this subparagraph as a condition of granting the extension authorized by the previous sentence.

(B) An existing source which achieves the reduction referred to in subparagraph (A) after the proposal of an applicable standard but before January 1, 1994, may qualify under subparagraph (A), if the source makes an enforceable commitment to achieve such reduction before the proposal of the standard. Such commitment shall be enforceable to the same extent as a regulation under this section.

(C) The reduction shall be determined with respect to verifiable and actual emissions in a base year not earlier than calendar year 1987, provided that, there is no evidence that emissions in the base year are artificially or substantially greater than emissions in other years prior to implementation of emissions reduction measures. The Administrator may allow a source to use a baseline year of 1985 or 1986 provided that the source can demonstrate to the satisfaction of the Administrator that emissions data for the source reflects verifiable data based on information for such source, received by the Administrator prior to the enactment of the Clean Air Act Amendments of 1990, pursuant to an information request issued under section 114 .

(D) For each source granted an alternative emission limitation under this paragraph there shall be established by a permit issued pursuant to title V an enforceable emission limitation for hazardous air pollutants reflecting the reduction which qualifies the source for an alternative emission limitation under this paragraph. An alternative emission limitation under this paragraph shall not be available with respect to standards or requirements promulgated pursuant to subsection (f) and the Administrator shall, for the purpose of determining whether a standard under subsection (f) is necessary, review emissions from sources granted an alternative emission limitation under this paragraph at the same time that other sources in the category or subcategory are reviewed.

(E) With respect to pollutants for which high risks of adverse public health effects may be associated with exposure to small quantities including, but not limited to, chlorinated dioxins and furans, the Administrator shall by regulation limit the use of offsetting reductions in emissions of other hazardous air pollutants from the source as counting toward the 90 per centum reduction in such high-risk pollutants qualifying for an alternative emissions limitation under this paragraph.

(6) Other reductions. — Notwithstanding the requirements of this section, no existing source that has installed—

(A) best available control technology (as defined in section 169(3)), or

(B) technology required to meet a lowest achievable emission rate (as defined in section 171), prior to the promulgation of a standard under this section applicable to such source and the same pollutant (or stream of pollutants) controlled pursuant to an action described in subparagraph (A) or (B) shall be required to comply with such standard under this section until the date 5 years after the date on which such installation or reduction has been achieved, as determined by the Administrator. The Administrator may issue such rules and guidance as are necessary to implement this paragraph.

(7) Extension for new sources. — A source for which construction or reconstruction is commenced after the date an emission standard applicable to such source is proposed pursuant to subsection (d) but before the date an emission standard applicable to such source is proposed pursuant to subsection (f) shall not be required to comply with the emission standard under subsection (f) until the date 10 years after the date construction or reconstruction is commenced.

(8) Coke ovens.

(A) Any coke oven battery that complies with the emission limitations established under subsection (d)(8)(C), subparagraph (B), and subparagraph (C), and complies with the provisions of subparagraph (E) shall not be required to achieve emission limitations promulgated under subsection (f) until January 1, 2020.

(B) (i) Not later than December 31, 1992, the Administrator shall promulgate emission limitations for coke oven emissions from coke oven batteries. Notwithstanding paragraph (3) of this subsection, the compliance date for such emission limitations for existing coke oven batteries shall be January 1, 1998. Such emission limitations shall reflect the lowest achievable emission rate as defined in section 171 for a coke oven battery that is rebuilt or a replacement at a coke oven plant for an existing battery. Such emission limitations shall be no less stringent than—

(I) 3 per centum leaking doors (5 per centum leaking doors for six meter batteries);

(II) 1 per centum leaking lids;

(III) 4 per centum leaking offtakes; and

(IV) 16 seconds visible emissions per charge,

with an exclusion for emissions during the period after the closing of self-sealing oven doors (or the total mass emissions equivalent). The rulemaking in which such emission limitations are promulgated shall also establish an appropriate measurement methodology for determining compliance with such emission limitations, and shall establish such emission limitations in terms of an equivalent level of mass emissions reduction from a coke oven battery, unless the Administrator finds that such a mass emissions standard would not be practicable or enforceable. Such measurement methodology, to the extent it measures leaking doors, shall take into consideration alternative test methods that reflect the best technology and practices actually applied in the affected industries, and shall assure that the final test methods are consistent with the performance of such best technology and practices.

(ii) If the Administrator fails to promulgate such emission limitations under this subparagraph prior to the effective date of such emission limitations, the emission limitations applicable to coke oven batteries under this subparagraph shall be—

(I) 3 per centum leaking doors (5 per centum leaking doors for six meter batteries);

(II) 1 per centum leaking lids;

(III) 4 per centum leaking offtakes; and

(IV) 16 seconds visible emissions per charge, or the total mass emissions equivalent (if the total mass emissions equivalent is determined to be practicable and enforceable), with no exclusion for emissions during the period after the closing of self-sealing oven doors.

(C) Not later than January 1, 2007, the Administrator shall review the emission limitations promulgated under subparagraph (B) and revise, as necessary, such emission limitations to reflect the lowest achievable emission rate as defined in section 171 at the time for a coke oven battery that is rebuilt or a replacement at a coke oven plant for an existing battery. Such emission limitations shall be no less stringent than the emission limitation promulgated under subparagraph (B). Notwithstanding paragraph (2) of this subsection, the compliance date for such emission limitations for existing coke oven batteries shall be January 1, 2010.

(D) At any time prior to January 1, 1998, the owner or operator of any coke oven battery may elect to comply with emission limitations promulgated under subsection (f) by the date such emission limitations would otherwise apply to such coke oven battery, in lieu of the emission limitations and the compliance dates provided under subparagraphs (B) and (C) of this paragraph. Any such owner or operator shall be legally bound to comply with such emission limitations promulgated under subsection (f) with respect to such coke oven battery as of January 1, 2003. If no such emission limitations have been promulgated for such coke oven battery, the Administrator shall promulgate such emission limitations in accordance with subsection (f) for such coke oven battery.

(E) Coke oven batteries qualifying for an extension under subparagraph (A) shall make available not later than January 1, 2000, to the surrounding communities the results of any risk assessment performed by the Administrator to determine the appropriate level of any emission standard established by the Administrator pursuant to subsection (f).

(F) Notwithstanding the provisions of this section, reconstruction of any source of coke oven emissions qualifying for an extension under this paragraph shall not subject such source to emission limitations under subsection (f) more stringent than those established under subparagraphs (B) and (C) until January 1, 2020. For the purposes of this subparagraph, the term "reconstruction" includes the replacement of existing coke oven battery capacity with new coke oven batteries of comparable or lower capacity and lower potential emissions.

(j) Equivalent Emission Limitation by Permit. —

(1) Effective Date. — The requirements of this subsection shall apply in each State beginning on the effective date of a permit program established pursuant to title V in such State, but not prior to the date 42 months after the date of enactment of the Clean Air Act Amendments of 1990.

(2) Failure to Promulgate a Standard. —In the event that the Administrator fails to promulgate a standard for a category of subcategory of major sources by the date established pursuant to subsection (e)(1) and (3), and beginning 18 months after such date (but not prior to the effective date of a permit program under title V), the owner or operator of any major source in such category or subcategory shall submit a permit application under paragraph (3) and such owner or operator shall also comply with paragraphs (5) and (6).

(3) Applications. — By the date established by paragraph (2), the owner or operator of a major source subject to this subsection shall file an application for a permit. If the owner or operator of a source has submitted a timely and complete application for a permit required by this subsection, any failure to have a permit shall not be a violation of paragraph (2), unless the delay in final action is due to the failure of the applicant to timely submit information required or requested to process the application. The Administrator shall not later than 18 months after the date of enactment of the Clean Air Act Amendments of 1990, and after notice and opportunity for comment, establish requirements for applications under this subsection including a standard application form and criteria for determining in a timely manner the completeness of applications.

(4) Review and Approval. — Permit applications submitted under this subsection shall be reviewed and approved or disapproved according to the provisions of section 505 . In the event that the Administrator (or the State) disapproves a permit application submitted under this subsection or determines that the application is incomplete, the applicant shall have up to 6 months to revise the application to meet the objections of the Administrator (or the State).

(5) Emission Limitation. — The permit shall be issued pursuant to title V and shall contain emission limitations for the hazardous air pollutants subject to regulation under this section and emitted by the source that the Administrator (or the State) determines, on a case-by-case basis, to be equivalent to the limitation that would apply to such source if an emission standard had been promulgated in a timely manner under subsection (d). In the alternative, if the applicable criteria are met, the permit may contain an emissions limitation established according to the provisions of subsection (i)(5). For purposes of the preceding sentence, the reduction required by subsection (i)(5)(A) shall be achieved by the date on which the relevant standard should have been promulgated under subsection (d). No such pollutant may be emitted in amounts exceeding an emission limitation contained in a permit immediately for new sources and, as expeditiously as practicable, but not later than the date 3 years after the permit is issued for existing sources or such other compliance date as would apply under subsection (i).

(6) Applicability of Subsequent Standards. — If the Administrator promulgates an emission standard that is applicable to the major source prior to the date on which a permit application is approved, the emission limitation in the permit shall reflect the promulgated standard rather than the emission limitation determined pursuant to paragraph (5), provided that the source shall have the compliance period provided under subsection (i). If the Administrator promulgates a standard under subsection (d) that would be applicable to the source in lieu of the emission limitation established by permit under this subsection after the date on which the permit has been issued, the Administrator (or the State) shall revise such permit upon the next renewal to reflect the standard promulgated by the Administrator providing such source a reasonable time to comply, but no longer than 8 years after such standard is promulgated or 8 years after the date on which the source is first required to comply with the emissions limitation established by paragraph (5), whichever is earlier.

(k) Area Source Program. —

(1) Findings and Purpose. — The Congress finds that emissions of hazardous air pollutants from area sources may individually, or in the aggregate, present significant risks to public health in urban areas. Considering the large number of persons exposed and the risks of carcinogenic and other adverse health effects from hazardous air pollutants, ambient concentrations characteristic of large urban areas should be reduced to levels substantially below those currently experienced. It is the purpose of this subsection to achieve a substantial reduction in emissions of hazardous air pollutants from area sources and an equivalent reduction in the public health risks associated with such sources including a reduction of not less than 75 per centum in the incidence of cancer attributable to emmissions from such sources.

(2) Research Program. — The Administrator shall, after consultation with State and local air pollution control officials, conduct a program of research with respect to sources of hazardous air pollutants in urban areas and shall include within such program—

(A) ambient monitoring for a broad range of hazardous air pollutants (including, but not limited to, volatile organic compounds, metals, pesticides and products of incomplete combustion) in a representative number of urban locations;

(B) analysis to characterize the sources of such pollution with a focus on area sources and the contribution that such sources make to public health risks from hazardous air pollutants; and

(C) consideration of atmospheric transformation and other factors which can elevate public health risks from such pollutants.

Health effects considered under this program shall include, but not be limited to, carcinogenicity, mutagenicity, teratogenicity, neurotoxicity, reproductive dysfunction and other acute and chronic effects including the role of such pollutants as precursors of ozone or acid aerosol formation. The Administrator shall report the preliminary results of such research not later than 3 years after the date of enactment of the Clean Air Act Amendments of 1990.

(3) National Strategy. —

(A) Considering information collected pursuant to the monitoring program authorized by paragraph (2), the Administrator shall, not later than 5 years after the date of enactment of the Clean Air Act Amendments of 1990 and after notice and opportunity for public comment, prepare and transmit to the Congress a comprehensive strategy to control emissions of hazardous air pollutants from area sources in urban areas.

(B) The strategy shall—

(i) identify not less than 30 hazardous air pollutants which, as the result of emissions from area sources, present the greatest threat to public health in the largest number of urban areas and that are or will be listed pursuant to subsection (b), and

(ii) identify the source categories or subcategories emitting such pollutants that are or will be listed pursuant to subsection (c). When identifying categories and subcategories of sources under this subparagraph, the Administrator shall assure that sources accounting for 90 per centum or more of the aggregate emissions of each of the 30 identified hazardous air pollutants are subject to standards pursuant to subsection (d).

(C) The strategy shall include a schedule of specific actions to substantially reduce the public health risks posed by the release of hazardous air pollutants from area sources that will be implemented by the Administrator under the authority of this or other laws (including, but not limited to, the Toxic Substances Control Act, the Federal Insecticide, Fungicide and Rodenticide Act and the Resource Conservation and Recovery Act) or by the States. The strategy shall achieve a reduction in the incidence of cancer attributable to exposure to hazardous air pollutants emitted by stationary sources of not less than 75 per centum, considering control of emissions of hazardous air pollutants from all stationary sources and resulting from measures implemented by the Administrator or by the States under this or other laws.

(D) The strategy may also identify research needs in monitoring, analytical methodology, modeling or pollution control techniques and recommendations for changes in law that would further the goals and objectives of this subsection.

(E) Nothing in this subsection shall be interpreted to preclude or delay implementation of actions with respect to area sources of hazardous air pollutants under consideration pursuant to this or any other law and that may be promulgated before the strategy is prepared.

(F) The Administrator shall implement the strategy as expeditiously as practicable assuring that all sources are in compliance with all requirements not later than 9 years after the date of enactment of the Clean Air Act Amendments of 1990.

(G) As part of such strategy the Administrator shall provide for ambient monitoring and emissions modeling in urban areas as appropriate to demonstrate that the goals and objectives of the strategy are being met.

(4) Areawide Activities. — In addition to the national urban air toxics strategy authorized by paragraph (3), the Administrator shall also encourage and support areawide strategies developed by State or local air pollution control agencies that are intended to reduce risks from emissions by area sources within a particular urban area. From the funds available for grants under this section, the Administrator shall set aside not less than 10 per centum to

support areawide strategies addressing hazardous air pollutants emitted by area sources and shall award such funds on a demonstration basis to those States with innovative and effective strategies. At the request of State or local air pollution control officials, the Administrator shall prepare guidelines for control technologies or management practices which may be applicable to various categories or subcategories of area sources.

(5) Report. — The Administrator shall report to the Congress at intervals not later than 8 and 12 years after the date of enactment of the Clean Air Act Amendments of 1990 on actions taken under this subsection and other parts of this Act to reduce the risk to public health posed by the release of hazardous air pollutants from area sources. The reports shall also identify specific metropolitan areas that continue to experience high risks to public health as the result of emissions from area sources.

(l) State Programs. —

(1) In General. — Each State may develop and submit to the Administrator for approval a program for the implementation and enforcement (including a review of enforcement delegations previously granted) of emission standards and other requirements for air pollutants subject to this section or requirements for the prevention and mitigation of accidental releases pursuant to subsection (r). A program submitted by a State under this subsection may provide for partial or complete delegation of the Administrator's authorities and responsibilities to implement and enforce emissions standards and prevention requirements but shall not include authority to set standards less stringent than those promulgated by the Administrator under this Act.

(2) Guidance. — Not later than 12 months after the date of enactment of the Clean Air Act Amendments of 1990, the Administrator shall publish guidance that would be useful to the States in developing programs for submittal under this subsection. The guidance shall also provide for the registration of all facilities producing, processing, handling or storing any substance listed pursuant to subsection (r) in amounts greater than the threshold quantity. The Administrator shall include as an element in such guidance an optional program begun in 1986 for the review of high-risk point sources of air pollutants including, but not limited to, hazardous air pollutants listed pursuant to subsection (b).

(3) Technical Assistance. — The Administrator shall establish and maintain an air toxics clearinghouse and center to provide technical information and assistance to State and local agencies and, on a cost recovery basis, to others on control technology, health and ecological risk assessment, risk analysis, ambient monitoring and modeling, and emissions measurement and monitoring. The Administrator shall use the authority of section 103 to examine methods for preventing, measuring, and controlling emissions and evaluating associated health and ecological risks. Where appropriate, such activity shall be conducted with not-for-profit organizations. The Administrator may conduct research on methods for preventing measuring and controlling emissions and evaluating associated health and environment risks. All information collected under this paragraph shall be available to the public.

(4) Grants. — Upon application of a State, the Administrator may make grants, subject to such terms and conditions as the Administrator deems appropriate, to such State for the purpose of assisting the State in developing and implementing a program for submittal and approval under the subsection. Programs assisted under this paragraph may include program elements addressing air pollutants or extremely hazardous substances other than those specifically subject to this section. Grants under this paragraph may include support for high-risk point source review as provided in paragraph (2) and support for the development and implementation of areawide area source programs pursuant to subsection (k).

(5) Approval or Disapproval. — Not later than 180 days after receiving a program submitted by a State, and after notice and opportunity for public comment, the Administrator shall either approve or disapprove such program. The Administrator shall disapprove any program submitted by a State, if the Administrator determine that—

(A) the authorities contained in the program are not adequate to assure compliance by all sources within the State with each applicable standard, regulation or requirement established by the Administrator under this section;

(B) adequate authority does not exist, or adequate resources are not available, to implement the program;

(C) the schedule for implementing the program and assuring compliance by affected sources is not sufficiently expeditious; or

(D) the program is otherwise not in compliance with the guidance issued by the Administrator under paragraph (2) or is not likely to satisfy, in whole or in part, the objectives of this Act.

If the Administrator disapproves a State program, the Administrator shall notify the State of any revisions or modifications necessary to obtain approval. The State may revise and resubmit the proposed program for review and approval pursuant to the provisions of this subsection.

(6) Withdrawal. — Whenever the Administrator determines, after public hear ing, that a State is not administering and enforcing a program approved pursuant to this subsection in accordance with the guidance published pursuant to paragraph (2) or the requirements of paragraph (5), the Administrator shall so notify the State and, if action which will assure prompt compliance is not taken within 90 days, the Administrator shall withdraw approval of the program. The Administrator shall not withdraw approval of any program unless the State shall have been notified and the reasons for withdrawal shall have been stated in writing and made public.

(7) Authority to Enforce. — Nothing in this subsection shall prohibit the Administrator from enforcing any applicable emission standard or requirement under this section.

(8) Local Program. — The Administrator may, after notice and opportunity for public comment, approve a program developed and submitted by a local air pollution control agency (after consultation with the State) pursuant to this subsection and any such agency implementing an approved program may take any action authorize to be taken by a State under this section.

(9) Permit Authority. — Nothing in this subsection shall affect the authorities and obligations of the Administrator or the State under title V.

(m) Atmospheric Deposition to Great Lakes and Coastal Waters. —

(1) The Administrator, in cooperation with the Under Secretary of Commerce for Oceans and Atmosphere, shall conduct a program to identify and assess the extent of atmospheric deposition of hazardous air pollutants (and in the discretion of the Administrator, other air pollutants) to the Great Lakes, the Chesapeake Bay, Lake Champlain and coastal waters. As part of such program, the Administrator shall—

(A) monitor the Great Lakes, the Chesapeake Bay, Lake Champlain and coastal waters, including monitoring of the Great Lakes through the monitoring network established pursuant to paragraph (2) of this subsection and designing and deploying an atmospheric monitoring network for coastal water pursuant to paragraph (4);

(B) investigate the sources and deposition rates of atmospheric deposition of air pollutants (and their atmospheric transformation precursors);

(C) conduct research to develop and improve monitoring methods and to determine the relative contribution of atmospheric pollutants to total pollution loadings to the Great Lakes, the Chesapeake Bay, Lake Champlain, and coastal waters;

(D) evaluate any adverse effects to public health or the environment caused by such deposition (including effects resulting from indirect exposure pathways) and assess the contribution of such deposition to violations of water quality standards established pursuant to the Federal Water Pollution Control Act and drinking water standards established pursuant to the Safe Drinking Water Act; and

(E) sample for such pollutants in biota, fish, and wildlife of the Great Lakes, the Chesapeake Bay, Lake Champlain and coastal waters and characterize the sources of such pollutants.

(2) Great Lake Monitoring Network. —The administrator shall oversee, in accordance with Annex 15 of the Great Lakes Water Quality Agreement, the establishment and operation of a Great Lakes atmospheric deposition network to monitor atmospheric deposition of hazardous air pollutants (and in the Administrator's discretion, other air pollutants) to the Great Lakes.

(A) As part of the network provided for in this paragraph, and not later than December 31, 1991, the Administrator shall establish in each of the 5 Great Lakes at least 1 facility capable of monitoring the atmospheric deposition of hazardous air pollutants in both dry and wet conditions.

(B) The Administrator shall use the date provided by the network to identify and track the movement of hazardous air pollutants through the Great Lakes, to determine the portion of water pollution loadings attributable to atmospheric deposition of such pollutants, and to support development of remedial action plans and other management plans as required by the Great Lakes Water Quality Agreement.

(C) The Administrator shall assure that the data collected by the Great Lakes atmospheric deposition monitoring network is in a format compatible with databases sponsored by the International Joint Commission, Canada, and the several States of the Great Lakes region.

(3) Monitoring for the Chesapeake Bay and Lake Champlain. — The Administrator shall establish at the Chesapeake Bay and Lake Champlain atmospheric deposition stations to monitor deposition of hazardous air pollutants (and in the Administrator's discretion, other air pollutants) within the Chesapeake Bay and Lake Champlain watersheds. The Administrator shall determine the role of air deposition in the pollutant loadings of the Chesapeake Bay and Lake Champlain, investigate the sources of air pollutants deposited in the watersheds, evaluate the health and environmental effects of such pollutant loadings, and shall sample such pollutants in biota, fish and wildlife within the watersheds, as necessary to characterize such effects.

(4) Monitoring for Coastal Waters. — The Administrator shall design and deploy atmospheric deposition monitoring networks for coastal waters and their watersheds and shall make any information collected through such networks available to the public. As part of this effort, the Administrator shall conduct research to develop and improve deposition monitoring methods, and to determine the relative contribution of atmospheric pollutants to pollutant loadings. For purposes of this subsection, 'coastal waters' shall mean estuaries selected pursuant to section 320(a)(2)(A) of the Federal Water Pollution Control Act or listed pursuant to section 320(a)(2)(B) of such Act or estuarine research reserves designated pursuant to section 315 of the Coastal Zone Management Act (16 U.S.C. 1461).

(5) Report. — Within 3 years of the date of enactment of the Clean Air Act Amendments of 1990 and biennially thereafter, the Administrator, in cooperation with the Under Secretary of Commerce for Oceans and Atmosphere, shall submit to the Congress a report on the results of any monitoring, studies, and investigations conducted pursuant to this subsection. Such report shall include, at a minimum, an assessment of—

(A) the contribution of atmospheric deposition to pollutant loadings in the Great Lakes, the Chesapeake Bay, Lake Champlain and coastal waters;

(B) the environmental and public health effects of any pollution which is attributable to atmospheric deposition to the Great Lakes, the Chesapeake Bay, Lake Champlain and coastal waters;

(C) the source or sources of any pollution to the Great Lakes, the Chesapeake Bay, Lake Champlain and coastal waters which is attributable to atmospheric deposition;

(D) whether pollution loadings in the Great Lakes, the Chesapeake Bay, Lake Champlain or coastal waters cause or contribute to exceedances of drinking water standards pursuant to the Safe Drinking Water Act or water quality standards pursuant to the Federal Water Pollution Control Act or, with respect to the Great Lakes, exceedances of the specific objectives of the Great Lakes Water Quality Agreement; and

(E) a description of any revisions of the requirements, standards, and limitations pursuant to this Act and other applicable Federal laws as are necessary to assure protection of human health and the environment.

(6) Additional Regulation. — As part of the report to Congress, the Administrator shall determine whether the other provisions of this section are adequate to prevent serious adverse effects to public health and serious or widespread environmental effects, including such effects resulting from indirect exposure pathways, associated with atmospheric deposition to the Great Lakes, the Chesapeake Bay, Lake Champlain and coastal waters of hazardous air pollutants (and their atmospheric transformation products). The Administrator shall take into consideration the tendency of such pollutants to bioaccumulate. Within 5 years after the date of enactment of the Clean Air Act Amendments of 1990, the Administrator shall, based on such report and determination, promulgate, in accordance with this section, such further emission standards or control measures as may be necessary and appropriate to prevent such effects, including effects due to bioaccumulation and indirect exposure pathways. Any requirements promulgated pursuant to this paragraph with respect to coastal waters shall only apply to the

coastal waters of the States which are subject to section 328(a) .

(n) Other Provisions. —

(1) Electric Utility Steam Generating Units. —

(A) The Administrator shall perform a study of the hazards to public health reasonably anticipated to occur as a result of emissions by electric utility steam generating units of pollutants listed under subsection (b) after imposition of the requirements of this Act. The Administrator shall report the results of this study to the Congress within 3 years after the date of the enactment of the Clean Air Act Amendments of 1990. The Administrator shall develop and describe in the Administrator's report to Congress alternative control strategies for emissions which may warrant regulation under this section. The Administrator shall regulate electric utility steam generating units under this section, if the Administrator finds such regulation is appropriate and necessary after considering the results of the study required by this subparagraph.

(B) The Administrator shall conduct, and transmit to the Congress not later than 4 years after the date of enactment of the Clean Air Act Amendments of 1990, a study of mercury emissions from electric utility steam generating units, municipal waste combustion units, and other sources, including area sources. Such study shall consider the rate and mass of such emissions, the health and environmental effects of such emissions, technologies which are available to control such emissions, and the costs of such technologies.

(C) The National Institute of Environmental Health Sciences shall conduct, and transmit to the Congress not later than 3 years after the date of enactment of the Clean Air Act Amendments of 1990, a study to determine the threshold level of mercury exposure below which adverse human health effects are not expected to occur. Such study shall include a threshold for mercury concentrations in the tissue of fish which may be consumed (including consumption by sensitive populations) without adverse effects to public health.

(2) Coke Oven Production Technology Study. —

(A) The Secretary of the Department of Energy and the Administrator shall jointly undertake a 6–year study to assess coke oven production emission control technologies and to assist in the development and commercialization of technically practicable and economically viable control technologies which have the potential to significantly reduce emissions of hazardous air pollutants from coke oven production facilities. In identifying control technologies, the Secretary and the Administrator shall consider the range of existing coke oven operations and battery design and the availability of sources of materials for such coke ovens as well as alternatives to existing coke oven production design.

(B) The Secretary and the Administrator are authorized to enter into agreements with persons who propose to develop, install and operate coke production emission control technologies which have the potential for significant emissions reductions of hazardous air pollutants provided that Federal funds shall not exceed 50 per centum of the cost of any project assisted pursuant to this paragraph.

(C) The Secretary shall prepare annual reports to Congress on the status of the research program and at the completion of the study shall make recommendations to the Administrator identifying practicable and economically viable control technologies for coke oven production facilities to reduce residual risks remaining after implementation of the standard under subsection (d).

(D) There are authorized to be appropriated $5,000,000 for each of the fiscal years 1992 through 1997 to carry out the program authorized by this paragraph.

(3) Publicly Owned Treatment Works. —The Administrator may conduct, in cooperation with the owners and operators of publicly owned treatment works, studies to characterize emissions of hazardous air pollutants emitted by such facilities, to identify industrial, commercial and residential discharges that contribute to such emissions and to demonstrate control measures for such emissions. When promulgating any standard under this section applicable to publicly owned treatment works, the Administrator may provide for control measures that include pretreatment of discharges causing emissions of hazardous air pollutants and process or product substitutions or limitations that may be effective in reducing such emissions. The Administrator may prescribe uniform sampling, modeling and risk assessment methods for use in implementing this subsection.

(4) Oil and Gas Wells; Pipeline Facilities. —

(A) Notwithstanding the provisions of subsection (a), emissions from any oil or gas exploration or production well (with its associated equipment) and emissions from any pipeline compressor or pump station shall not be aggregated with emissions from other similar units, whether or not such units are in a contiguous area or under common control, to determine whether such units or stations are major sources, and in the case of any oil or gas exploration or production well (with its associated equipment), such emissions shall not be aggregated for any purpose under this section.

(B) The Administrator shall not list oil and gas production wells (with its associated equipment) as an area source category under subsection (c), except that the Administrator may establish an area source category for oil and gas production wells located in any metropolitan statistical area or consolidated metropolitan statistical area with a population in excess of 1 million, if the Administrator determines that emissions of hazardous air pollutants from such wells present more than a negligible risk of adverse effects to public health.

(5) Hydrogen Sulfide. — The Administrator is directed to assess the hazards to public health and the environment resulting from the emission of hydrogen sulfide associated with the extraction of oil and natural gas resources. To the extent practicable, the assessment shall build upon and not duplicate work conducted for an assessment pursuant to section 8002(m) of the Solid Waste Disposal Act and shall reflect consultation with the States. The assessment shall include a review of existing State and industry control standards, techniques and enforcement. The Administrator shall report to the Congress within 24 months after the date of enactment of the Clean Air Act Amendments of 1990 with the findings of such assessment, together with any recommendations, and shall, as appropriate, develop and implement a control strategy for emissions of hydrogen sulfide to protect human health and the environment, based on the findings of such assessment, using authorities under this Act including sections 111 and this section.

(6) Hydrofluoric Acid. — Not later than 2 years after the date of enactment of the Clean Air Act Amendments of 1990, the Administrator shall, for those regions of the country which do not have comprehensive health and safety regulations with respect to hydrofluoric acid, complete a study of the potential hazards of hydrofluoric acid and the uses of hydrofluoric acid in industrial and commercial applications to public health and the environment considering a range of events including worst-case accidental releases and shall make recommendations to the Congress for the reduction of such hazards, if appropriate.

(7) RCRA Facilities. — In the case of any category or subcategory of sources the air emissions of which are regulated under subtitle C of the Solid Waste Disposal Act, the Administrator shall take into account any regulations of such emissions which are promulgated under such subtitle and shall, to the maximum extent practicable and consistent with the provisions of this section, ensure that the requirements of such subtitle and this section are consistent.

(o) National Academy of Sciences Study. —

(1) Request of the Academy. — Within 3 months of the date of enactment of the Clean Air Act Amendments of 1990, the Administrator shall enter into appropriate arrangements with the National Academy of Sciences to conduct a review of—

(A) risk assessment methodology used by the Environmental Protection Agency to determine the carcinogenic risk associated with exposure to hazardous air pollutants from source categories and subcategories subject to the requirements of this section; and

(B) improvements in such methodology.

(2) Elements to be Studied. — In conducting such review, the National Academy of Sciences should consider, but not be limited to, the following—

(A) the techniques used for estimating and describing the carcinogenic potency to humans of hazardous air pollutants; and

(B) the techniques used for estimating exposure to hazardous air pollutants (for hypothetical and actual maximally exposed individuals as well as other exposed individuals).

(3) Other Health Effects of Concern. —To the extent practicable, the Academy shall evaluate and report on the methodology for assessing the risk of adverse human health effects other than cancer for which safe thresholds of exposure may not exist, including, but not limited to, inheritable genetic mutations, birth defects, and reproductive dysfunctions.

(4) Report. — A report on the results of such review shall be submitted to the Senate Com-

mittee on Environment and Public Works, the House Committee on Energy and Commerce, the Risk Assessment and Management Commission established by section 303 of the Clean Air Act Amendments of 1990 and the Administrator not later than 30 months after the date of enactment of the Clean Air Act Amendments of 1990.

(5) Assistance. — The Administrator shall assist the Academy in gathering any information the Academy deems necessary to carry out this subsection. The Administrator may use any authority under this Act to obtain information from any person, and to require any person to conduct tests, keep and produce records, and make reports respecting research or other activities conducted by such person as necessary to carry out this subsection.

(6) Authorization. — Of the funds authorized to be appropriated to the Administrator by this Act, such amounts as are required shall be available to carry out this subsection.

(7) Guidelines for Carcinogenic Risk Assessment. — The Administrator shall consider, but need not adopt, the recommendations contained in the report of the National Academy of Sciences prepared pursuant to this subsection and the views of the Science Advisory Board, with respect to such report. Prior to the promulgation of any standard under subsection (f), and after notice and opportunity for comment, the Administrator shall publish revised Guidelines for Carcinogenic Risk Assessment or a detailed explanation of the reasons that any recommendations contained in the report of the National Academy of Sciences will not be implemented. The publication of such revised Guidelines shall be a final Agency action for purposes of section 307 .

(p) Mickey Leland Urban Air Toxics Research Center —

(1) Establishment. — The Administrator shall oversee the establishment of a National Urban Air Toxics Research Center, to be located at a university, a hospital, or other facility capable of undertaking and maintaining similar research capabilities in the areas of epidemiology, oncology, toxicology, pulmonary medicine, pathology, and biostatistics. The center shall be known as the Mickey Leland National Urban Air Toxics Research Center. The geographic site of the National Urban Air Toxics Research Center should be further directed to Harris County, Texas, in order to take full advantage of the well developed scientific community presence on-site at the Texas Medical Center as well as the extensive data previously compiled for the comprehensive monitoring system currently in place.

(2) Board of Directors. — The National Urban Air Toxics Research Center shall be governed by a Board of Directors to be comprised of 9 members, the appointment of which shall be allocated pro rata among the Speaker of the House, the Majority Leader of the Senate and the President. The members of the Board of Directors shall be selected based on their respective academic and professional backgrounds and expertise in matters relating to public health, environmental pollution and industrial hygiene. The duties of the Board of Directors shall be to determine policy and research guidelines, submit views from center sponsors and the public and issue periodic reports of center findings and activities.

(3) Scientific Advisory Panel. — The Board of Directors shall be advised by a Scientific Advisory Panel, the 13 members of which shall be appointed by the Board, and to include eminent members of the scientific and medical communities. The Panel membership may include scientists with relevant experience from the National Institute of Environmental Health Sciences, the Center for Disease Control, the Environmental Protection Agency, the National Cancer Institute, and others, and the Panel shall conduct peer review and evaluate research results. The Panel shall assist the Board in developing the research agenda, reviewing proposals and applications, and advise on the awarding of research grants.

(4) Funding. — The center shall be established and funded with both Federal and private source funds.

(q) Savings Provision. —

(1) Standards Previously Promulgated. —Any standard under this section in effect before the date of enactment of the Clean Air Act Amendments of 1990 shall remain in force and effect after such date unless modified as provided in this section before the date of enactment of such Amendments or under such Amendments. Except as provided in paragraph (4), any standard under this section which has been promulgated, but has not taken effect, before such date shall not be affected by such Amendments unless modified as provided in this section before such date or under such Amendments. Each such standard shall be reviewed and if appropriate, revised, to comply with the requirements of subsection (d) within 10 years after the date of enactment

of the Clean Air Act Amendments of 1990. If a timely petition for review of any such standard under section 307 is pending on such date of enactment, the standard shall be upheld if it complies with this section as in effect before that date. If any such standard is remanded to the Administrator, the Administrator may in the Administrator's discretion apply either the requirements of this section, or those of this section as in effect before the date of enactment of the Clean Air Act Amendments of 1990.

(2) Special Rule. — Notwithstanding paragraph (1), no standard shall be established under this section, as amended by the Clean Air Act Amendments of 1990, for radionuclide emissions from (A) elemental phosphorous plants, (B) grate calcination elemental phosphorous plants, (C) phosphogypsum stacks, or (D) any subcategory of the foregoing. This section, as in effect prior to the date of enactment of the Clean Air Act Amendments of 1990, shall remain in effect for radionuclide emissions from such plants and stacks.

(3) Other Categories. — Notwithstanding paragraph (1), this section, as in effect prior to the date of enactment of the Clean Air Act Amendments of 1990, shall remain in effect for radionuclide emissions from non-Department of Energy Federal facilities that are not licensed by the Nuclear Regulatory Commission, coal-fired utility and industrial boilers, underground uranium mines, surface uranium mines, and disposal of uranium mill tailings piles, unless the Administrator, in the Administrator's discretion, applies the requirements of this section as modified by the Clean Air Act Amendments of 1990 to such sources of radionuclides.

(4) Medical Facilities. — Notwithstanding paragraph (1), no standard promulgated under this section prior to the date of enactment of the Clean Air Act Amendments of 1990 with respect to medical research or treatment facilities shall take effect for two years following the date of enactment of the Clean Air Act Amendments of 1990, unless the Administrator makes a determination pursuant to a rulemaking under section 112(d)(9). If the Administrator determines that the regulatory program established by the Nuclear Regulatory Commission for such facilities does not provide an ample margin of safety to protect public health, the requirements of section 112 shall fully apply to such facilities. If the Administrator determines that such regulatory program does provide an ample margin of safety to protect the public health, the Administrator is not required to promulgate a standard under this section for such facilities, as provided in section 112(d)(9) .

(r) Prevention of Accidental Releases.

(1) Purpose and General Duty. — It shall be the objective of the regulations and programs authorized under this subsection to prevent the accidental release and to minimize the consequences of any such release of any substance listed pursuant to paragraph (3) or any other extremely hazardous substance. The owners and operators of stationary sources producing, processing, handling or storing such substances have a general duty in the same manner and to the same extent as section 654, title 29 of the United States Code, to identify hazards which may result from such releases using appropriate hazard assessment techniques, to design and maintain a safe facility taking such steps as are necessary to prevent releases, and to minimize the consequences of accidental releases which do occur. For purposes of this paragraph, the provisions of section 304 shall not be available to any person or otherwise be construed to be applicable to this paragraph. Nothing in this section shall be interpreted, construed, implied or applied to create any liability or basis for suit for compensation for bodily injury or any other injury or property damages to any person which may result from accidental releases of such substances.

(2) Definitions. —

(A) The term 'accidental release' means an unanticipated emission of a regulated substance or other extremely hazardous substance into the ambient air from a stationary source.

(B) The term 'regulated substance' means a substance listed under paragraph (3).

(C) The term 'stationary source' means any buildings, structures, equipment, installations or substance emitting stationary activities (i) which belong to the same industrial group, (ii) which are located on one or more contiguous properties, (iii) which are under the control of the same person (or persons under common control), and (iv) from which an accidental release may occur.

(3) List of Substances. — The Administrator shall promulgate not later than 24 months after enactment of the Clean Air Act Amendments of 1990 an initial list of 100 substances which, in the case of an accidental release, are known

to cause or may reasonably be anticipated to cause death, injury, or serious adverse affects to human health or the environment. For purposes of promulgating such list, the Administrator shall use, but is not limited to, the list of extremely hazardous substances published under the Emergency Planning and Community Right-to-Know Act of 1986, with such modifications as the Administrator deems appropriate. The initial list shall include chlorine, anhydrous ammonia, methyl chloride, ethylene oxide, vinyl chloride, methyl isocyanate, hydrogen cyanide, ammonia, hydrogen sulfide, toluene diisocyanate, phosgene, bromine, anhydrous hydrogen chloride, hydrogen fluoride, anhydrous sulfur dioxide, and sulfur trioxide. The initial list shall include at least 100 substances which pose the greatest risk of causing death, injury or serious adverse effects to human health or the environment from accidental releases. Regulations establishing the list shall include an explanation of the basis for establishing the list. The list may be revised from time to time by the Administrator on the Administrator's own motion or by petition and shall be reviewed at least every 5 years. No air pollutant for which a national primary ambient air quality standard has been established shall be included on any such list. No substance, practice, process, or activity regulated under title VI shall be subject to regulations under this subsection. The Administrator shall establish procedures for the addition and deletion of substances from the list established under this paragraph consistent with those applicable to the list in subsection (b).

(4) Factors to be Considered. — In listing substances under paragraph (3), the Administrator shall consider each of the following criteria—

(A) the severity of any acute adverse health effects associated with accidental releases of the substance;

(B) the likelihood of accidental releases of the substance; and

(C) the potential magnitude of human exposure to accidental releases of the substance.

(5) Threshold Quantity. — At the time any substance is listed pursuant to paragraph (3), the Administrator shall establish by rule, a threshold quantity for the substance, taking into account the toxicity, reactivity, volatility, dispersibility, combustibility, or flammability of the substance and the amount of the substance which, as a result of an accidental release, is known to cause or may reasonably be anticipated to cause death, injury or serious adverse effects to human health for which the substance was listed. The Administrator is authorized to establish a greater threshold quantity for, or to exempt entirely, any substance that is a nutrient used in agriculture when held by a farmer.

(6) Chemical Safety Board. —

(A) There is hereby established an independent safety board to be known as the Chemical Safety and Hazard Investigation Board.

(B) The Board shall consist of 5 members, including a Chairperson, who shall be appointed by the President, by and with the advice and consent of the Senate. Members of the Board shall be appointed on the basis of technical qualification, professional standing, and demonstrated knowledge in the fields of accident reconstruction, safety engineering, human factors, toxicology, or air pollution regulation. The terms of office of members of the Board shall be 5 years. Any member of the Board, including the Chairperson, may be removed for inefficiency, neglect of duty, or malfeasance in office. The Chairperson shall be the Chief Executive Officer of the Board and shall exercise the executive and administrative functions of the Board.

(C) The Board shall—

(i) investigate (or cause to be investigated), determine and report to the public in writing the facts, conditions, and circumstances and the cause or probable cause of any accidental release resulting in a fatality, serious injury or substantial property damages;

(ii) issue periodic reports to the Congress, Federal, State and local agencies, including the Environmental Protection Agency and the Occupational Safety and Health Administration, concerned with the safety of chemical production, processing, handling and storage, and other interested persons recommending measures to reduce the likelihood or the consequences of accidental releases and proposing corrective steps to make chemical production, processing, handling and storage as safe and free from risk of injury as is possible and may include in such reports proposed rules or orders which should be issued by the Administrator under the authority of this section or the Secretary of Labor under the Occupational Safety and Health Act to prevent or minimize the consequences of any release of substances that may cause death, injury or other serious adverse effects on human health or substantial property damage as the result of an accidental release; and

(iii) establish by regulation requirements binding on persons for reporting accidental releases into the ambient air subject to the Board's investigatory jurisdiction. Reporting releases to the National Response Center, in lieu of the Board directly, shall satisfy such regulations. The National Response Center shall promptly notify the Board of any releases which are within the Board's jurisdiction.

(D) The Board may utilize the expertise and experience of other agencies.

(E) The Board shall coordinate its activities with investigations and studies conducted by other agencies of the United States having a responsibility to protect public health and safety. The Board shall enter into a memorandum of understanding with the National Transportation Safety Board to assure coordination of functions and to limit duplication of activities which shall designate the National Transportation Safety Board as the lead agency for the investigation of releases which are transportation related. The Board shall not be authorized to investigate marine oil spills, which the National Transportation Safety Board is authorized to investigate. The Board shall enter into a memorandum of understanding with the Occupational Safety and Health Administration so as to limit duplication of activities. In no event shall the Board forego an investigation where an accidental release causes a fatality or serious injury among the general public, or had the potential to cause substantial property damage or a number of deaths or injuries among the general public.

(F) The Board is authorized to conduct research and studies with respect to the potential for accidental releases, whether or not an accidental release has occurred, where there is evidence which indicates the presence of a potential hazard or hazards. To the extent practicable, the Board shall conduct such studies in cooperation with other Federal agencies having emergency response authorities, State and local governmental agencies and associations and organizations from the industrial, commercial, and nonprofit sectors.

(G) No part of the conclusions, findings, or recommendations of the Board relating to any accidental release or the investigation thereof shall be admitted as evidence or used in any action or suit for damages arising out of any matter mentioned in such report.

(H) Not later than 18 months after the date of enactment of the Clean Air Act Amendments of 1990, the Board shall publish a report accompanied by recommendations to the Administrator on the use of hazard assessments in preventing the occurrence and minimizing the consequences of accidental releases of extremely hazardous substances. The recommendations shall include a list of extremely hazardous substances which are not regulated substances (including threshold quantities for such substances) and categories of stationary sources for which hazard assessments would be an appropriate measure to aid in the prevention of accidental releases and to minimize the consequences of those releases that do occur. The recommendations shall also include a description of the information and analysis which would be appropriate to include in any hazard assessment. The Board shall also make recommendations with respect to the role of risk management plans as required by paragraph (8)(B) in preventing accidental releases. The Board may from time to time review and revise its recommendations under this subparagraph.

(I) Whenever the Board submits a recommendation with respect to accidental releases to the Administrator, the Administrator shall respond to such recommendation formally and in writing not later than 180 days after receipt thereof. The response to the Board's recommendation by the Administrator shall indicate whether the Administrator will—

(i) initiate a rulemaking or issue such orders as are necessary to implement the recommendation in full or in part, pursuant to any timetable contained in the recommendation;

(ii) decline to initiate a rulemaking or issue orders as recommended.

Any determination by the Administrator not to implement a recommendation of the Board or to implement a recommendation only in part, including any variation from the schedule contained in the recommendation, shall be accompanied by a statement from the Administrator setting forth the reasons for such determination.

(J) The Board may make recommendations with respect to accidental releases to the Secretary of Labor. Whenever the Board submits such recommendation, the Secretary shall respond to such recommendation formally and in writing not later than 180 days after receipt thereof. The response to the Board's recommendation by the Administrator shall indicate whether the Secretary will—

(i) initiate a rulemaking or issue such orders as are necessary to implement the recommendation in full or in part, pursuant to any timetable contained in the recommendation;

(ii) decline to initiate a rulemaking or issue orders as recommended.

Any determination by the Secretary not to implement a recommendation or to implement a recommendation only in part, including any variation from the schedule contained in the recommendation, shall be accompanied by a statement from the Secretary setting forth the reasons for such determination.

(K) Within 2 years after enactment of the Clean Air Act Amendments of 1990, the Board shall issue a report to the Administrator of the Environmental Protection Agency and to the Administrator of the Occupational Safety and Health Administration recommending the adoption of regulations for the preparation of risk management plans and general requirements for the prevention of accidental releases of regulated substances into the ambient air (including recommendations for listing substances under paragraph (3)) and for the mitigation of the potential adverse effect on human health or the environment as a result of accidental releases which should be applicable to any stationary source handling any regulated substance in more than threshold amounts. The Board may include proposed rules or orders which should be issued by the Administrator under authority of this subsection or by the Secretary of Labor under the Occupational Safety and Health Act. Any such recommendations shall be specific and shall identify the regulated substance or class of regulated substances (or other substances) to which the recommendations apply. The Administrator shall consider such recommendations before promulgating regulations required by paragraph (7)(B).

(L) The Board, or upon authority of the Board, any member thereof, any administrative law judge employed by or assigned to the Board, or any officer or employee duly designated by the Board, may for the purpose of carrying out duties authorized by subparagraph (C)—

(i) hold such hearings, sit and act at such times and places, administer such oaths, and require by subpoena or otherwise attendance and testimony of such witnesses and the production of evidence and may require by order that any person engaged in the production, processing, handling, or storage of extremely hazardous substances submit written reports and responses to requests and questions within such time and in such form as the Board may require; and

(ii) upon presenting appropriate credentials and a written notice of inspection authority, enter any property where an accidental release causing a fatality, serious injury or substantial property damage has occurred and do all things therein necessary for a proper investigation pursuant to subparagraph (C) and inspect at reasonable times records, files, papers, processes, controls, and facilities and take such samples as are relevant to such investigation. Whenever the Administrator or the Board conducts an inspection of a facility pursuant to this subsection, employees and their representatives shall have the same rights to participate in such inspections as provided in the Occupational Safety and Health Act.

(M) In addition to that described in subparagraph (L), the Board may use any information gathering authority of the Administrator under this Act, including the subpoena power provided in section 307(a)(1) of this Act.

(N) The Board is authorized to establish such procedural and administrative rules as are necessary to the exercise of its functions and duties. The Board is authorized without regard to section 5 of title 41 of the United States Code to enter into contracts, leases, cooperative agreements or other transactions as may be necessary in the conduct of the duties and functions of the Board with any other agency, institution, or person.

(O) After the effective date of any reporting requirement promulgated pursuant to subparagraph (C)(iii) it shall be unlawful for any person to fail to report any release of any extremely hazardous substance as required by such subparagraph. The Administrator is authorized to enforce any regulation or requirements established by the Board pursuant to subparagraph (C)(iii) using the authorities of sections 113 and 114 . Any request for information from the owner or operator of a stationary source made by the Board or by the Administrator under this section shall be treated, for purposes of sections 113, 114, 116, 120, 303, 304 and 307 and any other enforcement provisions of this Act, as a request made by the Administrator under section 114 and may be enforced by the Chairperson of the Board or by the Administrator as provided in such section.

(P) The Administrator shall provide to the Board such support and facilities as may be necessary for operation of the Board.

(Q) Consistent with subsection (G) and section 114(c) any records, reports or information obtained by the Board shall be available to the Administrator, the Secretary of Labor, the Congress and the public, except that upon a showing satisfactory to the Board by any person that records, reports, or information, or particular part thereof (other than release or emissions data) to which the Board has access, if made public, is likely to cause substantial harm to the person's competitive position, the Board shall consider such record, report, or information or particular portion thereof confidential in accordance with section 1905 of title 18 of the United States Code, except that such record, report, or information may be disclosed to other officers, employees, and authorized representatives of the United States concerned with carrying out this Act or when relevant under any proceeding under this Act. This subparagraph does not constitute authority to withhold records, reports, or information from the Congress.

(R) Whenever the Board submits or transmits any budget estimate, budget request, supplemental budget request, or other budget information, legislative recommendation, prepared testimony for congressional hearings, recommendation or study to the President, the Secretary of Labor, the Administrator, or the Director of the Office of Management and Budget, it shall concurrently transmit a copy thereof to the Congress. No report of the Board shall be subject to review by the Administrator or any Federal agency or to judicial review in any court. No officer or agency of the United States shall have authority to require the Board to submit its budget requests or estimates, legislative recommendations, prepared testimony, comments, recommendations or reports to any officer or agency of the United States for approval or review prior to the submission of such recommendations, testimony, comments or reports to the Congress. In the performance of their functions as established by this Act, the members, officers and employees of the Board shall not be responsible to or subject to supervision or direction, in carrying out any duties under this subsection, of any officer or employee or agent of the Environmental Protection Agency, the Department of Labor or any other agency of the United States except that the President may remove any member, officer or employee of the Board for inefficiency, neglect of duty or malfeasance in office. Nothing in this section shall affect the application of title 5, United States Code to officers or employees of the Board.

(S) The Board shall submit an annual report to the President and to the Congress which shall include, but not be limited to, information on accidental releases which have been investigated by or reported to the Board during the previous year, recommendations for legislative or administrative action which the Board has made, the actions which have been taken by the Administrator or the Secretary of Labor or the heads of other agencies to implement such recommendations, an identification of priorities for study and investigation in the succeeding year, progress in the development of risk-reduction technologies and the response to and implementation of significant research findings on chemical safety in the public and private sector.

(7) Accident Prevention. —

(A) In order to prevent accidental releases of regulated substances, the Administrator is authorized to promulgate release prevention, detection, and correction requirements which may include monitoring, record-keeping, reporting, training, vapor recovery, secondary containment, and other design, equipment, work practice, and operational requirements. Regulations promulgated under this paragraph may make distinctions between various types, classes, and kinds of facilities, devices and systems taking into consideration factors including, but not limited to, the size, location, process, process controls, quantity of substances handled, potency of substances, and response capabilities present at any stationary source. Regulations promulgated pursuant to this subparagraph shall have an effective date, as determined by the Administrator, assuring compliance as expeditiously as practicable.

(B) (i) Within 3 years after the date of enactment of the Clean Air Act Amendments of 1990, the Administrator shall promulgate reasonable regulations and appropriate guidance to provide, to the greatest extent practicable, for the prevention and detection of accidental releases of regulated substances and for response to such releases by the owners or operators of the sources of such releases. The Administrator shall utilize the expertise of the Secretaries of Transportation and Labor in promulgating such regulations. As appropriate, such regulations shall cover the use, operation, repair, replacement, and maintenance of equipment to monitor, detect, inspect, and control such releases, including training of persons in the use and maintenance of such equipment and in the conduct of periodic inspections. The regulations shall include procedures and measures for emergency response after an accidental release of a regulated substance in order to protect human health and the environment. The regulations shall cover storage, as well as operations. The regulations shall, as appropriate, recognize differences in size, operations, processes, class and categories of sources and the voluntary actions of such sources to prevent such releases and respond to such releases. The regulations shall be applicable to a stationary source 3 years after the date of promulgation, or 3 years after the date on which a regulated substance present at the source in more than threshold amounts is first listed under paragraph (3), whichever is later.

(ii) The regulations under this subparagraph shall require the owner or operator of stationary sources at which a regulated substance is present in more than a threshold quantity to prepare and implement a risk management plan to detect and prevent or minimize accidental releases of such substances from the stationary source, and to provide a prompt emergency response to any such releases in order to protect human health and the environment. Such plan shall provide for compliance with the requirements of this subsection and shall also include each of the following:

(I) a hazard assessment to assess the potential effects of an accidental release of any regulated substance. This assessment shall include an estimate of potential release quantities and a determination of downwind effects, including potential exposures to affected populations. Such assessment shall include a previous release history of the past 5 years, including the size, concentration, and duration of releases, and shall include an evaluation of worst case accidental releases;

(II) a program for preventing accidental releases of regulated substances, including safety precautions and maintenance, monitoring and employee training measures to be used at the source; and

(III) a response program providing for specific actions to be taken in response to an accidental release of a regulated substance so as to protect human health and the environment, including procedures for informing the public and local agencies responsible for responding to accidental releases, emergency health care, and employee training measures. At the time regulations are promulgated under this subparagraph, the Administrator shall promulgate guidelines to assist stationary sources in the preparation of risk management plans. The guidelines shall, to the extent practicable, include model risk management plans.

(iii) The owner or operator of each stationary source covered by clause (ii) shall register a risk management plan prepared under this subparagraph with the Administrator before the effective date of regulations under clause (i) in such form and manner as the Administrator shall, by rule, require. Plans prepared pursuant to this subparagraph shall also be submitted to the Chemical Safety and Hazard Investigation Board, to the State in which the stationary source is located, and to any local agency or entity having responsibility for planning for or responding to accidental releases which may occur at such source, and shall be available to the public under section 114(c). The Administrator shall establish, by rule, an auditing system to regularly review and, if necessary, require revision in risk management plans to assure that the plans comply with this subparagraph. Each such plan shall be updated periodically as required by the Administrator, by rule.

(C) Any regulations promulgated pursuant to this subsection shall to the maximum extent practicable, consistent with this subsection, be consistent with the recommendations and standards established by the American Society of Mechanical Engineers

(ASME), the American National Standards Institute (ANSI) or the American Society of Testing Materials (ASTM). The Administrator shall take into consideration the concerns of small business in promulgating regulations under this subsection.

(D) In carrying out the authority of this paragraph, the Administrator shall consult with the Secretary of Labor and the Secretary of Transportation and shall coordinate any requirements under this paragraph with any requirements established for comparable purposes by the Occupational Safety and Health Administration or the Department of Transportation. Nothing in this subsection shall be interpreted, construed or applied to impose requirements affecting, or to grant the Administrator, the Chemical Safety and Hazard Investigation Board, or any other agency any authority to regulate (including requirements for hazard assessment), the accidental release of radionuclides arising from the construction and operation of facilities licensed by the Nuclear Regulatory Commission.

(E) After the effective date of any regulation or requirement imposed under this subsection, it shall be unlawful for any person to operate any stationary source subject to such regulation or requirement in violation of such regulation or requirement. Each regulation or requirement under this subsection shall for purposes of sections 113, 114, 116, 120, 304, and 307 and other enforcement provisions of this Act, be treated as a standard in effect under subsection (d).

(F) Notwithstanding the provisions of title V or this section, no stationary source shall be required to apply for, or operate pursuant to, a permit issued under such title solely because such source is subject to regulations or requirements under this subsection.

(G) In exercising any authority under this subsection, the Administrator shall not, for purposes of section 653(b)(1) of title 29 of the United States Code, be deemed to be exercising statutory authority to prescribe or enforce standards or regulations affecting occupational safety and health.

(8) Research on Hazard Assessments. —The Administrator may collect and publish information on accident scenarios and consequences covering a range of possible events for substances listed under paragraph (3). The Administrator shall establish a program of long-term research to develop and disseminate information on methods and techniques for hazard assessment which may be useful in improving and validating the procedures employed in the preparation of hazard assessments under this subsection.

(9) Order Authority. —

(A) In addition to any other action taken, when the Administrator determines that there may be an imminent and substantial endangerment to the human health or welfare or the environment because of an actual or threatened accidental release of a regulated substance, the Administrator may secure such relief as may be necessary to abate such danger or threat, and the district court of the United States in the district in which the threat occurs shall have jurisdiction to grant such relief as the public interest and the equities of the case may require. The Administrator may also, after notice to the State in which the stationary source is located, take other action under this paragraph including, but not limited to, issuing such orders as may be necessary to protect human health. The Administrator shall take action under section 303 rather than this paragraph whenever the authority of such section is adequate to protect human health and the environment.

(B) Orders issued pursuant to this paragraph may be enforced in an action brought in the appropriate United States district court as if the order were issued under section 303 .

(C) Within 180 days after enactment of the Clean Air Act Amendments of 1990, the Administrator shall publish guidance for using the order authorities established by this paragraph. Such guidance shall provide for the coordinated use of the authorities of this paragraph with other emergency powers authorized by section 106 of the Comprehensive Environmental Response, Compensation and Liability Act, sections 311(c), 308, 309 and 504(a) of the Federal Water Pollution Control Act, sections 3007, 3008, 3013, and 7003 of the Solid Waste Disposal Act, sections 1445 and 1431 of the Safe Drinking Water Act, sections 5 and 7 of the Toxic Substances Control Act, and sections 113, 114, and 303 of this Act.

(10) Presidential Review. — The President shall conduct a review of release prevention, mitigation and response authorities of the various Federal agencies and shall clarify and coordinate agency responsibilities to assure the most effective and efficient implementation of such

authorities and to identify any deficiencies in authority or resources which may exist. The President may utilize the resources and solicit the recommendations of the Chemical Safety and Hazard Investigation Board in conducting such review. At the conclusion of such review, but not later than 24 months after the date of enactment of the Clean Air Act Amendments of 1990, the President shall transmit a message to the Congress on the release prevention, mitigation and response activities of the Federal Government making such recommendations for change in law as the President may deem appropriate. Nothing in this paragraph shall be interpreted, construed or applied to authorize the President to modify or reassign release prevention, mitigation or response authorities otherwise established by law.

(11) State authority. — Nothing in this subsection shall preclude, deny or limit any right of a State or political subdivision thereof to adopt or enforce any regulation, requirement, limitation or standard (including any procedural requirement) that is more stringent than a regulation, requirement, limitation or standard in effect under this subsection or that applies to a substance not subject to this subsection.

(s) Periodic Report. — Not later than January 15, 1993 and every 3 years thereafter, the Administrator shall prepare and transmit to the Congress a comprehensive report on the measures taken by the Agency and by the States to implement the provisions of this section. The Administrator shall maintain a database on pollutants and sources subject to the provisions of this section and shall include aggregate information from the database in each annual report. The report shall include, but not be limited to—

(1) a status report on standard-setting under subsections (d) and (f);

(2) information with respect to compliance with such standards including the costs of compliance experienced by sources in various categories and subcategories;

(3) development and implementation of the national urban air toxics program; and

(4) recommendations of the Chemical Safety and Hazard Investigation Board with respect to the prevention and mitigation of accidental releases.

§7413. Federal Enforcement [Sec. 113]

[§113 revised by PL 101–549]

(a) In General.—

(1) Order to comply with SIP.—Whenever, on the basis of any information available to the Administrator, the Administrator finds that any person has violated or is in violation of any requirements or prohibition of an applicable implementation plan or permit, the Administrator shall notify the person and the State in which the plan applies of such finding. At any time after the expiration of 30 days following the date on which such notice of a violation is issued, the Administrator may, without regard to the period of violation (subject to section 2462 of title 28 of the United States Code)—

(A) Issue an order requiring such person to comply with the requirements or prohibitions of such plan or permit,

(B) Issue an administrative penalty order in accordance with subsection (d), or

(C) Bring a civil action in accordance with subsection (b).

(2) Whenever, on the basis of information available to the Administrator, the Administrator finds that violations of an applicable implementation plan or an approved permit program under title V are so widespread that such violations appear to result from a failure of the State in which the plan or permit program applies to enforce the plan or permit program effectively, the Administrator shall so notify the State. In the case of a permit program, the notice shall be made in accordance with title V. If the Administrator finds such failure extends beyond the 30th day after such notice (90 days in the case of such permit program), the Administrator shall give public notice of such finding. During the period beginning with such public notice and ending when such State satisfied the Administrator that it will enforce such plan or permit program (hereafter referred to in this section as "period of federally assumed enforcement"), the Administrator may enforce any requirement or prohibition of such plan or permit program with respect to any person by —

(A) issuing an order requiring such person to comply with such requirement or prohibition,

(B) issuing an administrative penalty order in accordance with subsection (d), or

(C) bringing a civil action in accordance with subsection (b).

(3) EPA Enforcement of Other Requirements. — Except for a requirement or prohibition enforceable under the preceding provisions of

this subsection, whenever, on the basis of any information available to the Administrator, the Administrator finds that any person has violated, or is in violation of, any other requirement or prohibition of this title, section 303 of title III, title IV, title V, or title VI, including, but not limited to, a requirement or prohibition of any rule, plan, order, waiver, or permit promulgated, issued, or approved under those provisions or titles, or for the payment of any fee owed to the United States under this Act (other than title II), the Administrator may —

(A) issue an administrative penalty order in accordance with subsection (d),

(B) issue an order requiring such person to comply with such requirement or prohibition,

(C) bring a civil action in accordance with subsection (b) or section 305 , or

(D) request the Attorney General to commence a criminal action in accordance with subsection (c).

(4) Requirements for Orders. An order issued under this subsection (other than an order relating to a violation of section 112) shall not take effect until the person to whom it is issued has had an opportunity to confer with the Administrator concerning the alleged violation. A copy of any order issued under this subsection shall be sent to the State air pollution control agency of any State in which the violation occurs. Any order issued under this subsection shall state with reasonable specificity the nature of the violation and specify a time for compliance which the Administrator determines is reasonable, taking into account the seriousness of the violation and any good faith efforts to comply with applicable requirements. In any case in which an order under this subsection (or notice to a violator under paragraph (1)) is issued to a corporation, a copy of such order (or notice) shall be issued to appropriate corporate officers. An order issued under this subsection shall require the person to whom it was issued to comply with the requirement as expeditiously as practicable, but in no event longer than one year after the date the order was issued, and shall be nonrenewable. No order issued under this subsection shall prevent the State or the Administrator from assessing any penalties nor otherwise affect or limit the State's or the United States authority to enforce under other provisions of this Act, nor affect any person's obligations to comply with any section of this Act or with a term or condition of any permit or applicable implementation plan promulgated or approved under this Act.

(5) Failure to Comply with New Source Requirements.— Whenever, on the basis of any available information, the Administrator finds that a State is not acting in compliance with any requirement or prohibition of the Act relating to the construction of new sources or the modification of existing sources, the Administrator may —

(A) issue an order prohibiting the construction or modification of any major stationary source in any area to which such requirement applies;

(B) issue an administrative penalty order in accordance with subsection (d), or

(C) bring a civil action under subsection (b).

Nothing in this subsection shall preclude the United States from commencing a criminal action under section 113(c) at any time for any such violation.

(b) Civil Judicial Enforcement. — The Administrator shall, as appropriate, in the case of any person that is the owner of operator of an affected source, a major emitting facility, or a major stationary source, and may, in the case of any other person, commence a civil action for a permanent or temporary injunction, or to assess and recover a civil penalty of not more than $25,000 per day for each violation, or both, in any of the following instances:

(1) Whenever such person has violated, or is in violation of, any requirement or prohibition of an applicable implementation plan or permit. Such an action shall be commenced (A) during any period of federally assumed enforcement, or (B) more than 30 days following the date of the Administrator's notification under subsection (a)(1) that such person has violated, or is in violation of, such requirement or prohibition.

(2) Whenever such person has violated, or is in violation of, any other requirement or prohibition of this title, section 303 of title III, title IV, title V, or title VI, including, but not limited to, a requirement or prohibition of any rule, order, waiver or permit promulgated, issued, or approved under this Act, or for the payment of any fee owed the United States under this Act (other than title II).

(3) Whenever such person attempts to construct or modify a major stationary source in any area with respect to which a finding under subsection (a)(5) has been made. Any action under this subsection may be brought in the

district court of the United States for the district in which the violation is alleged to have occurred, or is occurring, or in which the defendant resides, or where the defendant's principal place of business is located, and such court shall have jurisdiction to restrain such violation, to require compliance, to assess such civil penalty, to collect any fees owed the United States under this Act (other than title II) and any noncompliance assessment and nonpayment penalty owed under section 120 , and to award any other appropriate relief. Notice of the commencement of such action shall be given to the appropriate State air pollution control agency. In the case of any action brought by the Administrator under this subsection, the court may award costs of litigation (including reasonable attorney and expert witness fees) to the party or parties against whom such action was brought if the court finds that such action was unreasonable.

(c) Criminal Penalties. —

(1) Any person who knowingly violates any requirement or prohibition of an applicable implementation plan (during any period of federally assumed enforcement or more than 30 days after having been notified under subsection (a)(1) by the Administrator that such person is violating such requirement or prohibition), any order under subsection (a) of this section, requirement or prohibition of section 111(e) of this title (relating to new source performance standards), section 112 of this title, section 114 of this title (relating to inspections, etc.), section 129 of this title (relating to solid waste combustion), section 165(a) of this title (relating to preconstruction requirements), an order under section 167 of this title (relating to preconstruction requirements), an order under section 303 of title III (relating to emergency orders), section 502(a) or 503(c) of title V (relating to permits), or any requirement or prohibition of title IV (relating to acid deposition control), or title VI (relating to stratospheric ozone control), including a requirement of any rule, order, waiver, or permit promulgated or approved under such sections or titles, and including any requirement for the payment of any fee owed the United States under this Act (other than title II) shall, upon conviction, be punished by a fine pursuant to title 18 of the United States Code, or by imprisonment for not to exceed 5 years, or both. If a conviction of any person under this paragraph is for a violation committed after a first conviction of such person under this paragraph, the maximum punishment shall be doubled with respect to both the fine and imprisonment.

(2) Any person who knowingly —

(A) makes any false material statement, representation, or certification in, or omits material information from, or knowingly alters, conceals, or fails to file or maintain any notice, application, record, report, plan, or other document required pursuant to this Act to be either filed or maintained (whether with respect to the requirements imposed by the Administrator or by a State);

(B) fails to notify or report as required under this Act; or

(C) falsifies, tampers, with, renders inaccurate, or fails to install any monitoring device or method required to be maintained or followed under this Act shall, upon conviction, be punished by a fine pursuant to title 18 of the United States Code, or by imprisonment for not more than 2 years, or both. If a conviction of any person under this paragraph is for a violation committed after a first conviction of such person under this paragraph, the maximum punishment shall be doubled with respect to both the fine and imprisonment.

(3) Any person who knowingly fails to pay any fee owed the United States under this title, title III, IV, V, or VI shall, upon conviction, be punished by a fine pursuant to title 18 of the United States Code, or by imprisonment for not more than 1 year, or both. If a conviction of any person under this paragraph is for a violation committed after a first conviction of such person under this paragraph, the maximum punishment shall be doubled with respect to both the fine and imprisonment.

(4) Any person who negligently releases into the ambient air any hazardous air pollutant listed pursuant to section 112 of this Act or any extremely hazardous substance listed pursuant to section 302(a)(2) of the Superfund Amendments and Reauthorization Act of 1986 (42 U.S.C. 11002(a)(2)) that is not listed in section 112 of this Act, and who at the time negligently places another person in imminent danger of death or serious bodily injury shall, upon conviction, be punished by a fine under title 18 of the United States Code, or by imprisonment for not more than 1 year, or both. If a conviction of any person under this paragraph is for a violation committed after a first conviction of such person under this paragraph, the maximum punishment shall be doubled with respect to both the fine and imprisonment.

(5) (A) Any person who knowingly releases into the ambient air any hazardous air pollutant listed pursuant to section 112 of this Act or any extremely hazardous substance listed pursuant to section 302(a)(2) of the Superfund Amendments and Reauthorization Act of 1986 (42 U.S.C. 11002(a)(2)) that is not listed in section 112 of this Act, and who knows at the time that he thereby places another person in imminent danger of death or serious bodily injury shall, upon conviction, be punished by a fine under title 18 of the United States Code, or by imprisonment of not more than 15 years, or both. Any person committing such violation which is an organization shall, upon conviction under this paragraph, be subject to a fine of not more than $1,000,000 for each violation. If a conviction of any person under this paragraph is for a violation committed after a first conviction of such person under this paragraph, the maximum punishment shall be doubled with respect to both the fine and imprisonment. For any air pollutant for which the Administrator has set an emissions standard or for any source for which a permit has been issued under title V, a release of such pollutant in accordance with that standard or permit shall not constitute a violation of this paragraph or paragraph (4).

(B) In determining whether a defendant who is an individual knew that the violation placed another person in imminent danger of death or serious bodily injury—

(i) the defendant is responsible only for actual awareness or actual belief possessed; and

(ii) knowledge possessed by a person other than the defendant, but not by the defendant, may not be attributed to the defendant; except that in proving a defendant's possession of actual knowledge, circumstantial evidence may be used, including evidence that the defendant took affirmative steps to be shielded from relevant information.

(C) It is an affirmative defense to a prosecution that the conduct charged was freely consented to by the person endangered and that the danger and conduct charged were reasonably foreseeable hazards of—

(i) an occupation, a business, or a profession; or

(ii) medical treatment or medical or scientific experimentation conducted by professionally approved methods and such other person had been made aware of the risks involved prior to giving consent.

The defendant may establish an affirmative defense under this subparagraph by a preponderance of the evidence.

(D) All general defenses, affirmative defenses, and bars to prosecution that may apply with respect to other Federal criminal offenses may apply under subparagraph (A) of this paragraph and shall be determined by the courts of the United States according to the principles of common law as they may be interpreted in the light of reason and experience. Concepts of justification and excuse applicable under this section may be developed in the light of reason and experience.

(E) The term 'organization' means a legal entity, other than a government, established or organized for any purpose, and such term includes a corporation, company, association, firm, partnership, joint stock company, foundation, institution, trust, society, union, or any other association of persons.

(F) The term 'serious bodily injury' means bodily injury which involves a substantial risk of death, unconsciousness, extreme physical pain, protracted and obvious disfigurement or protracted loss or impairment of the function of a bodily member, organ, or mental faculty.

(6) For the purpose of this subsection, the term 'person' includes, in addition to the entities referred to in section 302(e) , any responsible corporate officer.

(d) Administrative Assessment of Civil Penalties. —

(1) The Administrator may issue an administrative order against any person assessing a civil administrative penalty of up to $25,000, per day of violation, whenever, on the basis of any available information, the Administrator finds that such person—

(A) has violated or is violating any requirement or prohibition of an applicable implementation plan (such order shall be issued (i) during any period of federally assumed enforcement, or (ii) more than thirty days following the date of the Administrator's notification under subsection (a)(1) of this section of a finding that such person has violated or is violating such requirement or prohibition); or

(B) has violated or is violating any other requirement or prohibition of title I, III, IV, V, or VI, including, but not limited to, a requirement or prohibition of any rule, order, waiver, permit, or plan promulgated, issued, or approved under this Act, or for the payment of any fee owed the United States under this Act (other than title II); or

(C) attempts to construct or modify a major stationary source in any area with respect to which a finding under subsection (a)(5) of this section has been made. The Administrator's authority under this paragraph shall be limited to matters where the total penalty sought does not exceed $200,000 and the first alleged date of violation occurred no more than 12 months prior to the initiation of the administrative action, except where the Administrator and the Attorney General jointly determine that a matter involving a larger penalty amount or longer period of violation is appropriate for administrative penalty action. Any such determination by the Administrator and the Attorney General shall not be subject to judicial review.

(2) (A) An administrative penalty assessed under paragraph (1) shall be assessed by the Administrator by an order made after opportunity for a hearing on the record in accordance with sections 554 and 556 of title 5 of the United States Code. The Administrator shall issue reasonable rules for discovery and other procedures for hearings under this paragraph. Before issuing such an order, the Administrator shall give written notice to the person to be assessed an administrative penalty of the Administrator's proposal to issue such order and provide such person an opportunity to request such a hearing on the order, within 30 days of the date the notice is received by such person.

(B) The Administrator may compromise, modify, or remit, with or without conditions, any administrative penalty which may be imposed under this subsection.

(3) The Administrator may implement, after consultation with the Attorney General and the States, a field citation program through regulations establishing appropriate minor violations for which field citations assessing civil penalties not to exceed $5,000 per day of violation may be issued by officers or employees designated by the Administrator. Any person to whom a field citation is assessed may, within a reasonable time as prescribed by the Administrator through regulation, elect to pay the penalty assessment or to request a hearing on the field citation. If a request for a hearing is not made within the time specified in the regulation, the penalty assessment in the field citation shall be final. Such hearing shall not be subject to section 554 or 556 of title 5 of the United States Code, but shall provide a reasonable opportunity to be heard and to present evidence. Payment of a civil penalty required by a field citation shall not be a defense to further enforcement by the United States or a State to correct a violation, or to assess the statutory maximum penalty pursuant to other authorities in the Act, if the violation continues.

(4) Any person against whom a civil penalty is assessed under paragraph (3) of this subsection or to whom an administrative penalty order is issued under paragraph (1) of this subsection may seek review of such assessment in the United States District Court for the District of Columbia or for the district in which the violation is alleged to have occurred, in which such person resides, or where such person's principal place of business is located, by filing in such court within 30 days following the date the administrative penalty order becomes final under paragraph (2), the assessment becomes final under paragraph (3), or a final decision following a hearing under paragraph (3) is rendered, and by simultaneously sending a copy of the filing by certified mail to the Administrator and the Attorney General. Within 30 days thereafter, the Administrator shall file in such court a certified copy, or certified index, as appropriate, of the record on which the administrative penalty order or assessment was issued. Such court shall not set aside or remand such order or assessment unless there is not substantial evidence in the record, taken as a whole, to support the finding of a violation or unless the order or penalty assessment constitutes an abuse of discretion. Such order or penalty assessment shall not be subject to review by any court except as provided in this paragraph. In any such proceedings, the United States may seek to recover civil penalties ordered or assessed under this section.

(5) If any person fails to pay an assessment of a civil penalty or fails to comply with an administrative penalty order—

(A) After the order or assessment has become final, or

(B) after a court in an action brought under paragraph (4) has entered a final judgment in favor of the Administrator, the Administrator shall request the Attorney General to bring a civil action in an appropriate district court to enforce the order or to recover the amount ordered or assessed (plus interest at rates established pursuant to section 6621(a)(2) of the Internal Revenue Code of 1986 from the date of the final order or decision or the date of the final judgment, as the case may be). In such an action, the validity, amount, and appropriateness of such order or assessment shall not be subject to review. Any person who fails to pay on a timely basis a civil penalty ordered or assessed under this section shall be required to pay, in addition to such penalty and interest, the United States enforcement expenses, including but not limited to attorneys fees and costs incurred by the United States for collection proceedings and a quarterly nonpayment penalty for each quarter during which such failure to pay persists. Such nonpayment penalty shall be 10 percent of the aggregate amount of such person's outstanding penalties and nonpayment penalties accrued as of the beginning of such quarter.

(e) Penalty Assessment Criteria. —

(1) In determining the amount of any penalty to be assessed under this section or section 304(a), the Administrator or the court, as appropriate, shall take into consideration (in addition to such other factors as justice may require) the size of the business, the economic impact of the penalty on the business, the violator's full compliance history and good faith efforts to comply, the duration of the violation as established by any credible evidence (including evidence other than the applicable test method), payment by the violator of penalties previously assessed for the same violation, the economic benefit of noncompliance, and the seriousness of the violation. The court shall not assess penalties for noncompliance with administrative subpoenas under section 307(a), or actions under section 114 of this Act, where the violator had sufficient cause to violate or fail or refuse to comply with such subpoena or action.

(2) A penalty may be assessed for each day of violation. For purposes of determining the number of days of violation for which a penalty may be assessed under subsection (b) or (d)(1) of this section, or section 304(a), or an assessment may be made under section 120, where the Administrator or an air pollution control agency has notified the source of the violation, and the plaintiff makes a prima facie showing that the conduct or events giving rise to the violation are likely to have continued or recurred past the date of notice, the days of violation shall be presumed to include the date of such notice and each and every day thereafter until the violator establishes that continuous compliance has been achieved, except to the extent that the violator can prove by a preponderance of the evidence that there were intervening days during which no violation occurred or that the violation was not continuing in nature.

(f) Awards. — The Administrator may pay an award, not to exceed $10,000, to any person who furnishes information or services which lead to a criminal conviction or a judicial or administrative civil penalty for any violation of this title or title III, IV, V, or VI of this Act enforced under this section. Such payment is subject to available appropriations for such purposes as provided in annual appropriation Acts. Any officer, or employee of the United States or any State or local government who furnishes information or renders service in the performance of an official duty is ineligible for payment under this subsection. The Administrator may, by regulation, prescribe additional criteria for eligibility for such an award.

(g) Settlements; Public Participation. —At least 30 days before a consent order or settlement agreement of any kind under this Act to which the United States is a party (other than enforcement actions under section 113, 120 , or title II, whether or not involving civil or criminal penalties, or judgments subject to Department of Justice policy on public participation) is final or filed with a court, the Administrator shall provide a reasonable opportunity by notice in the Federal Register to persons who are not named as parties or intervenors to the action or matter to comment in writing. The Administrator or the Attorney General, as appropriate, shall promptly consider any such written comments and may withdraw or withhold his consent to the proposed order or agreement if the comments disclose facts or considerations which indicate that such consent is inappropriate, improper, inadequate, or inconsistent with the requirements of this Act. Nothing in this subsection shall apply to civil or criminal penalties under this Act.

(h) Operator— For purposes of the provisions of this section and section 120, the term 'operator', as used in such provisions, shall include any person who is senior management personnel or a corporate officer. Except in the case of knowing and willful violations, such term shall not include any person who is a stationary engineer or technician responsible for the operation, maintenance, repair, or monitoring of equipment and facilities and who often has supervisory and training duties but who is not senior management personnel or a corporate officer. Except in the case of knowing and willful violations, for purposes of subsection (c)(4) of this section, the term 'a person' shall not include an employee who is carrying out his normal activities and who is not a part of senior management personnel or a corporate officer. Except in the case of knowing and willful violations, for purposes of paragraphs (1), (2), (3), and (5) of subsection (c) of this section the term 'a person' shall not include an employee who is carrying out his normal activities and who is acting under orders from the employer.

[Editor's Note: §114(a)(i) was amended by two different sections of PL 101–549. Both versions of the amended section appear below.]

[Text of (i) as amended by §302 of PL 101–549]

§7414. Recordkeeping, Inspections, Monitoring, and Entry [Sec. 114]

(a) For the purpose (i) of developing or assisting in the development of any implementation plan under section 110 or 111(d) , any standard of performance under section 111, any emission standard under section 112, or any regulation of solid waste combustion under section 129, (ii) of determining whether any person is in violation of any such standard or any requirement of such a plan, of (iii) carrying out any provision of this Act (except a provision of Title II with respect to a manufacturer of new motor vehicles or new motor vehicle engines)—

[Text of (i) as amended by §702 of PL 101–549]

(a) For the purpose (i) of developing or assisting in the development of any implementation plan under section 110 or 111(d), any standard of performance under section 111, any emission standard under section 112 or any regulation under section 129 (relating to solid waste combustion), (ii) of determining whether any person is in violation of any such standard or any requirement of such a plan, of (iii) carrying out any provision of this Act (except a provision of Title II with respect to a manufacturer of new motor vehicles or new motor vehicle engines)—

[§114(a) amended by PL 95–95; PL 95–190; PL 101–549]

(1) the Administrator may require any person who owns or operates any emission source, who manufactures emission control equipment or process equipment, who the Administrator believes may have information necessary for the purposes set forth in this section, or who is subject to any requirement of this Act (other than a manufacturer subject to the provisions of section 206(c) or 208 with respect to a provision of title II) on a one-time, periodic or continuous basis to—

(A) establish and maintain such records;

(B) make such reports;

(C) install, use, and maintain such monitoring equipment, and use such audit procedures, or methods;

(D) sample such emissions (in accordance with such procedures or methods, at such locations, at such intervals, during such periods and in such manner as the Administrator shall prescribe);

(E) keep records on control equipment parameters, production variables or other indirect data when direct monitoring of emissions is impractical;

(F) submit compliance certifications in accordance with section 114(a)(3); and

(G) provide such other information as the Administrator may reasonably require; and

[§114(a)(1) revised by PL 95–95; PL 95–190; PL 101–549]

(2) the Administrator or his authorized representative, upon presentation of his credentials—

(A) shall have a right of entry to, upon or through any premises of such person or in which any records required to be maintained under paragraph (1) of this section are located, and

[§114(a)(2)(A) amended by PL 95–95]

(B) may at reasonable times have access to and copy of any records, inspect any monitoring equipment or methods required under paragraph (1), and sample any emissions which such person is required to sample under paragraph (1)

[§114(a)(2)(B) amended by PL 95–95]

(3) The Administrator shall in the case of any person which is the owner or operator of a major stationary source, and may, in the case of any other person, require enhanced monitoring and submission of compliance certifications. Compliance certifications shall include (A) identification of the applicable requirement that is the basis of the certification, (B) the method used for determining the compliance status of the source, (C) the compliance status, (D) whether compliance is continuous or intermittent, (E) esuch other facts as the Administrator may require. Compliance certi-

fications and monitoring data shall be subject to subsection (c) of this section. Submission of a compliance certification shall in no way limit the Administrator's authorities to investigate or otherwise implement this Act. The Administrator shall promulgate rules to provide guidance and to implement this paragraph within 2 years after the enactment of the Clean Air Act Amendments of 1990.

[§114(a)(3) added by PL 101–549]

(b) (1) Each State may develop and submit to the Administrator a procedure for carrying out this section in such State. If the Administrator finds the State procedure is adequate, he may delegate to such State any authority he has to carry out this section.

[§114(b)(1) amended by PL 95–95]

(2) Nothing in this subsection shall prohibit the Administrator from carrying out this section in a State.

(c) Any records, reports or information obtained under subsection (a) shall be available to the public, except that upon a showing satisfactory to the Administrator by any person that records, reports, or information, or particular part thereof, (other than emission data) to which the Administrator has access under this section if made public would divulge methods or processes entitled to protection as trade secrets of such person, the Administrator shall consider such record, report, or information or particular portion thereof confidential in accordance with the purposes of section 1905 of title 18 of the United States Code, except that such record, report, or information may be disclosed to other officers, employees, or authorized representatives of the United States concerned with carrying out this Act or when relevant in any proceeding under this Act.

(d) (1) In the case of any emission standard or limitation or other requirement which is adopted by a State, as part of an applicable implementation plan or as part of an order under section 113(d) , before carrying out an entry, inspection, or monitoring under paragraph (2) of subsection (a) with respect to such standard, limitation, or other requirement, the Administrator (or his representatives) shall provide the State air pollution control agency with reasonable prior notice of such action, indicating the purpose of such action. No State agency which receives notice under this paragraph of an action proposed to be taken may use the information contained in the notice to inform the person whose property is proposed to be affected of the proposed action. If the Administrator has reasonable basis for believing that a State agency is so using or will so use such information, notice to the agency under this paragraph is not required until such time as the Administrator determines the agency will no longer so use information contained in a notice under this paragraph. Nothing in this section shall be construed to require notification to any State agency of any action taken by the Administrator with respect to any standard, limitation, or other requirement which is not part of an applicable implementation plan or which was promulgated by the Administrator under section 110(c) .

(2) Nothing in paragraph (1) shall be construed to provide that any failure of the Administrator to comply with the requirements of such paragraph shall be a defense in any enforcement action brought by the Administrator or shall make inadmissable as evidence in any such action any information or material obtained notwithstanding such failure to comply with such requirements.

[§114(d) added by PL 95–95]

§7415. International Air Pollution [Sec. 115]

(a) Whenever the Administrator, upon receipt of reports, surveys or studies from any duly constituted international agency has reason to believe that any air pollutant or pollutants emitted in the United States cause or contribute to air pollution which may reasonably be anticipated to endanger public health or welfare in a foreign country or whenever the Secretary of State requests him to do so with respect to such pollution which the Secretary of State alleges is of such a nature the Administrator shall give formal notification thereof to the Governor of the State in which such emissions originate.

(b) The notice of the Administrator shall be deemed to be a finding under section 110(a)(2)(H)(ii) which requires a plan revision with respect to so much of the applicable implementation plan as is inadequate to prevent or eliminate the endangerment referred to in subsection (a). Any foreign country so affected by such emission of pollutant or pollutants shall be invited to appear at any public hearing associated with any revision of the appropriate portion of the applicable implementation plan.

(c) This section shall apply only to a foreign country which the Administrator determines has given the United States essentially the same rights with respect to the prevention or control of air pollution occurring in that country as is given that country by this section.

(d) Recommendations issued following any abatement conference conducted prior to the enactment of the Clean Air Act Amendments of 1977 shall remain in effect with respect to any pollutant for which no national ambient air quality standard has been established under section 109 of this Act unless the Administrator, after consultation with all agencies which were party to the conference, rescinds any such recommendation on grounds of obsolescence.

[§115 revised by PL 95–95]

§7416. Retention of State Authority [Sec. 116]

Except as otherwise provided in sections 119(c), (e) and (f) (as in effect before the date of the enactment of the Clean Air Act Amendments of 1977), 209.211(c)(4), and 233 (preempting certain State regulation of moving sources) nothing in this Act shall preclude or deny the right of any State or political subdivision thereof to adopt or enforce (1) any standard or limitation respecting emissions of air pollutants or (2) any requirement respecting control or abatement of air pollution; except that if an emission standard or limitation is in effect under an applicable implementation plan or under section 111 or 112 , such State or political subdivision may not adopt or enforce any emission standard or limitation which is less stringent than the standard or limitation under such plan or section.

[§116 amended by PL 93–319; PL 95–190]

§7417. President's Air Quality Advisory Board and Advisory Committees [Sec. 117]

(a) In order to obtain assistance in the development and implementation of the purposes of this Act including air quality criteria, recommended control techniques, standards, research and development, and to encourage the continued efforts on the part of industry to improve air quality and to develop economically feasible methods for the control and abatement of air pollution, the Administration shall from time to time establish advisory committees. Committee members shall include, but not be limited to, persons who are knowledgeable concerning air quality from the standpoint of health, welfare, economics, or technology.

[Former §117(d) amended and redesignated as (a) by PL 95–95]

(b) The members of any other advisory committees appointed pursuant to this Act who are not officers or employees of the United States while attending conferences or meeting or while otherwise serving at the request of the Administrator, shall be entitled to receive compensation at a rate to be fixed by the Administrator, but not exceeding $100 per diem, including travel-time, and while away from their homes or regular places of business they may be allowed travel expenses, including per diem in lieu of subsistence, as authorized by section 5703 of title 5 of the United States Code for persons in the Government service employed intermittently.

[Former §117(e) amended and redesignated as (b) by PL 95–95]

[Editor's Note: The following note appears in the 1988 Edition of the U.S. Code after 42 U.S.C. 7417(c): "subsec. (c) was originally enacted as subsec (f) but has been redesignated (c) for purposes of codification in view of the failure of Pub. L. 95–95 to redesignated subsec. (f) as (c) after repealing former subsecs. (a) and (b) and redesignating former subsecs. (d) and (e) as (a) and (b)."]

(f) Prior to—

(1) issuing criteria for an air pollutant under section 108(a)(2),

(2) publishing any list under section 111(b)(1)(A) or 112(b)(1)(A) ,

(3) publishing any standard under section 111 or section 112, or

[§117(f) amended by PL 95–623]

(4) publishing any regulation under section 202(a), the Administrator shall, to the maximum extent practicable within the time provided, consult with appropriate advisory committees, independent experts, and Federal departments and agencies.

§7418. Control of Pollution from Federal Facilities [Sec. 118]

(a) Each department, agency, and instrumentality of the executive, legislative, and judicial branches of the Federal Government (1) having jurisdiction over any property or facility, or (2) engaged in any activity resulting, or which may result, in the discharge of air pollutants, and each officer, agent, or employee, thereof, shall be subject to, and comply with, all Federal, State, interstate, and local requirements, administrative authority, and process and sanctions respecting the control and abatement of air pollution in the same manner, and to the same extent as any non-governmental entity. The preceding sentence shall apply (A) to any requirement whether substantive or procedural (including any recordkeeping or reporting requirement, any requirement respecting permits and any other requirement whatsoever), (B) to any requirement to pay a fee or charge imposed by any State or local agency to defray the costs of its air pollution regulatory program, (C) to the exercise of any Federal, State, or local administrative authority, and (D) to any process and sanction, whether enforced in Federal, State, or local courts, or in any other manner. This subsection shall apply notwithstanding any immunity of such agencies, officers, agents, or employees under any law or rule of law. No officer, agent, or employee of the United States shall be personally liable for any civil penalty for which he is not otherwise liable.

(b) The President may exempt any emission source of any department, agency, or instrumentality in the executive branch from compliance with such a requirement if he determines it to be in the paramount interest of the United States to do so, except that no exemption may be granted from section 111 , and an exemption from section 112 may be granted only in accordance with section 112(i)(4) . No such exemption shall be granted due to lack of appropriation unless the President shall have specifically requested such appropriation as a part of the budgetary process and the Congress shall have failed to make available such requested appropriation. Any exemption shall be for a period not in excess of one year, but additional exemptions may be granted for periods of not to exceed one year upon the President's making a new determination. In addition to any such exemption of a particular emission source, the President may, if he determines it to be in the paramount interest of the United States to do so, issue regulations exempting from compliance with the requirements of this section any weaponry, equipment, aircraft, vehicles, or other classes or categories of property which are owned or operated by the Armed Forces of the United States (including the Coast Guard) or by the National Guard of any State and which are uniquely military in nature. The President shall reconsider the need for such regulations at three-year intervals. The President shall report each January to the Congress all exemptions from the requirements of this section granted during the preceding calendar year, together with his reason for granting each such exemption.

[§118(b) amended by PL 101–549]

(c) Government Vehicles. — Each department, agency, and instrumentality of executive, legislative, and judicial branches of the Federal Government shall comply with all applicable provisions of a valid inspection and maintenance program established under the provisions of subpart 2 of part D or subpart 3 of part D except for such vehicles that are considered military tactical vehicles.

[§118(c) added by PL 101–549]

(d) Vehicles Operated on Federal Installations. — Each department, agency, and instrumentality of executive, legislative, and judicial branches of the Federal Government having jurisdiction over any property or facility shall require all employees which operate motor vehicles on the property or facility to furnish proof of compliance with the applicable requirements of any vehicle inspection and maintenance program established under the provisions of subpart 2 of part D or subpart 3 of part D for the State in which such property or facility is located (without regard to whether such vehicles are registered in the State). The installation shall use one of the following methods to establish proof of compliance—

(1) presentation by the vehicle owner of a valid certificate of compliance from the vehicle inspection and maintenance program;

(2) presentation by the vehicle owner of proof of vehicle registration within the geographic area covered by the vehicle inspection and maintenance program (except for any program whose enforcement mechanism is not through the denial of vehicle registration);

(3) another method approved by the vehicle inspection and maintenance program administrator.

[§118(d) added by PL 101–549]

[Editor's Note: Section 112(b)(1) of PL 95–95, The Clean Air Act Amendments of 1977, repealed section 119 of the Clean Air Act (Energy-Related Authority, added by PL 93–319). Section 117(b) of PL 95–95 added a new section 119 — relating to primary nonferrous smelters —to the Clean Air Act. The provisions of 112(b) follow.]

[Sec. 112]

(b) (1) section 119 of [the Clean Air Act] is hereby repealed. All references to such section 119 or subsections thereof in section 2 of the Energy Supply and Environmental Coordination Act of 1974 (Public Law 93–319) or any amendment thereto, or any subsequent enactment which supersedes such Act, shall be construed to refer to section 113(d) of the Clean Air Act and to paragraph (5) thereof in particular. Any certification or notification required to be given by the Administrator of the Environmental Protection Agency under section 2 of the Energy Supply and Environmental Coordination Act of 1974 or any amendment thereto, or any sub-

sequent enactment which supersedes such Act, shall be given only when the Governor of the State in which is located the source to which the proposed order under section 113(d)(5) of the Clean Air Act is to be issued gives his prior written concurrence.

(2) In the case of any major stationary source to which any requirement is applicable under section 113(d)(5)(B) of the Clean Air Act and for which certification is required under section 2 of the Energy Supply and Environmental Coordination Act of 1974 or any amendment thereto, or any subsequent enactment which supersedes such Act, the Administrator of the Environmental Protection Agency shall certify the date which he determines is the earliest date that such source will be able to comply with all such requirements. In the case of any plant or installation which the Administrator of the Environmental Protection Agency determines (after consultation with the State) will not be subject to an order under section 113(d) of the Clean Air Act and for which certification is required under section 2 of the Energy Supply and Environmental Coordination Act of 1974 or any amendment thereto, or any subsequent enactment which supersedes such Act, the Administrator of the Environmental Protection Agency shall certify the date which he determines is the earliest date that such plant or installation will be able to burn coal in compliance with all applicable emission limitations under the implementation plan.

(3) Any certification required under section 2 of the Energy Supply and Environmental Coordination Act of 1974 or any amendment thereto, or any subsequent enactment which supersedes such Act, or under this subsection may be provided in an order under section 113(d) of the Clean Air Act.

§7419. Primary Nonferrous Smelter Orders
[Sec. 119]

(a) (1) Upon application by the owner or operator of a primary nonferrous smelter, a primary nonferrous smelter order under subsection (b) may be issued—

(A) by the Administrator, after thirty days' notice to the State, or

(B) by the State in which such source is located, but no such order issued by the State shall take effect until the Administrator determines that such order has been issued in accordance with the requirements of this Act.

Not later than ninety days after submission by the State to the Administrator of notice of the issuance of a primary nonferrous smelter order under this section, the Administrator shall determine whether or not such order has been issued by the State in accordance with the requirements of this Act. If the Administrator determines that such order has not been issued in accordance with such requirements, he shall conduct a hearing respecting the reasonable control technology for primary nonferrous smelters.

(2) (A) An order issued under this section to a primary nonferrous smelter shall be referred to as a 'primary nonferrous smelter order'. No primary nonferrous smelter may receive both an enforcement order under section 113(d) and a primary nonferrous smelter order under this section.

(B) Before any hearing conducted under this section in the case of an application made by the owner or operator of a primary nonferrous smelter for a second order under this section, the applicant shall furnish the Administrator (or the State as the case may be) with a statement of the grounds on which such application is based (including all supporting documents and information). The statement of the grounds for the proposed order shall be provided by the Administrator or the State in any case in which such State or Administrator is acting on its own initiative. Such statement (including such documents and information) shall be made available to the public for a thirty- day period before such hearing and shall be considered as part of such hearing. No primary nonferrous smelter order may be granted unless the applicant establishes that he meets the conditions required for the issuance of such order (or the Administrator or State establishes the meeting of such conditions when acting on their own initiative).

(C) Any decision with respect to the issuance of a primary nonferrous smelter order shall be accompanied by a concise statement of the findings and of the basis of such findings.

(3) For the purposes of section 110, 304, and 307 of this Act, any order issued by the State and in effect pursuant to this subsection shall become part of the applicable implementation plan.

[§119(a)(3) added by PL 95–190]

(b) A primary nonferrous smelter order under this section may be issued to a primary nonferrous smelter if—

(1) such smelter is in existence on the date of the enactment of this section;

(2) the requirement of the applicable implementation plan with respect to which the order is issued is an emission limitation or standard

for sulfur oxides which is necessary and intended to be itself sufficient to enable attainment and maintenance of national primary and secondary ambient air quality standards for sulfur oxides, and

(3) such smelter is unable to comply with such requirement by the applicable date for compliance because no means of emission limitation applicable to such smelter which will enable it to achieve compliance with such requirement has been adequately demonstrated to be reasonably available (as determined by the Administrator, taking into account the cost of compliance, non-air quality health and environmental impact, and energy consideration).

(c) (1) A second order issued to a smelter under this section shall set forth compliance schedules containing increments of progress which require compliance with the requirement postponed as expeditiously as practicable. The increments of progress shall be limited to requiring compliance with subsection (d) and, in the case of a second order, to procuring, installing, and operating the necessary means of emission limitation as expeditiously as practicable after the Administrator determines such means have been adequately demonstrated to be reasonably available within the meaning of subsection (b)(3).

(2) Not in excess of two primary nonferrous smelter orders may be issued under this section to any primary nonferrous smelter. The first such order issued to a smelter shall not result in the postponement of the requirement with respect to which such order is issued beyond January 1, 1983. The second such order shall not result in the postponement of such requirement beyond January 1, 1988.

(d) (1) (A) Each primary nonferrous smelter to which an order is issued under this section shall be required to use such interim measures for the period during which such order is in effect as may be necessary in the judgment of the Administrator to assure attainment and maintenance of the national primary and secondary ambient air quality standards during such period, taking into account the aggregate effect on air quality of such order together with all variances, extensions, waivers, enforcement orders, delayed compliance orders and primary nonferrous smelter orders previously issued under this Act.

(B) Such interim requirements shall include—

(i) a requirement that the source to which the order applies comply with such reporting requirements and conduct such monitoring as the Administrator determines may be necessary, and

(ii) such measures as the Administrator determines are necessary to avoid an imminent and substantial endangerment to health of persons.

(C) Such interim measures shall also, except as provided in paragraph (2), include continuous emission reduction technology. The Administrator shall condition the use of any such interim measures upon the agreement of the owner or operator of the smelter—

(i) to comply with such conditions as the Administrator determines are necessary to maximize the reliability and enforceability of such interim measures, as applied to the smelter, in attaining and maintaining the national ambient air quality standards to which the order relates, and

(ii) to commit reasonable resources to research and development of appropriate emission control technology.

(2) The requirement of paragraph (1) for the use of continuous emission reduction technology may be waived with respect to a particular smelter by the State or the Administrator, after notice and a hearing on the record, and upon a showing by the owner or operator of the smelter that such requirement would be so costly as to necessitate permanent or prolonged temporary cessation of operations of the smelter. Upon application for such waiver, the Administrator shall be notified and shall, within ninety days, hold a hearing on the record in accordance with section 554 of title 5 of the United States Code. At such hearing the Administrator shall require the smelter involved to present information relating to any alleged cessation of operations and the detailed reasons or justifications therefor. On the basis of such hearing the Administrator shall make findings of fact as to the effect of such requirement and on the alleged cessation of operations and shall make recommendations as he deems appropriate. Such report, findings, and recommendations shall be available to the public, and shall be taken into account by the State or the Administrator in making the decision whether or not to grant such waiver.

(3) In order to obtain information for purposes of a waiver under paragraph (2), the Administrator may, on his own motion, conduct an

investigation and use the authority under section 321.

[§119(d)(3) amended by PL 95–190]

(4) In the case of any smelter which on the date of enactment of this section uses continuous emission reduction technology and supplemental controls and which receives an initial primary nonferrous smelter order under this section, no additional continuous emission reduction technology shall be required as a condition of such order unless the Administrator determines, at any time, after notice and public hearing, that such additional continuous emission reduction technology is adequately demonstrated to be reasonably available for the primary nonferrous smelter industry.

(e) At any time during which an order under this section applies, the Administrator may enter upon a public hearing respecting the availability of technology. Any order under this section shall be terminated if the Administrator determines on the record, after notice and public hearing, that the conditions upon which the order was based no longer exist. If the owner or operator of the smelter to which the order is issued demonstrates that prompt termination of such order would result in undue hardship, the termination shall become effective at the earliest practicable date on which such undue hardship would not result, but in no event later than the date required under subsection (c).

[§119(e) amended by PL 95–190]

(f) If the Administrator determines that a smelter to which an order is issued under this section is in violation of any requirement of subsection (c) or (d), he shall—

(1) enforce such requirement under section 113,

(2) (after notice and opportunity for public hearing) revoke such order and enforce compliance with the requirement with respect to which such order was granted.

(3) give notice of noncompliance and commence action under section 120 , or

(4) take any appropriate combination of such actions.

[§119 added by PL 95–95]

§7420. Noncompliance Penalty [Sec. 120]

(a) (1) (A) Not later than 6 months after the date of enactment of this section, and after notice and opportunity for a public hearing, the Administrator shall promulgate regulations requiring the assessment and collection of a noncompliance penalty against persons referred to in paragraph (2)(A).

(B) (i) Each State may develop and submit to the Administrator a plan for carrying out this section in such State. If the Administrator finds that the State plan meets the requirements of this section, he may delegate to such State any authority he has to carry out this section.

(ii) Notwithstanding a delegation to a State under clause (i), the Administrator may carry out this section in such State under the circumstances described in subsection (b)(2)(B).

(2) (A) Except as provided in subparagraph (B) or (C) of this paragraph, the State or the Administrator shall assess and collect a noncompliance penalty against every person who owns or operates—

(i) a major stationary source (other than a primary nonferrous smelter which has received a primary nonferrous smelter order under section 119) which is not in compliance with any emission limitation, emission standard or compliance schedule under any applicable implementation plan (whether or not such source is subject to a Federal or State consent decree), or

(ii) a stationary source which is not in compliance with an emission limitation, emission standard, standard of performance, or other requirement established under section 111, 167, 303, or 112 of this Act, or

[§120(a)(2)(A)(ii) amended by PL 101–549]

(iii) a stationary source which is not in compliance with any requirement of title IV, V, or VI of this Act, or

[New §120 (a)(2)(A)(iii) added, former (iii) amended and redesignated as new (iv) by PL 101–549]

(iv) any source referred to in clause (i), (ii), or (iii) (for which an extension, order, or suspension referred to in subparagraph (B), or Federal or State consent decree is in effect), or a primary nonferrous smelter which has received a primary non-ferrous smelter order under section 119 which is not in compliance with any interim emission control requirement or schedule of compliance under such extension, order, suspension, or consent decree.

For purposes of subsection (d)(2), in the case of a penalty assessed with respect to a source referred to in clause (iii) of this subparagraph, the costs referred to in such subsection (d)(2) shall be the economic value of noncompliance with the interim emission control requirement or the remaining steps in the schedule of compliance referred to in such clause.

(B) Notwithstanding the requirements of subparagraph (A)(i) and (ii), the owner or operator of any source shall be exempted from the duty to pay a noncompliance penalty under such requirements with respect to that source if, in accordance with the procedures in subsection (b) (5), the owner or operator demonstrates that the failure of such source to comply with any such requirement is due solely to—

(i) a conversion by such source from the burning of petroleum products or natural gas, or both, as the permanent primary energy source to the burning of coal pursuant to an order under section 113(d)(5) or section 119 (as in effect before the date of enactment of the Clean Air Act Amendments of 1977);

(ii) in the case of a coal-burning source granted an extension under the second sentence of section 119(c)(1) (as in effect before the date of the enactment of the Clean Air Act Amendments of 1977) a prohibition from using petroleum products or natural gas or both, by reason of an order under the provisions of section 2 (a) and (b) of the Energy Supply and Environmental Coordination Act of 1974 or under any legislation which amends or supersedes such provisions;

(iii) the use of innovative technology sanctioned by an enforcement order under section 113(d)(4);

(iv) an inability to comply with any such requirement, for which inability the source has received an order under section 113(d) (or an order under section 113 issued before the date of enactment of this section) which has the effect of permitting a delay or violation of any requirement of this Act (including a requirement of an applicable implementation plan) which inability results from reasons entirely beyond the control of the owner or operator of such source or of any entity controlling, controlled by, or under common control with the owner or operator of such source, or

(v) the conditions by reason of which a temporary emergency suspension is authorized under section 110(f) or (g).

An exemption under this subparagraph shall cease to be effective if the source fails to comply with the interim emission control requirements or schedules of compliance (including increments of progress) under any such extension, order, or suspension.

[§120(a)(2)(B) amended by PL 95–190]

(C) The Administrator may, after notice and opportunity for public hearing, exempt any source from the requirements of this section with respect to a particular instance of noncompliance if he finds that such instance of noncompliance is de minimis in nature and in duration.

(b) Regulations under subsection (a) shall—

(1) permit the assessment and collection of such penalty by the State if the State has a delegation of authority in effect under subsection (a)(1)(B)(i);

(2) provide for the assessment and collection of such penalty by the Administrator, if—

(A) the State does not have a delegation of authority in effect under subsection (a)(1)(B)(i), or

[§120(b)(2)(A) amended by PL 95–190]

(B) the State has such a delegation in effect but fails with respect to any particular person or source to assess or collect the penalty in accordance with the requirements of this section;

(3) require the States, or in the event the States fail to do so, the Administrator, to give a brief but reasonably specific no tice of noncompliance under this section to each person referred to in subsection (a)(2)(A) with respect to each source owned or operated by such person which is not in compliance as provided in such subsection, not later than July 1, 1979, or thirty days after the discovery of such noncompliance, whichever is later;

(4) require each person to whom notice is given under paragraph (3) to—

(A) calculate the amount of the penalty owed (determined in accordance with subsection (d)(2) and the schedule of payments (determined in accordance with subsection (d)(3) for each such source and, within forty-five days after the issuance of such notice or after the denial of a petition under subparagraph (B), to submit that calculation and proposed schedule, together with the information necessary for an independent verification thereof, to the State and to the Administrator, or

(B) submit a petition, within forty-five days after the issuance of such notice, challenging such notice of noncompliance or alleging entitlement to an exemption under subsection (a)(2)(B) with respect to a particular source;

(5) require the Administrator to provide a hearing on the record (within the meaning of subchapter II of chapter 5 of title 5, United States Code) and to make a decision on such petition (including findings of fact and conclusions of law) not later than ninety days after the receipt of any petition under paragraph (4)(B) unless the State agrees to provide a hearing which is substantially similar to such a hearing on the record and to make a decision on such petition (including such findings and conclusions) within such ninety- day period;

(6) (A) authorize the Administrator on his own initiative to review the decision of the State under paragraph (5) and disapprove it if it is not in accordance with the requirements of this section, and

(B) require the Administrator to do so not later than sixty days after receipt of a petition under this subparagraph, notice, and public hearing and a showing by such petitioner that the State decision under paragraph (5) is not in accordance with the requirements of this section;

(7) require payment, in accordance with subsection (d), of the penalty by each person to whom notice of noncompliance is given under paragraph (3) with respect to each noncomplying source for which such notice is given unless there has been a final determination granting a petition under paragraph (4)(B) with respect to such source;

(8) authorize the State or the Administrator to adjust (and from time to time to readjust) the amount of the penalty assessment calculated or the payment schedule proposed by such owner or operator under paragraph (4), if the Administrator finds after notice and opportunity for a hearing on the record that the penalty or schedule does meet the requirements of this section; and

[§120(b)(8) amended by PL 95–190]

(9) require a final adjustment of the penalty within 180 days after such source comes into compliance in accordance with subsection (d)(4).

In any case in which the State established a noncompliance penalty under this section, the State shall provide notice thereof to the Administrator. A noncompliance penalty established by a State under this section shall apply unless the Administrator, within ninety days after the date of receipt of notice of the State penalty assessment under this section, objects in writing to the amount of the penalty as less than would be required to comply with guidelines established by the Administrator. If the Administrator objects under this subsection, he shall immediately establish a substitute noncompliance penalty applicable to such source.

[§120(b) closing paragraph amended by PL 95–190]

(c) If the owner or operator of any stationary source to whom a notice is issued under subsection (b)(3)—

(1) does not submit a timely petition under subsection (b)(4)(B), or

(2) submits a petition under subsection (b)(4)(B) which is denied, and fails to submit a calculation of the penalty assessment, a schedule for payment, and the information necessary for independent verification thereof, the State (or the Administrator, as the case may be) may enter into a contract with any person who has no financial interest in the owner or operator of the source (or in any person controlling, controlled by or under common control with such source) to assist in determining the amount of the penalty assessment or payment schedule with respect to such source. The cost of carrying out such contract may be added to the penalty to be assessed against the owner or operator of such source.

(d) (1) All penalties assessed by the Administrator under this section shall be paid to the United States Treasury. All penalties assessed by the State under this section shall be paid to such State.

(2) The amount of the penalty which shall be assessed and collected with respect to any source under this section shall be equal to—

(A) the amount determined in accordance with regulations promulgated by the Administrator under subsection (a), which is no less than the economic value which a delay in compliance beyond July 1, 1979, may have for the owner of such source, including the quarterly equivalent of the capital costs of compliance and debt service over a normal amortization period, not to exceed ten years, operation and maintenance costs foregone as a result of noncompliance, and any additional economic value which such a delay may have for the owner or operator of such source, minus

[§120(d)(2)(A) amended by PL 95–190]

(B) the amount of any expenditure made by the owner or operator of that source during any such quarter for the purpose of bringing that source into, and maintaining compliance with, such requirement to the extent that such expenditures have not been taken into account in the calculation of the penalty under subparagraph (A). To the extent that any expenditure under subparagraph (B) made during any quarter is not subtracted for such quarter from the costs under subparagraph (A), such expenditure may be subtracted for any subsequent quarter from such costs, except that in no event shall the amount paid be less than the quarterly payment minus the amount attributed to actual cost of construction.

(3) (A) The assessed penalty required under this section shall be paid in quarterly installments for the period of covered noncompliance. All quarterly payments (determined without regard to any adjustment or any subtraction under paragraph (2)(B) after the first payment shall be equal.

(B) The first payment shall be due on the date six months after the date of issuance of the notice of non-compliance under subsection (b)(3) with respect to any source or on January 1, 1980, whichever is later. Such first payment shall be in the amount of the quarterly installment for the upcoming quarter, plus the amount owed for any preceding period within the period of covered noncompliance for such source.

(C) For the purpose of this section, the term 'period of covered noncompliance' means the period which begins—

(i) two years after the date of enactment of this section, in the case of a source for which notice of noncompliance under subsection (b)(3) is issued on or before the date two years after such date of enactment, or

(ii) on the date of issuance of the notice of noncompliance under subsection (b)(3), in the case of a source for which such notice is issued after July 1, 1979,

and ending on the date on which such source comes into (or for the purpose of establishing the schedule of payments, is estimated to come into) compliance with such requirement.

(4) Upon making a determination that a source with respect to which a penalty has been paid under this section is in compliance and is maintaining compliance with the applicable requirement, the State (or the Administrator as the case may be) shall review the actual expenditures made by the owner or operator of such source for the purpose of attaining and maintaining compliance, and shall within 180 days after such source comes into compliance—

(A) provide reimbursement with interest (to be paid by the State or Secretary of the Treasury, as the case may be) at appropriate prevailing rates (as determined by the Secretary of the Treasury) for any overpayment by such person, or

(B) assess and collect an additional payment with interest at appropriate prevailing rates (as determined by the Secretary of the Treasury) for any underpayment by such person.

(5) Any person who fails to pay the amount of any penalty with respect to any source under this section on a timely basis shall be required to pay in addition a quarterly nonpayment penalty for each quarter during which such failure to pay persists. Such nonpayment penalty shall be in an amount equal to 20 percent of the aggregate amount of such person's penalties and nonpayment penalties with respect to such source which are unpaid as of the beginning of such quarter.

(e) Any action pursuant to this section, including any objection of the Administration under the last sentence of subsection (b), shall be considered a final action for purposes of judicial review of any penalty under section 307 of this Act.

(f) Any orders, payments, sanctions, or other requirements under this section shall be in addition to any other permits, orders, payments, sanctions, or other requirements established under this Act, and shall in no way affect any civil or criminal enforcement proceedings brought under any provision of this Act or State or local law.

(g) In the case of any emission limitation or other requirement approved or promulgated by the Administrator under this Act after the enactment of the Clean Air Act Amendments of 1977 which is more stringent than the emission limitation or requirement for the source in effect prior to such approval or promulgation, if any, or where there was no emission limitation or requirement approved or promulgated before enactment of the Clean Air Act Amendments of 1977, the date for imposition of the non-compliance penalty under this section, shall be either July 1, 1979, or the date on which the source is required to be in full compliance with such emission limitation or requirement, whichever is later, but in no event later than three years after the approval or promulgation of such emission limitation or requirement.

[§120 added by PL 95–95]

§7421. Consultation [Sec. 121]

In carrying out the requirements of this Act requiring applicable implementation plans to contain—

(1) any transportation controls, air quality maintenance plan requirements or preconstruction review of direct sources of air pollution, or

(2) any measure referred to—

(A) in part D (pertaining to nonattainment requirements), or

(B) in part C (pertaining to prevention of significant deterioration),

and in carrying out the requirements of section 113(d) (relating to certain enforcement orders), the State shall provide a satisfactory process of consultation with general purpose local governments, designated organizations of elected officials of local governments and any Federal land manager having authority over Federal land to which the State plan applies, effective with respect to any such requirement which is adopted more than one year after the date of enactment of the Clean Air Act amendments of 1977 as part of such plan. Such process shall be in accordance with regulations promulgated by the Administrator to assure adequate consultation. The Administrator shall update as necessary the original regulations required and promulgated under this section (as in effect immediately before the date of the enactment of the Clean Air Act Amendments of 1990) to ensure adequate consultation. Only a general purpose unit of local government, regional agency, or council of governments adversely affected by action of the Administrator approving any portion of a plan referred to in this subsection may petition for judicial review of such action on the basis of a violation of the requirements of this section.

[§121 added by PL 95–95; amended by PL 101-549]

§7422. Listing of Certain Unregulated Pollutants [Sec. 122]

(a) Not later than one year after date of enactment of this section (two years for radioactive pollutants) and after notice and opportunity for public hearing, the Administrator shall review all available relevant information and determine whether or not emissions of radioactive pollutants (including source material, special nuclear material, and byproduct material), cadmium, arsenic and polycyclic organic matter into the ambient air will cause, or contribute to, air pollution which may reasonably be anticipated to endanger public health. If the Administrator makes an affirmative determination with respect to any such substance, he shall simultaneously with such determination include such substance in the list published under section 108(a)(1) or 112(b)(1)(A) (in the case of a substance which, in the judgment of the Administrator, causes, or contributes to, air pollution which may reasonably be anticipated to result in an increase in mortality or an increase in serious irreversible, or incapacitating reversible, illness), or shall include each category of stationary sources emitting such substance in significant amounts in the list published under section 111(b)(1)(A) , or take any combination of such actions.

(b) Nothing in subsection (a) shall be construed to affect the authority of the Administrator to revise any list referred to in subsection (a) with respect to any substance (whether or not enumerated in subsection (a)).

(c) (1) Before listing any source material, special nuclear, or byproduct material (or component or derivative thereof) as provided in subsection (a), the Administrator shall consult with the Nuclear Regulatory Commission.

(2) Not later than six months after listing any such material (or component or derivative thereof) the Administrator and the Nuclear Regulatory Commission shall enter into an interagency agreement with respect to those sources or facilities which are under the jurisdiction of the Commission. This agreement shall, to the maximum extent practicable consistent with this Act, minimize duplication of effort and conserve administrative resources in the establishment, implementation, and enforcement of emission limitations, standards of performance, and other requirements and authorities (substantive and procedural) under this Act respecting the emission of such material (or component or derivative thereof) from such sources or facilities.

(3) In case of any standard or emission limitation promulgated by the Administrator, under this Act or by any State (or the Administrator) under any applicable implementation plan

under this Act, if the Nuclear Regulatory Commission determines, after notice and opportunity for public hearing that the application of such standard or limitation to a source or facility within the jurisdiction of the Commission would endanger public health or safety, such standard or limitation shall not apply to such facilities or sources unless the President determines otherwise within ninety days from the date of such finding.

[Editor's Note: PL 95–95, Section 120(a) added a new section 122 to the Clean Air Act. Section 120(b) of PL 95–95 further provides: (b) The Administrator of the Environmental Protection Agency shall conduct a study, in conjunction with other appropriate agencies, concerning the effect on the public health and welfare of sulfates, radioactive pollutants, cadmium, arsenic, and polycyclic organic matter which are present or may reasonably be anticipated to occur in the ambient air. Such study shall include a thorough investigation of how sulfates are formed and how to protect public health and welfare from the injurious effects, if any, of sulfates, cadmium, arsenic, and polycyclic organic matter.]

[§122 added by PL 95–95]

§7423. Stack Heights [Sec. 123]

(a) The degree of emission limitation required for control of any air pollutant under an applicable implementation plan under this title shall not be affected in any manner by—

(1) so much of the stack height of any source as exceeds good engineering practice (as determined under regulations promulgated by the Administrator), or

(2) any other dispersion technique.

The preceding sentence shall not apply with respect to stack heights in existence before the date of enactment of the Clean Air Amendments of 1970 or dispersion techniques implemented before such date. In establishing an emission limitation for coal-fired steam electric generating units which are subject to the provisions of section 118 and which commenced operation before July 1, 1957, the effect of the entire stack height of stacks for which a construction contract was awarded before February 8, 1974, may be taken into account.

(b) For the purpose of this section, the term 'dispersion technique' includes any intermittent or supplemental control of air pollutants varying with atmospheric conditions.

(c) No later than six months after the date of enactment of this section, the Administrator, shall after notice and opportunity for public hearing, promulgate regulations to carry out this section. For purposes of this section, good engineering practice means, with respect to stack heights, the height necessary to insure that emissions from the stack do not result in excessive concentrations of any air pollutant in the immediate vicinity of the source as a result of atmospheric down- wash, eddies and wakes which may be created by the source itself, nearby structures or nearby terrain obstacles (as determined by the Administrator). For purposes of this section such height shall not exceed two and a half times the height of such source unless the owner or operator of the source demonstrates, after notice and opportunity for public hearing, to the satisfaction of the Administrator, that a greater height is necessary as provided under the preceding sentence. In no event may the administrator prohibit any increase in any stack height or restrict in any manner the stack height of any source.

[§123 added by PL 95–95]

§7424. Assurance of Adequacy of State Plans [Sec. 124]

(a) As expeditiously as practicable but not later than one year after date of enactment of this section, each State shall review the provisions of its implementation plan which relate to major fuel burning sources and shall determine—

(1) the extent to which compliance with requirements of such plan is dependent upon the use by major fuel burning stationary sources of petroleum products or natural gas,

(2) the extent to which such plan may reasonably be anticipated to be inadequate to meet the requirements of this Act in such State on a reliable and long- term basis by reason of its dependence upon the use of such fuels, and

(3) the extent to which compliance with the requirements of such plan is dependent upon use of coal or coal derivatives which is not locally or regionally available.

Each State shall submit the results of its review and its determination under this paragraph to the Administrator promptly upon completion thereof.

(b) (1) Not later than eighteen months after the date of enactment of this section, the Administrator shall review the submissions of the States under subsection (a) and shall require each State to revise its plan if, in the judgment of the Administrator, such plan revision is necessary to assure that such plan will be adequate to assure compliance with the requirements of this Act in such State on a reliable and long-term basis, taking into account the actual or potential prohibitions on use of petroleum products or natural gas, or both, under any other authority of law.

(2) Before requiring a plan revision under this subsection, with respect to any State the Administrator shall take into account the report of the review conducted by such State under paragraph (1) and shall consult with the Governor of the State respecting such required revision.

[§124 added by PL 95–95]

§7425. Measures to Prevent Economic Disruption or Unemployment [Sec. 125]

(a) After notice and opportunity for a public hearing—

(1) the Governor of any State in which a major fuel burning stationary source referred to in this subsection (or class or category thereof) is located.

(2) the Administrator, or

(3) the President (or his designee), may determine that action under subsection (b) is necessary to prevent or minimize significant local or regional economic disruption or unemployment which would otherwise result from use by such source (or class or category) of—

(A) coal or coal derivatives other than locally or regionally available coal,

(B) petroleum products,

(C) natural gas, or

(D) any combination of fuels referred to in subparagraphs (A) through (C). To comply with the requirements of a State implementation plan.

(b) Upon a determination under subsection (a)—

(1) such Governor, with the written consent of the President or his designee,

(2) the President's designee with the written consent of such Governor, or

(3) the President may by rule or order prohibit any such major fuel burning stationary source (or class or category thereof) from using fuels other than locally or regionally available coal or coal derivatives to comply with implementation plan requirements. In taking any action under this subsection, the Governor, the President, or the President's designee as the case may be, shall take into account, the final cost to the consumer of such an action.

(c) The Governor, in the case of action under subsection (b)(1), or the Administrator, in the case of an action under subsection (b)(2) or (3) shall, by rule or order, require each source to which such action applies to—

(1) enter into long-term contracts of at least ten years in duration (except as the President or his designee may otherwise permit or require by rule or order for good cause) for supplies of locally or regionally available coal or coal derivatives,

(2) enter into contracts to acquire any additional means of emission limitation which the Administrator or the State determines may be necessary to comply with the requirements of this Act while using such coal or coal derivatives as fuel, and

(3) comply with such schedules (including increments of progress), timetables and other requirements as may be necessary to assure compliance with the requirements of this Act. Requirements under this subsection shall be established simultaneously with, and as a condition of, any action under subsection (b).

(d) This section applies only to existing or new major fuel burning stationary sources—

(1) which have the design capacity to produce 250,000,000 Btu's per hour (or its equivalent), as determined by the Administrator, and

(2) which are not in compliance with the requirements of an applicable implementation plan or which are prohibited from burning oil or natural gas, or both, under any other authority of law.

(e) Except as may otherwise be provided by rule by the State or the Administrator for good cause, any action required to be taken by a major fuel burning stationary source under this section shall not be deemed to constitute a modification for purposes of section 111(a)(2) and (4) of this Act.

(f) For purposes of sections 113 and 120 a prohibition under subsection (b), and a corresponding rule or order under subsection (c), shall be treated as a requirement of section 113 . For purposes of any plan (or portion thereof) promulgated under section 110(c), any rule or order under subsection (c) corresponding to a prohibition under subsection (b), shall be treated as a part of such plan. For purposes of section 113 , a prohibition under subsection (b), applicable to any source, and a corresponding rule or order under subsection (c), shall be treated as part of the applicable implementation plan for the State in which subject source is located.

(g) The President may delegate his authority under this section to an officer or employee of the United States designated by him on a case-by-case basis or in any other manner he deems suitable.

(h) For the purpose of this section — the term 'locally or regionally available coal or coal derivatives' means coal or coal derivatives which is, or can in the judgment of the State or the Administrator feasibly be, mined or produced in the local or regional area (as determined by the Administrator) in which the major fuel burning stationary source is located.

[§125 added by PL 95–95]

[Editor's Note: Section 661 of the National Energy Conservation Policy Act, PL 95–619, amends the Energy Policy and Conservation Act in line with Section 125 of the Clean Air Act. See page 71:2501.]

§7426. Interstate Pollution Abatement [Sec. 126]

(a) Each applicable implementation plan shall—

(1) require each major proposed new (or modified source—

(A) subject to part C (relating to significant deterioration of air quality) or

(B) which may significantly contribute to levels of air pollution in excess of the national ambient air quality standards in any air quality control region outside the State in which such source intends to locate (or make such modification), to provide written notice to all nearby States the air pollution levels of which may be affected by such source at least sixty days prior to the date on which commencement of construction is to be permitted by the State providing notice, and

(2) identify all major existing stationary sources which may have the impact described in paragraph (1) with respect to new or modified sources and provide notice to all nearby States of the identity of such sources not later than three months after the date of enactment of the Clean Air Act Amendments of 1977.

(b) Any State or political subdivision may petition the Administrator for a finding that any major source or group of stationary sources emits or would emit any air pollutant in violation of the prohibition of section 110(a)(2)(D)(ii) . Within 60 days after receipt of any petition under this subsection and after public hearing, the Administrator shall make such a finding or deny the petition.

[§126(b) amended by PL 101–549]

(c) Notwithstanding any permit which may have been granted by the State in which the source is located (or intends to locate), it shall be a violation of this section and the applicable implementation plan in such State—

(1) for any major proposed new (or modified) source with respect to which a finding has been made under subsection (b) to be constructed or to operate in violation of the prohibition of section 110(a)(2)(D)(ii) , or

(2) for any major existing source to operate more than three months after such finding has been made with respect to it. The Administrator may permit the continued operation of a source referred to in paragraph (2) beyond the expiration of such three-month period if such source complies with such emission limitations and compliance schedules (containing increments of progress) as may be provided by the Administrator to bring about compliance with the requirement contained in section 110(a)(2)(D)(ii) as expeditiously as practicable, but in no case later than three years after the date of such finding. Nothing in the preceding sentence shall be construed to preclude any such source from being eligible for an enforcement order under section 113(d) after the expiration of such period during which the Administrator has permitted continuous operation.

[§126 added by PL 95–95; amended by PL 101–549]

§7427. Public Notification [Sec. 127]

(a) Each State plan shall contain measures which will be effective to notify the public during any calendar year on a regular basis of instances or areas in which any national primary ambient air quality standard is exceeded or was exceeded during any portion of the preceding calendar year to advise the public of the health hazards associated with such pollution, and to enhance public awareness of the measures which can be taken to prevent such standards from being exceeded and the ways in which the public can participate in regulatory and other efforts to improve air quality. Such measures may include the posting of warning signs on interstate highway access points to metropolitan areas or television, radio, or press notices or information.

(b) The Administrator is authorized to make grants to States to assist in carrying out the requirements of subsection (a).

[§127 added by PL 95–95]

§7428. State Boards [Sec. 128]

(a) Not later than the date one year after the date of the enactment of this section, each applicable implementation plan shall contain requirements that—

(1) any board or body which approves permits or enforcement orders under this Act shall have at least a majority of members who represent the public interest and do not derive any significant portion of their income from persons subject to permits or enforcement orders under this Act, and

(2) any potential conflicts of interest by members of such board or body or the head of an executive agency with similar power be adequately disclosed. A State may adopt any requirement respecting conflicts of interest for such boards or bodies or heads of executive agencies, or any other entities which are more stringent than the requirements of paragraph (1) and (2), and the Administrator shall approve any such more stringent requirements submitted as part of an implementation plan.

[§128 added by PL 95–95]

§7429. Solid Waste Combustion [Sec. 129]

(a) New Source Performance Standards.—

(1) In General.—

(A) The Administrator shall establish performance standards and other requirements pursuant to section 111 and this section for each category of solid waste incineration units. Such standards shall include emissions limitations and other requirements applicable to new units and guidelines (under section 111(d) and this section) and other requirements applicable to existing units.

(B) Standards under section 111 and this section applicable to solid waste incineration units with capacity greater than 250 tons per day combusting municipal waste shall be promulgated not later than 12 months after the date of enactment of the Clean Air Act Amendments of 1990. Nothing in this subparagraph shall alter any schedule for the promulgation of standards applicable to such units under section 111 pursuant to any settlement and consent decree entered by the Administrator before the date of enactment of the Clean Air Act Amendments of 1990: *Provided*,That, such standards are subsequently modified pursuant to the schedule established in this subparagraph to include each of the requirements of this section.

(C) Standards under section 111 and this section applicable to solid waste incineration units with capacity equal to or less than 250 tons per day combusting municipal waste and units combusting hospital waste, medical waste and infectious waste shall be promulgated not later than 24 months after the date of enactment of the Clean Air Act Amendments of 1990.

(D) Standards under section 111 and this section applicable to solid waste incineration units combusting commercial or industrial waste shall be proposed not later than 36 months after the date of enactment of the Clean Air Act Amendments of 1990 and promulgated not later than 48 months after such date of enactment.

(E) Not later than 18 months after the date of enactment of the Clean Air Act Amendments of 1990, the Administrator shall publish a schedule for the promulgation of standards under section 111 and this section applicable to other categories of solid waste incineration units.

(2) Emissions Standard.—Standards applicable to solid waste incineration units promulgated under section 111 and this section shall reflect the maximum degree of reduction in emissions of air pollutants listed under section (a)(4) that the Administrator, taking into consideration the cost of achieving such emission reduction, and any non-air quality health and environmental impacts and energy requirements, determines is achievable for new or existing units in each category. The Administrator may distinguish among classes, types (including mass- burn, refuse-derived fuel, modular and other types of units), and sizes of units within a category in establishing such standards. The degree of reduction in emissions that is deemed achievable for new units in a category shall not be less stringent than the emissions control that is achieved in practice by the best controlled similar unit, as determined by the Administrator. Emissions standards for existing units in a category may be less stringent than standards for new units in the same category but shall not be less stringent than the average emissions limitation achieved by the best performing 12 percent of units in the category (excluding units which first met lowest achievable emissions rates 18 months before the date such standards are proposed or 30 months before the date such standards are promulgated, whichever is later.)

(3) Control Methods and Technologies.—Standards under section 111 and this section applicable to solid waste incineration units shall be based on methods and technologies for removal or destruction of pollutants before, during, or after combustion, and shall incorporate for new units siting requirements that minimize, on a site specific basis, to the maximum extent practicable, potential risks to public health or the environment.

(4) Numerical Emissions Limitations.—The performance standards promulgated under section 111 and this section and applicable to solid waste incineration units shall specify numerical emission limitations for the following substances or mixtures: particulate matter (total and fine), opacity (as appropriate), sulfur dioxide, hydrogen chloride, oxides of nitrogen, carbon monoxide, lead, cadmium, mercury, and dioxins and dibenzofurans. The Administrator may promulgate numerical emissions limitations or provide for the monitoring of postcombustion concentrations of surrogate substances, parameters or periods of residence time in excess of stated temperatures with respect to pollutants other than those listed in this paragraph.

(5) Review and Revision.—Not later than 5 years following the initial promulgation of any performance standards and other requirements under this section and section 111 applicable to a category of solid waste incineration units, and at 5 year intervals thereafter, the Administrator shall review, and in accordance with this section and section 111 , revise such standards and requirements.

(b) Existing Units.—

(1) Guidelines.—Performance standards under this section and section 111 for solid waste incineration units shall include guidelines promulgated pursuant to section 111(d) and this section applicable to existing units. Such guidelines shall include, as provided in this section, each of the elements required by subsection (a) (emissions limitations, notwithstanding any restriction in section 111(d) regarding issuance of such limitations), subsection (c) (monitoring), subsection (d) (operator training), subsection (e) (permits), and subsection (h)(4) (residual risk).

(2) State Plans.—Not later than 1 year after the Administrator promulgates guidelines for a category of solid waste incineration units, each State in which units in the category are operating shall submit to the Administrator a plan to implement and enforce the guidelines with respect to such units. The State plan shall be at least as protective as the guidelines promulgated by the Administrator and shall provide that each unit subject to the guidelines shall be in compliance with all requirements of this section not later than 3 years after the State plan is approved by the Administrator but not later than 5 years after the guidelines were promulgated. The Administrator shall approve or disapprove any State plan within 180 days of the submission, and if a plan is disapproved, the Administrator shall state the reasons for disapproval in writing. Any State may modify and resubmit a plan which has been disapproved by the Administrator.

(3) Federal Plan. — The Administrator shall develop, implement and enforce a plan for existing solid waste incineration units within any category located in any State which has not submitted an approvable plan under this subsection with respect to units in such category within 2 years after the date on which the Administrator promulgated the relevant guidelines. Such plan shall assure that each unit subject to the plan is in compliance with all provisions of the guidelines not later than 5 years after the date the relevant guidelines are promulgated.

(c) Monitoring. — The Administrator shall, as part of each performance standard promulgated pursuant to subsection (a) and section 111 , promulgate regulations requiring the owner or operator of each solid waste incineration unit—

(1) to monitor emissions from the unit at the point at which such emissions are emitted into the ambient air (or within the stack, combustion chamber or pollution control equipment, as appropriate) and at such other points as necessary to protect public health and the environment;

(2) to monitor such other parameters relating to the operation of the unit and its pollution control technology as the Administrator determines are appropriate; and

(3) to report the results of such monitoring. Such regulations shall contain provisions regarding the frequency of monitoring, test methods and procedures validated on solid waste incineration units, and the form and frequency of reports containing the results of monitoring and shall require that any monitoring reports or test results indicating an exceedance of any standard under this section shall be reported separately and in a manner that facilitates review for purposes of enforcement actions. Such regulations shall require that

copies of the results of such monitoring be maintained on file at the facility concerned and that copies shall be made available for inspection and copying by interested members of the public during business hours.

(d) Operator Training. — Not later than 24 months after the enactment of the Clean Air Act Amendments of 1990, the Administrator shall develop and promote a model State program for the training and certification of solid waste incineration unit operators and high-capacity fossil fuel fired plant operators. The Administrator may authorize any State to implement a model program for the training of solid waste incineration unit operators and high capacity fossil fuel fired plant operators, if the State has adopted a program which is at least as effective as the model program developed by the Administrator. Beginning on the date 36 months after the date on which performance standards and guidelines are promulgated under subsection (a) and section 111 for any category of solid waste incineration units it shall be unlawful to operate any unit in the category unless each person with control over processes affecting emissions from such unit has satisfactorily completed a training program meeting the requirements established by the Administrator under this subsection.

(e) Permits. — Beginning (1) 36 months after the promulgation of a performance standard under subsection (a) and section 111 applicable to a category of solid waste incineration units, or (2) the effective date of a permit program under title V in the State in which the unit is located, whichever is later, each unit in the category shall operate pursuant to a permit issued under this subsection and title V. Permits required by this subsection may be renewed according to the provisions of title V. Notwithstanding any other provision of this Act, each permit for a solid waste incineration unit combusting municipal waste issued under this Act shall be issued for a period of up to 12 years and shall be reviewed every 5 years after date of issuance or reissuance. Each permit shall continue in effect after the date of issuance until the date of termination, unless the Administrator or State determines that the unit is not in compliance with all standards and conditions contained in the permit. Such determination shall be made at regular intervals during the term of the permit, such intervals not to exceed 5 years, and only after public comment and public hearing. No permit for a solid waste incineration unit may be issued under this Act by an agency, instrumentality or person that is also responsible, in whole or part, for the design and construction or operation of the unit. Notwithstanding any other provision of this subsection, the Administrator or the State shall require the owner or operator of any unit to comply with emissions limitations or implement any other measures, if the Administrator or the State determines that emissions in the absence of such limitations or measures may reasonably be anticipated to endanger public health or the environment. The Administrator's determination under the preceding sentence is a discretionary decision.

(f) Effective Date and Enforcement. —

(1) New Units. — Performance standards and other requirements promulgated pursuant to this section and section 111 and applicable to new solid waste incineration units shall be effective as of the date 6 months after the date of promulgation.

(2) Existing Units. — Performance standards and other requirements promulgated pursuant to this section and section 111 and applicable to existing solid waste incineration units shall be effective as expeditiously as practicable after approval of a State plan under subsection (b)(2) (or promulgation of a plan by the Administrator under subsection (b)(3)) but in no event later than 3 years after the State plan is approved or 5 years after the date such standards or requirements are promulgated, whichever is earlier.

(3) Prohibition. — After the effective date of any performance standard, emission limitation or other requirement promulgated pursuant to this section and section 111 , it shall be unlawful for any owner or operator of any solid waste incineration unit to which such standard, limitation or requirement applies to operate such unit in violation of such limitation, standard or requirement or for any other person to violate an applicable requirement of this section.

(4) Coordination with Other Authorities. — For purposes of sections 111(e), 113, 114, 116, 120, 303, 304, 307 and other provisions for the enforcement of this Act, each performance standard, emission limitation or other requirement established pursuant to this section by the Administrator or a State or local government, shall be treated in the same manner as a standard of performance under section 111 which is an emission limitation.

(g) Definitions. — For purposes of section 306 of the Clean Air Act Amendments of 1990 and this section only—

(1) Solid Waste Incineration Unit.—The term 'solid waste incineration unit' means a distinct operating unit of any facility which combusts any solid waste material from commercial or industrial establishments or the general public (including single and multiple residences, hotels, and motels). Such term does not include incinerators or other units required to have a permit under section 3005 of the Solid Waste Disposal Act. The term 'solid waste incineration unit' does not include (A) materials recovery facilities (including primary or secondary smelters) which combust waste for the primary purpose of recovering metals, (B) qualifying small power production facilities, as defined in section 3(17)(C) of the Federal Power Act (16 U.S.C. 769(17)(C)), or qualifying cogeneration facilities, as defined in section 3(18)(B) of the Federal Power Act (16 U.S.C. 796(18)(B)), which burn homogeneous waste (such as units which burn tires or used oil, but not including refuse-derived fuel) for the production of electric energy or in the case of qualifying cogeneration facilities which burn homogeneous waste for the production of electric energy and steam or forms of useful energy (such as heat) which are used for industrial, commercial, heating or cooling purposes, or (C) air curtain incinerators provided that such incinerators only burn wood wastes, yard wastes and clean lumber and that such air curtain incinerators comply with opacity limitations to be established by the Administrator by rule.

(2) New Solid Waste Incineration Unit.—The term 'new solid waste incineration unit' means a solid waste incineration unit the construction of which is commenced after the Administrator proposes requirements under this section establishing emissions standards or other requirements which would be applicable to such unit or a modified solid waste incineration unit.

(3) Modified Solid Waste Incineration Unit.—The term 'modified solid waste incineration unit' means a solid waste incineration unit at which modifications have occurred after the effective date of a standard under subsection (a) if (A) the cumulative cost of the modifications, over the life of the unit, exceed 50 per centum of the original cost of construction and installation of the unit (not including the cost of any land purchased in connection with such construction or installation) updated to current costs, or (B) the modification is a physical change in or change in the method of operation of the unit which increases the amount of any air pollutant emitted by the unit for which standards have been established under this section or section 111.

(4) Existing Solid Waste Incineration Unit. — The term 'existing solid waste incineration unit' means a solid waste unit which is not a new or modified solid waste incineration unit.

(5) Municipal Waste. — The term 'municipal waste' means refuse (and refuse- derived fuel) collected from the general public and from residential, commercial, institutional, and industrial sources consisting of paper, wood, yard wastes, food wastes, plastics, leather, rubber, and other combustible materials and non-combustible materials such as metal, glass and rock, provided that: (A) the term does not include industrial process wastes or medical wastes that are segregated from such other wastes; and (B) an incineration unit shall not be considered to be combusting municipal waste for purposes of section 111 or this section if it combusts a fuel feed stream, 30 percent or less of the weight of which is comprised, in aggregate, of municipal waste.

(6) Other Terms.—The terms 'solid waste' and 'medical waste' shall have the meanings established by the Administrator pursuant to the Solid Waste Disposal Act.

(h) Other Authority.—

(1) State Authority.—Nothing in this section shall preclude or deny the right of any State or political subdivision thereof to adopt or enforce any regulation, requirement, limitation or standard relating to solid waste incineration units that is more stringent than a regulation, requirement, limitation or standard in effect under this section or under any other provision of this Act.

(2) Other Authority under this Act.— Nothing in this section shall diminish the authority of the Administrator or a State to establish any other requirements applicable to solid waste incineration units under any other authority of law, including the authority to establish for any air pollutant a national ambient air quality standard, except that no solid waste incineration unit subject to performance standards under this section and section 111 shall be subject to standards under section 112(d) of this Act.

(3) Residual Risk.—The Administrator shall promulgate standards under section 112(f) for a category of solid waste incineration units, if promulgation of such standards is required

under section 112(f) . For purposes of this preceding sentence only—

(A) the performance standards under subsection (a) and section 111 applicable to a category of solid waste incineration units shall be deemed standards under section 112(d)(2), and

(B) the Administrator shall consider and regulate, if required, the pollutants listed under subsection (a)(4) and no others.

(4) Acid Rain.—A solid waste incineration unit shall not be a utility unit as defined in title IV: *Provided,*That, more than 80 per centum of its annual average fuel consumption measured on a Btu basis, during a period or periods to be determined by the Administrator, is from a fuel (including any waste burned as a fuel) other than a fossil fuel.

(5) Requirements of Parts C and D.—No requirement of an applicable implementation plan under section 165 (relating to construction of facilities in regions identified pursuant to section 107(d)(1)(A)(ii) or (iii) or under section 172(c)(5) (relating to permits for construction and operation in nonattainment areas) may be used to weaken the standards in effect under this section.

[§129 added by PL 101–549]

[Editor's Note: §§305 and 306 of PL 101–549 detail provisions relating to acid gas scrubbing requirements and ash from solid waste incineration units. Those provisions follow.]

[Sec. 305]

(c) Review of Acid Gas Scrubbing Requirements.—Prior to the promulgation of any performance standard for solid waste incineration units combusting municipal waste under section 111 or section 129 of the Clean Air Act, the Administrator shall review the availability of acid gas scrubbers as a pollution control technology for small new units and for existing units (as defined in 54 Federal Register 52190 (December 20, 1989), taking into account the provisions of subsection (a)(2) of section 129 of the Clean Air Act.

[Sec. 306]

For a period of 2 years after the date of enactment of the Clean Air Act Amendments of 1990, ash from solid waste incineration units burning municipal waste shall not be regulated by the Administrator of the Environmental Protection Agency pursuant to section 3001 of the Solid Waste Disposal Act. Such reference and limitation shall not be construed to prejudice, endorse or otherwise affect any activity by the Administrator following the 2–year period from the date of enactment of the Clean Air Act Amendments of 1990.

§7430. Emission Factors [Sec. 130]

Within 6 months after enactment of the Clean Air Act Amendments of 1990, and at least every 3 years thereafter, the Administrator shall review and, if necessary, revise, the methods ("emission factors") used for purposes of this Act to estimate the quantity of emissions of carbon monoxide, volatile organic compounds, an oxides of nitrogen from sources of such air pollutants (including area sources and mobile sources). In addition, the Administrator shall establish emission factors for sources for which no such methods have previously been established by the Administrator. The Administrator shall permit any person to demonstrate improved emissions estimating techniques, and following approval of such techniques, the Administrator shall authorize the use of such techniques. Any such technique may be approved only after appropriate public participation. Until the Administrator has completed the revision required by this section, nothing in this section shall be construed to affect the validity of emission factors established by the Administrator before the date of the enactment of the Clean Air Act Amendments of 1990.

[§130 added by PL 101–549]

§7431. Land Use Authority [Sec. 131]

Nothing in this Act constitutes an infringement on the existing authority of counties and cities to plan or control land use, and nothing in this Act provides or transfers authority over such land use.

[§131 added by PL 101–549]

PART B — OZONE PROTECTION

[Repealed by PL 101–549]

PART C — PREVENTION OF SIGNIFICANT DETERIORATION OF AIR QUALITY

SUBPART I

§7470. Purposes [Sec. 160]

The purposes of this part are as follows:

(1) to protect public health and welfare from any actual or potential adverse effect which in the Administrator's judgment may reasonably be anticipated to occur from air pollution (or from exposures to pollutants in other media, which pollutants originate as emissions to the ambient air), notwithstanding attainment and maintenance of all national ambient air quality standards;

(2) to preserve, protect, and enhance the air quality in national parks, national wilderness areas, national monuments, national seashores, and other areas of special national or regional natural recreational, scenic, or historic value;

(3) to insure that economic growth will occur in a manner consistent with the preservation of existing clean air resources;

(4) to assure that emissions from any source in any State will not interfere with any portion of the applicable implementation plan to prevent significant deterioration of air quality for any other State; and

(5) to assure that any decision to permit increased air pollution in any area to which this section applies is made only after careful evaluation of all the consequences of such a decision and after adequate procedural opportunities for informed public participation for the decision-making process.

§7471. Plan Requirements [Sec. 161]

In accordance with the policy of section 101(b)(1) , each applicable implementation plan shall contain emission limitations and such other measures as may be necessary, as determined under regulations promulgated under this part, to prevent significant deterioration of air quality in each region (or portion thereof) designated pursuant to section 107 as attainment or unclassifiable.

[§161 amended by PL 101–549]

§7472. Initial Classifications [Sec. 162]

(a) Upon the enactment of this part, all—

(1) international parks,

(2) national wilderness areas which exceed 5,000 acres in size,

(3) national memorial parks which exceed 5,000 acres in size, and

(4) national parks which exceed six thousand acres in size, and which are in existence on the date of enactment of the Clean Air Act Amendments of 1977 shall be class I areas and may not be redesignated. All areas which were redesignated as class I under regulations promulgated before such date of enactment shall be class I areas which may be redesignated as provided in this part.

The extent of the areas designated as Class I under this section shall conform to any changes in the boundaries of such areas which have occurred subsequent to the date of the enactment of the Clean Air Act Amendments of 1977, or which may occur subsequent to the date of the enactment of the Clean Air Act Amendments of 1990.

[§162(a) amended by PL 101–549]

(b) All areas in such State designated pursuant to section 107(d) as attainment or unclassifiable which are not established as class I under subsection (a) shall be class II areas unless redesignated under section 164.

[§162(b) amended by PL 101–549]

§7473. Increments and Ceilings [Sec. 163]

(a) In the case of sulfur oxides and particulates, each applicable implementation plan shall contain measures assuring that maximum allowable increases over baseline concentrations of, and maximum allowable concentrations of, such pollutant shall not be exceeded. In the case of any maximum allowable increase (except an allowable increase specified under 165(d)(2)(C)(iv)) for a pollutant based on concentrations permitted under national ambient air quality standards for any period other than an annual period, such regulations shall permit such maximum allowable increase to be exceeded during one such period per year.

(b) (1) For any class I area, the maximum allowable increase in concentrations of sulfur dioxide and particulate matter over the baseline concentration of such pollutants shall not exceed the following amounts:

Pollutants:	Maximum allowable increase (in micrograms per cubic meter
Particulate matter:	
Annual geometric mean	5
Twenty-four-hour maximum	10
Sulfur dioxide:	
Annual arithmetic mean	2
Twenty-four-hour maximum	5
Three-hour maximum	25

(2) For any class II area, the maximum allowable increase in concentrations of sulfur dioxide and particulate matter over the baseline

concentration of such pollutants shall not exceed the following amounts:

Pollutants	Maximum allowable increase (in micrograms per cubic meter)
Particulate matter:	
Annual geometric mean	19
Twenty-four-hour maximum	37
Sulfur dioxide:	
Annual arithmetic mean	20
Twenty-four-hour maximum	91
Three-hour maximum	512

(3) For each class III area, the maximum allowable increase in concentrations of sulfur dioxide and particulate matter over the baseline concentration of such pollutants shall not exceed the following amounts:

Pollutants	Maximum allowable increase (in micrograms per cubic meter)
Particulate matter:	
Annual geometric mean	37
Twenty-four-hour maximum	75
Sulfur dioxide:	
Annual arithmetic mean	40
Twenty-four-hour maximum	182
Three-hour maximum	700

(4) The maximum allowable concentrations of any air pollutant in any area to which this part applies shall not exceed a concentration for such pollutant for each period of exposure equal to—

(A) the concentration permitted under the national secondary ambient air quality standards, or

(B) the concentration permitted under the national primary ambient air quality standard. whichever concentration is lowest for such pollutant for such period of exposure.

(c) (1) In the case of any State which has a plan approved by the Administrator for purposes of carrying out this part, the Governor of such State may, after notice and opportunity for public hearing, issue orders or promulgate rules providing that for purposes of determining compliance with the maximum allowable increases in ambient concentrations of an air pollutant, the following concentrations of such pollutant shall not be taken into account:

(A) concentrations of such pollutant attributable to the increase in emissions from stationary sources which have converted from the use of petroleum products, or natural gas, or both, by reason of an order which is in effect under the provisions of section 2(a) and (b) of the Energy Supply and Environmental Coordination Act of 1974 (or any subsequent legislation which supersedes such provisions) over the emissions from such sources before the effective date of such order.

(B) the concentrations of such pollutant attributable to the increase in emissions from stationary sources which have converted from using natural gas by reason of a natural gas curtailment pursuant to a natural gas curtailment plan in effect pursuant to the Federal Power Act over the emissions from such sources before the effective date of such plan,

(C) concentrations of particulate matter attributable to the increase in emissions from construction or other temporary emission-related activities, and

(D) the increase in concentrations attributable to new sources outside the United States over the concentrations attributable to existing sources which are included in the baseline concentration determined in accordance with section 169(4) .

(2) No action taken with respect to a source under paragraph (1)(A) or (1)(B) shall apply more than five years after the effective date of the order referred to in paragraph (1)(A) or the plan referred to in paragraph (1)(B), whichever is applicable. If both such order and plan are applicable, no such action shall apply more than five years after the later of such effective dates.

(3) No action under this subsection shall take effect unless the Governor submits the order or rule providing for such exclusion to the Administrator and the Administrator determines that such order or rule is in compliance with the provisions of this subsection.

§7474. Area Redesignation [Sec. 164]

(a) Except as otherwise provided under subsection (c), a State may redesignate such areas as it deems appropriate as class I areas. The following areas may be redesignated only as class I or II:

(1) an area which exceeds ten thousand acres in size and is a national monument, a national primitive area, a national preserve, a national recreation area, a national wild and scenic river, national wildlife refuge, a national lakeshore or seashore, and

(2) a national park or national wilderness area established after the date of enactment of this Act which exceeds ten thousand acres in size. The extent of the areas referred to in paragraph (1) and (2) shall conform to any changes in the boundaries of such areas which have occurred subsequent to the date of the enactment of the Clean Air Act Amendments of 1977, or which may occur subsequent to the date of the enactment of the Clean Air Act Amendments of 1990. Any area (other than an area referred to in paragraph (1) or (2) or an area established as class I under section 162(a)) may be redesignated by the State as class III if—

[§164(a)(2) introductory paragraph amended by PL 101–549]

(A) such redesignation has been specifically approved by the Governor of the State, after consultation with the appropriate Committees of the legislature if it is in session or with the leadership of the legislature if it is not in session (unless State law provides that such redesignation must be specifically approved by State legislation) and if general purpose units of local government representing a majority of the residents of the area so redesignated enact legislation (including for such units of local government resolutions where appropriate) concurring in the State's redesignation;

(B) such redesignation will not cause, or contribute to, concentrations of any air pollutant which exceed any maximum allowable increase or maximum allowable concentration permitted under the classification of any other area; and

(C) such redesignation otherwise meets the requirements of this part.

Subparagraph (A) of this paragraph shall not apply to area redesignation by Indian tribes.

(b) (1) (A) Prior to redesignation of any area under this part, notice shall be afforded and public hearings shall be conducted in areas proposed to be redesignated and in areas which may be affected by the proposed redesignation. Prior to any such public hearing a satisfactory description and analysis of the health, environmental, economic, social, and energy effects of the proposed redesignation shall be prepared and made available for public inspection and prior to any such redesignation, the description and analysis of such effects shall be reviewed and examined by the redesignating authorities.

(B) Prior to the issuance of notice under subparagraph (A) respecting the redesignation of any area under this subsection, if such area includes any Federal lands, the State shall provide written notice to the appropriate Federal land manager and afford adequate opportunity (but not in excess of 60 days) to confer with the State respecting the intended notice of redesignation and to submit written comments and recommendations with respect to such intended notice of redesignation. In redesignating any area under this section with respect to which any Federal land manager has submitted written comments and recommendations, the State shall publish a list of any inconsistency between such recommendations and an explanation of such inconsistency (together with the reasons for making such redesignation against the recommendation of the Federal land manager).

(C) The Administrator shall promulgate regulations not later than six months after date of enactment of this part, to assure, insofar as practicable, that prior to any public hearing on redesignation of any area, there shall be available for public inspection any specific plans for any new or modified major emitting facility which may be permitted to be constructed and operated only if the area in question is designated or redesignated as class III.

(2) The Administrator may disapprove the redesignation of any area only if he finds, after notice and opportunity for public hearing, that such redesignation does not meet the procedural requirements of this section or is inconsistent with the requirements of section 162(a) or of subsection (a) of this section. If any such disapproval occurs, the classification of the area shall be that which was in effect prior to the redesignation which was disapproved.

[§164(b)(2) amended by PL 95–190]

(c) Lands within the exterior boundaries of reservations of federally recognized Indian tribes may be redesignated only by the appropriate

Indian governing body. Such Indian governing body shall be subject in all respects to the provisions of subsection (e).

(d) The Federal Land Manager shall review all national monuments, primitive areas, and national preserves, and shall recommend any appropriate areas for redesignation as class I where air quality related values are important attributes of the area. The Federal Land Manager shall report such recommendations, with supporting analysis, to the Congress and the affected States within one year after enactment of this section. The Federal Land Manager shall consult with the appropriate States before making such recommendations.

(e) If any State affected by the redesignation of an area by an Indian tribe or any Indian tribe affected by the redesignation of an area by a State disagrees with such redesignation of any area, or if a permit is proposed to be issued for any new major emitting facility proposed for construction in any State which the Governor of an affected State or governing body of an affected Indian tribe determines will cause or contribute to a cumulative change in air quality in excess of that allowed in this part within the affected State or tribal reservation, the Governor or ruling body may request the Administrator to enter into negotiations with the parties involved to resolve such dispute. If requested by any State or Indian tribe involved, the Administrator shall make a recommendation to resolve the dispute and protect the air quality related values of the lands involved. If the parties involved do not reach agreement, the Administrator shall resolve the dispute and his determination, or the results of agreements reached through other means, shall become part of the applicable plan and shall be enforceable as part of such plan. In resolving such disputes relating to area redesignation, the Administrator shall consider the extent to which the lands involved are of sufficient size to allow effective air quality management or have air quality related values of such an area.

§7475. Preconstruction Requirements [Sec. 165]

(a) No major emitting facility on which construction is commenced after the date of the enactment of this part may be constructed in any area to which this part applies unless—

(1) a permit has been issued for such proposed facility in accordance with this part setting forth emission limitations for such facility which conform to the requirements of this part;

(2) the proposed permit has been subject to a review in accordance with this section, the required analysis has been conducted in accordance with regulations promulgated by the Administrator, and a public hearing has been held with opportunity for interested persons including representatives of the Administrator to appear and submit written or oral presentations on the air quality impact of such source, alternatives thereto, control technology requirements, and other appropriate considerations;

(3) the owner or operator of such facility demonstrates, as required pursuant to section 110(j), that emissions from construction or operation of such facility will not cause, or contribute to, air pollution in excess of any (A) maximum allowable increase or maximum allowable concentration for any pollutant in any area to which this part applies more than one time per year, (B) national ambient air quality standard in any air quality control region, or (C) any other applicable emission standard or standard of performance under this Act;

[§165(a)(3) amended by PL 95–190]

(4) the proposed facility is subject to the best available control technology for each pollutant subject to regulation under this Act emitted from, or which results from, such facility;

(5) the provisions of subsection (d) with respect to protection of class I areas have been complied with for such facility;

(6) there has been an analysis of any air quality impacts projected for the area as a result of growth associated with such facility;

(7) the person who owns or operates, or proposes to own or operate, a major emitting facility for which a permit is required under this part agrees to conduct such monitoring as may be necessary to determine the effect which emissions from any such facility may have, or is having, on air quality in any area which may be affected by emissions from such source; and

(8) in the case of a source which proposes to construct in a class III area, emissions from which would cause or contribute to exceeding the maximum allowable increments applicable in a class II area and where no standard under section 111 of this Act has been promulgated subsequent to enactment of the Clean Air Act Amendments of 1977 for such source category, the Administrator has approved the determination of best available technology as set forth in the permit.

(b) The demonstration pertaining to maximum allowable increases required under section (a)(3) shall not apply to maximum allowable increases for class II areas in the case of an expansion or modification of a major emitting facility which is in existence on the date of enactment of the Clean Air Act Amendment of 1977, whose allowable emissions of air pollutants, after compliance with subsection (a)(4), will be less than fifty tons per year and for which the owner or operator of such facility demonstrates that emissions of particulate matter and sulfur oxides will not cause or contribute to ambient air quality levels in excess of the national secondary ambient air quality standard for either of such pollutants.

[§165(b) amended by PL 95–190]

(c) Any completed permit application under section 100 for a major emitting facility in any area to which this part applies shall be granted or denied not later than one year after the date of filing of such completed application.

(d) (1) Each State shall transmit to the Administrator a copy of each permit application relating to a major emitting facility received by such State and provided notice to the Administrator of every action related to the consideration of such permit.

(2) (A) The Administrator shall provide notice of the permit application to the Federal Land Manager and the Federal official charged with direct responsibility for management of any lands within a class I area which may be affected by emissions from the proposed facility.

(B) The Federal Land Manager and the Federal official charged with direct responsibility for management of such lands shall have an affirmative responsibility to protect the air quality related values (including visibility) of such lands within a class I area and to consider, in consultation with the Administrator, whether a proposed major emitting facility will have an adverse impact on such values.

(C) (i) In any case where the Federal official charged with direct responsibility for management of any lands within a class I area or the Federal Land Manager of such lands, or the Administrator, or the Governor of an adjacent State containing such a class I area files a notice alleging that emissions from a proposed major emitting facility may cause or contribute to a change in the air quality in such area and identifying the potential adverse impact of such change, a permit shall not be issued unless the owner or operator of such facility demonstrates that emissions of particulate matter and sulfur dioxide will not cause or contribute to concentrations which exceed maximum allowable increases for a class I area.

(ii) In any case where the Federal Land Manager demonstrates to the satisfaction of the State that the emissions from such facility will have an adverse impact on the air quality-related values (including visibility) of such lands, notwithstanding the fact that the change in air quality resulting from emissions from such facility will not cause or contribute to concentrations which exceed the maximum allowable increases for a class I area, a permit shall not be issued.

(iii) In any case where the owner or operator of such facility demonstrates to the satisfaction of the Federal Land Managers, and the Federal Land Manager so certifies, that the emissions from such facility will have no adverse impact on the air quality related values of such lands (including visibility), notwithstanding the fact that the change in air quality result ing from emissions from such facility will cause or contribute to concentrations which exceed the maximum allowable increases for class I areas, the State may issue a permit.

(iv) In the case of a permit issued pursuant to clause (iii), such facility shall comply with such emission limitations under such permit as may be necessary to assure that emissions of sulfur oxides and particulates from such facility, will not cause or contribute to concentrations of such pollutant which exceed the following maximum allowable increases over the baseline concentration for such pollutants.

[§165(d)(2)(C) amended by PL 95–190]

Pollutants	Maximum allowable increase (in micrograms per cubic meter)
Particulate matter:	
Annual geometric mean	19
Twenty-four-hour maximum	37
Sulfur dioxide:	
Annual arithmetic means	20
Twenty-four-hour maximum	91

Pollutants	Maximum allowable increase (in micrograms per cubic meter)
Three-hour maximum	325

(D) (i) In any case where the owner or operator of a proposed major emitting facility who has been denied a certification under subparagraph (C)(iii) demonstrates to the satisfaction of the Governor, after notice and public hearing, and the Governor finds, that the facility cannot be constructed by reason of any maximum allowable increase for sulfur dioxide for periods of 24 hours or less applicable to any class I area and, in the case of Federal mandatory class I areas, that a variance under this clause will not adversely affect the air quality related values of the area (including visibility), the Governor, after consideration of the federal land manager's recommendation (if any) and subject to his concurrence, may grant a variance from such maximum allowable increase. If such variance is granted, a permit may be issued to such source pursuant to the requirements of this subparagraph.

(ii) In any case in which the Governor recommends a variance under this subparagraph in which the Federal land manager does not concur, the recommendations of the Governor and the Federal land manager shall be transmitted to the President. The President may approve the Governor's recommendation if he finds that such variance is in the national interest. No Presidential finding shall be reviewable in any court. The variance shall take effect if the President approves the Governor's recommendations. The President shall approve or disapprove such recommendation within 90 days after his receipt of the recommendations of the Governor and the Federal land manager.

(iii) In the case of a permit issued pursuant to this subparagraph, such facility shall comply with such emission limitations under such permit as may be necessary to assure that emissions of sulfur oxides from such facility will not (during any day on which the otherwise applicable maximum allowable increases are exceeded) cause or contribute to concentrations which exceed the following maximum allowable increases for such areas over the baseline concentration for such pollutant and to assure that such emissions will not cause or contribute to concentrations which exceed the otherwise applicable maximum allowable increases for periods of exposure of 24 hours or less on more than 18 days during any annual period:

MAXIMUM ALLOWABLE INCREASE
[In micregrams per cubic meter]

Period of exposure	Low terrain areas	High terrain areas
24-hr maximum	36	62
3-hr maximum	130	221

(iv) For purposes of clause (iii), the term 'high terrain area' means with respect to any facility, any area having an elevation of 900 feet or more above the base of the stack of such facility, and the term 'low terrain area' means any area other than a high terrain area.

[§165(d)(2)(D) amended by PL 95–190]

(e) (1) The review provided for in subsection (a) shall be preceded by an analysis in accordance with regulations of the Administrator, promulgated under this subsection, which may be conducted by the State (or any general purpose unit of local government) or by the major emitting facility applying for such permit, of the ambient air quality at the proposed site and in areas which may be affected by emissions from such facility for each pollutant subject to regulation under this Act which will be emitted from such facility.

(2) Effective one year after date of enactment of this part, the analysis required by this subsection shall include continuous air quality monitoring data gathered for purposes of determining whether emissions from such facility will exceed the maximum allowable increases or the maximum allowable concentration permitted under this part. Such data shall be gathered over a period of one calendar year preceding the date of application for a permit under this part unless the State, in accordance with regulations promulgated by the Administrator, determines that a complete and adequate analysis for such purposes may be accomplished in a shorter period. The results of such analysis shall be available at the time of the public hearing on the application for such permit.

(3) The Administrator shall within six months after the date of enactment of this part promulgate regulations respecting the analysis required under this subsection which regulations—

(A) shall not require the use of any automatic or uniform buffer zone or zones,

(B) shall require an analysis of the ambient air quality, climate and meteorology, terrain, soils and vegetation, and visibility at the site of the proposed major emitting facility and in the area potentially affected by the emissions from such facility for each pollutant regulated under this Act which will be emitted from, or which results from the construction or operation of, such facility, the size and nature of the proposed facility, the degree of continuous emission reduction which could be achieved by such facility, and such other factors as may be relevant in determining the effect of emissions from a proposed facility on any air quality control region,

(C) shall require the results of such analysis shall be available at the time of the public hearing on the application for such permit, and

(D) shall specify with reasonable particularity each air quality model or models to be used under specified sets of conditions for purposes of this part. Any model or models designated under such regulations may be adjusted upon a determination, after notice and opportunity for public hearing, by the Administrator that such adjustment is necessary to take into account unique terrain or meteorological characteristics of an area potentially affected by emissions from a source applying for a permit required under this part.

§7476. Other Pollutants [Sec. 166]

(a) In the case of the pollutants hydrocarbons, carbon monoxide, photochemical oxidants, and nitrogen oxides, the Administrator shall conduct a study and not later than two years after the date of enactment of this part, promulgate regulations to prevent the significant deterioration of air quality which would result from the emissions of such pollutants. In the case of pollutants for which national ambient air quality standards are promulgated after the date of the enactment of this part, he shall promulgate such regulations not more than 2 years after the date of promulgation of such standards.

(b) Regulations referred to in subsection (a) shall become effective one year after the date of promulgation. Within 21 months after such date of promulgation such plan revision shall be submitted to the Administrator who shall approve or disapprove the plan within 25 months after such date or promulgation in the same manner as required under section 110 .

(c) Such regulations shall provide specific numerical measures against which permit applications may be evaluated, a framework for stimulating improved control technology, protection of air quality values, and fulfill the goals and purposes set forth in section 101 and section 160.

(d) The regulations of the Administrator under subsection (a) shall provide specific measures at least as effective as the increments established in section 163 to fulfill such goals and purposes, and may contain air quality increments, emission density requirements, or other measures.

(e) With respect to any air pollutant for which a national ambient air quality standard is established other than sulfur oxides or particulate matter, an area classification plan shall not be required under this section if the implementation plan adopted by the State and submitted for the Administrator's approval or promulgated by the Administrator under section 110(c) contains other provisions which when considered as a whole, the Administrator finds will carry out the purposes in section 160 at least as effectively as an area classification plan for such pollutant. Such other provisions referred to in the preceding sentence need not require the establishment of maximum allowable increases with respect to such pollutant for any area to which this section applies.

(f) PM–10 Increments.—The Administrator is authorized to substitute, for the maximum allowable increases in particulate matter specified in section 163(b) and section 165(d)(2)(C)(iv), maximum allowable increases in particulate matter with an aerodynamic diameter smaller than or equal to 10 micrometers. Such substituted maximum allowable increases shall be of equal stringency in effect as those specified in the provisions for which they are substituted. Until the Administrator promulgates regulations under the authority of this subsection, the current maximum allowable increases in concentrations of particulate matter shall remain in effect.

[§166(f) added by PL 101–549]

§7477. Enforcement [Sec. 167]

The Administrator shall, and a State may take such measures, including issuance of an order, or seeking injunctive relief, as necessary to prevent the construction or modification of a major emitting facility which does not conform to the requirements of this part, or which is proposed to be constructed in any area designated pursuant to section 107(d) as attainment or unclassifiable and which is not subject to an implementation plan which meets the requirements of this part.

[§167 amended by PL 101–549]

§7478. Period Before Plan Approval [Sec. 168]

(a) Until such time as an applicable implementation plan is in effect for any area, which plan meets the requirements of this part to prevent significant deterioration of air quality with respect to any air pollutant, applicable regulations under this act prior to enactment of this part shall remain in effect to prevent significant deterioration of air quality in any such area for any such pollutant except as otherwise provided in subsection (b).

(b) If any regulation in effect prior to enactment of this part to prevent significant deterioration of air quality would be inconsistent with the requirements of section 162(a) , section 163(b) or section 164(a) , then such regulations shall be deemed amended so as to conform with such requirements. In the case of a facility on which construction was commended (in accordance with the definition of 'commenced' in section 169(2)) after June 1, 1975, and prior to the enactment of the Clean Air Act Amendments of 1977, the review and permitting of such facility shall be in accordance with the regulations for the prevention of significant deterioration in effect prior to the enactment of the Clean Air Act Amendments of 1977.

[§168(b) amended by PL 95–190]

§7479. Definitions [Sec. 169]

For purposes of this part—

(1) The term 'major emitting facility' means any of the following stationary sources of air pollutants which emit, or have the potential to emit, one hundred tons per year or more of any air pollutant from the following types of stationary sources; fossil-fuel fired steam electric plants of more than two hundred and fifty million British thermal units per hour heat input, coal cleaning plants (thermal dryers), kraft pulp mills, Portland Cement plants, primary zinc smelters, iron and steel mill plants, primary aluminum ore reduction plants, primary copper smelters, municipal incinerators capable of charging more than fifty tons of refuse per day, hydrofluoric, sulfuric, and nitric acid plants, petroleum refineries, lime plants, phosphate rock processing plants, coke oven batteries, sulfur recovery plants, carbon black plants (furnace process), primary lead smelters, fuel conversion plants, sintering plants, secondary metal production facilities, chemical process plants, fossil-fuel boilers of more than two hundred and fifty million British thermal units per hour heat input, petroleum storage and transfer facilities with a capacity exceeding three hundred thousand barrels, taconite ore processing facilities, glass fiber processing plants, charcoal production facilities. Such term also includes any other source with the potential to emit two hundred and fifty tons per year or more of any air pollutant. This term shall not include new or modified facilities which are nonprofit health or education institutions which have been exempted by the State.

(2) (A) The term 'commenced' as applied to construction of a major emitting facility means that the owner or operator has obtained all necessary preconstruction approvals or permits required by Federal, State, or local air pollution emissions and air quality laws or regulations and either has (i) begun, or caused to begin, a continuous program of physical onsite con struction of the facility or (ii) entered into binding agreements or contractual obligations, which cannot be canceled or modified without substantial loss to the owner or operator, to undertake a program of construction of the facility to be completed within a reasonable time.

(B) The term 'necessary preconstruction approvals or permits' means those permits or approvals, required by the permitting authority as a precondition to undertaking any activity under clauses (i) or (ii) of subparagraph (A) of this paragraph.

(C) The term 'construction' when used in connection with any source or facility, includes the modification (as defined in section 111(a)) of any source or facility.

[§169(2)(C) added by PL 95–190]

(3) The term 'best available control technology' means an emission limitation based on the maximum degree of reduction of each pollutant subject to regulation under this Act emitted from or which results from any major emitting facility, which the permitting authority, on a case- by-case basis, taking into account energy, environmental, and economic impacts and other costs, determines is achievable for such facility through application of production, processes and available methods, systems, and techniques, including fuel cleaning, clean fuels, or treatment or innovative fuel combustion techniques for control of each such pollutant. In no event shall application of 'best available control technology' result in emissions of any pollutants which will exceed the emissions allowed by any applicable standard established pursuant to section 111 or 112 of this Act. Emissions from any

source utilizing clean fuels, or any other means, to comply with this paragraph shall not be allowed to increase above levels that would have been required under this paragraph as it existed prior to enactment of the Clean Air Act Amendments of 1990.

[§169(3) amended by PL 101–549]

(4) The term 'baseline concentration' means, with respect to a pollutant, the ambient concentration levels which exist at the time of the first application for a permit in an area subject to this part, based on air quality data available in the Environmental Protection Agency or a State air pollution control agency and on such monitoring data as the permit applicant is required to submit. Such ambient concentration levels shall take into account all projected emissions in, or which may affect, such area from any major emitting facility on which construction commenced prior to January 6, 1975, but which has not begun operation by the date of the baseline air quality concentration determination. Emissions of sulfur oxides and particulate matter from any major emitting facility on which construction commenced after January 6, 1975, shall not be included in the baseline and shall be counted against the maximum allowable increases in pollutant concentrations established under this part.

SUBPART 2

§7491. Visibility Protection for Federal Class I Areas [Sec. 169A]

(a) (1) Congress hereby declares as a national goal the prevention of any future, and the remedying of any existing, impairment of visibility in mandatory class I Federal areas which impairment results from manmade air pollution.

(2) Not later than six months after the date of the enactment of this section, the Secretary of the Interior in consultation with other Federal land managers shall review all mandatory class I Federal areas and identify those where visibility is an important value of the area. From time to time the Secretary of the Interior may revise such identification. Not later than one year after such date of enactment, the Administrator shall, after consultation with the Secretary of the Interior, promulgate a list of mandatory class I Federal areas in which he determines visibility is an important value.

(3) Not later than eighteen months after the date of enactment of this section, the Administrator shall complete a study and report to Congress on available methods for implementing the national goal set forth in paragraph (1). Such report shall include recommendations for—

(A) methods for identifying, characterizing, determining, quantifying, and measuring visibility impairment in Federal areas referred to in paragraph (1), and

(B) modeling techniques (or other methods) for determining the extent to which manmade air pollution may reasonably be anticipated to cause or contribute to such impairment, and

(C) methods for preventing and remedying such manmade air pollution and resulting visibility impairment. Such report shall also identify the classes or categories of sources and the types of air pollutants which, alone or in conjunction with other sources or pollutants, may reasonably be anticipated to cause or contribute significantly to impairment of visibility.

(4) Not later than twenty-four months after the date of enactment of this section, and after notice and public hearing, the Administrator shall promulgate regulations to assure (A) reasonable progress toward meeting the national goal specified in paragraph (1), and (B) compliance with the requirements of this section.

(b) Regulations under subsection (a)(4) shall—

(1) provide guidelines to the States, taking into account the recommendations under subsection (a)(3) on appropriate techniques and methods for implementing this section (as provided in subparagraphs (A) through (C) of such subsection (a)(3)), and

(2) require each applicable implementation plan for a State in which any area listed by the Administrator under subsection (a)(2) is located (or for a State the emissions from which may reasonably be anticipated to cause or contribute to any impairment of visibility in any such area) to contain such emission limits, schedules of compliance and other measures as may be necessary to make reasonable progress toward meeting the national goal specified in subsection (a), including—

(A) except as otherwise provided pursuant to subsection (c), a requirement that each major stationary source which is in existence on the date of enactment of this section, but which has not been in operation for more than fifteen years as of such date, and which, as determined by the State (or the Administrator in the case of a plan promulgated under section 110(c)) emits any air pollutant which may reasonably be anticipated to cause or contribute to any impairment of visibility in any such area, shall procure, install, and operate, as expeditiously as practicable (and maintain thereafter) the best available retrofit technology, as determined by the State (or the Administrator in the case of a plan promulgated under section 110(c)) for controlling emissions from such source for the purpose of eliminating or reducing any such impairment, and

(B) a long-term (ten to fifteen years) strategy for making reasonable progress toward meeting the national goal specified in subsection (a). In the case of a fossil- fuel fired generating powerplant having a total generating capacity in excess of 750 megawatts, the emission limitations required under this paragraph shall be determined pursuant to guidelines, promulgated by the Administrator under paragraph (1).

(c) (1) The Administrator may, by rule, after notice and opportunity for public hearing, exempt any major stationary source from the requirement of subsection (b)(2)(A), upon his determination that such source does not or will not, by itself or in combination with other sources, emit any air pollutant which may reasonably be anticipated to cause or contribute to a significant impairment of visibility in any mandatory class I Federal area.

(2) Paragraph (1) of this subsection shall not be applicable to any fossil-fuel fired powerplant with total design capacity of 750 megawatts or more, unless the owner or operator of any such plant demonstrates to the satisfaction of the Administrator that such power-plant is located at such distance from all areas listed by the Administrator under subsection (a)(2) that such powerplant does not or will not, by itself or in combination with other sources, emit any air pollutant which may reasonably be anticipated to cause or contribute to significant impairment of visibility in any such area.

(3) An exemption under this subsection shall be effective only upon concurrence by the appropriate Federal land manager or managers with the Administrator's determination under this subsection.

(d) Before holding the public hearing on the proposed revision of an applicable implementation plan to meet the requirements of this section, the State (or the Administrator, in the case of a plan promulgated under section 110(c) shall consult in person with the appropriate Federal land manager or managers and shall include a summary of the conclusions and recommendations of the Federal land managers in the notice to the public.

(e) In promulgating regulations under this section, the Administrator shall not require the use of any automatic or uniform buffer zone or zones.

(f) For purposes of section 304(a)(2) , the meeting of the national goal specified in subsection (a)(1) by any specific date or dates shall not be considered a 'non- discretionary duty' of the Administrator.

(g) For the purpose of this section—

(1) in determining reasonable progress there shall be taken into consideration the costs of compliance, the time necessary for compliance, and the energy and non- air quality environmental impacts of compliance, and the remaining useful life of any existing source subject to such requirements;

(2) in determining best available retrofit technology the State (or the Administrator in determining emission limitations which reflect such technology) shall take into consideration the costs of compliance, the energy and non-air quality environmental impacts of compliance, any existing pollution control technology in use at the source, the remaining useful life of the source, and the degree of improvement in visibility which may reasonably be anticipated to result from the use of such technology;

(3) the term 'manmade air pollution' means air pollution which results directly or indirectly from human activities;

(4) the term 'as expeditiously as practicable' means as expeditiously as practicable but in no event later than five years after the date of approval of a plan revision under this section (or the date of promulgation of such a plan revision in the case of action by the Administrator under section 110(c) for purposes of this section);

(5) the term 'mandatory class I Federal areas' means Federal areas which may not be designated as other than class I under this part.

(6) the terms 'visibility impairment' and impairment of visibility' shall include reduction in visual range and atmospheric discoloration; and

(7) the term 'major stationary source' means the following types of stationary sources with the potential to emit 250 tons or more of any pollutant; fossil-fuel fired steam electric plants of more than 250 million British thermal units

per hour heat input, coal cleaning plants (thermal dryers), kraft pulp mills, Portland Cement plants, primary zinc smelters, iron and steel mill plants, primary aluminum ore reduction plants, primary coppers smelters, municipal incinerators capable of charging more than 250 tons of refuse per day, hydrofluoric, sulfuric, and nitric acid plants, petroleum refineries, lime plants, phosphate rock processing plants, coke oven batteries, sulfur recovery plants, carbon black plants (furnace process), primary lead smelters, fuel conversion plants, sintering plants, secondary metal production facilities, chemical process plants, fossil-fuel boilers of more than 250 million British thermal units per hour heat input, petroleum storage and transfer facilities with a capacity exceeding 300,000 barrels, taconite ore processing facilities, glass fiber processing plants, charcoal production facilities.

§7492. Visibility [Sec. 169B]

(a) Studies.—

(1) The Administrator, in conjunction with the National Park Service and other appropriate Federal agencies, shall conduct research to identify and evaluate sources and source regions of both visibility impairment and regions that provide predominantly clean air in class I areas. A total of $8,000,000 per year for 5 years is authorized to be appropriated for the Environmental Protection Agency and the other Federal agencies to conduct this research. The research shall include—

(A) expansion of current visibility related monitoring in class I areas;

(B) assessment of current sources of visibility impairing pollution and clean air corridors;

(C) adaption of regional air quality models for the assessment of visibility;

(D) studies of atmospheric chemistry and physics of visibility.

(2) Based on the findings available from the research required in subsection (a)(1) as well as other available scientific and technical data, studies, and other available information pertaining to visibility source-receptor relationships, the Administrator shall conduct an assessment and evaluation that identifies, to the extent possible, sources and source regions of visibility impairment including natural sources as well as source regions of clear air for class I areas. The Administrator shall produce interim findings from this study within 3 years after enactment of the Clean Air Act Amendments of 1990.

(b) Impacts of Other Provisions.—Within 24 months after enactment of the Clean Air Act Amendments of 1990, the Administrator shall conduct an assessment of the progress and improvements in visibility in class I areas that are likely to result from the implementation of the provisions of the Clean Air Act Amendments of 1990 other than the provisions of this section. Every 5 years thereafter the Administrator shall conduct an assessment of actual progress and improvement in visibility in class I areas. The Administrator shall prepare a written report on each assessment and transmit copies of these reports to the appropriate committees of Congress.

(c) Establishment of Visibility Transport Regions and Commissions.—

(1) Authority to establish visibility transport regions.—Whenever, upon the Administrator's motion or by petition from the Governors of at least two affected States, the Administrator has reason to believe that the current or projected interstate transport of air pollutants from one or more States contributes significantly to visibility impairment in class I areas located in the affected States, the Administrator may establish a transport region for such pollutants that includes such States. The Administrator, upon the Administrator's own motion or upon petition from the Governor of any affected State, or upon the recommendations of a transport commission established under subsection (b) of this section may—

(A) add any State or portion of a State to a visibility transport region when the Administrator determines that the interstate transport of air pollutants from such State significantly contributes to visibility impairment in a class I area located within the transport region, or

(B) remove any State or portion of a State from the region whenever the Administrator has reason to believe that the control of emissions in that State or portion of the State pursuant to this section will not significantly contribute to the protection or enhancement of visibility in any class I area in the region.

(2) Visibility transport commissions.—Whenever the Administrator establishes a transport region under subsection (c)(1), the Administrator shall establish a transport commission comprised of (as a minimum) each of the following members:

(A) the Governor of each State in the Visibility Transport Region, or the Governor's designee;

(B) The Administrator or the Administrator's designee; and

(C) A representative of each Federal agency charged with the direct management of each class I area or areas within the Visibility Transport Region.

(3) All representatives of the Federal Government shall be ex officio members.

(4) The visibility transport commissions shall be exempt from the requirements of the Federal Advisory Committee Act (5 U.S.C. Appendix 2, Section 1).

(d) Duties of Visibility Transport Commissions.—A Visibility Transport Commission—

(1) shall assess the scientific and technical data, studies, and other currently available information, including studies conducted pursuant to subsection (a)(1), pertaining to adverse impacts on visibility from potential or projected growth in emissions from sources located in the Visibility Transport Region; and

(2) shall, within 4 years of establishment, issue a report to the Administrator recommending what measures, if any, should be taken under the Clean Air Act to remedy such adverse impacts. The report required by this subsection shall address at least the following measures:

(A) the establishment of clean air corridors, in which additional restrictions on increases in emissions may be appropriate to protect visibility in affected class I areas;

(B) the imposition of the requirements of part D of this title affecting the construction of new major stationary sources or major modifications to existing sources in such clean air corridors specifically including the alternative siting analysis provisions of section 173(a)(5) ; and

(C) the promulgation of regulations under section 169A to address long range strategies for addressing regional haze which impairs visibility in affected class I areas.

(e) Duties of the Administrator.—

(1) The Administrator shall, taking into account the studies pursuant to subsection (a)(1) and the reports pursuant to subsection (d)(2) and any other relevant information, within eighteen months of receipt of the report referred to in subsection (d)(2) of this section, carry out the Administrator's regulatory responsibilities under section 169A , including criteria for measuring 'reasonable progress' toward the national goal.

(2) Any regulations promulgated under section 169A of this title pursuant to this subsection shall require affected States to revise within 12 months their implementation plans under section 110 of this title to contain such emission limits, schedules of compliance, and other measures as may be necessary to carry out regulations promulgated pursuant to this subsection.

(f) Grand Canyon Visibility Transport Commission.—The Administrator pursuant to subsection (c)(1) shall, within 12 months, establish a visibility transport commission for the region affecting the visibility of the Grand Canyon National Park.

[§169B added by PL 101-549]

PART D—PLAN REQUIREMENTS FOR NON-ATTAINMENT AREAS

SUBPART 1—NONATTAINMENT AREAS IN GENERAL

[Subpart 1 designated by PL 101–549]

§7501. Definitions [Sec. 171]

For the purpose of this part—

(1) Reasonable Further Progress.—The term 'reasonable further progress' means such annual incremental reductions in emissions of the relevant air pollutant as are required by this part or may reasonably be required by the Administrator for the purpose of ensuring attainment of the applicable national ambient air quality standard by the applicable date.

(2) Nonattainment Area.—The term 'nonattainment area' means, for any air pollutant, an area which is designated 'nonattainment' with respect to that pollutant within the meaning of section 107(d) .

[§171(1) and (2) amended by PL 101–549]

(3) The term 'lowest achievable emission rate' means for any source that rate of emissions which reflects—

(A) the most stringent emission limitation which is contained in the implementation plan of any State for such class or category of source, unless the owner or operator of the proposed source demonstrates that such limitations are not achievable, or

(B) the most stringent emission limitation which is achieved in practice by such class or category of source, whichever is more stringent.

In no event shall the application of this term permit a proposed new or modified source to emit any pollutant in excess of the amount allowable under applicable new source standards of performance.

(4) The terms 'modification' and 'modified' mean the same as the term 'modification' as used in section 111(a)(4) of this Act.

§7502. Nonattainment Plan Provisions In General [Sec. 172]

(a) Classifications and Attainment Dates.—

(1) Classifications.—

(A) On or after the date the Administrator promulgates the designation of an area as a nonattainment area pursuant to section 107(d) with respect to any national ambient air quality standard (or any revised standard, including a revision of any standard in effect on the date of the enactment of the Clean Air Act Amendments of 1990), the Administrator may classify the area for the purpose of applying an attainment date pursuant to paragraph (2), and for other purposes. In determining the appropriate classification, if any, for a nonattainment area, the Administrator may consider such factors as the severity of nonattainment in such area and the availability and feasibility of the pollution control measures that the Administrator believes may be necessary to provide for attainment of such standard in such area.

(B) The Administrator shall publish a notice in the Federal Register announcing each classification under subparagraph (A), except the Administrator shall provide an opportunity for at least 30 days for written comment. Such classification shall not be subject to the provisions of sections 553 through 557 of title 5 of the United States Code (concerning notice and comment) and shall not be subject to judicial review until the Administrator takes final action under subsection (k) or (l) of section 110 (concerning action on plan submissions) or section 179 (concerning sanctions) with respect to any plan submissions required by virtue of such classification.

(C) This paragraph shall not apply with respect to nonattainment areas for which classifications are specifically provided under other provisions of this part.

(2) Attainment Dates for Nonattainment Areas.—

(A) The attainment date for an area designated nonattainment with respect to a national primary ambient air quality standard shall be the date by which attainment can be achieved as expeditiously as practicable, but no later than 5 years from the date such area was designated nonattainment under section 107(d) , except that the Administrator may extend the attainment date to the extent the Administrator determines appropriate, for a period no greater than 10 years from the date of designation as nonattainment, considering the severity of nonattainment and the availability, and feasibility of pollution control measures.

(B) The attainment date for an area designated nonattainment with respect to a secondary national ambient air quality standard shall be the date by which attainment can be achieved as expeditiously as practicable after the date such area was designated nonattainment under section 107(d) .

(C) Upon application by any State, the Administrator may extend for 1 additional year (hereinafter referred to as the "Extension year") the attainment date determined by the Administrator under subparagraph (A) or (B) if—

(i) the State has complied with all requirements and commitments pertaining to the area in the applicable implementation plan, and

(ii) in accordance with guidance published by the Administrator, no more than a minimal number of exceedances of the relevant national ambient air quality standard has occurred in the area in the year preceding the Extension Year. No more than 2 one-year extensions may be issued under this subparagraph for a single nonattainment area.

(D) This paragraph shall not apply with respect to nonattainment areas for which attainment dates are specifically provided under other provisions of this part.

(b) Schedule for Plan Submissions.—At the time the Administrator promulgates the designation of an area as nonattainment with respect to a national ambient air quality standard under section 107(d) , the Administrator shall establish a schedule according to which the State containing such area shall submit a plan or plan revision (including the plan items) meeting the applicable requirements of subsection (c) and section 110(a)(2) . Such schedule shall at a minimum, include a date or dates, extending no later than 3 years from the date of the nonattainment designation, for the submission of a plan or plan revision (including the plan items) meeting the applicable requirements of subsection (c) and section 110(a)(2) .

(c) Nonattainment Plan Provisions.—The plan provisions (including plan items) required to be submitted under this part shall comply with each of the following:

(1) In General.—Such plan provisions shall provide for the implementation of all reasonably available control measures as expeditiously as practicable (including such reduction in emissions from existing sources in the area as may be obtained through the adoption, at a minimum, of reasonably available control technology) and shall provide for attainment of the national primary ambient air quality standards.

(2) RFP.—Such plan provisions shall require reasonable further progress.

(3) Inventory.—Such plan provisions shall include a comprehensive, accurate, current inventory of actual emissions from all sources of the relevant pollutant or pollutants in such area, including such periodic revisions as the Administrator may determine necessary to assure that the requirements of this part are met.

(4) Identification and Quantification.—Such plan provisions shall expressly identify and quantify the emissions, if any, of any such pollutant or pollutants which will be allowed, in accordance with section 173(a)(1)(B) , from the construction and operation of major new or modified stationary sources in each such area. The plan shall demonstrate to the satisfaction of the Administrator that the emissions quantified for this purpose will be consistent with the achievement of reasonable further progress and will not interfere with attainment of the applicable national ambient air quality standard by the applicable attainment date.

(5) Permits for New and Modified Major Stationary Sources.—Such plan provisions shall require permits for the construction and operation of new or modified major stationary sources anywhere in the nonattainment area, in accordance with section 173 .

(6) Other Measures.—Such plan provisions shall include enforceable emission limitations, and such other control measures, means or techniques (including economic incentives such as fees, marketable permits, and auctions of emission rights), as well as schedules and timetables for compliance, as may be necessary or ap propriate to provide for attainment of such standard in such area by the applicable attainment date specified in this part.

(7) Compliance with Section 110(a)(2) .—Such plan provisions shall also meet the applicable provisions of section 110(a)(2) .

(8) Equivalent Techniques.—Upon application by any State, the Administrator may allow the use of equivalent modeling, emission inventory, and planning procedures, unless the Administrator determines that the proposed techniques are, in the aggregate, less effective than the methods specified by the Administrator.

(9) Contingency Measures.—Such plan shall provide for the implementation of specific measures to be undertaken if the area fails to make reasonable further progress, or to attain the national primary ambient air quality standard by the attainment date applicable under this part. Such measures shall be included in the plan revision as contingency measures to take effect in any such case without further action by the State or the Administrator.

(d) Plan Revisions Required in Response to Finding of Plan Inadequacy.—Any plan revision for a nonattainment area which is required to be submitted in response to a finding by the Administrator pursuant to section 110(k)(5) (relating to calls for plan revisions) must correct the plan deficiency (or deficiencies) specified by the Administrator and meet all other applicable plan requirements of section 110 and this part. The Administrator may reasonably adjust the dates otherwise applicable under such requirements to such revision (except for attainment dates that have not yet elapsed), to the extent necessary to achieve a consistent application of such requirements. In order to facilitate submittal by the States of adequate and approvable plans consistent with the applicable requirements of this Act, the Administrator shall, as appropriate and from time to time, issue written guidelines, interpretations, and information to the States which shall be available to the public, taking into consideration any such guidelines, interpretations, or information provided before the date of the enactment of the Clean Air Act Amendments of 1990.

(e) Future Modification of Standard.—If the Administrator relaxes a national primary ambient air quality standard after the date of the enactment of the Clean Air Act Amendments of 1990, the Administrator shall, within 12 months after the relaxation, promulgate requirements applicable to all areas which have not attained that standard as of the date of such relaxation. Such requirements shall provide for controls which are not less stringent than the controls applicable to areas designated nonattainment before such relaxation.

[§172 revised by PL 101–549]

§7503. Permit Requirements [Sec. 173]

(a) In General—The permit program required by section 172(b)(6) shall provide that permits to construct and operate may be issued if—

(1) in accordance with regulations issued by the Administrator for the determination of baseline emissions in a manner consistent with the assumptions underlying the applicable implementation plan approved under section 110 and this part, the permitting agency determines that—

(A) by the time the source is to commence operation, sufficient offsetting emissions reductions have been obtained, such that total allowable emissions from existing sources in the region, from new or modified sources which are not major emitting facilities, and from the proposed source will be sufficiently less than total emissions from existing sources (as determined in accordance with the regulations under this paragraph) prior to the application for such permit to construct or modify so as to represent (when considered together with the plan provisions required under section 172) reasonable further progress (as defined in section 171); or

(B) in the case of a new or modified major stationary source which is located in a zone (within the nonattainment area) identified by the Administrator, in consultation with the Secretary of Housing and Urban Development, as a zone to which economic development should be targeted, that emissions of such pollutant resulting from the proposed new or modified major stationary source will not cause or contribute to emissions levels which exceed the allowance permitted for such pollutant for such area from new or modified major stationary sources under section 172(c) ;

(2) the proposed source is required to comply with the lowest achievable emission rate;

(3) the owner or operator of the proposed new or modified source has demonstrated that all major stationary sources owned or operated by such person (or by any entity controlling, controlled by, or under common control with such person) in such State are subject to emission limitations and are in compliance, or on a schedule for compliance, with all applicable emission limitations and standards under this Act; and

(4) the Administrator has not determined that the applicable implementation plan is not being adequately implemented for the nonattainment area in which the proposed source is to be constructed or modified in accordance with the requirements of this part; and

(5) an analysis of alternative sites, sizes, production processes, and environmental control techniques for such proposed source demonstrates that benefits of the proposed source significantly outweigh the environmental and social costs imposed as a result of its location, construction, or modification.

Any emission reductions required as a precondition of the issuance of a permit under paragraph (1) shall be federally enforceable before such permit may be issued.

[§173(a) designated and revised by PL 101–549]

(b) Prohibition on Use of Old Growth Allowances.—Any growth allowance included in an applicable implementation plan to meet the requirements of section 172(b)(5) (as in effect immediately before the date of the enactment of the Clean Air Act Amendments of 1990) shall not be valid for use in any area that received or receives a notice under section 110(a)(2)(H)(ii) (as in effect immediately before the date of the enactment of the Clean Air Act Amendments of 1990) or under section 110(k)(1) that its applicable implementation plan containing such allowance is substantially inadequate.

[§173(b) added by PL 101–549]

(c) Offsets.—

(1) The owner or operator of a new or modified major stationary source may comply with any offset requirement in effect under this part for increased emissions of any air pollutant only by obtaining emission reductions of such air pollutant from the same source or other sources in the same nonattainment area, except that the State may allow the owner or operator of a source to obtain such emission reductions in another nonattainment area if (A) the other area has an equal or higher nonattainment classification than the area in which the source is located and (B) emissions from such other area contribute to a violation of the national ambient air quality standard in the nonattainment area in which the source is located. Such emission reductions shall be, by the time a new or modified source commences operation, in effect and enforceable and shall assure that the total tonnage of increased emissions of the air

pollutant from the new or modified source shall be offset by an equal or greater reduction, as applicable in the actual emissions of such air pollutant from the same or other sources in the area.

(2) Emission reductions otherwise required by this Act shall not be creditable as emissions reductions for purposes of any such offset requirement. Incidental emission reductions which are not otherwise required by this Act shall be creditable as emission reductions for such purposes if such emission reductions meet the requirements of paragraph (1).

[§173(c) added by PL 101–549]

(d) Control Technology Information.—The State shall provide that control technology information from permits issued under this section will be promptly submitted to the Administrator for purposes of making such information available through the RACT/BACT/LAER clearing house to other States and to the general public.

[§173(d) added by PL 101–549]

(e) Rocket Engines or Motors.—The permitting authority of a State shall allow a source to offset by alternative or innovative means emission increases from rocket engine and motor firing, and cleaning related to such firing, at an existing or modified major source that tests rocket engines or motors under the following conditions:

(1) Any modification proposed is solely for the purpose of expanding the testing of rocket engines or motors at an existing source that is permitted to test such engines on the date of enactment of this subsection.

(2) The source demonstrates to the satisfaction of the permitting authority of the State that it has used all reasonable means to obtain and utilize offsets, as determined on an annual basis, for the emissions increases beyond allowable levels, that all available offsets are being used, and that sufficient offsets are not available to the source.

(3) The source has obtained a written finding from the Department of Defense, Department of Transportation, National Aeronautics and Space Administration or other appropriate Federal agency, that the testing of rocket motors or engines at the facility is required for a program essential to the national security.

(4) The source will comply with an alternative measure imposed by the permitting authority, designed to offset any emission increases beyond permitted levels not directly offset by the source. In lieu of imposing any alternative offset measures, the permitting authority may impose an emissions fee to be paid to such authority of a State which shall be an amount no greater than 1.5 times the average cost of stationary source control measures adopted in that area during the previous 3 years. The permitting authority shall utilize the fees in a manner that maximizes the emissions reductions in that area.

[§173(e) added by PL 101–549]

§7504. Planning Procedures [Sec. 174]

[§174 revised by PL 101–549]

(a) In General.—For any ozone, carbon monoxide, or PM–10 nonattainment area, the State containing such area and elected officials of affected local governments shall, before the date required for submittal of the inventory described under sections 182(a)(1) and 187(a)(1), jointly review and update as necessary the planning procedures adopted pursuant to this subsection as in effect immediately before the date of the enactment of the Clean Air Act Amendments of 1990, or develop new planning procedures pursuant to this subsection, as appropriate. In preparing such procedures the State and local elected officials shall determine which elements of a revised implementation plan will be developed, adopted, and implemented (through means including enforcement) by the State and which by local governments or regional agencies, or any combination of local governments, regional agencies, or the State. The implementation plan required by this part shall be prepared by an organization certified by the State, in consultation with elected officials of local governments and in accordance with the determination under the second sentence of this subsection. Such organization shall include elected officials of local governments in the affected area, and representatives of the State air quality planning agency, the State transportation planning agency, the metropolitan planning organization designated to conduct the continuing, cooperative and comprehensive transportation planning process for the area under section 134 of title 23, United States Code, the organization responsible for the air quality maintenance planning process under regulations implementing this Act, and any other organization with responsibilities for developing, submitting, or implementing the plan required by this part. Such organization may be one that carried out these functions before the date of the enactment of the Clean Air Act Amendments of 1990.

(b) Coordination.—The preparation of implementation plan provisions and subsequent plan revisions under the continuing transportation-air quality planning process described in section 108(e) shall be coordinated with the continuing, cooperative and comprehensive transportation planning process required under section 134 of title 23, United States Code, and such planning processes shall take into account the requirements of this part.

(c) Joint Planning.—In the case of a nonattainment area that is included within more than one State, the affected States may jointly, through interstate compact or otherwise, undertake and implement all or part of the planning procedures described in this section.

§7505. Environmental Protection Agency Grants [Sec. 175]

(a) The Administrator shall make grants to any organization of local elected officials with transportation or air quality maintenance planning responsibilities recognized by the State under section 174(a) for payment of the reasonable costs of developing a plan revision under this part.

(b) The amount granted to any organization under subsection (a) shall be 100 percent of any additional costs of developing a plan revision under this part for the first two fiscal years following receipt of the grant under this paragraph, and shall supplement any funds available under Federal law to such organization for transportation or air quality maintenance planning. Grants under this section shall not be used for construction.

§7505a. Maintenance Plans [Sec. 175A]

(a) Plan Revision.—Each State which submits a request under section 107(d) for redesignation of a nonattainment area for any air pollutant as an area which has attained the national primary ambient air quality standard for that air pollutant shall also submit a revision of the applicable State implementation plan to provide for the maintenance of the national primary ambient air quality standard for such air pollutant in the area concerned for at least 10 years after the redesignation. The plan shall contain such additional measures, if any, as may be necessary to ensure such maintenance.

(b) Subsequent Plan Revisions.—8 years after redesignation of any area as an attainment area under section 107(d) , the State shall submit to the Administrator an additional revision of the applicable State implementation plan for maintaining the national primary ambient air quality standard for 10 years after the expiration of the 10-year period referred to in subsection (a).

(c) Nonattainment Requirements Applicable Pending Plan Approval.—Until such plan revision is approved and an area is redesignated as attainment for any area designated as a nonattainment area, the requirements of this part shall continue in force and effect with respect to such area.

(d) Contingency Provisions.—Each plan revision submitted under this section shall contain such contingency provisions as the Administrator deems necessary to assure that the State will promptly correct any violation of the standard which occurs after the redesignation of the area as an attainment area. Such provisions shall include a requirement that the State will implement all measures with respect to the control of the air pollutant concerned which were contained in the State implementation plan for the area before redesignation of the area as an attainment area. The failure of any area redesignated as an attainment area to maintain the national ambient air quality standard concerned shall not result in a requirement that the State revise its State implementation plan unless the Administrator, in the Administrator's discretion, requires the State to submit a revised State implementation plan.

[§175A added by PL 101–549]

§7506. Limitations on Certain Federal Assistance [Sec. 176]

(a) [Repealed by PL 101–549]

(b) [Repealed by PL 101–549]

(c) (1) No department, agency, or instrumentality of the Federal Government shall engage in, support in any way or provide financial assistance for, license or permit, or approve, any activity which does not conform to an implementation plan after it has been approved or promulgated under section 110 . No metropolitan planning organization designated under section 134 of title 23, United States Code, shall give its approval to any project, program, or plan which does not conform to an implementation plan approved or promulgated under section 110 . The assurance of conformity to such an implementation plan shall be an affirmative responsibility of the head of such department, agency, or instrumentality. Conformity to an implementation plan means—

(A) conformity to an implementation plan's purpose of eliminating or reducing the severity and number of violations of the national ambient air quality standards and achieving expeditious attainment of such standards; and

(B) that such activities will not—

(i) cause or contribute to any new violation of any standard in any area;

(ii) increase the frequency or severity of any existing violation of any standard in any area; or

(iii) delay timely attainment of any standard or any required interim emission reductions or other milestones in any area. The determination of conformity shall be based on the most recent estimates of emissions, and such estimates shall be determined from the most recent population, employment, travel and congestion estimates as determined by the metropolitan planning organization or other agency authorized to make such estimates.

(2) Any transportation plan or program developed pursuant to title 23, United States Code, or the Urban Mass Transportation Act shall implement the transportation provisions of any applicable implementation plan approved under this Act applicable to all or part of the area covered by such transportation plan or program. No Federal agency may approve, accept or fund any transportation plan, program or project unless such plan, program or project has been found to conform to any applicable implementation plan in effect under this Act. In particular—

(A) no transportation plan or transportation improvement program may be adopted by a metropolitan planning organization designated under title 23, United States Code, or the Urban Mass Transportation Act, or be found to be in conformity by a metropolitan planning organization until a final determination has been made that emissions expected from implementation of such plans and programs are consistent with estimates of emissions from motor vehicles and necessary emissions reductions contained in the applicable implementation plan, and that the plan or program will conform to the requirements of paragraph (1)(B);

(B) no metropolitan planning organization or other recipient of funds under title 23, United States Code, or the Urban Mass Transportation Act shall adopt or approve a transportation improvement program of projects until it determines that such program provides for timely implementation of transportation control measures consistent with schedules included in the applicable implementation plan;

(C) a transportation project may be adopted or approved by a metropolitan planning organization or any recipient of funds designated under title 23, United States Code, or the Urban Mass Transportation Act, or found in conformity by a metropolitan planning organization or approved, accepted, or funded by the Department of Transportation only if it meets either the requirements of subparagraph (D) or the following requirements—

(i) such a project comes from a conforming plan and program;

(ii) the design concept and scope of such project have not changed significantly since the conformity finding regarding the plan and program from which the project derived; and

(iii) the design concept and scope of such project at the time of the conformity determination for the program was adequate to determine emissions.

(D) Any project not referred to in subparagraph (C) shall be treated as conforming to the applicable implementation plan only if it is demonstrated that the projected emissions from such project, when considered together with emissions projected for the conforming transportation plans and programs within the nonattainment area, do not cause such plans and programs to exceed the emission reduction projections and schedules assigned to such plans and programs in the applicable implementation plan.

(3) Until such time as the implementation plan revision referred to in paragraph (4)(C) is approved, conformity of such plans, programs, and projects will be demonstrated if—

(A) the transportation plans and programs—

(i) are consistent with the most recent estimates of mobile source emissions;

(ii) provide for the expeditious implementation of transportation control measures in the applicable implementation plan; and

(iii) with respect to ozone and carbon monoxide nonattainment areas, contribute to annual emissions reductions consistent with sections 182(b)(1) and 187(a)(7) ; and

(B) the transportation projects—

(i) come from a conforming transportation plan and program as defined in subparagraph (A) or for 12 months after the date of the enactment of the Clean Air Act Amendments of 1990, from a transportation program found to conform within 3 years prior to such date of enactment; and

(ii) in carbon monoxide nonattainment areas, eliminate or reduce the severity and number of violations of the carbon monoxide standards in the area substantially affected by the project. With regard to subparagraph (B)(ii), such determination may be made as part of either the conformity determination for the transportation program or for the individual project taken as a whole during the environmental review phase of project development.

(4) (A) No later than one year after the date of enactment of the Clean Air Act Amendments of 1990, the Administrator shall promulgate criteria and procedures for determining conformity (except in the case of transportation plans, programs, and projects) of, and for keeping the Administrator informed about, the activities referred to in paragraph (1). No later than one year after such date of enactment, the Administrator, with the concurrence of the Secretary of Transportation, shall promulgate criteria and procedures for demonstrating and assuring conformity in the case of transportation plans, programs, and projects. A suit may be brought against the Administrator and the Secretary of Transportation under section 304 to compel promulgation of such criteria and procedures and the Federal district court shall have jurisdiction to order such promulgation.

(B) The procedures and criteria shall, at a minimum—

(i) address the consultation procedures to be undertaken by metropolitan planning organizations and the Secretary of Transportation with State and local air quality agencies and State departments of transportation before such organizations and the Secretary make conformity determinations;

(ii) address the appropriate frequency for making conformity determinations, but in no case shall such determinations for transportation plans and programs be less frequent than every three years; and

(iii) address how conformity determinations will be made with respect to maintenance plans.

(C) Such procedures shall also include a requirement that each State shall submit to the Administrator and the Secretary of Transportation within 24 months of such date of enactment, a revision to its implementation plan that includes criteria and procedures for assessing the conformity of any plan, program, or project subject to the conformity requirements of this subsection.

[§176(c) amended by PL 101–549]

(d) Each department, agency, or instrumentality of the Federal Government having authority to conduct or support any program with air-quality related transportation consequences shall give priority in the exercise of such authority, consistent with statutory requirements for allocation among States or other jurisdictions, to the implementation of those portions of plans prepared under this section to achieve and maintain the national primary ambient air quality standards. This paragraph extends to, but is not limited to, authority exercised under the Urban Mass Transportation Act, title 23 of the United States Code, and the Housing and Urban Development Act.

§7506a. Interstate Transport Commissions
[Sec. 176A]

(a) Authority to Establish Interstate Transport Regions.—Whenever, on the Administrator's own motion or by petition from the Governor of any State, the Administrator has reason to believe that the interstate transport of air pollutants from one or more States contributed significantly to a violation of a national ambient air quality standard in one or more other States, the Administrator may establish, by rule, a transport region for such pollutant that includes such States. The Administrator, on the Administrator's own motion or upon petition from the Governor of any State, or upon the recommendation of a transport commission established under subsection (b), may—

(1) add any State or portion of a State to any region established under this subsection whenever the Administrator has reason to believe that the interstate transport of air pollutants from such State significantly contributes to a violation of the standard in the transport region, or

(2) remove any State or portion of a State from the region whenever the Administrator has reason to believe that the control of emissions in that State or portion of the State pursuant to this section will not significantly contribute to the attainment of the standard in any area in the region. The Administrator shall approve or disapprove any such petition or recommendation within 18 months of its receipt. The Administrator shall establish appropriate proceedings for public participation regarding

such petitions and motions, including notice and comment.

(b) Transport Commissions.—

(1) Establishment.—Whenever the Administrator establishes a transport region under subsection (a), the Administrator shall establish a transport commission comprised of (at a minimum) each of the following members:

(A) The Governor of each State in the region or the designee of each such Governor.

(B) The Administrator or the Administrator's designee.

(C) The Regional Administrator (or the Administrator's designee) for each Regional Office for each Environmental Protection Agency Region affected by the transport region concerned.

(D) An air pollution control official representing each State in the region, appointed by the Governor. Decisions of, and recommendations and requests to, the Administrator by each transport commission may be made only by a majority vote of all members other than the Administrator and the Regional Administrators (or designees thereof).

(2) Recommendations.—The transport commission shall assess the degree of interstate transport of the pollutant or precursors to the pollutant throughout the transport region, assess strategies for mitigating the interstate pollution, and recommend to the Administrator such measures as the Commission determines to be necessary to ensure that the plans for the relevant States meet the requirements of section 110(a)(2)(D) . Such commission shall not be subject to the provisions of the Federal Advisory Committee Act (5 U.S.C. App.).

(c) Commission Requests.—A transport commission established under subsection (b) may request the Administrator to issue a finding under section 110(k)(5) that the implementation plan for one or more of the States in the transport region is substantially inadequate to meet the requirements of section 110(a)(2)(D) . The Administrator shall approve, disapprove, or partially approve and partially disapprove such a request within 18 months of its receipt and, to the extent the Administrator approves such request, issue the finding under section 110(k)(5) at the time of such approval. In acting on such request, the Administrator shall provide an opportunity for public participation and shall address each specific recommendation made by the commission. Approval or disapproval of such a request shall constitute final agency action within the meaning of section 307(b) .

[§176A added by PL 101–549]

§7507. New Motor Vehicle Emission Standards in Nonattainment Areas [Sec. 177]

Notwithstanding section 209(a), any State which has plan provisions approved under this part may adopt and enforce for any model year standards relating to control of emissions from new motor vehicles or new motor vehicle engines and take such other actions as are referred to in section 209(a) respecting such vehicles if—

(1) such standards are identical to the California standards for which a waiver has been granted for such model year, and

(2) California and such State adopt such standards at least two years before commencement of such model year (as determined by regulations of the Administrator). Nothing in this section or in title II of this Act shall be construed as authorizing any such State to prohibit or limit, directly or indirectly, the manufacture or sale of a new motor vehicle or motor vehicle engine that is certified in California as meeting California standards, or to take any action of any kind to create, or have the effect of creating, a motor vehicle or motor vehicle engine different than a motor vehicle or engine certified in California under California standards (a "third vehicle") or otherwise create such a "third vehicle".

[§177 amended by PL 101–549]

§7508. Guidance Documents [Sec. 178]

The Administrator shall issue guidance documents under section 108 for purposes of assisting States in implementing requirements of this part respecting the lowest achievable emission rate. Such a document shall be published not later than nine months after the date of enactment of this part and shall be revised at least every two years thereafter.

Sanctions and Consequences of Failure to Attain [Sec. 179]

(a) State Failure.—For any implementation plan or plan revision required under this part (or required in response to a finding of substantial inadequacy as described in section 110(k)(5)), if the Administrator—

(1) finds that a State has failed, for an area designated nonattainment under section 107(d) , to submit a plan, or to submit 1 or more of the elements (as determined by the Administrator) required by the provisions of this Act applicable to such an area, or has failed to make a sub-

mission for such an area that satisfies the minimum criteria established in relation to any such element under section 110(k) .

(2) disapproves a submission under section 110(k) , for an area designated nonattainment under section 107 , based on the submission's failure to meet one or more of the elements required by the provisions of this Act applicable to such an area,

(3) (A) determines that a State has failed to make any submission as may be required under this Act, other than one described under paragraph (1) or (2), including an adequate maintenance plan, or has failed to make any submission, as may be required under this Act, other than one described under paragraph (1) or (2), that satisfies the minimum criteria established in relation to such submission under section 110(k)(1)(A) , or

(B) disapproves in whole or in part a submission described under subparagraph (A), or

(4) finds that any requirement of an approved plan (or approved part of a plan) is not being implemented, unless such deficiency has been corrected within 18 months after the finding, disapproval, or determination referred to in paragraphs (1), (2), (3), and (4), one of the sanctions referred to in subsection (b) shall apply, as selected by the Administrator, until the Administrator determines that the State has come into compliance, except that if the Administrator finds a lack of good faith, sanctions under both paragraph (1) and paragraph (2) of subsection (b) shall apply until the Administrator determines that the State has come into compliance. If the Administrator has selected one of such sanctions and the deficiency has not been corrected within 6 months thereafter, sanctions under both paragraph (1) and paragraph (2) of subsection (b) shall apply until the Administrator determines that the State has come into compliance. In addition to any other sanction applicable as provided in this section, the Administrator may withhold all or part of the grants for support of air pollution planning and control programs that the Administrator may award under section 105 .

(b) Sanctions.—The sanctions available to the Administrator as provided in subsection (a) are as follows:

(1) Highway Sanctions.—

(A) The Administrator may impose a prohibition, applicable to a nonattainment area, on the approval by the Secretary of Transportation of any projects or the awarding by the Secretary of any grants, under title 23, United States Code, other than projects or grants for safety where the Secretary determines, based on accident or other appropriate data submitted by the State, that the principal purpose of the project is an improvement in safety to resolve a demonstrated safety problem and likely will result in a significant reduction in, or avoidance of, accidents. Such prohibition shall become effective upon the selection by the Administrator of this sanction.

(B) In addition to safety, projects or grants that may be approved by the Secretary, notwithstanding the prohibition in subparagraph (A), are the following—

(i) capital programs for public transit;

(ii) construction or restriction of certain roads or lanes solely for the use of passenger buses or high occupancy vehicles;

(iii) planning for requirements for employers to reduce employee work-trip-related vehicle emissions;

(iv) highway ramp metering, traffic signalization, and related programs that improve traffic flow and achieve a net emission reduction;

(v) fringe and transportation corridor parking facilities serving multiple occupancy vehicle programs or transit operations;

(vi) programs to limit or restrict vehicle use in downtown areas or other areas of emission concentration particularly during periods of peak use, through road use charges, tolls, parking surcharges, or other pricing mechanisms, vehicle restricted zones or periods, or vehicle registration programs;

(vii) programs for breakdown and accident scene management, nonrecurring congestion, and vehicle information systems, to reduce congestion and emissions; and

(viii) such other transportation-related programs as the Administrator, in consultation with the Secretary of Transportation, finds would improve air quality and would not encourage single occupancy vehicle capacity. In considering such measures, the State should seek to ensure adequate access to downtown, other commercial, and residential areas, and avoid increasing or relocating emissions and congestion rather than reducing them.

(2) Offsets.—In applying the emissions offset requirements of section 173 to new or modified sources or emissions units for which a permit

is required under part D, the ratio of emission reductions to increased emissions shall be at least 2 to 1.

(c) Notice of Failure to Attain.—

(1) As expeditiously as practicable after the applicable attainment date for any nonattainment area, but not later than 6 months after such date, the Administrator shall determine, based on the area's air quality as of the attainment date, whether the area attained the standard by that date.

(2) Upon making the determination under paragraph (1), the Administrator shall publish a notice in the Federal Register containing such determination and identifying each area that the Administrator has determined to have failed to attain. The Administrator may revise or supplement such determination at any time based on more complete information or analysis concerning the area's air quality as of the attainment date.

(d) Consequences for Failure to Attain.—

(1) Within 1 year after the Administrator publishes the notice under subsection (c)(2) (relating to notice of failure to attain), each State containing a nonattainment area shall submit a revision to the applicable implementation plan meeting the requirements of paragraph (2) of this subsection.

(2) The revision required under paragraph (1) shall meet the requirements of section 110 and section 172 . In addition, the revision shall include such additional measures as the Administrator may reasonably prescribe, including all measures that can be feasibly implemented in the area in light of technological achievability, costs, and any nonair quality and other air quality-related health and environmental impacts.

(3) The attainment date applicable to the revision required under paragraph (1) shall be the same as provided in the provisions of section 172(a)(2), except that in applying such provisions the phrase 'from the date of the notice under section 179(c)(2)' shall be substituted for the phrase 'from the date such area was designated nonattainment under section 107(d)' and for the phrase 'from the date of designation as nonattainment'.

[§179 added by PL 101–549]

§7509a. International Border Areas [Sec. 179B]

(a) Implementation Plans and Revisions.—Notwithstanding any other provision of law, an implementation plan or plan revision required under this Act shall be approved by the Administrator if—

(1) such plan or revision meets all the requirements applicable to it under the Act other than a requirement that such plan or revision demonstrate attainment and maintenance of the relevant national ambient air quality standards by the attainment date specified under the applicable provision of this Act, or in a regulation promulgated under such provision, and

(2) the submitting State establishes to the satisfaction of the Administrator that the implementation plan of such State would be adequate to attain and maintain the relevant national ambient air quality standards by the attainment date specified under the applicable provision of this Act, or in a regulation promulgated under such provision, but for emissions emanating from outside of the United States.

(b) Attainment of Ozone Levels.—Notwithstanding any other provision of law, any State that establishes to the satisfaction of the Administrator that, with respect to an ozone nonattainment area in such State, such State would have attained the national ambient air quality standard for ozone by the applicable attainment date, but for emissions emanating from outside of the United States, shall not be subject to the provisions of section 181(a)(2) or (5) or section 185 .

(c) Attainment of Carbon Monoxide Levels.—Notwithstanding any other provision of law, any State that establishes to the satisfaction of the Administrator, with respect to a carbon monoxide nonattainment area in such State, that such State has attained the national ambient air quality standard for carbon monoxide by the applicable attainment date, but for emissions emanating from outside of the United States, shall not be subject to the provisions of section 186(b)(2) or (9) .

(d) Attainment of PM–10 Levels.—Notwithstanding any other provision of law, any State that establishes to the satisfaction of the Administrator that, with respect to a PM–10 nonattainment area in such State, such State would have attained the national ambient air quality standard for carbon monoxide by the applicable attainment date, but for emissions emanating from outside the United States shall not be subject to the provisions of section 188(b)(2) .

[§179B added by PL 101–549]

SUBPART 2—ADDITIONAL PROVISIONS FOR OZONE NONATTAINMENT AREAS

§7511. Classification and Attainment Dates [Sec. 181]

(a) Classification and Attainment Dates for 1989 Nonattainment Areas.—

(1) Each area designated nonattainment for ozone pursuant to section 107(d) shall be classified at the time of such designation under table 1, by operation of law, as a Marginal Area, a Moderate Area, a Serious Area, a Severe Area, or an Extreme Area based on the design value for the area. The design value shall be calculated according to the interpretation methodology issued by the Administrator most recently before the date of the enactment of the Clean Air Act Amendments of 1990. For each area classified under this subsection, the primary standard attainment date for ozone shall be as expeditiously as practicable but not later than the date provided in table 1.

TABLE 1

Area class	Design value*	Primary standard attainment date**
Marginal	0.121 up to 0.138	3 years after enactment
Moderate	0.138 up to 0.160	6 years after enactment
Serious	0.160 up to 0.180	9 years after enactment
Severe	0.180 up to 0.280	15 years after enactment
Extreme	0.280 and above	20 years after enactment

* The design value is measured in parts per million (ppm).

** The primary standard attainment date is measured from the date of the enactment of the Clean Air Amendments of 1990.

(2) Notwithstanding table 1, in the case of a severe area with a 1988 ozone design value between 0.190 and 0.280 ppm, the attainment date shall be 17 years (in lieu of 15 years) after the date of the enactment of the Clean Air Amendments of 1990.

(3) At the time of publication of the notice under section 107(d)(4) (relating to area designations) for each ozone nonattainment area, the Administrator shall publish a notice announcing the classification of such ozone nonattainment area. The provisions of section 172(a)(1)(B) (relating to lack of notice and comment and judicial review) shall apply to such classification.

(4) If an area classified under paragraph (1) (Table 1) would have been classified in another category if the design value in the area were 5 percent greater or 5 percent less than the level on which such classification was based, the Administrator may, in the Administrator's discretion, within 90 days after the initial classification, by the procedure required under paragraph (3), adjust the classification to place the area in such other category. In making such adjustment, the Administrator may consider the number of exceedances of the national primary ambient air quality standard for ozone in the area, the level of pollution transport between the area and other affected areas, including both intrastate and interstate transport, and the mix of sources and air pollutants in the area.

(5) Upon application by any State, the Administrator may extend for 1 additional year (hereinafter the date specified in table 1 of paragraph (1) of this subsection if—

(A) the State has complied with all requirements and commitments pertaining to the area in the applicable implementation plan, and

(B) no more than 1 exceedance of the national ambient air quality standard level for ozone has occurred in the area in the year preceding the Extension Year. No more than 2 one-year extensions may be issued under this paragraph for a single nonattainment area.

(b) New Designations and Reclassifications.—

(1) New designations to nonattainment.—Any area that is designated attainment or unclassifiable for ozone under section 107(d)(4) , and that is subsequently redesignated to nonattainment for ozone under section 107(d)(3) , shall, at the time of the redesignation, be classified by operation of law in accordance with table 1 under subsection (a). Upon its classification, the area shall be subject to the same requirements under section 110 , subpart 1 of this part, and this subpart that would have applied had the area been so classified at the time of the notice under subsection (a)(3), except that any absolute, fixed date applicable in connection with any such requirement is extended by operation of law by a period equal to the length of time between the date of the enactment of the Clean Air Act Amendments of 1990 and the date the area is classified under this paragraph.

(2) Reclassification upon failure to attain.—

(A) Within 6 months following the applicable attainment date (including any extension thereof) for an ozone nonattainment area, the Administrator shall determine, based on the area's design value (as of the attainment date), whether the area attained the standard by that date. Except for any Severe or Extreme area, any area that the Administrator finds has not attained the standard by that date shall be reclassified by operation of law in accordance with table 1 of subsection (a) to the higher of—

(i) the next higher classification for the area, or

(ii) the classification applicable to the area's design value as determined at the time of the notice required under subparagraph (B). No area shall be reclassified as Extreme under clause (ii).

(B) The Administrator shall publish a notice in the Federal Register, no later than 6 months following the attainment date, identifying each area that the Administrator has determined under subparagraph (A) as having failed to attain and identifying the reclassification, if any, described under subparagraph (A).

(3) Voluntary reclassification.—The Administrator shall grant the request of any State to reclassify a nonattainment area in that State in accordance with table 1 of subsection (a) to a higher classification. The Administrator shall publish a notice in the Federal Register of any such request and of action by the Administrator granting the request.

(4) Failure of severe areas to attain standard.—

(A) If any Severe Area fails to achieve the national primary ambient air quality standard for ozone by the applicable attainment date (including any extension thereof), the fee provisions under section 185 shall apply within the area, the percent reduction requirements of section 182(c)(2)(B) and (C) (relating to reasonable further progress demonstration and NOx control) shall continue to apply to the area, and the State shall demonstrate that such percent reduction has been achieved in each 3–year interval after such failure until the standard is attained. Any failure to make such a demonstration shall be subject to the sanctions provided under this part.

(B) In addition to the requirements of subparagraph (A), if the ozone design value for a Severe Area referred to in subparagraph (A) is above 0.140 ppm for the year of the applicable attainment date, or if the area has failed to achieve its most recent milestone under section 182(g), the new source review requirements applicable under this subpart in Extreme Areas shall apply in the area and the term 'major source' and 'major stationary source' shall have the same meaning as in Extreme Areas.

(C) In addition to the requirements of subparagraph (A) for those areas referred to in subparagraph (A) and not covered by subparagraph (B), the provisions referred to in subparagraph (B) shall apply after 3 years from the applicable attainment date unless the area has attained the standard by the end of such 3–year period.

(D) If, after the date of the enactment of the Clean Air Act Amendments of 1990, the Administrator modifies the method of determining compliance with the national primary ambient air quality standard, a design value or other indicator comparable to 0.140 in terms of its relationship to the standard shall be used in lieu of 0.140 for purposes of applying the provisions of subparagraphs (B) and (C).

(c) References to Terms.—

(1) Any reference in this subpart to a 'Marginal Area', a 'Moderate Area', a 'Serious Area', a 'Severe Area', or an 'Extreme Area' shall be considered a reference to a Marginal Area, a Moderate Area, a Serious Area, a Severe Area, or an Extreme Area as respectively classified under this section.

(2) Any reference in this subpart to 'next higher classification' or comparable terms shall be considered a reference to the classification related to the next higher set of design values in table 1.

§7511a. Plan Submissions And Requirements [Sec. 182]

(a) Marginal Areas.—Each State in which all or part of a Marginal Area is located shall, with respect to the Marginal Area (or portion thereof, to the extent specified in this subsection), submit to the Administrator the State implementation plan revisions (including the plan items) described under this subsection except to the extent the State has made such submissions as of the date of the enactment of the Clean Air Act Amendments of 1990.

(1) Inventory.—Within 2 years after the date of the enactment of the Clean Air Act Amendments of 1990, the State shall submit a comprehensive, accurate, current inventory of actual emissions from all sources, as described in sec-

tion 172(c)(3) , in accordance with guidance provided by the Administrator.

(2) Corrections to the State Implementation Plan.—Within the periods prescribed in this paragraph, the State shall submit a revision to the State implementation plan that meets the following requirements—

(A) Reasonably Available Control Technology Corrections.—For any Marginal Area (or, within the Administrator's discretion, portion thereof) the State shall submit, within 6 months of the date of classification under section 181(a) , a revision that includes such provisions to correct requirements in (or add requirements to) the plan concerning reasonably available control technology as were required under section 172(b) (as in effect immediately before the date of the enactment of the Clean Air Act Amendments of 1990), as interpreted in guidance issued by the Administrator under section 108 before the date of the enactment of the Clean air Act Amendments of 1990.

(B) Savings Clause for Vehicle Inspection and Maintenance.—

(i) For any Marginal Area (or, within the Administrator's discretion, portion thereof), the plan for which already includes, or was required by section 172(b)(11)(B) (as in effect immediately before the date of the enactment of the Clean Air Act Amendments of 1990) to have included, a specific schedule for implementation of a vehicle emission control inspection and maintenance program, the State shall submit, immediately after the date of the enactment of the Clean Air Act Amendments 1990, a revision that includes any provisions necessary to provide for a vehicle inspection and maintenance program of no less stringency than that of either the program defined in House Report Numbered 95–294, 95th Congress, 1st Session, 281–291 (1977) as interpreted in guidance of the Administrator issued pursuant to section 172(b)(11)(B) (as in effect immediately before the date of the enactment of the Clean Air Act Amendments of 1990) or the program already included in the plan, whichever is more stringent.

(ii) Within 12 months after the date of the enactment of the Clean Air Act Amendments of 1990, the Administrator shall review, revise, update, and republish in the Federal Register the guidance for the States for motor vehicle inspection and maintenance programs required by this Act, taking into consideration the Administrator's investigations and audits of such program. The guidance shall, at a minimum, cover the frequency of inspections, the types of vehicles to be inspected (which shall include leased vehicles that are registered in the nonattainment area), vehicle maintenance by owners and operators, audits by the State, the test method and measures, including whether centralized or decentralized, inspection methods and procedures, quality of inspection, components covered, assurance that a vehicle subject to a recall notice from a manufacturer has complied with that notice, and effective implementation and enforcement, including ensuring that any retesting of a vehicle after a failure shall include proof of corrective action and providing for denial of vehicle registration in the case of tampering or misfueling. The guidance which shall be incorporated in the applicable State implementation plans by the States shall provide the States with continued reasonable flexibility to fashion effective, reasonable, and fair programs for the affected consumer. No later than 2 years after the Administrator promulgates regulations under section 202(m)(3) (relating to emission control diagnostics), the State shall submit a revision to such program to meet any requirements that the Administrator may prescribe under that section.

(C) Permit Programs.—Within 2 years after the date of the enactment of the Clean Air Act Amendments of 1990, the State shall submit a revision that includes each of the following:

(i) Provisions to require permits, in accordance with sections 172(c)(5) and 173 , for the construction and operation of each new or modified major stationary source (with respect to ozone) to be located in the area.

(ii) Provisions to correct requirements in (or add requirements to) the plan concerning permit programs as were required under section 172(b)(6) (as in effect immediately before the date of the enactment of the Clean Air Act Amendments of 1990), as interpreted in regulations of the Administrator promulgated as of the date of the enactment of the Clean Air Act Amendments of 1990.

(3) Periodic Inventory.—

(A) General Requirements.—No later than the end of each 3-year period after submission of the inventory under paragraph (1) until the area is redesignated to attainment, the State shall submit a revised inventory meeting the requirements of subsection (a)(1).

(B) Emissions Statements.—

(i) Within 2 years after the date of the enactment of the Clean Air Act Amendments of 1990, the State shall submit a revision to the State implementation plan to require that the owner or operator of each stationary source of oxides of nitrogen or volatile organic compounds provide the State with a statement, in such form as the Administrator may prescribe (or accept an equivalent alternative developed by the State), for classes or categories of sources, showing the actual emissions of oxides of nitrogen and volatile organic compounds from that source. The first such statement shall be submitted within 3 years after the date of the enactment of the Clean Air Act Amendments of 1990. Subsequent statements shall be submitted at least every year thereafter. The statement shall contain a certification that the information contained in the statement is accurate to the best knowledge of the individual certifying the statement.

(ii) The State may waive the application of clause (i) to any class or category of stationary sources which emit less than 25 tons per year of volatile organic compounds or oxides of nitrogen if the State, in its submissions under subparagraphs (1) or (3)(A), provides an inventory of emissions from such class or category of sources, based on the use of the emission factors established by the Administrator or other methods acceptable to the Administrator.

(4) General Offset Requirement.—For purposes of satisfying the emission offset requirements of this part, the ratio of total emission reductions of volatile organic compounds to total increased emissions of such air pollutant shall be at least 1.1 to 1. The Administrator may, in the Administrator's discretion, require States to submit a schedule for submitting any of the revisions or other items required under this subsection. The requirements of this subsection shall apply in lieu of any requirement that the State submit a demonstration that the applicable implementation plan provides for attainment of the ozone standard by the applicable attainment date in any Marginal Area. section 172(c)(9) (relating to contingency measures) shall not apply to Marginal Areas.

(b) Moderate Areas.—Each State in which all or part of a Moderate Area is located shall, with respect to the Moderate Area, make the submissions described under subsection (a) (relating to Marginal Areas), and shall also submit the revisions to the applicable implementation plan described under this subsection.

(1) Plan Provisions for Reasonable Further Progress.—

(A) General Rule.—

(i) By no later than 3 years after the date of the enactment of the Clean Air Act Amendments of 1990, the State shall submit a revision to the applicable implementation plan to provide for volatile organic compound emission reductions, within 6 years after the date of the enactment of the Clean Air Act Amendments of 1990, of at least 15 percent from baseline emissions, accounting for any growth in emissions after the year in which the Clean Air Act Amendments of 1990 are enacted. Such plan shall provide for such specific annual reductions in emissions of volatile organic compounds and oxides of nitrogen as necessary to attain the national primary ambient air quality standard for ozone by the attainment date applicable under this Act. This subparagraph shall not apply in the case of oxides of nitrogen for those areas for which the Administrator determines (when the Administrator approves the plan or plan revision) that additional reductions of oxides of nitrogen would not contribute to attainment.

(ii) A percentage less than 15 percent may be used for purposes of clause (i) in the case of any State which demonstrates to the satisfaction of the Administrator that—

(I) new source review provisions are applicable in the nonattainment areas in the same manner and to the same extent as required under subsection (e) in the case of Extreme Areas (with the exception that, in applying such provisions, the terms 'major source' and 'major stationary source' shall include (in addition to the sources described in section 302) any stationary source or group of sources located within a contiguous area and under common control that emits, or has the potential to emit, at least 5 tons per year of volatile organic compounds);

(II) reasonably available control technology is required for all existing major sources (as defined in subclause (I)); and

(III) the plan reflecting a lesser percentage than 15 percent includes all measures that can feasibly be implemented in the area, in light of technological achievability. To qualify for a lesser percentage under this clause, a State must demonstrate to the satisfaction of the Administrator that the plan for the area includes the measures that are achieved in practice by sources in the same source category in nonattainment areas of the next higher category.

(B) Baseline Emissions.—For purposes of subparagraph (A), the term 'baseline emissions' means the total amount of actual VOC or NO_xemissions from all anthropogenic sources in the area during the calendar year of the enactment of the Clean Air Act Amendments of 1990, excluding emissions that would be eliminated under the regulations described in clauses (i) and (ii) of subparagraph (D).

(C) General Rule for Creditability of Reductions.—Except as provided under subparagraph (D), emissions reductions are creditable toward the 15 percent required under subparagraph (A) to the extent they have actually occurred, as of 6 years after the date of the enactment of the Clean Air Act Amendments of 1990, from the implementation of measures required under the applicable implementation plan, rules promulgated by the Administrator, or a permit under title V.

(D) Limits on Creditability of Reductions.—Emission reductions from the following measures are not creditable toward the 15 percent reductions required under subparagraph (A):

(i) Any measure relating to motor vehicle exhaust or evaporative emissions promulgated by the Administrator by January 1, 1990.

(ii) Regulations concerning Reid Vapor Pressure promulgated by the Administrator by the date of the enactment of the Clean Air Act Amendments of 1990 or required to be promulgated under section 211(h) .

(iii) Measures required under subsection (a)(2)(A) (concerning corrections to implementation plans prescribed under guidance by the Administrator).

(iv) Measures required under subsection (a)(2)(B) to be submitted immediately after the date of the enactment of the Clean Air Act Amendments of 1990 (concerning corrections to motor vehicle inspection and maintenance programs).

(2) Reasonably Available Control Technology.—The State shall submit a revision to the applicable implementation plan to include provisions to require the implementation of reasonably available control technology under section 172(c)(1) with respect to each of the following:

(A) Each category of VOC sources in the area covered by a CTG document issued by the Administrator between the date of the enactment of the Clean Air Act Amendments of 1990 and the date of attainment.

(B) All VOC sources in the area covered by any CTG issued before the date of the enactment of the Clean Air Act Amendments of 1990.

(C) All other major stationary sources of VOCs that are located in the area. Each revision described in subparagraph (A) shall be submitted within the period set forth by the Administrator in issuing the relevant CTG document. The revisions with respect to sources described in subparagraphs (B) and (C) shall be submitted by 2 years after the date of the enactment of the Clean Air Act Amendments of 1990, and shall provide for the implementation of the required measures as expeditiously as practicable but no later than May 31, 1995.

(3) Gasoline Vapor Recovery.—

(A) General Rule.—Not later than 2 years after the date of the enactment of the Clean Air Act Amendments of 1990, the State shall submit a revision to the applicable implementation plan to require all owners or operators of gasoline dispensing systems to install and operate, by the date prescribed under subparagraph (B), a system for gasoline vapor recovery of emissions from the fueling of motor vehicles. The Administrator shall issue guidance as appropriate as to the effectiveness of such system. This subparagraph shall apply only to facilities which sell more than 10,000 gallons of gasoline per month (50,000 gallons per month in the case of an independent small business marketer of gasoline as defined in section 325).

(B) Effective Date.—The date required under subparagraph (A) shall be—

(i) 6 months after the adoption date, in the case of gasoline dispensing facilities for which construction commenced after the date of the enactment of the Clean Air Act Amendments of 1990;

(ii) one year after the adoption date, in the case of gasoline dispensing facilities which dispense at least 100,000 gallons of gasoline per month, based on average monthly sales for the 2–year period before the adoption date; or

(iii) 2 years after the adoption date, in the case of all other gasoline dispensing facilities. Any gasoline dispensing facility described under both clause (i) and clause (ii) shall meet the requirements of clause (i).

(C) Reference to Terms.—For purposes of this paragraph, any reference to the term 'adoption date' shall be considered a reference to the date of adoption by the State of requirements for the installation and operation of a system for gasoline vapor recovery of emissions from the fueling of motor vehicles.

(4) Motor Vehicle Inspection and Maintenance.—For all Moderate Areas, the State shall submit, immediately after the date of the enactment of the Clean Air Act Amendments of 1990, a revision to the applicable implementation plan that includes provisions necessary to provide for a vehicle inspection and maintenance program as described in subsection (a)(2)(B) (without regard to whether or not the area was required by section 172(b)(11)(B) (as in effect immediately before the date of the enactment of the Clean Air Act Amendments of 1990) to have included a specific schedule for implementation of such a program).

(5) General Offset Requirement.—For purposes of satisfying the emission offset requirements of this part, the ratio of total emission reductions of volatile organic compounds to total increase emissions of such air pollutant shall be at least 1.15 to 1.

(c) Serious Areas.—Except as otherwise specified in paragraph (4), each State in which all or part of a Serious Area is located shall, with respect to the Serious Area (or portion thereof, to the extent specified in this subsection), make the submissions described under subsection (b) (relating to Moderate Areas), and shall also submit the revisions to the applicable implementation plan (including the plan items) described under this subsection. For any Serious Area, the terms 'major source' and 'major stationary source' include (in addition to the sources described in section 302) any stationary source or group or sources located within a contiguous area and under common control that emits, or has the potential to emit, at least 50 tons per year of volatile organic compounds.

(1) Enhanced Monitoring.—In order to obtain more comprehensive and representative data on ozone air pollution, not later than 18 months after the date of the enactment of the Clean Air Act Amendments of 1990 the Administrator shall promulgate rules, after notice and public comment, for enhanced monitoring of ozone, oxides of nitrogen, and volatile organic compounds. The rules shall, among other things, cover the location and maintenance of monitors. Immediately following the promulgation of rules by the Administrator relating to enhanced monitoring, the State shall commence such actions as may be necessary to adopt and implement a program based on such rules, to improve monitoring for ambient concentrations of ozone, oxides of nitrogen and volatile organic compounds and to improve monitoring of emissions of oxides of nitrogen and volatile organic compounds. Each State implementation plan for the area shall contain measures to improve the ambient monitoring of such air pollutants.

(2) Attainment and Reasonable Further Progress Demonstrations.—Within 4 years after the date of the enactment of the Clean Air Act Amendments of 1990, the State shall submit a revision to the applicable implementation plan that includes each of the following:

(A) Attainment Demonstration.—A demonstration that the plan, as revised, will provide for attainment of the ozone national ambient air quality standard by the applicable attainment date. This attainment demonstration must be based on photochemical grid modeling or any other analytical method determined by the Administrator, in the Administrator's discretion, to be at least as effective.

(B) Reasonable Further Progress Demonstration.—A demonstration that the plan, as revised, will result in VOC emissions reductions from the baseline emissions described in subsection (b)(1)(B) equal to the following amount averaged over each consecutive 3–year period beginning 6 years after the date of the enactment of the Clean Air Act Amendments of 1990, until the attainment date:

(i) at least 3 percent of baseline emissions each year; or

(ii) an amount less than 3 percent of such baseline emissions each year, if the State demonstrates to the satisfaction of the Administrator that the plan reflecting such lesser amount includes all measures that can feasibly be implemented in the area, in light of technological achievability. To lessen the 3 percent requirement under clause (ii), a State must demonstrate to the satisfaction of the Administrator that the plan for the area includes the measures that are achieved in practice by sources in the same source category in nonattainment areas of the next higher classification. Any determination to lessen the 3 percent requirement shall be reviewed at each milestone under section 182(g) and revised to reflect such new measures (if any) achieved in practice by sources in the same category in any State, allowing a reasonable time to implement such measures. The emission reductions described in this subparagraph shall be calculated in accordance with subsection (b)(1)(C) and (D) (concerning creditability of reductions). The reductions creditable for the period beginning 6 years after the date of the enactment of the Clean Air Act Amendments of 1990, shall include reductions that occurred before such period, computed in accordance with subsection (b)(1), that exceed the 15–percent amount of reductions required under subsection (b)(1)(A).

(C) NO_x Control. The revision may contain, in lieu of the demonstration required under subparagraph (B), a demonstration to the satisfaction of the Administrator that the applicable implementation plan, as revised, provides for reductions of emissions of VOC's and oxides of nitrogen (calculated according to the creditability provisions of subsection (b)(1)(C) and (D)), that would result in a reduction in ozone concentrations at least equivalent to that which would result from the amount of VOC emission reductions required under subparagraph (B). Within 1 year after the date of the enactment of the Clean Air Act Amendments of 1990, the Administrator shall issue guidance concerning the conditions under which NOx control may be substituted for VOC control or may be combined with VOC control in order to maximize the reduction in ozone air pollution. In accord with such guidance, a lesser percentage of VOCs may be accepted as an adequate demonstration for purposes of this subsection.

(3) Enhanced Vehicle Inspection and Maintenance Program.—

(A) Requirement For Submission.—Within 2 years after the date of the enactment of the Clean Air Act Amendments of 1990, the State shall submit a revision to the applicable implementation plan to provide for an enhanced program to reduce hydrocarbon emissions and NOx emissions from in-use motor vehicles registered in each urbanized area (in the nonattainment area), as defined by the Bureau of the Census, with a 1980 population of 200,000 or more.

(B) Effective Date of State Programs; Guidance.—The State program required under subparagraph (A) shall take effect no later than 2 years from the date of the enactment of the Clean Air Act Amendments of 1990, and shall comply in all respects with guidance published in the Federal Register (and from time to time revised) by the Administrator for enhanced vehicle inspection and maintenance programs. Such guidance shall include—

(i) a performance standard achievable by a program combining emission testing, including on-road emission testing, with inspection to detect tampering with emission control devices and misfueling for all light-duty vehicles and all light-duty trucks subject to standards under section 202 ; and

(ii) program administration features necessary to reasonably assure that adequate management resources, tools, and practices are in place to attain and maintain the performance standard. Compliance with the performance standard under clause (i) shall be determined using a method to be established by the Administrator.

(C) State Program.—The State program required under subparagraph (A) shall include, at a minimum, each of the following elements—

(i) Computerized emission analyzers, including on-road testing devices.

(ii) No waivers for vehicles and parts covered by the emission control performance warranty as provided for in section 207(b) unless a warranty remedy has been denied in writing, or for tampering- related repairs.

(iii) In view of the air quality purpose of the program, if, for any vehicle, waivers are permitted for emissions-related repairs not covered by warranty, an expenditure to qualify for the waiver of an amount of $450 or more for such repairs (adjusted annually as determined by the Administrator on the basis of the Consumer Price Index in the same manner as provided in title V).

(iv) Enforcement through denial of vehicle registration (except for any program in operation before the date of the enactment of the Clean Air Act Amendments of 1990 whose enforcement mechanism is demonstrated to the Administrator to be more effective than the applicable vehicle registration program in assuring that noncomplying vehicles are not operated on public roads).

(v) Annual emission testing and necessary adjustment, repair, and maintenance, unless the State demonstrates to the satisfaction of the Administrator that a biennial inspection, combination with other features of the program which exceed the requirements of this Act, will result in emission reductions which equal or exceed the reductions which can be obtained through such annual inspections.

(vi) Operation of the program on a centralized basis, unless the State demonstrates to the satisfaction of the Administrator that a decentralized program will be equally effective. An electronically connected testing system, a licensing system, or other measures (or any combination thereof) may be considered, in accordance with criteria established by the Administrator, as equally effective for such purposes.

(vii) Inspection of emission control diagnostic systems and the maintenance or repair of malfunctions or system deterioration identified by or affecting such diagnostics systems. Each State shall biennially prepare a report to the Administrator which assesses the emission reductions achieved by the program required under this paragraph based on data collected during inspection and repair of vehicles. The methods used to assess the emission reductions shall be those established by the Administrator.

(4) Clean-Fuel Vehicle Programs.—

(A) Except to the extent that substitute provisions have been approved by the Administrator under subparagraph (B), the State shall submit to the Administrator, within 42 months of the date of the enactment of the Clean Air Act Amendments of 1990, a revision to the applicable implementation plan for each area described under part C of title II to include such measures as may be necessary to ensure the effectiveness of the applicable provisions of the clean-fuel vehicle program prescribed under part C of title II, including all measures necessary to make the use of clean alternative fuels in clean-fuel vehicles (as defined in part C of title II) economic from the standpoint of vehicle owners. Such a revision shall also be submitted for each area that opts into the clean fuel-vehicle program as provided in part C of title II.

(B) The Administrator shall approve, as a substitute for all or a portion of the clean-fuel vehicle program prescribed under part C of title II, any revision to the relevant applicable implementation plan that in the Administrator's judgment will achieve long-term reductions in ozone- producing and toxic air emissions equal to those achieved under part C of title II, or the percentage thereof attributable to the portion of the clean-fuel vehicle program for which the revision is to substitute. The Administrator may approve such revision only if it consists exclusively of provisions other than those required under this Act for the area. Any State seeking approval of such revision must submit the revision to the Administrator within 24 months of the date of the enactment of the Clean Air Act Amendments of 1990. The Administrator shall approve or disapprove any such revision within 30 months of the date of the enactment of the Clean Air Act Amendments of 1990. The Administrator shall publish the revision submitted by a State in the Federal Register upon receipt. Such notice shall constitute a notice of proposed rulemaking on whether or not to approve such revision and shall be deemed to comply with the requirements concerning notices of proposed rulemaking contained in sections 553 through 557 of title 5 of the United States Code (related to notice and comment). Where the Administrator approves such revision for any area, the State need not submit the revision required by subparagraph (A) for the area with respect to the portions of the Federal clean-fuel vehicle program for which the Administrator has approved the revision as a substitute.

(C) If the Administrator determines, under section 179 , that the State has failed to submit any portion of the program required under subparagraph (A), then, in addition to any sanctions available under section 179 , the State may not receive credit, in any demonstration of attainment or reasonable further progress for the area, for any emission reductions from implementation of the corresponding aspects of the Federal clean-fuel vehicle requirements established in part C of title II.

(5) Transportation Control.—

(A) Beginning 6 years after the date of the enactment of the Clean Air Act Amendments of 1990 and each third year thereafter, the State shall submit a demonstration as to whether current aggregate vehicle mileage, aggregate vehicle emissions, congestion levels, and other relevant parameters are consistent with those used for the area's demonstration of attainment. Where such parameters and emissions levels exceed the levels projected for purposes of the area's attainment demonstration, the State shall within 18 months develop and submit a revision of the applicable implementation plan that includes a transportation control measures program consisting of measures from, but not limited to, section 108(f) that will reduce emissions to levels that are consistent with emission levels projected in such demonstration. In considering such measures, the State should ensure adequate access to downtown, other commercial, and residential areas and should avoid measures that increase or relocate emissions and congestion rather than reduce them. Such revision shall be developed in accordance with guidance issued by the Administrator pursuant to section 108(e) and with the requirements of section 174(b) and shall include implementation and funding schedules that achieve expeditious emissions reductions in accordance with implementation plan projections.

(6) De Minimis Rule.—The new source review provisions under this part shall ensure that increased emissions of volatile organic compounds resulting from any physical change in, or change in the method of operation of, a stationary source located in the area shall not be considered de minimis for purposes of determining the applicability of the permit requirements established by this Act unless the increase in net emissions of such air pollutant from such source does not exceed 25 tons when aggregated with all other net increases in emissions from the source over any period of 5 consecutive calendar years which includes the calendar year in which such increase occurred.

(7) Special Rule for Modifications of Sources Emitting Less Than 100 Tons.—In the case of any major stationary source of volatile organic compounds located in the area (other than a source which emits or has the potential to emit 100 tons or more of volatile organic compounds per year), whenever any change (as described in section 111(a)(4)) at that source results in any increase (other than a de minimis increase) in emissions of volatile organic compounds from any discrete operation, unit, or other pollutant emitting activity at the source, such increase shall be considered a modification for purposes of section 172(c)(5) and section 173(a) , except that such increase shall not be considered a modification for such purposes if the owner or operator of the source elects to offset the increase by a greater reduction in emissions of volatile organic compounds concerned from other operations, units, or activities within the source at an internal offset ratio of at least 1.3 to 1. If the owner or operator does not make such election, such change shall be considered a modification for such purposes, but in applying section 173(a)(2) in the case of any such modification, the best available control technology (BACT), as defined in section 169 , shall be substituted for the lowest achievable emission rate (LAER). The Administrator shall establish and publish policies and procedures for implementing the provisions of this paragraph.

(8) Special Rule for Modification of Sources Emitting 100 Tons or More.—In the case of any major stationary source of volatile organic compounds located in the area which emits or has the potential to emit 100 tons or more of volatile organic compounds per year, whenever any change (as described in section 111(a)(4)) at that source results in any increase (other than a de minimis increase) in emissions of volatile organic compounds from any discrete operation, unit, or other pollutant emitting activity at the source, such increase shall be considered a modification for purposes of section 172(c)(5) and section 173(a) , except that if the owner or operator of the source elects to offset the increase by a greater reduction in emissions of volatile organic compounds from other operations, units, or activities within the source at an internal offset ratio of at least 1.3 to 1, the requirements of section 173(a)(2) (concerning the lowest achievable emission rate (LAER)) shall not apply.

(9) Contingency Provisions.—In addition to the contingency provisions required under section 172(c)(9) , the plan revision shall provide for the implementation of specific measures to be undertaken if the area fails to meet any applicable milestone. Such measures shall be included in the plan revision as contingency measures to take effect without further action by the State or the Administrator upon a failure by the State to meet the applicable milestone.

(10) General Offset Requirement.—For purposes of satisfying the emission offset require-

ments of this part, the ratio of total emission reductions of volatile organic compounds to total increase emissions of such air pollutant shall be at least 1.2 to 1. Any reference to 'attainment date' in subsection (b), which is incorporated by reference into this subsection, shall refer to the attainment date for serious areas.

(d) Severe Areas.—Each State in which all or part of a Severe Area is located shall, with respect to the Severe Area, make the submissions described under subsection (c) (relating to Serious Areas), and shall also submit the revisions to the applicable implementation plan (including the plan items) described under this subsection. For any Severe Area, the terms 'major source' and 'major stationary source' include (in addition to the sources described in section 302) any stationary source or group of sources located within a contiguous area and under common control that emits, or has the potential to emit, at least 25 tons per year of volatile organic compounds.

(1) Vehicle Miles Traveled.—

(A) Within 2 years after the date of enactment of the Clean Air Act Amendments of 1990, the State shall submit a revision that identifies and adopts specific enforceable transportation control strategies and transportation control measures to offset any growth in emissions from growth in vehicle miles traveled or numbers of vehicle trips in such area and to attain reduction in motor vehicle emissions as necessary, in combination with other emission reduction requirements of this subpart, to comply with the requirements of subsection (b)(2)(B) and (c)(2)(B) (pertaining to periodic emissions reduction requirements). The State shall consider measures specified in section 108(f) , and choose from among and implement such measures as necessary to demonstrate attainment with the national ambient air quality standards; in considering such measures, the State should ensure adequate access to downtown, other commercial, and residential areas and should avoid measures that increase or relocate emissions and congestion rather than reduce them.

(B) Within 2 years after the date of enactment of the Clean Air Act Amendments of 1990, the State shall submit a revision requiring employers in such area to implement programs to reduce work- related vehicle trips and miles traveled by employees. Such revision shall be developed in accordance with guidance issued by the Administrator pursuant to section 108(f) and shall, at a minimum, require that each employer of 100 or more persons in such area increase average passenger occupancy per vehicle in commuting trips between home and the workplace during peak travel periods by not less than 25 percent above the average vehicle occupancy for all such trips in the area at the time the revision is submitted. The guidance of the Administrator may specify average vehicle occupancy rates which vary for locations within a nonattainment area (suburban, center city, business district) or among nonattainment areas reflecting existing occupancy rates and the availability of high occupancy modes. The revision shall provide that each employer subject to a vehicle occupancy requirement shall submit a compliance plan within 2 years after the date the revision is submitted which shall convincingly demonstrate compliance with the requirements of this paragraph not later than 4 years after such date.

(2) Offset Requirement.—For purposes of satisfying the offset requirements pursuant to this part, the ratio of total emission reductions of VOCs to total increased emissions of such air pollutant shall be at least 1.3 to 1, except that if the State plan requires all existing major sources in the nonattainment area to use best available control technology (as defined in section 169(3)) for the control of volatile organic compounds, the ratio shall be at least 1.2 to 1.

(3) Enforcement under section 185.—By December 31, 2000, the State shall submit a plan revision which includes the provisions required under section 185 . Any reference to the term 'attainment date' in subsection (b) or (c), which is incorporated by reference into this subsection (d), shall refer to the attainment date for Severe Areas.

(e) Extreme Areas.—Each State in which all or part of an Extreme Area is located shall, with respect to the Extreme Area, make the submissions described under subsection (d) (relating to Severe Areas), and shall also submit the revisions to the applicable implementation plan (including the plan items) described under this subsection. The provisions of clause (ii) of subsection (c)(2)(B) (relating to reductions of less than 3 percent), the provisions of paragraphs (6), (7) and (8) of subsection (c) relating to de minimus rule and modification of sources), and the provisions of clause (ii) of subsection (b)(1)(A) (relating to reductions of less than 15 percent) shall not apply in the case of an Extreme Area. For any Extreme Area, the terms 'major source' and 'major stationary source' includes (in addition to the sources described in section 302) any stationary source or group of sources located within a contiguous area and under common control that emits, or has the potential to emit, at least 10 tons per year of volatile organic compounds.

(1) Offset Requirement.—For purposes of satisfying the offset requirements pursuant to this part, the ratio of total emission reductions of VOCs to total increased emissions of such air pollutant shall be at least 1.5 to 1, except that if the State plan requires all existing major sources in the nonattainment area to use best available control technology (as defined in section 169(3)) for the control of volatile organic compounds, the ratio shall be at least 1.2 to 1.

(2) Modifications—Any change (as described in section 111(a)(4)) at a major stationary source which results in any increase in emissions from any discrete operation, unit, or other pollutant emitting activity at the source shall be considered a modification for purposes of section 172(c)(5) and section 173(a) , except that for purposes of complying with the offset requirement pursuant to section 173(a)(1) , any such increase shall not be considered a modification if the owner or operator of the source elects to offset the increase by a greater reduction in emissions of the air pollutant concerned from other discrete operations, units, or activities within the source at an internal offset ratio of at least 1.3 to 1. The offset requirements of this part shall not be applicable in Extreme Areas to a modification of an existing source if such modification consists of installation of equipment required to comply with the applicable implementation plan, permit, or this Act.

(3) Use of Clean Fuels or Advanced Control Technology.—For Extreme Areas, a plan revision shall be submitted within 3 years after the date of the enactment of the Clean Air Act Amendments of 1990 to require, effective 8 years after such date, that each new, modified, and existing electric utility and industrial and commercial boiler which emits more than 25 tons per year of oxides of nitrogen—

(A) burn as its primary fuel natural gas, methanol, or ethanol (or a comparably low polluting fuel), or

(B) use advanced control technology (such as catalytic control technology or other comparably effective control methods) for reduction of emissions of oxides of nitrogen. For purposes of this subsection, the term 'primary fuel' means the fuel which is used 90 percent or more of the operating time. This paragraph shall not apply during any natural gas supply emergency (as defined in title III of the Natural Gas Policy Act 1978).

(4) Traffic Control Measures During Heavy Traffic Hours.—For Extreme Areas, each implementation plan revision under this subsection may contain provisions establishing traffic control measures applicable during heavy traffic hours to reduce the use of high polluting vehicles or heavy-duty vehicles, notwithstanding any other provision of law.

(5) New Technologies.—The Administrator may, in accordance with section 110 , approve provisions of an implementation plan for an Extreme Area which anticipate development of new control techniques or improvement of existing control technologies, and an attainment demonstration based on such provisions, if the State demonstrates to the satisfaction of the Administrator that—

(A) such provisions are not necessary to achieve the incremental emission reductions required during the first 10 years after the date of the enactment of the Clean Air Act Amendments of 1990; and

(B) the State has submitted enforceable commitments to develop and adopt contingency measures to be implemented as set forth herein if the anticipated technologies do not achieve planned reductions. Such contingency measures shall be submitted to the Administrator no later than 3 years before proposed implementation of the plan provisions and approved or disapproved by the Administrator in accordance with section 110. The contingency measures shall be adequate to produce emission reductions sufficient, in conjunction with other approved plan provisions, to achieve the periodic emission reductions required by subsection (b)(1) or (c)(2) and attainment by the applicable dates. If the Administrator determines that an Extreme Area has failed to achieve an emission reduction requirement set forth in subsection (b)(1) or (c)(2), and that such failure is due in whole or part to an inability to fully implement provisions approved pursuant to this subsection, the Administrator shall require the State to implement the contingency measures to the extent necessary to assure compliance with subsections (b)(1) and (c)(2). Any reference to the term 'attainment date' in subsection (b), (c), or (d) which is incorporated by reference into this subsection, shall refer to the attainment date for Extreme Areas.

(f) NO_x Requirements.—

(1) The plan provisions required under this subpart for major stationary sources of volatile organic compounds shall also apply to major stationary sources (as defined in section 302 and subsections (c), (d), and (e) of this section) of oxides of nitrogen. This subsection shall not apply in the case of oxides of nitrogen for those sources for which the Administrator determines (when the Administrator approves a plan or plan revision) that net air quality benefits are greater in the absence of reductions of oxides of nitrogen from the sources concerned. This subsection shall also not apply in the case of oxides of nitrogen for—

(A) nonattainment areas not within an ozone transport region under section 184 if the Administrator determines (when the Administrator approves a plan or plan revision) that additional reductions of oxides of nitrogen would not contribute to attainment of the national ambient air quality standard for ozone in the area, or

(B) nonattainment areas within such an ozone transport region if the Administrator determines (when the Administrator approves a plan or plan revision) that additional reductions of oxides of nitrogen would not produce net ozone air quality benefits in such region. The Administrator shall, in the Administrator's determinations, consider the study required under section 185B .

(2) (A) If the Administrator determines that excess reductions in emissions of NO_xwould be achieved under paragraph (1), the Administrator may limit the application of paragraph (1) to the extent necessary to avoid achieving such excess reductions.

(B) For purposes of this paragraph, excess reductions in emissions of $NO_x$are emission reductions for which the Administrator determines that net air quality benefits are greater in the absence of such reductions. Alternatively, for purposes of this paragraph, excess reductions in emissions of $NO_x$are, for—

(i) nonattainment areas not within an ozone transport region under section 184 , emission reductions that the Administrator determines would not contribute to attainment of the national ambient air quality standard for ozone in the area, or

(ii) nonattainment areas within such ozone transport region, emission reductions that the Administrator determines would not produce net ozone air quality benefits is such region.

(3) At any time after the final report under section 185B is submitted to Congress, a person may petition the Administrator for a determination under paragraph (1) or (2) with respect to any nonattainment area or any ozone transport region under section 184 . The Administrator shall grant or deny such petition within 6 months after its filing with the Administrator.

(g) Milestones.—

(1) Reductions In Emissions.—6 years after the date of the enactment of the Clean Air Amendments of 1990 and at intervals of every 3 years thereafter, the State shall determine whether each nonattainment area (other than an area classified as Marginal or Moderate) has achieved a reduction in emissions during the preceding intervals equivalent to the total emission reductions required to be achieved by the end of such interval pursuant to subsection (b)(1) and the corresponding requirements of subsections (c)(2) (B) and (C), (d), and (e). Such reduction shall be referred to in this section as an applicable milestone.

(2) Compliance Demonstration.—For each nonattainment area referred to in paragraph (1), not later 90 days after the date on which an applicable milestone occurs (not including an attainment date on which a milestone occurs in cases where the standard has been attained), each State in which all or part of such area is located shall submit to the Administrator a demonstration that the milestone has been met. A demonstration under this paragraph shall be submitted in such form and manner, and shall contain such information and analysis, as the Administrator shall require, by rule. The Administrator shall determine whether or not a State's demonstration is adequate within 90 days after the Administrator's receipt of a demonstration which contains the information and analysis required by the Administrator.

(3) Serious and Severe Areas; State Election.—If a State fails to submit a demonstration under paragraph (2) for any Serious or Severe Area within the required period or if the Administrator determines that the area has not met any applicable milestone, the State shall elect,

within 90 days after such failure or determination—

(A) to have the area reclassified to the next higher classification,

(B) to implement specific additional measures adequate, as determined by the Administrator, to meet the next milestone as provided in the applicable contingency plan, or

(C) to adopt an economic incentive program as described in paragraph (4). If the State makes an election under subparagraph (B), the Administrator shall, within 90 days after the election, review such plan and shall, if the Administrator finds the contingency plan inadequate, require further measures necessary to meet such milestone. Once the State makes an election, it shall be deemed accepted by the Administrator as meeting the election requirement. If the State fails to make an election required under this paragraph within the required 90-day period or within 6 months thereafter, the area shall be reclassified to the next higher classification by operation of law at the expiration of such 6-month period. Within 12 months after the date required for the State to make an election, the State shall submit a revision of the applicable implementation plan for the area that meets the requirements of this paragraph. The Administrator shall review such plan revision and approve or disapprove the revision within 9 months after the date of its submission.

(4) Economic Incentive Program.—

(A) An economic incentive program under this paragraph shall be consistent with rules published by the Administrator and sufficient, in combination with other elements of the State plan, to achieve the next milestone. The State program may include a nondiscriminatory system, consistent with applicable law regarding interstate commerce, of State established emissions fees or a system of marketable permits, or a system of State fees on sale or manufacture of products the use of which contributes to ozone information, or any combination of the foregoing or other similar measures. The program may also include incentives and requirements to reduce vehicle emissions and vehicle miles traveled in the area, including any of the transportation control measures identified in section 108(f) .

(B) Within 2 years after the date of the enactment of the Clean Air Act Amendments of 1990, the Administrator shall publish rules for the programs to be adopted pursuant to subparagraph (A). Such rules shall include model plan provisions which may be adopted for reducing emissions from permitted stationary sources, area sources, and mobile sources. The guidelines shall require that any revenues generated by the plan provisions adopted pursuant to subparagraph (A) shall be used by the State for any of the following:

(i) Providing incentives for achieving emission reductions.

(ii) Providing assistance for the development of innovative technologies for the control of ozone air pollution and for the development of lower-polluting solvents and surface coatings. Such assistance shall not provide for the payment of more than 75 percent of either the costs of any project to develop such a technology or the costs of development of a lower-polluting solvent or surface coating.

(iii) Funding the administrative costs of State programs under this Act. Not more than 50 percent of such revenues may be used for purposes of this clause.

(5) Extreme Areas.—If a State fails to submit a demonstration under paragraph (2) for any Extreme Area within the required period, or if the Administrator determines that the area has not met any applicable milestone, the State shall, within 9 months after such failure or determination, submit a plan revision to implement an economic incentive program which meets the requirements of paragraph (4). The Administrator shall review such plan revision and approve or disapprove the revision within 9 months after the date of its submission.

(h) Rural Transport Areas.—

(1) Notwithstanding any other provision of section 181 or this section, a State containing an ozone nonattainment area that does not include, and is not adjacent to, any part of a Metropolitan Statistical Area or, where one exists, a Consolidated Metropolitan Statistical Area (as defined by the United States Bureau of the Census), which area is treated by the Admin istrator, in the Administrator's discretion, as a rural transport area within the meaning of paragraph (2), shall be treated by operation of law as satisfying the requirements of this section if it makes the submissions required under subsection (a) of this section (relating to marginal areas).

(2) The Administrator may treat an ozone nonattainment area as a rural transport area if the Administrator finds that sources of VOC (and, where the Administrator determines relevant, NO_x) emissions within the area do not make a significant contribution to the ozone concentrations measured in the area or in other areas.

(i) Reclassified Areas.—Each State containing an ozone non-attainment area reclassified under section 181(b)(2) shall meet such requirements of subsections (b) through (d) of this section as may be applicable to the area as reclassified, according to the schedules prescribed in connection with such requirements, except that the Administrator may adjust any applicable deadlines (other than attainment dates) to the extent such adjustment is necessary or appropriate to assure consistency among the required submissions.

(j) Multi-State Ozone Nonattainment Areas.—

(1) Coordination Among States.—Each State in which there is located a portion of a single ozone nonattainment area which covers more than one State (hereinafter in this section referred to as "multi-State ozone nonattainment area") shall—

(A) take all reasonable steps to coordinate, substantively and procedurally, the revisions and implementation of State implementation plans applicable to the nonattainment area concerned; and

(B) use photochemical grid modeling or any other analytical method determined by the Administrator, in his discretion, to be at least as effective. The Administrator may not approve any revision of a State implementation plan submitted under this part for a State in which part of a multi- State ozone nonattainment area is located if the plan revision for that State fails to comply with the requirements of this subsection.

(2) Failure to Demonstrate Attainment.—If any State in which there is located a portion of a multi-State ozone nonattainment area fails to provide a demonstration of attainment of the national ambient air quality standard for ozone in that portion within the required period, the State may petition the Administrator to make a finding that the State would have been able to make such demonstration but for the failure of one or more other States in which other portions of the area are located to commit to the implementation of all measures required under section 182 (relating to plan submissions and requirements for ozone nonattainment areas). If the Administrator makes such finding, the provisions of section 179 (relating to sanctions) shall not apply, by reason of the failure to make such demonstration, in the portion of the multi-State ozone nonattainment area within the State submitting such petition.

§7511b. Federal Ozone Measures [Sec. 183]

(a) Control Techniques Guidelines for VOC Sources.—Within 3 years after the date of the enactment of the Clean Air Act Amendments of 1990, the Administrator shall issue control techniques guidelines, in accordance with section 108 , for 11 categories of stationary sources of VOC emissions for which such guidelines have not been issued as of such date of enactment, not including the categories referred to in paragraphs (3) and (4) of subsection (b) of this section. The Administrator may issue such additional control techniques guidelines as the Administrator deems necessary.

(b) Existing and New CTGS.—

(1) Within 36 months after the date of the enactment of the Clean Air Act Amendments of 1990, and periodically thereafter, the Administrator shall review and, if necessary, update control technique guidance issued under section 108 before the date of the enactment of the Clean Air Act Amendments of 1990.

(2) In issuing the guidelines the Administrator shall give priority to those categories which the Administrator considers to make the most significant contribution to the formation of ozone air pollution in ozone nonattainment areas, including hazardous waste treatment, storage, and disposal facilities which are permitted under subtitle C of the Solid Waste Disposal Act. Thereafter the Administrator shall periodically review and, if necessary, revise such guidelines.

(3) Within 3 years after the date of the enactment of the Clean Air Act Amendments of 1990, the Administrator shall issue control techniques guidelines in accordance with section 108 to reduce the aggregate emissions of volatile organic compounds into the ambient air from aerospace coatings and solvents. Such control techniques guidelines shall, at a minimum, be adequate to reduce aggregate emissions of volatile organic compounds into the ambient air from the application of such coatings and solvents to such level as the Administrator determines may be achieved through the adoption of best available control measures. Such control technology guidance shall pro-

vide for such reductions in such increments and on such schedules as the Administrator determines to be reasonable, but in no event later than 10 years after the final issuance of such control technology guidance. In developing control technology guidance under this subsection, the Administrator shall consult with the Secretary of Defense, the Secretary of Transportation, and the Administrator of the National Aeronautics and Space Administration with regard to the establishment of specifications for such coatings. In evaluating VOC reduction strategies, the guidance shall take into account the applicable requirements of section 112 and the need to protect stratospheric ozone.

(4) Within 3 years after the date of the enactment of the Clean Air Act Amendments of 1990, the Administrator shall issue control techniques guidelines in accordance with section 108 to reduce the aggregate emissions of volatile organic compounds and PM–10 into the ambient air from paints, coatings, and solvents used in shipbuilding operations and ship repair. Such control techniques guidelines shall, at a minimum, be adequate to reduce aggregate emissions of volatile organic compounds and PM-10 into the ambient air from the removal or application of such paints, coatings, and solvents to such level as the Administrator determines may be achieved through the adoption of the best available control measures. Such control techniques guidelines shall provide for such reductions in such increments and on such schedules as the Administrator determines to be reasonable, but in no event later than 10 years after the final issuance of such control technology guidance. In developing control techniques guidelines under this sub section, the Administrator shall consult with the appropriate Federal agencies.

(c) Alternative Control Techniques.—Within 3 years after the date of the enactment of the Clean Air Act Amendments of 1990, the Administrator shall issue technical documents which identify alternative controls for all categories of stationary sources of volatile organic compounds and oxides of nitrogen which emit, or have the potential to emit 25 tons per year or more of such air pollutant. The Administrator shall revise and update such documents as the Administrator determines necessary.

(d) Guidance for Evaluating Cost-Effectiveness.—Within 1 year after the date of the enactment of the Clean Air Act Amendments of 1990, the Administrator shall provide guidance to the States to be used in evaluating the relative cost-effectiveness of various options for the control of emissions from existing stationary sources of air pollutants which contribute to nonattainment of the national ambient air quality standards for ozone.

(e) Control of Emissions from Certain Sources.—

(1) Definitions.—For purposes of this subsection—

(A) Best Available Controls.—The term 'best available controls' means the degree of emissions reduction that the Administrator determines, on the basis of technological and economic feasibility, health, environmental, and energy impacts, is achievable through the application of the most effective equipment, measures, processes, methods, systems or techniques, including chemical reformulation, product or feedstock substitution, repackaging, and directions for use, consumption, storage, or disposal.

(B) Consumer or Commercial Product.—Then term 'consumer or commercial product' means any substance, product (including paints, coatings, and solvents), or article (including any container or packaging) held by any person, the use, consumption, storage, disposal, destruction, or decomposition of which may result in the release of volatile organic compounds. The term does not include fuels or fuel additives regulated under section 211 , or motor vehicles, non-road vehicles, and non-road engines as defined under section 216 .

(C) Regulated Entities.—The term 'regulated entities' means—

(i) manufacturers, processors, wholesale distributors, or importers of consumer or commercial products for sale or distribution in interstate commerce in the United States; or

(ii) manufacturers, processors, wholesale distributors, or importers that supply the entities listed under clause (i) with such products for sale or distribution in interstate commerce in the United States.

(2) Study and Report.—

(A) Study.—The Administrator shall conduct a study of the emissions of volatile organic compounds into the ambient air from consumer and commercial products (or any combination thereof) in order to—

(i) determine their potential to contribute to ozone levels which violate the national ambient air quality standard for ozone; and

(ii) establish criteria for regulating consumer and commercial products or classes or categories thereof which shall be subject to control under this subsection. The study shall be completed and a report submitted to Congress not later than 3 years after the date of the enactment of the Clean Air Act Amendments of 1990.

(B) Consideration of Certain Factors.—In establishing the criteria under subparagraph (A)(ii), the Administrator shall take into consideration each of the following:

(i) The uses, benefits, and commercial demand of consumer and commercial products.

(ii) The health or safety functions (if any) served by such consumer and commercial products.

(iii) Those consumer and commercial products which emit highly reactive volatile organic compounds into the ambient air.

(iv) Those consumer and commercial products which are subject to the most cost-effective controls.

(v) The availability of alternatives (if any) to such consumer and commercial products which are of comparable costs, considering health, safety, and environmental impacts.

(3) Regulations to Require Emission Reductions.—

(A) In General.—Upon submission of the final report under paragraph (2), the Administrator shall list those categories of consumer or commercial products that the Administrator determines, based on the study, account for at least 80 percent of the VOC emissions, on a reactivity-adjusted basis, from consumer or commercial products in areas that violate the NAAQS for ozone. Credit toward the 80 percent emissions calculation shall be given for emission reductions from consumer or commercial products made after the date of enactment of this section. At such time, the Administrator shall divide the list into 4 groups establishing priorities for regulation based on the criteria established in paragraph (2). Every 2 years after promulgating such list, the Administrator shall regulate one group of categories until all 4 groups are regulated. The regulations shall require best available controls as defined in this section. Such regulations may exempt health use products for which the Administrator determines there is no suitable substitute. In order to carry out this section, the Administrator may, by regulation, control or prohibit any activity, including the manufacture or introduction into commerce, offering for sale, or sale of any consumer or commercial product which results in emission of volatile organic compounds into the ambient air.

(B) Regulated Entities.—Regulations under this subsection may be imposed only with respect to regulated entities.

(C) Use of CTGS.—For any consumer or commercial product the Adminstrator may issue control techniques guidelines under this Act in lieu of regulations required under subparagraph (A) if the Administrator determines that such guidance will be substantially as effective as regulations in reducing emissions of volatile organic compounds which contribute to ozone levels in areas which violate the national ambient air quality standard for ozone.

(4) Systems of Regulation.—The regulations under this subsection may include any system or systems of regulation as the Administrator may deem appropriate, including requirements for registration and labeling, self-monitoring and reporting, prohibitions, limitations, or economic incentives (including marketable permits and auctions of emissions rights) concerning the manufacture, processing, distribution, use, consumption, or disposal of the product.

(5) Special Fund.—Any amounts collected by the Administrator under such regulations shall be deposited in a special fund in the United States Treasury for licensing and other services, which thereafter shall be available until expended, subject to annual appropriation Acts, solely to carry out the activities of the Administrator for which such fees, charges, or collections are established or made.

(6) Enforcement.—Any regulation established under this subsection shall be treated, for purposes of enforcement of this Act, as a standard under section 111 and any violation of such regulation shall be treated as a violation of a requirement of section 111(e) .

(7) State Administration.—Each State may develop and submit to the Administrator a procedure under State law for implementing and enforcing regulations promulgated under this subsection. If the Administrator finds the State procedure is adequate, the Administrator shall approve such procedure. Nothing in this paragraph shall prohibit the Administrator from enforcing any applicable regulations under this subsection.

(8) Size, etc.—No regulations regarding the size, shape, or labeling of a product may be promulgated, unless the Administrator determines such regulations to be useful in meeting any national ambient air quality standard.

(9) State Consultation.—Any State which proposes regulations other than those adopted under this subsection shall consult with the Administrator regarding whether any other State or local subdivision has promulgated or is promulgating regulations on any products covered under this part. The Administrator shall establish a clearinghouse of information, studies, and regulations proposed and promulgated regarding products covered under this subsection and disseminate such information collected as requested by State or local subdivisions.

(f) Tank Vessel Standards.—

(1) Schedule For Standards.—

(A) Within 2 years after the date of the enactment of the Clean Air Act Amendments of 1990, the Administrator, in consultation with the Secretary of the Department in which the Coast Guard is operating, shall promulgate standards applicable to the emission of VOCs and any other air pollutant from loading and unloading of tank vessels (as that term is defined in section 2101 of title 46 of the United States Code) which the Administrator finds causes, or contributes to, air pollution that may be reasonably anticipated to endanger public health or welfare. Such standards shall require the application of reasonably available control technology, considering costs, any nonair- quality benefits, environmental impacts, energy requirements and safety factors associated with alternative control techniques. To the extent practicable such standards shall apply to loading and unloading facilities and not to tank vessels.

(B) Any regulation prescribed under this subsection (and any revision thereof) shall take effect after such period as the Administrator finds (after consultation with the Secretary of the department in which the Coast Guard is operating) necessary to permit the development and application of the requisite technology, giving appropriate consideration to the cost of compliance within such period, except that the effective date shall not be more than 2 years after promulgation of such regulations.

(2) Regulations on Equipment Safety.—Within 6 months after the date of the enactment of the Clean Air Act Amendments of 1990, the Secretary of the Department in which the Coast Guard is operating shall issue regulations to ensure the safety of the equipment and operations which are to control emissions from the loading and unloading of tank vessels, under section 3703 of title 46 of the United States Code and section 6 of the Ports and Waterways Safety Act (33 U.S.C. 1225). The standards promulgated by the Administrator under paragraph (1) and the regulations issued by a State or political subdivision regarding emissions from the loading and unloading of tank vessels shall be consistent with the regulations regarding safety of the Department in which the Coast Guard is operating.

(3) Agency Authority.—

(A) The Administrator shall ensure compliance with the tank vessel emission standards prescribed under paragraph (1)(A). The Secretary of the Department in which the Coast Guard is operating shall also ensure compliance with the tank vessel standards prescribed under paragraph (1)(A).

(B) The Secretary of the Department in which the Coast Guard is operating shall ensure compliance with the regulations issued under paragraph (2).

(4) State or Local Standards.—After the Administrator promulgates standards under this section, no State or political subdivision thereof may adopt or attempt to enforce any standard respecting emissions from tank vessels subject to regulation under paragraph (1) unless such standard is no less stringent than the standards promulgated under paragraph (1).

(5) Enforcement.—Any standard established under paragraph (1)(A) shall be treated, for purposes of enforcement of this Act, as a standard under section 111 and any violation of such standard shall be treated as a violation of a requirement of section 111(e) .

(g) Ozone Design Value Study.—The Administrator shall conduct a study of whether the methodology in use by the Environmental Protection Agency as of the date of the enactment of the Clean Air Act Amendments of 1990 for establishing a design value for ozone provides a reasonable indicator of the ozone air quality of ozone nonattainment areas. The Administrator shall obtain input from States, local subdivisions thereof, and others. The study shall be completed and a report submitted to Congress not later than 3 years after the date of the enactment of the Clean Air Act Amendments of 1990. The results of the study shall be subject to peer and public review before submitting it to Congress.

§7511c. Control of Interstate Ozone Air Pollution [Sec. 184]

(a) Ozone Transport Regions.—A single transport region for ozone (within the meaning of section 176A(a)), comprised of the States of Connecticut, Delaware, Maine, Maryland, Massachusetts, New Hampshire, New Jersey, New York, Pennsylvania, Rhode Island, Vermont, and the Consolidated Metropolitan Statistical Area that includes the District of Columbia, is hereby established by operation of law. The provisions of section 176A(a)(1) and (2) shall apply with respect to the transport region established under this section and any other transport region established for ozone, except to the extent inconsistent with the provisions of this section. The Administrator shall convene the commission required (under section 176A(b)) as a result of the establishment of such region within 6 months of the date of the enactment of the Clean Air Act Amendments of 1990.

(b) Plan Provisions for States in Ozone Transport Regions.—

(1) In accordance with section 110 , not later than 2 years after the date of the enactment of the Clean Air Act Amendments of 1990 (or 9 months after the subsequent inclusion of a State in a transport region established for ozone), each State included within a transport region established for ozone shall submit a State implementation plan or revision thereof to the Administrator which requires the following—

(A) that each area in such State that is in an ozone transport region, and that is a metropolitan statistical area or part thereof with a population of 100,000 or more comply with the provisions of section 182(c)(2)(A) (pertaining to enhanced vehicle inspection and maintenance programs); and

(B) implementation of reasonably available control technology with respect to all sources of volatile organic compounds in the State covered by a control techniques guideline issued before or after the date of the enactment of the Clean Air Act Amendments of 1990.

(2) Within 3 years after the date of the enactment of the Clean Air Act Amendments of 1990, the Administrator shall complete a study identifying control measures capable of achieving emission reductions comparable to those achievable through vehicle refueling controls contained in section 182(b)(3) , and such measures or such vehicle refueling controls shall be implemented in accordance with the provisions of this section. Notwithstanding other deadlines in this section, the applicable implementation plan shall be revised to reflect such measures within 1 year of completion of the study. For purposes of this section any stationary source that emits or has the potential to emit at least 50 tons per year of volatile organic compounds shall be considered a major stationary source and subject to the requirements which would be applicable to major stationary sources if the area classified as a Moderate nonattainment area.

(c) Additional Control Measures.—

(1) Recommendations.—Upon petition of any State within a transport region established for ozone, and based on a majority vote of the Governors on the Commission (or their designees), the Commission may, after notice and opportunity for public comment, develop recommendations for additional control measures to be applied within all or a part of such transport region if the commission determines such measures are necessary to bring any area in such region into attainment by the dates provided by this subpart. The commission shall transmit such recommendations to the Administrator.

(2) Notice and Review.—Whenever the Administrator receives recommendations prepared by a commission pursuant to paragraph (1) (the date of receipt of which shall hereinafter in this section be referred to as the "receipt date"), the Administrator shall—

(A) immediately publish in the Federal Register a notice stating that the recommendations are available and provide an opportunity for public hearing within 90 days beginning on the receipt date; and

(B) commence a review of the recommendations to determine whether the control measures in the recommendations are necessary to bring any area in such region into attainment by the dates provided by this subpart and are otherwise consistent with this Act.

(3) Consultation.—In undertaking the review required under paragraph (2)(B), the Administrator shall consult with members of the commission of the affected States and shall take into account the data, views, and comments received pursuant to paragraph (2)(A).

(4) Approval and Disapproval.—Within 9 months after the receipt date, the Administra-

tor shall (A) determine whether to approve, disapprove, or partially disapprove and partially approve the recommendations; (B) notify the commission in writing of such approval, disapproval, or partial disapproval; and (C) publish such determination in the Federal Register. If the Administrator disapproves or partially disapproves the recommendations, the Administrator shall specify—

(i) why any disapproved additional control measures are not necessary to bring any area in such region into attainment by the dates provided by this subpart or are otherwise not consistent with the Act; and

(ii) recommendations concerning equal or more effective actions that could be taken by the commission to conform the disapproved portion of the recommendations to the requirements of this section.

(5) Finding.—Upon approval or partial approval of recommendations submitted by a commission, the Administrator shall issue to each State which is included in the transport region and to which a requirement of the approved plan applies, a finding under section 110(k)(5) that the implementation plan for such State is inadequate to meet the requirements of section 110(a)(2)(D) . Such finding shall require each such State to revise its implementation plan to include the approved additional control measures within one year after the finding is issued.

(d) Best Available Air Quality Monitoring and Modeling.—For purposes of this section, not later than 6 months after the date of the enactment of the Clean Air Act Amendments of 1990, the Administrator shall promulgate criteria for purposes of determining the contribution of sources in one area to concentrations of ozone in another area which is a nonattainment area for ozone. Such criteria shall require that the best available air quality monitoring and modeling techniques be used for purposes of making such determinations.

§7511d. Enforcement for Severe and Extreme Ozone Nonattainment Areas for Failure to Attain [Sec. 185]

(a) General Rule.—Each implementation plan revision required under section 182(d) and (e) (relating to the attainment plan for Severe and Extreme ozone nonattainment areas) shall provide that, if the area to which such plan revision applies has failed to attain the national primary ambient air quality standard for ozone by the applicable attainment date, each major stationary source of VOCs located in the area shall, except as otherwise provided under subsection (c), pay a fee to the State as a penalty for such failure, computed in accordance with subsection (b), for each calendar year beginning after the attainment date, until the area is redesignated as an attainment area for ozone. Each such plan revision should include procedures for assessment and collection of such fees.

(b) Computation of Fee.—

(1) Fee Amount.—The fee shall equal $5,000, adjusted in accordance with paragraph (3), per ton of VOC emitted by the source during the calendar year in excess of 80 percent of the baseline amount, computed under paragraph (2).

(2) Baseline Amount.—For purposes of this section, the baseline amount shall be computed, in accordance with such guidance as the Administrator may provide, as the lower of the amount of actual VOC emissions ('actuals') or VOC emissions allowed under the permit applicable to the source (or, if no such permit has been issued for the attainment year, the amount of VOC emissions allowed under the applicable implementation plan ('allowables')) during the attainment year. Notwithstanding the preceding sentence, the Administrator may issue guidance authorizing the baseline amount to be determined in accordance with the lower of average actuals or average allowables, determined over a period of more than one calendar year. Such guidance may provide that such average calculation for a specific source may be used if that source's emissions are irregular, cyclical, or otherwise vary significantly from year to year.

(3) Annual Adjustment.—The fee amount under paragraph (1) shall be adjusted annually, beginning in the year beginning after the year of enactment, in accordance with section 502(b)(3)(B)(v) (relating to inflation adjustment).

(c) Exception.—Notwithstanding any provision of this section, no source shall be required to pay any fee under subsection (a) with respect to emissions during any year that is treated as an Extension Year under section 181(a)(5) .

(d) Fee Collection by the Administrator.—If the Administrator has found that the fee provisions of the implementation plan do not meet the requirements of this section, or if the Administrator makes a finding that the State is not administering and enforcing the fee required under this section, the Administrator shall, in addition to any other action authorized under this title, collect, in accordance with procedures promulgated by the Administrator, the unpaid fees required under subsection (a). If the Administrator makes such a finding under section 179(a)(4) , the Administrator may collect fees for periods before the determination, plus interest computed in accordance with section 6621(a)(2) of the Internal Revenue Code of 1986 (relating to computation of interest on underpayment of Federal taxes), to the extent the Administrator finds such fees have not been paid to the State. The provisions of clauses (ii) through (iii) of section 502(b)(3)(C) (relating to penalties and use of the funds, respectively) shall apply with respect to fees collected under this subsection.

(e) Exemption for Certain Small Areas.—For areas with a total population under 200,000 which fail to attain the standard by the applicable attainment date, no sanction under this section or under any other provision of this Act shall apply if the area can demonstrate, consistent with guidance issued by the Administrator, that attainment in the area is prevented because of ozone or ozone precursors transported from other areas. The prohibition applies only in cases in which the area has met all requirements and implemented all measures applicable to the area under this Act.

§7511e. Transitional Areas [Sec. 185A]

If an area designated as an ozone nonattainment area as of the date of enactment of the Clean Air Act Amendments of 1990 has not violated the national primary ambient air quality standard for ozone for the 36-month period commencing on January 1, 1987, and ending on December 31, 1989, the Administrator shall suspend the application of the requirements of this subpart to such area until December 31, 1991. By June 30, 1992, the Administrator shall determine by order, based on the area's design value as of the attainment date, whether the area attained such standard by December 31, 1991. If the Administrator determines that the area attained the standard, the Administrator shall require, as part of the order, the State to submit a maintenance plan for the area within 12 months of such determination. If the Administrator determines that the area failed to attain the standard, the Administrator shall, by June 30, 1992, designate the area as nonattainment under section 107(d)(4) .

§7511f. NO_x and VOC Study [Sec. 185B]

The Administrator, in conjunction with the National Academy of Sciences, shall conduct a study on the role of ozone precursors in tropospheric ozone formation and control. The study shall examine the roles of NO_x and VOC emission reductions, the extent to which NO_x reductions may contribute (or be counterproductive) to achievement of attainment in different nonattainment areas, the sensitivity of ozone to the control of NO_x, the availability and extent of controls for NO_x, the role of biogenic VOC emissions, and the basic information required for air quality models. The study shall be completed and a proposed report made public for 30 days comment within 1 year of the date of the enactment of the Clean Air Act Amendments of 1990, and a final report shall be submitted to Congress within 15 months after such date of enactment. The Administrator shall utilize all available information and studies, as well as develop additional information, in conducting the study required by this section.

SUBPART 3—ADDITIONAL PROVISIONS FOR CARBON MONOXIDE NONATTAINMENT AREAS

[Subpart 3 added by PL 101-549]

§7512. Classification and Attainment Dates [Sec. 186]

(a) Classification by Operation of Law and Attainment Dates for Nonattainment Areas.—

(1) Each area designated non-attainment for carbon monoxide pursuant to section 107(d) shall be classified at the time of such designation under table 1, by operation of law, as a Moderate Area or a Serious Area based on the design value for the area. The design value shall be calculated according to the interpretation methodology issued by the Administrator most recently before the date of the enactment of the Clean Air Act Amendments of 1990. For each area classified under this subsection, the primary standard attainment date for carbon monoxide shall be as expeditiously as practicable but not later than the date provided in table 1:

TABLE 3

Area classification	Design value	Primary standard attainment date
Moderate	9.1-16.4 ppm	December 31, 1995
Serious	16.5 and above	December 31, 2000

[Editor's Note: The table is referred to in the law as Table 1 but is numbered Table 3.]

(2) At the time of publication of the notice required under section 107 (designating car-

bon monoxide nonattainment areas), the Administrator shall publish a notice announcing the classification of each such carbon monoxide nonattainment area. The provisions of section 172(a)(1)(B) (relating to lack of notice-and-comment and judicial review) shall apply with respect to such classification.

(3) If an area classified under paragraph (1), table 1, would have been classified in another category if the design value in the area were 5 percent greater or 5 percent less than the level on which such classification was based, the Administrator may, in the Administrator's discretion, within 90 days after the date of the enactment of the Clean Air Act Amendments of 1990 by the procedure required under paragraph (2), adjust the classification of the area. In making such adjustment, the Administrator may consider the number of exceedances of the national primary ambient air quality standard for carbon monoxide in the area, the level of pollution transport between the area and the other affected areas, and the mix of sources and air pollutants in the area. The Administrator may make the same adjustment for purposes of paragraphs (2), (3), (6), and (7) of section 187(a) .

(4) Upon application by any State, the Administrator may extend for 1 additional year (hereinafter in this subpart referred to as the 'Extension Year') the date specified in table 1 of subsection (a) if—

(A) the State has complied with all requirements and commitments pertaining to the area in the applicable implementation plan, and

(B) no more than one exceedance of the national ambient air quality standard level for carbon monoxide has occurred in the area in the year preceding the Extension Year.

No more than 2 one-year extensions may be issued under this paragraph for a single nonattainment area.

(b) New Designations and Reclassifications.—

(1) New Designations to Nonattainment.—Any area that is designated attainment or unclassifiable for carbon monoxide under section 107(d)(4), and that is subsequently redesignated to nonattainment for carbon monoxide under section 107(d)(3) , shall, at the time of the redesignation, be classified by operation of law in accordance with table 1 under subsections (a)(1) and (a)(4). Upon its classification, the area shall be subject to the same requirements under section 110, subpart 1 of this part, and this subpart that would have applied had the area been so classified at the time of the notice under subsection (a)(2), except that any absolute, fixed date applicable in connection with any such requirement is extended by operation of law by a period equal to the length of time between the date of the enactment of the Clean Air Act Amendments of 1990 and the date the area is classified.

(2) Reclassification of Moderate Areas Upon Failure to Attain.—

(A) General Rule.—Within 6 months following the applicable attainment date for a carbon monoxide nonattainment area, the Administrator shall determine, based on the area's design value as of the attainment date, whether the area has attained the standard by that date. Any Moderate Area that the Administrator finds has not attained the standard by that date shall be reclassified by operation of law in accordance with table 1 of subsection (a)(1) as a Serious Area.

(B) Publication of Notice.—The Administrator shall publish a notice in the Federal Register, no later than 6 months following the attainment date, identifying each area that the Administrator has determined, under subparagraph (A), as having failed to attain and identifying the reclassification, if any, described under subparagraph (A).

(c) References to Terms.—Any reference in this subpart to a 'Moderate Area' or a 'Serious Area' shall be considered a reference to a Moderate Area or a Serious Area, respectively, as classified under this section.

§7512a. Plan Submissions and Requirements [Sec. 187]

(a) Moderate Areas.—Each State in which all or part of a Moderate Area is located shall, with respect to the Moderate Area (or portion thereof, to the extent specified in guidance of the Administrator issued before the date of the enactment of the Clean Air Act Amendments of 1990), submit to the Administrator the State implementation plan revisions (including the plan items) described under this subsection, within such periods as are prescribed under this subsection, except to the extent the State has made such submissions as of such date of enactment:

(1) Inventory.—No later than 2 years from the date of the enactment of the Clean Air Act Amendments of 1990, the State shall submit a comprehensive, accurate, current inventory of actual emissions from all sources, as described

in section 172(c)(3) , in accordance with guidance provided by the Administrator.

(2) (A) Vehicle Miles Traveled.—No later than 2 years after the date of the enactment of the Clean Air Act Amendments of 1990, for areas with a design value above 12.7 ppm at the time of classification, the plan revision shall contain a forecast of vehicle miles traveled in the nonattainment area concerned for each year before the year in which the plan projects the national ambient air quality standard for carbon monoxide to be attained in the area. The forecast shall be based on guidance which shall be published by the Administrator, in consultation with the Secretary of Transportation, within 6 months after the date of the enactment of the Clean Air Act Amendments of 1990. The plan revision shall provide for annual updates of the forecasts to be submitted to the Administrator together with annual reports regarding the extent to which such forecasts proved to be accurate. Such annual reports shall contain estimates of actual vehicle miles traveled in each year for which a forecast was required.

(B) Special Rule for Denver.—Within 2 years after the date of the enactment of the Clean Air Act Amendments of 1990, in the case of Denver, the State shall submit a revision that includes the transportation control measures as required in section 182(d)(1)(A) except that such revision shall be for the purpose of reducing CO emissions rather than volatile organic compound emissions. If the State fails to include any such measure, the implementation plan shall contain an explanation of why such measures was not adopted and what emissions reduction measure was adopted to provide a comparable reduction in emissions, or reasons why such reduction is not necessary to attain the national primary ambient air quality standard for carbon monoxide.

(3) Contingency Provisions.—No later than 2 years after the date of the enactment of the Clean Air Act Amendments of 1990, for areas with a design value above 12.7 ppm at the time of classification, the plan revision shall provide for the implementation of specific measures to be undertaken if any estimate of vehicle miles traveled in the area which is submitted in an annual report under paragraph (2) exceeds the number predicted in the most recent prior forecast or if the area fails to attain the national primary ambient air quality standard for carbon monoxide by the primary standard attainment date. Such measures shall be included in the plan revision as contingency measures to take effect without further action by the State or the Administrator if the prior forecast has been exceeded by an updated forecast or if the national standard is not attained by such deadline.

(4) Savings Clause for Vehicle Inspection and Maintenance Provisions of the State Implementation Plan.—Immediately after the date of the enactment of the Clean Air Act Amendments of 1990, for any Moderate Area (or, within the Administrator's discretion, portion thereof), the plan for which is of the type described in section 182(a)(2)(B) any provisions necessary to ensure that the applicable implementation plan includes the vehicle inspection and maintenance program described in section 182(a)(2)(B) .

(5) Periodic Inventory.—No later than September 30, 1995, and no later than the end of each 3 year period thereafter, until the area is redesignated to attainment a revised inventory meeting the requirements of subsection (a)(1).

(6) Enhanced Vehicle Inspection and Maintenance.—No later than 2 years after the date of the enactment of the Clean Air Act Amendments of 1990 in the case of Moderate Areas with a design value greater than 12.7 ppm at the time of classification, a revision that includes provisions for an enhanced vehicle inspection and maintenance program as required in section 182(c)(3) (concerning serious ozone nonattainment areas), except that such program shall be for the purpose of reducing carbon monoxide rather than hydrocarbon emissions.

(7) Attainment Demonstration and Specific Annual Emission Reductions.—In the case of Moderate Areas with a design value greater than 12.7 ppm at the time of classification, no later than 2 years after the date of the enactment of the Clean Air Act Amendments if 1990, a revision to provide, and a demonstration that the plan as revised will provide, for attainment of the carbon monoxide NAAQS by the applicable attainment date and provisions for such specific annual emission reductions as are necessary to attain the standard by that date. The Administrator may, in the Administrator's discretion, require States to submit to schedule for submitting any of the revisions or other items required under this subsection. In the case of Moderate Areas with a design value of 12.7 ppm or lower at the time of classification, the requirements of this subsection shall

apply in lieu of any requirement that the State submit a demonstration that the applicable implementation plan provides for attainment of the carbon monoxide standard by the applicable attainment date.

(b) Serious Areas.—

(1) In general.—Each State in which all or part of a Serious Area is located shall, with respect to the Serious Area, make the submissions (other than those required under subsection (a)(1)(B) applicable under subsection (a) to Moderate Areas with a design value of 12.7 ppm or greater at the time of classification, and shall also submit the revision and other items described under this subsection.

(2) Vehicle Miles Traveled.—Within 2 years after the date of the enactment of the Clean Air Act Amendments of 1990 the State shall submit a revision that includes the transportation control measures as required in section 182(d)(1) except that such revision shall be for the purpose of reducing CO emissions rather than volatile organic compound emissions. In the case of any such area (other than an area in New York State) which is a covered area (as defined in section 246(a)(2)(B)) for purposes of the Clean Fuel Fleet program under part C of title II, if the State fails to include any such measure, the implementation plan shall contain an explanation of why such measure was not adopted and what emissions reduction measure was adopted to provide a comparable reduction in emissions, or reasons why such reduction is not necessary to attain the national primary ambient air quality standard for carbon monoxide.

(3) Oxygenated Gasoline.—

(A) Within 2 years after the date of the enactment of the Clean Air Act Amendments of 1990, the State shall submit a revision to require that gasoline sold, supplied, offered for sale or supply, dispensed, transported or introduced into commerce in the larger of—

(i) the Consolidated Metropolitan Statistical Area (as defined by the United States Office of Management and Budget) (CMSA) in which the area is located, or

(ii) if the area is not located in a CMSA, the Metropolitan Statistical Area (as defined by the United States Office of Management and Budget) in which the area is located, be blended, during the portion of the year in which the area is prone to high ambient concentrations of carbon monoxide (as determined by the Administrator), with fuels containing such level of oxygen as is necessary, in combination with other measures, to provide for attainment of the carbon monoxide national ambient air quality standard by the applicable attainment date and maintenance of the national ambient air quality standard thereafter in the area. The revision shall provide that such requirement shall take effect no later than October 1, 1993, and shall include a program for implementation and enforcement of the requirement consistent with guidance to be issued by the Administrator.

(B) Notwithstanding subparagraph (A), the revision described in this para graph shall not be required for an area if the State demonstrates to the satisfaction of the Administrator that the revision is not necessary to provide for attainment of the carbon monoxide national ambient air quality standard by the applicable attainment date and maintenance of the national ambient air quality standard thereafter in the area.

(c) Areas With Significant Stationary Source Emissions of CO.—

(1) Serious Areas.—In the case of Serious Areas in which stationary sources contribute significantly to carbon monoxide levels (as determined under rules issued by the Administrator), the State shall submit a plan revision within 2 years after the date of the enactment of the Clean Air Act Amendments of 1990, which provides that the term 'major stationary source' includes (in addition to the sources described in section 302) any stationary source which emits, or has the potential to emit, 50 tons per year or more of carbon monoxide.

(2) Waivers for Certain Areas.—The Administrator may, on a case-by-case basis, waive any requirements that pertain to transportation controls, inspection and maintenance, or oxygenated fuels where the Administrator determines by rule that mobile sources of carbon monoxide do not contribute significantly to carbon monoxide levels in the area.

(3) Guidelines.—Within 6 months after the date of the enactment of the Clean Air Act Amendments of 1990, the Administrator shall issue guidelines for and rules determining whether stationary sources contribute significantly to carbon monoxide levels in an area.

(d) CO Milestone.—

(1) Milestone Demonstration.—By March 31, 1996, each State in which all or part of a Seri-

ous Area is located shall submit to the Administrator a demonstration that the area has achieved a reduction in emissions of CO equivalent to the total of the specific annual emission reductions required by December 31, 1995. Such reductions shall be referred to in this subsection as the milestone.

(2) Adequacy of Demonstration.—A demonstration under this paragraph shall be submitted in such form and manner, and shall contain such information and analysis, as the Administrator shall require. The Administrator shall determine whether or not a State's demonstration is adequate within 90 days after the Administrator's receipt of a demonstration which contains the information and analysis required by the Administrator.

(3) Failure to Meet Emission Reduction Milestone.—If a State fails to submit a demonstration under paragraph (1) within the required period, or if the Administrator notifies the State that the State has not met the milestone, the State shall, within 9 months after such a failure or notification, submit a plan revision to implement an economic incentive and transportation control program as described in section 182(g)(4) . Such revision shall be sufficient to achieve the specific annual reductions in carbon monoxide emissions set forth in the plan by the attainment date.

(e) Multi-State CO Nonattainment Areas.—

(1) Coordination Among States.—Each State in which there is located a portion of a single nonattainment area for carbon monoxide which covers more than one State ('multi-State nonattainment reasonable steps to coordinate, substantively and procedurally, the revisions and implementation of State implementation plans applicable to the nonattainment area concerned. The Administrator may not approve any revision of a State implementation plan submitted under this part for a State in which part of a multi-State nonattainment area is located if the plan revision for that State fails to comply with the requirements of this subsection.

(2) Failure to Demonstrate Attainment.—If any State in which there is located a portion of a multi-State nonattainment area fails to provide a demonstration of attainment of the national ambient air quality standard for carbon monoxide in that portion within the period required under this part the State may petition the Administrator to make a finding that the State would have been able to make such demonstration but for the failure of one or more other States in which other portions of the area are located to commit to the implementation of all measures required under section 187 (relating to plan submissions for carbon monoxide nonattainment areas). If the Administrator makes such finding, in the portion of the nonattainment area within the State submitting such petition, no sanction shall be imposed under section 179 or under any other provision of this Act, by reason of the failure to make such demonstration.

(f) Reclassified Areas.—Each State containing a carbon monoxide nonattainment area reclassified under section 186(b)(2) shall meet the requirements of subsection (b) of this section, as may be applicable to the area as reclassified, according to the schedules prescribed in connection with such requirements, except that the Administrator may adjust any applicable deadlines (other than the attainment date) where such deadlines are shown to be infeasible.

(g) Failure of Serious Area to Attain Standards.—If the Administrator determines under section 186(b)(2) that the national primary ambient air quality standard for carbon monoxide has not been attained in a Serious Area by the applicable attainment date, the State shall submit a plan revision for the area within 9 months after the date of such determination. The plan revision shall provide that a program of incentives and requirements as described in section 182(g)(4) shall be applicable in the area, and such program, in combination with other elements of the revised plan, shall be adequate to reduce the total tonnage of emissions of carbon monoxide in the area by at least 5 percent per year in each year after approval of the plan revision and before attainment of the national primary ambient air quality standard for carbon monoxide.

SUBPART 4—ADDITIONAL PROVISIONS FOR PARTICULATE MATTER NONATTAINMENT AREAS

[Subpart 4 added by PL 101–549]

§7513. Classifications and Attainment Dates

[Sec. 188]

(a) Initial Classifications.—Every area designated nonattainment for PM–10 pursuant to section 107(d) shall be classified at the time of such designation, by operation of law, as a moderate PM–10 nonattainment area (also referred to in this of such designation. At the time of publication of the notice under section 107(d)(4) (relating to area designations) for each PM–10 nonattainment area, the Administrator shall publish a notice announcing the classification of such area. The provisions of section 172(a)(1)(B) (relating to lack of notice-and-comment and judicial review) shall apply with respect to such classification.

(b) Reclassification as Serious.—

(1) Reclassification Before Attainment Date.—The Administrator may reclassify as a Serious PM–10 nonattainment area (identified in this subpart that the Administrator determines cannot practicably attain the national ambient air quality standard for PM–10 by the attainment date (as prescribed in subsection (c)) for Moderate Areas. The Administrator shall reclassify appropriate areas as Serious by the following dates:

(A) For areas designated nonattainment for PM–10 under section 107(d)(4), the Administrator shall propose to reclassify appropriate areas by June 30, 1991, and take final action by December 31, 1991.

(B) For areas subsequently designated nonattainment, the Administrator shall reclassify appropriate areas within 18 months after the required date for the State's submission of a SIP for the Moderate Area.

(2) Reclassification upon failure to attain.—Within 6 months following the applicable attainment date for a PM–10 nonattainment area, the Administrator shall determine whether the area attained the standard by that date. If the Administrator finds that any Moderate Area is not in attainment after the applicable attainment date—

(A) the area shall be reclassified by operation of law as a Serious Area; and

(B) the Administrator shall publish a notice in the Federal Register no later than 6 months following the attainment date, identifying the area as having failed to attain and identifying the reclassification described under subparagraph (A).

(c) Attainment Dates.—Except as provided under subsection (d), the attainment dates for PM–10 nonattainment areas shall be as follows:

(1) Moderate Areas.—For a Moderate Area, the attainment date shall be as expeditiously as practicable but no later than the end of the sixth calendar year after the area's designation as nonattainment, except that, for areas designated nonattainment for PM–10 under section 107(d)(4), the attainment date shall not extend beyond December 31, 1994.

(2) Serious Areas.—For a Serious Area, the attainment date shall be as expeditiously as practicable but no later than the end of the tenth calendar year beginning after the area's designation as nonattainment, except that, for areas designated nonattainment for PM–10 under section 107(d)(4), the date shall not extend beyond December 31, 2001.

(d) Extension of Attainment Date for Moderate Areas.—Upon application by any State, the Administrator may extend for 1 additional year (hereinafter) the date specified in paragraph (c)(1) if—

(1) the State has complied with all requirements and commitments pertaining to the area in the applicable implementation plan; and

(2) no more than one exceedance of the 24-hour national ambient air quality standard level for PM–10 has occurred in the area in the year preceding the Extension Year, and the annual mean concentration of PM–10 in the area for such year is less than or equal to the standard level.

No more than 2 one-year extensions may be issued under the subsection for a single nonattainment area.

(e) Extension of Attainment Date for Serious Areas.—Upon application by any State, the Administrator may extend the attainment date for a Serious Area beyond the date specified under subsection (c), if attainment by the date established under subsection (c) would be impracticable, the State has complied with all requirements and commitments pertaining to that area in the implementation plan, and the State demonstrates to the satisfaction of the Administrator that the plan for that area includes the most stringent measures that are included in the implementation plan of any State or are achieved in practice in any State, and can feasibly be implemented in the area. At the time of such application, the State must submit a revision to the implementation plan that includes a demonstration of attainment by the most expeditious alternative date practicable. In determining whether to grant an extension, and the appropriate length of time for any such extension, the Administrator may consider the nature and extent of nonattainment, the types and numbers of sources or other emitting activities in the area (including the influence of uncontrollable natural sources and transboundary emissions from foreign countries), the population exposed to concentrations in excess of the standard, the presence and concentration of potentially toxic substances in the mix of particulate emissions in the area, and the technological and economic feasibility of various control measures. The Administrator may not approve an extension until the State submits an attainment demonstration for the area. The Administrator may grant at most one such extension for an area, of no more than 5 years.

(f) Waivers for Certain Areas.—The Administrator may, on a case-by-case basis, waive any requirement applicable to any Serious Area under this subpart where the Administrator determines that anthropogenic sources of PM–10 do not contribute significantly to the violation of the PM–10 standard in the area. The Administrator may also waive a specific date for attainment of the standard where the Administrator determines that nonanthropogenic sources of PM–10 contribute significantly to the violation of the PM–10 standard in the area.

§7513a. Plan Provisions and Schedules for Plan Submissions [Sec. 189]

(a) Moderate Areas.—

(1) Plan Provisions.—Each State in which all or part of a Moderate Area is located shall submit, according to the applicable schedule under paragraph (2), an implementation plan that includes each of the following:

(A) For the purpose of meeting the requirements of section 172(c)(5) , a permit program providing that permits meeting the requirements of section 173 are required for the construction and operation of new and modified major stationary sources of PM–10.

(B) Either (i) a demonstration (including air quality modeling) that the plan will provide for attainment by the applicable attainment date; or (ii) a demonstration that attainment by such date is impracticable.

(C) Provisions to assure that reasonably available control measures for the control of PM–10 shall be implemented no later than December 10, 1993, or 4 years after designation in the case of an area classified as moderate after the date of the enactment of the Clean Air Act Amendments of 1990.

(2) Schedule for Plan Submissions.—A State shall submit the plan required under subparagraph (1) no later that the following:

(A) Within 1 year of the date of the enactment of the Clean Air Act Amendments of 1990, for areas designated nonattainment under section 107(D)(4) , except that the provision required under subparagraph (1)(A) shall be submitted no later than June 30, 1992.

(B) 18 months after the designations as nonattainment, for those areas designated nonattainment after the designations prescribed under section 107(d)(4) .

(b) Serious Areas.—

(1) Plan Provisions.—In addition to the provisions submitted to meet the requirements of paragraph (a)(1) (relating to Moderate Areas), each State in which all or part of a Serious Area is located shall submit an implementation plan for such area that includes each of the following:

(A) A demonstration (including air quality modeling)—

(i) that the plan provides for attainment of the PM–10 national ambient air quality standard by the applicable attainment date, or

(ii) for any area for which the State is seeking, pursuant to section 188(e) , an extension of the attainment date beyond the date set forth in section 188(c) , that attainment by that date would be impracticable, and that the plan provides for attainment by the most expeditious alternative date practicable.

(B) Provisions to assure that the best available control measures for the control of PM–10 shall be implemented no later than 4 years after the date the area is classified (or reclassified) as a Serious Area.

(2) Schedule for Plan Submission.—A State shall submit the demonstration required for an area under paragraph (1)(A) no later than 4 years after reclassification of the area to Serious, except that for areas reclassified under section 188(b)(2) , the State shall submit the attainment demonstration within 18 months after reclassification to Serious. A State shall submit the provisions described under paragraph (1)(B) no later than 18 months after reclassification of the area as a Serious Area.

(3) Major Sources.—For any Serious Area, the terms "major source" and "major stationary source" include any stationary source of group of stationary sources located within a contiguous area and under common control that emits, or has the potential to emit, at least 70 tons per year of PM–10.

(c) Milestones.—

(1) Plan revisions demonstrating attainment submitted to the Administrator for approval under this subpart shall contain quantitative milestone which are to be achieve every 3 years until the area is redesignated attainment

and which demonstrate reasonable further progress, as defined in section 171(1) , toward attainment by the applicable date.

(2) No later than 90 days after the date on which a milestone applicable to the area occurs, each State in which all or part of such area is located shall submit to the Administrator a demonstration that all measures in the plan approved under this section have been implemented and that the milestone has been met. A demonstration under this subsection shall be submitted in such form and manner, and shall contain such information and analysis, as the Administrator shall require. The Administrator shall determine whether or not a State's demonstration under this subsection is adequate within 90 days after the Administrator's receipt of a demonstration which contains the information and analysis required by the Administrator.

(3) If a State fails to submit a demonstration under paragraph (2) with respect to a milestone within the required period or if the Administrator determines that the area has not met any applicable milestone, the Administrator shall require the State, within 9 months after such failure or determination to submit a plan revision that assures that the State will achieve the next milestone (or attain the national ambient air quality standard for PM–10, if there is no next milestone) by the applicable date.

(d) Failure to Attain.—In the case of a Serious PM–10 nonattainment area in which the PM–10 standard is not attained by the applicable attainment date, the State in which such area is located shall, after notice and opportunity for public comment, submit within 12 months after the applicable attainment date, plan revisions which provide for attainment of the PM–10 air quality standard and, from the date of such submission until attainment, for an annual reduction in PM–10 or PM–10 precursor emissions within the area of not less than 5 percent of the amount of such emissions as reported in the most recent inventory prepared for such area.

(e) PM–10 Precursors.—The control requirements applicable under plans in effect under this part for major stationary sources of PM–10 shall also apply to major stationary sources of PM–10 precursors, except where the Administrator determines that such sources do not contribute significantly to PM–10 levels which exceed the standard in the area. The Administrator shall issue guidelines regarding the application of the preceding sentence.

§7513b. Issuance of RACM and BACM Guidance [Sec. 190]

The Administrator shall issue, in the same manner and according to the same procedure as guidance is issued under section 108(c) , technical guidance on reasonably available control measures and best available control measures for urban fugitive dust, and emissions from residential wood combustion (including curtailments and exemptions from such curtailments) and prescribed silvicultural and agricultural burning, no later than 18 months following the date of the enactment of the Clean Air Act Amendments of 1990. The Administrator shall also examine other categories of sources contributing to nonattainment of the PM–10 standard, and determine whether additional guidance on reasonably available control measures and best available control measures is needed, and issue any such guidance no later than 3 years after the date of the enactment of the Clean Air Act Amendments of 1990. In issuing guidelines and making determinations under this section, the Administrator (in consultation with the State) shall take into account emission reductions achieved, or expected to be achieved, under title IV and other provisions of this Act.

SUBPART 5—ADDITIONAL PROVISIONS FOR AREAS DESIGNATED NONATTAINMENT FOR SULFUR OXIDES, NITROGEN DIOXIDE, OR LEAD

[Subpart 5 added by PL 101–549]

§7514. Plan Submission Deadlines [Sec. 191]

(a) Submission.—Any State containing an area designated or redesignated under section 107(d) as nonattainment with respect to the national primary ambient air quality standards for sulfur oxides, nitrogen dioxide, or lead subsequent to the date of the enactment of the Clean Air Act Amendments of 1990 shall submit to the Administrator, within 18 months of the designation, an applicable implementation plan meeting the requirements of this part.

(b) States Lacking Fully Approved State Implementation Plans.—Any State containing an area designated nonattainment with respect to national primary ambient air quality standards for sulfur oxides or nitrogen dioxide under section 107(d)(1)(C)(i), but lacking a fully approved implementation plan complying with the requirements of this Act (including part D) as in effect immediately before the date of the enactment of the Clean Air Act Amendments of 1990, shall submit to the Administrator, within 18 months of the date of the enactment of the Clean

Air Act Amendments of 1990, an implementation plan meeting the requirements of subpart 1 (except as otherwise prescribed by section 192).

§7514a. Attainment Dates [Sec. 192]

(a) Plans under section 191(a).— Implementation plans required under section 191(a) shall provide for attainment of the relevant primary standard as expeditiously as practicable but no later than 5 years from the date of the nonattainment designation.

(b) Plans under section 191(b).— Implementation plans required under section 191(b) shall provide for attainment of the relevant primary national ambient air quality standard within 5 years after the date of the enactment of the Clean Air Act Amendments of 1990.

(c) Inadequate Plans.— Implementation plans for nonattainment areas for sulfur oxides or nitrogen dioxide with plans that were approved by the Administrator before the date of the enactment of the Clean Air Act Amendments of 1990 but, subsequent to such approval, were found by the Administrator to be substantially inadequate, shall provide for attainment of the relevant primary standard within 5 years from the date of such finding.

SUBPART 6—SAVINGS PROVISIONS

[Subpart 6 added by PL 101-549]

§7515. General Savings Clause [Sec. 193]

Each regulation, standard, rule, notice, order and guidance promulgated or issued by the Administrator under this Act, as in effect before the date of the enactment of the Clean Air Act Amendments of 1990 shall remain in effect according to its terms, except to the extent otherwise provided under this Act, inconsistent with any provision of this Act, or revised by the Administrator. No control requirement in effect, or required to be adopted by an order, settlement agreement, or plan in effect before the date of the enactment of the Clean Air Act Amendments of 1990 in any area which is a nonattainment area for any air pollutant may be modified after such enactment in any manner unless the modification insures equivalent or greater emission reductions of such air pollutant.

TITLE II—EMISSION STANDARDS FOR MOVING SOURCES

PART A—MOTOR VEHICLE EMISSION AND FUEL STANDARDS

Short Title [Sec. 201]

This part may be cited as the 'National Emission Standards Act.'

§7521. Establishment of Standards [Sec. 202]

(a) Except as otherwise provided in subsection (b)—

(1) The Administration shall by regulation prescribe (and from time to time revise) in accordance with the provisions of this section, standards applicable to the emission of any air pollution from any class or classes of new motor vehicles or new motor vehicle engines, which in his judgment cause or contribute to, air pollution which may reasonably be anticipated to endanger public health or welfare. Such standards shall be applicable to such vehicles and engines for their useful life (as determined under subsection (d), relating to useful life of vehicles for purposes of certification), whether such vehicles and engines are designed as complete systems or incorporate devices to prevent or control such pollution.

[§202(a)(1) designated by PL 95–190]

(2) Any regulation prescribed under paragraph (1) of this subsection (and any revision thereof) shall take effect after such period as the Administrator finds necessary to permit the development and application of the requisite technology, giving appropriate consideration to the cost of compliance within such period.

Emission Standards For Heavy Duty Vehicles Or Engines And Certain Other Vehicles Or Engines

(3) (A) In General.—

(i) Unless the standard is changed as provided in subparagraph (B), regulations under paragraph (1) of this subsection applicable to emissions of hydrocarbons, carbon monoxide, oxides of nitrogen, and particulate matter from classes or categories of heavy-duty vehicles or engines manufactured during or after model year 1983 shall contain standards which reflect the greatest degree of emission reduction achievable through the application of technology which the Administrator determines will be available for the model year to which such standards apply, giving appropriate consideration to cost, energy, and safety factors associated with the application of such technology.

(ii) In establishing classes or categories of vehicles or engines for purposes of regulations under this paragraph, the Administrator may base such classes or categories on gross vehicle weight, horsepower, type of fuel used, or other appropriate factors.

[§202(a)(3)(A) revised by PL 101–549]

(B) Revised Standards for Heavy Duty Trucks.—

(i) On the basis of information available to the Administrator concerning the effects of air pollutants emitted from heavy-duty vehicles or engines and from other sources of mobile source related pollutants on the public health and welfare, and taking costs into account, the Administrator may promulgate regulations under paragraph (1) of this subsection revising any standard promulgated under, or before the date of, the enactment of the Clean Air Act Amendments of 1990 (or previously revised under this subparagraph) and applicable to classes or categories of heavy-duty vehicles or engines.

(ii) Effective for the model year 1998 and thereafter, the regulations under paragraph (1) of this subsection applicable to emissions of oxides of nitrogen (NO_x) from gasoline and diesel-fueled heavy duty trucks shall contain standards which provide that such emissions may not exceed 4.0 grams per brake horsepower hour (gbh).

[§202(a)(3)(B) revised by PL 101–549]

(C) Lead Time and Stability.—Any standard promulgated or revised under this paragraph and applicable to classes or categories of heavy-duty vehicles or engines shall apply for a period of no less than 3 model years beginning no earlier than the model year commencing 4 years after such revised standard is promulgated.

[§202(a)(3)(C) revised by PL 101–549]

(D) Rebuilding Practices.—The Administrator shall study the practice of rebuilding heavy-duty engines and the impact rebuilding has on engine emissions. On the basis of that study and other information available to the Administrator, the Administrator may prescribe requirements to control rebuilding practices, including standards applicable to emissions from any rebuilt heavy-duty engines (whether or not the engine is past its statutory useful life), which in the Administrator's judgment cause, or contribute to, air pollution which may reasonably be anticipated to endanger public health or welfare taking costs into account. Any regulation shall take effect after a period the Administrator finds necessary to permit the development and application of the requisite control measures, giving appropriate consideration to the cost of compliance within the period and energy and safety factors.

[§202(a)(3)(D) revised by PL 101–549]

(E) Motorcycles.—For purposes of this paragraph, motorcycles and motorcycle engines shall be treated in the same manner as heavy-duty vehicles and engines (except as otherwise permitted under section 206(f)(1)) unless the Administrator promulgates a rule reclassifying motorcycles as light-duty vehicles within the meaning of this section or unless the Administrator promulgates regulations under subsection (a) applying standards applicable to the emission of air pollutants from motorcycles as a separate class or category. In any case in which such standards are promulgated for such emissions from motorcycles as a separate class or category, the Administrator promulgating such standards, shall consider the need to achieve equivalency of emission reductions between motorcycles and other vehicles to the maximum extent practicable.

[Former §202(a)(3)(E) deleted and former (F) redesignated as (E) by PL 101–549]

(4) (A) Effective with respect to vehicles and engines manufactured after model year 1978, no emission control device, system, or element of design shall be used in a new motor vehicle or new motor vehicle engine for purposes of complying with requirements prescribed under this title if such device, system, or element of design will cause or contribute to an unreasonable risk to public health, welfare, or safety in its operation or function.

(B) In determining whether an unreasonable risk exists under subparagraph (A), the Administrator shall consider, among other factors, (i) whether and to what extent the use of any device, system, or element of design causes, increases, reduces, or eliminates emissions of any unregulated pollutants; (ii) available methods for reducing or eliminating any risk to public health, welfare, or safety which may be associated with the use of such device, system, or element of design, and (iii) the availability of other devices, systems, or elements of design which may be used to conform to requirements prescribed under this title without causing or contributing to such unreasonable risk. The Administrator shall include in the consideration required by this paragraph all relevant information developed pursuant to section 214 .

[§202(a)(4) amended by PL 101–549]

Pipe Standards

(5) (A) If the Administrator promulgates final regulations which define the degree of control required and the test procedures by which compliance could be determined for gasoline vapor recovery of uncontrolled emissions from the fueling of motor vehicles, the Administrator shall, after consultation with the Secretary of Transportation with respect to motor vehicle safety prescribe, by regulation, fill pipe standards for new motor vehicles in order to insure effective connection between such fill pipe and any vapor recovery system which the Administrator determines may be required to comply with such vapor recovery regulations. In promulgating such standards the Administrator shall take into consideration limits on fill pipe diameter, minimum design criteria for nozzle retainer lips, limits on the location of the unleaded fuel restrictors, a minimum access zone surrounding a fill pipe, a minimum fill pipe or nozzle insertion angle, and such other factors as he deems pertinent.

(B) Regulations prescribing standards under subparagraph (A) shall not become effective until the introduction of the model year for which it would be feasible to implement such standards, taking into consideration the restraints of an adequate leadtime for design and production.

(C) Nothing in subparagraph (A) shall (i) prevent the Administrator from specifying different nozzle and fill neck sizes for gasoline with additives and gasoline without additives or (ii) permit the Administrator to require a specific location, configuration, modeling, or styling of the motor vehicle body with respect to the fuel tank fill neck or fill nozzle clearance envelope.

(D) For the purpose of this paragraph, the term 'fill pipe' shall include the fuel tank fill pipe, fill neck, fill inlet, and closure.

Onboard Hydrocarbon Technology

(6) Onboard Vapor Recovery.—Within 1 year after the date of the enactment of the Clean Air

Act Amendments of 1990, the Administrator shall, after consultation with the Secretary of Transportation regarding the safety of vehicle-based ('onboard') systems for the control of vehicle refueling emissions, promulgate standards under this section requiring that new light-duty vehicles manufactured beginning in the fourth model year after the model year in which the standards are promulgated and thereafter shall be equipped with such systems. The standards required under this paragraph shall apply to a percentage of each manufacturer's fleet of new light-duty vehicles beginning with the fourth model year after the model year in which the standards are promulgated. The percentage shall be as specified in the following table:

IMPLEMENTATION SCHEDULE FOR ONBOARD VAPOR RECOVERY REQUIREMENTS

Model year commencing after standards promulgated	Percentage*
Fourth	40
Fifth	80
After Fifth	100

* Percentages in the table refer to a percentage of the manufacturer'sales volume.

The standards shall require that such systems provide a minimum evaporative emission capture efficiency of 95 percent. The requirements of section 182(b)(3) (relating to stage II gasoline vapor recovery) for areas classified under section 181 as moderate for ozone shall not apply after promulgation of such standards and the Administrator may, be rule, revise or waive the application of the requirements of such section 182(b)(3) for areas classified under section 181 as Serious, Severe, or Extreme for ozone, as appropriate, after such time as the Administrator determines that onboard emissions control systems required under this paragraph are in widespread use throughout the motor vehicle fleet.

[§202(a)(6) revised by PL 101–549]

Light Duty Motor Vehicle Emissions

(b) (1) (A) The regulations under subsection (a) applicable to emissions of carbon monoxide and hydrocarbons from light-duty vehicles and engines manufactured during models years 1977 through 1979 shall contain standards which provide that such emissions from such vehicles and engines may not exceed 1.5 grams per vehicle mile of hydrocarbons and 15.0 grams per vehicle mile of carbon monoxide. The regulations under subsection (a) applicable to emissions of carbon monoxide from light-duty vehicles and engines manufactured during the model year 1980 shall contain standards which provide that such emissions may not exceed 7.0 grams per vehicle mile. The regulations under subsection (a) applicable to emissions of hydrocarbons from light- duty vehicles and engines manufactured during or after model year 1980 shall contain standards which require a reduction of at least 90 percent from emissions of such pollutant allowable under the standards under this section applicable to light-duty vehicles and engines manufactured in model year 1970. Unless waived as provided in paragraph (5), regulations under subsection (a) applicable to emissions of carbon monoxide from light-duty vehicles and engines manufactured during or after the model year 1981 shall contain standards which require a reduction of at least 90 percent from emissions of such pollutants allowable under the standards under this section applicable to light-duty vehicles and engines manufactured in model year 1970.

(B) The regulations under subsection (a) applicable to emissions of oxides of nitrogen from light-duty vehicles and engines manufactured during model years 1977 through 1980 shall contain standards which provide that such emissions from such vehicles and engines may not exceed 2.0 grams per vehicle mile. The regulations under subsection (a) applicable to emissions of oxides of nitrogen from light-duty vehicles and engines manufactured during the model year 1981 and thereafter shall contain standards which provide that such emissions from such vehicles and engines may not exceed 1.0 gram per vehicle mile. The Administrator shall prescribe standards in lieu of those required by the preceding sentence, which provide that emissions of oxides of nitrogen may not exceed 2.0 grams per vehicle mile for any light-duty vehicle manufactured during model years 1981 and 1982 by any manufacturer whose production, by corporate identity, for calendar year 1976 was less than 300,000 light-duty motor vehicles worldwide if the Administrator determines that—

[§202(b)(1)(B) amended by PL 95–190]

(i) the ability of such manufacturer to meet emission standards in the 1975 and subsequent model years was, and is, primarily dependent upon technology developed by other manufacturers and purchased from such manufacturers; and

[§202(b)(1)(B)(i) amended by PL 95–190]

(ii) such manufacturer lacks the financial resources and technological ability to develop such technology.

Test Procedures For Measuring Evaporative Emissions

(C) The Administrator may promulgate regulations under subsection (a)(1) revising any standard prescribed or previously revised under this subsection, as needed to protect public health or welfare, taking costs, energy, and safety into account. Any revised standard shall require a reduction of emissions from the standard that was previously applicable. Any such revision under this title may provide for a phase-in of the standard. It is the intent of Congress that the numerical emission standards specified in subsections (a)(3)(B)(ii), (g), (h), and (i) shall not be modified by the Administrator after the enactment of the Clean Air Act Amendments of 1990 for any model year before the model year 2004.

[§202(b)(1)(C) revised by PL 101–549]

(2) Emission standards under paragraph (1), and measurement techniques on which such standards are based (if not promulgated prior to the date of the enactment of the Clean Air Act Amendments of 1990), shall be promulgated by regulation within 180 days after such date.

[§202(b)(2) amended by PL 101–549]

(3) For purposes of this part

(A) (i) The term 'model year' with reference to any specific calendar year means the manufacturer's annual production period (as determined by the Administrator) which includes January 1 of such calendar year. If the manufacturer has no annual production period, the term 'model year' shall mean the calendar year.

(ii) For the purpose of assuring that vehicles and engines manufactured before the beginning of a model year were not manufactured for purposes of circumventing the effective date of a standard required to be prescribed by subsection (b), the Administrator may prescribe regulations defining 'model year' otherwise than as provided in clause (i).

(B) [Repealed]

[§202(b)(3)(B) repealed by PL 101–549]

(C) The term 'heavy duty vehicle' means a truck, bus, or other vehicle manufactured primarily for use on the public streets, roads, and highways (not including any vehicle operated exclusively on a rail or rails) which has a gross vehicle weight (as determined under regulations promulgated by the Administrator) in excess of six thousand pounds. Such term includes any such vehicle which has special features enabling off-street or off- highway operation and use.

[§202(b)(6) revised and redesignated as the second (3) by PL 101–549]

(3) Upon the petition of any manufacturer, the Administrator, after notice and opportunity for public hearing, may waive the standard required under sub- paragraph (B) of paragraph (1) to not exceed 1.5 grams of oxides of nitrogen per vehicle mile for any class or category of light-duty vehicles or engines manufactured by such manufacturer during any period of up to four model years beginning after the model year 1980 if the manufacturer demonstrates that such waiver is necessary to permit the use of an innovative power train technology, or innovative emission control device or system, in such class or category of vehicles or engines and that such technology or system was not utilized by more that 1 percent of the light-duty vehicles sold in the United States in the 1975 model year. Such waiver may be granted only if the Administrator determines—

(A) that such waiver would not endanger public health,

(B) that there is a substantial likelihood that the vehicles or engines will be able to comply with the applicable standard under this section at the expiration of the waiver, and

(C) that the technology or system has a potential for long-term air quality benefit and has the potential to meet or exceed the average fuel economy standard applicable under the Energy Policy and Conservation Act upon the expiration of the waiver. No waiver under this subparagraph granted to any manufacturer shall apply to more than 5 percent of such manufacturer's production or 50,000 vehicles or engines, whichever is greater.

[§202(b)(4), (5), (7) deleted by PL 101–549]

(c) (1) The Administrator shall undertake to enter into appropriate arrangements with the National Academy of Sciences to conduct a comprehensive study and investigation of the technology feasibility of meeting the emissions standards required to be prescribed by the Administrator by subsection (b) of this section.

(2) Of the funds authorized to be appropriated to the Administrator by this Act, such amounts as are required shall be available to carry out the study and investigation authorized by paragraph (1) of this subsection.

(3) In entering into any arrangement with the National Academy of Sciences for conducting the study and investigation authorized by paragraph (1) of this subsection, the Administrator shall request the National Academy of Sciences to submit semiannual reports on the progress of its study and investigation to the Administrator and the Congress, beginning not later than July 1, 1971, and continuing until such study and investigation is completed.

(4) The Administrator shall furnish to such Academy at its request any information which the Academy deems necessary for the purpose of conducting the investigation and study authorized by paragraph (1) of this subsection. For the purpose of furnishing such information, the Administrator may use any authority he has under this Act

(A) to obtain information from any person, and (B) to require such person to conduct such tests, keep such records, and make such reports respecting research or other activities conducted by such person as may be reasonably necessary to carry out this subsection.

(d) The Administrator shall prescribe regulations under which the useful life of vehicles and engines shall be determined for purposes of subsection (a)(1) of this section and section 207 . Such regulations shall provide that, except where a different useful life period is specified in this title, useful life shall—

[§202(d) intro. para. amended by PL 101–549]

(1) in the case of light duty vehicles and light duty vehicle engines and light- duty trucks up to 3,750 lbs. LVW and up to 6,000 lbs. GVWR, be a period of use of five years or of fifty thousand miles (or the equivalent), whichever first occurs, except that in the case of any requirement of this section which first becomes applicable after the enactment of the Clean Air Act Amendments of 1990 where the useful life period is not otherwise specified for such vehicles and engines, the period shall be 10 years or 100,000 miles (or the equivalent), whichever first occurs, with testing for purposes of in-use compliance under section 207 up to (but not beyond) 7 years or 75,000 miles (or the equivalent), whichever first occurs;

[§202 (d)(1) amended by PL 101–549]

(2) in the case of any other motor vehicle or motor vehicle engine (other than motorcycles or motorcycle engines) be a period of use set forth in paragraph (1) unless the Administrator determines that a period of use of greater duration or mileage is appropriate in lieu thereof; and

(3) in the case of any motorcycle or motorcycle engine, be a period of use the Administrator shall determine.

[§202(d)(3) added by PL 95–95]

(e) In the event a new power source or propulsion system for new motor vehicles or new motor vehicle engines is submitted for certification pursuant to section 206(a) , the Administrator may postpone certification until he has prescribed standards for any air pollutants emitted by such vehicle or engine which in his judgment cause, or contribute to, air pollution which may reasonably be anticipated to endanger the public health or welfare but for which standards have not been prescribed under subsection (a).

[§202(e) amended by PL 95–95]

(f) (1) The high altitude regulation in effect with respect to model year 1977 motor vehicles shall not apply to the manufacture, distribution, or sale of 1978 and later model year motor vehicles. Any future regulation affecting the sale or distribution of motor vehicles or engines manufactured before the model year 1984 in high altitude areas of the country shall take effect no earlier than model year 1981.

(2) Any future regulation applicable to high altitude vehicles or engines shall not require a percentage of reduction in the emissions of such vehicles which is greater than the required percentage of reduction in emissions from motor vehicles as set forth in section 202(b). This percentage reduction shall be determined by comparing any proposed high altitude emission standards to high altitude emissions from vehicles manufactured during model year 1970. In no event shall regulations applicable to high altitude vehicles manufactured before the model year 1984 establish a numerical standard which is more stringent than that applicable to vehicles certified under non-high altitude conditions.

(3) Section 307 (d) shall apply to any high altitude regulation referred to in paragraph (2) and before promulgating any such regulation, the Administrator shall consider and make a finding with respect to—

(A) the economic impact upon consumers, individual high altitude dealers, and the automobile industry of any such regulation, including the economic impact which was experienced as a result of the regulation imposed during model year 1977 with respect to high altitude certification requirements:

(B) the present and future availability of emission control technology capable of meeting the applicable vehicle and engine emission requirements without reducing model availability; and

(C) the likelihood that the adoption of such a high altitude regulation will result in any significant improvement in air quality in any area to which it shall apply, be used to conform to standards prescribed under this subsection without causing or contributing to such unreasonable risk. The Administrator shall include in the consideration required by this paragraph all relevant information developed pursuant to section 214 .

[§202(f) added by PL 95–95]

[Editor's Note: §207(b) of PL 101–549 added a second subsection (f) to §202.]

(f) Model Years After 1990.—For model years prior to model year 1994, the regulations under section 202(a) applicable to buses other than those subject to standards under section 219 shall contain a standard which provides that emissions of particulate matter (PM) from such buses may not exceed the standards set forth in the following table:

PM STANDARD FOR BUSES

Model year	Standard*
1991	0.25
1992	0.25
1993 and thereafter	0.10

* Standards are expressed in grams per brake horsepower hour (g/bhp/hr).

Emission Standards For Conventional Motor Vehicles

(g) Light-Duty Trucks up to 6,000 lbs. GVWR and Light-Duty Vehicles; Standards for Model Years After 1993.—

(1) NMHC, CO, and NO_x.—Effective with respect to the model year 1994 and thereafter, the regulations under subsection (a) applicable to emissions of nonmethane hydrocarbons (NMHC), carbon monoxide (CO), and oxides of nitrogen (NO_x) from light-duty trucks (LDTs) of up to 6,000 lbs. gross vehicle weight rating (GVWR) and light-duty vehicles (LDVs) shall contain standards which provide that emissions from a percentage of each manufacturer's sales volume of such vehicles and trucks shall comply with the levels specified in table G.

[Editor's Note: Table G listed on following page].

The percentage shall be as specified in the implementation schedule below:

IMPLEMENTATION SCHEDULE FOR TABLE G STANDARDS

Model year	Percentage*
1994	40
1995	80
after 1995	100

* Percentages in the table refer to a percentage of each manufacturer'sales volume.

(2) PM Standard.—Effective with respect to model year 1994 and thereafter in the case of light-duty vehicles and effective with respect to the model year 1995 and thereafter in the case of light- duty trucks (LDTs) of up to 6,000 lbs. gross vehicle weight rating (GVWR), the regulations under subsection (a) applicable to emissions of particulate matter (PM) from such vehicles and trucks shall contain standards which provide that such emissions from a percentage of each man ufacturer's sales volume of such vehicles and trucks shall not exceed the levels specified in the table below. The percentage shall be as specified in the Implementation Schedule below.

PM STANDARDS FOR LDT'S OF UP TO 6,000 LBS. GVWR

Useful Life Period	Standard
5/50,000	0.08 gpm
10/100,000	0.10 gpm

The applicable useful life, for purposes of certification under section 206 and for purposes of in-use compliance under section 207, shall be 5 years or 50,000 miles (or the equivalent), whic ever first occurs, in the case of the 5/50,000 standard.

The applicable useful life, for purposes of certification under section 206 and for purposes of in-use compliance under section 207, shall be 5 years or 50,000 miles (or the equivalent), whic ever first occurs, in the case of the 5/100,000 standard.

IMPLEMENTATION SCHEDULE FOR PM STANDARDS

Model year	Light-duty vehicles	LDTs
1994	40%*	
1995	80%*	40%*
1996	100%*	80%*

TABLE G—EMISSION STANDARDS FOR NMHC, CO, AND NO_X FROM LIGHT-DUTY TRUCKS OF UP TO 6,000 LBS. GVWR AND LIGHT-DUTY VEHICLES

Vehicle type	Column A (5 yrs/50,000 mi)			Column B (10 yrs/100,000 mi)		
	NMHC	CO	NO_x	NMHC	CO	NO_x
LDT's (0-3,750 lbs. LVW) and light-duty vehicles	0.25	3.4	0.4*	0.31	4.2	0.6*
LDT's (3,750-5,750 lbs. LVW)	0.32	4.4	0.7**	0.40	5.5	0.97

Standards are expressed in grams per mile (gpm).

For standards under column A, for purposes of certification under section 206, the applicable useful life shall be 5 years or 50,000 miles (or the equivalent), whichever first occurs.

For standards under Column B, for purposes of certification under section 206, the applicable useful life shall be 10 years or 100,000 miles (or equivalent), whichever first occurs.

*In the case of diesel-fueled LDT's (0-3,750 lvw) and light-duty vehicles, before the model year 2004, in lieu of the 0.4 and 0.6 standards for NO_X, the applicable standards for NO_X shall be 1.0 gpm for a useful life of 5 years or 50,000 miles (or equivalent), whichever first occurs, and 1.25 gpm for a useful life of 10 years or 100,000 miles (or equivalent) whichever first occurs.

**This standard does not apply to diesel-feuled LDT's (3,750-5,750 lbs. LVW).

TABLE H—EMISSION STANDARDS FOR NMHC AND CO FROM GASOLINE AND DIESEL FUELED LIGHT-DUTY TRUCKS OF MORE THAN 6,000 LBS. GVWR

LDT Test weight	Column A (5 yrs/50,000 mi)			Column B (11 yrs/120,000 mi)			
	NMHC	CO	NO_x	NMHC	CO	NO_x	PM
3,750-5,750 lbs. TW	0.32	4.4	0.7*	0.46	6.4	0.98	0.10
Over 5,750 lbs. TW	0.39	5.0	1.1*	0.56	7.3	1.53	0.12

Standards are expressed in grams per mile (GPM).

For standards under column A, for purposes of certification under section 206, the applicable useful life shall be 5 years or 50,000 miles (or equivalent) whichever first occurs.

For standards under column B, for purposes of certification under section 206, the applicable useful life shall be 11 years or 120,000 miles (or equivalent), whichever first occurs.

*Not applicable to diesel-fueled LDT's.

IMPLEMENTATION SCHEDULE FOR PM STANDARDS

Model year	Light-duty vehicles	LDTs
after 1996	100%*	100%*

* Percentages in the table refer to a percentage of each manufacturer'sales volume.

[§202(g) added by PL 101–549]

(h) Light-Duty Trucks of More Than 6,000 lbs. GVWR; Standards for Model Years After 1995.— Effective with respect to the model year 1996 and thereafter, the regulations under subsection (a) applicable to emissions of nonmethane hydrocarbons (NMHC), carbon monoxide (CO), oxides of nitrogen (NO_x), and particulate matter (PM) from light-duty trucks (LDTs) of more than 6,000 lbs. gross vehicle weight rating (GVWR) shall contain standards which provide that emissions from a specified percentage of each manufacturer's sales volume of such trucks shall comply with the levels specified in table H.

[Editor's Note: Table H listed on previous page]..

The specified percentage shall be 50 percent in model year 1996 and 100 percent thereafter.

[§202(h) added by PL 101–549]

(i) Phase II Study for Certain Light- Duty Vehicles and Light-Duty Trucks.—

(1) The Administrator, with the participation of the Office of Technology Assessment, shall study whether or not further reductions in emissions from light-duty vehicles and light-duty trucks should be required pursuant to this title. The study shall consider whether to establish with respect to model years commencing after January 1, 2003, the standards and useful life period for gasoline and diesel-fueled light-duty vehicles and light-duty trucks with a loaded vehicle weight (LVW) of 3,750 lbs. or less specified in the following table:

TABLE 3—PENDING EMISSION STANDARDS FOR GASOLINE AND DIESEL FUELED LIGHT-DUTY VEHICLES AND LIGHT-DUTY TRUCKS 3,750 LBS. LVW OR LESS

Pollutant	Emission level*
NMHC	0.125 GPM
NO_x	0.2 GPM
CO	1.7 GPM

* Emission levels are expressed in grams per mile (GPM). For vehicles and engines subject to this subsection for purposes of section 202(d) and any reference thereto, the useful life of such vehicles and engines shall be a period of 10 years or 100,000 miles (or the equivalent), whichever first occurs.

Such study shall also consider other standards and useful life periods which are more stringent or less stringent than those set forth in table 3 (but more stringent than those referred to in subsections (g) and (h)).

(2) (A) As part of the study under paragraph (1), the Administrator shall examine the need for further reductions in emissions in order to attain or maintain the national ambient air quality standards, taking into consideration the waiver provisions of section 209(b) . As part of such study, the Administrator shall also examine—

(i) the availability of technology (including the costs thereof), in the case of light-duty vehicles and light-duty trucks with a loaded vehicle weight (LVW) of 3,750 lbs. or less, for meeting more stringent emission standards than those provided in subsections (g) and (h) for model years commencing not earlier than after January 1, 2003, and not later than model year 2006, including the lead time and safety and energy impacts of meeting more stringent emission standards; and

(ii) the need for, and cost effectiveness of, obtaining further reductions in emissions from such light-duty vehicles and light-duty trucks, taking into consideration alternative means of attaining or maintaining the national primary ambient air quality standards pursuant to State implementation plans and other requirements of this Act, including their feasibility and cost effectiveness.

(B) The Administrator shall submit a report to Congress no later than June 1, 1997, containing the results of the study under this subsection, including the results of the examination conducted under subparagraph (A). Before submittal of such report the Administrator shall provide a reasonable opportunity for public comment and shall include a summary of such comments in the report to Congress.

(3) (A) Based on the study under paragraph (1) the Administrator shall determine, by rule, within 3 calendar years after the report is submitted to Congress, but not later than December 31, 1999, whether—

(i) there is a need for further reductions in emissions as provided in paragraph (2)(A);

(ii) the technology for meeting more stringent emission standards will be available, as provided in paragraph (2)(A)(i), in the case of light-duty vehicles and light- duty trucks with a loaded vehicle weight (LVW) of 3,750 lbs. or less, for model years commencing not earlier than January 1, 2003, and not later than model year 2006, considering the factors listed in paragraph (2)(A)(i); and

(iii) obtaining further reductions in emissions from such vehicles will be needed and cost effective, taking into consideration alternatives as provided in paragraph (2)(A)(ii). The rulemaking under this paragraph shall commence within 3 months after submission of the report to Congress under paragraph (2)(B).

(B) If the Administrator determines under subparagraph (A) that—

(i) there is no need for further reductions in emissions as provided in paragraph (2)(A);

(ii) the technology for meeting more stringent emission standards will not be available as provided in paragraph (2)(A)(i), in the case of light-duty vehicles and light-duty trucks with a loaded vehicle weight (LVW) of 3,750 lbs. or less, for model years commencing not earlier than January 1, 2003, and not later than model year 2006, considering the factors listed in paragraph (2)(A)(i); or

(iii) obtaining further reductions in emissions from such vehicles will not be needed or cost effective, taking into consideration alternatives as provided in paragraph (2)(A)(ii), the Administrator shall not promulgate more stringent standards than those in effect pursuant to subsections (g) and (h). Nothing in this paragraph shall prohibit the Administrator from exercising the Administrator's authority under subsection (a) to promulgate more stringent standards for light- duty vehicles and light-duty trucks with a loaded vehicle weight (LVW) of 3,750 lbs. or less at any other time thereafter in accordance with subsection (a).

(C) If the Administrator determines under subparagraph (A) that—

(i) there is a need for further reductions in emissions as provided in paragraph (2)(A);

(ii) the technology for meeting more stringent emission standards will be available, as provided in paragraph (2)(A)(i), in the case of light-duty vehicles and light- duty trucks with a loaded vehicle weight (LVW) of 3,750 lbs. or less, for model years commencing not earlier than January 1, 2003, and not later than model year 2006, considering the factors listed in paragraph (2)(A)(i); and

(iii) obtaining further reductions in emissions from such vehicles will be needed and cost effective, taking into consideration alternatives as provided in paragraph (2)(A)(ii), the Administrator shall either promulgate the standards (and useful life periods) set forth in Table 3 in paragraph (1) or promulgate alternative standards (and useful life periods) which are more stringent than those referred to in subsections (g) and (h). Any such standards (or useful life periods) promulgated by the Administrator shall take effect with respect to any such vehicles or engines no earlier than the model year 2003 but not later than model year 2006, as determined by the Administrator in the rule.

(D) Nothing in this paragraph shall be construed by the Administrator or by a court as a presumption that any standards (or useful life period) set forth in Table 3 shall be promulgated in the rule-making required under this paragraph. The action required of the Administrator in accordance with this paragraph shall be treated as a nondiscretionary duty for purposes of section 304(a)(2) (relating to citizen suits).

(E) Unless the Administrator determines not to promulgate more stringent standards as provided in subparagraph (B) or to postpone the effective date of standards referred to in Table 3 in paragraph (1) or to establish alternative standards as provided in subparagraph (C), effective with respect to model years commencing after January 1, 2003, the regulations under subsection (a) applicable to emissions of nonmethane hydrocarbons (NMHC), oxides of nitrogen (NO_x), and carbon monoxide (CO) from motor vehicles and motor vehicle engines in the classes specified in Table 3 in paragraph (1) above shall contain standards which provide that emissions may not exceed the pending emission levels specified in Table 3 in paragraph (1).

[§202(i) added by PL 101–549]

Carbon Monoxide Emissions At Cold Temperatures

(j) Cold CO Standard.—

(1) Phase I.—Not later than 12 months after the date of the enactment of the Clean Air Act Amendments of 1990, the Administrator shall promulgate regulations under subsection (a) of this section applicable to emissions of carbon

monoxide from 1994 and later model year light- duty vehicles and light-duty trucks when operated at 20 degrees Fahrenheit. The regulations shall contain standards which provide that emissions of carbon monoxide from a manufacturer's vehicles when operated at 20 degrees Fahrenheit may not exceed, in the case of light-duty vehicles, 10.0 grams per mile, and in the case of light-duty trucks, and a level comparable in stringency to the standard applicable to light-duty vehicles. The standards shall take effect after model year 1993 according to a phase-in schedule which requires a percentage of each manufacturer's sales volume of light-duty vehicles and light-duty trucks to comply with applicable standards after model year 1993. The percentage shall be as specified in the following table:

Phase-In Schedule for Cold Start Standards

Model Year	Percentage
1994	40
1995	80
1996 and after	100

(2) Phase II.—

(A) Not later than June 1, 1997, the Administrator shall complete a study assessing the need for further reductions in emissions of carbon monoxide and the maximum reductions in such emissions achievable from model year 2001 and later model year light-duty vehicles and light-duty trucks when operated at 20 degrees Fahrenheit.

(B) (i) If as of June 1, 1997, 6 or more nonattainment areas have a carbon monoxide design value of 9.5 ppm or greater, the regulations under subsection (a)(1) of this section applicable to emissions of carbon monoxide from model year 2002 and later model year light-duty vehicles and light-duty trucks shall contain standards which provide that emissions of carbon monoxide from such vehicles and trucks when operated at 20 degrees Fahrenheit may not exceed 3.4 grams per mile (gpm) in the case of light-duty vehicles and 4.4 grams per mile (gpm) in the case of light- duty trucks up to 6,000 GVWR and a level comparable in stringency in the case of light-duty trucks 6,000 GVWR and above.

(ii) In determining for purposes of this subparagraph whether 6 or more nonattainment areas have a carbon monoxide design value of 9.5 ppm or greater, the Administrator shall exclude the areas of Steubenville, Ohio, and Oshkosh, Wisconsin.

(3) Useful-Life for Phase I and Phase II Standards.—In the case of the standards referred to in paragraphs (1) and (2), for purposes of certification under section 206 and in-use compliance under section 207 , the applicable useful life period shall be 5 years or 50,000 miles, whichever first occurs, except that the Administrator may extend such useful life period (for purposes of section 206 , or section 207 , or both) if he determines that it is feasible for vehicles and engines subject to such standards to meet such standards for a longer useful life. If the Administrator extends such useful life period, the Administrator may make an appropriate adjustment of applicable standards for such extended useful life. No such extend useful life shall extend beyond the useful life period provided in regulations under subsection (d).

(4) Heavy-duty Vehicles and Engines.—The Administrator may also promulgate regulations under subsection (a)(1) applicable to emissions of carbon monoxide from heavy-duty vehicles and engines when operated at cold temperatures.

[§202(j) added by PL 101–549]

Evaporative Emissions

(k) Control of Evaporative Emissions.—The Administrator shall promulgate (and from time to time revise) regulations applicable to evaporative emissions of hydrocarbons from all gasoline fueled motor vehicles—

(1) during operation; and

(2) over 2 or more days of nonuse; under ozone-prone summertime conditions (as determined by regulations of the Administrator). The regulations shall take effect as expeditiously as possible and shall require the greatest degree of emission reduction achievable by means reasonably expected to be available for production during any model year to which the regulations apply, giving appropriate consideration to fuel volatility, and to cost, energy, and safety factors associated with the application of the appropriate technology. The Administrator shall commence a rulemaking under this subsection within 12 months after the date of the enactment of the Clean Air Act Amendments of 1990. If final regulations are not promulgated under this subsection within 18 months after the date of the enactment of the Clean Air Act Amendments of 1990, the Administrator shall submit a statement to the

Congress containing an explanation of the reasons for the delay and a date certain for promulgation of such final regulations in accordance with this Act. Such date certain shall not be later than 15 months after the expiration of such 18 months deadline.

[§202(k) added by PL 10–549]

Mobile Source-Related Air Toxics

(l) Mobile Source-Related Air Toxics.—

(1) Study.—Not later than 18 months after the date of the enactment of the Clean Air Act Amendments of 1990, the Administrator shall complete a study of the need for, and feasibility of, controlling emissions of toxic air pollutants which are unregulated under this Act and associated with motor vehicles and motor vehicle fuels, and the need for, and feasibility of, controlling such emissions and the means and measures for such controls. The study shall focus on those categories of emissions that pose the greatest risk to human health or about which significant uncertainties remain, including emissions of benzene, formaldehyde, and 1, 3 butadiene. The proposed report shall be available for public review and comment and shall include a summary of all comments.

(2) Standards.—Within 54 months after the date of the enactment of the Clean Air Act Amendments of 1990, the Administrator shall, based on the study under paragraph (1), promulgate (and from time to time revise) regulations under subsection (a)(1) or section 211(c)(1) containing reasonable requirements to control hazardous air pollutants from motor vehicles and motor vehicle fuels. The regulations shall contain standards for such fuels or vehicles, or both, which the Administrator determines reflect the greatest degree of emission reduction achievable through the application of technology which will be available, taking into consideration the standards established under subsection (a), the availability and costs of the technology, and noise, energy, and safety factors, and lead time. Such regulations shall not be inconsistent with standards under section 202(a) . The regulations shall, at a minimum, apply to emissions of benzene and formaldehyde.

[§202(l) added by PL 101–549]

Emission Control Diagnostics Systems and Buses

(m) Emissions Control Diagnostics.—

(1) Regulations.—Within 18 months after the enactment of the Clean Air Act Amendments of 1990, the Administrator shall promulgate regulations under subsection (a) requiring manufacturers to install on all new light duty vehicles and light duty trucks diagnostics systems capable of—

(A) accurately identifying for the vehicle's useful life as established under this section, emission-related systems deterioration or malfunction, including, at a minimum, the catalytic converter and oxygen sensor, which could cause or result in failure of the vehicles to comply with emission standards established under this section,

(B) alerting the vehicle's owner or operator to the likely need for emission-related components or systems maintenance or repair,

(C) storing and retrieving fault codes specified by the Administrator, and

(D) providing access to stored information in a manner specified by the Administrator. The Administrator may, in the Administrator's discretion, promulgate regulations requiring manufacturers to install such onboard diagnostic systems on heavy-duty vehicles and engines.

(2) Effective Date.—The regulations required under paragraph (1) of this subsection shall take effect in model year 1994, except that the Administrator may waive the application of such regulations for model year 1994 or 1995 (or both) with respect to any class or category of motor vehicles if the Administrator determines that it would be infeasible to apply the regulations to that class or category in such model year or years, consistent with corresponding regulations or policies adopted by the California Air Resources Board for such systems.

(3) State Inspection.—The Administrator shall by regulation require States that have implementation plans containing motor vehicle inspection and maintenance programs to amend their plans within 2 years after promulgation of such regulations to provide for inspection of onboard diagnostics systems (as prescribed by regulations under paragraph (1) of this subsection) and for the maintenance or repair of malfunctions or system deterioration identified by or affecting such diagnostics systems. Such regulations shall not be inconsistent with the provisions for warranties promulgated under section 207(a) and (b) .

(4) Specific Requirements.—In promulgating regulations under this subsection, the Administrator shall require—

(A) that any connectors through which the emission control diagnostics system is accessed for inspection, diagnosis, service, or repair shall be standard and uniform on all motor vehicles and motor vehicle engines;

(B) that access to the emission control diagnostics system through such connectors shall be unrestricted and shall not require any access code or any device which is only available from a vehicle manufacturer; and

(C) that the output of the data from the emission control diagnostics system through such connectors shall be usable without the need for any unique decoding information or device.

(5) Information Availability.—The Administrator, by regulation, shall require (subject to the provisions of section 208(c) regarding the protection of methods or processes entitled to protection as trade secrets) manufacturers to provide promptly to any person engaged in the repairing or servicing of motor vehicles or motor vehicle engines, and the Administrator for use by any such persons, with any and all information needed to make use of the emission control diagnostics system prescribed under this subsection and such other information including instructions for making emission related diagnosis and repairs. No such information may be withheld under section 208(c) if that information is provided (directly or indirectly) by the manufacturer to franchised dealers or other persons engaged in the repair, diagnosing, or servicing of motor vehicles or motor vehicle engines. Such information shall also be available to the Administrator, subject to section 208(c) , in carrying out the Administrator's responsibilities under this section.

[§202(m) added by PL 101–549]

§7522. Prohibited Acts [Sec. 203]

(a) The following acts and the causing thereof are prohibited—

(1) in the case of a manufacturer of new motor vehicles or new motor vehicles engines for distribution in commerce, the sale, or the offering for sale, or the introduction, or delivery for introduction, into commerce, or (in the case of any person, except as provided by regulation of the Administrator), the importation into the United States, of any new motor vehicle or new motor vehicle engine, manufactured after the effective date of regulations under this part which are applicable to such vehicle or engine unless such vehicle or engine is covered by a certificate of conformity issued (and in effect) under regulations prescribed under this part or part C in the case of clean-fuel vehicles (except as provided in subsection (b)).

[§203(a)(1) amended by PL 101–549]

(2) (A) for any person to fail or refuse to permit access to or copying of records or to fail to make reports to provide information required under section 208 ;

(B) for any person to fail or refuse to permit entry, testing or inspection authorized under section 206(c) or section 208 ;

(C) for any person to fail or refuse to perform tests, or have tests performed as required under section 208 ;

(D) for any manufacturer to fail to make information available as provided by regulation under section 202(m)(5) ;

[§203(a)(2) revised by PL 101–549]

(3) (A) for any person to remove or render inoperative any device or element of design installed on or in a motor vehicle or motor vehicle engine in compliance with regulations under this title prior to its sale and delivery to the ultimate purchaser, or for any person knowingly to remove or render inoperative any such device or element of design after such sale and delivery to the ultimate purchaser; or

(B) for any person to manufacture or sell, or offer to sell, or install, any part or component intended for use with, or as part of, any motor vehicle or motor vehicle engine, where a principal effect of the part or component is to bypass, defeat, or render inoperative any device or element of design installed on or in a motor vehicle or motor vehicle engine in compliance with regulations under this title, and where the person knows or should know that such part or component is being offered for sale or installed for such use or put to such use; or

[§203(a)(3) amended by PL 101–549]

(4) For any manufacturer of a new motor vehicle or new motor vehicle engine subject to standards prescribed under section 202 or part C—

(A) to sell or lease any such vehicle or engine unless such manufacturer has complied with (i) the requirements of section 207(a) and (b) with respect to such vehicle or engine, and unless a label or tag is affixed to such vehicle or engine in accordance with section 207(c)(3), or (ii) the corresponding requirements of part C in the case of clean fuel vehicles unless the manufacturer has complied with the corresponding requirements of part C,

(B) to fail or refuse to comply with the requirements of section 207(c) or (e) or the corresponding requirements of part C in the case of clean fuel vehicles.

Warranties

(C) except as provided in subsection (c)(3) of section 207 and the corresponding requirements of part C in the case of clean fuel vehicles, to provide directly or indirectly in any communication to the ultimate purchaser or any subsequent purchaser that the coverage of any warranty under this Act is conditioned upon use of any part, component, or system manufactured by such manufacturer or any person acting for such manufacturer or under his control, or conditioned upon service performed by any such person, or

(D) to fail or refuse to comply with the terms and conditions of the warranty under section 207 (a) or (b) or the corresponding requirements of part C in the case of clean fuel vehicles with respect to any vehicle.

[§203(a)(4) amended by PL 101–549]

High Altitude Performance Adjustments

(5) for any person to violate section 218, 219, or part C of this title or any regulations under section 218, 219, or part C.

[§203(a)(5) added by PL 101–549]

No action with respect to any element of design referred to in paragraph (3) (including any adjustment or alteration of such element) shall be treated as a prohibited act under such paragraph (3) if such action is in accordance with section 215. Nothing in paragraph (3) shall be construed to require the use of manufacturer parts in maintaining or repairing any motor vehicle or motor vehicle engine. For the purpose of the preceding sentence, the term 'manufacturer parts' means, with respect to a motor vehicle engine, parts produced or sold by the manufacturer of the motor vehicle or motor vehicle engine.

No action with respect to any device or element of design referred to in paragraph (3) shall be treated as a prohibited act under that paragraph if (i) the action is for the purpose of repair or replacement of the device or element, or is a necessary and temporary procedure to repair or replace any other item and the device or element is replaced upon completion of the procedure, and (ii) such action thereafter results in the proper functioning of the device or element referred to in paragraph (3). No action with respect to any device or element of design referred to in paragraph (3) shall be treated as a prohibited act under that paragraph if the action is for the purpose of a conversion of a motor vehicle for use of a clean alternative fuel (as defined in this title) and if such vehicle complies with the applicable standard under section 202 when operating on such fuel, and if in the case of a clean alternative fuel vehicle (as defined by rule by the Administrator), the device or element is replaced upon completion of the conversion procedure and such action results in proper functioning of the device or element when the motor vehicle operates on conventional fuel.

(b) (1) The Administrator may exempt any new motor vehicle or new motor vehicle engine, from subsection (a) upon such terms and conditions as he may find necessary for the purpose of research, investigations, studies, demonstrations, or training, or for reasons of national security.

(2) A new motor vehicle or new motor vehicle engine offered for importation or imported by any person in violation of subsection (a) shall be refused admission into the United States, but the Secretary of the Treasury and the Administrator may, by joint regulation, provide for deferring final determination as to admission and authorizing the delivery of such a motor vehicle or engine offered for import to the owner or consignee thereof upon such terms and conditions (including the furnishing of a bond) as may appear to them appropriate to insure that any such motor vehicle or engine will be brought into conformity with the standards, requirements, and limitations applicable to it under this title. The Secretary of the Treasury shall, if a motor vehicle or engine is finally refused admission under this paragraph, cause disposition thereof in accordance with the customs laws unless it is exported, under regulations prescribed by such Secretary, within ninety days of the date of notice of such refusal or such additional time as may be permitted pursuant to such regulations, except that disposition in accordance with the customs laws may not be made in such manner as may result, directly or indirectly, in the sale, to the ultimate consumer, of a new motor vehicle or new motor vehicle engine that fails to comply with applicable standards of the Administrator under this part.

(3) A new motor vehicle or new motor vehicle engine intended solely for export, and so

labeled or tagged on the outside of the container and on the vehicle or engine itself, shall be subject to the provisions of subsection (a), except that if the country which is to receive such vehicle or engine has emission standards which differ from the standards prescribed under section 202 , then such vehicle or engine shall comply with the standards of such country which is to receive such vehicle or engine.

[§203(b)(3) amended by PL 95–95]

(c) [Deleted]

[§203(c) deleted by PL 101–549]

[Editor's Note: PL 95–95, the Clean Air Act Amendments of 1977, Section 203, provides: §203 Study And Report Of Fuel Consumption. Following each motor vehicle model year, the Administrator of the Environmental Protection Agency shall report to the Congress respecting the motor vehicle fuel consumption associated with the standards applicable for the immediately preceding model year.]

§7523. Injunction Proceedings [Sec. 204]

(a) The district courts of the United States shall have jurisdiction to restrain violations of section 203(a) .

[§204(a) amended by PL 95–95]

(b) Actions to restrain such violations shall be brought by and in the name of the United States. In any such action, subpoenas for witnesses who are required to attend a district court in any district may run into another district.

§7524. Civil Penalties [Sec. 205]

[§205 revised by PL 101–549]

(a) Violations.—Any person who violates sections 203(a)(1), 203(a)(4), or 203(a)(5) or any manufacturer or dealer who violates section 203(a)(3)(A) shall be subject to a civil penalty of not more than $25,000. Any person other than a manufacture or dealer who violates section 203(a)(3)(A) or any person who violates section 203(a)(3)(B) shall be subject to a civil penalty of not more than $2,500. Any such violation with respect to paragraph (1), (3)(A), or (4) of section 203(a) shall constitute a separate offense with respect to each motor vehicle or motor vehicle engine. Any such violation with respect to section 203(a)(3)(B) shall constitute a separate offense with respect to each part or component. Any person who violates section 203(a)(2) shall be subject to a civil penalty of not more than $25,000 per day of violation.

(b) Civil Actions.—The Administrator may commence a civil action to assess and recover any civil penalty under subsection (a) of this section, section 211(d) , or section 213(d) . Any action under this subsection may be brought in the district court of the United States for the district in which the violation is alleged to have occurred or in which the defendant resides or has the Administrator's principal place of business, and the court shall have jurisdiction to assess a civil penalty. In determining the amount of any civil penalty to be assessed under this subsection, the court shall take into account the gravity of the violation, the economic benefit or savings (if any) resulting from the violation, the size of the violator's business, the violator's history of compliance with this title, action taken to remedy the violation, the effect of the penalty on the violator's ability to continue in business, and such other matters as justice may require. In any such action, subpoenas for witnesses who are required to attend a district court in any district may run into any other district.

(c) Administrative Assessment of Certain Penalties.—

(1) Administrative Penalty Authority.—In lieu of commencing a civil action under subsection (b), the Administrator may assess any civil penalty prescribed in subsection (a) of this section, section 211(d) , or section 213(d) , except that the maximum amount of penalty sought against each violator in a penalty assessment proceeding shall not exceed $200,000, unless the Administrator and the Attorney General jointly determine that a matter involving a larger penalty amount is appropriate for administrative penalty assessment. Any such determination by the Administrator and the Attorney General shall not be subject to judicial review. Assessment of a civil penalty under this subsection shall be by an order made on the record after opportunity for a hearing in accordance with sections 554 and 556 of title 5 of the United States Code. The Administrator shall issue reasonable rules for discovery and other procedures for hearings under this paragraph. Before issuing such an order, the Administrator shall give written notice to the person to be assessed an administrative penalty of the Administrator's proposal to issue such order and provide such person an opportunity to request such a hearing on the order, within 30 days of the date the notice is received by such person. The Administrator may compromise, or remit, with or without conditions, any administrative penalty which may be imposed under this section.

(2) Determining Amount.—In determining the amount of any civil penalty assessed under

this subsection, the Administrator shall take into account the gravity of the violation, the economic benefit or savings (if any) resulting from the violation, the size of the violator's business, the violator's history of compliance with this title, action taken to remedy the violation, the effect of the penalty on the violator's ability to continue in business, and such other matters as justice may require.

(3) Effect of Administrator's Action.—

(A) Action by the Administrator under this subsection shall not affect or limit the Administrator's authority to enforce any provision of this Act, except that any violation,

(i) with respect to which the Administrator has commenced and is diligently prosecuting an action under this subsection, or

(ii) for which the Administrator has issued a final order not subject to further judicial review and the violator has paid a penalty assessment under this subsection, shall not be the subject of civil penalty action under subsection (b).

(B) No action by the Administrator under this subsection shall affect any person's obligation to comply with any section of this Act.

(4) Finality of Order.—An order issued under this subsection shall become final 30 days after its issuance unless a petition for judicial review is filed under paragraph (5).

(5) Judicial Review.—Any person against whom a civil penalty is assessed in accordance with this subsection may seek review of the assessment in the United States District Court for the District of Columbia, or for the district in which the violation is alleged to have occurred, in which such person resides, or where such person's principal place of business is located, within the 30-day period beginning on the date a civil penalty order is issued. Such person shall simultaneously send a copy of the filing by certified mail to the Administrator and the Attorney General. The Administrator shall file in the court a certified copy, or certified index, as appropriate, of the record on which the order was issued within 30 days. The court shall not set aside or remand any order issued in accordance with the requirements of this subsection unless there is not substantial evidence in the record, taken as a whole, to support the finding of a violation or unless the Administrator's assessment of the penalty constitutes an abuse of discretion, and the court shall not impose additional civil penalties unless the Administrator's assessment of the penalty constitutes an abuse of discretion. In any proceedings, the United States may seek to recover civil penalties assessed under this section.

(6) Collection.—If any person fails to pay an assessment of a civil penalty imposed by the Administrator as provided in this subsection—

(A) after the order making the assessment has become final, or

(B) after a court in an action brought under paragraph (5) had entered a final judgment in favor of the Administrator, the Administrator shall request the Attorney General to bring a civil action in an appropriate district court to recover the amount assessed (plus interest at rates established pursuant to section 6621(a)(2) of the Internal Revenue Code of 1986 from the date of the final order or the date of the final judgment, as the case may be). In such an action, the validity, amount, and appropriateness of the penalty shall not be subject to review. Any person who fails to pay on a timely basis the amount of an assessment of a civil penalty as described in the first sentence of this paragraph shall be required to pay, in addition to that amount and interest, the United States' enforcement expenses, including attorneys fees and costs for collection proceedings, and a quarterly nonpayment penalty for each quarter during which such failure to pay persists. The nonpayment penalty shall be in an amount equal to 10 percent of the aggregate amount of that person's penalties and nonpayment penalties which are unpaid as of the beginning of such quarter.

[Editor's Note: §711 of the Clean Air Act Amendments of 1990 details savings provisions and effective dates.]

[Sec. 711]

(a) Savings Provisions.—Except as otherwise expressly provided in this Act, no suit, action, or other proceeding lawfully commenced by the Administrator or any other officer or employee of the United States in his official capacity or in relation to the discharge of his official duties under the Clean Air Act, as in effect immediately prior to the date of enactment of this Act, shall abate by reason of the taking effect of the amendments made by this Act.

(b) Effective Dates.—(1) Except as otherwise expressly provided, the amendments made by this Act shall be effective on the date of enactment of this Act.

(2) The Administrator's authority to assess civil penalties under section 205(c) of the Clean Air Act, as amended by this Act, shall apply to violations that

occur or continue on or after the date of enactment of this Act. Civil penalties for violations that occur prior to such date and do not continue after such date shall be assessed in accordance with the provisions of the Clean Air Act in effect immediately prior to the date of enactment of this Act.

(3) The civil penalties prescribed under sections 205(a) and 211(d)(1) of the Clean Air Act, as amended by this Act, shall apply to violations that occur on or after the date of enactment of this Act. Violations that occur prior to such date shall be subject to the civil penalty provisions prescribed in sections 205(a) and 211(d) of the Clean Air Act in effect immediately prior to the enactment of this Act. The injunctive authority prescribed under section 211(d)(2) of the Clean Air Act, as amended by this Act, shall apply to violations that occur or continue on or after the date of enactment of this Act.

(4) For purposes of paragraphs (2) and (3), where the date of a violation cannot be determined it will be assumed to be the date on which the violation is discovered.

§7525. Motor Vehicle and Motor Vehicle Engine Compliance Testing and Certification

[Sec. 206]

(a) (1) The Administrator shall test, or require to be tested in such manner as he deems appropriate, any new motor vehicle or new motor vehicle engine submitted by a manufacturer to determine whether such vehicle or engine conforms with the regulations prescribed under section 202 of this Act. If such vehicle or engine conforms to such regulations, the Administrator shall issue a certificate of conformity upon such terms, and for such period (not in excess of one year), as he may prescribe.

Testing By Small Manufacturers

In case of any original equipment manufacturer (as defined by the Administrator in regulations promulgated before the date of the enactment of the Clean Air Act Amendments of 1990) of vehicles or vehicle engines whose projected sales in the United States for any model year (as determined by the Administrator) will not exceed 300, the Administrator shall not require, for purposes of determining compliance with regulations under section 202 for the useful life of the vehicle or engine, operation of any vehicle or engine manufactured during such model year for more than 5,000 miles or 160 hours, respectively, unless the Administrator, by regulation, prescribes otherwise. The Administrator shall apply any adjustment factors that the Administrator deems appropriate to assure that each vehicle or engine will comply during its useful life (as determined under section 202(d)) with the regulations prescribed under section 202 .

[§206(a)(1) revised by PL 101–549]

(2) The Administrator shall test any emission control system incorporated in a motor vehicle or motor vehicle engine submitted to him by any person, in order to determine whether such system enables such vehicle or engine to conform to the standards required to be prescribed under section 202(b) of this Act. If the Administrator finds on the basis of such tests that such vehicle or engine conforms to such standards, the Administrator shall issue a verification of compliance with emission standards for such system when incorporated in vehicles of a class of which the tested vehicle is representative. He shall inform manufacturers and the National Academy of Sciences, and make available to the public, the results of such tests. Tests under this paragraph shall be conducted under such terms and conditions (including requirements for preliminary testing by qualified independent laboratories) as the Administrator may prescribe by regulations.

(3) (A) A Certificate of conformity may be issued under this section only if the Administrator determines that the manufacturer (or in the case of a vehicle or engine for import, any person) has established to the satisfaction of the Administrator that any emission control device, system, or element of design installed on, or incorporated in, such vehicle or engine conforms to applicable requirements of section 202(a)(4) .

(B) The Administrator may conduct such tests and may require the manufacturer (or any such person) to conduct such tests and provide such information as is necessary to carry out subparagraph (A) of this paragraph. Such requirements shall include a requirement for prompt reporting of the emission of any unregulated pollutant from a system, device, or element of design if such pollutant was not emitted, or was emitted in significantly lesser amounts, from the vehicle or engine without use of the system, device, or element of design.

[§206(a)(3) added by PL 95–95]

(4) (A) Not later than 12 months after the date of the enactment of the Clean Air Act Amendments of 1990, the Administrator shall revise the regulations promulgated under this subsection to add test procedures capable of determining whether model year 1994 and later model year light-duty vehicles

and light-duty trucks, when properly maintained and used, will pass the inspection methods and procedures established under section 207(b) for that model year, under conditions reasonably likely to be encountered in the conduct of inspection and maintenance programs, but which those programs cannot reasonably influence or control. The conditions shall include fuel characteristics, ambient temperature, and short (30 minutes or less) waiting periods before tests are conducted. The Administrator shall not grant a certificate of conformity under this subsection for any 1994 or later model year vehicle or engine that the Administrator concludes cannot pass the test procedures established under this paragraph.

(B) From time to time, the Administrator may revise the regulations promulgated under subparagraph (A), as the Administrator deems appropriate.

[§206(a)(4) added by PL 101–549]

(b) (1) In order to determine whether new motor vehicles or new motor vehicle engines being manufactured by a manufacturer do in fact conform with the regulations with respect to which the certificate of conformity was issued, the Administrator is authorized to test such vehicles or engines. Such tests may be conducted by the Administrator directly or, in accordance with conditions specified by the Administrator, by the manufacturer.

(2) (A) (i) If, based on tests conducted under paragraph (1) on a sample of new vehicles or engines covered by a certificate of conformity, the Administrator determines that all or part of the vehicles or engines so covered do not conform with the regulations with respect to which the certificate of conformity was issued and with the requirements of section 202(a)(4) , he may suspend or revoke such certificate in whole or in part, and shall so notify the manufacturer. Such suspension or revocation shall apply in the case of any new motor vehicles or new motor vehicle engines manufactured after the date of such notification (or manufactured before such date if still in the hands of the manufacturer), and shall apply until such time as the Administrator finds that vehicles and engines manufactured by the manufacturer do conform to such regulations and requirements. If, during any period of suspension or revocation, the Administrator finds that a vehicle or engine actually conforms to such regulations and requirements, he shall issue a certificate of conformity applicable to such vehicle or engine.

(ii) If, based on tests conducted under paragraph (1) on any new vehicle or engine, the Administrator determines that such vehicle or engine does not conform with such regulations and requirements, he may suspend or revoke such certificate insofar as it applies to such vehicle or engine until such time as he finds such vehicle or engine actually so conforms with such regulations and requirements, and he shall so notify the manufacturer.

[§206(b)(2)(A) amended by PL 95–95]

(B) (i) At the request of any manufacturer the Administrator shall grant such manufacturer a hearing as to whether the tests have been properly conducted or any sampling methods have been properly applied, and make a determination on the record with respect to any suspension or revocation under subparagraph (A); but suspension or revocation under subparagraph (A) shall not be stayed by reason of such hearing.

(ii) In any case of actual controversy as to the validity of any determination under clause (i), the manufacturer may at any time prior to the 60th day after such determination is made file a petition with the United States court of appeals for the circuit wherein such manufacturer resides or has his principal place of business for a judicial review of such determination. A copy of the petition shall be forthwith transmitted by the clerk of the court to the Administrator or other officer designated by him for that purpose. The Administrator thereupon shall file in the court record of the proceedings on which the Administrator based his determination, as provided in section 2112 of title 28 of the United States Code.

(iii) If the petitioner applies to the court for leave to adduce additional evidence, and shows to the satisfaction of the court that such additional evidence is material and that there were reasonable grounds for the failure to adduce such evidence in the proceeding before the Administrator, the court may order such additional evidence (and evidence in rebuttal thereof) to be taken before the Administrator, in such manner and upon such terms and conditions as the court may deem proper. The Administrator may modify his findings as to the facts, or make new findings, by reason of the additional evidence so taken and he shall file such modified or new findings, and his recommendation, if any, for the modification or setting aside of his original determination, with the return of such additional evidence.

(iv) Upon the filing of the petition referred to in clause (ii), court shall have jurisdiction to review the order in accordance with chapter 7 of title 5, United States Code, and to grant appropriate relief as provided in such chapter.

(c) For purposes of enforcement of this section, officers or employees duly designated by the Administrator, upon presenting appropriate credentials to the manufacturer or person in charge, are authorized (1) to enter, at reasonable times, any plan or other establishment of such manufacturer, for the purpose of conducting tests of vehicles or engines in the hands of the manufacturer, or, (2) to inspect at reasonable times, records, files, papers, processes, controls, and facilities used by such manufacturer in conducting tests under regulations of the Administrator. Each such inspection shall be commenced and completed with reasonable promptness.

(d) The Administrator shall by regulation establish methods and procedures for making tests under this section.

(e) The Administrator shall make available to the public the results of his tests of any motor vehicle or motor vehicle engine submitted by a manufacturer under subsection (a) as promptly as possible after the enactment of the Clean Air Act Amendments of 1970 and at the beginning of each model year which begins thereafter. Such results shall be described in such nontechnical manner as will reasonably disclose to prospective ultimate purchasers of new motor vehicles and new motor vehicle engines the comparative performance of the vehicle and engines tested in meeting the standards prescribed under section 202 of this Act.

[§206(e) amended by PL 101–549]

(f) All light duty vehicles and engines manufactured during or after model year 1984 and all light-duty trucks manufactured during or after model year 1995 shall comply with the requirements of section 202 of this Act regardless of the altitude at which they are sold.

[Former §206(f)(1) amended and redesignated as (f) by PL 101–549]

(2) [Deleted]

[§206(f)(2) deleted by PL 101–549]

(g) (1) In the case of any class or category of heavy-duty vehicles or engines to which a standard promulgated under section 202(a) of this Act applies, except as provided in paragraph (2), a certificate of conformity shall be issued under subsection (a) and shall not be suspended or revoked under subsection (b) for such vehicles or engines manufactured by a manufacturer notwithstanding the failure of such vehicles or engines to meet such standard if such manufacturer pays a nonconformance penalty as provided under regulations promulgated by the Administrator after notice and opportunity for public hearing. In the case of motorcycles to which such standard applies, such a certificate may be issued notwithstanding such failure if the manufacturer pays such a penalty.

(2) No certificate of conformity may be issued under paragraph (1) with respect to any class or category of vehicle or engine if the degree by which the manufacturer fails to meet any standard promulgated under section 202(a) with respect to such class or category exceeds the percentage determined under regulations promulgated by the Administrator to be practicable. Such regulations shall require such testing of vehicles or engines being produced as may be necessary to determine the percentage of the classes or categories of vehicles or engines which are not in compliance with the regulations with respect to which a certificate of conformity was issued and shall be promulgated not later than one year after the date of enactment of the Clean Air Act Amendments of 1977.

(3) The regulations promulgated under paragraph (1) shall, not later than one year after the date of enactment of the Clean Air Act Amendments of 1977, provide for nonconformance penalties in amounts determined under a formula established by the Administrator. Such penalties under such formula—

(A) may vary from pollutant-to-pollutant;

(B) may vary by class or category of vehicle or engine;

(C) shall take into account the extent to which actual emissions of any air pollutant exceed allowable emissions under the standards promulgated under section 202 ;

(D) shall be increased periodically in order to create incentives for the development of production vehicles or engines which achieve the required degree of emission reduction; and

[§206(g)(3)(D) amended by PL 95–190]

(E) shall remove any competitive disadvantage to manufacturers whose engines or vehicles achieve the required degree of emission reduction (including any such disadvantage arising from the application of paragraph (4).

(4) In any case in which a certificate of conformity has been issued under this subsection, any warranty required under section 207(b)(2) and any action under section 207(c) shall be required to be effective only for the emission levels which the Administrator determines that such certificate was issued and not for the emission levels required under the applicable standard.

(5) The authorities of section 208(a) shall apply, subject to the conditions of section 208(b) , for purposes of this subsection.

[§206(g) added by PL 95–95]

(h) Within 18 months after the enactment of the Clean Air Act Amendments of 1990, the Administrator shall review and revise as necessary the regulations under subsection (a) and (b) of this section regarding the testing of motor vehicles and motor vehicle engines to insure that vehicles are tested under circumstances which reflect the actual current driving conditions under which motor vehicles are used, including conditions relating to fuel, temperature, acceleration, and altitude.

[§206(h) added by PL 101–549]

§7541. Compliance by Vehicle and Engines in Acutal Use [Sec. 207]

[§207(a) revised by PL 95–190]

(a) (1) Effective with respect to vehicles and engines manufactured in model years beginning more than 60 days after the date of the enactment of the Clean Air Act Amendments of 1970, the manufacturer of each new motor vehicle and new motor vehicle engine shall warrant to the ultimate purchaser and each subsequent purchaser that such vehicle or engine is (A) designed, built, and equipped so as to conform at the time of sale with applicable regulations under section 202, and (B) free from defects in materials and workmanship which cause such vehicle or engine to fail to conform with applicable regulations for its useful life (as determined under section 202(d)). In the case of vehicles and engines manufactured in the model year 1995 and thereafter such warranty shall require that the vehicle or engine is free from any such defects for the warranty period provided under subsection (i).

[§207(a)(1) amended by PL 101–549]

(2) In the case of a motor vehicle part or motor vehicle engine part, the manufacturer or rebuilder of such part may certify that use of such part will not result in a failure of the vehicle or engine to comply with emission standards promulgated under section 202 . Such certification shall be made only under such regulations as may be promulgated by the Administrator to carry out the purposes of subsection (b). The Administrator shall promulgate such regulations no later than two years following the date of the enactment of this paragraph.

Cost Of Certain Emission Control Parts

(3) The cost of any part, device, or component of any light-duty vehicle that is designed for emission control and which in the instructions issued pursuant to subsection (c)(3) of this section is scheduled for replacement during the useful life of the vehicle in order to maintain compliance with regulations under section 202 of this Act, the failure of which shall not interfere with the normal performance of the vehicle, and the expected retail price of which, including installation costs, is greater than 2 percent of the suggested retail price of such vehicle, shall be borne or reimbursed at the time of replacement by the vehicle manufacturer and such replacement shall be provided without cost to the ultimate purchaser, subsequent purchaser, or dealer. The term 'designed for emission control' as used in the preceding sentence means a catalytic converter, thermal reactor, or other component installed on or in vehicle for the sole or primary purpose reducing vehicle emissions (not including those vehicle components which were in general use prior to model year 1968 and the primary function of which is not related to emission control).

(b) If the Administrator determines that (i) there are available testing methods and procedures to ascertain whether, when in actual use throughout its the warrant period (as determined under subsection (i)), each vehicle and engine to which regulations under section 202 apply complies with the emission standards of such regulations, (ii) such methods and procedures are in accordance with good engineering practices, and (iii) such methods and procedures are reasonably capable of being correlated with tests conducted under 206(a)(1) , then—

(1) he shall establish such methods and procedures by regulation, and

(2) at such time as he determines that inspection facilities or equipment are available for purposes of carrying out testing methods and procedures established under paragraph (1), he shall prescribe regulations which shall require manufacturers to warrant the emission control device or system of each motor vehicle or new motor vehicle engine to which a regulation under section 202 applies and which is manufactured in a model year beginning after the Administrator first prescribes warranty regulations under this paragraph (2). The warranty under such regulations shall run to the ultimate purchaser and each subsequent purchaser and shall provide that if—

(A) the vehicle or engine is maintained and operated in accordance with instructions under subsection (c)(3),

(B) it fails to conform at any time during its the warranty period life (as determined under subsection (i)) to the regulations prescribed under section 202 , and

(C) such nonconformity results in the ultimate purchaser (or any subsequent purchaser) of such vehicle or engine having to bear any penalty or other sanction (including the denial of the right to use such vehicle or engine) under State or Federal law, then such manufacturer shall remedy such nonconformity under such warranty with the cost thereof to be borne by the manufacturer. No such warranty shall be invalid on the basis of any part used in the maintenance or repair of a vehicle or engine if such part was certified as provided under subsection (a)(2).

[§207(b) amended by PL 95–95; PL 101–549]

(c) Effective with respect to vehicles and engines manufactured during model year beginning more than 60 days after the date of enactment of the Clean Air Amendments of 1970—

(1) If the Administrator determines that a substantial number of any class or category of vehicles or engines, although properly maintained and used, do not conform to the regulations prescribed under section 202 , when in actual use throughout their useful life (as determined under section 202(d) , he shall immediately notify the manufacturer to submit a plan for remedying the nonconformity of the vehicles or engines with respect to which such notification is given. The plan shall provide that the nonconformity of any such vehicles or engines which are properly used and maintained will be remedied at the expense of the manufacturer. If the manufacturer disagrees with such determination of nonconformity and so advises the Administrator, the Administrator shall afford the manufacturer and other interested persons an opportunity to present their views and evidence in support thereof at a public hearing. Unless, as a result of such hearing the Administrator withdraws such determination of nonconformity, he shall, within 60 days after completion of such hearing, order the manufacturer to provide prompt notification of such nonconformity in accordance with paragraph (2).

(2) Any notification required by paragraph (1) with respect to any class or category of vehicles or engines shall be given to dealers, ultimate purchasers, and subsequent purchasers (if known) in such manner and containing such information as the Administrator may by regulations require.

Maintenance Instructions

(3) (A) The manufacturer shall furnish with each new motor vehicle or motor vehicle engine written instructions for the proper maintenance and use of the vehicle or engine by the ultimate purchaser and such instructions shall correspond to regulations which the Administrator shall promulgate. The manufacturer shall provide in bold-face type on the first page of the written maintenance instructions notice that maintenance, replacement, or repair of the emission control devices and systems may be performed by any automotive repair establishment or individual using any automotive part which has been certified as provided in subsection (a)(2).

(B) The instruction under subparagraph (A) of this paragraph shall not include any condition on the ultimate purchaser's using, in connection with such vehicle or engine, any component or service (other than a component or service provided without charge under the terms of the purchase agreement) which is identified by brand, trade, or corporate name; or directly or indirectly distinguishing between service performed by the franchised dealers of such manufacturer or any other service establishments with which such manufacturer has a commercial relationship, and service performed by independent automotive repair facilities with which such manufacturer has no commercial relationships; except that the prohibition of this subsection may be waived by the Administrator if—

(i) the manufacturer satisfies the Administrator that the vehicle or engine will function properly only if the component or service so identified is used in connection with such vehicle or engine, and

(ii) the Administrator finds that such a waiver is in the public interest.

(C) In addition, the manufacturer shall indicate by means of a label or tag permanently affixed to such vehicle or engine that such vehicle or engine is covered by a certificate of conformity issued for the purpose of assuring achievement of emissions standards prescribed under section 202 of this Act. Such label or tag shall contain such other information relating to control of motor vehicle emissions as the Administrator shall prescribe by regulation.

[§207(c)(3) amended by PL 95–95]

(4) Intermediate In-Use Standards.—

(A) Model Years 1994 and 1995.—For light-duty trucks of up to 6,000 lbs. gross vehicle weight rating (GVWR) and light- duty vehicles which are subject to standards under table G of section 202(g)(1) in model years 1994 and 1995 (40 percent of the manufacturer's sales volume in model year 1994 and 80 percent in model year 1995), the standards applicable to NMHC, CO, and NO_x for purposes of this subsection shall be those set forth in table A below in lieu of the standards for such air pollutants otherwise applicable under this title:

TABLE A—INTERMEDIATE IN-USE STANDARDS LDT'S UP TO 6,000 LBS. GVWR AND LIGHT-DUTY VEHICLES

Vehicle type	NMHC	CO	NO_x
Light-duty vehicles	0.32	3.4	0.4*
LDT's (0-3,750 LVW)	0.32	5.2	0.4*
LDT's (3,750-5,750 LVW)	0.41	6.7	0.7*

* Not applicable to diesel-fueled vehicles.

(B) Model Years 1996 and Thereafter.—

(i) In the model years 1996 and 1997, light-duty trucks (LDTs) up to 6,000 lbs. gross vehicle weight rating (GVWR) and light-duty vehicles which are not subject to final in-use standards under paragraph (5) (60 percent of the manufacturer's sales volume in model year 1996 and 20 percent in model year 1997) shall be subject to the standards set forth in table A of subparagraph (A) for NMHC, CO, and NO_x for purposes of this subsection in lieu of those set forth in paragraph (5).

(ii) For LDTs of more than 6,000 lbs. GVWR—

(I) in model year 1996 which are subject to the standards set forth in Table H of section 202(h) (50%);

(II) in model year 1997 (100%); and

(III) in model year 1998 which are not subject to final in-use standards under paragraph (5) (50%); the standards for NMHC, CO, and NO_x for purposes of this subsection shall be those set forth in Table B below in lieu of the standards for such air pollutants otherwise applicable under this title.

TABLE B—INTERMEDIATE IN-USE STANDARDS LDT'S MORE THAN 6,000 LBS. GVWR

Vehicle type	NMHC	CO	NO_x
LDTs (3,751-5,750 lbs. TW)	0.40	5.5	0.88*
LDTs (over 5,750 lbs. TW)	0.49	6.2	1.38*

* Not applicable to diesel-fueled vehicles.

(C) Useful Life.—In the case of the in-use standards applicable under this paragraph, for purposes of applying this subsection, the applicable useful life shall be 5 years or 50,000 miles or the equivalent (whichever first occurs).

[§207(c)(4) added by PL 101–549]

(5) Final In-Use Standards.—

(A) After the model year 1995, for purposes of applying this subsection, in the case of the percentage specified in the implementation schedule below of each manufacturer's sales volume of light-duty trucks of up to 6,000 lbs. gross vehicle weight rating (GVWR) and light duty vehicles, the standards for NMHC, CO, and NO_x shall be as provided in Table G in section 202(g) , except that in applying the standards set forth in Table G for purposes of determining compliance with this subsection, the applicable useful life shall be (i) 5 years or 50,000 miles (or the equivalent) whichever first occurs in the case of standards applicable for purposes of certification at 50,000 miles; and (ii) 10 years or 100,000 miles (or the equivalent), whichever first occurs in the case of standards applicable for purposes of certification at 100,000 miles, except that no testing shall be done beyond 7 years or 75,000 miles, or the equivalent whichever first occurs.

LDT's UP TO 6,000 LBS. GVWR AND LIGHT-DUTY VEHICLE SCHEDULE FOR IMPLEMENTATION OF FINAL IN-USE STANDARDS

Model year	Percent
1996	40
1997	80
1998	100

(B) After the model year 1997, for purposes of applying this subsection, in the case of the percentage specified in the implementation schedule below of each manufacturer's sales volume of light-duty trucks of more than 6,000 lbs. gross vehicle weight rating (GVWR), the standards for NMHC, CO, and NO_xshall be as provided in Table H in section 202(h), except that in applying the standards set forth in Table H for purposes of determining compliance with this subsection, the applicable useful life shall be (i) 5 years or 50,000 miles (or the equivalent) whichever first occurs in the case of standards applicable for purposes of certification at 50,000 miles: and (ii) 11 years or 120,000 miles (or the equivalent), whichever first occurs in the case of standards applicable for purposes of certification at 120,000 miles, except that no testing shall be done beyond 7 years or 90,000 miles (or the equivalent) whichever first occurs.

LDT's OF MORE THAN 6,000 LBS. GVWR IMPLEMENTATION SCHEDULE FOR IMPLEMENTATION OF FINAL IN-USE STANDARDS

Model year	Percent
1998	50
1999	100

[§207(c)(5) added by PL 101–549]

(6) Diesel Vehicles; In-Use Useful Life and Testing.—

(A) In the case of diesel-fueled light- duty trucks up to 6,000 lbs. GVWR and light-duty vehicles, the useful life for purposes of determining in-use compliance with the standards under section 202(g) for NO_xshall be a period of 10 years or 100,000 miles (or the equivalent), whichever first occurs, in the case of standards applicable for purposes of certification at 100,000 miles, except that testing shall not be done for a period beyond 7 years or 75,000 miles (or the equivalent) whichever first occurs.

(B) In the case of diesel-fueled light- duty trucks of 6,000 lbs. GVWR or more, the useful life for purposes of determining in-use compliance with the standards under section 202(h) for NO_xshall be a period of 11 years or 120,000 miles (or the equivalent), whichever first occurs, in the case of standards applicable for purposes of certification at 120,000 miles, except that testing shall not be done for a period beyond 7 years or 90,000 miles (or the equivalent) whichever first occurs.

[§207(c)(6) added by PL 101–549]

(d) Any cost obligation of any dealer incurred as a result of any requirement imposed by subsection (a), (b), or (c) shall be borne by the manufacturer. The transfer of any such cost obligation from a manufacturer to any dealer through franchise or other agreement is prohibited.

(e) If a manufacturer includes in any advertisement a statement respecting the cost or value of emission control devices or systems, such manufacturer shall set forth in such statement the cost or value attributed to such devices or systems by the Secretary of Labor (through the Bureau of Labor Statistics). The Secretary of Labor, and his representatives, shall have the same access for this purpose to the books, documents, papers, and records of a manufacturer as the Comptroller General has to those of a recipient of assistance for the purposes of section 311 .

(f) Any inspection of a motor vehicle or a motor vehicle engine for purposes of subsection (c)(1), after its sale to the ultimate purchaser, shall be made only if the owner of such vehicle or engine voluntarily permits such inspection to be made, except as may be provided by any State or local inspection program.

Repair At Owner's Place Of Choosing

(g) For the purposes of this section, the owner of any motor vehicle or motor vehicle engine warranted under this section is responsible in the proper maintenance of such vehicle or engine to replace and to maintain, at his expense at any service establishment or facility of his choosing, such items as spark plugs, points, condensors, and any other part, item, or device related to emission control (but not designed for emission control under the terms of the last three sentences of section 207(a)(3) , unless such part, item, or device is covered by any warranty not mandated by this Act.

[§207(g) added by PL 95–95; amended by PL 101–549]

Dealer Certification

(h) (1) Upon the sale of each new light- duty motor vehicle by a dealer, the dealer shall furnish to the purchaser a certificate that such motor vehicle conforms to the applicable regulations under section 202 including notice of the purchaser's rights under paragraph (2).

(2) If at any time during the period for which the warranty applies under subsection (b), a motor vehicle fails to conform to the applicable regulations under section 202 as determined under subsection (b) of this section such nonconformity shall be remedied by the manufacturer at the cost of the manufacturer pursuant to such warranty as provided in section 207(b)(2) (without regard to subparagraph (C) thereof).

[§207(h)(2) amended by PL 95–190]

(3) Nothing in section 209(a) shall be construed to prohibit a State from testing, or requiring testing of, a motor vehicle after the date of sale of such vehicle to the ultimate purchaser (except that no new motor vehicle manufacturer or dealer may be required to conduct testing under this paragraph).

[Former §207(f) redesignated as (h) by PL 95–190, August 7, 1977]

(i) Warranty Period.—

(1) In General.—For purposes of subsection (a)(1) and subsection (b), the warranty period, effective with respect to new light-duty trucks and new light-duty vehicles and engines, manufactured in the model year 1995 and thereafter, shall be the first 2 years or 24,000 miles of use (whichever first occurs), except as provided in paragraph (2). For purposes of subsection (a)(1) and subsection (b), for other vehicles and engines the warranty period shall be the period established by the Administrator by regulation (promulgated prior to the enactment of the Clean Air Act Amendments of 1990) for such purposes unless the Administrator subsequently modifies such regulation.

(2) Specified Major Emission Control Components.—In the case of a specified major emission control component, the warranty period for new light-duty trucks and new light-duty vehicles and engines manufactured in the model year 1995 and thereafter for purposes of subsection (a)(1) and subsection (b) shall be 8 years or 80,000 miles of use (whichever first occurs). As used in this paragraph, the term 'specified major emission control component' means only a catalytic converter, an electronic emissions control unit, and an onboard emissions diagnostic device, except that the Administrator may designate any other pollution control device or component as a specified major emission control component if—

(A) the device or component was not in general use on vehicles and engines manufactured prior to the model year 1990; and

(B) the Administrator determines that the retail cost (exclusive of installation costs) of such device or component exceeds $200 (in 1989 dollars), adjusted for inflation or deflation as calculated by the Administrator at the time of such determination. For purposes of this paragraph, the term 'onboard emissions diagnostic device' means any device installed for the purpose of storing or processing emissions related diagnostic information, but not including any parts or other systems which it monitors except specified major emissions control components. Nothing in this Act shall be construed to provide that any part (other than a part referred to in the preceding sentence) shall be required to be warranted under this Act for the period of 8 years or 80,000 miles referred to in this paragraph.

(3) Instructions.—Subparagraph (A) of subsection (b)(2) shall apply only where the Administrator has made a determination that the instructions concerned conform to the requirements of subsection (c)(3).

§7542. Information Collection [Sec. 208]

[§208 revised by PL 101–549]

(a) Manufacturer's Responsibility.—Every manufacturer of new motor vehicles or new motor vehicle engines, and every manufacturer of new motor vehicle or engine parts or components, and other persons subject to the requirements of this part or part C, shall establish and maintain records, perform tests where such testing is not otherwise reasonably available under this part and part C (including fees for testing), make reports and provide information the Administrator may reasonably require to determine whether the manufacturer or other person has acted or is acting in compliance with this part and part C and regulations thereunder, or to otherwise carry out the provision of this part and part C, and shall, upon request of an officer or employee duly designated by the Administrator, permit such officer or employee at reasonable times to have access to and copy such records.

(b) Enforcement Authority.—For the purposes of enforcement of this section, officers or employees duly designated by the Administrator upon presenting appropriate credentials are authorized—

(1) to enter, at reasonable times, any establishment of the manufacturer, or of any person whom the manufacturer engages to perform any activity required by subsection (a), for the purposes of inspecting or observing any activity conducted pursuant to subsection (a), and

(2) to inspect records, files, papers, processes, controls, and facilities used in performing any activity required by subsection (a), by such manufacturer or by any person whom the manufacturer engages to perform any such activity.

(c) Availability to the Public; Trade Secrets.—Any records, reports, or information obtained under this part or part C shall be available to the public, except that upon a showing satisfactory to the Administrator by any person that records, reports, or information, or a particular portion thereof (other than emission data), to which the Administrator has access under this section, if made public, would divulge methods or processes entitled to protection as trade secrets of that person, the Administrator shall consider the record, report, or information or particular portion thereof confidential in accordance with the purposes of section 1905 of title 18 of the United States Code. Any authorized representative of the Administrator shall be considered an employee of the United States for purposes of section 1905 of title 18 of the Untied States Code. Nothing in this section shall prohibit the Administrator or authorized representative of the Administrator from disclosing records, reports or information to other officers, employees or authorized representatives of the United States concerned with carrying out this Act or when relevant in any proceeding under this Act. Nothing in this section shall authorize the withholding of information by the Administrator or any officer or employee under the Administrator's control from the duly authorized committees of the Congress.

§7543. State Standards [Sec. 209]

(a) No State or any political subdivision thereof shall adopt or attempt to enforce any standard relating to the control emissions from new motor vehicles or new motor vehicle engines subject to this part. No State shall require certification, inspection, or any other approval relating to the control of emissions from any new motor vehicle or new motor vehicle engine as conditions precedent to the initial retail sale, titling (if any), or registration of such motor vehicle, motor vehicles engine or equipment.

California Waiver

(b) (1) The Administrator shall, after notice and opportunity for public hearing, waive application of this section to any State which has adopted standards (other than crankcase emission standards) for the control of emissions from new motor vehicles or new motor vehicle engines prior to March 30, 1966, if the State determines that the State standards will be, in the aggregate, at least as protective of public health and welfare as applicable Federal standards. No such waiver shall be granted if the Administrator finds that—

(A) the determination of the State is arbitrary and capricious,

(B) such State does not need such State standards to meet compelling and extraordinary conditions, or

(C) such State standards and accompanying enforcement procedures are not consistent with section 202(a) of this part.

(2) If each State standard is at least as stringent as the comparable applicable Federal standard, such State standards shall be deemed to be at least as protective of health and welfare as such Federal standards for purposes of paragraph (1).

(3) In the case of any new motor vehicle or new motor vehicle engine to which State standards apply pursuant to a waiver granted under paragraph (1), compliance with such State standards shall be treated as compliance with applicable Federal standards for purposes of this title.

[§209(b) amended by PL 95–95]

Parts Standards; Preemption Of State Law

(c) Whenever a regulation with respect to any motor vehicle part or motor vehicle engine part is in effect under section 207 (a)(2), no State or political subdivision thereof shall adopt or attempt to enforce any standard or any requirement of certification, inspection or approval which relates to motor vehicle emissions and is applicable to the same aspect of such part. The preceding sentence shall not apply in the case of a State with respect to which a waiver is in effect under subsection (b).

[§209(c) added by PL 95–95]

(d) Nothing in this part shall preclude or deny to any State or political subdivision thereof the right otherwise to control, regulate, or restrict the use, operation, or movement of registered or licensed motor vehicles.

[Former §209(c) redesignated as (d) by PL 95–95]

(e) Nonroad Engines or Vehicles.—

(1) Prohibition on Certain State Standards.—No State or any political subdivision thereof shall adopt or attempt to enforce any standard or other requirement relating to the control of emissions from either of the following new nonroad engines or nonroad vehicles subject to regulation under this Act—

(A) New engines which are used in construction equipment or vehicles or used in farm equipment or vehicles and which are smaller than 175 horsepower.

(B) New locomotives or new engines used in locomotives. Subsection (b) shall not apply for purposes of this paragraph.

(2) Other Nonroad Engines or Vehicles.—

(A) In the case of any nonroad vehicles or engines other than those referred to in subparagraph (A) or (B) of paragraph (1), the Administrator shall, after notice and opportunity for public hearing, authorize California to adopt and enforce standards and other requirements relating to the control of emissions from such vehicles or engines if California determines that California standards will be, in the aggregate, at least as protective of public health and welfare as applicable Federal standards. No such authorization shall be granted if the Administrator finds that—

(i) the determination of California is arbitrary and capricious,

(ii) California does not need such California standards to meet compelling and extraordinary conditions, or

(iii) California standards and accompanying enforcement procedures are not consistent with this section.

(B) Any State other than California which has plan provisions approved under part D of title I may adopt and enforce, after notice to the Administrator, for any period, standards relating to control of emissions from nonroad vehicles or engines (other than those referred to in subparagraph (A) or (B) of paragraph (1)) and take such other actions as are referred to in subparagraph (A) of this paragraph respecting such vehicles or engines if—

(i) such standards and implementation and enforcement are identical, for the period concerned, to the California standards authorized by the Administrator under subparagraph (A), and

(ii) California and such State adopt such standards at least 2 years before commencement of the period for which the standards take effect. The Administrator shall issue regulations to implement this subsection.

[§209(e) added by PL 101–549]

§7544. State Grants [Sec. 210]

The Administrator is authorized to make grants to appropriate State agencies in an amount up to two-thirds of the cost of developing and maintaining effective vehicle emission devices and systems inspection and emission testing and control programs, except that—

(1) no such grant shall be made for any part of any State vehicle inspection program which does not directly relate to the cost of the air pollution control aspects of such a program;

(2) no such grant shall be made unless the Secretary of Transportation has certified to the Administrator that such program is consistent with any highway safety program developed pursuant to section 402 of title 23 of the United States Code; and

(3) no such grant shall be made unless the program includes provisions designed to insure that emission control devices and systems on vehicles in actual use have not been discontinued or rendered inoperative.

Grants may be made under this section by way of reimbursement in any case in which amounts have been expended by the State before the date on which any such grant was made.

[§210 amended by PL 95–95]

§7545. Regulations Of Fuels [Sec. 211]

(a) The Administrator may by regulation designate any fuel or fuel additive (including any fuel or fuel additive used exclusively in nonroad engines or nonroad engines or nonroad vehicles) and, after such date or dates as may be prescribed by him, no manufacturer or processor of any such fuel or additive (including any fuel or fuel additive used exclusively in nonroad engines, or nonroad engines or nonroad vehicles) may sell, offer for sale, or introduce into commerce such fuel or additive (including any fuel or fuel additive used exclusively in nonroad engines, or nonroad engines or nonroad vehicles) unless the Administrator has registered such fuel or additive in accordance with subsection (b) of this section.

[§211(a) amended by PL 101–549]

(b) (1) For the purpose of registration of fuels and fuel additives, the Administrator shall require—

(A) the manufacturer of any fuel to notify him as to the commercial identifying name and manufacturer of any additive contained in such fuel; the range of concentration of any additive in the fuel; and the purpose-in-use of any such additive; and

(B) the manufacture of any additive to notify him as to the chemical composition of such additive.

(2) For the purpose of registration of fuels and fuel additives, the Administrator may also require the manufacturer of any fuel or fuel additive—

(A) to conduct tests to determine potential public health effects of such fuel or additive (including, but not limited to, carcinogenic, teratogenic, or mutagenic effects), and

(B) to furnish the description of any analytical technique that can be used to detect and measure any additive in such fuel, the recommended range of concentration of such additive, and the recommended purpose-in-use of such additive, and such other information as is reasonable and necessary to determine the emissions resulting from the use of the fuel or additive contained in such fuel, the effect of such fuel or additive on the emission control performance of any vehicle, vehicle engine, nonroad engine or nonroad vehicle, or the extent to which such emissions affect the public health or welfare.

[§211(b)(2)(B) amended by PL 101–549]

Tests under subparagraph (A) shall be conducted in conformity with test procedures and protocols established by the Administrator. The result of such tests shall not be considered confidential.

(3) Upon compliance with the provision of this subsection, including assurances that the Administrator will receive changes in the information required, the Administrator shall register such fuel or fuel additive.

(c) (1) The Administrator may, from time to time on the basis of information obtained under subsection (b) of this section or other information available to him, by regulation, control or prohibit the manufacture, introduction into commerce, offering for sale, or sale of any fuel additive for use in a motor vehicle, motor vehicle engine, or nonroad engine or nonroad vehicle (A) if in the judgment of the Administrator any emission product of such fuel or fuel additives causes, or contributes to, air pollution which may reasonably be anticipated to endanger the public health or welfare, or (B) if emission products of such fuel or fuel additive will impair to a significant degree the performance of any emission control device or system which is in general use, or which the Administrator finds has been developed to a point where in a reasonable time it would be in general use were such regulation to be promulgated.

[§211(c)(1)(A) amended by PL 95–95; PL 101–549]

(2) (A) No fuel, class of fuels, or fuel additive may be controlled or prohibited by the Administrator pursuant to clause (A) of paragraph (1) except after consideration of all relevant medical and scientific evidence available to him, including consideration of other technologically or economically feasible means of achieving emission standards under section 202 .

(B) No fuel or fuel additive may be controlled or prohibited by the Administrator pursuant to clause (B) of paragraph (1) except after consideration of available scientific and economic data, including a cost benefit analysis comparing emission control devices or systems which are or will be in general use and require the proposed control or prohibition with emission control devices or systems which are or will be in general use and do not require the proposed control or prohibition. On request of a manufacturer of motor vehicles, motor vehicle engines, fuels, or fuel additives submitted within 10 days of notice of proposed rulemaking, the Administrator shall hold a public hearing and publish his findings with respect to any matter he is required to consider under this subparagraph. Such findings shall be published at the time of promulgation of final regulations.

(C) No fuel or fuel additive may be prohibited by the Administrator under paragraph (1) unless he finds, and publishes such finding, that in his judgment such prohibition will not cause the use of any other fuel or fuel additive which will produce emissions which will endanger the public health or welfare to the same or greater degree than the use of the fuel or fuel additive proposed to be prohibited.

(3) (A) For the purpose of obtaining evidence and data to carry out paragraph (2), the Administrator may require the manufacturer of any motor vehicle engine to furnish any

information which has been developed concerning the emissions from motor vehicles resulting from the use of any fuel additive, or the effect of such use on the performance of any emission control device or system.

(B) In obtaining information under subparagraph (A), section 307(a) (relating to subpoenas) shall be applicable.

(4) (A) Except as otherwise provided in subparagraph (B) or (C), no State (or political subdivision thereof) may prescribe or attempt to enforce, for purposes of motor vehicle emission control, any control or prohibition respecting any characteristic or component of a fuel or fuel additive in a motor vehicle or motor vehicle engine—

(i) if the Administrator has found that no control or prohibition of the characteristic or component of a fuel or fuel additive under paragraph (1) is necessary and has published his finding in the Federal Register, or

(ii) if the Administrator has prescribed under paragraph (1) a control or prohibition applicable to such characteristic or component of a fuel or fuel additive, unless State prohibition or control is identical to the prohibition or control prescribed by the Administrator.

[§211 (c)(4)(A) amended by PL 101–549]

(B) Any State for which application of section 209(a) has at anytime been waived under section 209(b) may at any time prescribe and enforce, for the purpose of motor vehicle emission control, a control or prohibition respecting any fuel or fuel additive.

(C) A State may prescribe and enforce, for the purposes of motor vehicle emission control, a control or prohibition respecting the use of a fuel or fuel additive in a motor vehicle or motor vehicle engine if an applicable implementation plan for such State under section 110 so provides. The Administrator may approve such provision in an implementation plan, or promulgate an implementation plan containing such a provision, only if he finds that the State control or prohibition is necessary to achieve the national primary or secondary ambient air quality standard which the plan implements. The Administrator may find that a State control or prohibition is necessary to achieve that standard if no other measures that would bring about timely attainment exist, or if other measures exist and are technically possible to implement, but are unreasonable or impracticable. The Administrator may make a finding of necessity under this subparagraph even if the plan for the area does not contain an approved demonstration of timely attainment.

[§211(c)(4)(C) amended by PL 101–549]

(d) Penalties and Injunctions.—

(1) Civil Penalties.—Any person who violates subsection (a), (f), (g), (k), (l), (m), or (n) of this section or the regulations prescribed under subsection (c), (h), (i), (k), (l), (m), or (n) of this section or who fails to furnish any information or conduct any tests required by the Administrator under subsection (b) of this section shall be liable to the United States for a civil penalty of not more than the sum of $25,000 for every day of such violation and the amount of economic benefit or savings resulting from the violation. Any violation with respect to a regulation prescribed under subsection (c), (k), (l), or (m) of this section which establishes a regulatory standard based upon a multiday averaging period shall constitute a separate day of violation for each and every day in the averaging period. Civil penalties shall be assessed in accordance with subsections (b) and (c) of section 205 .

(2) Injunctive Authority.—The district courts of the United States shall have jurisdiction to restrain violations of subsections (a), (f), (g), (k), (l), (m), and (n) of this section and of the regulations prescribed under subsections (c), (h), (i), (k), (1), (m), and (n) of this section, to award other appropriate relief, and to compel the furnishing of information and the conduct of tests required by the Administrator under subsection (b) of this section. Actions to restrain such violations and compel such actions shall be brought by and in the name of the United States. In any such action, subpoenas for witnesses who are required to attend a district court in any district may run into any other district.

[§211(d) revised by PL 101–549]

(e) Testing of Fuels and Fuel Additives

(1) Not later than one year after the date of enactment of this subsection and after notice and opportunity for a public hearing, the Administrator shall promulgate regulations which implement the authority under subsection (b)(2)(A) and (B) with respect to each fuel or fuel additive which is registered on the date of promulgation of such regulations and with respect to each fuel or fuel additive for which

an application for registration is filed thereafter.

(2) Regulations under subsection (b) to carry out this subsection shall require that the requisite information be provided to the Administrator by each such manufacturer—

(A) prior to registration, in the case of any fuel or fuel additive which is not registered on the date of promulgation of such regulations; or

(B) not later than three years after the date of promulgation of such regulations, in the case of any fuel or fuel additive which is registered on such date.

(3) In promulgating such regulations, the Administrator may—

(A) exempt any small business (as defined in such regulations) from or defer or modify the requirements of, such regulations with respect to any such small business;

(B) provide for cost-sharing with respect to the testing of any fuel or fuel additive which is manufactured or processed by two or more persons or otherwise provide for shared responsibility to meet the requirements of this section without duplication; or

(C) exempt any person from such regulations with respect to a particular fuel or fuel additive upon a finding that any additional testing of such fuel or fuel additive would be duplicative of adequate existing testing.

[§211(e) added by PL 95–95]

(f) (1) (A) Effective upon March 31, 1977, it shall be unlawful for any manufacturer of any fuel or fuel additive to first introduce into commerce, or to increase the concentration in use of, any fuel or fuel additive for general use in light duty motor vehicles manufactured after model year 1974 which is not substantially similar to any fuel or fuel additive utilized in the certification of any model year 1975, or subsequent model year, vehicle or engine under section 206 .

[§211(f)(1) redesignated as (1)(A) and (B) added by PL 101–549]

(B) Effective upon the date of the enactment of the Clean Air Act Amendments of 1990, it shall be unlawful for any manufacturer of any fuel or fuel additive to first introduce into commerce, or to increase the concentration in use of, any fuel or fuel additive for use by any person in motor vehicles manufactured after model year 1974 which is not substantially similar to any fuel or fuel additive utilized in the certification of any model year 1975, or subsequent model year, vehicle or engine under section 206.

(2) Effective November 30, 1977, it shall be unlawful for any manufacturer of any fuel to introduce into commerce any gasoline which contains a concentration of manganese in excess of .0625 grams per gallon of fuel, except as otherwise provided pursuant to a waiver under paragraph (4).

[§211(f)(2) amended by PL 95–190]

(3) Any manufacturer of any fuel or fuel additive which prior to March 31, 1977, and after January 1, 1974, first introduced into commerce or increased the concentration in use of a fuel or fuel additive that would otherwise have been prohibited under paragraph (1)(A) if introduced on or after March 31, 1977 shall, not later than September 15, 1978, cease to distribute such fuel or fuel additive in commerce. During the period beginning 180 days after the date of the enactment of this subsection and before September 15, 1978, the Administrator shall prohibit or restrict the concentration of any fuel additive which he determines will cause or contribute to the failure of an emission control device or system (over the useful life of any vehicle in which such device or system is used) to achieve compliance by the vehicle with the emission standards with respect to which it has been certified under section 206 .

[§211(f)(3) amended by PL 101–549]

(4) The Administrator, upon application of any manufacturer of any fuel or fuel additive, may waive the prohibitions established under paragraph (1) or (3) of this subsection or the limitation specified in paragraph (2) of this subsection, if he determines that the applicant has established that such fuel or fuel additive or a specified concentration thereof, and the emission products of such fuel or additive or specified concentration thereof, will not cause or contribute to a failure of any emission control device or system (over the useful life of any vehicle in which such device or system is used) to achieve compliance by the vehicle with the emission standards with respect to which it has been certified pursuant to section 206 . If the Administrator has not acted to grant or deny an application under this paragraph within one hundred and eighty days of receipt of such application, the waiver authorized by this paragraph shall be treated as granted.

[§211(f)(4) amended by PL 95–190]

(5) No action of the Administrator under this section may be stayed by any court pending judicial review of such action.

[§211(f) added by PL 95–95]

(g) Misfueling.—

(1) No person shall introduce, or cause or allow the introduction of, leaded gasoline into any motor vehicle which is labeled 'unleaded gasoline only,' which is equipped with a gasoline tank filler inlet designed for the introduction of unleaded gasoline, which is a 1990 or later model year motor vehicle, or which such person knows or should know is a vehicle designed solely for the use of unleaded gasoline.

(2) Beginning October 1, 1993, no person shall introduce or cause or allow the introduction into any motor vehicle of diesel fuel which such person knows or should know contains a concentration of sulfur in excess of 0.05 percent (by weight) or which fails to meet a cetane index minimum of 40 or such equivalent alternative aromatic level as prescribed by the Administrator under subsection (i)(2).

[§211(g) revised by PL 101–549]

Fuel Volatility

(h) Reid Vapor Pressure Requirements.—

(1) Prohibition.—Not later than 6 months after the date of the enactment of the Clean Air Act Amendments of 1990, the Administrator shall promulgate regulations making it unlawful for any person during the high ozone season (as defined by the Administrator) to sell, offer for sale, dispense, supply, offer for supply, transport, or introduce into commerce gasoline with a Reid Vapor Pressure in excess of 9.0 pounds per square inch (psi). Such regulations shall also establish more stringent Reid Vapor Pressure standards in a nonattainment area as the Administrator finds necessary to generally achieve comparable evaporative emissions (on a per-vehicle basis) in nonattainment areas, taking into consideration the enforceability of such standards, the need of an area for emission control, and economic factors.

(2) Attainment Areas.—The regulations under this subsection shall not make it unlawful for any person to sell, offer for supply, transport, or introduce into commerce gasoline with a Reid Vapor Pressure of 9.0 pounds per square inch (psi) or lower in any area designated under section 107 as an attainment area. Notwithstanding the preceding sentence, the Administrator may impose a Reid vapor pressure requirement lower than 9.0 pounds per square inch (psi) in any area, formerly an ozone nonattainment area, which has been redesignated as an attainment area.

(3) Effective Date; Enforcement.—The regulations under this subsection shall provide that the requirements of this subsection shall take effect not later than the high ozone season for 1992, and shall include such provisions as the Administrator determines are necessary to implement and enforce the requirements of this subsection.

(4) Ethanol Waiver.—For fuel blends containing gasoline and 10 percent denatured anhydrous ethanol, the Reid vapor pressure limitation under this subsection shall be one pound per square inch (psi) greater than the applicable Reid vapor pressure limitations established under paragraph (1); Provided, however, That a distributor, blender, marketer, reseller, carrier, retailor, or wholesale purchaser- consumer shall be deemed to be in full compliance with the provisions of this subsection and the regulations promulgated thereunder if it can demonstrate (by showing receipt of a certification or other evidence acceptable to the Administrator) that—

(A) the gasoline portion of the blend complies with the Reid vapor pressure limitations promulgated pursuant to this subsection;

(B) the ethanol portion of the blend does not exceed its waiver condition under subsection (f)(4); and

(C) no additional alcohol or other additive has been added to increase the Reid Vapor Pressure of the ethanol portion of the blend.

(5) Areas Covered.—The provisions of this subsection shall apply only to the 48 contiguous States and the District of Columbia.

[§211(h) added by PL 101–549]

(i) Sulfur Content Requirements for Diesel Fuel.—

(1) Effective October 1, 1993, no person shall manufacture, sell, supply, offer for sale or supply, dispense, transport, or introduce into commerce motor vehicle diesel fuel which contains a concentration of sulfur in excess of 0.05 percent (by weight) or which fails to meet a cetane index minimum of 40.

(2) Not later than 12 months after the date of the enactment of the Clean Air Act Amendments of 1990, the Administrator shall promulgate regulations to implement and enforce the requirements of paragraph (1). The Administrator may require manufacturers and importers of diesel fuel not intended for use in motor

vehicles to dye such fuel in a particular manner in order to segregate it from motor vehicle diesel fuel. The Administrator may establish an equivalent alternative aromatic level to the cetane index specification in paragraph (1).

(3) The sulfur content of fuel required to be used in the certification of 1991 through 1993 model year heavy-duty diesel vehicles and engines shall be 0.10 percent (by weight). The sulfur content and cetane index minimum of fuel required to be used in the certification of 1994 and later model year heavy-duty diesel vehicles and engines shall comply with the regulations promulgated under paragraph (2).

(4) The States of Alaska and Hawaii may be exempted from the requirements of this subsection in the same manner as provided in section 324 . The Administrator shall take final action on any petition filed under section 324 or this paragraph for an exemption from the requirements of this subsection, within 12 months from the date of the petition.

[§211(i) added by PL 101–549]

(j) Lead Substitute Gasoline Additives.—

(1) After the date of the enactment of the Clean Air Act Amendments of 1990, any person proposing to register any gasoline additive under subsection (a) or to use any previously registered additive as a lead substitute may also elect to register the additive as a lead substitute gasoline additive for reducing valve seat wear by providing the Administrator with such relevant information regarding product identity and composition as the Administrator deems necessary for carrying out the responsibilities of paragraph (2) of this subsection (in addition to other information which may be required under subsection (b)).

(2) In addition to the other testing which may be required under subsection (b), in the case of the lead substitute gasoline additives referred to in paragraph (1), the Administrator shall develop and publish a test procedure to determine the additives' effectiveness in reducing valve seat wear and the additives' tendencies to produce engine deposits and other adverse side effects. The test procedures shall be developed in cooperation with the Secretary of Agriculture and with the input of additive manufacturers, engine and engine components manufacturers, and other interested persons. The Administrator shall enter into arrangements with an independent laboratory to conduct tests of each additive using the test procedures developed and published pursuant to this paragraph. The Administrator shall publish the results of the tests by company and additive name in the Federal Register along with, for comparison purposes, the results of applying the same test procedures to gasoline containing 0.1 gram of lead per gallon in lieu of the lead substitute gasoline additive. The Administrator shall not rank or otherwise rate the lead substitute additives. Test procedures shall be established within 1 year after the date of the enactment of the Clean Air Act Amendments of 1990. Additives shall be tested within 18 months of the date of the enactment of the Clean Air Act Amendments of 1990 or 6 months after the lead substitute additives are identified to the Administrator, whichever is later.

(3) The Administrator may impose a user fee to recover the costs of testing of any fuel additive referred to in this subsection. The fee shall be paid by the per son proposing to register the fuel additive concerned. Such fee shall not exceed $20,000 for a single fuel additive.

(4) There are authorized to be appropriated to the Administrator not more than $1,000,000 for the second full fiscal year after the date of the enactment of the Clean Air Act Amendments of 1990 to establish test procedures and conduct engine tests as provided in this subsection. Not more than $500,000 per year is authorized to be appropriated for each of the 5 subsequent fiscal years.

(5) Any fees collected under this subsection shall be deposited in a special fund in the United States Treasury for licensing and other services which thereafter shall be available for appropriation, to remain available until expended, to carry out the Agency's activities for which the fees were collected.

[§211(j) added by PL 101–549]

(k) Reformulated Gasoline for Conventional Vehicles.—

(1) EPA Regulations.—Within 1 year after the enactment of the Clean Air Act Amendments of 1990, the Administrator shall promulgate regulations under this section establishing requirements for reformulated gasoline to be used in gasoline-fueled vehicles in specified nonattainment areas. Such regulations shall require the greatest reduction in emissions of ozone forming volatile organic compounds (during the high ozone season) and emissions of toxic air pollutants (during the entire year) achievable through the reformulation of conventional gasoline, taking into consideration

the cost of achieving such emission reductions, any nonair- quality and other air-quality related health and environmental impacts and energy requirements.

(2) General Requirements.—The regulations referred to in paragraph (1) shall require that reformulated gasoline comply with paragraph (3) and with each of the following requirements (subject to paragraph (7)):

(A) NO_x Emissions.—The emissions of oxides of nitrogen (NO_x) from baseline vehicles when using the reformulated gasoline shall be no greater than the level of such emissions from such vehicles when using baseline gasoline. If the Administrator determines that compliance with the limitation on emissions of oxides of nitrogen under the preceding sentence is technically infeasible, considering the other requirements applicable under this subsection to such gasoline, the Administrator may, as appropriate to ensure compliance with this subparagraph, adjust (or waive entirely), any other requirements of this paragraph (including the oxygen content requirement contained in subparagraph (B)) or any requirements applicable under paragraph (3)(A).

(B) Oxygen Content.—The oxygen content of the gasoline shall equal or exceed 2.0 percent by weight (subject to a testing tolerance established by the Administrator) except as otherwise required by this Act. The Administrator may waive, in whole or in part, the application of this subparagraph for any ozone nonattainment area upon a determination by the Administrator that compliance with such requirement would prevent or interfere with the attainment by the area of a national primary ambient air quality standard.

(C) Benzene Content.—The benzene content of the gasoline shall not exceed 1.0 percent by volume.

(D) Heavy Metals.—The gasoline shall have no heavy metals, including lead or manganese. The Administrator may waive the prohibition contained in this subparagraph for a heavy metal (other than lead) if the Administrator determines that addition of the heavy metal to the gasoline will not increase, on an aggregate mass or cancer-risk basis, toxic air pollutant emissions from motor vehicles.

(3) More Stringent of Formula or Performance Standards.—The regulations referred to in paragraph (1) shall require compliance with the more stringent of either the requirements set forth in subparagraph (A) or the requirements of subparagraph (B) of this paragraph. For purposes of determining the more stringent provision, clause (i) and clause (ii) of subparagraph (B) shall be considered independently.

(A) Formula.—

(i) Benzene.—The benzene content of the reformulated gasoline shall not exceed 1.0 percent by volume.

(ii) Aromatics.—The aromatic hydrocarbon content of the reformulated gasoline shall not exceed 25 percent by volume.

(iii) Lead.—The reformulated gasoline shall have no lead content.

(iv) Detergents.—The reformulated gasoline shall contain additives to prevent the accumulation of deposits in engines or vehicle fuel supply systems.

(v) Oxygen Content.—The oxygen content of the reformulated gasoline shall equal or exceed 2.0 percent by weight (subject to a testing tolerance established by the Administrator) except as otherwise required by this Act.

(B) Performance Standard.—

(i) VOC Emissions.—During the high ozone season (as defined by the Administrator), the aggregate emissions of ozone forming volatile organic compounds from baseline vehicles when using the reformulated gasoline shall be 15 percent below the aggregate emissions of ozone forming volatile organic compounds from such vehicles when using baseline gasoline. Effective in calendar year 2000 and thereafter, 25 percent shall be substituted for 15 percent in applying this clause, except that the Administrator may adjust such 25 percent requirement to provide for a lesser or greater reduction based on technological feasibility, considering the cost of achieving such reductions in VOC emissions. No such adjustment shall provide for less than a 20 percent reduction below the aggregate emissions of such air pollutants from such vehicles when using baseline gasoline. The reductions required under this clause shall be on a mass basis.

(ii) Toxics.—During the entire year, the aggregate emissions of toxic air pollutants from baseline vehicles when using the reformulated gasoline shall be 15 percent below the aggregate emissions of toxic air pollutants from such vehicles when using baseline gasoline. Effective in calendar year

2000 and thereafter, 25 percent shall be substituted for 15 percent in applying this clause, except that the Administrator may adjust such 25 percent requirement to provide for a lesser or greater reduction based on technological feasibility, considering the cost of achieving such reductions in toxic air pollutants. No such adjustment shall provide for less than a 20 percent reduction below the aggregate emissions of such air pollutants from such vehicles when using baseline gasoline. The reductions required under this clause shall be on a mass basis. Any reduction greater than a specific percentage reduction required under this subparagraph shall be treated as satisfying such percentage reduction requirement.

(4) Certification Procedures.—

(A) Regulations.—The regulations under this subsection shall include procedures under which the Administrator shall certify reformulated gasoline as complying with the requirements established pursuant to this subsection. Under such regulations, the Administrator shall establish procedures for any person to petition the Administrator to certify a fuel formulation, or slate of fuel formulations. Such procedures shall further require that the Administrator shall approve or deny such petition within 180 days of receipt. If the Administrator fails to act within such 180-day period, the fuel shall be deemed certified until the Administrator completes action on the petition.

(B) Certification; Equivalency.—The Administrator shall certify a fuel formulation or slate of fuel formulations as complying with this subsection if such fuel or fuels—

(i) comply with the requirements of paragraph (2), and

(ii) achieve equivalent or greater reductions in emissions of ozone forming volatile organic compounds and emissions of toxic air pollutants than are achieved by a reformulated gasoline meeting the applicable requirements of paragraph (3).

(C) EPA Determination of Emissions Level.—Within 1 year after the enactment of the Clean Air Act Amendments of 1990, the Administrator shall determine the level of emissions of ozone forming volatile organic compounds and emissions of toxic air pollutants emitted by baseline vehicles when operating on baseline gasoline. For purposes of this subsection, within 1 year after the enactment of the Clean Air Act Amendments of 1990, the Administrator shall, by rule, determine appropriate measures of, and methodology for, ascertaining the emissions of air pollutants (including calculations, equipment, and testing tolerances).

(5) Prohibition.—Effective beginning January 1, 1995, each of the following shall be a violation of this subsection:

(A) The sale or dispensing by any person of conventional gasoline to ultimate consumers in any covered area.

(B) The sale or dispensing by any refiner, blender, importer, or marketer of conventional gasoline for resale in any covered area, without (i) segregating such gasoline from reformulated gasoline, and (ii) clearly marking such conventional gasoline as "conventional gasoline, not for sale to ultimate consumer in a covered area". Any refiner, blender, importer or marketer who purchases property segregated and marked conventional gasoline, and thereafter labels, represents, or wholesales such gasoline as reformulated gasoline shall also be in violation of this subsection. The Administrator may impose sampling, testing, and recordkeeping requirements upon any refiner, blender, importer, or marketer to prevent violations of this section.

(6) Opt-In Areas.—

(A) Upon the application of the Governor of a State, the Administrator shall apply the prohibition set forth in paragraph (5) in any area in the State classified under subpart 2 of part D of title I as a Marginal, Moderate, Serious, or Severe Area (without regard to whether or not the 1980 population of the area exceeds 250,000). In any such case, the Administrator shall establish an effective date for such prohibition as he deems appropriate, not later than January 1, 1995, or 1 year after such application is received, whichever is later. The Administrator shall publish such application in the Federal Register upon receipt.

(B) If the Administrator determines, on the Administrator's own motion or on petition of any person, after consultation with the Secretary of Energy, that there is insufficient domestic capacity to produce gasoline certified under this subsection, the Administrator shall, by rule, extend the effective date of such prohibition in Marginal, Moderate, Serious, or Severe Areas referred to in subparagraph (A) for one additional year, and may, by rule, renew such extension for 2 additional one- year periods. The Administrator shall act on any petition submitted under this paragraph within 6 months after receipt of the petition. The Administrator shall issue such extensions for areas with a lower ozone classification before issuing any such extension for areas with a higher classification.

(7) Credits.—

(A) The regulations promulgated under this subsection shall provide for the granting of an appropriate amount of credits to a person who refines, blends, or imports and certifies a gasoline or slate of gasoline that—

(i) has an oxygen content (by weight) that exceeds the minimum oxygen content specified in paragraph (2);

(ii) has an aromatic hydrocarbon content (by volume) that is less than the maximum aromatic hydrocarbon content required to comply with paragraph (3); or

(iii) has a benzene content (by volume) that is less than the maximum benzene content specified in paragraph (2).

(B) The regulations described in subparagraph (A) shall also provide that a person who is granted credits may use such credits, or transfer all or a portion of such credits to another person for use within the same nonattainment area, for the purpose of complying with this subsection.

(C) The regulations promulgated under subparagraphs (A) and (B) shall ensure the enforcement of the requirements for the issuance, application, and transfer of the credits. Such regulations shall prohibit the granting or transfer of such credits for use with respect to any gasoline in a nonattainment area, to the extent the use of such credits would result in any of the following:

(i) An average gasoline aromatic hydrocarbon content (by volume) for the nonattainment (taking into account all gasoline sold for use in conventional gasoline-fueled vehicles in the nonattainment area) higher than the average fuel aromatic hydrocarbon content (by volume) that would occur in the absence of using any such credits.

(ii) An average gasoline oxygen content (by weight) for the nonattainment area (taking into account all gasoline sold for use in conventional gasoline-fueled vehicles in the nonattainment area) lower than the average gasoline oxygen content (by weight) that would occur in the absence of using any such credits.

(iii) An average benzene content (by volume) for the nonattainment area (taking into account all gasoline sold for use in conventional gasoline-fueled vehicles in the nonattainment area) higher than the average benzene content (by volume) that would occur in the absence of using any such credits.

(8) Anti-Dumping Rules.—

(A) In General.—Within 1 year after the enactment of the Clean Air Act Amendments of 1990, the Administrator shall promulgate regulations applicable to each refiner, blender, or importer of gaso line ensuring that gasoline sold or introduced into commerce by such refiner, blender, or importer (other than reformulated gasoline subject to the requirements of paragraph (1)) does not result in average per gallon emissions (measured on a mass basis) of (i) volatile organic compounds, (ii) oxides of nitrogen, (iii) carbon monoxide, and (iv) toxic air pollutants in excess of such emissions of such pollutants attributable to gasoline sold or introduced into commerce in calendar year 1990 by that refiner, blender, or importer. Such regulations shall take effect beginning January 1, 1995.

(B) Adjustments.—In evaluating compliance with the requirements of subparagraph (A), the Administrator shall make appropriate adjustments to insure that no credit is provided for improvement in motor vehicle emissions control in motor vehicles sold after the calendar year 1990.

(C) Compliance Determined for Each Pollutant Independently.—In determining whether there is an increase in emissions in violation of the prohibition contained in subparagraph (A) the Administrator shall consider an increase in each air pollutant referred to in clauses (i) through (iv) as a separate violation of such prohibition, except that the Administrator shall promulgate regulations to provide that any increase in emissions of oxides of nitrogen resulting from adding oxygenates to gasoline may be offset by an equivalent or greater reduction (on a mass basis) in emissions of volatile organic compounds, carbon monoxide, or toxic air pollutants, or any combination of the foregoing.

(D) Compliance Period.—The Administrator shall promulgate an appropriate compliance period or appropriate compliance periods to be used for assessing compliance with the prohibition contained in subparagraph (A).

(E) Baseline for Determining Compliance.—If the Administrator determines that no adequate and reliable data exists regarding the composition of gasoline sold or introduced into commerce by a refiner, blender, or importer in calendar year 1990, for such refiner, blender, or importer, baseline gasoline shall be substituted for such 1990 gasoline in determining compliance with subparagraph (A).

(9) Emissions from Entire Vehicle.—In applying the requirements of this subsection, the Administrator shall take into account emissions from the entire motor vehicle, including evaporative, running, refueling, and exhaust emissions.

(10) Definitions.—For purposes of this subsection—

(A) Baseline Vehicles.—The term 'baseline vehicles' means representative model year 1990 vehicles.

(B) Baseline Gasoline.—

(i) Summertime.—The term 'baseline gasoline' means in the case of gasoline sold during the high ozone period (as defined by the Administrator) a gasoline which meets the following specifications:

Baseline Gasoline Fuel Properties

API Gravity	57.4
Sulfur, ppm	339
Benzene, %	1.53
RVP, psi	8.7
Octane, R+M/2	87.3
IBP, F	91
10%, F	128
50%, F	218
90%, F	330
End Point, F	415
Aromatics, %	32.0
Olefins, %	9.2
Saturates, %	58.8

(ii) Wintertime.—The Administrator shall establish the specifications of 'baseline gasoline' for gasoline sold at times other than the high ozone period (as defined by the Administrator). Such specifications shall be the specifications of 1990 industry average gasoline sold during such period.

(C) Toxic Air Pollutants.—The term 'toxic air pollutants' means the aggregate emissions of the following:

Benzene

1,3 Butadiene

Polycyclic organic matter (POM)

Acetaldehyde

Formaldehyde.

(D) Covered Area.—The 9 ozone nonattainment areas having a 1980 population in excess of 250,000 and having the highest ozone design value during the period 1987 through 1989 shall be 'covered areas' for purposes of this subsection. Effective one year after the reclassification of any ozone nonattainment area as a Severe ozone nonattainment area under section 181(b), such Severe area shall also be a 'covered area' for purposes of this subsection.

(E) Reformulated Gasoline.—The term 'reformulated gasoline' means any gasoline which is certified by the Administrator under this section as complying with this subsection.

(F) Conventional Gasoline.—The term 'conventional gasoline' means any gasoline which does not meet specifications set by a certification under this subsection.

[§211(k) added by PL 101–549]

(l) Detergents.—Effective beginning January 1, 1995, no person may sell or dispense to an ultimate consumer in the United States, and no refiner or marketer may directly or indirectly sell or dispense to persons who sell or dispense to ultimate consumers in the United States any gasoline which does not contain additives to prevent the accumulation of deposits in engines or fuel supply systems. Not later than 2 years after the date of the enactment of the Clean Air Act Amendments of 1990, the Administrator shall promulgate a rule establishing specifications for such additives.

[§211(l) added by PL 101–549]

(m) Oxygenated Fuels.—

(1) Plan Revisions For CO Nonattainment Areas.

(A) Each State in which there is located all or part of an area which is designated under title I as a nonattainment area for carbon monoxide and which has a carbon monoxide design value of 9.5 parts per million (ppm) or above based on data for the 2-year period of 1988 and 1989 and calculated according to the most recent interpretation methodology issued by the Administrator prior to the enactment of the Clean Air Act Amendments of 1990 shall submit to the Administrator a State implementation plan revision under section 110 and part D of title I for such area which shall contain the provisions specified under this subsection regarding oxygenated gasoline.

(B) A plan revision which contains such provisions shall also be submitted by each State in which there is located any area which, for any 2-year period after 1989 has a carbon monoxide design value of 9.5 ppm or above. The revision shall be submitted within 18 months after such 2-year period.

(2) Oxygenated Gasoline in CO Nonattainment Areas.—Each plan revision under this subsection shall contain provisions to require that any gasoline sold, or dispensed, to the ultimate consumer in the carbon monoxide nonattainment area or sold or dispensed directly or indirectly by fuel refiners or marketers to persons who sell or dispense to ultimate consumers, in the larger of —

(A) the Consolidated Metropolitan Statistical Area (CMSA) in which the area is located, or

(B) if the area is not located in a CMSA, the Metropolitan Statistical Area in which the area is located,

be blended, during the portion of the year in which the area is prone to high ambient concentrations of carbon monoxide to contain not less than 2.7 percent oxygen by weight (subject to a testing tolerance established by the Administrator). The portion of the year in which the area is prone to high ambient concentrations of carbon monoxide shall be as determined by the Administrator, but shall not be less than 4 months. At the request of a State with respect to any area designated as nonattainment for carbon monoxide, the Administrator may reduce the period specified in the preceding sentence if the State can demonstrate that because of meteorological conditions, a reduced period will assure that there will be no exceedances of the carbon monoxide standard outside of such reduced period. For areas with a carbon monoxide design value of 9.5 ppm or more of the date of enactment of the Clean Air Act Amendments of 1990, the revision shall provide that such requirement shall take effect no later than November 1, 1992, (or at such other date during 1992 as the Administrator establishes under the preceding provisions of this paragraph). For other areas, the revision shall provide that such requirement shall take effect no later than November 1 of the third year after the last year of the applicable 2-year period referred to in paragraph (1) (or at such other date during such third year as the Administrator establishes under the preceding provisions of this paragraph) and shall include a program for implementation and enforcement of the requirement consistent with guidance to be issued by the Administrator.

(3) Waivers.—

(A) The Administrator shall waive, in whole or in part, the requirements of paragraph (2) upon a demonstration by the State to the satisfaction of the Administrator that the use of oxygenated gasoline would prevent or interfere with the attainment by the area of a national primary ambient air quality standard (or a State or local ambient air quality standard) for any air pollutant other than carbon monoxide.

(B) The Administrator shall, upon demonstration by the State satisfactory to the Administrator, waive the requirement of paragraph (2) where the Administrator determines that mobile sources of carbon monoxide do not contribute significantly to carbon monoxide levels in an area.

(C) (i) Any person may petition the Administrator to make a finding that there is, or is likely to be, for any area, an inadequate domestic supply of, or distribution capacity for, oxygenated gasoline meeting the requirements of paragraph (2) or fuel additives (oxygenates) necessary to meet such requirements. The Administrator shall act on such petition within 6 months after receipt of the petition.

(ii) If the Administrator determines, in response to a petition under clause (i), that there is an inadequate supply or capacity described in clause (i), the Administrator shall delay the effective date of paragraph (2) for 1 year. Upon petition, the Administrator may extend such effective date for one additional year. No partial delay or lesser waiver may be granted under this clause.

(iii) In granting waivers under this subparagraph the Administrator shall consider distribution capacity separately from the adequacy of domestic supply and shall grant such waivers in such manner as will assure that, if supplies of oxygenated gasoline are limited, areas having the highest design value for carbon monoxide will have a priority in obtaining oxygenated gasoline which meets the requirements of paragraph (2).

(iv) As used in this subparagraph, the term distribution capacity includes capacity for transportation, storage, and blending.

(4) Fuel Dispensing Systems.—Any person selling oxygenated gasoline at retail pursuant to this subsection shall be required under regulations promulgated by the Administrator to label the fuel dispensing system with a notice that the gasoline is oxygenated and will reduce the carbon monoxide emissions from the motor vehicle.

(5) Guidelines for Credit.—The Administrator shall promulgate guidelines, within 9 months after the date of the enactment of the Clean Air Act Amendments of 1990, allowing the use of marketable oxygen credits from gasolines during that portion of the year specified in paragraph (2) with higher oxygen content than required to offset the sale or use of gasoline with a lower oxygen content than required. No credits may be transferred between nonattainment areas.

(6) Attainment Areas.—Nothing in this subsection shall be interpreted as requiring an oxygenated gasoline program in an area which is in attainment for carbon monoxide, except that in a carbon monoxide nonattainment area which is redesignated as attainment for carbon monoxide, the requirements of this subsection shall remain in effect to the extent such program is necessary to maintain such standard thereafter in the area.

(7) Failure to Attain CO Standard.—If the Administrator determines under section 186(b)(2) that the national primary ambient air quality standard for carbon monoxide has not been attained in a Serious Area by the applicable attainment date, the State shall submit a plan revision for the area within 9 months after the date of such determination. The plan revision shall provide that the minimum oxygen content of gasoline referred to in paragraph (2) shall be 3.1 percent by weight unless such requirement is waived in accordance with the provisions of this subsection.

[§211(m) added by PL 101–549]

(n) Prohibition on Leaded Gasoline for Highway Use.—After December 31, 1995, it shall be unlawful for any person to sell, offer for sale, supply, offer for supply, dispense, transport, or introduce into commerce, for use as fuel in any motor vehicle (as defined in section 219(2)) any gasoline which contains lead or lead additives.

[§211(n) added by PL 101–549]

(o) Fuel and Fuel Additive Importers and Importation.—For the purposes of this section, the term 'manufacturer' includes an importer and the term 'manufacture' includes importation.

[§211(o) added by PL 101–549]

Development of Low-Emission Vehicles

[Editor's Note: PL 96–209, March 14, 1980 provides: "The Low-Emission Vehicle Certification Board established by Act of December 31, 1970 (84 Stat. 1700; 42 U.S.C. 1857f–6e), is hereby abolished."]

§7546. [Sec. 212]

[Repealed by PL 101–549]

§7547. Nonroad Engines and Vehicles [Sec. 213]

(a) Emissions Standards.—

(1) The Administrator shall conduct a study of emissions from nonroad engines and nonroad vehicles (other than locomotives or engines used in locomotives) to determine if such emissions cause, or significantly contribute to, air pollution which may reasonably be anticipated to endanger public health or welfare. Such study shall be completed within 12 months of the date of the enactment of the Clean Air Act Amendments of 1990.

(2) After notice and opportunity for public hearing, the Administrator shall determine within 12 months after completion of the study under paragraph (1), based upon the results of such study, whether emissions of carbon monoxide, oxides of nitrogen, and volatile organic compounds from new and existing nonroad engines or nonroad vehicles (other than locomotives or engines used in locomotives) are significant contributors to ozone or carbon monoxide concentrations in more than 1 area which has failed to attain the national ambient air quality standards for ozone or carbon monoxide. Such determination shall be included in the regulations under paragraph (3).

(3) If the Administrator makes an affirmative determination under paragraph (2) the Administrator shall, within 12 months after completion of the study under paragraph (1), promulgate (and from time to time revise) regulations containing standards applicable to emissions from those classes or categories of new nonroad engines and new nonroad vehicles (other than locomotives or engines used in locomotives) which in the Administrator's judgment cause, or contribute to, such air pollution. Such standards shall achieve the greatest degree of emission reduction achievable through the application of technology which the Administrator determines will be available for the engines or vehicles to which such stan-

dards apply, giving appropriate consideration to the cost of applying such technology within the period of time available to manufacturers and to noise, energy, and safety factors associated with the application of such technology. In determining what degree of reduction will be available, the Administrator shall first consider standards equivalent in stringency to standards for comparable motor vehicles or engines (if any) regulated under section 202 , taking into account the technological feasibility, costs, safety, noise, and energy factors associated with achieving, as appropriate, standards of such stringency and lead time. The regulations shall apply to the useful life of the engines or vehicles (as determined by the Administrator).

(4) If the Administrator determines that any emissions not referred to in paragraph (2) from new nonroad engines or vehicles significantly contribute to air pollution which may reasonably be anticipated to endanger public health or welfare, the Administrator may promulgate (and from time to time revise) such regulations as the Administrator deems appropriate containing standards applicable to emissions from those classes or categories of new nonroad engines and new nonroad vehicles (other than locomotives or engines used in locomotives) which in the Administrator's judgment cause, or contribute to, such air pollution, taking into account costs, noise, safety, and energy factors associated with the application of technology which the Administrator determines will be available for the engines and vehicles to which such standards apply. The regulations shall apply to the useful life of the engines or vehicles (as determined by the Administrator).

(5) Within 5 years after the enactment of the Clean Air Act Amendments of 1990, the Administrator shall promulgate regulations containing standards applicable to emissions from new locomotives and new engines used in locomotives. Such standards shall achieve the greatest degree of emission reduction achievable through the application of technology which the Administrator determines will be available for the locomotives or engines to which such standards apply, giving appropriate consideration to the cost of applying such technology within the period of time available to manufacturers and to noise, energy, and safety factors associated with the application of such technology.

(b) Effective Date.—Standards under this section shall take effect at the earliest possible date considering the lead time necessary to permit the development and application of the requisite technology, giving appropriate consideration to the cost of compliance within such period and energy and safety.

(c) Safe Controls.—Effective with respect to new engines or vehicles to which standards under this section apply, no emission control device, system, or element of design shall be used in such a new nonroad engine or new nonroad vehicle for purposes of complying with such standards if such device, system, or element of design will cause or contribute to an unreasonable risk to public health, welfare, or safety in its operation or function. In determining whether an unreasonable risk exists, the Administrator shall consider factors including those described in section 202(a)(4)(B) .

(d) Enforcement.—The standards under this section shall be subject to sections 206, 207, 208, and 209, with such modifications of the applicable regulations implementing such sections as the Administrator deems appropriate, and shall be enforced in the same manner as standards prescribed under section 202 . The Administrator shall revise or promulgate regulations as may be necessary to determine compliance with, and enforce, standards in effect under this section.

[§213 revised by PL 101–549]

§7548. Study of Particulate Emissions from Motor Vehicles [Sec. 214]

(a) (1) The Administrator shall conduct a study concerning the effects on health and welfare of particulate emissions from motor vehicles or motor vehicle engines to which section 202 applies. Such study shall characterize and quantify such emissions and analyze the relationship of such emissions to various fuels and fuel additives.

(2) The study shall also include an analysis of particulate emissions from mobile sources which are not related to engine emissions (including, but not limited to tire debris, and asbestos from brake lining).

(b) The Administrator shall report to the Congress the findings and results of the study conducted under subsection (a) not later than two years after the date of the enactment of the Clean Air Act Amendments of 1977. Such report shall also include recommendations for stan dards or methods to regulate particulate emissions described in paragraph (2) of subsection (a).

[§214 added by PL 95–95]

§7549. High Altitude Performance Adjustments [Sec. 215]

(a) (1) Any action taken with respect to any element of design installed on or in a motor vehicle or motor vehicle engine in compliance with regulations under this title (including any alteration or adjustment of such element), shall be treated as not in violation of section 203(a) if such action is performed in accordance with high altitude adjustment instructions provided by the manufacturer under subsection (b) and approved by the Administrator.

(2) If the Administrator finds that adjustments or modifications made pursuant to instructions of the manufacturer under paragraph (1) will not insure emission control performance with respect to each standard under section 202 at least equivalent to that which would result if no such adjustments or modifications were made, he shall disapprove such instructions. Such finding shall be based upon minimum engineering evaluations consistent with good engineering practice.

(b) (1) Instructions respecting each class or category of vehicles or engines to which this title applies providing for such vehicle and engine adjustments and modifications as may be necessary to insure emission control performance at different altitudes shall be submitted by the manufacturer to the Administrator pursuant to regulations promulgated by the Administrator.

(2) Any knowing violation by a manufacturer of requirements of the Administrator under paragraph (1) shall be treated as a violation by such manufacturer of section 203(a)(3) for purposes of the penalties contained in section 205 .

(3) Such instructions shall provide, in addition to other adjustments, for adjustments for vehicles moving from high altitude areas to low altitude areas after the initial registration of such vehicles.

(c) No instructions under this section respecting adjustments or modifications may require the use of any manufacturer parts (as defined in section (203(a)) unless the manufacturer demonstrates to the satisfaction of the Administrator that the use of such manufacturer parts is necessary to insure emission control per- formance.

(d) Before January 1, 1981 the authority provided by this section shall be available in any high altitude State (as determined under regulations of the Adminis- trator under regulations promulgated before the date of the enactment of this Act) but after December 31, 1980, such authority shall be available only in any such State in which an inspection and maintenance program for the testing of motor vehicle emissions has been instituted for the portions of the State where any national ambient air quality standard for auto-related pollutants has not been attained.

[§215(d) amended by PL 95–190]

(e) High Altitude Testing.—

(1) The Administrator shall promptly establish at least one testing center (in addition to the testing centers existing on the date of the enactment of the Clean Air Act Amendments of 1990) located at a site that represents high altitude conditions, to ascertain in a reasonable manner whether, when in actual use throughout their useful life (as determined under section 202(d)), each class or category of vehicle and engines to which regulations under section 202 apply conforms to the emissions standards established by such regulations. For purposes of this subsection, the term 'high altitude conditions' refers to high altitude as defined in regulations of the Administrator in effect as of the date of the enactment of the Clean Air Act Amendments of 1990.

(2) The Administrator, in cooperation with the Secretary of Energy and the Administrator of the Urban Mass Transportation Administration, and such other agencies as the Administrator deems appropriate, shall establish a research and technology assessment center to provide for the development and evaluation of less polluting heavy-duty engines and fuels for use in buses, heavy-duty trucks, and non- road engines and vehicles, which shall be located at a high-altitude site that represents high-altitude conditions. In establishing and funding such a center, the Administrator shall give preference to proposals which provide for local cost-sharing of facilities and recovery of costs of operation through utilization of such facility for the purposes of this section.

(3) The Administrator shall designate at least one center at high-altitude conditions to provide research on after-market emission components, dual-fueled vehicles and conversion kits, the effects of tampering on emissions equipment, testing of alternate fuels and conversion kits, and the development of curricula, training courses, and materials to maximize the effectiveness of inspection and maintenance programs as they relate to promoting effective control of vehicle emissions at high-altitude elevations. Preference shall be given to existing vehicle emissions testing and research centers that have established reputations for

vehicle emissions research and development and training, and that possess in-house Federal Test Procedure capacity.

[§215(e) added by PL 101–549]

§7550. Definitions for Part A [Sec. 216]

As used in this title—

(1) The term 'manufacturer' as used in sections 202, 203, 206, 207, and 208 means any person engaged in the manufacturing or assembling of new motor vehicles, new motor vehicle engines, new nonroad vehicles or new nonroad engines or importing such vehicles or engines for resale, or who acts for and is under the control of any such person in connection with the distribution of new motor vehicles, new motor vehicle engines, new nonroad vehicles or new nonroad engines, but shall not include any dealer with respect to new motor vehicles, new motor vehicle engines, new nonroad vehicles or new nonroad engines received by him in commerce.

[§216(1) amended by PL 101–549]

(2) The term 'motor vehicle' means any self-propelled vehicle designed for transporting persons or property on a street or highway.

(3) Except with respect to vehicles or engines imported or offered for importation, the term 'new motor vehicle' means a motor vehicle the equitable or legal title to which has never been transferred to an ultimate purchaser; and the term 'new motor vehicle engine' means an engine in a new motor vehicle or a motor vehicle engine the equitable or legal title to which has never been transferred to the ultimate purchaser; and with respect to imported vehicles or engines, such terms mean a motor vehicle and engine, respectively, manufactured after the effective date of a regulation issued under section 202 which is applicable to such vehicle or engine (or which would be applicable to such vehicle or engine had it been manufactured for importation into the United States).

(4) The term 'dealer' means any person who is engaged in the sale or the distribution of new motor vehicles or new motor vehicle engines to the ultimate purchaser.

(5) The term 'ultimate purchaser' means, with respect to any new motor vehicle or new motor vehicle engine, the first person who in good faith purchases such new motor vehicle or new engine for purposes other than resale.

(6) the term 'commerce' means (A) commerce between any place in any State and any place outside thereof; and (B) commerce wholly within the District of Columbia.

(7) Vehicle Curb Weight, Gross Vehicle Weight Rating, Light-Duty Truck, Light-Duty Vehicle, And Loaded Vehicle Weight.—The terms 'vehicle curb weight', 'gross vehicle weight rating' (GVWR), 'light-duty truck' (LDT), light- duty vehicle, and 'loaded vehicle weight' (LVW) have the meaning provided in regulations promulgated by the Administrator and in effect as of the enactment of the Clean Air Act Amendments of 1990. The abbreviations in parentheses corresponding to any term referred to in this paragraph shall have the same meaning as the corresponding term.

[§216(7) added by PL 101–549]

(8) Test Weight.—The term 'test weight' and the abbreviation 'tw' mean the vehicle curb weight added to the gross vehicle weight rating (gvwr) and divided by 2.

[§216(8) added by PL 101–549]

(9) Motor Vehicle Or Engine Part Manufacturer.—The term 'motor vehicle or engine part manufacturer' as used in sections 207 and 208 means any person engaged in the manufacturing, assembling or rebuilding of any device, system, part, component or element of design which is installed in or on motor vehicles or motor vehicle engines.

[§216(9) added by PL 101–549]

(10) Nonroad Engine.—The term 'nonroad engine' means an internal combustion engine (including the fuel system) that is not used in a motor vehicle or a vehicle used solely for competition, or that is not subject to standards promulgated under section 111 or section 202 .

[§216(10) added by PL 101–549]

(11) Nonroad Vehicle.—The term 'nonroad vehicle' means a vehicle that is powered by a nonroad engine and that is not a motor vehicle or a vehicle used solely for competition.

[§216(11) added by PL 101–549]

§7552. Motor Vehicle Compliance Program Fees [Sec. 217]

(a) Fee Collection.—Consistent with section 9701 of title 31, United States Code, the Administrator may promulgate (and from time to time revise) regulations establishing fees to recover all reasonable costs to the Administrator associated with—

(1) new vehicle or engine certification under section 206(a) or part C,

(2) new vehicle or engine compliance monitoring and testing under section 206(b) or part C, and

(3) in-use vehicle or engine compliance monitoring and testing under section 207(c) or part C. The Administrator may establish for all foreign and domestic manufacturers a fee schedule based on such factors as the Administrator finds appropriate and equitable and nondiscriminatory, including the number of vehicles or engines produced under a certificate of conformity. In the case of heavy- duty engine and vehicle manufacturers, such fees shall not exceed a reasonable amount to recover an appropriate portion of such reasonable costs.

(b) Special Treasury Fund.—Any fees collected under this section shall be deposited in a special fund in the United States Treasury for licensing and other services which thereafter shall be available for appropriation, to remain available until expended, to carry out the Agency's activities for which the fees were collected.

(c) Limitation on Fund Use.—Moneys in the special fund referred to in subsection (b) shall not be used until after the first fiscal year commencing after the first July 1 when fees are paid into the fund.

(d) Administrator's Testing Authority.—Nothing in this subsection shall be construed to limit the Administrator's authority to require manufacturer or confirmatory testing as provided in this part.

[§217 added by PL 101–549]

§7553. Prohibition on Production of Engines Requiring Leaded Gasoline [Sec. 218]

The Administrator shall promulgate regulations applicable to motor vehicle engines and nonroad engines manufactured after model year 1992 that prohibit the manufacture, sale, or introduction into commerce of any engine that requires leaded gasoline.

[§218 added by PL 101–549]

§7554. Urban Bus Standards [Sec. 219]

(a) Standards for Model Years After 1993.—Not later than January 1, 1992, the Administrator shall promulgate regulations under section 202(a) applicable to urban buses for the model year 1994 and thereafter. Such standards shall be based on the best technology that can reasonably be anticipated to be available at the time such measures are to be implemented, taking costs, safety, energy, lead time, and other relevant factors into account. Such regulations shall require that such urban buses comply with the provisions of subsection (b) of this section (and subsection (c) of this subsection, if applicable) in addition to compliance with the standards applicable under section 202(a) for heavy-duty vehicles of the same type and model year.

(b) PM Standard.—

(1) 50 Percent Reduction.—The standards under section 202(a) applicable to urban buses shall require that, effective for the model year 1994 and thereafter, emissions of particulate matter (PM) from urban buses shall not exceed 50 percent of the emissions of particulate matter (PM) allowed under the emission standard applicable under section 202(a) as of the date of the enactment of the Clean Air Act Amendments of 1990 for particulate matter (PM) in the case of heavy- duty diesel vehicles and engines manufactured in the model year 1994.

(2) Revised Reduction.—The Administrator shall increase the level of emissions of particulate matter allowed under the standard referred to in paragraph (1) if the Administrator determines that the 50 percent reduction referred to in paragraph (1) is not technologically achievable, taking into account durability, costs, lead time, safety, and other relevant factors. The Administrator may not increase such level of emissions above 70 percent of the emissions of particulate matter (PM) allowed under the emission standard applicable under section 202(a) as of the date of the enactment of the Clean Air Act Amendments of 1990 for particulate matter (PM) in the case of heavy-duty diesel vehicles and engines manufactured in the model year 1994.

(3) Determination as Part of Rule.—As part of the rulemaking under subsection (a), the Administrator shall make a determination as to whether the 50 percent reduction referred to in paragraph (1) is technologically achievable, taking into account durability, costs, lead time, safety, and other relevant factors.

(c) Low-Polluting Fuel Requirement.—

(1) Annual Testing.—Beginning with model year 1994 buses, the Administrator shall conduct annual tests of a representative sample of operating urban buses subject to the particulate matter (PM) standard applicable pursuant to subsection (b) to determine whether such buses comply with such standard in use over their full useful life.

(2) Promulgation of Additional Low- Polluting Fuel Requirement.—

(A) If the Administrator determines, based on the testing under paragraph (1), that urban buses subject to the particulate matter (PM) standard applicable pursuant to subsection (b) do not comply with such standard in use over their full useful life, he shall revise the standards applicable to such buses to require (in addition to compliance with the PM standard applicable pursuant to subsection (b)) that all new urban buses purchased or placed into service by owners or operators of urban buses in all metropolitan statistical areas or consolidated metropolitan statistical areas with a 1980 population of 750,000 or more shall be capable of operating, and shall be exclusively operated, on low-polluting fuels. The Administrator shall establish the pass-fail rate for purposes of testing under this subparagraph.

(B) The Administrator shall promulgate a schedule phasing in any low-polluting fuel requirement established pursuant to this paragraph to an increasing percentage of new urban buses purchased or placed into service in each of the first 5 model years commencing 3 years after the determination under subparagraph (A). Under such schedule 100 percent of new urban buses placed into service in the fifth model year commencing 3 years after the determination under subparagraph (A) shall comply with the low-polluting fuel requirement established pursuant to this paragraph.

(C) The Administrator may extend the requirements of this paragraph to metropolitan statistical areas or consolidated metropolitan statistical areas with a 1980 population of less than 750,000, if the Administrator determines that a significant benefit to public health could be expected to result from such extension.

(d) Retrofit Requirements.—Not later than 12 months after the enactment of the Clean Air Act Amendments of 1990, the Administrator shall promulgate regulations under section 202(a) requiring that urban buses which—

(1) are operating in areas referred to in subparagraph (A) of subsection (c)(2) (or subparagraph (C) of subsection (c)(2) if the Administrator has taken action under that subparagraph);

(2) were not subject to standards in effect under the regulations under subsection (a); and

(3) have their engines replaced or rebuilt after January 1, 1995, shall comply with an emissions standard or emissions control technology requirement established by the Administrator in such regulations. Such emissions standard or emissions control technology requirement shall reflect the best retrofit technology and maintenance practices reasonably achievable.

(e) Procedures for Administration and Enforcement.—The Administrator shall establish, within 18 months after the enactment of the Clean Air Act Amendments to 1990, and in accordance with section 206(h) , procedures for the administration and enforcement of standards for buses subject to standards under this section, testing procedures, sampling protocols, in-use compliance requirements, and criteria governing evaluation of buses. Procedures for testing (including, but not limited to, certification testing) shall reflect actual operating conditions.

(f) Definitions.—For purposes of this section—

(1) Urban Bus.—The term 'urban bus' has the meaning provided under regulations of the Administrator promulgated under section 202(a) .

(2) Low-Polluting Fuel.—The term 'low-polluting fuel' means methanol, ethanol, propane, or natural gas, or any comparably low-polluting fuel. In determining whether a fuel is comparably low-polluting, the Administrator shall consider both the level of emissions of air pollutants from vehicles using the fuel and the contribution of such emissions to ambient levels of air pollutants. For purposes of this paragraph, the term 'methanol' includes any fuel which contains at least 85 percent methanol unless the Administrator increases such percentage as he deems appropriate to protect public health and welfare.

[§219 added by PL 101–549]

PART B—AIRCRAFT EMISSION STANDARDS

§7571. Establishment of Standards [Sec. 231]

(a) (1) Within 90 days after the date of enactment of the Clean Air Act Amendments of 1970, the Administrator shall commence a study and investigation of emissions of air pollutants from aircraft in order to determine—

(A) the extent to which such emissions affect air quality in air quality control regions throughout the United States, and

(B) the technological feasibility of controlling such emissions.

(2) The Administrator shall, from time to time, issue proposed emission standards applicable to emissions of any air pollution from any class or classes of aircraft or aircraft engines which in his judgment causes, or contributes to, air

pollution which may reasonably be anticipated to endanger the public health or welfare.

[§231(a)(2) amended by PL 95–95]

(3) The Administrator shall hold public hearings with respect to such proposed standards. Such hearings shall, to the extent practicable, be held in air quality control regions which are most seriously affected by aircraft emissions. Within 90 days after the issuance of such proposed regulations, he shall issue such regulations with such modifications as he deems appropriate. Such regulations may be revised from time to time.

(b) Any regulation prescribed under this section (and any revision thereof) shall take effect after such period as the Administrator finds necessary (after consultation with the Secretary of Transportation) to permit the development and application of the requisite technology, giving appropriate consideration to the cost of compliance within such period.

(c) Any regulations in effect under this section on date of enactment of the Clean Air Act Amendments of 1977 or proposed or promulgated thereafter, or amendments thereto, with respect to aircraft shall not apply if disapproved by the President, after notice and opportunity for public hearing, on the basis of a finding by the Secretary of Transportation that any such regulation would create a hazard to aircraft safety. Any such finding shall include a reasonably specific statement of the basis upon which the finding was made.

[§231(c) amended by PL 95–95]

§7572. Enforcement of Standards [Sec. 232]

(a) The Secretary of Transportation, after consultation with the Administrator, shall prescribe regulations to insure compliance with all standards prescribed under section 231 by the Administrator. The regulations of the Secretary of Transportation shall include provisions making such standards applicable in the issuance, amendment, modification, suspension, or revocation of any certificate authorized by the Federal Aviation Act or the Department of Transportation Act. Such Secretary shall insure that all necessary inspections are accomplished, and, may execute any power or duty vested in him by any other provision of law in the execution of all powers and duties vested in him under this section.

(b) In any action to amend, modify, suspend, or revoke a certificate in which violation of an emission standard prescribed under section 231 or of a regulation prescribed under subsection (a) is at issue, the certificate holder shall have the same notice and appeal rights as are prescribed for such holders in the Federal Aviation Act of 1958 or the Department of Transportation Act, except that in any appeal to the National Transportation Safety Board, the Board may amend, modify, or revoke the order of the Secretary of Transportation only if it finds no violation of such standard or regulation and that such amendment, modification, or revocation is consistent with safety in air transportation.

§7573. State Standards and Controls [Sec. 233]

No State or political subdivision thereof may adopt or attempt to enforce any standard respecting emissions of any air pollutant from any aircraft or engine thereof unless such standard is identical to a standard applicable to such aircraft under this part.

§7574. Definitions [Sec. 234]

Terms used in this part (other than Administrator) shall have the same meaning as such terms have under section 101 of the Federal Aviation Act of 1958.

PART C—CLEAN FUEL VEHICLES

[Part C added by PL 101–549]

§7581. Definitions [Sec. 241]

For purposes of this part—

(1) Terms defined in part A.—The definitions applicable to part A under section 216 shall also apply for purposes of this part.

(2) Clean alternative fuel.— The term 'clean alternative fuel' means any fuel (including methanol, ethanol, or other alcohols (including any mixture thereof containing 85 percent or more by volume of such alcohol with gasoline or other fuels), reformulated gasoline, diesel, natural gas, liquefied petroleum gas, and hydrogen) or power source (including electricity) used in a clean-fuel vehicle that complies with the standards and requirements applicable to such vehicle under this title when using such fuel or power source. In the case of any flexible fuel vehicle or dual fuel vehicle, the term 'clean alternative fuel' means only a fuel with respect to which such vehicle was certified as a clean-fuel vehicle meeting the standards applicable to clean-fuel vehicles under section 243(d)(2) when operating on clean alternative fuel (or any CARB standards which replaces such standards pursuant to section 243(e)).

(3) NMOG.—The term nonmethane organic gas ('NMOG') means the sum of nonoxygenated and oxygenated hydrocarbons contained in a gas sample, including, at a minimum, all oxy-

genated organic gases containing 5 or fewer carbon atoms (i.e., aldehydes, ketones, alcohols, ethers, etc.), and all known alkanes, alkenes, alkynes, and aromatics containing 12 or fewer carbon atoms. To demonstrate compliance with a NMOG standard, NMOG emissions shall be measured in accordance with the 'California Non-Methane Organic Gas Test Procedures'. In the case of vehicles using fuels other than base gasoline, the level of NMOG emissions shall be adjusted based on the reactivity of the emissions relative to vehicles using base gasoline.

(4) Base Gasoline.—The term 'base gasoline' means gasoline which meets the following specifications:

Specifiactions of Base Gasoline Used as Basis for Reactivity

Readjustment:	
API gravity	57.8
Sulfur, ppm	317
Color	Purple
Benzene, vol. %	1.35
Reid vapor pressure	8.7
Drivability	11195
Antiknock index	87.3
Distillation, D-86° F	
IBP	92
10%	126
50%	219
90%	327
EP	414
Hydrocarbon Type, Vol. % FIA:	
Aromatics	30.9
Olefins	8.2
Saturates	60.9

The Administrator shall modify the definitions of NMOG, base gasoline, and the methods for making reactivity adjustments, to conform to the definitions and method used in California under the Low- Emission Vehicle and Clean Fuel Regulations of the California Air Resources Board, so long as the California definitions are, in the aggregate, at least as pro tective of public health and welfare as the definitions in this section.

(5) Covered Fleet.—The term 'covered fleet' means 10 or more motor vehicles which are owned or operated by a single person. In determining the number of vehicles owned or operated by a single person for purposes of this paragraph, all motor vehicles owned or operated, leased or otherwise controlled by such person, by any person who controls such person, by any person controlled by such person, and by any person under common control with such person shall be treated as owned by such person. The term 'covered fleet' shall not include motor vehicles held for lease or rental to the general public, motor vehicles held for sale by motor vehicle dealers (including demonstration vehicles), motor vehicles used for motor vehicle manufacturer product evaluations or tests, law enforcement and other emergency vehicles, or nonroad vehicles (including farm and construction vehicles).

(6) Covered Fleet Vehicle.—The term 'covered fleet vehicle' means only a motor vehicle which is—

(i) in a vehicle class for which standards are applicable under this part; and

(ii) in a covered fleet which is centrally fueled (or capable of being centrally fueled). No vehicle which under normal operations is garaged at a personal residence at night shall be considered to be a vehicle which is capable of being centrally fueled within the meaning of this paragraph.

(7) Clean-fuel Vehicle.—The term 'clean fuel vehicle' means a vehicle in a class or category of vehicles which has been certified to meet for any model year the clean-fuel vehicle standards applicable under this part for that model year to clean-fuel vehicles in that class or category.

§7582. Requirements Applicable to Clean Fuel Vehicles [Sec. 242]

(a) Promulgation of Standards.—Not later than 24 months after the enactment of the Clean Air Act Amendments of 1990, the Administrator shall promulgate regulations under this part containing clean-fuel vehicle standards for the clean- fuel vehicles specified in this part.

(b) Other Requirements.—Clean-fuel vehicles of up to 8,500 gvwr subject to standards set forth in this part shall comply with all motor vehicle requirements of this title (such as requirements relating to on-board diagnostics, evaporative emissions, etc.) which are applicable to conventional gasoline-fueled vehicles of the same category and model year, except as provided in section 244 with respect to administration and enforcement, and except to the extent that any such requirement is in conflict with the provisions of this part. Clean-fuel vehicles of 8,500 gvwr or greater subject to standards set forth in this part shall comply with all requirements of this title which are applicable in the case of conventional gasoline- fueled or diesel fueled vehicles of the same category and model year, except as provided in section 244 with respect to administration and enforcement, and except to the extent that any such requirement is in conflict with the provisions of this part.

(c) In-use Useful Life and Testing.—

(1) In the case of light-duty vehicles and light-duty trucks up to 6,000 lbs gvwr, the useful life for purposes of determining in-use compliance with the standards under section 243 shall be—

(A) a period of 5 years or 50,000 miles (or the equivalent) whichever first occurs, in the case of standards applicable for purposes of certification at 50,000 miles; and

(B) a period of 10 or 100,000 miles (or the equivalent) whichever first occurs, in the case of standards applicable for purposes of certification at 100,000 miles, except that in-use testing shall not be done for a period beyond 7 years or 75,000 miles (or the equivalent) whichever first occurs.

(2) In the case of light-duty trucks of more than 6,000 lbs gvwr, the useful life for purposes of determining in-use compliance with the standards under section 243 shall be—

(A) a period of 5 years or 50,000 miles (or the equivalent) whichever first occurs, in the case of standards applicable for purposes of certification at 50,000 miles; and

(B) a period of 11 years or 120,000 miles (or the equivalent) whichever first occurs in the case of standards applicable for purposes of certification at 120,000 miles, except that in-use testing shall not be done for a period beyond 7 years or 90,000 miles (or the equivalent) whichever first occurs.

§7583. Standards for Light-duty Clean Fuel Vehicles [Sec. 243]

(a) Exhaust Standards for Light-duty Vehicles and Certain Light-duty Trucks.—The standards set forth in this subsection shall apply in the case of clean- fuel vehicles which are light-duty trucks of up to 6,000 lbs. gross vehicle weight rating (gvwr) (but not including light-duty trucks of more than 3,750 lbs. loaded vehicle weight (lvw)) or light-duty vehicles:

(1) Phase I.—Beginning with model year 1996, for the air pollutants specified in the following table, the clean-fuel vehicle standards under this section shall provide that vehicle exhaust emissions shall not exceed the levels specified in the following table:

[Editor's Note: Refer to Table 1 on following page].

(2) Phase II.—Beginning with model year 2001, for air pollutants specified in the following table, the clean-fuel vehicle standards under this section shall provide that vehicle exhaust emissions shall not exceed the levels specified in the following table.

[Editor's Note: Refer to Table 2 on following page].

(b) Exhaust Standards for Light-Duty Trucks of More Than 3,750 Lbs. LVW and up to 5,750 Lbs. LVW and up to 6,000 Lbs. GVWR.—The standards set forth in this paragraph shall apply in the case of clean-fuel vehicles which are light-duty trucks of more than 3,750 lbs. loaded vehicle weight (lvw) but not more than 5,750 lbs. lvw and not more 6,000 lbs. gross weight rating (GVWR):

(1) Phase I.—Beginning with model year 1996, for the air pollutants specified in the following table, the clean-fuel vehicle standards under this section shall provide that vehicle exhaust emissions shall not exceed the levels specified in the following table.

[Editor's Note: Refer to Table 3 on following page].

(2) Phase II.—Beginning with model year 2001, for the air pollutants specified in the following table, the clean-fuel vehicle standards under this section shall provide that vehicle exhaust emissions shall not exceed the levels specified in the following table.

[Editor's Note: Refer to Table 4 on following page].

(c) Exhaust Standards for Light-Duty Trucks Greater Than 6,000 Lbs. GVWR.—The standards set forth in this subsection shall apply in the case of clean- fuel vehicles which are light-duty trucks of more than 6,000 lbs. gross weight rating (GVWR) and less than or equal to 8,500 lbs. GVWR, beginning with model year 1998. For the air pollutants specified in the following table, the clean-fuel vehicle standards under this section shall provide that vehicle exhaust emissions of vehicles within the test weight categories specified in the following table shall not exceed the levels specified in such table.

[Editor's Note: Refer to Table 5 on following page].

(d) Flexible and Dual-Fuel Vehicles.—

(1) In general.—The Administrator shall establish standards and requirements under this section for the model year 1996 and thereafter for vehicles weighing not more than 8,500 lbs. gvwr which are capable of operating on more than one fuel. Such standards shall require that

Table 1: Phase I Clean Vehicle Emission Standards for Light-Duty Trucks of up to 3,750 Lbs. LVW and up to 6,000 Lbs. GVWR and Light-Duty Vehicles

Pollutant	NMOG	CO	NO_x	PM	HCHO (formaldehyde)
50,000 mile standard	0.125	3.4	0.4		0.015
100,000 mile standard	0.156	4.2	0.6	0.08*	0.018

Table 2: Phase II Clean Vehicle Emission Standards for LIght-Duty Trucks of More Than 3,750 Lbs. LVW and up to 6,000 Lbs. GVWR and Light-Duty Vehicles

Pollutant	NMOG	CO	NO_x	PM*	HCHO (formaldehyde)
50,000 mile standard	0.075	3.4	0.2		0.015
100,000 mile standard	0.090	4.2	0.3	0.08	0.018

Table 3: Phase I Clean Fuel Vehicle Emission Standards for Light-Duty Trucks of More Than 3,750 Lbs. and up to 5,750 Lbs. LVW and up to 6,000 Lbs. GVWR

Pollutant	NMOG	CO	NO_x	PM*	HCHO (formaldehyde)
50,000 mile standard	0.160	4.4	0.7		0.018
100,000 mile standard	0.200	5.5	0.9	0.08	0.023

Table 4: Phase II Clean Fuel Vehicle Emission Standards for Light-Duty Trucks of More Than 3,750 Lbs. LVW and up to 5,750 Lbs. LVW and up to 6,000 Lbs. GVWR

Pollutant	NMOG	CO	NO_x	PM*	HCHO (formaldehyde)
50,000 mile standard	0.100	4.4	0.4		0.018
120,000 mile standard	0.130	5.5	0.5	0.08	0.023

Standards are expressed in grams per mile (gpm).}

*Standards for particulates (PM) shall apply only to diesel-fueled vehicles.

In the case of the 50,000 mile standards and the 100,000 mile standards, for purposes of certificatoin, the applicable useful life shall be 50,000 miles or 100,000 miles, respectively.

Table 5: CLEAN FUEL VEHICLE EMISSION STANDARDS FOR LIGHT DUTY TRUCKS GREATER THAN 6,000 LBS. GVWR

Test Weight Category: Up to 3,750 lbs. tw

Pollutant	NMOG	CO	NO_x	PM*	HCHO (formaldehyde)
50,000 mile standard	0.125	3.4	0.4**		0.015
100,000 mile standard	0.180	5.0	0.6	0.08	0.022

Standards are expressed in grams per mile (gpm).}

*Standards for particulates (PM) shall apply only to diesel-fueled vehicles.

**Standard not applicable to diesel-fueled vehicles.

In the case of the 50,000 mile standards and the 120,000 mile standards, for purposes of certificatoin, the applicable useful life shall be 50,000 miles or 120,000 miles, respectively.

Continued on next page

Test Weight Category: Above 3,750 but not above 5,750 lbs. tw

Pollutant	NMOG	CO	NO_X	PM*	HCHO (formaldehyde)
50,000 mile standard	0.160	4.4	0.7**		0.018
120,000 mile standard	0.230	6.4	1.0	0.08	0.027

Test Weight Category: Above 5,750 tw but not above 8,500 lbs. gvwr

Pollutant	NMOG	CO	NO_X	PM*	HCHO (formaldehyde)
50,000 mile standard	0.195	5.0	1.1**		0.022
120,000 mile standard	.0280	7.3	1.5	0.12	0.032

Standards are expressed in grams per mile (gpm).
*Standards for particulates (PM) shall apply only to diesel-fueled vehicles.
**Standard not applicable to diesel-fueled vehicles.
In the case of the 50,000 mile standards and the 120,000 mile standards, for purposes of certificatoin, the applicable useful life shall be 50,000 miles or 120,000 miles, respectively.

such vehicles meet the exhaust standards applicable under subsection (a), (b), and (c) for CO, NO_x, and HCHO, and if appropriate, PM for single-fuel vehicles of the same vehicle category and model year.

(2) Exhaust NMOG standard for operation on clean alternative fuel.—In addition to standards for the pollutants referred to in paragraph (1), the standards established under paragraph (1) shall require that vehicle exhaust emissions of NMOG not exceed the levels (expressed in grams per mile) specified in the tables below when the vehicle is operated on the clean alternative fuel for which such vehicle is certified:

NMOG Standards for Flexible- and Dual-Fueled Vehicles When Operating on Clean Alternative Fuel

Vehicle Type	Column A (50,000 mi.) Standard (gpm)	Column B (100,000 mi.) Standard (gpm)
Beginning MY 1996:		
LDT's (0-3,750 lbs. LVW) and light-duty vehicles	0.125	0.156
LDT's (3,751-5,750 lbs. LVW)	0.160	0.20
Beginning MY 2001:		

Vehicle Type	Column A (50,000 mi.) Standard (gpm)	Column B (100,000 mi.) Standard (gpm)
LDT's (0-3,750 lbs. LVW) and light-duty vehicles	0.075	0.090
LDT's (3,751-5750 lbs. LVW)	0.100	0.130

For standards under column A, for purposes of certification under section 206, the applicable useful life shall be 50,000 miles.
For standards under column B, for purposes of certification under section 206, the applicable useful life shall be 100,000 miles.

Light-duty Trucks More than 6,000 lbs. GVWR

Vehicle Type	Column A (50,000 mi.) Standard	Column B (120,000 mi.) Standard
Beginning MY 1998:		
LDT's (0-3,750 lbs. TW)	0.125	0.180
LDT's (3,751-5,750 lbs. TW)	0.160	0.230
LDT's (above 5,750 lbs. TW)	0.195	0.280

For standards under column A, for purposes of certification under section 206, the applicable useful life shall be 50,000 miles.
For standards under column B, for purposes of certification under section 206, the applicable useful life shall be 120,000 miles.

(3) NMOG standard for operation on conventional fuel.—In addition to the standards referred to in paragraph (1), the standards established under paragraph (1) shall require that vehicle exhaust emissions of NMOG not exceed the levels (expressed in grams per mile) specfied in the tables below:

NMOG STANDARDS FOR FLEXIBLE- AND DUAL-FUELED VEHICLES WHEN OPERATING ON CONVENTIONAL FUEL

Light-duty Trucks of up to 6,000 lbs. GVWR and Light-duty vehicles

Vehicle Type	Column A (50,000 mi.) Standard	Column B (100,000 mi.) Standard
Beginning MY 1996:		
LDT's (0-3,750 lbs. LVW) and light-duty vehicles	0.25	0.31
LDT's (3,751-5,750 lbs. LVW)	0.32	0.40
Beginning MY 2001:		
LDT's (0-3,750 lbs. LVW) and light-duty vehicles	0.125	0.156
LDT's (3,751-5,750 lbs. LVW)	0.160	0.200

For standards under column A, for purposes of certification under section 206, the applicable useful life shall be 50,000 miles.

For standards under column B, for purposes of certification under section 206, the applicable useful life shall be 100,000 miles.

Light-duty Trucks of up to 6,000 lbs. GVWR

Vehicle Type	Column A (50,000 mi.) Standard	Column B (120,000 mi.) Standard
Beginning MY 1998:		
LDT's (0-3,750 lbs. TW)	0.25	0.36
LDT's (3,751-5,750 lbs. TW)	0.32	0.46
LDT's (above 5,750 lbs. TW)	0.39	0.56

For standards under column A, for purposes of certification under section 206, the applicable useful life shall be 50,000 miles.

For standards under column B, for purposes of certification under section 206, the applicable useful life shall be 120,000 miles.

(e) Replacement by CARB Standards.—

(1) Single set of CARB Standards.—If the State of California promulgates regulations establishing and implementing a single set of standards applicable in California pursuant to a waiver approved under section 209 to any category of vehicles referred to in subsection (a), (b), (c), or (d) of this section and such set of standards is, in the aggregate, at least as protective of public health and welfare as the otherwise applicable standards set forth in section 242 and subsection (a), (b), (c), or (d) of this section, such set of California standards shall apply to clean-fuel vehicles in such category in lieu of the standards otherwise applicable under section 242 and subsection (a), (b), (c), or (d) of this section, as the case may be.

(2) Multiple Sets of CARB Standards.—If the State of California promulgates regulations establishing and implementing several different sets of standards applicable in California pursuant to a waiver approved under section 209 to any category of vehicles referred to in subsection (a), (b), (c), or (d) of this section and each of such sets of California standards is, in the aggregate, at least as protective of public health and welfare as the otherwise applicable standards set forth in section 242 and subsection (a), (b), (c), or (d) of this section, such standards shall be treated as 'qualifying California standards' for purposes of this paragraph. Where more than one set of qualifying standards are established and administered by the State of California, the least stringent set of qualifying California standards shall apply to the clean-fuel vehicles concerned in lieu of the standards otherwise applicable to such vehicles under section 242 and this section.

(f) Less Stringent CARB Standards.—If the Low-Emission Vehicle and Clean Fuels Regulations of the California Air Resources Board applicable to any category of vehicles referred to in subsection (a), (b), (c), or (d) of this section are modified after the enactment of the Clean Air Act of 1990 to provide an emissions standard which is less stringent than the otherwise applicable standard set forth in subsection (a), (b), (c), or (d), or if any effective date contained in such regula tions is delayed, such modified standards or such delay (or both, as the case may be) shall apply, for an interim period, in lieu of the standard or effective date otherwise applicable under subsection (a), (b), (c), or (d) to any vehicles covered by such modified standard or delayed effective date. The interim period shall be a period of not more than 2 model years from the effective date otherwise applicable under subsection (a), (b), (c), or (d). After such interim period, the otherwise applicable standard set forth in subsection (a), (b), (c), or (d) shall take effect with respect to such vehicles (unless subsequently replaced under subsection (e).

(g) Not Applicable to Heavy-Duty Vehicles.—Notwithstanding any provision of the Low-Emission Vehicle and Clean Fuels Regulations of the California Air Resources Board nothing in this section shall apply to heavy-duty engines in vehicles of more than 8,500 lbs. GVWR.

§7584. Administration and Enforcement as per California Standards [Sec. 244]

Where the numerical clean-fuel vehicle standards applicable under this part to vehicles of not more than 8,500 lbs. GVWR are the same as numerical emission standards applicable in California under the Low-Emission Vehicle and Clean Fuels Regulations of the California Air Resources Board ('CARB'), such standards shall be administered and enforced by the Administrator—

(1) in the same manner and with the same flexibility as the State of California administers and enforces corresponding standards applicable under the Low-Emission Vehicle and Clean Fuels Regulations of the California Air Resources Board ('CARB'); and

(2) subject to the same requirements, and utilizing the same interpretations and policy judgments, as are applicable in the case of such CARB standards, including, but not limited to, requirements regarding certification, production-line testing, and in-use compliance, unless the Administrator determines (in promulgating the rules establishing the clean fuel vehicle program under this section) that any such administration and enforcement would not meet the criteria for a waiver under section 209. Nothing in this section shall apply in the case of standards under section 245 for heavy-duty vehicles.

§7585. Standards for Heavy-duty Clean-fuel Vehicles (GVWR Above 8,500 up to 26,000 LBS). [Sec. 245]

(a) Model Years After 1997; Combined $NO_x$and NMHC Standard.—For classes or categories of heavy-duty vehicles or engines manufactured for the model year 1998 or thereafter and having a GVWR greater than 8,500 lbs. and up to 26,000 lbs. GVWR, the standards under this part for clean-fuel vehicles shall require that combined emissions of oxides of nitrogen (NO_x) and non-methane hydrocarbons (NMHC) shall not exceed 3.15 grams per brake horsepower hour (equivalent to 50 percent of the combined emission standards applicable under section 202 for such air pollutants in the case of a conventional model year 1994 heavy-duty diesel-fueled vehicle or engine). No standard shall be promulgated as provided in this section for any heavy-duty vehicle of more than 26,000 lbs. GVWR.

(b) Revised Standards that are Less Stringent.—

(1) The Administrator may promulgate a revised less stringent standard for the vehicles or engines referred to in subsection (a) if the Administrator determines that the 50 percent reduction required under subsection (a) is not technologically feasible for clean diesel-fueled vehicles and engines, taking into account durability, costs, lead time, safety, and other relevant factors. To provide adequate lead time the Administrator shall make a determination with regard to the technological feasibility of such 50 percent reduction before December 31, 1993.

(2) Any person may at any time petition the Administrator to make a determination under paragraph (1). The Administrator shall act on such a petition within 6 months after the petition is filed.

(3) Any revised less stringent standards promulgated as provided in this subsection shall require at least a 30 percent reduction in lieu of the 50 percent reduction referred to in paragraph (1).

§7586. Centrally Fueled Fleets [Sec. 246]

(a) Fleet Program Required for Certain Nonattainment Areas.—

(1) SIP Revision.—Each State in which there is located all or part of a covered area (as defined in paragraph (2)) shall submit, within 42 months after the enactment of the Clean Air Act Amendments of 1990, a State implementation plan revision under section 110 and part D of title I to establish a clean-fuel vehicle program for fleets under this section.

(2) Covered Areas.—For purposes of this subsection, each of the following shall be a 'covered area':

(A) Ozone Nonattainment Areas.—Any ozone nonattainment area with a 1980 population of 250,000 or more classified under subpart 2 of part D of title I of this Act as Serious, Severe, or Extreme based on data for the calendar years 1987, 1988, and 1989. In determinating the ozone nonattainment areas to be treated as covered areas pursuant to this subparagraph, the Administrator shall use the most recent interpretation methodology issued by the Administrator prior to the enactment of the Clean Air Act Amendments of 1990.

(B) Carbon Monoxide Nonattainment Areas.—Any carbon monoxide nonattainment area with a 1980 population of 250,000 or more and a carbon monoxide design value at or above 16.0 parts per million based on data for calendar years 1988 and 1989 (as calculated according to the most recent interpretation methodology issued prior to enactment of the Clean Air Act Amendments of 1990 by the United States Environmental Protection Agency), excluding those carbon monoxide nonattainment areas in which mobile sources do not contribute significantly to carbon monoxide exceedances.

(3) Plan revisions for reclassified areas.—In the case of ozone nonattainment areas reclassified as Serious, Severe, or Extreme under part D of title I with a 1980 population of 250,000 or more, the State shall submit a plan revision meeting the requirements of this subsection within 1 year after reclassification. Such plan revision shall implement the requirements applicable under this subsection at the time of reclassification and thereafter, except that the Administrator may adjust for a limited period the deadlines for compliance where compliance with such deadlines would be infeasible.

(4) Consultation; consideration of factors.—Each State required to submit an implementation plan revision under this subsection shall develop such revision in consultation with fleet operators, vehicle manufacturers, fuel producers and distributors, motor vehicle fuel, and other interested parties, taking into consideration operational range, specialty uses, vehicle and fuel availability, costs, safety, resale values of vehicles and equipment and other relevant factors.

(b) Phase-in of requirements.—The plan revision required under this section shall contain provisions requiring that at least a specified percentage of all new covered fleet vehicles in model year 1998 and thereafter purchased by each covered fleet operator in each covered area shall be clean-fuel vehicles and shall use clean alternative fuels when operating in the covered area. For the applicable model years (MY) specified in the following table and thereafter, the specified percentage shall be as provided in the table for the vehicle types set forth in the table:

CLEAN FUEL VEHICLE PHASE-IN REQUIREMENTS FOR FLEETS

Vehicle Type	MY1998	MY1999	MY2000
Light-duty trucks up to 6,000 lbs. GVWR and light-duty vehicles	30%	50%	70%
Heavy-duty trucks above 8,500 lbs. GVWR	50%	50%	50%

The term MY refers to model year.

(c) Accelerated standard for light-duty trucks up to 6,000 lbs. GVWR and light- duty vehicles.—Notwithstanding the model years for which clean-fuel vehicle standards are applicable as provided in section 243 , for purposes of this section, light duty trucks of up to 6,000 lbs. GVWR and light-duty vehicles manufactured in model years 1998 through model year 2000 shall be treated as clean-fuel vehicles only if such vehicles comply with the standards applicable under section 243 for vehicles in the same class for the model year 2001. The requirements of subsection (b) shall take effect on the earlier of the following:

(1) The first model year after model year 1997 in which new light-duty trucks up to 6,000 lbs. GVWR and light-duty vehicles which comply with the model year 2001 standards under section 243 are offered for sale in California.

(2) Model year 2001.— Whenever the effective date of subsection (b) is delayed pursuant to paragraph (1) of this subsection, the phase-in schedule under subsection (b) shall be modified to commence with the model year referred to in paragraph (1) in lieu of model year 1998.

(d) Choice of Vehicles and Fuel.—The plan revision under this subsection shall provide that the choice of clean-fuel vehicles and clean alternative fuels shall be made by the covered fleet operator subject to the requirements of this subsection.

(e) Availability of Clean Alternative Fuel.—The plan revision shall require fuel providers to make clean alternative fuel available to covered fleet operators at locations at which covered fleet vehicles are centrally fueled.

(f) Credits.—

(1) Issuance of Credits.—The State plan revision required under this section shall provide for the issuance by the State of appropriate

credits to a fleet operator for any of the following (or any combination thereof):

(A) The purchase of more clean-fuel vehicles than required under this section.

(B) The purchase of clean fuel vehicles which meet more stringent standards established by the Administrator pursuant to paragraph (4).

(C) The purchase of vehicles in categories which are not covered by this section but which meet standards established for such vehicles under paragraph (4).

(2) Use of Credits; Limitations Based on Weight Classes.—

(A) Use of Credits.—Credits under this subsection may be used by the person holding such credits to demonstrate compliance with this section or may be traded or sold for use by any other person to demonstrate compliance with other requirements applicable under this section in the same nonattainment area. Credits obtained at any time may be held or banked for use at any later time, and when so used, such credits shall maintain the same value as if used at an earlier date.

(B) Limitations Based on Weight Classes.—Credits issued with respect to the purchase of vehicles of up to 8,500 lbs. GVWR may not be used to demonstrate compliance by any person with the requirements applicable under this subsection to vehicles of more than 8,500 lbs. GVWR. Credits issued with respect to the purchase of vehicles of more than 8,500 lbs. GVWR may not be used to demonstrate compliance by any person with the requirements applicable under this subsection to vehicles weighing up to 8,500 lbs. GVWR.

(C) Weighting.—Credits issued for purchase of a clean fuel vehicle under this subsection shall be adjusted with appropriate weighting to reflect the level of emission reduction achieved by the vehicle.

(3) Regulations and Administration.—Within 12 months after the enactment of the Clean Air Act Amendments of 1990, the Administrator shall promulgate regulations for such credit program. The State shall administer the credit program established under this subsection.

(4) Standards for Issuing Credits for Cleaner Vehicles.—Solely for purposes of issuing credits under paragraph (1)(B), the Administrator shall establish under this paragraph standards for Ultra-Low Emission Vehicles ('ULEV's) and Zero Emissions Vehicles ('ZEV's) which shall be more stringent than those otherwise applicable to clean-fuel vehicles under this part. The Administrator shall certify clean fuel vehicles as complying with such more stringent standards, and administer and enforce such more stringent standards, in the same manner as in the case of the otherwise applicable clean-fuel vehicle standards established under this section. The standards established by the Administrator under this paragraph for vehicles under 8,500 lbs. GVWR or greater shall conform as closely as possible to standards which are established by the State of California for ULEV and ZEV vehicles in the same class. For vehicles of 8,500 lbs. GVWR or more, the Administrator shall promulgate comparable standards for purposes of this subsection.

(5) Early Fleet Credits.—The State plan revision shall provide credits under this subsection to fleet operators that pur chase vehicles certified to meet clean- fuel vehicle standards under this part during any period after approval of the plan revision and prior to the effective date of the fleet program under this section.

(g) Availability to the Public.—At any facility owned or operated by a department, agency, or instrumentality of the United States where vehicles subject to this subsection are supplied with clean alternative fuel, such fuel shall be offered for sale to the public for use in other vehicles during reasonable business times and subject to national security concerns, unless such fuel is commercially available for vehicles in the vicinity of such Federal facilities.

(h) Transportation Control Measures.—The Administrator shall by rule, within 1 year after the enactment of the Clean Air Act Amendments of 1990, ensure that certain transportation control measures including time-of-day or day-of- week restrictions, and other similar measures that restrict vehicle usage, do not apply to any clean-fuel vehicle that meets the requirements of this section. This subsection shall apply notwithstanding title I.

§7587. Vehicle Conversions [Sec. 247]

(a) Conversion of Existing any New Conventional Vehicles to Clean-Fuel Vehicles.—The requirements of section 246 may be met through the conversion of existing or new gasoline or diesel-powered vehicles to clean-fuel vehicles which comply with the applicable requirements of that section. For purposes of such provisions the conversion of a vehicle to clean fuel vehicle shall be treated as the purchase of a clean fuel vehicle. Nothing in this part shall be construed to provide that any covered fleet operator subject to fleet vehicle purchase requirements under section 246 shall be required to convert existing or new gasoline or diesel-powered vehicles to clean-fuel vehicles or to purchase converted vehicles.

(b) Regulations.—The Administrator shall, within 24 months after the enactment of the Clean Air Act Amendments of 1990, consistent with the requirements of this title applicable to new vehicles, promulgate regulations governing conversions of conventional vehicles to clean-fuel vehicles. Such regulations shall establish criteria for such conversions which will ensure that a converted vehicle will comply with the standards applicable under this part to clean-fuel vehicles. Such regulations shall provide for the application to such conversions of the same provisions of this title (including provisions relating to administration enforcement) as are applicable to standards under section 242, 243, 244, and 245, except that in the case of conversions the Administrator may modify the applicable regulations implementing such provisions as the Administrator deems necessary to implement this part.

(c) Enforcement.—Any person who converts conventional vehicles to clean fuel vehicles pursuant to subsection (b), shall be considered a manufacturer for purposes of sections 206 and 207 and related enforcement provisions. Nothing in the preceding sentence shall require a person who performs such conversions to warrant any part or operation of a vehicle other than as required under this part. Nothing in this paragraph shall limit the applicability of any other warranty to unrelated parts or operations.

(d) Tampering.—The conversion from a vehicle capable of operating on gasoline or diesel fuel only to a clean-fuel vehicle shall not be considered a violation of section 203(a)(3) if such conversion complies with the regulations promulgated under subsection (b).

(e) Safety.—The Secretary of Transportation shall, if necessary, promulgate rules under applicable motor vehicle laws regarding the safety of vehicles converted from existing and new vehicles to clean- fuel vehicles.

§7588. Federal Agency Fleets [Sec. 248]

(a) Additional Provisions Applicable.—The provisions of this section shall apply, in addition to the other provisions of this part, in the case of covered fleet vehicles owned or operated by an agency, department, or instrumentality of the United States, except as otherwise provided in subsection (e).

(b) Cost of Vehicles to Federal Agency.—Notwithstanding the provisions of section 211 of the Federal Property and Administrative Services Act of 1949, the Administrator of General Services shall not include the incremental costs of clean- fuel vehicles in the amount to be reimbursed by Federal agencies if the Administrator of General Services determines that appropriations provided pursuant to this paragraph are sufficient to provide for the incremental cost of such vehicles over the cost of comparable conventional vehicles.

(c) Limitations on Appropriations.—Funds appropriated pursuant to the authorization under this paragraph shall be applicable only—

(1) to the portion of the cost of acquisition, maintenance and operation of vehicles acquired under this subparagraph which exceeds the cost of acquisition, maintenance and operation of comparable conventional vehicles;

(2) to the portion of the costs of fuel storage and dispensing equipment attributable to such vehicles which exceeds the costs for such purposes required for conventional vehicles; and

(3) to the portion of the costs of acquisition of clean-fuel vehicles which represents a reduction in revenue from the disposal of such vehicles as compared to revenue resulting from the disposal of comparable conventional vehicles.

(d) Vehicle Costs.—The incremental cost of vehicles acquired under this part over the cost of comparable conventional vehicles shall not be applied to any calculation with respect to a limitation under law on the maximum cost of individual vehicles which may be required by the United States.

(e) Exemptions.—The requirements of this part shall not apply to vehicles with respect to which the Secretary of Defense has certified to the Administrator that an exemption is needed based on national security consideration.

(f) Acquisition Requirement.—Federal agencies, to the extent practicable, shall obtain clean-fuel vehicles from original equipment manufacturers.

(g) Authorization of Appropriations.—There are authorized to be appropriated such sums as may be required to carry out the provisions of this section: *Provided,* That such sums as are appropriated for the Administrator of General Services pursuant to the authorization under this section shall be added to the General Supply Fund established in section 109 of the Federal Property and Administrative Services Act of 1949.

§7589. California Pilot Test Program [Sec. 249]

(a) Establishment.—The Administrator shall establish a pilot program in the State of California to demonstrate the effectiveness of clean-fuel vehicles in con trolling air pollution in ozone nonattainment areas.

(b) Applicability.—The provisions of this section shall only apply to light-duty trucks and light-duty vehicles, and such provisions shall apply only in the State of California, except as provided in subsection (f).

(c) Program Requirements.—Not later than 24 months after the enactment of the Clean Air Act Amendments of 1990, the Administrator shall promulgate regulations establishing requirements under this section applicable in the State of California. The regulations shall provide the following:

(1) Clean-Fuel Vehicles.—Clean fuel vehicles shall be produced, sold, and distributed (in accordance with normal business practices and applicable franchise agreements) to ultimate purchasers in California (including owners of covered fleets referred to in section 246) in numbers that meet or exceed the following schedule:

Model Years	Number of Clean-Fuel Vehicles
1996, 1997, 1998	150,000 vehicles
1999 and thereafter	300,000 vehicles

(2) Clean Alternative Fuels.—

(A) Within 2 years after the enactment of the Clean Air Act Amendments of 1990, the State of California shall submit a revision of the applicable implementation plan under part D of title I and section 110 containing a clean fuel plan that requires that clean alternative fuels on which the clean-fuel vehicles required under this paragraph can operate shall be produced and distributed by fuel suppliers and made available in California. At a minimum, sufficient clean alternative fuels shall be produced, distributed and made available to assure that all clean- fuel vehicles required under this section can operate, to the maximum extent practicable, exclusively on such fuels in California. The State shall require that clean alternative fuels be made available and offered for sale at an adequate number of locations with sufficient geographic distribution to ensure convenient refueling with clean alternative fuels, considering the number of, and type of, such vehicles sold and the geographic distribution of such vehicles within the State. The State shall determine the clean alternative fuels to be produced, distributed, and made available based on motor vehicle manufacturers' projections of future sales of such vehicles and consultations with the affected local governments and fuel suppliers.

(B) The State may by regulation grant persons subject to the requirements prescribed under this paragraph an appropriate amount of credits for exceeding such requirements, and any person granted credits may transfer some or all of the credits for use by one or more persons in demonstrating compliance with such requirements. The State may make the credits available for use after consideration of enforceability, environmental, and economic factors and upon such terms and conditions as the State finds appropriate.

(C) The State may also by regulation establish specifications for any clean alternative fuel produced and made available under this paragraph as the State finds necessary to reduce or eliminate an unreasonable risk to public health, welfare, or safety associated with its use or to ensure acceptable vehicle maintenance and performance characteristics.

(D) If a retail gasoline dispensing facility would have to remove or replace one or more motor vehicle fuel underground storage tanks and accompanying piping in order to comply with the provisions of this section, and it had removed and replaced such tank or tanks and accompanying piping in order to comply with subtitle I of the Solid Waste Disposal Act prior to the date of the enactment of the Clean Air Act Amendments of 1990, it shall not be required to comply with this subsection until a period of 7 years has passed from the date of the removal and replacement of such tank or tanks.

(E) Nothing in this section authorizes any State other than California to adopt provisions regarding clean alternative fuels.

(F) If the State of California fails to adopt a clean fuel program that meets the requirements of this paragraph, the Administrator shall, within 4 years after the enactment of the Clean Air Act Amendments of 1990, establish a clean fuel program for the State of California under this paragraph and section

110(c) that meets the requirements of this paragraph.

(d) Credits for Motor Vehicle Manufacturers.—

(1) The Administrator may (by regulation) grant a motor vehicle manufacturer an appropriate amount of credits toward fulfillment of such manufacturer's share of the requirements of subsection (c)(1) of this section for any of the following (or any combination thereof):

(A) The sale of more clean-fuel vehicles than required under subsection (c)(1) of this section.

(B) The sale of clean fuel vehicles which meet standards established by the Administrator as provided in paragraph (3) which are more stringent than the clean-fuel vehicle standards otherwise applicable to such clean-fuel vehicle. A manufacturer granted credits under this paragraph may transfer some or all of the credits for use by one or more other manufacturers in demonstrating compliance with the requirements prescribed under this paragraph. The Administrator may make the credits available for use after consideration of enforceability, environmental, and economic factors and upon such terms and conditions as he finds appropriate. The Administrator shall grant credits in accordance with this paragraph, notwithstanding any requirements of State law or any credits granted with respect to the same vehicles under any State law, rule, or regulation.

(2) Regulations and Administration.—The Administrator shall administer the credit program established under this subsection. Within 12 months after the enactment of the Clean Air Act Amendments of 1990, the Administrator shall promulgate regulations for such credit program.

(3) Standards for Issuing Credits for Cleaner Vehicles.—The more stringent standards and other requirements (including requirements relating to the weighting of credits) established by the Administrator for purposes of the credit program under 245(e) (relating to credits for clean fuel vehicles in the fleets program) shall also apply for purposes of the credit program under this paragraph.

(e) Program Evaluation.—

(1) Not later than June 30, 1994 and again in connection with the report under paragraph (2), the Administrator shall provide a report to the Congress on the status of the California Air Resources Board Low-Emissions Vehicles and Clean Fuels Program. Such report shall examine the capability, from a technological standpoint, of motor vehicle manufacturers and motor vehicle fuel suppliers to comply with the requirements of such program and with the requirements of the California Pilot Program under this section.

(2) Not later than June 30, 1998, the Administrator shall complete and submit a report to Congress on the effectiveness of the California pilot program under this section. The report shall evaluate the level of emission reductions achieved under the program, the costs of the program, the advantages and disadvantages of extending the program to other nonattainment areas, and desirability of continuing or expanding the program in California.

(3) The program under this section cannot be extended or terminated by the Administrator except by Act of Congress enacted after the date of the Clean Air Act Amendments of 1990. Section 177 of this Act does not apply to the program under this section.

(f) Voluntary Opt-In for Other States.—

(1) EPA Regulations.—Not later than 2 years after the enactment of the Clean Air Act Amendments of 1990, the Administrator shall promulgate regulations establishing a voluntary opt-in program under this subsection pursuant to which—

(A) clean-fuel vehicles which are required to be produced, sold, and distributed in the State of California under this section, and

(B) clean alternative fuels required to be produced and distributed under this section by fuel suppliers and made available in California

may also be sold and used in other States which submit plan revisions under paragraph (2).

(2) Plan Revisions.—Any State in which there is located all or part of an ozone nonattainment area classified under subpart D of title I as Serious, Severe, or Extreme may submit a revision of the applicable implementation plan under part D of title I and section 110 to provide incentives for the sale or use in such an area or State of clean-fuel vehicles which are required to be produced, sold, and distributed in the State of California, and for the use in such an area or State of clean alternative fuels required to be produced and distributed by fuel suppliers and made available in California. Such plan provisions shall not take effect until 1 year after the State has provided notice of such

provisions to motor vehicle manufacturers and to fuel suppliers.

(3) Incentives.—The incentives referred to in paragraph (2) may include any or all of the following:

(A) A State registration fee on new motor vehicles registered in the State which are not clean-fuel vehicles in the amount of at least 1 percent of the cost of the vehicle. The proceeds of such fee shall be used to provide financial incentives to purchasers of clean-fuel vehicles and to vehicle dealers who sell high volumes or high percentages of clean-fuel vehicles and to defray the administrative costs of the incentive program.

(B) Provisions to exempt clean-fuel vehicles from high occupancy vehicle or trip reduction requirements.

(C) Provisions to provide preference in the use of existing parking spaces for clean-fuel vehicles. The incentives under this paragraph shall not apply in the case of covered fleet vehicles.

(4) No Sales or Production Mandate.—The regulations and plan revisions under paragraphs (1) and (2) shall not include any production or sales mandate for clean-fuel vehicles or clean alternative fuels. Such regulations and plan revisions shall also provide that vehicle manufacturers and fuel suppliers may not be subject to penalties or sanctions for failing to produce or sell clean-fuel vehicles or clean alternative fuels.

§7590. General Provisions [Sec. 250]

(a) State Refueling Facilities.—If any State adopts enforceable provisions in an implementation plan applicable to a nonattainment area which provides that existing State refueling facilities will be made available to the public for the purchase of clean alternative fuels or that State-operated refueling facilities for such fuels will be constructed and operated by the State and made available to the public at reasonable times, taking into consideration safety, costs, and other relevant factors, in approving such plan under section 110 and part D, the Administrator may credit a State with the emission reductions for purposes of part D attributable to such actions.

(b) No Production Mandate.—The Administrator shall have no authority under this part to mandate the production of clean-fuel vehicles except as provided in the California pilot test program or to specify as applicable the models, lines, or types of, or marketing or price practices, policies, or strategies for, vehicles subject to this part. Nothing in this part shall be construed to give the Administrator authority to mandate marketing or pricing practices, policies, or strategies for fuels.

(c) Tank and Fuel System Safety.—The Secretary of Transportation shall, in accordance with the National Motor Vehicle Traffic Safety Act of 1966, promulgate applicable regulations regarding the safety and use of fuel storage cylinders and fuel systems, including appropriate testing and retesting, in conversions of motor vehicles.

(d) Consultation with Department of Energy and Department of Transportation.—The Administrator shall coordinate with the Secretaries of the Department of Energy and the Department of Transportation in carrying out the Administrator's duties under this part.

[Editor's Note: Sections 231, 233, and 234 of PL 101–549 did not specifically amend this Act but contain relevant provisions and the text follows.]

Ethanol Substitute for Diesel [Sec. 231]

Within one year after the enactment of the Clean Air Act Amendments of 1990, the Administrator shall contract with a laboratory which has done research on alcohol esters of rapeseed oil to evaluate the feasibility, engine performance, emissions, and production capability associated with an alternative to diesel fuel composed of ethanol and high erucic rapeseed oil. The Administrator shall submit a report on the results of this research to Congress within 3 years of the issuance of such contract.

States Authority to Regulate [Sec. 233]

(a) Study.—The Administrator of the Environmental Protection Agency and the Secretary of Transportation, in consultation with the Secretary of Defense, shall commence a study and investigation of the testing of uninstalled aircraft engines in enclosed test cells that shall address at a minimum the following issues and such other issues as they shall deem appropriate—

(1) whether technologies exist to control some or all emissions of oxides of nitrogen from test cells;

(2) the effectiveness of such technologies;

(3) the cost of implementing such technologies;

(4) whether such technologies affect the safety, design, structure, operation, or performance of aircraft engines;

(5) whether such technologies impair the effectiveness and accuracy of aircraft engine safety design, and performance tests conducted in test cells; and

(6) the impact of not controlling such oxides of nitrogen in the applicable nonattainment areas and on

other sources, stationary and mobile, on oxides of nitrogen in such areas.

(b) Report, Authority to Regulate.—Not later than 24 months after enactment of the Clean Air Act Amendments of 1990, the Administrator of the Environmental Protection Agency and the Secretary of Transportation shall submit to Congress a report of the study conducted under this section. Following the completion of such study, any of the States may adopt or enforce any standard for emissions of oxides of nitrogen from test cells only after issuing a public notice stating whether such standards are in accordance with the findings of the study.

Fugitive Dust [Sec. 234]

(a) Prior to any use of the Industrial Source Complex (ISC) Model using AP- 42 Compilation of Air Pollutant Emission Factors to determine the effect on air quality of fugitive particulate emissions from surface coal mines, for purposes of new source review or for purposes of demonstrating compliance with national ambient air quality standards for particulate matter applicable to periods of 24 hours or less, under section 110 or parts C or D of title I of the Clean Air Act, the Administrator shall analyze the accuracy of such model and emission factors and make revisions as may be necessary to eliminate any significant over-prediction of air quality effect of fugitive particulate emissions from such sources. Such revisions shall be completed not later than 3 years after the date of enactment of the Clean Air Act Amendments of 1990. Until such time as the Administrator develops a revised model for surface mine fugitive emissions, the States may use alternative empirical based modeling approaches pursuant to guidelines issued by the Administrator.

TITLE III—GENERAL

§7601. Administration [Sec. 301]

(a) (1) The Administrator is authorized to prescribe such regulations as are necessary to carry out his functions under this Act. The Administrator may delegate to any officer or employee of the Environmental Protection Agency such of his powers and duties under this Act, except the making of regulations subject to section 307(d) , as he may deem necessary or expedient.

[§301(a)(1) designated by PL 95–95; amended by PL 101–549]

(2) Not later than one year after the date of enactment of this paragraph, the Administrator shall promulgate regulations establishing general applicable procedures and policies for regional officers and employees (including the Regional Administrator) to follow in carrying out a delegation under paragraph (1), if any. Such regulations shall be designed—

(A) to assure fairness and uniformity in the criteria, procedures, and policies applied by the various regions implementing and enforcing the Act;

(B) to assure at least an adequate quality audit of each State's performance and adherence to the requirements of this Act in implementing and enforcing the Act, particularly in the review of new sources and in enforcement of the Act; and

(C) to provide a mechanism for identifying and standardizing inconsistent or varying criteria, procedures, and policies being employed by such officers and employees in implementing and enforcing the Act.

[§301(a)(2)(C) amended by PL 95–95]

(b) Upon the request of an air pollution control agency, personnel of the Environmental Protection Agency may be detailed to such agency for the purpose of carrying out the provisions of this Act.

(c) Payments under grants made under this Act may be made in installments, and in advance or by way of reimbursement, as may be determined by the Administrator.

(d) Tribal Authority.—

(1) Subject to the provisions of paragraph (2), the Administrator—

(A) is authorized to treat Indian tribes as States under this Act, except for purposes of the requirement that makes available for application by each State no less than one-half of 1 percent of annual appropriations under section 105 ; and

(B) may provide any such Indian tribe grant and contract assistance to carry out functions provided by this Act.

(2) The Administrator shall promulgate regulations within 18 months after the date of the enactment of the Clean Air Act Amendments of 1990, specifying those provisions of this Act for which it is appropriate to treat Indian tribes as States. Such treatment shall be authorized only if—

(A) the Indian tribe has a governing body carrying out substantial governmental duties and powers;

(B) the functions to be exercised by the Indian tribe pertain to the management and protection of air resources within the exterior boundaries of the reservation or other areas within the tribe's jurisdiction; and

(C) the Indian tribe is reasonably expected to be capable, in the judgment of the Administrator, of carrying out the functions to be exercised in a manner consistent with the terms and purposes of this Act and all applicable regulations.

(3) The Administrator may promulgate regulations which establish the elements of tribal implementation plans and procedures for approval or disapproval of tribal implementation plans and portions thereof.

(4) In any case in which the Administrator determines that the treatment of Indian tribes as identical to States is inappropriate or administratively infeasible, the Administrator may provide, by regulation, other means by which the Administrator will directly administer such pro visions so as to achieve the appropriate purpose.

(5) Until such time as the Administrator promulgates regulations pursuant to this subsection, the Administrator may continue to provide financial assistance to eligible Indian tribes under section 105 .

[§301(d) added by PL 101–549]

§7602. Definitions [Sec. 302]

When used in this Act—

(a) The term 'Administrator' means the Administrator of the Environmental Protection Agency.

(b) The term 'air pollution control agency' means any of the following:

(1) A single State agency designated by the Governor of that State as the official State air

pollution control agency for purposes of this Act.

[§302(b)(1) amended by PL 101–549]

(2) An agency established by two or more States and having substantial powers or duties pertaining to the prevention and control of air pollution.

[§302(b)(2) amended by PL 101–549]

(3) A city, county, or other local government health authority, or, in the case of any city, county, or other local government in which there is an agency other than the health authority charged with responsibility for enforcing ordinances or laws relating to the prevention and control of air pollution, such other agency.

[§302(b)(3) amended by PL 101–549]

(4) An agency of two or more municipalities located in the same State or in different States and having substantial powers or duties pertaining to the prevention and control of air pollution.

(5) An agency of an Indian tribe.

[§302(b)(5) added by PL 101–549]

(c) The term 'interstate air pollution control agency' means—

(1) an air pollution control agency established by two or more States, or

(2) an air pollution control agency of two or more municipalities located in different States.

(d) The term 'state' means a State, the District of Columbia, the Commonwealth of Puerto Rico, the Virgin Islands, Guam, and American Samoa and includes the Commonwealth of the Northern Mariana Islands.

[§302(d) amended by PL 95–95]

(e) The term 'person' includes an individual, corporation, partnership, association, State, municipality, political subdivision of a State, and any agency, department, or instrumentality of the United States and any officer, agent, or employee thereof.

[§302(e) amended by PL 95–95; PL 95–190]

(f) The term 'municipality' means a city, town, borough, county, parish, district, or other public body created by or pursuant to State law.

[Editor's Note: Sec. 101(d) of PL 101–549 amended Sec. 302(g) and (h) but the language applies to Sec. 110(g) and (h).]

(g) The term 'air pollutant' means any air pollution agent or combination of such agents, including any physical, chemical, biological, radioactive (including source material, special nuclear material, and byproduct material) substance or matter which is emitted into or otherwise enters the ambient air. Such term includes any precursors to the formation of any air pollutant, to the extent the Administrator has identified such precursor or precursors for the particular purpose for which the term 'air pollutant' is used.

[§302(g) amended by PL 95–95; PL 101–549]

(h) All language referring to effects on welfare includes, but is not limited to, effects on soils, water, crops, vegetation, manmade materials, animals, wildlife, weather, visibility, and climate, damage to and deterioration of property, and hazards to transportation, as well as effects on economic values and on personal comfort and well-being, whether caused by transformation, conversion, or combination with other air pollutants.

[§302(h) amended by PL 101–549]

(i) The term 'Federal land manager' means with respect to any lands in the United States the Secretary of the department with authority over such lands.

(j) Except as otherwise expressly provided, the terms 'major stationary source' and 'major emitting facility' mean any stationary facility or source of air pollutants which directly emits, or has the potential to emit, one hundred tons per year or more of any air pollutant (including any major emitting facility or source of fugitive emissions of any such pollutant, as determined by rule by the Administrator).

(k) The terms 'emission limitation' and 'emission standard' mean a requirement established by the State or the Administrator which limits the quantity, rate, or concentration of emissions of air pollutants on a continuous basis including any requirement relating to the operation or maintenance of a source to assure continuous emission reduction, and any design, equipment, work practice or operational standard promulgated under this Act.

[§302(k) amended by PL 101–549]

(l) The term 'standard of performance' means a requirement of continuous emission reduction, including any requirement relating to the operation or maintenance of a source to assure continuous emission reduction.

(m) The term 'means of emission limitation' means a system of continuous emission reduction (including the use of specific technology or fuels with specified pollution characteristics).

(n) The term 'primary standard attainment date' means the date specified in the applicable implementation plan for the attainment of a national primary ambient air quality standard for any air pollutant.

(o) The term 'delayed compliance order' means an order issued by the State or by the Administrator to an existing stationary source, postponing the date required under an applicable implementation plan for compliance by such source with any requirement of such plan.

(p) The term 'schedule and timetable of compliance' means a schedule of remedial measures including an enforceable sequence of actions or operations leading to compliance with an emission limitation, other limitation, prohibition, or standard.

(q) For purposes of this Act, the term 'applicable implementation plan' means the portion (or portions) of the implementation plan, or most recent revision thereof, which has been approved under section 110 , or promulgated under section 110(c) , or promulgated or approved pursuant to regulations promulgated under section 301(d) and which implements the relevant requirements of this Act.

[§302(q) added by PL 101–549]

(r) Indian Tribe.—The term 'Indian tribe' means any Indian tribe, band, nation, or other organized group or community, including any Alaska Native village, which is Federally recognized as eligible for the special programs and services provided by the United States to Indians because of their status as Indians.

[§302(r) added by PL 101–549]

(s) VOC.—The term 'VOC' means volatile organic compound, as defined by the Administrator.

[§302(s) added by PL 101–549]

(t) PM–10.—The term 'PM–10' means particulate matter with an aerodynamic diameter less than or equal to a nominal ten micrometers, as measured by such method as the Administrator may determine.

[§302(t) added by PL 101–549]

(u) NAAQS And CTG.—The term 'NAAQS' means national ambient air quality standard. The term 'CTG' means a Control Technique Guideline published by the Administrator under section 108.

[§302(u) added by PL 101–549]

(v) NO_x.—The term 'NO_x' means oxides of nitrogen.

[§302(v) added by PL 101–549]

(w) CO.—The term 'CO' means carbon monoxide.

[§302(w) added by PL 101–549]

(x) Small Source.—The term 'small source' means a source that emits less than 100 tons of regulated pollutants per year, or any class of persons that the Administrator determines, through regulation, generally lack technical ability or knowledge regarding control of air pollution.

[§302(x) added by PL 101–549]

(y) Federal Implementation Plan.—The term 'Federal implementation plan' means a plan (or portion thereof) promulgated by the Administrator to fill all or a portion of a gap or otherwise correct all or a portion of an inadequacy in a State implementation plan, and which includes enforceable emission limitations or other control measures, means or techniques (including economic incentives, such as marketable permits or auctions of emissions allowances), and provides for attainment of the relevant national ambient air quality standard.

[§302(y) added by PL 101–549]

(z) Stationary Source.—The term 'stationary source' means generally any source of an air pollutant except those emissions resulting directly from an internal combustion engine for transportation purposes or from a nonroad engine or nonroad vehicle as defined in section 216 .

[§302(z) added by PL 101–549]

§7603. Emergency Powers [Sec. 303]

Notwithstanding any other provision of this Act, the Administrator, upon receipt of evidence that a pollution source or combination of sources (including moving sources) is presenting an imminent and substantial endangerment to public health or welfare, or the environment, may bring suit on behalf of the United States in the appropriate United States district court to immediately restrain any person causing or contributing to the alleged pollution to stop the emission of air pollutants causing or contributing to such pollution or to take such other action as may be necessary. If it is not practicable to assure prompt protection of public health or welfare or the environment by commencement of such a civil action, the Administrator may issue such orders as may be necessary to protect public health or welfare or the environment. Prior to taking any action under this section, the Administrator shall consult with appropriate

State and local authorities and attempt to confirm the accuracy of the information on which the action proposed to be taken is based. Any order issued by the Administrator under this section shall be effective upon issuance and shall remain in effect for a period of not more than 60 days, unless the Administrator brings an action pursuant to the first sentence of this section before the expiration of that period. Whenever the Administrator brings such an action within the 60–day period, such order shall remain in effect for an additional 14 days or for such longer period as may be authorized by the court in which such action is brought.

[§303 amended by PL 95–95; revised by PL 101–549]

(b) [Repealed]

[§303(b) repealed by PL 101–549]

§7604. Citizen Suits [Sec. 304]

(a) Except as provided in subsection (b), any person may commence a civil action on his own behalf—

(1) against any person (including (i) the United States, and (ii) any other governmental instrumentality or agency to the extent permitted by the Eleventh Amendment to the Constitution) who is alleged to have violated (if there is evidence that the alleged violation has been repeated) or to be in violation of (A) an emission standard or limitation under this Act or (B) an order issued by the Administrator or a State with respect to such a standard or limitation,

(2) against the Administrator where there is alleged a failure of the Administrator to perform any act or duty under this Act which is not discretionary with the Administrator, or

(3) against any person who proposes to construct or constructs any new or modified major emitting facility without a permit required under part C of title I (relating to significant deterioration of air quality) or part D of title I (relating to nonattainment) or who is alleged to have violated (if there is evidence that the alleged violation has been repeated) or to be in violation of any condition of such permit.

[Editor's Note: Section 707(g) of PL 101–549 amending Sec. 304(a)(1) and (3) also states that "the amendment made by this subsection shall take effect with respect to actions brought after the date 2 years after the enactment of the clean Air Act Amendments of 1990."]

The district courts shall have jurisdiction, without regard to the amount in controversy or the citizenship of the parties, to enforce such an emission standard or limitation, or such an order, or to order the Administrator to perform such act or duty, as the case may be, and to apply any appropriate civil penalties (except for actions under paragraph (2)). The district courts of the United States shall have jurisdiction to compel (consistent with paragraph (2) of this subsection) agency action unreasonably delayed, except that an action to compel agency action referred to in section 307(b) which is unreasonably delayed may only be filed in a United States District Court within the circuit in which such action would be reviewable under section 307(b). In any such action for unreasonable delay, notice to the entities referred to in subsection (b)(1)(A) shall be provided 180 days before commencing such action.

[§304(a) amended by PL 95–95; PL 95–190; PL 101–549]

(b) No action may be commenced—

(1) under subsection (a)(1)—

(A) prior to 60 days after the plaintiff has given notice of the violation (i) to the Administrator, (ii) to the State in which the violation occurs, and (iii) to any alleged violator of the standard, limitation, or order, or

(B) if the Administrator or State has commenced and is diligently prosecuting a civil action in a court of the United States or a State to require compliance with the standard, limitation, or order, but in any such action in a court of the United States any person may intervene as a matter of right.

(2) under subsection (a)(2) prior to 60 days after the plaintiff has given notice of such action to the Administrator, except that such action may be brought immediately after such notification in the case of an action under this section respecting a violation of section 112(i)(3)(A) or (f)(4) or an order issued by the Administrator pursuant to section 113(a) . Notice under this subsection shall be given in such manner as the Administrator shall prescribe by regulation.

[§304(b)(2) amended by PL 101–549]

(c) (1) Any action respecting a violation by a stationary source of an emission standard or limitation or an order respecting such standard or limitation may be brought only in the judicial district in which such source is located.

(2) In any action under this section, the Administrator, if not a party, may intervene as a matter of right at any time in the proceeding. A judgment in an action under this section to

which the United States is not a party shall not, however, have any binding effect upon the United States.

[§304(c)(2) amended by PL 101–549]

(3) Whenever any action is brought under this section the plaintiff shall serve a copy of the complaint on the Attorney General of the United States and on the Administrator. No consent judgment shall be entered in an action brought under this section in which the United States is not a party prior to 45 days following the receipt of a copy of the proposed consent judgment by the Attorney General and the Administrator during which time the Government may submit its comments on the proposed consent judgment to the court and parties or may intervene as a matter of right.

[§304(c)(3) added by PL 101–549]

(d) The court, in issuing any final order in any action brought pursuant to subsection (a) of this section, may award costs of litigation (including reasonable attorney and expert witness fees) to any party, whenever the court determines such award is appropriate. The court may, if a temporary restraining order or preliminary injunction is sought, require the filing of a bond or equivalent security in accordance with the Federal Rules of Civil Procedure.

(e) Nothing in this section shall restrict any right which any person (or class of persons) may have under any statute or common law to seek enforcement of any emission standard or limitation or to seek any other relief (including relief against the Administrator or a State agency). Nothing in this section or in any other law of the United States shall be construed to prohibit, exclude, or restrict any State, local, or interstate authority from—

(1) bringing any enforcement action or obtaining any judicial remedy or sanction in any State or local court, or

(2) bringing any administrative enforcement action or obtaining any administrative remedy or sanction in any State or local administrative agency, department or instrumentality, against the United States, any department, agency, or instrumentality thereof, or any officer, agent, or employee thereof under State or local law respecting control and abatement of air pollution. For provisions requiring compliance by the United States, departments, agencies, instrumentalities, officers, agents, and employees in the same manner as non-governmental entities, see section 118 .

[§304(e) amended by PL 95–95]

(f) For purposes of this section, the term 'emission standard or limitation under this Act' means—

(1) a schedule or timetable of compliance, emission limitation, standard of performance or emission standard,

(2) a control or prohibition respecting a motor vehicle fuel or fuel additive, which is in effect under this Act (including a requirement applicable by reason of section 118) or under an applicable implementation plan, or

(3) any condition or requirement of a permit under part C of title I (relating to significant deterioration of air quality) or part D of title I (relating to nonattainment), 119 (relating to primary nonferrous smelter orders), any condition or requirement under an applicable implementation plan relating to transportation control measures, air quality maintenance plans, vehicle inspection and maintenance programs, or vapor recovery requirements, section 211 (e) and (f) (relating to fuels and fuel additives), section 169A (relating to visibility protection), any condition or requirement under title VI (relating to ozone protection), or any requirement under section 111 or 112 without regard to whether such requirement is expressed as an emission standard or otherwise); or

[§304(f)(3) added by PL 95–95; PL 95–190; PL 101–549]

(4) any other standard, limitation, or schedule established under any permit issued pursuant to title V or under any applicable State implementation plan approved by the Administrator, any permit term or condition, and any requirement to obtain a permit as a condition of operations.

which is in effect under this title (including a requirement applicable by reason of section 118) or under an applicavle implementation plan.

[§304(f)(4) added by PL 101–549]

(g) Penalty Fund.—

(1) Penalties received under subsection (a) shall be deposited in a special fund in the United States Treasury for licensing and other services. Amounts in such fund are authorized to be appropriated and shall remain available until expended, for use by the Administrator to finance air compliance and enforcement activities. The Administrator shall annually report to the Congress about the sums deposited into the fund, the sources thereof, and the actual and proposed uses thereof.

(2) Notwithstanding paragraph (1) the court in any action under this subsection to apply civil penalties shall have discretion to order that such civil penalties, in lieu of being deposited in the fund referred to in paragraph (1), be used in beneficial mitigation projects which are consistent with this Act and enhance the public health or the environment. The court shall obtain the view of the Administrator in exercising such discretion and selecting any such projects. The amount of any such payment in any such action shall not exceed $100,000.

[§304(g) added by PL 101–549]

§7605. Representation in Litigation [Sec. 305]

(a) The Administrator shall request the Attorney General to appear and represent him in any civil action instituted under this Act to which the Administrator is a party. Unless the Attorney General notifies the Administrator that he will appear in such action, within a reasonable time, attorneys appointed by the Administrator shall appear and represent him.

(b) In the event the Attorney General agrees to appear and represent the Administrator in any such action, such representation shall be conducted in accordance with, and shall include participation by attorneys appointed by the Administrator to the extent authorized by, the memorandum of understanding between the Department of Justice and the Environmental Protection Agency, dated June 13, 1977, respecting representation of the agency by the department in civil litigation.

[§305 amended by PL 95–95]

§7606. Federal Procurement [Sec. 306]

(a) No Federal agency may enter into any contract with any person who is convicted of any offense under section 113(c) for the procurement of goods, materials, and services to perform such contract at any facility at which the violation which gave rise to such conviction occurred if such facility is owned, leased, or supervised by such person. The prohibition in the preceding sentence shall continue until the Administrator certifies that the condition giving rise to such a conviction has been corrected. For convictions arising under section 113(c)(2) , the condition giving rise to the conviction also shall be considered to include any substantive violation of this Act associated with the violation of 113(c)(2). The Administrator may extend this prohibition to other facilities owned or operated by the convicted person.

[§306(a) amended by PL 101–549]

(b) The Administrator shall establish procedures to provide all Federal agencies with the notification necessary for the purposes of subsection (a).

(c) In order to implement the purposes and policy of this Act to protect and enhance the quality of the Nation's air the President shall, not more than 180 days after enactment of the Clean Air Amendments of 1970 cause to be issued an order (1) requiring each Federal agency authorized to enter into contracts and each Federal agency which is empowered to extend Federal assistance by way of grant, loan, or contract to effectuate the purpose and policy of this Act in such contracting or assistance activities, and (2) setting forth procedures, sanctions, penalties, and such other provisions, as the President determines necessary to carry out such requirement.

(d) The President may exempt any contract, loan, or grant from all or part of the provisions of this section where he determines such exemption is necessary in the paramount interest of the United States and he shall notify the Congress of such exemption.

(e) The President shall annually report to the Congress on measures taken toward implementing the purpose and intent of this section, including but not limited to the progress and problems associated with implementation of this section.

§7607. General Provision Relating to Administrative Proceedings and Judicial Review [Sec. 307]

(a) In connection with any determination under section 110(f) , or for purposes of obtaining information under section 202(b)(4) or 211(c)(3), any investigation, monitoring, reporting requirement, entry, compliance inspection, or administrative enforcement proceeding under the Act (including but not limited to section 113, section 114, section 120, section 129, section 167, section 205, section 206, section 208, section 303, or section 306), the Administrator may issue subpoenas for the attendance and testimony of witnesses and the production of relevant papers, books, and documents, and he may administer oaths. Except for emission data, upon a showing satisfactory to the Administrator by such owner or operator that such papers, books documents, or information or particular part thereof, if made public, would divulge trade secrets or secret processes of such owner or operator, the Administrator shall consider such record, report, or information or particular portion thereof confidential in accordance with the purposes of section 1905 of title 18 of the United

States Code, except that such paper, book, document, or information may be disclosed to other officers, employees, or authorized representatives of the United States concerned with carrying out this Act, to persons carrying out the National Academy of Sciences' study and investigation provided for in section 202(c), or when relevant in any proceeding under this Act. Witnesses summoned shall be paid the same fees and mileage that are paid witnesses in the courts of the United States. In case of contumacy or refusal to obey a subpoena served upon any person under this subparagraph, the district court of the United States for any district in which such person is found or resides or transacts business, upon application by the United States and after notice to such person, shall have jurisdiction to issue an order requiring such person to appear and give testimony before the Administrator to appear and produce papers, books, and documents before the Administrator, or both, and any failure to obey such order of the court may be punished by such court as a contempt thereof.

[§307(a) amended by PL 101-549]

(b) (1) A petition for review of action of the Administrator in promulgating any national primary or secondary ambient air quality standard, any emission standard or requirement under section 112, any standard of performance or requirement under 111; any standard under section 202 (other than a standard required to be prescribed under section 202(b)(1)), any determination under section 202(b)(5) , any control or prohibition under section 211 , any standard under section 231 or any rule issued under section 113, 119, or under section 120 or any other nationally applicable regulations promulgated, or final action taken, by the Administrator under this Act may be filed only in the United States Court of Appeals for the District of Columbia. A petition for review of the Administrator's action in approving or promulgating any implementation plan under section 110 or section 111(d) , any order under section 111(j) , under section 112, under section 119, or under section 120, or his action under section 119(c)(2)(A), (B), or (C) (as in effect before the enactment of the Clean Air Act Amendments of 1977) or under regulations thereunder, or revising regulations for enhanced monitoring and compliance certification programs under section 114(a)(3) of this Act, or any other final action of the Administrator under this (including any denial or disapproval by the Administrator under Title I) Act which is locally or regionally applicable may be filed only in the United States Court of Appeals for the appropriate circuit. Notwithstanding the preceding sentence a petition for review of any action referred to in such sentence may be filed only in the United States Court of Appeals for the District of Columbia if such action is based on a determination of nationwide scope or effect and if in taking such action the Administrator finds and publishes that such action is based on such a determination. Any petition for review under this subsection shall be filed within sixty days from the date notice of such promulgation, approval, or action appears in the Federal Register, except that if such petition is based solely on grounds arising after such sixtieth day, then any petition for review under this subsection shall be filed within sixty days after such grounds arise. The filing of a petition for reconsideration by the Administrator of any otherwise final rule or action shall not affect the finality of such rule or action for purposes of judicial review nor extend the time within which a petition for judicial review of such rule or action under this section may be filed, and shall not postpone the effectiveness of such rule or action; and

[§307(b)(1) amended by PL 93–319; PL 95–95; PL 95–190; PL 101–549]

(2) Action of the Administrator with respect to which review could have been obtained under paragraph (1) shall not be subject to judicial review in civil or criminal proceedings for enforcement. Where a final decision by the Administrator defers performance of any nondiscretionary statutory action to a later time, any person may challenge the deferral pursuant to paragraph (1).

[§307(b)(2) amended by PL 101–549]

(c) In any judicial proceeding in which review is sought of a determination under this Act required to be made on the record after notice and opportunity for hearing, if any part applies to the court for leave to adduce additional evidence, and shows to the satisfaction of the court that such additional evidence is material and that there were reasonable grounds for the failure to adduce such evidence in the proceeding before the Administrator the court may order such additional evidence (and evidence in rebuttal thereof) to be taken before the Administrator, in such manner and upon such terms and conditions as to the court may deem proper. The Administrator may modify his findings as to the facts, or make new findings, by reason of the additional evidence so taken and he shall file such modified or new findings, and his recommendation, if any, for the modification or setting aside of his original determination, with the return of such additional evidence.

(d) (1) This subsection applies to—

[§307(d)(1) revised by PL 101–549]

(A) the promulgation or revision of any national ambient air quality standard under section 109,

(B) the promulgation or revision of an implementation plan by the Administrator under section 110(c),

(C) the promulgation or revision of any standard of performance under section 111, or emission standard or limitation under section 112(d) , any standard under section 112(f) , or any regulation under section 112(g)(1)(D) and (F), or any regulation under section 112(m) or (n),

(D) the promulgation of any requirement for solid waste combustion under section 129,

(E) the promulgation or revision of any regulation pertaining to any fuel or fuel additive under section 211.

(F) the promulgation or revision of any aircraft emission standard under section 231.

(G) the promulgation or revision of any regulation under title IV (relating to control of acid deposition),

(H) promulgation or revision of regulation pertaining to primary nonferrous smelter orders under section 119 (but not including the granting or denying of any such order),

(I) promulgation or revision of regulations under title VI (relating to stratosphere and ozone protection),

(J) promulgation or revision of regulations under subtitle C of title I (relating to prevention of significant deterioration of air quality and protection of visibility),

(K) promulgation or revision of regulations under section 202 and test procedures for new motor vehicles or engines under section 206, and the revision of a standard, under section 202(a)(3),

(L) promulgation or revision of regulations for noncompliance penalties under section 120,

(M) promulgation or revision of any regulations promulgated under section 207 (relating to warranties and compliance by vehicles in actual use),

(N) action of the Administrator under section 126 (relating to interstate pollution abatement),

(O) the promulgation or revision of any regulation pertaining to consumer and commercial products under section 183(e),

(P) the promulgation or revision of any regulation pertaining to field citations under section 113(d)(3),

(Q) the promulgation or revision of any regulation pertaining to urban buses or the clean-fuel vehicle, clean-fuel fleet, and clean fuel programs under part C of title II,

(R) the promulgation or revision of any regulation pertaining to nonroad engines or nonroad vehicles under section 213,

(S) the promulgation or revision of any regulation relating to motor vehicle compliance program fees under section 217,

(T) the promulgation or revision of any regulation under title IV (relating to acid deposition),

(U) the promulgation or revision of any regulation under section 183(f) pertaining to marine vessels, and

(V) Such other actions as the Administrator may determine. The provisions of section 553 through 557 and section 706 of title 5 of the United States Code shall not, except as expressly provided in this subsection, apply to actions to which this subsection applies. This subsection shall not apply in the case of any rule or circumstance referred to in subparagraphs (A) or (B) of subsection 553(b) of title 5 of the United States Code;

(2) Not later than the date of proposal of any action to which this subsection applies, the Administrator shall establish a rulemaking docket for such action (hereinafter in this subsection referred to as a "rule"). Whenever a rule applies only within a particular State, a second (identical) docket shall be simultaneously established in the appropriate regional office of the Environmental Protection Agency.

(3) In the case of any rule to which this subsection applies, notice of proposed rulemaking shall be published in the Federal Register, as provided under section 553(b) of title 5, United States Code, shall be accompanied by a statement of its basis and purpose and shall specify the period available for public comment (hereinafter referred to as the "comment period"). The notice of proposed rulemaking shall also state the docket number, the location or locations of the docket, and the times it will be

open to public inspection. The statement of basis and purpose shall include a summary of—

(A) the factual data on which the proposed rule is based;

(B) the methodology used in obtaining the data and in analyzing the data; and

(C) the major legal interpretations and policy considerations underlying the proposed rule. The statement shall also set forth or summarize and provide a reference to any pertinent findings, recommendations, and comments by the Scientific Review Committee established under section 109(d) and the National Academy of Sciences, and, if the proposed differs in any important respect from any of these recommendations, an explanation of the reasons for such differences. All data, information, and documents referred to in this paragraph on which the proposed rule relies shall be included in the docket on the date of publication of the proposed rule.

(4) (A) The rulemaking docket required under paragraph (2) shall be open for inspection by the public at reasonable times specified in the notice of proposed rulemaking. Any person may copy documents contained in the docket. The Administrator shall provide copying facilities which may be used at the expense of the person seeking copies, but the Administrator may waive or reduce such expenses in such instances as the public interest requires. Any person may request copies by mail if the person pays the expenses, including personnel costs to do the copying.

(B) (i) Promptly upon receipt by the agency, all written comments and documentary information on the proposed rule received from any person for inclusion in the docket during the comment period shall be placed in the docket. The transcript of public hearings, if any, on the proposed rule shall also be included in the docket promptly upon receipt from the person who transcribed such hearings. All documents which become available after the proposed rule has been published and which the Administrator determines are of central relevance to the rulemaking shall be placed in the docket as soon as possible after their availability.

(ii) The drafts of proposed rules submitted by the Administrator to the Office of Management and Budget for any interagency review process prior to proposal of any such rule, all documents accompanying such drafts, and all written comments thereon by other agencies and all written responses to such written comments by the Administrator shall be placed in the docket no later than the date of proposal of the rule. The drafts of the final rule submitted for such review process prior to promulgation and all such written comments thereon, all documents accompanying such drafts, and written responses thereto shall be placed in the docket no later than the date of promulgation.

(5) In promulgating a rule to which this subsection applies (i) the Administrator shall allow any person to submit written comments, data, or documentary information; (ii) the Administrator shall give interested persons an opportunity for the oral presentation of data, views, or arguments, in addition to an opportunity to make written submissions; (iii) a transcript shall be kept of any oral presentation; and (iv) the Administrator shall keep the record of such proceeding open for thirty days after completion of the proceeding to provide an opportunity for submission of rebuttal and supplementary information.

(6) (A) The promulgated rule shall be accompanied by (i) a statement of basis and purpose like that referred to in paragraph (3) with respect to a proposed rule and (ii) an explanation of the reasons for any major changes in the promulgated rule from the proposed rule.

(B) The promulgated rule shall also be accompanied by a response to each of the significant comments, criticisms, and new data submitted, in written or oral presentations during the comment period.

(C) The promulgated rule may not be based (in part or whole) on any information or data which has not been placed in the docket as of the date of such promulgation.

(7) (A) The record for judicial review shall consist exclusively of the material referred to in paragraph (3), clause (i) of paragraph (4)(B), and subparagraphs (A) and (B) of paragraph (6).

(B) Only an objection to a rule or procedure which was raised with reasonable specificity during the period for public comment (including any public hearing) may be raised during judicial review. If the person raising an objection can demonstrate to the Administrator that it was impracticable to raise such objection within such time or if the grounds for such objection arose after the period for public comment (but within the time specified for judicial review) and if such objection is of central relevance to the outcome of the rule, the Administrator shall convene a proceeding for reconsideration of the rule and provide the same procedural rights as would have been afforded had the information been available at the time the rule was proposed. If the Administrator refuses to convene such a proceeding, such person may seek review of such refusal in the United States court of appeals for the appropriate circuit (as provided in subsection (b)). Such reconsideration shall not postpone the effectiveness of the rule. The effectiveness of the rule may be stayed during such reconsideration, however, by the Administrator or the court for a period not to exceed three months.

(8) The sole forum for challenging procedural determinations made by the Administrator under this subsection shall be in the United States court of appeals for the appropriate circuit (as provided in subsection (b)) at the time of the substantive review of the rule. No interlocutory appeals shall be permitted with respect to such procedural determinations. In reviewing alleged procedural errors, the court may invalidate the rule only if the errors were so serious and related to matters of such central relevance to the rule that there is a substantial likelihood that the rule would have been significantly changed if such errors had not been made.

(9) In the case of review of any action of the Administrator to which this subsection applies, the court may reverse any such action found to be—

(A) arbitrary, capricious, an abuse of discretion, or otherwise not in accordance with law;

(B) contrary to constitutional right, power, privilege, or immunity;

(C) in excess of statutory jurisdiction, authority, or limitations, or short of statutory right; or

(D) without observance of procedure required by law if (i) such failure to observance such procedure is arbitrary or capricious, (ii) the requirement of paragraph (7)(B) has been met, and (iii) the condition of the last sentence of paragraph (8) is met.

(10) Each statutory deadline for promulgation of rules to which this subsection applies which requires promulgation less than six months after date of proposal may be extended to not more than six months after date of proposal by the Administrator upon a determination that such extension is necessary to afford the public, and the agency, adequate opportunity to carry out the purposes of this subsection.

(11) The requirements of this subsection shall take effect with respect to any rule the proposal of which occurs after ninety days after the date of enactment of the Clean Air Act Amendments of 1977.

(e) Nothing in this Act shall be construed to authorize judicial review of regulations or orders of the Administrator under this Act, except as provided in this section.

[§307(e) added by PL 95-95]

(f) In any judicial proceeding under this section, the court may award costs of litigation (including reasonable attorney and expert witness fees) whenever it determines that such award is appropriate.

[§307(f) added by PL 95-95]

(g) In any action respecting the promulgation of regulations under section 120 or the administration or enforcement of section 120 no court shall grant any stay, injunctive, or similar relief before final judgment by such court in such action.

[§307(g) added by PL 95-95]

(h) Public Participation.—It is the intent of Congress that, consistent with the policy of the Administrative Procedures Act, the Administrator in promulgating any regulation under this Act, including a regulation subject to a deadline, shall ensure a reasonable period for public participation of at least 30 days, except as otherwise expressly provided in section 107(d), 172(a), 181(a) and (b), and 186(a) and (b).

[§307(h) added by PL 101-549]

§7608. Mandatory Licensing [Sec. 308]

Whenever the Attorney General determines, upon application of the Administrator—

(1) that—

(A) in the implementation of the requirements of section 111, 112, or 202 of this Act, a right under any United States letters patent, which is being used or intended for public or commercial use and not otherwise reasonably available, is necessary to enable any person required to comply with such limitation to so comply, and

(B) there are no reasonable alternative methods to accomplish such purpose, and

(2) that the unavailability of such right may result in a substantial lessening of competition or tendency to create monopoly in any

line of commerce in any section of the country,

the Attorney General may so certify to a district court of the United States, which may issue an order requiring the person who owns such patent to license it on such reasonable terms and conditions as the court, after hearing, may determine. Such certification may be made to the district court for the district in which the person owning the patent resides, does business, or is found.

§7609. Policy Review [Sec. 309]

(a) The Administrator shall review and comment in writing on the environmental impact of any matter relating to duties and responsibilities granted pursuant to this Act or other provisions of the authority of the Administrator, contained in any (1) legislation proposed by any Federal department or agency, (2) newly authorized Federal projects for construction and any major Federal agency action (other than a project for construction) to which section 102(2)(C) of Public Law 91–190 applies and (3) proposed regulations published by any department or agency of the Federal Government. Such written comment shall be made public at the conclusion of any such review.

(b) In the event the Administrator determines that any such legislation, action, or regulation is unsatisfactory from the standpoint of public health or welfare or environmental quality he shall publish his determination and the matter shall be referred to the Council on Environmental Quality.

§7610. Other Authority Not Affected [Sec. 310]

(a) Except as provided in subsection (b) of this section, this Act shall not be construed as superseding or limiting the authorities and responsibilities, under any other provision of law, of the Administrator or any other Federal officer, department, or agency.

(b) No appropriation shall be authorized or made under section 301, 311, or 314 of the Public Health Service Act for any fiscal year after the fiscal year ending June 30, 1964, for any purpose for which appropriations may be made under authority of this Act.

§7611. Records and Audit [Sec. 311]

(a) Each recipient of assistance under this Act shall keep records as the Administrator shall prescribe, including records which fully disclose the amount and disposition by such recipient of the proceeds of such assistance, the total cost of the project or undertaking in connection with which such assistance is given or used, and the amount of that portion of the cost of the project or undertaking supplied by other sources, and such other records as will facilitate an effective audit.

(b) The Administrator and the Comptroller General of the United States, or any of their duly authorized representatives, shall have access for the purpose of audit and examinations to any books, documents, papers, and records of the recipients that are pertinent to the grants received under this Act.

§7612. Economic Impact Analyses [Sec. 312]

[§312 revised by PL 101–549]

(a) The Administrator, in consultation with the Secretary of Commerce, the Secretary of Labor, and the Council on Clean Air Compliance Analysis (as established under subsection (f) of this section), shall conduct a comprehensive analysis of the impact of this Act on the public health, economy, and environment of the United States. In performing such analysis, the Administrator should consider the costs, benefits and other effects associated with compliance with each standard issued for—

(1) a criteria air pollutant subject to a standard issued under section 109 ;

(2) a hazardous air pollutant listed under section 112 , including any technology- based standard and any risk-based standard for such pollutant;

(3) emissions from mobile sources regulated under title II of this Act;

(4) a limitation under this Act for emissions of sulfur dioxide or nitrogen oxides;

(5) a limitation under title VI of this Act on the production of any ozone-depleting substance; and

(6) any other section of this Act.

(b) In describing the benefits of a standard described in subsection (a), the Administrator shall consider all of the economic, public health, and environmental benefits of efforts to comply with such standard. In any case where numerical values are assigned to such benefits, a default assumption of zero value shall not be assigned to such benefits unless supported by specific data. The Administrator shall assess how benefits are measured in order to assure that damage to human health and the environment is more accurately measured and taken into account.

(c) In describing the costs of a standard described in subsection (a), the Administrator shall consider the effects of such standard on employment, productivity, cost of living, economic growth, and the overall economy of the United States.

(d) Not later than 12 months after the date of enactment of the Clean Air Act Amendments of 1990, the Administrator, in consultation with the Secretary of Commerce, the Secretary of Labor, and the Council on Clean Air Compliance Analysis, shall submit a report to the Congress that summarizes the results of the analysis described in subsection (a), which reports—

(1) all costs incurred previous to the date of enactment of the Clean Air Act Amendments of 1990 in the effort to comply with such standards; and

(2) all benefits that have accrued to the United States as a result of such costs.

(e) Not later than 24 months after the date of enactment of the Clean Air Act Amendments of 1990, and every 24 months thereafter, the Administrator, in consultation with the Secretary of Commerce, the Secretary of Labor, and the Council on Clean Air Compliance Analysis, shall submit a report to the Congress that updates the report issued pursuant to subsection (d), and which, in addition, makes projections into the future regarding expected costs, benefits, and other effects of compliance with standards pursuant to this Act as listed in subsection (a).

(f) Not later than 6 months after the date of enactment of the Clean Air Act Amendments of 1990, the Administrator, in consultation with the Secretary of Commerce and the Secretary of Labor, shall appoint an Advisory Council on Clean Air Compliance Analysis of not less than nine members (hereafter in this section referred to mem- bers, the Administrator shall appoint recognized experts in the fields of the health and environmental effects of air pollution, economic analysis, environmental sciences, and such other fields that the Administrator determines to be appropriate.

(g) The Council shall—

(1) review the data to be used for any analysis required under this section and make recommendations to the Administrator on the use of such data;

(2) review the methodology used to analyze such data and make recommendations to the Administrator on the use of such methodology; and

(3) prior to the issuance of a report required under subsection (d) or (e), review the findings of such report, and make recommendations to the Administrator concerning the validity and utility of such findings.

[Editor's Note: Sec. 812 of PL 101–549 also provides: (b) "GAO Reports on Costs and Benefits.— Commencing on the second year after the date of the enactment of the Clean Air Act Amendments of 1990 and annually thereafter, the Comptroller General of the General Accounting Office, in consultation with other agencies, such as the Environmental Protection Agency, the Department of Labor, the Department of Commerce, the United States Trade Representative, the National Academy of Sciences, the Office of Technology Assessment, the National Academy of Engineering, the Council on Environmental Quality, and the Surgeon General, shall provide a report to the Congress on the incremental human health and environmental benefits, and incremental costs beyond current clean air requirements of the new control strategies and technologies required by this Act. The report shall include, for such strategies and technologies, an analysis of the actual emissions reductions beyond existing practice, the effects on human life, human health and the environment (including both positive impacts and those that may be detrimental to jobs and communities resulting from loss of employers and employment, etc.), the energy security impacts, and the effect on United States products and industrial competitiveness in national and international markets."]

§7613. [Sec. 313]

[§313 repealed by PL 101–549]

§7614. Labor Standards [Sec. 314]

The Administrator shall take such action as may be necessary to insure that all laborers and mechanics employed by contractors or subcontractors on projects assisted under this Act shall be paid wages at rates not less than those prevailing for the same type of work on similar construction in the locality as determined by the Secretary of Labor, in accordance with the Act of March 3, 1931, as amended, known as the Davis-Bacon Act (46 Stat. 1494; 40 U.S.C. 276a–276a–5). The Secretary of Labor shall have, with respect to the labor standards specified in this subsection, the authority and functions set forth in Reorganization Plan Numbered 14 of 1950 (15 F.R. 3176; 64 Stat. 1267) and section 2 of the Act of June 13, 1934, as amended (48 Stat. 948; 40 U.S.C. 276c).

§7615. Separability [Sec. 315]

If any provision of this Act, or the application of any provision of this Act to any person or circumstance, is held invalid, the application of such provision to other persons or circumstances, and the remainder of this Act, shall not be affected thereby.

§7616. Sewage Treatment Grants [Sec. 316]

(a) No grant which the Administrator is authorized to make to any applicant for construction of sewage treatment works in any area in any State may be withheld, conditioned, or restricted by the Administrator on the basis of any requirement of this Act except as provided in subsection (b).

(b) The Administrator may withhold, condition, or restrict the making of any grant for construction referred to in subsection (a) only if he determines that—

(1) such treatment works will not comply with applicable standards under section 111 or 112 ,

(2) the State does not have in effect, or is not carrying out, a State implementation plan approved by the Administrator which expressly quantifies and provides for the increase in emissions of each air pollutant (from stationary and mobile sources in any area to which either part C or Part D of title I applies for such pollutant) which increase may reasonably be anticipated to result directly or indirectly from the new sewage treatment capacity which would be created by such construction,

(3) the construction of such treatment works would create new sewage treatment capacity which—

(A) may reasonably be anticipated to cause or contribute to, directly or indirectly, an increase in emissions of any air pollutant in excess of the increase provided for under the provisions referred to in paragraph (2) for any such area, or

(B) would otherwise not be in conformity with the applicable implementation plan, or

(4) such increase in emissions would interfere with, or be inconsistent with, the applicable implementation plan for any other State. In the case of construction of a treatment works which would result, directly or indirectly, in an increase in emissions of any air pollutant from stationary and mobile sources in an area to which part D of title I applies, the quantification of emissions referred to in paragraph (2) shall include the emissions of any such pollutant resulting directly or indirectly from areawide and nonmajor stationary source growth (mobile and stationary) for each such area.

(c) Nothing in this section shall be construed to amend or alter any provision of the National Environmental Policy Act or to affect any determination as to whether or not the requirements of such Act have been met in the case of the construction of any sewage treatment works.

[§316 added by PL 95–95]

§7617. Economic Impact Assessment [Sec. 317]

(a) This section applies to action of the Administrator in promulgating or revising—

(1) any new source standard of performance under section 111.

[§317(a)(1) amended by PL 95–623]

(2) any regulation under section 111(d) ,

(3) any regulation under part B of title I (relating to ozone and stratosphere protection),

(4) any regulation under Part C of title I (relating to prevention of significant deterioration of air quality),

(5) any regulation establishing emission standards under section 202 and any other regulation promulgated under that section,

(6) any regulation controlling or prohibiting any fuel or fuel additive under section 211(c) , and

(7) any aircraft emission standard under section 231 . Nothing in this section shall apply to any standard or regulation described in paragraphs (1) through (7) of this subsection unless the notice of proposed rulemaking in connection with such standard or regulation is published in the Federal Register after the date ninety days after the date of enactment of this section. In the case of revisions of such standards or regulations, this section shall apply only to revisions which the Administrator determines to be substantial revisions.

(b) Before publication of notice of proposed rulemaking with respect to any standard or regulation to which this section applies, the Administrator shall prepare an economic impact assessment respecting such standard or regulation. Such assessment shall be included in the docket required under section 307(d)(2) and shall be available to the public as provided in section 307(d)(4). Notice of proposed rulemaking shall include notice of such availability together with an explanation of the extent and manner in which the Administrator has considered the analysis contained in such economic impact assessment in proposing the action. The Administrator shall also provide such an explanation in his notice of promulgation of any regulation or standard referred to in subsection (a). Each such explanation shall be part of the statements of basis and purpose required under sections 307(d)(3) and 307(d)(6) .

(c) Subject to subsection (d), the assessment required under this section with respect to any standard or regulation shall contain an analysis of—

(1) the costs of compliance with any such standard or regulation, including extent to which the costs of compliance will vary depending on (A) the effective date of the standard or regulation, and (B) the development of less expensive, more efficient means or methods of compliance with the standard or regulation;

(2) the potential inflationary or recessionary effects of the standard or regulation;

(3) the effects on competition of the standard or regulation with respect to small business;

(4) the effects of the standard or regulation on consumer costs; and

(5) the effects of the standard or regulation on energy use. Nothing in this section shall be construed to provide that the analysis of the factors specified in this subsection affects or alters the factors which the Administrator is required to consider in taking any action referred to in subsection (a).

(d) The assessment require under this section shall be as extensive as practicable, in the judgment of the Administrator taking into account the time and resources available to the Environmental Protection Agency and other duties and authorities which the Administrator is required to carry out under this Act.

(e) Nothing in this section shall be construed—

(1) to alter the basis on which a standard or regulation is promulgated under this Act;

(2) to preclude the Administrator from carrying out his responsibility under this Act to protect public health and welfare; or

(3) to authorize or require any judicial review of any such standard or regulation, or any stay or injunction of the proposal, promulgation, or effectiveness of such standard or regulation on the basis of failure to comply with this section.

(f) The requirements imposed on the Administrator under this section shall be treated as nondiscretionary duties for purposes of section 304(a)(2), relating to citizen suits. The sole method for enforcement of the Administrator's duty under this section shall be by bringing a citizen suit under such section 304(a)(2) for a court order to compel the Administrator to perform such duty. Violation of any such order shall subject the Administrator to penalties for contempt of court.

(g) In the case of any provision of this Act in which costs are expressly required to be taken into account, the adequacy or inadequacy of any assessment required under this section may be taken into consideration, but shall not be treated for purposes of judicial review of any such provision as conclusive with respect to compliance or noncompliance with the requirement of such provision to take cost into account.

[§317 added by PL 95–95]

§7618. [Sec. 318]

[§318 repealed by PL 101–549]

§7619. Air Quality Monitoring [Sec. 319]

Not later than one year after the date of enactment of the Clean Air Act Amendments of 1977 and after notice and opportunity for public hearing, the Administrator shall promulgate regulations establishing an air quality monitoring system throughout the United States which—

(1) utilizes uniform air quality monitoring criteria and methodology and measures such air quality according to a uniform air quality index.

(2) provides for air quality monitoring stations in major urban areas and other appropriate areas throughout the United States to provide monitoring such as will supplement (but not duplicate) air quality monitoring carried out by the States required under any applicable implementation plan.

(3) provides for daily analysis and reporting of air quality based upon such uniform air quality index, and

(4) provides for recordkeeping with respect to such monitoring data and for periodic analysis and reporting to the general public by the Administrator with respect to air quality based upon such data.

The operation of such air quality monitoring system may be carried out by the Administrator or by such other departments, agencies, or entities of the Federal Government (including the National Weather Service) as the President may deem appropriate. Any air quality monitoring system required under any applicable implementation plan under section 110 shall, as soon as practicable following promulgation of regulations under this section, utilize the standard criteria and methodology, and measure air quality according to the standard index, established under such regulations.

[§319 added by PL 95–95]

§7620. Standardized Air Quality Modeling [Sec. 320]

(a) Not later than six months after the date of the enactment of the Clean Air Act Amendments of 1977, and at least every three years thereafter, the Administrator shall conduct a conference on air quality modeling. In conducting such conference, special attention shall be given to appropriate modeling necessary for carrying out part C of title I (relating to prevention of significant deterioration of air quality).

(b) The conference conducted under this section shall provide for participation by the National Academy of Sciences, representatives of State and local air pollution control agencies, and appropriate Federal agencies, including the National Science Foundation; the National Oceanic and Atmospheric Administration, and the National Institute of Standards and Technology.

[§320(b) amended by PL 100–418]

(c) Interested persons shall be permitted to submit written comments and a verbatim transcript of the conference proceedings shall be maintained.

(d) The comments submitted and the transcript maintained pursuant to subsection (c) shall be included in the docket required to be established for purposes of promulgating or revising any regulation relating to air quality modeling under part C of title I.

[§320 added by PL 95–95]

§7621. Employment Effects [Sec. 321]

(a) The Administrator shall conduct continuing evaluations of potential loss or shifts of employment which may result from the administration or enforcement of the provision of this Act and applicable implementation plans, including where appropriate, investigating threatened plant closures or reductions in employment allegedly resulting from such administration or enforcement.

(b) Any employee, or any representative of such employee, who is discharged or laid off, threatened with discharge or layoff, or whose employment is otherwise adversely affected or threatened to be adversely affected because of the alleged results of any requirement imposed or proposed to be imposed under this Act, including any requirement applicable to Federal facility and any requirement imposed by a State or political subdivision thereof, may request the Administrator to conduct a full investigation of the matter. Any such request shall be reduced to writing, shall set forth with reasonable particularity the grounds for the request, and shall be signed by the employee, or representative of such employee, making the request. The Administrator shall thereupon investigate the matter and, at the request of any party, shall hold public hearings on not less than five days notice. At such hearings, the Administrator shall require the parties, including the employer involved, to present information relating to the actual or potential effect of such requirements on employment and the detailed reasons or justification thereof. If the Administrator determines that there are no reasonable grounds for conducting a public hearing he shall notify (in writing), the party requesting such hearing of such determination and the reasons therefor. If the Administrator does convene such a hearing, the hearing shall be on the record. Upon receiving the report of such investigation, the Administrator shall make findings of fact as to the effect of such requirements on employment and on the alleged actual or potential discharge, layoff, or other adverse effect on employment, and shall make such recommendations as he deems appropriate. Such report, findings, and recommendations shall be available to the public.

(c) In connection with any investigation or public hearing conducted under subsection (b) of this section or as authorized in section 119 (relating to primary nonferrous smelter orders), the Administrator may issue subpoenas for the attendance and testimony of witnesses and the production of relevant papers, books, and documents, and he may administer oaths. Except for emission data, upon a showing satisfactory to the Administrator by such owner or operator that such papers, books, documents, or information or particular part thereof, if made public, would divulge trade secrets or secret processes of such owner, or operator, the Administrator shall consider such record, report, or information or particular portion thereof confidential in accordance with the purposes of section 1905 of title 18 of the United States Code, except that such paper, book, document, or information may be disclosed to other officers, employees, or authorized representatives of the United States concerned with carrying out this Act, or when relevant in any proceeding under this Act. Witnesses summoned shall be paid the same fees and mileage that are paid witnesses in the courts of the United States. In cases of contumacy or refusal to obey a subpoena served upon any person under this subparagraph, the district court of the United States for any district in which such person is found or resides or transacts business, upon application by the United States and after notice to such person, shall have jurisdiction to issue an order requiring such person to appear and give testimony before the Administrator, to appear and produce papers, books, and documents before the Administrator, or both, and any failure to obey such order of the court may be punished by such court as a contempt thereof.

(d) Nothing in this section shall be construed to require or authorize the Administrator, the States, or political subdivisions thereof, to modify or withdraw any requirement imposed or proposed to be imposed under this Act.

[§321 added by PL 95–95]

§7622. Employee Protection [Sec. 322]

(a) No employer may discharge any employee or otherwise discriminate against any employee with respect to his compensation, terms conditions, or privileges or employment because the employee (or any person acting pursuant to a request of the employee)—

(1) commenced, caused to be commenced, or is about to commence or cause to be commenced a proceeding under this Act or a proceeding for the administration or enforcement of any requirement imposed under this Act or under any applicable implementation plan,

(2) testified or is about to testify in such proceeding, or

(3) assisted or participated or is about to assist or participate in any manner in such a proceeding or in any other action to carry out the purposes of this Act.

(b) (1) Any employee who believes that he has been discharged or otherwise discriminated against by any person in violation of subsection (a) may, within thirty days after such violation occurs, file (or have any person file on his behalf) a complaint with the Secretary of Labor (hereinafter in this subsection referred to as or discrimination. Upon receipt of such a complaint, the Secretary shall notify the person named in the complaint of the filing of the complaint.

(2) (A) Upon receipt of a complaint filed under paragraph (1), the Secretary shall conduct an investigation of the violation alleged in the complaint. Within thirty days of the receipt of such complaint, the Secretary shall complete such investigation and shall notify in writing the complainant (and any person acting in his behalf) and the person alleged to have committed such violation of the results of the investigation conducted pursuant to this subparagraph. Within ninety days of the receipt of such complaint the Secretary shall, unless the proceeding on the complaint is terminated by the Secretary on the basis of a settlement entered into by the Secretary and the person alleged to have committed such violation, issue an order either providing the relief prescribed by subparagraph (B) or denying the complaint. An order of the Secretary shall be made on the record after notice and opportunity for public hearing. The Secretary may not enter into a settlement terminating a proceeding on a complaint without the participation and consent of the complainant.

(B) If, in response to a complaint filed under paragraph (1), the Secretary determines that a violation of subsection (a) has occurred, the Secretary shall order the person who committed such violation to (i) take affirmative action to abate the violation, and (ii) reinstate the complainant to his former position together with the compensation (including back pay), terms, conditions, and privileges of his employment, and the Secretary may order such person to provide compensatory damages to the complainant. If an order is issued under this paragraph, the Secretary, at the request of the complainant, shall assess against the person against whom the order is issued a sum equal to the aggregate amount of all costs and expenses (including attorneys' and expert witness fees) reasonably incurred, as determined by the Secretary, by the complainant for, or in connection with, the bringing of the complaint upon which the order was issued.

(c) (1) Any person adversely affected or aggrieved by an order issued under subsection (b) may obtain review of the order in the United States court of appeals for the circuit in which the violation, which respect to which the order was issued, allegedly occurred. The petition for review must be filed within sixty days from the issuance of the Secretary's order. Review shall conform to chapter 7 of title 5 of the United States Code. The commencement of proceedings under this subparagraph shall not, unless ordered by the court, operate as a stay of the Secretary's order.

(2) An order of the Secretary with respect to which review could have been obtained under paragraph (1) shall not be subject to judicial review in any criminal or other civil proceeding.

(d) Whenever a person has failed to comply with an order issued under subsection (b)(2), the Secretary may file a civil action in the United States district court for the district in which the violation was found to occur to enforce such order. In actions brought under this subsection, the district courts shall have jurisdiction to grant all appropriate relief including, but not limited to, injunctive relief, compensatory, and exemplary damages.

(e) (1) Any person on whose behalf an order was issued under paragraph (2) of subsection (b) may commence a civil action against the person to whom such order was issued to require compliance with such order. The appropriate United States district court shall have jurisdiction, without regard to the amount in controversy or the citizenship of the parties, to enforce such order.

(2) The court, in issuing any final order under this subsection, may award costs of litigation (including reasonable attorney and expert witness fees) to any party whenever the court determines such award is appropriate.

(f) Any nondiscretionary duty imposed by this section shall be enforceable in a mandamus proceeding brought under section 1361 of title 28 of the United States Code.

(g) Subsection (a) shall not apply with respect to any employee who, acting without direction from his employer (or the employer's agent), deliberately causes a violation of any requirement of this Act.

[§322 added by PL 95–95]

[Editor's Note: The National Commission on Air Quality expired in 1981 in accordance with PL 96–300. Sections (c) and (d) of PL 96–300 also provide that: (c) "Effective on the date on which the National Commission on Air Quality ceases to exist pursuant to section 323(g) of the Clean Air Act, section 323 of the Clean Air Act is repealed and sections 324, 325, 326, and 327 of such Act are redesignated as sections 323, 324, 325, and 326 respectively.(d) Nothing in any other authority of law shall be construed to authorize or permit the extension of the National Commission on Air Quality pursuant to any Executive order or other Executive agency action." Therefore, the aforementioned sections have been redesignated accordingly.]

§7624. Cost of Emission Control for Certain Vapor Recovery to be Borne by Owner of Retail Outlet [Sec. 323]

(a) The regulations under this Act applicable to vapor recovery with respect to mobile source fuels at retail outlets of such fuels shall provide that the cost of procurement and installation of such vapor recovery shall be borne by the owner of such outlet (as determined under such regulations). Except as provided in subsection (b), such regulations shall provide that no lease of a retail outlet by the owner thereof which is entered into or renewed after the date of enactment of the Clean Air Act Amendments of 1977 may provide for a payment by the lessee of the cost of procurement and installation of vapor recovery equipment. Such regulations shall also provide that the cost of procurement and installation of vapor recovery equipment may be recovered by the owner of such outlet by means of price increases in the cost of any product sold by such owner, notwithstanding any provision of law.

(b) The regulations of the Administrator referred to in subsection (a) shall permit a lease of a retail outlet to provide for payment by the lessee of the cost of procurement and installation of vapor recovery equipment over a reasonable period (as determined in accordance with such regulations), if the owner of such outlet does not sell, trade in, or otherwise dispense any product at wholesale or retail at such outlet.

[Former §324 added by PL 95–95;amended and redesignated as §323 by PL 96–300]

§7625. Vapor Recovery for Small Business Marketers of Petroleum Products [Sec. 324]

(a) The regulations under this Act applicable to vapor recovery from fueling of motor vehicles at retail outlets of gasoline shall not apply to any outlet owned by an independent small business marketer of gasoline having monthly sales of less than 50,000 gallons. In the case of any other outlet owned by an independent small business marketer, such regulations shall provide, with respect to independent small business marketers of gasoline, for a three-year phase-in period for the installation of such vapor recovery equipment at such outlets under which such marketers shall have—

(1) 33 percent of such outlets in compliance at the end of the first year during which such regulations apply to such marketers.

(2) 66 percent at the end of such second year, and

(3) 100 percent at the end of the third year.

(b) Nothing in subsection (a) shall be construed to prohibit any State from adopting or enforcing, with respect to independent small business marketers of gasoline having monthly sales of less than 50,000 gallons, any vapor recovery requirements for mobile source fuels at retail outlets. Any vapor recovery requirement which is adopted by a State and submitted to the Administrator as part of its implementation plan may be approved and enforced by the Administrator as part of the applicable implementation plan for that State.

(c) For purposes of this section, an independent small business marketer of gasoline is a person engaged in the marketing of gasoline who would be required to pay for procurement and installation of vapor recovery equipment under section 324 of this Act or under regulations of the Administrator, unless such person—

(1) (A) is a refiner, or

(B) controls, is controlled by, or is under common control with, a refiner,

(C) is otherwise directly or indirectly affiliated (as determined under the regulations of the Administrator) with a refiner or with a person who controls, is controlled by, or is under a common control with a refiner (unless the sole affiliation referred to herein is by means of a supply contract or an agreement or contract to use a trademark, trade name, service mark, or other identifying symbol or name owned by such refiner or any such person), or

(2) receives less than 50 percent of his annual income from refining or marketing of gasoline. For the purpose of this section, the term "refiner" shall not include any refiner whose total refinery capacity (including the refinery capacity of any person who controls, is controlled by, or is under common control with, such refiner) does not exceed 65,000 barrels per day. For purposes of this section, "control" of a corporation means ownership of more than 50 percent of its stock.

[Former §325 redesignated as §324 by PL 96–300]

§7625. Exemptions for Certain Territories [Sec. 325]

(a) (1) Upon petition by the governor of Guam, American Samoa, the Virgin Islands, or the Commonwealth of the Northern Mariana Islands, the Administrator is authorized to exempt any person or source or class of persons or sources in such territory from any requirement under this Act other than section 112 or any requirement under section 110 or part D necessary to attain or maintain a national primary ambient air quality standard. Such exemption may be granted if the Administrator finds that compliance with such requirement is not feasible or is unreasonable due to unique geographical, meteorological, or economic factors of such territory, or such other local factors as the Administrator deems significant. Any such petition shall be considered in accordance with section 307(d) and any exemption under this subsection shall be considered final action by the Administrator for the purposes of section 307(b) .

[§325(a)(1) amended by PL 101–549]

(2) The Administrator shall promptly notify the Committees on Energy and Commerce and on Interior and Insular Affairs of the House of Representatives and the Committees on Environment and Public Works and on Energy and Natural Resources of the Senate upon receipt of any petition under this subsection and of the approval or rejection of such petition and the basis for such action.

(b) Notwithstanding any other provision of this Act, any fossil fuel fired steam electric power plant operating within Guam as of the date of enactment of this section is hereby exempted from:

(1) any requirement of the new source performance standards relating to sulfur dioxide promulgated under section 111 as of such date of enactment; and

(2) any regulation relating to sulfur dioxide standards or limitations contained in a State implementation plan approved under section 110 as of such date of enactment: Provided, That such exemption shall expire eighteen months after such date of enactment unless the Administrator determines that such plant is making all emissions reductions practicable to prevent exceedances of the national ambient air quality standards for sulfur dioxide.

§7625a. Construction of Certain Clauses [Sec. 326]

The parenthetical cross references in any provision of this Act to other provisions of the Act, or other provisions of law, where the words "relating to" or "pertaining to" are used, are made only for convenience, and shall be given no legal effect.

[Another former §325 redesignated as §326 by PL 98–213]

§7626. Authorization of Appropriations [Sec. 327]

(a) In General.—There are authorized to be appropriated to carry out this Act such sums as may be necessary for the 7 fiscal years commencing after the enactment of the Clean Air Act Amendments of 1990.

(b) Grants for Planning.—There are authorized to be appropriated (1) not more than $50,000,000 to carry out section 175 beginning in fiscal year 1991, to be available until expended, to develop plan revisions required by subpart 2, 3, or 4 of part D of title I, and (2) not more than $15,000,000 for each of the 7 fiscal years commencing after the enactment of the Clean Air Act Amendments of 1990 to make grants to the States to prepare implementation plans as required by subpart 2, 3, or 4 of part D of title I.

[Former §326 redesignated as §327 by PL 98–213; amended by PL 101–549]

[§327 revised by PL 101–549]

§7627. Air Pollution from Outer Continental Shelf Activities [Sec. 328]

(a) (1) Applicable Requirements for Certain Areas.—Not later than 12 months after the enactment of the Clean Air Act Amendments of 1990, following consultation with the Secretary of the Interior and the Commandant of the United States Coast Guard, the Administrator, by rule, shall establish requirements to control air pollution from Outer Continental Shelf sources located offshore of the States along the Pacific, Arctic and Atlantic Coasts, and along the United States Gulf Coast off the State of Florida eastward of longitude 87 degrees and 30 maintain Federal and State ambient air quality standards and to comply with the provisions of part C of title I. For such sources located within 25 miles of the seaward boundary of such States, such requirements shall be the same as would be applicable if the source were located in the corresponding onshore area, and shall include, but not be limited to, State and local requirements for emission controls, emission limitations, offsets, permitting, monitoring, testing, and reporting. New OCS sources shall comply with such requirements on the date of promulgation and existing OCS sources shall comply on the date 24 months thereafter. The Administrator shall update such requirements as necessary to maintain consistency with onshore regulations. The authority of this subsection shall supersede section 5(a)(8) of the Outer Continental Shelf Lands Act but shall not repeal or modify any other Federal, State, or local authorities with respect to air quality. Each requirement established under this section shall be treated, for purposes of sections 113, 114, 116, 120, and 304, as a standard under section 111 and a violation of any such requirement shall be considered a violation of section 111(e) .

(2) Exemptions.—The Administrator may exempt an OCS source from a specific requirement in effect under regulations under this subsection if the Administrator finds that compliance with a pollution control technology requirement is technically infeasible or will cause an unreasonable threat to health and safety. The Administrator shall make written findings explaining the basis of any exemption issued pursuant to this subsection and shall impose another requirement equal to or as close in stringency to the original requirement as possible. The Administrator shall ensure that any increase in emissions due to the granting of an exemption is offset by reductions in actual emissions, not otherwise required by this Act, from the same source or other sources in the area or in the corresponding onshore area. The Administrator shall establish procedures to provide for public notice and comment on exemptions proposed pursuant to this subsection.

(3) State Procedures.—Each State adjacent to an OCS source included under this subsection may promulgate and submit to the Administrator regulations for implementing and enforcing the requirements of this subsection. If the Administrator finds that the State regulations are adequate, the Administrator shall delegate to that State any authority the Administrator has under this Act to implement and enforce such requirements. Nothing in this subsection shall prohibit the Administrator from enforcing any requirement of this section.

(4) Definitions.—For purposes of subsections (a) and (b)—

(A) Outer Continental Shelf.—The term 'Outer Continental Shelf has the meaning provided by section 2 of the Outer Continental Shelf Lands Act (43 U.S.C. 1331).

(B) Corresponding Onshore Area.—The term 'corresponding onshore area' means, with respect to any OCS source, the onshore attainment or nonattainment area that is closest to the source, unless the Administrator determines that another area with more stringent requirements with respect to the control and abatement of air pollution may reasonably be expected to be affected by such emissions. Such determination shall be based on the potential for air pollutants from the OCS source to reach the other onshore area and the potential of such air pollutants to affect the efforts of the other onshore area to attain or maintain any Federal or State ambient air quality standard or to comply with the provisions of part C of title I.

(C) Outer Continental Shelf Source.—The terms 'Outer Continental Shelf source' and 'OCS source' include any equipment, activity, or facility which—

(i) emits or has the potential to emit any air pollutant,

(ii) is regulated or authorized under the Outer Continental Shelf Lands Act, and

(iii) is located on the Outer Continental Shelf or in or on waters above the Outer Continental Shelf. Such activities include, but are not limited to, platform and drill ship exploration, construction, development, production, processing, and transportation. For purposes of this subsection, emissions from any vessel servicing or associated with an OCS source, including emissions while at the OCS source or en route to or from the OCS source within 25 miles of the OCS source, shall be considered direct emissions from the OCS source.

(D) New and Existing OCS Sources.—The term 'new OCS source' means an OCS source which is a new source within the meaning of section 111(a) . The term 'existing OCS source' means any OCS source other than a new OCS source.

(b) Requirements for Other Offshore Areas.—For portions of the United States Gulf Coast Outer Continental Shelf that are adjacent to the States not covered by subsection (a) which are Texas, Louisiana, Mississippi, and Alabama, the Secretary shall consult with the Administrator to assure coordination of air pollution control regulation for Outer Continental Shelf emissions and emissions in adjacent onshore areas. Concurrently with this obligation, the Secretary shall complete within 3 years of enactment of this section a research study examining the impacts of emissions from Outer Continental Shelf activities in such areas that fail to meet the national ambient air quality standards for either ozone or nitrogen dioxide. Based on the results of this study, the Secretary shall consult with the Administrator and determine if any additional actions are necessary. There are authorized to be appropriated such sums as may be necessary to provide funding for the study required under this section.

(c) (1) Coastal Waters.—The study report of section 112(n) of the Clean Air Act shall apply to the coastal waters of the United States to the same extent and in the same manner as such requirements apply to the Great Lakes, the Chesapeake Bay, and their tributary waters.

(2) The regulatory requirements of section 112(n) of the Clean Air Act shall apply to the coastal waters of the States which are subject to subsection (a) of this section, to the same extent and in the same manner as such requirements apply to the Great Lakes, the Chesapeake Bay, and their tributary waters.

[§328 added by PL 101–549]

TITLE IV—NOISE POLLUTION

[Title IV added by PL 91–604]

This title may be cited as the "Noise Pollution and Abatement Act of 1970".

§7641. Noise abatement [Sec. 402]

(a) The Administrator shall establish within the Environmental Protection Agency an Office of Noise Abatement and Control, and shall carry out through such Office a full and complete investigation and study of noise and its effect on the public health and welfare in order to

(1) identify and classify causes and sources of noise, and

(2) determine—

(A) effects at various levels;

(B) projected growth of noise levels in urban areas through the year 2000;

(C) the psychological and physiological effect on humans;

(D) effects of sporadic extreme noise (such as jet noise near airports) as compared with constant noise;

(E) effect on wildlife and property (including values);

(F) effect of sonic booms on property (including values); and

(G) such other matters as may be of interest in the public welfare.

(b) In conducting such investigation, the Administrator shall hold public hearings, conduct research, experiments, demonstrations, and studies. The Administrator shall report the results of such investigation and study, together with his recommendations for legislation or other action, to the President and the Congress not later than one year after the date of enactment of this title.

(c) in any case where any Federal department or agency is carrying out or sponsoring any activity resulting in noise which the Administrator determines amounts to a public nuisance or is otherwise objectionable, such department or agency shall consult with the Administrator to determine possible means of abating such noise.

§7642. Authorization of appropriations [Sec. 403]

There is authorized to be appropriated such amount not to exceed $30,000,000 as may be necessary for the purposes of this title.

TITLE IV—ACID DEPOSITION CONTROL

[A second Title IV was added by PL 101–549]

§7651. Findings and Purposes [Sec. 401]

(a) Findings.—The Congress finds that—

(1) the presence of acidic compounds and their precursors in the atmosphere and in deposition from the atmosphere represents a threat to natural resources, ecosystems, materials, visibility, and public health;

(2) the principal sources of the acidic compounds and their precursors in the atmosphere are emissions of sulfur and nitrogen oxides from the combustion of fossil fuels;

(3) the problem of acid deposition is of national and international significance;

(4) strategies and technologies for the control of precursors to acid deposition exist now that are economically feasible, and improved methods are expected to become increasingly available over the next decade;

(5) current and future generations of Americans will be adversely affected by delaying measures to remedy the problem;

(6) reduction of total atmospheric loading of sulfur dioxide and nitrogen oxides will enhance protection of the public health and welfare and the environment; and

(7) control measures to reduce precursor emissions from steam-electric generating units should be initiated without delay.

(b) Purposes.—The purpose of this title is to reduce the adverse effects of acid deposition through reductions in annual emissions of sulfur dioxide of ten million tons from 1980 emission levels, and, in combination with other provisions of this Act, of nitrogen oxides emissions of approximately two million tons from 1980 emission levels, in the forty-eight contiguous States and the District of Columbia. It is the intent of this title to effectuate such reductions by requiring compliance by affected sources with prescribed emission limitations by specified deadlines, which limitations may be met through alternative methods of compliance provided by an emission allocation and transfer system. It is also the purpose of this title to encourage energy conservation, use of renewable and clean alternative technologies, and pollution prevention as a long- range strategy, consistent with the provisions of this title, for reducing air pollution and other adverse impacts of energy production and use.

§7651a. Definitions [Sec. 402]

As used in this title:

(1) The term 'affected source' means a source that includes one or more affected units.

(2) The term 'affected unit' means a unit that is subject to emission reduction requirements or limitations under this title.

(3) The term 'allowance' means an authorization, allocated to an affected unit by the Administrator under this title, to emit, during or after a specified calendar year, one ton of sulfur dioxide.

(4) The term 'baseline' means the annual quantity of fossil fuel consumed by an affected unit, measured in millions of British Thermal Units ('mmBtu's' follows:

(A) For each utility unit that was in commercial operation prior to January 1, 1985, the baseline shall be the annual average quantity of mmBtu's consumed in fuel during calendar years 1985, 1986, and 1987, as recorded by the Department of Energy pursuant to Form 767. For any utility unit for which such form was not filed, the baseline shall be the level specified for such unit in the 1985 National Acid Precipitation Assessment Program (NAPAP) Emissions Inventory, Version 2, National Utility Reference File (NURF) or in a corrected data base as established by the Administrator pursuant to paragraph (3). For non-utility units, the baseline is the NAPAP Emissions Inventory, Version 2. The Administrator, in the Administrator's sole discretion, may exclude periods during which a unit is shutdown for a continuous period of four calendar months or longer, and make appropriate adjustments under this paragraph. Upon petition of the owner or operator of any unit, the Administrator may make appropriate baseline adjustments for accidents that caused prolonged outages.

(B) For any other nonutility unit that is not included in the NAPAP Emissions Inventory, Version 2, or a corrected data base as established by the Administrator pursuant to paragraph (3), the baseline shall be the annual average quantity, in mmBtu consumed in fuel by that unit, as calculated pursuant to a method which the administrator shall prescribe by regulation to be promulgated not later than eighteen months after enactment of the Clean Air Act Amendments of 1990.

(C) The Administrator shall, upon application or on his own motion, by December 31, 1991, supplement data needed in support of this title and correct any factual errors in data from which affected Phase II units' baselines or actual 1985 emission rates have been calculated. Corrected data shall be used for purposes of issuing allowances under the title. Such corrections shall not be subject to judicial review, nor shall the failure of the Administrator to correct an alleged factual error in such reports be subject to judicial review.

(5) The term 'capacity factor' means the ratio between the actual electric output from a unit and the potential electric output from that unit.

(6) The term 'compliance plan' means, for purposes of the requirements of this title, either—

(A) a statement that the source will comply with all applicable requirements under this title, or

(B) where applicable, a schedule and description of the method or methods for compliance and certification by the owner or operator that the source is in compliance with the requirements of this title.

(7) The term 'continuous emission monitoring system' (CEMS) means the equipment as required by section 412 , used to sample, analyze, measure, and provide on a continuous basis a permanent record of emissions and flow (expressed in pounds per million British thermal units (lbs/mmBtu), pounds per hour (lbs/hr) or such other form as the Administrator may prescribe by regulations under section 412).

(8) The term 'existing unit' means a unit (including units subject to section 111) that commenced commercial operation before the date of enactment of the Clean Air Act Amendments of 1990. Any unit that commenced commercial operation before the date of enactment of the Clean Air Act Amendments of 1990 which is modified, reconstructed, or repowered after the date of enactment of the Clean Air Act Amendments of 1990 shall continue to be an existing unit for the purposes of this title. For the purposes of this title, existing units shall not include simple combustion turbines, or units which serve a generator with a nameplate capacity of 25MWe or less.

(9) The term 'generator' means a device that produces electricity and which is reported as a generating unit pursuant to Department of Energy Form 860.

(10) The term 'new unit' means a unit that commences commercial operation on or after the date of enactment of the Clean Air Act Amendments of 1990.

(11) The term 'permitting authority' means the Administrator, or the State or local air pollution control agency, with an approved permitting program under part B of title III of the Act.

(12) The term 'repowering' means replacement of an existing coal-fired boiler with one of the

following clean coal technologies: atmospheric or pressurized fluidized bed combustion, integrated gasification combined cycle, magnetohydrodynamics, direct and indirect coal-fired turbines, integrated gasification fuel cells, or as determined by the Administrator, in consultation with the Secretary of Energy, a derivative of one or more of these technologies, and any other technology capable of controlling multiple combustion emissions simultaneously with improved boiler or generation efficiency with significantly greater waste reduction relative to the performance of technology in widespread commercial use as of the date of enactment of the Clean Air Act Amendments of 1990. Notwithstanding the provisions of section 409(a) , for the purpose of this title, the term 'repowering' shall also include any oil and/or gas-fired unit which has been awarded clean coal technology demonstration funding as of January 1, 1991, by the Department of Energy.

(13) The term 'reserve' means any bank of allowances established by the Administrator under this title.

(14) The term 'State' means one of the 48 contiguous States and the District of Columbia.

(15) The term 'unit' means a fossil fuel- fired combustion device.

(16) The term 'actual 1985 emission rate', for electric utility units means the annual sulfur dioxide or nitrogen oxides emission rate in pounds per million Btu as reported in the NAPAP Emissions Inventory, Version 2, National Utility Refer ence File. For nonutility units, the term 'actual 1985 emission rate' means the annual sulfur dioxide or nitrogen oxides emission rate in pounds per million Btu as reported in the NAPAP Emission Inventory, Version 2.

(17) (A) The term 'utility unit' means—

(i) a unit that serves a generator in any State that produces electricity for sale, or

(ii) a unit that, during 1985, served a generator in any State that produced electricity for sale.

(B) Notwithstanding subparagraph (A), a unit described in subparagraph (A)—

(i) was in commercial operation during 1985, but

(ii) did not, during 1985, serve a generator in any State that produced electricity for sale shall not be a utility unit for purposes of this title.

(C) A unit that cogenerates steam and electricity is not a 'utility unit' for purposes of this title unless the unit is constructed for the purpose of supplying, or commences construction after the date of enactment of this title and supplies, more than one-third of its potential electric output capacity and more than 25 megawatts electrical output to any utility power distribution system for sale.

(18) The term 'allowable 1985 emissions rate' means a federally enforceable emissions limitation for sulfur dioxide or oxides of nitrogen, applicable to the unit in 1985 or the limitation applicable in such other subsequent year as determined by the Administrator if such a limitation for 1985 does not exist. Where the emissions limitation for a unit is not expressed in pounds of emissions per million Btu, or the averaging period of that emissions limitation is not expressed on an annual basis, the Administrator shall calculate the annual equivalent of that emissions limitation in pounds per million Btu to establish the allowable 1985 emissions rate.

(19) The term 'qualifying phase I technology' means a technological system of continuous emission reduction which achieves a 90 percent reduction in emissions of sulfur dioxide from the emissions that would have resulted from the use of fuels which were not subject to treatment prior to combustion.

(20) The term 'alternative method of compliance' means a method of compliance in accordance with one or more of the following authorities:

(A) a substitution plan submitted and approved in accordance with subsections 404(b) and (c);

(B) a Phase I extension plan approved by the Administrator under section 404(d), using qualifying phase I technology as determined by the Administrator in accordance with that section; or

(C) repowering with a qualifying clean coal technology under section 409.

(21) The term 'commenced' as applied to construction of any new electric utility unit means that an owner or operator has undertaken a continuous program of construction or that an owner or operator has entered into a contractual obligation to undertake and complete, within a reasonable time, a continuous program of construction.

(22) The term 'commenced commercial operation' means to have begun to generate electricity for sale.

(23) The term 'construction' means fabrication, erection, or installation of an affected unit.

(24) The term 'industrial source' means a unit that does not serve a generator that produces electricity, a 'nonutility unit' as defined in this section, or a process source as defined in section 410(e) .

(25) The term 'nonutility unit' means a unit other than a utility unit.

(26) The term 'designated representative' means a responsible person or official authorized by the owner or operator of a unit to represent the owner or operator in matters pertaining to the holding, transfer, or disposition of allowances allocated to a unit, and the submission of and compliance with permits, permit applications, and compliance plans for the unit.

(27) The term 'life-of-the-unit, firm power contractual arrangement' means a unit participation power sales agreement under which a utility or industrial customer reserves, or is entitled to receive, a specified amount or percentage of capacity and associated energy generated by a specified generating unit (or units) and pays its proportional amount of such unit's total costs, pursuant to a contract either—

(A) for the life of the unit;

(B) for a cumulative term of no less than 30 years, including contracts that permit an election for early termination; or

(C) for a period equal to or greater than 25 years or 70 percent of the economic useful life of the unit determined as of the time the unit was built, with option rights to purchase or release some portion of the capacity and associated energy generated by the unit (or units) at the end of the period.

(28) The term 'basic Phase II allowance allocations' means:

(A) For calendar years 2000 through 2009 inclusive, allocations of allowances made by the Administrator pursuant to section 403 and subsections (b)(1), (3), and (4); (c)(1), (2), (3), and (5); (d)(1), (2), (4), and (5); (e); (f); (g)(1), (2), (3), (4), and (5); (h)(1); (i) and (j) of section 405 .

(B) For each calendar year beginning in 2010, allocations of allowances made by the Administrator pursuant to section 403 and subsections (b)(1), (3), and (4); (c)(1), (2), (3), and (5); (d)(1), (2), (4) and (5); (e); (f); (g)(1), (2), (3), (4), and (5); (h)(1) and (3); (i) and (j) of section 405 .

(29) The term 'Phase II bonus allowance allocations' means, for calendar year 2000 through 2009, inclusive, and only for such years, allocations made by the Administrator pursuant to section 403 , subsections (a)(2), (b)(2), (c)(4), (d)(3) (except as otherwise provided therein), and (h)(2) of section 405 , and section 406 .

§7651b. Sulfur Dioxide Allowance Program for Existing and New Units [Sec. 403]

(a) Allocations of Annual Allowances for Existing and New Units.—

(1) For the emission limitation programs under this title, the Administrator shall allocate annual allowances for the unit, to be held or distributed by the designated representative of the owner or operator of each affected unit at an affected source in accordance with this title, in an amount equal to the annual tonnage emission limitation calculated under section 404, 405, 406, 409, or 410 except as otherwise specifically provided elsewhere in this title. Except as provided in sections 405(a)(2) , 405(a)(3), 409 and 410, beginning January 1, 2000, the Administrator shall not allocate annual allowances to emit sulfur dioxide pursuant to section 405 in such an amount as would result in total annual emissions of sulfur dioxide from utility units in excess of 8.90 million tons except that the Administrator shall not take into account unused allowances carried forward by owners and operators of affected units or by other persons holding such allowances, following the year for which they were allocated. If necessary to meeting the restrictions imposed in the preceding sentence, the Administrator shall reduce, pro rata, the basic Phase II allowance allocations for each unit subject to the requirements of section 405 . Subject to the provisions of section 416 , the Administrator shall allocate allowances for each affected unit at an affected source annually, as provided in paragraphs (2) and (3) and section 408 . Except as provided in sections 409 and 410 , the removal of an existing affected unit or source from commercial operation at any time after the date of the enactment of the Clean Air Act Amendments of 1990 (whether before or after January 1, 1995, or January 1, 2000) shall not terminate or otherwise affect the allocation of allowances pursuant to section 404 or 405 to which the unit is entitled. Allowances shall be allocated by the Administrator without cost to the recipient, except for allowances sold by the Administrator pursuant to section 416 . Not later than December 31, 1991, the Administrator shall publish a pro-

posed list of the basic Phase II allowance allocations, the Phase II bonus allowance allocations and, if applicable, allocations pursuant to section 405(a)(3) for each unit subject to the emissions limitation requirements of section 405 for the year 2000 and the year 2010. After notice and opportunity for public comment, but not later than December 31, 1992, the Administrator shall publish a final list of such allocations, subject to the provisions of section 405(a)(2) . Any owner or operator of an existing unit subject to the requirements of section 405(b) or (c) who is considering applying for an extension of the emission limitation requirement compliance deadline for that unit from January 1, 2000, until not later than December 31, 2000, pursuant to section 409 , shall notify the Administrator no later than March 31, 1991. Such notification shall be used as the basis for estimating the basic Phase II allowances under this subsection. Prior to June 1, 1998, the Administrator shall publish a revised final statement of allowance allocations, subject to the provisions of section 405(a)(2) and taking into account the effect of any compliance date extensions granted pursuant to section 409 on such allocations. Any person who may make an election concerning the amount of allowances to be allocated to a unit or units shall make such election and so inform the Administrator not later than March 31, 1991, in the case of an election under section 405 (or June 30, 1991, in the case of an election under section 406) . If such person fails to make such election, the Administrator shall set forth for each unit owned or operated by such person, the amount of allowances reflecting the election that would, in the judgment of the Administrator, provide the greatest benefit for the owner or operator of the unit. If such person is a Governor who may make an election under section 406 and the Governor fails to make an election, the Administrator shall set forth for each unit in the State the amount of allowances reflecting the election that would, in the judgment of the Administrator, provide the greatest benefit for units in the State.

(b) Allowance Transfer System.—Allowances allocated under this title may be transferred among designated representatives of the owners or operators of affected sources under this title and any other person who holds such allowances, as provided by the allowance system regulations to be promulgated by the Administrator not later than eighteen months after the date of enactment of the Clean Air Act Amendments of 1990. Such regulations shall establish the allowance system prescribed under this section, including, but not limited to, requirements for the allocation, transfer, and use of allowances under this title. Such regulations shall prohibit the use of any allowance prior to the calendar year for which the allowance was allocated, and shall provide, consistent with the purposes of this title, for the identification of unused allowances, and for such unused allowances to be carried forward and added to allowances allocated in subsequent years, including allowances allocated to units subject to Phase I requirements (as described in section 404) which are applied to emissions limitations requirements in Phase II (as described in section 405). Transfers of allowances shall not be effective until written certification of the transfer, signed by a responsible official of each party to the transfer, is received and recorded by the Administrator. Such regulations shall permit the transfer of allowances prior to the issuance of such allowances. Recorded pre-allocation transfers shall be deducted by the Administrator from the number of allowances which would otherwise be allocated to the transferor, and added to those allowances allocated to the transferee. Pre-allocation transfers shall not affect the prohibition contained in this subsection against the use of allowances prior to the year for which they are allocated.

(c) Interpollutant Trading.—Not later than January 1, 1994, the Administrator shall furnish to the Congress a study evaluating the environmental and economic consequences of amending this title to permit trading sulfur dioxide allowances for nitrogen oxides allowances.

(d) Allowance Tracking System.—

(1) The Administrator shall promulgate, not later than 18 months after the date of enactment of the Clean Air Act Amendments of 1990, a system for issuing, recording, and tracking allowances, which shall specify all necessary procedures and requirements for an orderly and competitive functioning of the allowance system. All allowance allocations and transfers shall, upon recordation by the Administrator, be deemed a part of each unit's permit requirements pursuant to section 408, without any further permit review and revision.

(2) In order to insure electric reliability, such regulations shall not prohibit or affect temporary increases and decreases in emissions within utility systems, power pools, or utilities entering into allowance pool agreements, that result from their operations, including emer-

gencies and central dispatch, and such temporary emissions increases and decreases shall not require transfer of allowances among units nor shall it require recordation. The owners or operators of such units shall act through a designated representative. Notwithstanding the preceding sentence, the total tonnage of emissions in any calendar year (calculated at the end thereof) from all units in such a utility system, power pool, or allowance pool agreements shall not exceed the total allowances for such units for the calendar year concerned.

(e) New Utility Units.—After January 1, 2000, it shall be unlawful for a new utility unit to emit an annual tonnage of sulfur dioxide in excess of the number of allowances to emit held for the unit by the unit's owner or operator. Such new utility units shall not be eligible for an allocation of sulfur dioxide allowances under subsection (a)(1), unless the unit is subject to the provisions of subsection (g)(2) or (3) of section 405 . New utility units may obtain allowances from any person, in accordance with this title. The owner or operator of any new utility unit in violation of this subsection shall be liable for fulfilling the obligations specified in section 411 of this title.

(f) Nature of Allowances.—An allowance allocated under this title is a limited authorization to emit sulfur dioxide in accordance with the provisions of this title. Such allowance does not constitute a property right. Nothing in this title or in any other provision of law shall be construed to limit the authority of the United States to terminate or limit such authorization. Nothing in this section relating to allowances shall be construed as affecting the application of, or compliance with, any other provision of this Act to an affected unit or source, including the provisions related to applicable National Ambient Air Quality Standards and State implementation plans. Nothing in this section shall be construed as requiring a change of any kind in any State law regulating electric utility rates and charges or affecting any State law regarding such State regulation or as limiting State regulation (including any prudency review) under such a State law. Nothing in this section shall be construed as modifying the Federal Power Act or as affecting the authority of the Federal Energy Regulatory Commission under that Act. Nothing in this title shall be construed to interfere with or impair any program for competitive bidding for power supply in a State in which such program is established. Allowances, once allocated to a person by the Administrator, may be received, held, and temporarily or permanently transferred in accordance with this title and the regulations of the Administrator without regard to whether or not a permit is in effect under title V or section 408 with respect to the unit for which such allowance was originally allocated and recorded. Each permit under this title and each permit issued under title V for any affected unit shall provide that the affected unit may not emit an annual tonnage of sulfur dioxide in excess of the allowances held for that unit.

(g) Prohibition.—It shall be unlawful for any person to hold, use, or transfer any allowance allocated under this title, except in accordance with regulations promulgated by the Administrator. It shall be unlawful for any affected unit to emit sulfur dioxide in excess of the number of allowances held for that unit for that year by the owner or operator of the unit. Upon the allocation of allowances under this title, the prohibition contained in the preceding sentence shall supersede any other emission limitation applicable under this title to the units for which such allowances are allocated. Allowances may not be used prior to the calendar year for which they are allocated. Nothing in this section or in the allowance system regulations shall relieve the Administrator of the Administrator's permitting, monitoring and enforcement obligations under this Act, nor relieve affected sources of their requirements and liabilities under this Act.

(h) Competitive Bidding for Power Supply.—Nothing in this title shall be construed to interfere with or impair any program for competitive bidding for power supply in a State in which such program is established.

(i) Applicability of the Antitrust Laws.—

(1) Nothing in this section affects—

(A) the applicability of the antitrust laws to the transfer, use, or sale of allowances, or

(B) the authority of the Federal Energy Regulatory Commission under any provision of law respecting unfair methods of competition or anticompetitive acts or practices.

(2) As used in this section, 'antitrust laws' means those Acts set forth in section 1 of the Clayton Act (15 U.S.C. 12), as amended.

(j) Public Utility Holding Company Act.—The acquisition or disposition of allowances pursuant to this title including the issuance of securities or the undertaking of any other financing transaction in connection with such allowances shall not be subject to the provisions of the Public Utility Holding Company Act of 1935.

§7651c. Phase I Sulfur Dioxide Requirements
[Sec. 404]

(a) Emission Limitations.—

(1) After January 1, 1995, each source that includes one or more affected units listed in table A is an affected source under this section. After January 1, 1995, it shall be unlawful for any affected unit (other than an eligible phase I unit under section 404(d)(2)) to emit sulfur dioxide in excess of the tonnage limitation stated as a total number of allowances in table A for phase I, unless (A) the emissions reduction requirements applicable to such unit have been achieved pursuant to subsection (b) or (d), or (B) the owner or operator of such unit holds allowances to emit not less than the unit's total annual emissions, except that, after January 1, 2000, the emissions limitations established in this section shall be superseded by those established in section 405 . The owner or operator of any unit in violation of this section shall be fully liable for such violation including, but not limited to, liability for fulfilling the obligations specified in section 411 .

(2) Not later than December 31, 1991, the Administrator shall determine the total tonnage of reductions in the emissions of sulfur dioxide from all utility units in calendar year 1995 that will occur as a result of compliance with the emissions limitation requirements of this section, and shall establish a reserve of allowances equal in amount to the number of tons determined thereby not to exceed a total of 3.50 million tons. In making such a determination, the Administrator shall compute for each unit subject to the emissions limitation requirements of this section the difference between:

(A) the product of its baseline multiplied by the lesser of each unit's allowable 1985 emissions rate and its actual 1985 emissions rate, divided by 2,000, and

(B) the product of each unit's baseline multiplied by 2.50 lbs/mmBtu divided by 2,000, and sum the computations. The Administrator shall adjust the foregoing calculation to reflect projected calendar year 1995 utilization of the units subject to the emissions limitations of this title that the Administrator finds would have occurred in the absence of the imposition of such requirements. Pursuant to subsection (d), the Administrator shall allocate allowances from the reserve established hereinunder until the earlier of such time as all such allowances in the reserve are allocated or December 31, 1999.

(3) In addition to allowances allocated pursuant to paragraph (1), in each calendar year beginning in 1995 and ending in 1999, inclusive, the Administrator shall allocate for each unit on Table A that is located in the States of Illinois, Indiana, or Ohio (other than units at Kyger Creek, Clifty Creek and Joppa Steam), allowances in an amount equal to 200,000 multiplied by the units's pro rata share of the total number of allowances allocated for all units on Table A in the 3 States (other than units at Kyger Creek, Clifty Creek, and Joppa Steam) pursuant to paragraph (1). Such allowances shall be excluded from the calculation of the reserve under paragraph (2).

(b) Substitutions.—The owner or operator of an affected unit under subsection (a) may include in its section 408 permit application and proposed compliance plan a proposal to reassign, in whole or in part, the affected unit's sulfur dioxide reduction requirements to any other unit(s) under the control of such owner or operator. Such proposal shall specify—

(1) the designation of the substitute unit or units to which any part of the reduction obligations of subsection (a) shall be required, in addition to, or in lieu of, any original affected units designated under such subsection;

(2) the original affected unit's baseline, the actual and allowable 1985 emissions rate for sulfur dioxide, and the authorized annual allowance allocation stated in table A;

(3) calculation of the annual average tonnage for calendar years 1985, 1986, and 1987, emitted by the substitute unit or units, based on the baseline for each unit, as defined in section 402(d) , multiplied by the lesser of the unit's actual or allowable 1985 emissions rate;

(4) The emissions rate and tonnage limitations that would be applicable to the original and substitle affected units under the substitution proposal;

(5) documentation, to the satisfaction of the Administrator, that the reassigned tonnage limits will, in total, achieve the same or greater emissions reduction than would have been achieved by the original affected unit and the substitle unit or units without such substitution; and

(6) such other information as the Administrator may require.

(c) Administrator's Action on Substitution Proposals.—

(1) The Administrator shall take final action on such substitution proposal in accordance with

section 408(c) if the substitution proposal fulfills the requirements of this subsection. The Administrator may approve a substitution proposal in whole or in part and with such modifications or conditions as may be consistent with the orderly functioning of the allowance system and which will ensure the emissions reductions contemplated by this title. If a proposal does not meet the requirements of subsection (b), the Administrator shall disapprove it. The owner or operator of a unit listed in table A shall not substitle another unit or units without the prior approval of the Administrator.

(2) Upon approval of a substitution proposal, each substitute unit, and each source with such unit, shall be deemed affected under this title, and the Administrator shall issue a permit to the original and substitute affected source and unit in accordance with the approved substitution plan and section 408 . The Administrator shall allocate allowances for the original and substitute affected units in accordance with the approved substitution proposal pursuant to section 403 . It shall be unlawful for any source or unit that is allocated allowances pursuant to this section to emit sulfur dioxide in excess of the emissions limitation provided for in the approved substitution permit and plan unless the owner or operator of each unit governed by the permit and approved substitution plan holds allowances to emit not less than the units total annual emissions. The owner or operator of any original or substitute affected unit operated in violation of this subsection shall be fully liable for such violation, including liability for fulfilling the obligations specified in section 411 of this title. If a substitution proposal is disapproved, the Administrator shall allocate allowances to the original affected unit or units in accordance with subsection (a).

(d) Eligible Phase I Extension Units.—

(1) The owner or operator of any affected unit subject to an emissions limitation requirement under this section may petition the Administrator in its permit application under section 408 for an extension of 2 years of the deadline for meeting such requirement, provided that the owner or operator of any such unit holds allowances to emit not less than the unit's total annual emissions for each of the 2 years of the period of extension. To qualify for such an extension, the affected unit must either employ a qualifying phase I technology, or transfer its phase I emissions reduction obligation to a unit employing a qualifying phase I technology. Such transfer shall be accomplished in accordance with a compliance plan, submitted and approved under section 408 , that shall govern operations at all units included in the transfer, and that specifies the emissions reduction requirements imposed pursuant to this title.

(2) Such extension proposal shall—

(A) specify the unit or units proposed for designation as an eligible phase I extension unit;

(B) provide a copy of an executed contract, which may be contingent upon the Administrator approving the proposal, for the design engineering, and construction of the qualifying phase I technology for the extension unit, or for the unit or units to which the extension unit's emission reduction obligation is to be transferred;

(C) specify the unit's or units' baseline, actual 1985 emissions rate, allowable 1985 emissions rate, and projected utilization for calendar years 1995 through 1999;

(D) require CEMS on both the eligible phase I extension unit or units and the transfer unit or units beginning no later than January 1, 1995; and

(E) specify the emission limitation and number of allowances expected to be necessary for annual operation after the qualifying phase I technology has been installed.

(3) The Administrator shall review and take final action on each extension proposal in order of receipt, consistent with section 408, and for an approved proposal shall designate the unit or units as an eligible phase I extension unit. The Administrator may approve an extension proposal in whole or in part, and with such modifications or conditions as may be necessary, consistent with the orderly functioning of the allowance system, and to ensure the emissions reductions contemplated by the title.

(4) In order to determine the number of proposals eligible for allocations from the reserve under subsection (a)(2) and the number of allowances remaining available after each proposal is acted upon, the Administrator shall reduce the total number of allowances remaining available in the reserve by the number of allowances calculated according to subparagraphs (A), (B) and (C) until either no allowances remain available in the reserve for further allocation or all approved proposals have been acted upon. If no allowances remain

available in the reserve for further allocation before all proposals have been acted upon by the Administrator, any pending proposals shall be disapproved. The Administrator shall calculate allowances equal to—

(A) the difference between the lesser of the average annual emissions in calendar years 1988 and 1989 or the projected emissions tonnage for calendar year 1995 or each eligible phase I extension unit, as designated under paragraph (3), and the product of the unit's baseline multiplied by an emission rate of 2.50 lbs/mmBtu, divided by 2,000;

(B) the difference between the lesser of the average annual emissions in calendar years 1988 and 1989 or the projected emissions tonnage for calendar year 1996 of each eligible phase I extension unit, as designated under paragraph (3), and the product of the unit's baseline multiplied by an emission rate of 2.50 lbs/mmBtu, divided by 2,000; and

(C) the amount by which (i) the product of each unit's baseline multiplied by an emission rate of 1.20 lbs/mmBtu, divided by 2,000, exceeds (ii) the tonnage level specified under subparagraph (E) of paragraph (2) of this subsection multiplied by a factor of 3.

(5) Each eligible Phase I extension unit shall receive allowances determined under subsection (a)(1) or (c) of this section. In addition, for calendar year 1995, the Administrator shall allocate to each eligible Phase I extension unit, from the allowance reserve created pursuant to subsection (a)(2), allowances equal to the difference between the lesser of the average annual emissions in calendar years 1988 and 1989 or its projected emissions tonnage for calendar year 1995 and the product of the unit's baseline multiplied by an emission rate of 2.50 lbs/mmBtu, divided by 2,000. In calendar year 1996, the Administrator shall allocate for each eligible unit, from the allowance reserve created pursuant to subsection (a)(2), allowances equal to the difference between the lesser of the average annual emissions in calendar years 1988 and 1989 or its projected emissions tonnage for calendar year 1996 and the product of the unit's baseline multiplied by an emission rate of 2.50 lbs/mmBtu, divided by 2,000. It shall be unlawful for any source or unit subject to an approved extension plan under this subsection to emit sulfur dioxide in excess of the emissions limitations provided for in the permit and approved extension plan, unless the owner or operator of each unit governed by the permit and approved plan holds allowances to emit not less than the unit's total annual emissions.

(6) In addition to allowances specified in paragraph (5), the Administrator shall allocate for each eligible Phase I extension unit employing qualifying Phase I technology, for calendar years 1997, 1998, and 1999, additional allowances, from any remaining allowances in the reserve created pursuant to subsection (a)(2), following the reduction in the reserve provided for in paragraph (4), not to exceed the amount by which (A) the product of each eligible unit's baseline times an emission rate of 1.20 lbs/mmBtu, divided by 2,000, exceeds (B) the tonnage level specified under subparagraph (E) of paragraph (2) of this subsection.

(7) After January 1, 1997, in addition to any liability under this Act, including under section 411, if any eligible phase I extension unit employing qualifying phase I technology or any transfer unit under this subsection emits sulfur dioxide in excess of the annual tonnage limitation specified in the extension plan, as approved in paragraph (3) of this subsection, the Administrator shall, in the calendar year following such excess, deduct allowances equal to the amount of such excess from such unit's annual allowance allocation.

(e) (1) In the case of a unit that receives authorization from the Governor of the State in which such unit is located to make reductions in the emissions of sulfur dioxide prior to calendar year 1995 and that is part of a utility system that meets the following requirements: (A) the total coal-fired generation within the utility system as a percentage of total system generation decreased by more than 20 percent between January 1, 1980, and December 31, 1985; and (B) the weighted capacity factor of all coal-fired units within the utility system averaged over the period from January 1, 1985, through December 31, 1987, was below 50 percent, the Administrator shall allocate allowances under this paragraph for the unit pursuant to this subsection. The Administrator shall allocate allowances for a unit that is an affected unit pursuant to section 405 (but is not also an affected unit under this section) and part of a utility system that includes 1 or more affected units under section 405 for reductions in the emissions of sulfur dioxide made during the period 1995–1999 if the unit meets the requirements of this subsection and the requirements of the preceding sentence, except that for the purposes of applying this subsection to any such unit, the prior year concerned as specified below, shall be any year after January 1, 1995 but prior to January 1, 2000.

(2) In the case of an affected unit under this section described in subparagraph (A), the allowances allocated under this subsection for early reductions in any prior year may not exceed the amount which (A) the product of the unit's baseline multiplied by the unit's 1985 actual sulfur dioxide emission rate (in lbs. per mmBtu), divided by 2,000, exceeds (B) the allowances specified for such unit in Table A. In the case of an affected unit under section 405 described in subparagraph (A), the allowances awarded under this subsection for early reductions in any prior year may not exceed the amount by which (i) the product of the quantity of fossil fuel consumed by the unit (in mmBtu) in the prior year multiplied by the lesser of 2.50 or the most stringent emission rate (in lbs. per mmBtu) applicable to the unit under the applicable implementation plan, divided by 2,000, exceeds (ii) the unit's actual tonnage of sulfur dioxide emission for the prior year concerned. Allowances allocated under this subsection for units referred to in subparagraph (A) may be allocated only for emission reductions achieved as a result of physical changes or changes in the method of operation made after the date of enactment of the Clean Air Act Amendments of 1990, including changes in the type or quality of fossil fuel consumed.

(3) In no event shall the provisions of this paragraph be interpreted as an event of force majeur or a commercial impractibility or in any other way as a basis for excused nonperformance by a utility system under a coal sales contract in effect before the date of enactment of the Clean Air Act Amendments of 1990.

TABLE A—AFFECTED SOURCES AND UNITS IN PHASE I AND THEIR SULFUR DIOXIDE ALLOWANCES (TONS)

State	Plant Name	Generator	Phase I Allowances
Alabama	Colbert	1	13,570
		2	15,310
		3	15,400
		4	15,410
		5	37,180
	E.C. Gaston	1	18,100
		2	18,540
		3	18,310
		4	19,280

State	Plant Name	Generator	Phase I Allowances
		5	59,840
Florida	Big Bend	1	28,410
		2	27,100
		3	26,740
	Crist	6	19,200
		7	31,680
Georgia	Bowen	1	56,320
		2	54,770
		3	71,750
		4	71,740
	Hammond	1	8,780
		2	9,220
		3	8,910
		4	37,640
	J. McDonough	1	19,910
		2	20,600
	Wansley	1	70,770
		2	65,430
	Yates	1	7,210
		2	7,040
		3	6,950
		4	8,910
		5	9,410
		6	24,760
		7	21,480
Illinois	Baldwin	1	42,010
		2	44,420
		3	42,550
	Coffees	1	11,790
		2	35,670
	Grand Tower	4	5,910
	Hennepin	2	18,410
	Joppa Steam	1	12,590
		2	10,770
		3	12,270
		4	11,860
		5	11,420
		6	10,620
	Kincaid	1	31,580
		2	33,810
	Meredosia	3	13,890
	Vermilion	2	8,880
Indiana	Bailly	7	11,180
		8	15,630
	Breed	1	18,500
	Cayuga	1	33,370
		2	34,130
	Clifty Creek	1	20,150

State	Plant Name	Generator	Phase I Allowances
		2	19,810
		3	20,410
		4	20,080
		5	19,360
		6	20,380
	E. W. Stout	5	3,880
		6	4,770
		7	28,610
	F.B. Culley	2	4,290
		3	16,970
	F. E. Ratts	1	8,330
		2	8,480
	Gibson	1	40,400
		2	41,010
		3	41,080
		4	40,320
	H. T. Pritchard	6	5,770
	Michigan City	12	23,310
	Petersburg	1	16,430
		2	32,380
	R. Gallagher	1	6,490
		2	7,280
		3	6,530
		4	7,650
	Tanners Creek	4	24,820
	Wabash River	1	4,000
		2	2,860
		3	3,750
		5	3,670
		6	12,280
	Warrick	4	26,980
Iowa	Burlington	1	10,710
	Des Moines	7	2,320
	George Neal	1	1,290
	M.L. Kapp	2	13,800
	Prairie Creek	4	8,180
	Riverside	5	3,990
Kansas	Quindaro	2	4,220
Kentucky	Coleman	1	11,250
		2	12,840
		3	12,340
	Cooper	1	7,450
		2	15,320
	E.W. Brown	1	7,110
		2	10,910
		3	26,100
	Elmer Smith	1	6,520
		2	14,410
	Ghent	1	28,410
	Green River	4	7,820
	H.L. Spurlock	1	22,780
	Henderson II	1	13,340
		2	12,310
	Paradise	3	59,170
	Shawnee	10	10,170
Maryland	Chalk Point	1	21,910
		2	24,330
	C.P. Crane	1	10,330
		2	9,230
	Morgantown	1	35,260
		2	38,480
Michigan	J.H. Campbell	1	19,280
		2	23,060
Minnesota	High Bridge	6	4,270
Mississippi	Jack Watson	4	17,910
		5	36,700
Missouri	Asbury	1	16,190
	James River	5	4,850
	Labadie	1	40,110
		2	37,710
		3	40,310
		4	35,940
	Montrose	1	7,390
		2	8,200
		3	10,090
	New Madrid	1	28,240
		2	82,480
	Sibley	3	15,580
	Sioux	1	22,570
		2	23,690
	Thomas Hill	1	10,250
		2	19,390
New Hampshire	Merrimack	1	10,190
		2	22,000
New Jersey	B.L. England	1	9,060
		2	11,720
New York	Dunkirk	3	12,600
		4	14,060
	Greenidge	4	7,540
	Milliken	1	11,170
		2	12,410

State	Plant Name	Generator	Phase I Allowances
	Northport	1	19,810
		2	24,110
		3	26,480
	Port Jefferson	3	10,470
		4	12,330
Ohio	Ashtabula	5	16,740
	Avon Lake	8	11,650
		9	30,480
	Cardinal	1	34,270
		2	38,320
	Conesville	1	4,210
		2	4,890
		3	5,500
		4	48,770
	Eastlake	1	7,800
		2	8,640
		3	10,020
		4	14,510
		5	34,070
	Edgewater	4	5,050
	Gen J.M. Gavin	1	79,080
		2	80,560
	Kyger Creek	1	19,280
		2	18,560
		3	17,910
		4	18,710
		5	18,740
	Miami Fort	5	760
		6	11,380
		7	38,510
	Muskingum River	1	14,880
		2	14,170
		3	13,950
		4	11,780
		5	40,470
	Niles	1	6,940
		2	9,100
	Picway	5	4,930
	R.E. Burger	3	6,150
		4	10,780
		5	12,430
	W.H. Sammis	5	24,170
		6	39,930
		7	43,220
	W.C. Beck-jord	5	8,950
		6	23,020
Pennsylva-nia	Armstrong	1	14,410
		2	15,430
	Brunner Island	1	27,760
		2	31,100
		3	53,820
	Cheswick	1	39,170
	Conemaugh	1	59,790
		2	66,450
	Hatfield's Ferry	1	37,830
		2	37,320
		3	40,270
	Martins Creek	1	12,660
		2	12,820
	Portland	1	5,940
		2	10,230
	Shawville	1	10,320
		2	10,320
		3	14,220
		4	14,070
	Sunbury	3	8,760
		4	11,450
Tennessee	Allen	1	15,320
		2	16,770
		3	15,670
	Cumberland	1	86,700
		2	94,840
	Gallatin	1	17,870
		2	17,310
		3	20,020
		4	21,260
	Johnsonville	1	7,790
		2	8,040
		3	8,410
		4	7,990
		5	8,240
		6	7,890
		7	8,980
		8	8,700
		9	7,080
		10	7,550
West Virginia	Albright	3	12,000
	Fort Martin	1	41,590
		2	41,200
	Harrison	1	48,620

State	Plant Name	Generator	Phase I Allowances
		2	46,150
		3	41,500
	Kammer	1	18,740
		2	19,460
		3	17,390
	Mitchell	1	43,980
		2	45,510
	Mount Storm	1	43,720
		2	35,580
		3	42,430
Wisconsin	Edgewater	4	24,750
	La Crosse/ Genoa	3	22,700
	Nelson Dewey	1	6,010
		2	6,680
	N. Oak Creek	1	5,220
		2	5,140
		3	5,370
		4	6,320
	Pulliam	8	7,510
	S. Oak Creek	5	9,670
		6	12,040
		7	16,180
		8	15,790

(f) Energy Conservation and Renewable Energy.—

(1) Definitions.—As used in this subsection:

(A) Qualified Energy Conservation Measure.—The term 'qualified energy conservation measure' means a cost effective measure, as identified by the Administrator in consultation with the Secretary of Energy, that increases the efficiency of the use of electricity provided by an electric utility to its customers.

(B) Qualified Renewable Energy.—The term 'qualified renewable energy' means energy derived from biomass, solar, geothermal, or wind as identified by the Administrator in consultation with the Secretary of Energy.

(C) Electric Utility.—The term 'electric utility' means any person, State agency, or Federal agency, which sells electric energy.

(2) Allowances for Emissions Avoided Through Energy Conservation and Renewable Energy.—

(A) In General.—The regulations under paragraph (4) of this subsection shall provide that for each ton of sulfur dioxide emissions avoided by an electric utility, during the applicable period, through the use of qualified energy conservation measures or qualified renewable energy, the Administrator shall allocate a single allowance to such electric utility, on a first- come-first-served basis from the Conservation and Renewable Energy Reserve established under subsection (g), up to a total of 300,000 allowances for allocation from such Reserve.

(B) Requirements for Issuance.—The Administrator shall allocate allowances to an electric utility under this subsection only if all of the following requirements are met:

(i) Such electric utility is paying for the qualified energy conservation measures or qualified renewable energy directly or through purchase from another person.

(ii) The emissions of sulfur dioxide avoided through the use of qualified energy conservation measures or qualified renewable energy are quantified in accordance with regulations promulgated by the Administrator under this subsection.

(iii) (I) Such electric utility has adopted and is implementing a least cost energy conservation and electric power plan which evaluates a range of resources, including new power supplies, energy conservation, and renewable energy resources, in order to meet expected future demand at the lowest system cost.

(II) The qualified energy conservation measures or qualified renewable energy, or both, are consistent with that plan.

(III) Electric utilities subject to the jurisdiction of a State regulatory authority must have such plan approved by such authority. For electric utilities not subject to the jurisdiction of a State regulatory authority such plan shall be approved by the entity with ratemaking authority for such utility.

(iv) In the case of qualified energy conservation measures undertaken by a State regulated electric utility, the Secretary of energy certifies that the State regulatory authority with jurisdiction over the electric rates of such electric utility has established rates and charges which ensure that the net income of such electric utility after implementation of specific cost effective energy conservation measures is at least as high as such net income would have been if the energy conservation measures had not been implemented. Upon the date of any such certification by the Secretary of Energy, all allowances which, but for this paragraph, would have been allocated under subparagraph (A) before such date, shall be allocated to the electric utility. This clause is not a requirement for qualified renewable energy.

(v) Such utility or any subsidiary of the utility's holding company owns or operates at least one affected unit.

(C) Period of Applicability.—Allowances under this subsection shall be allocated only with respect to kilowatt hours of electric energy saved by qualified energy conservation measures or generated by qualified renewable energy after January 1, 1992 and before the earlier of (i) December 31, 2000, or (ii) the date on which any electric utility steam generating unit owned or operated by the electric utility to which the allowances are allocated becomes subject to this title (including those sources that elect to become affected by this title, pursuant to section 410).

(D) Determination of Avoided Emissions.—

(i) Application.— In order to receive allowances under this subsection, an electric utility shall make an application which—

(I) designates the qualified energy conservation measures implemented and the qualified renewable energy sources used for purposes of avoiding emissions,

(II) calculates, in accordance with subparagraphs (F) and (G), the number of tons of emissions avoided by reason of the implementation of such measures or the use of such renewable energy sources; and

(III) demonstrates that the requirements of subparagraph (B) have been met. Such application for allowances by a State-regulated electric utility shall require approval by the State regulatory authority with jurisdiction over such electric utility. The authority shall review the application for accuracy and compliance with this subsection and the rules under this subsection. Electric utilities whose retail rates are not subject to the jurisdiction of a State regulatory authority shall apply directly to the Administrator for such approval.

(E) Avoided Emissions from Qualified Energy Conservation Measures.—For the purposes of this subsection, the emission tonnage deemed avoided by reason of the implementation of qualified energy conservation measures for any calendar year shall be a tonnage equal to the product of multiplying—

(i) the kilowatt hours that would otherwise have been supplied by the utility during such year in the absence of such qualified energy conservation measures, by

(ii) 0.004, and dividing by 2,000.

(F) Avoided Emissions From the Use of Qualified Renewable Energy.—The emissions tonnage deemed avoided by reason of the use of qualified renewable energy by an electric utility for any calendar year shall be a tonnage equal to the product of multiplying—

(i) the actual kilowatt hours generated by, or purchased from, qualified renewable energy, by

(ii) 0.004, and dividing by 2,000.

(G) Prohibitions.—

(i) No allowances shall be allocated under this subsection for the implementation of programs that are exclusively informational or educational in nature.

(ii) No allowances shall be allocated for energy conservation measures or renewable energy that were operational before January 1, 1992.

(3) Savings Provision.—Nothing in this subsection precludes a State or State regulatory authority from providing additional incentives to utilities to encourage investment in demand-side resources.

(4) Regulations.—Not later than 18 months after the date of the enactment of the Clean Air Act Amendments of 1990 and in conjunction with the regulations required to be promulgated under subsections (b) and (c), the Administrator shall, in consultation with the Secretary of Energy, promulgate regulations under this subsection. Such regulations shall list energy conservation measures and renewable energy sources which may be treated as qualified energy conservation measures and qualified renewable energy for purposes of this subsection. Allowances shall only be allocated if all requirements of this subsection and the rules promulgated to implement this subsection are complied with. The Administrator shall review the determinations of each State regulatory authority under this subsection to encourage consistency from electric utility to electric utility and from State to State in accordance with the Administrator's rules. The Administrator shall publish the findings of this review no less than annually.

(g) Conservation and Renewable Energy Reserve.—The Administrator shall establish a Conservation and Renewable Energy Reserve under this subsection. Beginning on January 1, 1995, the Administrator may allocate from the Conservation and Renewable Energy Reserve an amount equal to a total of 300,000 allowances for emissions of sulfur dioxide pursuant to section 403. In order to provide 300,000 allowances for such reserve, in each year beginning in calendar year 2000 and until calendar year 2009, inclusive, the Administrator shall reduce each unit's basic Phase II allowance allocation on the basis of its pro rata share of 30,000 allowances. If allowances remain in the reserve after January 2, 2010, the Administrator shall allocate such allowances for affected units under section 405 on a pro rata basis. For purposes of this subsection, for any unit subject to the emissions limitation requirements of section 405 , the term 'pro rata basis' refers to the ratio which the reductions made in such unit's allowances in order to establish the reserve under this subsection bears to the total of such reductions for all such units.

(h) Alternative Allowance Allocation for Units in Certain Utility Systems with Optional Baseline.—

(1) Optional baseline for units in certain systems.—In the case of a unit subject to the emissions limitation requirements of this section which (as of the date of the enactment of the Clean Air Act Amendments of 1990)—

(A) has an emission rate below 1.0 lbs/mmBtu,

(B) has decreased its sulfur dioxide emissions rate by 60 percent or greater since 1980, and

(C) is part of a utility system which has a weighted average sulfur dioxide emissions rate for all fossil fueled-fired units below 1.0 lbs/mmBtu, at the election of the owner or operator of such unit, the unit's baseline may be calculated (i) as provided under section 402(d), or (ii) by utilizing the unit's average annual fuel consumption at a 60 percent capacity factor. Such election shall be made no later than March 1, 1991.

(2) Allowance Allocation.—Whenever a unit referred to in paragraph (1) elects to calculate its baseline as provided in clause (ii) of paragraph (1), the Administrator shall allocate allowances for the unit pursuant to section 403(a)(1), this section, and section 405 (as basic Phase II allowance allocations) in an amount equal to the baseline selected multiplied by the lower of the average annual emission rate for such unit in 1989, or 1.0 lbs./mmBtu. Such allowance allocation shall be in lieu of any allocation of allowances under this section and section 405 .

§7651d. Phase II Sulfur Dioxide Requirements [Sec. 405]

(a) Applicability.—

(1) After January 1, 2000, each existing utility unit as provided below is subject to the limitations or requirements of this section. Each utility unit subject to an annual sulfur dioxide tonnage emission limitation under this section is an affected units is an affected source. In the case of an existing unit that was not in operation during calendar year 1985, the emission rate for a calendar year after 1985, as determined by the Administrator, shall be used in lieu of the 1985 rate. The owner or operator of any unit operated in violation of this section shall be fully liable under this Act for fulfilling the obligations specified in section 411 of this title.

(2) In addition to basic Phase II allowance allocations, in each year beginning in calendar year 2000 and ending in calendar year 2009, inclusive, the Administrator shall allocate up to 530,00 Phase II bonus allowances pursuant to subsections (b)(2), (c)(4), (d)(3)(A) and (B), and (h)(2) of this section and section 406. Not later than June 1, 1998, the Administrator shall calculate, for each unit granted an extension pursuant to section 409 the difference between (A) the number of allowances allocated for the unit in calendar year 2000, and (B) the product of the unit's baseline multiplied by 1.20 lbs/mmBtu, divided by 2000, and sum the computations. In each year, beginning in calendar year 2000 and ending in calendar year 2009, inclusive, the Administrator shall deduct from each unit's basic Phase II allowance allocation its pro rata share of 10 percent of the sum calculated pursuant to the preceding sentence.

(3) In addition to basic Phase II allowance allocations and Phase II bonus allowance allocations, beginning January 1, 2000, the Administrator shall allocate for each unit listed on Table A in section 404 (other than units at Kyger Creek, Clifty Creek, and Joppa Steam) and located in the States of Illinois, Indiana, Ohio, Georgia, Alabama, Missouri, Pennsylvania, West Virginia, Kentucky, or Tennessee allowances in an amount equal to 50,000 multiplied by the unit's pro rata share of the total number of basic allowances allocated for all units listed on Table A (other than units at Kyger Creek, Clifty Creek, and Joppa Steam). Allowances allocated pursuant to this paragraph shall not be subject to the 8,900,000 ton limitation in section 403(a) .

(b) Units equal to, or Above, 75 MWe and 1.20 lbs/mmBtu.—

(1) Except as otherwise provided in paragraph (3), after January 1, 2000, it shall be unlawful for any existing utility unit that serves a generator with name plate capacity equal to, or greater, than 75 MWe and an actual 1985 emission rate equal to or greater than 1.20 lbs/mmBtu to exceed an annual sulfur dioxide tonnage emission limitation equal to the product of the unit's baseline multiplied by an emission rate equal to 1.20 lbs/mmBtu, divided by 2,000, unless the owner or operator of such unit holds allowances to emit not less than the unit's total annual emissions.

(2) In addition to allowances allocated pursuant to paragraph (1) and section 403(a)(1) as basic Phase II allowance allocations, beginning January 1, 2000, and for each calendar year thereafter until and including 2009, the Administrator shall allocate annually for each unit subject to the emissions limitation requirements of paragraph (1) with an actual 1985 emissions rate greater than 1.20 lbs/mmBtu and less than 2.50 lbs/mmBtu and a baseline capacity factor of less than 60 percent, allowances from the reserve created pursuant to subsection (a)(2) in an amount equal to 1.20 lbs/mmBtu multiplied by 50 percent of the difference, on a Btu basis, between the unit's baseline and the unit's fuel consumption at a 60 percent capacity factor.

(3) After January 1, 2000, it shall be unlawful for any existing utility unit with an actual 1985 emissions rate equal to or greater than 1.20 lbs/mmBtu whose annual average fuel consumption during 1985, 1986, and 1987 on a Btu basis exceeded 90 percent in the form of lignite coal which is located in a State in which, as of July 1, 1989, no county or portion of a county was designated nonattainment under section 107 of this Act for any pollutant subject to the requirements of section 109 of this Act to exceed an annual sulfur dioxide tonnage limitation equal to the product of the unit's baseline multiplied by the lesser of the unit's actual 1985 emissions rate or its allowable 1985 emissions rate, divided by 2,000, unless the owner or operator of such unit holds allowances to emit not less than the unit's total annual emissions.

(4) After January 1, 2000, the Administrator shall allocate annually for each unit, subject to the emissions limitation requirements of paragraph (1), which is located in a State with an installed electrical generating capacity of more 30,000,000 kw in 1988 and for which was issued a prohibition order or a proposed prohibition order (from burning oil), which unit subsequently converted to coal between January 1, 1980 and December 31, 1985, allowances equal to the difference between (A) the product of the unit's annual fuel consumption, on a Btu basis, at a 65 percent capacity factor multiplied by the lesser of its actual or allowable emissions rate during the first full calendar year after conversion, divided by 2,000, and (B) the number of allowances allocated for the unit pursuant to paragraph (1): *Provided,*That the number of allowances allocated pursuant to this paragraph shall not exceed an annual total five thousand. If necessary to meeting the restriction imposed in the preceding sentence the Administrator shall reduce, pro rata, the annual allowances allocated for each unit under this paragraph.

(c) Coal Or Oil-Fired Units Below 75 MWe And Above 1.20 lbs/mmBtu.—

(1) Except as otherwise provided in paragraph (3), after January 1, 2000, it shall be unlawful for a coal or oil-fired existing utility unit that serves a generator with nameplate capacity of less than 75 MWe and an actual 1985 emission rate equal to, or greater than, 1.20 lbs/mmBtu and which is a unit owned by a utility operating company whose aggregate nameplate fossil fuel steam-electric capacity is, as of December 31, 1989, equal to, or greater than, 250 MWe to exceed an annual sulfur dioxide emissions limitation equal to the product of the unit's baseline multiplied by an emission rate equal to 1.20 lbs/mmBtu, divided by 2,000, unless the owner or operator of such unit holds allowances to emit not less than the unit's total annual emissions.

(2) After January 1, 2000, it shall be unlawful for a coal or oil-fired existing utility unit that serves a generator with nameplate capacity of less than 75 MWe and an actual 1985 emission rate equal to, or greater than, 1.20 lbs/mmBtu (excluding units subject to section 111 of the Act or to a federally enforceable emissions limitation for sulfur dioxide equivalent to an annual rate of less than 1.20 lbs/mmBtu) and which is a unit owned by a utility operating company whose aggregate nameplate fossil fuel steam-electric capacity is, as of December 31, 1989, less than 250 MWe, to exceed an annual sulfur dioxide tonnage emissions limitation equal to the product of the unit's baseline multiplied by the lesser of its actual 1985 emissions rate or its allowable 1985 emissions

rate, divided by 2,000, unless the owner or operator of such unit holds allowances to emit not less than the unit's total annual emissions.

(3) After January 1, 2000, it shall be unlawful for any existing utility unit with a nameplate capacity below 75 MWe and an actual 1985 emissions rate equal to, or greater than, 1.20 lbs/mmBtu which became operational on or before December 31, 1965, which is owned by a utility operating company with, as of December 31, 1989, a total fossil fuel steam-electric generating capacity greater than 250 MWe, and less than 450 MWe which serves fewer than 78,000 electrical customers as of the date of enactment of the Clean Air Act Amendments of 1990 to exceed an annual sulfur dioxide emissions tonnage limitation equal to the product of its baseline multiplied by the lesser of its actual or allowable 1985 emission rate, divided by 2,000, unless the owner or operator holds allowances to emit not less than the units total annual emissions. After January 1, 2010, it shall be unlawful for each unit subject to the emissions limitation requirements of this paragraph to exceed an annual emissions tonnage limitation equal to the product of its baseline multiplied by an emissions rate of 1.20 lbs/mmBtu, divided by 2,000, unless the owner or operator holds allowances to emit not less than the unit's total annual emissions.

(4) In addition to allowance allocated pursuant to paragraph (1) and section 403(a)(1) as basic Phase II allowance allocations, beginning January 1, 2000, and for each calendar year thereafter until and including 2009, inclusive, the Administrator shall allocate annually for each unit subject to the emissions limitation requirements of paragraph (1) with an actual 1985 emissions rate equal to, or greater than, 1.20 lbs/mmBtu and less 2.50 lbs/mmBtu and a baseline capacity factor of less than 60 percent, allowances from the reserve created pursuant to subsection (a)(2) in an amount equal to 1.20 lbs/mmBtu multiplied by 50 percent of the difference, on a Btu basis, between the unit's baseline and the unit's fuel consumption at a 60 percent capacity factor.

(5) After January 1, 2000, it shall be unlawful for any existing utility unit with a nameplate capacity below 75 MWe and an actual 1985 emissions rate equal to, or greater than, 1.20 lbs/mmBtu which is part of an electric utility system which, as the date of the enactment of the Clean Air Act Amendments of 1990, (A) has at least 20 percent of its fossil-fuel capacity controlled by flue gas desulfurization devices, (B) has more than 10 percent of its fossil-fuel capacity consisting of coal-fired units of less than 75 MWe, and (C) has large units (greater than 400 MWe) all of which have difficult or very difficult FGD Retrofit Cost Factors (according to the Emissions and the FGD Retrofit Feasibility at the 200 Top Emitting Generating Stations, prepared for the United States Environmental Protection Agency on January 10, 1986) to exceed an annual sulfur dioxide emissions tonnage limitation equal to the product of its baseline multiplied by an emissions rate of 2.5 lbs/mmBtu, divided by 2,000, unless the owner or operator holds allowances to emit not less than the unit's total annual emissions. After January 1, 2010, it shall be unlawful for each unit subject to the emissions limitations requirements of this paragraph to exceed an annual emissions tonnage limitations equal to the product of its baseline multiplied by an emissions rate of 1.20 lbs/mmBtu, divided by 2,000, unless the owner or operator holds for use allowances to emit not less than the unit's total annual emissions.

(d) Coal-Fired Units Below 1.20 lbs/mmBtu.—

(1) After January 1, 2000, it shall be unlawful for any existing coal-fired utility unit the lesser of whose actual or allowable 1985 sulfur dioxide emissions rate is less than 0.60 lbs/mmBtu to exceed an annual sulfur dioxide tonnage emission limitation equal to the product of the unit's baseline multiplied by (A) the lesser of 0.60 lbs/mmBtu or the units allowable 1985 emissions rate, and (B) a numerical factor of 120 percent, divided by 2,000, unless the owner or operator of such unit holds allowances to emit not less than the unit's total annual emissions.

(2) After January 1, 2000, it shall be unlawful for any existing coal-fired utility unit the lesser of whose actual or allowable 1985 sulfur dioxide emissions rate is equal to, or greater than, 0.60 lbs/mmBtu and less than 1.20 lbs/mmBtu to exceed an annual sulfur dioxide tonnage emissions limitation equal to the product of the unit's baseline multiplied by (A) the lesser of its actual 1985 emissions rate or its allowable 1985 emissions rate, and (B) a numerical factor of 120 percent, divided by 2,000, unless the owner or operator of such unit holds allowances to emit not less than the unit's total annual emissions.

(3) (A) In addition to allowances allocated pursuant to paragraph (1) and section 403(a)(1) as basic Phase II allowance allocations, at the election of the designated representative of

the operating company, beginning January 1, 2000, and for each calendar year thereafter until and including 2009, the Administrator shall allocate annually for each unit subject to the emissions limitation requirements of paragraph (1) allowances from the reserve created pursuant to subsection (a)(2) in an amount equal to the amount by which (i) the product of the lesser of 0.60 lbs/mmBtu or the unit's allowable 1985 emissions rate multiplied by the units baseline adjusted to reflect operation at a 60 percent capacity factor, divided by 2,000, exceeds (ii) the number of allowances allocated for the unit pursuant to paragraph (1) and section 403(a)(1) as basic Phase II allowance allocations.

(B) In addition to allowances allocated pursuant to paragraph (2) and section 403(a)(1) as basic Phase II allowance allocations, at the election of the designated representative of the operating company, beginning January 1, 2000, and for each calendar year thereafter until and including 2009, the Administrator shall allocate annually for each unit subject to the emissions limitation requirements of paragraph (2) allowances from the reserve created pursuant to subsection (a)(2) in an amount equal to the amount by which (i) the product of the lesser of the units actual 1985 emission rate or its allowable 1985 emissions rate multiplied by the unit's baseline adjusted to reflect operation at a 60 percent capacity factor, divided by 2,000, exceeds (ii) the number of allowances allocated for the unit pursuant to paragraph (2) and section 403(a)(1) as basic Phase II allowance allocations.

(C) An operating company with units subject to the emissions limitation requirements of this subsection may elect the allocation of allowances as provided under subparagraphs (A) and (B). Such election shall apply to the annual allowance allocation for each and every unit in the operating company subject to the emissions limitation requirements of this subsection. The Administrator shall allocate allowances pursuant to subparagraphs (A) and (B) only in accordance with this subparagraph.

(4) Notwithstanding any other provision of this section, at the election of the owner or operator, after January 1, 2000, the Administrator shall allocate in lieu of allocation, pursuant to paragraph (1), (2), (3), (5), or (6), allowances for a unit subject to the emissions limitation requirements of this subsection which commenced commercial operation on or after January 1, 1981 and before December 31, 1985, which was subject to, and in compliance with, section 111 of the Act in an amount equal to the unit's annual fuel consumption, on a Btu basis, at a 65 percent capacity factor multiplied by the unit's allowable 1985 emissions rate, divided by 2,000.

(5) For the purposes of this section, in the case of an oil- and gas-fired unit which has been awarded a clean coal technology demonstration grant as of January 1, 1991, by the United States Department of Energy, beginning January 1, 2000, the Administrator shall allocate for the unit allowances in an amount equal to the unit's baseline multiplied by 1.20 lbs/mmBtu, divided by 2,000.

(e) Oil and Gas-fired Units Equal to or Greater Than 0.60 lbs/mmBtu and Less Than 1.20 lbs/mmBtu.—After January 1, 2000, it shall be unlawful for any existing oil and gas-fired utility unit the lesser of whose actual or allowable 1985 sulfur dioxide emission rate is equal to, or greater than, 0.60 lbs/mmBtu, but less than 1.20 lbs/mmBtu to exceed an annual sulfur dioxide tonnage limitation equal to the product of the unit's baseline multiplied by (A) the lesser of the unit's allowable 1985 emissions rate or its actual 1985 emissions rate and (B) a numerical factor of 120 percent divided by 2,000 unless the owner or operator of such unit holds allowances to emit not less than the unit's total annual emissions.

(f) Oil and Gas-fired Units Less Than 0.60 lbs/mmBtu.—

(1) After January 1, 2000, it shall be unlawful for any oil and gas-fired existing utility unit the lesser of whose actual or allowable 1985 emission rate is less than 0.60 lbs/mmBtu and whose average annual fuel consumption during the period 1980 through 1989 on a Btu basis was 90 percent or less in the form of natural gas to exceed an annual sulfur dioxide tonnage emissions limitation equal to the product of the unit's baseline multiplied by (A) the lesser of 0.60 lbs/mmBtu or the unit's allowable 1985 emissions, and (B) a numerical factor of 120 percent, divided by 2,000 unless the owner or operator of such unit holds allowances to emit not less than the unit's total annual emissions.

(2) In addition to allowances allocated pursuant to paragraph (1) as basic Phase II allowance allocations and section 403(a)(1) , beginning January 1, 2000, the Administrator shall, in the case of any unit operated by a utility that furnishes electricity, electric energy, steam, and natural gas within an area consist-

ing of a city and 1 contiguous county, and in the case of any unit owned by a State authority, the output of which unit is furnished within that same area consisting of a city and 1 contiguous county, the Administrator shall allocate for each unit in the utility its pro rata share of 7,000 allowances and for each unit in the State authority its pro rata share of 2,000 allowances.

(g) Units That Commence Operation Between 1986 and December 31, 1995.—

(1) After January 1, 2000, it shall be unlawful for any utility unit that has commenced commercial operation on or after January 1, 1986, but not later than September 30, 1990 to exceed an annual tonnage emission limitation equal to the product of the unit's annual fuel consumption, on a Btu basis, at a 65 percent capacity factor multiplied by the unit's allowable 1985 sulfur dioxide emission rate (converted, if necessary, to pounds per mmBtu), divided by 2,000 unless the owner or operator of such unit holds allowances to emit not less than the unit's total annual emissions.

(2) After January 1, 2000, the Administrator shall allocate allowances pursuant to section 403 to each unit which is listed in table B of this paragraph in an annual amount equal to the amount specified in table B.

TABLE B

Unit	Allowances
Brandon Shores	8,907
Miller 4	9,197
TNP One 2	4,000
Zimmer 1	18,458
Spruce 1	7,647
Clover 1	2,796
Clover 2	2,796
Twin Oak 2	1,760
Twin Oak 1	9,158
Cross 1	6,401
Malakoff 1	1,759

Notwithstanding any other paragraph of this subsection, for units subject to this paragraph, the Administrator shall not allocate allowances pursuant to any other paragraph of this subsection, Provided that the owner or operator of a unit listed on Table B may elect an allocation of allowances under another paragraph of this subsection in lieu of an allocation under this paragraph.

(3) Beginning January 1, 2000, the Administrator shall allocate to the owner or operator of any utility unit that commences commercial operation, or has commenced commercial operation, on or after October 1, 1990, but not later than December 31, 1992 allowances in an amount equal to the product of the unit's annual fuel consumption, on a Btu basis, at a 65 percent capacity factor multiplied by the lesser of 0.30 lbs/mmBtu or the unit's allowable sulfur dioxide emission rate (converted, if necessary, to pounds per mmBtu), divided by 2,000.

(4) Beginning January 1, 2000, the Administrator shall allocate to the owner or operator of any utility unit that has commenced construction before December 31, 1990 and that commences commercial operation between January 1, 1993 and December 31, 1995, allowances in an amount equal to the product of the unit's annual fuel consumption, on a Btu basis, at a 65 percent capacity factor multiplied by the lesser of 0.30 lbs/mmBtu or the unit's allowable sulfur dioxide emission rate (converted, if necessary, to pounds per mmBtu), divided by 2,000.

(5) After January 1, 2000, it shall be unlawful for any existing utility unit that has completed conversion from predominantly gas fired existing operation to coal fired operation between January 1, 1985 and December 31, 1987, for which there has been allocated a proposed or final prohibition order pursuant to section 301(b) of the Powerplant and Industrial Fuel Use Act of 1978 (42 U.S.C. 8301 et seq, repealed 1987) to exceed an annual sulfur dioxide tonnage emissions limitation equal to the product of the unit's annual fuel consumption, on a Btu basis, at a 65 percent capacity factor multiplied by the lesser of 1.20 lbs/mmBtu or the unit's allowable 1987 sulfur dioxide emissions rate, divided by 2,000, unless the owner or operator of such unit has obtained allowances equal to its actual emissions.

(6) (A) Unless the Administrator has approved a designation of such facility under section 410, the provisions of this title shall not apply to a 'qualifying small power production facility' or 'qualifying cogeneration facility' (within the meaning of section 3(17)(C) or 3(18)(B) of the Federal Power Act) or to a 'new independent power production facility' as defined in section 416 except that clause (iii) of such definition in section 416 shall not apply for purposes of this paragraph if, as of the date of enactment,

(i) an applicable power sales agreement has been executed;

(ii) the facility is the subject of a State regulatory authority order requiring an electric utility to enter into a power sales agreement with, purchase capacity from, or (for purposes of establishing terms and conditions of the electric utility's purchase of power) enter into arbitration concerning, the facility;

(iii) an electric utility has issued a letter of intent or similar instrument committing to purchase power from the facility at a previously offered or lower price and a power sales agreement is executed within a reasonable period of time; or

(iv) the facility has been selected as a winning bidder in a utility competitive bid solicitation.

(h) Oil and Gas-fired Units Less Than 10 Percent Oil Consumed.—

(1) After January 1, 2000, it shall be unlawful for any oil- and gas-fired utility unit whose average annual fuel consumption during the period 1980 through 1989 on a Btu basis exceeded 90 percent in the form of natural gas to exceed an annual sulfur dioxide tonnage limitation equal to the product of the unit's baseline multiplied by the unit's actual 1985 emissions rate divided by 2,000 unless the owner or operator of such unit holds allowances to emit not less than the unit's total annual emissions.

(2) In addition to allowances allocated pursuant to paragraph (1) and section 403(a)(1) as basic Phase II allowance allocations, beginning January 1, 2000, and for each calendar year thereafter until and including 2009, the Administrator shall allocate annually for each unit subject to the emissions limitation requirements of paragraph (1) allowances from the reserve created pursuant to subsection (a)(2) in an amount equal to the unit's baseline multiplied by 0.050 lbs/mm Btu, divided by 2,000.

(3) In addition to allowances allocated pursuant to paragraph (1) and section 403(a)(1) , beginning January 1, 2010, the Administrator shall allocate annually for each unit subject to the emissions limitation requirements of paragraph (1) allowances in an amount equal to the unit's baseline multiplied by 0.050 lbs/mmBtu, divided by 2,000.

(i) Units in High Growth States.—

(1) In addition to allowances allocated pursuant to this section and section 403(a)(1) as basic Phase II allowance allocations, beginning January 1, 2000, the Administrator shall allocate annually allowances for each unit, subject to an emissions limitation requirement under this section, and located in a State that—

(A) has experienced a growth in population in excess of 25 percent between 1980 and 1988 according to State Population and Household Estimates, With Age, Sex, and Components of Change: 1981–1988 allocated by the United States Department of Commerce, and

(B) had an installed electrical generating capacity of more than 30,000,000 kw in 1988, in an amount equal to the difference between (A) the number of allowances that would be allocated for the unit pursuant to the emissions limitation requirements of this section applicable to the unit adjusted to reflect the unit's annual average fuel consumption on a Btu basis of any three consecutive calendar years between 1980 and 1989 (inclusive) as elected by the owner or operator and (B) the number of allowances allocated for the unit pursuant to the emissions limitation requirements of this section: *Provided,*That the number of allowances allocated pursuant to this subsection shall not exceed an annual total of 40,000. If necessary to meeting the 40,000 allowance restriction imposed under this subsection the Administrator shall reduce, pro rata, the additional annual allowances allocated to each unit under this subsection.

(2) Beginning January 1, 2000, in addition to allowances allocated pursuant to this section and section 403(a)(1) as basic Phase II allowance allocations, the Administrator shall allocate annually for each unit subject to the emissions limitation requirements of subsection (b)(1), (A) the lesser of whose actual or allowable 1980 emissions rate has declined by 50 percent or more as of the date of enactment of the Clean Air Act Amendments of 1990, (B) whose actual emissions rate is less than 1.2 lbs/mmBtu as of January 1, 2000, (C) which commenced operation after January 1, 1970, (D) which is owned by a utility company whose combined commercial and industrial kilowatt- hour sales have increased by more than 20 percent between calendar year 1980 and the date of enactment of the Clean Air Act Amendments of 1990, and (E) whose company-wide fossil-fuel sulfur dioxide emissions rate has declined 40 per centum or more from 1980 to 1988, allowances in an amount equal to the difference between (i) the number of allowances that would be allocated for the unit pursuant to the emissions limitation requirements of subsection (b)(1) adjusted to reflect the unit's annual average fuel consumption on a

Btu basis for any three consecutive years between 1980 and 1989 (inclusive) as elected by the owner or operator and (ii) the number of allowances allocated for the unit pursuant to the emissions limitation requirements of subsection (b)(1): *Provided,* That the number of allowances allocated pursuant to this paragraph shall not exceed an annual total of 5,000. If necessary to meeting the 5,000-allowance restriction imposed in the last clause of the preceding sentence the Administrator shall reduce, pro rata, the additional allowances allocated to each unit pursuant to this paragraph.

(j) Certain Municipally Owned Power Plants.—Beginning January 1, 2000, in addition to allowances allocated pursuant to this section and section 403(a)(1) as basic Phase II allowance allocations, the Administrator shall allocate annually for each existing municipally owned oil and gas-fired utility unit with nameplate capacity equal to, or less than, 40 MWe, the lesser of whose actual or allowable 1985 sulfur dioxide emission rate is less than 1.20 lbs/mmBtu, allowances in an amount equal to the product of the unit's annual fuel consumption on a Btu basis at a 60 percent capacity factor multiplied by the lesser of its allowable 1985 emission rate or its actual 1985 emission rate, divided by 2,000.

§7651e. Allowances for States with Emissions Rates at or Below 0.80 Lbs/MMBTU [Sec. 406]

(a) Election of Governor.—In addition to basic Phase II allowance allocations, upon the election of the Governor of any State, with a 1985 statewide annual sulfur dioxide emissions rate equal to or less than, 0.80 lbs/mmBtu, averaged over all fossil fuel-fired utility steam generating units, beginning January 1, 2000, and for each calendar year thereafter until and including 2009, the Administrator shall allocate, in lieu of other Phase II bonus allowance allocations, allowances from the reserve created pursuant to section 405(a)(2) to all such units in the State in an amount equal to 125,000 multiplied by the unit's pro rata share of electricity generated in calendar year 1985 at fossil fuel- fired utility steam units in all States eligible for the election.

(b) Notification of Administrator.— Pursuant to section 403(a)(1), each Governor of a State eligible to make an election under paragraph (a) shall notify the Administrator of such election. In the event that the Governor of any such State fails to notify the Administrator of the Governor's elections, the Administrator shall allocate allowances pursuant to section 405

(c) Allowances After January 1, 2010.—After January 1, 2010, the Administrator shall allocate allowances to units subject to the provisions of this section pursuant to section 405 .

§7651f. Nitrogen Oxides Emission Reduction Program [Sec. 407]

(a) Applicability.—On the date that a coal-fired utility unit becomes an affected unit pursuant to sections 404 , 405, 409, or on the date a unit subject to the provisions of section 404(d) or 409(b), must meet the SO_2 reduction requirements, each such unit shall become an affected unit for purposes of this section and shall be subject to the emission limitations for nitrogen oxides set forth herein.

(b) Emission Limitations.—

(1) Not later than eighteen months after enactment of the Clean Air Act Amendments of 1990, the Administrator shall by regulation establish annual allowable emission limitations for nitrogen oxides for the types of utility boilers listed below, which limitations shall not exceed the rates listed below: *Provided,*That the Administrator may set a rate higher than that listed for any type of utility boiler if the Administrator finds that the maximum listed rate for that boiler type cannot be achieved using low NO_xburner technology. The maximum allowable emission rates are as follows:

(A) for tangentially fired boilers, 0.45 lb/mmBtu;

(B) for dry bottom wall-fired boilers (other than units applying cell burner technology), 0.50 lb/mmBtu. After January 1, 1995, it shall be unlawful for any unit that is an affected unit on that date and is of the type listed in this paragraph to emit nitrogen oxides in excess of the emission rates set by the Administrator pursuant to this paragraph.

(2) Not later than January 1, 1997, the Administrator shall, by regulation, establish allowable emission limitations on a lb/mmBtu, annual average basis, for nitrogen oxides for the following types of utility boilers:

(A) wet bottom wall-fired boilers;

(B) cyclones;

(C) units applying cell burner technology;

(D) all other types of utility boilers. The Administrator shall base such rates on the degree of reduction achievable through the retrofit application of the best system of continuous emission reduction, taking into account available technology, costs and energy and environmental impacts; and which is comparable to the costs of nitrogen oxides controls set pursuant to subsection (b)(1). Not later than January 1, 1997, the Administrator may revise the applicable emission limitations for tangentially fired and dry bottom, wall-fired boilers (other than cell burners) to be more stringent if the Administrator determines that more effective low NO_x burner technology is available: *Provided,* That, no unit that is an affected unit pursuant to section 404 and that is subject to the requirements of subsection (b)(1), shall be subject to the revised emission limitations, if any.

(c) Revised Performance Standards.—

(1) Not later than January 1, 1993, the Administrator shall propose revised standards of performance to section 111 for nitrogen oxides emissions from fossil-fuel fired steam generating units, including both electric utility and nonutility units. Not later than January 1, 1994, the Administrator shall promulgate such revised standards of performance. Such revised standards of performance shall reflect improvements in methods for the reduction of emissions of oxides of nitrogen.

(d) Alternative Emission Limitations.—The permitting authority shall, upon request of an owner or operator of a unit subject to this section, authorize an emission limitation less stringent than the applicable limitation established under subsection (b)(1) or (b)(2) upon a determination that—

(1) a unit subject to subsection (b)(1) cannot meet the applicable limitation using low NO_x burner technology; or

(2) a unit subject to subsection (b)(2) cannot meet the applicable rate using the technology on which the Administrator based the applicable emission limitation.

The permitting authority shall base such determination upon a showing satisfactory to the permitting authority, in accordance with regulations established by the Administrator not later than eighteen months after enactment of the Clean Air Act Amendments of 1990, that the owner or operator—

(1) has properly installed appropriate control equipment designed to meet the applicable emission rate;

(2) has properly operated such equipment for a period of fifteen months (or such other period of time as the Administrator determines through the regulations), and provides operating and monitoring data for such period demonstrating that the unit cannot meet the applicable emission rate; and

(3) has specified an emission rate that such unit can meet on an annual average basis.

The permitting authority shall issue an operating permit for the unit in question, in accordance with section 408 and part B of title III—

(i) that permits the unit during the demonstration period referred to in subparagraph (2) above, to emit at a rate in excess of the applicable emission rate;

(ii) at the conclusion of the demonstration period to revise the operating permit to reflect the alternative emission rate demonstrated in paragraphs (2) and (3) above.

Units subject to subsection (b)(1) for which an alternative emission limitation is established shall not be required to install any additional control technology beyond low NO_x burners. Nothing in this section shall preclude an owner or operator from installing and operating an alternative NO_x control technology capable of achieving the applicable emission limitation. If the owner or operator of a unit subject to the emissions limitation requirements of subsection (b)(1) demonstrates to the satisfaction of the Administrator that the technology necessary to meet such requirements is not in adequate supply to enable its installation and operation at the unit, consistent with system reliability, by January 1, 1995, then the Administrator shall extend the deadline for compliance for the unit by a period of 15 months. Any owner or operator may petition the Administrator to make a determination under the previous sentence. The Administrator shall grant or deny such petition within 3 months of submittal.

(e) Emissions Averaging.—In lieu of complying with the applicable emissions limitations under subsection (b)(1), (2), or (d), the owner or operator of two or more units subject to one or more of the applicable emission limitations set pursuant to these sections, may petition the permitting authority for alternative contemporaneous annual emission limitations for such units that ensure that (1) the actual annual emission rate in pounds of nitrogen oxides per million Btu averaged over the units in question is a rate that is less than or equal to (2) the Btu-weighted average annual emission rate for the same units if they had been operated, during the same period of time, in compliance with limitations set in accordance with the applicable emission rates set pursuant to subsections (b)(1) and (2).

If the permitting authority determines, in accordance with regulations issued by the Administrator not later than eighteen months after enactment of the Clean Air Act Amendments of 1990; that the conditions in the paragraph above can be met, the permitting authority shall issue operating permits for such units, in accordance with section 408 and part B of title III, that allow alternative contemporaneous annual emission limitations. Such emission limitations shall only remain in effect while both units continue operation under the conditions specified in their respective operating permits.

§7651g. Permits and Compliance Plans [Sec. 408]

(a) Permit Program.—The provisions of this title shall be implemented, subject to section 403, by permits issued to units subject to this title (and enforced) in accordance with the provisions of title V, as modified by this title. Any such permit issued by the Administrator, or by a State with an approved permit program, shall prohibit—

(1) annual emissions of sulfur dioxide in excess of the number of allowances to emit sulfur dioxide the owner or operator, or the designated representative of the owners or operators, of the unit hold for the unit,

(2) exceedances of applicable emissions rates,

(3) the use of any allowance prior to the year for which it was allocated, and

(4) contravention of any other provision of the permit.

Permits issued to implement this title shall be issued for a period of 5 years, notwithstanding title V. No permit shall be issued that is inconsistent with the requirements of this title, and title V as applicable.

(b) Compliance Plan.—Each initial permit application shall be accompanied by a compliance plan for the source to comply with its requirements under this title. Where an affected source consists of more than one affected unit, such plan shall cover all such units, and for purposes of section 502(c) , such source shall be considered a 'facility'. Nothing in this section regarding compliance plans or in title V shall be construed as affecting allowances. Except as provided under subsection (c)(1)(B), submission of a statement by the owner or operator, or the designated representative of the owners and operators, of a unit subject to the emissions limitation requirements of sections 404, 405, and 407 , that the unit will meet the applicable emissions limitation requirements of such sections in a timely manner or that, in the case of the emissions limitation requirements of sections 404 and 405, the owners and operators will hold allowances to emit not less than the total annual emissions of the unit, shall be deemed to meet the proposed and approved compliance planning requirements of this section and title V, except that, for any unit that will meet the requirmeents of this title by means of an alternative method of compliance authorized under section 404(b), (c), (d), or (f) section 407(d) or (e), section 409 and section 410 , the proposed and approved compliance plan, permit application and permit shall include, pursuant to regulations promulgated by the Administrator, for each alternative method of compliance a comprehensive description of the schedule and means by which the unit will rely on one or more alternative methods of compliance in the manner and time authorized under this title. Recordation by the Administrator of transfers of allowances shall amend automatically all applicable proposed or approved permit applications, compliance plans and permits. The Administrator may also require—

(1) for a source, a demonstration of attainment of national ambient air quality standards and

(2) from the owner or operator of two or more affected sources, an integrated compliance plan providing an overall plan for achieving compliance at the affected sources.

(c) First Phase Permits.—The Administrator shall issue permits to affected sources under sections 404 and 407 .

(1) Permit Application and Compliance Plan.—

(A) Not later than 27 months after the date of the enactment of the Clean Air Act Amendments of 1990, the designated representative of the owners or operators, or the owner and operator, of each affected source under sections 404 and 407 shall submit a permit application and compliance plan for that source in accordance with regulations issued by the Administrator under paragraph (3). The permit application and the compliance plan shall be binding on the owner or operator or the designated representative of owners and operators for purposes of this title and section 402(a), and shall be enforceable in lieu of a permit until a permit is issued by the Administrator for the source.

(B) In the case of a compliance plan for an affected source under sections 404 and 407 for which the owner or operator proposes to meet the requirements of that section by reducing utilization of the unit as compared with its baseline or by shutting down the unit, the owner or operator shall include in the proposed compliance plan a specification of the unit or units that will provide electrical generation to compensate for the reduced output at the affected source, or a demonstration that such reduced utilization will be accomplished through energy conservation or improved unit efficiency. The unit to be used for such compensating generation, which is not otherwise an affected unit under sections 404 and 407, shall be deemed an affected unit under section 404, subject to all of the requirements for such units under this title, except that allowances shall be allocated to such compensating unit in the amount of an annual limitation equal to the product of the unit's baseline multiplied by the lesser of the unit's actual 1985 emissions rate or its allowable 1985 emissions rates, divided by 2,000.

(2) EPA Action on Compliance Plans.—The Administrator shall review each proposed compliance plan to determine whether it satisfies the requirements of this title, and shall approve or disapprove such plan within 6 months after receipt of a complete submission. If a plan is disapproved, it may be resubmitted for approval with such changes as the Administrator shall require consistent with the requirements of this title and within such period as the Administrator prescribes as part of such disapproval.

(3) Regulations; Issuance of Permits.—Not later than 18 months after the date of the enactment of the Clean Air Act Amendments of 1990, the Administrator shall promulgate regulations, in accordance with title V, to implement a Federal permit program to issue permits for affected sources under this title. Following promulgation, the Administrator shall issue a permit to implement the requirements of section 404 and the allowances provided under section 403 to the owner or operator of each affected source under section 404 . Such a permit shall supersede any permit application and compliance plan submitted under paragraph (1).

(4) Fees.—During the years 1995 through 1999 inclusive, no fee shall be required to be paid under section 502(b)(3) or under section 110(a)(2)(L) with respect to emissions from any unit which is an affected unit under section 404

(d) Second Phase Permits.—

(1) To provide for permits for (A) new electric utility steam generating units required under section 403(e) to have allowances, (B) affected units or sources under section 405, and (C) existing units subject to nitrogen oxide emission reductions under section 407 , each State in which one or more such units or sources are located shall submit in accordance with title V, a permit program for approval as provided by that title. Upon approval of such program, for the units or sources subject to such approved program the Administrator shall suspend the issuance of permits as provided in title V.

(2) The owner or operator or the designated representative of each affected source under section 405 shall submit a permit application and compliance plan for that source to the permitting authority, not later than January 1, 1996.

(3) Not later than December 31, 1997, each State with an approved permit program shall issue permits to the owner or operator, or the designated representative of the owners and operators, of affected sources under section 405 that satisfy the requirements of title V and this title and that submitted to such State a permit application and compliance plan pursuant to paragraph (2). In the case of a State without an approved permit program by July 1, 1996, the Administrator shall, not later than January 1, 1998, issue a permit to the owner or operator or the designated representative of each such affected source. In the case of affected sources for which applications and plans are timely received under paragraph (2), the permit application and the compliance plan, including amendments thereto, shall be binding on the owner or operator or the designated representative of the owners or operators and shall be enforceable as a permit for purposes of this title and title V until a permit is issued by the permitting authority for the affected source. The provisions of section 558(c) of title V of the United States Code (relating to renewals) shall apply to permits issued by a permitting authority under this title and title V.

(4) The permit issued in accordance with this subsection for an affected source shall provide that the affected units at the affected source may not emit an annual tonnage of sulfur dioxide in excess of the number of allowances to emit sulfur dioxide the owner or operator or designated representative hold for the unit.

(e) New Units.—The owner or operator of each source that includes a new electric utility steam generating unit shall submit a permit application and compliance plan to the permitting authority not later than 24 months before the later of (1) January 1, 2000, or (2) the date on which the unit commences operation. The permitting authority shall issue a permit to the owner or operator, or the designated representative thereof, of the unit that satisfies the requirements of title V and this title.

(f) Units Subject to Certain Other Limits.—The owner or operator or designated representative thereof, of any unit subject to an emission rate requirement under section 407 shall submit a permit application and compliance plan for such unit to the permitting authority, not later than January 1, 1998. The permitting authority shall issue a permit to the owner or operator that satisfies the requirements of title V and this title, including any appropriate monitoring and reporting requirements.

(g) Amendment of Application and Compliance Plan.—At any time after the submission of an application and compliance plan under this section, the applicant may submit a revised application and compliance plan, in accordance with the requirements of this section. In considering any permit application and compliance plan under this title, the permitting authority shall endure coordination with the applicable electric ratemaking authority, in the case of regulated utilities, and with unregulated public utilities.

(h) Prohibition.—

(1) It shall be unlawful for an owner or operator or designated representative, required to submit a permit application or compliance plan under this title to fail to submit such application or plan in accordance with the deadlines specified in this section or to otherwise fail to comply with regulations implementing this section.

(2) It shall be unlawful for any person to operate any source subject to this title except in compliance with the terms and requirements of a permit application and compliance plan (including amendments thereto) or permit issued by the Administrator or a State with an approved permit program. For purposes of this subsection, compliance, as provided in section 504(f) , with a permit issued under title V which complies with this title for sources subject to this title shall be deemed compliance with this subsection as well as section 502(a) .

(3) In order to ensure reliability of electric power, nothing in this title or title V shall be construed as requiring termination of operations of an electric utility steam generating unit for failure to have an approved permit or compliance plan, except that any such unit may be subject to the applicable enforcement provisions of section 113 .

(i) Multiple Owners.—No permit shall be issued under this section to an affected unit until the designated representative of the owners or operators has filed a certificate of representation with regard to matters under this title, including the holding and distribution of allowances and the proceeds of transactions involving allowances. Where there are multiple holders of a legal or equitable title to, or a leasehold interest in, such a unit, or where a utility or industrial customer purchases power from an affected unit (or units) under life-of-the-unit, firm power contractual arrangements, the certificate shall state (1) that allowances and the proceeds of transactions involving allowances will be deemed to be held or distributed in proportion to each holder's legal, equitable, leasehold, or contractual reservation or entitlement, or (2) if such multiple holders have expressly provided for a different distribution of allowances by contract, that allowances and the proceeds of transactions involving allowances will be deemed to be held or distributed in accordance with the contract. A passive lessor, or a person who has an equitable interest through such lessor, whose rental payments are not based, either directly or indirectly, upon the revenues or income from the affected unit shall not be deemed to be a holder of a legal, equitable, leasehold, or contractual interest for the purpose of holding or distributing allowances as provided in this subsection, during either the term of such leasehold or thereafter, unless expressly provided for in the leasehold agreement. Except as otherwise provided in this subsection, where all legal or equitable title to or interest in an affected unit is held by a single person, the certification shall state that all allowances received by the unit are deemed to be held for that person.

§7651h. Repowered Sources [Sec. 409]

(a) Availability.—Not later than December 31, 1997, the owner or operator of an existing unit subject to the emissions limitation requirements of section 405(b) and (c) may demonstrate to the permitting authority that one or more units will be repowered with a qualifying clean coal technology to comply with the require ments under section 405 . The owner or operator shall, as part of any such demonstration, provide, not later than January 1, 2000, satisfactory documentation of a preliminary design and engineering effort for such repowering and an executed and binding contract for the majority of the equipment to repower such unit and such other information as the Administrator may require by regulation. The replacement of an existing utility unit with a new utility unit using a repowering technology referred to in section 402(2) which is located at a different site, shall be treated as repowering of the existing unit for purposes of this title, if—

(1) The replacement unit is designated by the owner or operator to replace such existing unit, and

(2) the existing unit is retired from service on or before the date on which the designated replacement unit enters commercial operation.

(b) Extension.—

(1) An owner or operator satisfying the requirements of subsection (a) shall be granted an extension of the emission limitation requirement compliance date for that unit from January 1, 2000, to December 31, 2003. The extension shall be specified in the permit issued to the source under section 408 , together with any compliance schedule and other requirements necessary to meet second phase requirements by the extended date. Any unit that is granted an extension under this section shall not be eligible for a waiver under section 111(j) of this Act, and shall continue to be subject to requirements under this title as if it were a unit subject to section 405 .

(2) If (A) the owner or operator of an existing unit has been granted an extension under paragraph (1) in order to repower such unit with a clean coal unit, and (B) such owner or operator demonstrates to the satisfaction of the Administrator that the repowering technology to be utilized by such unit has been properly constructed and tested on such unit, but nevertheless has been unable to achieve the emission reduction limitations and is economically or technologically infeasible, such existing unit may be retrofitted or repowered with equipment or facilities utilizing another clean coal technology or other available control technology.

(c) Allowances.—

(1) For the period of the extension under this section, the Administrator shall allocate to the owner or operator of the affected unit, annual allowances for sulfur dioxide equal to the affected unit's baseline multiplied by the lesser of the unit's federally approved State Implementation Plan emissions limitation or its actual emission rate for 1995 in lieu of any other allocation. Such allowances may not be transferred or used by any other source to meet emission requirements under this title. The source owner or operator shall notify the Administrator sixty days in advance of the date on which the affected unit for which the extension has been granted is to be removed from operation to install the repowering technology.

(2) Effective on that date, the unit shall be subject to the requirements of section 405 . Allowances for the year in which the unit is removed from operation to install the repowering technology shall be calculated as the product of the unit's baseline multiplied by 1.20 lbs/mmBtu, divided by 2,000, and prorated accordingly, and are transferable.

(3) Allowances for such existing utility units for calendar years after the year the repowering is complete shall be calculated as the product of the existing unit's baseline multiplied by 1.20 lbs/mmBtu, divided by 2,000.

(4) Notwithstanding the provisions of section 403(a) and (e), allowances shall be allocated under this section for a designated replacement unit which replaces an existing unit (as provided in the last sentence of subsection (a)) in lieu of any further allocations of allowances for the existing unit.

(5) For the purpose of meeting the aggregate emissions limitation requirement set forth in section 403(a)(1), the units with an extension under this subsection shall be treated in each calendar year during the extension period as holding allowances allocated under paragraph (3).

(d) Control Requirements.—Any unit qualifying for an extension under this section that does not increase actual hourly emissions for any pollutant regulated under the Act shall not be subject to any standard of performance under section 111 of this Act. Notwithstanding the provisions of this subsection, no new unit (1) designated as a replacement for an existing unit, (2) qualifying for the extension under subsection (b), and (3) located at a different site than the existing unit shall receive an exemption from the requirements imposed under section 111 .

(e) Expedited Permitting.—State permitting authorities and, where applicable, the Administrator, are encouraged to give expedited consideration to permit applications under parts C and D of title I of this Act for any source qualifying for an extension under this section.

(f) Prohibition.—It shall be unlawful for the owner or operator of a repowered source to fail to comply with the requirement of this section, or any regulations of permit requirements to implement this section, including the prohibition against emitting sulfur dioxide in excess of allowances held.

§7651i. Election for Additional Sources [Sec. 410]

(a) Applicability.—The owner or operator of any unit that is not, nor will become, an affected unit under section 403(e), 404, or 405, or that is a process source under subsection (d), that emits sulfur dioxide, may elect to designate that unit or source to become an affected unit and to receive allowances under this title. An election shall be submitted to the Administrator for approval, along with a permit application and proposed compliance plan in accordance with section 408 . The Administrator shall approve a designation that meets the requirements of this section, and such designated unit, or source, shall be allocated allowances, and be an affected unit for purposes of this title.

(b) Establishment of Baseline.—The baseline for a unit designated under this section shall be established by the Administrator by regulation, based on fuel consumption and operating data for the unit for calendar years 1985, 1986, and 1987, or if such data is not available, the Administrator may prescribe a baseline based on alternative representative data.

(c) Emission Limitations.—Annual emissions limitations for sulfur dioxide shall be equal to the product of the baseline multiplied by the lesser of the unit's 1985 actual or allowable emission rate in lbs/mmBtu, or, if the unit did not operate in 1985, by the lesser of the unit's actual or allowable emission rate for a calendar year after 1985 (as determined by the Administrator), divided by 2,000.

(d) Process Sources.—Not later than 18 months after enactment of the Clean Air Act Amendments of 1990, the Ad ministrator shall establish a program under which the owner or operator of a process source that emits sulfur dioxide may elect to designate that source as an affected unit for the purpose of receiving allowances under this title. The Administrator shall, by regulation, define the sources that may be designated; specify the emissions limitation; specify the operating, emission baseline and other data requirements; prescribe CEMS or other monitoring requirements; and promulgate permit, reporting, and any other requirements necessary to implement such a program.

(e) Allowances and Permits.—The Administrator shall issue allowances to an affected unit under this section in an amount equal to the emissions limitation calculated under subsection (c) or (d), in accordance with section 403 . Such allowance may be used in accordance with, and shall be subject to, the provisions of section 403 . Affected sources under this section shall be subject to the requirements of sections 403, 408, 411, 412, 413, and 414 .

(f) Limitation.—Any unit designated under this section shall not transfer or bank allowances produced as a result of reduced utilization or shutdown, except that, such allowances may be transferred or carried forward for use in subsequent years to the extent that the reduced utilization or shutdown results from the replacement of thermal energy from the unit designated under this section, with thermal energy generated by any other unit or units subject to the requirements of this title, and the designated unit's allowances are transferred or carried forward for use at such other replacement unit or units. In no case may the Administrator allocate to a source designated under this section allowances in an amount greater than the emissions resulting from operation of the source in full compliance with the requirements of this Act. No such allowances shall authorize operation of a unit in violation of any other requirements of this Act.

(g) Implementation.—The Administrator shall issue regulations to implement this section not later than eighteen months after enactment of the Clean Air Act Amendments of 1990.

(h) Small Diesel Refineries.—The Administrator shall issue allowances to owners or operators of small diesel refineries who produce diesel fuel after October 1, 1993, meeting the requirements of subsection 211(i) of this Act.

(1) Allowance Period.—Allowances may be allocated under this subsection only for the period from October 1, 1993, through December 31, 1999.

(2) Allowance Determination.—The number of allowances allocated pursuant to this paragraph shall equal the annual number of pounds of sulfur dioxide reduction attributable to desulfurization by a small refinery divided by 2,000. For the purposes of this calculation, the concentration of sulfur removed from diesel fuel shall be the difference between 0.274 percent (by weight) and 0.050 percent (by weight).

(3) Refinery Eligibility.—As used in this subsection, the term 'small refinery' shall mean a refinery or portion of a refinery—

(A) which, as of the date of enactment of the Clean Air Act Amendments of 1990, has bona fide crude oil throughput of less than 18,250,000 barrels per year, as reported to the Department of Energy, and

(B) which, as of the date of enactment of the Clean Air Act Amendments of 1990, is owned or controlled by a refiner with a total combined bona fide crude oil throughput of less than 50,187,500 barrels per year as reported to the Department of Energy.

(4) Limitation per Refinery.—The maximum number of allowances that can be annually allocated to a small refinery pursuant to this subsection is one thousand and five hundred.

(5) Limitation on Total.—In any given year, the total number of allowances allocated pursuant to this subsection shall not exceed thirty-five thousand.

(6) Required Certification.—The Administrator shall not allocate any allowances pursuant to this subsection unless the owner or operator of a small diesel refinery shall have certified, at a time and in a manner prescribed by the Administrator, that all motor diesel fuel produced by the refinery for which allowances are claimed, including motor diesel fuel for off-highway use, shall have met the requirements of subsection 211(i) of this Act.

§7651j. Excess Emissions Penalty [Sec. 411]

(a) Excess Emissions Penalty.—The owner or operator of any unit or process source subject to the requirements of sections 403, 404, 405, 406, 407 or 409 , or designated under section 410, that emits sulfur dioxide or nitrogen oxides for any calendar year in excess of the unit's emissions limitation requirement or, in the case of sulfur dioxide, of the allowances the owner or operator holds for use for the unit for that calendar year shall be liable for the payment of an excess emissions penalty, except where such emissions were authorized pursuant to section 110(f) . That penalty shall be calculated on the basis of the number of tons emitted in excess of unit's emissions limitation requirement or, in the base of sulfur dioxide, of the allowances the operator holds for use for the unit for that year, multiplied by \$2,000. Any such penalty shall be due and payable without demand to the Administrator as provided in regulations to be issued by the Administrator by no later than eighteen months after the date of enactment of the Clean Air Act Amendments of 1990. Any such payment shall be deposited in the United States Treasury pursuant to the Miscellaneous Receipts Act. Any penalty due and payable under this section shall not diminish the liability of the unit's owner or operator for any fine, penalty or assessment against the unit for the same violation under any other section of this Act.

(b) Excess Emissions Offset.—The owner or operator of any affected source that emits sulfur dioxide during any calendar year in excess of the unit's emissions limitation requirement or of the allowances held for the unit for the calendar year, shall be liable to offset the excess emissions by an equal tonnage amount in the following calendar year, or such longer period as the Administrator may prescribe. The owner or operator of the source shall, within sixty days after the end of the year in which the excess emissions occurred, submit to the Administrator, and to the State in which the source is located, a proposed plan to achieve the required offsets. Upon approval of the proposed plan by the Administrator, as submitted, modified or conditioned, the plan shall be deemed at a condition of the operating permit for the unit without further review or revision of the permit. The Administrator shall also deduct allowances equal to the excess tonnage from those allocated for the source for the calendar year, or succeeding years during which offsets are required, following the year in which the excess emissions occurred.

(c) Penalty Adjustment.—The Administrator shall, by regulation, adjust the penalty specified in subsection (a) for inflation, based on the Consumer Price Index, on the date of enactment and annually thereafter.

(d) Prohibition.—It shall be unlawful for the owner or operator of any source liable for a penalty and offset under this section to fail (1) to pay the penalty under subsection (a), (2) to provide, and thereafter comply with, a compliance plan as required by subsection (b), or (3) to offset excess emissions as required by subsection (b).

(e) Savings Provision.—Nothing in this title shall limit or otherwise affect the application of section 113, 114, 120, or 304 except as otherwise explicitly provided in this title.

§7651k. Monitoring, Reporting, and Recordkeeping Requirements [Sec. 412]

(a) Applicability.—The owner and operator of any source subject to this title shall be required to install and operate CEMS on each affected unit at the source, and to quality assure the data for sulfur dioxide, nitrogen oxides, opacity and volumetric flow at each such unit. The Administrator shall, by regulations issued not later than eighteen months after enactment of the Clean Air Act Amendments of 1990, specify the requirements for CEMS, for any alternative monitoring system that is demonstrated as providing information with the same precision, reliability, accessibility, and timeliness as that provided by CEMS, and for recordkeeping and reporting of information from such systems. Such regulations may include limitations or the use of alternative compliance methods by units equipped with an alternative monitoring system as may be necessary to preserve the orderly functioning of the allowance system, and which will ensure the emissions reductions contemplated by this title. Where 2 or more units utilize a single stack, a separate CEMS shall not be required for each unit, and for such units the regulations shall require that the owner or operator collect sufficient information to permit reliable compliance determinations for each such unit.

(b) First Phase Requirements.—Not later than thirty-six months after enactment of the Clean Air Act Amendments of 1990, the owner or operator of each affected unit under section 404 , including, but not limited to, units that become affected units pursuant to subsections (b) and (c) and eligible units under subsection (d), shall install and operate CEMS, quality assure the data, and keep records and reports in accordance with the regulations issued under subsection (a).

(c) Second Phase Requirements.—Not later than January 1, 1995, the owner or operator of each affected unit that has not previously met the requirements of subsections (a) and (b) shall install and operate CEMS, quality assure the data, and keep records and reports in accordance with the regulations issued under subsection (a). Upon commencement of commercial operation of each new utility unit, the unit shall comply with the requirements of subsection (a).

(d) Unavailability of Emissions Data.—If CEMS data or data from an alternative monitoring system approved by the Administrator under subsection (a) is not available for any affected unit during any period of a calendar year in which such data is required under this title, and the owner or operator cannot provide information, satisfactory to the Administrator, on emissions during that period, the Administrator shall deem the unit to be operating in an uncontrolled manner during the entire period for which the data was not available and shall, by regulation which shall be issued not later than eighteen months after enactment of the Clean Air Act Amendments of 1990, prescribe means to calculate emissions for that period. The owner or operator shall be liable for excess emissions fees and offsets under section 411 in accordance with such regulations. Any fee due and payable under this subsection shall not diminish the liability of the unit's owner or operator for any fine, penalty, fee or assessment against the unit for the same violation under any other section of this Act.

(e) Prohibition.—It shall be unlawful for the owner or operator of any source subject to this title to operate a source without complying with the requirements of this section, and any regulations implementing this section.

§7651l. General Compliance With Other Provisions [Sec. 413]

Except as expressly provided, compliance with the requirements of this title shall not exempt or exclude the owner or operator of any source subject to this title from compliance with any other applicable requirements of this Act.

§7651m. Enforcement [Sec. 414]

It shall be unlawful for any person subject to this title to violate any prohibition of, requirement of, or regulation promulgated pursuant to this title shall be a violation of this Act. In addition to the other requirements and prohibitions provided for in this title, the operation of any affected unit to emit sulfur dioxide in excess of allowances held for such unit shall be deemed a violation, with each ton emitted in excess of allowances held constituting a separate violation.

§7651n. Clean Coal Technology Regulatory Incentives [Sec. 415]

(a) Definition.—For purposes of this section, 'clean coal technology' means any technology, including technologies applied at the precombustion, combustion or post combustion stage, at a new or existing facility which will achieve significant reductions in air emissions of sulfur dioxide or oxides of nitrogen associated with the utilization of coal in the generation of electricity, process steam, or industrial products, which is not in widespread use as of the date of enactment of this title.

(b) Revised Regulations for Clean Coal Technology Demonstrations.—

(1) Applicability.—This subsection applies to physical or operational changes to existing

facilities for the sole purpose of installation, operation, cessation, or removal of a temporary or permanent clean coal technology demonstration project. For the purposes of this section, a clean coal technology demonstration project shall mean a project using funds appropriated under the heading 'Department of Energy—Clean Coal Technology', up to a total amount of $2,500,000,000 for commercial demonstration of clean coal technology, or similar projects funded through appropriations for the Environmental Protection Agency. The Federal contribution for a qualifying project shall be at least 20 percent of the total cost of the demonstration project.

(2) Temporary projects.—Installation, operation, cessation, or removal of a temporary clean coal technology demonstration project that is operated for a period of five years or less, and which complies with the State implementation plans for the State in which the project is located and other requirements necessary to attain and maintain the national ambient air quality standards during and after the project is terminated, shall not subject such facility to the requirements of section 111 or part C or D of title I.

(3) Permanent projects.—For permanent clean coal technology demonstration projects that constitute repowering as defined in section 402(l) of this title, any qualifying project shall not be subject to standards of performance under section 111 or to the review and permitting requirements of part C for any pollutant the potential emissions of which will not increase as a result of the demonstration project.

(4) EPA regulations.—Not later than 12 months after the date of enactment, the Administrator shall promulgate regulations or interpretive rulings to revise requirements under section 111 and parts C and D, as appropriate, to facilitate projects consistent in this subsection. With respect to parts C and D, such regulations or rulings shall apply to all areas in which EPA is the permitting authority. In those instances in which the State is the permitting authority under part C or D, any State may adopt and submit to the Administrator for approval revisions to its implementation plan to apply the regulations or rulings promulgated under this subsection.

(c) Exemption for Reactivation of Very Clean Units.—Physical changes or changes in the method of operation associated with the commencement of commercial operations by a coal-fired utility unit after a period of discontinued operation shall not subject the unit to the requirements of section 111 or part C of the Act where the unit (1) has not been in operation for the two-year period prior to the enactment of the Clean Air Act Amendments of 1990, and the emissions from such unit continue to be carried in the permitting authority's emissions inventory at the time of enactment, (2) was equipped prior to shut-down with a continuous system of emissions control that achieves a removal efficiency for sulfur dioxide of no less than 85 percent and a removal efficiency for particulates of no less than 98 percent, (3) is equipped with low-NO_x burners prior to the time of commencement, and (4) is otherwise in compliance with the requirements of this Act.

§7651o. Contingency Guarantee: Auctions, Reserve [Sec. 416]

(a) Definitions.—For purposes of this section—

(1) The term 'independent power producer' means any person who owns or operates, in whole or in part, one or more new independent power production facilities.

(2) The term 'new independent power production facility' means a facility that—

(A) is used for the generation of electric energy, 80 percent or more of which is sold at wholesale;

(B) is nonrecourse project-financed (as such term is defined by the Secretary of Energy within 3 months of the date of the enactment of the Clean Air Act Amendments of 1990);

(C) does not generate electric energy sold to any affiliate (as defined in section 2(a)(11) of the Public Utility Holding Company Act of 1935) of the facility's owner or operator unless the owner or operator of the facility demonstrates that it cannot obtain allowances from the affiliate; and

(D) is a new unit required to hold allowances under this title.

(3) The term 'required allowances' means the allowances required to operate such unit for so much of the unit's useful life as occurs after January 1, 2000.

(b) Special Reserve of Allowances.—Within 36 months after the date of the enactment of the Clean Air Act Amendments of 1990, the Administrator shall promulgate regulations establishing a Special Allowance Reserve containing allowances to be sold under this section. For purposes of establishing the Special Allowance Reserve, the Administrator shall withhold—

(1) 2.8 percent of the allocation of allowances for each year from 1995 through 1999 inclusive; and

(2) 2.8 percent of the basic Phase II allowance allocation of allowances for each year beginning in the year 2000 which would (but for this subsection) be used for each affected unit at an affected source. The Administrator shall record such withholding for purposes of transferring the proceeds of the allowance sales under this subsection. The allowances so withheld shall be deposited in the Reserve under this section.

(c) Direct Sale at $1,500 Per Ton.—

(1) Subaccount for Direct Sales.—In accordance with regulations under this section, the Administrator shall establish a Direct Sale Subaccount in the Special Allowance Reserve established under this section. The Direct Sale Subaccount shall contain allowances in the amount of 50,000 tons per year for each year beginning in the year 2000.

(2) Sales.—Allowances in the subaccount shall be offered for direct sale to any person at the times and in the amounts specified in table 1 at a price of $1,500 per allowance, adjusted by the Consumer Price Index in the same manner as provided in paragraph (3). Requests to purchase allowances from the Direct Sale Subaccount established under paragraph (1) shall be approved in the order of receipt until no allowances remain in such subaccount, except that an opportunity to purchase such allowances shall be provided to the independent power producers referred to in this subsection before such allowances are offered to any other person. Each applicant shall be required to pay 50 percent of the total purchase price of the allowances within 6 months after the approval of the request to purchase. The remainder shall be paid on or before the transfer of the allowances.

TABLE 1—NUMBER OF ALLOWANCES AVAILABLE FOR SALE AT $1,500 PER TON

Year of Sale	Spot Auction (same year)	Advance Sale
1993-1999		25,000
2000 and after	25,000	25,000

Allowances sold in the spot sale in any year are allowances which may only be used in that year (unless banked for use in a later year). Allowances sold in the advance sale in any year are allowances which may only be used in the 7th year after the year in which they are first offered for sale (unless banked for use in a later year).

(3) Entitlement To Written Guarantee.—Any independent power producer that submits an application to the Administrator establishing that such independent power producer—

(A) proposes to construct a new independent power production facility for which allowances are required under this title;

(B) will apply for financing to construct such facility after January 1, 1990, and before the date of the first auction under this section;

(C) has submitted to each owner or operator of an affected unit listed in table A (in section 404) a written offer to purchase the required allowances for $750 per ton; and

(D) has not received (within 180 days after submitting offers to purchase under subparagraph (C)) an acceptance of the offer to purchase the required allowances. shall, within 30 days after submission of such application, be entitled to receive the Administrator's written guarantee (subject to the eligibility requirements set forth in paragraph (4)) that such required allowances will be made available for purchase from the Direct Sale Subaccount established under this subsection and at a guaranteed price. The guaranteed price at which such allowances shall be made available for purchase shall be $1,500 per ton, adjusted by the percentage, if any, by which the Consumer Price Index (as determined under section 502(b)(3)(B)(v)) for the year in which the allowance is purchased exceeds the Consumer Price Index for the calendar year 1990.

(4) Eligibility Requirements.—The guarantee issued by the Administrator under paragraph (3) shall be subject to a demonstration by the independent power producer, satisfactory to the Administrator, that—

(A) the independent power producer has—

(i) made good faith efforts to purchase the required allowances from the owners or operators of affected units to which allowances will be allocated, including efforts to purchase at annual auctions under this section, and from industrial sources that have elected to become affected units pursuant to section 410 ; and

(ii) such bids and efforts were unsuccessful in obtaining the required allowances; and

(B) the independent power producer will continue to make good faith efforts to purchase the required allowances from the owners or operators of affected units and from industrial sources.

(5) Issuance of Guaranteed Allowances From Direct Sale Subaccount Under This Section.—

From the allowances available in the Direct Sale Subaccount established under this subsection, upon payment of the guaranteed price, the Administrator shall issue to any person exercising the right to purchase allowances pursuant to a guarantee under this subsection the allowances covered by such guarantee. Persons to which guarantees under this subsection have been issued shall have the opportunity to purchase allowances pursuant to such guarantee from such subaccount before the allowances in such reserve are offered for sale to any other person.

(6) Proceeds.—Notwithstanding section 3302 of title 31 of the United States Code or any other provision of law, the Administrator shall require that the proceeds of any sale under this subsection be transferred, within 90 days after the sale, without charge, on a pro rata basis to the owners or operators of the affected units from whom the allowances were withheld under subsection (b) and that any unsold allowances be transferred to the Subaccount for Auction Sales established under subsection (d). No proceeds of any sale under this subsection shall be held by any officer or employee of the United States or treated for any purpose as revenue to the United States or to the Administrator.

(7) Termination of Subaccount.—If the Administrator determines that, during any period of 2 consecutive calendar years, less than 20 percent of the allowances available in the subaccount for direct sales established under this subsection have been purchased under this paragraph, the Administrator shall terminate the subaccount and transfer such allowances to the Auction Subaccount under subsection (d).

(d) Auction Sales.—

(1) Subaccount for Auctions.—The Administrator shall establish an Auction Subaccount in the Special Reserve established under this section. The auction Subaccount shall contain allowances to be sold at auction under this section in the amount of 150,000 tons per year for each year from 1995 through 1999, inclusive and 250,000 tons per year for each year beginning in the calendar year 2000.

(2) Annual Auctions.—Commencing in 1993 and in each year thereafter, the Administrator shall conduct auctions at which the allowances refereed to in paragraph (1) shall be offered for sale in accordance with regulations promulgated by the Administrator in consultation with the Secretary of the Treasury, within 12 months of enactment of the Clean Air Act Amendments of 1990. The allowances referred to in paragraph (1) shall be offered for sale at auction in the amounts specified in table 2. The auction shall be open to any person. A person wishing to bid for such allowances shall submit (by a date set by the administrator) to the Administrator (on a sealed bid schedule provided by the Administrator) offers to purchase specified number of allowances at specified prices. Such regulations shall specify that the auctioned allowances shall be allocated and sold on the basis of bid price, starting with the highest priced bid and continuing until all allowances for sale at such auction have been allocated. The regulations shall not permit that a minimum price be set for the purchase of withheld allowances. Allowances purchased at the auction may be used for any purpose and at any time after the auction, subject to the provisions of this title.

TABLE 2—NUMBER OF ALLOWANCES AVAILABLE FOR AUCTION

Year of Sale	Spot Auction (same year)	Advance Sale
1993	50,000*	100,000
1994	50,000*	100,000
1995	50,000*	100,000
1996	150,000	100,000
1997	150,000	100,000
1998	150,000	100,000
1999	150,000	100,000
2000 and after	100,000	100,000

Allowances sold in the spot sale in any year are allowances which may only be used in that year (unless banked for use in a later year), except as otherwise noted. Allowances sold in the advance auction in any year are allowances which may only be used in the 7th year after the year in which they are first offered for sale (unless banked for use in a later year).

* Available for use only in 1995 (unless banked for use in a later year).

(3) Proceeds.—

(A) Notwithstanding section 3302 of title 31 of the United States Code or any other provision of law, within 90 days of receipt, the Administrator shall transfer the proceeds from the auction under this section, on a pro rata basis, to the owners or operators of the affected units at an affected source from whom allowances were withheld under subsection (b). No funds transferred from a purchaser to a seller of allowances under this paragraph shall be held by any officer or employee of the United States or treated for any purpose as revenue to the United States or the Administrator.

(B) At the end of each year, any allowances offered for sale but not sold at the auction shall be returned without charge, on a pro rata basis, to the owner or operator of the affected units from the whose allocation the allowances were withheld.

(4) Additional Auction Participants.—Any person holding allowances or to home allowances are allocated by the Administrator may submit those allowances to the Administrator to be offered for sale at auction under this subsection. The proceeds of any such sale shall be transferred at the time of sale by the purchaser to the person submitting such allowances for sale. The holder of allowances offered for sale under this paragraph may specify a minimum sale price. Any person may purchase allowances offered for auction under this paragraph. Such allowances shall be allocated and sold to purchasers on the basis of bid price after the auction under paragraph (2) is complete. No funds transferred from a purchaser to a seller of allowances under this paragraph shall be held by any officer or employee of the United States or treated for any purpose as revenue to the United States or the Administrator.

(5) Recording By EPA.—The Administrator shall record and publicly report the nature, prices and results of each auction under this subsection, including the prices of successful bids, and shall record the transfers of allowances as a result of each auction in accordance with the requirements of this section. The transfer of allowances at such auction shall be recorded in accordance with the regulations promulgated by the Administrator under this title.

(e) Changes in sales, auctions, and withholding.—Pursuant to rulemaking after public notice and comment the Administrator may at any time after the year 1998 (in the case of advance sales or advance auctions) and 2005 (in the case of spot sales or spot auctions) decrease the number of allowances withheld and sold under this section.

(f) Termination of auctions.—The Administrator may terminate the withholding of allowances and the auction sales under this section if the Administrator determines that, during any period of 3 consecutive calendar years after 2002, less than 20 percent of the allowances available in the auction subaccount have been purchased. Pursuant to regulations under this section, the Administrator may by delegation or contract provide for the conduct of sales or auctions under the Administrator's supervision by other departments or agencies of the United States Government or by non-governmental agencies, groups, or organizations.

TITLE V—PERMITS

[Title V added by PL 101–549]

§7661. Definitions [Sec. 501]

As used in this title—

(1) Affected sources.—The term 'affected source' shall have the meaning given such term in title IV.

(2) Major source.—The term 'major source' means any stationary source (or any group of stationary sources located within a contiguous area and under common control) that is either of the following:

(A) A major source as defined in section 112 .

(B) A major stationary source and defined in section 302 or part D of title I.

(3) Schedule of compliance.—The term 'schedule of compliance' means a schedule of remedial measures, including an enforceable sequence of actions or operations, leading to compliance with an applicable implementation plan, emission standard, emission limitation, or emission prohibition.

(4) Permitting authority.—The term 'permitting authority' means the Administrator or the air pollution control agency authorized by the Administrator to carry out a permit program under this title.

§7661a. Permit Programs [Sec. 502]

(a) Violations.—After the effective date of any permit program approved or promulgated under this title, it shall be unlawful for any person to violate any requirement of a permit issued under this title, or to operate an affected source (as provided in title IV), a major source, any other source (including an area source) subject to standards or regulations under section 111 or 112, any other source required to have a permit under parts C or D of title I, or any other stationary source in a category designated (in whole or in part) by regulations promulgated by the Administrator (after notice and public comment) which shall include a finding setting forth the basis for such designation, except in compliance with a permit issued by a permitting authority under this title. (Nothing in this subsection shall be construed to alter the applicable requirements of this Act that a permit be obtained before construction or modification.) The Administrator may, in the Administrator's discretion and consistent with the applicable provisions of this Act, promulgate regulations to exempt one or more source categories (in whole or in part) from the requirements of this subsection if the Administrator finds that compliance with such requirements is impracticable, infeasible, or unnecessarily burdensome on such categories, except that the Administrator may not exempt any major source from such requirements.

(b) Regulations.—The Administrator shall promulgate within 12 months after the date of the enactment of the Clean Air Act Amendments of 1990 regulations establishing the minimum elements of a permit program to be administered by any air pollution control agency. These elements shall include each of the following:

(1) Requirements for permit applications, including a standard application form and criteria for determining in a timely fashion the completeness of applications.

(2) Monitoring and reporting requirements.

(3) (A) A requirement under State or local law or interstate compact that the owner or operator of all sources subject to the requirement to obtain a permit under this title pay an annual fee, or the equivalent over some other period, sufficient to cover all reasonable (direct and indirect) costs required to develop and administer the permit program requirements of this title, including section 507 , including the reasonable costs of—

(i) reviewing and acting upon any application for such a permit,

(ii) if the owner or operator receives a permit for such source, whether before or after the date of the enactment of the Clean Air Act Amendments of 1990, implementing and enforcing the terms and conditions of any such permit (not including any court costs or other costs associated with any enforcement action),

(iii) emissions and ambient monitoring,

(iv) preparing generally applicable regulations, or guidance,

(v) modeling, analyses, and demonstrations, and

(vi) preparing inventories and tracking emissions.

(B) The total amount of fees collected by the permitting authority shall conform to the following requirements:

(i) The Administrator shall not approve a program as meeting the requirements of this paragraph unless the State demonstrates that, except as otherwise provided in subparagraphs (ii) through (v) of this subparagraph, the program will result in the collection, in the aggregate, from all sources subject to subparagraph (A), of an amount not less than $25 per ton of each regulated pollutant, or such other amount as the Administrator may determine adequately reflects the reasonable costs of the permit program.

(ii) As used in this subparagraph, the term 'regulated pollutant' shall mean (I) a volatile organic compound; (II) each pollutant regulated under section 111 or 112; and (III) each pollutant for which a national primary ambient air quality standard has been promulgated (except that carbon monoxide shall be excluded from this reference).

(iii) In determining the amount under clause (i), the permitting authority is not required to include any amount of regulated pollutant emitted by any source in excess of 4,000 tons per year of that regulated pollutant.

(iv) The requirements of clause (i) shall not apply if the permitting authority demonstrates that collecting an amount less than the amount specified under clause (i) will meet the requirements of subparagraph (A).

(v) The fee calculated under clause (i) shall be increased (consistent with the need to cover the reasonable costs authorized by subparagraph (A)) in each year beginning after the year of the enactment of the clean Air Act Amendments of 1990 by the percentage, if any, by which the Consumer Price Index for the most recent calendar year ending before the beginning of such year exceeds the Consumer Price Index for the calendar year 1989. For purposes of this clause—

(I) the Consumer Price Index for any calendar year is the average of the Consumer Price Index for all-urban consumers published by the Department of Labor, as of the close of the 12-month period ending on August 31 of each calendar year, and

(II) the revision of the Consumer Price Index which is most consistent with the Consumer Price Index for calendar year 1989 shall be used.

(C) (i) If the Administrator determines, under subsection (d), that the fee provisions of the operating permit program do not meet the requirements of this paragraph, or if the Administrator makes a determination, under subsection (i), that the permitting authority is not adequately administering or enforcing an approved fee program, the Administrator may, in addition to taking any other action authorized under this title, collect reasonable fees from the sources identified under subparagraph (A). Such fees shall be designed solely to cover the Administrator's costs of administering the provisions of the permit program promulgated by the Administrator.

(ii) Any source that fails to pay fees lawfully imposed by the Administrator under this subparagraph shall pay a penalty of 50 percent of the fee amount, plus interest on the fee amount computed in accordance with section 6621(a)(2) of the Internal Revenue Code of 1986 (relating to computation of interest on underpayment of Federal taxes).

(iii) Any fees, penalties, and interest, collected under this subparagraph shall be deposited in a special fund in the United States Treasury for licensing and other services, which thereafter shall be available for appropriation, to remain available until expended, subject to appropriation, to carry out the Agency's activities for which the fees were collected. Any fee required to be collected by a State, local, or interstate agency under this subsection shall be utilized solely to cover all reasonable (direct and indirect) costs required to support the permit program as set forth in subparagraph (A).

(4) Requirements for adequate personnel and funding to administer the program.

(5) A requirement that the permitting authority have adequate authority to:

(A) issue permits and assure compliance by all sources required to have a permit under this title with each applicable standard, regulation or requirement under this Act;

(B) issue permits for a fixed term, not to exceed 5 years;

(C) assure that upon issuance or renewal permits incorporate emission limitations and other requirements in an applicable implementation plan;

(D) terminate, modify, or revoke and reissue permits for cause;

(E) enforce permits, permit fee requirements, and the requirement to obtain a permit, including authority to recover civil penalties in a maximum amount of not less than $10,000 per day for each violation, and provide appropriate criminal penalties; and

(F) assure that no permit will be issued if the Administrator objects to its issuance in a timely manner under this title.

(6) Adequate, streamlined, and reasonable procedures for expeditiously determining when applications are complete, for processing such applications, for public notice, including offering an opportunity for public comment and a hearing, and for expeditious review of permit actions, including applications, renewals, or revisions, and including an opportunity for judicial review in State court of the final permit action by the applicant, any person who participated in the public comment process, and any other person who could obtain judicial review of that action under applicable law.

(7) To ensure against unreasonable delay by the permitting authority, adequate authority and procedures to provide that a failure of such permitting authority to act on a permit application or permit renewal application (in accordance with the time periods specified in section 503 or, as appropriate, title IV) shall be treated as a final permit action solely for purposes of obtaining judicial review in State court of an action brought by any person referred to in paragraph (6) to require that action be taken by the permitting authority on such application without additional delay.

(8) Authority, and reasonable procedures consistent with the need for expeditious action by the permitting authority on permit applications and related matters, to make available to the public any permit application, compliance plan, permit, and monitoring or compliance report under section 503(e), subject to the provisions of section 114(c) of this Act.

(9) A requirement that the permitting authority, in the case of permits with a term of 3 or more years for major sources, shall require revisions to the permit to incorporate applicable standards and regulations promulgated under this Act after the issuance of such permit. Such revisions shall occur as expeditiously as practicable and consistent with the procedures established under paragraph (6) but not later than 18 months after the promulgation of such standards and regulations. No such revision shall be required if the effective date of the standards or regulations is a date after the expiration of the permit term. Such permit revision shall be treated as a permit renewal if it complies with the requirements of this title regarding renewals.

(10) Provisions to allow changes within a permitted facility (or one operating pursuant to section 503(d)) without requiring a permit revision, if the changes are not modifications under any provision of title I and the changes do not exceed the emissions allowable under the permit (whether expressed therein as a rate of emissions or in terms of total emissions: *Provided,* That the facility provides the Administrator and the permitting authority with written notification in advance of the proposed changes which shall be a minimum of 7 days, unless the permitting authority provides in its regulations a different timeframe for emergencies.

(c) Single Permit.—A single permit may be issued for a facility with multiple sources.

(d) Submission and Approval.—

(1) Not later than 3 years after the date of the enactment of the Clean Air Act Amendments of 1990, the Governor of each State shall develop and submit to the Administrator a permit program under State or local law or under an interstate compact meeting the requirements of this title. In addition, the Governor shall submit a legal opinion from the attorney general (or the attorney for those State air pollution control agencies that have independent legal counsel), or from the chief legal officer of an interstate agency, that the laws of the State, locality, or the interstate compact provide adequate authority to carry out the program. Not later than 1 year after receiving a program, and after notice and opportunity for public comment, the Administrator shall approve or disapprove such program, in whole or in part. The Administrator may approve a program to the extent that the program meets the requirements of this Act, including the regulations issued under subsection (b). If the program is disapproved, in whole or in part, the Administrator shall notify the Governor of any revisions or modifications necessary to obtain approval. The Governor shall revise and resubmit the program for review under this section within 180 days after receiving notification.

(2) (A) If the Governor does not submit a program as required under paragraph (1) or if the Administrator disapproves a program submitted by the Governor under paragraph (1), in whole or in part, the Administrator may, prior to the expiration of the 18-month period referred to in subparagraph (B), in the Administrator's discretion, apply any of the sanctions specified in section 179(b) .

(B) If the Governor does not submit a program as required under paragraph (1), or if the Administrator disapproves any such program submitted by the Governor under paragraph (1), in whole or in part, 18 months after the date required for such submittal or the date of such disapproval, as the case may be, the Administrator shall apply sanctions under section 179(b) in the same manner and subject to the same deadlines and other conditions as are applicable in the case of a determination, disapproval, or finding under section 179(a).

(C) The sanctions under section 179(b)(2) shall not apply pursuant to this paragraph in any area unless the failure to submit or the disapproval referred to in subparagraph (A) or (B) relates to an air pollutant for which such area has been designated a nonattainment area (as defined in part D of title I).

(3) If a program meeting the requirements of this title has not been approved in whole for any State, the Administrator shall, 2 years after the date required for submission of such a program under paragraph (1), promulgate, administer, and enforce a program under this title for that State.

(e) Suspension.—The Administrator shall suspend the issuance of permits promptly upon publication of notice of approval of a permit program under this section, but may, in such notice, retain juris diction over permits that have been federally issued, but for which the administrative or judicial review process is not complete. The Administrator shall continue to administer and enforce federally issued permits under this title until they are replaced by a permit issued by a permitting program. Nothing in this subsection should be construed to limit the Administrator's ability to enforce permits issued by a State.

(f) Prohibition.—No partial permit program shall be approved unless, at a minimum, it applies, and ensures compliance with, this title and each of the following:

(1) All requirements established under title IV applicable to 'affected sources.'

(2) All requirements established under section 112 applicable to 'major sources,' 'area sources,' and 'new sources'.

(3) All requirements of title I (other than section 112) applicable to sources required to have a permit under this title. Approval of a partial program shall not relieve the State of its obligation to submit a complete program, nor from the application of any sanctions under this Act for failure to submit an approvable permit program.

(g) Interim Approval.—If a program (including a partial permit program) submitted under this title substantially meets the requirements of this title, but is not fully approvable, the Administrator may by rule grant the program interim approval. In the notice of final rulemaking, the Administrator shall specify the changes that must be made before the program can receive full approval. An interim approval under this subsection shall expire on a date set by the Administrator not later than 2 years after such approval, and may not be renewed. For the period of any such interim approval, the provisions of subsection (d)(2), and the obligation of the Administrator to promulgate a program under this title for the State pursuant to subsection (d)(3), shall be suspended. Such provisions and such obligation of the Administrator shall apply after the expiration of such interim approval.

(h) Effective Date.—The effective date of a permit program, or partial or interim program, approved under this title, shall be the effective date of approval by the Administrator. The effective date of a permit program, or partial permit program, promulgated by the Administrator shall be the date of promulgation.

(i) Administration and Enforcement.—

(1) Whenever the Administrator makes a determination that a permitting authority is not adequately administering and enforcing a program, or portion thereof, in accordance with the requirements of this title, the Administrator shall provide notice to the State and may, prior to the expiration of the 18-month period referred to in paragraph (2), in the Administrator's discretion, apply any of the sanctions specified in section 179(b).

(2) Whenever the Administrator makes a determination that a permitting authority is not adequately administering and enforcing a program, or portion thereof, in accordance with the requirements of this title, 18 months after the date of the notice under paragraph (1), the Administrator shall apply the sanctions under section 179(b) in the same manner and subject to the same deadline and other conditions as are applicable in the case of a determination, disapproval, or finding under section 179(a).

(3) The sanctions under section 179(b)(2) shall not apply pursuant to this subsection in any area unless the failure to adequately enforce and administer the program relates to an air pollutant for which such area has been designated a nonattainment area.

(4) Whenever the Administrator has made a finding under paragraph (1) with respect to any State, unless the State has corrected such deficiency within 18 months after the date of such finding, the Administrator shall, 2 years after the date of such finding, promulgate, administer, and enforce a program under this title for that State. Nothing in this paragraph shall be construed to affect the validity of a program which has been approved under this title or the authority of any permitting authority acting under such program until such time as such program is promulgated by the Administrator under this paragraph.

§7661b. Permit Applications [Sec. 503]

(a) Applicable Date.—Any source specified in section 502(a) shall become subject to a permit program, and required to have a permit, on the later of the following dates—

(1) the effective date of a permit program or partial or interim permit program applicable to the source; or

(2) the date such source becomes subject to section 502(a) .

(b) Compliance Plan.—

(1) The regulations required by section 502(b) shall include a requirement that the applicant submit with the permit application a compliance plan describing how the source will comply with all applicable requirements under this Act. The compliance plan shall include a schedule of compliance, and a schedule under which the permittee will submit progress reports to the permitting authority no less frequently than every 6 months.

(2) The regulations shall further require the permittee to periodically (but no less frequently than annually) certify that the facility is in compliance with any applicable requirements of the permit, and to promptly report any deviations from permit requirements to the permitting authority.

(c) Deadline.—Any person required to have a permit shall, not later than 12 months after the date on which the source becomes subject to a permit program approved or promulgated under this title, or such earlier date as the permitting authority may establish, submit to the permitting authority a compliance plan and an application for a permit signed by a responsible official, who shall certify the accuracy of the information submitted. The permitting authority shall approve or disapprove a completed application (consistent with the procedures established under this title for consideration of such applications), and shall issue or deny the permit, within 18 months after the date of receipt thereof, except that the permitting authority shall establish a phased schedule for acting on permit applications submitted within the first full year after the effective date of a permit program (or a partial or interim program). Any such schedule shall assure that at least one-third of such permits will be acted on by such authority annually over a period of not to exceed 3 years after such effective date. Such authority shall establish reasonable procedures to prioritize such approval or disapproval actions in the case of applications for construction or modification under the applicable requirements of this Act.

(d) Timely and Complete Applications.—Except for sources required to have a permit before construction or modification under the applicable requirements of this Act, if an applicant has submitted a timely and complete application for a permit required by this title (including renewals), but final action has not been taken on such application, the source's failure to have a permit shall not be a violation of this Act, unless the delay in final action was due to the failure of the applicant timely to submit information required or requested to process the application. No source required to have a permit under this title shall be in violation of section 502(a) before the date on which the source is required to submit an application under subsection (c).

(e) Copies; Availability.—A copy of each permit application, compliance plan (including the schedule of compliance), emissions or compliance monitoring report, certification, and each permit issued under this title, shall be available to the public. If an applicant or permittee is required to submit information entitled to protection from disclosure under section 114(c) of this Act, the applicant or permittee may submit such information separately. The requirements of section 114(c) shall apply to such information. The contents of a permit shall not be entitled to protection under section 114(c) .

§7661c. Permit Requirements and Conditions [Sec. 504]

(a) Conditions.—Each permit issued under this title shall include enforceable emission limitations and standards, a schedule of compliance, a requirement that the permittee submit to the permitting authority, no less often than every 6 months, the results of any required monitoring, and such other conditions as are necessary to assure compliance with applicable requirements of this Act, including the requirements of the applicable implementation plan.

(b) Monitoring and Analysis.—The Administrator may by rule prescribe procedure and methods for determining compliance and for monitoring and analysis of pollutants regulated under this Act, but continuous emissions monitoring need not be required if alternative methods are available that provide sufficiently reliable and timely information for determining compliance. Nothing in this subsection shall be construed to affect any continuous emissions monitoring requirement of title IV, or where required elsewhere in this Act.

(c) Inspection, Entry, Monitoring, Certification, and Reporting.—Each permit issued under this title shall set forth inspection, entry, monitoring, compliance certification, and reporting requirements to assure compliance with the permit terms and conditions. Such monitoring and reporting requirements shall conform to any applicable regulation under subsection (b). Any report required to be submitted by a permit issued to a corporation under this title shall be signed by a responsible corporate official, who shall certify its accuracy.

(d) General Permits.—The permitting authority may, after notice and opportunity for public hearing, issue a general permit covering numerous similar sources. Any general permit shall comply with all requirements applicable to permits under this title. No source covered by a general permit shall thereby be relieved from the obligation to file an application under section 503 .

(e) Temporary Sources.—The permitting authority may issue a single permit authorizing emissions from similar operations at multiple temporary locations. No such permit shall be issued unless it includes conditions that will assure compliance with all the requirements of this Act at all authorized locations, including, but not limited to, ambient standards and compliance with any applicable increment or visibility requirements under part C of title I. Any such permit shall in addition require the owner or operator to notify the permitting authority in advance of each change in location. The permitting authority may require a separate permit fee for operations at each location.

(f) Permit Shield.—Compliance with a permit issued in accordance with this title shall be deemed compliance with section 502 . Except as otherwise provided by the Administrator by rule, the permit may also provide that compliance with the permit shall be deemed compliance with other applicable provisions of this Act that relate to the permittee if—

(1) the permit includes the applicable requirements of such provisions, or

(2) the permitting authority in acting on the permit application makes a determination relating to the permittee that such other provisions (which shall be referred to in such determination) are not applicable and the permit includes the determination or a concise summary thereof. Nothing in the preceding sentence shall alter or affect the provisions of section 303 , including the authority of the Administrator under that section.

§7661d. Notification to Administrator and Contiguous States [Sec. 505]

(a) Transmission and Notice.—

(1) Each permitting authority—

(A) shall transmit to the Administrator a copy of each permit application (and any application for a permit modification or renewal) or such portion thereof, including any compliance plan, as the Administrator, may require to effectively review the application and otherwise to carry out the Administrator's responsibilities under this Act, and

(B) shall provide to the Administrator a copy of each permit proposed to be issued and issued as a final permit.

(2) The permitting authority shall notify all States—

(A) whose air quality may be affected and that are contiguous to the State in which the emission originates, or

(B) that are within 50 miles of the source, of each permit application or proposed permit forwarded to the Administrator under this section, and shall provide an opportunity for such States to submit written recommendations respecting the issuance of the permit and its terms and conditions. If any part of those recommendations are not accepted by the permitting authority, such authority shall notify the State submitting the recommendations and the Administrator in writing of its failure to accept those recommendations and the reasons therefor.

(b) Objection by EPA.—

(1) If any permit contains provisions that are determined by the Administrator as not in compliance with the applicable requirements of this Act, including the requirements of an applicable implementation plan, the Administrator shall, in accordance with this subsection,

object to its issuance. The permitting authority shall respond in writing if the Administrator (A) within 45 days after receiving a copy of the proposed permit under subsection (a)(1), or (B) within 45 days after receiving notification under subsection (a)(2), objects in writing to its issuance as not in compliance with such requirements. With the objection, the Administrator shall provide a statement of the reasons for the objection. A copy of the objection and statement shall be provided to the applicant.

(2) If the Administrator does not object in writing to the issuance of a permit pursuant to paragraph (1), any person may petition the Administrator within 60 days after the expiration of the 45–day review period specified in paragraph (1) to take such action. A copy of such petition shall be provided to the permitting authority and the applicant by the petitioner. The petition shall be based only on objections to the permit that were raised with reasonable specificity during the public comment period provided by the permitting agency (unless the petitioner demonstrates in the petition to the Administrator that it was impracticable to raise such objections within such period or unless the grounds for such objection arose after such period). The petition shall identify all such objections. If the permit has been issued by the permitting agency, such petition shall not postpone the effectiveness of the permit. The Administrator shall grant or deny such petition within 60 days after the petition is filed. The Administrator shall issue an objection within such period if the petitioner demonstrates to the Administrator that the permit is not in compliance with the requirements of this Act, including the requirements of the applicable implementation plan. Any denial of such petition shall be subject to judicial review under section 307. The Administrator shall include in regulations under this title provisions to implement this paragraph. The Administrator may not delegate the requirements of this paragraph.

(3) Upon receipt of an objection by the Administrator under this subsection, the permitting authority may not issue the permit unless it is revised and issued in accordance with subsection (c). If the permitting authority has issued a permit prior to receipt of an objection by the Administrator under paragraph (2) of this subsection, the Administrator shall modify, terminate, or revoke such permit and the permitting authority may thereafter only issue a revised permit in accordance with subsection (c).

(c) Issuance or Denial.—If the permitting authority fails, within 90 days after the date of an objection under subsection (b), to submit a permit revised to meet the objection, the Administrator shall issue or deny the permit in accordance with the requirements of this title. No objection shall be subject to judicial review until the Administrator takes final action to issue or deny a permit under this subsection.

(d) Waiver of Notification Requirements.—

(1) The Administrator may waive the requirements of subsections (a) and (b) at the time of approval of a permit program under this title for any category (including any class, type, or size within such category) of sources covered by the program other than major sources.

(2) The Administrator may, by regulation, establish categories of sources (including any class, type, or size within such category) to which the requirements of subsections (a) and (b) shall not apply. The preceding sentence shall not apply to major sources.

(3) The Administrator may exclude from any waiver under this subsection notification under subsection (a)(2). Any waiver granted under this subsection may be revoked or modified by the Administrator by rule.

(e) Refusal of Permitting Authority to Terminate, Modify, or Revoke and Reissue.—If the Administrator finds that cause exists to terminate, modify, or revoke and reissue a permit under this title, the Administrator shall notify the permitting authority and the source of the Administrator's finding. The permitting authority shall, within 90 days after receipt of such notification, forward to the Administrator under this section a proposed determination of termination, modification, or revocation and reissuance, as appropriate. The Administrator may extend such 90 day period for an additional 90 days if the Administrator finds that a new or revised permit application is necessary, or that the permitting authority must require the permittee to submit additional information. The Administrator may review such proposed determination under the provisions of subsections (a) and (b). If the permitting authority fails to submit the required proposed determination, or if the Administrator objects and the permitting authority fails to resolve the objection within 90 days, the Administrator may, after notice and in accordance with fair and reasonable procedures, terminate, modify, or revoke and reissue the permit.

§7661e. Other Authorities [Sec. 506]

(a) In General.—Nothing in this title shall prevent a State, or interstate permitting authority, from establishing additional permitting requirements not inconsistent with this Act.

(b) Permits Implementing Acid Rain Provisions.—The provisions of this title, including provisions regarding schedules for submission and approval or disapproval of permit applications, shall apply to permits implementing the requirements of title IV except as modified by that title.

§7661f. Small Business Stationary Source Technical and Environmental Compliance Assistance Program [Sec. 507]

(a) Plan Revisions.—Consistent with sections 110 and 112 , each State shall, after reasonable notice and public hearings, adopt and submit to the Administrator as part of the State implementation plan for such State or as a revision to such State implementation plan under section 110 , plans for establishing a small business stationary source technical and environmental compliance assistance program. Such submission shall be made within 24 months after the date of the enactment of the Clean Air Act Amendments of 1990. The Administrator shall approve such program if it includes each of the following:

(1) Adequate mechanisms for developing, collecting, and coordinating information concerning compliance methods and technologies for small business stationary sources, and programs to encourage lawful cooperation among such sources and other persons to further compliance with this Act.

(2) Adequate mechanisms for assisting small business stationary sources with pollution prevention and accidental release detection and prevention, including providing information concerning alternative technologies, process changes, products, and methods of operation that help reduce air pollution.

(3) A designated State office within the relevant State agency to serve as ombudsman for small business stationary sources in connection with the implementation of this Act.

(4) A compliance assistance program for small business stationary sources which assists small business stationary sources in determining applicable requirements and in receiving permits under this Act in a timely and efficient manner.

(5) Adequate mechanisms to assure that small business stationary sources receive notice of their rights under this Act in such manner and form as to assure reasonably adequate time for such sources to evaluate compliance methods and any relevant or applicable proposed or final regulation or standard issued under this Act.

(6) Adequate mechanisms for informing small business stationary sources of their obligations under this Act, including mechanisms for referring such sources to qualified auditors or, at the option of the State, for providing audits of the operations of such sources to determine compliance with this Act.

(7) Procedures for consideration of requests from a small business stationary source for modification of—

(A) any work practice or technological method of compliance, or

(B) the schedule of milestones for implementing such work practice or method of compliance preceding any applicable compliance date, based on the technological and financial capability of any such small business stationary source. No such modification may be granted unless it is in compliance with the applicable requirements of this Act, including the requirements of the applicable implementation plan. Where such applicable requirements are set forth in Federal regulations, only modifications authorized in such regulations may be allowed.

(b) Program.—The Administrator shall establish within 9 months after the date of the enactment of the Clean Air Act Amendments of 1990 a small business stationary source technical and environmental compliance assistance program. Such program shall—

(1) assist the States in the development of the program required under subsection (a) (relating to assistance for small business stationary sources);

(2) issue guidance for the use of the States in the implementation of these programs that includes alternatve control technologies and pollution prevention methods applicable to small business stationary sources; and

(3) provide for implementation of the program provisions required under subsection (a)(4) in any State that fails to isubmit such a program under that subsection.

(c) Eligibility.—

(1) Except as provided in paragraphs (2) and (3), for purposes of this section, the term 'small

business stationary source" means a stationary source that—

(A) is owned or operated by a person that employs 100 or fewer individuals;

(B) is a small business concern as defined in the Small Business Act;

(C) is not a major stationary source;

(D) does not emit 50 tons or more per year of any regulated pollutant; and

(E) emits less than 75 tons per year of all regulated pollutants.

(2) Upon petition by a source, the State may, after notice and opportunity for public comment, include as a small business stationary source for purposes of this section any stationary source which does not meet the criteria of subparagraphs (C), (D), or (E) of paragraph (1) but which does not emit more than 100 tons per year of all regulated pollutants.

(3) (A) The Administrator, in consultation with the Administrator of the Small Business Administration and after providing notice and opportunity for public comment, may exclude from the small business stationary source definition under this section any category or subcategory of sources that the Administrator determines to have sufficient technical and financial capabilities to meet the requirements of this Act without the application of this subsection.

(B) The State, in consultation with the Administrator and the Administrator of the Small Business Administration and after providing notice and opportunity for public hearing, may exclude from the small business stationary source definition under this section any category or subcategory of sources that the State determines to have sufficient technical and financial capabilities to meet the requirements of this Act without the application of this subsection.

(d) Monitoring.—The Administrator shall direct the Agency's Office of Small and Disadvantaged Business Utilization through the Small Business Ombudsman (hereinafter in this section referred to as the "Ombudsman") to monitor the small business stationary source technical and environmental compliance assistance program under this section. In carrying out such monitoring activities, the Ombudsman shall—

(1) render advisory opinions on the overall effectiveness of the Small Business Stationary Source Technical and Environmental Compliance Assistance Program, difficulties encountered, and degree and severity of enforcement;

(2) make periodic reports to the Congress on the compliance of the Small Business Stationary Source Technical and Environmental Compliance Assistance Program with the requirements of the Paperwork Reduction Act, the Regulatory Flexibility Act, and the Equal Access to Justice Act;

(3) review information to be issued by the Small Business Stationary Source Technical and Environmental Compliance Assistance Program for small business stationary sources to ensure that the information is understandable by the layperson; and

(4) have the Small Business Stationary Source Technical and Environmental Compliance Assistance Program serve as the secretariat for the development and dissemination of such reports and advisory opinions.

(e) Compliance Advisory Panel.—

(1) There shall be created a Compliance Advisory Panel (hereinafter referred to as the "Panel") on the State level of not less than 7 individuals. This Panel shall—

(A) render advisory opinions concerning the effectiveness of the small business stationary source technical and environmental compliance assistance program, difficulties encountered, and degree and severity of enforcement;

(B) make periodic reports to the Administrator concerning the compliance of the State Small Business Stationary Source Technical and Environmental Compliance Assistance Program with the requirements of the Paperwork Reduction Act, the Regulatory Flexibility Act, and the Equal Access to Justice Act;

(C) review information for small business stationary sources to assure such information is understandable by the layperson; and

(D) have the Small Business Stationary Source Technical and Environmental Compliance Assistance Program serve as the secretariat for the development and dissemination of such reports and advisory opinions.

(2) The Panel shall consist of—

(A) 2 members, who are not owners, or representatives of owners, of small business stationary sources, selected by the Governor to represent the general public;

(B) 2 members selected by the State legislature who are owners, or who represent owners, of small business stationary sources (1 member each by the majority and minority leadership of the lower house, or in the case of a unicameral State legislature, 2 members each shall be selected by the majority leadership and the minority leadership, respectively, of such legislature, and subparagraph (C) shall not apply);

(C) 2 members selected by the State legislature who are owners, or who represent owners, of small business stationary sources (1 member each by the majority and minority leadership of the upper house, or the equivalent State entity); and

(D) 1 member selected by the head of the department or agency of the State responsible for air pollution permit programs to represent that agency.

(f) Fees.—The State (or the Administrator) may reduce any fee required under this Act to take into account the financial resources of small business stationary sources.

(g) Continuous Emission Monitors.—In developing regulations and CTGs under this Act that contain continuous emission monitoring requirements, the Administrator, consistent with the requirements of this Act, before applying such requirements to small business stationary sources, shall consider the necessity and appropriateness of such requirements for such sources. Nothing in this subsection shall affect the applicability of title IV provisions relating to continuous emissions monitoring.

(h) Control Technique Guidelines.—The Administrator shall consider, consistent with the requirements of this Act, the size, type, and technical capabilities of small business stationary sources (and sources which are eligible under subsection (c)(2) to be treated as small business stationary sources) in developing CTGs applicable to such sources under this Act.

TITLE VI—STRATOSPHERIC OZONE PROTECTION

[Title VI added by PL 101–549]

§7671. Definitions [Sec. 601]

As used in this title—

(1) Appliance.—The term 'appliance' means any device which contains and uses a class I or class II substance as a refrigerant and which is used for household or commercial purposes, including any air conditioner, refrigerator, chiller, or freezer.

(2) Baseline year.—The term 'baseline year' means—

(A) the calendar year 1986, in the case of any class I substance listed in group I or II under section 602(a) ,

(B) the calendar year 1989, in the case of any class I substance listed in Group III, IV, or V under section 602(a) , and

(C) a representative calendar year selected by the Administrator, in the case of—

(i) any substance added to the list of class I substances after the publication of the initial list under section 602(a) , and

(ii) any class II substance.

(3) Class I Substance.—The term 'class I substance' means each of the substances listed as provided in section 602(a) .

(4) Class II Substance.—The term 'class II substance' means each of the substances listed as provided in section 602(b) .

(5) Commissioner.—The term 'Commissioner' means the Commissioner of the Food and Drug Administration.

(6) Consumption.—The term 'consumption' means, with respect to any substance, the amount of that substance produced in the United States, plus the amount imported, minus the amount exported to Parties to the Montreal Protcool. Such term shall be construed in a manner consistent with the Montreal Protocol.

(7) Import.—The term 'import' means to land on, bring into, or introduce into, or attempt to land on, bring into, or introduce into, any place subject to the jurisdiction of the United States, whether or not such landing, bringing, or introduction constitutes an importation within the meaning of the customs laws of the United States.

(8) Medical Device.—The term 'medical device' means any device (as defined in the Federal Food, Drug, and Cosmetic Act (21 U.S.C. 321)), diagnostic product, drug (as defined in the Federal Food, Drug, and Cosmetic Act), and drug delivery system—

(A) if such device, product, drug, or drug delivery system utilizes a class I or class II substance for which no safe and effective alternative has been developed, and where necessary, approved by the Commissioner; and

(B) if such device, product, drug, or drug delivery system, has, after notice and opportunity for public comment, been approved and determined to be essential by the Commissioner in consultation with the Administrator.

(9) Montreal Protocol.—The terms 'Montreal Protocol' and 'the Protocol' mean the Montreal Protocol on Substances that Deplete the Ozone Layer, a protocol to the Vienna Convention for the Protection of the Ozone Layer, including adjustments adopted by Parties thereto and amendments that have entered into force.

(10) Ozone-Depletion Potential.—The term 'ozone-depletion potential' means a factor established by the Administrator to reflect the ozone-depletion potential of a substance, on a mass per kilogram basis, as compared to chlorofluorocarbon-11 (CFC-11). Such factor shall be based upon the substance's atmospheric lifetime, the molecular weight of bromine and chlorine, and the substance's ability to be photolytically disassociated, and upon other factors determined to be an accurate measure of relative ozone-depletion potential.

(11) Produce, Produced, and Production.—The terms 'produce', 'produced', and 'production', refer to the manufacture of a substance from any raw material or feedstock chemical, but such terms do not include—

(A) the manufacture of a substance that is used and entirely consumed (except for trace quantities) in the manufacture of other chemicals, or

(B) the reuse or recycling of a substance.

§7671a. Listing of Class I and Class II Substances [Sec. 602]

(a) List of Class I Substances.—Within 60 days after enactment of the Clean Air Act Amendments of 1990, the Administrator shall publish an initial list of class I substances, which list shall contain the following substances:

Group I

chlorofluorocarbon-11 (CFC-11)

chlorofluorocarbon-12 (CFC-12)

chlorofluorocarbon-113 (CFC-113)
chlorofluorocarbon-114 (CFC-114)
chlorofluorocarbon-115 (CFC-115)

Group II

halon-1211
halon-1301
halon-2402

Group III

chlorofluorocarbon-13 (CFC-13)
chlorofluorocarbon-111 (CFC-111)
chlorofluorocarbon-112 (CFC-112)
chlorofluorocarbon-211 (CFC-211)
chlorofluorocarbon-212 (CFC-212)
chlorofluorocarbon-213 (CFC-213)
chlorofluorocarbon-214 (CFC-214)
chlorofluorocarbon-215 (CFC-215)
chlorofluorocarbon-216 (CFC-216)
chlorofluorocarbon-217 (CFC-217)

Group IV

carbon tetrachloride

Group V

methyl chloroform

The initial list under this subsection shall also include the isomers of the substances listed above, other than 1,1,2- trichloroethane (an isomer of methyl chloroform). Pursuant to subsection (c), the Administrator shall add to the list of class I substances any other substance that the Administrator finds causes or contributes significantly to harmful effects on the stratospheric ozone layer. The Administrator shall, pursuant to subsection (c), add to such list all substances that the Administrator determines have an ozone depletion potential of 0.2 or greater.

(b) List of Class II Substances.—Simultaneously with publication of the initial list of class I substances, the Administrator shall publish an initial list of class II substances, which shall contain the following substances:

hydrochlorofluorocarbon-21 (HCFC-21)
hydrochlorofluorocarbon-22 (HCFC-22)
hydrochlorofluorocarbon-31 (HCFC-31)
hydrochlorofluorocarbon-121 (HCFC- 121)
hydrochlorofluorocarbon-122 (HCFC- 122)
hydrochlorofluorocarbon-123 (HCFC- 123)
hydrochlorofluorocarbon-124 (HCFC- 124)
hydrochlorofluorocarbon-131 (HCFC- 131)
hydrochlorofluorocarbon-132 (HCFC- 132)
hydrochlorofluorocarbon-133 (HCFC- 133)
hydrochlorofluorocarbon-141 (HCFC- 141)
hydrochlorofluorocarbon-142 (HCFC- 142)
hydrochlorofluorocarbon-221 (HCFC- 221)
hydrochlorofluorocarbon-222 (HCFC- 222)
hydrochlorofluorocarbon-223 (HCFC- 223)
hydrochlorofluorocarbon-224 (HCFC- 224)
hydrochlorofluorocarbon-225 (HCFC- 225)
hydrochlorofluorocarbon-226 (HCFC- 226)
hydrochlorofluorocarbon-231 (HCFC- 231)
hydrochlorofluorocarbon-232 (HCFC- 232)
hydrochlorofluorocarbon-233 (HCFC- 233)
hydrochlorofluorocarbon-234 (HCFC- 234)
hydrochlorofluorocarbon-235 (HCFC- 235)
hydrochlorofluorocarbon-241 (HCFC- 241)
hydrochlorofluorocarbon-242 (HCFC- 242)
hydrochlorofluorocarbon-243 (HCFC- 243)
hydrochlorofluorocarbon-244 (HCFC- 244)
hydrochlorofluorocarbon-251 (HCFC- 251)
hydrochlorofluorocarbon-252 (HCFC- 252)
hydrochlorofluorocarbon-253 (HCFC- 253)
hydrochlorofluorocarbon-261 (HCFC- 261)
hydrochlorofluorocarbon-262 (HCFC- 262)
hydrochlorofluorocarbon-271 (HCFC- 271)

The initial list under this subsection shall also include the isomers of the substances listed above. Pursuant to subsection (c), the Administrator shall add to the list of class II substances any other substance that the Administrator finds is known or may reasonably be anticipated to cause or contribute to harmful effects on the stratospheric ozone layer.

(c) Additions to the Lists.—

(1) The Administrator may add, by rule, in accordance with the criteria set forth in subsection (a) or (b), as the case may be, any substance to the list of class I or class II substances under subsection (a) or (b). For purposes of exchanges under section 507 , whenever a substance is added to the list of class I substances the Administrator shall, to the extent consistent with Montreal Protocol, assign such substance to existing Group I, II, III, IV, or V or place such substance in a new Group.

(2) Periodically, but not less frequently than every 3 years after the enactment of the Clean Air Act Amendments of 1990, the Administrator shall list, by rule, as additional class I or class II substances those substances which the

Administrator finds meet the criteria of subsection (a) or (b), as the case may be.

(3) At any time, any person may petition the Administrator to add a substance to the list of class I or class II substances. Pursuant to the criteria set forth in subsection (a) or (b) as the case may be, within 180 days after receiving such a petition, the Administrator shall either propose to add the substance to such list or publish an explanation of the petition denial. In any case where the Administrator proposes to add a substance to such list, the Administrator shall add, by rule, (or make a final determination not to add) such substance to such list within 1 year after receiving such petition. Any petition under this paragraph shall include a showing by the petitioner that there are data on the substance adequate to support the petition. If the Administrator determines that information on the substance is not sufficient to make a determination under this paragraph, the Administrator shall use any authority available to the Administrator, under any law administered by the Administrator, to acquire such information.

(4) Only a class II substance which is added to the list of class I substances may be removed from the list of class II substances. No substance referred to in subsection (a), including methyl chloroform, may be removed from the list of class I substances.

(d) New Listed Substances.—In the case of any substance added to the list of class I or class II substances after publication of the initial list of such substances under this section, the Administrator may extend any schedule or compliance deadline contained in section 604 or 605 to a later date than specified in such sections if such schedule or deadline is unattainable, considering when such substance is added to the list. No extension under this subsection may extend the date for termination of production of any class I substance to date more than 7 years after January 1 of the year after the year in which the substance is added to the list of class I substances. No extension under his subsection may extend the date for termination of production of any class II substance to a date more than 10 years after January 1 of the year after the year in which the substance is added to the list of class II substances.

(e) Ozone-Depletion and Global Warming Potential.—Simultaneously with publication of the lists under this section and simultaneously with any addition to either of such lists, the Administrator shall assign to each listed substance a numerical value representing the substance's ozone-depletion potential. In addition, the Administrator shall publish the chlorine and bromine loading potential and the atmospheric lifetime lifetime of each listed substance. One year after enactment of the Clean Air Act Amendments of 1990 (one year after the addition of a substance to either of such lists in the case of a substance added after the publication of the initial lists of such substances), and after notice and opportunity for public comment, the Administrator shall publish the global warming potential of each listed substance. The preceding sentence shall not be construed to be the basis of any additional regulation under this Act. In the case of the substances referred to in table 1, the ozone-depletion potential shall be as specified in table 1, unless the Administrator adjusts the substance's ozone-depletion potential based on criteria referred to in section 601(10):

Table 1

Substance	Ozone-depletion potential
chlorofluorocarbon–11 (CFC–11)	1.0
chlorofluorocarbon–12 (CFC–12)	1.0
chlorofluorocarbon–13 (CFC–13)	1.0
chlorofluorocarbon–111 (CFC–111)	1.0
chlorofluorocarbon–112 (CFC–112)	1.0
chlorofluorocarbon–113 (CFC–113)	0.8
chlorofluorocarbon–114 (CFC–114)	1.0
chlorofluorocarbon–115 (CFC–115)	0.6
chlorofluorocarbon–211 (CFC–211)	1.0
chlorofluorocarbon–212 (CFC–212)	1.0
chlorofluorocarbon–213 (CFC–213)	1.0
chlorofluorocarbon–214 (CFC–214)	1.0
chlorofluorocarbon–215 (CFC–215)	1.0
chlorofluorocarbon–216 (CFC–216)	1.0

Substance	Ozone-depletion potential
chlorofluorocarbon–217 (CFC–217)	1.0
halon–1211	3.0
halon–1301	10.0
halon–2402	6.0
carbon tetrachloride	1.1
methyl chloroform	0.1
hydrochlorofluorocarbon–22 (HCFC–22)	0.05
hydrochlorofluorocarbon–123 (HCFC–123)	0.02
hydrochlorofluorocarbon–124 (HCFC–124)	0.02
hydrochlorofluorocarbon–141(b) (HCFC–141(b))	0.1
hydrochlorofluorocarbon–142(b) (HCFC–142(b))	0.06

Where the ozone-depletion potential of a substance is specified in the Montreal Protocol, the ozone-depletion potential specified for that substance under this section shall be consistent with the Montreal Protocol.

§7671b. Monitoring and Reporting Requirements [Sec. 603]

(a) Regulations.—Within 270 days after the enactment of the Clean Air Act Amendments of 1990, the Administrator shall amend the regulations of the Administrator in effect on such date regarding monitoring and reporting of class I and class II substances. Such amendments shall conform to the requirements of this section. The amended regulations shall include requirements with respect to the time and manner of monitoring and reporting as required under this section.

(b) Production, Import, and Export Level Reports. —On a quarterly basis, or such other basis (not less than annually) as determined by the Administrator, each person who produced, imported, or exported a class I or class II substance shall file a report with the Administrator setting forth the amount of the substance that such person produced, imported, and exported during the preceding reporting period. Each such report shall be signed and signed and attested by a responsible officer. No such report shall be required from a person after April 1 of the calendar year after such person permanently ceases production, importation, and exportation of the substance and so notifies the Administrator in writing.

(c) Baseline Reports for Class I Substances.—Unless such information has previously been reported to the. Administrator, on the date on which the first report under subsection (b) is required to be filed, each person who produced, import ed, or exported a class I substance (other than a substance added to the list of class I substances alter the publication of the initial list of such substances under this section) shall file a report with the Administrator setting forth the amount of such substance that such person produced, imported, and exported during the baseline year. In the case of a substance added to the list of class I substances alter publication of the initial list of such substances under this section, the regulations shall require that each person who produced, imported, or exported such substance shall file a report with the Administrator within 180 days alter the date on which such substance is added 'to the list, setting forth the amount of the substance that such person produced, 'imported, and exported in the baseline year.

(d) Monitoring and Reports to Congress.—

(1) The Administrator shall monitor and, not less often than every 3 years following enactment of the Clean Air Act Amendments of 1990, submit a report to Congress on the production, use and consumption of class I and class II substances. Such report shall include data on domestic production, use and consumption, and an estimate of worldwide production, use and consumption of such substances. Not less frequently than every 6 years the Administrator shall report to Congress on the environmental and economic effects of any stratospheric ozone depletion.

(2) The Administrators of the National Aeronautics and Space Administration and the National manic and Atmospheric Administration shall monitor, and not less often than every 3 years following enactment of the Clean Air Act Amendments of 1990, submit a report to Congress on the current average tropospheric concentration of chlorine and bromine and on the level of straps spheric ozone depletion. Such reports shall include updated projections of—

(A) peak chlorine loading

(B) the rate at which the atmospheric abundance of chlorine to decrease alter the year 2000; and

(C) the date by which the atmospheric abundance of chlorine projected to return to a level of two parts per billion.

Such updated projections shall be made on the basis of current international and domestic controls on substances covered by this title as well as on the basis of such controls supplemented by a year 2000 global phase out of all halocarbon emissions (the base case). It is the purpose of the Congress through the provisions of this section to monitor closely the production and consumption of class II substances to assure that the production and consumption of such substances will not:

(i) increase significantly the peak chlorine loading that is projected to occur under the base case established for purposes of this section;

(ii) reduce significantly the rate at which the atmospheric abundance of chlorine is projected to decrease under the base case; or

(iii) delay the date by which the average atmospheric concentration of chlorine is projected under the base case to return to a level of two parts per billion.

(e) Technology Status Report in 2015.—The Administrator shall review, on a periodic basis, the progress being made in the development of alternative systems or products necessary to manufacture and operate appliances without class II substances. If the Administrator finds, after notice and opportunity for public comment, that as a result of technological development problems, the development of such alternative systems or products will not occur within the time necessary to provide for the manufacture of such equipment without such substances prior to the applicable deadlines under section 605 , the Administrator shall, not later than January 1, 2015, so inform the Congress.

(f) Emergency Report.—If, in consultation with the Administrators of the National Aeronautics and Space Administration and the National Oceanic and Atmospheric Administration, and after notice and opportunity for public comment, the Administrator determines that the global production, consumption, and use of class II substances are projected to contribute to an atmospheric chlorine loading in excess of the base case projections by more than 5/10ths parts per billion, the Administrator shall so inform the Congress immediately. The determination referred to in the preceding sentence shall be based on the monitoring under subsection (d) and updated not less often than every 3 years.

§7671c. Phase-Out of Production and Consumption of Class I Substances [Sec. 604]

(a) Production Phase-Out.—Effective on January 1 of each year specified in Table 2, it shall be unlawful for any person to produce any class I substance in an annual quantity greater than the relevant percentage specified in Table 2. The percentages in Table 2 refer to a maximum allowable production as a percentage of the quantity of the substance produced by the person concerned in the baseline year.

Table 2

Date	Carbon tetrachloride	Methyl chloroform	Other class I substances
1991	100%	100%	85%
1992	90%	100%	80%
1993	80%	90%	75%
1994	70%	85%	65%
1995	15%	70%	50%
1996	15%	50%	40%
1997	15%	50%	15%
1998	15%	50%	15%
1999	15%	50%	15%
2000		20%	
2001		20%	

(b) Termination of Production of Class I Substances.—Effective January 1, 2000 (January 1, 2002 in the case of methyl chloroform), it shall be unlawful for any person to produce any amount of a class I substance.

(c) Regulations Regarding Production and Consumption of Class I Substances.—The Administrator shall promulgate regulations within 10 months after the enactment of the Clean Air Act Amendments of 1990 phasing out the production of class I substances in accordance with this section and other applicable provisions of this title. The Administrator shall also promulgate regulations to insure that the consumption of class I substances in the United States is phased out and terminated in accordance with the same schedule (subject to the same exceptions and other provisions) as is applicable to the phase-out and termination of production of class I substances under this title.

(d) Exceptions for Essential Uses of Methyl Chloroform, Medical Devices, and Aviation Safety.—

(1) Essential uses of methyl chloroform.—Notwithstanding the termination of production required by subsection (b), during the period beginning on January 1, 2002, and ending on January 1, 2005, the Administrator, after notice

and opportunity for public comment, may, to the extent such action is consistent with the Montreal Protocol, authorize the production of limited quantities of methyl chloroform solely for use in essential applications (such as nondestructive testing for metal fatigue and corrosion of existing airplane engines and airplane parts susceptible to metal fatigue) for which no safe and effective substitute is available. Notwithstanding this paragraph, the authority to produce methyl chloroform for use in medical devices shall be provided in accordance with paragraph (2).

(2) Medical devices.—Notwithstanding the termination of production required by subsection (b), the Administrator, after notice and opportunity for public comment, shall, to the extent such action is consistent with the Montreal Protocol, authorize the production of limited quantities of class I substances solely for use in medical devices if such authorization is determined by the Commissioner, in consultation with the Administrator, to be necessary for use in medical devices.

(3) Aviation safety.—

(A) Notwithstanding the termination of production required by subsection (b), the Administrator, after notice and opportunity for public comment, may, to the extent such action is consistent with the Montreal Protocol, authorize the production of limited quantities of halon–1211 (bromochlorodifluoromethane), halon–1301 (bromotrifluoromethane), and halon–2402 (dibromotetrafluoroethane) solely for purposes of aviation safety if the Administrator of the Federal Aviation Administration, in consultation with the Administrator, determines that no safe and effective substitute has been developed and that such authorization is necessary for aviation safety purposes.

(B) The Administrator of the Federal Aviation Administration shall, in consultation with the Administrator, examine whether safe and effective substitutes for methyl chloroform or alternative techniques will be available for nondestructive testing for metal fatigue and corrosion of existing airplane engines and airplane parts susceptible to metal fatigue and whether an exception for such uses of methyl chloroform under this paragraph will be necessary for purposes of airline safety after January 1, 2005 and provide a report to Congress in 1998.

(4) Cap on certain exceptions.—Under no circumstances may the authority set forth in paragraphs (1), (2), and (3) of subsection (d) be applied to authorize any person to produce a class I substance in annual quantities greater than 10 percent of that produced by such person during the baseline year.

(e) Developing Countries.—

(1) Exception.—Notwithstanding the phase-out and termination of production required under subsections (a) and (b), the Administrator, after notice and opportunity for public comment, may, consistent with the Montreal Protocol, authorize the production of limited quantities of a class I substance in excess of the amounts otherwise allowable under subsection (a) or (b), or both, solely for export to, and use in, developing countries that are Parties to the Montreal Protocol and are operating under article 5 of such Protocol. Any production authorized under this paragraph shall be solely for purposes of satisfying the basic domestic needs of such countries.

(2) Cap on exception.—

(A) Under no circumstances may the authority set forth in paragraph (1) be applied to authorize any person to produce a class I substance in any year for which a production percentage is specified in Table 2 of subsection (a) in an annual quantity greater than the specified percentage, plus an amount equal to 10 percent of the amount produced by such person in the baseline year.

(B) Under no circumstances may the authority set forth in paragraph (1) be applied to authorize any person to produce a class I substance in the applicable termination year referred to in subsection (b), or in any year thereafter, in an annual quantity greater than 15 percent of the baseline quantity of such substance produced by such person.

(C) An exception authorized under this subsection shall terminate no later than January 1, 2010 (2012 in the case of methyl chloroform).

(f) National Security.—The President may, to the extent such action is consistent with the Montreal Protocol, issue such orders regarding production and use of CFC–114 (chlorofluorocarbon–114), halon–1211, halon–1301, and halon–2402, at any specified site or facility or on any vessel as may be necessary to protect the national security interests of the United States if the President finds that adequate substitutes are not available and that the production and use of such substance are necessary to protect such national security interest.

Such orders may include, where necessary to protect such interests, an exemption from any prohibition or requirement contained in this title. The President shall notify the Congress within 30 days of the issuance of an order under this paragraph providing for any such exemption. Such notification shall include a statement of the reasons for the granting of the exemption. An exemption under this paragraph shall be for a specified period which may not exceed one year. Additional exemptions may be granted, each upon the President's issuance of a new order under this paragraph. Each such additional exemption shall be for a specified period which may not exceed one year. No exemption shall be granted under this paragraph due to lack of appropriation unless the President shall have specifically requested such appropriation as a part of the budgetary process and the Congress shall have failed to make available such requested appropriation.

(g) Fire Suppression and Explosion Prevention.—

(1) Notwithstanding the production phase-out set forth in subsection (a), the Administrator, after notice and opportunity for public comment, may, to the extent such action is consistent with the Montreal Protocol, authorize the production of limited quantities of halon–1211, halon–1301, and halon–2402 in excess of the amount otherwise permitted pursuant to the schedule under subsection (a) solely for purposes of fire suppression or explosion prevention if the Administrator, in consultation with the Administrator of the United States Fire Administration, determines that no safe and effective substitute has been developed and that such authorization is necessary for fire suppression or explosion prevention purposes. The Administrator shall not authorize production under this paragraph for purposes of fire safety or explosion prevention training or testing of fire suppression or explosion prevention equipment. In no event shall the Administrator grant an exception under this paragraph that permits production after December 31, 1999.

(2) The Administrator shall periodically monitor and assess the status of efforts to obtain substitutes for the substances referred to in paragraph (1) for purposes of fire suppression or explosion prevention and the probability of such substitutes being available by December 31, 1999. The Administrator, as part of such assessment, shall consider any relevant assessments under the Montreal Protocol and the actions of the Parties pursuant to Article 2B of the Montreal Protocol in identifying essential uses and in permitting a level of production or consumption that is necessary to satisfy such uses for which no adequate alternatives are available after December 31, 1999. The Administrator shall report to Congress the results of such assessment in 1994 and again in 1998.

(3) Notwithstanding the termination of production set forth in subsection (b), the Administrator, after notice and opportunity for public comment, may, to the extent consistent with the Montreal Protocol, authorize the production of limited quantities of halon–1211, halon–1301, and halon–2402 in the period after December 31, 1999, and before December 31, 2004, solely for purposes of fire suppression or explosion prevention in association with domestic production of crude oil and natural gas energy supplies on the North Slope of Alaska, if the Administrator, in consultation with the Administrator of the United States Fire Administration, determines that no safe and effective substitute has been developed and that such authorization is necessary for fire suppression and explosion prevention purposes. The Administrator shall not authorize production under the paragraph for purposes of fire safety or explosion prevention training or testing of fire suppression or explosion prevention equipment. In no event shall the Administrator authorize under this paragraph any person to produce any such halon in an amount greater than 3 percent of that produced by such person during the baseline year.

§7671d. Phase-Out of Production and Consumption of Class II Substances [Sec. 605]

(a) Restriction of Use of Class II Substances.— Effective January 1, 2015, it shall be unlawful for any person to introduce into interstate commerce or use any class II substance unless such substance—

(1) has been used, recovered, and recycled;

(2) is used and entirely consumed (except for trace quantities) in the production of other chemicals; or

(3) is used as a refrigerant in appliances manufactured prior to January 1, 2020. As used in this subsection, the term 'refrigerant' means any class II substance used for heat transfer in a refrigerating system.

(b) Production Phase-Out.—

(1) Effective January 1, 2015, it shall be unlawful for any person to produce any class II substance in an annual quantity greater than the

quantity of such substance produced by such person during the baseline year.

(2) Effective January 1, 2030, it shall be unlawful for any person to produce any class II substance.

(c) Regulation Regarding Production and Consumption of Class II Substances.—By December 31, 1999, the Administrator shall promulgate regulations phasing out the production, and restricting the use, of class II substances in accordance with this section, subject to any acceleration of the phase-out of production under section 606 . The Administrator shall also promulgate regulations to insure that the consumption of class II substances in the United States is phased out and terminated in accordance with the same schedule (subject to the same exceptions and other provisions) as is applicable to the phase-out and termination of production of class II substances under this title.

(d) Exceptions.—

(1) Medical Devices.—

(A) In General.—Notwithstanding the termination of production required under subsection (b)(2) and the restriction on use referred to in subsection (a), the Administrator, after notice and opportunity for public comment, shall, to the extent such action is consistent with the Montreal Protocol, authorize the production and use of limited quantities of class II substances solely for purposes of use in medical devices if such authorization is determined by the Commissioner, in consultation with the Administrator, to be necessary for use in medical devices.

(B) Cap on Exception.—Under no circumstances may the authority set forth in subparagraph (A) be applied to authorize any person to produce a class II substance in annual quantities greater than 10 percent of that produced by such person during the baseline year.

(2) Developing Countries.—

(A) In General.—Notwithstanding the provisions of subsection (a) or (b), the Administrator, after notice and opportunity for public comment, may authorize the production of limited quantities of a class II substance in excess of the quantities otherwise permitted under such provisions solely for export to and use in developing countries that are Parties to the Montreal Protocol, as determined by the Administrator. Any production authorized under this subsection shall be solely for purposes of satisfying the basic domestic needs of such countries.

(B) Cap on Exception.—

(i) Under no circumstances may the authority set forth in subparagraph (A) be applied to authorize any person to produce a class II substance in any year following the effective date of subsection (b)(1) and before the year 2030 in annual quantities greater than 110 percent of the quantity of such substance produced by such person during the baseline year.

(ii) Under no circumstances may the authority set forth in subparagraph (A) be applied to authorize any person to produce a class II substance in the year 2030, or any year thereafter, in an annual quantity greater than 15 percent of the quantity of such substance produced by such person during the baseline year.

(iii) Each exception authorized under this paragraph shall terminate no later than January 1, 2040.

§7671e. Accelerated Schedule [Sec. 606]

(a) In General.—The Administrator shall promulgate regulations, after notice and opportunity for public comment, which establish a schedule for phasing out the production and consumption of class I and class II substances (or use of class II substances) that is more stringent than set forth in section 604 or 605, or both, if—

(1) based on an assessment of credible current scientific information (including any assessment under the Montreal Protocol) regarding harmful effects on the stratospheric ozone layer associated with a class I or class II substance, the Administrator determines that such more stringent schedule may be necessary to protect human health and the environment against such effects,

(2) based on the availability of substitutes for listed substances, the Administrator determines that such more stringent schedule is practicable, taking into account technological achievability, safety, and other relevant factors, or

(3) the Montreal Protocol is modified to include a schedule to control or reduce production, consumption, or use of any substance more rapidly than the applicable schedule under this title. In making any determination under paragraphs (1) and (2), the Administrator shall consider the status of the period

remaining under the applicable schedule under this title.

(b) Petition.—Any person may petition the Administrator to promulgate regulations under this section. The Administrator shall grant or deny the petition within 180 days after receipt of any such petition. If the Administrator denies the petition, the Administrator shall publish an explanation of why the petition was denied. If the Administrator grants such petition, such final regulations shall be promulgated within 1 year. Any petition under this subsection shall include a showing by the petitioner that there are data adequate to support the petition. If the Administrator determines that information is not sufficient to make a determination under this subsection, the Administrator shall use any authority available to the Administrator, under any law administered by the Administrator, to acquire such information.

§7671f. Exchange Authority [Sec. 607]

(a) Transfers.—The Administrator shall, within 10 months after the enactment of the Clean Air Act Amendments of 1990, promulgate rules under this title providing for the issuance of allowances for the production of class I and II substances in accordance with the requirements of this title and governing the transfer of such allowances. Such rules shall insure that the transactions under the authority of this section will result in greater total reductions in the production in each year of class I and class II substances than would occur in that year in the absence of such transactions.

(b) Interpollutant Transfers.—

(1) The rules under this section shall permit a production allowance for a substance for any year to be transferred for a production allowance for another substance for the same year on an ozone depletion weighted basis.

(2) Allowances for substances in each group of class I substances (as listed pursuant to section 602) may only be transferred for allowances for other substances in the same Group.

(3) The Administrator shall, as appropriate, establish groups of class II substances for trading purposes and assign class II substances to such groups. In the case of class II substances, allowances may only be transferred for allowances for other class II substances that are in the same Group.

(c) Trades With Other Persons.—The rules under this section shall permit 2 or more persons to transfer production allowances (including interpollutant transfers which meet the requirements of subsections (a) and (b)) if the transferor of such allowances will be subject, under such rules, to an enforceable and quantifiable reduction in annual production which—

(1) exceeds the reduction otherwise applicable to the transferor under this title,

(2) exceeds the production allowances transferred to the transferee, and

(3) would not have occurred in the absence of such transaction.

(d) Consumption.—The rules under this section shall also provide for the issuance of consumption allowances in accordance with the requirements of this title and for the trading of such allowances in the same manner as is applicable under this section to the trading of production allowances under this section.

§7671g. National Recycling and Emission Reduction Program [Sec. 608]

(a) In General.—

(1) The Administrator shall, by not later than January 1, 1992, promulgate regulations establishing standards and requirements regarding the use and disposal of class I substances during the service, repair, or disposal of appliances and industrial process refrigeration. Such standards and requirements shall become effective not later than July 1, 1992.

(2) The Administrator shall, within 4 years after the enactment of the Clean Air Act Amendments of 1990, promulgate regulations establishing standards and requirements regarding use and disposal of class I and II substances not covered by paragraph (1), including the use and disposal of class II substances during service, repair, or disposal of appliances and industrial process refrigeration. Such standards and requirements shall become effective not later than 12 months after promulgation of the regulations.

(3) The regulations under this subsection shall include requirements that—

(A) reduce the use and emission of such substances to the lowest achievable level, and

(B) maximize the recapture and recycling of such substances. Such regula tions may include requirements to use alternative substances (including substances which are not class I or class II substances) or to minimize use of class I or class II substances, or to promote the use of safe alternatives pursuant to section 612 or any combination of the foregoing.

(b) Safe Disposal.—The regulations under subsection (a) shall establish standards and requirements for the safe disposal of class I and II substances. Such regulations shall include each of the following—

(1) Requirements that class I or class II substances contained in bulk in appliances, machines or other goods shall be removed from each such appliance, machine or other good prior to the disposal of such items or their delivery for recycling.

(2) Requirements that any appliance, machine or other good containing a class I or class II substance in bulk shall not be manufactured, sold, or distributed in interstate commerce or offered for sale or distribution in interstate commerce unless it is equipped with a servicing aperture or an equally effective design feature which will facilitate the recapture of such substance during service and repair or disposal of such item.

(3) Requirements that any product in which a class I or class II substance is incorporated so as to constitute an inherent element of such product shall be disposed of in a manner that reduces, to the maximum extent practicable, the release of such substance into the environment. If the Administrator determines that the application of this paragraph to any product would result in producing only insignificant environmental benefits, the Administrator shall include in such regulations an exception for such product.

(c) Prohibitions.—

(1) Effective July 1, 1992, it shall be unlawful for any person, in the course of maintaining, servicing, repairing, or disposing of an appliance or industrial process refrigeration, to knowingly vent or otherwise knowingly release or dispose of any class I or class II substance used as a refrigerant in such appliance (or industrial process refrigeration) in a manner which permits such substance to enter the environment. De minimis releases associated with good faith attempts to recapture and recycle or safely dispose of any such substance shall not be subject to the prohibition set forth in the preceding sentence.

(2) Effective 5 years after the enactment of the Clean Air Act Amendments of 1990, paragraph (1) shall also apply to the venting, release, or disposal of any substitute substance for a class I or class II substance by any person maintaining, servicing, repairing, or disposing of an appliance or industrial process refrigeration which contains and uses as a refrigerant any such substance, unless the Administrator determines that venting, releasing, or disposing of such substance does not pose a threat to the environment. For purposes of this paragraph, the term 'appliance' includes any device which contains and uses as a refrigerant a substitute substance and which is used for household or commercial purposes, including any air conditioner, refrigerator, chiller, or freezer.

§7671h. Servicing of Motor Vehicle Air Conditioners [Sec. 609]

(a) Regulations.—Within 1 year after the enactment of the Clean Air Act Amendments of 1990, the Administrator shall promulgate regulations in accordance with this section establishing standards and requirements regarding the servicing of motor vehicle air conditioners.

(b) Definitions.—As used in this section—

(1) The term 'refrigerant' means any class I or class II substance used in a motor vehicle air conditioner. Effective 5 years after the enactment of the Clean Air Act Amendments of 1990, the term 'refrigerant' shall also include any substitute substance.

(2) (A) The term 'approved refrigerant recycling equipment' means equipment certified by the Administrator (or an independent standards testing organization approved by the Administrator) to meet the standards established by the Administrator and applicable to equipment for the extraction and reclamation of refrigerant from motor vehicle air conditioners. Such standards shall, at a minimum, be at least as stringent as the standards of the Society of Automotive Engineers in effect as of the date of the enactment of the Clean Air Act Amendments of 1990 and applicable to such equipment (SAE standard J-1990).

(B) Equipment purchased before the proposal of regulations under this section shall be considered certified if it is substantially identical to equipment certified as provided in subparagraph (A).

(3) The term 'properly using' means, with respect to approved refrigerant recycling equipment, using such equipment in conformity with standards established by the Administrator and applicable to the use of such equipment. Such standards shall, at a minimum, be at least as stringent as the standards of the Society of Automotive Engineers in effect as of the date of the enactment of the

Clean Air Act Amendments of 1990 and applicable to the use of such equipment (SAE standard J-1989).

(4) The term 'properly trained and certified' means training and certification in the proper use of approved refrigerant recycling equipment for motor vehicle air conditioners in conformity with standards established by the Administrator and applicable to the performance of service on motor vehicle air conditioners. Such standards shall, at a minimum, be at least as stringent as specified, as of the date of the enactment of the Clean Air Act Amendments of 1990, in SAE standard J-1989 under the certification program of the National Institute for Automotive Service Excellence (ASE) or under a similar program such as the training and certification program of the Mobile Air Conditioning Society (MACS).

(c) Servicing Motor Vehicle Air Conditioners.—Effective January 1, 1992, no person repairing or servicing motor vehicles for consideration may perform any service on a motor vehicle air conditioner involving the refrigerant for such air conditioner without properly using approved refrigerant recycling equipment and no such person may perform such service unless such person has been properly trained and certified. The requirements of the previous sentence shall not apply until January 1, 1993 in the case of a person repairing or servicing motor vehicles for consideration at an entity which performed service on fewer than 100 motor vehicle air conditioners during calendar year 1990 and if such person so certifies, pursuant to subsection (d)(2), to the Administrator by January 1, 1992.

(d) Certification.—

(1) Effective 2 years after the enactment of the Clean Air Act Amendments of 1990, each person performing service on motor vehicle air conditioners for consideration shall certify to the Administrator either—

(A) that such person has acquired, and is properly using, approved refrigerant recycling equipment in service on motor vehicle air conditioners involving refrigerant and that each individual authorized by such person to perform such service is properly trained and certified; or

(B) that such person is performing such service at an entity which serviced fewer than 100 motor vehicle air conditioners in 1991.

(2) Effective January 1, 1993, each person who certified under paragraph (1)(B) shall submit a certification under paragraph (1)(A).

(3) Each certification under this subsection shall contain the name and address of the person certifying under this subsection and the serial number of each unit of approved recycling equipment acquired by such person and shall be signed and attested by the owner or another responsible officer. Certifications under paragraph (1)(A) may be made by submitting the required information to the Administrator on a standard form provided by the manufacturer of certified refrigerant recycling equipment.

(e) Small Containers of Class I or Class II Substances.—Effective 2 years after the date of the enactment of the Clean Air Act Amendments of 1990, it shall be unlawful for any person to sell or distribute, or offer for sale or distribution, in interstate commerce to any person (other than a person performing service for consideration on motor vehicle air-conditioning systems in compliance with this section) any class I or class II substance that is suitable for use as a refrigerant in a motor vehicle air-conditioning system and that is in a container which contains less than 20 pounds of such refrigerant.

§7671i. Nonessential Products Containing Chlorofluoro Carbons [Sec. 610]

(a) Regulations.—The Administrator shall promulgate regulations to carry out the requirements of this section within 1 year after the enactment of the Clean Air Act Amendments of 1990.

(b) Nonessential Products.—The regulations under this section shall identify nonessential products that release class I substances into the environment (including any release occurring during manufacture, use, storage, or disposal) and prohibit any person from selling or distributing any such product, or offering any such product for sale or distribution, in interstate commerce. At a minimum, such prohibition shall apply to—

(1) chlorofluorocarbon-propelled plastic party streamers and noise horns,

(2) chlorofluorocarbon-containing cleaning fluids for noncommercial electronic and photographic equipment, and

(3) other consumer products that are determined by the Administrator—

(A) to release class I substances into the environment (including any release occurring during manufacture, use, storage, or disposal), and

(B) to be nonessential. In determining whether a product is nonessential, the

Administrator shall consider the purpose or intended use of the product, the technological availability of substitutes for such product and for such class I substance, safety, health, and other relevant factors.

(c) Effective Date.—Effective 24 months after the enactment of the Clean Air Act Amendments of 1990, it shall be unlawful for any person to sell or distribute, or offer for sale or distribution, in interstate commerce any nonessential product to which regulations under subsection (a) implementing subsection (b) are applicable.

(d) Other Products.—

(1) Effective January 1, 1994, it shall be unlawful for any person to sell or distribute, or offer for sale or distribution, in interstate commerce—

(A) any aerosol product or other pressurized dispenser which contains a class II substance; or

(B) any plastic foam product which contains, or is manufactured with, a class II substance.

(2) The Administrator is authorized to grant exceptions from the prohibition under subparagraph (A) of paragraph (1) where—

(A) the use of the aerosol product or pressurized dispenser is determined by the Administrator to be essential as a result of flammability or worker safety concerns, and

(B) the only available alternative to use of a class II substance is use of a class I substance which legally could be substituted for such class II substance.

(3) Subparagraph (B) of paragraph (1) shall not apply to—

(A) a foam insulation product, or

(B) an integral skin, rigid, or semi-rigid foam utilized to provide for motor vehicle safety in accordance with Federal Motor Vehicle Safety Standards where no adequate substitute substance (other than a class I or class II substance) is practicable for effectively meeting such Standards.

(d) Medical Devices.—Nothing in this section shall apply to any medical device as defined in section 601(8) .

§7671j. Labeling [Sec. 611]

(a) Regulations.—The Administrator shall promulgate regulations to implement the labeling requirements of this section within 18 months after enactment of the Clean Air Act Amendments of 1990, after notice and opportunity for public comment.

(b) Containers Containing Class I or Class II Substances and Products Containing Class I Substances.—Effective 30 months after the enactment of the Clean Air Act Amendments of 1990, no container in which a class I or class II substance is stored or transported, and no product containing a class I substance, shall be introduced into interstate commerce unless it bears a clearly legible and conspicuous label stating:

"Warning: Contains [insert name of substance], a substance which harms public health and environment by destroying ozone in the upper atmosphere."

(c) Products Containing Class II Substances.—

(1) After 30 months after the enactment of the Clean Air Act Amendments of 1990, and before January 1, 2015, no product containing a class II substance shall be introduced into interstate commerce unless it bears the label referred to in subsection (b) if the Administrator determines, after notice and opportunity for public comment, that there are substitute products or manufacturing processes (A) that do not rely on the use of such class II substance, (B) that reduce the overall risk to human health and the environment, and (C) that are currently or potentially available.

(2) Effective January 1, 2015, the requirements of subsection (b) shall apply to all products containing a class II substance.

(d) Products Manufactured with Class I And Class II Substances.—

(1) In the case of a class II substance, after 30 months after the enactment of the Clean Air Act Amendments of 1990, and before January 1, 2015, if the Administrator, after notice and opportunity for public comment, makes the determination referred to in subsection (c) with respect to a product manufactured with a process that uses such class II substance, no such product shall be introduced into interstate commerce unless it bears a clearly legible and conspicuous label stating:

"Warning: Manufactured with [insert name of substance], a substance which harms public health and environment by destroying ozone in the upper atmosphere."

(2) In the case of a class I substance, effective 30 months after the enactment of the Clean Air Act Amendments of 1990, and before January 1, 2015, the labeling requirements of this subsection shall apply to all products manufactured with a process that uses such class I substance unless the Administrator determines that there are no substitute products or

manufacturing processes that (A) do not rely on the use of such class I substance, (B) reduce the overall risk to human health and the environment, and (C) are currently or potentially available.

(e) Petitions.—

(1) Any person may, at any time after 18 months after the enactment of the Clean Air Act Amendments of 1990, petition the Administrator to apply the requirements of this section to a product containing a class II substance or a product manufactured with a class I or II substance which is not otherwise subject to such requirements. Within 180 days after receiving such petition, the Administrator shall, pursuant to the criteria set forth in subsection (c), either propose to apply the requirements of this section to such product or publish an explanation of the petition denial. If the Administrator proposes to apply such requirements to such product, the Administrator shall, by rule, render a final determination pursuant to such criteria within 1 year after receiving such petition.

(2) Any petition under this paragraph shall include a showing by the petitioner that there are data on the product adequate to support the petition.

(3) If the Administrator determines that information on the product is not sufficient to make the required determination the Administrator shall use any authority available to the Administrator under any law administered by the Administrator to acquire such information.

(4) In the case of a product determined by the Administrator, upon petition or on the Administrator's own motion, to be subject to the requirements of this section, the Administrator shall establish an effective date for such requirements. The effective date shall be 1 year after such determination or 30 months after the enactment of the Clean Air Act Amendments of 1990, whichever is later.

(5) Effective January 1, 2015, the labeling requirements of this subsection shall apply to all products manufactured with a process that uses a class I or class II substance.

(f) Relationship to Other Law.—

(1) The labeling requirements of this section shall not constitute, in whole or part, a defense to liability or a cause for reduction in damages in any suit, whether civil or criminal, brought under any law, whether Federal or State, other than a suit for failure to comply with the labeling requirements of this section.

(2) No other approval of such label by the Administrator under any other law administered by the Administrator shall be required with respect to the labeling requirements of this section.

§7671k. Safe Alternatives Policy [Sec. 612]

(a) Policy.—To the maximum extent practicable, class I and class II substances shall be replaced by chemicals, product substitutes, or alternative manufacturing processes that reduce overall risks to human health and the environment.

(b) Reviews and Reports.—The Administrator shall—

(1) in consultation and coordination with interested members of the public and the heads of relevant Federal agencies and departments, recommend Federal research programs and other activities to assist in identifying alternatives to the use of class I and class II substances as refrigerants, solvents, fire retardants, foam blowing agents, and other commercial applications and in achieving a transition to such alternatives, and, where appropriate, seek to maximize the use of Federal research facilities and resources to assist users of class I and class II substances in identifying and developing alternatives to the use of such substances as refrigerants, solvents, fire retardants, foam blowing agents, and other commercial applications;

(2) examine in consultation and coordination with the Secretary of Defense and the heads of other relevant Federal agencies and departments, including the General Services Administration, Federal procurement practices with respect to class I and class II substances and recommend measures to promote the transition by the Federal Government, as expeditiously as possible, to the use of safe substitutes;

(3) specify initiatives, including appropriate intergovernmental, international, and commercial information and technology transfers, to promote the development and use of safe substitutes for class I and class II substances, including alternative chemicals, product substitutes, and alternative manufacturing processes; and

(4) maintain a public clearinghouse of alternative chemicals, product substitutes, and alternative manufacturing processes that are available for products and manufacturing processes which use class I and class II substances.

(c) Alternatives for Class I or II Substances.—Within 2 years after enactment of the Clean Air

Act Amendments of 1990, the Administrator shall promulgate rules under this section providing that it shall be unlawful to replace any class I or class II substance with any substitute substance which the Administrator determines may present adverse effects to human health or the environment, where the Administrator has identified an alternative to such replacement that—

(1) reduces the overall risk to human health and the environment; and

(2) is currently or potentially available. The Administrator shall publish a list of (A) the substitutes prohibited under this subsection for specific uses and (B) the safe alternatives identified under this subsection for specific uses.

(d) Right to Petition.—Any person may petition the Administrator to add a substance to the lists under subsection (c) or to remove a substance from either of such lists. The Administrator shall grant or deny the petition within 90 days after receipt of any such petition. If the Administrator denies the petition, the Administrator shall publish an explanation of why the petition was denied. If the Administrator grants such petition the Administrator shall publish such revised list within 6 months thereafter. Any petition un der this subsection shall include a showing by the petitioner that there are data on the substance adequate to support the petition. If the Administrator determines that information on the substance is not sufficient to make a determination under this subsection, the Administrator shall use any authority available to the Administrator, under any law administered by the Administrator, to acquire such information.

(e) Studies and Notification.—The Administrator shall require any person who produces a chemical substitute for a class I substance to provide the Administrator with such person's unpublished health and safety studies on such substitute and require producers to notify the Administrator not less than 90 days before new or existing chemicals are introduced into interstate commerce for significant new uses as substitutes for a class I substance. This subsection shall be subject to section 114(c) .

§7671l. Federal Procurement [Sec. 613]

Not later than 18 months after the enactment of the Clean Air Act Amendments of 1990, the Administrator, in consultation with the Administrator of the General Services Administration and the Secretary of Defense, shall promulgate regulations requiring each department, agency, and instrumentality of the United States to conform its procurement regulations to the policies and requirements of this title and to maximize the substitution of safe alternatives identified under section 612 for class I and class II substances. Not later than 30 months after the enactment of the Clean Air Act Amendments of 1990, each department, agency, and instrumentality of the United States shall so conform its procurement regulations and certify to the President that its regulations have been modified in accordance with this section.

§7671m. Relationship to Other Laws [Sec. 614]

(a) State Laws.—Notwithstanding section 116, during the 2-year period beginning on the enactment of the Clean Air Act Amendments of 1990, no State or local government may enforce any requirement concerning the design of any new or recalled appliance for the purpose of protecting the stratospheric ozone layer.

(b) Montreal Protocol.—This title as added by the Clean Air Act Amendments of 1990 shall be construed, interpreted, and applied as a supplement to the terms and conditions of the Montreal Protocol, as provided in Article 2, paragraph 11 thereof, and shall not be construed, interpreted, or applied to abrogate the responsibilities or obligations of the United States to implement fully the provisions of the Montreal Protocol. In the case of conflict between any provision of this title and any provision of the Montreal Protocol, the more stringent provision shall govern. Nothing in this title shall be construed, interpreted, or applied to affect the authority or responsibility of the Administrator to implement Article 4 of the Montreal Protocol with other appropriate agencies.

(c) Technology Export and Overseas Investment.—Upon enactment of this title, the President shall—

(1) prohibit the export of technologies used to produce a class I substance;

(2) prohibit direct or indirect investments by any person in facilities designed to produce a class I or class II substance in nations that are not parties to the Montreal Protocol; and

(3) direct that no agency of the government provide bilateral or multilateral subsidies, aids, credits, guarantees, or insurance programs, for the purpose of producing any class I substance.

§7671n. Authority of Administrator [Sec. 615]

If, in the Administrator's judgment, any substance, practice, process, or activity may reasonably be anticipated to affect the stratosphere, especially ozone in the stratosphere, and such effect may reasonably be anticipated to endanger public health or welfare, the Administrator shall promptly promulgate regulations respecting the control of such substance, practice, process, or activity, and shall submit notice of the proposal and promulgation of such regulation to the Congress.

§7671o. Transfers Among Parties to Montreal Protocol [Sec. 616]

(a) In General.—Consistent with the Montreal Protocol, the United States may engage in transfers with other Parties to the Protocol under the following conditions:

(1) The United States may transfer production allowances to another Party if, at the time of such transfer, the Administrator establishes revised production limits for the United States such that the aggregate national United States production permitted under the revised production limits equals the lesser of (A) the maximum production level permitted for the substance or substances concerned in the transfer year under the Protocol minus the production allowances transferred, (B) the maximum production level permitted for the substance or substances concerned in the transfer year under applicable domestic law minus the production allowances transferred, or (C) the average of the actual national production level of the substance or substances concerned for the 3 years prior to the transfer minus the production allowances transferred.

(2) The United States may acquire production allowances from another Party if, at the time of such transfer, the Administrator finds that the other Party has revised its domestic production limits in the same manner as provided with respect to transfers by the United States in subsection (a).

(b) Effect of Transfers on Production Limits.—The Administrator is authorized to reduce the production limits established under this Act as required as a prerequisite to transfers under paragraph (1) of subsection (a) or to increase production limits established under this Act to reflect production allowances acquired under a transfer under paragraph (2) of subsection (a).

(c) Regulations.—The Administrator shall promulgate, within 2 years after the date of enactment of the Clean Air Act Amendments of 1990, regulations to implement this section.

(d) Definition.—In the case of the United States, the term 'applicable domestic law' means this Act.

§7671p. International Cooperation [Sec. 617]

(a) In General.—The President shall undertake to enter into international agreements to foster cooperative research which complements studies and research authorized by this title, and to develop standards and regulations which protect the stratosphere consistent with regulations applicable within the United States. For these purposes the President through the Secretary of State and the Assistant Secretary of State for Oceans and International Environmental and Scientific Affairs, shall negotiate multilateral treaties, conventions, resolutions, or other agreements, and formulate, present, or support proposals at the United Nations and other appropriate international forums and shall report to the Congress periodically on efforts to arrive at such agreements.

(b) Assistance to Developing Countries.—The Administrator, in consultation with the Secretary of State, shall support global participation in the Montreal Protocol by providing technical and financial assistance to developing countries that are Parties to the Montreal Protocol and operating under article 5 of the Protocol. There are authorized to be appropriated not more than $30,000,000 to carry out this section in fiscal years 1991, 1992 and 1993 and such sums as may be necessary in fiscal years 1994 and 1995. If China and India become Parties to the Montreal Protocol, there are authorized to be appropriated not more than an additional $30,000,000 to carry out this section in fiscal years 1991, 1992, and 1993.

§7671q. Miscellaneous Provisions [Sec. 618]

For purposes of section 116, requirements concerning the areas addressed by this title for the protection of the stratosphere against ozone layer depletion shall be treated as requirements for the control and abatement of air pollution. For purposes of section 118, the requirements of this title and corresponding State, interstate, and local requirements, administrative authority, and process, and sanctions respecting the protection of the stratospheric ozone layer shall be treated as requirements for the control and abatement of air pollution within the meaning of section 118.

ADDITIONAL PROVISIONS

[Editor's Note: The text of sections of the Clean Air Amendments of 1990 that did not directly amend the Clean Air Act, but are pertinent follow.]

Risk Assessment and Management Commission[Sec. 303]

(a) Establishment.—There is hereby established a Risk Assessment and Management Commission (hereafter referred to in this section as the "Commission"), which shall commence proceedings not later than 18 months after the date of enactment of the Clean Air Act Amendments of 1990 and which shall make a full investigation of the policy implications and appropriate uses of risk assessment and risk management in regulatory programs under various Federal laws to prevent cancer and other chronic human health effects which may result from exposure to hazardous substances.

(b) Charge.—The Commission shall consider—

(1) the report of the National Academy of Sciences authorized by section 112(o) of the Clean Air Act, the use and limitations of risk assessment in establishing emission or effluent standards, ambient standards, exposure standards, acceptable concentration levels, tolerances or other environmental criteria for hazardous substances that present a risk of carcinogenic effects or other chronic health effects and the suitability of risk assessment for such purposes;

(2) the most appropriate methods for measuring and describing cancer risks or risks of other chronic health effects from exposure to hazardous substances considering such alternative approaches as the lifetime risk of cancer or other effects to the individual or individuals most exposed to emissions from a source or sources on both an actual and worst case basis, the range of such risks, the total number of health effects avoided by exposure reductions, effluent standards, ambient standards, exposures standards, acceptable concentration levels, tolerances and other environmental criteria, reductions in the number of persons exposed at various levels of risk, the incidence of cancer, and other public health factors;

(3) methods to reflect uncertainties in measurement and estimation techniques, the existence of synergistic or antagonistic effects among hazardous substances, the accuracy of extrapolating human health risks from animal exposure data, and the existence of unquantified direct or indirect effects on human health in risk assessment studies;

(4) risk management policy issues including the use of lifetime cancer risks to individuals most exposed, incidence of cancer, the cost and technical feasibility of exposure reduction measures and the use of site-specific actual exposure information in setting emissions standards and other limitations applicable to sources of exposure to hazardous substances; and

(5) and comment on the degree to which it is possible or desirable to develop a consistent risk assessment methodology, or a consistent standard of acceptable risk, among various Federal programs.

(c) Membership.—Such Commission shall be composed of ten members who shall have knowledge or experience in fields of risk assessment or risk management, including three members to be appointed by the President, two members to be appointed by the Speaker of the House of Representatives, one member to be appointed by the Minority Leader of the House of Representatives, two members to be appointed by the Majority Leader of the Senate, one member to be appointed by the Minority Leader of the Senate, and one member to be appointed by the President of the National Academy of Sciences. Appointments shall be made not later than 18 months after the date of enactment of the Clean Air Act Amendments of 1990.

(d) Assistance from Agencies.—The Administrator of the Environmental Protection Agency and the heads of all other departments, agencies, and instrumentalities of the executive branch of the Federal Government shall, to the maximum extent practicable, assist the Commission in gathering such information as the Commission deems necessary to carry out this section subject to other provisions of law.

(e) Staff and Contracts.—

(1) In the conduct of the study required by this section, the Commission is authorized to contract (in accordance with Federal contract law) with nongovernmental entities that are competent to perform research or investigations within the Commission's mandate, and to hold public hearings, forums, and workshops to enable full public participation.

(2) The Commission may appoint and fix the pay of such staff as it deems necessary in accordance with the provisions of title 5, United States Code. The Commission may request the temporary assignment of personnel from the Environmental Protection Agency or other Federal agencies.

(3) The members of the Commission who are not officers or employees of the United States, while attending conferences or meetings of the Commission or while otherwise serving at the request of the Chair, shall be entitled to receive compensation at a rate not in excess of the maximum rate of pay for Grade GS–18, as provided in the General Schedule under section 5332 of title 5 of the United States Code, including travel time, and while away from

their homes or regular places of business they may be allowed travel expenses, including per diem in lieu of substances as authorized by law for persons in the Government service employed intermittently.

(f) Report.—A report containing the results of all Commission studies and investigations under this section, together with any appropriate legislative recommendations or administrative recommendations, shall be made available to the public for comment not later than 42 months after the date of enactment of the Clean Air Act Amendments of 1990 and shall be submitted to the President and to the Congress not later than 48 months after such date of enactment. In the report, the Commission shall make recommendations with respect to the appropriate use of risk assessment and risk management in Federal regulatory programs to prevent cancer or other chronic health effects which may result from exposure to hazardous substances. The Commission shall cease to exist upon the date determined by the Commission, but not later than 9 months after the submission of such report.

(g) Authorization.—There are authorized to be appropriated such terms as are necessary to carry out the activities of the Commission established by this section.

Chemical Process Safety Management [Sec. 304]

(a) Chemical Process Safety Standards.—The Secretary of Labor shall act under the Occupational Safety and Health Act of 1970 (29 U.S.C. 653) to prevent accidental releases of chemicals which could pose a threat to employees. Not later than 12 months after the date of enactment of the Clean Air Act Amendments of 1990, the Secretary of Labor, in coordination with the Administrator of the Environmental Protection Agency, shall promulgate, pursuant to the Occupational Safety and Health Act, a chemical process safety standard designed to protect employees from hazards associated with accidental releases of highly hazardous chemicals in the work-place.

(b) List of Highly Hazardous Chemicals.—The Secretary shall include as part of such standard a list of highly hazardous chemicals, which include toxic, flammable, highly reactive and explosive substances. The list of such chemicals may include those chemicals listed by the Administrator under section 302 of the Emergency Planning and Community Right to Know Act of 1986. The Secretary may make additions to such list when a substance is found to pose a threat of serious injury or fatality in the event of an accidental release in the workplace.

(c) Elements of Safety Standard.—Such standard shall, at minimum, require employers to—

(1) develop and maintain written safety information identifying workplace chemical and process hazards, equipment used in the processes, and technology used in the processes;

(2) perform a workplace hazard assessment, including, as appropriate, identification of potential sources of accidental releases, an identification of any previous release within the facility which had a likely potential for catastrophic consequences in the workplace, estimation of workplace effects of a range of releases, estimation of the health and safety effects of such range on employees;

(3) consult with employees and their representatives on the development and conduct of hazard assessments and the development of chemical accident prevention plans and provide access to these and other records required under the standard;

(4) establish a system to respond to the workplace hazard assessment findings, which shall address prevention, mitigation, and emergency responses;

(5) periodically review the workplace hazard assessment and response system;

(6) develop and implement written operating procedures for the chemical process including procedures for each operating phase, operating limitations, and safety and health considerations;

(7) provide written safety and operating information to employees and train employees in operating procedures, emphasizing hazards and safe practices;

(8) ensure contractors and contract employees are provided appropriate information and training;

(9) train and educate employees and contractors in emergency response in a manner as comprehensive and effective as that required by the regulation promulgated pursuant to section 126(d) of the Superfund Amendments and Reauthorization Act;

(10) establish a quality assurance program to ensure that initial process related equipment, maintenance materials, and spare parts are fabricated and installed consistent with design specifications;

(11) establish maintenance systems for critical process related equipment including written procedures, employee training, appropriate inspections, and testing of such equipment to ensure ongoing mechanical integrity;

(12) conduct pre-start-up safety reviews of all newly installed or modified equipment;

(13) establish and implement written procedures to manage change to process chemicals, technology, equipment and facilities; and

(14) investigate every incident which results in or could have resulted in a major accident in the workplace, with any findings to be reviewed by operating personnel and modifications made if appropriate.

(d) State Authority.—Nothing in this section may be construed to diminish the authority of the States and political subdivisions thereof as described in section 112(r)(11) of the Clean Air Act.

Fossil Fuel Use [Sec. 402]

(a) Contracts for Hydroelectric Energy.—Any person who, after the date of the enactment of the Clean Air Act Amendments of 1990, enters into a contract under which such person receives hydroelectric energy in return for the provision of electric energy by such person shall use allowances held by such person as necessary to satisfy such person's obligations under such contract.

(b) Federal Power Marketing Administration.—A Federal Power Marketing Administration shall not be subject to the provisions and requirements of this title with respect to electric energy generated by hydroelectric facilities and marketed by such Power Marketing Administration. Any person who sells or provides electric energy to a Federal Power Marketing Administration shall comply with the provisions and requirements of this title.

Acid Deposition Standards [Sec. 404]

Not later than 36 months after the date of enactment of this Act, the Administrator of the Environmental Protection Agency shall transmit to the Committee on Environment and Public Works of the Senate and the Committee on Energy and Commerce of the House of Representatives a report on the feasibility and effectiveness of an acid deposition standard or standards to protect sensitive and critically sensitive aquatic and terrestrial resources. The study required by this section shall include, but not be limited to, consideration of the following matters:

(1) identification of the sensitive and critically sensitive aquatic and terrestrial resources in the United States and Canada which may be affected by the deposition of acidic compounds;

(2) description of the nature and numerical value of a deposition standard or standards that would be sufficient to protect such resources;

(3) description of the use of such standard or standards in other Nations or by any of the several States in acid deposition control programs;

(4) description of the measures that would need to be taken to integrate such standard or standards with the control program required by title IV of the Clean Air Act;

(5) description of the state of knowledge with respect to source-receptor relationships necessary to develop a control program on such standard or standards and the additional research that is on-going or would be needed to make such a control program feasible; and

(6) description of the impediments to implementation of such control program and the cost-effectiveness of deposition standards compared to other control strategies including ambient air quality standards, new source performance standards and the requirements of title IV of the Clean Air Act.

National Acid Lakes Registry [Sec. 405]

The Administrator of the Environmental Protection Agency shall create a National Acid Lakes Registry that shall list, to the extent practical, all lakes that are known to be acidified due to acid deposition, and shall publish such list within one year of the enactment of this Act. Lakes shall be added to the registry as they become acidic or as data becomes available to show they are acidic. Lakes shall be deleted from the registry as they become nonacidic.

Industrial SO_2 Emissions [Sec. 406]

(a) Report.—Not later than January 1, 1995 every 5 years thereafter, the Administrator of the Environmental Protection Agency shall transmit to the Congress a report containing an inventory of national annual sulfur dioxide emissions from industrial sources (as defined in title IV of the Act), including units subject to section 405(g)(6) of the Clean Air Act, for all years for which data are available, as well as the likely trend in such emissions over the following twenty-year period. The reports shall also contain estimates of the actual emission reduction in each year resulting from promulgation of the diesel fuel desulfurization regulations under section 214 .

(b) 5.60 Million Ton Cap.—Whenever the inventory required by this section indicates that sulfur dioxide emissions from industrial sources, including units subject to section 405(g)(5) of the Clean Air Act, may reasonably be expected to reach levels greater than 5.60 million tons per year, the Administrator of the Environmental Protection Agency shall take such actions under the Clean Air Act as may be appropriate to ensure that such emissions do not exceed 5.60 million tons per year. Such actions may include the promulgation of new and revised standards of performance for new sources, including units subject to section 405(g)(5) of the Clean Air Act, under section 111(b) of the Clean Air Act, as well as promulgation of standards of performance for existing sources, including units subject to section 405(g)(5) of the Clean Air Act, under authority of this section. For an existing source regulated under this section, "standard of performance" means a standard which the Administrator determines is applicable to that source and which reflects the degree of emission reduction achievable through the application of the best system of continuous emission reduction which (taking into consideration the cost of achieving such emission reduction, and any nonair quality health and envi-

ronmental impact and energy requirements) the Administrator determines has been adequately demonstrated for that category of sources.

(c) Election.—Regulations promulgated under section 405(b) of the Clean Air Act shall not prohibit a source from electing to become an affected unit under section 410 of the Clean Air Act.

Sense of the Congress on Emission Reductions Costs [Sec. 407]

It is the sense of the Congress that the Clean Air Act Amendments of 1990, through the allowance program, allocates the costs of achieving the required reductions in emissions of sulfur dioxide and oxides of nitrogen among sources in the United States. Broad based taxes and emissions fees that would provide for payment of the costs of achieving required emissions reductions by any party or parties other than the sources required to achieve the reductions are undesirable.

Monitor Acid Rain Program in Canada [Sec. 408]

(a) Reports to Congress.—The Administrator of the Environmental Protection Agency, in consultation with the Secretary of State, the Secretary of Energy, and other persons the Administrator deems appropriate, shall prepare and submit a report to Congress on January 1, 1994, January 1, 1999, and January 1, 2005.

(b) Contents.—The report to Congress shall analyze the current emission levels of sulfur dioxide and nitrogen oxides in each of the provinces participating in Canada's acid rain control program, the amount of emission reductions of sulfur dioxide and oxides of nitrogen achieved by each province, the methods utilized by each province in making those reductions, the costs to each province and the employment impacts in each province of making and maintaining those reductions.

(c) Compliance.—Beginning on January 1, 1999, the reports shall also assess the degree to which each province is complying with its stated emissions cap.

Report on Clean Coal Technologies Export Programs [Sec. 409]

The Secretary of Energy in consultation with the Secretary of Commerce shall provide a report to the Congress within one year of enactment of this legislation which will identify, inventory and analyze clean coal technologies export programs within United States Government agencies including the Departments of State, Commerce, and Energy and at the Export-Import Bank and the Overseas Private Investment Corporation. The study shall address the effectiveness of interagency coordination of export promotion and determine the feasibility of establishing an interagency commission for the purpose of promoting the export and use of clean coal technologies.

Acid Deposition Research by the United States Fish And Wildlife Service [Sec. 410]

There are authorized to be appropriated to the United States Fish and Wildlife Service of the Department of the Interior an amount equal to $500,000 to fund research related to acid deposition and the monitoring of high altitude mountain lakes in the Wind River Reservation, Wyoming, to be conducted through the Management Assistance Office of the United States Fish and Wildlife Service located in Lander, Wyoming and the University of Wyoming.

Study of Buffering and Neutralizing Agents [Sec. 411]

There are authorized to be appropriated to the United States Fish and Wildlife Service of the Department of the Interior an amount equal to $250,000 to fund a study to be conducted in conjunction with the University of Wyoming of the effectiveness of various buffering and neutralizing agents used to restore lakes and streams damaged by acid deposition.

Special Clean Coal Technology Project [Sec. 413]

(a) Demonstration Project.—The Secretary of Energy shall, subject to appropriation, as part of the Secretary's activities with respect to fossil energy research and development under the Department of Energy Organization Act (Public Law 95–91) consider funding at least 50 percent of the cost of a demonstration project to design, construct, and test a technology system for a cyclone boiler that will serve as a model for sulfur dioxide and nitrogen oxide reductions technology at a combustion unit required to meet the emissions reduction prescribed in this bill. The Secretary shall expedite approval and funding to enable such project to be completed no later than January 1, 1995. The unit selected for this project shall be in a utility plan that (1) is among the top 10 emitters of sulfur dioxide as identified on Table A of section 404; (2) has 3 or more units, 2 of which are cyclone boiler units; and (3) has no existing scrubbers.

(b) Authorization.—There are authorized to be appropriated such sums as may be necessary to carry out this section, to remain available until expended.

Methane Studies [Sec. 603]

(a) Economically Justified Actions.—Not later than 2 years after enactment of this Act, the Administrator shall prepare and submit a report to the Congress that identifies activities, substances, processes, or combinations thereof that could reduce methane emissions and that are economically and technologically justified with and without consideration of environmental benefit.

(b) Domestic Methane Source Inventory and Control.—Not later than 2 years after the enactment of this Act, the Administrator, in consultation and coordination with the Secretary of Energy and the Secretary of Agriculture, shall prepare and submit to the Congress reports on each of the following:

(1) Methane emissions associated with natural gas extraction, transportation, distribution, storage, and use. Such report shall include an inventory of methane emissions associated with such activities within the United States. Such emissions include, but are not limited to, accidental and intentional releases from natural gas and oil wells, pipelines, processing facilities, and gas burners. The report shall also include an inventory of methane generation with such activities.

(2) Methane emissions associated with coal extraction, transportation, distribution, storage, and use. Such report shall include an inventory of methane emissions associated with such activities within the United States. Such emissions include, but are not limited to, accidental and intentional releases from mining shafts, degasification wells, gas recovery wells and equipment, and from the processing and use of coal. The report shall also include an inventory of methane generation with such activities.

(3) Methane emissions associated with management of solid waste. Such report shall include an inventory of methane emissions associated with all forms of waste management in the United States, including storage, treatment, and disposal.

(4) Methane emissions associated with agriculture. Such report shall include an inventory of methane emissions associated with rice and livestock production in the United States.

(5) Methane emissions associated with biomass burning. Such report shall include an inventory of methane emissions associated with the intentional burning of agricultural wastes, wood, grasslands, and forests.

(6) Other methane emissions associated with human activities. Such report shall identify and inventory other domestic sources of methane emissions that are deemed by the Administrator and other such agencies to be significant.

(c) International Studies.—

(1) Methane emissions.—Not later than 2 years after the enactment of this Act, the Administrator shall prepare and submit to the Congress a report on methane emissions from countries other than the United States. Such report shall include inventories of methane emissions associated with the activities listed in subsection (b).

(2) Preventing increases in methane concentrations.—Not later than 2 years after the enactment of this Act, the Administrator shall prepare and submit to the Congress a report that analyzes the potential for preventing an increase in atmospheric concentrations of methane from activities and sources in other countries. Such report shall identify and evaluate the technical options for reducing methane emission from each of the activities listed in subsection (b), as well as other activities or sources that are deemed by the Administrator in consultation with other relevant Federal agencies and departments to be significant and shall include an evaluation of costs. The report shall identify the emissions reductions that would need to be achieved to prevent increasing atmospheric concentrations of methane. The report shall also identify technology transfer programs that could promote methane emissions reductions in lesser developed countries.

(d) Natural Sources.—Not later than 2 years after the enactment of this Act, the Administrator shall prepare and submit to the Congress a report on—

(1) methane emissions from biogenic sources such as (A) tropical, temperate, and subarctic forests, (B) tundra, and (C) freshwater and saltwater wetlands; and

(2) the changes in methane emissions from biogenic sources that may occur as a result of potential increases in temperatures and atmospheric concentrations of carbon dioxide.

(e) Study of Measures To Limit Growth in Methane Concentrations.—Not later than 2 years after the completion of the studies in subsections (b), (c), and (d), the Administrator shall prepare and submit to the Congress a report that presents options outlining measures that could be implemented to stop or reduce the growth in atmospheric concentrations of methane from sources within the United States referred to in paragraphs (1) through (6) of subsection (b). This study shall identify and evaluate the technical options for reducing methane emissions from each of the activities listed in subsection (b), as well as other activities or sources deemed by such agen cies to be significant, and shall include an evaluation of costs, technology, safety, energy, and other factors. The study shall be based on the other studies under this section. The study shall also identify programs of the United States and international lending agencies that could be used to induce lesser developed countries to undertake measures that will reduce methane emissions and the resource needs of such programs.

(f) Information Gathering.—In carrying out the studies under this section, the provisions and requirements of section 114 of the Clean Air Act shall be available for purposes of obtaining information to carry out such studies.

(g) Consultation and Coordination.—In preparing the studies under this section the Administrator shall consult and coordinate with the Secretary of Energy, the Administrators of the National Aeronautics and Space Administration and the National Oceanic and Atmospheric Administration, and the heads of other relevant Federal agencies and departments. In the case of the studies under subsections (a), (b), and (e), such consultation and coordination shall include the Secretary of Agriculture.

Hydrogen Fuel Cell Vehicle Study and Test Program [Sec. 807]

The Administrator of the Environmental Protection Agency, in conjunction with the National Aeronautics and Space Administration and the Department of Energy, shall conduct a study and test program on the development of a hydrogen fuel cell electric vehicle. The study and test program shall determine how best to transfer existing NASA hydrogen fuel cell technology into the form of a mass-producible, cost effective hydrogen fuel cell vehicle. Such study and test program shall include at a minimum a feasibility-design study, the construction of a prototype, and a demonstration. This study and test program should be completed and a report submitted to Congress within 3 years after the enactment of the Clean Air Act Amendments of 1990. This study and test program should be performed in the university or universities which are best exhibiting the facilities and expertise to develop such a fuel cell vehicle.

Renewable Energy and Energy Conservation Incentives [Sec. 808]

(a) Definition.—For purposes of this section, "renewable energy" means energy from photovoltaic, solar thermal, wind, geothermal, and biomass energy production technologies.

(b) Rate Incentives Study.—Within 18 months after enactment, the Federal Energy Regulatory Commission, in consultation with the Environmental Protection Agency, shall complete a study which calculates the net environmental benefits of renewable energy, compared to nonrenewable energy, and assigns numerical values to them. The study shall include, but not be limited to, environmental impacts on air, water, land use, water use, human health, and waste disposal.

(c) Model Regulations.—In conjunction with the study in subsection (b), the Commission shall propose one or more models for incorporating the net environmental benefits into the regulatory treatment of renewable energy in order to provide economic compensation for those benefits.

(d) Report.—The Commission shall transmit the study and the model regulations to Congress, along with any recommendations on the best ways to reward renewable energy technologies for their environmental benefits, in a report no later than 24 months after enactment.

Clean Air Study of Southwestern New Mexico [Sec. 809]

The Administrator shall conduct a study of the causes of degraded visibility in southwestern New Mexico. The Administrator, in consultation with the Secretary of State, is encouraged to cooperate with the Government of Mexico, other Federal agencies, and any other appropriate organizations in conducting the study. Nothing in this section shall be construed as contravening or superseding the provisions of any international agreement in force for the United States as of the date of enactment of this section, or any relevant Federal statute.

Impact on Small Communities [Sec. 810]

Before implementing a provision of this Act, the Administrator of the Environmental Protection Agency shall consult with the Small Communities Coordinator of the Environmental Protection Agency to determine the impact of such provision on small communities, including the estimated cost of compliance with such provision.

Equivalent Air Quality Controls Among Trading Nations [Sec. 811]

(a) Findings.—The Congress finds that—

(1) all nations have the responsibility to adopt and enforce effective air quality standards and requirements and the United States, in enacting this Act, is carrying out its responsibility in this regard;

(2) as a result of complying with this Act, businesses in the United States will make significant capital investments and incur incremental costs in implementing control technology standards;

(3) such compliance may impair the competitiveness of certain United States jobs, production, processes, and products if foreign goods are produced under less costly environmental standards and requirements than are United States goods; and

(4) mechanisms should be sought through which the United States and its trading partners can agree to eliminate or reduce competitive disadvantages.

(b) Action by the President.—

(1) In general.—Within 18 months after the date of the enactment of the Clean Air Act Amendments of 1990, the President shall submit to the Congress a report—

(A) identifying and evaluating the economic effects of—

(i) the significant air quality standards and controls required under this Act, and

(ii) the differences between the significant standards and controls required under this Act and similar standards and controls adopted and enforced by the major trading partners of the United States, on the international competitiveness of United States manufacturers; and

(B) containing a strategy for addressing such economic effects through trade consultations and negotiations.

(2) Additional Reporting Requirements.—

(A) The evaluation required under paragraph (1)(A) shall examine the extent to which the significant air quality standards and controls required under this Act are comparable to existing internationally-agreed norms.

(B) The strategy required to be developed under paragraph (1)(B) shall include recommended options (such as the harmonization of standards and trade adjustment measures) for reducing or eliminating competitive disadvantages caused by differences in standards and controls between the United States and each of its major trading partners.

(3) Public comment.—Interested parties shall be given an opportunity to submit comments regarding the evaluations and strategy required in the report under paragraph (1). The President shall take any such comment into account in preparing the report.

(4) Interim report.—Within 9 months after the date of the enactment of the Clean Air Act Amendments of 1990, the President shall submit to the Congress an interim report on the progress being made in complying with paragraph (1).

Combustion of Contaminated Used Oil in Ships [Sec. 813]

Within 2 years after the enactment of the Clean Air Act Amendments of 1990, the Administrator of the Environmental Protection Agency shall complete a study and submit a report to Congress evaluating the health and environmental impacts of the combustion of contaminated used oil in ships, the reasons for using such oil for such purposes, the alternatives to such use, the costs of such alternatives, and other relevant factors and impacts. In preparing such study, the Administrator shall obtain the view and comments of all interested persons and shall consult with the Secretary of Transportation and the Secretary of the department in which the Coast Guard is operating.

American Made Products [Sec. 814]

It is the sense of the Congress that—

(1) existing equipment and machinery retrofitted to comply with the Clean Air Act's "Best Available Control Technology" language and all other specifications within the Act be produced in the United States and purchased from American manufacturers.

(2) The construction of new industrial and utility facilities comply to the Act's specifications through the incorporation of American made equipment and technology.

(3) Individuals, groups, and organizations in the pubic sector strive to purchase and produce American made products that improve our nation's air quality.

Establishment of Program to Monitor and Improve Air Quality in Regions Along the Border Between the United States and Mexico[Sec. 815]

(a) In General.—The Administrator of the Environmental Protection Agency (hereinafter referred to as the "Administrator") is authorized, in cooperation with the Department of State and the affected States, to negotiate with representatives of Mexico to authorize a program to monitor and improve air quality in regions along the border between the United States and Mexico. The program established under this section shall not extend beyond July 1, 1995.

(b) Monitoring and Remediation.—

(1) Monitoring.—The monitoring component of the program conducted under this section shall identify and determine sources of pollutants for which national ambient air quality standards (hereinafter referred to as "NAAQS") and other air quality goals have been established in regions along the border between the United States and Mexico. Any such monitoring component of the program shall include, but not be limited to, the collection of meteorological data, the measurement of air quality, the compilation of an emissions inventory, and shall be sufficient to the extent necessary to successfully support the use of a state-of-the-art mathematical air modeling analysis. Any such monitoring component of the program shall collect and produce data projecting the level of emission reductions necessary in both Mexico and the United States to bring about attainment of both primary and secondary NAAQS, and other air quality goals, in regions along the border in the United States. Any such monitoring component of the program shall include to the extent possible, data from monitoring programs undertaken by other parties.

(2) Remediation.—The Administrator is authorized to negotiate with appropriate representatives of Mexico to develop joint remediation measures to reduce the level of airborne pollutants to achieve and maintain primary and secondary NAAQS, and other air quality goals, in regions along the border

between the United States and Mexico. Such joint remediation measures may include, but not be limited to measures included in the Environmental Protection Agency's Control Techniques and Control Technology documents. Any such remediation program shall also identify those control measures implementation of which in Mexico would be expedited by the use of material and financial assistance of the United States.

(c) Annual Reports.—The Administrator shall, each year the program authorized in this section is in operation, report to Congress on the progress of the program in bringing nonattainment areas along the border of the United States into attainment with primary and secondary NAAQS. The report issued by the Administrator under this paragraph shall include recommendations on funding mechanisms to assist in implementation of monitoring and remediation efforts.

(d) Funding and Personnel.—The Administrator may, where appropriate, make available, subject to the appropriations, such funds, personnel, and equipment as may be necessary to implement the provisions of this section. In those cases where direct financial assistance of the United States is provided to implement monitoring and remediation programs in Mexico, the Administrator shall develop grant agreements with appropriate representatives of Mexico to assure the accuracy and completeness of monitoring data and the performance of remediation measures which are financed by the United States. With respect to any control measures within Mexico funded by the United States, the Administrator shall, to the maximum extent practicable, utilize resources of Mexico where such utilization would reduce costs to the United States. Such funding agreements shall include authorization for the Administrator to—

(1) review and agree to plans for monitoring and remediation;

(2) inspect premises, equipment and records to insure compliance with the agreements established under and the purposes set forth in this section; and

(3) where necessary, develop grant agreements with affected States to carry out the provisions of this section.

Role of Secondary Standards [Sec. 817]

(a) Report.—The Administrator shall request the National Academy of Sciences to prepare a report to the Congress on the role of national secondary ambient air quality standards in protecting welfare and the environment. The report shall:

(1) include information on the effects on welfare and the environment which are caused by ambient concentrations of pollutants listed pursuant to section 108 and other pollutants which may be listed;

(2) estimate welfare and environmental costs incurred as a result of such effects;

(3) examine the role of secondary standards and the State implementation planning process in preventing such effects;

(4) determine ambient concentrations of each such pollutant which would be adequate to protect welfare and the environment from such effects;

(5) estimate the costs and other impacts of meeting secondary standards; and

(6) consider other means consistent with the goals and objectives of the Clean Air Act which may be more effective than secondary standards in preventing or mitigating such effects.

(b) Submission to Congress; Comments; Authorization.—

(1) The report shall be transmitted to the Congress not later than 3 years after the date of enactment of the Clean Air Act Amendments of 1990.

(2) At least 90 days before issuing a report the Administrator shall provide an opportunity for public comment on the proposed report. The Administrator shall include in the final report a summary of the comments received on the proposed report.

(3) There are authorized to be appropriated such sums as are necessary to carry out this section.

Exemptions for Stripper Wells [Sec. 819]

Notwithstanding any other provision of law, the amendments to the Clean Air Act made by section 103 of the Clean Air Act Amendments of 1990 (relating to additional provisions for ozone nonattainment areas), by section 104 of such amendments (relating to additional provisions for carbon monoxide nonattainment areas), by section 105 of such amendments (relating to additional provisions for PM–10 nonattainment areas), and by section 106 of such amendments (relating to additional provisions for areas designated as nonattainment for sulfur oxides, nitrogen dioxide, and lead) shall not apply with respect to the production of and equipment used in the exploration, production, development, storage or processing of—

(1) oil from a stripper well property, within the meaning of the June 1979 energy regulations (within the meaning of section 4996(b)(7) of the Internal Revenue Code of 1986, as in effect before the repeal of such section); and

(2) stripper well natural gas, as defined in section 108(b) of the Natural Gas Policy Act of 1978 (15 U.S.C. 3318(b)) except to the extent that provisions of such amendments cover areas designated as Serious pursuant to part D of title I of the Clean Air Act and having a population of 350,000 or more, or

areas designated as Severe or Extreme pursuant to such part D.

EPA Report on Magnetic Levitation [Sec. 820]

The Administrator of the Environmental Protection Agency shall, not later than 6 months after the date of enactment of this Act, submit to the Congress and the President a report of the Administrator's activities under any agreement with the Department of Transportation entered into prior to such date of enactment providing for an analysis of the health and environmental aspects of magnetic levitation technology.

Information Gathering on Greenhouse Gases Contributing to Global Climate Change [Sec. 821]

(a) Monitoring.—The Administrator of the Environmental Protection Agency shall promulgate regulations within 18 months after the enactment of the Clean Air Act Amendments of 1990 to require that all affected sources subject to title V of the Clean Air Act shall also monitor carbon dioxide emissions according to the same timetable as in section 511(b) and (c) . The regulations shall require that such data be reported to the Administrator. The provisions of section 511(e) of title V of the Clean Air Act shall apply for purposes of this section in the same manner and to the same extent as such provision applies to the monitoring and data referred to in section 511 .

(b) Public Availability of Carbon Dioxide Information.—For each unit required to monitor and provide carbon dioxide data under subsection (a), the Administrator shall compute the unit's aggregate annual total carbon dioxide emissions, incorporate such data into a computer data base, and make such aggregate annual data available to the public.

TITLE X—DISADVANTAGED BUSINESS CONCERNS

Disadvantaged Business Concerns[Sec. 1001]

(a) In General.—In providing for any research relating to the requirements of the amendments made by the Clean Air Act Amendments of 1990 which uses funds of the Environmental Protection Agency, the Administrator of the Environmental Protection Agency shall, to the extent practicable, require that not less than 10 percent of total Federal funding for such research will be made available to disadvantaged business concerns.

(b) Definition.—

(1) (A) For purposes of subsection (a), the term "disadvantaged business concern" means a concern—

(i) which is at least 51 percent owned by one or more socially and economically disadvantaged individuals or, in the case of a publicly traded company, at least 51 percent of the stock of which is owned by one or more socially and economically disadvantaged individuals; and

(ii) the management and daily business operations of which are controlled by such individuals.

(B) (i) A for-profit business concern is presumed to be a disadvantaged business concern for purposes of subsection (a) if it is at least 51 percent owned by, or in the case of a concern which is a publicly traded company at least 51 percent of the stock of the company is owned by, one or more individuals who are members of the following groups:

(I) Black Americans.

(II) Hispanic Americans.

(III) Native Americans.

(IV) Asian Americans.

(V) Women.

(VI) Disabled Americans.

(ii) The presumption established by clause (i) may be rebutted with respect to a particular business concern if it is reasonably established that the individual or individuals referred to in that clause with respect to that business concern are not experiencing impediments to establishing or developing such concern as a result of the individual's identification as a member of a group specified in that clause.

(C) The following institutions are presumed to be disadvantaged business concerns for purposes of subsection (a):

(i) Historically black colleges and universities, and colleges and universities having a student body in which 40 percent of the students are Hispanic.

(ii) Minority institutions (as that term is defined by the Secretary of Education pursuant to the General Education Provision Act (20 U.S.C. 1221 et seq.)).

(iii) Private and voluntary organizations controlled by individuals who are socially and economically disadvantaged.

(D) A joint venture may be considered to be a disadvantaged business concern under subsection (a), notwithstanding the size of such joint venture, if—

(i) a party to the joint venture is a disadvantaged business concern; and

(ii) that party owns at least 51 percent of the joint venture. A person who is not an economically disadvantaged individual or a disadvantaged business concern, as a party to a joint venture, may not be a party to more than 2

awarded contracts in a fiscal year solely by reason of this subparagraph.

(E) Nothing in this paragraph shall prohibit any member of a racial or ethnic group that is not listed in subparagraph (B)(i) from establishing that they have been impeded in establishing or developing a business concern as a result of racial or ethnic discrimination.

Use of Quotas Prohibited. [Sec. 402]

Nothing in this title shall permit or require the use of quotas or a requirement that has the effect of a quota in determining eligibility under section 1001.

[Editor's Note: §16 of the PL 91–604 did not directly amend the Clean Air Act, but is pertinent, and follows. Provisions of the Amendments relating solely to federal personnel under the Civil Service Act and the Public Health Service Act are not included here.]

Savings Provisions [Sec. 16]

(a) (1) Any implementation plan adopted by any State and submitted to the Secretary of Health, Education and Welfare, or to the Administrator pursuant to the Clean Air Act prior to enactment of this Act may be approved under section 110 of the Clean Air Act (as amended by this Act) and shall remain in effect, unless the Administrator determines that such implementation plan or any portion thereof, is not consistent with the applicable requirements of the Clean Air Act (as amended by this Act) and will not provide for the attainment of national primary ambient air quality standards in the time required by such Act. If the Administrator so determines, he shall, within 90 days after promulgation of any national ambient air quality standards pursuant to section 109(a) of the Clean Air Act, notify the State and specify in what respects changes are needed to meet the additional requirements of such Act, including requirements to implement national secondary ambient air quality standards. If such changes are not adopted by the State after public hearings and within six months after such notification, the Administrator shall promulgate such changes pursuant to section 110(c) of such Act.

(2) The amendments made by section 4(b) shall not be construed as repealing or modifying the powers of the Administrator with respect to any conference convened under section 108(d) of the Clean Air Act before the date of enactment of this Act.

(b) Regulations or standards issued under title II of the Clean Air Act prior to the enactment of this Act shall continue in effect until revised by the Administrator consistent with the purposes of such Act.

[Editor's Note: §§ 402–406 of PL 95–95 are also relevant. Those provisions follow.]

Interagency Cooperation of Prevention of Environmental Cancer and Heart and Lung Disease [Sec. 402]

(a) Not later than three months after the date of enactment of this section, there shall be established a Task Force on Environmental Cancer and Heart and Lung Disease (hereinafter referred to as the 'Task Force'). The Task Force shall include representatives of the Environmental Protection Agency, the National Cancer Institute, the National Heart, Lung, and Blood Institute, the National Institute of Occupational Safety and Health, and the National Institute on Environmental Health Sciences, and shall be chaired by the Administrator (or his delegate).

(b) The Task Force shall—

(1) recommend a comprehensive research program to determine and quantify the relationship between environmental pollution and human cancer and heart and lung disease;

(2) recommend comprehensive strategies to reduce or eliminate the risks of cancer or such other diseases associated with environmental pollution;

(3) recommend research and such other measures as may be appropriate to prevent or reduce the incidence of environmentally related cancer and heart and lung diseases;

(4) coordinate research by, and stimulate cooperation between, the Environmental Protection Agency, the Department of Health, Education, and Welfare, and such other agencies as may be appropriate to prevent environmentally related cancer and heart and lung diseases; and

(5) report to Congress, not later than one year after the date of enactment of this section and annually thereafter, on the problems and progress in carrying out this section.

Studies [Sec. 403]

(a) Not later than eighteen months after the date of the enactment of the Clean Air Act Amendments of 1977, the Administrator of the Environmental Protection Agency, in cooperation with the National Academy of Sciences, shall study and report to Congress on (1) the relationship between the size, weight, and chemical composition of suspended particulate matter and the nature and degree of the endangerment to public health or welfare presented by such particulate matter (especially with respect to fine particulate matter) and (2) the availability of technology for controlling such particulate matter.

(b) The Administrator of the Environmental Protection Agency shall conduct a study and report to the Congress not later than January 1, 1979, on the effects on public health and welfare of odors or odorous emissions, the sources of such emissions, the

technology or other mea sures available for control of such emissions and the costs of such technology or measures, and the costs and benefits of alternative measures or strategies to abate such emissions. Such report shall include an evaluation of whether air quality criteria or national ambient air quality standards should be published under the Clean Air Act for odors, and what other strategies or authorities under the Clean Air Act are available or appropriate for abating such emissions.

(c) (1) Not later than twelve months after the date of enactment of this Act the Administrator of the Environmental Protection Agency shall publish throughout the United States a list of all known chemical contaminants resulting from environmental pollution which have been found in human tissue including blood, urine, breast milk, and all other human tissue. Such list shall be prepared for the United States and shall indicate the approximate number of cases, the range of levels found, and the mean levels found.

(2) Not later than eighteen months after the date of enactment of this Act the Administrator shall publish in the same manner an explanation of what is known about the manner in which the chemicals described in paragraph (1) entered the environment and thereafter human tissue.

(3) The Administrator, in consultation with the National Institutes of Health, the National Center for Health Statistics, and the National Center for Health Services Research and Development, shall, if feasible, conduct an epidemiological study to demonstrate the relationship between levels of chemicals in the environment and in human tissue. Such study shall be made in appropriate regions or areas of the United States in order to determine any different results in such regions or areas. The results of such study shall, as soon as practicable, be reported to the appropriate committees of the Congress.

(d) The Administrator of the Environmental Protection Agency shall conduct a study of air quality in various areas throughout the country including the gulf coast region. Such study shall include analysis of liquid and solid aerosols and other fine particulate matter and the contribution of such substances to visibility and public health problems in such areas. For the purposes of this study, the Administrator shall use environmental health experts from the National Institutes of Health and other outside agencies and organizations.

(e) (1) The Secretary of Labor, in consultation with the Administrator, shall conduct a study of potential dislocation of employees due to implementation of laws administered by the Administrator. Such study shall estimate the number of employees so affected, identify existing sources of assistance available to such employees, assess the adequacy of such assistance, and recommend additional adjustment measures, if justified.

(2) The Secretary shall submit to Congress the results of the study conducted under paragraph (1) not more than one year after the date of enactment of this section.

(f) The Administrator of the Environmental Protection Agency shall undertake to enter into appropriate arrangements with the National Academy of Sciences to conduct continuing comprehensive studies and investigations of the effects on public health and welfare of emission subject to section 202(a) of the Clean Air Act (including sulfur compounds) and the technological feasibility of meeting emission standards required to be prescribed by the Administrator by section 202(b) of such Act. The Administrator shall report to the Congress within six months of the date of enactment of this section and each year thereafter regarding the status of the contractual arrangements and conditions necessary to implement this paragraph.

(g) The Administrator of the Environmental Protection Agency shall conduct a study and report to Congress by the date one year after the date of the enactment of this section, on the emission of sulfur-bearing compounds from motor vehicles and motor vehicle engines and aircraft engines. Such study and report shall include but not be limited to a review of the effects of such emissions on public health and welfare and an analysis of the costs and benefits of alternatives to reduce or eliminate such emissions (including desulfurization of fuel, short-term allocation of low sulfur crude oil, technological devices used in conjunction with current engine technologies, alternative engine technologies, and other methods) as may be required to achieve any proposed or promulgated emission standards for sulfur compounds.

Railroad Emission Study[Sec. 404]

(a) The Administrator of the Environmental Protection Agency shall conduct a study and investigation of emissions of air pollutants from railroad locomotives, locomotive engines, and secondary power sources on railroad rolling stock, in order to determine—

(1) The extent to which such emissions affect air quality in air quality control regions throughout the United States,

(2) the technological feasibility and the current state of technology for controlling such emissions, and

(3) the status and effect of current and proposed State and local regulations affecting such emissions.

(b) Within one hundred and eighty days after commencing such study and investigation, the Administrator shall submit a report of such study and investigation, together with recommendations for appropriate legislation to the Senate Committee on Environment and Public Works and the House Committee on Interstate and Foreign Commerce.

Study and Report Concerning Economic Approaches to Controlling Air Pollution [Sec. 405]

(a) The Administrator, in conjunction with the Council of Economic Advisors (hereinafter in this section referred to as 'the Council'), shall undertake a study and assessment of economic measures for the control of air pollution which could—

(1) strengthen the effectiveness of existing methods of controlling air pollution,

(2) provide incentives to abate air pollution to a greater degree than is required by existing provisions of the Clean Air Act (and regulations thereunder), and

(3) serve as the primary incentive for controlling air pollution problems not addressed by any provision of the Clean Air Act (or any regulation thereunder).

(b) The study of measures referred to in paragraph (1) of subsection (a) shall concentrate on (1) identification of air pollution problems for which existing methods of control are not effective because of economic incentives to delay compliance and (2) formulation of economic measures which could be taken with respect to each such air pollution problem which would provide an incentive to comply without interfering with such existing methods of control.

(c) The study of measures referred to in paragraph (2) of subsection (a) shall concentrate on (1) identification of air pollution problems for which existing methods of control may not be sufficiently extensive to achieve all desired environmental goals and (2) formulation of economic measures for each such air pollution problem which would provide additional incentives to reduce air pollution without—

(A) interfering with the effectiveness of existing methods of control, or

(B) creating problems similar to those which prevent alternative regulatory methods from being used to reach such environmental goals.

(d) The study of the measures referred to in paragraph (3) of subsection (a) shall concentrate on (1) identification of air pollution problems for which no existing methods of control exist, (2) formulation of economic measures to reduce such pollution, and (3) comparison of the environmental and economic impacts of the economic measures with those of any alternative regulatory methods which can be identified.

(e) In conducting the study under this section, a preliminary screening should be made of the problems referred to in subsections (b)(1), (c)(1), and (d)(1) and economic measures should be formulated under sections (b)(2), (c)(2). and (d)(2) in the most promising cases, giving special attention to structural and administrative problems. In formulating any such measure which provides for a charge, the appropriate level of the charge should be determined, if possible, and the environmental and economic impacts should be identified.

(f) Within one year after the date of enactment of this Act, the Administrator shall complete a study and report to the Congress on the advantages and disadvantages (including an analysis of the feasibility) of establishing a system of penalties for stationary sources on emissions of oxides of nitrogen and make recommendations regarding the establishment of such a system. Such study shall determine if such a system will effectively encourage the development of more effective systems and technologies for control of emissions of oxide of nitrogen for new major emitting facilities, or existing major emitting facilities, or both. In any case in which a proposed penalty system is recommended by the Administrator, the report should include—

(1) a recommendation respecting the appropriate period during which such system of penalties should apply and the appropriate termination date or dates for such system, if any, taking into account—

(A) the time at which adequate technology may reasonably be anticipated to be available to control oxides of nitrogen for that category of facilities,

(B) the degree to which such technology can be expected to be used on such facilities, and

(C) the Administrator's authorities to require the use of such technology, and

(2) recommendations respecting the compilation of records by facilities subject to such penalties for purposes of determining the applicability and amount of such penalty.

(g) Not later than two years after the date of the enactment of this section, the Administrator and the Council shall conclude the study and assessment under this section and submit a report containing the results thereof to the President and to the Congress. Interim reports on specific pollution problems and solutions recommended shall be made available to the

President and the Congress by the Administrator whenever available.

Savings Provision; Effective Dates [Sec. 406]

(a) No suit, action, or other proceeding lawfully commenced by or against the Administrator or any other officer or employee of the United States in his official capacity or in relation to the discharge of his official duties under the Clean Air Act, as in effect immediately prior to the date of enactment of this Act shall abate by reason of the taking effect of the amendments made by this Act. The court may, on its own motion or that of any party made at any time within twelve months after such taking effect, allow the same to be maintained by or against the Administrator or such officer or employee.

(b) All rules, regulations, orders, determinations, contacts, certifications, authorizations, delegations, or other actions duly issued, made, or taken by or pursuant to the Clean Air Act as in effect immediately prior to the date of enactment of this Act, and pertaining to any functions, powers, requirements, and duties under the Clean Air Act, as in effect immediately prior to the date of enactment of this Act, and not suspended by the Administrator or the courts, shall continue in full force and effect after the date of enactment of this Act until modified or rescinded in accordance with the Clean Air Act as amended by this Act.

(c) Nothing in this Act nor any action taken pursuant to this Act shall in any way affect any requirement of an approved implementation plan in effect under section 110 of the Clean Air Act or any other provision of the Act in effect under the Clean Air Act before the date of enactment of this section until modified or rescinded in accordance with the Clean Air Act as amended by this Act.

[§406(c) amended by PL 95–190]

(d) (1) Except as otherwise expressly provided, the amendments made by this Act shall be effective on date of enactment.

(2) Except as otherwise expressly provided, each State required to revise its applicable implementation plan by reason of any amendment made by this Act shall adopt and submit to the Administrator of the Environmental Protection Agency such plan revision before the later of the date—

(A) one year after the date of enactment of this Act, or

(B) nine months after the date of promulgation by the Administrator of the Environmental Protection Agency of any regulations under an amendment made by this Act which are necessary for the approval of such plan revision.

2

Clean Water Act

INTRODUCTION

The Clean Water Act's roots stretch back to 1948, when Congress provided the first trickle of money to help municipalities construct sewage treatment facilities. However, the 1948 law contained no federal requirements concerning the control of water pollution. Its stated policy was simply "to recognize, preserve, and protect the primary responsibilities and rights of the states in controlling water pollution."

The next two decades saw numerous amendments to the 1948 law. But it was not until 1972, when Congress passed the Federal Water Pollution Control Act Amendments of 1972 (PL 92-500), that federal water pollution law was essentially rewritten.

The 1972 law set optimistic and ambitious goals. By 1983, Congress envisioned fishable, swimmable waters throughout the nation. By 1985, it was the act's goal that the discharge of pollutants to waterways be eliminated. The law embodied two major strategies for achieving these objectives. First, it expanded the limited federal assistance of the past into a giant, $5 billion per year federal grants program to finance construction of local sewage treatment systems.

Second, the Act required all municipal and industrial waste water to be treated before being discharged into waterways. The Environmental Protection Agency was required to establish federal limits on the amounts of specific pollutants that could be released by municipal and industrial facilities. These "effluent limitations" were to be based on the level of cleanup that could be achieved using existing technologies and were to take into account costs to the regulated community. The limits were to be written into "national pollutant discharge elimination system" permits issued to all dischargers.

The technology-based approach of the 1972 Clean Water Act is regarded as a success. Discharges of pollutants from industrial facilities have largely been brought under control, and while more work is needed to bring municipalities into compliance, substantial progress has been made.

Nevertheless, many waterways, notably marine estuaries, lakes, and rivers in heavily populated areas, still suffer from degradation. In amending the Clean Water Act in 1987, the basic issue lawmakers had to confront was that after most technology standards called for in the 1970s had been issued, and the final push to get cities to provide a minimum of secondary treatment for sewage was at hand, some stubborn water pollution problems still remained. The most serious of these remaining problems are excessive levels of toxic pollutants in some waters—even where dischargers have installed required pollution control technologies—and contaminated runoff from "non-point" sources such as farmland and city streets.

The Water Quality Act of 1987, passed by Congress over a presidential veto on February 4, 1987, sought to correct these problems. The amendments direct EPA and state officials to supplement existing, nationwide technology-based standards with a water-quality-based approach to control persistent pollution problems. Essentially, Congress said, regulators should identify waterways that are still polluted and do what is needed to restore them.

For example, under non-point source pollution control provisions in the 1987 amendments, states are required to identify waters that are not expected to meet water quality standards because of non-point source pollution and develop programs for reducing the polluted runoff. In similar toxic control provisions, states must identify waters that are not expected to meet water quality standards, even after technology-based controls have been put into effect, because of the presence of toxic pollutants. States must identify the sources responsible for the toxic pollution and propose strategies for reducing discharges of toxic pollutants from these facilities.

The other major change made by the 1987 amendments involved the phase-out of federal assistance for municipal waste water treatment plant construction. Under the new law, the existing construction grants program was reauthorized through fiscal year 1990 at a total level of $9.6 billion. Afterwards, the grants program was replaced by a new federal program that provides a total of $8.4 billion through fiscal year 1994 in seed money for states to establish permanent, state-run revolving loan fund programs. The revolving funds, which states must also contribute to, will be used to provide loans and other forms of non-grant assistance to local areas for construction of sewage treatment systems, with loan repayments to be channeled back into the state funds and reused.

This $18 billion funding scheme was seen as accomplishing two desired purposes: ending the federal government's role in financing the construction of local sewage treatment plants, but at the same time providing a continuing source of money for construction of those facilities, thereby ensuring progress toward the Clean Water Act's goal of fishable, swimmable waters.

In other important provisions, the 1987 amendments added a new section to the law directing EPA to solve pollution problems in estuaries, the coastal water bodies where fresh river water and salty ocean water meet.

Another new section was meant to bolster U.S. efforts to comply with the 1978 Great Lakes Water Quality Agreement. Under the agreement, the United States and Canada made a commitment "to eliminate or reduce to the maximum extent practicable the discharge of pollutants into the Great Lakes system." Specific steps called for in the agreement include construction of sewage treatment facilities and control of pesticide runoff and toxic industrial discharges.

Other provisions of the amendments strengthened an existing program to improve water quality in lakes, with authorizations totaling $85 million, including $15 million to aid lakes that have been damaged by acid rain.

In other key changes, the amendments:

• Required permits for all discharges of storm water from industrial facilities, and set deadlines for cities to obtain permits for storm water discharges;

• Limited the ability of industrial facilities to get exemptions, or "variances," from federal pollution control regulations;

• Prohibited, except in certain narrowly defined circumstances, "backsliding" on permits, or the weakening of treatment requirements when industrial and municipal discharge permits are renewed or reissued;

• Extended deadlines for industries to comply with national pollution control standards to account for the fact that EPA has not yet finished issuing some of these regulations;

• Specified deadlines for EPA to issue remaining needed industrial effluent limitations;

• Required EPA to promulgate regulations to control toxic pollutants in sewage sludge; and

• Limited availability of modifications of federal treatment standards for nonconventional pollutants to five well-understood substances.

In August 1990, President Bush signed the Oil Pollution Act of 1990 P.L. 101-380, which established new liability limits for owners and operators of tankers that cause damaging oil spills. Enacted largely in response to the 1989 spill from the Exxon Valdez in Prince William Sound, Alaska, the new law also amended the Clean Water Act, principally Section 311 (33 U.S.C. 1321), relating to liability for spills of oil and hazardous substances in U.S. waters. Jail penalties under Section 311(b)(5) for failure to provide prompt notification of spills were increased to a maximum of five years. Administrative penalties under Section 311(b)(6) were similarly increased.

The Great Lakes Critical Programs Act of 1990 (P.L. 101-596) amended Section 118(c) (33 U.S.C. 1268). Its basic requirement was that EPA propose, by June 30, 1991, the Great Lakes Water Quality Guidance, and issue the final guidance a year later. In October 1992, the National Wildlife Federation sued the agency for failing to issue the guidance by the statutory deadlines (*National Wildlife Federation v. EPA*, DC DC, No. 92-2338). The U.S. District Court for the District of Columbia ordered EPA to issue the guidance by April 15, 1993. On March 31, 1993, the agency announced the proposal, which was published in the Federal Register on April 16 (58 FR 20802).

The proposal, the first regional approach taken by the agency to water pollution problems, is seen as the first step toward the development of uniform water quality standards for persistent toxic chemicals in the Great Lakes. The three basic parts of the proposed guidance are water quality criteria that apply throughout the Great Lakes basin to protect human health, aquatic life, and wildlife; a standard antidegradation procedure to protect existing levels of water quality; and procedures for translating the water quality criteria into enforceable limits on the discharge of pollutants.

Reauthorization of the Clean Water Act was considered but went nowhere in the 102nd Congress. Sen. Max S. Baucus (D-Mont) introduced legislation (S 1081) in May 1991; but, except for hearings, the measure was not even considered by the Senate Environment and Public Works Committee. Legislation affecting the act on the House side included a measure (HR 2029) introduced by Rep. Gerry Studds (D-Mass). Ultimately, however, disagreements over controversial issues such as wetlands and contaminated sediments derailed congressional action in the 102nd Congress.

In the 103rd Congress, Baucus again introduced comprehensive reauthorization legislation (S 1114); but, unlike with S 1081 in the previous Congress, bipartisanship was stressed. Sen. John Chafee (R-R.I.), the ranking Republican on the Environment and Public Works Committee, was a co-sponsor of the legislation, and Baucus said the bill "moves more toward cooperation." The bill would authorize $2.5 billion for the waste water state revolving loan fund and would create another fund for non-point source pollution control grants. S 1114 also would create new initiatives to prevent and control pollution by toxic chemicals, establish new authority for watershed planning and expand authorities for controlling pollution from diffuse sources, improve programs for controlling pollution from municipal sources, and strengthen the act's enforcement provisions.

In July 1993, Baucus and Chafee introduced S 1304, aimed at the protection and restoration of wetlands. They said the measure probably would be incorporated into S 1114. Broadly, the bill would make the protection and restoration of wetlands a national goal. To achieve this goal it would authorize the creation of wetland mitigation banks under the oversight of the Army Corps of Engineers. It also would require the use of the Corps of Engineers' 1987 manual for the identification of wetlands until a new manual is prepared. In August, the Clinton Administration revealed its plan for reform of the U.S. wetlands program, including proposed changes to the Clean Water Act.

In hearings on the bills, many witnesses said the basic Clean Water Act was in good shape and did not need dramatic revision. The largest remaining problem to be tackled, they said, was control of non-point source pollution. Other senators as well as state officials and legislators encouraged a greater emphasis on regional water quality provisions. Representatives of the Clinton Administration Environmental Protection Agency stressed EPA Administrator Carol M. Browner's focus on watershed approaches to dealing with water quality problems. The Association of State and Interstate Water Pollution Control Administrators (ASIWPCA) expressed concerns about the bill's provisions on the state revolving loan fund, overall program funding, watershed management, and non-point source pollution. An industry group, the Clean Water Industry Coalition, said it saw problems with provisions relating to effluent guidelines, pollution prevention, prohibitions on the discharge of toxic chemicals, and the domestic sewage exclusion.

At a hearing in October, a representative of ASIWPCA said the bill would "significantly federalize" the current clean water program and hamper state action. In fact, he said, the bill "is fixing a lot of things that aren't broken."

In February 1994, the Senate Environment and Public Works Committee approved a new version of Baucus' legislation (S 2093), but early estimates that the Senate could begin floor consideration of the measure by April proved overly optimistic. Considerable opposition was voiced to specific provisions in the legislation, and one congressional aide said the bill would not reach the floor unless members could resolve the issue of polluted runoff and other major issues.

House legislation (HR 3948) was introduced by Rep. Norman Mineta (D-Calif) in March 1994 and revised by him in April. As in the Senate, however, considerable opposition developed over specific provisions, including polluted runoff, ground water protection, water quality standards, and enforcement. With opposition growing, and a number of legislators announcing plans to introduce amendments to correct what they perceived as deficiencies in the bill, Mineta held off markup. Mineta also said he would hold the bill back if any attempt was made to add provisions that would specifically mandate compensation to landowners for a "taking" of private property by regulatory requirements.

At mid-summer, few observers gave Clean Water Act reauthorization much chance approval in the 103rd Congress. Mineta said in late July that superfund reform would take precedence over markup of the Clean Water Act.

FINDING LIST

FEDERAL WATER POLLUTION CONTROL ACT, AS AMENDED BY THE CLEAN WATER ACT OF 1977

Public Law 92–500, approved Oct. 18, 1972, 86 Stat. 816.

33 U.S.C. §§1251 et seq.

Amended by PL 93–207, Dec. 28, 1973; PL 93–243, Jan. 2, 1974; PL 93–592, Jan. 2, 1975; PL 94–238, March 23, 1976; PL 94–273, April 21, 1976; PL 94–558, Oct. 19, 1976; PL 95–217, Dec. 28, 1977; PL 95–576, Nov. 2, 1978; PL 96–148, Dec. 16, 1979; PL 96–483, Oct. 21, 1980; PL 96–510, Dec. 11, 1980; PL 96–561, Dec. 22, 1980; PL 97–35, Aug. 13, 1981; PL 97–117, Dec. 29, 1981; PL 97–164, April 2, 1982; PL 97–440, Jan. 8, 1983; PL 100–4, Feb. 4, 1987; PL 100–202, Dec. 22, 1987; PL 100–236, Jan. 8, 1988; PL 100–581, Nov. 1, 1988; PL 100–653, Nov. 14, 1988; PL 100–688, Nov. 18, 1988; PL 101–380, Aug. 18, 1990; PL 101–596, Nov. 16, 1990; PL 102–285, May 18, 1992; PL 102–388, Oct. 6, 1992; PL 102–572, Oct. 29, 1992; PL 102–580, Oct. 31, 1992.

TITLE I—RESEARCH AND RELATED PROGRAMS

§1251. Declaration of Goals and Policy

[Sec. 101]

(a) The objective of this Act is to restore and maintain the chemical, physical, and biological integrity of the Nation's waters. In order to achieve this objective it is hereby declared that, consistent with the provisions of this Act—

(1) it is the national goal that the discharge of pollutants into the navigable waters be eliminated by 1985;

(2) it is the national goal that wherever attainable, an interim goal of water quality which provides for the protection and propagation of fish, shellfish, and wildlife and provides for recreation in and on the water be achieved by July 1, 1983;

(3) it is the national policy that the discharge of toxic pollutants in toxic amounts be prohibited;

(4) it is the national policy that Federal financial assistance be provided to construct publicly owned waste treatment works;

(5) it is the national policy that areawide waste treatment management planning processes be developed and implemented to assure adequate control of sources of pollutants in each State;

(6) it is the national policy that a major research and demonstration effort be made to develop technology necessary to eliminate the discharge of pollutants into the navigable waters, waters of the contiguous zone, and the oceans; and

(7) it is the national policy that programs for the control of nonpoint sources of pollution be developed and implemented in an expeditious manner so as to enable the goals of this Act to be met through the control of both point and nonpoint sources of pollution.

[§101(a)(7) added by PL 100–41]

(b) It is the policy of the Congress to recognize, preserve, and protect the primary responsibilities and rights of States to prevent, reduce, and eliminate pollution, to plan the development and use (including restoration, preservation, and enhancement) of land and water resources, and to consult with the Administrator in the exercise of his authority under this Act. It is the policy of Congress that the States manage the construction grant program under this Act and implement the permit programs under sections 402 and 404 of this Act. It is further the policy of the Congress to support and aid research relating to the prevention, reduction, and elimination of pollution, and to provide Federal technical services and financial aid to State and interstate agencies and municipalities in connection with the prevention, reduction, and elimination of pollution.

(c) It is further the policy of Congress that the President, acting through the Secretary of State and such national and international organizations as he determines appropriate, shall take such action as may be necessary to insure that to the fullest extent possible all foreign countries shall take meaningful action for the prevention, reduction, and elimination of pollution in their waters and in international waters and for the achievement of goals regarding the elimination of discharge of pollutants and the improvement of water quality to at least the same extent as the United States does under its laws.

(d) Except as otherwise expressly provided in this Act, the Administrator of the Environmental Protection Agency (hereinafter in this Act called "Administrator") shall administer this Act.

(e) Public participation in the development, revision, and enforcement of any regulation, standard, effluent limitation, plan, or program established by the Administrator or any State under this Act shall be provided for, encouraged, and assisted by the Administrator and the States. The Administrator, in cooperation with the States, shall develop and publish regulations specifying minimum guidelines for public participation in such processes.

(f) It is the national policy that to the maximum extent possible the procedures utilized for implementing this Act shall encourage the drastic minimization of paperwork and interagency decision procedures, and the best use of available manpower and funds, so as to prevent needless duplication and unnecessary delays at all levels of government.

(g) It is the policy of Congress that the authority of each State to allocate quantities of water within its jurisdiction shall not be superseded, abrogated or otherwise impaired by this Act. It is the further policy of Congress that nothing in this Act shall be construed to supersede or abrogate rights to quantities of water which have been established by any State. Federal agencies shall co-operate with State and local agencies to' develop comprehensive solutions to prevent, reduce and eliminate pollution in concert with programs for managing water resources.

§1252. Comprehensive Programs for Water Pollution Control [Sec. 102]

(a) The Administrator shall, after careful investigation, and in cooperation with other Federal agencies, State water pollution control agencies, interstate agencies, and the municipalities and industries involved, prepare or develop comprehensive programs for preventing, reducing, or eliminating the pollution of the navigable waters and ground waters and improving the sanitary condition of surface and underground waters. In the development of such comprehensive programs due regard shall be given to the improvements which are necessary to conserve such waters for the protection and propagation of fish and aquatic life and wildlife, recreational purposes, and the withdrawal of such waters for public water supply, agricultural, industrial, and other purposes. For the purpose of this section, the Administrator is authorized to make joint investigations with any such agencies of the condition of any waters in any State or States, and of the discharges of any sewage, industrial wastes, or substance which may adversely affect such waters.

(b) (1) In the survey of planning of any reservoir by the Corps of Engineers, Bureau of Reclamation, or other Federal agency, consideration shall be given to inclusion of storage for regulation of streamflow, except that any such storage and water releases shall not be provided as a substitute for adequate treatment or other methods of controlling waste at the source.

(2) The need for and the value of storage or regulation of streamflow (other than for water quality) including but not limited to navigation, salt water intrusion, recreation, esthetics, and fish and wildlife, shall be determined by the Corps of Engineers, Bureau of Reclamation, or other Federal agencies.

(3) The need for, the value of, and the impact of, storage for water quality control shall be determined by the Administrator, and his views on these matters shall be set forth in any report or presentation to Congress proposing authorization or construction of any reservoir including such storage.

(4) The value of such storage shall be taken into account in determining the economic value of the entire project of which it is a part, and costs shall be allocated to the purpose of regulation of streamflow in a manner which will insure that all project purposes, share equitably in the benefits of multiple-purpose construction.

(5) Costs of regulation of streamflow features incorporated in any Federal reservoir or other impoundment under the provisions of this Act shall be determined and the beneficiaries identified and if the benefits are widespread or national in scope, the costs of such features shall be nonreimbursable.

(6) No license granted by the Federal Power Commission for a hydroelectric power project shall include storage for regulation of stream flow for the purpose of water quality control unless the Administrator shall recommend its inclusion and such reservoir storage capacity shall not exceed such proportion of the total storage required for the water quality control plan as the drainage area of such reservoir bears to the drainage area of the river basin or basins involved in such water quality control plan.

(c) (1) The Administrator shall, at the request of the Governor of a State, or a majority of the Governors when more than one State is involved, make a grant to pay not to exceed 50 per centum of the administrative expenses of a planning agency for a period not to exceed three years, which period shall begin after the date of enactment of the Federal Water Pollution Control Act Amendments of 1972, if such agency provides for adequate representation of appropriate State, interstate, local, or (when appropriate) international interests in the basin or portion thereof involved and is capable of developing an effective, comprehensive water quality control plan for a basin or portion thereof.

(2) Each planning agency receiving a grant under this subsection shall develop a comprehensive pollution control plan for the basin or portion thereof which—

(A) is consistent with any applicable water quality standards, effluent and other limitations, and thermal discharge regulations established pursuant to current law within the basin;

(B) recommends such treatment works as will provide the most effective and economical means of collection, storage, treatment, and elimination of pollutants and recommends means to encourage both municipal and industrial use of such works;

(C) recommends maintenance and improvement of water quality within the basin or portion thereof and recommends methods of adequately financing those facilities as may be necessary to implement the plan; and

(D) as appropriate, is developed in cooperation with, and is consistent with any comprehensive plan prepared by the Water Resources Council, any areawide waste management plans developed pursuant to section 208 of this Act, and any State plan developed pursuant to section 303(e) of this Act.

(3) For the purposes of this subsection the term "basin" includes, but is not limited to, rivers and their tributaries, streams, coastal waters, sounds, estuaries, bays, lakes, and portions thereof, as well as the lands drained thereby.

(d) The Administrator, after consultation with the States, and River Basin Commissions established under the Water Resources Planning Act, shall submit a report to Congress on or before July 1, 1978, which analyzes the relationship between programs under this Act, and the programs by which State and Federal agencies allocate quantities of water. Such report shall include recommendations concerning the policy in section 101(g) of the Act to improve coordination of efforts to reduce and eliminate pollution in concert with programs for managing water resources.

§1253. Interstate Cooperation and Uniform Laws [Sec. 103]

(a) The Administrator shall encourage cooperative activities by the States for the prevention, reduction, and elimination of pollution, encourage the enactment of improved and, so far as practicable,uniform State laws relating to the prevention, reduction, and elimination of pollution; and encourage compacts between States for the prevention and control of pollution.

(b) The consent of the Congress is hereby given to two or more States to negotiate and enter into agreements or compacts, not in conflict with any law or treaty of the United States, for

(1) cooperative effort and mutual assistance for the prevention and control of pollution and the enforcement of their respective laws relating thereto, and (2) the establishment of such agencies, joint or otherwise, as they may deem desirable for making effective such agreements and compacts. No such agreement or compact shall be binding or obligatory upon any State a party thereto unless and until it has been approved by the Congress.

§1254. Research, Investigations, Training, and Information [Sec. 104]

(a) The Administrator shall establish national programs for the prevention, reduction, and elimination of pollution and as part of such programs shall—

(1) in cooperation with other Federal, State, and local agencies, conduct and promote the coordination and acceleration of, research, investigations, experiments, training, demonstrations, surveys, and studies relating to the causes, effects, extent, prevention, reduction, and elimination of pollution;

(2) encourage, cooperate with, and render technical services to pollution control agencies and other appropriate public or private agencies, institutions, and organizations, and individuals, including the general public, in the conduct of activities referred to in paragraph (1) of this subsection;

(3) conduct, in cooperation with State water pollution control agencies and other interested agencies, organizations and persons, public investigations conerning the pollution of any navigable waters, and report on the results of such investigations;

(4) establish advisory committees composed of recognized experts in various aspects of pollution and representatives of the public to assist in the examination and evaluation of research progress and proposals and to avoid duplication of research;

(5) in cooperation with the States, and their political subdivisions, and other Federal agencies establish, equip, and maintain a water quality surveillance system for the purpose of monitoring the quality of the navigable waters and ground waters and the contiguous zone

and the oceans and the Administrator shall, to the extent practicable, conduct such surveillance by utilizing the resources of the National Aeronautics and Space Administration, the National Oceanic and Atmospheric Administration, the United States Geological Survey, and the Coast Guard, and shall report on such quality in the report required under subsection (a) of section 516; and

[§104(a)(5) amended by PL 102–285]

(6) initiate and promote the coordination and acceleration of research designed to develop the most effective practicable tools and techniques for measuring the social and economic costs and benefits of activities which are subject to regulation under this Act; and shall transmit a report on the results of such research to the Congress not later than January 1, 1974.

(b) In carrying out the provisions of subsection (a) of this section the Administrator is authorized to—

(1) collect and make available, through publications and other appropriate means, the results of and other information, including appropriate recommendations by him in connection therewith, pertaining to such research and other activities referred to in paragraph (1) of subsection (a);

(2) cooperate with other Federal departments and agencies, State water pollution control agencies, interstate agencies, other public and private agencies, institutions, organizations, industries involved, and individuals, in the preparation and conduct of such research and other activities referred to in paragraph (1) of subsection (a);

(3) make grants to State water pollution control agencies, interstate agencies, other public or nonprofit private agencies, institutions, organizations, and individuals, for purposes stated in paragraph (1) of subsection (a) of this section;

(4) contract with public or private agencies, institutions, organizations, and individuals, without regard to sections 3648 and 3709 of the Revised Statutes (31 U.S.C. 529; 41 U.S.C. 5), referred to in paragraph (1) of subsection (a);

(5) establish and maintain research fellowships at public or nonprofit private educational institutions or research organizations;

(6) collect and disseminate, in cooperation with other Federal departments and agencies, and with other public or private agencies, institutions, and organizations having related responsibilities, basic data on chemical, physical, and biological effects of varying water quality and other information pertaining to pollution and the prevention, reduction, and elimination thereof; and

(7) develop effective and practical processes, methods, and prototype devices for the prevention, reduction, and elimination of pollution.

(c) In carrying out the provisions of subsection (a) of this section the Administrator shall conduct research on, and survey the results of other scientific studies on, the harmful effects on the health or welfare of persons caused by pollutants. In order to avoid duplication of effort, the Administrator shall, to the extent practicable, conduct such research in cooperation with and through the facilities of the Secretary of Health, Education, and Welfare.

(d) In carrying out the provisions of this section the Administrator shall develop and demonstrate under varied conditions (including conducting such basic and applied research, studies, and experiments as may be necessary:

(l) Practicable means of treating municipal sewage, and other waterborne wastes to implement the requirements of section 201 of this Act;

(2) Improved methods and procedures to identify and measure the effects of pollutants including those pollutants created by new technological developments; and

(3) Methods and procedures for evaluating the effects on water quality of augmented streamflows to control pollution not susceptible to other means of prevention, reduction, or elimination.

(e) The Administrator shall establish, equip, and maintain field laboratory and research facilities, including, but not limited to, one to be located in the northeastern area of the United States, one in the Middle Atlantic area, one in the southeastern area, one in the midwestern area, one in the southwestern area, one in the Pacific Northwest, and one in the State of Alaska, for the conduct of research, investigations, experiments, field demonstrations and studies, and training relating to the prevention, reduction and elimination of pollution. Insofar as practicable, each such facility shall be located near institutions of higher learning in which graduate training in such research might be carried out. In conjunction with the development of criteria under section 403 of this Act, the Administrator shall construct the facilities authorized for the National Marine

Water Quality Laboratory established under this subsection.

(f) The Administrator shall conduct research and technical development work, and make studies, with respect to the quality of the waters of the Great Lakes, including an analysis of the present and projected future water quality of the Great Lakes under varying conditions of waste treatment and disposal, an evaluation of the water quality needs of those to be served by such waters, an evaluation of municipal, industrial, and vessel waste treatment and disposal practices with respect to such waters, and a study of alternate means of solving pollution problems (including additional waste treatment measures) with respect to such waters.

(g) (1) For the purpose of providing an adequate supply of trained personnel to operate and maintain existing and future treatment works and related activities, and for the purpose of enhancing substantially the proficiency of those engaged in such activities, the Administrator shall finance pilot programs, in cooperation with State and interstate agencies, municipalities, educational institutions, and other organizations and individuals, of manpower development and training and retraining of persons in, on entering into, the field of operation and maintenance of treatment works and related activities. Such program and any funds expended for such a program shall supplement, not supplant, other manpower and training programs and funds available for the purposes of this paragraph. The Administrator is authorized under such terms and conditions as he deems appropriate, to enter into agreements with one or more States, acting jointly or severally, or with other public or private agencies or institutions for the development and implementation of such a program.

(2) The Administrator is authorized to enter into agreements with public and private agencies and institutions, and individuals to develop and maintain an effective system for forecasting the supply of, and demand for, various professional and other occupational categories needed for the prevention, reduction, and elimination of pollution in each region, State, or area of the United States and; from time to time, to publish the results of such forecasts.

(3) In furtherance of the purposes of this Act, the Administrator is authorized to—

(A) make grants to public or private agencies and institutions and to individuals for training projects, and provide for the conduct of training by contract with public or private agencies and institutions and with individuals without regard to sections 3648 and 3709 of the Revised Statutes;

(B) establish and maintain research fellowships in the Environmental Protection Agency with such stipends and allowances, including traveling and subsistence expenses, as he may deem necessary to procure the assistance of the most promising research fellows; and

(C) provide, in addition to the program established under paragraph (1) of this subsection, training in technical matters relating to the causes, prevention, reduction, and elimination of pollution for personnel of public agencies and other persons with suitable qualifications.

(4) The Administrator shall submit, through the President, a report to the Congress not later than December 31, 1973, summarizing the actions taken under this subsection and the effectiveness of such actions, and setting forth the number of persons trained, the occupational categories for which training was provided, the effectiveness of other Federal, State, and local training programs in this field, together with estimates of future needs, recommendations on improving training programs, and such other information and recommendations, including legislative recommendations, as he deems appropriate.

(h) The Administrator is authorized to enter into contracts with, or make grants to, public or private agencies and organizations and individuals for (A) the purpose of developing and demonstrating new or improved methods for the prevention, removal, reduction, and elimination of pollution in lakes, including the undesirable effects of nutrients and vegetation, and (B) the construction of publicly owned research facilities for such purpose.

(i) The Administrator, in cooperation with the Secretary of the department in which the Coast Guard is operating, shall—

(1) engage in such research, studies, experiments, and demonstrations as he deems appropriate, relative to the removal of oil from any waters and to the prevention, control, and elimination of oil and hazardous substances pollution;

(2) publish from time to time the results of such activities; and

(3) from time to time, develop and publish in the Federal Register specifications and other

technical information on the various chemical compounds used in the control of oil and hazardous substances spills.

In carrying out this subsection, the Administrator may enter into contracts with, or make grants to, public or private agencies and organizations and individuals.

(j) The Secretary of the department in which the Coast Guard is operating shall engage in such research, studies, experiments, and demonstrations as he deems appropriate relative to equipment which is to be installed on board a vessel and is designed to receive, retain, treat, or discharge human body wastes and the wastes from toilets and other receptacles intended to receive or retain body wastes with particular emphasis on equipment to be installed on small recreational vessels. The Secretary of the department in which the Coast Guard is operating shall report to Congress the results of such research, studies, experiments, and demonstrations prior to the effective date of any regulations established under section 312 of this Act. In carrying out this subsection the Secretary of the department in which the Coast Guard is operating may enter into contracts with, or make grants to, public or private organizations and individuals.

(k) In carrying out the provisions of this section relating to the conduct by the Administrator of demonstration projects and the development of field laboratories and research facilities, the Administrator may acquire land and interests therein by purchase, with appropriated or donated funds, by donation, or by exchange for acquired or public lands under his jurisdiction which he classifies as suitable for disposition. The values of the properties so exchanged either shall be approximately equal, or if they are not approximately equal, the values shall be equalized by the payment of cash to the grantor or to the Administrator as the circumstances require.

(l) (1) The Administrator shall, after consultation with appropriate local, State, and Federal agencies, public and private organizations, and interested individuals, as soon as practicable but not later than January 1, 1973, develop and issue to the States for the purpose of carrying out this Act the latest scientific knowledge available in indicating the kind and extent of effects on health and welfare which may be expected from the presence of pesticides in the water in varying quantities. He shall revise and add to such information whenever necessary to reflect developing scientific knowledge.

(2) The President shall, in consultation with appropriate local, State, and Federal agencies, public and private organizations, and interested individuals, conduct studies and investigations of methods to control the release of pesticides into the environment which study shall include examination of the persistency of pesticides in the water environment and alternatives thereto. The President shall submit reports, from time to time, on such investigations to Congress together with his recommendations for any necessary legislation.

(m) (1) The Administrator shall, in an effort to prevent degradation of the environment from the disposal of waste oil, conduct a study of (A) the generation of used engine, machine, cooling, and similar waste oil, including quantities generated, the nature and quality of such oil, present collecting methods and disposal practices, and alternate uses of such oil; (B) the long-term, chronic biological effects of the disposal of such waste oil; and (C) the potential market for such oils, including the economic and legal factors relating to the sale of products made from such oils, the level of subsidy, if any, needed to encourage the purchase by public and private nonprofit agencies of products from such oil, and the practicability of Federal procurement, on a priority basis, of products made from such oil. In conducting such study, the Administrator shall consult with affected industries and other persons.

(2) The Administrator shall report the preliminary results of such study to Congress within six months after the date of enactment of the Federal Water Pollution Control Act Amendments of 1972, and shall submit a final report to Congress within 18 months after such date of enactment.

(n) (1) The Administrator shall, in cooperation with the Secretary of the Army, the Secretary of Agriculture, the Water Resources Council, and with other appropriate Federal, State, interstate, or local public bodies and private organizations, institutions, and individuals, conduct and promote, encourage contributions to, continuing comprehensive studies of the effects of pollution, including sedimentation, in the estuaries and estuarine zones of the United States on fish and wildlife, on sport and commercial fishing, on recreation, on water supply and water power, and on other beneficial purposes. Such studies shall also consider the effect of demographic trends, the exploitation of mineral resources and fossil fuels, land and industrial development, navigation, flood and erosion control, and other uses of estuaries and estuarine zones upon the pollution of the waters therein.

(2) In conducting such studies, the Administrator shall assemble, coordinate, and organize all existing pertinent information on the Nation's estuaries and estuarine zones; carry out a program of investigations and surveys to supplement existing information in representative estuaries and estuarine zones; and identify the problems and areas where further research and study are required.

(3) The Administrator shall submit to Congress, from time to time, reports of the studies authorized by this subsection but at least one such report during any six-year period. Copies of each such report shall be made available to all interested parties, public and private.

(4) For the purpose of this subsection, the term "estuarine zones" means an environmental system consistting of an estuary and those transitional areas which are consistently influenced or affected by water from an estuary such as, but not limited to, salt marshes, coastal and intertidal areas, bays, harbors, lagoons, inshore waters, and channels, and the term "estuary" means all or part of the mouth of a river or stream or other body of water having unimpaired natural connection with open sea and within which the sea water is measurably diluted with fresh water derived from land drainage.

(o) (1) The Administrator shall conduct research and investigations on devices, systems, incentives, pricing policy, and other methods of reducing the total flow of sewage, including, but not limited to, unnecessary water consumption in order to reduce the requirements for, and the costs of, sewage and waste treatment services. Such research and investigations shall be directed to develop devices, systems, policies, and methods capable of achieving the maximum reduction of unnecessary water consumption.

(2) The Administrator shall report the preliminary results of such studies and investigations to the Congress within one year after the date of enactment of the Federal Water Pollution Control Act Amendments of 1972, and annually thereafter in the report required under subsection (a) of section 516. Such report shall include recommendations for any legislation that may be required to provide for the adoption and use of devices, systems, policies, or other methods of reducing water consumption and reducing the total flow of sewage. Such report shall include an estimate of the benefits to be derived from adoption and use of such devices, systems, policies, or other methods and also shall reflect estimates of any increase in private, public, or other cost that would be occasioned thereby.

(p) In carrying out the provisions of subsection (a) of this section the Administrator shall, in cooperation with the Secretary of Agriculture, other Federal agencies, and the States, carry out a comprehensive study and research program to determine new and improved methods and the better application of existing methods of preventing, reducing, and eliminating pollution from agriculture, including the legal, economic, and other implications of the use of such methods.

(q) (1) The Administrator shall conduct a comprehensive program of research and investigation and pilot project implementation into new and improved methods of preventing reducing, storing, collecting, treating, or otherwise eliminating pollution from sewage in rural and other areas where collection of sewage in conventional, community-wide sewage collection systems is impractical, uneconomical, or otherwise infeasible, or where soil conditions or other factors preclude the use of septic tank and drainage field systems.

(2) The Administrator shall conduct a comprehensive program of research and investigation and pilot project implementation into new and improved methods for the collection and treatment of sewage and other liquid wastes combined with the treatment and disposal of solid wastes.

(3) The Administrator shall establish, either within the Environmental Protection Agency, or through contract with an appropriate public or private non-profit organization, a national clearinghouse which shall (A) receive reports and information resulting from research, demonstrations, and other projects funded under this Act related to paragraph (1) of this subsection and to subsection (e)(2) of section 105; (B) coordinate and disseminate such reports and information for use by Federal and Staie agencies, municipalities, institutions, and persons in developing new and improved methods pursuant to this subsection; and (C) provide for the collection and dissemination of reports and information relevant to this subsection from other Federal and State agencies, institutions, universities, and persons.

(4) Small Flows Clearinghouse.— Notwithstanding section 205(d) of this Act, from amounts t:iat are set aside for a fiscal year

under section 205(i) of this Act and are not obligated by the end of the 24-month period of availability for such amounts under section 205(d), the Administrator shall make available $1,000,000 or such unobligated amount, whichever is less, to support a national clearinghouse within the Environmental Protection Agency to collect and disseminate information on small flows of sewage and innovative or alternative wastewater treatment processes and techniques, consistent with paragraph (3). This paragraph shall apply with respect to amounts set aside under section 205(i) for which the 24–month period of availability referred to in the preceding sentence ends on or after September 30, 1986.

[§104(q)(4) added by PL 100–41]

(r) The Administrator is authorized to make grants to colleges and universities to conduct basic research into the structure and function of fresh water aquatic ecosystems, and to improve understanding of the ecological characteristics necessary to the maintenance of the chemical, physical, and biological integrity of freshwater aquatic ecosystems.

(s) The Administrator is authorized to make grants to one or more institutions of higher education (regionally located and to be designated as "River Study Centers") for the purpose of conducting and reporting on interdisciplinary studies on the nature of river systems, including, hydrology, biology, ecology, economics, the relationship between river uses and land uses, and the effects of development within river basins on river systems and on the value of water resources and water related activities. No such grant in any fiscal year shall exceed $1,000,000.

(t) The Administrator shall, in cooperation with State and Federal agencies and public and private organizations, conduct continuing comprehensive studies of the effects and methods of control of thermal discharges. In evaluating alternative methods of control the studies shall consider (1) such data as are available on the latest available technology, economic feasibility including cost-effectivness analysis, and (2) the total impact on the environment, considering not only water quality but also air quality, land use, and effective utilization and conservation of fresh water and other natural resources. Such studies shall consider methods of minimizing adverse effects and maximizing beneficial effects of thermal discharges. The results of these studies shall be reported by the Administrator as soon as practicable, but not later than 270 days after enactment of this subsection, and shall be made available to the public and the States, and considered as they become available by the Administrator in carrying out section 316 of this Act and by the States in proposing thermal water quality standards.

(u) There is authorized to be appropriated (1) not to exceed $100,000,000 per fiscal year ending June 30, 1973, the fiscal year ending June 30, 1974, and the fiscal year ending June 30, 1975, not to exceed $14,039,000 for the fiscal year ending September 30, 1980, not to exceed $20,697,000 for the fiscal year ending September 30, 1981, not to exceed $22,770,000 for the fiscal year ending September 30, 1982, such sums as may be necessary for fiscal years 1983 through 1985, and not to exceed $22,770,000 per fiscal year for each of the fiscal years 1986 through 1990, for carrying out the provisions of this section, other than subsections (g)(1) and (2), (p), (r), and (t), except that such authorizations are not for any research, development, or demonstration activity pursuant to such provisions; (2) not to exceed $7,500,000 for fiscal years 1973, 1974, and 1975, $2,000,000 for fiscal year 1977, $3,000,000 for fiscal year 1978, $3,000,000 for fiscal year 1979, $3,000,000 for fiscal year 1980, $3,000,000 for fiscal year 1981, $3,000,000 for fiscal year 1982, such sums as may be necessary for fiscal years 1983 through 1985, and $3,000,000 per fiscal year for each of the fiscal years 1986 through 1990, for carrying out the provisions of subsection (g)(1); (3) not to exceed $2,500,000 for fiscal year 1973, 1974, and 1975. $1,000,000 for fiscal year 1977, $1,500,000 for fiscal year 1978, $1,500,000 for fiscal year 1979, $1,500,000 for fiscal year 1980, $1,500,000 for fiscal year 1981, $1,500,000 for fiscal year 1982, such sums as may be necessary for fiscal years 1983 through 1985, and $1,500,000 per fiscal year for each of the fiscal years 1986 through 1990, for carrying out the provisions of subsection (g)(2); (4) not to exceed $10,000,000 for each of the fiscal years ending June 30, 1973, June 30, 1974, and June 30, 1975, for carrying out the provisions of subsection (p); (5) not to exceed $15,000,000 per fiscal year for the fiscal years ending June 30, 1973, June 30, 1974, and June 30, 1975, for carrying out the provisions of subsection (r); and (6) not to exceed $10,000,000 per fiscal year for the fiscal years ending June 30, 1973, June 30, 1974, and June 30, 1975, for carrying out the provisions of subsection (t).

[§104(u) amended by PL 95–576; PL 96–483; PL 100–4]

[Editor's Note: §105 of PL 100–4 required further research by the EPA. The provisions follow.]

Research on Effects of Pollutants [Sec. 105]

In carrying out the provisions of section 104(a) of the Federal Water Pollution Control Act, the Administrator shall conduct research on the harmful effects on the health and welfare of persons caused by pollutants in water, in conjunction with the United States Fish and Wildlife Service, the National Oceanic and Atmospheric Administration, and other Federal, State, and interstate agencies carrying on such research. Such research shall include, and shall place special emphasis on, the effect that bioaccumulation of these pollutants in aquatic species has upon reducing the value of aquatic commercial and sport industries. Such research shall further study methods to reduce and remove these pollutants from the relevant affected aquatic species so as to restore and enhance these valuable resources.

§1255. Grants for Research and Development [Sec. 105]

(a) The Administrator is authorized to conduct in the Environmental Protection Agency, and to make grants to any State, municipality, or intermunicipal or interstate agency for the purpose of assisting in the development of—

(1) any project which will demonstrate a new or improved method of preventing, reducing, and eliminating the discharge into any waters of pollutants from sewers which carry storm water or both storm water and pollutants; or

(2) any project which will demonstrate advanced waste treatment and water purification methods (including the temporary use of new or improved chemical additives which provide substantial immediate improvement to existing treatment processes), or new or improved methods of joint treatment systems for municipal and industrial wastes; and to include in such grants such amounts as are necessary for the purpose of reports, plans, and specifications in connection therewith.

(b) The Administrator is authorized to make grants to any State or States or interstate agency to demonstrate, in river basins or portions thereof, advanced treatment and environmental enhancement techniques to control pollution from all sources, within such basins or portions thereof, including nonpoint sources, together with in stream water quality improvement techniques.

(c) In order to carry out the purposes of section 301 of this Act, the Administrator is authorized to (1) conduct in the Environmental Protection Agency, (2) make grants to persons, and (3) enter into contracts with persons, for research and demonstration projects for prevention of pollution of any waters by industry including, but not limited to, the prevention, reduction, and elimination of the discharge of pollutants. No grant shall be made for any project under this subsection unless the Administrator determines that such project will develop or demonstrate a new or improved method of treating industrial wastes or otherwise prevent pollution by industry, which method shall have industry-wide application.

(d) In carrying out the provisions of this section, the Administrator shall conduct, on a priority basis, an accelerated effort to develop, refine, and achieve practical application of:

(1) waste management methods applicable to point and nonpoint sources of pollutants to eliminate the discharge of pollutants, including, but not limited to, elimination of runoff of pollutants and the effects of pollutants from inplace or accumulated sources;

(2) advanced waste treatment methods applicable to point and nonpoint sources, including inplace or accumulated sources of pollutants, and methods for reclaiming and recycling water and confining pollutants so they will not migrate to cause water or other environmental pollution; and

(3) improved methods and procedures to identify and measure the effects of pollutants on the chemical, physical, and biological integrity of water, including those pollutants created by new technological developments.

(e)(1) The Administrator is authorized to (A) make, in consultation with the Secretary of Agriculture, grants to persons for research and demonstration projects with respect to new and improved methods of preventing, reducing, and eliminating pollution from agriculture, and (B) disseminate, in cooperation with the Secretary of Agriculture, such information obtained under this subsection, section 104(p), and section 304 as will encourage and enable the adoption of such methods in the agricultural industry.

(2) The Administrator is authorized, (A) in consultation with other interested Federal agencies, to make grants for demonstration projects with respect to new and improved methods of preventing, reducing, storing, collecting, treating, or otherwise eliminating pollution from sewage in rural and other areas where collection of sewage in conventional, community-wide sewage collection systems is

impractical, uneconomical, or otherwise infeasible, or where soil conditions or other factors preclude the use of septic tank and drainage field systems, and (B) in cooperation with other interested Federal and State agencies, to disseminate such information obtained under this subsection as will encourage and enable the adoption of new and improved methods developed pursuant to this subsection.

(f) Federal grants under subsection (a) of this section shall be subject to the following limitations:

(1) No grant shall be made for any project unless such project shall have been approved by the appropriate State water pollution control agency or agencies and by the Administrator;

(2) No grant shall be made for any project in an amount exceeding 75 per centum of cost thereof as determined by the Administrator; and

(3) No grant shall be made for any project unless the Administrator determines that such project will serve as a useful demonstration for the purpose set forth in clause (1) or (2) of subsection (a).

(g) Federal grants under subsections (c) and (d) of this section shall not exceed 75 per centum of the cost of the project.

(h) For the purpose of this section there is authorized to be appropriated $75,000,000 per fiscal year for the fiscal year ending June 30, 1973, the fiscal year ending June 30, 1974, and the fiscal year ending June 30, 1975, and from such appropriations at least 10 per centum of the funds actually appropriated in each fiscal year shall be available only for the purposes of subsection (e).

(i) The Administrator is authorized to make grants to a municipality to assist in the costs of operating and maintaining a project which received a grant under this section, section 104, or section 113 of this Act prior to the date of enactment of this subsection so as to reduce the operation and maintenance costs borne by the recipients of services from such project to costs comparable to those for projects assisted under title II of this Act.

(j) The Administrator is authorized to make a grant to any grantee who received an increased grant pursuant to section 202(a)(2) of this Act. Such grant may pay up to 100 per centum of the costs of technical evaluation of the operation of the treatment works, costs of training of persons (other than employees of the grantee), and costs of disseminating technical information on the operation of the treatment works.

§1256. Grants for Pollution Control Programs [Sec. 106]

(a) There are hereby authorized to be appropriated the following sums, to remain available until expended, to carry out the purposes of this section—

(1) $60,000,000 for the fiscal year ending June 30, 1973; and

(2) $75,000,000 for the fiscal year ending June 30, 1974, and the fiscal year ending June 30, 1975, $100,000,000 per fiscal year for the fiscal years 1977, 1978, 1979, 1980, $75,000,000 per fiscal year for the final years 1981 and 1982, such sums as may be necessary for fiscal years 1983 through 1985, and $75,000,000 per fiscal year for each of the fiscal years 1986 through 1990; for grants to States and to interstate agencies to assist them in administering programs for the prevention, reduction, and elimination of pollution, including enforcement directly or through appropriate State law enforcement officers or agencies.

[§106(a)(2) amended by PL 96-483; PL 100-4]

(b) From the sums appropriated in any fiscal year, the Administrator shall make allotments to the several States and interstate agencies in accordance with regulations promulgated by him on the basis of the extent of the pollution problem in the respective States.

(c) The Administrator is authorized to pay each State and interstate agency each fiscal year either—

(1) the allotment of such State or agency for such fiscal year under subsection (b), or

(2) the reasonable costs as determined by the Administrator of developing and carrying out a pollution program by such State or agency during such fiscal year, whichever amount is the lesser.

(d) No grant shall be made under this section to any State or interstate agency for any fiscal year when the expenditure of non-Federal funds by such State or interstate agency during such fiscal year for the recurrent expenses of carrying out its pollution control program are less than the expenditure by such State or interstate agency of non-Federal funds for such recurrent program expenses during the fiscal year ending June 30, 1971.

(e) Beginning in fiscal year 1974 the Administrator shall not make any grant under this section to any State which has not provided or is not carrying out as a part of its program—

(1) the establishment and operation of appropriate devices, methods, systems, and procedures necessary to monitor, and to compile and analyze data on (including classification according to eutrophic condition), the quality of navigable waters and to the extent practIcable, ground waters including biological monitoring; and provision for annually updating such data and including it in the report required under section 305 of this Act;

(2) authority comparable to that in section 504 of this Act and adequate contingency plans to implement such authority.

(f) Grants shall be made under this section on condition that—

(1) Such State (or interstate agency) filed with the Administrator within one hundred and twenty days after the date of enactment of this section:

(A) a summary report of the current status of the State pollution control program, including the criteria used by the State in determining priority of treatment works; and

(B) such additional information, data, and reports as the Administrator may require.

(2) No federally assumed enforcement as defined in section 309(a)(2) is in effect with respect to such State or interstate agency.

(3) Such State (or interstate agency) submits within one hundred and twenty days after the date of enactment of this section and before October 1 of each year thereafter for the Administrator's approval of its program for the prevention, reduction, and elimination of pollution in accordance with purposes and provisions of this Act in such form and content as the Administrator may prescribe.

[§106(f)(3) amended by PL 94–273]

(g) Any sums allotted under subsection (b) in any fiscal year which are not paid shall be reallotted by the Administrator in accordance with regulations promulgated by him.

§1257. Mine Water Pollution Control Demonstrations [Sec. 107]

(a) The Administrator in cooperation with the Appalachian Regional Commission and other Federal agencies is authorized to conduct, to make grants for, or to contract for, projects to demonstrate comprehensive approaches to the elimination or control of acid or other mine water pollution resulting from active or abandoned mining operations and other environmental pollution affecting water quality within all or part of a watershed or river basin, including siltation from surface mining. Such projects shall demonstrate the engineering and economic feasibility and practicality of various abatement techniques which will contribute substantially to effective and practical methods of acid or other mine water pollution elimination or control, and other pollution affecting water quality, including techniques that demonstrate the engineering and economic feasibility and practicality of using sewage sludge materials and other municipal wastes to diminish or prevent pollution affecting water quality from acid, sedimentation, or other pollutants and in such projects to restore affected lands to usefulness for forestry, agriculture, recreation, or other beneficial purposes.

(b) Prior to undertaking any demonstration project under this section in the Appalachian region (as defined in section 403 of the Appalachian Regional Development Act of 1965, as amended), the Appalachian Regional Commission shall determine that such demonstration project is consistent with the objectives of the Appalachian Regional Development Act of 1965, as amended.

(c) The Administrator, in selecting watersheds for the purposes of this section, shall be satisfied that the project area will not be affected adversely by the influx of acid or other mine water pollution from nearby sources.

(d) Federal participation in such projects shall be subject to the conditions—

(1) that the State shall acquire any land or interests therein necessary for such project; and

(2) that the State shall provide legal and practical protection to the project area to insure against any activities which will cause future acid or other mine water pollution.

(e) There is authorized to be appropriated $30,000,000 to carry out the provisions of this section, which sum shall be available until expended.

§1258. Pollution Control in Great Lakes [Sec. 108]

(a) The Administrator, in cooperation with other Federal departments, agencies, and instrumentalities is authorized to enter, into agreements with any State, political subdivision, interstate agency, or other public agency, or combination thereof, to carry out one or more projects to demonstrate new methods and techniques and to develop preliminary plans for the elimination or control of pollution, within all or any part of the watersheds of the Great Lakes. Such projects shall demonstrate the engineering and economic feasibility and practicality of removal of pollutants and prevention of any polluting matter from entering into the Great Lakes in the future and other reduction and remedial techniques which will contribute substantially to effective and practical methods of pollution prevention, reduction, or elimination.

(b) Federal participation in such projects shall be subject to the condition that the State, political subdivision, interstate agency, or other public agency, or combination thereof, shall pay not less than 25 per centum of the actual project costs, which payment may be in any form, including, but not limited to, land or interests therein that is needed for the project, and personal property or services the value of which shall be determined by the Administrator.

(c) There is authorized to be appropriated $20,000,000 to carry out the provisions of subsections (a) and (b) of this section, which sum shall be available until expended.

(d) (1) In recognition of the serious conditions which exist in Lake Erie, the Secretary of the Army, acting through the Chief of Engineers, is directed to design and develop a demonstration waste water management program for the rehabilitation and environmental repair of Lake Erie. Prior to the initiation of detailed engineering and design, the program, along with the specific recommendations shall be submitted to the Congress for statutory approval. This authority is in addition to, and not in lieu of, other waste water studies aimed at eliminating pollution emanating from select sources around Lake Erie.

(2) This program is to be developed in cooperation with the Environmental Protection Agency, other interested departments, agencies, and instrumentalities of the Federal Government, and the States and their political subdivisions. This program shall set forth alternative systems for managing waste water on a regional basis and shall provide local and State governments with a range of choice as to the type of system to be used for the treatment of waste water. These alternative systems shall include both advanced waste treatment technology and land disposal systems including aerated treatment-spray irrigation technology and will also include provisions for the disposal of solid wastes, including sludge. Such program should include measures to control point sources of pollution, area sources of pollution, including acid-mine drainage, urban runoff and rural runoff, and in place sources of pollution, including bottom loads, sludge banks, and polluted harbor dredgings.

(e) There is authorized to be appropriated $5,000,000 to carry out the provisions of subsection (d) of this section, which sum shall be available until expended.

§1259. Training Grants and Contracts [Sec. 109]

(a) The Administrator is authorized to make grants to or contracts with institutions of higher education, or combinations of such institutions, to assist them in planning, developing, strengthening, improving, or carrying out programs or projects for the preparation of undergraduate students to enter an occupation which involves the design, operation, and maintenance of treatment works. and other facilities whose purpose is water quality control. Such grants or contracts may include payment of all or part of the cost of programs or projects such as—

(A) planning for the development or expansion of programs or projects for training persons in the operation and maintenance of treatment works:

(B) training and retraining of faculty members;

(C) conduct of short-term or regular session institutes for study by persons engaged in, or preparing to engage in, the preparation of students preparing to enter an occupation involving the operation and maintenance of treatment works;

(D) carrying out innovative and experimental programs of cooperative education involving alternate periods of full-time or part-time academic study at the institution and periods of full-time or part-time employment involving the operation and maintenance of treatment works; and

(E) research into, and development of, methods of training students or faculty, including the preparation of teaching materials and the planning of curriculum.

(b) (1) The Administrator may pay 100 per centum of any additional cost of construction of treatment works required for a facility to train and upgrade waste treatment works operation and maintenance personnel and for the costs of other State treatment works operator training programs, including mobile training units, classroom rental, specialized instructors, and instructional material.

(2) The Administrator shall make no more than one grant for such additional construction in

any State (to serve a group of States, where, in his judgment, efficient training programs require multi- State programs), and shall make such grant after consultation with and approval by the State or States on the basis of (A) the suitability of such facility for training operation and maintenance personnel for treatment works throughout such State or States; and (B) a commitment by the State agency or agencies to carry out at such facility a program of training approved by the Administrator. In any case where a grant is made to serve two or more States, the Administrator is authorized to make an additional grant for a supplemental facility in each such State.

(3) The Administrator may make such grant out of the sums allocated to a State under section 205 of this Act, except that in no event shall the Federal cost of any such training facilities exceed $500,000.

(4) The Administrator may exempt a grant under thIs section from any requirement under section 204(a)(3) of this Act. Any grantee who received a grant under this section prior to enactment of the Clean Water Act of 1977 shall be eligible to have its grant increased by funds made available under such Act.

§1260. Application for Training Grant or Contract; Allocation of Grants or Contracts [Sec. 110]

(1) A grant or contract authorized by section 109 may be made only upon application to the Administrator at such time or times and containing such information as he may prescribe, except that no such application shall be approved unless it—

(A) sets forth programs, activities, research, or development for which a grant is authorized under section 109 and describes the relation to any program set forth by the applicant in an application, if any, submitted pursuant to section 111;

(B) provides such fiscal control and fund accounting procedures as may be necessary to assure proper disbursement of and accounting for Federal funds paid to the applicant under this section; and

(C) provides for making such reports, in such form and containing such information, as the Administrator may require to carry out his functions under this section, and for keeping such records and for affording such access thereto as the Administrator may find necessary to assure the correctness and verification of such reports.

(2) The Administrator shall allocate grants or contracts under section 109 in such manner as will most nearly provide an equitable distribution of the grants or contracts throughout the United States among institutions of higher education which show promise of being able to use funds effectively for the purpose of this section.

(3) (A) Payments under this section may be used in accordance with regulations of the Administrator, and subject to the terms and conditions set forth in an application approved under paragraph (1), to pay part of the compensation of students employed in connection with the operation and maintenance of treatment works, other than as an employee in connection with the operation and maintenance of treatment works or as an employee in any branch of the Government of the United States, as part of a program for which a grant has been approved pursuant to this section.

(B) Departments and agencies of the United States are encouraged, to the extent consistent with efficient administration, to enter into arrangements with institutions of higher education for the full- time, part-time, or temporary employment, whether in the competitive or excepted service, of students enrolled in programs set forth in applications approved under paragraph (1).

§1261. Award of Scholarships [Sec. 111]

(1) The Administrator is authorized to award scholarships in accordance with the provisions of this section for undergraduate study by persons who plan to enter an occupation involving the operation and maintenance of treatment works. Such scholarships shall be awarded for such periods as the Administrator may determine but not to exceed four academic years.

(2) The Administrator shall allocate scholarships under this section among institutions of higher educationwith programs approved under the provisions of this section for the use of individuals accepted into such programs, in such manner and accordance to such plan as will insofar as practicable—

(A) provide an equitable distribution of such scholarships throughout the United States; and

(B) attract recent graduates of secondary schools to enter an occupation involving the operation and mainte nance of treatment works.

(3) The Administrator shall approve a program of any institution of higher education for the purposes ofthis section only upon application by the institution and only upon his finding—

(A) that such program has a principal objective the education and training of persons in the operation and maintenance of treatment works;

(B) that such program is in effect and of high quality, or can be readily put into effect and may reasonably be expected to be of high quality;

(C) that the application describes the relation of such program to any program, activity, research, or development set forth by the applicant in an application, if any, submitted pursuant to section 110 of this Act; and

(D) that the application contains satisfactory assurances that (i) the institution will recommend to the Administrator for the award of scholarships under this section, for study in such program, only persons who have demonstrated to the satisfaction of the institution a serious intent, upon completing the program, to enter an occupation involving the operation and maintenance of treatment works, and (ii) the institution will make reasonable continuing efforts to encourage recipients of scholarships under this section, enrolled in such program, to enter occupations involving the operation and maintenance of treatment works upon completing the program.

(4) (A) The Administrator shall pay to persons awarded scholarships under this section such stipends (including such allowances for subsistence and other expenses for such persons and their dependents) as he may determine to be consistent with prevailing practices under comparable federally supported programs.

(B) The Administrator shall (in addition to the stip ends paid to persons under paragraph (1)) pay to the institution of higher education at which such person is pursuing his course of study such amount as he may determine to be consistent with prevailing practices under comparable federally support programs.

(5) A person awarded a scholarship under the provisions of this section shall continue to receive the payments provided in this section only during such periods as the Administrator finds that he is maintaining satisfactory proficiency and devoting full time to study or research in the field in which such scholarship was awarded in an institution of higher education, and is no engaging in gainful employment other than employment approved by the Administrator by or pursuant to regulation.

(6) The Administrator shall by regulation provide that any person awarded a scholarship under this section shall agree in writing to enter and remain in an occupation involving the design, operation, or maintenance of treatment works for such period after completion of this course of studies as the Administrator determines appropriate.

§1262. Definitions and Authorizations
[Sec. 112]

(a) As used in sections 109 through 112 of this Act—

(1) The term "institution of higher education" means an education institution described in the first sentence of section 1201 of the Higher Education Act of 1965 (other than an institution of any agency of the United States) which is accredited by a nationally recognized accrediting agency of association approved by the Administrator for this purpose. For purposes of this subsection, the Administrator shall publish a list of nationally recognized accrediting agencies or associations which he determines to be reliable authority as to the quality of training offered.

(2) The term "academic year" means an academic year or its equivalent, as determined by the Administrator.

(b) The Administrator shall annually report his activities under section 109 through 112 of this Act, including recommendations for needed revisions in the provisions thereof.

(c) There are authorized to be appropriated $25,000,000 per fiscal year for the fiscal years ending June 30, 1973, June 30, 1974, and June 30, 1975, $6,000,000 for the fiscal year ending September 30, 1977, $7,000,000 for the fiscal year ending September 30, 1978, $7,000,000 for the fiscal year ending September 30, 1979, $7,000,000 for the fiscal year ending September 30, 1980, $7,000,000 for the fiscal year ending September 30, 1981, $7,000,000 for the fiscal year ending September 30, 1982, such sums as may be necessary for fiscal years 1983 through 1985, and $7,000,00 per fiscal year for each of the fiscal years 1986 through 1990, to carry out sections 109 through 112 of this Act.

[§112(c) amended by PL 96–483; PL 100–4]

§1263. Alaska Village Demonstration Projects
[Sec. 113]

(a) The Administrator is authorized to enter into agreements with the State of Alaska to carry out one or more projects to demonstrate methods to provide for central community facilities for safe water andelimination or control of pollution in those native villages of Alaska without such facilities. Such project shall include provisions for community safe water supply systems, toilets, bathing and laundry facilities, sewage disposal facilities, and other similar facilities, and educational and informational facilities and programs relating to health and hygiene. Such demonstration projects shall be for the further purpose of developing preliminary plans for providing such safe water and such elimination or control of pollution for all native villages in such State.

(b) In carrying out this section the Administrator shall cooperate with the Secretary of Health, Education, and Welfare for the purpose of utilizing such of the personnel and facilities of that Department as may be appropriate.

(c) The Administrator shall report to Congress not later than July 1, 1973, the rcsults of the demonstration projects authorized by this section together with his recommendations, including any necessary legislation, relating to the establishment of a statewide program.

(d) There is authorized to be appropriated not to exceed $2,000,000 to carry out this section. In addition, there is authorized to be appropriated to carry out this section not to exceed $200,000 for the fiscal year ending September 30, 1978 and $220,000 for the fiscal year ending September 30, 1979.

(e) The Administrator is authorized to coordinate with the Secretary of the Department of Health, Education, and Welfare, the Secretary of the Department of Housing and Urban Development, the Secretary of the Department of the Interior, the Secretary of the Department of Agriculture, and the heads of any other departments or agencies he may deem appropriate to conduct a joint study with representatives of the State of Alaska and the appropriate Native organizations (as defined in Public Law 92–203) to develop a comprehensive program for achieving adequate sanitation services in Alaska villages. This study shall be coordinated with the programs and projects authorized by sections 104(q) and 105(e)(2) of this Act. The Administrator shall submit a report of the results of the study, together with appropriate supporting data and such recommendations as he deems desirable, to the Committee on Environment and Public Works of the Senate and to the Committee on Public Works and Transportation of the House of Representatives not later than December 31, 1979. The Administrator shall also submit recommended administrative actions, procedures, and any proposed legislation necessary to implement the recommendations of the study no later than June 30, 1980.

(f) The Administrator is authorized to provide technical, financial and management assistance for operation and maintenance of the demonstration projects constructed under this section, until such time as the recommendations of subsection (e) are implemented.

(g) For the purpose of this section, the term "village" shall mean an incorporated or unincorporated community with a population of ten to six hundred people living within a two-mile radius. The term "sanitation services" shall mean water supply, sewage disposal, solid waste disposal and other services necessary to maintain generally accepted standards of personal hygiene and public health.

§1264. Lake Tahoe Study [Sec. 114]

(a) The Administrator, in consultation with the Tahoe Regional Planning Agency, the Secretary of Agriculture, other Federal agencies, representatives of State and local governments, and members of the public, shall conduct a thorough and complete study on the adequacy of and need for extending Federal oversight and control in order to preserve the fragile ecology of Lake Tahoe.

(b) Such study shall include an examination of the interrelationships and responsibilities of the various agencies of the Federal Government and State and local governments with a view to establishing the necessity for redefinition of legal and other arrangements between these various governments, and making specific legislative recommendations to Congress. Such study shall consider the effect of various actions in terms of their environmental impact on the Tahoe Basin, treated as an ecosystem.

(c) The Administrator shall report on such study to Congress not later than one year after the date of enactment of this subsection.

(d) There is authorized to be appropriated to carry out this section not to exceed $500,000.

§1265. In-Place Toxic Pollutants [Sec. 115]

The Administrator is directed to identify the location of in-place pollutants with emphasis on toxic pollutants in harbors and navigable waterways and is authorized, acting through the Secretary of the Army, to make contracts for the removal and appropriate disposal of such materials from critical port and harbor areas. There is authorized to be appropriated $15,000,000 to carry out the provisions of this section, which sum shall be available until expended.

§1266. Hudson River PCB Reclamation Demonstration Project [Sec. 116]

(a) The Administrator is authorized to enter into contracts and other agreements with the State of New York to carry out a project to demonstrate methods for the selective removal of polychlorinated biphenyls contaminating bottom sediments of the Hudson River, treating such sediments as required, burying such sediments in secure landfills, and installing monitoring systems for such landfills. Such demonstration project shall be for the purpose of determining the feasibility of indefinite storage in secure landfills of toxic substances and of ascertaining the improvement of the rate of recovery of a toxic contaminated national waterway. No pollutants removed pursuant to this paragraph shall be placed in any landfill unless the Administrator first determines that disposal of the pollutants in such landfill would provide a higher standard of protection of the public health, safety, and welfare than disposal of such pollutants by any other method including, but not limited to, incineration or a chemical destruction process.

(b) The Administrator is authorized to make grants to the State of New York to carry out this section from funds allotted to such State under section 205(a) of this Act, except that the amount of any such grant shall be equal to 75 per centum of the cost of the project and such grant shall be made on condition that non-Federal sources provide the remainder of the cost of such project. The authority of this section shall be available until September 30, 1983. Funds allotted to the State of New York under section 205(a) shall be available under this subsection only to the extent that funds are not available, as determined by the Administrator, to the State of New York for the work authorized by this section under section 115 or 311 of this Act or a comprehensive hazardous substance response and clean up fund. Any funds used under the authority of this subsection shall be deducted from any estimate of the needs of the State of New York prepared under section 616(b) of this Act. The Administrator may not obligate or expend more than $20,000,000 to carry out this section.

[§116 added by PL 96–483]

§1267. Chesapeake Bay [Sec. 117]

(a) Office.—The Administrator shall continue the Chesapeake Bay Program and shall establish and maintain in the Environmental Protection Agency an office, division, or branch of Chesapeake Bay Programs to—

(1) collect and make available, through publications and other appropriate means, information pertaining to the environmental quality of the Chesapeake Bay (hereinafter in this subsection referred to as the "Bay");

(2) coordinate Federal and State efforts to improve the water quality of the Bay;

(3) determine the impact of sediment deposition in the Bay and identify the sources, rates, routes, and distribution patterns of such sediment deposition; and

(4) determine the impact of natural and man-induced environmental changes on the living resources of the Bay and the relationships among such changes, with particular emphasis placed on the impact of pollutant loadings of nutrients, chlorine, acid precipitation, dissolved oxygen, and toxic pollutants, including organic chemicals and heavy metals, and with special attention given to the impact of such changes on striped bass.

(b) Interstate Development Plan Grants.—

(1) Authority.—The Administrator shall, at the request of the Governor of a State affected by the interstate management plan developed pursuant to the Chesapeake Bay Program (hereinafter in this section referred to as the "plan"), make a grant for the purpose of implementing the management mechanisms contained in the plan if such State has, within 1 year after the date of the enactment of this section, approved and committed to implement all or substantially all aspects of the plan. Such grants shall be made subject to such terms and conditions as the Administrator considers appropriate.

(2) Submission of Proposal.—A State or combination of States may elect to avail itself of the benefits of this subsection by submitting to the Administrator a comprehensive proposal to implement management mechanisms contained in the plan which shall include (A) a description of proposed abatement actions which the State or combination of States commits to take within a specified time period to reduce pollution in the Bay and to meet applicable water quality standards, and (B) the estimated cost of the abatement actions proposed to be taken during the next fiscal year. If the Administrator finds that such proposal is consistent with the national policies set forth in section 101(a) of this Act and will contribute to the achievement of the national goals set forth in such section, the Administrator shall approve such proposal and shall finance the

costs of implementing segments of such proposal.

(3) Federal share.—Grants under this subsection shall not exceed 50 percent of the costs of implementing the management mechanims contained in the plan in any fiscal year and shall be made on condition that non-Federal sources provide the remainder of the cost of implementing the management mechanisms contained in the plan during such fiscal year.

(4) Administrative costs.—Administrative costs in the form of salaries, overhead, or indirect costs for services provided and charged against programs or projects supported by funds made available under this subsection shall not exceed in any one fiscal year 10 percent of the annual Federal grant made to a State under this subsection.

(c) Reports.—Any State or combination of States that receives a grant under subsection (b) shall, within 18 months after the date of receipt of such grant and biennially thereafter, report to the Adminstrator on the progress made in implementing the interstate management plan developed pursuant to the Chesapeake Bay Program. The Administrator shall transmit each such report along with the comments of the administrator on such report to Congress.

(d) Authorization of Appropriations.— There are hereby authorized to be appropriated the following sums, to remain available until expended, to carry out the purposes of this section:

(1) $3,000,000 per fiscal year for each of the fiscal years 1987, 1988, 1989, and 1990, to carry out subsection (a); and

(2) $10,000,000 per fiscal year for each of the fiscal years 1987, 1988, 1989, and 1990, for grants to States under subsction (b).

[§117 added by PL 100-4]

§1268. Great Lakes [Sec. 118]

[§118 added by PL 100–4;amended by PL 100–688]

(a) Findings, Purpose, and Definitions.—

(1) Findings.—The Congress finds that—

(A) the Great Lakes are a valuable national resource, continuously serving the people of the United States and other nations as an important source of food, fresh water, recreation, beauty, and enjoyment;

(B) the United States should seek to attain the goals embodied in the Great Lakes Water Quality Agreement of 1978, as amended by the Water Quality Agreement of 1987 and any other agreements and amendments, with particular emphasis on goals related to toxic pollutants; and

[§118(a)(1)(B) amended by PL 100–688]

(C) the Environmental Protection Agency should take the lead in the effort to meet those goals, working with other Federal agencies and State and local authorities.

(2) Purpose.—It is the purpose of this section to achieve the goals embodied in the Great Lakes Water Quality Agreement of 1978, as amended by the Water Quality Agreement of 1987 and any other agreements and amendments, through improved organization and definition of mission on the part of the Agency, funding of State grants for pollution control in the Great Lakes area, and improved accountability for implementation of such agreement.

[§118(a)(2) amended by PL 100–688]

(3) Definitions.—For purposes of this section, the term—

(A) "Agency" means the Environmental Protection Agency;

(B) "Great Lakes" means Lake Ontario, Lake Erie, Lake Huron (including Lake St. Clair), Lake Michigan, and Lake Superior, and the connecting channels (Saint Mary's River, Saint Clair River, Detroit River, Niagara River, and Saint Lawrence River to the Canadian Border);

(C) "Great Lakes System" means all the streams, rivers, lakes, and other bodies of water within the drainage basin of the Great Lakes:

(D) "Program Office" means the Great Lakes National Program Office established by this section;

[§118(a)(3)(D) amended by PL 101-596]

(E) "Research Office" means the Great Lakes Research Office established by subsection (d);

[§118(a)(3)(E) amended by PL 101-596]

(F) "area of concern" means a geographic area located within the Great Lakes, in which beneficial uses are impaired and which has been officially designated as such under Annex 2 of the Great Lakes Water Quality Agreement;

[§118(a)(2)(F) added by PL 101-596]

(G) "Great Lakes States" means the States of Illinois, Indiana, Michigan, Minnesota, New York, Ohio, Pennsylvania, and Wisconsin;

[§118(a)(2)(G) added by PL 101-596]

(H) "Great Lakes Water Quality Agreement" means the bilateral agreement, between the United States and Canada which was signed in 1978 and amended by the Protocol of 1987;

[§118(a)(2)(H) added by PL 101-596]

(I) "Lakewide Management Plan" means a written document which embodies a systematic and comprehensive ecosystem approach to restoring and protecting the beneficial uses of the open waters of each of the Great Lakes, in accordance with article VI and Annex 2 of the Great Lakes Water Quality Agreement; and

[§118(a)(2)(I) added by PL 101-596]

(J) "Remedial Action Plan" means a written document which embodies a systematic and comprehensive ecosystem approach to restoring and protecting the beneficial uses of areas of concern, in accordance with article VI and Annex 2 of the Great Lakes Water Quality Agreement.

[§118(a)(2)(J) added by PL 101-596]

(b) Great Lakes National Program Office.—The Great Lakes National Program Office (previously established by the Administrator) is hereby established within the Agency. The Program Office shall be headed by a Director who, by reason of management experience and technical expertise relating to the Great Lakes, is highly qualified to direct the development of programs and plans on a variety of Great Lakes issues. The Great Lakes National Program Office shall be located in a Great Lakes State.

(c) Great Lakes Management.—

(1) Functions.—The Program Office shall—

(A) in cooperation with appropriate Federal, State, tribal, and international agencies, and in accordance with section 101(e) of this Act, develop and implement specific action plans to carry out the responsibilities of the United States under the Great Lakes Water Quality Agreement of 1978, as amended by the Water Quality Agreement of 1987 and any other agreements and amendments;

[§118(c)(1)(A) amended by PL 100–688]

(B) establish a Great Lakes system- wide surveillance network to monitor the water quality of the Great Lakes, with specific emphasis on the monitoring of toxic pollutants;

(C) serve as the liaison with, and provide information to, the Canadian members of the International Joint Commission and the Canadian counterpart to the Agency;

(D) coordinate actions of the Agency (including actions by headquarters and regional offices thereof) aimed at improving Great Lakes water quality; and

(E) coordinate actions of the Agency with the actions of other Federal agencies and State and local authorities, so as to ensure the input of those agencies and authorities in developing water quality strategies and obtain the support of those agencies and authorities in achieving the objectives of such agreement.

[New §118(c)(2)–(5) added and former (2)–(6) redesignated as new (6)–(10) by PL 101–596]

(2) Great Lakes Water Quality Guidance.—

(A) By June 30, 1991, the Administrator, after consultation with the Program Office, shall publish in the Federal Register for public notice and comment proposed water quality guidance for the Great Lakes System. Such guidance shall conform with the objectives and provisions of the Great Lakes Water Quality Agreement, shall be no less restrictive than the provisions of this Act and national water quality criteria and guidance, shall specify numerical limits on pollutants in ambient Great Lakes water to protect human health, aquatic life, and wildlife, and shall provide guidance to the Great Lakes States on minimum water quality standard, antidegradation policies, and implementation procedures for the Great Lakes System.

(B) By June 30, 1992, the Administrator, in consultation with the Program Office, shall publish in the Federal Register, pursuant to this section and the Administrator's authority under this chapter, final water quality guidance for the Great Lakes System.

(C) Within two years after such Great Lakes guidance is published, the Great Lakes States shall adopt water quality standards, antidegradation policies, and implementation procedures for waters within the Great Lakes System which are consistent with such guidance. If a Great Lakes State fails to adopt such standards, policies, and procedures, the Administrator shall promulgate them not later than the end of such two-year period. When reviewing any Great Lakes State's water quality plan, the agency shall consider the extent to which the State has complied with the Great Lakes guidance issued pursuant to this section.

(3) Remedial Action Plans.—

(A) For each area of concern for which the United States has agreed to draft a Remedial Action Plan, the Program Office shall ensure that the Great Lakes State in which such area of concern is located—

(i) submits a Remedial Action Plan to the Program Office by June 30, 1991;

(ii) submits such Remedial Action Plan to the International Joint Commission by January 1, 1992; and

(iii) includes such Remedial Action Plans within the State's water quality plan by January 1, 1993.

(B) For each area of concern for which Canada has agreed to draft a Remedial Action Plan, the Program Office shall, pursuant to subparagraph (c)(1)(C) of this section, work with Canada to assure the submission of such Remedial Action Plans to the International Joint Commission by June 30, 1991, and to finalize such Remedial Action Plans by January 1, 1993.

(C) For any area of concern designated as such subsequent to the enactment of this Act, the Program Office shall (i) if the United States has agreed to draft the Remedial Action Plan, ensure that the Great Lakes State in which such area of concern is located submits such Plan to the Program Office within two years of the area's designation, submits it to the International Joint Commission no later than six months after submitting it to the Program Office, and includes such Plan in the State's water quality plan no later than one year after submitting it to the Commission; and (ii) if Canada has agreed to draft the Remedial Action Plan, work with Canada, pursuant to subparagraph (c)(1)(C) of this section, to ensure the submission of such Plan to the International Joint Commission within two years of the area's designation and the finalization of such Plan no later than eighteen months after submitting it to such Commission.

(D) The Program Office shall compile formal comments on individual Remedial Action Plans made by the International Joint Commission pursuant to section 4(d) of Annex 2 of the Great Lakes Water Quality Agreement and, upon request by a member of the public, shall make such comments available for inspection and copying. The Program Office shall also make available, upon request, formal comments made by the Environmental Protection Agency on individual Remedial Action Plans.

(4) Lakewide Management Plans.— The Administrator, in consultation with the Program Office shall—

(A) by January 1, 1992, publish in the Federal Register a proposed Lakewide Management Plan for Lake Michigan and solicit public comments;

(B) by January 1, 1993, submit a proposed Lakewide Management Plan for Lake Michigan to the International Joint Commission for review; and

(C) by January 1, 1994, publish in the Federal Register a final Lakewide Management Plan for Lake Michigan and begin implementation. Nothing in this subparagraph shall preclude the simultaneous development of Lakewide Management Plans for the other Great Lakes.

(5) Spills of Oil and Hazardous Materials.— The Program Office, in consultation with the Coast Guard, shall identify areas within the Great Lakes which are likely to experience numerous or voluminous spills of oil or other hazardous materials from land based facilities, vessels, or other sources and, in consultation with the Great Lakes States, shall identify weaknesses in Federal and State programs and systems to prevent and respond to such spills. This information shall be included on at least a biennial basis in the report required by this section.

(6) 5-Year Plan and Program.—The Program Office shall develop, in consultation with the States, a five-year plan and program for reducing the amount of nutrients introduced into the Great Lakes. Such program shall incorporate any management program for reducing nutrient runoff from nonpoint sources established under section 319 of this Act and shall include a program for monitoring nutrient runoff into, and ambient levels in, the Great Lakes.

(7) 5-Year Study and Demonstration Projects.—

(A) The Program Office shall carry out a five-year study and demonstration projects relating to the control and removal of toxic pollutants in the Great Lakes, with emphasis on the removal of toxic pollutants from bottom sediments. In selecting locations for conducting demonstration projects under this paragraph, priority consideration shall be given to projects at the following locations: Saginaw Bay, Michigan; Sheboygan Harbor, Wisconsin; Grand Calumet River, Indiana; Ashtabula River, Ohio; and Buffalo River, New York.

[§118(c)(7) designated as (A) by PL 101–596]

(B) The Program Office shall—

(i) by December 31, 1990, complete chemical, physical, and biological assessments of the contaminated sediments at the locations selected for the study and demonstration projects;

(ii) by December 31, 1990, announce the technologies that will be demonstrated at each location and the numerical standard of protection intended to be achieved at each location;

(iii) by December 31, 1992, complete full or pilot scale demonstration projects on site at each location of promising technologies to remedy contaminated sediments; and

(iv) by December 31, 1993, issue a final report to Congress on its findings.

[§118(c)(7)(B) added by PL 101-596]

(C) The Administrator, after providing for public review and comment, shall publish information concerning the public health and environmental consequences of contaminants in Great Lakes sediment. Information published pursuant to this subparagraph shall include specific numerical limits to protect health, aquatic life, and wildlife from the bioaccumulation of toxins. The Administrator shall, at a minimum, publish information pursuant to this subparagraph within 2 years of the date of the enactment of this title.

[§118(c)(7)(C) added by PL 101-596]

(8) Administrator's Responsibility.— The Administrator shall ensure that the Program Office enters into agreements with the various organizational elements of the Agency involved in Great Lakes activities and the appropriate State agencies specifically delineating—

(A) the duties and responsibilities of each such element in the Agency with respect to the Great Lakes;

(B) the time periods for carrying out such duties and responsibilities; and

(C) the resources to be committed to such duties and responsibilities.

(9) Budget Item.—The Administrator shall, in the Agency's annual budget submission to Congress, include a funding request for the Program Office as a separate budget line item.

(10) Comprehensive Report.—Within 90 days after the end of each fiscal year, the Administrator shall submit to Congress a comprehensive report which—

(A) describes the achievements in the preceding fiscal year in implementing the Great Lakes Water Quality Agreement of 1978, as amended by the Water Quality Agreement of 1987 and any other agreements and amendments, and shows by categories (including judicial enforcement, research, State cooperative efforts, and general administration) the amounts expended on Great Lakes water quality initiatives in such proceeding fiscal year;

[§118(c)(6)(A) amended by PL 100–688]

(B) describes the progress made in such preceding fiscal year in implementing the system of surveillance of the water quality in the Great Lakes System, including the monitoring of groundwater and sediment, with particular reference to toxic pollutants;

(C) describes the long-term prospects for improving the condition of the Great Lakes; and

(D) provides a comprehensive assessment of the planned efforts to be pursued in the succeeding fiscal year for implementing the Great Lakes Water Quality Agreement of 1978, as amended by the Water Quality Agreement of 1987 and any other agreements and amendments, which assessment shall—

(i) show by categories (including judicial enforcement, research, State cooperative efforts, and general administration) the amount anticipated to be expended on Great Lakes water quality initiatives in the fiscal year to which the assessment relates; and

(ii) include a report of current programs administered by other Federal agencies which make available resources to the Great Lakes water quality management efforts.

[§118(c)(6)(D) amended by PL 100–688]

(11) Confined Disposal Facilities.—

(A) The Administrator, in consultation with the Assistant Secretary of the Army for Civil Works, shall develop and implement, within one year of the date of enactment of this paragraph, management plans for every Great Lakes confined disposal facility.

(B) The plan shall provide for monitoring of such facilities, including—

(i) water quality at the site and in the area of the site;

(ii) sediment quality at the site and in the area of the site;

(iii) the diversity, productivity, and stability of aquatic organisms at the site and in the area of the site; and

(iv) such other conditions as the Administrator deems appropriate.

(C) The plan shall identify the anticipated use and management of the site over the following twenty-year period including the expected termination of dumping at the site, the anticipated need for site management, including pollution control, following the termination of the use of the site.

(D) The plan shall identify a schedule for review and revision of the plan which shall not be less frequent than five years after adoption of the plan and every five years thereafter.

[§118(c)(11) added by PL 101–596]

(d) Great Lakes Research.—

(1) Establishment of Research Office.—There is established within the National Oceanic and Atmospheric Administration the Great Lakes Research Office.

(2) Identification of Issues.—The Research Office shall identify issues relating to the Great Lakes resources on which research is needed. The Research Office shall submit a report to Congress on such issues before the end of each fiscal year which shall identify any changes in the Great Lakes system with respect to such issues.

(3) Inventory.—The Research Office shall identify and inventory Federal, State, university, and tribal environmental research programs (and, to the extent feasible, those of private organizations and other nations) relating to the Great Lakes system, and shall update that inventory every four years.

(4) Research Exchange.—The Research Office shall establish a Great Lakes research exchange for the purpose of facilitating the rapid identification, acquisition, retrieval, dissemination, and use of information concerning research projects which are ongoing or completed and which affect the Great Lakes System.

(5) Research Program.—The Research Office shall develop, in cooperation with the Coordination Office, a comprehensive environmental research program and data base for the Great Lakes system. The data base shall include, but not be limited to, data relating to water quality, fisheries, and biota.

(6) Monitoring.—The Research Office shall conduct, through the Great Lakes Environmental Research Laboratory, the National Sea Grant College program, other Federal laboratories, and the private sector, appropriate research and monitoring activities which address priority issues and current needs relating to the Great Lakes.

(7) Location.—The Research Office shall be located in a Great Lakes State.

(e) Research and Management Coordination.—

(1) Joint Plan. Before October 1 of each year, the Program Office and the Research Office shall prepare a joint research plan for the fiscal year which begins in the following calendar year.

(2) Contents of Plan.—Each plan prepared under paragraph (1) shall—

(A) identify all proposed research dedicated to activities conducted under the Great Lakes Water Quality Agreement of 1978, as amended by the Water Quality Agreement of 1987 and any other agreements and amendments;

(B) include the Agency's assessment of priorities for research needed to fulfill the terms of such Agreement; and

(C) identify all proposed research that may be used to develop a comprehensive environmental data base for the Great Lakes System and establish priorities for development of such data base.

(3) Health Research Report.—

(A) Not later than September 30, 1994, the Program Office, in consultation with the Research Office, the Agency for Toxic Substances and Disease Registry, and Great Lakes States shall submit to the Congress a report assessing the adverse effects of water pollutants in the Great Lakes System on the health of persons in Great Lakes States and the health of fish, shellfish, and wildlife in the Great Lakes System. In conducting research in support of this report, the Administrator may, where appropriate, provide for research to be conducted under cooperative agreements with Great Lakes States.

(B) There is authorized to be appropriated to the Administrator to carry out this section not to exceed $3,000,000 for each of fiscal years 1992, 1993, and 1994.

[§118(e)(3) added by PL 101–596]

(f) Interagency Cooperation.—The head of each department, agency, or other instrumentality of the Federal Government which is engaged in, is concerned with, or has authority over programs relating to research, monitoring, and planning to maintain, enhance, preserve, or rehabilitate the environmental quality and natural resources of the Great Lakes, including the Chief of Engineers of the Army, the Chief of the Soil Conservation Service, the Commandant of the Coast Guard, the Director of the Fish and Wildlife Service, and the Administrator of the National Oceanic and Atmospheric Administration, shall submit an annual report to the Administrator with respect to the activities of that agency or office affecting compliance with the Great Lakes Water Quality Agreement of 1978, as amended by the Water Quality Agreement of 1987 and any other agreements and amendments;

[§118(f) amended by PL 100–688]

(g) Relationship to Existing Federal and State Laws and International Treaties.—Nothing in this section shall be construed to affect the jurisdiction, powers, or prerogatives of any department, agency, or officer of the Federal Government or of any State government, or of any tribe, nor any powers, jurisdiction, or prerogatives of any international body created by treaty with authority relating to the Great Lakes.

(h) Authorizations of Great Lakes Appropriations.—There are authorized to be appropriated to the Administrator to carry out this section not to exceed $ 11,000,000 per fiscal year for the fiscal years 1987, 1988, 1989 and 1990, and $25,000,000 for fiscal year 1991. Of the amounts appropriated each fiscal year—

(1) 40 percent shall be used by the Great Lakes National Program Office on demonstration projects on the feasibility of controlling and removing toxic pollutants;

(2) 37 percent shall be used by the Great Lakes National Program Office for the program of nutrient monitoring; and

(3) 30 percent or $3,300,000 whichever is the lesser, shall be transferred to the National Oceanic and Atmospheric Administration for use by the Great Lakes Research Office.

[§118(h) amended by PL 101–596]

§1269. Long Island Sound [Sec. 119]

(a) The Administrator shall continue the Management Conference of the Long Island Sound Study (hereinafter referred to as the "Conference") as established pursuant to section 320 of this Act, and shall establish an office (hereinafter referred to as the "Office") to be located on or near Long Island Sound.

(b) Administration and Staffing of Office.—The Office shall be headed by a Director, who shall be detailed by the Administrator, following consultation with the Administrators of EPA regions I and II, from among the employees of the Agency who are in civil service. The Administrator shall delegate to the Director such authority and detail such additional staff as may be necessary to carry out the duties of the Director under this section.

(c) Duties of the Office.—The Office shall assist the Management Conference of the Long Island Sound Study in carrying out its goals. Specifically, the Office shall—

(1) assist and support the implementation of the Comprehensive Conservation and Management Plan for Long Island Sound developed pursuant to section 320 of this Act;

(2) conduct or commission studies deemed necessary for strengthened implementation of the Comprehensive Conservation and Management Plan including, but not limited to—

(A) population growth and the adequacy of wastewater treatment facilities,

(B) the use of biological methods for nutrient removal in sewage treatment plants,

(C) contaminated sediments, and dredging activities,

(D) nonpoint source pollution abatement and land use activities in the Long Island Sound watershed,

(E) wetland protection and restoration,

(F) atmospheric deposition of acidic and other pollutants into Long Island Sound,

(G) water quality requirements to sustain fish, shellfish, and wildlife populations, and the use of indicator species to assess environmental quality,

(H) State water quality programs, for their adequacy pursuant to implementation of the Comprehensive Conservation and Management Plan, and

(I) options for long-term financing of wastewater treatment projects and water pollution control programs.

(3) coordinate the grant, research and planning programs authorized under this section;

(4) coordinate activities and implementation responsibilities with other Federal agencies which have jurisdiction over Long Island Sound and with national and regional marine monitoring and research programs established pursuant to the Marine Protection, Research, and Sanctuaries Act;

(5) provide administrative and technical support to the conference;

(6) collect and make available to the public publications, and other forms of information the conference determines to be appropriate, relating to the environmental quality of Long Island Sound;

(7) not more than two years after the date of the issuance of final Comprehensive Conservation and Management Plan for Long Island Sound under section 320 this Act, and biennially thereafter, issue a report to theCongress which—

(A) summarizes the progress made by the States in implementing the Comprehensive Conservation and Management Plan;

(B) summarizes any modifications to the Comprehensive Conservation and Management Plan in the twelve month period immediately preceding such report; and

(C) incorporates specific recommendations concerning the implementation of the Comprehensive Conservation and Management Plan; and

(8) convene conferences and meetings for legislators from State governments and political subdivisions thereof for the purpose of making recommendations for coordinating legislative efforts to facilitate the environmental restoration of Long Island Sound and the implementation of the Comprehensive Conservation and Management Plan.

(d) Grants.—

(1) The Administrator is authorized to make grants for projects and studies which will help implement the Long Island Sound Comprehensive Conservation and Management Plan. Special emphasis shall given be to implementation, research and planning, enforcement, and citizen involvement and education.

(2) State, interstate, and regional water pollution control agencies, and other public or nonprofit private agencies, institutions, and organizations held to be eligible for grants pursuant to this subsection.

(3) Citizen involvement and citizen education grants under this subsection shall not exceed 95 per centum of the costs of such work. All other grants under this subsection shall not exceed 50 per centum of the research, studies, or work. All grants shall be made on the condition that the non-Federal share of such costs are provided from non-Federal sources.

(e) Authorizations.—

(1) There is authorized to be appropriated to the Administrator for the implementation of this section, other than subsection (d), such sums as may be necessary for each of the fiscal years 1991 through 1996.

(2) There is authorized to be appropriated to the Administrator for the implementation of subsection (d) not to exceed $3,000,000 for each of the fiscal years 1991 through 1996.

[§119 added by PL 101–596]

Lake Champlain Management Conference
[Sec. 120]

There is established a Lake Champlain Management Conference to develop a comprehensive pollution prevention, control, and restoration plan for Lake Champlain. The Administrator shall convene the management conference within ninety days of the date of enactment of this section.

(b) Membership.—The Members of the Management Conference shall be comprised of—

(1) the Governors of the States of Vermont and New York;

(2) each interested Federal agency, not to exceed a total of five members;

(3) the Vermont and New York Chairpersons of the Vermont, New York, Quebec Citizens Advisory Committee for the Environmental Management of Lake Champlain;

(4) four representatives of the State legislature of Vermont;

(5) four representatives of the State legislature of New York;

(6) six persons representing local governments having jurisdiction over any land or water within the Lake Champlain basin, as determined appropriate by the Governors; and

(7) eight persons representing affected industries, nongovernmental organizations, public and private educational institutions, and the general public, as determined appropriate by the trigovernmental Citizens Advisory Committee for the Environmental Management of Lake Champlain, but not to be current members of the Citizens Advisory Committee.

(c) Technical Advisory Committee.—

(1) The Management Conference shall, not later than one hundred and twenty days after the date of enactment of this section, appoint a Technical Advisory Committee.

(2) Such Technical Advisory Committee shall consist of officials of: appropriate departments and agencies of the Federal Government; the State governments of New York and Vermont; and governments of political subdivisions of

such States; and public and private research institutions.

(d) Research Program.—

(1) The Management Conference shall establish a multi-disciplinary environmental research program for Lake Champlain. Such research program shall be planned and conducted jointly with the Lake Champlain Research Consortium.

(e) Pollution Prevention, Control, and Restoration Plan.—

(1) Not later than three years after the date of the enactment of this section, the Management Conference shall publish a pollution prevention, control, and restoration plan (hereafter in this section referred to as the "Plan") for Lake Champlain.

(2) The Plan developed pursuant to this section shall—

(A) identify corrective actions and compliance schedules addressing point and nonpoint sources of pollution necessary to restore and maintain the chemical, physical, and biological integrity of water quality, a balanced, indigenous population of shellfish, fish and wildlife, recreational, and economic activities in and on the lake;

(B) incorporate environmental management concepts and programs established in State and Federal plans and programs in effect at the time of the development of such plan;

(C) clarify the duties of Federal and State agencies in pollution prevention and control activities, and to the extent allowable by law, suggest a timetable for adoption by the appropriate Federal and State agencies to accomplish such duties within a reasonable period of time;

(D) describe the methods and schedules for funding of programs, activities, and projects identified in the Plan, including the use of Federal funds and other sources of funds; and

(E) include a strategy for pollution prevention and control that includes the promotion of pollution prevention and management practices to reduce the amount of pollution generated in the Lake Champlain basin.

(3) The Administrator, in cooperation with the Management Conference, shall provide for public review and comment on the draft Plan. At a minimum, the Management Conference shall conduct one public meeting to hear comments on the draft plan in the State of New York and one such meeting in the State of Vermont.

(4) Not less than one hundred and twenty days after the publication of the Plan required pursuant to this section, the Administrator shall approve such plan if the plan meets the requirements of this section and the Governors of the States of New York and Vermont concur.

(5) Upon approval of the plan, such plan shall be deemed to be an approved management program for the purposes of section 319(h) of this Act and such plan shall be deemed to be an approved comprehensive conservation and management plan pursuant to section 320 of this Act.

(f) Grant Assistance.—

(1) The Administrator may, in consultation with the Management Conference, make grants to State, interstate, and regional water pollution control agencies, and public or nonprofit agencies, institutions, and organizations.

(2) Grants under this subsection shall be made for assisting research, surveys, studies, and modeling and technical and supporting work necessary for the development of the Plan and for retaining expert consultants in support of litigation undertaken by the State of New York and the State of Vermont to compel cleanup or obtain cleanup damage costs from persons responsible for pollution of Lake Champlain.

(3) The amount of grants to any person under this subsection for a fiscal year shall not exceed 75 per centum of the costs of such research, survey, study and work and shall be made available on the condition that non-Federal share of such costs are provided from non-Federal sources.

(4) The Administrator may establish such requirements for the administration of grants as he determines to be appropriate.

(g) Definition.—For the purposes of this section, the term "Lake Champlain drainage basin" means all or part of Clinton, Franklin, Warren, Essex, and Washington counties in the State of New York and all or part of Franklin, Grand Isle, Chittenden, Addison, Rutland, Lamoille, Orange, Washington, Orleans, and Caledonia counties in Vermont, that contain all of the streams, rivers, lakes, and other bodies of water, including wetlands, that drain into Lake Champlain.

(h) Statutory Interpretation.—Nothing in this section shall be construed so as to affect the jurisdiction or powers of—

(1) any department or agency of the Federal Government or any State government; or

(2) any international organization or entity related to Lake Champlain created by treaty or memorandum to which the United States is a signatory.

(i) Authorization.—There are authorized to be appropriated to the Environmental Protection Agency to carry out this section $2,000,000 for each of fiscal years 1991, 1992, 1993, 1994, and 1995.

[§120 added by PL 101-596]

[Editor's Note: Section 304 of PL 101–596 did not amend the Federal Water Pollution Control Act directly, but has some impact on its implementation. Those provisions follow.]

Federal Program Coordination [Sec. 304]

(a) Designation of Lake Champlain as a Special Project Area Under the Agricultural Conservation Program.—

(1) In General.—Notwithstanding any other provision of law, the Lake Champlain basin, as defined under section 120(h) of the Federal Water Pollution Control Act, shall be designated by the Secretary of Agriculture as a special project area under the Agricultural Conservation Program established under section 8(b) of the Soil Conservation and Domestic Allotment Act (16 U.S.C. 590h(b)).

(2) Technical Assistance Reimbursement.—To carry out the purposes of this subsection, the technical assistance reimbursement from the Agricultural Stabilization and Conservation Service authorized under the Soil Conservation and Domestic Allotment Act, shall be inreased from 5 per centum to 10 per centum.

(3) Comprehensive Agricultural Monitoring.—The Secretary, in consultation with the Management Conference and appropriate State and Federal agencies, shall develop a comprehensive agricultural monitoring and evaluation network for all major drainages within the Lake Champlain basin.

(4) Allocation of Funds.—In allocating funds under this subsection, the Secretary of Agriculture shall consult with the Management Conference established under section 120 of the Federal Water Pollution Control Act and to the extent allowable by law, allocate funds to those agricultural enterprises located at sites that the Management Conference determines to be priority sites, on the basis of a concern for ensuring implementation of point source pollution controls throughout the Lake champlain basin.

(b) Cooperation of the United States Geological Survey of the Department of the Interior.—For the purpose of enhancing and expanding basic data collection and monitoring in operation in the Lake Champlain basin, as defined under section 120 of the Federal Water Pollution Control Act, the Secretary of the Interior, acting through the heads of water resources divisions of the New York and New England districts of the United States Geological Survey, shall—

(1) in cooperation with appropriate universities and private research institutions, and the appropriate officials of the appropriate departments and agencies of the States of New York and Vermont, develop an integrated geographic information system of the Lake Champlain basin;

(2) convert all partial recording sites in the Lake Champlain basin to continuous monitoring stations with full gauging capabilities and status; and

(3) establish such additional continuous monitoring station sites in the Lake Champlain basin as are necessary to carry out basic data collection and monitoring, as defined by the Secretary of the Interior, including groundwater mapping, and water quality and sediment data collection.

(c) Cooperation of the United States Fish and Wildlife Service of The Department of the Interior.—

(1) Resource Conservation Program.—The Secretary of the Interior, acting through the United States Fish and Wildlife Service, in cooperation with the Lake Champlain Fish and Wildlife Management Cooperative and the Management Conference established pursuant to this subsection shall—

(A) establish and implement a fisheries resources restoration, development and conservation program, including dedicating a level of hatchery production within the Lake Champlain basin at or above the level that existed immediately preceding the date of enactment of this Act; and

(B) conduct a wildlife species and habitat assessment survey in the Lake Champlain basin, including—

(i) a survey of Federal threatened and endangered species, listed or proposed for listing under the Endangered Species Act of 1973 (16 U.S.C. 1531 et seq.), New York State and State of Vermont threatened and endangered species and other species of special concern, migratory nongame species of management concern, and national resources plan species;

(ii) a survey of wildlife habitats such as islands, wetlands, and riparian areas; and

(iii) a survey of migratory bird populations breeding, migrating and wintering within the Lake Champlain basin.

(2) To accomplish the purposes of paragraph (1), the Director of the United States Fish and Wildlife Service is authorized to carry out activities related to—

(A) controlling sea lampreys and other nonindigenous aquatic animal nuisances;

(B) improving the health of fishery resources;

(C) conducting investigations about and assessing the status of fishery resources, and disseminating that information to all interested parties; and

(D) conducting and periodically updating a survey of the fishery resources and their habitats and food chains in the Lake Champlain basin.

(d) Authorizations.—

(1) There is authorized to be appropriated to the Department of Agriculture $2,000,000 for each of fiscal years 1991, 1992, 1993, 1994, and 1995 to carry out subsection (a) of this section.

(2) There is authorized to be appropriated to the Department of Interior $1,000,000 for each of fiscal years 1991, 1992, 1993, 1994, and 1995 to carry out subsections (b) and (c) of this section.

TITLE II—GRANTS FOR CONSTRUCTION OF TREATMENT WORKS

§1281. Purpose [Sec. 201]

(a) It is the purpose of this title to require and to assist the development and implementation of waste treatment management plans and practices which will achieve the goals of this Act.

(b) Waste treatment management plans and practices shall provide for the application of the best practicable waste treatment technology before any discharge into receiving waters, including reclaiming and recycling of water, and confined disposal of pollutants so they will not migrate to cause water or other environmental pollution and shall provide for consideration of advanced waste treatment techniques.

(c) To the extent practicable, waste treatment management shall be on an areawide basis and provide control or treatment of all point and nonpoint sources of pollution, including in place or accumulated pollution sources.

(d) The Administrator shall encourage waste treatent management which results in the construction of revenue producing facilities providing for—

(1) the recycling of potential sewage pollutants through the production of agriculture, silviculture, or aquaculture products, or any combination thereof;

(2) the confined and contained disposal of pollutants not recycled;

(3) the reclamation of wastewater; and

(4) the ultimate disposal of sludge in a manner that will not result in environmental hazards.

(e) The Administrator shall encourage waste treatment management which results in integrating facilities for sewage treatment and recycling with facilities to treat, dispose of, or utilize other industrial and municipal wastes, including but not limited to solid waste and waste heat and thermal discharges. Such integrated facilities shall be designed and operated to produce revenues in excess of capital and operation and maintenance costs and such revenues shall be used by the designated regional management agency to aid in financing other environmental improvement programs.

(f) The Administrator shall encourage waste treatment management which combines "open space" and recreational considerations with such management.

(g) (1) The Administrator is authorized to make grants to any State, municipality, or intermunicipal or interstate agency for the construction of publicly owned treatment works. On and after October 1, 1984, grants under this title shall be made only for projects for secondary treatment or more stringent treatment, or any cost effective alternative thereto, new interceptors and appurtenances, and infiltration-in-flow correction., Notwithstanding the preceding sentences, the Administrator may make grants on and after October 1, 1984, for (A) any project within the definition set forth in section 212(2) of this Act, other than for a project referred to in the preceding sentence, and (B) any purpose for which a grant may be made under sections 319(h) and (i) of this Act (including any innovative and alternative approaches for the control of nonpoint sources of pollution), except that not more than 20 per centum (as determined by the Governor of the State) of the amount allotted to a State under section 205 of this Act for any fiscal year shall be obligated in such State under authority of this sentence.

[§201(g)(1) revised by PL 97–117;amended by PL 100–4]

(2) The Administrator shall not make grants from funds authorized for any fiscal year beginning after June 30, 1974, to any State, municipality, or intermunicipal or interstate agency for the erection, building, acquisition, alteration, remodeling, improvement, or exten-

sion of treatment works unless the grant applicant has satisfactorily demonstrated to the Administrator that—

(A) alternative waste management techniques have been studied and evaluated and the works proposed for grant assistance will provide for the application of the best practicable waste treatment technology over the life of the works consistent with the purposes of this title;

(B) as appropriate, the works proposed for grant assistance will take into account and allow to the extent practicable the application of technology at a later date which will provide for the reclaiming or recycling of water or otherwise eliminate the discharge of pollutants.

(3) The Administrator shall not approve any grant after July 1, 1973, for treatment works under this section unless the applicant shows to the satisfaction of the Administrator that each sewer collection system discharging into such treatment works is not subject to excessive infiltration.

(4) The Administrator is authorized to make grants to applicants for treatment works grants under this section for such sewer system evaluation studies as may be necessary to carry out the requirements of paragraph (3) of this subsection. Such grants shall be made in accordance with rules and regulations promulgated by the Administrator. Initial rules and regulations shall be promulgated under this paragraph not later than 120 days after the date of enactment of the Federal Water Pollution Control Act Amendments of 1972.

(5) The Administrator shall not make grants from funds authorized for any fiscal year beginning after September 30, 1978, to any State, municipality, or intermunicipal or interstate agency for the erection, building, acquisition, alteration, remodeling, improvement, or extension of treatment works unless the grant applicant has satisfactorily demonstrated to the Administrator that innovative and alternative wastewater treatment processes and techniques which provide for the reclaiming and reuse of water, otherwise eliminate the discharge of pollutants, and utilize recycling techniques, land treatment, new or improved methods of waste treatment management for municipal and industrial waste (discharged into municipal systems) and the confined disposal of pollutants, so that pollutants will not migrate to cause water or other environmental pollution, have been fully studied and evaluated by the applicant taking into account section 201(d) of this Act and taking into account and allowing to the extent practicable the more efficient use of energy and resources.

(6) The Administrator shall not make grants from funds authorized for any fiscal year beginning after September 30, 1978, to any State, municipality, or intermunicipal or interstate agency for the erection, building, acquisition, alteration, remodeling, improvement, or extension of treatment works unless the grant applicant has satisfactorily demonstrated to the Administrator that the applicant has analyzed the potential recreation and open space opportunities in the planning of the proposed treatment works.

(h) A grant may be made under this section to construct a privately owned treatment works serving one or more principal residences or small commercial establishments constructed prior to, and inhabited on the date of enactment of this subsection where the Administrator finds that—

(1) a public body otherwise eligible for a grant under subsection (g) of this section has applied on behalf of a number of such units and certified that public ownership such works is not feasible;

(2) such public body has entered into an agreement with the Administrator which guarantees that such treatment works will be properly operated and maintained and will comply with all other requirements of section 204 of this Act and includes a system of charges to assure that each recipient of waste treatment services under such a grant will pay its proportionate share of the cost of operation and maintenance (including replacement); and

(3) the total cost and environmental impact of providing waste treatment services to such residences or commercial establishments will be less than the cost of providing a system of collection and central treatment of such wastes.

(i) The Administrator shall encourage waste treatment management methods, processes, and techniques which will reduce total energy requirements.

(j) The Administrator is authorized to make a grant for any treatment works utilizing processes and techniques meeting the guidelines promulgated under section 304(d)(3) of this Act, if the Administrator determines it is in the public interest and if in the cost effectiveness study made of the construction grant application for the purpose of evaluating alternative treatment works, the life cycle cost of the treatment works for which the grant is to be made does not exceed the life cycle cost of the most effective alternative by more than 15 per centum.

(k) No grant made after November 15, 1981, for a publicly owned treatment works, other than for facility planning and the preparation of construction plans and specifications, shall be used to treat, store, or convey the flow of any industrial user into such treatment works in excess of a flow per day equivalent to fifty thousand gallons per day of sanitary waste. This subsection shall not apply to any project proposed by a grantee which is carryingout an approved project to prepare construction plans and specifications for a facility to treat wastewater, which received its grant approval before May 15, 1980. This subsection shall not be in effect after November 15, 1981.

[§201(k) added by PL 96–483; amended by PL 97–117]

(l) (1) After the date of enactment of this subsection, Federal grants shall not be made for the purpose of providing assistance solely for facility plans, or plans, specifications, and estimates for any proposed project for the construction of treatment works. In the event that the proposed project receives a grant under this section for construction, the Administrator shall make an allowance in such grant for non-Federal funds expended during the facility planning and advanced engineering and design phase at the prevailing Federal share under section 202(a) of this Act, based on the percentage of total project costs which the Administrator determines is the general experience for such projects.

(2) (A) Each State shall use a portion of the funds allotted to such State each fiscal year, but not to exceed 10 per centum of such funds, to advance to potential grant applicants under this title the costs of facility planning or the preparation of plans, specifications, and estimates.

(B) Such an advance shall be limited to the allowance for such costs which the Administrator establishes under paragraph (1) of this subsection, and shall be provided only to a potential grant applicant which is a small community and which in the judgment of the State would otherwise be unable to prepare a request for a grant for construction costs under this section.

(C) In the event a grant for construction costs is made under this section for a project for which an advance has been made under this paragraph, the Administrator shall reduce the amount of such grant by the allowance established under paragraph (1) of this subsection. In the event no such grant is made, the State is authorized to seek repayment of such advance on such terms and conditions as it may determine.

[§201(l) added by PL 97–117]

(m) (1) Notwithstanding any other provisions of this title, the Administrator is authorized to make a grant from any funds otherwise allotted to the State of California under section 205 of this Act to the project (and in the amount) specified in Order WQG 81–1 of the California State Water Resources Control Board.

(2) Notwithstanding any other provisions of this Act, the Administrator shall make a grant from any funds otherwise allotted to the State of California to the city of Eureka, California, in connection with project numbered C–06–2772, for the purchase of one hundred and thirty nine acres of property as environmental mitigation for siting of the proposed treatment plant.

(3) Notwithstanding any other provision of this Act, the Administrator shall make a grant from any funds otherwise allotted to the State of California to the city of San Diego, California, in connection with that city's aquaculture sewage process (total resources recover: system) as an innovative and alternative waste treatment process.

[§201(m) added by PL 97–117]

(n)(1) On and after October 1, 1984, upon the request of the Governor of an affected State, the Administrator is authorized to use funds available to such State under section 205 to address water quality problems due to the impacts of discharges from combined storm water and sanitary sewer overflows, which are not otherwise eligible under this subsection, were correction of such discharges is a major priority for such State.

(2) Beginning fiscal year 1983, the Administrator shall have available $200,000,000 per fiscal year in addition to those funds authorized in section 207 of this Act to be utilized to address water quality problems of marine bays and estuaries subject to lower levels of water quality due to the impacts of discharges from combined storm water and sanitary sewer overflows from adjacent urban complexes, not otherwise eligible under this subsection. Such sums may be used as deemed appropriate by the Administrator as provided in paragraphs

(1) and (2) of this subsection, upon the request of and demonstration of water quality benefits by the Governor of an affected State.

[§201(n) added by PL 97–117]

(o) The Administrator shall encourage and assist applicants for grant assistance under this title to develop and file with the Administrator a capital financing plan which, at a minimum —

(1) projects the future requirements for waste treatment services within the applicant's jurisdiction for a period of no less than ten years;

(2) projects the nature, extent, timing, and costs of future expansion and reconstruction of treatment works which will be necessary to satisfy the applicant's projected future requirements for waste treatment services; and

(3) sets forth with specificity the manner in which the applicant intends to finance such future expansion and reconstruction.

[§201(o) added by PL 97–117]

(p) Time Limit on Resolving Certain Disputes. — In any case in which a dispute arises with respect to the awarding of a contract for construction of treatment works by a grantee of funds under this title and a party to such dispute files an appeal with the Administrator under this title for resolution of such dispute, the Administrator shall make a final decision on such appeal within 90 days of the filing of such appeal.

[§201(p) added by PL 100–4]

§1282. Federal Share [Sec. 202]

(a) (1) The amount of any grant for treatment works made under this Act from funds authorized for any fiscal year beginning after June 30, 1971, and ending before October 1, 1984, shall be 75 per centum of the cost of construction thereof (as approved by the Administrator), and for any fiscal year beginning on or after October 1, 1984, shall be 55 per centum of the cost of construction thereof (as approved by the Administrator), unless modified to a lower percentage rate uniform throughout a State by the Governor of that State with the concurrence of the Administrator. Within ninety days after the enactment of this sentence the Administrator shall issue guidelines for concurrence in any such modification, which shall provide for the consideration of the unobligated balance of sums allocated to the State under section 205 of this Act, the need for assistance under this title in such State, and the availability of State grant assistance to replace the Federal share reduced by such modification. The payment of any such reduced Federal share shall not constitute an obligation on the part of the United States or a claim on the part of any State or grantee to reimbursement for the portion of the Federal share reduced in any such State. Any grant (other than for reimbursement) made prior to the date of enactment of the Federal Water Pollution Control Act Amendments of 1972 from any funds authorized for any fiscal year beginning after June 30, 1971, shall, upon the request of the applicant, be increased to the applicable percentage under this section. Notwithstanding the first sentence of this paragraph, in any case where a primary, secondary, or advanced waste treatment facility or its related interceptors or a project for infiltration-in-flow correction has received a grant for erection, building, acquisition, alteration, remodeling, improvement, extension, or correction before October 1, 1984, all segments and phases of such facility, interceptors, and project for infiltration-in-flow correction shall be eligible for grants at 75 per centum of the cost of construction thereof for any grant made pursuant to a State obligation which obligation occurred before October 1, 1990. Notwithstanding the first sentence of this paragraph, in the case of a project for which an application for a grant under this title has been made to the Administrator before October 1, 1984, and which project is under judicial injunction on such date prohibiting its construction, such project shall be eligible for grants at 75 percent of the cost of construction thereof. Notwithstanding the first sentence of this paragraph, in the case of the Wyoming Valley Sanitary Authority project mandated by judicial order under a proceeding begun prior to October 1, 1984, and a project for wastewater treatment for Altoona, Pennsylvania, such projects shall be eligible for grants at 75 percent of the cost of construction thereof.

[§202(a)(1) amended by PL 96–483; PL 97–117; PL 100–4]

(2) The amount of any grant made after September 30, 1978, and before October 1, 1981, for any eligible treatment works or significant portion thereof utilizing innovative or alternative wastewater treatment processes and techniques referred to in section 201(g)(5) shall be 85 per centum of the cost of construction thereof unless modified by the Governor of the State with the concurrence of the Administrator to a percentage rate no less than is percentum greater than the modified uniform percentage rate in which the Administrator

has concurred pursuant to paragraph (1) of this subsection. The amount of any grant made after September 30, 1981, for any eligible treatment works or unit processes and techniques thereof utilizing innovative or alternative wastewater treatment processes and techniques referred to in section 201(g)(5) shall be a percentage of the cost of construction thereof equal to 20 per centum greater than the percentage in effect under paragraph (1) of this subsection for such works or unit processes and techniques, but in no event greater than 85 per centum of the cost of construction thereof. No grant shall be made under this paragraph for construction of a treatment works in any State unless the proportion of the State contribution to the non-Federal share of construction costs for all treatment works in such State receiving a grant under this paragraph is the same as or greater than the proportion of the State contribution (if any) to the non-Federal share of construction costs for all treatment works receiving grants in such State under paragraph (1) of this subsection.

[§202(a)(2) amended by PL 96–483; PL 97–117]

(3) In addition to any grant made pursuant to paragraph (2) of this subsection, the Administrator is authorized to make a grant to fund all of the costs of the modification or replacement of any facilities constructed with a grant made pursuant to paragraph (2) if the Administrator finds that such facilities have not met design performance specifications unless such failure is attributable to negligence on the part of any person and if such failure has significantly increased capital or operating and maintenance expenditures. In addition, the Administrator is authorized to make a grant to fund all of the costs of the modification or replacement of biodisc equipment (rotating biological contractors) in any publicly owned treatment works if the Administrator finds that such equipment has failed to meet design performance specifications, unless such failure is attributable to negligence on the part of any person, and if such failure has significantly increased capital or operating and maintenance expenditures.

[§202(a)(3) amended by PL 100–4]

(4) For the purposes of this section, the term "eligible treatment works" means those treatment works in each State which meet the requirements of section 201(g)(5) of this Act and which can be fully funded from funds available for such purpose in such State.

[§202(a)(4) amended by PL–117]

(b) The amount of the grant for any project approved by the Administrator after January 1, 1971, and before July 1, 1971, for the construction of treatment works, the actual erection, building or acquisition of which was not commenced prior to July 1, 1971, shall, upon the request of the applicant, be increased to the applicable percentage under subsection (a) of this section for grants for treatment works from funds for fiscal years beginning after June 30, 1971, with respect to the cost of such actual erection, building, or acquisition. Such increased amount shall be paid from any funds allocated to the State in which the treatment works is located without regard to the fiscal year for which such funds were authorized. Such increased amount shall be paid for such project only if—

(1) a sewage collection system that is a part of the same total waste treatment system as the treatment works for which such grant was approved is under construction or is to be constructed for use in conjunction with such treatment works, and if the cost of such sewage collection system exceeds the cost of such treatment works, and

(2) the State water pollution control agency or other appropriate State authority certifies that the quantity of available ground water will be insufficient, inadequate, or unsuitable for public use, including the ecological preservation and recreational use of surface water bodies, unless effluents from publicly owned treatment works after adequate treatment are returned to the ground water consistent with acceptable technological standards.

§1283. Plans, Specifications, Estimates, and Payments [Sec. 203]

(a) (1) Each applicant for a grant shall submit to the Administrator for his approval, plans, specifications, and estimates for each proposed project for the construction of treatment works for which a grant is applied for under section 201(g)(1) from funds allotted to the State under section 205 and which otherwise meets the requirements of this Act. The Administrator shall act upon such plans, specifications, and estimates as soon as practicable after the same have been submitted, and his approval of any such plans, specifications, and estimates shall be deemed a contractual obligation of the United States for the payment of its proportional contribution to such project.

[§203(a) amended by PL 96–483;(a)(1) designated by PL 100–4]

(2) Agreement on Eligible Costs.—

(A) Limitation on Modifications. — Before taking final action on any plans, specifications, and estimates submitted under this subsection after the 60th day following the date of the enactment of the Water Quality Act of 1987, the Administrator shall enter into a written agreement with the applicant which establishes and specifies which items of the proposed project are eligible for Federal payments under this section. The Administrator may not later modify such eligibility determinatons unless they are found to have been made in violation of applicable Federal statutes and regulations.

(B) Limitation on Effect. — Eligibility determinations under this paragraph shall not preclude the Administrator from auditing a project pursuant to section 501 of this Act, or other authority, or from withholding or recovering Federal funds for costs which are found to be unreasonable, unsupported by adequate documentation, or otherwise unallowable under applicable Federal cost principles, or which are incurred on a project which fails to meet the design specifications or effluent limitations contained in the grant agreement and permit pursuant to section 402 of this Act for such project.

[§203(a)(2) added by PL 100–4]

(3) In the case of a treatment works that has an estimated total cost of $8,000,000 or less (as determined by the Administrator), and the population of the applicant municipality is twenty-five thousand or less (according to the most recent United States census), upon completion of an approved facility plan, a single grant may be awarded for the combined Federal sharc of the cost of preparing construction plans and specifications, and the building and erection of the treatment works.

[§203(a)(3) designated by PL 100–4]

(b) The Administrator shall, from time to time as the work progresses, make payments to the recipient of a grant for costs of construction incurred on a project. These payments shall at no time exceed the Federal share of the cost of construction incurred to the date of the voucher covering such payment plus the Federal share of the value of the materials which have been stockpiled in the vicinity of such construction in conformity to plans and specifications for the project.

(c) After completion of a project and approval of the final voucher by the Administrator, he shall pay out of the appropriate sums the unpaid balance of the Federal share payable on account of such project.

(d) Nothing in this Act shall be construed to require, or to authorize the Administrator to require, that grants under this Act for construction of treatment works be made only for projects which are operable units usable for sewage collection, transportation, storage, waste treatment, or for similar purposes without additional construction.

(e) At the request of a grantee under this title, the Administrator is authorized to provide technical and legal assistance in the administration and enforcement of any contract in connection with treatment works assisted under this title, and to intervene in any civil action involving the enforcement of such a contract.

(f) Design/Build Projects.—

(1) Agreement. — Consistent with State law, an applicant who proposes to construct waste water treatment works may enter into an agreement with the Administrator under this subsection providing for the preparation of construction plans and specifications and the erection of such treatment works, in lieu of proceeding under the other provisions of this section.

(2) Limitation on Projects. — Agreements under this subsection shall be limited to projects under an approved facility plan which projects are—

(A) treatment works that have an estimated total cost of $8,000,000 or less; and

(B) any of the following types of waste water treatment systems: aerated lagoons, trickling filters, stabilization ponds, land application systems, sand filters, and subsurface disposal systems.

(3) Required Terms. — An agreement entered into under this subsection shall—

(A) set forth an amount agreed to as the maximum Federal contribution to the project, based upon a competitively bid document of basic design data and applicable standard construction specifications and a determination of the federally eligible costs of the project at the applicable Federal share under section 202 of this Act;

(B) set forth dates for the start and completion of construction of the treatment works by the applicant and a schedule of payments of the Federal contribution to the project:

(C) contain assurances by the applicant that (i) engineering and management assistance will be provided to manage the project; (ii) the proposed treatment works will be an operable unit and will meet all the requirements of this title; and (iii) not later than I year after the date specified as the date of completion of cunstruction of the treatment works, the treatment works will beoperating so as to meet the requirements of any applicable permit for such treatment works under section 402 of this Act;

(D) require the applicant to obtain a bond from the contractor in an amount determined necessary by the Administrator to protect the Federal interest in the project; and

(E) contain such other terms and conditions as are necessary to assure compliance with this title (except as provided in paragraph (4) of this subsection).

(4) Limitation on Application. — Subsections (a), (b), and (c) of this section shall not apply to grants made pursuant to this subsection.

(5) Reservation to Assure Compliance. —The Administrator shall reserve a portion of the grant to assure contract compliance until final project approval as defined by the Administrator. If the amount agreed to under paragraph (3)(A) exceeds the cost of designing and constructing the treatment works, the Administrator shall reallot the amount of the excess to the State in which such treatment works are located for the fiscal year in which such audit is completed.

(6) Limitation on Obligations. — The Administrator shall not obligate more than 20 percent of the amount allotted to a State for a fiscal year under section 205 of this Act for grants pursuant to this subsection.

(7) Allowance. — The Administrator shall determine an allowance for facilities planning for projects constructed under this subsection in accordance with section 201(l) .

(8) Limitation on Federal Contributions. — In no event shall the Federal contribution for the cost of preparing construction plans and specifications and the building and erection of treatment works pursuant to this subsection exceed the amount agreed upon under paragraph (3).

(9) Recovery Action. — In any case in which the recipient of a grant made pursuant to this subsection does not comply with the terms of the agreement entered into under paragraph (3), the Administrator is authorized to take such action as may be necessary to recover the amount of the Federal contribution to the project.

(10) Prevention of Double Benefits. — A recipient of a grant made pursuant to this subsection shall not be eligible for any other grants under this title for the same project.

[§203(f) added by PL 100-4]

§1283. Limitations and Conditions [Sec. 204]

(a) Before approving grants for any project for any treatment works under section 201(g)(1) the Administrator shall determine—

(1) that any required areawide waste treatment management plan under section 208 of this Act (A) is being implemented for such area and the proposed treatment works are included in such plan, or (B) is being developed for such area and reasonable progress is being made toward its implementation and the proposed treatment works will be included in such plan;

[§204(a)(1) revised by PL 100-4]

(2) that (A) the State in which the project is to be located (i) is implementing any required plan under section 303(e) of this Act and the proposed treatment works are in conformity with such plan, or (ii) is developing such a plan and the proposed treatment works will be in conformity with such plan, and (B) such State is in compliance with section 305(b) of this Act;

[§204(a)(2) revised by PL 100-4]

(3) that such works have been certified by the appropriate State water pollution control agency as entitled to priority over such other works in the State in accordance with any applicable State plan under section 303(e) of this Act, except that any priority list developed pursuant to section 303(e)(3)(H) may be modified by such State in accordance with regulations promulgated by the Administrator to give higher priority for grants for the Federal share of the cost of preparing construction drawings and specifications for any treatment works utilizing processes and techniques meeting the guidelines promulgated under section 304(d)(3) of this Act and for grants for the combined Federal share of the cost of preparing construction drawings and specifications and the building and erection of any treatment works meeting the requirements of the next to the last sentence of section 203(a) of this Act which utilizes processes and techniques meeting the guidelines promulgated under section 304(d)(3) of this Act;

(4) that the applicant proposing to construct such works agrees to pay the non- Federal costs of such works and has made adequate provisions satisfactory to the Administrator for assuring proper and efficient operation, including the employment of trained management and operations personnel, and the maintenance of such works in accordance with a plan of operation approved by the State water pollution control agency or, as appropriate, the interstate agency, after construction thereof;

(5) that the size and capacity of such works relate directly to the needs to be served by such works, including sufficient reserve capacity. The amount of reserve capacity provided shall be approved by the Administrator on the basis of a comparison of the cost of constructing such reserves as a part of the works to be funded and the anticipated cost of providing expanded capacity at a date when such capacity will be required after taking into account, in accordance with regulations promulgated by the Administrator, efforts to reduce total flow of sewage and unnecessary water consumption. The amount of reserve capacity eligible for a grant under this title shall be determined by the Administrator taking into account the projected population and associated commercial and industrial establishments within the jurisdiction of the applicant to be served by such treatment works as identified in an approved facilities plan, an areawide plan under section 208; or an applicable municipal master plan of development. For the purpose of this paragraph, section 208, and any such plan, projected population shall be determined on the basis of the latest information available from the United States Department of Commerce or from the States as the Administrator, by regulation, determines appropriate. Beginning October 1, 1984, no grant shall be made under this title to construct that portion of any treatment works providing reserve capacity in excess of existing needs (including existing needs of residential, commercial, industrial, and other users) on the date of approval of a grant for the erection, building, acquisition, alteration, remodeling, improvement, or extension of a project for secondary treatment or more stringent treatment or new interceptors and appurtenances, except that in no event shall reserve capacity of a facility and its related interceptors to which this subsection applies be in excess of existing needs on October 1, 1990. In any case in which an applicant proposes to provide reserve capacity greater than that eligible for Federal financial assistance under this title, the incremental costs of the additional reserve capacity shall be paid by the applicant;

[§204(a)(5) amended by PL 97–117]

(6) that no specification for bids in connection with such works shall be written in such a manner as to contain proprietary, exclusionary, or discriminatory requirements other than those based upon performance, unless such requirements are necessary to test or demonstrate a specific thing or to provide for necessary interchangeability of parts and equipment. When in the judgment of the grantee, it is impractical or uneconomical to make a clear and accurate description of the technical requirements, a "brand name or equal" description may be used as a means to define the performance or other salient requirements of a procurement, and in doing so the grantee need not establish the existence of any source other than the brand or source so named.

[§204(a)(6) amended by PL 97–117]

(b) (1) Notwithstanding any other provision of this title, the Administrator shall not approve any grant for any treatment works under section 201(g)(1) after March 1, 1973, unless he shall first have determined that the applicant (A) has adopted or will adopt a system of charges to assure that each recipient of waste treatment services within the applicant's jurisdiction, as determined by the Administrator, will pay its proportionate share (except as otherwise provided in this paragraph) of the costs of operation and maintenance (including replacement) of any waste treatment services provided by the applicant; and (B) has legal, institutional, managerial, and financial capability to insure adequate construction, operation, and maintenance of treatment works throughout the applicant's jurisdiction, as determined by the Administrator. In any case where an applicant which, as of the date of enactment of this sentence, uses a system of dedicated ad valorem taxes and the Administrator determines that the applicant has a system of charges which results in the distribution of operation and maintenance costs for treatment works within the applicant's jurisdiction, to each user class, in proportion to the contribution to the total cost of operation and maintenance of such works by each user class (taking into account total waste water loading of such works, the constituent elements of the waste, and other appropriate factors) and such applicant is otherwise in compliance with clause (A) of this paragraph with respect to each industrial user, then such dedicated ad valorem tax system shall be deemed to be the user charge system meeting the requirements of clause (A) of this paragraph for the residential user class and such small non- residential user classes as defined by the Administrator. In defining small non-residential users, the Administrator shall consider the volume of wastes discharged into the treatment works by such users and the constituent elements of such wastes as well as such other factors as he deems appropriate. A system of user charges which imposes a lower charge for low-income residential users (as defined by the Administrator) shall be deemed to be a user charge system meeting the requirements of clause (A) of this paragraph if the Administrator determines that such system was adopted after public notice and hearing.

[§204(b)(1) amended by PL 96–483; PL 100–4]

(2) The Administrator shall, within one hundred and eighty days after the date of enactment of the Federal Water Pollution Control Act Amendments of 1972, and after consultation with appropriate State, interstate, municipal, and intermunicipal agencies, issue guidelines applicable to payment of waste treatment costs by industrial and nonindustrial recipients of waste treatment services which shall establish (A) classes of users of such services, including categories of industrial users; (B) criteria against which to determine the adequacy of charges imposed on classes and categories of users reflecting all factors that influence the cost of waste treatment, including strength, volume, and delivery flow rate characteristics of waste; and (C) model systems and rates of user charges typical of various treatment works serving municipal-industrial communities.

(3) Approval by the Administrator of a grant to an interstate agency established by interstate compact for any treatment works shall satisfy any other requirement that such works be authorized by Act of Congress.

[Former §204(b)(3) repealed and (4) redesignated as (3) by PL 96–483]

(4) A system of charges which meets the requirement of clause (A) of paragraph (1) of this subsection may be based on something other than metering the sewage or water supply flow of residential recipients of waste treatment services, including ad valorem taxes. If the system of charges is based on something other than metering the Administrator shall require (A) the applicant to establish a system by which maintenance of the treatment works; and (B) the applicant to establish a procedure under which the residential user will be notified as to that portion of his total payment which will be allocated to the costs of the waste treatment services.

[Former §204(b)(5) redesignated as (4) and §204(b)(6) repealed by PL 96–483]

(c) The next to the last sentence of paragraph (5) of subsection (a) of this section shall not apply in any case where a primary, secondary, or advanced waste treatment facility or its related interceptors has received a grant for erection, building, acquisition, alteration, remodeling, improvement, or extension before October 1, 1984, and all segments and phases of such facility and interceptors shall be funded based on a 20-year reserve capacity in the case of such facility and a 20-year reserve capacity in the case of such interceptors, except that, if a grant for such interceptors has heen approved prior to the date of enactment of the Municipal Wastewater Treatment Construction Grant Amendments of 1981, such interceptors shall be funded based on the approved reserve capacity not to exceed 40 years.

[§204(c) added by PL 97–117]

(d) (1) A grant for the construction of treatment works under this title shall provide that the engineer or engineering firm supervising construction or providing architect engineering services during construction shall continue its relationship to the grant applicant for a period of one year after the completion of construction and initial operation of such treatment works. During such period such engineer or engineering firm shall supervise operation of the treatment works, train operating personnel, and prepare curricula and training material for operating personnel. Costs associated with the implementation of this paragraph shall be eligible for Federal assistance in accordance with this title.

(2) On the date one year after the completion of construction and initial operation of such treatment works, the owner and operator of such treatment works shall certify to the Administrator whether or not such treatment works meet the design specifications and effluent limitations contained in the grant agreement and permit pursuant to section 402 of the Act for such works. If the owner and operator of such treatment works cannot certify that such treatment works meet such design specifications and effluent limitations, any failure to

meet such design specifications and effluent limitations shall be corrected in a timely manner, to allow such affirmative certification, at other than Federal expense.

(3) Nothing in this section shall be construed to prohibit a grantee under this title from requiring more assurances, guarantees, or indemnity or other contractual requirements from any party to a contract pertaining to a project assisted under this title, than those provided under this subsection.

[§204(d) added by PL 97–117]

§1285. Allotment [Sec. 205]

(a) Sums authorized to be appropriated pursuant to section 207 for each fiscal year beginning after June 30, 1972, and before September 30, 1977, shall be allotted by the Administrator not later than the January 1st immediately preceding the beginning of the fiscal year for which authorized, except that the allotment for fiscal year 1973 shall be made not later than 30 days after the date of enactment of the Federal Water Pollution Control Act Amendments of 1972. Such sums shall be allotted among the States by the Administrator in accordance with regulations promulgated by him, in the ratio that the estimated cost of constructing all needed publicly owned treatment works in each State bears to the estimated cost of construction of all needed publicly owned treatment works in all of the States. For the fiscal years ending June 30, 1973, and June 30, 1974, such ratio shall be determined on the basis of the table III of House Public Works Committee Print No. 92–50.

For the fiscal year ending June 30, 1975, such ratio shall be determined one- half on the basis of table I of House Public Works Committee Print Numbered 93–28 and one-half on the, basis of table II of such print, except that no State shall receive an allotment less than that which it received for the fiscal year ending June 30, 1972, as set forth in table III of such print Allotments for fiscal years which begin after the fiscal year ending June 30, 1975 shall be made only in accordance with a revised cost estimate made and submitted to Congress in accordance with section 516(b) of this Act and only after such revised cost estimate shall have been approved by law specifically enacted hereafter.

(b) (1) Any sums allotted to a State under subsection (a) shall be available for obligation under section 203 on and after the date of such allotment. Such sums shall continue available for obligation in such State for a period of one year after the close of the fiscal year for which such sums are authorized. Any amount so allotted which are not obligated by the end of such one-year period shall be immediately reallotted by the Administrator, in accordance with regulations promulgated by him, generally on the basis of the ratio used in making the last allotment of sums under this section. Such reallotted sums shall be added to the last allotments made to the States. Any sum made available to a State by reallotment under this subsection shall be in addition to any funds otherwise allotted to such State for grants under this title during any fiscal year.

(2) Any sums which have been obligated under section 203 and which are released by the payment of the final voucher for the project shall be immediately credited to the State to which such sums were last allotted. Such released sums shall be added to the amounts last allotted to such State and shall be immediately available for obligation in the same manner and to the same extent as such last allotment.

(c) (1) Sums authorized to be appropriated pursuant to section 207 for the fiscal years during the period beginning October 1, 1977, and ending September 30, 1981, shall be allotted for each such year by the Administrator not later than the tenth day which begins after the date of enactment of the Clean Water Act of 1977. Notwithstanding any other provision of law, sums authorized for the fiscal years ending September 30, 1978, September 30, 1979, September 30, 1980, and September 30, 1981, shall be allotted in accordance with table 3 of Committee Print Numbered 95–30 of the Committee on Public Works and Transportation of the House of Representatives.

(2) Sums authorized to be appropriated pursuant to section 207 for the fiscal years 1982, 1983, 1984, and 1985 shall be allotted for each such year by the Administrator not later than the tenth day which begins after the date of enactment of the Municipal Wastewater Treatment Construction Grant Amendments of 1981. Notwithstanding any other provision of law, sums authorized for the fiscal year ending September 30, 1982, shall be allotted in accordance with table 3 of Committee Print Numbered 95–30 of the Committee on Public Works and Transportation of the House of Representatives. Sums authorized for the fiscal years ending September 30, 1983, September 30, 1984, September 30, 1985, and September 30, 1986,

shall be alloted in accordance with the following table:

States:	Fiscal years 1983 through 1985
Alabama	.011398
Alaska	.006101
Arizona	.006885
Arkansas	.006668
California	.072901
Colorado	.008154
Connecticut	.012487
Delaware	.004965
District of Columbia	.004965
Florida	.034407
Georgia	.017234
Hawaii	007895
Idaho	.004965
Illinois	.046101
Indiana	.024566
Iowa	.013796
Kansas	.009201
Kentucky	.012973
Louisiana	.011205
Maine	.007788
Maryland	.024653
Massachusetts	.034608
Michigan	.043829
Minnesota	.018735
Mississippi	.009184
Missouri	.028257
Montana	.004965
Nebraska	.005214
Nevada	.004965
New Hampshire	.010186
New Jersey	.041654
New Mexico	.004965
New York	.113097
North Carolina	.018396
North Dakota	.004965
Ohio	.057383
Oklahoma	.008235
Oregon	.011515
Pennsylvania	.040377
Rhode Island	.006750
South Carolina	.010442
South Dakota	.004965
Tennessee	.014807
Texas	.038726
Utah	.005371
Vermont	.004965
Virginia	.020861
Washington	.017726
West Virginia	.015890
Wisconsin	.027557
Wyoming	.004965
Samoa	.000915
Guam	.000662
Northern Marianas	.000425
Puerto Rico	.013295
Pacific Trust Territories	.001305
Virgin Islands	.000531
United States totals	.399996

[§205(c)(2) added by PL 97–117;amended by PL 100–4]

(3) Fiscal years 1987–1990. — Sums authorized to be appropriated pursuant to section 207 for the fiscal years 1987, 1988, 1989, and 1990 shall be allotted for each such year by the Administrator not later than the 10th day which begins after the date of the enactment of this paragraph. Sums authorized for such fiscal years shall be allotted in accordance with the following table:

States:	Fiscal years 1987 through 1990
Alabama	.011309
Alaska	.006053
Arizona	.006831
Arkansas	.006616

States:	Fiscal years 1987 through 1990
California	.072333
Colorado	.008090
Connecticut	.012390
Delaware	.004965
District of Columbia	.004965
Florida	.034139
Georgia	.017100
Hawaii	.007833
Idaho	.004965
Illinois	.045741
Indiana	.024374
Iowa	.013688
Kansas	.009129
Kentucky	.012872
Louisiana	.011118
Maine	.007829
Maryland	.024461
Massachusetts	.034338
Michigan	.043487
Minnesota	.018589
Mississippi	.009112
Missouri	.028037
Montana	.004965
Nebraska	.005173
Nevada	.004965
New Hampshire	.010107
New Jersey	.041329
New Mexico	.004965
New York	.111632
North Carolina	.018253
North Dakota	.056936
Ohio	.056936
Oklahoma	.008171
Oregon	.011425
Pennsylvania	.040062
Rhode Island	.006791
South Carolina	.010361
South Dakota	.004965
Tennessee	.014692
Texas	.046226
Utah	.005329
Vermont	.004965
Virginia	.020698
Washington	.017588
West Virginia	.015766
Wisconsin	.027342
Wyoming	.004965
American Samoa	.000908
Guam	.000657
Northern Marianas	.000422
Puerto Rico	.013191
Pacific Trust Territories	.001295
Virginia Islands	.000527
United States totals	.999996

[§205(c)(3) added by PL 100–4]

(d) Sums allotted to the States for a fiscal year shall remain available for obligation for the fiscal year for which authorized and for the period of the next succeeding twelve months. The amount of any allotment not obligated by the end of such twenty-four-month period shall be immediately reallotted by the Administrator on the basis of the same ratio as applicable to sums allotted for the then current fiscal year, except that none of the funds reallotted by the Administrator for fiscal year 1978 and for fiscal years thereafter shall be allotted to any State which failed to obligate any of the funds being reallotted. Any sum made available to a State by reallotment under this subsection shall be in addition to any funds otherwise allotted to such State for grants under this title during any fiscal year.

(e) For the fiscal years, 1978, 1979, 1980, 1981, 1982, 1983, 1984, 1985, 1986, 1987, 1988, 1989, and 1990, no State shall receive less than one-half of 1 per centum of the total allotment under subsection (c) of this section, except that in the case of Guam, Virgin Islands, American Samoa, and the Trust Territories not more than thirty-three one-hundredths of 1 per centum on the aggregate shall be allotted to all four of these jurisdictions. For the purpose of carrying out this subsection there are authorized to be appropriated, subject to such amounts as are provided in appropriation Acts, not to exceed $75,000,000 for each of fiscal years 1978, 1979, 1980, 1981, 1982, 1983, 1984, 1985, 1986, 1987, 1988, 1989, and 1990. If for any fiscal year the amount appropriated under authority of this subsection is less than the amount necessary to carry out this subsection, the amount each State receives under this subsection for such year shall bear the same ratio to the amount such State would have received under this subsection in such year if the amount necessary to carry it out had been appropriated as the amount appropriated for such year bears to the amount necessary to carry out this subsection for such year.

[§205(e) amended by PL 97–117; PL 100–4]

(f) Notwithstanding any other provision of this section, sums made available between January 1, 1975, and March 1, 1975, by the Administrator for obligation shall be available for obligation until September 30, 1978.

(g) (1) The Administrator is authorized to reserve each fiscal year not to exceed 2 percentum of the amount authorized under section 207 of this title for purposes of the allotment made to each State under this section on or after October 1, 1977, except in the case of any fiscal year beginning on or after October 1, 1981, and ending before October 1, 1994, in which case the percentage authorized to be reserved shall not exceed 4 per centum or $400,000 whichever amount is the greater. Sums so reserved shall be available for making grants to such State under paragraph (2) of this subsection for the same period as sums are available from such allotment under subsection (d) of this section, and any such grant shall be available for obligation only during such period. Any grant made from sums reserved under this subsection which has not been obligated by the end of the period for which available shall be added to the amount last allotted to such State under this section and shall be immediately available for obligation in the same manner and to the same extent as such last allotment. Sums authorized to be reserved by this paragraph shall be in addition to and not in lieu of any other funds which may be authorized to carry out this subsection.

[§205(g)(1) amended by PL 96–483; PL 97–117; PL 100–4]

(2) The Administrator is authorized to grant to any State from amounts reserved to such State under this subsection, the reasonable costs of administering any aspects of sections 201, 203, 204, and 212 of this Act the responsibility for administration of which the Administrator has delegated to such State. The Administrator may increase such grant to take into account the reasonable costs of administering an approved program under section 402 or 404 , administering a statewide waste treatment management planning program under section 208(b)(4), and managing waste treatment construction grants for small communities.

(h) The Administrator shall set aside from funds authorized for each fiscal year beginning on or after October 1, 1978, a total (as determined by the Governor of the State) of not less than 4 percent nor more than 7½ percent of the sums allotted to any State with a rural population of 25 per centum or more of the total population of such State, as determined by the Bureau of the Census. The Administrator may set aside no more than 7½ of the sums allotted to any other State for which the Governor requests such action. Such sums shall be available only for alternatives to conventional sewage treatment works for municipalities having a population of three thousand five hundred or less, or for the highly dispersed sections of larger municipalities, as defined by the Administrator.

[§205(h) amended by PL 100–4]

(i) Set-Aside for Innovative and Alternative Projects. — Not less than ½ of 1 percent of funds allotted to a State for each of the fiscal years ending September 30, 1979, through September 30, 1990, under subsection (c) of this section shall be expended only for increasing the Federal share of grants for construction of treatment works utilizing innovative processes and techniques pursuant to section 202(a)(2) of this Act. Including the expenditures authorized by the preceding sentence, a total of 2 percent of the funds allotted to a State for each of the fiscal years ending September 30, 1979, and September 30, 1980, and 3 percent of the funds allotted to a State for the fiscal year ending September 30, 1981, under subsection (c) of this section shall be expended only for increasing grants for construction of treatment works pursuant to section 202(a)(2) of this Act. Including the expenditures authorized by the first sentence of this subsection, a total (as determined by the Governor of the State) of not less than 4 percent nor more than 7½ percent of the funds allotted to such State under subsection (c) of this section for each of the fiscal years ending September 30, 1982, through September 30, 1990, shall be expended only for increasing the

Federal share of grants for construction of treatment works pursuant to section 202(a)(2) of this Act.

[§205(i) amended by PL 97–117; PL 100–4]

(j) (1) The Administrator shall reserve each fiscal year not to exceed 1 per centum of the sums allotted and available for obligation to each State under this section for each fiscal year beginning on or after October 1, 1981, or $100,000, whichever amount is the greater.

[§205(j) added by PL 97–117]

(2) Such sums shall be used by the Administrator to make grants to the States to carry out water quality management planning, including, but not limited to—

(A) identifying most cost effective and locally acceptable facility and non-point measures to meet and maintain water quality standards;

(B) developing an implementation plan to obtain State and local financial and regulatory commitments to implement measures developed under subparagraph (A);

(C) determining the nature, extent, and causes of water quality problems in various areas of the State and interstate region, and reporting on these annually; and

(D) determining those publicly owned treatment works which should be constructed with assistance under this title, in which areas and in what sequence, taking into account the relative degree of effluent reduction attained, the relative contributions to water quality of other point or nonpoint sources, and the consideration of alternatives to such construction, and implementing section 303(e) of this Act.

(3) In carrying out planning with grants made under paragraph (2) of this subsection, a State shall develop jointly with local, regional, and interstate entities, a plan for carrying out the program and give funding priority to such entities and designated or undesignated public comprehensive planning organizations to carry out the purposes of this subsection. In giving such priority, the State shall allocate at least 40 percent of the amount granted to such State for a fiscal year under paragraph (2) of this subsection to regional public comprehensive planning organizations in such State and appropriate interstate organizations for the development and implementation of the plan described in this paragraph. In any fiscal year for which the Governor, in consultation with such organizations and with the approval of the Administrator, determines that allocation of at least 40 percent of such amount to such organizations will not result in significant participation by such organizations in water quality management planning and not significantly assist in development and implementation of the plan described in this paragraph and achieving the goals of this Act, the allocation to such organization may be less than 40 percent of such amount.

[§205(j)(3) amended by PL 100–4]

(4) All activities undertaken under this subsection shall be in coordination with other related provisions of this Act.

(5) Nonpoint Source Reservation. — In addition to the sums reserved under paragraph (1), the Administrator shall reserve each fiscal year for each State 1 percent of the sums allotted and available for obligation to such State under this section for each fiscal year beginning on or after October 1, 1986, or $100,000, whichever is greater, for the purpose of carrying out section 319 of this Act. Sums so reserved in a State in any fiscal year for which such State does not request the use of such sums, to the extent such sums exceed $100,000, may be used by such State for other purposes under this title.

[§205(j)(5) added by PL 100–4]

(k) The Administrator shall allot to the State of New York from sums authorized to be appropriated for the fiscal year ending September 30, 1982, an amount necessary to pay the entire cost of conveying sewage from the Convention Center of the city of New York to the Newtown sewage treatment plant, Brooklyn-Queens area, New York. The amount allotted under this subsection shall be in addition to and not in lieu of any other amounts authorized to be allotted to such State under this Act.

[§205(k) added by PL 97–117]

(l) Marine Estuary Reservation.—

(1) Reservation of Funds.—

(A) General Rule. — Prior to making allotments among the States under subsection (c) of this section, the Administrator shall reserve funds from sums appropriated pursuant to section 207 for each fiscal year beginning after September 30, 1986.

(B) Fiscal Years 1987 and 1988. — For each of fiscal years 1987 and 1988 the reservation shall be 1 percent of the sums appropriated pursuant to section 207 for such fiscal year.

(C) Fiscal Years 1989 and 1990. — For each of fiscal years 1989 and 1990 the reservation shall be 1½ percent of the funds appropriated pursuant to section 207 for such fiscal year.

(2) Use of Funds. — Of the sums reserved under this subsection, two-thirds shall be available to address water quality problems of marine bays and estuaries subject to lower levels of water quality due to the impacts of discharges from combined storm water and sanitary sewer overflows from adjacent urban complexes, and one-third shall be available for the implementation of section 320 of this Act, relating to the national estuary program.

(3) Period of availability. — Sums reserved under this subsection shall be subject to the period of availability for obligation established by subsection (d) of this section.

(4) Treatment of Certain Body of Water. — For purposes of this section and section 201(n), Newark Bay, New Jersey, and the portion of the Passaic River up to Little Falls, in the vicinity of Beatties Dam, shall be treated as a marine bay and estuary.

[§205(l) added by PL 100–4]

(m) Discretionary Deposits Into State Water Pollution Control Revolving Funds.—

(1) From Construction Grant Allotments. — In addition to any amounts deposited in a water pollution control revolving fund established by a State under title VI, upon request of the Governor of such State, the Administrator shall make available to the State for deposit, as capitalization grants, in such fund in any fiscal year beginning after September 30, 1986, such portion of the amounts allotted to such State under this section for such fiscal year as the Governor considers appropriate; except that (A) in fiscal year 1987, such deposit may not exceed 50 percent of the amounts allotted to such State under this section for such fiscal year, and (B) in fiscal year 1988, such deposit may not exceed 75 percent of the amounts allotted to such State under this section for this fiscal year.

(2) Notice Requirement. — The Governor of a State may make a request under paragraph (1) for a deposit into the water pollution control revolving fund of such State—

(A) in fiscal year 1987 only if no later than 90 days after the date of the enactment of this subsection, and

(B) in each fiscal year thereafter only if 90 days before the first day of such fiscal year,the State provides notice of its intent to make such deposit.

(3) Exception. — Sums reserved under section 205(j) of this Act shall not be available for obligation under this subsection.

[§205(m) added by PL 100–4]

§1286. Reimbursement and Advanced Construction [Sec. 206]

(a) Any publicly owned treatment works in a State on which construction was initiated after June 30, 1966, but before July 1, 1973, which was approved by the appropriate State water pollution control agency and which the Administrator finds meets the requirements of section 8 of this Act in effect at the time of the initiation of construction shall be reimbursed a total amount equal to the difference between the amount of Federal financial assistance, if any, received under such section 8 for such project and 50 per centum of the cost of such project, or 55 per centum of the project cost where the Administrator also determines that such treatment works was constructed in conformity with a comprehensive metropolitan treatment plan as described in section 8(f) of the Federal Water Pollution Control Act as in effect immediately prior to the date of enactment of the Federal Water Pollution Control Act Amendments of 1972. Nothing in this subsection shall result in any such works receiving Federal grants from all sources in excess of 80 per centum of the cost of such project.

(b) Any publicly owned treatment works constructed with or eligible for Federal financial assistance under this Act in a State between June 30, 1956, and June 30, 1966, which was approved by the State water pollution control agency and which the Administrator finds meets the requirements of section 8 of this Act prior to the date of enactment of the Federal Water Pollution Control Act Amendments of 1972 but which was constructed without assistance under such section 8 or which received such assistance in an amount less than 30 per centum of the cost of such project shall qualify for payments and reimbursement of State or local funds used for such project from sums allocated to such State under this section in an amount which shall not exceed the difference between the amount of such assistance, if any, received for such project and 30 per centum of the cost of such project.

(c) No publicly owned treatment works shall receive any payment or reimbursement under subsection (a) or (b) of this section unless an application for such assistance is filed with the Administrator within the one year period which begins on the date of enactment of the Federal Water Pollution Control Act Amendments of 1972. Any application filed within such one year period may be revised from time to time, as may be necessary.

(d) The Administrator shall allocate to each qualified project under subsection (a) of this section each fiscal year for which funds are appropriated under subsection (e) of this section an amount which bears the same ratio to the unpaid balance of the reimbursement due such project as the total of such funds for such year bears to the total unpaid balance of reimbursement due all such approved projects on the date of enactment of such appropriations. The Administrator shall allocate to each qualified project under subsection (b) of this section each fiscal year for which funds are appropriated under subsection (e) of this section an amount which bears the same ratio to the unpaid balance of the reimbursement due such project as the total of such funds for such years bears to the total unpaid balance of reimbursement due all such approved projects on the date of enactment of such appropriation.

(e) There is authorized to be appropriated to carry out subsection (a) of this section not to exceed $2,600,000,000 and to carry out subsection (b) of this section, not to exceed $750,000,000. The authorizations contained in this subsection shall be the sole source of funds for reimbursements authorized by this section.

(f) (1) In any case where a substantial portion of the funds allotted to a State for the current fiscal year under this title have been obligated under section 201(g) , or will be so obligated in a timely manner (as determined by the Administrator), and there is construction of any treatment work project without the aid of Federal funds and in accordance with all procedures and all requirements applicable to treatment works projects, except those procedures and requirements which limit construction of projects to those constructed with the aid of previously allotted Federal funds, the Administrator, upon his approval of an application made under this subsection therefor, is authorized to pay the Federal share of the cost of construction of such project when additional funds are allotted to the State under this title if prior to the construction of the project the Administrator approves plans, specifications, and estimates therefor in the same manner as other treatment works projects. The Administrator may not approve an application under this subsection unless an authorization is in effect for the first fiscal year in the period for which the application requests payment and such requested payment for that fiscal year does not exceed the State's expected allotment from such authorization. The Administrator shall not be required to make such requested payment for any fiscal year —

(A) to the extent that such payment would exceed such State's allotment of the amount appropriated for such fiscal year; and

(B) unless such payment is for a project which, on the basis of an approved funding priority list of such State, is eligible to receive such payment based on the allotment and appropriation for such fiscal year. To the extent that sufficient funds are not appropriated to pay the full Federal share with respect to a project for which obligations under the provisions of this subsection have been made, the Administrator shall reduce the Federal share to such amount less than 75 percentum as such appropriations do provide.

[§206 (f)(1) amended by PL 96–483]

(2) In determining the allotment for any fiscal year under this title, any treatment works project constructed in accordance with this section and without the aid of Federal funds shall not be considered completed until an application under the provisions of this subsection with respect to such project has been approved by the Administrator, or the availability of funds from which this project is eligible for reimbursement has expired, whichever first occurs.

§1287. Authorization [Sec. 207]

There is authorized to be appropriated to carry out this title, other than sections 206 (e), 208 and 209 , for the fiscal year ending June 30, 1973, not to exceed $5,000,000,000, for the fiscal year ending June 30, 1974, not to exceed $6,000,000,000, and for the fiscal year ending June 30, 1975, not tO exceed $7,000,000,000, and, subject to such amounts as are provided in appropriation Acts, for the fiscal year ending September 30, 1977, $1,000,000,000 for the fiscal year ending September 30, 1978, $4,500,000,000 and for the fiscal years ending September 30, 1979, September 30, 1980, not to exceed $5,000,000,000; for the fiscal year ending September 30, 1981, not to exceed $2,548,837,000; and for the fiscal years ending September 30, 1982, September 30, 1983, September 30, 1984, and September 30, 1985, not to exceed $2,400,000,000 per fiscal year; and for each of the fiscal years ending September 30, 1986, September 30, 1987, and September 30, 1988, not to exceed $2,400,000,000; and for each of the fiscal years ending September 30, 1989, and September 30, 1990, not to exceed $1,200,000,000.

[§207 amended by PL 97–35; PL 97–117; PL 100–4]

§1288. Areawide Waste Treatment Management [Sec. 208]

(a) For the purpose of encouraging and facilitating the development and implementation of area wide waste treatment management plans—

(1) The Administrator, within ninety days after the date of enactment of this Act and after consultation with appropriate Federal, State, and local authorities, shall by regulation publish guidelines for the identification of those areas which, as a result of urban-industrial concentrations or other factors, have substantial water quality control problems.

(2) The Governor of each State, within sixty days after publication of the guidelines issued pursuant to paragraph (1) of this subsection, shall identify each area within the State which, as a result of urban-industrial concentrations or other factors, has substantial water quality control problems. Not later than one hundred and twenty days following such identification and after consultation with appropriate elected and other officials of local governments having jurisdiction in such areas, the Governor shall designate (A) the boundaries of each such area, and (B) a single representative organization, including elected officials from local governments or their designees, capable of developing effective area wide waste treatment management plans for such area. The Governor may in the same manner at any later time identify any additional area (or modify an existing area) for which he determines areawide waste treatment management to be appropriate, designate the boundaries of such area, and designate an organization capable of developing effective areawide waste treatment management plans for such area.

(3) With respect to any area which, pursuant to the guidelines published under paragraph (1) of this subsection, is located in two or more States, the Governors of the respective States shall consult and cooperate in carrying out the provisions of paragraph (2), with a view toward designating the boundaries of the interstate area having common water quality control problems and for which areawide waste treatment management plans would be most effective, and toward designating, within one hundred and eighty days after publication of guidelines issued pursuant to paragraph (1) of this subsection, of a single representative organization capable of developing effective areawide waste treatment management plans for such area.

(4) If a Governor does not act, either by designating or determining not to make a designation under paragraph (2) of this subsection, within the time required by such paragraph, or if, in the case of an interstate area, the Governors of the States involved do not designate a planning organization within the time required by paragraph (3) of this subsection, the chief elected officials of local governments within an area may by agreement designate (A) the boundaries for such an area, and (B) a single representative organization including elected officials from such local governments, or their designees, capable of developing an areawide waste treatment management plan for such area.

(5) Existing regional agencies may be designated under paragraphs (2), (3), and (4) of this subsection.

(6) The State shall act as a planning agency for all portions of such State which are not designated under paragraphs (2), (3), or (4) of this subsection.

(7) Designations under this subsection shall be subject to the approval of the Administrator.

(b) (1) (A) Not later than one year after the date of designation of any organization under subsection (a) of this section such organization shall have in operation a continuing areawide waste treatment management planning process consistent with section 201 of this Act. Plans prepared in accordance with this process shall contain alternatives for waste treatment management, and be applicable to all wastes generated within the area involved. The initial plan prepared in accordance with such process shall be certified by the Governor and submitted to the Administrator not later than two years after the planning process is in operation.

(B) For any agency designated after 1975 under subsection (a) of this section and for all portions of a State for which the State is required to act as the planning agency in accordance with subsection (a)(6), the initial plan prepared in accordance with such process shall be certified by the Governor and submitted to the Administrator not later than three years after the receipt of the initial grant award authorized under subsection (f) of this section.

(2) Any plan prepared under such process shall include, but not be limited to—

(A) the identification of treatment works necessary to meet the anticipated municipal and industrial waste treatment needs of the area over a twenty-year period, annually updated (including an analysis of alternative waste treatment systems), including any requirements for the acquisition of land for treatment purposes; the necessary waste water collection and urban storm water runoff systems; and a program to provide the necessary financial arrangements for the development of such treatment works, and an identification of open space and recreation opportunities that can be expected to result from improved water quality, including consideration of potential use of lands associated with treatment works and increased access to water-based recreation;

(B) the establishment of construction priorities for such treatment works and time schedules for the initiation and completion of all treatment works;

(C) the establishment of a regulatory program to—

(i) implement the waste treatment management requirements of section 201(c) ,

(ii) regulate the location, modification, and construction of any facilities within such area which may result in any discharge in such area, and

(iii) assure that any industrial or commercial waste discharged into any treatment works in such area meet applicable pretreatment requirements;

(D) the identification of those agencies necessary to construct, operate, and maintain all facilities required by the plan and otherwise to carry out the plan;

(E) the identification of the measures necessary to carry out the plan (including financing), the period of time necessary to carry out the plan, the costs of carrying out the plan within such time, and the economic, social, and environmental impact of carrying out the plan within such time;

(F) a process to (i) identify, if appropriate, agriculturally and silviculturally related nonpoint sources of pollution, including return flows from irrigated agriculture, and their cumulative effects, runoff from manure disposal areas, and from land used for livestock and crop production, and (ii) set forth procedures and methods (including land use requirements) to control to the extent feasible such sources;

(G) a process of (i) identify, if appropriate, mine-related sources of pollution including new, current, and abandoned surface and underground mine runoff, and (ii) set forth procedures and methods (including land use requirements) to control to the extent feasible such sources;

(H) a process to (i) identify construction activity related sources of pollution, and (ii) set forth procedures and methods (including land use requirements) to control to the extent feasible such sources;

(I) a process to (i) identify, if appropriate, salt water intrusion into rivers, lakes, and estuaries resulting from reduction of fresh water flow from any cause, including irrigation, obstruction, ground water extraction, and diversion, and (ii) set forth procedures and methods to control such intrusion to the extent feasible where such procedures and methods are otherwise a part of the waste treatment management plan;

(J) a process to control the disposition of all residual waste generated in such area which could affect water quality; and

(K) a process to control the disposal of pollutants on land or in subsurface excavations within such area to protect ground and surface water quality.

(3) Areawide waste treatment management plans shall be certified annually by the Governor or his designee (or Governors or their designees, where more than one State is involved) as being consistent with applicable basin plans and such areawide waste treatment management plans shall be submitted to the Administrator for his approval.

(4) (A) Whenever the Governor of any State determines (and notifies the Administrator) that consistency with a statewide regulatory program under section 303 so requires, the requirements of clauses (F) through (K) of paragraph (2) of this subsection shall be developed and submitted by the Governor to the Administrator for approval for application to a class or category of activity throughout each State.

(B) Any program submitted under subparagraph (A) of this paragraph which, in whole or in part, is to control the discharge or other placement of dredged or fill material into the navigable waters shall include the following:

(i) A consultation process which includes the State agency with primary jurisdiction over fish and wildlife resources.

(ii) A process to identify and manage the discharge or other placement of dredged or fill material which adversely affects navigable waters, which shall complement and be coordinated with a State program under section 404 conducted pursuant to this Act.

(iii) A process to assure that any activity conducted pursuant to a best management practice will comply with the guidelines established under section 404(b)(1), and sections 307 and 403 of this Act.

(iv) A process to assure that any activity conducted pursuant to a best management practice can be terminated or modified for cause including, but not limited to, the following:

(I) violation of any condition of the best management practice;

(II) change in any activity that requires either a temporary or permanent reduction or elimination of the discharge pursuant to the best management practice.

(v) A process to assure continued coordination with Federal and Federal-State water-related planning and reviewing processes, including the National Wetlands Inventory.

(C) If the Governor of a State obtains approval from the Administrator of a statewide regulatory program which meets the requirements of subparagraph (B) of this paragraph and if such State is administering a permit program under section 404 of this Act, no person shall be required to obtain an individual permit pursuant to such section, or to comply with a general permit issued pursuant to such section, with respect to any appropriate activity within such State for which a best management practice has been approved by the Administrator under the program approved by the Administrator pursuant to this paragraph.

(D) (i) Whenever the Administrator determines after public hearing that a State is not administering a program approved under this section in accordance with the requirements of this section, the Administrator shall so notify the State, and if appropriate corrective action is not taken within a reasonable time, not to exceed ninety days, the Administrator shall withdraw approval of such program. The Administrator shall not withdraw approval of any such program unless he shall first have notified the State, and made public, in writing, the reasons for such withdrawal.

(ii) In the case of a State with a program submitted and approved under this paragraph, the Administrator shall withdraw approval of such program under this subparagraph only for a substantial failure of the State to administer its program in accordance with the requirements of this paragraph.

(c) (1) The Governor of each State, in consultation with the planning agency designated under subsection (a) of this section, at the time a plan is submitted to the Administrator, shall designate one or more waste treatment management agencies (which may be an existing or newly created local, regional or State agency or potential subdivision) for each area designated under subsection (a) of this section and submit such designations to the Administrator.

(2) The Administrator shall accept any such designation, unless, within 120 days of such designation, he finds that the designated management agency (or agencies) does not have adequate authority—

(A) to carry out appropriate portions of an areawide waste treatment management plan developed under subsection (b) of this section;

(B) to manage effectively waste treatment works and related facilities serving such area in conformance with any plan required by subsection (b) of this section;

(C) directly or by contract, to design and construct new works, and to operate and maintain new and existing works as required by any plan developed pursuant to subsection (b) of this section;

(D) to accept and utilize grants, or other funds from any source, for waste treatment management purposes;

(E) to raise revenues, including the assessment of waste treatment charges;

(F) to incur short- and long-term indebtedness;

(G) to assure in implementation of an areawide waste treatment management plan that each participating community pays its proportionate share of treatment costs;

(H) to refuse to receive any wastes from any municipality or subdivision thereof, which does not comply with any provisions of an approved plan under this section applicable to such area; and

(I) to accept for treatment industrial wastes.

(d) After a waste treatment management agency having the authority required by subsection (c) has been designated under such subsection for an area and a plan for such area has been approved under subsection (b) of this section, the Administrator shall not make any grant for construction of a publicly owned treatment works under section 201(g)(1) within such area except to such designated agency and for works in conformity with such plan.

(e) No permit under section 402 of this Act shall be issued for any point source which is in conflict with a plan approved pursuant to subsection (b) of this section.

(f) (1) The Administrator shall make grants to any agency designated under subsection (a) of this section for payment of the reasonable costs of developing and operating a continuing areawide waste treatment management planning process under subsection (b) of this section.

(2) For the two-year period beginning on the date the first grant is made under paragraph (1) of this subsection to an agency, if such first grant is made before October 1, 1977, the amount of each such grant to such agency shall be 100 per centum of the costs of developing and operating a continuing areawide waste treatment management planning process under subsection (b) of this section, and thereafter the amount granted to such agency shall not exceed 75 per centum of such costs in each succeeding one-year period. In the case of any other grant made to an agency under such paragraph (1) of this subsection, the amount of such grant shall not exceed 75 per centum of the costs of developing and operating a continuing areawide waste treatment management planning process in any year.

(3) Each applicant for a grant under this subsection shall submit to the Administrator for his approval each proposal for which a grant is applied for under this subsection. The Administrator shall act upon such proposal as soon as practicable after it has been submitted, and his approval of that proposal shall be deemed a contractual obligation of the United States for the payment of its contribution to such proposal, subject to such amounts as are provided in appropriation Acts. There is authorized to be appropriated to carry out this subsection not to exceed $50,000,000 for the fiscal year ending June 30, 1973, not to exceed $100,000,000 for the fiscal year ending June 30, 1974, not to exceed $150,000,000 per fiscal year for the fiscal years ending June 30, 1975, September 30, 1977, September 30, 1978, September 30, 1979, and September 30, 1980, not to exceed $100,000,000 per fiscal year for the fiscal years ending September 30, 1981, and September 30, 1982, and such sums as may be necessary for fiscal years 1983 through 1990.

[§208(f)(3) amended by PL 96–483; PL 100–4]

(g) The Administrator is authorized, upon request of the Governor or the designated planning agency, and without reimbursement, to consult with, and provide technical assistance to, any agency designated under subsection (a) of this section in the development of areawide waste treatment management plans under subsection (b) of this section.

(h) (1) The Secretary of the Army, acting through the Chief of Engineers, in cooperation with the Administrator is authorized and directed, upon request of the Governor or the designated planning organization, to consult with, and provide technical assistance to, any agency designed under subsection (a) of this section in developing and operating a continuing areawide waste treatment management planning process under subsection (b) of this section.

(2) There is authorized to be appropriated to the Secretary of the Army, to carry out this subsection, not to exceed $50,000,000 per fiscal year for the fiscal years ending June 30, 1973, and June 30, 1974.

(i) (1) The Secretary of the Interior, acting through the Director of the United States Fish and Wildlife Service, shall, upon request of the Governor of a State, and without reimbursement, provide technical assistance to such State in developing a statewide program for submission to the Administrator under subsection (b)(4)(B) of this section and in implementing such program after its approval.

(2) There is authorized to be appropriated to the Secretary of the Interior $6,000,000 to complete the National Wetlands Inventory of the United States, by December 31, 1981, and to provide information from such Inventory to States as it becomes available to assist such States in the development and operation of programs under this Act.

(j) (1) The Secretary of Agriculture, with the concurrence of the Administrator, and acting through the Soil Conservation Service and such other agencies of the Department of Agriculture as the Secretary may designate, is authorized and directed to establish and administer a program to enter into contracts of not less than five years nor more than ten years with owners and operators having control of rural land for the purpose of installing and maintaining measures incorporating best management practices to control nonpoint source pollution for improved water quality in those States or areas for which the Administrator has approved a plan under subsection (b) of this section where the practices to which the contracts apply are certified by the management agency designated under subsection (c)(1) of this section to be consistent with such plans and will result in improved water quality. Such contracts may be entered into during the period ending not later than September 31, 1988. Under such contracts the land owner or operator shall agree—

(i) to effectuate a plan approved by a soil conservation district, where one exists, under this section for his farm, ranch, or other land substantially in accordance with the schedule outlined therein unless any requirement thereof is waived or modified by the Secretary;

(ii) to forfeit all rights to further payments or grants under the contract and refund to the United States all payments and grants received thereunder, with interest, upon his violation of the contract at any stage during the time he has control of the land if the Secretary, after considering the recommendations of the soil conservation district where one exists, and the Administrator, determines that such violation is of such a nature as to warrant termination of the contract, or to make refunds or accept such payment adjustments as the Secretary may deem appropriate if he determines that the violation by the owner or operator does not warrant termination of the contract;

(iii) upon transfer of his right and interest in the farm, ranch, or other land during the contract period to forfeit all rights to further payments or grants under the contract and refund to the United States all payments or grants received thereunder, with interest, unless the transferee of any such land agrees with the Secretary to assume all obligations of the contract;

(iv) not to adopt any practice specified by the Secretary on the advice of the Administrator in the contract as a practice which would tend to defeat the purposes of the contract;

(v) to such additional provisions as the Secretary determines are desirable and includes in the contract to effectuate the purposes of the program or to facilitate the practical administration of the program.

(2) In return for such agreement by the landowner or operator the Secretary shall agree to provide technical assistance and share the cost of carrying out those conservation practices and measures set forth in the contract for which he determines that cost sharing is appropriate and in the public interest and which are approved for cost sharing by the agency designated to implement the plan developed under subsection (b) of this section. The portion of such cost (including labor) to be shared shall be that part which the Secretary determines is necessary and appropriate to effectuate the installation of the water quality management practices and measures under the contract, but not to exceed 50 per centum of the total cost of the measures set forth in the contract; except the Secretary may increase the matching cost share where he determines that (1) the main benefits to be derived from the measures are related to improving offsite water quality, and (2) the matching share requirement would place a burden on the landowner which would probably prevent him from participating in the program.

(3) The Secretary may terminate any contract with a landowner or operator by mutual agreement with the owner or operator if the Secretary determines that such termination would be in the public interest, and may agree to such modification of contracts previously entered into as he may determine to be desirable to carry out the purposes of the program or facilitate the practical administration thereof or to accomplish equitable treatment with respect to other conservation, land use, or water quality programs.

(4) In providing assistance under this subsection the Secretary will give priority to those areas and sources that have the most significant effect upon water quality. Additional investigations or plans may be made, where necessary, to supplement approved water quality management plans, in order to determine priorities.

(5) The Secretary shall, where practicable, enter into agreements with soil conservation districts, State soil and water conservation agencies, or State water quality agencies to administer all or part of the program established in this subsection under regulations developed by the Secretary. Such agreements shall provide for the submission of such reports as the Secretary deems necessary, and

for payment by the United States of such portion of the costs incurred in the administration of the program as the Secretary may deem appropriate.

(6) The contracts under this subsection shall be entered into only in areas where the management agency designated under subsection (c)(1) of this section assures an adequate level of participation by owners and operators having control of rural land in such areas. Within such areas the local soil conservation district, where one exists, together with the Secretary of Agriculture, will determine the priority of assistance among individual landowners and operators to assure that the most critical water quality problems are addressed.

(7) The Secretary, in consultation with the Administrator and subject to section 304(k) of this Act, shall, not later than September 30, 1978, promulgate regulations for carrying out this subsection and for support and cooperation with other Federal and non-Federal agencies for implementation of this subsection.

(8) This program shall not be used to authorize or finance projects that would otherwise be eligible for assistance under the terms of Public Law 83–566.

(9) There are hereby authorized to be appropriated to the Secretary of Agriculture $200,000,000 for fiscal year 1979, $400,000,000 for fiscal year 1980, $100,000,000 for fiscal year 1981, $100,000,000 for fiscal year 1982, and such sums as may be necessary for fiscal years 1983 through 1990, to carry out this subsection. The program authorized under this subsection shall be in addition to, and not in substitution of, other programs in such area authorized by this or any other public law.

[§208(j)(9) amended by PL 96–483; PL 100–4]

§1289. Basin Planning [Sec. 209]

(a) The President, acting through the Water Resources Council, shall, as soon as practicable, prepare a Level B plan under the Water Resources Planning Act for all basins in the United States. All such plans shall be completed not later than January 1, 1980, except that priority in the preparation of such plans shall be given to those basins and portions thereof which are within those areas designated under paragraphs (2), (3), and (4) of subsection (a) of section 208 of this Act.

(b) The President, acting through the Water Resources Council, shall report annually to Congress on progress being made in carrying out this section. The first such report shall be submitted not later than January 31, 1973.

(c) There is authorized to be appropriated to carry out this section not to exceed $200,000,000.

§1290. Annual Survey [Sec. 210]

The Administrator shall annually make a survey to determine the efficiency of the operation and maintenance of treatment works constructed with grants made under this Act, as compared to the efficiency planned at the time the grant was made. The results of such annual survey shall be included in the report required under section 516(a) of this Act.

§1291. Sewage Collection Systems [Sec. 211]

(a) No grant shall be made for a sewage collection system under this title unless such grant (1) is for replacement or major rehabilitation of an existing collection system and is necessary to the total integrity and performance of the waste treatment works servicing such community, or (2) is for a new collection system in an existing community with sufficient existing or planned capacity adequately to treat such collected sewage and is consistent with section 201 of this Act.

(b) If the Administrator uses population density as a test for determining the eligibility of a collector sewer for assistance it shall be only for the purpose of evaluating alternatives and determining the needs for such system in relation to ground or surface water quality impact.

(c) No grant shall be made under this title from funds authorized for any fiscal year during the period beginning October 1, 1977, and ending September 30, 1990, for treatment works for control of pollutant discharges from separate storm sewer systems.

[§211(c) amended by PL 97–117; PL 100–4]

§1292. Definitions [Sec. 212]

As used in this title—

(1) The term "construction" means any one or more of the following: preliminary planning to determine the feasibility of treatment works, engineering, architectural, legal, fiscal, or economic investigations or studies, surveys, designs, plans, working drawings, specifications, procedures, field testing of innovative or alternative waste water treatment processes and techniques meeting guidelines promulgated under section 304(d)(3) of this Act, or other necessary actions, erection, building, acquisition, alteration, remodeling, improvement, or extension of treatment works, or the inspection or supervision of any of the foregoing items.

[§212(1) amended by PL 97–117]

(2) (A) The term "treatment works" means any devices and systems used in the storage, treatment, recycling, and reclamation of municipal sewage or industrial wastes of a liquid nature to implement section 201 of this act, or necessary to recycle or reuse water at the most economical cost over the estimated life of the works, including intercepting sewers, outfall sewers, sewage collection systems, pumping, power, and other equipment, and their appurtenances; extensions, improvements, remodeling, additions, and alterations thereof; elements essential to provide a reliable recycled supply such as standby treatment units and clear well facilities; and any works, including site acquisition of the land that will be an integral part of the treatment process (including land use for the storage of treated wastewater in land treatment systems prior to land application) or is used for ultimate disposal of residues resulting from such treatment.

(B) In addition to the definition contained in subparagraph (A) of this paragraph, "treatment works" means any other method or system for preventing, abating, reducing, storing, treating, separating, or disposing of municipal waste, including storm water runoff, or industrial waste, including waste in combined storm water and sanitary sewer systems. Any application for construction grants which includes wholly or in part such methods or systems shall, in accordance with guidelines published by the Administrator pursuant to subparagraph (C) of this paragraph, contain adequate data and analysis demonstrating such proposal to be, over the life of such works, the most cost efficient alternative to comply with sections 301 or 302 of this act, or the requirements of section 201 of this act.

(C) For the purposes of subparagraph (B) of this paragraph, the Administrator shall, within one hundred and eighty days after the date of enactment of this title, publish and thereafter revise no less often than annually, guidelines for the evaluation of methods, including cost effective analysis, described in subparagraph (B) of this paragraph.

(3) The term "replacement" as used in this title means those expenditures for obtaining and installing equipment, accessories, or appurtenances during the useful life of the treatment works necessary to maintain the capacity and performance for which such works are designed and constructed.

§1293. Loan Guarantees for Construction of Treatment Works [Sec. 213]

(a) Subject to the conditions of this section and to such terms and conditions as the Administrator determines to be necessary to carry out the purposes of this title, the Administrator is authorized to guarantee, and to make commitments to guarantee, the principal and interest (including interest accruing between the date of default and the date of the payment in full of the guarantee) of any loan, obligation, or participation therein of any State, municipality, or intermunicipal or interstate agency issued directly and exclusively to the Federal Financing Bank to finance that part of the cost of any grant- eligible project for the construction of publicly owned treatment works not paid for with Federal financial assistance under this title (other than this section), which project the Administrator has determined to be eligible for such financial assistance under this title, including, but not limited to, projects eligible for reimbursement under section 206 of this title.

(b) No guarantee, or commitment to make a guarantee, may be made pursuant to this section—

(1) unless the Administrator certifies that the issuing body is unable to obtain on reasonable terms sufficient credit to finance its actual needs without such guarantee; and

(2) unless the Administrator determines that there is a reasonable assurance of repayment of the loan, obligation, or participation therein.

A determination of whether financing is available at reasonable rates shall be made by the Secretary of the Treasury with relationship to the current average yield on outstanding marketable obligations of municipalities of comparable maturity.

(c) The Administrator is authorized to charge reasonable fees for the investigation of an application for a guarantee and for the issuance of a commitment to make a guarantee.

(d) The Administrator, in determining whether there is a reasonable assurance of repayment, may require a commitment which would apply to such repayment. Such commitment may include, but not be limited to, any funds received by such grantee from the amounts appropriated under section 206 of this act.

[§213(d) amended by PL 96–483]

§1294. Public Information [Sec. 214]

The Administrator shall develop and operate within one year of the date of enactment of this section, a continuing program of public information and education on recycling and reuse of wastewater (including sludge), the use of land treatment, and methods for the reduction of wastewater volume.

§1295. Requirements for American Materials [Sec. 215]

Notwithstanding any other provision of law, no grant for which application is made after February 1, 1978, shall be made under this title for any treatment works unless only such unmanufactured articles, materials, and supplies as have been mined or produced in the United States, and only such manufactured articles, materials, and supplies as have been manufactured in the United States, substantially all from articles, materials, or supplies mined, produced, or manufactured, as the case may be, in the United States will be used in such treatment works. This section shall not apply in any case where the Administrator determines, based upon those factor the Administrator deems relevant, including the available resources of the agency, it to be inconsistent with the public interest (including multilateral government procurement agreements) or the cost to be unreasonable, or if articles, materials, or supplies of the class or kind to be used or the articles, material, or supplies from which they are manufactured are not mined, produced, or manufactured, as the case may be, in the United States in sufficient and reasonably available commercial quantities and of a satisfactory quality.

§1295. Determination of Priority [Sec. 216]

Notwithstanding any other provision of this Act, the determination of the priority to be given each category of projects for construction of publicly owned treatment works within each State shall be made solely by that State, except that if the Administrator, after a public hearing, determines that a specific project will not result in compliance with the enforceable requirements of this Act, such project shall be removed from the State's priority list and such State shall submit a revised priority list. These categories shall include, but not be limited to (A) secondary treatment, (B) more stringent treatment, (C) infiltration-in-flow correction,(D) major sewer system rehabilitation, (E) new collector sewers and appurtenances, (F) new interceptors and appurtenances, and (G) correction of combined sewer overflows. Not less than 25 per centum of funds allocated to a State in any fiscal year under this title for construction of publicly owned treatment works in such State shall be obligated for those types of projects referred to in clauses (D, (E), (F), and (G) of this section, if such projects are on such State's priority list for that year and are otherwise eligible for funding in that fiscal year. It is the policy of Congress that projects for wastewater treatment and management undertaken with Federal financial assistance under this Act by any State, municipality, or intermunicipal or interstate agency shall be projects which, in the estimation of the State, are designed to achieve optimum water quality management, consistent with the public health and water quality goals and requirements of the Act.

[§216 amended by PL 97–117]

§1297. Cost-Effectiveness Guidelines [Sec. 217]

Any guidelines for cost-effectiveness analysis published by the Administrator under this title shall provide for the identification and selection of cost effective alternatives to comply with the objective and goals of this Act and sections 201(b), 201(d), 201(g)(2)(A), and 301(b)(2)(B) of this Act.

§1298. Cost Effectiveness [Sec. 218]

(a) It is the policy of Congress that a project for waste treatment and management undertaken with Federal financial assistance under this Act by any State, municipality, or intermunicipal or interstate agency shall be considered as an overall waste treatment system for waste treatment and management, and shall be that system which constitutes the most economical and cost-effective combination of devices and systems used in the storage, treatment, recycling, and reclamation of municipal sewage or industrial wastes of a liquid nature to implement section 201 of this Act, or necessary to recycle or reuse water at the most economical cost over the estimated life of the works, including intercepting sewers, outfall sewers, sewage collection systems, pumping power, and other equipment, and their appurtenances; extension, improvements, remodeling, additions, and alterations thereof; elements essential to provide a reliable recycled supply such as standby treatment units and clear well facilities; and any works, including site acquisition of the land that will be an integral part of the treatment process (including land use for the storage of treated wastewater in land treatment systems prior to land application) or which is used for ultimate disposal of residues resulting from such treatment; water efficiency measures and devices; and any other method or system for preventing, abating, reducing, storing, treating, separating, or disposing of municipal waste, including storm water runoff, or industrial waste, including waste in combined storm water and sanitary sewer systems; to meet the requirements of this Act.

(b) In accordance with the policy set forth in subsection (a) of this section, before the Administrator approves any grant to any State, municipality, or inter municipal or interstate agency for the erection, building, acquisition, alteration, remodeling, improvement, or extension of any treatment works the Administrator shall determine that the facilities plan of which such treatment works are a part constitutes the most economical and cost- effective combination of treatment works over the life of the project to meet the requirements of this Act, including, but not limited to, consideration of construction costs, operation, maintenance, and replacement costs.

(c) In furtherance of the policy set forth in subsection (a) of this section, the Administrator shall require value engineering review in connection with any treatment works, prior to approval of any grant for the erection, building, acquisition, alteration, remodeling, improvement, or extension of such treatment works, in any case in which the cost of such erection, building, acquisition, alteration, remodeling, improvement, or extension is projected to be in excess of $10,000,000. For purposes of this subsection, the term 'value engineering review" means a specialized cost control technique which uses a systematic and creative approach to identify and to focus on unnecessarily high cost in a project in order to arrive at a cost saving without sacrificing the reliability or efficiency of the project.

(d) This section applies to projects for waste treatment and management for which no treatment works including a facilities plan for such project have received Federal financial assistance for the preparation of construction plans and specifications under this Act before the date of enactment of this section.

[§218 added by PL 97–117]

§1299. State Certification of Projects [Sec. 219]

Whenever the Governor of a State which has been delegated sufficient authority to administer the construction grant program under this title in that State certifies to the Administrator that a grant application meets applicable requirements of Federal and State law for assistance under this title, the Administrator shall approve or disapprove such application within 45 days of the date of receipt of such application. If the Administrator does not approve or disapprove such application within 45 days of receipt, the application shall be deemed approved. If the Administrator disapproves such application the Administrator shall state in writing the reasons for such disapproval. Any grant approved or deemed approved under this section shall be subject to amounts provided in appropriation Acts.

[§219 added by PL 97–117]

TITLE III—STANDARDS AND ENFORCEMENT

§1311. Effluent Limitations [Sec. 301]

(a) Except as in compliance with this section and sections 302, 306, 307, 318, 402, and 404 of this Act, the discharge of any pollutant by any person shall be unlawful.

(b) In order to carry out the objective of this Act there shall be achieved—

(1) (A) not later than July 1, 1977, effluent limitations for point sources, other than publicly owned treatment works, (i) which shall require the application of the best practicable control technology currently available as defined by the Administrator pursuant to section 304(b) of this Act, or (ii) in the case of a discharge into a publicly owned treatment works which meets the requirements of subparagraph (B) of this paragraph, which shall require compliance with any applicable pretreatment requirements and any requirements under section 307 of this Act; and

(B) for publicly owned treatment works in existence on July 1, 1977, or approved pursuant to section 203 of this Act prior to June 30, 1974 (for which construction must be completed within four years of approval), effluent limitations based upon secondary treatment as defined by the Administrator pursuant to section 304(d)(1) of this Act; or,

(C) not later than July 1, 1977, any more stringent limitation, including those necessary to meet water quality standards, treatment standards, or schedule of compliance, established pursuant to any State law or regulations, (under authority preserved by section 510) or any other Federal law or regulation, or required to implement any applicable water quality standard established pursuant to this Act.

(2) (A) for pollutants identified in subparagraphs (C), (D), and (F) of this paragraph, effluent limitations for categories and classes of point sources, other than publicly owned treatment works, which (i) shall require

application of the best available technology economically achievable for such category or class, which will result in reasonable further progress toward the national goal of eliminating the discharge of all pollutants, as determined in accordance with regulations issued by the Administrator pursuant to section 304(b)(2) of this Act, which such effluent limitations shall require the elimination of discharges of all pollutants if the Administrator finds, on the basis of information available to him (including information developed pursuant to section 315), that such elimination is technologically and economically achievable for category or class of point sources as determined in accordance with regulations issued by the Administrator pursuant to section 304(b)(2) of this Act or (ii) in the case of the introduction of a pollutant into a publicly owned treatment works which meets the requirements of subparagraph (b) of this paragraph, shall require compliance with any applicable pretreatment requirements and any other requirement under section 307 of this Act;

(B) [Repealed]

[§301(b)(2)(B) repealed by PL 97–117]

(C) with respect to all toxic pollutants referred to in table 1 of Committee Print Number 95–30 of the Committee on Public Works and Transportation of the House of Representatives compliance with effluent limitations in accordance with subparagraph (A) of this paragraph as expeditiously as practicable but in no case later than three years after the date such limitations are promulgated under section 304(b), and in no case later than March 31, 1989.

[§301(b)(2)(C) amended by PL 100–4]

(D) for all toxic pollutants listed under paragraph (1) of subsection (a) of section 307 of this Act which are not referred to in subparagraph (C) of this paragraph compliance with effluent limitation in accordance with subparagraph (A) of this paragraph as expeditiously as practicable, but in no case later than three years after date such limitations are promulgated under section 304(b), and in no case later than March 31, 1989;

[§301(b)(2)(D) amended by PL 100–4]

(E) as expeditiously as practicable but in no case later than three years after the date such limitations are promulgated under section 304(b), and in no case later than March 31, 1989, compliance with effluent limitations for categories and classes of point sources, other than publicly owned treatment works, which in the case of pollutants identified pursuant to section 304(a)(4) of this Act shall require application of the best conventional pollutant control technology as determined in accordance with regulations issued by the Administrator pursuant to section 304(b)(4) of this Act; and

[§301(b)(2)(E) amended by PL 100–4]

(F) for all pollutants (other than those subject to subparagraphs (C), (D), or (E) of this paragraph) compliance with effluent limitations in accordance with subparagraph (A) of this paragraph as expeditiously as practicable but in no case later than 3 years after the date such limitations are established, and in no case later than March 31, 1989.

[§301(b)(2)(F) amended by PL 100–4]

(3) (A) for effluent limitations under paragraph (1)(A)(i) of this subsection promulgated after January 1, 1982, and requiring a level of control substantially greater or based on fundamentally different control technology than under permits for an industrial category issued before such date, compliance as expeditiously as practicable but in no case later than three years after the date such limitations are promulgated under section 304(b), and in no case later than March 31, 1989; and

(B) for any effluent limitation in accordance with paragraph (1)(A)(i), (2)(A)(i), or (2)(E) of this subsection established only on the basis of section 402(a)(1) in a permit issued after enactment of the Water Quality Act of 1987, compliance as expeditiously as practicable but in no case later than three years after the date such limitations are established, and in no case later than March 31, 1989.

[§301(b)(3) added by PL 100–4]

(c) The Administrator may modify the requirements of subsection (b)(2)(A) of this section with respect to any point source for which a permit application is filed after July 1, 1977, upon a showing by the owner or operator of such point source satisfactory to the Administrator that such modified requirements (1) will represent the maximum use of technology within the economic capability of the owner or operator; and (2) will result in reasonable further progress toward the elimination of the discharge of pollutants.

(d) Any effluent limitation required by paragraph (2) of subsection (b) of this section shall be reviewed at least every five years and, if appropriate, revised pursuant to the procedure established under such paragraph.

(e) Effluent limitations established pursuant to this section or section 302 of this Act shall be applied to all point sources of discharge of pollutants in accordance with the provisions of this Act.

(f) Notwithstanding any other provisions of this Act it shall be unlawful to discharge any radiological, chemical, or biological warfare agent, any high-level radioactive waste, or any medical waste, into the navigable waters.

[§301(f) amended by PL 100–688]

(g) Modifications for Certain Nonconventional Pollutants.—

(1) General Authority. — The Administrator, with the concurrence of the State, may modify the requirements of subsection (b)(2)(A) of this section with respect to the discharge from any point source of ammonia, chlorine, color, iron, and total phenols (4AAP) (when determined by the Administrator to be a pollutant covered by subsection (b)(2)(F)) and any other pollutant which the Administrator lists under paragraph (4) of this subsection.

[Former §301(g)(1) deleted and new (1) and (2) added by PL 100–4]

(2) Requirements for Granting Modifications. — A modification under this subsection shall be granted only upon a showing by the owner or operator of a point source satisfactory to the Administrator that—

(A) such modified requirements will result at a minimum in compliance with the requirements of subsection (b)(1)(A) or (C) of this section, whichever is applicable;

(B) such modified requirements will not result in any additional requirements on any other point or nonpoint source; and

(C) such modification will not interfere with the attainment of maintenance of that water quality which shall assure protection of public water supplies, and the protection and propagation of a balanced population of shellfish, fish, and wildlife, and allow recreational activities, in and on the water and such modification will not result in the discharge of pollutants in quantities which may reasonably be anticipated to pose an unacceptable risk to human health or the environment because of bioaccumulation, persistency in the environment, acute toxicity, chronic toxicity (including carcinogenicity, mutagenicity or teratogenicity), or synergistic propensities.

(3) Limitation on Authority to Apply for Subsection (c) Modification — If an owner or operator of a point source applies for a modification under this subsection with respect to the discharge of any pollutant, such owner or operator shall be eligible to apply for modification under subsection (c) of this section with respect to such pollutant only during the same time-period as he is eligible to apply for a modification under this subsection.

[Former §301(g)(2) amended and redesignated as (3) by PL 100–4]

(4) Procedures for Listing Additional Pollutants.—

(A) General Authority. — Upon petition of any person, the Administrator may add any pollutant to the list of pollutants for which modification under this section is authorized (except for pollutants identified pursuant to section 304(a)(4) of this Act, toxic pollutants subject to section 307(a) of this Act, and the thermal component of discharges) in accordance with the provisions of this paragraph.

(B) Requirements for Listing.—

(i) Sufficient Information. — The person petitioning for listing of an additional pollutant under this subsection shall submit to the Administrator sufficient information to make the determinations required by this subparagraph.

(ii) Toxic Criteria Determination. — The Administrator shall determine whether or not the pollutant meets the criteria for listing as a toxic pollutant under section 307(a) of this Act.

(iii) Listing as Toxic Pollutant. — If the Administrator determines that the pollutant meets the criteria for listing as a toxic pollutant under section 307(a) , the Administrator shall list the Pollutant as a toxic pollutant under section 307(a) .

(iv) Nonconventional Criteria Determination. — If the Administrator determines that the pollutant does not meet the criteria for listing as a toxic pollutant under such section and determines that adequate test methods and sufficient data are available to make the determinations required by paragraph (2) of this subsection with respect to the pollutant, the Administrator shall add the pollutant to the list of pollutants specified in paragraph (1) of this subsection for which modifications are authorized under this subsection.

(C) Requirements for Filing of Petitions. — A petition for listing of a pollutant under this paragraph—

(i) must be filed not later than 270 days after the date of promulgation of an applicable effluent guideline under section 304 ;

(ii) may be filed before promulgation of such guideline; and

(iii) may be filed with an application for a modification under paragraph (1) with respect to the discharge of such pollutant.

(D) Deadline for Approval of Petition. —A decision to add a pollutant to the list of pollutants for which modifications under this subsection are authorized must be made within 270 days after the date of promulgation of an applicable effluent guideline under section 304.

(E) Burden of Proof. — The burden of proof for making the determinations under subparagraph (B) shall be on the petitioner.

[§301(g)(4) added by PL 100–4]

(5) Removal of Pollutants. — The Administrator may remove any pollutant from the list of pollutants for which modifications are authorized under this subsection if the Administrator determines that adequate test methods and sufficient data are no longer available for determining whether or not modifications may be granted with respect to such pollutant under paragraph (2) of this subsection.

[§301(g)(5) added by PL 100–4]

(h) The Administrator, with the concurrence of the State, may issue a permit under section 402 which modifies the requirements of subsection (b)(1)(B) of this section with respect to the discharge of any pollutant from a publicly owned treatment works into marine waters, if the applicant demonstrates to the satisfaction of the Administrator that—

(1) there is an applicable water quality standard specific to the pollutant for which the modification is requested, which has been identified under section 304(a)(6) of this Act;

(2) the discharge of pollutants in accordance with such modified requirements will not interfere, alone or in combination with pollutants from other sources, with the attainment or maintenance of that water quality which assures protection of public water supplies and protection and propagation of a balanced, indigenous population of shellfish, fish and wildlife, and allows recreational activities, in and on the water;

(3) the applicant has established a system for monitoring the impact of such discharge on a representative sample of aquatic biota, to the extent practicable, and the scope of such monitoring is limited to include only those scientific investigations which are necessary to study the effects of the proposed discharge;

[§301(h)(3) amended by PL 100–4]

[Editor's Note: Section 303(b)(2) of PL 100–4 states the amendment to 301(h)(3) "shall only apply to modifications and renewals of modifications which are tentatively or finally approved after the date of the enactment of this Act."]

(4) such modified requirements will not result in any additional requirements on any other point or nonpoint source;

(5) all applicable pretreatment requirements for sources introducing waste into such treatment works will be enforced;

(6) in the case of any treatment works serving a population of 50,000 or more, with respect to any toxic pollutant introduced into such works by an industrial discharger for which pollutant there is no applicable pretreatment requirement in effect, sources introducing waste into such works are in compliance with all applicable pretreatment requirements, the applicant will enforce such requirements, and the applicant has in effect a pretreatment program which, in combination with the treatment of discharges from such works, removes the same amount of such pollutant as would be removed if such works were to apply secondary treatment to discharges and if such works had no pretreatment program with respect to such pollutant;

[New §301(h)(6) added by PL 100–4]

(7) to the extent practicable, the applicant has established a schedule of activities designed to eliminate the entrance of toxic pollutants from nonindustrial sources into such treatment works;

[Former §301(h)(8) deleted by PL 97–117;former (6) and (7) redesignated as (7) and (8) by PL 100–4]

(8) there will be no new or substantially increased discharges from the point source of the pollutant to which the modification applies above that volume of discharge specified in the permit;

(9) the applicant at the time such modification becomes effective will be discharging effluent which has received at least primary or equivalent treatment and which meets the criteria

established under section 304(a)(1) of this Act after initial mixing in the waters surrounding or adjacent to the point at which such effluent is discharged.

[§301(h)(9) added by PL 100–4]

For the purposes of this subsection the phrase "the discharge of any pollutant into marine waters" refers to a discharge into deep waters of the territorial sea or the waters of the contiguous zone, or into saline estuarine waters where there is strong tidal movement and other hydrological and geological characteristics which the Administrator determines necessary to allow compliance with paragraph (2) of this subsection, and section 101(a)(2) of this Act. For the purposes of paragraph (9), "primary or equivalent treatment" means treatment by screening, sedimentation, and skimming adequate to remove at least 30 percent of the biological oxygen demanding material and of the suspending solids in the treatment works influent, and disinfection, where appropriate. A municipality which applies secondary treatment shall be eligible to receive a permit pursuant to this subsection which modifies the requirements of subsection (b)(1)(B) of this section with respect to the discharge of any pollutant from any treatment works owned by such municipality into marine waters. No permit issued under this subsection shall authorize the discharge of sewage sludge into marine waters. In order for a permit to be issued under this subsection for the discharge of a pollutant into marine waters, such marine waters must exhibit characteristics assuring that water providing dilution does not contain significant amounts of previously discharged effluent from such treatment works. No permit issued under this subsection shall authorize the discharge of any pollutant into saline estuarine waters which at the time of application do not support a balanced indigenous population of shellfish, fish and wildlife, or allow recreation in and on the waters or which exhibit ambient water quality below applicable water quality standards adopted for the protection of public water supplies, shellfish, fish and wildlife or recreational activities or such other standards necessary to assure support and protection of such uses. The prohibition contained in the preceding sentence shall apply without regard to the presence or absence of a causal relationship between such characteristics and the applicant's current or proposed discharge. Notwithstanding any other provisions of this subsection, no permit may be issued under this subsection for discharge of a pollutant into the New York Bight Apex consisting of the ocean waters of the Atlantic Ocean westward of 73 degrees 30 minutes west longitude and northward of 40 degrees 10 minutes north latitude.

[§301(h) amended by PL 97–117; PL 100–4]

(i) (1) Where construction is required in order for a planned or existing publicly owned treatment works to achieve limitations under subsection (b)(1)(B) or (b)(1)(C) of this section, but (A) construction cannot be completed within the time required in such subsection, or (B) the United States has failed to make financial assistance under this Act available in time to achieve such limitations by the time specified in such subsection, the owner or operator of such treatment works may request the Administrator (or if appropriate the State) to issue a permit pursuant to section 402 of this Act or to modify a permit issued pursuant to that section to extend such time for compliance. Any such request shall be filed with the Administrator (or if appropriate the State) within 180 days after the date of enactment of the Water Quality Act of 1987. The Administrator (or if appropriate the State) may grant such request and issue or modify such a permit, which shall contain a schedule of compliance for the publicly owned treatment works based on the earliest date by which such financial assistance will be available from the United States and construction can be completed, but in no event later than July 1, 1988, and shall contain such other terms and conditions, including those necessary to carry out subsections (b) through (g) of section 201 of this Act, section 307 of this Act, and such interim effluent limitations applicable to that treatment works as the Administrator determines are necessary to carry out the provisions of this Act.

[§301(i)(1) amended by PL 100–4]

[Editor's Note: Section 304(b) of PL 100–4 states the amendment to 301(i)(1) "shall not apply to those treatment works which are subject to a compliance schedule established before the date of the enactment of this Act by a court order or a final administrative order."]

(2) (A) Where a point source (other than a publicly owned treatment works) will not achieve the requirements of subsections (b)(1)(A) and (b)(1)(C) of this section and—

(i) if a permit issued prior to July 1, 1977, to such point source is based upon a discharge into a publicly owned treatment works; or

(ii) if such point source (other than a publicly owned treatment works) had before July 1, 1977, a contract (enforceable against such point source) to discharge into a publicly owned treatment works; or

(iii) if either an application made before July 1, 1977, for a construction grant under this Act for a publicly owned treatment works, or engineering or architectural plans or working drawings made before July 1, 1977, for a publicly owned treatment works, show that such point source was to discharge into such publicly owned treatment works, and such publicly owned treatment works is presently unable to accept such discharge without construct ion, and in the case of a discharge to an existing publicly owned treatment works, such treatment works has an extension pursuant to paragraph (1) of this subsection, the owner or operator of such point source may request the Administrator (or if appropriate the State) to issue or modify such a permit pursuant to such section 402 to extend such time for compliance. Any such request shall be filed with the Administrator (or if appropriate the State) within 180 days after the date of enactment of this subsection or the filing of a request by the appropriate publicly owned treatment works under paragraph (1) of this subsection, whichever is later. If the Administrator (or if appropriate the State) finds that the owner or operator of such point source has acted in good faith, he may grant such request and issue or modify such a permit, which shall contain a schedule of compliance for the point source to achieve the requirements of subsections (b)(1)(A) and (C) of this section and shall contain such other terms and conditions, including pretreatment and interim effluent limitations and water conservation requirements applicable to that point source, as the Administrator determines are necessary to carry out the provisions of this Act.

(B) No time modification granted by the Administrator (or if appropriate the State) pursuant to paragraph (2)(A) of this subsection shall extend beyond the earliest date practicable for compliance or beyond the date of any extension granted to the appropriate publicly owned treatment works pursuant to paragraph (1) of this subsection, but in no event shall it extend beyond July 1, 1988; and no such time modification shall be granted unless (i) the publicly owned treatment works will be in operation and available to the point source before July 1, 1988, and will meet the requirements to subsections (b)(1)(B) and (C) of this section after receiving the discharge from that point source; and (ii) the point source and the publicly owned treatment works have entered into an enforceable contract requiring the point source to discharge into the publicly owned treatment works, the owner or operator of such point source to pay the costs required under section 204 of this Act, and the publicly owned treatment works to accept the discharge from the point source; and (iii) the permit for such point source requires point source to meet all requirements under section 307(a) and (b) during the period of such time modification.

[§301(i) amended by PL 97–117]

(j) (1) Any application filed under this section for a modification of the provisions of—

(A) subsection (b)(1)(B) under subsection (h) of this section shall be filed not later that[n] the 365th day which begins after the date of enactment of the Municipal Wastewater Treatment Construction Grant Amendments of 1981, except that a publicly owned treatment works which prior to December 31, 1982, had a contractual arrangement to use a portion of the capacity of an ocean outfall operated by another publicly owned treatment works which has applied for or received modification under subsection (h), may apply for a modification of subsection (h) in its own right not later than 30 days after the date of the enactment of the Water Quality Act of 1987;

[§301(j)(1)(A) revised by PL 97–117; amended by PL 100-4]

(B) Subsection (b)(2)(A) as it applies to pollutants identified in subsection (b)(2)(F) shall be filed not later than 270 days after the date of promulgation of an applicable effluent guideline under section 304 or not later than 270 days after the date of enactment of the Clean Water Act of 1977, whichever is later.

(2) Subject to paragraph (3) of this section, any application for a modification filed under subsection (g) of this section shall not operate to stay any requirement under this Act, unless in the judgment of the Administrator such a stay or the modification sought will not result in the discharge of pollutants in quantities which may reasonably be anticipated to pose an unacceptable risk to human health or the environment because of bioaccumulation, persistency in the environment, acute toxicity, chronic toxicity (including carcinogenicity, mutagenicity or teratogenicity), or synergistic propensities, and that there is a substantial

likelihood that the applicant will succeed on the merits of such application. In the case of an application filed under subsection (g) of this section, the Administrator may condition any stay granted under this paragraph on requiring the filing of a bond or other appropriate security to assure timely compliance with the requirements from which a modification is sought.

(3) Compliance Requirements Under Subsection (g).—

(A) Effect of Filing. — An application for a modification under subsection (g) and a petition for listing of a pollutant as a pollutant for which modifications are authorized under such subsection shall not stay the requirement that the person seeking such modification or listing comply with effluent limitations under this Act for all pollutants not the subject of such application or petition.

(B) Effect of Disapproval. — Disapproval of an application for a modification under subsection (g) shall not stay the requirement that the person seeking such modification comply with all applicable effluent limitations under this Act.

[§301(j)(3) added by PL 100–4]

(4) Deadline for Subsection (g) Decision. — An application for a modification with respect to a pollutant filed under subsection (g) must be approved or disapproved not later than 365 days after the date of such filing; except that in any case in which a petition for listing such pollutant as a pollutant for which modifications are authorized under such subsection is approved, such application must be approved or disapproved not later than 365 days after the date of approval of such petition.

[§301(j)(4) added by PL 100–4]

(k) In the case of any facility subject to a permit under section 402 which proposes to comply with the requirements of subsection (b)(2)(A) or (b)(2)(E) of this section by replacing existing production capacity with an innovative production process which will result in an effluent reduction significantly greater than that required by the limitation otherwise applicable to such facility and moves toward the national goal of eliminating the discharge of all pollutants, or with the installation of an innovative control technique that has a substantial likelihood for enabling the facility to comply with the applicable effluent limitation by achieving a significantly greater effluent reduction than that required by the applicable effluent limitation and moves toward the national goal of eliminating the discharge of all pollutants, or by achieving the required reduction with an innovative system that has the potential for significantly lower costs than the systems which have been determined by the Administrator to be economically achievable, the Administrator (or the State with an approved program under section 402 , in consultation with the Administrator) may establish a date for compliance under subsection (b)(2)(A) or (b)(2)(E) of this section no later than two years after the date for compliance with such effluent limitation which would otherwise be applicable under such subsection, if it is also determined that such innovative system has the potential for industrywide application.

[§301(k) amended by PL 100–4]

(l) Other than as provided in subsection (n) of this section, the Administrator may not modify any requirement of this section as it applies to any specific pollutant which is on the toxic pollutant list under section 307(a)(1) of this Act.

[§301(l) amended by PL 100–4]

(m) (1) The Administrator, with the concurrence of the State, may issue a permit under section 402 which modifies the requirements of subsections (b)(1)(A) and (b)(2)(E) of this section, and of section 403 , with respect to effluent limitations to the extent such limitations relate to biochemical oxygen demand and pH from discharges by an industrial discharger in such State into deep waters of the territorial seas, if the applicant demonstrates and the Administrator finds that—

(A) the facility for with modification is sought is covered at the time of the enactment of this subsection by National Pollutant Discharge Elimination System permit number CA0005894 or CA0005282;

(B) the energy and environmental costs of meeting such requirements of subsections (b)(1)(A) and (b)(2)(E) and section 403 exceed by an unreasonable amount the benefits to be obtained, including the objectives of this Act;

(C) the applicant has established a system for monitoring the impact of such discharges on a representative sample of aquatic biota;

(D) such modified requirements will not result in any additional requirements on any other point or nonpoint source;

(E) there will be no new or substantially increased discharges from the point source of the pollutant to which the modification applies above that volume of discharge specified in the permit;

(F) the discharge is into waters where there is strong tidal movement and other hydrological and geological characteristics which are necessary to allow compliance with this subsection and section 101(a)(2) of this Act;

(G) the applicant accepts as a condition to the permit a contractural obligation to use funds in the amount required (but not less than $250,000 per year for ten years) for research and development of water pollution control technology, including but not limited to closed cycle technology;

(H) the facts and circumstances present a unique situation which, if relief is granted, will not establish a precedent or the relaxation of the requirements of this Act applicable to similarly situated discharges; and

(I) no owner or operator of a facility comparable to that of the applicant situated in the United States has demonstrated that it would be put at a competitive disadvantage to the applicant (or the parent company or any subsidiary thereof) as a result of the issuance of a permit under this subsection.

(2) The effluent limitations established under a permit issued under paragraph (1) shall be sufficient to implement the applicable State water quality standards, to assure the protection of public water supplies and protection and propagation of a balanced, indigenous population of shellfish, fish, fauna, wildlife, and other aquatic organisms, and to allow recreational activities in and on the water. In setting such limitations, the Administrator shall take into account any seasonal variations and the need for an adequate margin of safety, considering the lack of essential knowledge concerning the relationship between effluent limitations and water quality and the lack of essential knowledge of the effects of discharges on beneficial uses of the receiving waters.

(3) A permit under this subsection may be issued for a period not to exceed five years, and such a permit may be renewed for one additional period not to exceed five years upon a demonstration by the applicant and a finding by the Administrator at the time of application for any such renewal that the provisions of this subsection are met.

(4) The Administrator may terminate a permit issued under this subsection if the Administrator determines that there has been a decline in ambient water quality of the receiving waters during the period of the permit even if a direct cause and effect relationship cannot be shown: Provided, That if the effluent from a source with a permit issued under this subsection is contributing to a decline in ambient water quality of the receiving waters, the Administrator shall terminate such permit.

[§301(m) added by PL 97–440]

(n) Fundamentally Different Factors.—

(1) General Rule. — The Administrator, with the concurrence of the State, may establish an alternative requirement under subsection (b)(2) or section 307(b) for a facility that modifies the requirements of national effluent limitation guidelines or categorical pretreatment standards that would otherwise be applicable to such facility, if the owner or operator of such facility demonstrates to the satisfaction of the Administrator that—

(A) the facility is fundamentally different with respect to the factors (other than cost) specified in section 304(b) or 304(g) and considered by the Administrator in establishing such national effluent limitation guidelines or categorical pretreatment standards;

(B) the application—

(i) is based solely on information and supporting data submitted to the Administrator during the rulemaking for establishment of the applicable national effluent limitation guidelines or categorical pretreatment standard specifically raising the factors that are fundamentally different for such facility; or

(ii) is based on information and supporting data referred to in clause (i) and information and supporting data the applicant did not have a reasonable opportunity to submit during such rulemaking;

(C) the alternative requirement is no less stringent than justified by the fundamental difference: and

(D) the alternative requirement will not result in a non-water quality environmental impact which is markedly more adverse than the impact considered by the Administrator in establishing such national effluent limitation guideline or categorical pretreatment standard.

(2) Time Limit for Applications. — An application for an alternative requirement which modifies the requirements of an effluent limitation or pretreatment standard under this subsection must be submitted to the Administrator within 180 days after the date on which such limitation or standard is established or revised, as the case may be.

(3) Time Limit for Decision. — The Administrator shall approve or deny by final agency

action an application submitted under this subsection within 180 days after the date such application is filed with the Administrator.

(4) Submission of Information. — The Administrator may allow an applicant under this subsection to submit information and supporting data until the earlier of the date the application is approved or denied or the last day that the Administrator has to approve or deny such application.

(5) Treatment of Pending Applications. —For the purposes of this subsection, an application for an alternative requirement based on fundamentally different factors which is pending on the date of the enactment of this subsection shall be treated as having been submitted to the Administrator on the 180th day following such date of enactment. The applicant may amend the application to take into account the provisions of this subsection.

(6) Effect of Submission of Application. — An application for an alternative requirement under this subsection shall not stay the applicant's obligation to comply with the effluent limitation guideline or categorical pretreatment standard which is the subject of the application.

(7) Effect of Denial. — If an application for an alternative requirement which modifies the requirements of an effluent limitation or pretreatment standard under this subsection is denied by the Administrator, the applicant must comply with such limitation or standard as established or revised, as the case may be.

(8) Reports. — Every 6 months after the date of the enactment of this subsection, the Administrator shall submit to the Committee on Environment and Public Works of the Senate and the Committee on Public Works and Transportation of the House of Representatives a report on the status of applications for alternative requirements which modify the requirements of effluent limitations under section 301 or 304 of this Act or any national categorical pretreatment standard under section 307(b) of this Act filed before, on, or after such date of enactment.

[§301(n) added by PL 100–4]

(o) Application Fees. — The Administrator shall prescribe and collect from each applicant fees reflecting the reasonable administrative costs incurred in reviewing and processing applications for modifications submitted to the Administrator pursuant to subsections (c), (g), (i), (k), (m), and (n) of section 301, section 304(d)(4), and section 316(a) of this Act. All amounts collected by the Administrator under this subsection shall be deposited into a special fund of the Treasury entitled "Water Permits and Related Services" which shall thereafter be available for appropriation to carry out activities of the Environmental Protection Agency for which such fees were collected.

[§301(o) added by PL 100–4]

(p) Modified Permit for Coal Refining Operations.—

(1) In General. — Subject to paragraphs (2) through (4) of this subsection, the Administrator, or the State in any case which the State has an approved permit pro gram under section 402(b) , may issue a permit under section 402 which modifies the requirements of subsection (b)(2)(A) of this section with respect to the pH level of any pre-existing discharge, and with respect to preexisting discharges of iron and manganese from the remined area of any coal remining operation or with respect to the pH level or level of iron or manganese in any preexisting discharge affected by the remining operation. Such modified requirements shall apply the best available technology economically achievable on a case- by-case basis, using best professional judgment, to set specific numerical effluent limitations in each permit.

(2) Limitations. — The Administrator or the State may only issue a permit pursuant to paragraph (l) if the applicant demonstrates to the satisfaction of the Administrator or the State, as the case may be, that the coal remining operation will result in the potential for improved water quality from the remining operation but in no event shall such a permit allow the pH level of any discharge, and in no event shall such a permit allow the discharges of iron and manganese, to exceed the levels being discharged from the remined area before the coal remining operation begins. No discharge from, or affected by, the remining operation shall exceed State water quality standards established under section 303 of this Act.

(3) Definitions. — For purposes of this subsection—

(A) Coal Remining Operation. — The term "coal remining operation" means a coal mining operation which begins after the date of the enactment of this subsection at a site on which coal mining was conducted before the effective date of the Surface Mining Control and Reclamation Act of 1977,

(B) Remined Area. — The term "remined area" means only that area of any coal remining operation on which coal mining was conducted before the effective date of the Surface Mining Control and Reclamation Act of 1977,

(C) Pre-existing Discharge. — The term "pre-existing discharge" means any discharge at the time of permit application under this subsection.

(4) Applicability of Strip Mining Laws. — Nothing in this subsection shall affect the application of the Surface Mining Control and Reclamation Act of 1977 to any coal remining operation, including the application of such Act to suspended solids.

[§301(p) added by PL 100–4]

§1312. Water Quality Related Effluent Limitations [Sec. 302]

(a) Whenever, in the judgment of the Administrator or as identified under section 304(1) discharges of pollutants from a point source or group of point sources, with the application of effluent limitations required under section 301 (b)(2) of this Act, would interfere with the attainment or maintenance of that water quality in a specific portion of the navigable waters which shall assure protection of public health, public water supplies, agricultural and industrial uses, and the protection and propagation of a balanced population of shellfish, fish and wildlife, and allow recreational activities in and on the water, effluent limitations (including alternative effluent control strategies) for such point source or sources shall be established which can reasonably be expected to contribute to the attainment or maintenance of such water quality.

[§302(a) amended by PL 100–4]

(b) Modifications of Effluent Limitations.—

(1) Notice and Hearing. — Prior to establishment of any effluent limitation pursuant to subsection (a) of this section, the Administrator shall publish such proposed limitation and within 90 days of such publication hold a public hearing.

(2) Permits.—

(A) No Reasonable Relationship. — The Administrator, with the concurrence of the State, may issue a permit which modifies the effluent limitations required by subsection (a) of this section for pollutants other than toxic pollutants if the applicant demonstrates at such hearing that (whether or not technology or other alternative control strategies are available) there is no reasonable relationship between the economic and social costs and the benefits to be obtained (including attainment of the objective of this Act) from achieving such limitation.

(B) Reasonable Progress. — The Administrator, with the concurrence of the State, may issue a permit which modifies the effluent limitations required by subsection (a) of this section for toxic pollutants for a single period not to exceed 5 years if the applicant demonstrates to the satisfaction of the Administrator that such modified requirements (i) will represent the maximum degree of control within the economic capability of the owner and operator of the source, and (ii) will result in reasonable further progress beyond the requirements of section 301(b)(2) toward the requirements of subsection (a) of this section.

[§302(b) revised by PL 100–4]

(c) The establishment of effluent limitations under this section shall not operate to delay the application of any effluent limitation established under section 301 of this Act.

§1313. Water Quality Standards and Implementation Plans [Sec. 303]

(a) (1) In order to carry out the purpose of this Act, any water quality standard applicable to interstate waters which was adopted by any State and submitted to, and approved by, or is awaiting approval by, the Administrator pursuant to this Act as in effect immediately prior to the date of enactment of the Federal Water Pollution Control Act Amendments of 1972, shall remain in effect unless the Administrator determined that such standard is not consistent with the applicable requirements of this Act as in effect immediately prior to the date of enactment of the Federal Water Pollution Control Act Amendments of 1972. If the Administrator makes such a determination he shall, within three months after the date of enactment of the Federal Water Pollution Control Act Amendments of 1972, notify the State and specify the changes needed to meet such requirements. If such changes are not adopted by the State within ninety days after the date of such notification, the Administrator shall promulgate such changes in accordance with subsection (b) of this section.

(2) Any State which, before the date of enactment of the Federal Water Pollution Control Act Amendments of 1972, has adopted pursuant to its own law, water quality standards applicable to intrastate waters shall submit

such standards to the Administrator within thirty days after the date of enactment of the Federal Water Pollution Control Act Amendments of 1972. Each such standard shall remain in effect, in the same manner and to the same extent as any other water quality standard established under this Act unless the Administrator determines that such standard is inconsistent with the applicable requirements of this Act as in effect immediately prior to the date of enactment of the Federal Water Pollution Control Act Amendments of 1972. If the Administrator makes such a determination he shall not later than the one hundred and twentieth day after the date of submission of such standards, notify the State and specify the changes needed to meet such requirements. If such changes are not adopted by the State within ninety days after such notification, the Administrator shall promulgate such changed in accordance with subsection (b) of this section.

(3) (A) Any State which prior to the date of enactment of the Federal Water Pollution Control Act Amendments of 1972 has not adopted pursuant to its own laws water quality standards applicable to intrastate waters shall, not later than one hundred and eighty days after the date of enactment of the Federal Water Pollution Control Act Amendments of 1972, adopt and submit such standards to the Administrator.

(B) If the Administrator determines that any such standards are consistent with the applicable requirements of this Act as in effect immediately prior to the date of enactment of the Federal Water Pollution Control Act Amendments of 1972, he shall approve such standards.

(C) If the Administrator determines that any such standards are not consistent with the applicable requirements of this Act as in effect immediately prior to the date of enactment of the Federal Water Pollution Control Act Amendments of 1972, he shall, not later than the ninetieth day after the date of submission of such standards, notify the State and specify the changes to meet such requirements. If such changes are not adopted by the State within ninety days after the date of notification, the Administrator shall promulgate such standards pursuant to subsection (b) of this section.

(b) (1) The Administrator shall promptly prepare and publish proposed regulations setting forth water quality standards for a State in accordance with the applicable requirements of this Act as in effect immediately prior to the date of enactment of the Federal Water Pollution Control Act Amendments of 1972, if—

(A) the State fails to submit water quality standards within the times prescribed in subsection (a) of this section,

(B) a water quality standard submitted by such State under subsection (a) of this section is determined by the Administrator not to be consistent with the applicable requirements of subsection (a) of this section.

(2) The Administrator shall promulgate any water quality standard published in a proposed regulation not later than one hundred and ninety days after the date he publishes any such proposed standard, unless prior to such promulgation, such State has adopted a water quality standard which the Administrator determines to be in accordance with subsection (a) of this section.

(c) (1) The Governor of a State or the State water pollution control agency of such State shall from time to time (but at least once each three year period beginning with the date of enactment of the Federal Water Pollution Control Act Amendments of 1972) hold public hearings for the purpose of reviewing applicable water quality standards and, as appropriate, modifying and adopting standards. Results of such review shall be made available to the Administrator.

(2) (A) Whenever the State revises or adopts a new standard, such revised or new standard shall be submitted to the Administrator. Such revised or new water quality standard shall consist of the designated uses of the navigable waters involved and the water quality criteria for such waters based upon such uses. Such standards shall be such as to protect the public health or welfare, enhance the quality of water and serve the purposes of this Act. Such standards shall be established taking into consideration their use and value for public water supplies, propagation of fish and wildlife, recreational purposes, and agricultural, industrial, and other purposes, and also taking into consideration their use and value for navigation.

[§303(c)(2)(A) designated by PL 100–4]

(B) Whenever a State reviews water quality standards pursuant to paragraph (1) of this subsection, or revises or adopts new standards pursuant to this paragraph, such State shall adopt criteria for all toxic pollutants listed pursuant to section 307(a)(1) of this Act for which criteria have been published under section 304(a) , the discharge or presence of which in the affected waters could reasonably be expected to interfere with those designated uses adopted by the State, as necessary to support such designated uses. Such criteria shall be specific numerical criteria for such toxic pollutants. Where such numerical criteria are not available, whenever a State reviews water quality standards pursuant to paragraph (1), or revises or adopts new standards pursuant to this paragraph, such State shall adopt criteria based on biological monitoring or assessment methods consistent with information published pursuant to section 304(a)(8) . Nothing in this section shall be construed to limit or delay the use of effluent limitations or other permit conditions based on or involving biological monitoring or assessment methods or previously adopted numerical criteria.

[§303(c)(2)(B) added by PL 100–4]

(3) If the Administrator, within sixty days after the date of submission of the revised or new standard, determines that such standard meets the requirements of this Act, such standard shall thereafter be the water quality standard for the applicable waters of that State. If the Administrator determines that any such revised or new standard is not consistent with the applicable requirements of this Act, he shall not later than the ninetieth day after the date of submission of such standard notify the State and specify the changes to meet such requirements. If such changes are not adopted by the State within ninety days after the date of notification, the Administrator shall promulgate such standard pursuant to paragraph (4) of this subsection.

(4) The Administrator shall promptly prepare and publish proposed regulations setting forth a revised or new water quality standard for the navigable waters involved—

(A) if a revised or new water quality standard submitted by such State under paragraph (3) of this subsection for such waters is determined by the Administrator not to be consistent with the applicable requirements of this Act, or

(B) in any case where the Administrator determines that a revised or new standard is necessary to meet the requirements of this Act. The Administrator shall promulgate any revised or new standard under this paragraph not later than ninety days after he publishes such proposed standards, unless prior to such promulgation, such State has adopted a revised or new water quality standard which the Administrator determines to be in accordance with this Act.

(d) (1) (A) Each state shall identify those waters within its boundaries for which the effluent limitations required by section 301(b)(1)(A) and section 301(b)(1)(B) are not stringent enough to implement any water quality standard applicable to such waters. The State shall establish a priority ranking for such waters, taking into account the severity of the pollution and the uses to be made of such waters.

(B) Each State shall identify those waters or parts thereof within its boundaries for which controls on thermal discharges under section 301 are not stringent enough to assure protection and propagation of a balanced indigenous population of shellfish, fish, and wildlife.

(C) Each State shall establish for the waters identified in paragraph (1)(A) of this subsection, and in accordance with the priority ranking, the total maximum daily load, for those pollutants which the Administrator identifies under section 304(a)(2) as suitable for such calculation. Such load shall be established at a level necessary to implement the applicable water quality standards with seasonal variations and a margin of safety which takes into account any lack of knowledge concerning the relationship between effluent limitations and water quality.

(D) Each State shall estimate for the waters identified in paragraph (1)(d) of this subsection the total maximum daily thermal load required to assure protection and propagation of a balanced, indigenous population of shellfish, fish and wildlife. Such estimates shall take into account the normal water temperatures, flow rates, seasonal variations, existing sources of heat input, and the dissipative capacity of the identified waters or parts thereof. Such estimates shall include a calculation of the maximum heat input that can be made into each such part and shall include a margin of safety which takes into account any lack of knowledge concerning the development of thermal water quality criteria for such protection and propagation in the identified waters or parts thereof.

(2) Each State shall submit to the Administrator from time to time, with the first such submission not later than one hundred and eighty

days after the date of publication of the first identification of pollutants under section 304(a)(2)(D) , for his approval the waters identified and the loads established under paragraphs (1)(A), (1)(B), (1)(C), and (1)(D) of this subsection. The Administrator shall either approve or disapprove such identification and load not later than thirty days after the date of submission. If the Administrator approves such identification and load, such State shall incorporate them into its current plan under subsection (e) of this section. If the Administrator disapproves such identification and load, he shall not later than thirty days after the date of such disapproval identify such waters in such State and establish such loads for such waters as he determines necessary to implement the water quality standards applicable to such waters and upon such identification and establishment the State shall incorporate them into its current plan under subsection (e) of this section.

(3) For the specific purpose of developing information, each State shall identify all waters within its boundaries which it has not identified under paragraph (1)(A) and (1)(B) of this subsection and estimate for such waters the total maximum daily load with seasonal variations and margins of safety, for those pollutants which the Administrator identifies under section 304(a)(2) as suitable for such calculation and for thermal discharges, at a level that would assure protection and propagation of a balanced indigenous population of fish, shellfish and wildlife.

(4) Limitations on Revision of Certain Effluent Limitations.—

(A) Standard Not Attained. — For waters identified under paragraph (1)(A) where the applicable water quality standard has not yet been attained, any effluent limitation based on a total maximum daily load or other waste load allocation established under this section may be revised only if (i) the cumulative effect of all such revised effluent limitations based on such total maximum daily load or waste load allocation will assure the attainment of such water quality standard, or (ii) the designated use which is not being attained is removed in accordance with regulations established under this section.

(B) Standard Attained. — For waters identified under paragraph (1)(A) where the quality of such waters equals or exceeds levels necessary to protect the designated use for such waters or otherwise required by applicable water quality standards, any effluent limitation based on a total maximum daily load or other waste load allocation established under this section, or any water quality standard established under this section, or any other permitting standard may be revised only if such revision is subject to and consistent with the antidegradation policy established under this section.

[§303(d)(4) added by PL 100–4]

(e) (1) Each State shall have a continuing planning process approved under paragraph (2) of this subsection which is consistent with this Act.

(2) Each State shall submit not later than 120 days after the date of the enactment of the Water Pollution Control Amendments of 1972 to the Administrator for his approval a proposed continuing planning process which is consistent with this Act. Not later than thirty days after the date of submission of such a process the Administrator shall either approve or disapprove such process. The Administrator shall from time to time review each State's approved planning process for the purpose of insuring that such planning process is at all times consistent with this Act. The Administrator shall not approve any State permit program under title IV of this Act for any State which does not have an approved continuing planning process under this section.

(3) The Administrator shall approve any continuing planning process submitted to him under this section which will result in plans for all navigable waters within such State, which include, but are not limited to, the following:

(A) effluent limitations and schedules of compliance at least as stringent as those required by section 301(b)(1), section 301(b)(2), section 306, and section 307, and at least as stringent as any requirements contained in any applicable water quality standard in effect under authority of this section;

(B) the incorporation of all elements of any applicable areawide waste management plans under section 208 , and applicable basin plans under section 209 of this Act;

(C) total maximum daily load for pollutants in accordance with subsection (d) of this section;

(D) procedures for revision;

(E) adequate authority for intergovernmental cooperation;

(F) adequate implementation, including schedules of compliance, for revised or new water quality standards, under subsection (c) of this section;

(G) controls over the disposition of all residual waste from any water treatment processing;

(H) an inventory and ranking, in order of priority, of needs for construction of waste treatment works required to meet the applicable requirements of sections 301 and 302 .

(f) Nothing in this section shall be construed to affect any effluent limitation, or schedule of compliance required by any State to be implemented prior to the dates set forth in sections 301(b)(1) and 301(b)(2) nor to preclude any State from requiring compliance with any effluent limitation or schedule of compliance at dates earlier than such dates.

(g) Water quality standards relating to heat shall be consistent with the requirements of section 316 of this Act.

(h) For the purposes of this Act the term "water quality standards" includes thermal water quality standards.

§1314. Information and Guidelines [Sec. 304]

(a) (1) The Administrator, after consultation with appropriate Federal and State agencies and other interested persons, shall develop and publish, within one year after the date of enactment of this title (and from time to time thereafter revise) criteria for water quality accurately reflecting the latest scientific knowledge (A) on the kind and extent of all identifiable effects on health and welfare including, but not limited to, plankton, fish, shellfish, wildlife, plant life, shore lines, beaches, esthetics, and recreation which may be expected from the presence of pollutants in any body of water, including ground water; (B) on the concentration and dispersal of pollutants, or their byproducts, through biological, physical, and chemical processes; and (C) on the effects of pollutants on biological community diversity, productivity, and stability, including information on the factors affecting rates of eutrophication and rates of organic and inorganic sedimentation for varying types of receiving waters.

(2) The Administrator, after consultation with appropriate Federal and State agencies and other interested persons, shall develop and publish, within one year after the date of enactment of this title (and from time to time thereafter revise) information (A) on the factors necessary to restore and maintain the chemical, physical, and biological integrity of all navigable waters, ground waters, waters of the contiguous zone, and the oceans; (B) on the factors necessary for the protection and propagation of shellfish, fish, and wildlife for classes and categories of receiving waters and to allow recreational activities in and on the water; and (C) on the measurement and classification of water quality; and (D) for the purpose of section 303, on and the identification of pollutants suitable for maximum daily load measurement correlated with the achievement of water quality objectives.

(3) Such criteria and information and revisions thereof shall be issued to the States and shall be published in the Federal Register and otherwise made available to the public.

(4) The Administrator shall, within 90 days after the date of enactment of the Clean Water Act of 1977 and from time to time thereafter, publish and revise as appropriate information identifying conventional pollutants, including but not limited to, pollutants classified as biological oxygen demanding, suspended solids, fecal coliform, and pH. The thermal component of any discharge shall not be identified as a conventional pollutant under this paragraph.

(5) (A) The Administrator, to the extent practicable before consideration of any request under section 301(g) of this Act and within six months after the date of enactment of the Clean Water Act of 1977, shall develop and publish information on the factors necessary for the protection of public water supplies, and the protection and propagation of a balanced population of shellfish, fish and wildlife, and to allow recreational activities, in and on the water.

(B) The Administrator, to the extent practicable before consideration of any application under section 301(h) of this Act and within six months after the date of enactment of the Clean Water Act of 1977, shall develop and publish information on the factors necessary for the protection of public water supplies, and the protection and propagation of a balanced indigenous population of shellfish, fish and wildlife, and to allow recreational activities, in and on the water.

(6) The Administrator shall, within three months after enactment of the Clean Water Act of 1977 and annually thereafter, for purposes of section 301(h) of this Act publish and revise as appropriate information identifying each water quality standard in effect under this Act of State law, the specific pollutants associated with such water quality standard, and the par-

ticular waters to which such water quality standard applies.

(7) Guidance to States. — The Administrator, after consultation with appropriate State agencies and on the basis of criteria and information published under paragraphs (1) and (2) of this subsection, shall develop and publish, within 9 months after the date of the enactment of the Water Quality Act of 1987, guidance to the States on performing the identification required by section 304(1)(l) of this Act.

[§304(a)(7) added by PL 100–4]

(8) Information on Water Quality Criteria. — The Administrator, after consultation with appropriate State agencies and within 2 years after the date of the enactment of the Water Quality Act of 1987, shall develop and publish information on methods for establishing and measuring water quality criteria for toxic pollutants on other bases than pollutant-by- pollutant criteria, including biological monitoring and assessment methods.

[§304(a)(8) added by PL 100–4]

(b) For the purpose of adopting or revising effluent limitations under this Act the Administrator shall, after consultation with appropriate Federal and State agencies and other interested persons, publish within one year of enactment of this title, regulations, providing guidelines for effluent limitations, and, at least annually thereafter, revise, if appropriate, such regulations. Such regulations shall—

(1) (A) identify, in terms of amounts of constituents and chemical, physical, and biological characteristics of pollutants, the degree of effluent reduction attainable through the application of the best practicable control technology currently available for classes and categories of point sources (other than publicly owned treatment works); and

(B) specify factors to be taken into account in determining the control measures and practices to be applicable to point sources (other than publicly owned treatment works) within such categories or classes. Factors relating to the assessment of best practicable control technology currently available to comply with subsection (b)(1) of section 301 of this Act shall include consideration of the total cost of application of technology in relation to the effluent reduction benefits to be achieved from such application, and shall also take into account the age of equipment and facilities involved, the process employed, the engineering aspects of the application of various types of control techniques, process changes, non-water quality environmental impact (including energy requirements), and such other factors as the Administrator deems appropriate;

(2) (A) identify, in terms of amounts of constituents and chemical, physical, and biological characteristics of pollutants, the degree of effluent reduction attainable through the application of the best control measures and practices achievable including treatment techniques, process and procedure innovations, operating methods, and other alternatives for classes and categories of point sources (other than publicly owned treatment works); and

(B) specify factors to be taken into account in determining the best measures and practices available to comply with subsection (b)(2) of section 301 of this Act to be applicable to any point source (other than publicly owned treatment works) within such categories of classes. Factors relating to the assessment of best available technology shall take into account the age of equipment and facilities involved, the process employed, the engineering aspects of the application of various types of control techniques, process changes, the cost of achieving such effluent reduction, non-water quality environmental impact (including energy requirements), and such other factors as the Administrator deems appropriate;

(3) identify control measures and practices available to eliminate the discharge of pollutants from categories and classes of point sources, taking into account the cost of achieving such elimination of the discharge of pollutants; and

(4) (A) identify, in terms of amounts of constituents and chemical, physical, and biological characteristics of pollutants, the degree of effluent reduction attainable through the application of the best conventional pollutant control technology (including measures and practices) for classes and categories of point sources (other than publicly owned treatment works); and

(B) specify factors to be taken into account in determining the best conventional pollutant control technology measures and practices to comply with section 301(b)(2)(E) of this Act to be applicable to any point source (other than publicly owned treatment works) within such categories or classes. Factors relating to the assessment of best conventional pollutant control technology (including measures and practices) shall include consideration of the reasonableness of the relationship between the costs of attaining a reduction in effluents and the effluent reduction benefits derived, and the comparison of the cost and level of reduction of such pollutants from the discharge from publicly owned treatment works to the cost and level of reduction of such pollutants from a class or category of industrial sources, and shall take into account the age of equipment and facilities involved, the process employed, the engineering aspects of the application of various types of control techniques, process changes, non-water quality environmental impact (including energy requirements), and such other factors as the Administrator deems appropriate.

(c) The Administrator, after consultation, with appropriate Federal and State agencies and other interested persons, shall issue to the States and appropriate water pollution control agencies within 270 days after enactment of this title (and from time to time thereafter) information on the processes, procedures, or operating methods which result in the elimination or reduction of the discharge of pollutants to implement standards of performance under section 306 of this Act. Such information shall include technical and other data, including costs, as are available on alternative methods of elimination or reduction of the discharge of pollutants. Such information, and revisions thereof, shall be published in the Federal Register and otherwise shall be made available to the public.

(d) (1) The Administrator, after consultation with appropriate Federal and State agencies and other interested persons, shall publish within sixty days after enactment of this title (and from time to time thereafter) information, in terms of amounts of constituents and chemical, physical, and biological characteristics of pollutants, on the degree of effluent reduction attainable through the application of secondary treatment.

(2) The Administrator, after consultation with appropriate Federal and State agencies and other interested persons, shall publish within nine months after the date of enactment of this title (and from time to time thereafter) information on alternative waste treatment management techniques and systems available to implement section 201 of this Act.

(3) The Administrator, after consultation with appropriate Federal and State agencies and other interested persons, shall promulgate within one hundred and eighty days after the date of enactment of this subsection guidelines for identifying and evaluating innovative and alternative wastewater treatment processes and techniques referred to in section 201(g)(5) of this Act.

(4) For the purposes of this subsection, such biological treatment facilities as oxidation ponds, lagoons, and ditches and trickling filters shall be deemed the equivalent of secondary treatment. The Administrator shall provide guidance under paragraph (1) of this subsection on design criteria for such facilities, taking into account pollutant removal efficiencies and, consistent with the objective of the Act, assuring that water quality will not be adversely affected by deeming such facilities as the equivalent of secondary treatment.

[§304(d)(4) added by PL 97–117]

(e) The Administrator, after consultation with appropriate Federal and State agencies and other interested persons, may publish regulations, supplemental to any effluent limitations specified under subsections (b) and (c) of this section for a class or category of point sources, for any specific pollutant which the Administrator is charged with a duty to regulate as a toxic or hazardous pollutant under section 307(a)(1) or 311 of this Act, to control plant site runoff, spillage or leaks, sludge or waste disposal, and drainage from raw material storage which the Administrator determines are associated with or ancillary to the industrial manufacturing or treatment process within such class or category of point sources and may contribute significant amounts of such pollutants to navigable waters. Any applicable controls established under this subsection shall be included as a requirement for the purposes of section 301, 302, 306, 307, or 403 , as the case may be, in any permit issued to a point source pursuant to section 402 of this Act.

(f) The Administrator, after consultation with appropriate Federal and State agencies and other interested persons, shall issue to appropriate Federal agencies, the States, water pollution control agencies, and agencies designated under section 208 of this Act, within one year after the effective date of this subsection (and from time to time thereafter) information including (1) guidelines for identifying and evaluating the nature and extent of nonpoint sources of pollutants, and (2) processes, procedures, and methods to control pollution resulting from—

(A) agricultural and silvicultural activities, including runoff from fields and crop and forest lands;

(B) mining activities, including runoff and siltation from new, currently operating, and abandoned surface and underground mines;

(C) all construction activity, including runoff from the facilities resulting from such construction;

(D) the disposal of pollutants in wells or in subsurface excavations;

(E) salt water intrusion resulting from reductions of fresh water flow from any cause, including extraction of ground water, irrigation, obstruction, and diversion; and

(F) changes in the movement, flow, or circulation of any navigable waters or ground waters, including changes caused by the construction of dams, levees, channels, causeways, or flow diversion facilities. Such information and revisions thereof shall be published in the Federal Register and otherwise made available to the public.

(g) (1) For the purpose of assisting States in carrying out programs under section 402 of this Act, the Administrator shall publish, within one hundred and twenty days after the date of enactment of this title, and review at least annually thereafter and, if appropriate, revise guidelines for pretreatment of pollutants which he determines are not susceptible to treatment by publicly owned treatment works. Guidelines under this subsection shall be established to control and prevent the discharge into the navigable waters, the contiguous zone, or the ocean (either directly or through publicly owned treatment works) of any pollutant which interferes with, passes through, or otherwise is incompatible with such works.

(2) When publishing guidelines under this subsection, the Administrator shall designate the category or categories of treatment works to which the guidelines shall apply.

(h) The Administrator shall, within one hundred and eighty days from the date of enactment of this title, promulgate guidelines establishing test procedures for the analysis of pollutants that shall include the factors which must be provided in any certification pursuant to section 401 of this Act or permit application pursuant to section 402 of this Act.

(i) The Administrator shall (1) within sixty days after the enactment of this title promulgate guidelines for the purpose of establishing uniform application forms and other minimum requirements for the acquisition of information from owners and operators of point-sources of discharge subject to any State program under section 402 of this Act, and (2) within sixty days from the date of enactment of this title promulgate guidelines establishing the minimum procedural and other elements of any State program under section 402 of this Act which shall include:

(A) monitoring requirements;

(B) reporting requirements (including procedures to make information available to the public);

(C) enforcement provisions; and

(D) funding, personnel qualifications, and manpower requirements (including a requirement that no board or body which approves permit applications or portions thereof shall include, as a member, any person who receives, or has during the previous two years received, a significant portion of his income directly or indirectly from permit holders or applicants for a permit).

(j) Lake Restoration Guidance Manual —The Administrator shall, within 1 year after the date of the enactment of the Water Quality Act of 1987 and biennially thereafter, publish and disseminate a lake restoration guidance manual describing methods, procedures, and processes to guide State and local efforts to improve, restore, and enhance water quality in the Nation's publicly owned lakes.

[§304(j) revised by PL 100–4]

(k) (1) The Administrator shall enter into agreements with the Secretary of Agriculture, the Secretary of the Army, and the Secretary of the Interior, and the heads of such other departments, agencies, and instrumentalities of the United States as the Administrator determines, to provide for the maximum utilization of other Federal laws and programs for the purpose of achieving and maintaining water quality through appropriate implementation of plans approved under section 208 of this Act and nonpoint source pollution management programs approved under section 319 of this Act.

[§304(k)(1) amended by PL 100–4]

(2) The Administrator is authorized to transfer to the Secretary of Agriculture, the Secretary of the Army, and the Secretary of the Interior and

the heads of such other departments, agencies, and instrumentalities of the United States as the Administrator determines, any funds appropriated under paragraph (3) of this subsection to supplement funds otherwise appropriated to programs authorized pursuant to any agreement under paragraph (1).

(3) There is authorized to be appropriated to carry out the provisions of this subsection, $100,000,000 per fiscal year for the fiscal years 1979 through 1983 and such sums as may be necessary for fiscal years 1984 through 1990.

[§304(k)(3) amended by PL 100–4]

(l) Individual Control Strategies for Toxic Pollutants.—

(1) State List of Navigable Waters and Development of Strategies. — Not later than 2 years after the date of the enactment of this subsection, each State shall submit to the Administrator for review, approval, and implementation under this subsection—

(A) a list of those waters within the State which after the application of effluent limitations required under section 301(b)(2) of this Act cannot reasonably be anticipated to attain or maintain (i) water quality standards for such waters reviewed, revised, or adopted in accordance with section 303(c)(2)(B) of this Act, due to toxic pollutants, or (ii) that water quality which shall assure protection of public health, public water supplies, agricultural and industrial uses, and the protection and propagation of a balanced population of shellfish, fish and wildlife, and allow recreational activities in and on the water;

(B) a list of all navigable waters in such State for which the State does not expect the applicable standard under section 303 of this Act will be achieved after the requirements of sections 301(b), 306, and 307(b) are met, due entirely or substantially to discharges from point sources of any toxic pollutants listed pursuant to section 307(a) ;

(C) for each segment of the navigable waters included on such lists, a determination of the specific point sources discharging any such toxic pollutant which is believed to be preventing or impairing such water quality and the amount of each such toxic pollutant discharged by each such source; and

(D) for each such segment, an individual control strategy which the State determines will produce a reduction in the discharge of toxic pollutants from point sources identified by the State under this paragraph through the establishment of effluent limitations under section 402 of this Act and water quality standards under section 303(c)(2)(B) of this Act, which reduction is sufficient, in combination with existing controls on point and nonpoint sources of pollution, to achieve the applicable water quality standard as soon as possible, but not later than 3 years after the date of the establishment of such strategy.

(2) Approval or Disapproval. — Not later than 120 days after the last day of the 2–year period referred to in paragraph (1), the Administrator shall approve or disapprove the control strategies submitted under paragraph (1) by any State.

(3) Administrator's Action. — If a State fails to submit control strategies in accordance with paragraph (1) or the Administrator does not approve the control strategies submitted by such State in accordance with paragraph (1), then, not later than 1 year after the last day of the period referred to in paragraph (2), the Administrator, in cooperation with such State and after notice and opportunity for public comment, shall implement the requirements of paragraph (1) in such State. In the implementation of such requirements, the Administrator shall, at a minimum, consider for listing under this subsection any navigable waters for which any person submits a petition to the Administrator for listing not later than 120 days after such last day.

[§304(l) added by PL 100–4]

(m) Schedule for Review of Guidelines.—

(1) Publication. — Within 12 months after the date of the enactment of the Water Quality Act of 1987, and biennially thereafter, the Administrator shall publish in the Federal Register a plan which shall—

(A) establish a schedule for the annual review and revision of promulgated effluent guidelines, in accordance with subsection (b) of this section;

(B) identify categories of sources discharging toxic or nonconventional pollutants for which guidelines under subsection (b)(2) of this section and section 306 have not previously been published; and

(C) establish a schedule for promulgation of effluent guidelines for categories identified in subparagraph (B), under which promulgation of such guidelines shall be no later than 4 years after such date of enactment for categories identified in the first published plan or

3 years after the publication of the plan for categories identified in later published plans.

(2) Public Review. — The Administrator shall provide for public review and comment on the plan prior to final publication.

[§304(m) added by PL 100–4]

§1315. Water Quality Inventory [Sec. 305]

(a) The Administrator, in cooperation with the States and with the assistance of appropriate Federal agencies shall prepare a report to be submitted to the Congress on or before January 1, 1974, which shall—

(1) describe the specific quality, during 1973, with appropriate supplemental descriptions as shall be required to take into account seasonal, tidal, and other variations, of all navigable waters and the waters of the contiguous zone;

(2) include an inventory of all point sources of discharge (based on a qualitative and quantitative analysis of discharges) of pollutants, into all navigable waters and the waters of the contiguous zone; and

(3) identify specifically those navigable waters, the quality of which—

(A) is adequate to provide for the protection and propagation of a balanced population of shellfish, fish, and wildlife and allow recreational activities in and on the water;

(B) can reasonably be expected to attain such level by 1977 or 1983; and

(C) can reasonably be expected to attain such level by any later date.

(b) (1) Each State shall prepare and submit to the Administrator by April 1, 1975, and shall bring up to date by April 1, 1976, and biennially thereafter, a report which shall include—

(A) a description of the water quality of all navigable waters in such State during the preceding year, with appropriate supplemental descriptions as shall be required to take into account seasonal, tidal, and other variations, correlated with the quality of water required by the objective of this Act (as identified by the Administrator pursuant to criteria published under section 304(a) of this Act) and the water quality described in subparagraph (B) of this paragraph;

(B) an analysis of the extent to which all navigable waters of such State provide for the protection and propagation of a balanced population of shellfish, fish, and wildlife, and allow recreational activities in and on the water;

(C) an analysis of the extent to which the elimination of the discharge of pollutants and a level of water quality which provides for the protection and propagation of a balanced population of shellfish, fish, and wildlife and allows recreational activities in and on the water, have been or will be achieved by the requirements of this Act, together with recommendations as to additional action necessary to achieve such objectives and for what waters such additional action is necessary;

(D) an estimate of (i) the environmental impact, (ii) the economic and social costs necessary to achieve the objective of this Act in such State, (iii) the economic and social benefits of such achievement, and (iv) an estimate of the date of such achievement; and

(E) a description of the nature and extent of non-point sources of pollutants, and recommendations as to the programs which must be undertaken to control each category of such sources, including an estimate of the costs of implementing such programs.

(2) The Administrator shall transmit such State reports, together with an analysis thereof, to Congress on or before October 1, 1975, and October 1, 1976, and biennially thereafter.

§1316. National Standards of Performance [Sec. 306]

(a) For purposes of this section:

(1) The term "standard of performance" means a standard for the control of the discharge of pollutants which reflects the greatest degree of effluent reduction which the Administrator determines to be achievable through application of the best available demonstrated control technology, processes, operating methods, or other alternatives, including, where practicable, a standard permitting no discharge of pollutants.

(2) The term "new source" means any source, the construction of which is commenced after the publication of proposed regulations prescribing a standard of performance under this section which will be applicable to such source, if such standard is thereafter promulgated in accordance with this section.

(3) The term "source" means any building, structure, facility, or installation from which there is or may be the discharge of pollutants.

(4) The term "owner or operator" means any person who owns, leases, operates, controls, or supervises a source.

(5) The term "construction" means any placement, assembly, or installation of facilities or equipment (including contractual obligations to purchase such facilities or equipment) at the premises where such equipment will be used, including preparation work at such premises.

(b) (1) (A) The Administrator shall, within ninety days after the date of enactment of this title publish (and from time to time thereafter shall revise) a list of categories of sources, which shall, at the minimum, include:

(B) As soon as practicable, but in no case more than one year, after a category of sources is included in a list under subparagraph (A) of this paragraph, the Administrator shall propose and publish regulations establishing Federal standards of performance for new sources within such category. The Administrator shall afford interested persons an opportunity for written comment on such proposed regulations. After considering such comments, he shall promulgate, within one hundred and twenty days after publication of such proposed regulations, such standards with such adjustments as he deems appropriate. The Administrator shall, from time to time, as technology and alternatives change, revise such standards following the procedure required by this subsection for promulgation of such standards. Standards of performance, or revisions thereof, shall become effective upon promulgation. In establishing or revising Federal standards of performance for new sources under this section, the Administrator shall take into consideration the cost of achieving such effluent reduction, and any non- water quality environmental impact and energy requirements.

(2) The Administrator may distinguish among classes, types, and sizes within categories of new sources for the purpose of establishing such standards and shall consider the type of process employed (including whether batch or continuous).

(3) The provisions of this section shall apply to any new source owned or operated by the United States.

(c) Each State may develop and submit to the Administrator a procedure under State law for applying and enforcing standards of performance for new sources located in such State. If the Administrator finds that the procedure and the law of any State require the application and enforcement of standards of performance to at least the same extent as required by this section, such State is authorized to apply and enforce such standards of performance (except with respect to new sources owned or operated by the United States).

(d) Notwithstanding any other provision of this Act, any point source the construction of which is commenced after the date of enactment of the Federal Water Pollution Control Act Amendments of 1972 and which is so constructed as to meet all applicable standards of performance shall not be subject to any more stringent standard of performance during a ten-year period beginning on the date of completion of such construction or during the period of depreciation or amortization of such facility for the purposes of section 167 or 169 (or both) of the Internal Revenue Code of 1954, whichever period ends first.

(e) After the effective date of standards of performance promulgated under this section, it shall be unlawful for any owner or operator of any new source to operate such source in violation of any standard of performance applicable to such source.

§1317. Toxic and Pretreatment Effluent Standards [Sec. 307]

(a) (1) On and after the date of enactment of the Clean Water Act of 1977, the list of toxic pollutants or combination of pollutants subject to this Act shall consist of those toxic pollutants listed in table 1 of Committee Print Numbered 95–30 of the Committee on Public Works and Transportation of the House of Representatives, and the Administrator shall publish, not later than the thirtieth day after date of enactment of the Clean Water Act of 1977, that list. From time to time thereafter, the Administrator may revise such list and the Administrator is authorized to add to or remove from such list any pollutant. The Administrator in publishing any revised list, including the addition or removal of any pollutant from such list, shall take into account the toxicity of the pollutant, its persistence, degradability, the usual or potential presence of the affected organisms in any waters, the importance of the affected organisms, and the nature and extent of the effect of the toxic pollutant on such organisms. A determination of the Administrator under this paragraph shall be final except that if, on judicial review, such determination was based on arbitrary and capricious action of the Administrator, the Administrator shall make a redetermination.

[Editor's Note: The current version of Table 1, as revised by the EPA, is published in Environment

Reporter (BNA), *Federal Regulations Binder, p. 135:0501.]*

(2) Each toxic pollutant listed in accordance with paragraph (1) of this subsection shall be subject to effluent limitations resulting from the application of the best available technology economically achievable for the applicable category or class of point sources established in accordance with section 301(b)(2)(A) and 304(b)(2) of this Act. The Administrator, in his discretion, may publish in the Federal Register a proposed effluent standard (which may include a prohibition) establishing requirements for a toxic pollutant which, if an effluent limitation is applicable to a class or category of point sources, shall be applicable to such category or class only if such standard imposes more stringent requirements. Such published effluent standard (or prohibition) shall take into account the toxicity of the pollutant, its persistence, degradability, the usual or potential presence of the affected organisms in any waters, the importance of the affected organisms and the nature and extent of the effect of the toxic pollutant on such organisms, and the extent to which effective control is being or may be achieved under other regulatory authority. The Administrator shall allow a period of not less than sixty days following publication of any such proposed effluent standard (or prohibition) for written comment by interested persons on such proposed standard. In addition, if within thirty days of publication of any such proposed effluent standard (or prohibition) any interested person so requests, the Administrator shall hold a public hearing in connection therewith. Such a public hearing shall provide an opportunity for oral and written presentations, such cross-examination as the Administrator determines is appropriate on disputed issues of material fact, and the transcription of a verbatim record which shall be available to the public. After consideration of such comments and any information and material presented at any public hearing held on such proposed standard or prohibition, the Administrator shall promulgate such standards (or prohibition) with such modifications as the Administrator finds are justified. Such promulgation by the Administrator shall be made within two hundred and seventy days after publication of proposed standard (or prohibition). Such standard (or prohibition) shall be final except that if, on judicial review, such standard was not based on substantial evidence, the Administrator shall promulgate a revised standard. Effluent limitations shall be established in accordance with sections 301(b)(2)(A) and 304(b)(2) for every toxic pollutant referred to in table 1 of Committee Print Numbered 95–30 of the Committee on Public Works and Transportation of the House of Representatives as soon as practicable after the date of enactment of the Clean Water Act of 1977, but no later than July 1, 1980. Such effluent limitations or effluent standards (or prohibitions) shall be established for every other toxic pollutant listed under paragraph (1) of this subsection as soon as practicable after it is so listed.

(3) Each such effluent standard (or prohibition) shall be reviewed and, if appropriate, revised at least every three years.

(4) Any effluent standard promulgated under this section shall be at that level which the Administrator determines provides an ample margin of safety.

(5) When proposing or promulgating any effluent standard (or prohibition) under this section, the Administrator shall designate the category or categories of sources to which the effluent standard (or prohibition) shall apply. Any disposal of dredged material may be included in such a category of sources after consultation with the Secretary of the Army.

(6) Any effluent standard (or prohibition) established pursuant to this section shall take effect on such date or dates as specified in the order promulgating such standard, but in no case, more than one year from the date of such promulgation. If the Administrator determines that compliance within one year from the date of promulgation is technologically infeasible for a category of sources, the Administrator may establish the effective date of the effluent standard (or prohibition) for such category at the earliest date upon which compliance can be feasibly attained by sources within such category, but in no event more than three years after the date of such promulgation.

(7) Prior to publishing any regulations pursuant to this section the Administrator shall, to the maximum extent practicable within the time provided, consult with appropriate advisory committees, States, independent experts, and Federal departments and agencies.

(b) (1) The Administrator shall, within one hundred and eighty days after the date of enactment of this title and from time to time thereafter, publish proposed regulations establishing pretreatment standards for introduction of pollutants into treatment works (as defined in section 212 of this Act) which are publicly owned for those pollutants which are determined not to be susceptible to treatment by such treatment works or which would interfere with the operation of such treatment works. Not later than ninety days after such publication, and after opportunity for public hearing, the Administrator shall promulgate such pretreatment standards. Pretreatment standards under this subsection shall specify a time for compliance not to exceed three years from the date of promulgation and shall be established to prevent the discharge of any pollutant through treatment works (as defined in section 212 of this Act) which are publicly owned, which pollutant interferes with, passes through, or otherwise is incompatible with such works. If, in the case of any toxic pollutant under subsection (a) of this section introduced by a source into a publicly owned treatment works, the treatment by such works removes all or any part of such toxic pollutant and the discharge from such works does not violate that effluent limitation or standard which would be applicable to such toxic pollutant if it were discharged by such source other than through a publicly owned treatment works, and does not prevent sludge use or disposal by such works in accordance with section 405 of this Act, then the pretreatment requirements for the sources actually discharging such toxic pollutant into such publicly owned treatment works may be revised by the owner or operator of such works to reflect the removal of such toxic pollutant by such works.

(2) The Administrator shall, from time to time, as control technology, processes, operating methods, or other alternative change, revise such standards following the procedure established by this subsection for promulgation of such standards.

(3) When proposing or promulgating any pretreatment standard under this section, the Administrator shall designate the category or categories of sources to which such standard shall apply.

(4) Nothing in this subsection shall affect any pretreatment requirement established by any State or local law not in conflict with any pretreatment standard established under this subsection.

(c) In order to insure that any source introducing pollutants into a publicly owned treatment works, which source would be a new source subject to section 306 if it were to discharge pollutants, will not cause a violation of the effluent limitations established for any such treatment works, the Administrator shall promulgate pretreatment standards for the category of such sources simultaneously with the promulgation of standards of performance under section 306 for the equivalent category of new sources. Such pretreatment standards shall prevent the discharge of any pollutant into such treatment works, which pollutant may interfere with, pass through, or otherwise be incompatible with such works.

(d) After the effective date of any effluent standard or prohibition or pretreatment standard promulgated under this section, it shall be unlawful for any owner or operator of any source to operate any source in violation of any such effluent standard or prohibition or pretreatment standard.

(e) Compliance Date Extension for Innovative Pretreatment Systems. — In the case of any existing facility that proposes to comply with the pretreatment standards of subsection (b) of this section by applying an innovative system that meets the requirements of section 301(k) of this Act, the owner or operator of the publicly owned treatment works receiving the treated effluent from such facility may extend the date for compliance with the applicable pretreatment standard established under this section for a period not to exceed 2 years—

(1) if the Administrator determines that the innovative system has the potential for industrywide application, and

(2) if the Administrator (or the State in consultation with the Administrator, in any case in which the State has a pretreatment program approved by the Administrator)—

(A) determines that the proposed extension will not cause the publicly owned treatment works to be in violation of its permit under section 402 or of section 405 or to contribute to such a violation, and B concurs with the proposed extension.

[§307(e) added by PL 100–4]

§1318. Inspections, Monitoring and Entry
[Sec. 308]

(a) Whenever required to carry out the objective of this Act, including but not limited to

(1) developing or assisting in the development of any effluent limitation, or other limitation, prohibition, or effluent standard, pretreatment standard, or standard of performance under this Act;

(2) determining whether any person is in violation of any such effluent limitation, or other limitation, prohibition or effluent standard, pretreatment standard, or standard of performance,

(3) any requirement established under this Section, or

(4) carrying out sections 305, 311, 402, 404 (relating to State permit programs), 405, and 504 of this Act—

[§308(a)(4) amended by PL 100–4]

(A) the Administrator shall require the owner or operator of any point source to (i) establish and maintain such records, (ii) make such reports, (iii) install, use, and maintain such monitoring equipment or methods (including where appropriate, biological monitoring methods), (iv) sample such effluents (in accordance with such methods, at such locations, at such intervals, and in such manner as the Administrator shall prescribe), and (v) provide such other information as he may reasonably require; and

(B) the Administrator or his authorized representative (including an authorized contractor acting as a representative of the Administrator), upon presentation of his credentials—

(i) shall have a right of entry to, upon, or through any premises in which an effluent source is located or in which any records required to be maintained under clause (A) of this subsection are located, and

(ii) may at reasonable times have access to and copy any records, inspect any monitoring equipment or method required under clause (A), and sample any effluents which the owner or operator of such source is required to sample under such clause.

[§308(a)(4)(B) amended by PL 100–4]

(b) Any records, reports, or information obtained under this section (1) shall, in the case of effluent data, be related to any applicable effluent limitations, toxic, pretreatment, or new source performance standards, and (2) shall be available to the public, except that upon a showing satisfactory to the Administrator by any person that records, reports, or information, or particular part thereof (other than effluent data), to which the Administrator has access under this section, if made public would divulge methods or processes entitled to protection as trade secrets of such person, the Administrator shall consider such record, report, or information, or particular portion thereof confidential in accordance with the purposes of section 1905 of title 18 of the United States Code. Any authorized representative of the Administrator (including an authorized contractor acting as a representative of the Administrator) who knowingly or willfully publishes, divulges, discloses, or makes known in any manner or to any extent not authorized by law any information which is required to be considered confidential under this subsection shall be fined not more than $1,000 or imprisoned not more than 1 year, or both. Nothing in this subsection shall prohibit the Administrator or an authorized representative of the Administrator (including any authorized contractor acting as a representative of the Administrator) from disclosing records, reports, or information to other officers, employees, or authorized representatives of the United States concerned with carrying out this Act or when relevant in any proceeding under this Act.

[§308(b) amended by PL 100–4]

(c) Each State may develop and submit to the Administrator procedures under State law for inspection, monitoring, and entry with respect to point sources located in such State. If the Administrator finds that the procedures and the law of any State relating to inspection, monitoring, and entry are applicable to at least the same extent as those required by this section, such State is authorized to apply and enforce its procedures for inspection, monitoring, and entry with respect to point sources located in such State (except with respect to point sources owned or operated by the United States).

(d) Access by Congress. — Notwithstanding any limitation contained in this section or any other provision of law, all information reported to or otherwise obtained by the Administrator (or any representative of the Administrator) under this Act shall be made available, upon written request of any duly authorized committee of Congress, to such committee.

[§308(d) added by PL 100–4]

§1319. Federal Enforcement [Sec. 309]

[Editor's Note: See also Section 318 of PL 100–4, published at the end of this Act, for applicability of this Section to the Unconsolidated Quarternary Aquifer, Rockaway River Basin, New Jersey.]

(a) (1) Whenever, on the basis of any information available to him, the Administrator finds that any person is in violation of any condition or limitation which implements section 301, 302, 306, 307, 308, 318, or 405 of this Act in a permit issued by a State under an approved permit program under section 402 or 404 of this Act, he shall proceed under his authority in paragraph (3) of this subsection or he shall notify the person in alleged violation and such State of such finding. If beyond the thirtieth day after the Administrator's notification the State has not commenced appropriate enforcement action, the Administrator shall issue an order requiring such person to comply with such condition or limitation or shall bring a civil action in accordance with subsection (b) of this section.

(2) Whenever, on the the basis of information available to him, the Administrator finds that violations of permit conditions or limitations as set forth in paragraph (1) of this subsection are so widespread that such violations appear to result from a failure of the State to enforce such permit conditions or limitations effectively, he shall so notify the State. If the Administrator finds such failure extends beyond the thirtieth day after such notice, he shall give public notice of such finding. During the period beginning with such public notice and ending when such State satisfies the Administrator that it will enforce such conditions and limitations (hereafter referred to in this section as the period of "federally assumed enforcement"), except where an extension has been granted under paragraph (5)(B) of this subsection, the Administrator shall enforce any permit condition or limitation with respect to any person—

(A) by issuing an order to comply with such condition or limitation, or

(B) by bringing a civil action under subsection (b) of this section.

(3) Whenever on the basis of any information available to him the Administrator finds that any person is in violation of section 301, 306, 307, 308, 318, or 405 of this Act, or is in violation of any permit condition or limitation implementing any of such sections in a permit issued under section 402 of this Act by him or by a State or in a permit issued under section 404 of this Act by a State, he shall issue an order requiring such person to comply with such section or requirement, or he shall bring a civil action in accordance with subsection (b) of this section.

(4) A copy of any order issued under this subsection shall be sent immediately by the Administrator to the State in which the violation occurs and other affected States. In any case in which an order under this subsection (or notice to a violator under paragraph (1) of this subsection) is issued to a corporation, a copy of such order (or notice) shall be served on any appropriate corporate officers. An order issued under this subsection relating to a violation of section 308 of this Act shall not take effect until the person to whom it is issued has had an opportunity to confer with the Administrator concerning the alleged violation.

(5) (A) Any order issued under this subsection shall be by personal service, shall state with reasonable specificity the nature of the violation, and shall specify a time for compliance not to exceed thirty days in the case of a violation of an interim compliance schedule or operation and maintenance requirement and not to exceed a time the Administrator determines to be reasonable in the case of a violation of a final deadline, taking into account the seriousness of the violation and any good faith efforts to comply with applicable requirements.

(B) The Administrator may, if he determines (i) that any person who is a violator of, or any person who is otherwise not in compliance with, the time requirements under this Act or in any permit issued under this Act, has acted in good faith, and has made a commitment (in the form of contracts or other securities) of necessary resources to achieve compliance by the earliest possible date after July 1, 1977, but not later than April 1, 1979; (ii) that any extension under this provision will not result in the imposition of any additional controls on any other point or nonpoint source; (iii) that an application for a permit under section 402 of this Act was filed for such person prior to December 31, 1974; and (iv) that the facilities necessary for compliance with such requirements are under construction, grant an extension of the date referred to in section 301(b)(1)(A) to a date which will achieve compliance at the earliest time possible but not later than April 1, 1979.

(6) Whenever, on the basis of information available to him, the Administrator finds (A) that any person is in violation of section 301(b)(1)(A) or (C) of this Act, (B) that such person cannot meet the requirements for a time extension under section 301(i)(2) of this Act, and (C) that the most expeditious and appropriate means of compliance with this Act by such person is to discharge into a publicly owned treatment works, then, upon request of such person, the Administrator may issue an order requiring such person to comply with this Act at the earliest date practicable, but not

later than July 1, 1983, by discharging into a publicly owned treatment works if such works concur with such order. Such order shall include a schedule of compliance.

(b) The Administrator is authorized to commence a civil action for appropriate relief, including a permanent or temporary injunction, for any violation for which he is authorized to issue a compliance order under subsection (a) of this section. Any action under this subsection may be brought in the district court of the United States for the district in which the defendant is located or resides or is doing business, and such court shall have jurisdiction to restrain such violation and to require compliance. Notice of the commencement of such action shall be given immediately to the appropriate State.

(c) Criminal Penalties.—

[309(c) revised by PL 100–4;amended by PL 101–380]

(1) Negligent Violations. — Any person who—

(A) negligently violates section 301, 302, 306, 307, 308, 311(b)(3), 318 or 405 of this Act, or any permit condition or limitation implementing any of such sections in a permit issued under section 402 of this Act by the Administrator or by a State, or any requirement imposed in a pretreatment program approved under section 402(a)(3) or 402(b)(8) of this Act or in a permit issued under section 404 of this Act by the Secretary of the Army or by a State; or

[§309(c)(1)(A) amended by PL 101–380]

(B) negligently introduces into a sewer system or into a publicly owned treatment works any pollutant or hazardous substance which such person knew or reasonably should have known could cause personal injury or property damage or, other than in compliance with all applicable Federal, State, or local requirements or permits, which causes such treatment works to violate any effluent limitation or condition in any permit issued to the treatment works under section 402 of this Act by the Administrator or a State; shall be punished by a fine of not less than $2,500 nor more than $25,000 per day of violation, or by imprisonment for not more than 1 year, or by both. If a conviction of a person is for a violation committed after a first conviction of such person under this paragraph, punishment shall be by a fine of not more than $50,000 per day of violation, or by imprisonment of not more than 2 years, or by both.

(2) Knowing Violations. — Any person who—

(A) knowingly violates section 301, 302, 306, 307, 308, 311(b)(3), 318 or 405 of this Act, or any permit condition or limitation implementing any of such sections in a permit issued under section 402 of this Act by the Administrator or by a State, or any requirement imposed in a pretreatment program approved under section 402(a)(3) or 402(b)(8) of this Act or in a permit issued under section 404 of this Act by the Secretary of the Army or by a State; or

[§309(c)(2)(A) amended by PL 101–380]

(B) knowingly introduces into a sewer system or into a publicly owned treatment works any pollutant or hazardous substance which such person knew or reasonably should have known could cause personal injury or property damage or, other than in compliance with all applicable Federal, State, or local requirements or permits, which causes such treatment work to violate any effluent limitation or condition in a permit issued to the treatment works under section 402 of this Act by the Administrator or a State; shall be punished by a fine of not less than $5,000 nor more than $50,000 per day of violation, or by imprisonment for not more than 3 years, or by both. If a conviction of a person is for a violation committed after a first conviction of such person under this paragraph, punishment shall be a fine of not more than $100,000 per day of violation, or by imprisonment of not more than 6 years, or by both.

(3) Knowing Endangerment.—

(A) General Rule. — Any person who knowingly violates section 301, 302, 303, 306, 307, 308, 311(b)(3), 318 or 405 of this Act, or any permit condition or limitation implementing any of such sections in a permit issued under section 402 of this Act by the Administrator or by a State, or in a permit issued under section 404 of this Act by the Secretary of the Army or by a State, and who knows at that time that he thereby places another person in imminent danger of death or serious bodily injury, shall, upon conviction, be subject to a fine of not more than $250,000 or imprisonment of not more than 15 years, or both. A person which is an organization shall, upon conviction of violating this subparagraph, be subject to a fine of not more than $1,000,000. If a conviction of a person is for a violation committed after a first conviction of such person under this paragraph, the maximum punishment shall be doubled with respect to both fine and imprisonment.

[§309(c)(3)(A) amended by PL 101–380]

(B) Additional Provisions. — For the purpose of subparagraph (A) of this paragraph—

(i) in determining whether a defendant who is an individual knew that his conduct placed another person in imminent danger of death or serious bodily injury—

(I) the person is responsible only for actual awareness or actual belief that he possessed; and

(II) knowledge possessed by a person other than the defendant but not by the defendant himself may not be attributed to the defendant; except that in proving the defendant's possession of actual knowledge, circumstantial evidence may be used, including evidence that the defendant took affirmative steps to shield himself from relevant information;

(ii) it is an affirmative defense to prosecution that the conduct charged was consented to by the person endangered and that the danger and conduct charged were reasonably foreseeable hazards of—

(I) an occupation, a business, or a profession; or

(II) medical treatment or medical or scientific experimentation conducted by professionally approved methods and such other person had been made aware of the risks involved prior to giving consent; and such defense may be established under this subparagraph by a preponderance of the evidence;

(iii) the term "organization" means a legal entity, other than a government, established or organized for any purpose, and such term includes a corporation, company, association, firm, partnership, joint stock company, foundation, institution, trust, society, union, or any other association of persons; and

(iv) the term "serious bodily injury" means bodily injury which involves a substantial risk of death, unconsciousness, extreme physical pain, protracted and obvious disfigurement, or protracted loss or impairment of the function of a bodily member, organ, or mental faculty.

(4) False Statements. — Any person who knowingly makes any false material statement, representation, or certification in any application, record, report, plan, or other document filed or required to be maintained under this Act or who knowingly falsifies, tampers with, or renders inaccurate any monitoring device or method required to be maintained under this Act, shall upon conviction, be punished by a fine of not more than $10,000, or by imprisonment for not more than 2 years, or by both. If a conviction of a person is for a violation committed after a first conviction of such person under this paragraph, punishment shall be by a fine of not more than $20,000 per day of violation, or by imprisonment of not more than 4 years, or by both.

(5) Treatment of Single Operational Upset. — For purposes of this subsection, a single operational upset which leads to simultaneous violations of more than one pollutant parameter shall be treated as a single violation.

(6) Responsible Corporate Officer as "Person". — For the purpose of this subsection, the term "person" means, in addition to the definition contained in section 502(5) of this Act, any responsible corporate officer.

(7) Hazardous Substance Defined. — For the purpose of this subsection, the term "hazardous substance" means (A) any substance designated pursuant to section 311(b)(2)(A) of this Act, (B) any element, compound, mixture, solution, or substance designated pursuant to section 102 of the Comprehensive Environmental Response, Compensation, and Liability Act of 1980, (C) any hazardous waste having the characteristics identified under or listed pursuant to section 3001 of the Solid Waste Disposal Act (but not including any waste the regulation of which under the Solid Waste Disposal Act has been suspended by Act of Congress), (D) any toxic pollutant listed under section 307(a) of this Act, and (E) any imminently hazardous chemical substance or mixture with respect to which the Administrator has taken action pursuant to section 7 of the Toxic Substances Control Act.

(d) Any person who violates section 301, 302, 306, 307, 308, 318, or 405 of this Act, or any permit condition or limitation implementing any of such sections in a permit issued under section 402 of this Act by the Administrator, or by a State, or in a permit issued under section 404 of this Act by a State, or any requirement imposed in a pretreatment program approved under section 402(a)(3) or 402(b)(8) of this Act, and any person who violates any order issued by the Administrator under subsection (a) of this section, shall be subject to a civil penalty not to exceed $25,000 per day for each violation. In determining the amount of a civil penalty the court shall consider the seriousness of the violation or violations, the economic benefit (if any) resulting from the violation, any history of such violations, any good-faith efforts to comply with the applicable requirements, the economic impact of the penalty on the violator, and such other matters as justice may require. For purposes of this subsection, a single operational upset which leads to simultaneous violations of more than one pollutant parameter shall be treated as a single violation.

[§309(d) amended by PL 100–4]

(e) Whenever a municipality is a party to a civil action brought by the United States under this section, the State in which such municipality is located shall be joined as a party. Such State shall be liable for payment of any judgment, or any expenses incurred as a result of complying with any judgment, entered against the municipality in such action to the extent that the laws of that State prevent the municipality from raising revenues needed to comply with such judgment.

(f) Whenever, on the basis of an information available to him, the Administrator finds that an owner or operator of any source is introducing a pollutant into a treatment works in violation of subsection (d) of section 307 , the Administrator may notify the owner or operator of such treatment works and the State of such violation. If the owner or operator of the treatment works does not commence appropriate enforcement action within 30 days of the date of such notification, the Administrator may commence a civil action for appropriate relief, including but not limited to, a permanent or temporary injunction, against the owner or operator of such treatment works. In any such civil action the Administrator shall join the owner or operator of such source as a party to the action. Such action shall be brought in the district court of the United States in the district in which the treatment works is located. Such court shall have jurisdiction to restrain such violation and to require the owner or operator of the treatment works and the owner or operator of the source to take such action as may be necessary to come into compliance with this Act. Notice of commencement of any such action shall be given to the State. Nothing in this subsection shall be construed to limit or prohibit any other authority the Administrator may have under this Act.

(g) Administrative Penalties.—

(1) Violations. — Whenever on the basis of any information available—

(A) the Administrator finds that any person has violated section 301, 302, 306, 307, 308, 318, or 405 of this Act, or has violated any permit condition or limitation implementing any of such sections in a permit issued under section 402 of this Act by the Administrator or by a State, or in a permit issued under section 404 by a State, or

(B) the Secretary of the Army (hereinafter in this subsection referred to as the "Secretary") finds that any person has violated any permit condition or limitation in a permit issued under section 404 of this Act by the Secretary. the Administrator or Secretary, as the case may be, may, after consultation with the State in which the violation occurs, assess a class I civil penalty or a class II civil penalty under this subsection.

(2) Classes of Penalties.—

(A) Class I. — The amount of a class I civil penalty under paragraph (1) may not exceed $10,000 per violation, except that the maximum amount of any class I civil penalty under this subparagraph shall not exceed $25,000. Before issuing an order assessing a civil penalty under this subparagraph, the Administrator or the Secretary, as the case may be, shall give to the person to be assessed such penalty written notice of the Administrator's or Secretary's proposal to issue such order and the opportunity to request, within 30 days of the date the notice is received by such person, a hearing on the proposed order. Such hearing shall not be subject to section 554 or 556 of title 5, United States Code, but shall provide a reasonable opportunity to be heard and to present evidence.

(B) Class II. — The amount of a class II civil penalty under paragraph (1) may not exceed $10,000 per day for each day during which the violation continues; except that the maximum amount of any class II civil penalty under this subparagraph shall not exceed $125,000. Except as otherwise provided in this subsection, a class II civil penalty shall be assessed and collected in the same manner, and subject to the same provisions, as in the case of civil penalties assessed and collected after notice and opportunity for a hearing on the record in accordance with section 554 of title 5, United States Code. The Administrator and the Secretary may issue rules for discovery procedures for hearings under this subparagraph.

(3) Determining Amount. — In determining the amount of any penalty assessed under this subsection, the Administrator or the Secretary, as the case may be, shall take into account the nature, circumstances, extent and gravity of the violation, or violations, and, with respect to the violator, ability to pay, any prior history of such violations, the degree of culpability, economic benefit or savings (if any) resulting from the violation, and such other matters as justice may require. For purposes of this subsection, a single operational upset which leads to simultaneous violations of more than one pollutant parameter shall be treated as a single violation.

(4) Rights of Interested Persons.—

(A) Public Notice. — Before issuing an order assessing a civil penalty under this subsection the Administrator or Secretary, as the case may be, shall provide public notice of and reasonable opportunity to comment on the proposed issuance of such order.

(B) Presentation of Evidence. — Any person who comments on a proposed assessment of a penalty under this subsection shall be given notice of any hearing held under this subsection and of the order assessing such penalty. In any hearing held under this subsection, such person shall have a reasonable opportunity to be heard and to present evidence.

(C) Rights of Interested Persons to a Hearing. — If no hearing is held under paragraph (2) before issuance of an order assessing a penalty under this subsection, any person who commented on the proposed assessment may petition, within 30 days after the issuance of such order, the Administrator or Secretary, as the case may be, to set aside such order and to provide a hearing on the penalty. If the evidence presented by the petitioner in support of the petition is material and was not considered in the issuance of the order, the Administrator or Secretary shall immediately set aside such order and provide a hearing in accordance with paragraph (2)(A) in the case of a class I civil penalty and paragraph (2)(B) in the case of a class II civil penalty. If the Administrator or Secretary denies a hearing under this subparagraph, the Administrator or Secretary shall provide to the petitioner, and publish in the Federal Register, notice of and the reasons for such denial.

(5) Finality of Order. — An order issued under this subsection shall become final 30 days after its issuance unless a petition for judicial review is filed under paragraph (8) or a hearing is requested under paragraph (4)(C). If such a hearing is denied, such order shall become final 30 days after such denial.

(6) Effect of Order.—

(A) Limitation on Actions Under Other Sections.— Action taken by the Administrator or the Secretary, as the case may be, under this subsection shall not affect or limit the Administrator's or Secretary's authority to enforce any provision of this Act; except that any violation—

(i) with respect to which the Administrator or the Secretary has commenced and is diligently prosecuting an action under this subsection,

(ii) with respect to which a State has commenced and is diligently prosecuting an action under a State law comparable to this subsection, or

(iii) for which the Administrator, the Secretary, or the State has issued a final order not subject to further judicial review and the violator has paid a penalty assessed under this subsection, or such comparable State law, as the case may be, shall not be the subject of a civil penalty action under subsection (d) of this section or section 311(b) or section 505 of this Act.

(B) Applicability of Limitation With Respect to Citizen Suits. — The limitations contained in subparagraph (A) on civil penalty actions under section 505 of this Act shall not apply with respect to any violation for which—

(i) a civil action under section 505(a)(1) of this Act has been filed prior to commencement of an action under this subsection, or

(ii) notice of an alleged violation of section 505(a)(1) of this Act has been given in accordance with section 505(b)(1)(A) prior to commencement of an action under this subsection and an action under section 505(a)(1) with respect to such alleged violation is filed before the 120th day after the date on which such notice is given.

(7) Effect of Action on Compliance. — No action by the Administrator or the Secretary under this subsection shall affect any person's obligation to comply with any section of this Act or with the terms and conditions of any permit issued pursuant to section 402 or 404 of this Act.

(8) Judicial Review. — Any person against whom a civil penalty is assessed under this subsection or who commented on the proposed assessment of such penalty in accor-

dance with paragraph (4) may obtain review of such assessment—

(A) in the case of assessment of a class I civil penalty, in the United States District Court for the District of Columbia or in the district in which the violation is alleged to have occurred, or

(B) in the case of assessment of a class II civil penalty, in United States Court of Appeals for the District of Columbia Circuit or for any other circuit in which such person resides or transacts business, by filing a notice of appeal in such court within the 30–day period beginning on the date the civil penalty order is issued and by simultaneously sending a copy of such notice by certified mail to the Administrator or the Secretary, as the case may be, and the Attorney General. The Administrator or the Secretary shall promptly file in such court a certified copy of the record on which the order was issued, Such court shall not set aside or remand such order unless there is not substantial evidence in the record, taken as a whole, to support the finding of a violation or unless the Administrator's or Secretary's assessment of the penalty constitutes an abuse of discretion and shall not impose additional civil penalties for the same violation unless the Administrator's or Secretary's assessment of the penalty constitutes an abuse of discretion.

(9) Collection. — If any person fails to pay an assessment of a civil penalty—

(A) after the order making the assessment has become final, or

(B) after a court in an action brought under paragraph (8) has entered a final judgment in favor of the Administrator or the Secretary, as the case may be, the Administrator or the Secretary shall request the Attorney General to bring a civil action in an appropriate district court to recover the amount assessed (plus interest at currently prevailing rates from the date of the final order or the date of the final judgment, as the case may be). In such an action, the validity, amount, and appropriateness of such penalty shall not be subject to review. Any person who fails to pay on a timely basis the amount of an assessment of a civil penalty as described in the first sentence of this paragraph shall be required to pay, in addition to such amount and interest, attorneys fees and costs for collection proceedings and a quarterly nonpayment penalty for each quarter during which such failure to pay persists. Such nonpayment penalty shall be in an amount equal to 20 percent of the aggregate amount of such person's penalties and nonpayment penalties which are unpaid as of the beginning of such quarter.

(10) Subpoenas. — The Administrator or Secretary, as the case may be, may issue subpoenas for the attendance and testimony of witnesses and the production of relevant papers, books, or documents in connection with hearings under this subsection. In case of contumacy or refusal to obey a subpoena issued pursuant to this paragraph and served upon any person. the district court of the United States for any district in which such person is found, resides, or transacts business, upon application by the United States and after notice to such person, shall have jurisdiction to issue an other requiring such person to appear and give testimony before the administrative law judge or to appear and produce documents before the administrative law judge or both, and any failure to obey such order of the court may be punished by such court as a contempt thereof.

(11) Protection of Existing Procedures. —Nothing in this subsection shall change the procedures existing on the day before the date of the enactment of the Water Quality Act of 1987 under other subsections of this section for issuance and enforcement of orders by the Administrator.

[§309(g) added by PL 100-4]

§1320. International Pollution Abatement
[Sec. 310]

(a) Whenever the Administrator, upon receipts of reports, surveys, or studies from any duly constituted international agency, has reason to believe that pollution is occurring which endangers the health or welfare of persons in a foreign country, and the Secretary of State requests him to abate such pollution, he shall give formal notification thereof to the State water pollution control agency of the State or States in which such discharge or discharges originate and to the appropriate interstate agency, if any. He shall also promptly call such a hearing, if he believes that such pollution is occurring in sufficient quantity to warrant such action, and if such foreign country has given the United States essentially the same rights with respect to the prevention and control of pollution occurring in that country as is given that country by this subsection. The Administrator, through the Secretary of State, shall invite the foreign country which may be adversely affected by the pollution to attend and participate in the hearing, and the representative of such country shall, for the purpose of the hearing and any further proceeding resulting from such hearing, have all the rights of a State water pollution control agency. Nothing in this subsection shall be construed to modify, amend, repeal, or otherwise affect the provisions of the 1909 Boundary Waters Treaty between Canada and the United States or the Water Utilization Treaty of 1944 between Mexico and the United States (59 Stat. 1219), relative to the control and abatement of pollution in waters covered by those treaties.

(b) The calling of a hearing under this section shall not be construed by the courts, the Administrator, or any person as limiting, modifying, or otherwise affecting the functions and responsibilities of the Administrator under this section to establish and enforce water quality requirements under this Act.

(c) The Administrator shall publish in the Federal Register a notice of a public hearing before a hearing board of five or more persons appointed by the Administrator. A majority of the members of the board and the chairman who shall be designated by the Administrator shall not be officers or employees of Federal, State, or local governments. On the basis of the evidence presented at such hearing, the board shall within sixty days after completion of the hearing make findings of fact as to whether or not such pollution is occurring and shall thereupon by decision, incorporating its findings therein, make such recommendations to abate the pollution as may be appropriate and shall transmit such decision and the record of the hearings to the Administrator. All such decisions shall be public. Upon receipt of such decision, the Administrator shall promptly implement the board's decision in accordance with the provisions of this Act.

(d) In connection with any hearing called under this subsection, the board is authorized to require any person whose alleged activities result in discharges causing or contributing to pollution to file with it in such forms as it may prescribe, a report based on existing data, furnishing such information as may reasonably be required as to the character, kind, and quantity of such discharges and the use of facilities or other means to prevent or reduce such discharges by the person filing such a report. Such report shall be made under oath or otherwise, as the board may prescribe, and shall be filed with the board within such reasonable period as it may prescribe, unless additional time is granted by it. Upon a showing satisfactory to the board by the person filing such report that such report or portion thereof (other than effluent data), to which the Administrator has access under this section, if made public would divulge trade secrets or secret processes of such person, the board shall consider such report or portion thereof confidential for the purposes of section 1905 of title 18 of the United States Code. If any person required to file any report under this paragraph shall fail to do so within the time fixed by the board for filing the same, and such failure shall continue for thirty days after notice of such default, such person shall forfeit to the United States the sum of $1,000 for each and every day of the continuance of such failure, which forfeiture shall be payable into the Treasury of the United States, and shall be recoverable in a civil suit in the name of the United States in the district court of the United States where such person has his principal office or in any district in which he does business. The Administrator may upon application therefor remit or mitigate any forfeiture provided for under this subsection.

(e) Board members, other than officers or employees of Federal, State, or local governments, shall be for each day (including traveltime) during which they are performing board business, entitled to receive compensation at a rate fixed by the Administrator but not in excess of the maximum rate of pay for grade GS–18, as provided in the General Schedule under section 5332 of title 5 of the United States Code, and shall, notwithstanding the limitations of sections 5703 and 5704 of title 5 of the United States Code, be fully reimbursed for travel, subsistence, and related expenses.

(f) When any such recommendation adopted by the Administrator involves the institution of enforcement proceedings against any person to obtain the abatement of pollution subject to such recommendation, the Administrator shall institute such proceedings if he believes that the evidence warrants such proceedings. The district court of the United States shall consider and determine de novo all relevant issues, but shall receive in evidence the record of the proceedings before the conference or hearing board. The court shall have jurisdiction to enter such judgment and orders enforcing such judgment as it deems appropriate or to remand such proceedings to the Administrator for such further action as it may direct.

§1321. Oil and Hazardous Substance Liability
[Sec. 311]

(a) For the purpose of this section, the term—

(1) "oil" means oil of any kind or in any form, including, but not limited to, petroleum, fuel oil, sludge, oil refuse, and oil mixed with wastes other than dredged spoil;

(2) "discharge" includes, but is not limited to, any spilling, leaking, pumping, pouring, emitting, emptying or dumping, but excludes (A) discharges in compliance with a permit under section 402 of this Act, (B) discharges resulting from circumstances identified and reviewed and made a part of the public record 'with respect to a permit issued or modified under section 402 of this Act, and subject to a condition in such permit, and (C) continuous or anticipated intermittent discharges from a point source, identified in a permit or permit application under section 402 of this Act, which are caused by events occurring within the scope of relevant operating or treatment systems.

[§311(a)(2) amended by PL 95–576]

(3) "vessel" means every description of watercraft or other artificial contrivance used, or capable of being used, as a means of transportation on water other than a public vessel;

(4) "public vessel" means a vessel owned or bare-boat-chartered and operated by the United States, or by a State or political subdivision thereof, or by a foreign nation, except when such vessel is engaged in commerce;

(5) "United States" means the States, the District of Columbia, the Commonwealth of Puerto Rico, the Commonwealth of the Northern Mariana Islands, Guam, American Samoa, the Virgin Islands and the Trust Territory of the Pacific Islands;

[§311(a)(5)amended by PL 100–4]

(6) "owner or operator" means (A) in the case of a vessel, any person owning, operating, or chartering by demise, such vessel, and (B) in the ease of an onshore facility, and an offshore facility, any person owning or operating such onshore facility or offshore facility, and (C) in the ease of any abandoned offshore facility, the person who owned or operated such facility immediately prior to such abandonment;

(7) "person" includes an individual, firm, corporation, association, and a partnership;

(8) "remove" or "removal" refers to containment and removal of the oil or hazardous substances from the water and shorelines or the taking of such other actions as may be necessary to minimize or mitigate damage to the public health or welfare, including, but not limited to, fish, shellfish, wildlife, and public and private property, shorelines, and beaches;

[§311(a)(8) amended by PL 101–380]

(9) "contiguous zone" means the entire zone established or to be established by the United States under article 24 of the Convention on the Territorial Sea and the Contiguous Zone;

(10) "onshore facility" means any facility (including, but not limited to, motor vehicles and rolling stock) of any kind located in, on, or under, any land within the United States other than submerged land;

(11) "offshore facility" means any facility of any kind located in, on, or under, any of the navigable waters of the United States, and any facility of any kind which is subject to the jurisdiction of the United States and is located in, on, or under any other waters, other than a vessel or a public vessel;

(12) "act of God" means an act occasioned by an unanticipated grave natural disaster;

(13) "barrel" means 42 United States gallons at 60 degrees Fahrenheit;

(14) "hazardous substance" means any substance designated pursuant to subsection (b)(2) of this section;

(15) "inland oil barge" means a non- self-propelled vessel carrying oil in bulk as cargo and certificated to operate only in the inland waters of the United States, while operating in such waters;

(16) "inland waters of the United States" means those waters of the United States lying inside the baseline from which the territorial sea is measured and those waters outside such baseline which are a part of the Gulf Intracoastal Waterway;

[§311(a)(16) amended by PL 101–380]

(17) "otherwise subject to the jurisdiction of the United States" means subject to the jurisdiction of the United States by virtue of United States citizenship, United States vessel documentation or numbering, or as provided for by international agreement to which the United States is a party;

[§311(a)(17) added by PL 95–576;amended by PL 101–380]

(18) "Area Committee" means an Area Committee established under subsection (j);

[§311(a)(18) added by PL 101–380]

(19) "Area Contingency Plan" means an Area Contingency Plan prepared under subsection (j);

[§311(a)(19) added by PL 101–380]

(20) "Coast Guard District Response Group" means a Coast Guard District Response Group established under subsection (j);

[§311(a)(20) added by PL 101–380]

(21) "Federal On-Scene Coordinator" means a Federal On-Scene Coordinator designated in the National Contingency Plan;

[§311(a)(21) added by PL 101–380]

(22) "National Contingency Plan" means the National Contingency Plan prepared and published under subsection (d);

[§311(a)(22) added by PL 101–380]

(23) "National Response Unit" means the National Response Unit established under subsection (j); and

[§311(a)(23) added by PL 101–380]

(24) "worst case discharge" means—

(A) in the case of a vessel, a discharge in adverse weather conditions of its entire cargo; and

(B) in the case of an offshore facility or onshore facility, the largest foreseeable discharge in adverse weather conditions.

[§311(a)(24) added by PL 101–380]

(b) (1) The Congress hereby declares that it is the policy of the United States that there should be no discharges of oil or hazardous substances into or upon the navigable waters of the United States, adjoining shorelines, or into or upon the waters of the contiguous zone, or in connection with activities under the Outer Continental Shelf Lands Act or the Deepwater Port Act of 1977, or which may affect natural resources belonging to, appertaining to, or under the exclusive management authority of the United States (including resources under the Magnuson Fishery Conservation and Management Act of 1976).

[§311(b)(1) amended by PL 96–561]

(2) (A) The Administrator shall develop, promulgate, and revise as may be appropriate, regulations designating as hazardous substances, other than oil as defined in this section, such elements and compounds which, when discharged in any quantity into or upon the navigable waters of the United States or adjoining shorelines or the waters of the contiguous zone or in connection with activities under the Outer Continental Shelf Lands Act or the Deepwater Port Act of 1974, or which may affect natural resources belonging to, appertaining to, or under the exclusive management authority of the United States (including resources under the Magnuson Fishery Conservation and Management Act of 1976), present an imminent and substantial danger to the public health or welfare, including, but not limited to, fish, shellfish, wildlife, shorelines, and beaches.

[§311(b)(2)(A) amended by PL 96–561]

(B) The Administrator shall within 18 months after the date of enactment of this paragraph, conduct a study and report to the Congress on methods, mechanisms, and procedures to create incentives to achieve a higher standard of care in all aspects of the management and movement of hazardous substances on the part of owners, operators, or persons in charge of onshore facilities, offshore facilities or vessels. The Administrator shall include in such study (1) limits of liability, (2) liability for third party damages, (3) penalties and fees, (4) spill prevention plans, (5) current practices in the insurance and banking industries, and (6) whether the penalty enacted in subclause (bb) of clause (iii) of subparagraph (B) of subsection (b)(2) of section 311 of Public Law 92–500 should be enacted.

(3) The discharge of oil or hazardous substances (i) into or upon the navigable waters of the United States, adjoining shorelines, or into or upon the waters of the contiguous zone, or (ii) in connection with activities under the Outer Continental Shelf Lands Act or the Deepwater Port Act of 1974, or which may affect natural resources belonging to, appertaining to, or under the exclusive management authority of the United States (including resources under the Magnuson Fishery Conservation and Management Act of 1976), in such quantities as may be harmful as determined by the President under paragraph (4) of this subsection, is prohibited, except (A) in the case of such discharges into the waters of the contiguous zone or which may affect natural resources belonging to, appertaining to, or under the exclusive management authority of the United States (including resources under the Magnuson Fishery Conservation and Management Act of 1976), where permitted under the Protocol of 1978 Relating to the International Convention for the Prevention of Pollution from Ships, 1973 and (B) where permitted in quantities and at times and locations or under such circumstances or conditions as the President may, by regulation, determine not to be harmful. Any regulations issued under this subsection shall be consistent with maritime

safety and with marine and navigation laws and regulations and applicable water quality standards.

[§311(b)(3) revised by PL 95–576; amended by PL 96–478; PL 96–561]

(4) The President shall by regulation determine for the purposes of this section those quantities of oil and any hazardous substances the discharge of which may be harmful to the public health or welfare or the environment of the United States, including but not limited to fish, shellfish, wildlife, and public and private property. shorelines, and beaches.

[§311(b)(4) amended by PL 95–576; PL 101–380]

(5) Any person in charge of a vessel or of an onshore facility or an offshore facility shall, as soon as he has knowledge of any discharge of oil or a hazardous substance from such vessel or facility in violation of paragraph (3) of this subsection, immediately notify the appropriate agency of the United States Government of such discharge. The Federal agency shall immediately notify the appropriate State agency of any State which is, or may reasonably be expected to be, affected by the discharge of oil or a hazardous substance. Any such person (A) in charge of a vessel from which oil or a hazardous substance is discharged in violation of paragraph (3)(i) of this subsection, or (B) in charge of a vessel from which oil or a hazardous substance is discharged in violation of paragraph (3)(ii) of this subsection and who is otherwise subject to the jurisdiction of the United States at the time of the discharge, or (C) in charge of an onshore facility or an offshore facility, who fails to notify immediately such agency of such discharge shall, upon conviction, be fined in accordance with title 18, United States Code, or imprisoned for not more than 5 years, or both. Notification received pursuant to this paragraph shall not be used against any such natural person in any criminal case, except a prosecution for perjury or for giving a false statement.

[§311(b)(5) amended by PL 95–576; PL 101–380]

(6) Administrative Penalties.—

(A) Violations. — Any owner, operator, or person in charge of any vessel, onshore facility, or offshore facility—

(i) from which oil or a hazardous substance is discharged in violation of paragraph (3), or

(ii) who fails or refuses to comply with any regulation issued under subsection (j) to which that owner, operator, or person in charge is subject, may be assessed a class I or class II civil penalty by the Secretary of the department in which the Coast Guard is operating or the Administrator.

(B) Classes of Penalties.—

(i) Class I. — The amount of a class I civil penalty under subparagraph (A) may not exceed $10,000 per violation, except that the maximum amount of any class I civil penalty under this subparagraph shall not exceed $25,000. Before assessing a civil penalty under this clause, the Administrator or Secretary, as the case may be, shall give to the person to be assessed such penalty written notice of the Administrator's or Secretary's preposal to assess the penalty and the opportunity to request, within 30 days of the date the notice is received by such person, a hearing on the proposed penalty. Such hearing shall not be subject to section 554 or 556 of title 5, United States Code, but shall provide a reasonable opportunity to be heard and to present evidence.

(ii) Class II. — The amount of a class II civil penalty under subparagraph (A) may not exceed $10,000 per day for each day during which the violation continues; except that the maximum amount of any class II civil penalty under this subparagraph shall not exceed $125,000. Except as otherwise provided in this subsection, a class II civil penalty shall be assessed and collected in the same manner, and subject to the same provisions, as in the case of civil penalties assessed and collected after notice and opportunity for a hearing on the record in accordance with section 554 of title 5, United States Code. The Administrator and Secretary may issue rules for discovery procedures for hearings under this paragraph.

(C) Rights of Interested Persons.—

(i) Public Notice. — Before issuing an order assessing a class II civil penalty under this paragraph the Administrator or Secretary, as the case may be, shall provide public notice of and reasonable opportunity to comment on the proposed issuance of such order.

(ii) Presentation of Evidence. — Any person who comments on a proposed assessment of a class II civil penalty under this paragraph shall be given notice of any hearing held under this paragraph and of the order assessing such penalty. In any hearing held under this paragraph, such person shall have a reasonable opportunity to be heard and to present evidence.

(iii) Rights of Interested Persons to a Hearing.— If no hearing is held under subparagraph (B) before issuance of an order assessing a class II civil penalty under this paragraph, any person who commented on the proposed assessment may petition, within 30 days after the issuance of such order, the Administrator or Secretary, as the case may be, to set aside such order and to provide a hearing on the penalty. If the evidence presented by the petitioner in support of the petition is material and was not considered in the issuance of the order, the Administrator or Secretary shall immediately set aside such order and provide a hearing in accordance with subparagraph (B)(ii). If the Administrator or Secretary denies a hearing under this clause, the Administrator or Secretary shall provide to the petitioner, and publish in the Federal Register, notice of and the reasons for such denial.

(D) Finality of Order. — An order assessing a class II civil penalty under this paragraph shall become final 30 days after its issuance unless a petition for judicial review is filed under subparagraph (G) or a hearing is requested under subparagraph (C)(iii). If such a hearing is denied, such order shall become final 30 days after such denial.

(E) Effect of Order.— Action taken by the Administrator or Secretary, as the case may be, under this paragraph shall not affect or limit the Administrator's or Secretary's authority to enforce any provision of this Act; except that any violation—

(i) with respect to which the Administrator or Secretary has commenced and is diligently prosecuting an action to access a class II civil penalty under this paragraphs or

(ii) for which the Administrator or Secretary has issued a final order assessing a class II civil penalty not subject to further judicial review and the violator has paid a penalty assessed under this paragraph, shall not be the subject of a civil penalty action under section 309(d), 309(g), or 505of this Act or under paragraph (7).

(F) Effect of Action on Compliance.— No action by the Administrator or Secretary under this paragraph shall affect any person's obligation to comply with any section of this Act.

(G) Judicial Review.—Any person against whom a civil penalty is assessed under this paragraph or who commented on the proposed assessment of such penalty in accordance with subparagraph (C) may obtain review of such assessment—

(i) in the case of assessment of a class I civil penalty, in the United States District Court for the District of Columbia or in the district in which the violation is alleged to have occurred, or

(ii) in the case of assessment of a class II civil penalty, in United States Court of Appeals for the District of Columbia Circuit or for any other circuit in which such person resides or transacts business, by filing a notice of appeal in such court within the 30–day period beginning on the date the civil penalty order is issued and by simultaneously sending a copy of such notice by certified mail to the Administrator or Secretary, as the case may be, and the Attorney General. The Administrator or Secretary shall promptly file in such court a certified copy of the record on which the order was issued. Such court shall not set aside or remand such order unless there is not substantial evidence in the record, taken as a whole, to support the finding of a violation or unless the Administrator's or Secretary's assessment of the penalty constitutes an abuse of discretion and shall not impose additional civil penalties for the same violation unless the Administrator's or Secretary's assessment of the penalty constitutes an abuse of discretion.

(H) Collection.—If any person fails to pay an assessment of a civil penalty—

(i) after the assessment has become final, or

(ii) after a court in an action brought under subparagraph (G) has entered a final judgment in favor of the Administrator or Secretary, as the case may be, the Administrator or Secretary shall request the Attorney General to bring a civil action in an appropriate district court to recover the amount assessed (plus interest at currently prevailing rates from the date of the final order or the date of the final judgment, as the case may be). In such an action, the validity, amount, and appropriateness of such penalty shall not be subject to review. Any person who fails to pay on a timely basis the amount of an assessment of a civil penalty as described in the first sentence of this subparagraph shall be required to pay, in addition to such amount and interest, attorneys fees and costs for collection proceedings and a quarterly nonpayment penalty for each quarter during which such failure to pay persists. Such nonpayment penalty shall be in an amount equal to 20 percent of the aggregate amount of such person's penalties and nonpayment penalties which are unpaid as of the beginning of such quarter.

(I) Subpoenas.—The Administrator or Secretary, as the case may be, may issue subpoenas for the attendance and testimony of witnesses and the production of relevant papers, books, or documents in connection with hearings under this paragraph. In case of contumacy or refusal to obey a subpoena issued pursuant to this subparagagph and served upon any person, the district court of the United States for any district in which such person is found, resides, or transacts business, upon application by the United States and after notice to such person, shall have jurisdiction to issue an order requiring such person to appear and give testimony before the administrative law judge or to appear and produce documents before the administrative law judge, or both, and any failure to obey such order of the court may be punished by such court as a contempt thereof.

[Former §311(b)(6) repealed and new (b)(6) added by PL 101-380]

(7) Civil Penalty Action.—

(A) Discharge, Generally.—Any person who is the owner, operator, or person in charge of any vessel, onshore facility, or offshore facility from which oil or a hazardous substance is discharged in violation of paragraph (3), shall be subject to a civil penalty in an amount up to $25,000 per day of violation or an amount up to $1,000 per barrel of oil or unit of reportable quantity of hazardous substances discharged.

(B) Failure to Remove or Comply.— Any person described in subparagraph (A) who, without sufficient cause—

(i) fails to properly carry out removal of the discharge under an order of the President pursuant to subsection (c); or

(ii) fails to comply with an order pursuant to subsection (e)(1)(B); shall be subject to a civil penalty in an amount up to $25,000 per day of violation or an amount up to 3 times the costs incurred by the Oil Spill Liability Trust Fund as a result of such failure.

(C) Failure to comply with Regulation.—Any person who fails or refuses to comply with any regulation issued under subsection (j) shall be subject to a civil penalty in an amount up to $25,000 per day of violation.

(D) Gross Negligence.—In any case in which a violation of paragraph (3) was the result of gross negligence or willful misconduct of a person described in subparagraph (A), the person shall be subject to a civil penalty of not less than $100,000, and not more than $3,000 per barrel of oil or unit of reportable quantity of hazardous substance discharged.

(E) Jurisdiction.—An action to impose a civil penalty under this paragraph may be brought in the district court of the United States for the district in which the defendant is located, resides, or is doing business, and such court shall have jurisdiction to assess such penalty.

(F) Limitation.—A person is not liable for a civil penalty under this paragraph for a discharge if the person has been assessed a civil penalty under paragraph (6) for the discharge.

[§311(b)(7) added by PL 101–380]

(8) Determination of Amount.—In determining the amount of a civil penalty under paragraphs (6) and (7), the Administrator, Secretary, or the court, as the case may be, shall consider the seriousness of the violation or violations, the economic benefit to the violator, if any, resulting from the violation, the degree of culpability involved, any other penalty for the same incident, any history of prior violations, the nature, extent, and degree of success of any efforts of the violator to minimize or mitigate the effects of the discharge, the economic impact of the penalty on the violator, and any other matters as justice may require.

[§311(b)(8) added by PL 101–380]

(9) Mitigation of Damage.—In addition to establishing a penalty for the discharge of oil or a hazardous substance, the Administrator or the Secretary of the department in which the Coast Guard is operating may act to mitigate the damage to the public health or welfare caused by such discharge. The cost of such mitigation shall be deemed a cost incurred under subsection (c) of this section for the removal of such substance by the United States Government.

[§311(b)(9) added by PL 101–380]

(10) Recovery of Removal Costs.— Any costs of removal incurred in connection with a dis-

charge excluded by subsection (a)(2)(C) of this section shall be recoverable from the owner or operator of the source of the discharge in an action brought under section 309(b) of this Act.

[§311(b)(10) added by PL 101–380]

(11) Limitation.—Civil penalties shall not be assessed under both this section and section 309 for the same discharge.

[§311(b)(11) added by PL 101–380]

(12) Withholding Clearance.—If any owner, operator, or person in charge of a vessel is liable for a civil penalty under this subsection, or if reasonsable cause exists to believe that the owner, operator, or person in charge may be subject to a civil penalty under this subsection, the Secretary of the Treasury, upon the request of the Secretary of the department in which the Coast Guard is operating or the Administrator, shall with respect to such vessel refuse or revoke—

(A) the clearance required by section 4197 of the Revised Statutes of the United States (46 U.S.C. App. 91);

(B) a permit to proceed under sectin 4367 of the Revised Statutes of the United States (46 U.S.C. App. 313); and

(C) a permit to depart required under section 443 of the Tariff Act of 1930 (19 U.S.C. 1443);

as applicable. Clearance or a permit refused or revoked under this paragraph may be granted upon the filing of a bond or other surety satisfactory to the Secretary of the department in which the Coast Guard is operating or the Administrator.

[§311(b)(12) added by PL 102–388]

(c) Federal Removal Authority.—

(1) General Removal Requirement.—

(A) The President shall in accordance with the National Contingency Plan and any appropriate Area Contingency Plan, ensure effective and immediate removal of a discharge, and mitigation or prevention of a substantial threat of a discharge, of oil or a hazardous substance—

(i) into or on the navigable waters;

(ii) on the adjoining shorelines to the navigable waters;

(iii) into or on the waters of the exclusive economic zone; or

(iv) that may affect natural resources belonging to, appertaining to, or under the exclusive management authority of the United States.

(B) In carrying out this paragraph, the President may—

(i) remove or arrange for the removal of a discharge, and mitigate or prevent a substantial threat of a discharge, at any time;

(ii) direct or monitor all Federal, State, and private actions to remove a discharge; and

(iii) remove and, if necessary, destroy a vessel discharging, or threatening to discharge, by whatever means are available.

(2) Discharge Posing Substantial Threat to Public Health or Welfare.—

(A) If a discharge, or a substantial threat of a discharge, of oil or a hazardous substance from a vessel, offshore facility, or onshore facility is of such 'a size or character as to be a substantial threat to the public health or welfare of the United States (including but not limited to fish, shellfish, wildlife, other natural resources, and the public and private beaches and shorelines of the United States), the President shall direct all Federal, State, and private actions to remove the discharge or to mitigate or prevent the threat of the discharge.

(B) In carrying out this paragraph, the President may, without regard to any other provision of law governing contracting procedures or employment of personnel by the Federal Government—

(i) remove or arrange for the removal of the discharge, or mitigate or prevent the substantial threat of the discharge; and

(ii) remove and, if necessary, destroy a vessel discharging. or threatening to discharge, by whatever means are available.

[§311(c) revised by PL 101–380]

[Editor's Note: Section 4201(c) of PL 101–380 (the Oil Pollution Act of 1990) included provisions concerning the National Contingency Plan. Those provisions follow.]

(c) (3) Actions in Accordance with National Contingency Plan.—

(A) Each Federal agency, State, owner or operator, or other person participating in efforts under this subsection shall act in accordance with the National Contingency Plan or as directed by the President.

(B) An owner or operator participating in efforts under this subsection shall act in accordance with the National Contingency Plan and the applicable response plan required under subsection (j), or as directed by the President.

(4) Exemption From Liability.—

(A) person is not liable for removal costs or damages which result from actions taken or omitted to be taken in the course of rendering care, assistance, or advice consistent with the National Contingency Plan or as otherwise directed by the President.

(B) Subparagraph (A) does not apply—

(i) to a responsible party;

(ii) to a response under the Comprehensive Environmental Response, Compensation, and Liability Act of 1980 (42 U.S.C. 9601 et seq.);

(iii) with respect to personal injury or wrongful death; or

(iv) if the person is grossly negligent or engages in willful misconduct.

(C) A responsible party is liable for any removal costs and damages that another person is relieved of under subparagraph (A).

(5) Obligation and Liability of Owner or Operator not Affected.—Nothing in this subsection affects—

(A) the obligation of an owner or operator to respond immediately to a discharge, or the threat of a discharge, of oil; or

(B) the liability of a responsible party under the Oil Pollution Act of 1990.

(6) Responsible Party Defined.—For purposes of this subsection, the term 'responsible party' has the meaning given that term under section 1001 of the Oil Pollution Act of 1990.

(d) National Contingency Plan.—

[§311(d) revised by PL 101–380]

(1) Preparation by President.—The President shall prepare and publish a National Contingency Plan for removal of oil and hazardous substances pursuant to this section.

(2) Contents.—The National Contingency Plan shall provide for efficient, coordinated, and effective action to minimize damage from oil and hazardous substance discharges, including containment, dispersal, and removal of oil and hazardous substances, and shall include, but not be limited to, the following:

(A) Assignment of duties and responsibilities among Federal departments and agencies in coordination with State and local agencies and port authorities including, but not limited to, water pollution control and conservation and trusteeship of natural resources (including conservation of fish and wildlife).

(B) Identification, procurement, maintenance, and storage of equipment and supplies.

(C) Establishment or designation of Coast Guard strike teams, consisting of—

(i) personnel who shall be trained, prepared, and available to provide necessary services to carry out the National Contingency Plan;

(ii) adequate oil and hazardous substance pollution control equipment and material; and

(iii) a detailed oil and hazardous substance pollution and prevention plan, including measures to protect fisheries and wildlife.

(D) A system of surveillance and notice designed to safeguard against as well as ensure earliest possible notice of discharges of oil and hazardous substances and imminent threats of such discharges to the appropriate State and Federal agencies.

(E) Establishment of a national center to provide coordination and direction for operations in carrying out the Plan.

(F) Procedures and techniques to be employed in identifying, containing, dispersing, and removing oil and hazardous substances.

(G) A schedule, prepared in cooperation with the States, identifying—

(i) dispersants, othei chemicals, and othcr spill mitigating devices and substances, if any, that may be used in carrying out the Plan,

(ii) the waters in which such dispersants. other chemicals, and other spill mitigating devices and substances may be used, and

(iii) the quantities of such dispersant, other chemicals, or other spill mitigating device or substance which can be used safely in such waters, which schedule shall provide in the case of any dispersant, chemical, spill mitigating device or substance, or waters not specifically identified in such schedule that the President, or his delegate, may, on a case-by-case basis, identify the dispersants, other chemicals, and other spill mitigating devices and substances which may be used, the waters in which they may be used and the quantities which can be used safely in such waters.

(H) A system whereby the State or States affected by a discharge of oil or hazardous substance may act where necessary to remove such discharge and such State or States may be reimbursed in accordance with the Oil Pollution Act of 1990, in the case of any discharge of oil from a vessel or facility, for the reasonable costs incurred for that removal, from the Oil Spill Liability Trust Fund.

(I) Establishment of criteria and procedures to ensure immediate and effective Federal identification of, and response to, a discharge, or the threat of a discharge, that results in a substantial threat to the public health or welfare of the United States, as required under subsection (c)(2).

(J) Establishment of procedures and standards for removing a worst case discharge of oil, and for mitigating or preventing a substantial threat of such a discharge.

(K) Designation of the Federal official who shall be the Federal On-Scene Coordinator for each area for which an Area Contingency Plan is required to be prepared under subsection (j).

(L) Establishment of procedures for the coordination of activities of—

(i) Coast Guard strike teams established under subparagraph (C);

(ii) Federal On-Scene Coordinators designated under subparagraph (K);

(iii) District Response Groups established under subsection (j); and

(iv) Area Committees established under subsection (j).

(M) A fish and wildlife response plan, developed in consultation with the United States Fish and Wildlife Service, the National Oceanic and Atmospheric Administration, and other interested parties (including State fish and wildlife conservation officials), for the immediate and effective protection, rescue, and rehabilitation of, and the minimization of risk of damage to, fish and wildlife resources and their habitat that are harmed or that may be jeopardized by a discharge.

(3) Revisions and Amendments.—The President may, from time to time, as the President deems advisable, revise or otherwise amend the National Contingency Plan.

(4) Actions in Accordance with National Contingency Plan.—After publication of the National Contingency Plan, the removal of oil and hazardous substances and actions to minimize damage from oil and hazardous substance discharges shall, to the greatest extent possible, be in accordance with the National Contingency Plan.

(e) Civil Enforcement.—

[§311(e) revised by PL 101–380]

(1) Orders Protecting Public Health.—In addition to any action taken by State or local government, when the President determines that there may be an imminent and substantial threat to the public health or welfare of the United States, including fish, shellfish, and wildlife, public and private property, shorelines, beaches, habitat, and other living and nonliving natural resources under the jurisdiction or control of the United States, because of an actual or threatened discharge of oil or a hazardous substance from a vessel or facility in violation of subsection (b), the President may—

(A) require the Attorney General to secure any relief from any person, including the owner or operator of the vessel or facility, as may be necessary to abate such endangerment; or

(B) after notice to the affected State, take any other action under this section, including issuing administrative orders, that may be necessary to protect the public health and welfare.

(2) Jurisdiction of District Courts.— The district courts of the United States shall have jurisdiction to grant any relief under this subsection that the public interest and the equities of the case may require.

(f) (1) Except where an owner or operator can prove that a discharge was caused solely by (A) an act of God, (B) an act of war, (C) negligence on the part of the United States Government, or (D) an act or omission of a third party without regard to whether any such act or omission was or was not negligent, or any combination of the foregoing clauses, such owner or operator of any vessel from which oil or a hazardous substance is discharged in violation of subsection (b)(3) of this section shall, notwithstanding any other provision of law, be liable to the United States Government for the actual costs incurred under subsection (c) for the removal of such oil or substance by the United States Government in an amount not to exceed, in the case of an inland oil barge $125 per gross ton of such barge, or $125,000, whichever is greater, and in the case of any other vessel, $150 per gross ton of such vessel (or, for a vessel carrying oil or hazardous substances as cargo, $250,000), whichever is greater, except that where the United States can show that such discharge was the result of willful negligence or willful misconduct within the privity and knowledge of the owner, such owner or operator shall be liable to the United States Government for the full amount of such costs. Such costs shall constitute a maritime lien on such vessel which may be recovered in an action in rem in the district court of the United States for any district within which any vessel may be found. The United States may also bring an action against the owner or operator of such vessel in any court of competent jurisdiction to recover such costs.

(2) Except where an owner or operator of an onshore facility can prove that a discharge was caused solely by (A) an act of God, (B) an act of war, (C) negligence on the part of the United States Government, or (D) an act or omission of a third party without regard to whether any such act or omission was or was not negligent, or any combination of the foregoing clauses, such owner or operator of any such facility from which oil or a hazardous substance is discharged in violation of subsection (b)(3) of this section shall be liable to the United States Government for the actual costs incurred under subsection (c) for the removal of such oil or substance by the United States Government in an amount not to exceed $50,000,000, except that where the United States can show that such discharge was the result of willful negligence or willful misconduct within the privity and knowledge of the owner, such owner or operator shall be liable to the United States Government for the full amount of such costs. The United States may bring an action against the owner or operator of such facility in any court of competent jurisdiction to recover such costs. The Administrator is authorized, by regulation, after consultation with the Secretary of Commerce and the Small Business Administration, to establish reasonable and equitable classifications of those onshore facilities having a total fixed storage capacity of 1,000 barrels or less which he determines because of size, type, and location do not present a substantial risk of the discharge of oil or a hazardous substance in violation of subsection (b)(3) of this section, and apply with respect to such classifications differing limits of liability which may be less than the amount contained in this paragraph.

(3) Except where an owner or operator of an offshore facility can prove that a discharge was caused solely by (A) an act of God, (B) an act of war, (C) negligence on the part of the United States Government, or (D) an act or omission of a third party without regard to whether any such act or omission was or was not negligent, or any combination of the foregoing clauses, such owner or operator of any such facility from which oil or a hazardous substance is discharged in violation of subsection (b)(3) of this section shall, notwithstanding any other provision of law, be liable to the United States Government for the actual costs incurred under subsection (c) for the removal of such oil or substance by the United States Government in an amount not to exceed $50,000,000, except that where the United States can show that such discharge was the result of willful negligence or willful misconduct within the privity and knowledge of the owner, such owner or operator shall be liable to the United States Government for the full amount of such costs. The United States may bring an action against the owner or operator of such a facility in any court of competent jurisdiction to recover such costs.

(4) The costs of removal of oil or a hazardous substance for which the owner or operator of a vessel or onshore or offshore facility is liable under subsection (f) of this section shall include any costs or expenses incurred by the Federal Government or any State government in the restoration or replacement of natural resources damaged or destroyed as a result of a discharge of oil or a hazardous substance in violation of subsection (b) of this section.

(5) The President, or the authorized representative of any State, shall act on behalf of the public as trustee of the natural resources to recover for the costs of replacing or restoring such resources. Sums recovered shall be used to restore, rehabilitate, or acquire the equivalent of such natural resources by the appropriate agencies of the Federal Government, or the State government.

(g) Where the owner or operator of a vessel (other than an inland oil barge) carrying oil or hazardous substances as cargo or an onshore or offshore facility which handles or stores oil or hazardous substances in bulk, from which oil or a hazardous substance is discharged in violation of subsection (b) of this section, alleges that such discharge was caused solely by an act or omission of a third party, such owner or operator shall pay to the United States Government the actual costs incurred under subsection (c) for removal of such oil or substance and shall be entitled by subrogation to all rights of the United States Government to recover such costs from such third party under this subsection. In any case where an owner or operator of a vessel, of an onshore facility, or of an offshore facility, from which oil or a hazardous substance is discharged in violation of subsection (b)(3) of this section, proves that such discharge of oil or hazardous substance was caused solely by an act or omission of a third party, or was caused solely by such an act or omission in combination with an act of God, an act of war, or negligence on the part of the United States Government, such third party shall, not withstanding any other provision of law, be liable to the United States Government for the actual costs incurred under subsection (c) for removal of such oil or substance by the United States Government, except where such third party can prove that such discharge was caused solely by (A) an act of God, (B) an act of war, (C) negligence on the part of the United States Government, or (D) an act or omission of another party without regard to whether such act or omission was or was not negligent, or any combination of the foregoing clauses. If such third party was the owner or operator of a vessel which caused the discharge of oil or a hazardous substance in violation of subsection (b)(3) of this section, the liability of such third party under this subsection shall not exceed, in the case of an inland oil barge, $125 per gross ton of such barge, $125,000, whichever is greater, and in the case of any other vessel, $150 per gross ton of such vessel (or, for a vessel carrying oil or hazardous substances as cargo, $250,000), whichever is greater. In any other case the liability of such third party shall not exceed the limitation which would have been applicable to the owner or operator of the vessel or the onshore or offshore facility from which the discharge actually occurred if such owner or operator were liable. If the United States can show that the discharge of oil or a hazardous substance in violation of subsection (b)(3) of this section was the result of willful negligence or willful misconduct within the privity and knowledge of such third party, such third party shall be liable to the United States Government for the full amount of such removal costs. The United States may bring an action against the third party in any court of competent jurisdiction to recover such removal costs.

(h) The liabilities established by this section shall in no way affect any rights which (1) the owner or operator of a vessel or of an onshore facility or an offshore facility may have against any third party whose acts may in any way have caused or contributed to such discharge, or (2) The United States Government may have against and third party whose actions may in any way have caused or contributed to the discharge of oil or hazardous substance.

(i) In any case where an owner or operator of a vessel or an onshore facility or an offshore facility from which oil or a hazardous substance is discharged in violation of subsection (b) of this section acts to remove such oil or substance in accordance with regulations promulgated pursuant to this section, such owner or operator shall be entitled to recover the reasonable costs incurred in such removal upon establishing, in a suit which may be brought against the United States Government in the United States Court of Federal Claims, that such discharge was caused solely by (A) an act of God, (B) an act of war, (C) negligence on the part of the United States Government or (D) an act or omission of a third party without regard to whether such act or omission was or was not negligent, or of any combination of the foregoing clauses.

[§311(i) amended by PL 102–572]

(2)-(3) [repealed]

[§311(i)(1) and (3) amended by PL 97–164; (i)(1) designation deleted and (2) and (3) repealed by PL 101–380]

[Editor's Note: Section 2002(a) of PL 101–380 provides: "(a) Application.—Subsections (f), (g), (h), and (i) of section 311 of the Federal Water Pollution Control Act (33 U.S.C. 1321) shall not apply with respect to any incident for which liability is established under section 1002 of this Act."]

(j) National Response System.—

(1) In General.—Consistent with the National Contingency Plan required by subsection (c)(2) of this section, as soon as practicable after the effective date of this section, and from time to time thereafter, the President shall issue regulations consistent with maritime safety and with marine and navigation laws (A) establishing methods and procedures for removal of discharged oil and hazardous substances, (B) establishing criteria for the development and implementation of local and regional oil and hazardous substance removal contingency plans, (C) establishing procedures, methods, and equipment and other requirements for equipment to prevent discharges of oil and hazardous substances from vessels and from onshore facilities and offshore facilities, and to contain such discharges, and (D) governing the inspection of vessels carrying cargoes of oil and hazardous substances and the inspection of such cargoes in order to reduce the likelihood of discharges of oil from vessels in violation of this section.

[§311(j) and (j)(1) heads added by PL 101–380]

(2) National Response Unit.—The Secretary of the department in which the Coast Guard is operating shall establish a National Response Unit at Elizabeth City, North Carolina. The Secretary, acting through the National Response Unit—

(A) shall compile and maintain a comprehensive computer list of spill removal resources, personnel, and equipment that is available worldwide and within the areas designated by the President pursuant to paragraph (4), which shall be available to Federal and State agencies and the public;

(B) shall provide technical assistance, equipment, and other resources requested by a Federal On-Scene Coordinator;

(C) shall coordinate use of private and public personnel and equipment to remove a worst case discharge, and to mitigate or prevent a substantial threat of such a discharge, from a vessel, offshore facility, or onshore facility operating in or near an area designated by the President pursuant to paragraph (4);

(D) may provide technical assistance in the preparation of Area Contingency Plans required under paragraph (4);

(E) shall administer Coast Guard strike teams established under the National Contingency Plan;

(F) shall maintain on file all Area Contingency Plans approved by the President under this subsection; and

(G) shall review each of those plans that affects its responsibilities under this subsection.

[Former §311(j)(2) repealed and new (j)(2) added by PL 101–380]

(3) Coast Guard District Response Groups.—

(A) The Secretary of the department in which the Coast Guard is operating shall establish in each Coast Guard district a Coast Guard District Response Group.

(B) Each Coast Guard District Response Group shall consist of—

(i) The Coast Guard personnel and equipment, including firefighting equipment, of each port within the district;

(ii) additional prepositioned equipment; and

(iii) a district response advisory staff.

(C) Coast Guard district response groups—

(i) shall provide technical assistance, equipment, and other resources when required by a Federal On-Scene Coordinator;

(ii) shall maintain all Coast Guard response equipment within its district;

(iii) may provide technical assistance in the preparation of Area Contingency Plans required under paragraph (4); and

(iv) shall review each of those plans that affect its area of geographic responsibility.

[§311(j)(3) added by PL 101–380]

(4) Area Committees and Area Contingency Plans.—

(A) There is established for each area designated by the President an Area Committee comprised of members appointed by the President from qualified personnel of Federal, State, and local agencies.

(B) Each Area Committee, under the direction of the Federal On-Scene Coordinator for its area, shall—

(i) prepare for its area the Area Contingency Plan required under subparagraph (C);

(ii) work with State and local officials to enhance the contingency planning of those officials and to assure preplanning of joint response efforts, including appropriate procedures for mechanical recovery, dispersal, shoreline cleanup, protection of sensitive environmental areas, and protection, rescue, and rehabilitation of fisheries and wildlife; and

(iii) work with State and local officials to expedite decisions for the use of dispersants and other mitigating substances and devices.

(C) Each Area Committee shall prepare and submit to the President for approval an Area Contingency Plan for its area. The Area Contingency Plan shall—

(i) when implemented in conjunction with the National Contingency Plan, be adequate to remove a worst case discharge, and to mitigate or prevent a substantial threat of such a discharge, from a vessel, offshore facility, or onshore facility operating in or near the area;

(ii) describe the area covered by the plan, including the areas of special economic or environmental importance that might be damaged by a discharge;

(iii) describe in detail the responsibilities of an owner or operator and of Federal, State, and local agencies in removing a discharge, and in mitigating or preventing a substantial threat of a discharge;

(iv) list the equipment (including firefighting equipment), dispersants or other mitigating substances and devices, and personnel available to an owner or operator and Federal, State, and local agencies, to ensure an effective and immediate removal of a discharge, and to ensure mitigation or prevention of a substantial threat of a discharge;

(v) describe the procedures to be followed for obtaining an expedited decision regarding the use of dispersants;

(vi) describe in detail how the plan is integrated into other Area Contingency Plans and vessel, offshore facility, and onshore facility response plans approved under this subsection, and into operating procedures of the National Response Unit;

(vii) include any other information the President requires; and

(viii) be updated periodically by the Area Committee.

(D) The President shall—

(i) review and approve Area Contingency Plans under this paragraph; and

(ii) periodically review Area Contingency Plans so approved.

[§311(j)(4) added by PL 101–380]

[Editor's Note: Section 4202(b)(1) of PL 101–380 states: "(b) Implementation.—(1) Area Committees and Contingency Plans.—(A) Not later than 6 months after the date of the enactment of this Act, the President shall designate the areas for which Area Committees are established under section 311(j)(4) of the Federal Water Pollution Control Act, as amended by this Act. In designating such areas, the President shall ensure that all navigable waters, adjoining shorelines, and waters of the exclusive economic zone are subject to an Area Contingency Plan under that section. (B) Not later than 18 months after the date of the enactment of this Act, each Area Committee established under that section shall submit to the President the Area Contingency Plan required under that section. (C) Not later than 24 months after the date of the enactment of this Act, the President shall—(i) promptly review each plan; (ii) require amendments to any plan that does not meet the requirements of section 311(j)(4) of the Federal Water Pollution Control Act; and (iii) approve each plan that meets the requirements of that section."]

(5) Tank Vessel and Facility Response Plans.—

(A) The President shall issue regulations which require an owner or operator of a tank vessel or facility described in subparagraph (B) to prepare and submit to the president a plan for responding, to the maximum extent practicable, to a worst case discharge, and to a substantial threat of such a discharge, of oil or a hazardous substance.

(B) The tank vessels and facilities referred to in subparagraph (A) are the following:

(i) A tank vessel, as defined under section 2101 of title 46, United States Code.

(ii) An offshore facility.

(iii) An onshore facility that, because of its location, could reasonably be expected to cause substantial harm to the environment by discharging into or on the navigable waters, adjoining shorelines, or the exclusive economic zone.

(C) A response plan required under this paragraph shall—

(i) be consistent with the requirements of the National Contingency Plan and Area Contingency Plans;

(ii) identify the qualified individual having full authority to implement removal actions, and require immediate communications between the individual and the appropriate Federal official and the persons providing personnel and equipment pursuant to clause (iii);

(iii) identify, and ensure by contract or other means approved by the President the availability of, private personnel and equipment necessary to remove to the maximum extent practicable a worst case discharge (including a discharge resulting from fire or explosion), and to mitigate or prevent a substantial threat of such a discharge;

(iv) describe the training, equipment testing, periodic unannounced drills, and response actions of persons on the vessel or at the facility, to be carried out under the plan to ensure the safety of the vessel or facility and to mitigate or prevent the discharge, or the substantial threat of a discharge;

(v) be updated periodically; and

(vi) be resubmitted for approval of each significant change.

(D) With respect to any response plan submitted under this paragraph for an onshore facility that, because of its location, could reasonably be expected to cause significant and substantial harm to the environment by discharging into or on the navigable waters or adjoining shorelines or the exclusive economic zone, and with respect to each response plan submitted under this paragraph for a tank vessel or offshore facility, the President shall—

(i) promptly review such response plan;

(ii) require amendments to any plan that does not meet the requirements of this paragraph;

(iii) approve any plan that meets the requirements of this paragraph; and

(iv) review each plan periodically thereafter.

(E) A tank vessel, offshore facility, or onshore facility required to prepare a response plan under this subsection may not handle, store, or transport oil unless—

(i) in the case of a tank vessel, offshore facility, or onshore facility for which a response plan is reviewed by the President under subparagraph (D), the plan has been approved by the President; and

(ii) the vessel or facility is operating in compliance with the plan.

(F) Notwithstanding subparagraph (E), the President may authorize a tank vessel, offshore facility, or onshore facility to operate without a response plan approved under this paragraph, until not later than 2 years after the date of the submission to the President of a plan for the tank vessel or facility, if the owner or operator certifies that the owner or operator has ensured by contract or other means approved by the President the availability of private personnel and equipment necessary to respond, to the maximum extent practicable, to a worst case discharge or a substantial threat of such a discharge.

(G) The owner or operator of a tank vessel, offshore facility, or onshore facility may not claim as a defense to liability under title I of the Oil Pollution Act of 1990 that the owner or operator was acting in accordance with an approved response plan.

(H) The Secretary shall maintain, in the Vessel Identification system established under chapter 125 of title 46, United States Code, the dates of approval and review of a response plan under this paragraph for each tank vessel that is a vessel of the United States.

[§311(j)(5) added by PL 101–380]

[Editor's Note: Section 4204(b)(4) of PL 101–380 provides: "(4) Tank Vessel and Facility Response Plans; Transition Provision; Effective Date of Prohibition.—(A) Not later than 24 months after the date of the enactment of this Act, the President shall issue regulations for tank vessel and facility response plans under section 311(j)(5) of the Federal Water Pollution Control Act, as amended by this Act. (B) During the period beginning 30 months after the date of the enactment of this paragraph and ending 36 months after the date of enactment, a tank vessel or facility for which a response plan is required to be prepared under section 311(j)(5) of the Federal Water Pollution Control Act, as amended by this Act, may not handle, store, or transport oil unless the owner or operator thereof has submitted such a plan to the President. (C) Subparagraph (E) of section 311(j)(5) of the Federal Water Pollution Control Act, as amended by this Act, shall take effect 36 months after the date of the enactment of this Act."]

(6) Equipment Requirements and Inspection.—Not later than 2 years after the date of enactment of this section, the President shall require—

(A) periodic inspection of containment booms, skimmers, vessels, and other major equipment used to remove discharges; and

(B) vessels operating on navigable waters and carrying oil or a hazardous substance in bulk as cargo to carry appropriate removal equipment that employs the best technology economically feasible and that is compatible with the safe operation of the vessel.

[§311(j)(6) added by PL 101–380]

(7) Area Drills.—The President shall periodically conduct drills of removal capability, without prior notice, in areas for which Area Contingency Plans are required under this subsection and under relevant tank vessel and facility response plans. The drills may include participation by Federal, State, and local agencies, the owners and operators of vessels and facilities in the area, and private industry. The President may publish annual reports on these drills, including assessments of the effectiveness of the plans and a list of amendments made to improve plans.

[§311(j)(7) added by PL 101-380]

(8) United States Government not Liable.—The United States Government is not liable for any damages arising from actions or omissions relating to any response plan required by this section.

[§311(j)(8) added by PL 101-380]

(k) [Repealed]

[§311(k) repealed by PL 101–380]

[Editor's Note: Section 2002(b)(2) of PL 101–380 repealed 311(k) of this Act and stipulated, "(2) ... Any amounts remaining in the revolving fund established under that subsection shall be deposited in the Fund. The Fund shall assume all liability incurred by the revolving fund established under that subsection."]

(l) The President is authorized to delegate the administration of this section to the heads of those Federal departments, agencies, and instrumentalities which he determines to be appropriate. Each such department, agency, and instrumentality, in order to avoid duplication of effort, shall, whenever appropriate, utilize the personnel, services, and facilities of other Federal departments, agencies, and instrumentalities.

[§311(l) amended by PL 101–380]

(m) Administrative Provisions.—

[§311(m) revised by PL 101–380]

(1) For Vessels.—Anyone authorized by the President to enforce the provisions of this section with respect to any vessel may, except as to public vessels—

(A) board and inspect any vessel upon the navigable waters of the United States or the waters of the contiguous zone,

(B) with or without a warrant, arrest any person who in the presence or view of the authorized person violates the provisions of this section or any regulation issued thereunder, and

(C) execute any warrant or other process issued by an officer or court of competent jurisdiction.

(2) For Facilities.—

(A) Recordkeeping.—Whenever, required to carry out the purposes of this section, the Administrator or the Secretary of the Department in which the Coast Guard is operating shall require the owner or operator of a facility to which this section applies to establish and maintain such records, make such reports, install, use, and maintain such monitoring equipment and methods, and provide such other information as the Administrator or Secretary, as the case may be, may require to carry out the objectives of this section.

(B) Entry and Inspection.—Whenever required to carry out the purposes of this section, the Administrator or the Secretary of the Department in which the Coast Guard is operating or an authorized representative of the Administrator or Secretary, upon presentation of appropriate credentials, may—

(i) enter and inspect any facility to which this section applies, including any facility at which any records are required to be maintained under subparagraph (A); and

(ii) at reasonable times, have access to and copy any records, take samples, and inspect any monitoring equipment or methods required under subparagraph (A).

(C) Arrests and Execution of Warrants.—Anyone authorized by the Administrator or the Secretary of the department in which the Coast Guard is operating to enforce the provisions of this section with respect to any facility may—

(i) with or without a warrant, arrest any person who violates the provisions of this section or any regulation issued thereunder in the presence or view of the person so authorized; and

(ii) execute any warrant or process issued by an officer or court of competent jurisdiction.

(D) Public Access.—Any records, reports, or information obtained under this paragraph shall be subject to the same public access and disclosure requirements which are applicable to records, reports, and information obtained pursuant to section 308.

(n) The several district courts of the United States are invested with jurisdiction for any actions, other than actions pursuant to subsection (i)(1), arising under this section. In the case of Guam and the Trust Territory of the Pacific Islands, such actions may be brought in the district court of Guam, and in the case of the Virgin Islands such actions may be brought in the district court of the Virgin Islands. In the case of American Samoa and the Trust Territory of the Pacific Islands, such actions may be brought in the District Court of the United States for the District of Hawaii and such court shall have jurisdiction of such actions. In the case of the Canal Zone, such actions may be brought in the United States District Court for the District of the Canal Zone.

(o) (1) Nothing in this section shall affect or modify in any way the obligations of any owner or operator of any vessel, or of any owner or operator of any onshore facility or offshore facility to any person or agency under any provision of law for damages to any publicly owned or privately owned property resulting from a discharge of any oil or hazardous substance or from the removal of any such oil or hazardous substance.

(2) Nothing in this section shall be construed as preempting any State or political subdivision thereof from imposing any requirement or liability with respect to the discharge of oil or hazardous substance into any waters within such State, or with respect to any removal activities related to such discharge.

[§311(o)(2) amended by PL 101–380]

(3) Nothing in this section shall be construed as affecting or modifying any other existing authority of any Federal department, agency, or instrumentality, relative to onshore or offshore facilities under this Act or any other provision of law, or to affect any State or local law not in conflict with this section.

(p) [Repealed]

[§311(p) repealed by PL 101–380]

(q) The President is authorized to establish, with respect to any class or category of onshore or offshore facilities, a maximum limit of liability under subsections (f)(2) and (3) of this section of less than $50,000,000, but not less than $8,000,000.

(r) Nothing in this section shall be construed to impose or authorize the imposition of any limitation on liability under the Outer Continental Shelf Lands Act or the Deepwater Port Act of 1974.

(s) The Oil Spill Liability Trust Fund established under section 9509 of the Internal Revenue Code of 1986 (26 U.S.C. 9509) shall be available to carry out subsections (b), (c), (d), (j), and (1) as those subsections apply to discharges, and substantial threats of discharges, of oil. Any amounts received by the United States under this section shall be deposited in the Oil Spill Liability Trust Fund.

[§311(s) added by PL 101–380]

§1322. Marine Sanitation Devices [Sec. 312]

(a) For the purpose of this section, the term—

(1) "new vessel" includes every description of water-craft or other artificial contrivance used, or capable of being used, as a means of transportation on the navigable waters, the construction of which is initiated after promulgation of standards and regulation under this section;

(2) "existing vessel" includes every description of watercraft or other artificial contrivance used, or capable of being used, as a means of transportation on the navigable waters, the construction of which is initiated before promulgation of standards and regulations under this section;

(3) "public vessel" means a vessel owned or bare-boat-chartered and operated by the United States, by a State or political subdivision thereof, or by a foreign nation, except when such vessel is engaged in commerce;

(4) "United States" includes the States, the District of Columbia, the Commonwealth of Puerto Rico, the Virgin Islands, Guam, American Samoa, the Canal Zone, and the Trust Territory of the Pacific Islands;

(5) "marine sanitation device" includes any equipment for installation on board a vessel which is designed to receive, retain, treat, or discharge sewage, and any process to treat such sewage;

(6) "sewage" means human body wastes and the wastes from toilets and other receptacles intended to receive or retain body wastes except that, with respect to commercial vessels on the Great Lakes such term shall include graywater;

(7) "manufacture" means any person engaged in the manufacturing, assembling, or importation of marine sanitation devices or of vessels subject to standards and regulations promulgated under this section;

(8) "person" means an individual, partnership, firm, corporation, or association, but does not include an individual on board a public vessel;

(9) "discharge" includes, but is not limited to, any spilling, leaking, pumping, pouring, emitting, emptying or dumping;

(10) "commercial vessels" means those vessels used in the business of transporting property for compensation or hire, or in transporting property in the business of the owner, lessee, or operator of the vessel;

(11) "graywater" means galley, bath, and shower water.

(b) (1) As soon as possible, after the enactment of this section and subject to the provisions of section 101(j) of this Act, the Administrator, after consultation with the Secretary of the department in which the Coast Guard is operating, after giving appropriate consideration to the economic costs involved, and within the limits of available technology, shall promulgate Federal standards of performance for marine sanitation devices (hereafter in this section referred to as "standards") which shall be designed to prevent the discharge of untreated or inadequately treated sewage into or upon the navigable waters from new vessels and existing vessels, except vessels not equipped with installed toilet facilities. Such standards and standards established under subsection (c)(1)(B) of this section shall be consistent with maritime safety and the marine and navigation laws and regulations and shall be coordinated with the regulations issued under this subsection by the Secretary of the department in which the Coast Guard is operating. The Secretary of the department in which the Coast Guard is operating shall promulgate regulations, which are consistent with standards promulgated under this subsection and subsection (c) of this section and with maritime safety and the marine and navigation laws and regulations governing the design, construction, installation, and operation of any marine sanitation device on board such vessels.

(2) Any existing vessel equipped with a marine sanitation device on the date of promulgation of initial standards and regulations under this section, which device is in compliance with such initial standards and regulations, shall be deemed in compliance with this section until such time as the device is replaced or is found not to be in compliance with such initial standards and regulations.

(c) (1) (A) Initial standards and regulations under this section shall become effective for new vessels two years after promulgation; and for existing vessels five years after promulgation. Revisions of standards and regulations shall be effective upon promulgation, unless another effective date is specified, except that no revision shall take effect before the effective date of the standard or regulation being revised.

(B) The Administrator shall, with respect to commercial vessels on the Great Lakes, establish standards which require at a minimum the equivalent of secondary treatment as defined under section 304(d) of this Act. Such standards and regulations shall take effect for existing vessels after such time as the Administrator determines to be reasonable for the upgrading of marine sanitation devices to attain such standard.

(2) The Secretary of the department in which the Coast Guard is operating with regard to his regulatory authority established by this section, after consultation with the Administrator, may distinguish among classes, types, and sizes of vessels as well as between new and existing vessels, and may waive applicability of standards and regulations as necessary or appropriate for such classes, types, and sizes of vessels (including existing vessels equipped with marine sanitation devices on the date of promulgation of the initial standards required by this section), and, upon application, for individual vessels.

(d) The provisions of this section and the standards and regulations promulgated hereunder apply to vessels owned and operated by the United States unless the Secretary of Defense finds that compliance would not be in the interest of national security. With respect to vessels owned and operated by the Department of Defense, regulations under the last sentence of subsection (b)(1) of this section and certifications under subsection (g)(2) of this section shall be promulgated and issued by the Secretary of Defense.

(e) Before the standards and regulations under this section are promulgated, the Administrator and the Secretary of the department in which the Coast Guard is operating shall consult with the Secretary of State; the Secretary of Health and Human Services; the Secretary of Defense; the Secretary of the Treasury; the Secretary of Commerce; other interested Federal agencies; and the States and industries interested; and otherwise comply with the requirements of section 553 of title 5 of the United States Code.

(f) (1) (A) Except as provided in subparagraph (B), after the effective date of the initial standards and regulations promulgated under this section, no State or political subdivision thereof shall adopt or enforce any statute or regulation of such State or political subdivision with respect to the design, manufacture, or installation or use of any marine sanitation devise on any vessel subject to the provisions of this section.

[§312(f)(1)(A) designated and amended by PL 100–4]

(B) A State may adopt and enforce a statute or regulation with respect to the design, manufacture, or installation or use of any marine sanitation device on a houseboat, if such statute or regulation is more stringent than the standards and regulations promulgated under this section. For purposes of this paragraph, the term 'houseboat' means a vessel which, for a period of time determined by the State in which the vessel is located, is used primarily as a residence and is not used primarily as a means of transportation.

[§312(f)(1)(B) added by PL 100–4]

(2) If after promulgation of the initial standards and regulations and prior to their effective date, a vessel is equipped with a marine sanitation device in compliance with such standards and regulations and the installation and operation of such device is in accordance with such standards and regulations, such standards and regulations shall, for the purposes of paragraph (1) of this subsection, become effective with respect to such vessel on the date of such compliance.

(3) After the effective date of the initial standards and regulations promulgated under this section, if any State determines that the protection and enhancement of the quality of some or all of the waters within such State require greater environmental protection, such State may completely prohibit the discharge from all vessels of any sewage, whether treated or not, into such waters, except that no such prohibition shall apply until the Administrator determines that adequate facilities for the safe and sanitary removal and treatment of sewage from all vessels are reasonably available for such water to which such prohibition would apply. Upon application of the State, the Administrator shall make such determination within 90 days of the date of such application.

(4) (A) If the Administrator determines upon application by a State that the protection and enhancement of the quality of specified waters within such State requires such a prohibition, he shall by regulation completely prohibit the discharge from a vessel of any sewage (whether treated or not) into such waters.

(B) Upon application by a State, the Administrator shall, by regulation, establish a drinking water intake zone in any waters within such State and prohibit the discharge of sewage from vessels within that zone.

(g) (1) No manufacturer of a marine sanitation device shall sell, offer for sale, or introduce or deliver for introduction in interstate commerce, or import into the United States for sale or resale any marine sanitation device manufactured after the effective date of the standards and regulations promulgated under this section unless such device is in all material respects substantially the same as a test device certified under this subsection.

(2) Upon application of the manufacturer, the Secretary of the department in which the Coast Guard is operating shall so certify a marine sanitation device if he determines, in accordance with the provisions of this paragraph, that it meets the appropriate standards and regulations promulgated under this section. The Secretary of the department in which the Coast Guard is operating shall test or require such testing of the device in accordance with procedures set forth by the Administrator as to standards of performance and for such other purposes as may be appropriate. If the Secretary of the department in which the Coast Guard is operating determines that the device is satisfactory from the standpoint of safety and any other requirements of maritime law or regulation, and after consideration of the design, installation, operation, material, or other appropriate factors, he shall certify the device. Any device manufactured by such manufacturer which is in all material respects substantially the same as the certified test device shall be deemed to be in conformity with the appropriate standards and regulations established under this section.

(3) Every manufacturer shall establish and maintain such records, make such reports, and provide such information as the Administrator or the Secretary of the department in which the Coast Guard is operating may reasonably require to enable him to determine whether such manufacturer has acted or is acting in compliance with this section and regulations issued thereunder and shall, upon request of an officer or employee duly designated by the Administrator or the Secretary of the department in which the Coast Guard is operating, permit such officer or employee at reasonable times to have access to and copy such records. All information reported to or otherwise obtained by the Administrator or the Secretary of the department in which the Coast Guard is operating or their representatives pursuant to this subsection which contains or relates to a trade secret or other matter referred in section 1905 of title 18 of the United States Code shall be considered confidential for the purpose of that section, except that such information may be disclosed to other officers or employees concerned with carrying out this section. This paragraph shall not apply in the case of the construction of a vessel by an individual for his own use.

(h) After the effective date of standards and regulations promulgated under this section, it shall be unlawful—

(1) for the manufacturer of any vessel subject to such standards and regulations to manufacture for sale, to sell or offer for sale, or to distribute for sale or resale any such vessel unless

it is equipped with a marine sanitation device which is in all material respects substantially the same as the appropriate test device certified pursuant to this section;

(2) for any person, prior to the sale or delivery of a vessel subject to such standards and regulations to the ultimate purchaser, wrongfully to remove or render inoperative any certified marine sanitation device or element of design of such device installed in such vessel;

(3) for any person to fail or refuse to permit access to or copying of records or to fail to make reports or provide information required under this section; and

(4) for a vessel subject to such standards and regulations to operate on the navigable waters of the United States, if such vessel is not equipped with an operable marine sanitation device certified pursuant to this section.

(i) The district courts of the United States shall have jurisdictions to restrain violations of subsection (g)(1) of this section and subsections (h)(1) through (3) of this section. Actions to restrain such violations shall be brought by, and in, the name of the United States. In case of contumacy or refusal to obey a subpena served upon any person under this subsection, the district court of the United States for any district in which such person is found or resides or transacts business, upon application by the United States and after notice to such person, shall have jurisdiction to issue an order requiring such person to appear and give testimony or to appear and produce documents, and any failure to obey such order of the court may be punished by such court as a contempt thereof.

(j) Any person who violates subsection (g)(1) of this section or clause (1) or (2) of subsection (h) of this section shall be liable to a civil penalty of not more than $5,000 for each violation. Any person who violates clause (4) of subsection (h) of this section or any regulation issued pursuant to this section shall be liable to a civil penalty of not more than $2,000 for each violation. Each violation shall be a separate offense. The Secretary of the department in which the Coast Guard is operating may assess and compromise any such penalty. No penalty shall be assessed until the person charged shall have been given notice and an opportunity for a hearing on such charge. In determining the amount of the penalty, or the amount agreed upon in compromise, the gravity of the violation, and the demonstrated good faith of the person charged in attempting to achieve rapid compliance, after notification of a violation, shall be considered by said Secretary.

(k) The provisions of this section shall be enforced by the Secretary of the department in which the Coast Guard is operating and he may utilize by agreement, with or without reimbursement, law enforcement officers or other personnel and facilities of the Administrator, other Federal agencies, or the States to carry out the provisions of this section. The provisions of this section may also be enforced by a State.

[§312(k) amended by PL 100–4]

(l) Anyone authorized by the Secretary of the department in which the Coast Guard is operating to enforce the provisions of this section may, except as to public vessels, (1) board and inspect any vessel upon the navigable waters of the United States and (2) execute any warrant or other process issued by an officer or court of competent jurisdiction.

(m) In the case of Guam and the Trust Territory of the Pacific Islands, actions arising under this section may be brought in the district court of Guam, and in the case of the Virgin Islands such actions may be brought in the district court of the Virgin Islands. In the case of American Samoa and the Trust Territory of the Pacific Islands, such actions may be brought in the District Court of the United States for the District of Hawaii and such court shall have jurisdiction of such actions. In the case of the Canal Zone, such action may be brought in the District Court for the District of the Canal Zone.

§1323. Federal Facilities Pollution Control
[Sec. 313]

(a) Each department, agency, or instrumentality of the executive, legislative, and judicial branches of the Federal Government (1) having jurisdiction over any property or facility, or (2) engaged in any activity resulting, or which may result, in the discharge or runoff of pollutants, and each officer, agent, or employee thereof in the performance of his official duties, shall be subject to, and comply with, all Federal, State, interstate, and local requirements, administrative authority, and process and sanctions respecting the control and abatement of water pollution in the same manner, and to the same extent as any nongovernmental entity including the payment of reasonable service charges. The preceding sentence shall apply (A) to any requirement whether substantive or procedural (including any recordkeeping or reporting requirement, any requirement respecting permits and any other requirement, whatsoever),

(B) to the exercise of any Federal, State, or local administrative authority, and (C) to any process and sanction, whether enforced in Federal, State, or local courts or in any other manner. This subsection shall apply notwithstanding any immunity of such agencies, officers, agents, or employees under any law or rule of law. Nothing in this section shall be construed to prevent any department, agency, or instrumentality of the Federal Government, or any officer, agent, or employee thereof in the performance of his official duties, from reporting to the appropriate Federal district court any proceeding to which the department, agency, or instrumentality or officer, agent, or employee thereof is subject pursuant to this section, and any such proceeding may be removed in accordance with 28 U.S.C. 1441 et seq. No officer, agent, or employee of the United States shall be personally liable for any civil penalty arising from the performance of his official duties, for which he is not otherwise liable, and the United States shall be liable only for those civil penalties arising under Federal law or imposed by a State or local court to enforce an order or the process of such court. The President may exempt any effluent source of any department, agency, or instrumentality in the executive branch from compliance with any such a requirement if he determines it to be in the paramount interest of the United States to do so; except that no exemption may be granted from the requirements of section 306 or 307 of this Act. No such exemptions shall be granted due to lack of appropriation unless the President shall have specifically requested such appropriation as a part of the budgetary process and the Congress shall have failed to make available such requested appropriation. Any exemption shall be for a period not in excess of one year, but additional exemptions may be granted for periods of not to exceed one year upon the President's making a new determination. The President shall report each January to the Congress all exemptions from the requirements of this section granted during the preceding calendar year, together with his reason for granting such exemption. In addition to any such exemption of a particular effluent source, the President may, if he determines it to be in the paramount interest of the United States to do so, issue regulations exempting from compliance with the requirements of this section any weaponry, equipment, aircraft, vessels, vehicles, or other classes or categories of property, and access to such property, which are owned or operated by the Armed Forces of the United States (including the Coast Guard) or by the National Guard of any State and which are uniquely military in nature. The President shall reconsider the need for such regulations at three-year intervals.

(b) (1) The Administrator shall coordinate with the head of each department, agency, or instrumentality of the Federal Government having jurisdiction over any property or facility utilizing federally owned wastewater facilities to develop a program of cooperation for utilizing wastewater control systems utilizing those innovative treatment processes and techniques for which guidelines have been promulgated under section 304(d)(3). Such program shall include an inventory of property and facilities which could utilize such processes and techniques.

(2) Construction shall not be initiated for facilities for treatment of wastewater at any Federal property or facility after September 30, 1979, if alternative methods for wastewater treatment at such property or facility utilizing innovative treatment processes and techniques, including but not limited to methods utilizing recycle and reuse techniques and land treatment are not utilized, unless the life cycle cost of the alternative treatment works exceeds the life cycle cost of the most cost effective alternative by more than 15 per centum. The Administrator may waive the application of this paragraph in any case where the Administrator determines it to be in the public interest, or that compliance with this paragraph would interfere with the orderly compliance with conditions of a permit issued pursuant to section 402 of this Act.

§1324. Clean Lakes [Sec. 314]

(a) Establishment and Scope of Program.—

[§314(a) revised by PL 100–4]

(1) State program requirements.— Each State on a biennial basis shall prepare and submit to the Administrator for his approval—

(A) an identification and classification according to eutrophic condition of all publicly owned lakes in such State;

(B) a description of procedures, processes, and methods (including land use requirements), to control sources of pollution of such lakes;

(C) a description of methods and procedures, in conjunction with appropriate Federal agencies, to restore the quality of such lakes;

(D) methods and procedures to mitigate the harmful effects of high acidity, including innovative methods of neutralizing and restoring buffering capacity of lakes and methods of removing from lakes toxic metals and other toxic substances mobilized by high acidity;

(E) a list and description of those publicly owned lakes in such State for which uses are known to be impaired, including those lakes which are known not to meet applicable water quality standards or which require implementation of control programs to maintain compliance with applicable standards and those lakes in which water quality has deteriorated as a result of high acidity that may reasonably be due to acid deposition; and

(F) an assessment of the status and trends of water quality in lakes in such State, including but not limited to, the nature and extent of pollution loading from point and nonpoint sources and the extent to which the use of lakes is impaired as a result of such pollution, particularly with respect to toxic pollution.

(2) Submission as Part of 305(b)(1) Report.—The information required under paragraph (1) shall be included in the report required under section 305(b)(1) of this Act, beginning with the report required under such section by April 1, 1988.

(3) Report of Administrator.—Not later than 180 days after receipt from the States of the biennial information required under paragraph (1), the Administrator shall submit to the Committee on Public Works and Transportation of the House of Representatives and the Committee on Environment and Public Works of the Senate a report on the status of water quality in lakes in the United States, including the effectiveness of the methods and procedures described in paragraph (1)(D).

(4) Eligibility Requirement.—Beginning after April 1, 1988, a State must have submitted the information required under paragraph (1) in order to receive grant assistance under this section.

(b) The Administrator shall provide financial assistance to States in order to carry out methods and procedures approved by him under subsection (a) of this section. The Administrator shall provide financial assistance to States to prepare the identification and classification surveys required in subsection (a)(1) of this section.

[§314(b) amended by PL 100–41]

(c) (1) The amount granted to any State for any fiscal year under subsection (b) of this section shall not exceed 70 per centum of the funds expended by such State in such year for carrying out approved methods and procedures under subsection (a) of this Section.

[§314(c)(1) amended by PL 100–4]

(2) There is authorized to be appropriated $50,000,000 for the fiscal year ending June 30, 1973; $100,000,000 for the fiscal year 1974; $150,000,000 for the fiscal year 1975, $50,000,000 for fiscal year 1977, $60,000,000 for fiscal year 1978, $60,000,000 for fiscal year 1979, $60,000,000 for fiscal year 1980, $30,000,000 for fiscal year 1981, $30,000,00 for fiscal year 1982, such sums as may be necessary for fiscal years 1983 through 1985, and $30,000,000 per fiscal year for each of the fiscal years 1986 through 1990 for grants to States under subsection (b) of this section which sums shall remain available until expended. The Administrator shall provide for an equitable distribution of such sums to the States with approved methods and procedures under subsection (a) of this section.

[§314(c)(2) amended by PL 100–4]

(d) Demonstration Program.—

[§314(d) added by PL 100–4]

(1) General Requirements.—The Administrator is authorized and directed to establish and conduct at locations throughout the Nation a lake water quality demonstration program. The program shall, at a minimum—

(A) develop cost effective technologies for the control of pollutants to preserve or enhance lake water quality while optimizing multiple lakes uses;

(B) control nonpoint sources of pollution which are contributing to the degradation of water quality in lakes;

(C) evaluate the feasibility of implementing regional consolidated pollution control strategies;

(D) demonstrate environmentally preferred techniques for the removal and disposal of contaminated lake sediments;

(E) develop improved methods for the removal of silt, stumps, aquatic growth, and other obstructions which impair the quality of lakes;

(F) construct and evaluate silt traps and other devices or equipment to prevent or abate the deposit of sediment in lakes; and

(G) demonstrate the costs and benefits of utilizing dredged material from lakes in the reclamation of despoiled land.

(2) Geographical Requirements.— Demonstration projects authorized by this subsection

shall be undertaken to reflect a variety of geographical and environmental conditions. As a priority, the Administrator shall undertake demonstration projects at Lake Champlain, New York and Vermont; Lake Houston, Texas; Beaver Lake, Arkansas; Greenwood Lake and Belcher Creek, New Jersey; Deal Lake, New Jersey; Alcyon Lake, New Jersey; Gorton's Pond, Rhode Island; Lake Washington, Rhode Island; Lake Bomoseen, Vermont; Sauk Lake, Minnesota; and Lake Worth, Texas.

[§314(d)(2) amended by PL 101–596]

(3) Reports.—The Administrator shall report annually to the Committee on Public Works and Transportation of the House of Representatives and the Committee on Environment and Public Works of the Senate on work undertaken pursuant to this subsection. Upon completion of the program authorized by this subsection, the Administrator shall submit to such committees a final report on the results of such program, along with recommendations for further measures to improve the water quality of the Nation's lakes.

(4) Authorization of Appropriations.—

(A) In General.—There is authorized to be appropriated to carry out this subsection not to exceed $40,000,000 for fiscal years beginning after September 30, 1986, to remain available until expended.

(B) Special Authorizations.—

(i) Amount.—There is authorized to be appropriated to carry out subsection (b) with respect to subsection (a)(1)(D) not to exceed $15,000,000 for fiscal years beginning after September 30, 1986, to remain available until expended.

(ii) Distribution of Funds.—The Administrator shall provide for an equitable distribution of sums appropriated pursuant to this subparagraph among States carrying out approved methods and procedures. Such distribution shall be based on the relative needs of each such State for the mitigation of the harmful effects on lakes and other surface waters of high acidity that may reasonably be due to acid deposition or acid mine drainage.

(iii) Grants as Additional Assistance.—The amount of any grant to a State under this subparagraph shall be in addition to, and not in lieu of, any other Federal financial assistance.

§1325. National Study Commission [Sec. 315]

(a) There is established a National Study Commission, which shall make a full and complete investigation and study of all of the technological aspects of achieving, and all aspects of the total economic, social, and environmental effects of achieving or not achieving, the effluent limitations and goals set forth for 1983 in section 301(b)(2) of this Act.

(b) Such Commission shall be composed of fifteen members, including five members of the Senate, who are members of the Public Works committee, appointed by the President of the Senate, five members of the House, who are members of the Public Works committee, appointed by the Speaker of the House, and five members of the public appointed by the President. The Chairman of such Commission shall be elected from among its members.

(c) In the conduct of such study, the Commission is authorized to contract with the National Academy of Sciences and the National Academy of Engineering (acting through the National Research Council), the National Institute of Ecology, Brookings Institution, and other nongovernmental entities, for the investigation of matters within their competence.

(d) The heads of the departments, agencies and instrumentalities of the executive branch of the Federal Government shall cooperate with the Commission in carrying out the requirements of this section, and shall furnish to the Commission such information as the Commission deems necessary to carry out this section.

(e) A report shall be submitted to the Congress of the results of such investigation and study, together with recommendations, not later than three years after the date of enactment of this title.

(f) The members of the Commission who are not officers or employees of the United States, while attending conferences or meetings of the Commission or while otherwise serving at the request of the Chairman shall be entitled to receive compensation at a rate not in excess of the maximum rate of pay for grade GS–18, as provided in the General Schedule under section 5332 of title V of the United States Code, including traveltime and while away from their homes or regular places of business they may be allowed travel expenses, including per diem in lieu of subsistence as authorized by law (5 U.S.C. 73b–2) for persons in the Government service employed intermittently.

(g) In addition to authority to appoint personnel subject to the provisions of title 5, United States Code, governing appointments in the competitive service, and to pay such personnel in accordance with the provisions of chapter 51 and subchapter III of chapter 53 of such title relating to classification and General Schedule pay rates, the Commission shall have authority to enter into contracts with private or public organizations who shall furnish the Commission with such administrative and technical personnel as may be necessary to carry out the purpose of this section. Personnel furnished by such organizations under this subsection are not, and shall not be considered to be, Federal employees for any purposes, but in the performance of their duties shall be guided by the standards which apply to employees of the legislative branches under rules 41 and 43 of the Senate and House of Representatives, respectively.

(h) There is authorized to be appropriated, for use in carrying out this section, not to exceed $17,250,000.

§1326. Thermal Discharges [Sec. 316]

(a) With respect to any point source otherwise subject to the provisions of section 301 or section 306 of this Act, whenever the owner or operator of any such source, after opportunity for public hearing, can demonstrate to the satisfaction of the Administrator (or, if appropriate, the State) that any effluent limitation proposed for the control of the thermal component of any discharge from such source will require effluent limitations more stringent than necessary to assure the projection and propagation of a balanced, indigenous population of shellfish, fish, and wildlife in and on the body of water into which the discharge is to be made, the Administrator (or, if appropriate, the State) may impose an effluent limitation under such sections for such plant, with respect to the thermal component of such discharge (taking into account the interaction of such thermal component with other pollutants), that will assure the protection and propagation of a balanced, indigenous population of shellfish, fish, and wildlife in and on that body of water.

(b) Any standard established pursuant to section 301 or section 306 of this Act and applicable to a point source shall require that the location, design, construction, and capacity of cooling water intake structures reflect the best technology available for minimizing adverse environmental impact.

(c) Notwithstanding any other provision of this Act, any point source of a discharge having a thermal component, the modification of which point source is commenced after the date of enactment of the Federal Water Pollution Control Act Amendments of 1972 and which, as modified, meets effluent limitations established under section 301, or, if more stringent, effluent limitations established under section 303 and which effluent limitations will assure protection and propagation of a balanced, indigenous population of shellfish, fish, and wildlife in or on the water into which the discharge is made, shall not be subject to any more stringent effluent limitation with respect to the thermal component of its discharge during a ten year period beginning on the date of completion of such modification or during the period of depreciation or amortization of such facility for the purpose of section 167 or 169 (or both) of the Internal Revenue Code of 1954, whichever period ends first.

§1327. Financing Study [Sec. 317]

(a) The Administrator shall continue to investigate and study the feasibility of alternate methods of financing the cost of preventing, controlling and abating pollution as directed in the Water Quality Improvement Act of 1970 (Public Law 91–224), including, but not limited to, the feasibility of establishing a pollution abatement trust fund. The results of such investigation and study shall be reported to the Congress not later than two years after enactment of this title, together with recommendations of the Administrator for financing the programs for preventing, controlling and abating pollution for the fiscal years beginning after fiscal year 1976, including any necessary legislation.

(b) There is authorized to be appropriated for use in carrying out this section, not to exceed $1,000,000.

§1328. Aquaculture [Sec. 318]

(a) The Administrator is authorized, after public hearings, to permit the discharge of a specific pollutant or pollutants under controlled conditions associated with an approved aquaculture project under Federal or State supervision pursuant to section 402 of this Act.

(b) The Administrator shall by regulation establish any procedures and guidelines which the Administrator deems necessary to carry out this section. Such regulations shall require the application to such discharge of each criterion, factor, procedure, and requirement applicable to a permit issued under section 402 of this title, as the Administrator determines necessary to carry out the objective of this Act.

(c) Each State desiring to administer its own permit program within its jurisdiction for discharge of a specific pollutant or pollutants under controlled conditions associated with an approved aquaculture project may do so if upon submission of such program the Administrator determines such program is adequate to carry out the objective of this Act.

§1329. Nonpoint Source Management Programs [Sec. 319]

(a) State Assessment Reports.—

(1) Contents.—The Governor of each State shall, after notice and opportunity for public comment, prepare and submit to the Administrator for approval, a report which—

(A) identifies those navigable waters within the State which, without additional action to control nonpoint sources of pollution, cannot reasonably be expected to attain or maintain applicable water quality standards or the goals and requirements of this Act;

(B) identifies those categories and subcategories of nonpoint sources or, where appropriate, particular nonpoint sources which add significant pollution to each portion of the navigable waters identified under subparagraph (A) in amounts which contribute to such portion not meeting such water quality standards or such goals and requirements;

(C) describes the process, including intergovernmental coordination and public participation, for identifying best management practices and measures to control each category and suhcategory of nonpoint sources and, where appropriate, particular non point sources identified under subparagraph (B) and to reduce, to the maximum extent practicable, the level of pollution resulting from such category, suhcategory, or source; and

(D) identifies and describes State and local programs for controlling pollution added from nonpoint sources to, and improving the quality of, each such portion of the navigable waters, including but not limited to those programs which are receiving Federal assistance under subsections (h) and (i).

(2) Information Used in Preparation.—In developing the report required by this section, the State (A) may rely upon information developed pursuant to sections 208, 303(e), 304(f), 305(b), and 314, and other information as appropriate, and (B) may utilize appropriate elements of the waste treatment management plans developed pursuant to sections 208(b) and 303, to the extent such elements are consistent with and fulfill the requirements of this section.

(b) State Management Programs.—

(1) In General.—The Governor of each State, for that State or in combination with adjacent States, shall, after notice and opportunity for public comment, prepare and submit to the Administrator for approval a management program which such State proposes to implement in the first four fiscal years beginning after the date of submission of such management program for controlling pollution added from nonpoint sources to the navigable waters within the State and improving the quality of such waters.

(2) Specific Contents.—Each management program proposed for implementation under this subsection shall include each of the following:

(A) An identification of the best management practices and measures which will be undertaken to reduce pollutant loadings resulting from each category, subcategory, or particular nonpoint source designated under paragraph (1)(B), taking into account the impact of the practice on ground water quality.

(B) An identification of programs (including, as appropriate, nonregulatory or regulatory programs for enforcement, technical assistance, financial assistance, education, training, technology transfer, and demonstration projects) to achieve implementation of the best management practices by the categories, subcategories, and particular nonpoint sources designated under subparagraph (A).

(C) A schedule containing annual milestones for (i) utilization of the program implementation methods identified in subparagraph (B), and (ii) implementation of the best management practices identified in subparagraph (A) by the categories, subcategories, or particular nonpoint sources designated under paragraph (1)(B). Such schedule shall provide for utilization of the best management practices at the earliest practicable date.

(D) A certification of the attorney general of the State or States (or the chief attorney of any State water pollution control agency which has independent legal counsel) that the laws of the State or States, as the case may be, provide adequate authority to implement such management program or, if there is not such adequate authority, a list of such additional authorities as will be necessary to implement such management program. A schedule and commitment by the State or

States to seek such additional authorities as expeditiously as practicable.

(E) Sources of Federal and other assistance and funding (other than assistance provided under subsections (h) and (i) which will be available in each of such fiscal years for supporting implementation of such practices and measures and the purposes for which such assistance will be used in each of such fiscal years.

(F) An identification of Federal financial assistance programs and Federal development projects for which the State will review individual assistance applications or development projects for their effect on water quality pursuant to the procedures set forth in Executive Order 12372 as in effect on September 17, 1983, to determine whether such assistance applications or development projects would be consistent with the program prepared under this subsection; for the purposes of this subparagraph, identification shall not be limited to the assistance programs or development projects subject to Executive Order 12372 but may include any programs listed in the most recent Catalog of Federal Domestic Assistance which may have an effect on the purposes and objectives of the State's nonpoint source pollution management program.

(3) Utilization of Local and Private Experts.— In development and implementing a management program under this subsection, a State shall, to the maximum extent practicable, involve local public and private agencies and organizations which have expertise in control of nonpoint sources of pollution.

(4) Development on Watershed Basis.—A State shall, to the maximum extent practicable, develop and implement a management program under this subsection on a watershed-by-watershed basis within such State.

(c) Administrative Provisions.—

(1) Cooperation Requirement.—Any report required by subsection (a) and any management program and report required by subsection (b) shall be developed in cooperation with local, substate regional, and interstate entities which are actively planning for the implementation of nonpoint source pollution controls and have either been certified by the Administrator in accordance with section 208, have worked jointly with the State on water quality management planning under section 205(j), or have been designated by the State legislative body or Governor as water quality management planning agencies for their geographic areas.

(2) Time Period for Submission of Reports and Management Programs.— Each report and management program shall be submitted to the Administrator during the 18–month period beginning on the date of the enactment of this section.

(d) Approval or Disapproval of Reports and Management Programs.—

(1) Deadline.—Subject to paragraph (2), not later than 180 days after the date of submission to the Administrator of any report or management program under this section (other than subsections (h), (i), and (k)), the Administrator shall either approve or disapprove such report or management program, as the case may be. The Administrator may approve a portion of a management program under this subsection. If the Administrator does not disapprove a report, management program, or portion of a management program in such 180–day period, such report, management program, or portion shall be deemed approved for purposes of this section.

(2) Procedure for Disapproval.—If, after notice and opportunity for public comment and consultation with appropriate Federal and State agencies and other interested persons, the Administrator determines that—

(A) the proposed management program or any portion thereof does not meet the requirements of subsection (b)(2) of this section or is not likely to satisfy, in whole or in part, the goals and requirements of this Act;

(B) adequate authority does not exist, or adequate resources are not available, to implement such program or portion;

(C) the schedule for implementing such program or portion is not sufficiently expeditious; or

(D) the practices and measures proposed in such program or portion are not adequate to reduce the level of pollution in navigable waters in the State resulting from nonpoint sources and to improve the quality of navigable waters in the State; the Administrator shall within 6 months of the receipt of the proposed program notify the State of any revisions or modifications necessary to obtain approval. The State shall thereupon have an additional 3 months to submit its revised management program and the Administrator shall approve or disapprove such revised program within three months of receipt.

(3) Failure of State to Submit Report.—If a Governor of State does not submit the report required by subsection (a) within the period specified by subsection (c)(2), the Administrator shall, within 30 months after the date of the enactment of this section, prepare a report for such State which makes the identifications required by paragraphs (1)(A) and (1)(B) of subsection (a). Upon completion of the requirement of the preceding sentence and after notice and opportunity for comment, the Administrator shall report to Congress on his actions pursuant to this section.

(e) Local Management Programs; Technical Assistance.—If a State fails to submit a management program under subsection (b) or the Administrator does not approve such a management program, a local public agency or organization which has expertise in, and authority to, control water pollution, resulting from nonpoint sources in any area of such State which the Administrator determines is of sufficient geographic size may, with approval of such State, request the Administrator to provide, and the Administrator shall provide, technical assistance to such agency or organization in developing for such area a management program which is described in subsection (b) and can be approved pursuant to subsection (d). After development of such management program, such agency or organization shall submit such management program to the Administrator for approval. If the Administrator approves such management program, such agency or organization shall be eligible to receive financial assistance under subsection (h) for implementation of such management program as if such agency or organization were a State for which a report submitted under subsection (a) and a management program submitted under subsection (b) were approved under this section. Such financial assistance shall be subject to the same terms and conditions as assistance provided to a State under subsection (h).

(f) Technical Assistance for States.— Upon request of a State, the Administrator may provide technical assistance to such State in developing a management program approved under subsection (b) for those portions of the navigable waters requested by such State.

(g) Interstate Management Conference.—

(1) Convening of Conference; Notification; Purpose.—If any portion of the navigable waters in any State which is implementing a management program approved under this section is not meeting applicable water quality standards or the goals and requirements of this Act as a result, in whole or in part, of pollution from nonpoint sources in another State, such State may petition the Administrator to convene, and the Administrator shall convene, a management conference of all States which contribute significant pollution resulting from nonpoint sources to such portion. If, on the basis of information available, the Administrator determines that a State is not meeting applicable water quality standards or the goals and requirements of this Act as a result, in whole or in part, of significant pollution from nonpoint sources in another State, the Administrator shall notify such States. The Administrator may convene a management conference under this paragraph not later than 180 days after giving such notification, whether or not the State which is not meeting such standards requests such conference. The purpose of such conference shall be to develop an agreement among such States to reduce the level of pollution in such portion resulting from nonpoint sources and to improve the water quality of such portion. Nothing in such agreement shall supersede or abrogate rights to quantities of water which have been established by interstate water compacts, Supreme Court decrees, or State water laws. This subsection shall not apply to any pollution which is subject to the Colorado River Basin Salinity Control Act. The requirement that the Administrator convene a management conference shall not be subject to the provisions of section 505 of this Act.

(2) State Management Program Requirement.—To the extent that the States reach agreement through such conference, the management programs of the States which are parties to such agreements and which contribute significant pollution to the navigable waters or portions thereof not meeting applicable water quality standards or goals and requirements of this Act will be revised to reflect such agreement. Such a management programs shall be consistent with Federal and State law.

(h) Grant Program.—

(1) Grants for Implementation of Management Programs.—Upon application of a State for which a report submitted under subsection (a) and a management program submitted under subsection (b) is approved under this section, the Administrator shall make grants, subject to such terms and conditions as the Administrator considers appropriate, under this subsec-

tion to such State for the purpose of assisting the State in implementing such management program. Funds reserved pursuant to section 205(j)(5) of this Act may be used to develop and implement such management program.

(2) Applications.—An application for a grant under this subsection in any fiscal year shall be in such form and shall contain such other information as the Administrator may require, including an identification and description of the best management practices and measures which the State proposes to assist, encourage, or require in such year with the Federal assistance to be provided under the grant.

(3) Federal Share.—The Federal share of the cost of each management program implemented with Federal assistance under this subsection in any fiscal year shall not exceed 60 percent of the cost incurred by the State in implementing such management program and shall be made on condition that the non-Federal share is provided from non-Federal sources.

(4) Limitation on Grant Amounts.— Notwithstanding any other provision of this subsection, not more than 15 percent of the amount appropriated to carry out this subsection may be used to make grants to any one State, including any grants to any local public agency or organization with authority to control pollution from nonpoint sources in any area of such State.

(5) Priority for Effective Mechanisms.—For each fiscal year beginning after September 30, 1987, the Administrator may give priority in making grants under this subsection, and shall give consideration in determining the Federal share of any such grant, to States which have implemented or are proposing to implement management programs which will—

(A) control particularly difficult or serious nonpoint source pollution problems, including, but not limited to, problems resulting from mining activities;

(B) implement innovative methods or practices for controlling nonpoint sources of pollution, including regulatory programs where the Administrator deems appropriate;

(C) control interstate nonpoint source pollution problems; or

(D) carry out ground water quality protection activities which the Administrator determines are part of a comprehensive nonpoint source pollution control program, including research, planning, ground water assessments, demonstration programs, enforcement, technical assistance, education, and training to protect ground water quality from nonpoint sources of pollution.

(6) Availability for Obligation.—The funds granted to each State pursuant to this subsection in a fiscal year shall remain available for obligation by such State for the fiscal year for which appropriated. The amount of any such funds not obligated by the end of such fiscal year shall be available to the Administrator for granting to other States under this subsection in the next fiscal year.

(7) Limitation on Use of Funds.— States may use funds from grants made pursuant to this section for financial assistance to persons only to the extent that such assistance is related to the costs of demonstration projects.

(8) Satisfactory Progress.—No grant may be made under this subsection in any fiscal year to a State which in the preceding fiscal year received a grant under this subsection unless the Administrator determines that such State made satisfactory progress in such preceding fiscal year in meeting the schedule specified by such State under subsection (b)(2).

(9) Maintenance of Effort.—No grant may be made to a State under this subsection in any fiscal year unless such State enters into such agreements with the Administrator as the Administrator may require to ensure that such State will maintain its aggregate expenditures from all other sources for programs for controlling pollution added to the navigable waters in such State from non- point sources and improving the quality of such waters at or above the average level of such expenditures in its two fiscal years preceding the date of enactment of this subsection.

(10) Request for Information.—The Administrator may request such information, data, and reports as he considers necessary to make the determination of continuing eligibility for grants under this section.

(11) Reporting and Other Requirements.—Each State shall report to the Administrator on an annual basis concerning (A) its progress in meeting the schedule of milestones submitted pursuant to subsection (b)(2)(C) of this section, and (B) to the extent that appropriate information is available, reductions in nonpoint source pollutant loading and improvements in water quality for those navigable waters or watersheds within the State which were identified pursuant to subsection (a)(1)(A) of this section

resulting from implementation of the management program.

(12) Limitation on Administrative Costs.—For purposes of this subsection, administrative costs in the form of salaries, overhead, or indirect costs for services provided and charged against activities and programs carried out with a grant under this subsection shall not exceed in any fiscal year 10 percent of the amount of the grant in such year, except that costs of implementing enforcement and regulatory activities, education, training, technical assistance, demonstration projects, and technology transfer programs shall not be subject to this limitation.

(i) Grants for Protecting Groundwater Quality.—

(1) Eligible Applicants and Activities.—Upon application of a State for which a report submitted under subsection (a) and a plan submitted under subsection (b) is approved under this section, the Administrator shall make grants under this subsection to such State for the purpose of assisting such State in carrying out groundwater quality protection activities which the Administrator determines will advance the State toward implementation of a comprehensive nonpoint source pollution control program. Such activities shall include, but not be limited to, research planning, groundwater assessments, demonstration programs, enforcement, technical assistance, education and training to protect the quality of groundwater and to prevent contamination of groundwater from nonpoint sources of pollution.

(2) Applications.—An application for a grant under this subsection shall be in such form and shall contain such information as the Administrator may require.

(3) Federal Share; Maximum Amount.—The Federal share of the cost of assisting a State in carrying out groundwater protection, activities in any fiscal year under this subsection shall be 50 percent of the costs incurred by the State in carrying out such activities, except that the maximum amount of Federal assistance which any State may receive under this subsection in any fiscal year shall not exceed $150,000.

(4) Report.—The Administrator shall include in each report transmitted under subsection (m) a report on the activities and programs implemented under this subsection during the preceding fiscal year.

(j) Authorization of Appropriations.— There is authorized to be appropriated to carry out subsections (h) and (i) not to exceed $70,000,000 for fiscal year 1988, $100,000,000 per fiscal year for each of fiscal years 1989 and 1990, and $130,000,000 for fiscal year 1991; except that for each of such fiscal years not to exceed $7,500,000 may be made available to carry out subsection (i). Sums appropriated pursuant to this subsection shall remain available until expended.

(k) Consistency of Other Programs and Projects With Management Programs.— The Administrator shall transmit to the Office of Management and Budget and the appropriate Federal departments and agencies a list of those assistance programs and development projects identified by each State under subsection (b)(2)(F) for which individual assistance applications and projects will be reviewed pursuant to the procedures set forth in Executive Order 12372 as in effect on September 17, 1983. Beginning not later than sixty days after receiving notification by the Administrator, each Federal department and agency shall modify existing regulations to allow States to review individual development projects and assistance applications under the identified Federal assistance programs and shall accommodate, according to the requirements and definitions of Executive Order 12372, as in effect on September 17, 1983, the concerns of the State regarding the consistency of such applications or projects with the State nonpoint source pollution management program.

(l) Collection of Information.—The Administrator shall collect and make available, through publications and other appropriate means, information pertaining to management practices and implementation methods, including, but not limited to, (1) information concerning the costs and relative efficiencies of best management practices for reducing nonpoint source pollution; and (2) available data concerning the relationship between water quality and implementation of various management practices to control nonpoint sources of pollution.

(m) Reports of Administrator.—

(1) Annual Reports.—Not later than January 1, 1988, and each January 1 thereafter, the Administrator shall transmit to the Committee on Public Works and Transportation of the House of Representatives and the Committee on Environment and Public Works of the Senate, a report for the preceding fiscal year on the activities and programs implemented under this section and the progress made in reducing pollution in the navigable waters resulting from nonpoint sources and improving the quality of such waters.

(2) Final Report.—Not later than January 1, 1990, the Administrator shall transmit to Congress a final report on the activities carried out under this section. Such report, at a minimum, shall—

(A) describe the management programs being implemented by the States by types and amount of affected navigable waters, categories and subcategories of nonpoint sources, and types of best management practices being implemented;

(B) describe the experiences of the States in adhering to schedules and implementing best management practices;

(C) describe the amount and purpose of grants awarded pursuant to subsections (h) and (i) of this section;

(D) identify, to the extent that information is available, the progress made in reducing pollutant loads and improving water quality in the navigable waters;

(E) indicate what further actions need to be taken to attain and maintain in those navigable waters (i) applicable water quality standards, and (ii) the goals and requirements of this Act;

(F) include recommendations of the Administrator concerning future programs (including enforcement programs) for controlling pollution from nonpoint sources; and

(G) identify the activities and programs of departments, agencies, and instrumentalities of the United States which are inconsistent with the management programs submitted by the States and recommend modifications so that such activities and programs are consistent with and assist the States in implementation of such management programs.

(n) Set Aside for Administrative Personnel.—Not less than 5 percent of the funds appropriated pursuant to subsection (j) for any fiscal year shall be available to the Administrator to maintain personnel levels at the Environmental Protection Agency at levels which are adequate to carry out this section in such year.

[§319 added by PL 100–4]

§1330. National Estuary Program [Sec. 320]

[§320 added by PL 100–4]

(a) Management Conference.—

(1) Nomination of Estuaries.—The Governor of any State may nominate to the Administrator an estuary lying in whole or in part within the State as an estuary of national significance and request a management conference to develop a comprehensive management plan for the estuary. The nomination shall document the need for the conference, the likelihood of success, and information relating to the factors in paragraph (2).

(2) Convening of Conference.—

(A) In General.—In any case where the Administrator determines, on his own initiative or upon nomination of a State under paragraph (1), that the attainment or maintenance of that water quality in an estuary which assures protection of public water supplies and the protection and propagation of a balanced, indigenous population of shellfish, fish, and wildlife, and allows recreational activities, in and on the water, requires the control of point and nonpoint sources of pollution to supplement existing controls of pollution in more than one State, the Administrator shall select such estuary and convene a management conference.

(B) Priority consideration.—The Administrator shall give priority consideration under this section to Long Island Sound, New York and Connecticut; Narragansett Bay, Rhode Island; Buzzards Bay, Massachusetts; Massachusetts Bay, Massachusetts (including Cape Cod Bay and Boston Harbor); Puget Sound, Washington; New York-New Jersey Harbor, New York and New Jersey; Delaware Bay, Delaware and New Jersey; Delaware Inland Bays, Delaware; Albermarle Sound, North Carolina; Sarasota Bay, Florida; San Francisco Bay, California; Santa Monica Bay, California; Galveston Bay, Texas; Barataria-Terrebonne Bay estuary complex, Louisiana; Indian River Lagoon, Florida; and Peconic Bay, New York.

[§320(a)(2)(B) amended by PL 100–202; PL 100–653; PL 100–688]

(3) Boundary Dispute Exception.—In any case in which a boundary between two States passes through an estuary and such boundary is disputed and is the subject of an action in any court, the Administrator shall not convene a management conference with respect to such estuary before a final adjudication has been made of such dispute.

(b) Purposes of Conference.—The purposes of any management conference convened with respect to an estuary under this subsection shall be to—

(1) assess trends in water quality, natural resources, and uses of the estuary;

(2) collect, characterize, and assess data on toxics, nutrients, and natural resources within the

estuarine zone to identify the causes of environmental problems;

(3) develop the relationship between the inplace loads and point and nonpoint loadings of pollutants to the estuarine zone and the potential uses of the zone, water quality, and natural resources;

(4) develop a comprehensive conservation and management plan that recommends priority corrective actions and compliance schedules addressing point and nonpoint sources of pollution to restore and maintain the chemical, physical, and biological integrity of the estuary, including restoration and maintenance of water quality, a balanced indigenous population of shellfish, fish and wildlife, and recreational activities in the estuary, and assure that the designated uses of the estuary are protected;

(5) develop plans for the coordinated implementation of the plan by the States as well as Federal and local agencies participating in the conference;

(6) monitor the effectiveness of actions taken pursuant to the plan; and

(7) review all Federal financial assistance programs and Federal development projects in accordance with the requirements of Executive Order 12372, as in effect on September 17, 1983, to determine whether such assistance program or project would be consistent with and further the purposes and objectives of the plan prepared under this section. For purposes of paragraph (7), such programs and projects shall not be limited to the assistance programs and development projects subject to Executive Order 12372, but may include any programs listed in the most recent Catalog of Federal Domestic Assistance which may have an effect on the purposes and objectives of the plan developed under this section.

(c) Members of Conference.—The members of a management conference convened under this section shall include, at a minimum, the Administrator and representatives of—

(1) each State and foreign nation located in whole or in part in the estuarine zone of the estuary for which the conference is convened;

(2) international, interstate, or regional agencies or entities having jurisdiction over all or a significant part of the estuary;

(3) each interested Federal agency, as determined appropriate by the Administrator;

(4) local governments having jurisdiction over any land or water within the estuarine zone, as determined appropriate by the Administrator; and

(5) affected industries, public and private educational institutions, and the general public, as determined appropriate by the Administrator.

(d) Utilization of Existing Data.—In developing a conservation and management plan under this section, the management conference shall survey and utilize existing reports, data, and studies relating to the estuary that have been developed by or made available to Federal, interstate, State, and local agencies.

(e) Period of Conference.—A management conference convened under this section shall be convened for a period not to exceed 5 years. Such conference may be extended by the Administrator, and if terminated after the initial period, may be reconvened by the Administrator at any time thereafter, as may be necessary to meet the requirements of this section.

(f) Approval and Implementation of Plans.—

(1) Approval.—Not later than 120 days after the completion of a conservation and management plan and after providing for public review and comment, the Administrator shall approve such plan if the plan meets the requirements of this section and the affected Governor or Governors concur.

(2) Implementation.—Upon approval of a conservation and management plan under this section, such plan shall be implemented. Funds authorized to be appropriated under titles II and VI and section 319 of this Act may be used in accordance with the applicable requirements of this Act to assist States with the implementation of such plan.

(g) Grants.—

(1) Recipients.—The Administrator is authorized to make grants to State, interstate, and regional water pollution control agencies and entities, State coastal zone management agencies, interstate agencies, other public or nonprofit private agencies, institutions, organizations, and individuals.

(2) Purposes.—Grants under this subsection shall be made to pay for assisting research, surveys, studies, and modeling and other technical work necessary for the development of a conservation and management plan under this section.

(3) Federal Share.—The amount of grants to any person (including a State, interstate, or

regional agency or entity) under this subsection for a fiscal year shall not exceed 75 percent of the costs of such research, survey, studies, and work and shall be made on condition that the non-Federal share of such costs are provided from non-Federal sources.

(h) Grant Reporting.—Any person (including a State, interstate, or regional agency or entity) that receives a grant under subsection (g) shall report to the Administrator not later than 18 months after receipt of such grant and biennially thereafter on the progress being made under this section.

(i) Authorization of Appropriations.— There are authorized to be appropriated to the Administrator not to exceed $12,000,000 per fiscal year for each of fiscal years 1987, 1988, 1989, 1990, and 1991 for—

(1) expenses related to the administration of management conferences under this section, not to exceed 10 percent of the amount appropriated under this subsection;

(2) making grants under subsection (g); and

(3) monitoring the implementation of a conservation and management plan by the management conference or by the Administrator, in any case in which the conference has been terminated. The Administrator shall provide up to $5,000,000 per fiscal year of the sums authorized to be appropriated under this subsection to the Administrator of the National Oceanic and Atmospheric Administration to carry out subsection (j).

(j) Research.—

(1) Programs.—In order to determine the need to convene a management conference under this section or at the request of such a management conference, the Administrator shall coordinate and implement through the National Marine Pollution Program Office and the National Marine Fisheries Service of the National Oceanic and Atmospheric Administration, as appropriate, for one or more estuarine zones—

(A) a long-term program of trend assessment monitoring measuring variations in pollutant concentrations, marine ecology, and other physical or biological environmental parameters which may affect estuarine zones, to provide the Administrator the capacity to determine the potential and actual effects of alternative management strategies and measures;

(B) a program of ecosystem assessment assisting in the development of (i) baseline studies which determine the state of estuarine zones and the effects of natural and anthropogenic changes, and (ii) predictive models capable of translating information on specific discharges or general pollutant loadings within estuarine zones into a set of probable effects on such zones;

(C) a comprehensive water quality sampling program for the continuous monitoring of nutrients, chlorine acid precipitation, dissolved oxygen, and potentially toxic pollutants (including organic chemicals and metals) in estuarine zones, after consultation with interested State, local, interstate, or international agencies and review and analysis of all environmental sampling data presently collected from estuarine zones; and

(D) a program of research to idcntify the movements of nutrients, sediments and pollutants through estuarine zones and the impact of nutrients, sediments, and pollutants on water quality, the ecosystem, and designated or potential uses of the estuarine zones.

(2) Reports.—The Administrator, in cooperation with the Administrator of the National Oceanic and Atmospheric Administration, shall submit to the Congress no less often than biennially a comprehensive report on the activities authorized under this subsection including—

(A) a listing of priority monitoring and research needs;

(B) an assessment of the state and health of the Nation's estuarine zones, to the extent evaluated under this subsection;

(C) a discussion of pollution problems and trends in pollutant concentrations with a direct or indirect effect on water quality, the ecosystem, and designated or potential uses of each estuarine zone, to the extent evaluated under this subsection; and

(D) an evaluation of pollution abatement activities and management measures so far implemented to determine the degree of improvement toward the objectives expressed in subsection (b)(4) of this section.

(k) Definitions.—For purposes of this section, the terms "estuary" and "estuarine zone" have the meanings such terms have in section 104(n)(4) of this Act, except that the term "estuarine zone" shall also include associated aquatic ecosystems and those portions of tributaries draining into the estuary up to the historic height of migration of anadromous fish or the historic head of tidal influence, whichever is higher.

TITLE IV—PERMITS AND LICENSES

§1341. Certification [Sec. 401]

(a) (1) Any applicant for a Federal license or permit to conduct any activity including, but not limited to, the construction or operation of facilities, which may result in any discharge into the navigable waters, shall provide the licensing or permitting agency a certification from the State in which the discharge originates or will originate, or, if appropriate, from the interstate water pollution control agency having jurisdiction over the navigable waters at the point where the discharge originates or will originate, that any such discharge will comply with the applicable provisions of sections 301, 302, 303, 306, and 307 of this Act. In the case of any such activity for which there is not an applicable effluent limitation or other limitation under sections 301(b) and 302, and there is not an applicable standard under sections 306 and 307, the State shall so certify, except that any such certification shall not be deemed to satisfy section 511(c) of this Act. Such State or interstate agency shall establish procedures for public notice in the case of all applications for certification by it and, to the extent it deems appropriate, procedures for public hearings in connection with specific applications. In any case where a State or interstate agency has no authority to give such a certification, such certification shall be from the Administrator. If the State, interstate agency, or Administrator, as the case may be, fails or refuses to act on a request for certification, within a reasonable period of time (which shall not exceed one year) after receipt of such request, the certification requirements of this subsection shall be waived with respect to such Federal application. No license or permit shall be granted until the certification required by this section has been obtained or has been waived as provided in the preceding sentence. No license or permit shall be granted if certification has been denied by the State, interstate agency, or the Administrator, as the case may be.

(2) Upon receipt of such application and certification the licensing or permitting agency shall immediately notify the Administrator of such application and certification. Whenever such a discharge may affect, as determined by the Administrator, the quality of the waters of any other State, the Administrator within thirty days of the date of notice of application for such Federal license or permit shall so notify such other State, the licensing or permitting agency, and the applicant. If, within sixty days after receipt of such notification, such other State determines that such discharge will affect the quality of its waters so as to violate any water quality requirement in such State, and within such sixty-day period notifies the Administrator and the licensing or permitting agency in writing of its objection to the issuance of such license or permit and requests a public hearing on such objection, the licensing or permitting agency shall hold such a hearing. The Administrator shall at such hearing submit his evaluation and recommendations with respect to any such objection to the licensing or permitting agency. Such agency, based upon the recommendations of such State, the Administrator, and upon any additional evidence, if any, presented to the agency at the hearing, shall condition such license or permit in such manner as may be necessary to insure compliance with applicable water quality requirements. If the imposition of conditions cannot insure such compliance such agency shall not issue such license or permit.

(3) The certification obtained pursuant to paragraph (1) of this subsection with respect to the construction of any facility shall fulfill the requirements of this subsection with respect to certification in connection with any other Federal license or permit required for the operation of such facility unless, after notice to the certifying State, agency, or Administrator, as the case may be, which shall be given by the Federal agency to whom application is made for such operating license or permit, the State, or if appropriate, the interstate agency or the Administrator, notifies such agency within sixty days after receipt of such notice that there is no longer reasonable assurance that there will be compliance with the applicable provisions of sections 301, 302, 303, 306, and 307 of this Act because of changes since the construction license or permit certification was issued in (A) the construction or operation of the facility, (B) the characteristics of the waters into which such discharge is made, (C) the water quality criteria applicable to such waters or (D) applicable effluent limitations or other requirements. This paragraph shall be inapplicable in any case where the applicant for such operating license or permit has failed to provide the certifying State, or, if appropriate, the interstate agency or the Administrator, with notice

of any proposed changes in the construction or operation of the facility with respect to which a construction license or permit has been granted, which changes may result in violation of section 301, 302, 303, 306, or 307 of this Act.

(4) Prior to the initial operation of any federally licensed or permitted facility or activity which may result in any discharge into the navigable waters and with respect to which a certification has been obtained pursuant to paragraph (1) of this subsection, which facility or activity is not subject to a Federal operating license or permit, the licensee or permittee shall provide an opportunity for such certifying State, or, if appropriate, the interstate agency or the Administrator to review the manner in which the facility or activity shall be operated or conducted for the purposes of assuring that applicable effluent limitations or other limitations or other applicable water quality requirements will not be violated. Upon notification by the certifying State, or if appropriate, the interstate agency or the Administrator that the operation of any such federally licensed or permitted facility or activity will violate applicable effluent limitations or other limitations or other water quality requirements such Federal agency may, after public hearing, suspend such license or permit. If such license or permit is suspended, it shall remain suspended until notification is received from the certifying State, agency, or Administrator, as the case may be, that there is reasonable assurance that such facility or activity will not violate the applicable provisions of section 301, 302, 303, 306, or 307 of this Act.

(5) Any Federal license or permit with respect to which a certification has been obtained under paragraph (1) of this subsection may be suspended or revoked by the Federal agency issuing such license or permit upon the entering of a judgment under this Act that such facility or activity has been operated in violation of the applicable provisions of section 301, 302, 303, 306, or 307 of this Act.

(6) Except with respect to a permit issued under section 402 of this Act, in any case where actual construction of a facility has been lawfully commenced prior to April 3, 1970, no certification shall be required under this subsection for a license or permit issued after April 3, 1970, to operate such facility, except that any such license or permit issued without certification shall terminate April 3, 1973, unless prior to such termination date the person having such license or permit submits to the Federal agency which issued such license or permit a certification and otherwise meets the requirements of this section.

(b) Nothing in this section shall be construed to limit the authority of any department or agency pursuant to any other provision of law to require compliance with any applicable water quality requirements. The Administrator shall, upon the request of any Federal department or agency, or State or interstate agency, or applicant, provide, for the purpose of this section, any relevant information on applicable effluent limitations, or other limitations, standards, regulations or requirements, or water quality criteria, and shall, when requested by any such department or agency or State or interstate agency, or applicant, comment on any methods to comply with such limitations, standards, regulations, requirements, or criteria.

(c) In order to implement the provisions of this section, the Secretary of the Army, acting through the Chief of Engineers, is authorized, if he deems it to be in the public interest, to permit the use of spoil disposal areas under his jurisdiction by Federal licensees or permittees, and to make an appropriate charge for such use. Moneys received from such licensees or permittees shall be deposited in the Treasury as miscellaneous receipts.

(d) Any certification provided under this section shall set forth any effluent limitations and other limitations, and monitoring requirements necessary to assure that any applicant for a Federal license or permit will comply with any applicable effluent limitations and other limitations, under section 301 or 302 of this Act, standard of performance under section 306 of this Act, or prohibition, effluent standard, or pretreatment standard under section 307 of this Act, and with any other appropriate requirement of State law set forth in such certification, and shall become a condition on any Federal license or permit subject to the provisions of this section.

§1342. National Pollutant Discharge Elimination System [Sec. 402]

(a) (1) Except as provided in sections 318 and 404 of this Act, the Administrator may, after opportunity for public hearing, issue a permit for the discharge of any pollutant, or combination of pollutants, notwithstanding section 301(a), upon condition that such discharge will meet either (A) all applicable requirements under sections 301, 302, 306, 307, 308 and 403 of this Act, or (B) prior to the taking of necessary implementing actions relating to all such requirements, such conditions as the Administrator determines are necessary to carry out the provisions of this Act.

[§402(a)(1)(A) and (B) designated by PL 100–4]

(2) The Administrator shall prescribe conditions for such permits to assure compliance with the requirements of paragraph (1) of this subsection, including conditions on data and information collection, reporting, and such other requirements as he deems appropriate.

(3) The permit program of the Administrator under paragraph (1) of this subsection, and permits issued thereunder, shall be subject to the same terms, conditions, and requirements as apply to a State permit program and permits issued thereunder under subsection (b) of this section.

(4) All permits for discharges into the navigable waters issued pursuant to section 13 of the Act of March 3, 1899, shall be deemed to be permits issued under this title, and permits issued under this title shall be deemed to be permits issued under section 13 of the Act of March 3, 1899, and shall continue in force and effect for their term unless revoked, modified, or suspended in accordance with the provisions of this Act.

(5) No permit for a discharge into the navigable waters shall be issued under section 13 of the Act of March 3, 1899, after the date of enactment of this title. Each application for a permit under section 13 of the Act of March 3, 1899, pending on the date of enactment of this Act shall be deemed to be an application for a permit under this section. The Administrator shall authorize a State, which he determines has the capability of administering a permit program which will carry out the objective of this Act, to issue permits for discharges into the navigable waters within the jurisdiction of such State. The Administrator may exercise the authority granted him by the preceding sentence only during the period which begins on the date of enactment of this Act and ends either on the ninetieth day after the date of the first promulgation of guidelines required by section 304(i)(2) of this Act, or the date of approval by the Administrator of a permit program for such State under subsection (b) of this section, whichever date first occurs, and no such authorization to a State shall extend beyond the last day of such period. Each such permit shall be subject to such conditions as the Administrator determines are necessary to carry out the provisions of this Act. No such permit shall issue if the Administrator objects to such issuance.

(b) At any time after the promulgation of the guidelines required by subsection (i)(2) of section 304 of this Act, the Governor of each State desiring to administer its own permit program for discharges into navigable waters within its jurisdiction may submit to the Administrator a full and complete description of the program it proposes to establish and administer under State law or under an interstate compact. In addition, such State shall submit a statement from the attorney general (or the attorney for those State water pollution control agencies which have independent legal counsel), or from the chief legal officer in the case of an interstate agency, that the laws of such State, or the interstate compact, as the case may be, provide adequate authority to carry out the described program. The Administrator shall approve each such submitted program unless he determines that adequate authority does not exist:

(1) To issue permits which—

(A) apply, and insure compliance with, any applicable requirements of sections 301, 302, 306, 307, and 403;

(B) are for fixed terms not exceeding five years; and

(C) can be terminated or modified for cause including, but not limited to, the following:

(i) violation of any condition of the permit;

(ii) obtaining a permit by misrepresentation, or failure to disclose fully all relevant facts;

(iii) change in any condition that requires either a temporary or permanent reduction or elimination of the permitted discharge;

(D) control the disposal of pollutants into wells;

(2) (A) To issue permits which apply, and insure compliance with, all applicable requirements of section 308 of this Act, or

(B) To inspect, monitor, enter, and require reports to at least the same extent as required in section 308 of this Act;

(3) To insure that the public, and any other State the waters of which may be affected, receive notice of each application for a permit and to provide an opportunity for public hearing before a ruling on each such application;

(4) To insure that the Administrator receives notice of each application (including a copy thereof) for a permit;

(5) To insure that any State (other than the permitting State), whose waters may be affected by the issuance of a permit may submit written

recommendations to the permitting State (and the Administrator) with respect to any permit application and, if any part of such written recommendations are not accepted by the permitting State, that the permitting State will notify such affected State (and the Administrator) in writing of its failure to so accept such recommendations together with its reasons for so doing;

(6) To insure that no permit will be issued if, in the judgment of the Secretary of the Army acting through the Chief of Engineers, after consultation with the Secretary of the department in which the Coast Guard is operating, anchorage and navigation of any of the navigable waters would be substantially impaired thereby;

(7) To abate violations of the permit or the permit program, including civil and criminal penalties and other ways and means of enforcement.

(8) To insure that any permit for a discharge from a publicly owned treatment works includes conditions to require the identification in terms of character and volume of pollutants of any significant source introducing pollutants subject to pretreatment standards under section 307(b) of this Act into such works and a program to assure compliance with such pretreatment standards by each such source, in addition to adequate notice to the permitting agency of (A) new introductions into such works of pollutants from any source which would be a new source as defined in section 306 if such source were discharging pollutants, (B) new introductions of pollutants into such works from a source which would be subject to section 301 if it were discharging such pollutants, or (C) a substantial change in volume or character of pollutants being introduced into such works by a source introducing pollutants into such works at the time of issuance of the permit. Such notice shall include information on the quality and quantity of effluent to be introduced into such treatment works and any anticipated impact of such change in the quantity or quality of effluent to be discharged from such publicly owned treatment works; and

(9) To insure that any industrial user of any publicly owned treatment works will comply with sections 204(b), 307, and 308.

(c) (1) Not later than ninety days after the date on which a State has submitted a program (or revision thereof) pursuant to subsection (b) of this section, the Administrator shall suspend the issuance of permits under subsection (a) of this section as to those discharges subject to such program unless he determines that the State permit program does not meet the requirements of subsection (b) of this section or does not conform to the guidelines issued under section 304(i)(2) of this Act. If the Administrator so determines, he shall notify the State of any revisions or modifications necessary to conform to such requirements or guidelines.

[§402(c)(1) amended by PL 100–4]

(2) Any State permit program under this section shall at all times be in accordance with this section and guidelines promulgated pursuant to section 304(i)(2) of this Act.

(3) Whenever the Administrator determines after public hearing that a State is not administering a program approved under this section in accordance with requirements of this section, he shall so notify the State and, if appropriate corrective action is not taken within a reasonable time, not to exceed ninety days, the Administrator shall withdraw approval of such program. The Administrator shall not withdraw approval of any such program unless he shall first have notified the State, and made public, in writing, the reasons for such withdrawal.

(4) Limitations on Partial Permit Program Returns and Withdrawals.—A State may return to the Administrator administration, and the Administrator may withdraw under paragraph (3) of this subsection approval, of—

(A) a State partial permit program approved under subsection (n)(4) only if the entire permit program being administered by the State department or agency at the time is returned or withdrawn; and

(B) a State partial permit program approved under subsection (n)(4) only if an entire phased component of the permit program being administered by the State at the time is returned or withdrawn.

[§402(c)(4) added by PL 100–4]

(d) (1) Each State shall transmit to the Administrator a copy of each permit application received by such State and provide notice to the Administrator of every action related to the consideration of such permit application, including each permit proposed to be issued by such State.

(2) No permit shall issue (A) if the Administrator within ninety days of the date of his notification under subsection (b)(5) of this section

objects in writing to the issuance of such permit, or (B) if the Administrator within ninety days of the date of transmittal of the proposed permit by the State objects in writing to the issuance of such permit as being outside the guidelines and requirements of this Act. Whenever the Administrator objects to the issuance of a permit under this paragraph such written objection shall contain a statement of the reasons for such objection and the effluent limitations and conditions which such permit would include if it were issued by the Administrator.

(3) The Administrator may, as to any permit application, waive paragraph (2) of this subsection.

(4) In any case where, after the date of enactment of this paragraph, the Administrator, pursuant to paragraph (2) of this subsection, objects to the issuance of a permit, or request of the State, a public hearing shall be held by the Administrator on such objection. If the State does not resubmit such permit revised to meet such objection within 30 days after completion of the hearing, or, if no hearing is requested within 90 days after the date of such objection, the Administrator may issue the permit pursuant to subsection (a) of this section for such source in accordance with the guidelines and requirements of this Act.

(e) In accordance with guidelines promulgated pursuant to subsection (i)(2) of section 304 of this Act, the Administrator authorized to waive the requirements of subsection (d) of this section at the time he approves a program pursuant to subsection (b) of this section for any category (including any class, type, or size within such category) of point sources within the State submitting such program.

(f) The Administrator shall promulgate regulations establishing categories of point sources which he determines shall not be subject to the requirements of subsection (d) of this section in any State with a program approved pursuant to subsection (b) of this section. The Administrator may distinguish among classes, types, and sizes within any category of point sources.

(g) Any permit issued under this section for the discharge of pollutants into the navigable waters from a vessel or other floating craft shall be subject to any applicable regulations promulgated by the Secretary of the Department in which the Coast Guard is operating, establishing specifications for safe transportation, handling, carriage, storage, and stowage of pollutants.

(h) In the event any condition of a permit for discharges from a treatment works (as defined in section 212 of this Act) which is publicly owned is violated, a State with a program approved under subsection (b) of this section or the Administrator, where no State program is approved or where the Administrator determines pursuant to section 309(a) of this Act that a State with an approved program has not commenced appropriate enforcement action with respect to such permit, may proceed in a court of competent jurisdiction to restrict or prohibit the introduction of any pollutant into such treatment works by a source not utilizing such treatment works prior to the finding that such condition was violated.

(i) Nothing in this section shall be construed to limit the authority of the Adminisfrator to take action pursuant to section 309 of this Act.

(j) A copy of each permit application and each permit issued under this section shall be available to the public. Such permit application or permit, or portion thereof, shall further be available on request for the purpose of reproduction.

(k) Compliance with a permit issued pursuant to this section shall be deemed compliance, for purposes of sections 309 and 505, with sections 301, 302, 306, 307, and 403, except any standard imposed under section 307for a toxic pollutant injurious to human health. Until December 31, 1974, in any case where a permit for discharge has been applied for pursuant to this section, but final administrative disposition of such application has not been made, such discharge shall not be a violation of (1) section 301, 306, and 402, of this Act, or (2) section 13 of the Act of March 3, 1899, unless the Administrator or other plaintiff proves that final administrative disposition of such application has not been made because of the failure of the applicant to furnish information reasonably required or requested in order to process the application. For the 180–day period beginning on the date of enactment of the Federal Water Pollution Control Act Amendments of 1972, in the case of any point source discharging any pollutant or combination of pollutants immediately prior to such date of enactment which source is not subject to section 13 of the Act of March 3, 1899, the discharge by such source shall not be a violation of this Act if such a source applies for a permit for discharge pursuant to this section within such 180–day period.

(l) Limitation on Permit Requirement.—

(1) Agricultural Return Flows.—The Administrator shall not require a permit under this sec-

tion, for discharge composed entirely of return flows from irrigated agriculture, nor shall the Administrator directly or indirectly, require any State to require such a permit.

[§402(l)(1) designated by PL 100–4]

(2) Stormwater Runoff From Oil, Gas, and Mining Operations.—The Administrator shall not require a permit under this section, nor shall the Administrator directly or indirectly require any State to require a permit, for discharges of stormwater runoff from mining operations or oil and gas exploration, production, precessing, or treatment operations or transmission facilities, composed entirely of flows which are from conveyances or systems of conveyances (including but not limited to pipes, conduits, ditches, and channels) used for collecting and conveying precipitation runoff and which are not contaminated by contact with, or do not come into contact with, any overburden, raw material, intermediate products, finished product, byproduct, or waste products located on the site of such operations.

[§402(l)(2) added by PL 100–4]

(m) Additional Pretreatment of Conventional Pollutants Not Required.—To the extent a treatment works (as defined in section 212 of this Act) which is publicly owned is not meeting the requirements of a permit issued under this section for such treatment works as a result of inadequate design or operation of such treatment works, the Administrator, in issuing a permit under this section, shall not require pretreatment by a person introducing conventional pollutants identified pursuant to section 304(a)(4) of this Act into such treatment works other than pretreatment required to assure compliance with pretreatment standards under subsection (b)(8) of this section and section 307(b)(1) of this Act. Nothing in this subsection shall affect the Administrator's authority under sections 307 and 309 of this Act, affect State and local authority under sections 307(b)(4) and 510 of this Act, relieve such treatment works of its obligations to meet requirements established under this Act, or otherwise preclude such works from pursuing whatever feasible options are available to meet its responsibility to comply with its permit under this section.

[§402(m) added by PL 100–4]

(n) Partial Permit Program.—

(1) State Submission.—The Governor of a State may submit under subsection (b) of this section a permit program for a portion of the discharges into the navigable waters in such State.

(2) Minimum Coverage.—A partial permit program under this subsection shall cover, at a minimum, administration of a major category of the discharges into the navigable waters of the State or a major component of the permit program required by subsection (b).

(3) Approval of Major Category Partial Permit Programs.—The Administrator may approve a partial permit program covering administration of a major category of discharges under this subsection if—

(A) such program represents a complete permit program and covers all of the discharges under the jurisdiction of a department or agency of the State; and

(B) the Administrator determines that the partial program represents a significant and identifiable part of the State program required by subsection (b).

(4) Approval of Major Component Partial Permit Programs.—The Administrator may approve under this subsection a partial and phased permit program covering administration of a major component (including discharge categories) of a State permit program required by subsection (b) if—

(A) the Administrator determines that the partial program represents a significant and identifiable part of the State program required by subsection (b); and

(B) the State submits, and the Administrator approves, a plan for the State to assume administration by phases of the remainder of the State program required by subsection (b) by a specified date not more than 5 years after submission of the partial program under this subsection and agrees to make all reasonable efforts to assume such administration by such date.

[§402(n) added by PL 100–4]

(o) Anti-Backsliding.—

(1) General Prohibition.—In the case of effluent limitations established on the basis of subsection (a)(1)(B) of this section, a permit may not be renewed, reissued, or modified on the basis of effluent guidelines promulgated under section 304(b) subsequent to the original issuance of such permit, to contain effluent limitations which are less stringent than the comparable effluent limitations in the previous permit. In the case of effluent limitations established on the basis of section 301(b)(1)(C) or section 303 (d) or (e), a permit may not be renewed, reissued, or modified to contain effluent limitations which are less stringent than the

comparable effluent limitations in the previous permit except in compliance with section 303(d)(4).

(2) Exceptions.—A permit with respect to which paragraph (1) applies may be renewed, reissued, or modified to contain a less stringent effluent limitation applicable to a pollutant if—

(A) material and substantial alterations or additions to the permitted facility occurred after permit issuance which justify the application of a less stringent effluent limitation;

(B) (i) information is available which was not available at the time of permit issuance (other than revised regulations, guidance, or test methods) and which would have justified the application of a less stringent effluent limitation at the time of permit issuance; or

(ii) the Administrator determines that technical mistakes or mistaken interpretations of law were made in issuing the permit under subsection (a)(1)(B);

(C) a less stringent effluent limitation is necessary because of events over which the permittee has no control and for which there is no reasonably available remedy;

(D) the permittee has received a permit modification under section 301(c), 301(g), 301(h), 301(i), 301(k), 301(n), or 316(a); or

(E) the permittee has installed the treatment facilities required to meet the effluent limitations in the previous permit and has properly operated and maintained the facilities but has nevertheless been unable to achieve the previous effluent limitations, in which case the limitations in the reviewed, reissued, or modified permit may reflect the level of pollutant control actually achieved (but shall not be less stringent than required by effluent guidelines in effect at the time of permit renewal, reissuance, or modification). Subparagraph (B) shall not apply to any revised waste load allocations or any alternative grounds for translating water quality standards into effluent limitations, except where the cumulative effect of such revised allocations results in a decrease in the amount of pollutants discharged into the concerned waters, and such revised allocations are not the result of a discharger eliminating or substantially reducing its discharge of pollutants due to complying with the requirements of this Act or for reasons otherwise unrelated to water quality.

(3) Limitations.—In no event may a permit with respect to which paragraph (1) applies be renewed, reissued, or modified to contain an effluent limitation which is less stringent than required by effluent guidelines in effect at the time the permit is renewed, reissued, or modified. In no event may such a permit to discharge into waters be renewed, reissued, or modified to contain a less stringent effluent limitation if the implementation of such limitation would result in a violation of a water quality standard under section 303 applicable to such waters.

[§402(o) added by PL 100-4]

(p) Municipal and Industrial Stormwater Discharges.—

(1) General Rule.—Prior to October 1, 1994, the Administrator or the State (in the case of a permit program approved under section 402 of this Act) shall not require a permit under this section for discharges composed entirely of stormwater.

[§402(p)(1) amended by PL 102–580]

(2) Exceptions.—Paragraph (1) shall not apply with respect to the following stormwater discharges:

(A) A discharge with respect to which a permit has been issued under this section before the date of the enactment of this subsection.

(B) A discharge associated with industrial activity.

(C) A discharge from a municipal separate storm sewer system serving a population of 250,000 or more.

(D) A discharge from a municipal separate storm sewer system serving a population of 100,000 or more but less than 250,000.

(E) A discharge for which the Administrator or the State, as the case may be, determines that the stormwater discharge contributes to a violation of a water quality standard or is a significant contributor of pollutants to waters of the United States.

(3) Permit Requirements.—

(A) Industrial Discharges.—Permits for discharges associated with industrial activity shall meet all applicable provisions of this section and section 301.

(B) Municipal Discharge.—Permits for discharges from municipal storm sewers—

(i) may be issued on a system—or jurisdiction-wide basis;

(ii) shall include a requirement to effectively prohibit non-stormwater discharges into the storm sewers; and

(iii) shall require controls to reduce the discharge of pollutants to the maximum extent practicable, including management practices, control techniques and system, design and engineering methods, and such other provisions as the Administrator or the State determines appropriate for the control of such pollutants.

(4) Permit Application Requirements.—

(A) Industrial and Large Municipal Discharges.—Not later than 2 years after the date of the enactment of this subsection, the Administrator shall establish regulations setting forth the permit application requirements for stormwater discharges described in paragraphs (2)(B) and (2)(C). Applications for permits for such discharges shall be filed no later than 3 years after such date of enactment. Not later than 4 years after such date of enactment, the Administrator or the State, as the case may be, shall issue or deny each such permit. Any such permit shall provide for compliance as expeditiously as practicable, but in no event later than 3 years after the date of issuance of such permit.

(B) Other Municipal Discharges.— Not later than 4 years after the date of the enactment of this subsection, the Administrator shall establish regulations setting forth the permit application requirements for stormwater discharges described in paragraph (2)(D). Applications for permits for such discharges shall be filed no later than 5 years after such date of enactment. Not later than 6 years after such date of enactment, the Administrator or the State, as the case may be, shall issue or deny each such permit. Any such permit shall provide for compliance as expeditiously as practicable, but in no event later than 3 years after the date of issuance of such permit.

(5) Studies.—The Administrator, in consultation with the States, shall conduct a study for the purposes of—

(A) identifying those stormwater discharges or classes of stormwater discharges for which permits are not required pursuant to paragraphs (1) and (2) of this subsection;

(B) determining, to the maximum extent practicable, the nature and extent of pollutants in such discharges; and

(C) establishing procedures and methods to control stormwater discharges to the extent necessary to mitigate impacts on water quality.

Not later than October 1, 1988, the Administrator shall submit to Congress a report on the results of the study described in subparagraphs (A) and (B). Not later than October 1, 1989, the Administrator shall submit to Congress a report on the results of the study described in subparagraph (C).

[§402(p)(6) amended by PL 102–580]

(6) Regulations.—Not later than October 1, 1994, the Administrator, in consultation with State and local officials, shall issue regulations (based on the results of the studies conducted under paragraph (5)) which designate stormwater discharges, other than those discharges described in paragraph (2), to be regulated to protect water quality and shall establish a comprehensive program to regulate such designated sources. The program shall, at a minimum, (A) establish priorities, (B) establish requirements for State stormwater management programs, and (C) establish expeditious deadlines. The program may include performance standards, guidelines, guidance, and management practices and treatment requirements, as appropriate.

[§402(p) added by PL 100-4]

§1343. Ocean Discharge Criteria [Sec. 403]

(a) No permit under section 402 of this Act for a discharge into the territorial sea, the waters of the contiguous zone, or the oceans shall be issued, after promulgation of guidelines established under subsection (c) of this section, except in compliance with such guidelines. Prior to the promulgation of such guidelines, a permit may be issued under such section 402 if the Administrator determines it to be in the public interest.

(b) The requirements of subsection (d) of section 402 of this Act may not be waived in the case of permits for discharges into the territorial sea.

(c) (1) The Administrator shall, within one hundred and eighty days after enactment of this Act (and from time to time thereafter), promulgate guidelines for determining the degradation of the waters of the territorial seas, the contiguous zone, and the oceans, which shall include:

(A) the effect of disposal of pollutants on human health or welfare, including but not limited to plankton, fish, shellfish, wildlife, shorelines, and beaches;

(B) the effect of disposal of pollutants on marine life including the transfer, concentration, and dispersal of pollutants or their byproducts through biological, physical, and chemical processes; changes in marine ecosystem diversity, productivity, and stability; and species and community population changes;

(C) the effect of disposal, of pollutants on esthetic, recreation, and economic values;

(D) the persistence and permanence of the effects of disposal of pollutants;

(E) the effect of the disposal at varying rates, of particular volumes and concentrations of pollutants;

(F) other possible locations and methods of disposal or recycling of pollutants including land-based alternatives; and

(G) the effect on alternate uses of the oceans, such as mineral exploitation and scientific study.

(2) In any event where insufficient information exists on any proposed discharge to make a reasonable judgment on any of the guidelines established pursuant to this subsection no permit shall be issued under section 402 of this Act.

§1344. Permits for Dredged or Fill Material
[Sec. 404]

(a) The Secretary may issue permits, after notice and opportunity for public hearings for the discharge of dredged or fill material into the navigable waters at specified disposal sites. Not later than the fifteenth day after the date an applicant submits all the information required to complete an application for a permit under this subsection, the Secretary shall publish the notice required by this subsection.

(b) Subject to subsection (c) of this section, each such disposal site shall be specified for each such permit by the Secretary (1) through the application of guidelines developed by the Administrator, in conjunction with the Secretary, which guidelines shall be based upon criteria comparable to the criteria applicable to the territorial seas, the contiguous zones, and the ocean under section 403(c), and (2) in any case where such guidelines under clause (1) alone would prohibit the specification of a site, through the application additionally of the economic impact of the site on navigation and anchorage.

(c) The Administrator is authorized to prohibit the specification (including the withdrawal of specification) of any defined area as a disposal site, and he is authorized to deny or restrict the use of any defined area for specification (including the withdrawal of specification) as a disposal site, whenever he determines, after notice and opportunity for public hearings, that the discharge of such materials into such area will have an unacceptable adverse effect on municipal water supplies, shellfish beds and fishery areas (including spawning and breeding areas), wildlife, or recreational areas. Before making such determination, the Administrator shall consult with the Secretary. The Administrator shall set forth in writing and make public his findings and his reasons for making any determination under this subsection.

(d) The term "Secretary" as used in this section means the Secretary of the Army, acting through the Chief of Engineers.

(e) (1) In carrying out his functions relating to the discharge of dredged or fill material under this section, the Secretary may, after notice and opportunity for public hearing, issue general permits on a State, regional, or nationwide basis for any category of activities involving discharges of dredged or fill material if the Secretary determines that the activities in such category are similar in nature, will cause only minimal adverse environmental effects when performed separately, and will have only minimal cumulative adverse effect on the environment. Any general permit issued under this subsection shall (A) be based on the guidelines described in subsection (b)(l) of this section, and (B) set forth the requirements and standards which shall apply to any activity authorized by such general permit.

(2) No general permit issued under this subsection shall be for a period of more than five years after the date of its issuance and such general permit may be revoked or modifed by the Secretary if, after opportunity for public hearing, the Secretary determines that the activities authorized by such general permit have an adverse impact on the environment or such activities are more appropriately authorized by individual permits.

(f) (1) Except as provided in paragraph (2) of this subsection, the discharge of dredge or fill material—

(A) from normal farming, silviculture, and ranching activities such as plowing, seeding, cultivating, minor drainage, harvesting for the production of food, fiber, and forest products, or upland soil and water conservation practices;

(B) for the purpose of maintenance, including emergency reconstruction of recently damaged parts, of currently serviceable structures such as dikes, dams, levees, groins, riprap, breakwaters, causeways, and bridge abutments or approaches, and transportation structures;

(C) for the purpose of construction or maintenance of farm or stock ponds or irrigation ditches, or the maintenance of drainage ditches;

(D) for the purpose of construction of temporary sedimentation basins on a construction site which does not include placement of fill material into the navigable waters;

(E) for the purpose of construction or maintenance of farm roads or forest roads, or temporary ioads for moving mining equipment, where such roads are constructed and maintained, in accordance with best management practices, to assure that flow and circulation patterns and chemical and biological characteristics of the navigable waters are not impaired, that the reach of the navigable waters is not reduced, and that any adverse effect on the aquatic environment will be otherwise minimized;

(F) resulting from any activity with respect to which a State has an approved program under section 208(b)(4) which meets the requirements of subparagraphs (B) and (C) of such section, is not prohibited by or otherwise subject to regulation under this section or section 301(a) or 402 of this Act (except for effluent standards or prohibitions under section 307).

(2) Any discharge of dredged or fill material into the navigable waters incidental to any activity having as its purpose bringing an area of the navigable waters into a use to which it was not previously subject, where the flow or circulation of navigable waters may be impaired or the reach of such waters be reduced, shall be required to have a permit under this section.

(g) (1) The Governor of any State desiring to administer its own individual and general permit program for the discharge of dredged or fill material into the navigable waters (other than those waters which are presently used, or are susceptible to use in their natural condition or by reasonable improvement as a means to transport interstate or foreign commerce shoreward to their ordinary high water mark, including all waters which are subject to the ebb and flow of the tide shoreward to their mean high water mark, or mean higher high water mark on the west coast, including wetlands adjacent thereto), within its jurisdiction may submit to the Administrator a full and complete description of the program it proposes to establish and administer under State law or under an interstate compact. In addition, such State shall submit a statement from the attorney general (or the attorney for those State agencies which have independent legal counsel), or from the chief legal officer in the case of an interstate agency, that the laws of such State, or the interstate compact, as the case may be, provide adequate authority to carry out the described program.

(2) Not later than the tenth day after the date of the receipt of the program and statement submitted by any State under paragraph (1) of this subsection, the Administrator shall provide copies of such program and statement to the Secretary and the Secretary of the Interior, acting through the Director of the United States Fish and Wildlife Service.

(3) Not later than the ninetieth day after the date of the receipt by the Administrator of the program and statement submitted by any State, under paragraph (1) of this subsection, the Secretary and the Secretary of the Interior, acting through the Director of the United States Fish and Wildlife Service, shall submit any comments with respect to such program and statement to the Administrator in writing.

(h) (1) Not later than the one-hundred- twentieth day after the date of the receipt by the Administrator of a program and statement submitted by any State under paragraph (1) of this subsection, the Administrator shall determine, taking into account any comments submitted by the Secretary and the Secretary of the Interior, acting through the Director of the United States Fish and Wildlife Service, pursuant to subsection (g) of this section, whether such State has the following authority with respect to the issuance of permits pursuant to such program:

(A) To issue permits which—

(i) apply and assure compliance with, any applicable requirements of this section, including, but not limited to, the guidelines established under section (b)(1) of this section, and sections 307 and 403 of this Act;

(ii) are for fixed terms not exceeding five years; and

(iii) can be terminated or modified for cause including, but not limited to, the following:

(I) violation of any condition of the permit;

(II) obtaining a permit by misrepresentation, or failure to disclose fully all relevant facts;

(III) change in any condition that requires either a temporary or permanent reduction or elimination of the permitted discharge.

(B) To issue permits which apply, and assure compliance with, all applicable requirements of section 308 of this Act, or to inspect, monitor, enter, and require reports to at least the same extent as required in section 308 of this Act.

(C) To assure that the public, and any other State the waters of which may be affected, receive notice of each application for a permit and to provide an opportunity for public hearing before a ruling on each such application.

(D) To assure that the Administrator receives notice of each application (including a copy thereof) for a permit.

(E) To assure that any State (other than the permitting State), whose waters may be affected by the issuance of a permit may submit written recommendation to the permitting State (and the Administrator) with respect to any permit application and, if any part of such written recommendations are not accepted by the permitting State, that the permitting State will notify such affected State (and the Administrator) in writing of its failure to so accept such recommendations together with its reasons for so doing.

(F) To assure that no permit will be issued if, in the judgment of the Secretary, after consultation with the Secretary of the department in which the Coast Guard is operating, anchorage and navigation of any of the navigable water would be substantially impaired thereby.

(G) To abate violations of the permit or the permit program, including civil and criminal penalties and other ways and means of enforcement.

(H) To assure continued coordination with Federal and Federal-State water-related planning and review processes.

(2) If, with respect to a State program submitted under subsection (g)(1) of this section, the Administrator determines that such State—

(A) has the authority set forth in paragraph (1) of this subsection, the Administrator shall approve the program and so notify (i) such State, and (ii) the Secretary, who upon subsequent notification from such State that it is administering such program, shall suspend the issuance of permits under subsection (a) and (e) of this section for activities with respect to which a permit may be issued pursuant to such State program; or

(B) does not have the authority set forth in paragraph (1) of this subsection, the Administrator shall so notify such State, which notification shall also describe the revisions or modifications necessary so that such State may resubmit such program for a determination by the Administrator under this subsection.

(3) If the Administrator fails to make a determination with respect to any program submitted by a State under subsection (g)(1) of this section within one-hundred-twenty days after the date of the receipt of such program, such program shall be deemed approved pursuant to paragraph (2)(A) of this subsection and the Administrator shall so notify such State and the Secretary who, upon subsequent notification from such State that it is administering such program, shall suspend the issuance of permits under subsection (a) and (e) of this section for activities with respect to which a permit may be issued by such State.

(4) After the Secretary receives notification from the Administrator under paragraph (2) or (3) of this subsection that a State permit program has been approved, the Secretary shall transfer any applications for permits before the Secretary for activities with respect to which a permit may be issued pursuant to such State program to such State for appropriate action.

(5) Upon notification from a State with a permit prcgram approved under this subsection that such State intends to administer and enforce the terms and conditions of a general permit issued by the Secretary under subsection (e) of this section with respect to activities in such State to which such general permit applies, the Secretary shall suspend the administration and enforcement of such general permit with respect to such activities.

(i) Whenever the Administrator determines after public hearing that a State is not administering a program approved under section (h)(2)(A) of this section, in accordance with this section, including, but not limited to, the guidelines established under subsection (b)(1) of this section, the Administrator shall so notify the State, and, if appropriate corrective action is not taken within a reasonable time, not to exceed ninety days after the date of the receipt of such notification, the Administrator shall (1) withdraw approval of such program until the Administrator determines such corrective action has been taken, and (2) notify the Secretary that the Secretary shall resume the program for the issuance of permits under subsections (a) and (e) of this section for activities with respect to which the State was issuing permits and that such authority of the Secretary shall continue in effect until such time as the Administrator makes the determination described in clause (l) of this subsection and such State again has an approved program.

(j) Each State which is administering a permit program pursuant to this section shall transmit to the Administrator (1) a copy of each permit application received by such State and provide notice to the Administrator of every action related to the consideration of such permit application, including each permit proposed to be issued by such State, and (2) a copy of each proposed general permit which such State intends to issue. Not later than the tenth day after the date of the receipt of such permit application or such proposed general permit, the Administrator shall provide copies of such permit application or such proposed general permit to the Secretary and the Secretary of the Interior, acting through the Director of the United States Fish and Wildlife Service. If the Administrator intends to provide written comments to such State with respect to such permit application or such proposed general permit, he shall so notify such State not later than the thirtieth day after the date of the receipt of such application or such proposed general permit and provide such written comments to such State, after consideration of any comments made in writing with respect to such application or such proposed general permit by the Secretary and the Secretary of the Interior, acting through the Director of the United States Fish and Wildlife Service, not later than the ninetieth day after the date of such receipt. If such State is so notified by the Administrator, it shall not issue the proposed permit until after the receipt of such comments from the Administrator, or after such ninetieth day, whichever first occurs. Such State shall not issue such proposed permit after such ninetieth day if it has received such written comments in which the Administrator objects (A) to the issuance of such proposed permit and such proposed permit is one that has been submitted to the Administrator pursuant to subsection (h)(1)(E), or (B) to the issuances of such proposed permit as being outside the requirements of this section, including, but not limited to, the guidelines developed under subsection (b)(1) of this section unless it modifies such proposed permit in accordance with such comments. Whenever the Administrator objects to the issuance of a permit under the preceding sentence such written objection shall contain a statement of the reasons for such objection and the conditions which such permit would include if it were issued by the Administrator. In any case where the Administrator objects to the issuance of a permit, on request of the State, a public hearing shall be held by the Administrator on such objection. If the State does not resubmit such permit revised to meet such objection within 30 days after completion of the hearing or, if no hearing is requested within 90 days after the date of such objection, the Secretary may issue the permit pursuant to subsection (a) or (e) of this section, as the case may be, for such source in accordance with the guidelines and requirements of this Act.

(k) In accordance with guidelines promulgated pursuant to subsection (h)(2) of section 304 of this Act, the Administrator is authorized to waive the requirements of subsection (j) of this section at the time of the approval of a program pursuant to subsection (h)(2)(A) of this section for any category (including any class, type, or size within such category) of discharge within the State submitting such program.

(l) The Administrator shall promulgate regulations establishing categories of discharges which he determines shall not be subject to the requirements of subsection (j) of this section in any State with a program approved pursuant to subsection (h)(2)(A) of this section. The Administrator may distinguish among classes, types, and sizes within any category of discharges.

(m) Not later than the ninetieth day after the date on which the Secretary notifies the Secretary of the Interior, acting through the Director of the United States Fish and Wildlife Service that (1) an application for a permit under subsection (a) of this section has been received by the Secretary, or (2) the Secretary proposes to issue a general permit under subsection (e) of this section, the Secretary of the Interior, acting through the Director of the United States Fish and Wildlife Service, shall submit any comments with respect to such application or such proposed general permit in writing to the Secretary.

(n) Nothing in this section shall be construed to limit the authority of the Administrator to take action pursuant to section 309 of this Act.

(o) A copy of each permit application and each permit issued under this section shall be available to the public. Such permit application or portion thereof, shall further be available on request for the purpose of reproduction.

(p) Compliance with a permit issued pursuant to this section, including any activity carried out pursuant to a general permit issued under this section, shall be deemed compliance, for purposes of sections 309 and 505, with sections 301, 307, and 403.

(q) Not later than the one-hundred- eightieth day after the date of enactment of this subsection, the Secretary shall enter into agreements with the Administrator, the Secretaries of the Departments of Agriculture, Commerce, Interior, and Transportation, and the heads of other appropriate Federal agencies to minimize, to the maximum extent practicable, duplication, needless paperwork, and delays in the issuance of permits under this section. Such agreements shall be developed to assure that, to the maximum extent practicable, a decision with respect to an application for a permit under subsection (a) of this section will be made not later than the ninetieth day after the date the notice of such application is published under subsection (a) of this section.

(r) The discharge of dredged or fill material as part of the construction of a Federal project specifically authorized by Congress, whether prior to or on or after the date of enactment of this subsection, is not prohibited by or otherwise subject to regulation under this section, or a State program approved under this section, or section 301(a) or 402 of the Act (except for effluent standards or prohibitions under section 307), if information on the effects of such discharge, including consideration of the guidelines developed under subsection (b)(1) of this section, is included in an environmental impact statement for such project pursuant to the National Environmental Policy Act of 1969 and such environmental impact statement has been submitted to Congress before the actual discharge of dredged or fill material in connection with the construction of such project and prior to either authorization of such project or an appropriation of funds for each construction.

(s) (1) Whenever on the basis of any information available to him the Secretary finds that any person is in violation of any condition or limitation set forth in a permit issued by the Secretary under this section, the Secretary shall issue an order requiring such persons to comply with such condition or limitation, or the Secretary shall bring a civil action in accordance with paragraph (3) of this subsection.

(2) A copy of any order issued under this subsection shall be sent immediately by the Secretary to the State in which the violation occurs and other affected States. Any order issued under this subsection shall be by personal service and shall state with reasonable specificity the nature of the violation, specify a time for compliance, not to exceed thirty days, which the Secretary determines is reasonable, taking into account the seriousness of the violation and any good faith efforts to comply with applicable requirements. In any case in which an order under this subsection is issued to a corporation, a copy of such order shall be served on any appropriate corporate officers.

(3) The Secretary is authorized to commence a civil action for appropriate relief, including a permanent or temporary injunction for any violation for which he is authorized to issue a compliance order under paragraph (1) of this subsection. Any action under this paragraph may be brought in the district court of the United States for the district in which the defendant is located or resides or is doing business, and such court shall have jurisdiction to restrain such violation and to require compliance. Notice of the commencement of such action shall be given immediately to the appropriate State.

(4) Any person who violates any condition or limitation in a permit issued by the Secretary under this section, and any person who violates any order issued by the Secretary under paragraph (1) of this subsection, shall be subject to a civil penalty not to exceed $25,000 per day for each violation. In determining the amount of a civil penalty the court shall consider the seriousness of the violation or violations, the economic benefit (if any) resulting from the violation, any history of such violations, any good-faith efforts to comply with the applicable requirements, the economic impact of the penalty on the violator, and such other matters as justice may require.

[Former §404(s)(4) deleted and (5) amended and redesignated as (4) by PL 100–4]

(t) Nothing in this section shall preclude or deny the right of any State or interstate agency to control the discharge of dredged or fill material in any portion of the navigable waters within the jurisdiction of such State, including any activity of any Federal agency, and each such agency shall comply with such State or interstate requirements both substantive and procedural to control the discharge of dredged or fill material to the same extent that any person is subject to such requirements. This section shall not be construed as affecting or impairing the authority of the Secretary to maintain navigation.

§1345. Disposal of Sewage Sludge [Sec. 405]

(a) Notwithstanding any other provision of this Act or of any other law, in the case where the disposal of sewage sludge resulting from the operation of a treatment works as defined in section 212 of this Act (including the removal of in-place sewage sludge from one location and its deposit at another location) would result in any pollutant from such sewage sludge entering the navigable waters, such disposal is prohibited except in accordance with a permit issued by the Administrator under section 402 of this Act.

(b) The Administrator shall issue regulations governing the issuance of permits for the disposal of sewage sludge subject to subsection (a) of this section and section 402 of this Act. Such regulations shall require the application to such disposal of each criterion, factor, procedure, and requirement applicable to a permit issued under section 402 of this title.

(c) Each State desiring to administer its own permit program for disposal of sewage sludge subject to subsection (a) of this section within its jurisdiction may do so in accordance with section 402 of this Act.

(d) Regulations.—

(1) Regulations.—The Administrator, after consultation with appropriate Federal and State agencies and other interested persons, shall develop and publish, within one year after the date of enactment of this subsection and from time to time thereafter, regulations providing guidelines for the disposal of sludge and the utilization of sludge for various purposes. Such regulations shall—

(A) identify uses for sludge, including disposal;

(B) specify factors to be taken into account in determining the measures and practices applicable to each such use or disposal (including publication of information on costs);

(C) identify concentrations of pollutants which interfere with each such use or disposal. The Administrator is authorized to revise any regulation issued under this subsection.

(2) Identification and Regulation of Toxic Pollutants.—

(A) On Basis of Available Information.—

(i) Proposed Regulations.—Not later than November 30, 1986, the Administrator shall identify those toxic pollutants which, on the basis of available information on their toxicity, persistence, concentration, mobility, or potential for exposure, may be present in sewage sludge in concentrations which may adversely affect public health or the environment, and propose regulations specifying acceptable management practices for sewage sludge containing each such toxic pollutant and establishing numerical limitations for each such pollutant for each use identified under paragraph (1)(A).

(ii) Final Regulations.—Not later than August 31, 1987, and after opportunity for public hearing, the Administrator shall promulgate the regulations required by subparagraph (A)(i).

(B) Others.—

(i) Proposed Regulations.—Not later than July 31, 1987, the Administrator shall identify those toxic pollutants not identified under subparagraph (A)(i) which may be present in sewage sludge in concentrations which may adversely affect public health or the environment, and propose regulations specifying acceptable management practices for sewage sludge containing each such toxic pollutant and establishing numerical limitations for each pollutant for each such use identified under paragraph (1)(A).

(ii) Final Regulations.—Not later than June 15, 1988, the Administrator shall promulgate the regulations required by subparagraph (B)(i).

(C) Review.—From time to time, but not less often than every 2 years, the Administrator shall review the regulations promulgated under this paragraph for the purpose of identifying additional toxic pollutants and promulgating regulations for such pollutants consistent with the requirements of this paragraph.

(D) Minimum Standards; Compliance Date.—The management practices and numerical criteria established under subparagraphs (A), (B), and (C) shall be adequate to protect public health and the environment from any reasonably anticipated adverse effects of each pollutant. Such regulations shall require compliance as expeditiously as practicable but in no case later than 12 months after their publication, unless such regulations require the construction of new pollution control facilities, in which case the regulations shall require compliance as expeditiously as practicable but in no case later than two years from the date of their publication.

[§405(d)(2)(5) added by PL 100–4]

(3) Alternative Standards.—For purposes of this subsection, if, in the judgment of the Administrator, it is not feasible to prescribe or enforce a numerical limitation for a pollutant identified under paragraph (2), the Administrator may instead promulgate a design, equipment, management practice, or operational standard, or combination thereof, which in the Administrator's judgment is adequate to protect public health and the environment from any reasonably anticipated adverse effects of such pollutant. In the event the Administrator promulgates a design or equipment standard under this subsection, the Administrator shall include as part of such standard such requirements as will assure the proper operation and maintenance of any such element of design or equipment.

[§405(d)(3) added by PL 100–4]

(4) Conditions on Permits.—Prior to the promulgation of the regulations required by paragraph (2), the Administrator shall impose conditions in permits issued to publicly owned treatment works under section 402 of this Act or take such other measures as the Administrator deems appropriate to protect public health and the environment from any adverse effects which may occur from toxic pollutants in sewage sludge.

[§405(d)(4) added by PL 100–4]

(5) Limitation on Statutory Construction.—Nothing in this section is intended to waive more stringent requirements established by this Act or any other law.

[§405(d)(5) added by PL 100–4]

(e) Manner of Sludge Disposal.—The determination of the manner of disposal or use of sludge is a local determination, except that it shall be unlawful for any person to dispose of sludge from a publicly owned treatment works or any other treatment works treating domestic sewage for any use for which regulations have been established pursuant to subsection (d) of this section, except in accordance with such regulations.

[§405(e) revised by PL 100–4]

(f) Implementation of Regulations.—

(1) Through Section 402 Permits.— Any permit issued under section 402 of this Act to a publicly owned treatment works or any other treatment works treating domestic sewage shall include requirements for the use and disposal of sludge that implement the regulations established pursuant to subsection (d) of this section, unless such requirements have been included in a permit issued under the appropriate provisions of subtitle C of the Solid Waste Disposal Act, part C of the Safe Drinking Water Act, the Marine Protection, Research, and Sanctuaries Act of 1972, or the Clean Air Act, or under State permit programs approved by the Administrator, where the Administrator determines that such programs assure compliance with any applicable requirements of this section. Not later than December 15, 1986, the Administrator shall promulgate procedures for approval of State programs pursuant to this paragraph.

(2) Through Other Permits.—In the case of a treatment works described in paragraph (1) that is not subject to section 402 of this Act and to which none of the other above listed permit programs nor approved State permit authority apply, the Administrator may issue a permit to such treatment works solely to impose requirements for the use and disposal of sludge that implement the regulations established pursuant to subsetion (d) of this section. The Administrator shall include in the permit appropriate requirements to assure compliance with the regulations established pursuant to subsetion (d) of this section. The Administrator shall establish procedures for issuing permits pursuant to this paragraph.

[§405(f) added by PL 100–4]

(g) Studies and Projects.—

(1) Grant Program; Information Gathering. The Administrator is authorized to conduct or initiate scientific studies, demonstration projects, and public information and education projects which are designed to promote the safe and beneficial management or use of sewage sludge for such purposes as aiding the restoration of abandoned mine sites, conditioning soil for parks and recreation areas, agricultural and horticultural uses, and other beneficial purposes. For the purposes of carrying out this subsection, the Administrator may make grants to State water pollution control agencies, other public or nonprofit agencies, institutions, organizations, and individuals. In cooperation with other Federal departments and agencies, other public and private agen-

cies, institutions, and organizations, the Administrator is authorized to collect and disseminate information pertaining to the safe and beneficial use of sewage sludge.

(2) Authorization of Appropriations.— For the purposes of carrying out the scientific studies, demonstration projects, and public information and education projects authorized in this section, there is authorized to be appropriated for fiscal years beginning after September 30, 1986, not to exceed $5,000,000.

[§405(g) added by PL 100–4]

TITLE V—GENERAL PROVISIONS

§1361. Administration [Sec. 501]

(a) The Administrator is authorized to prescribe such regulations as are necessary to carry out his functions under this Act.

(b) The Administrator, with the consent of the head of any other agency of the United States, may utilize such officers and employees of such agency as may be found necessary to assist in carrying out the purposes of this Act.

(c) Each recipient of financial assistance under this Act shall keep such records as the Administrator shall prescribe, including records which fully disclose the amount and disposition by such recipient of the proceeds of such assistance, the total cost of the project or undertaking in connection with which such assistance is given or used, and the amount of that portion of the cost of the project or undertaking supplied by other sources, and such other records as will facilitate an effective audit.

(d) The Administrator and the Comptroller General of the United States, or any of their duly authorized representatives, shall have access, for the purpose of audit and examination, to any books, documents, papers, and records of the recipients that are pertinent to the grants received under this Act. For the purpose of carrying out audits and examinations with respect to recipients of Federal assistance under this Act, the Administrator is authorized to enter into noncompetitive procurement contracts with independent State audit organizations, consistent with chapter 75 of title 31, United States Code. Such contracts may only be entered into to the extent and in such amounts as may be provided in advance in appropriation Acts.

[§501(d) amended by PL 100–4]

(e) (1) It is the purpose of this subsection to authorize a program which will provide official recognition by the United States Government to those industrial organizations and political subdivisions of States which during the preceding year demonstrated an outstanding technological achievement or an innovative process, method, or device in their waste treatment and pollution abatement programs. The Administrator shall, in consultation with the appropriate State water pollution control agencies, establish regulations under which such recognition may be applied for and granted, except that no applicant shall be eligible for an award under this subsection if such applicant is not in total compliance with all applicable water quality requirements under this Act, or otherwise does not have a satisfactory record with respect to environmental quality.

(2) The Administrator shall award a certificate or plaque of suitable design to each industrial organization or political subdivision which qualifies for such recognition under regulations established under this subsection.

(3) The President of the United States, the Governor of the appropriate State, the Speaker of the House of Representatives, and the President pro tempore of the Senate shall be notified of the award by the Administrator and the awarding of such recognition shall be published in the Federal Register.

(f) Upon the request of a State water pollution control agency, personnel of the Environmental Protection Agency may be detailed to such agency for the purpose of carrying out the provisions of this Act.

§1362. General Definitions [Sec. 502]

Except as otherwise specifically provided, when used in this Act:

(1) The term "State water pollution control agency" means the State agency designated by the Governor having responsibility for enforcing State laws relating to the abatement of pollution.

(2) The term "interstate agency" means an agency of two or more States established by or pursuant to an agreement of compact approved by the Congress, or any other agency of two or more. States, having substantial powers or duties pertaining to the control of pollution as determined and approved by the Administrator.

(3) The term "State" means a State, the District of Columbia, the Commonwealth of Puerto Rico, the Virgin Islands, Guam, American Samoa, the Commonwealth of the Northern Mariana Islands, and the Trust Territory of the Pacific Islands.

[§502(3) amended by PL 100–4]

(4) The term "municipality" means a city, town, borough, county, parish, district, association, or other public body created by or pursuant to State law and having jurisdiction over disposal of sewage, industrial wastes, or other wastes, or an Indian tribe or an authorized Indian tribal organization, or a designated and approved management agency under section 208 of this Act.

(5) The term "person" means an individual, corporation, partnership, association, State, municipality, commission, or political subdivision of a State, or any interstate body.

(6) The term "pollutant" means dredged spoil, solid waste, incinerator residue, sewage, garbage, sewage sludge, munitions, chemical wastes, biological materials, radioactive materials, heat, wrecked or discarded equipment, rock, sand, cellar dirt and industrial, municipal, and agricultural waste discharged into water. This term does not mean (A) "sewage from vessels" within the meaning of section 312 of this Act; or (B) water, gas, or other material which is injected into a well to facilitate production of oil or gas, or water derived in association with oil or gas production and disposed of in a well, if the well used either to facilitate production or for disposal purposes is approved by authority of the State in which the well is located, and if such State determines that such injection or disposal will not result in the degradation of ground or surface water resources.

(7) The term "navigable waters" means the waters of the United States, including the territorial seas.

(8) The term "territorial seas" means the belt of the seas measured from the line of ordinary low water along that portion of the coast which is in direct contact with the open sea and the line marking the seaward limit of inland waters, and extending seaward a distance of three miles.

(9) The term "contiguous zone" means the entire zone established or to be established by the United States under article 24 of the Convention of the Territorial Sea and the Contiguous Zone.

(10) The term "ocean" means any portion of the high seas beyond the contiguous zone.

(11) The term "effluent limitation" means any restriction established by a State or the Administrator on quantities, rates, and concentrations of chemical, physical, biological, and other constituents which are discharged from point sources into navigable waters, the waters of the contiguous zone, or the ocean, including schedules of compliance.

(12) The term "discharge of a pollutant" and the term "discharge of pollutants" each means (A) any addition of any pollutant to navigable waters from any point source, (B) any addition of any pollutant to the waters of the contiguous zone or the ocean from any point source other than a vessel or other floating craft.

(13) The term "toxic pollutant" means those pollutants, or combinations of pollutants, including disease-causing agents, which after discharge and upon exposure, ingestion, inhalation or assimilation into any organism, either directly from the environment or indirectly by ingestion through food chains, will, on the basis of information available to the Administrator, cause death, disease, behavioral abnormalities, cancer, genetic mutations, physiological malfunctions (including malfunctions in reproduction) or physical deformations, in such organisms or their offspring.

(14) The term "point source" means any discernible, confined and discrete conveyance, including but not limited to any pipe, ditch, channel, tunnel, conduit, well, discrete fissure, container, rolling stock, concentrated animal feeding operation, or vessel or other floating craft, from which pollutants are or may be discharged. This term does not include agricultural stormwater discharges and return flows from irrigated agriculture.

[§502(14) amended by PL 100–4]

[Editor's Note: Section 507 of PL 100–4 states: "Sec. 507. Definition of Point Source. For purposes of the Federal Water Pollution Control Act, the term "point source" includes a landfill leachate collection system."]

(15) The term "biological monitoring" shall mean the determination of the effects on aquatic life, including accumulation of pollutants in tissue, in receiving waters due to the discharge of pollutants (A) by techniques and procedures, including sampling of organisms representative of appropriate levels of the food chain appropriate to the volume and the physical, chemical, and biological characteristics of the effluent, and (B) at appropriate frequencies and locations.

(16) The term "discharge" when used without qualification includes a discharge of a pollutant, and a discharge of pollutants.

(17) The term "schedule of compliance" means a schedule of remedial measures including an enforceable sequence of actions or operations

leading to compliance with an effluent limitation, other limitation, prohibition, or standard.

(18) The term "industrial user" means those industries identified in the Standard Industrial Classification Manual, Bureau of the Budget, 1967, as amended and supplemented, under the category "Division D—Manufacturing" and such other classes of significant waste products as, by regulation, the Administrator deems appropriate.

(19) The term "pollution" means the man-made or man-induced alteration of the chemical, physical, biological and radiological integrity of water.

(20) The term "medical waste" means isolation wastes; infectious agents; human blood and blood products; pathological wastes; sharps; body parts; contaminated bedding; surgical wastes and potentially contaminated laboratory wastes; dialysis wastes; and such additional medical items as the Administrator shall prescribe by regulation.

[§502(20) added by PL 100–688]

§1363. Water Pollution Control Advisory Board [Sec. 503]

(a) (1) There is hereby established in the Environmental Protection Agency a Water Pollution Control Advisory Board, composed of the Administrator or his designee, who shall be Chairman, and nine members appointed by the President, none of whom shall be Federal officers or employees. The appointed members, having due regard for the purposes of this Act, shall be selected from among representatives of various State, interstate, and local governmental agencies, of public or private interests contributing to, affected by, or concerned with pollution, and of other public and private agencies, organizations, or groups demonstrating an active interest in the field of pollution prevention and control, as well as other individuals who are expert in this field.

(2) (A) Each member appointed by the President shall hold office for a term of three years, except that (i) any member appointed to fill a vacancy occurring prior to the expiration of the term for which his predecessor was appointed shall be appointed for the remainder of such term, and (ii) the terms of office of the members first taking office after June 30, 1956, shall expire as follows: three at the end of one year after such date, three at the end of two years after such date, and three at the end of three years after such date, as designated by the President at the time of appointment, and (iii) the term of any member under the preceding provisions shall be extended until the date on which his successor's appointment is effective. None of the members appointed by the President shall be eligible for reappointment within one year after the end of his preceding term.

(B) The members of the Board who are not officers or employees of the United States, while attending conferences or meetings of the Board or while otherwise serving at the request of the Administrator, shall be entitled to receive compensation at a rate to be fixed by the Administrator, but not exceeding $100 per diem, including travel-time, and while away from their homes or regular places of business they may be allowed travel expenses, including per diem in lieu of subsistence, as authorized by law (5 U.S.C. 73b–2) for persons in the Government service employed intermittently.

(b) The Board shall advise, consult with, and make recommendations to the Administrator on matters of policy relating to the activities and functions of the Administrator under this Act.

(c) Such clerical and technical assistance as may be necessary to discharge the duties of the Board shall be provided from the personnel of the Environmental Protection Agency.

§1364. Emergency Powers [Sec. 504]

(a) Notwithstanding any other provision of this Act, the Administrator upon receipt of evidence that a pollution source or combination of sources is presenting an imminent and substantial endangerment to the health of persons or to the welfare of persons where such endangerment is to the livelihood of such persons, such as inability to market shellfish, may bring suit on behalf of the United States in the appropriate district court to immediately restrain any person causing or contributing to the alleged pollution to stop the discharge of pollutants causing or contributing to such pollution or to take such other action as may be necessary.

(b) [Repealed]

[§504(b) repealed by PL 96–510]

§1365. Citizen Suits [Sec. 505]

(a) Except as provided in subsection (b) of this section, and section 309(g)(6) any citizen may commence a civil action on his own behalf—

[§505(a) amended by PL 100–4]

(1) against any person (including (i) the United States, and (ii) any other governmental instrumentality or agency to the extent permitted by

the eleventh amendment to the Constitution) who is alleged to be in violation of (A) an effluent standard or limitation under this Act or (B) an order issued by the Administrator or a State with respect to such a standard or limitation, or

(2) against the Administrator where there is alleged a failure of the Administrator to perform any act or duty under this Act which is not discretionary with the Administrator. The district courts shall have jurisdiction, without regard to the amount in controversy or the citizenship of the parties, to enforce such an effluent standard or limitation, or such an order, or to order the Administrator to perform such act or duty, as the case may be, and to apply any appropriate civil penalties under section 309(d) of this Act.

(b) No action may be commenced—

(1) under subsection (a)(1) of this section—

(A) prior to sixty days after the plaintiff has given notice of the alleged violation (i) to the Administrator, (ii) to the State in which the alleged violation occurs, and (iii) to any alleged violator of the standard, limitation, or order, or

(B) if the Administrator or State has commenced and is diligently prosecuting a civil or criminal action in a court of the United States, or a State to require compliance with the standard, limitation, or order, but in any such action in a court of the United States any citizen may intervene as a matter of right.

(2) under subsection (a)(2) of this section prior to sixty days after the plaintiff has given notice of such action to the Administrator, except that such action may be brought immediately after such notification in the case of an action under this section respecting a violation of sections 306 and 307(a) of this Act. Notice under this subsection shall be given in such manner as the Administrator shall prescribe by regulation.

(c) (1) Any action respecting a violation by a discharge source of an effluent standard or limitation or an order respecting such standard or limitation may be brought under this section only in the judicial district in which such source is located.

(2) In such action under this section, the Administrator, if not a party, may intervene as a matter of right.

(3) Protection of Interests of United States.—Whenever any action is brought under this section in a court of the United States, the plaintiff shall serve a copy of the complaint on the Attorney General and the Administrator. No consent judgment shall be entered in an action in which the United States is not a party prior to 45 days following the receipt of a copy of the proposed consent judgment by the Attorney General and the Administrator.

[§505(c)(3) added by PL 100–4]

(d) The court, in issuing any final order in any action brought pursuant to this section, may award costs of litigation (including reasonable attorney and expert witness fees) to any prevailing or substantially prevailing party, whenever the court determines such award is appropriate. The court may, if a temporary restraining order or preliminary injunction is sought, require the filing of a bond or equivalent security in accordance with the Federal Rules of Civil Procedure.

[§505(d) amended by PL 100–4]

(e) Nothing in this section shall restrict any right which any person (or class of persons) may have under any statute or common law to seek enforcement of any effluent standard or limitation or to seek any other relief (including relief against the Administrator or a State agency).

(f) For purposes of this section, the term "effluent standard or limitation under this Act" means (1) effective July 1, 1973, an unlawful act under subsection (a) of section 301 of this Act; (3) an effluent limitation or other limitation under section 301 or 302 of this Act; (4) standard of performance under section 306 of this Act; (3) prohibition, effluent standard or pretreatment standards under section 307 of this Act; (5) certification under section 401 of this Act; (6) a permit or condition thereof issued under section 402 of this Act, which is in effect under this Act (including a requirement applicable by reason of section 313 of this Act); or (7) a regulation under section 405(d) of this Act.

[§505(f) amended by PL 100–4]

(g) For the purposes of this section the term "citizen" means a person or persons having an interest which is or may be adversely affected.

(h) A Governor of a State may commmence a civil action under subsection (a), without regard to the limitations of subsection (b) of this section, against the Administrator where there is alleged a failure of the Administrator to enforce an effluent standard or limitation under this Act the violation of which is occurring in another State and is causing an adverse effect on the public health or welfare in his State, or is causing a violation of any water quality requirement in his State.

§1366. Appearance [Sec. 506]

The Administrator shall request the Attorney General to appear and represent the United States in any civil or criminal action instituted under this Act to which the Administrator is a party. Unless the Attorney General notifies the Administrator within a reasonable time, that he will appear in a civil action, attorneys who are officers or employees of the Environmental Protection Agency shall appear and represent the United States in such action.

§1367. Employee Protection [Sec. 507]

(a) No person shall fire, or in any other way discriminate against, or cause to be fired or discriminated against, any employee or any authorized representative of employees by reason of the fact that such employee or representative has filed, instituted, or caused to be filed or instituted any proceeding under this Act, or has testified or is about to testify in any proceeding resulting from the administration or enforcement of the provisions of this Act.

(b) Any employee or a representative of employees who believes that he has been fired or otherwise discriminated against by any person in violation of subsection (a) of this section may, within thirty days after such alleged violation occurs, apply to the Secretary of Labor for a review of such firing or alleged discrimination. A copy of the application shall be sent to such person who shall be the respondent. Upon receipt of such application, the Secretary of Labor shall cause such investigation to be made as he deems appropriate. Such investigation shall provide an opportunity for a public hearing at the request of any party to such review to enable the parties to present information relating to such alleged violation. The parties shall be given written notice of the time and place of the hearing at least five days prior to the hearing. Any such hearing shall be of record and shall be subject to section 554 of title 5 of the United States Code. Upon receiving the report of such investigation, the Secretary of Labor shall make findings of fact. If he finds that such violation did occur, he shall issue a decision, incorporating an order therein and his findings, requiring the party committing such violation to take such affirmative action to abate the violation as the Secretary of Labor deems appropriate, including, but not limited to, the rehiring or reinstatement of the employee or representative of employees to his former position with compensation. If he finds that there was no such violation, he shall issue an order denying the application. Such order issued by the Secretary of Labor under this subparagraph shall be subject to judicial review in the same manner as orders and decisions of the Administrator are subject to judicial review under this Act.

(c) Whenever an order is issued under this section to abate such violation, at the request of the applicant, a sum equal to the aggregate amount of all costs and expenses (including the attorney's fees), as determined by the Secretary of Labor, to have been reasonably incurred by the applicant for, or in connection with, the institution and prosecution of such proceedings, shall be assessed against the person committing such violation.

(d) This section shall have no application to any employee who, acting without direction from his employer (or his agent) deliberately violates any prohibition of effluent limitation or other limitation under section 301 or 302 of this Act, standards of performance under section 306 of this Act, effluent standard, prohibition or pretreatment standard under section 307 of this Act, or any other prohibition or limitation established under this Act.

(e) The Administrator shall conduct continuing evaluations of potential loss or shifts of employment which may result from the issuance of any effluent limitation or order under this Act, including, where appropriate, investigating threatened plant closures or reductions in employment allegedly resulting from such limitation or order. Any employee who is discharged or laid off, threatened with discharge or lay-off, or otherwise discriminated against by any person because of the alleged results of any effluent limitation or order issued under this Act, or any representative of such employee, may request the Administrator to conduct a full investigation of the matter. The Administrator shall thereupon investigate the matter and, at the request of any party, shall hold public hearings on not less than five days notice, and shall at such hearing require the parties, including the employer involved, to present information relating to the actual or potential effect of such limitation or order on employment and on any alleged discharge, lay off, or other discrimination and the detailed reasons or justification therefor. Any such hearing shall be of record and shall be subject to section 554 of title 5 of the United States Code. Upon receiving the report of such investigation, the Administrator shall make findings of fact as to the effect of such effluent limitation or order on employment and on the alleged discharge, lay-off, or discrimination and shall make such recommendations as he deems appropriate. Such report, findings, and recommendations shall be available to the public. Nothing in this subsection shall be construed to require or authorize the Administrator to modify or withdraw any effluent limitation or order issued under this Act.

§1368. Federal Procurement [Sec. 508]

(a) No Federal agency may enter into any contract with any person, who has been convicted of any offense under section 309(c) of this Act, for the procurement of goods, materials, and services if such contract is to be performed at any facility at which the violation which gave rise to such conviction occurred, and if such facility is owned, leased, or supervised by such person. The prohibition in the preceding sentence shall continue until the Administrator certifies that the condition giving rise to such conviction has been corrected.

(b) The Administrator shall establish procedures to provide all Federal agencies with the notification necessary for the purposes of subsection (a) of this section.

(c) In order to implement the purposes and policy of this Act to protect and enhance the quality of the Nation's water, the President shall, not more than one hundred and eighty days after enactment of this Act, cause to be issued an order (1) requiring each Federal agency authorized to enter into contracts and each Federal agency which is empowered to extend Federal assistance by way of grant, loan, or contract to effectuate the purpose and policy of this Act in such contracting or assistance activities, and (2) setting forth procedures, sanctions, penalties, and such other provisions, as the President determines necessary to carry out such requirement.

(d) The President may exempt any contract, loan, or grant from all or part of the provisions of this section where he determines such exemption is necessary in the paramount interest of the United States and he shall notify the Congress of such exemption.

(e) The President shall annually report to the Congress on measures taken in compliance with the purpose and intent of this section, including, but not limited to, the progress and problems associated with such compliance.

§1369. Administrative Procedure and Judicial Review [Sec. 509]

(a) (1) For the purposes of obtaining information under section 305 of this Act, or carrying out section 507(e) of this Act, the Administrator may issue subpenas for the attendance and testimony of witnesses and the production of relevant papers, books, and documents, and he may administer oaths. Except for effluent data, upon a showing satisfactory to the Administrator that such papers, books, documents, or information or particular part thereof, if made public, would divulge trade secrets or secret processes, the Administrator shall consider such record, report, or information or particular portion thereof confidential in accordance with the purposes of section 1905 of title 18 of the United States Code, except that such paper, book, document, or information may be disclosed to other officers, employees, or authorized representatives of the United States concerned with carrying out this Act, or when relevant in any proceeding under this Act. Witnesses summoned shall be paid the same fees and mileage that are paid witnesses in the courts of the United States. In case of contumacy or refusal to obey a subpena served upon any person under this subsection, the district court of the United States for any district in which such person is found or resides or transacts business, upon application by the United States and after notice to such person, shall have jurisdiction to issue an order requiring such person to appear and give testimony before the Administrator, to appear and produce papers, books, and documents before the Administrator, or both, and any failure to obey such order of the court may be punished by such court as a contempt thereof.

(2) The district courts of the United States are authorized, upon application by the Administrator, to issue subpenas for attendance and testimony of witnesses and the production of relevant papers, books, and documents, for purposes of obtaining information under sections 304(b) and (c) of this Act. Any papers, books, documents, or other information or part thereof, obtained by reason of such a subpena shall be subject to the same requirements as are provided in paragraph (1) of this subsection.

(b) (1) Review of the Administrator's action (A) in promulgating any standard of performance under section 306, (B) in making any determination pursuant to section 306(b)(1)(C), (C) in promulgating any effluent standard, prohibition, or pretreatment standard under section 307, (D) in making any determination as to a State permit program submitted under section 402(b), (E) in approving or promulgating any effluent limitation or other limitation under sections 301, 302, 306, or 405, [,] (F) in issuing or denying any permit under section 402, and (G) in promulgating any individual control strategy under section 304(l), may be had by any interested person in the Circuit Court of Appeals of the United States for the Federal judicial district in which such person resides or trapsacts business which is directly affected by such action upon application by such person. Any such application shall be made within 120 days from the date of such determination, approval, promulgation, issuance or denial, or after such date only if such application is based solely on grounds which arose after such 120th day.

[§509(b)(1) amended by PL 100–4]

(2) Action of the Administrator with respect to which review could have been obtained under paragraph (1) of this subsection shall not be subject to judicial review in any civil or criminal proceeding for enforcement.

(3) Award of Fees. In any judicial proceeding under this subsection, the court may award costs of litigation (including reasonable attorney and expert witness fees) to any prevailing or substantially prevailing party whenever it determines that such award is appropriate.

[Former §509(b)(3) repealed and §509(b)(4) as added by PL 100–4redesignated as (3) by PL 100–236]

(c) In any judicial proceeding brought under subsection (b) of this section in which review is sought of a determination under this Act required to be made on the record after notice and opportunity for hearing, if any party applies to the court for leave to adduce additional evidence, and shows to the satisfaction of the court that such additional evidence is material and that there were reasonable grounds for the failure to adduce such evidence in the proceeding before the Administrator, the court may order such additional evidence (and evidence in rebuttal thereof) to be taken before the Administrator in such manner and upon such terms and conditions as the court may deem proper. The Administrator may modify his findings as to the facts, or make new findings, by reason of the additional evidence so taken and he shall file such modified or new findings, and his recommendation, if any, for the modification or setting aside of his original determination, with the return of such additional evidence.

§1370. State Authority [Sec. 510]

Except as expressly provided in this Act, nothing in this Act shall (1) preclude or deny the right of any State or political subdivision thereof or interstate agency to adopt or enforce (A) any standard or limitation respecting discharges of pollutants, or (B) any requirement respecting control or abatement of pollution; except that if an effluent limitation, or other limitation, effluent standard, prohibition, pretreatment standard, or standard of performance is in effect under this Act, such State or political subdivision or interstate agency may not adopt or enforce any effluent limitation, or other limitation, effluent standard, prohibition, pretreatment standard, or standard of performance which is less stringent than the effluent limitation, or other limitation, effluent standard, prohibition, pretreatment standard, or standard of performance under this Act; or (2) be construed as impairing or in any manner affecting any right or jurisdiction of the States with respect to the waters (including boundary waters) of such States.

§1371. Other Affected Authority [Sec. 511]

(a) This act shall not be construed as (1) limiting the authority or functions of any officer or agency of the United States under any other law or regulation not inconsistent with this Act; (2) affecting or impairing the authority of the Secretary of the Army (A) to maintain navigation or (B) under the Act of March 3, 1899 (30 Stat. 1112); except that any permit issued under section 404 of this Act shall be conclusive as to the effect on water quality of any discharge resulting from any activity subject to section 10 of the Act of March 3, 1899, or (3) affecting or impairing the provisions of any treaty of the United States.

(b) Discharges of pollutants into the navigable waters subject to the Rivers and Harbors Act of 1910 (36 Stat. 593; 33 U.S.C. 421) and the Supervisory Harbors Act of 1888 (25 Stat. 209; 33 U.S.C. 441–451b) shall be regulated pursuant to this Act, and not subject to such Act of 1910 and the Act of 1888 except as to effect on navigation and anchorage.

(c) (1) Except for the provision of Federal financial assistance for the purpose of assisting the construction of publicly owned treatment works as authorized by section 201 of this Act, and the issuance of a permit under section 402 of this Act for the discharge of any pollutant by a new source as defined in section 306 of this Act, no action of the Administrator taken pursuant to this Act shall be deemed a major Federal action significantly affecting the quality of the human environment within the meaning of the National Environmental Policy Act of 1969 (83 Stat. 852); and

(2) Nothing in the National Environmental Policy Act of 1969 (83 Stat. 852) shall be deemed to—

(A) authorize any Federal agency authorized to license or permit the conduct of any activity which may result in the discharge of a pollutant into the navigable waters to review any effluent limitation or other requirement established pursuant to this Act or the adequacy of any certification under section 401 of this Act; or

(B) authorize any such agency to impose, as a condition precedent to the issuance of any license or permit, any effluent limitation other than any such limitation established pursuant to this Act.

(d) Notwithstanding this Act or any other provision of law, the Administrator (1) shall not require any State to consider in the development of the ranking in order of priority of needs for the construction of treatment works (as defined in title II of this Act), any water pollution control agreement which may have been entered into between the United States and any other nation, and (2) shall not consider any such agreement in the approval of any such priority ranking.

Separability [Sec. 512]

If any provision of this Act, or the application of any provision of this Act to any person or circumstance, is held invalid, the application of such provision to other persons or circumstances, and the remainder of this Act, shall not be affected thereby.

§1372. Labor Standards [Sec. 513]

The Administrator shall take such action as may be necessary to insure that all laborers and mechanics employed by contractors or subcontractors on treatment works for which grants are made under this Act shall be paid wages at rates not less than those prevailing for the same type of work on similar construction in the immediate locality, as determined by the Secretary of Labor, in accordance with the Act of March 3, 1931, as amended, known as the Davis-Bacon Act (46 Stat. 1494; 40 U.S.C., sec. 276a through 276a–5). The Secretary of Labor shall have, with respect to the labor standards specified in this subsection, the authority and functions set forth in Reorganization Plan Numbered 14 of 1950 (15 F.R. 3176) and section 2 of the Act of June 13, 1934, as amended (48 Stat. 948; 40 U.S.C. 276c).

§1373. Public Health Agency Coordination [Sec. 514]

The permitting agency under section 402 shall assist the applicant for a permit under such section in coordinating the requirements of this Act with those of the appropriate public health agencies.

§1374. Effluent Standards and Water Quality Information Advisory Committee [Sec. 515]

(a) (1) There is established an Effluent Standards and Water Quality Information Advisory Committee, which shall be composed of a Chairman and eight members who shall be appointed by the Administrator within sixty days after the date of enactment of this Act.

(2) All members of the Committee shall be selected from the scientific community, qualified by education, training, and experience to provide, assess, and evaluate scientific and technical information on effluent standards and limitations.

(3) Members of the Committee shall serve for a term of four years, and may be reappointed.

(b) (1) No later than one hundred and eight days prior to the date on which the Administrator is required to publish any proposed regulations required by section 304(b) of this Act, any proposed standard of performance for new sources required by section 306 of this Act, or any proposed toxic effluent standard required by section 307 of this Act, he shall transmit to the Committee a notice of intent to propose such regulations. The Chairman of the Committee within ten days after receipt of such notice may publish a notice of a public hearing by the Committee, to be held within thirty days.

(2) No later than one hundred and twenty days after receipt of such notice, the Committee shall transmit to the Administrator such scientific and technical information as is in its possession, including that presented at any public hearing, related to the subject matter contained in such notice.

(3) Information so transmitted to the Administrator shall constitute a part of the administrative record and comments on any proposed regulations or standards as information to be considered with other comments and information in making any final determinations.

(4) In preparing information for transmittal, the Committee shall avail itself of the technical and scientific services of any Federal agency, including the United States Geological Survey and any national environmental laboratories which may be established.

(c) (1) The Committee shall appoint and prescribe the duties of a Secretary, and such legal counsel as it deems necessary to exercise and fulfill its powers and responsibilities. The compensation of all employees appointed by the Committee shall be fixed in accordance with chapter 51 and subchapter III of chapter 53 of title V of the United States Code.

(2) Members of the Committee shall be entitled to receive compensation at a rate to be fixed by the President but not in excess of the maximum rate of pay for GS–18, as provided in the General Schedule under section 5332 of title V of the United States Code.

(d) Five members of the Committee shall constitute a quorum, and official actions of the Committee shall be taken only on the affirmative vote of at least five members. A special panel composed of one or more members upon order of the Committee shall conduct any hearing authorized by this section and submit the transcript of such hearing to the entire Committee for its action thereon.

(e) The Committee is authorized to make such rules as are necessary for the orderly transaction of its business.

§1375. Reports to Congress [Sec. 516]

(a) Within ninety days following the convening of each session of Congress, the Administrator shall submit to the Congress a report, in addition to any other report required by this Act, on measures taken toward implementing the objective of this Act, including, but not limited to, (1) the progress and problems associated with developing comprehensive plans under section 102 of this Act, area-wide plans under section 208 of this Act, basin plans under section 209 of this Act, and plans under section 303(e) of this Act; (2) a summary of actions taken and results achieved in the field of water pollution control research, experiments, studies, and related matters by the Administrator and other Federal agencies and by other persons and agencies under Federal grants or contracts; (3) the progress and problems associated with the development of effluent limitations and recommended control techniques; (4) the status State programs, including a detailed summary of the progress obtained as compared to that planned under State program plans for development and enforcement of water quality requirements; (5) the identification and status of enforcement actions pending or completed under such Act during the preceding year; (6) the status of State, interstate, and local pollution control programs established pursuant to, and assisted by, this Act; (7) a summary of the results of the survey required to be taken under section 210 of this Act; (8) his activities including recommendations under sections 109 through 111 of this Act; and (9) all reports and recommendations made by the Water Pollution Control Advisory Board.

(b) (1) The Administrator, in cooperation with the States, including water pollution control agencies and other water pollution control planning agencies, shall make (A) a detailed estimate of the cost of carrying out the provisions of this Act; (B) a detailed estimate, biennially revised, of the cost of construction of all needed publicly owned treatment works in all of the States and of the cost of construction of all needed publicly owned treatment works in each of the States; (C) a comprehensive study of the economic impact on affected units of government of the cost of installation of treatment facilities; and (D) a comprehensive analysis of the national requirements for and the cost of treating municipal, industrial, and other effluent to attain the water quality objectives as established by this Act or applicable State law. The Administrator shall submit such detailed estimate and such comprehensive study of such cost to the Congress no later than February 10 of each odd-numbered year. Whenever the Administrator, pursuant to this subsection, requests and receives an estimate of cost from a State, he shall furnish copies of such estimate together with such detailed estimate to Congress.

(2) Notwithstanding the second sentence of paragraph (1) of this subsection, the Administrator shall make a preliminary detailed estimate called for by subparagraph (B) of such paragraph and shall submit such preliminary detailed estimate to the Congress no later than September 3, 1974. The Administrator shall require each State to prepare an estimate of cost for such State, and shall utilize the survey form EPA–1, O.M.B. No. 158–R0017, prepared for the 1973 detailed estimate, except that such estimate shall include all costs of compliance with section 201(g)(2)(A) of this Act and water quality standards established pursuant to section 303 of this Act, and all costs of treatment works as defined in section 212(2), including all eligible costs of constructing sewage collection systems and correcting excessive infiltration or inflow and all eligible costs of correcting combined storm and sanitary sewer problems and treating storm water flows. The survey form shall be distributed by the Administrator to each State no later than January 31, 1974.

(c) The Administrator shall submit to the Congress by October 1, 1978, a report on the status of combined sewer overflows in municipal treatment works operations. The report shall include (1) the status of any projects funded under this Act to address combined sewer overflows, (2) a listing by State of combined sewer overflow needs identified in the 1977 State priority listings, (3) an estimate for each applicable municipality of the number of years necessary, assuming an annual authorization and appropriation for the construction grants program of $5,000,000,000 to correct combined sewer overflow problems, (4) an analysis using representative municipalities faced with major combined sewer overflow needs, of the annual discharges of pollutants from overflows in comparison to treated effluent discharges, (5) an analysis of the technological alternatives available to municipalities to correct major combined sewer overflow problems, and (6) any recommendations of the Administrator for legislation to address the problem of combined sewer overflows, including whether a separate authorization and grant program should be established by the Congress to address combined sewer overflows.

(d) The Administrator shall submit to the Congress by October 1, 1978, a report on the status of the use of municipal secondary effluent and sludge for agricultural and other purposes that utilize the nutrient value of treated wastewater effluent. The report shall include (1) a summary of results of research and development programs, grants, and contracts carried out by the Environmental Protection Agency pursuant to sections 104 and 105 of this Act, regarding alternatives to disposal, landfill, or incineration of secondary effluent of sludge, (2) an estimate of the amount of sludge generated by public treatment works and its disposition, including an estimate of annual energy costs to incinerate sludge, (3) an analysis of current technologies for the utilization, reprocessing, and other uses of sludge to utilize the nutrient value of sludge, (4) legal, institutional, public health, economic, and other impediments to the greater utilization of treated sludge, and (5) any recommendations of the Administrator for legislation to encourage or require the expanded utilization of sludge for agricultural and other purposes. In carrying out this subsection, the Administrator shall consult with, and use the services of the Tennessee Valley Authority and other departments, agencies and instrumentalities of the United States, to the extent it is appropriate to do so.

(e) The Administrator, in cooperation with the States, including water pollution control agencies, and other water pollution control planning agencies, and water supply and water resources agencies of the States and the United States shall submit to Congress, within two years of the date of enactment of this section, a report with recommendations for legislation on a program to require coordination between water supply and wastewater control plans as a condition to grants for construction of treatment works under this Act. No such report shall be submitted except after opportunity for public hearings on such proposed report.

[Editor's Note: Section 516(f) has not been enacted.]

(g) State Revolving Fund Report.—

(1) In General.—Not later than February 10, 1990, the Administrator shall submit to Congress a report on the financial status and operations of water pollution control revolving funds established by the States under title VI of this Act. The Administrator shall prepare such report in cooperation with the States, including water pollution control agencies and other water pollution control planning and financing agencies.

(2) Contents.—The report under this subsection shall also include the following:

(A) an inventory of the facilities that are in significant noncompliance with the enforceable requirements of this Act;

(B) an estimate of the cost of construction necessary to bring such facilities into compliance with such requirements;

(C) an assessment of the availability of sources of funds for financing such needed construction, including an estimate of the amount of funds available for providing assistance for such construction through September 30, 1999, from the water pollution control revolving funds established by the States under title VI of this Act;

(D) an assessment of the operations, loan portfolio, and loan conditions of such revolving funds;

(E) an assessment of the effect on user charges of the assistance provided by such revolving funds compared to the assistance provided with funds appropriated pursuant to section 207 of this Act; and

(F) an assessment of the efficiency of the operation and maintenance of treatment works constructed with assistance provided by such revolving funds compared to the efficiency of the operation and maintenance of treatment works constructed with assistance provided under section 201 of this Act.

[§516(g) added by PL 100–4]

§1376. General Authorization [Sec. 517]

There are authorized to be appropriated to carry out this Act, other than sections 104, 105, 106(a), 107, 108, 112, 113, 114, 115, 206, 207, 208 (f) and (h), 209, 304, 311(c), (d), (i), (l), and (k), 314, 315, and 317, $250,000,000 for the fiscal year ending June 30, 1973, $300,000,000 for the fiscal year ending June 30, 1974, $350,000,000 for the fiscal year ending June 30, 1975, $100,000,000 for the fiscal year ending September 30, 1977, $150,000,000 for the fiscal year ending September 30, 1978, $150,000,000 for the fiscal year ending September 30, 1979, $150,000,000 for the fiscal year ending September 30, 1980, $150,000,000 for the fiscal year ending September 30, 1981, $161,000,000 for the fiscal year ending September 30, 1982, such sums as may be necessary for fiscal years 1983 through 1985, and $135,000,000 per fiscal year for each of the fiscal years 1986 through 1990.

[§517 amended by PL 96–483; PL 100–4]

§1377. Indian Tribes [Sec. 518]

(a) Policy.—Nothing in this section shall be construed to affect the application of section 101(g) of this Act, and all of the provisions of this section shall be carried out in accordance with the provisions of such section 101(g). Indian tribes shall be treated as States for purposes of such section 101(g).

(b) Assessment of Sewage Treatment Needs; Report.—The Administrator, in cooperation with the Director of the Indian Health Service, shall assess the need for sewage treatment works to serve Indian tribes, the degree to which such needs will be met through funds allotted to States under section 205 of this Act and priority lists under section 216 of this Act, and any obstacles which prevent such needs from being met. Not later than one year after the date of the enactment of this section, the Administrator shall submit a report to Congress on the assessment under this subsection, along with recommendations specifying (1) how the Administrator intends to provide assistance to Indian tribes to develop waste treatment management plans and to construct treatment works under this Act, and (2) methods by which the participation in and administration of programs under this Act by Indian tribes can be maximized.

(c) Reservation of Funds.—The Administrator shall reserve each fiscal year beginning after September 30, 1986, before allotments to the States under section 205(e), one-half of one percent of the sums appropriated under section 207. Sums reserved under this subsection shall be available only for grants for the development of waste treatment management plans and for the construction of sewage treatment works to serve Indian tribes as defined in subsection (h) and former Indian reservations in Oklahoma (as determined by the Secretary of the Interior) and Alaska Native Villages as defined in Public Law 92–203.

[§518(c) added by PL 100–581]

(d) Cooperative Agreements.—In order to ensure the consistent implementation of the requirements of this Act, an Indian tribe and the State or States in which the lands of such tribe are located may enter into a cooperative agreement, subject to the review and approval of the Administrator, to jointly plan and administer the requirements of this Act.

(e) Treatment as States.—The Administrator is authorized to treat an Indian tribe as a State for purposes of title II and sections 104, 106, 303, 305, 308, 309, 314, 319, 401, 402, and 404 of this Act to the degree necessary to carry out the objectives of this section, but only if—

(1) the Indian tribe has a governing body carrying out substantial governmental duties and powers;

(2) the functions to be exercised by the Indian tribe pertain to the management and protection of water resources which are held by an Indian tribe, held by the United States in trust for Indians, held by a member of an Indian tribe if such property interest is subject to a trust restriction on alienation, or otherwise within the borders of an Indian reservation; and

(3) the Indian tribe is reasonably expected to be capable, in the Administrator's judgment, of carrying out the functions to be exercised in a manner consistent with the terms and purposes of this Act and of all applicable regulations. Such treatment as a State may include the direct provision of funds reserved under subsection (c) to the governing bodies of Indian tribes, and the determination of priorities by Indian tribes, where not determined by the Administrator in cooperation with the Director of the Indian Health Service. The Administrator, in cooperation with the Director of the Indian Health Service, is authorized to make grants under title 11 of this Act in an amount not to exceed 100 percent of the cost of a project. Not later than 18 months after the date of the enactment of this section, the Administrator shall, in consultation with Indian tribes, promulgate final regulations which specify how Indian tribes shall be treated as States for purposes of this Act. The Administrator shall, in promulgating such regulations, consult affected States sharing com-

mon water bodies and provide a mechanism for the resolution of any unreasonable consequences that may arise as a result of differing water quality standards that may be set by States and Indian tribes located on common bodies of water. Such mechanism shall provide for explicit consideration of relevant factors including, but not limited to, the effects of differing water quality permit requirements on upstream and downstream dischargers, economic impacts, and present and historical uses and quality of the waters subject to such standards. Such mechanism should provide for the avoidance of such unreasonable consequences in a manner consistent with the objective of this Act.

(f) Grants for Nonpoint Source Programs.—The Administrator shall make grants to an Indian tribe under section 319 of this Act as though such tribe was a State. Not more than one-third of one percent of the amount appropriated for any fiscal year under section 319 may be used to make grants under this subsection. In addition to the requirements of section 319, an Indian tribe shall be required to meet the requirements of paragraphs (1), (2), and (3) of subsection (d) of this section in order to receive such a grant.

(g) Alaska Native Organizations.— No provision of this Act shall be construed to—

(1) grant, enlarge, or diminish, or in any way affect the scope of the governmental authority, if any, of any Alaska Native organization, including any federally-recognized tribe, traditional Alaska Native council, or Native Council organized pursuant to the Act of June 18, 1934 (48 Stat. 987), over lands or persons in Alaska;

(2) create or validate any assertion by such organization or any form of governmental authority over lands or person in Alaska; or

(3) in any way affect any assertion that Indian country, as defined in section 1151 of title 18, United States Code, exists or does not exist in Alaska.

(h) Definitions.—For purposes of this section, the term—

(1) "Federal Indian reservation" means all land within the limits of any Indian reservation under the jurisdiction of the United States Government, notwithstanding the issuance of any patent, and including rights-of-way running through the reservation; and

(2) "Indian tribe" means any Indian tribe, band, group, or community recognized by the Secretary of the Interior and exercising governmental authority over a Federal Indian reservation.

[New §518 added by PL 100–4]

Short Title [Sec. 519]

This Act may be cited as the "Federal Water Pollution Control Act" (commonly referred to as the Clean Water Act).

[Former §518 redesignated as §519 by PL 100–4]

TITLE VI—STATE WATER POLLUTION CONTROL REVOLVING FUNDS

[Title VI added by PL 100–4]

§1381. Grants to States for Establishment of Revolving Funds [Sec. 601]

(a) General Authority. Subject to the provisions of this title, the Administrator shall make capitalization grants to each State for the purpose of establishing a water pollution control revolving fund for providing assistance (1) for construction of treatment works (as defined in section 212 of this Act) which are publicly owned, (2) for implementing a management program under section 319, and (3) for developing and implementing a conservation and management plan under section 320.

(b) Schedule of Grant Payments.— The Administrator and each State shall jointly establish a schedule of payments under which the Administrator will pay to the State the amount of each grant to be made to the State under this title. Such schedule shall be based on the State's intended use plan under section 606(c) of this Act, except that—

(1) such payments shall be made in quarterly installments, and

(2) such payments shall be made as expeditiously as possible, but in no event later than the earlier of—

(A) 8 quarters after the date such funds were obligated by the State, or

(B) 12 quarters after the date such funds were allotted to the State.

§1382. Capitalization Grant Agreements. [Sec. 602]

(a) General Rule.—To receive a capitalization grant with funds made available under this title and section 205(m) of this Act, a State shall enter into an agreement with the Administrator which shall include but not be limited to the specifications set forth in subsection (b) of this section.

(b) Specific Requirements.—The Administrator shall enter into an agreement under this section with a State only after the State has established to the satisfaction of the Administrator that—

(1) the State will accept grant payments with funds to be made available under this title and section 205(m) of this Act in accordance with a payment schedule established jointly by the Administrator under section 601(b) of this Act and will deposit all such payments in the water pollution control revolving fund established by the State in accordance with this title;

(2) the State will deposit in the fund from State moneys an amount equal to at least 20 percent of the total amount of all capitalization grants which will be made to the State with funds to be made available under this title and section 205(m) of this Act on or before the date on which each quarterly grant payment will be made to the State under this title;

(3) the State will enter into binding commitments to provide assistance in accordance with the requirements of this title in an amount equal to 120 percent of the amount of each such grant payment within 1 year after the receipt of such grant payment;

(4) all funds in the fund will be expended in an expeditious and timely manner;

(5) all funds in the fund as a result of capitalization grants under this title and section 205(m) of this Act will first be used to assure maintenance of progress, as determined by the Governor of the State, toward compliance with enforceable deadlines, goals, and requirements of this Act, including the municipal compliance deadlines;

(6) treatment works eligible under section 603(c)(1) of this Act which will be constructed in whole or in part before fiscal year 1995 with funds directly made available by capitalization grants under this title and section 205(m) of this Act will meet the requirements of, or otherwise be treated (as determined by the Governor of the State) under sections 201(b), 201(g)(1), 201(g)(2), 201(g)(3), 201(g)(5), 201(g)(6), 201(n)(1), 201(o), 204(a)(1), 204(a)(2), 204(b)(1), 204(d)(2), 211, 218, 511(c)(1), and 513 of this Act in the same manner as treatment works constructed with assistance under title II of this Act;

(7) in addition to complying with the requirements of this title, the State will commit or expend each quarterly grant payment which it will receive under this title in accordance with laws and procedures applicable to the commitment or expenditure of revenues of the State;

(8) in carrying out the requirements of section 606 of this Act, the State will use accounting, audit, and fiscal procedures conforming to generally accepted government accounting standards;

(9) the State will require as a condition of making a loan or providing other assistance, as described in section 603(d) of this Act, from the fund that the recipient of such assistance will maintain project accounts in accordance with generally accepted government accounting standards and

(10) the State will make annual reports to the Administrator on the actual use of funds in accordance with section 606(d) of this Act.

§1383. Water Pollution Control Revolving Loan Funds. [Sec. 603]

(a) Requirements for Obligation of Grant Funds. Before a State may receive a capitalization grant with funds made available under this title and section 205(m) of this Act, the State shall first establish a water pollution control revolving fund which complies with the requirements of this section.

(b) Administration.—Each State water pollution control revolving fund shall be administered by an instrumentality of the State with such powers and limitations as may be required to operate such fund in accordance with the requirements and objectives of this Act.

(c) Projects Eligible for Assistance.— The amounts of funds available to each State water pollution control revolving fund shall be used only for providing financial assistance (1) to any municipality intermunicipal, interstate, or State agency for construction of publicly owned treatment works (as defined in section 212 of this Act), (2) for the implementation of a management program established under section 319 of this Act, and (3) for development and implementation of a conservation and management plan under section 320 of this Act. The fund shall be established, maintained, and credited with repayments, and the fund balance shall be available in perpetuity for providing such financial assistance.

(d) Types of Assistance.—Except as otherwise limited by State law, a water pollution control revolving fund of a State under this section may be used only—

(1) to make loans, on the condition that—

(A) such loans are made at or below market interest rates, including interest free loans, at terms not to exceed 20 years;

(B) annual principal and interest payments will commence not later than 1 year after completion of any project and all loans will be fully amortized not later than 20 years after project completion;

(C) the recipient of a loan will establish a dedicated source of revenue for repayment of loans; and

(D) the fund will be credited with all payments of principal and interest on all loans;

(2) to buy or refinance the debt obligation of municipalities and intermunicipal and interstate agencies within the State at or below market rates, where such debt obligations were incurred after March 7, 1985;

(3) to guarantee, or purchase insurance for, local obligations where such action would improve credit market access or reduce interest rates;

(4) as a source of revenue or security for the payment of principal and interest on revenue or general obligation bonds issued by the State if the proceeds of the sale of such bonds will be deposited in the fund;

(5) to provide loan guarantees for similar revolving funds established by municipalities or intermunicipal agencies;

(6) to earn interest on fund accounts; and

(7) for the reasonable costs of administering the fund and conducting activities under this title, except that such amounts shall not exceed 4 percent of all grant awards to such fund under this title.

(e) Limitation to Prevent Double Benefits.—If a State makes, from its water pollution revolving fund, a loan which will finance the cost of facility planning and the preparation of plans, specifications, and estimates for construction of publicly owned treatment works, the State shall ensure that if the recipient of such loan receives a grant under section 201(g) of this Act for construction of such treatment works and an allowance under section 201(l)(1) of this Act for non-Federal funds expended for such planning and preparation, such recipient will promptly repay such loan to the extent of such allowance.

(f) Consistency With Planning Requirements.—A State may provide financial assistance from its water pollution control revolving fund only with respect to a project which is consistent with plans, if any, developed under sections 205(j), 208, 303(e), 319, and 320 of this Act.

(g) Priority List Requirement.—The State may provide financial assistance from its water pollution control revolving fund only with respect to a project for construction of a treatment works described in subsection (c)(1) if such project is on the State's priority list under section 216 of this Act. Such assistance may be provided regardless of the rank of such project on such list.

(h) Eligibility of Non-Federal Share of Construction Grant Projects.—A State water pollution control revolving fund may provide assistance (other than under subsection (d)(1) of this section) to a municipality or intermunicipal or interstate agency with respect to the non-Federal share of the costs of a treatment works project for which such municipality or agency is receiving assistance from the Administrator under any other authority only if such assistance is necessary to allow such project to proceed.

§1384. Allotment of Funds. [Sec. 604]

(a) Formula.—Sums authorized to be appropriated to carry out this section for each of fiscal years 1989 and 1990 shall be allotted by the Administrator in accordance with section 205(c) of this Act.

(b) Reservation of Funds for Planning.—Each State shall reserve each fiscal year 1 percent of the sums allotted to such State under this section for such fiscal year, or $100,000, whichever amount is greater, to carry out planning under section 205(j) and 303(e) of this Act.

(c) Allotment Period.—

(1) Period of Availability for Grant Award.—Sums allotted to a State under this section for a fiscal year shall be available for obligation by the State during the fiscal year for which sums are authorized and during the following fiscal year.

(2) Reallotment of Unobligated Funds.—The amount of any allotment not obligated by the State by the last day of the 2–year period of availability established by paragraph (1) shall be immediately reallotted by the Administrator on the basis of the same ratio as is applicable to sums allotted under title II of this Act for the second fiscal year of such 2–year period. None of the funds reallotted by the Administrator shall be reallotted to any State which has not obligated all sums allotted to such State in the first fiscal year of such 2–year period.

§1385. Corrective Action. [Sec. 605]

(a) Notification of Noncompliance.— If the Administrator determines that a State has not complied with its agreement with the Administrator under section 602 of this Act or any other requirement of this title, the Administrator shall notify the State of such noncompliance and the necessary corrective action.

(b) Withholding of Payments.—If a State does not take corrective action within 60 days after the date a State receives notification of such action under subsection (a), the Administrator shall withhold additional payments to the State until the Administrator is satisfied that the State has taken the necessary corrective action.

(c) Reallotment of Withheld Payments.—If the Administrator is not satisfied that adequate corrective actions have been taken by the State within 12 months after the State is notified of such actions under subsection (a), the payments withheld from the State by the Administrator under subsection (b) shall be made available for reallotment in accordance with the most recent formula for allotment of funds under this title.

§1384. Audits, Reports, and Fiscal Controls: Intended Use Plan. [Sec. 606]

(a) Fiscal Control and Auditing Procedure.—Each State electing to establish a water pollution control revolving fund under this title shall establish fiscal controls and accounting procedures sufficient to assure proper accounting during appropriate accounting periods for—

(1) payments received by the fund;

(2) disbursements made by the fund; and

(3) fund balances at the beginning and end of the accounting period.

(b) Annual Federal Audits.—The Administrator shall, at least on an annual basis, conduct or require each State to have independently conducted reviews and audits as may be deemed necessary or appropriate by the Administrator to carry out the objectives of this section. Audits of the use of funds deposited in the water pollution revolving fund established by such State shall be conducted in accordance with the auditing procedures of the General Accounting Office, including chapter 75 of title 31, United States Code.

(c) Intended Use Plan.—After providing for public comment and review, each State shall annually prepare a plan identifying the intended uses of the amounts available to its water pollution control revolving fund. Such intended use plan shall include, but not be limited to—

(1) a list of those projects for construction of publicly owned treatment works on the State's priority list developed pursuant to section 216 of this Act and a list of activities eligible for assistance under sections 319 and 320 of this Act;

(2) a description of the short- and long- term goals and objectives of its water pollution control revolving fund;

(3) information on the activities to be supported, including a description of project categories, discharge requirements under titles III and IV of this Act, terms of financial assistance, and communities served;

(4) assurances and specific proposals for meeting the requirements of paragraphs (3), (4), (5), and (6) of section 602(b) of this Act; and

(5) the criteria and method established for the distribution of funds.

(d) Annual Report.—Beginning the first fiscal year after the receipt of payments under this title, the State shall provide an annual report to the Administrator describing how the State has met the goals and objectives for the previous fiscal year as identified in the plan prepared for the previous fiscal year pursuant to subsection (c) including identification of loan recipients, loan amounts, and loan terms and similar details on other forms of financial assistance provided from the water pollution control revolving fund.

(e) Annual Federal Oversight Review.—The Administrator shall conduct an annual oversight review of each State plan prepared under subsection (c), each State report prepared under subsection (d), and other such materials as are considered necessary and appropriate in carrying out the purposes of this title. After reasonable notice by the Administrator to the State or the recipient of a loan from water pollution control revolving fund, the State or loan recipient shall make available to the Administrator such records as the Administrator reasonably requires to review and determine compliance with this title.

(f) Applicability of Title II Provisions. Except to the extent provided in this title, the provisions of title II shall not apply to grants under this title.

§1387. Authorization of Appropriations. [Sec. 607]

There is authorized to be appropriated to carry out the purposes of this title the following sums:

(1) $1,200,000,000 per fiscal year for each of fiscal years 1989 and 1990;

(2) $2,400,000,000 for fiscal year 1991;

(3) $1,800,000,000 for fiscal year 1992;

(4) $1,200,000,000 for fiscal year 1993; and

(5) $600,000,000 for fiscal year 1994.

3

The Resource Conservation and Recovery Act

INTRODUCTION

The regulation and cleanup of hazardous waste in the United States is one of the most important priorities of the Environmental Protection Agency. While much public attention focuses on the cleanup of inactive or abandoned waste sites under the Comprehensive Environmental Response, Compensation, and Liability Act, the law that has the most direct effect on the day-to-day management practices of the growing hazardous waste industry remains the Resource Conservation and Recovery Act. Perhaps even more importantly, given the United States' growing garbage crisis, RCRA also is the basic law regulating municipal solid waste disposal.

In recent years, hazardous and solid waste problems have become issues of growing national concern. Municipal landfills have become overburdened, many older landfills have been placed on the superfund national priorities list, public opposition has developed to wider use of incineration, widespread contamination by hazardous and radioactive wastes at federal facilities has been disclosed, medical wastes have washed up on U.S. beaches, and states have placed restrictions—and, in some cases, outright bans—on the treatment or disposal of out-of-state wastes within their borders. Some of these problems will have to be addressed in the RCRA reauthorization, but many already are being attacked at the local level as communities in ever-increasing numbers enact recycling ordinances. And industry representatives are starting to discuss process changes that could minimize the amount of waste they create.

This preoccupation with waste is of relatively recent origin. Waste management began at the federal level with the control of solid waste under the Solid Waste Disposal Act of 1965.

Carried out by the Department of Health, Education, and Welfare, the law focused on garbage, particularly on restricting open burning, which was considered a fire hazard. In 1970, then-President Nixon signed an amended version of the solid waste law and renamed it the Resource Recovery Act. This law provided funds for collecting and recycling materials and required a comprehensive investigation of hazardous waste management practices in the United States. Administration of the Act was given to the Environmental Protection Agency upon its creation. A Senate staff member said the sentiment at the time was that "we were drowning in our own garbage." Almost overnight, the law spawned an industry to recycle and incinerate waste, laying the foundations for the current waste disposal industry, a Senate staff aide said.

Two former EPA administrators, Douglas M. Costle and William D. Ruckelshaus, said that in the early 1970s some environmental professionals recognized the dangers of the toxic chemicals that were being generated by the chemical industry. But still it was not a particular concern for policy-makers at EPA or for the public, they said.

In 1976, the same year Congress enacted the Toxic Substances Control Act, it passed the Resource Conservation and Recovery Act of 1976 (P.L. 94-580), which completely replaced the language of the Resource Recovery Act.

The new law continued provisions on solid waste and resource recovery, including the disposal of used oil and waste, and it closed most open dumps; it redefined solid waste to include hazardous waste and ordered EPA to require "cradle to grave" tracking of hazardous waste and controls on hazardous waste facilities. The Act required standards to be set for hazardous waste treatment, storage, and disposal facilities to provide for "the maintenance of operation of such facilities and requiring such additional qualifications as to ownership, continuity of operation, training for personnel, and financial responsibility (including financial responsibility for corrective action) as may be necessary or desirable."

The agency gave little attention between 1976 and 1978 to drawing up rules to carry out the law. Steady pressure from the public and Congress focused the agency instead on revising and issuing regulations for the Clean Air Act and the Clean Water Act, Costle said.

That focus changed in August 1978, when then-President Carter declared a state of emergency in a neighborhood near Love Canal, where long-buried chemicals were seeping into homes and high incidences of health effects, from headaches to birth defects, were reported. The event triggered the discovery of thousands of other dumpsites, alarming the public and mobilizing the Administration and the Congress. "The dawning of knowledge in the minds of a few people is not enough to move our political system," Costle told BNA. "What our political system takes to move it is galvanizing events. And when Love Canal came along, bingo, that was a tremendously galvanizing event."

Under a court order, EPA issued the first two portions of the RCRA hazardous waste rules by May 5, 1980, in an attempt to prevent creation of more toxic waste dumps. The regulations define which wastes are hazardous and set standards for treatment, storage, and disposal facilities. Also in 1980, Congress passed what is a logical complement to RCRA, the Comprehensive Environmental Response, Compensation, and Liability Act of 1980 (PL 96-510), also known as the "superfund law," which ensures financial responsibility for the long-term maintenance of hazardous waste disposal facilities, and provides for the containment and cleanup of old, abandoned hazardous waste disposal sites that are leaking or endangering the public health.

Regulations governing the transport of hazardous wastes were developed jointly by EPA and the Department of Transportation (DOT). Wastes in transit are regulated by the labeling, packaging, and spill reporting provisions of the Hazardous Materials Transportation Act (HMTA), which is administered by DOT. Shippers must certify that they are in compliance with DOT regulations, and all hazardous wastes regulated by EPA, when shipped, must be accompanied by a uniform hazardous waste manifest. When the waste is received at the disposal facility, the facility must return a copy of the manifest to the generator, thereby letting the generator know that the waste was received. If no copy was received, the generator must notify EPA.

Meanwhile, another perception was surfacing: that the primary method of waste disposal envisioned by the new RCRA rules—land disposal—was going to result in an ever-increasing number of hazardous waste sites.

Major provisions of the 1984 RCRA amendments (P.L. 98-616) called for banning land disposal of untreated hazardous waste within five and one-half years of passage. Congress set schedules for the bans and made them automatic if the agency failed to act by certain dates.

The new law also closed "loopholes" in previous rules that allowed toxics to be burned in industrial and apartment furnaces. Increasing the breadth of EPA's regulatory program, the amendments require the agency for the first time to regulate an estimated 600,000 generators of small quantities of hazardous substances and petroleum products.

As of May 1990, the ban on land disposal of untreated hazardous wastes was final, even though standards for some wastes were deferred because treatment was not available for these wastes. However, in 1991 the U.S. Court of Appeals for the District of Columbia Circuit remanded on procedural grounds part of EPA's regulatory scheme for hazardous wastes (*Shell Oil Co. v. EPA*, 950 F.2d 741, 34 ER Cases 1049). The rules dealt with when RCRA Subchapter III (Subtitle C) applies to wastes that are mixed with other, non-hazardous wastes and to wastes that are derived from the treatment, storage, or disposal of wastes listed as hazardous under the act. The agency temporarily reinstated the rules, but was then challenged by Mobil Oil Corp., which filed suit in May 1992 on substantive grounds, arguing that EPA repeatedly has admitted that the mixture and derived-from rules cause materials that do not meet the definition of hazardous waste to be regulated under Subtitle C (*Mobil Oil Corp. v. EPA*, CA DC, No. 92-1211).

The agency's regulatory scheme was further complicated in September 1992 when the Court of Appeals for the District of Columbia Circuit, while approving EPA's decision to allow dilution as a treatment method for certain hazardous wastes, vacated treatment standards for ignitable and corrosive wastes (*Chemical Waste Management v. EPA*, 976 F.2d 2, 35 ER Cases 1329). The Supreme Court refused to hear a challenge to the decision in April 1993 (*Chemical Manufacturers Association v. EPA*, 61 U.S.L.W. 3731, 113 S.Ct. 1961, 36 ER Cases 1376). In May, EPA issued an emergency rule revising the rules and adding numerical treatment standards for the underlying hazardous constituents in these reactive wastes.

The agency is considering many of the underlying assumptions about the regulation of hazardous wastes through its advisory group, the Hazardous Waste Identification Rule (HWIR) Committee. Another advisory group, the Definition of Solid Waste Task Force, completed a series of public meetings in November 1993 and at year's end was working toward refining its recommendations to the agency on how to proceed on other key issues, such as recycling of hazardous wastes.

Medical wastes remain largely unregulated under RCRA. In 1988, toward the end of the 100th Congress, a measure (HR 3515) setting up a pilot tracking program for these wastes won approval. The legislation added a new Subtitle J to RCRA and required EPA to set up a tracking program in three Atlantic states—Connecticut, New Jersey, and New York—and the seven states bordering the Great Lakes, although these seven were given the option of choosing not to participate in the program. HR 3515 also required EPA to set up a limited regulatory program for these wastes, including labeling, segregation from other wastes, and proper packaging for disposal.

In March 1989, EPA issued its regulations. At the time, however, EPA officials expressed skepticism that the program would have any effect on the much-publicized beach washups of the previous summer. Sylvia Lowrance, director of the agency's Office of Solid Waste, said that most medical waste that washed up onto U.S. beaches could be attributed to "litter, poor solid waste practices, and combined sewer overflow problems." This latter problem is being dealt with under the Clean Water Act.

Incineration, once heralded as the answer to the solid waste problem, attracted intense public opposition. Citizens' groups and environmental organizations argued that the dangers of incineration—toxic air emissions and disposal of the ash produced—far outweighed any advantages. These groups said the answer was far greater use of recycling.

Meanwhile, opposition to waste incineration grew, and in 1993 several major waste management companies abandoned plans to build incinerators. One incinerator that began operation in 1993, operated by Waste Technologies Inc. in East Liverpool, Ohio, attracted national attention, as well as the attention of the new Clinton Administration. Although the facility received its required permits, citizens' groups continued their challenge. Incineration probably will continue to play a role in the management of waste in the United States, but that role will probably never be as great as proponents had originally hoped. In May 1993, EPA Administrator Carol M. Browner announced an 18-month freeze on new hazardous waste incinerators, along with new federal controls on incinerators and industrial furnaces that burn hazardous wastes. As a part of this new "Draft Strategy for the Combustion of Hazardous Waste," EPA also issued guidance to assist generators of hazardous waste and owners and operators of hazardous waste treatment, storage, and disposal facilities comply with the "waste minimization" certification requirements of Sections 3002(b) and 3005(h) of RCRA.

Another contentious issue is "flow control." Flow-control laws in states and localities designate a facility to which solid waste generated in the area must be sent for handling, treatment, or disposal. The U.S. Supreme Court, ruling in *C&A Carbone v. Clarkstown* (511 U.S. ____, 62 U.S.L.W. 4315, 38 ER Cases 1529, May 16, 1994), held that a municipal ordinance in the town of Clarkstown, N.Y., violated the Commerce Clause of the U.S. Constitution.

Responding to the Court's decision, several legislators began to draft legislation that would protect flow-control laws and other contractual agreements in effect as of January 1, 1994, as long as a facility had also been designated by that time.

In the House of Representatives, the Energy and Commerce Committee approved flow-control legislation (HR4683) that would let local governments retain most of their authority to operate or designate facilities that manage municipal solid waste within their borders. The Committee also approved legislation (HR 4779) that would let state governments freeze out-of-state waste shipments at 1993 levels if local governments asked them to.

Any amendment of RCRA in the 103rd Congress probably will be limited to a clearly defined and limited issue such as flow control or interstate transport. Most observers see little chance for a major overhaul of the law while more pressing issues such as reauthorization of CERCLA and the Clean Water Act still face Congress.

FINDING LIST

RESOURCE CONSERVATION AND RECOVERY ACT OF 1976

Public Law 94–580, effective Oct. 31, 1976, 90 Stat. 2795.

42 U.S.C. §§6901 et seq.

Amended by PL 95–609, Nov. 8, 1978; PL 96–463, Oct. 15, 1980; PL 96–482, Oct. 21, 1980; PL 96–510, Dec. 11, 1980; PL 97–272, Sept. 30, 1982; PL 97–375, Dec. 21, 1982; PL 98–45, July 12, 1983; PL 98–371, July 18, 1984; PL 98–616, Nov. 8, 1984; PL 99–339, June 19, 1986; PL 99–499, Oct. 17, 1986; PL 100–582, Nov. 1, 1988; PL 102–386, Oct. 6, 1992; PL 102–393, Oct. 6, 1992; PL 102–508, Oct. 24, 1992.

[Editor's Note: The Resource Conservation and Recovery Act of 1976, PL 94–580, completely replaced the previous language of the Solid Waste Disposal Act. Public Law 96–463 enacted the "Used Oil Recycling Act of 1980". Provisions that amended the Resource Conservation and Recovery Act directly have been incorporated into the Act. Other relevant sections that did not amend the Act directly are included where appropriate with an Editor's note. Provisions detailing EPA requirements on studies and reports due in 1981 have been omitted.]

Short Title [Sec. 1]

This Act may be cited as the "Resource Conservation and Recovery Act of 1976."

Amendment Of Solid Waste Disposal Act [Sec. 2]

The Solid Waste Disposal Act (42 U.S.C. 3251 and following) is amended to read as follows:

TITLE II—SOLID WASTE DISPOSAL

SUBTITLE A—GENERAL PROVISIONS

Short Title and Table of Contents [Sec. 1001]

This title (hereinafter in this title referred to as "this Act"), together with the following table of contents, may be cited as the "Solid Waste Disposal Act":

[Omitted]

[§2 amended by PL 102–386]

§6901. Congressional Findings [Sec. 1002]

(a) Solid Waste.—The Congress finds with respect to solid waste—

(1) that the continuing technological progress and improvement in methods of manufacture, packaging, and marketing of consumer products has resulted in an ever-mounting increase, and in a change in the characteristics, of the mass material discarded by the purchaser of such products;

(2) that the economic and population growth of our Nation, and the improvements in the standard of living enjoyed by our population, have required increased industrial production to meet our needs, and have made necessary the demolition of old buildings, the construction of new buildings, and the provision of highways and other avenues of transportation, which, together with related industrial, commercial, and agricultural operations, have resulted in a rising tide of scrap, discarded, and waste materials;

(3) that the continuing concentration of our population in expanding metropolitan and other urban areas has presented these communities with serious financial, management, intergovernmental, and technical problems in the disposal of solid wastes resulting from the industrial, commercial, domestic, and other activities carried on in such areas;

(4) that while the collection and disposal of solid wastes should continue to be primarily the function of State, regional, and local agencies, the problems of waste disposal as set forth above have become a matter national in scope and in concern and necessitate Federal action through financial and technical assistance and leadership in the development, demonstration, and application of new and improved methods and processes to reduce the amount of waste and unsalvageable materials and to provide for proper and economical solid waste disposal practices.

(b) Environment and Health. —The Congress finds with respect to the environment and health, that—

(1) although land is too valuable a national resource to be needlessly polluted by discarded materials, most solid waste is disposed of on land in open dumps and sanitary landfills;

(2) disposal of solid waste and hazardous waste in or on the land without careful planning and management can present a danger to human health and the environment;

(3) as a result of the Clean Air Act, the Water Pollution Control Act, and other Federal and State laws respecting public health and the environment, greater amounts of solid waste (in the form of sludge and other pollution treatment residues) have been created. Similarly, inadequate and environmentally unsound practices for the disposal or use of

solid waste have created greater amounts of air and water pollution and other problems for the environment and for health;

(4) open dumping is particularly harmful to health, contaminates drinking water from underground and surface supplies, and pollutes the air and the land;

(5) the placement of inadequate controls on hazardous waste management will result in substantial risks to human health and the environment;

[Former §1002(b)(5) deleted and new (5) added by PL 98–616]

(6) if hazardous waste management is improperly performed in the first instance, corrective action is likely to be expensive, complex, and time consuming;

[§1002(b)(6) added by PL 98–616]

(7) certain classes of land disposal facilities are not capable of assuring long-term containment of certain hazardous wastes, and to avoid substantial risk to human health and the environment, reliance on land disposal should be minimized or eliminated, and land disposal, particularly landfill and surface impoundment, should be the least favored method for managing hazardous wastes; and

[§1002(b)(7) added by PL 98–616]

(8) alternatives to existing methods of land disposal must be developed since many of the cities in the United States will be running out of suitable solid waste disposal sites within five years unless immediate action is taken.

[Former §1002(b)(6) redesignated as (8) by PL 98–616]

(c) Materials.—The Congress finds with respect to materials, that:

(1) millions of tons of recoverable material which could be used are needlessly buried each year;

(2) methods are available to separate usable materials from solid waste; and

(3) the recovery and conservation of such materials can reduce the dependence of the United States on foreign resources and reduce the deficit in its balance of payments.

(d) Energy.—The Congress finds with respect to energy, that—

(1) solid waste represents a potential source of solid fuel, oil, or gas that can be converted into energy;

(2) the need exists to develop alternative energy sources for public and private consumption in order to reduce our dependence on such sources as petroleum products, natural gas, nuclear and hydroelectric generation; and

(3) technology exists to produce usable energy from solid waste.

[Editor's Note: Section 2 of the "Used Oil Recycling Act of 1980," PL 96–463 detailed congressional concerns about used oil. The text of that section follows.]

§6901a. Findings. [Sec. 2]

(1) Used oil is a valuable source of increasingly scarce energy and materials;

(2) technology exists to re-refine, reprocess, reclaim, and otherwise recycle used oil;

(3) used oil constitutes a threat to public health and the environment when reused or disposed of improperly; and that, therefore, it is in the national interest to recycle used oil in a manner which does not constitute a threat to public health and the environment and which conserves energy and materials.

§6902. Objectives and National Policy [Sec. 1003]

[§1003 revised by PL 98–616]

(a) Objectives.—The objectives of this Act are to promote the protection of health and the environment and to conserve valuable material and energy resources by—

(1) providing technical and financial assistance to State and local governments and interstate agencies for the development of solid waste management plans (including resource recovery and resource conservation systems) which will promote improved solid waste management techniques (including more effective organizational arrangements), new and improved methods of collection, separation, and recovery of solid waste, and the environmentally safe disposal of nonrecoverable residues;

(2) providing training grants in occupations involving the design, operation, and maintenance of solid waste disposal systems;

(3) prohibiting future open dumping on the land and requiring the conversion of existing open dumps to facilities which do not pose a danger to the environment or to health;

(4) assuring that hazardous waste management practices are conducted in a manner which protects human health and the environment;

(5) requiring that hazardous waste be properly managed in the first instance thereby reducing the need for corrective action at a future date;

(6) minimizing the generation of hazardous waste and the land disposal of hazardous waste by encouraging process substitution, materials recovery, properly conducted recycling and reuse, and treatment;

(7) establishing a viable Federal-State partnership to carry out the purposes of this Act and insuring that the Administrator will, in carrying out the provisions of subtitle C of this Act, give a high priority to assisting and cooperating with States in obtaining full authorization of State programs under subtitle C;

(8) providing for the promulgation of guidelines for solid waste collection, transport, separation, recovery, and disposal practices and systems;

(9) promoting a national research and development program for improved solid waste management and resource conservation techniques, more effective organizational arrangements, and new and improved methods of collection, separation, and recovery, and recycling of solid wastes and environmentally safe disposal of nonrecoverable residues;

(10) promoting the demonstration, construction, and application of solid waste management, resource recovery, and resource conservation systems which preserve and enhance the quality of air, water, and land resources; and

(11) establishing a cooperative effort among the Federal, State, and local governments and private enterprise in order to recover valuable materials and energy from solid waste.

(b) National Policy.—The Congress hereby declares it to be the national policy of the United States that, wherever feasible, the generation of hazardous waste is to be reduced or eliminated as expeditiously as possible. Waste that is nevertheless generated should be treated, stored, or disposed of so as to minimize the present and future threat to human health and the environment.

§6903. Definitions [Sec. 1004]

As used in this Act:

(1) The term "Administrator" means the Administrator of the Environmental Protection Agency.

(2) The term "construction," with respect to any project of construction under this Act, means (A) the erection or building of new structures and acquisition of lands or interests therein, or the acquisition, replacement, expansion, remodeling, alteration, modernization, or extension of existing structures, and (B) the acquisition and installation of initial equipment of, or required in connection with, new or newly acquired structures or the expanded, remodeled, altered, modernized or extended part of existing structures (including trucks and other motor vehicles, and tractors, cranes, and other machinery) necessary for the proper utilization and operation of the facility after completion of the project; and includes preliminary planning to determine the economic and engineering feasibility and the public health and safety aspects of the project, the engineering, architectural, legal, fiscal, and economic investigations and studies, and any surveys, designs, plans, working drawings, specifications, and other action necessary for the carrying out of the project, and (C) the inspection and supervision of the process of carrying out the project to completion.

(2A) The term "demonstration" means the initial exhibition of a new technology process or practice or a significantly new combination or use of technologies, processes or practices, subsequent to the development stage, for the purpose of proving technological feasibility and cost effectiveness.

(3) The term "disposal" means the discharge, deposit, injection, dumping, spilling, leaking, or placing of any solid waste or hazardous waste into or on any land or water so that such solid waste or hazardous waste or any constituent thereof may enter the environment or be emitted into the air or discharged into any waters, including ground waters.

(4) The term "Federal agency" means any department, agency, or other instrumentality of the Federal Government, any independent agency or establishment of the Federal Government including any Government corporation, and the Government Printing Office.

(5) The term "hazardous waste" means a solid waste, or combination of solid wastes, which because of its quantity, concentration, or physical, chemical, or infectious characteristics may—

(A) cause, or significantly contribute to an increase in mortality or an increase in serious irreversible, or incapaciting reversible, illness; or

(B) pose a substantial present or potential hazard to human health or the environment when improperly treated, stored, transported, or disposed of, or otherwise managed.

(6) The term "hazardous waste generation" means the act or process of producing hazardous waste.

(7) The term "hazardous waste management" means the systematic control of the collection, source separation, storage, transportation, processing, treatment, recovery, and disposal of hazardous wastes.

(8) For purposes of Federal financial assistance (other than rural communities assistance), the term "implementation" does not include the acquisition, leasing, construction, or modification of facilities or equipment or the acquisition, leasing, or improvement of land.

(9) The term "intermunicipal agency" means an agency established by two or more municipalities with responsibility for planning or administration of solid waste.

(10) The term "interstate agency" means an agency of two or more municipalities in different States, or an agency established by two or more States, with authority to provide for the management of solid wastes and serving two or more municipalities located in different States.

(11) The term "long-term contract" means, when used in relation to solid waste supply, a contract of sufficient duration to assure the viability of a resource recovery facility (to the extent that such viability depends upon solid waste supply).

(12) The term "manifest" means the form used for identifying the quantity, composition, and the origin, routing, and destination of hazardous waste during its transportation from the point of generation to the point of disposal, treatment, or storage.

(13) The term "municipality" (A) means a city, town, borough, county, parish, district, or other public body created by or pursuant to State law, with responsibility for the planning or administration of solid waste management, or an Indian tribe or authorized tribal organization or Alaska Native village or organization, and (B) includes any rural community or unincorporated town or village or any other public entity for which an application for assistance is made by a State or political subdivision thereof.

(14) The term "open dump" means any facility or site where solid waste is disposed of which is not a sanitary landfill which meets the criteria promulgated under section 4004 and which is not a facility for disposal of hazardous waste.

[§1004(14) revised by PL 96–482]

(15) The term "person" means an individual, trust, firm, joint stock company, corporation (including a government corporation), partnership, association, State, municipality, commission, political subdivision of a State, or any interstate body and shall include each department agency, and instrumentality of the United States.

[§1004(15) amended by PL 102–386]

(16) The term "procurement item" means any device, good, substance, material, product, or other item whether real or personal property which is the subject of any purchase, barter, or other exchange made to procure such item.

(17) The term "procuring agency" means any Federal agency, or any State agency or agency of a political subdivision of a State which is using appropriated Federal funds for such procurement, or any person contracting with any such agency with respect to work performed under such contract.

(18) The term "recoverable" refers to the capability and likelihood of being recovered from solid waste for a commercial or industrial use.

(19) The term "recovered material" means waste material and byproducts which have been recovered or diverted from solid waste, but such terms does not include those materials and byproducts generated from, and commonly reused within, an original manufacturing process.

[§1004(19) revised by PL 96–482]

(20) The term "recovered resources" means material or energy recovered from solid waste.

(21) The term "resource conservation" means reduction of the amounts of solid waste that are generated, reduction of overall resource consumption, and utilization of recovered resources.

(22) The term "resource recovery" means the recovery of material or energy from solid waste.

(23) The term "resource recovery system" means a solid waste management system which provides for collection, separation, recycling, and recovery of solid wastes, including disposal of nonrecoverable waste residues.

(24) The term "resource recovery facility" means any facility at which solid waste is processed for the purpose of extracting, converting to energy, or otherwise separating and preparing solid waste for reuse.

(25) The term "regional authority" means the authority established or designated under section 4006.

(26) The term "sanitary landfill" means a facility for the disposal of solid waste which meets the criteria published under section 4004.

(26A) The term "sludge" means any solid, semisolid or liquid waste generated from a municipal, commercial, or industrial wastewater treatment plant, water supply treatment plant, or air pollution control facility or any other such waste having similar characteristics and effects.

(27) The term "solid waste" means any garbage, refuse, sludge from a waste treatment plant, water supply treatment plant, or air pollution control facility and other discarded material, including solid, liquid, semisolid, or contained gaseous material resulting from industrial, commercial, mining, and agricultural operations, and from community activities, but does not include solid or dissolved material in domestic sewage, or solid or dissolved materials in irrigation return flows or industrial discharges which are point sources subject to permits under section 402 of the Federal Water Pollution Control Act, as amended (86 Stat. 880), or source, special nuclear, or byproduct material as defined by the Atomic Energy Act of 1954, as amended (68 Stat. 923).

(28) The term "solid waste management" means the systematic administration of activities which provide for the collection, source separation, storage, transportation, transfer, processing, treatment, and disposal of solid waste.

(29) The term "solid waste management facility" includes (A) any resource recovery system or component thereof, (B) any system, program, or facility for resource conservation, and (C) any facility for the collection, source separation, storage, transportation, transfer, processing, treatment or disposal of solid wastes including hazardous wastes, whether such facility is associated with facilities generating such wastes or otherwise.

(30) The terms "solid waste planning," "solid waste management," and "comprehensive planning" include planning or management respecting resource recovery and resource conservation.

(31) The term "State" means any of the several States, the District of Columbia, the Commonwealth of Puerto Rico, the Virgin Islands, Guam, American Samoa, and the Commonwealth of the Northern Mariana Islands.

(32) The term "State authority" means the agency established or designated under section 4007.

(33) The term "storage," when used in connection with hazardous waste, means the containment of hazardous waste, either on a temporary basis or for a period of years, in such a manner as not to constitute disposal of such hazardous waste.

(34) The term "treatment", when used in connection with hazardous waste, means any method, technique, or process, including neutralization, designed to change the physical, chemical, or biological character or composition of any hazardous waste so as to neutralize such waste or so as to render such waste nonhazardous, safer for transport, amenable for recovery, amenable for storage, or reduced in volume. Such term includes any activity or processing designed to change the physical form or chemical composition of hazardous waste so as to render it nonhazardous.

(35) The term "virgin material" means a raw material, including previously unused copper, aluminum, lead, zinc, iron, or other metal or metal ore, any undeveloped resource that is, or with new technology will become, a source of raw materials.

(36) The term "used oil" means any oil which has been—

(A) refined from crude oil,

(B) used, and

(C) as a result of such use, contaminated by physical or chemical impurities.

[§1004(36) added by PL 96–463]

(37) The term "recycled oil" means any used oil which is reused, following its original use, for any purpose (including the purpose for which the oil was originally used). Such term includes oil which is re-refined, reclaimed, burned, or reprocessed.

[§1004(37) added by PL 96–463]

(38) The term "lubricating oil" means the fraction of crude oil which is sold for purposes of reducing friction in any industrial or mechanical device. Such term includes re-refined oil.

[§1004(38) added by PL 96–463]

(39) The term "re-refined oil" means used oil from which the physical and chemical contaminants acquired through previous use have been removed through a refining process.

[§1004(39) added by PL 96–463]

(40) Except as otherwise provided in this paragraph, the term "medical waste" means any solid waste which is generated in the diagnosis, treatment, or immunization of human beings or

animals in research pertaining thereto, or in the production or testing of biologicals. Such term does not include any hazardous waste identified or listed under subtitle C or any household waste as defined in regulations under subtitle C.

[§1004(40) added by PL 100–582]

(41) The term "mixed waste"' means waste that contains both hazardous waste and source, special nuclear, or by-product material subject to the Atomic Energy Act of 1954 (42 U.S.C. 2011 et seq.).

[§1004(41) added by PL 102–386]

§6904. Governmental Cooperation [Sec. 1005]

(a) Interstate Cooperation.—The provisions of this Act to be carried out by States may be carried out by interstate agencies and provisions applicable to States may apply to interstate regions where such agencies and regions have been established by the respective States and approved by the Administrator. In any such case, action required to be taken by the Governor of a State, respecting regional designation shall be required to be taken by the Governor of each of the respective States with respect to so much of the interstate region as is within the jurisdiction of that State.

(b) Consent of Congress to Compacts.—The Consent of the Congress is hereby given to two or more States to negotiate and enter into agreements or compacts, not in conflict with any law or treaty of the United States, for—

(1) cooperative effort and mutual assistance for the management of solid waste or hazardous waste (or both) and the enforcement of their respective laws relating thereto, and

(2) the establishment of such agencies, joint or otherwise, as they may deem desirable for making effective such agreements or compacts. No such agreement or compact shall be binding or obligatory upon any State a party thereto unless it is agreed upon by all parties to the agreement and until it has been approved by the Administrator and the Congress.

§6905. Application of Act and Integration with Other Acts [Sec. 1006]

(a) Application of Act.—Nothing in this Act shall be construed to apply to (or to authorize any State, interstate, or local authority to regulate) any activity or substance which is subject to the Federal Water Pollution Control Act (33 U.S.C. 1151 and following), the Safe Drinking Water Act (42 U.S.C. 300f and following), the Marine Protection, Research and Sanctuaries Act of 1972 (33 U.S.C. 1401 and following), or the Atomic Energy Act of 1954 (42 U.S.C. 2011 and following) except to the extent that such application (or regulation) is not inconsistent with the requirements of such Acts.

(b) Integration with Other Acts.—

(1) The Administrator shall integrate all provisions of this Act for purposes of administration and enforcement and shall avoid duplication, to the maximum extent practicable, with the appropriate provisions of the Clean Air Act (42 U.S.C. 1857 and following), the Federal Water Pollution Control Act (33 U.S.C. 1151 and following), the Federal Insecticide, Fungicide, and Rodenticide Act (7 U.S.C. 135 and following), the Safe Drinking Water Act (42 U.S.C. 300f and following), the Marine Protection, Research and Sanctuaries Act of 1972 (33 U.S.C. 1401 and following) and such other Acts of Congress as grant regulatory authority to the Administrator. Such integration shall be effected only to the extent that it can be done in a manner consistent with the goals and policies expressed in this Act and in the other acts referred to in this subsection.

[§1006(b)(1) designated by PL 98–616]

(2) (A) A promptly as practicable after the date of the enactment of the Hazardous and Solid Waste Amendments of 1984, the Administrator shall submit a report describing—

(i) the current data and information available on emissions of polychlorinated dibenzo-p-dioxins from resource recovery facilities burning municipal solid waste;

(ii) any significant risks to human health posed by these emissions; and

(iii) operating practices appropriate for controlling these emissions.

(B) Based on the report under subparagraph (A) and on any future information on such emissions, the Administrator may publish advisories or guidelines regarding the control of dioxin emissions from such facilities. Nothing in this paragraph shall be construed to preempt or otherwise affect the authority of the Administrator to promulgate any regulations under the Clean Air Act regarding emissions of polychlorinated dibenzo-p-dioxins.

[§1006(b)(2) added by PL 98–616]

(3) Notwithstanding any other provisions of law, in developing solid waste plans, it is the intention of this Act that in determining the size of a waste-to-energy facility, adequate provisions shall be given to the present and reasonably anticipated future needs, including

those needs created by thorough-implementation of section 6002(h), of the recycling and resource recovery interests within the area encompassed by the solid waste plan.

[§1006(b)(3) added by PL 98–616]

(c) Integration with the Surface Mining Control and Reclamation Act of 1977.—

(1) No later than 90 days after the date of enactment of the Solid Waste Disposal Act Amendments of 1980, the Administrator shall review any regulations applicable to the treatment, storage, or disposal of any coal mining wastes or overburden promulgated by the Secretary of the Interior under the Surface Mining and Reclamation Act of 1977. If the Administrator determines that any requirement of final regulations promulgated under any section of subtitle C relating to mining wastes or overburden is not adequately addressed in such regulations promulgated by the Secretary, the Administrator shall promptly transmit such determination, together with suggested revisions and supporting documentation, to the Secretary.

(2) The Secretary of the Interior shall have exclusive responsibility for carrying out any requirement of subtitle C of this Act with respect to coal mining wastes or overburden for which a surface coal mining and reclamation permit is issued or approved under the Surface Mining Control and Reclamation Act of 1977. The Secretary shall, with the concurrence of the Administrator, promulgate such regulations as may be necessary to carry out the purposes of this subsection and shall integrate such regulations with regulations promulgated under the Surface Mining Control and Reclamation Act of 1977.

[§1006(c) added by PL 96–482]

§6906. Financial Disclosure [Sec. 1007]

(a) Statement.—Each officer or employee of the Administrator who—

(1) performs any function or duty under this Act; and

(2) has any known financial interest in any person who applies for or receives financial assistance under this Act shall beginning on February 1, 1977, annually file with the Administrator a written statement concerning all such interests held by such officer or employee during the preceding calendar year. Such statement shall be available to the public.

(b) Action by Administrator.—The Administrator shall—

(1) act within ninety days after the date of enactment of this Act—

(A) to define the term "known financial interest" for purposes of subsection (a) of this section; and

(B) to establish the methods by which the requirement to file written statements specified in subsection (a) of this section will be monitored and enforced, including appropriate provision for the filing by such officers and employees of such statements and the review by the Administrator of such statements; and

(2) report to the Congress on June 1, 1978, and of each succeeding calendar year with respect to such disclosures and the actions taken in regard thereto during the preceding calendar year.

(c) Exemption.—In the rules prescribed under subsection (b) of this section, the Administrator may identify specific positions within the Environmental Protection Agency which are of a nonpolicymaking nature and provide that officers or employees occupying such positions shall be exempt from the requirements of this section.

(d) Penalty.—Any officer or employee who is subject to, and knowingly violates, this section shall be fined not more than $2,500 or imprisoned not more than one year, or both.

§6907. Solid Waste Management Information and Guidelines [Sec. 1008]

(a) Guidelines.—Within one year of enactment of this section, and from time to time thereafter, the Administrator shall, in cooperation with appropriate Federal, State, municipal, and intermunicipal agencies, and in consultation with other interested persons, and after public hearings, develop and publish suggested guidelines for solid waste management. Such suggested guidelines shall—

(1) provide a technical and economic description of the level of performance that can be attained by various available solid waste management practices (including operating practices) which provide for the protection of public health and the environment;

(2) not later than two years after the enactment of this section, describe levels of performance, including appropriate methods and degrees of control, that provide at a minimum for (A) protection of public health and welfare; (B) protection of the quality of ground waters and surface waters from leachates; (C) protection of the quality of surface waters from runoff through compliance with effluent limitations

under the Federal Water Pollution Control Act, as amended; (D) protection of ambient air quality through compliance with new source performance standards or requirements of air quality implementation plans under the Clean Air Act, as amended; (E) disease and vector control; (F) safety; and (G) esthetics; and

(3) provide minimum criteria to be used by the States to define those solid waste management practices which constitute the open dumping of solid waste or hazardous waste and are to be prohibited under subtitle D of this Act. Where appropriate, such suggested guidelines also shall include minimum information for use in deciding the adequate location, design, and construction of facilities associated with solid waste management practices, including the consideration of regional, geographic, demographic, and climatic factors.

(b) Notice.—The Administrator shall notify the Committee on Public Works of the Senate and the Committee on Interstate and Foreign Commerce of the House of Representatives a reasonable time before publishing any suggested guidelines or proposed regulations under this act of the content of such proposed suggested guidelines or proposed regulations under this Act.

SUBTITLE B—OFFICE OF SOLID WASTE; AUTHORITIES OF THE ADMINISTRATOR

§6911. Office of Solid Waste and Interagency Coordinating Committee [Sec. 2001]

(a) Office of Solid Waste.—The Administrator shall establish within the Environmental Protection Agency an Office of Solid Waste (hereinafter referred to as the "Office") to be headed by an Assistant Administrator of the Environmental Protection Agency. The duties and responsibilities (other than duties and responsibilities relating to research and development) of the Administrator under this Act (as modified by applicable reorganization plans) shall be carried out through the Office.

[§2001(a) designated by PL 96–482; amended by PL 96–510]

(b) Interagency Coordinating Committee.—

(1) There is hereby established an Interagency Coordinating Committee on Federal Resource Conservation and Recovery Activities which shall have the responsibility for coordinating all activities dealing with resource conservation and recovery from solid waste carried out by the Environmental Protection Agency, the Department of Energy, the Department of Commerce, and all other Federal agencies which conduct such activities pursuant to this or any other Act. For purposes of this subsection, the term "resource conservation and recovery activities" shall include, but not be limited to, all research, development and demonstration projects on resource conservation or energy, or material, recovery from solid waste, and all technical or financial assistance for State or local planning for, or implementation of, projects related to resource conservation or energy or material, recovery from solid waste. The Committee shall be chaired by the Administrator of the Environmental Protection Agency or such person as the Administrator may designate. Members of the Committee shall include representatives of the Department of Energy, the Department of Commerce, the Department of the Treasury, and each other Federal agency which the Administrator determines to have programs or responsibilities affecting resource conservation or recovery.

(2) The Interagency Coordinating Committee shall include oversight of the implementation of

(A) the May 1979 Memorandum of Understanding on Energy Recovery from Municipal Solid Waste between the Environmental Protection Agency and the Department of Energy;

(B) the May 30, 1978, Interagency Agreement between the Department of Commerce and the Environmental Protection Agency on the Implementation of the Resource Conservation and Recovery Act; and

(C) any subsequent agreements between these agencies or other Federal agencies which address Federal resource recovery or conservation activities.

(3) The Interagency Coordinating Committee shall submit to the Congress by March 1, 1981, and on March 1 each year thereafter, a five-year action plan for Federal resource conservation or recovery activities which shall identify means and propose programs to encourage resource conservation or material and energy recovery and increase private and municipal investment in resource conservation or recovery systems, especially those which provide for material conservation or recovery as well as energy conservation or recovery. Such plan shall describe, at a minimum, a coordinated and nonduplicatory plan for resource recovery and conservation activities for the Environmental Protection Agency, the Department of

Energy, the Department of Commerce, and all other Federal agencies which conduct such activities.

§6912. Authorities of Administrator [Sec. 2002]

(a) Authorities.—In carrying out this Act, the Administrator is authorized to—

(1) prescribe, in consultation with Federal, State, and regional authorities, such regulations as are necessary to carry out his functions under this Act;

(2) consult with or exchange information with other Federal agencies undertaking research, development, demonstration projects, studies, or investigations relating to solid waste;

(3) provide technical and financial assistance to States or regional agencies in the development and implementation of solid waste plans and hazardous waste management programs;

(4) consult with representatives of science, industry, agriculture, labor, environmental protection and consumer organizations, and other groups, as he deems advisable;

(5) utilize the information, facilities, personnel and other resources of Federal agencies, including the National Bureau of Standards and the National Bureau of the Census, on a reimbursable basis, to perform research and analyses and conduct studies and investigations related to resource recovery and conservation and to otherwise carry out the Administrator's functions under this Act; and

(6) to delegate to the Secretary of Transportation the performance of any inspection or enforcement function under this Act relating to the transportation of hazardous waste where such delegation would avoid unnecessary duplication of activity and would carry out the objectives of this Act and of the Hazardous Materials Transportation Act.

[§2002(a)(6) added by PL 96–482]

(b) Revision of Regulations.—Each regulation promulgated under this Act shall be reviewed and, where necessary, revised not less frequently than every three years.

(c) Criminal Investigations.—In carrying out the provisions of this Act, the Administrator, and duly-designated agents and employees of the Environmental Protection Agency, are authorized to initiate and conduct investigations under the criminal provisions of this Act, and to refer the results of these investigations to the Attorney General for prosecution in appropriate cases.

[§2002(c) added by PL 98–616]

§6913. Resource Recovery and Conservation Panels [Sec. 2003]

The Administrator shall provide teams of personnel, including Federal, State, and local employees or contractors (hereinafter referred to as "Resource Conservation and Recovery Panels") to provide Federal agencies, States and local governments upon request with technical assistance on solid waste management, resource recovery, and resource conservation. Such teams shall include technical, marketing, financial, and institutional specialists, and the services of such teams shall be provided without charge to States or local governments.

§6914. Grants for Discarded Tire Disposal [Sec. 2004]

(a) Grants.—The Administrator shall make available grants equal to 5 percent of the purchase price of tire shredders (including portable shredders attached to tire collection trucks) to those eligible applicants best meeting criteria promulgated under this section. An eligible applicant may be any private purchaser, public body, or public-private joint venture. Criteria for receiving grants shall be promulgated under this section and shall include the policy to offer any private purchaser the first option to receive a grant, the policy to develop widespread geographic distribution of tire shredding facilities, the need for such facilities within a geographic area, and the projected risk and viability of any such venture. In the case of an application under this section from a public body, the Administrator shall first make a determination that there are no private purchasers interested in making an application before approving a grant to a public body.

(b) Authorization.—There is authorized to be appropriated $750,000 for each of the fiscal years 1978 and 1979 to carry out this section.

§6914a. Labeling of Certain Oil [Sec. 2005]

For purposes of any provision of law which requires the labeling of commodities, lubricating oil shall be treated as lawfully labeled only if it bears the following statement, prominently displayed:*"DON'T POLLUTE — CONSERVE RESOURCES: RETURN USED OIL TO COLLECTION CENTERS"*

[§2005 added by PL 96–463]

[Editor's Note: Section 4(c) of PL 96–463 contains provisions on the labeling of recycled oil. Those provisions follow.]

[Sec. 4]

(c) Before the effective date of the labeling standards required to be prescribed under section 383(d)(1)(A) of the Energy Policy and Conservation Act, no requirement of any rule or order of the Federal Trade Commission may apply, or remain applicable, to any container of recycled oil (as defined in section 383(b) of such Act) if such requirement provides that the container must bear any label referring to the fact that it has been derived from previously used oil. Nothing in this subsection shall be construed to affect any labeling requirement applicable to recycled oil under any authority of law to the extent such requirement relates to fitness for intended use or any other performance characteristic of such oil or to any characteristic of such oil other than that referred to in the preceding sentence.

§6915. Annual Report [Sec. 2006]

The Administrator shall transmit to the Congress and the President, not later than ninety days after the end of each fiscal year, a comprehensive and detailed report on all activities of the Office during the preceding fiscal year. Each such report shall include—

(1) a statement of specific and detailed objectives for the activities and programs conducted and assisted under this Act;

[§2006(1) amended by PL 98–616]

(2) statements of the Administrator's conclusions as to the effectiveness of such activities and programs in meeting the stated objectives and the purposes of this Act, measured through the end of such fiscal year;

(3) a summary of outstanding solid waste problems confronting the Administrator, in order of priority;

(4) recommendations with respect to such legislation which the Administrator deems necessary or desirable to assist in solving problems respecting solid waste;

(5) all other information required to be submitted to the Congress pursuant to any other provision of this Act; and

(6) the Administrator's plans for activities and programs respecting solid waste during the next fiscal year.

[Former §2005 redesignated as §2006 by PL 96–463]

§6916. General Authorization [Sec. 2007]

(a) General Administration.—There are authorized to be appropriated to the Administrator for the purpose of carrying out the provisions of this Act, $35,000,000 for the fiscal year ending September 30, 1977, $38,000,000 for the fiscal year ending September 30, 1978, $42,000,000 for the fiscal year ending September 30, 1979, $70,000,000 for the fiscal year ending September 30, 1980, $80,000,000 for the fiscal year ending September 30, 1981, $80,000,000 for the fiscal year ending September 30, 1982, $70,000,000 for the fiscal year ending September 30, 1985, $80,000,000 for the fiscal year ending September 30, 1986, $80,000,000 for the fiscal year ending September 30, 1987, and $80,000,000 for the fiscal year 1988.

[§2007(a) amended by PL 98–616]

(b) Resource Recovery and Conservation Panels.—Not less than 20 percent of the amount appropriated under subsection (a), or $5,000,000 per fiscal year, whichever is less, shall be used only for purposes of Resource Recovery and Conservation Panels established under section 2003 (including travel expenses incurred by such panels in carrying out their functions under this Act).

(c) Hazardous Waste.—Not less than 30 percent of the amount appropriated under subsection (a) shall be used only for purposes of carrying out subtitle C of this Act (relating to hazardous waste) other than section 3011.

(d) State and Local Support.—Not less than 25 per centum of the total amount appropriated under this title, up to the amount authorized in section 4008(a)(1), shall be used only for purposes of support to State, regional, local, and interstate agencies in accordance with subtitle D of this Act other than section 4008(a)(2) or 4009.

[Editor's Note: PL 96–463 redesignated §2006 as §2007. However, PL 96–482 cites the former designation (§2006) in amending this section.]

(e) Criminal Investigators.—There is authorized to be appropriated to the Administrator $3,246,000 for the fiscal year 1985, $2,408,300 for the fiscal year 1986, $2,529,000 for the fiscal year 1987, and $2,529,000 for the fiscal year 1988 to be used—

(1) for additional officers or employees of the Environmental Protection Agency authorized by the Administrator to conduct criminal investigations (to investigate, or supervise the investigation of, any activity for which a criminal penalty is provided) under this Act; and

(2) for support costs for such additional officers or employees.

[§2007(e) added by PL 98–616]

(f) Underground Storage Tanks.—

(1) There are authorized to be appropriated to the Administrator for the purpose of carrying out the provisions of subtitle I (relating to regulation of underground storage tanks), $10,000,000 for each of the fiscal years 1985 through 1988.

(2) There is authorized to be appropriated $25,000,000 for each of the fiscal years 1985 through 1988 to be used to make grants to the States for purposes of assisting the States in the development and implementation of approved State underground storage tank release detection, prevention, and correction programs under subtitle I.

[§2007(f) added by PL 98–616]

§6917. Office of Ombudsman [Sec. 2008]

(a) Establishment; Functions.—The Administrator shall establish an Office of Ombudsman, to be directed by an Ombudsman. It shall be the function of the Office of Ombudsman to receive individual complaints, grievances, requests for information submitted by any person with respect to any program or requirement under this Act.

(b) Authority to Render Assistance.—The Ombusdsman shall render assistance with respect to the complaints, grievances, and requests submitted to the Office of Ombudsman, and shall make appropriate recommendation to the Administrator.

(c) Effect on Procedures for Grievances, Appeals, or Administrative Matters.—The establishment of the Office of Ombudsman shall not affect any procedures for grievances, appeals, or administrative matters in any other provision of this Act, any other provision of law, or any Federal regulation.

(d) Termination.—the Office of the Ombudsman shall cease to exist 4 years after the date of enactment of the Hazardous and Solid Waste Amendments of 1984.

[§2008 added by PL 98–616]

SUBTITLE C—HAZARDOUS WASTE MANAGEMENT

§6921. Identification and Listing of Hazardous Waste [Sec. 3001]

(a) Criteria for Identification or Listing—Not later than eighteen months after the date of the enactment of this Act, the Administrator shall, after notice and opportunity for public hearing, and after consultation with appropriate Federal and State agencies, develop and promulgate criteria for identifying the characteristics of hazardous waste, and for listing hazardous waste, which should be subject to the provisions of this subtitle, taking into account toxicity, persistence, and degradability in nature, potential for accumulation in tissue, and other related factors such as flammability, corrosiveness, and other hazardous characteristics. Such criteria shall be revised from time to time as may be appropriate.

(b) (1) Identification and Listing.—Not later than eighteen months after the date of enactment of this section, and after notice and opportunity for public hearing, the Administrator shall promulgate regulations identifying the characteristics of hazardous waste, and listing particular hazardous wastes (within the meaning of section 1004(5)), which shall be subject to the provisions of this subtitle. Such regulations shall be based on the criteria promulgated under subsection (a) and shall be revised from time to time thereafter as may be appropriate. The Administrator, in cooperation with the Agency for Toxic Substances and Disease Registry and the National Toxicology Program, shall also identify or list those hazardous wastes which shall be subject to the provisions of this subtitle solely because of the presence in such wastes of certain constituents (such as identified carcinogens, mutagens, or teratagens) at levels in excess of levels which endanger human health.

[§3001(b)(1) designated by PL 96–482; amended by PL 98–616]

(2) (A) Notwithstanding the provisions of paragraph (1) of this subsection, drilling fluids, produced waters, and other wastes associated with the exploration, development, or production of crude oil or natural gas or geothermal energy shall be subject only to existing State or Federal regulatory programs in lieu of subtitle C until at least 24 months after the date of enactment of the Solid Waste Disposal Act Amendments of 1980 and after promulgation of the regulations in accordance with subparagraphs (B) and (C) of this paragraph. It is the sense of the Congress that such State or Federal programs should include, for waste disposal sites which are to be closed, provisions requiring at least the following:

(i) The identification through surveying, platting, or other measures, together with recordation of such information on the public record, so as to assure that the location where such wastes are disposed of can be located in the future; except however, that no such surveying, platting, or other measure identifying the location of a disposal site for drilling fluids and associated wastes shall be required if the distance from the disposal site to the surveyed or platted location to the associated well is less than two hundred lineal feet; and

(ii) A chemical and physical analysis of a produced water and a composition of a drilling fluid suspected to contain a hazardous material, with such information to be acquired prior to closure and to be placed on the public record.

(B) Not later than six months after completion and submission of the study required by section 8002(m) of this Act, the Administrator shall, after public hearings and opportunity for comment, determine either to promulgate regulations under this subtitle for drilling fluids, produced waters, and other wastes associated with the exploration, development, or production of crude oil or natural gas or geothermal energy or that such regulations are unwarranted. The Administrator shall publish his decision in the Federal Register accompanied by an explanation and justification of the reasons for it. In making the decision under this paragraph, the Administrator shall utilize the information developed or accumulated pursuant to the study required under section 8002(m).

(C) The Administrator shall transmit his decision, along with any regulations, if necessary, to both Houses of Congress. Such regulations shall take effect only when authorized by Act of Congress.

[§3001(b)(2) added by PL 96–482]

(3) (A) Notwithstanding the provisions of paragraph (1) of this subsection, each waste listed below shall, except as provided in subparagraph (B) of this paragraph, be subject only to regulation under other applicable provisions of Federal or State law in lieu of this subtitle until at least six months after the date of submission of the applicable study required to be conducted under subsection (f), (n), (o), or (p) of section 8002 of this Act and after promulgation of regulations in accordance with subparagraph (C) of this paragraph:

(i) Fly ash waste, bottom ash waste, slag waste, and flue gas emission control waste generated primarily from the combustion of coal or other fossil fuels.

(ii) Solid waste from the extraction, beneficiation, and processing of ores and minerals, including phosphate rock and overburden from the mining of uranium ore.

(iii) Cement kiln dust waste.

(B) (i) Owners and operators of disposal sites for wastes listed in subparagraph (A) may be required by the Administrator, through regulations prescribed under authority of section 2002 of this Act —

(I) as to disposal sites for such wastes which are to be closed, to identify the locations of such sites through surveying, platting, or other measures, together with recordation of such information on the public record, to assure that the locations where such wastes are disposed of are known and can be located in the future, and

(II) to provide chemical and physical analysis and composition of such wastes, based on available information, to be placed on the public record.

(ii) (I) In conducting any study under subsection (f), (n), (o), or (p), of section 8002 of this Act, any officer, employee, or authorized representative of the Environmental Protection Agency, duly designated by the Administrator, is authorized, at reasonable times and as reasonably necessary for the purposes of such study, to enter any establishment where any waste subject to such study is generated, stored, treated, disposed of, or transported from; to inspect, take samples, and conduct monitoring and testing; and to have access to and copy records relating to such waste. Each such inspection shall be commenced and completed with reasonable promptness. If the officer, employee, or authorized representative obtains any samples prior to leaving the premises, he shall give to the owner, operator, or agent in charge a receipt describing the sample obtained and if requested a portion of each such sample equal in volume or weight to the portion retained. If any analysis is made of such samples, or monitoring and testing performed, a copy of the results shall be furnished promptly to the owner, operator, or agent in charge.

(II) Any records, reports, or information obtained from any person under subclause (I) shall be available to the public, except that upon a showing satisfactory to the Administrator by any person that records, reports, or information, or particular part thereof, to which the Administrator has access under this subparagraph if made public, would divulge information entitled to protection under section 1905 of title 18 of the United States Code, the Administrator shall consider such information or particular portion thereof confidential in accordance with the purposes of that section, except that such record, report, document, or information may be disclosed to other officers, employees, or authorized representatives of the United States concerned with carrying out this Act. Any person not subject to the provisions of section 1905 of title 18 of the United States Code who knowingly and willfully divulges or discloses any information entitled to protection under this subparagraph shall, upon conviction, be subject to a fine of not more than $5,000 or to imprisonment not to exceed one year, or both.

(iii) The Administrator may prescribe regulations, under the authority of this Act, to prevent radiation exposure which presents an unreasonable risk to human health from the use in construction or land reclamation (with or without revegetation) of (1) solid waste from the extraction, beneficiation, and processing of phosphate rock or (11) overburden from the mining of uranium ore.

(iv) Whenever on the basis of any information the Administrator determines that any person is in violation of any requirement of this subparagraph, the Administrator shall give notice to the violator of his failure to comply with such requirement. If such violation extends beyond the thirtieth day after the Administrator's notification, the Administrator may issue an order requiring compliance within a specified time period or the Administrator may commence a civil action in the United States district court in the district in which the violation occurred for appropriate relief, including a temporary or permanent injunction.

(C) Not later than six months after the date of submission of the applicable study required to be conducted under subsection (f), (n), (o), or (p), of section 8002 of this Act, the Administrator shall, after public hearings and opportunity for comment, either determine to promulgate regulations under this subtitle for each waste listed in subparagraph (A) of this paragraph or determine that such regulations are unwarranted. The Administrator shall publish his determination, which shall be based on information developed or accumulated pursuant to such study, public hearings, and comment, in the Federal Register accompanied by an explanation and justification of the reasons for it.

[§3001(b)(3) added by PL 96–482]

(c) Petition by State Governor.—At any time after the date eighteen months after the enactment of this title, the Governor of any State may petition the Administrator to identify or list a material as a hazardous waste. The Administrator shall act upon such petition within ninety days following his receipt thereof and shall notify the Governor of such action. If the Administrator denies such petition because of financial considerations, in providing such notice to the Governor he shall include a statement concerning such considerations.

(d) Small Quantity Generator Waste.—

(1) By March 31, 1986, the Administrator shall promulgate standards under sections 3002, 3003, and 3004 for hazardous waste generated by a generator in a total quantity of hazardous waste greater than one hundred kilograms but less than one thousand kilograms during a calendar month.

(2) The standards referred to in paragraph (1), including standards applicable to the legitimate use, reuse, recycling, and reclamation of such wastes, may vary from the standards applicable to hazardous waste generated by larger quantity generators, but such standards shall be sufficient to protect human health and the environment.

(3) Not later than two hundred and seventy days after the enactment of the Hazardous and Solid Waste Amendments of 1984 any hazardous waste which is part of a total quantity generated by a generator generating greater than one hundred kilograms but less than one thousand kilograms during one calendar month and which is shipped off the premises on which such waste is generated shall be accompanied by a copy of the Environmental Protection Agency Uniform Hazardous Waste Manifest form signed by the generator. This form shall contain the following information:

(A) the name and address of the generator of the waste;

(B) the United States Department of Transportation description of the waste, including the proper shipping name, hazard class, and identification number (UN/NA), if applicable;

(C) the number and type of containers;

(D) the quantity of waste being transported; and

(E) the name and address of the facility designated to receive the waste.

If subparagraph (B) is not applicable, in lieu of the description referred to in such subparagraph (B), the form shall contain the Environmental Protection Agency identification number, or a generic description of the waste, or a description of the waste by hazardous waste characteristic. Additional requirements related to the manifest form shall apply only if determined necessary by the Administrator to protect human health and the environment.

(4) The Administrator's responsibility under this subtitle to protect human health and the environment may require the promulgation of standards under this subtitle for hazardous wastes which are generated by any generator who does not generate more than one hundred kilograms of hazardous waste in a calendar month.

(5) Until the effective date of standards required to be promulgated under paragraph (1), any hazardous waste identified or listed under section 3001 generated by any generator during any calendar month in a total quantity greater than one hundred kilograms but less than one thousand kilograms, which is not treated, stored, or disposed of at a hazardous waste treatment, storage, or disposal facility with a permit under section 3005, shall be disposed of only in a facility which is permitted, licensed, or registered by a State to manage municipal or industrial solid waste.

(6) Standards promulgated as provided in paragraph (1) shall, at a minimum, require that all treatment, storage, or disposal of hazardous wastes generated by generators referred to in paragraph (1) shall occur at a facility with interim status or a permit under this subtitle, except that onsite storage of hazardous waste generated by a generator generating a total quantity of hazardous waste greater than one hundred kilograms, but less than one thousand kilograms during a calendar month, may occur without the requirement of a permit for up to one hundred and eighty days. Such onsite storage may occur without the requirement of a permit for not more than six thousand kilograms for up to two hundred and seventy days if such generator must ship or haul such waste over two hundred miles.

(7) (A) Nothing in this subsection shall be construed to affect or impair the validity of regulations promulgated by the Secretary of Transportation pursuant to the Hazardous Materials Transportation Act.

(B) Nothing in this subsection shall be construed to affect, modify, or render invalid any requirements in regulations promulgated prior to January 1, 1983 applicable to any acutely hazardous waste identified or listed under section 3001 which is generated by any generator during any calendar month in a total quantity less than one thousand kilograms.

(8) Effective March 31, 1986, unless the Administrator promulgates standards as provided in paragraph (1) of this subsection prior to such date, hazardous waste generated by any generator in a total quantity greater than one hundred kilograms but less than one thousand kilograms during a calendar month shall be subject to the following requirements until the standards referred to in paragraph (1) of this subsection have become effective:

(A) the notice requirements of paragraph (3) of this subsection shall apply and in addition, the information provided in the form shall include the name of the waste transporters and the name and address of the facility designated to receive the waste;

(B) except in the case of the onsite storage referred to in paragraph (6) of this subsection, the treatment, storage, or disposal of such waste shall occur at a facility with interim status or a permit under this subtitle;

(C) generators of such waste shall file manifest exception reports as required of generators producing greater amounts of hazardous waste per month except that such reports shall be filed by January 31, for any waste shipment occurring in the last half of the preceding calendar year, and by July 31, for any waste shipment occurring in the first half of the calendar year; and

(D) generators of such waste shall retain for three years a copy of the manifest signed by the designated facility that has received the waste. Nothing in this paragraph shall be construed as a determination of the standards appropriate under paragraph (1).

(9) The last sentence of section 3010(b) shall not apply to regulations promulgated under this subsection.

[§3001(d) added by PL 98-616]

(e) Specified Wastes.—

(1) Not later than 6 months after the date of enactment of the Hazardous and Solid Waste Amendments of 1984, the Administrator shall,

where appropriate, list under subsection (b)(1), additional wastes containing chlorinated dioxins or chlorinated-dibenzofurans. Not later than one year after the date of enactment of the Hazardous and Solid Waste Amendments of 1984, the Administrator shall, where appropriate, list under subsection (b)(1) wastes containing remaining halogenated dioxins and halogenated- dibenzofurans.

(2) Not later than fifteen months after the date of enactment of the Hazardous and Solid Waste Amendments of 1984, the Administrator shall make a determination of whether or not to list under subsection (b)(1) the following wastes: Chlorinated Aliphatics, Dioxin, Dimethyl Hydrazine, TDI (toluene diisocyanate), Carbamates, Bromacil, Linuron, Organo- bromines, solvents, refining wastes, chlorinated aromatics, dyes and pigments, inorganic chemical industry wastes, lithium batteries, coke byproducts, paint production wastes, and coal slurry pipeline effluent.

[§3001(e) added by PL 98–616]

(f) Delisting Procedures.—

(1) When evaluating a petition to exclude a waste generated at a particular facility from listing under this section, the Administrator shall consider factors (including additional constituents) other than those for which the waste was listed if the Administrator has a reasonable basis to believe that such additional factors could cause the waste to be a hazardous waste. The Administrator shall provide notice and opportunity for comment on these additional factors before granting or denying such petition.

(2) (A) To the maximum extent practicable the Administrator shall publish in the Federal Register a proposal to grant or deny a petition referred to in paragraph (1) within twelve months after receiving a complete application to exclude a waste generated at a particular facility from being regulated as a hazardous waste and shall grant or deny such a petition within twenty-four months after receiving a complete application.

(B) The temporary granting of such a petition prior to the enactment of the Hazardous and Solid Waste Amendments of 1984 without the opportunity for public comment and the full consideration of such comments shall not continue for more than twenty-four months after the date of enactment of the Hazardous and Solid Waste Amendments of 1984. If a final decision to grant or deny such a petition has not been promulgated after notice and opportunity for public comment within the time limit prescribed by the preceding sentence, any such temporary granting of such petition shall cease to be in effect.

[§3001(f) added by PL 98–616]

(g) EP Toxicity.—Not later than twenty-eight months after the date of enactment of the Hazardous and Solid Waste Amendments of 1984 the Administrator shall examine the deficiencies of the extraction procedure toxicity characteristic as a predictor of the leaching potential of wastes and make changes in the extraction procedure toxicity characteristic, including changes in the leaching media, as are necessary to insure that it accurately predicts the leaching potential of wastes which pose a threat to human health and the environment when mismanaged.

[§3001(g) added by PL 98–616]

(h) Additional Characteristics.—Not later than two years after the date of enactment of the Hazardous and Solid Waste Amendments of 1984, the Administrator shall promulgate regulations under this section identifying additional characteristics of hazardous waste, including measures or indicators of toxicity.

[§3001(h) added by PL 98–616]

(i) Clarification of Household Waste Exclusion.—A resource recovery facility recovering energy from the mass burning of municipal solid waste shall not be deemed to be treating, storing, disposing of, or otherwise managing hazardous wastes for the purposes of regulation under this subtitle, if—

(1) such facility—

(A) receives and burns only—

(i) household waste (from single and multiple dwellings, hotels, motels, and other residential sources), and

(ii) solid waste from commercial or industrial sources that does not contain hazardous waste identified or listed under this section, and

(B) does not accept hazardous wastes identified or listed under this section, and

(2) the owner or operator of such facility has established contractual requirements or other appropriate notification or inspection procedures to assure that hazardous wastes are not received at or burned in such facility.

[§3001(i) added by PL 98–616]

§6922. Standards Applicable to Generators of Hazardous Waste [Sec. 3002]

(a) In General — Not later than eighteen months after the date of the enactment of this section, and after notice and opportunity for public hearings and after consultation with appropriate Federal and State agencies, the Administrator shall promulgate regulations establishing such standards, applicable to generators of hazardous waste identified or listed under this subtitle, as may be necessary to protect human health and the environment. Such standards shall establish requirements respecting—

[§3002(a) designated by PL 98–616]

(1) recordkeeping practices that accurately identify the quantities of such hazardous waste generated, the constituents thereof which are significant in quantity or in potential harm to human health or the environment, and the disposition of such wastes;

(2) labeling practices for any containers used for the storage, transport, or disposal of such hazardous waste such as will identify accurately such waste;

(3) use of appropriate containers for such hazardous waste;

(4) furnishing of information on the general chemical composition of such hazardous waste to persons transporting, treating, storing, or disposing of such wastes;

(5) use of a manifiest system and any other reasonable means necessary to assure that all such hazardous waste generated is designated for treatment, storage, or disposal in, and arrives at treatment, storage, or disposal facilities (other than facilities on the premises where the waste is generated) for which a permit has been issued as provided in this subtitle, or pursuant to title I of the Marine Protection, Research, and Sanctuaries Act (86 Stat. 1052); and

(6) submission of reports to the Administrator (or the State agency in any case in which such agency carries out a permit program pursuant to this subtitle) at least once every two years, setting out—

(A) the quantities and nature of hazardous waste identified or listed under this subtitle that he has generated during the year;

(B) the disposition of all hazardous waste reported under subparagraph (A);

(C) the efforts undertaken during the year to reduce the volume and toxicity of waste generated; and

(D) the changes in volume and toxicity of waste actually achieved during the year in question in comparison with previous years, to the extent such information is available for years prior to enactment of the Hazardous and Solid Waste Amendments of 1984.

[§3002(a)(6) revised by PL 98–616]

(b) Waste Minimization. — Effective September 1, 1985, the manifest required by subsection (a)(5) shall contain a certification by the generator that—

(1) the generator of the hazardous waste has a program in place to reduce the volume or quantity and toxicity of such waste to the degree determined by the generator to be economically practicable; and

(2) the proposed method of treatment, storage, or disposal is that practicable method currently available to the generator which minimizes the present and future threat to human health and the environment.

[§3002(b) added by PL 98–616]

§6923. Standards Applicable to Transporters of Hazardous Waste [Sec. 3003]

(a) Standards. — Not later than eighteen months after the date of enactment of this section, and after opportunity for public hearings the Administrator, after consultation with the Secretary of Transportation and the States, shall promulgate regulations establishing such standards, applicable to transporters of hazardous waste identified or listed under this subtitle, as may be necessary to protect human health and the environment. Such standards shall include but need not be limited to requirements respecting—

(1) recordkeeping concerning such hazardous waste transported, and their source and delivery points;

(2) transportation of such waste only if properly labeled;

(3) compliance with the manifest system referred to in section 3002(5); and

(4) transportation of all such hazardous waste only to the hazardous waste treatment, storage, or disposal facilities which the shipper designates on the manifest form to be a facility holding a permit issued under this subtitle, or pursuant to title I of the Marine Protection, Research, and Sanctuaries act (86 Stat. 1052).

(b) Coordination With Regulations of Secretary of Transportation. — In case of any hazardous waste identified or listed under this subtitle which is subject to the Hazardous Materials

Transportation Act (88 Stat. 2156; 49 U.S.C. 1801 and following), the regulations promulgated by the Administrator under this section shall be consistent with the requirements of such Act and the regulations thereunder. The Administrator is authorized to make recommendations to the Secretary of Transportation respecting the regulations of such hazardous waste under the Hazardous Materials Transportation Act and for addition of materials to be covered by such Act.

(c) Fuel from Hazardous Waste. — Not later than two years after the date of enactment of the Hazardous and Solid Waste Amendments of 1984, and after opportunity for public hearing, the Administrator shall promulgate regulations establishing standards, applicable to transporters of fuel produced (1) from any hazardous waste identified or listed under section 3001, or (2) from any hazardous waste identified or listed under section 3001 and any other material, as may be necessary to protect human health and the environment. Such standards may include any of the requirements set forth in paragraphs (1) through (4) of subsection (a) as may be appropriate.

[§3003(c) added by PL 98–616]

§6924. Standards Applicable to Owners and Operators of Hazardous Waste Treatment, Storage, and Disposal Facilities [Sec. 3004]

(a) In General — Not later than eighteen months after the date of enactment of this section, and after opportunity for public hearing and after consultation with appropriate Federal and State agencies, the Administrator shall promulgate regulations establishing such performance standards, applicable to owners and operators of facilities for the treatment, storage, or disposal of hazardous waste identified or listed under this subtitle, as may be necessary to protect human health and the environment. In establishing such standards the Administrator shall, where appropriate, distinguish in such standards between requirements appropriate for new facilities and for facilities in existence on the date of promulgation of such regulations. Such standards shall include, but need not be limited to, requirements respecting—

[§3004 introductory paragraph amended by PL 96–482; designated as (a) by PL 98–616]

(1) maintaining records of all hazardous wastes identified or listed under this title which is treated, stored, or disposed of, as the case may be, and the manner in which such wastes were treated, stored, or disposed of;

(2) satisfactory reporting, monitoring, and inspection and compliance with the manifest system referred to in section 3002(5);

(3) treatment, storage, or disposal of all such waste received by the facility pursuant to such operating methods, techniques, and practices as may be satisfactory to the Administrator;

(4) the location, design, and construction of such hazardous waste treatment, disposal, or storage facilities;

(5) contingency plans for effective action to minimize unanticipated damage from any treatment, storage, or disposal of any such hazardous waste;

(6) the maintenance of operation of such facilities and requiring such additional qualifications as to ownership, continuity of operation, training for personnel, and financial responsibility (including financial responsibility for corrective action) as may be necessary or desirable; and

[§3004(a)(6) amended by PL 98–616]

(7) compliance with the requirements of section 3005 respecting permits for treatment, storage, or disposal.

No private entity shall be precluded by reason of criteria established under paragraph (6) from the ownership or operation of facilities providing hazardous waste treatment, storage, or disposal services where such entity can provide assurances of financial responsibility and continuity of operation consistent with the degree and duration of risks associated with the treatment, storage, or disposal of specified hazardous waste.

(b) Salt Dome Formations, Salt Bed Formations, Underground Mines and Caves.—

(1) Effective on the date of the enactment of the Hazardous and Solid Waste Amendments of 1984, the placement of any noncontainerized or bulk liquid hazardous waste in any salt dome formation, salt bed formation, underground mine, or cave is prohibited until such time as—

(A) the Administrator has determined, after notice and opportunity for hearings on the record in the affected areas, that such placement is protective of human health and the environment;

(B) the Administrator has promulgated performance and permitting standards for such facilities under this subtitle, and;

(C) a permit has been issued under section 3005(c) for the facility concerned.

(2) Effective on the date of enactment of the Hazardous and Solid Waste Amendments of 1984, the placement of any hazardous waste other than a hazardous waste referred to in paragraph (1) in a salt dome formation, salt bed formation, underground mine, or cave is prohibited until such time as a permit has been issued under section 3005(c) for the facility concerned.

(3) No determination made by the Administrator under subsection (d), (e), or (g) of this section regarding any hazardous waste to which such subsection (d), (e), or (g) applies shall affect the prohibition contained in paragraph (1) or (2) of this subsection.

(4) Nothing in this subsection shall apply to the Department of Energy Waste Isolation Pilot Project in New Mexico.

[§3004(b) added by PL 98–616]

(c) Liquids in Landfills.—

(1) Effective 6 months after the date of the enactment of the Hazardous and Solid Waste Amendments of 1984, the placement of bulk or noncontainerized liquid hazardous waste or free liquids contained in hazardous waste (whether or not absorbents have been added) in any landfill is prohibited. Prior to such date the requirements (as in effect on April 30, 1983) promulgated under this section by the Administrator regarding liquid hazardous waste shall remain in force and effect to the extent such requirements are applicable to the placement of bulk or noncontainerized liquid hazardous waste, or free liquids contained in hazardous waste, in landfills.

(2) Not later than fifteen months after the date of the enactment of the Hazardous and Solid Waste Amendments of 1984, the Administrator shall promulgate final regulations which—

(A) minimize the disposal of containerized liquid hazardous waste in landfills, and

(B) minimize the presence of free liquids in containerized hazardous waste to be disposed of in landfills. Such regulations shall also prohibit the disposal in landfills of liquids that have been absorbed in materials that biodegrade or that release liquids when compressed as might occur during routine landfill operations. Prior to the date on which such final regulations take effect, the requirements (as in effect on April 30, 1983) promulgated under this section by the Administrator shall remain in force and effect to the extent such requirements are applicable to the disposal of containerized liquid hazardous waste, or free liquids contained in hazardous waste, in landfills.

(3) Effective twelve months after the date of the enactment of the Hazardous and Solid Waste Amendments of 1984, the placement of any liquid which is not a hazardous waste in a landfill for which a permit is required under section 3005(c) or which is operating pursuant to interim status granted under section 3005(e) is prohibited unless the owner or operator of such landfill demonstrates to the Administrator, or the Administrator determines, that—

(A) the only reasonably available alternative to the placement in such landfill is placement in a landfill or unlined surface impoundment, whether or not permitted under section 3005(c) or operating pursuant to interim status under section 3005(e), which contains, or may reasonably be anticipated to contain, hazardous waste; and

(B) placement in such owner or operator's landfill will not present a risk of contamination of any underground source of drinking water.

As used in subparagraph (B), the term "underground source of drinking water" has the same meaning as provided in regulations under the Safe Drinking Water Act (title XIV of the Public Health Service Act).

(4) No determination made by the Administrator under subsection (d), (e), or (g) of this section regarding any hazardous waste to which such subsection (d), (e), or (g) applies shall affect the prohibition contained in paragraph (1) of this subsection.

[§3004(c) added by PL 98–616]

(d) Prohibitions on Land Disposal of Specified Wastes.—

(1) Effective 32 months after the enactment of the Hazardous and Solid Waste Amendments of 1984 (except as provided in subsection (f) with respect to underground injection into deep injection wells), the land disposal of the hazardous wastes referred to in paragraph (2) is prohibited unless the Administrator determines the prohibition on one or more methods of land disposal of such waste is not required in order to protect human health and the environment for as long as the waste remains hazardous, taking into account—

(A) the long-term uncertainties associated with land disposal,

(B) the goal of managing hazardous waste in an appropriate manner in the first instance, and

(C) the persistence, toxicity, mobility, and propensity to bioaccumulate of such hazardous wastes and their hazardous constituents.

For the purposes of this paragraph, a method of land disposal may not be determined to be protective of human health and the environment for a hazardous waste referred to in paragraph (2) (other than a hazardous waste which has complied with the pretreatment regulations promulgated under subsection (m)), unless, upon application by an interested person, it has been demonstrated to the Administrator, to a reasonable degree of certainty, that there will be no migration of hazardous constituents from the disposal unit or injection zone for as long as the wastes remain hazardous.

(2) Paragraph (1) applies to the following hazardous wastes listed or identified under section 3001:

(A) Liquid hazardous wastes, including free liquids associated with any solid or sludge, containing free cyanides at concentrations greater than or equal to 1,000 mg/l.

(B) Liquid hazardous wastes, including free liquids associated with any solid or sludge, containing the following metals (or elements) or compounds of these metals (or elements) at concentrations greater than or equal to those specified below:

(i) arsenic and/or compounds (as As) 500 mg/l;

(ii) cadmium and/or compounds (as Cd) 100 mg/l;

(iii) chromium (VI and/or compounds (as Cr VI)) 500 mg/l;

(iv) lead and/or compounds (as Pb) 500 mg/l;

(v) mercury and/or compounds (as Hg) 20 mg/l;

(vi) nickel and/or compounds (as Ni) 134 mg/l;

(vii) selenium and/or compounds (as Se) 100 mg/l; and

(viii) thallium and/or compounds (as Th) 130 mg/l.

(C) Liquid hazardous waste having a pH less than or equal to two (2.0).

(D) Liquid hazardous wastes containing polychlorinated biphenyls at concentrations greater than or equal to 50 ppm.

(E) Hazardous wastes containing halogenated organic compounds in total concentration greater than or equal to 1,000 mg/kg.

When necessary to protect human health and the environment, the Administrator shall substitute more stringent concentration levels than the levels specified in subparagraphs (A) through (E).

(3) During the period ending forty-eight months after the date of the enactment of the Hazardous and Solid Waste Amendments of 1984, this subsection shall not apply to any disposal of contaminated soil or debris resulting from a response action taken under section 104 or 106 of the Comprehensive Environmental Response, Compensation, and Liability Act of 1980 or a corrective action required under this subtitle.

[§3004(d) added by PL 98–616]

(e) Solvents and Dioxins.—

(1) Effective twenty-four months after the date of enactment of the Hazardous and Solid Waste Amendments of 1984 (except as provided in subsection (f) with respect to underground injection into deep injection wells), the land disposal of the hazardous wastes referred to in paragraph (2) is prohibited unless the Administrator determines the prohibition of one or more methods of land disposal of such waste is not required in order to protect human health and the environment for as long as the waste remains hazardous, taking into account the factors referred to in subparagraph (A) through (C) of subsection (d)(1). For the purposes of this paragraph, a method of land disposal may not be determined to be protective of human health and the environment for a hazardous waste referred to in paragraph (2)(other than a hazardous waste which has complied with the pretreatment regulations promulgated under subsection (m)), unless upon application by an interested person it has been demonstrated to the Administrator, to a reasonable degree of certainty, that there will be no migration of hazardous constituents from the disposal unit or injection zone for as long as the wastes remain hazardous.

(2) The hazardous wastes to which the prohibition under paragraph (1) applies are as follows—

(A) dioxin-containing hazardous wastes numbered F020, F021, F022, and F023 (as referred to in the proposed rule published by the Administrator in the Federal Register for April 4, 1983), and

(B) those hazardous wastes numbered F001, F002, F003, F004, and F005 in regulations promulgated by the Administrator under section

3001 (40 C.F.R. 261.31 (July 1, 1983)), as those regulations are in effect on July 1, 1983.

(3) During the period ending forty- eight months after the date of the enactment of the Hazardous and Solid Waste Amendments of 1984, this subsection shall not apply to any disposal of contaminated soil or debris resulting from a response action taken under section 104 or 106 of the Comprehensive Environmental Response, Compensation, and Liability Act of 1980 or a corrective action required under this subtitle.

[§3004(e) added by PL 98–616]

(f) Disposal into Deep Injection Wells: Specified Subsection (d) Wastes; Solvents and Dioxins.—

(1) Not later than forty-five months after the date of enactment of the Hazardous and Solid Waste Amendments of 1984, the Administrator shall complete a review of the disposal of all hazardous wastes referred to in paragraph (2) of subsection (d) and in paragraph (2) of subsection (e) by underground injection into deep injection wells.

(2) Within forty-five months after the date of the enactment of the Hazardous and Solid Waste Amendments of 1984, the Administrator shall make a determination regarding the disposal by underground injection into deep injection wells of the hazardous wastes referred to in paragraph (2) of subsection (d) and the hazardous wastes referred to in paragraph (2) of subsection (e). The Administrator shall promulgate final regulations prohibiting the disposal of such wastes into such wells if it may reasonably be determined that such disposal may not be protective of human health and the environment for as long as the waste remains hazardous, taking into account the factors referred to in subparagraphs (A) through (C) of subsection (d)(1). In promulgating such regulations, the Administrator shall consider each hazardous waste referred to in paragraph (2) of subsection (d) or in paragraph (2) of subsection (e) which is prohibited from disposal into such wells by any State.

(3) If the Administrator fails to make a determination under paragraph (2) for any hazardous waste referred to in paragraph (2) of subsection (d) or in paragraph (2) of subsection (e) within forty- five months after the date of enactment of the Hazardous and Solid Waste Amendments of 1984, such hazardous waste shall be prohibited from disposal into any deep injection well.

(4) As used in this subsection, the term "deep injection well" means a well used for the underground injection of hazardous waste other than a well to which section 7010(a) applies.

[§3004(f) added by PL 98–616]

(g) Additional Land Disposal Prohibition Determinations.—

(1) Not later than twenty-four months after the date of enactment of the Hazardous and Solid Waste Amendments of 1984, the Administrator shall submit a schedule to Congress for—

(A) reviewing all hazardous wastes listed (as of the date of the enactment of the Hazardous and Solid Waste Amendments of 1984) under section 3001 other than those wastes which are referred to in subsection (d) or (e); and

(B) taking action under paragraph (5) of this subsection with respect to each such hazardous waste.

(2) The Administrator shall base the schedule on a ranking of such listed wastes considering their intrinsic hazard and their volume such that decisions regarding the land disposal of high volume hazardous wastes with high intrinsic hazard shall, to the maximum extent possible, be made by the date forty-five months after the date of enactment of the Hazardous and Solid Waste Amendments of 1984. Decisions regarding low volume hazardous wastes with lower intrinsic hazard shall be made by the date sixty-six months after such date of enactment.

(3) The preparation and submission of the schedule under this subsection shall not be subject to the Paperwork Reduction Act of 1980. No hearing on the record shall be required for purposes of preparation or submission of the schedule. The schedule shall not be subject to judicial review.

(4) The schedule under this subsection shall require that the Administrator shall promulgate regulations in accordance with paragraph (5) or make a determination under paragraph (5)—

(A) for at least one-third of all hazardous wastes referred to in paragraph (1) by the date forty-five months after the date of enactment of the Hazardous and Solid Waste Amendments of 1984;

(B) for at least two-thirds of all such listed wastes by the date fifty-five months after the date of enactment of such Amendments; and

(C) for all such listed wastes and for all hazardous wastes identified under 3001 by the date sixty-six months after the date of enactment of such Amendments.

In the case of any hazardous waste identified or listed under section 3001 after the date of enactment of the Hazardous and Solid Waste Amendments of 1984, the Administrator shall determine whether such waste shall be prohibited from one or more methods of land disposal in accordance with paragraph (5) within six months after the date of such identification or listing.

(5) Not later than the date specified in the schedule published under this subsection, the Administrator shall promulgate final regulations prohibiting one or more methods of land disposal of the hazardous wastes listed on such schedule except for methods of land disposal which the Administrator determines will be protective of human health and the environment for as long as the waste remains hazardous, taking into account the factors referred to in subparagraph (A) through (C) of subsection (d)(1). For the purposes of this paragraph, a method of land disposal may not be determined to be protective of human health and the environment (except with respect to a hazardous waste which has complied with the pretreatment regulations promulgated under subsection (m) unless, upon application by an interested person, it has been demonstrated to the Administrator, to a reasonable degree of certainty, that there will be no migration of hazardous constituents from the disposal unit or injection zone for as long as the wastes remain hazardous.

(6) (A) If the Administrator fails (by the date forty-five months after the date of enactment of the Hazardous and Solid Waste Amendments of 1984) to promulgate regulations or make a determination under paragraph (5) for any hazardous waste which is included in the first one- third of the schedule published under this subsection, such hazardous waste may be disposed of in a landfill or surface impoundment only if—

(i) such facility is in compliance with the requirements of subsection (o) which are applicable to new facilities (relating to minimum technological requirements); and

(ii) prior to such disposal, the generator has certified to the Administrator that such generator has investigated the availability of treatment capacity and has determined that the use of such landfill or surface impoundment is the only practical alternative to treatment currently available to the generator.

The prohibition contained in this subparagraph shall continue to apply until the Administrator promulgates regulations or makes a determination under paragraph (5) for the waste concerned.

(B) If the Administrator fails (by the date 55 months after the date of enactment of the Hazardous and Solid Waste Amendments of 1984) to promulgate regulations or make a determination under paragraph (5) for any hazardous waste which is included in the first two-thirds of the schedule published under this subsection, such hazardous waste may be disposed of in a landfill or surface impoundment only if—

(i) such facility is in compliance with the requirements of subsection (o) which are applicable to new facilities (relating to minimum technological requirements); and

(ii) prior to such disposal, the generator has certified to the Administrator that such generator has investigated the availability of treatment capacity and has determined that the use of such landfill or surface impoundment is the only practical alternative to treatment currently available to the generator. The prohibition contained in this subparagraph shall continue to apply until the Administrator promulgates regulations or makes a determination under paragraph (5) for the waste concerned.

(C) If the Administrator fails to promulgate regulations, or make a determination under paragraph (5) for any hazardous waste referred to in paragraph (1) within 66 months after the date of enactment of the Hazardous and Solid Waste Amendments of 1984, such hazardous waste shall be prohibited from land disposal.

[§3004(g) added by PL 98–616]

(h) Variances From Land Disposal Prohibitions.—

(1) A prohibition in regulations under subsection (d), (e), (f), or (g) shall be effective immediately upon promulgation.

(2) The Administrator may establish an effective date different from the effective date which would otherwise apply under subsection (d), (e), (f), or (g) with respect to a specific hazardous waste which is subject to a prohibition under subsection (d), (e), (f), or (g) or under regulations under subsection (d), (e), (f),

or (g). Any such other effective date shall be established on the basis of the earliest date on which adequate alternative treatment, recovery, or disposal capacity which protects human health and the environment will be available. Any such other effective date shall in no event be later than 2 years after the effective date of the prohibition which would otherwise apply under subsection (d), (e), (f), or (g).

(3) The Administrator, after notice and opportunity for comment and after consultation with appropriate State agencies in all affected States, may on a case-by- case basis grant an extension of the effective date which would otherwise apply under subsection (d), (e), (f), or (g) or under paragraph (2) for up to one year, where the applicant demonstrates that there is a binding contractual commitment to construct or otherwise provide such alternative capacity but due to circumstances beyond the control of such applicant such alternative capacity cannot reasonably be made available by such effective date. Such extension shall be renewable once for no more than one additional year.

(4) Whenever another effective date (hereinafter referred to as a "variance") is established under paragraph (2), or an extension is granted under paragraph (3), with respect to any hazardous waste, during the period for which such variance or extension is in effect, such hazardous waste may be disposed of in a landfill or surface impoundment only if such facility is in compliance with the requirements of subsection (o).

[§3004(h) added by PL 98–616]

(i) Publication of Determination.—If the Administrator determines that a method of land disposal will be protective of human health and the environment, he shall promptly publish in the Federal Register notice of such determination, together with an explanation of the basis for such determination.

[§3004(i) added by PL 98–616]

(j) Storage of Hazardous Waste Prohibited from Land Disposal.—In the case of any hazardous waste which is prohibited from one or more methods of land disposal under this section (or under regulations promulgated by the Administrator under any provision of this section) the storage of such hazardous waste is prohibited unless such storage is solely for the purpose of the accumulation of such quantities of hazardous waste as are necessary to facilitate proper recovery, treatment or disposal.

[§3004(j) added by PL 98–616]

(k) Definition of Land Disposal.—For the purposes of this section, the term "land disposal", when used with respect to a specified hazardous waste, shall be deemed to include, but not be limited to, any placement of such hazardous waste in a landfill, surface impoundment, waste pile, injection well, land treatment facility, salt dome formation, salt bed formation, or underground mine or cave.

[§3004(k) added by PL 98–616]

(l) Ban on Dust Suppression.—The use of waste or used oil or other material, which is contaminated or mixed with dioxin or any other hazardous waste identified or listed under section 3001 (other than a waste identified solely on the basis of ignitability), for dust suppression or road treatment is prohibited.

[§3004(l) added by PL 98–616]

(m) Treatment Standards for Wastes Subject to Land Disposal Prohibition.—

(1) Simultaneously with the promulgation of regulations under subsection (d), (e), (f), or (g) prohibiting one or more methods of land disposal of a particular hazardous waste, and as appropriate thereafter, the Administrator shall, after notice and an opportunity for hearings and after consultation with appropriate Federal and State agencies, promulgate regulations specifying those levels or methods of treatment, if any, which substantially diminish the toxicity of the waste or substantially reduce the likelihood of migration of hazardous constituents from the waste so that short-term and long-term threats to human health and the environment are minimized.

(2) If such hazardous waste has been treated to the level or by a method specified in regulations promulgated under this subsection, such waste or residue thereof shall not be subject to any prohibition promulgated under subsection (d), (e), (f), or (g) and may be disposed of in a land disposal facility which meets the requirements of this subtitle. Any regulation promulgated under this subsection for a particular hazardous waste shall become effective on the same date as any applicable prohibition promulgated under subsection (d), (e), (f), or (g).

[§3004(m) added by PL 98–616]

(n) Air Emissions.—Not later than thirty months after the date of enactment of the Hazardous and Solid Waste Amendments of 1984, the Administrator shall promulgate such regulations for the monitoring and control of air emissions at hazardous waste treatment, storage, and disposal facilities, including but not limited to open tanks, surface impoundments, and landfills, as may be necessary to protect human health and the environment.

[§3004(n) added by PL 98–616]

(o) Minimum Technological Requirements.—

(1) The regulations under subsection (a) of this section shall be revised from time to time to take into account improvements in the technology of control and measurement. At a minimum, such regulations shall require, and a permit issued pursuant to section 3005(c) after the date of enactment of the Hazardous and Solid Waste Amendments of 1984 by the Administrator or a State shall require—

(A) for each new landfill or surface impoundment, each new landfill or surface impoundment unit at an existing facility, each replacement of an existing landfill or surface impoundment unit, and each lateral expansion of an existing landfill or surface impoundment for which an application for a final determination regarding issuance of a permit under section 3005(c) is received after the date of enactment of the Hazardous and Solid Waste Amendments of 1984—

(i) the installation of two or more liners and a leachate collection system above (in the case of a landfill) and between such liners; and

(ii) ground water monitoring; and

(B) for each incinerator which receives a permit under section 3005(c) after the date of enactment of the Hazardous and Solid Waste Amendments of 1984, the attainment of the minimum destruction and removal efficiency required by regulations in effect on June 24, 1982. The requirements of this paragraph shall apply with respect to all waste received after the issuance of the permit.

(2) Paragraph (1)(A)(i) shall not apply if the owner or operator demonstrates to the Administrator and the Administrator finds for such landfill or surface impoundment, that alternative design and operating practices, together with location characteristics, will prevent the migration of any hazardous constituents into the ground water or surface water at least as effectively as such liners and leachate collection systems.

(3) The double-liner requirement set forth in paragraph (1)(A)(i) may be waived by the Administrator for any monofill, if—

(A) such monofill contains only hazardous wastes from foundry furnace emission controls or metal casting molding sand,

(B) such wastes do not contain constituents which would render the wastes hazardous for reasons other than the Extraction Procedure ("EP") toxicity characteristics set forth in regulations under this subtitle, and

(C) such monofill meets the same requirements as are applicable in the case of a waiver under section 3005(j)(2) or (4).

(4) (A) Not later than thirty months after the date of enactment of the Hazardous and Solid Waste Amendments of 1984, the Administrator shall promulgate standards requiring that new landfill units, surface impoundment units, waste piles, underground tanks and land treatment units for the storage, treatment, or disposal of hazardous waste identified or listed under section 3001 shall be required to utilize approved leak detection systems.

(B) For the purposes of subparagraph (A)—

(i) the term "approved leak detection system" means a system or technology which the Administrator determines to be capable of detecting leaks of hazardous constituents at the earliest practicable time; and

(ii) the term "new units" means units on which construction commences after the date of promulgation of regulations under this paragraph.

(5) (A) The Administrator shall promulgate regulations or issue guidance documents implementing the requirements of paragraph (1)(A) within two years after the date of the enactment of the Hazardous and Solid Waste Amendments of 1984.

(B) Until the effective date of such regulations or guidance documents, the requirement for the installation of two or more liners may be satisfied by the installation of a top liner designed, operated, and constructed of materials to prevent the migration of any constituent into such liner during the period such facility remains in operation (including any post- closure monitoring period), and a lower liner designed, operated and constructed to prevent the migration of any constituent through such liner during such period. For the purpose of the preceding sentence, a lower liner shall be deemed to satisfy such requirement if it is constructed of at least a 3–foot thick layer of recompacted clay or other natural material with a permeability of no more than 1¥10^{-7}centimeter per second.

(6) Any permit under section 3005 which is issued for a landfill located within the State of Alabama shall require the installation of two or more liners and a leachate collection system above and between such liners, notwithstanding any other provision of this Act.

(7) In addition to the requirements set forth in this subsection, the regulations referred to in paragraph (1) shall specify criteria for the acceptable location of new and existing treatment, storage, or disposal facilities as necessary to protect human health and the environment. Within 18 months after the enactment of the Hazardous and Solid Waste Amendments of 1984, the Administrator shall publish guidance criteria identifying areas of vulnerable hydrogeology.

[§3004(o) added by PL 98–616]

(p) Ground Water Monitoring.—The standards under this section concerning ground water monitoring which are applicable to surface impoundments, waste piles, land treatment units, and landfills shall apply to such a facility whether or not—

(1) the facility is located above the seasonal high water table;

(2) two liners and a leachate collection system have been installed at the facility; or

(3) the owner or operator inspects the liner (or liners) which has been installed at the facility. This subsection shall not be construed to affect other exemptions or waivers from such standards provided in regulations in effect on the date of enactment of the Hazardous and Solid Waste Amendments of 1984 or as may be provided in revisions to those regulations, to the extent consistent with this subsection. The Administrator is authorized on a case-by-case basis to exempt from ground water monitoring requirements under this section (including subsection (o)) any engineered structure which the Administrator finds does not receive or contain liquid waste (nor waste containing free liquids), is designed and operated to exclude liquid from precipitation or other runoff, utilizes multiple leak detection systems within the outer layer of containment, and provides for continuing operation and maintenance of these leak detection systems during the operating period, closure, and the period required for post-closure monitoring and for which the Administrator concludes on the basis of such findings that there is a reasonable certainty hazardous constituents will not migrate beyond the outer layer of containment prior to the end of the period required for post-closure monitoring.

[§3004(p) added by PL 98–616]

(q) Hazardous Waste Used as Fuel.—

(1) Not later than two years after the date of the enactment of the Hazardous and Solid Waste Amendments of 1984, and after notice and opportunity for public hearing, the Administrator shall promulgate regulations establishing such—

(A) standards applicable to the owners and operators of facilities which produce a fuel—

(i) from any hazardous waste identified or listed under section 3001, or

(ii) from any hazardous waste identified or listed under section 3001 and any other material;

(B) standards applicable to the owners and operators of facilities which burn, for purposes of energy recovery, any fuel produced as provided in subparagraph (A) or any fuel which otherwise contains any hazardous waste identified or listed under section 3001; and

(C) standards applicable to any person who distributes or markets any fuel which is produced as provided in subparagraph (A) or any fuel which otherwise contains any hazardous waste identified or listed under section 3001; as may be necessary to protect human health and the environment. Such standards may include any of the requirements set forth in paragraphs (1) through (7) of subsection (a) as may be appropriate. Nothing in this subsection shall be construed to affect or impair the provisions of section 3001(b)(3). For purposes of this subsection, the term "hazardous waste listed under section 3001" includes any commercial chemical product which is listed under section 3001 and which, in lieu of its original intended use, is (i) produced for use as (or as a component of) a fuel, (ii) distributed for use as a fuel, or (iii) burned as a fuel.

(2) (A) This subsection, subsection (r), and subsection (s) shall not apply to petroleum refinery wastes containing oil which are converted into petroleum coke at the same facility at which such wastes were generated, unless the resulting coke product would exceed one or more characteristics by which a substance would be identified as a hazardous waste under section 3001.

(B) The Administrator may exempt from the requirements of this subsection, subsection (r), or subsection (s) facilities which burn de minimis quantities of hazardous waste as fuel, as defined by the Administrator, if the wastes are burned at the same facility at which such wastes are generated; the waste is burned to recover useful energy, as determined by the Administrator on the basis of the design and operating characteristics of the facility and the heating value and other characteristics of the waste, and the waste is burned in a type of device determined by the Administrator to be designed and operated at a destruction and removal efficiency sufficient such that protection of human health and environment is assured.

(C) (i) After the date of the enactment of the Hazardous and Solid Waste Amendments of 1984 and until standards are promulgated and in effect under paragraph (2) of this subsection, no fuel which contains any hazardous waste may be burned in any cement kiln which is located within the boundaries of any incorporated municipality with a population greater than five hundred thousand (based on the most recent census statistics) unless such kiln fully complies with regulations (as in effect on the date of the enactment of the Hazardous and Solid Waste Amendments of 1984) under this subtitle which are applicable to incinerators.

(ii) Any person who knowingly violates the prohibition contained in clause (i) shall be deemed to have violated section 3008(d)(2).

[§3004(q) added by PL 98–616]

(r) Labeling.—

(1) Notwithstanding any other provision of law, until such time as the Administrator promulgates standards under subsection (q) specifically superceding this requirement, it shall be unlawful for any person who is required to file a notification in accordance with paragraph (1) or (3) of section 3010 to distribute or market any fuel which is produced from any hazardous waste identified or listed under section 3001, or any fuel which otherwise contains any hazardous waste identified or listed under section 3001 if the invoice or the bill of sale fails—

(A) to bear the following statement: "WARNING: THIS FUEL CONTAINS HAZARDOUS WASTES", and

(B) to list the hazardous wastes contained therein. Beginning ninety days after the enactment of the Hazardous and Solid Waste Amendments of 1984, such statement shall be located in a conspicuous place on every such invoice or bill of sale and shall appear in conspicuous and legible type in contrast by typography, layouts, or color with other printed matter on the invoice or bill of sale.

(2) Unless the Administrator determines otherwise as may be necessary to protect human health and the environment, this subsection shall not apply to fuels produced from petroleum refining waste containing oil if—

(A) such materials are generated and reinserted onsite into the refining process;

(B) contaminants are removed; and

(C) such refining waste containing oil is converted along with normal process streams into petroleum-derived fuel products at a facility at which crude oil is refined into petroleum products and which is classified as a number SIC 2911 facility under the Office of Management and Budget Standard Industrial Classification Manual.

(3) Unless the Administrator determines otherwise as may be necessary to protect human health and the environment, this subsection shall not apply to fuels produced from oily materials, resulting from normal petroleum refining, production and transportation practices, if (A) contaminants are removed; and (B) such oily materials are converted along with normal process streams into petroleum-derived fuel products at a facility at which crude oil is refined into petroleum products and which is classified as a number SIC 2911 facility under the Office of Management and Budget Standard Classification Manual.

[§3004(r) added by PL 98–616]

(s) Recordkeeping.—Not later than fifteen months after the date of enactment of the Hazardous and Solid Waste Amendments of 1984, the Administrator shall promulgate regulations requiring that any person who is required to file a notification in accordance with subparagraph (1), (2), or (3), of section 3010(a) shall maintain such records regarding fuel blending, distribution, or use as may be necessary to protect human health and the environment.

[§3004(s) added by PL 98–616]

(t) Financial Responsibility Provisions.—

(1) Financial responsibility required by subsection (a) of this section may be established in accordance with regulations promulgated by the Administrator by any one, or any combination, of the following: insurance, guarantee,

surety bond, letter of credit, or qualification as a self-insurer. In promulgating requirements under this section, the Administrator is authorized to specify policy or other contractual terms, conditions, or defenses which are necessary or are unacceptable in establishing such evidence of financial responsibility in order to effectuate the purposes of this Act.

(2) In any case where the owner or operator is is bankruptcy, reorganization, or arrangement pursuant to the Federal Bankruptcy Code or where (with reasonable diligence) jurisdiction in any State court or any Federal Court cannot be obtained over an owner or operator likely to be solvent at the time of judgment, any claim arising from conduct for which evidence of financial responsibility must be provided under this section may be asserted directly against the guarantor providing such evidence of financial responsibility. In the case of any action pursuant to this subsection, such guarantor shall be entitled to invoke all rights and defenses which would have been available to the owner or operator if any action had been brought against the owner or operator by the claimant and which would have been available to the guarantor if an action had been brought against the guarantor by the owner or operator.

(3) The total liability of any guarantor shall be limited to the aggregate amount which the guarantor has provided as evidence of financial responsibility to the owner or operator under this Act. Nothing in this subsection shall be construed to limit any other State or Federal statutory, contractual or common law liability of a guarantor to its owner or operator including, but not limited to, the liability of such guarantor for bad faith either in negotiating or in failing to negotiate the settlement of any claim. Nothing in this subsection shall be construed to diminish the liability of any person under section 107 or 111 of the Comprehensive Environmental Response, Compensation and Liability Act of 1980 or other applicable law.

(4) For the purpose of this subsection, the term "guarantor" means any person, other than the owner or operator, who provides evidence of financial responsibility for an owner or operator under this section.

[§3004(t) added by PL 98–616]

(u) Continuing Releases at Permitted Facilities.—Standards promulgated under this section shall require, and a permit issued after the date of enactment of the Hazardous and Solid Waste Amendments of 1984 by the Administrator or a State shall require, corrective action for all releases of hazardous waste or constituents from any solid waste management unit at a treatment, storage, or disposal facility seeking a permit under this subtitle, regardless of the time at which waste was placed in such unit. Permits issued under section 3005 shall contain schedules of compliance for such corrective action (where such corrective action cannot be completed prior to issuance of the permit) and assurances of financial responsibility for completing such corrective action.

[§3004(u) added by PL 98–616]

(v) Corrective Actions Beyond Facility Boundary.—As promptly as practicable after the date of the enactment of the Hazardous and Solid Waste Amendments of 1984, the Administrator shall amend the standards under this section regarding corrective action required at facilities for the treatment, storage, or disposal, of hazardous waste listed or identified under section 3001 to require that corrective action be taken beyond the facility boundary where necessary to protect human health and the environment unless the owner or operator of the facility concerned demonstrates to the satisfaction of the Administrator that, despite the owner or operator's best efforts, the owner or operator was unable to obtain the necessary permission to undertake such action. Such regulations shall take effect immediately upon promulgation, notwithstanding section 3010(b), and shall apply to—

(1) all facilities operating under permits issued under subsection (c), and

(2) all landfills, surface impoundments, and waste pile units (including any new units, replacements of existing units, or lateral expansions of existing units) which receive hazardous waste after July 26, 1982.

Pending promulgation of such regulations, the Administrator shall issue corrective action orders for facilities referred to in paragraphs (1) and (2), on a case-by- case basis, consistent with the purposes of this subsection.

[§3004(v) added by PL 98–616]

(w) Underground Tanks.—Not later than March 1, 1985, the Administrator shall promulgate final permitting standards under this section for underground tanks that cannot be entered for inspection. Within forty-eight months after the date of the enactment of the Hazardous and Solid Waste Amendments of 1984, such standards shall be modified, if necessary, to cover at a minimum all requirements and standards described in section 9003.

[§3004(w) added by PL 98–616]

(x) If (1) solid waste from the extraction, beneficiation or procesing of ores and minerals, including phosphate rock and overburden from the mining of uranium, (2) fly ash waste, bottom ash waste, slage waste, and flue gas emission control waste generated primarily from the combustion of coal or other fossil fuels, or (3) cement kiln dust waste, is subject to regulation under this subtitle, the Administrator is authorized to modify the requirements of subsections (c), (d), (e), (f), (g), (o), and (u) and section 3005(j), in the case of landfills or surface impoundments receiving such solid waste, to take into account the special characteristics of such wastes, the practical difficulties associated with implementation of such requirements, and site-specific characteristics, including but not limited to the climate, geology, hydrology and soil chemistry at the site, so long as such modified requirements assure protection of human health and the environment.

[§3004(x) added by PL 98–616]

(y) Munitions.—

(1) Not later than 6 months after the date of the enactment of the Federal Facility Compliance Act of 1992, the Administrator shall propose, after consulting with the Secretary of Defense and appropriate State officials, regulations identifying when military munitions become hazardous waste for purposes of this subtitle and providing for the safe transportation and storage of such waste. Not later than 24 months after such date, and after notice and opportunity for comment, the Administrator shall promulgate such regulations. Any such regulations shall assure protection of human health and the environment.

(2) For purposes of this subsection, the term "military munitions" includes chemical and conventional munitions.

[§3004(y) added by PL 102–386]

§6925. Permits for Treatment, Storage, or Disposal of Hazardous Waste [Sec. 3005]

(a) Permit Requirements.—Not later than eighteen months after the date of the enactment of this section, the Administrator shall promulgate regulations requiring each person owning or operating an existing facility or planning to construct a new facility for the treatment, storage, or disposal of hazardous waste identified or listed under this subtitle to have a permit issued pursuant to this section. Such regulations shall take effect on the date provided in section 3010 and upon and after such date the treatment, storage, or disposal of any such hazardous waste and the construction of any new facility for the treatment, storage, or disposal of any such hazardous waste is prohibited except in accordance with such a permit. No permit shall be required under this section in order to construct a facility if such facility is constructed pursuant to an approval issued by the Administrator under section 6(e) of the Toxic Substances Control Act for the incineration of polycholorinated biphenyls and any person owning or operating such a facility may, at any time after operation or construction of such facility has begun, file an application for a permit pursuant to this section authorizing such facility to incinerate hazardous waste identified or listed under this subtitle.

[§3005(a) amended by PL 98–616]

(b) Requirements of Permit Application.—Each application for a permit under this section shall contain such information as may be required under regulations promulgated by the Administrator, including information respecting—

(1) estimates with respect to the composition, quantities, and concentrations of any hazardous waste identified or listed under this subtitle, or combinations of any such hazardous waste and any other solid waste, proposed to be disposed of, treated, transported, or stored, and the time, frequency, or rate of which such waste is proposed to be disposed of, treated, transported, or stored; and

(2) the site at which such hazardous waste or the products of treatment of such hazardous waste will be disposed of, treated, transported to, or stored.

(c) Permit Issuance.—

(1) Upon a determination by the Administrator (or a State, if applicable), of compliance by a facility for which a permit is applied for under this section with the requirements of this section and section 3004, the Administrator (or the State) shall issue a permit for such facilites. In the event permit applicants propose modification of their facilities, or in the event the Administrator (or the State) determines that modifications are necessary to conform to the requirements under this section and section 3004, the permit shall specify the time allowed to complete the modifications.

[§3005(c)(1) designated by PL 98–616]

(2) (A) (i) Not later than the date four years after the enactment of the Hazardous and

Solid Waste Amendments of 1984, in the case of each application under this subsection for a permit for a land disposal facility which was submitted before such date, the Administrator shall issue a final permit pursuant to such application or issue a final denial of such application.

(ii) Not later than the date five years after the enactment of the Hazardous and Solid Waste Amendments of 1984, in the case of each application for a permit under this subsection for an incinerator facility which was submitted before such date, the Administrator shall issue a final permit pursuant to such application or issue a final denial of such application.

(B) Not later than the date eight years after the enactment of the Hazardous and Solid Waste Amendments of 1984, in the case of each application for a permit under this subsection for any facility (other than a facility referred to in subparagraph (A)) which was submitted before such date, the Administrator shall issue a final permit pursuant to such application or issue a final denial of such application.

(C) The time periods specified in this paragraph shall also apply in the case of any State which is administering an authorized hazardous waste program under section 3006. Interim status under subsection (e) shall terminate for each facility referred to in subparagraph (A)(ii) or (B) on the expiration of the five- or eight-year period referred to in subparagraph (A) or (B), whichever is applicable, unless the owner or operator of the facility applies for a final determination regarding the issuance of a permit under this subsection within—

(i) two years after the date of the enactment of the Hazardous and Solid Waste Amendments of 1984 (in the case of a facility referred to in subparagraph (A)(ii)), or

(ii) four years after such date of enactment (in the case of a facility referred to in subparagraph (B)).

[§3005(c)(2) added by PL 98–616]

(3) Any permit under this section shall be for a fixed term, not to exceed 10 years in the case of any land disposal facility, storage facility, or incinerator or other treatment facility. Each permit for a land disposal facility shall be reviewed five years after date of issuance or reissuance and shall be modified as necessary to assure that the facility continues to comply with the currently applicable requirements of this section and section 3004. Nothing in this subsection shall preclude the Administrator from reviewing and modifying a permit at any time during its term. Review of any application for a permit renewal shall consider improvements in the state of control and measurement technology as well as changes in applicable regulations. Each permit issued under this section shall contain such terms and conditions as the Administrator (or the State) determines necessary to protect human health and the environment.

[§3005(c)(3) added by PL 98–616]

(d) Permit Revocation.—Upon a determination by the Administrator (or by a State, in the case of a State having an authorized hazardous waste program under section 3006) of noncompliance by a facility having a permit under this title with the requirements of this section or section 3004, the Administrator (or State, in the case of a State having an authorized hazardous waste program under section 3006) shall revoke such permit.

[§3005(e) revised by PL 98–616]

(e) Interim Status.—

(1) Any person who—

(A) owns or operates a facility required to have a permit under this section which facility—

(i) was in existence on November 19, 1980, or

(ii) is in existence on the effective date of statutory or regulatory changes under this Act that render the facility subject to the requirement to have a permit under this section,

(B) has complied with the requirements of section 3010(a), and

(C) has made an application for a permit under this section shall be treated as having been issued such permit until such time as final administrative disposition of such application is made, unless the Administrator or other plaintiff proves that final administrative disposition of such application has not been made because of the failure of the applicant to furnish information reasonably required or requested in order to process the application.

This paragraph shall not apply to any facility which has been previously denied a permit under this section or if authority to operate the facility under this section has been previously terminated.

(2) In the case of each land disposal facility which has been granted interim status under this subsection before the date of enactment of the Hazardous and Solid Waste Amendments of 1984, interim status shall terminate on the date twelve months after the date of the enactment of such Amendments unless the owner or operator of such facility—

(A) applies for a final determination regarding the issuance of a permit under subsection (c) for such facility before the date twelve months after the date of the enactment of such Amendments; and

(B) certifies that such facility is in compliance with all applicable groundwater monitoring and financial responsibility requirements.

(3) In the case of each land disposal facility which is in existence on the effective date of statutory or regulatory changes under this Act that render the facility subject to the requirement to have a permit under this section and which is granted interim status under this subsection, interim status shall terminate on the date twelve months after the date on which the facility first becomes subject to such permit requirement unless the owner or operator of such facility—

(A) applies for a final determination regarding the issuance of a permit under subsection (c) for such facility before the date twelve months after the date on which the facility first becomes subject to such permit requirement; and

(B) certifies that such facility is in compliance with all applicable groundwater monitoring and financial responsibility requirements.

(f) Coal Mining Wastes and Reclamation Permits.—Notwithstanding subsection (a) through (e) of this section, any surface coal mining and reclamation permit covering any coal mining wastes or overburden which has been issued or approved under the Surface Mining Control and Reclamation Act of 1977 shall be deemed to be a permit issued pursuant to this section with respect to the treatment, storage, or disposal of such wastes or overburden. Regulations promulgated by the Administrator under this subtitle shall not be applicable to treatment, storage, or disposal of coal mining wastes and overburden which are covered by such a permit.

[§3005(f) added by PL 96–482]

(g) Research, Development, and Demonstration Permits.—

(1) The Administrator may issue a research, development, and demonstration permit for any hazardous waste treatment facility which proposes to utilize an innovative and experimental hazardous waste treatment technology or process for which permit standards for such experimental activity have not been promulgated under this subtitle. Any such permit shall include such terms and conditions as will assure protection of human health and the environment. Such permits—

(A) shall provide for the construction of such facilities, as necessary, and for operation of the facility for not longer than one year (unless renewed as provided in paragraph (4)), and

(B) shall provide for the receipt and treatment by the facility of only those types and quantities of hazardous waste which the Administrator deems necessary for purposes of determining the efficacy and performance capabilities of the technology or process and the effects of such technology or process on human health and the environment, and

(C) shall include such requirements as the Administrator deems necessary to protect human health and the environment (including, but not limited to, requirements regarding monitoring, operation, insurance or bonding, financial responsibility, closure, and remedial action), and such requirements as the Administrator deems necessary regarding testing and providing of information to the Administrator with respect to the operation of the facility.

The Administrator may apply the criteria set forth in this paragraph in establishing the conditions of each permit without separate establishment of regulations implementing such criteria.

(2) For the purpose of expediting review and issuance of permits under this subsection, the Administrator may, consistent with the protection of human health and the environment, modify or waive permit application and permit issuance requirements established in the Administrator's general permit regulations except that there may be no modification or waiver of regulations regarding financial responsibility (including insurance) or of procedures established under section 7004(b)(2) regarding public participation.

(3) The Administrator may order an immediate termination of all operations at the facility at any time he determines that termination is necessary to protect human health and the environment.

(4) Any permit issued under this subsection may be renewed not more than three times. Each such renewal shall be for a period of not more than 1 year.

[§3005(g) added by PL 98–616]

(h) Waste Minimization.—Effective September 1, 1985, it shall be a condition of any permit issued under this section for the treatment, storage, or disposal of hazardous waste on the premises where such waste was generated that the permittee certify, no less often than annually, that—

(1) the generator of the hazardous waste has a program in place to reduce the volume or quantity and toxicity of such waste to the degree determined by the generator to be economically practicable; and

(2) the proposed method of treatment, storage, or disposal is that practicable method currently available to the generator which minimizes the present and future threat to human health and the environment.

[§3005(h) added by PL 98–616]

(i) Interim Status Facilities Receiving Wastes After July 26, 1982.—The standards concerning ground water monitoring, unsaturated zone monitoring, and corrective action, which are applicable under section 3004 to new landfills, surface impoundments, land treatment units, and waste-pile units required to be permitted under subsection (c) shall also apply to any landfill, surface impoundment, land treatment unit, or waste-pile unit qualifying for the authorization to operate under subsection (e) which receives hazardous waste after July 26, 1982.

[§3005(i) added by PL 98–616]

(j) Interim Status Surface Impoundments.—

(1) Except as provided in paragraph (2), (3), or (4), each surface impoundment in existence on the date of enactment of the Hazardous and Solid Waste Amendments of 1984 and qualifying for the authorization to operate under subsection (e) of this section shall not receive, store, or treat hazardous waste after the date four years after such date of enactment unless such surface impoundment is in compliance with the requirements of section 3004(o)(1)(A) which would apply to such impoundment if it were new.

(2) Paragraph (1) of this subsection shall not apply to any surface impoundment which (A) has at least one liner, for which there is no evidence that such liner is leaking; (B) is located more than one- quarter mile from an underground source of drinking water; and (C) is in compliance with generally applicable ground water monitoring requirements for facilities with permits under subsection (c) of this section.

(3) Paragraph (1) of this subsection shall not apply to any surface impoundment which (A) contains treated waste water during the secondary or subsequent phases of an aggressive biological treatment facility subject to a permit issued under section 402 of the Clean Water Act (or which holds such treated waste water after treatment and prior to discharge); (B) is in compliance with generally applicable ground water monitoring requirements for facilities with permits under subsection (c) of this section; and (C)(i) is part of a facility in compliance with section 301(b)(2) of the Clean Water Act, or (ii) in the case of a facility for which no effluent are guidelines required under section 304(b) (2) of the Clean Water Act in effect and no permit under section 402(a)(1) of such Act implementing section 301(b)(2) of such Act has been issued, is part of a facility in compliance with a permit under section 402 of such Act, which is achieving significant degradation of toxic pollutants and hazardous constituents contained in the untreated waste stream and which has identified those toxic pollutants and hazardous constituents in the untreated waste stream to the appropriate permitting authority.

(4) The Administrator (or the State, in the case of a State with an authorized program), after notice and opportunity for comment, may modify the requirements of paragraph (1) for any surface impoundment if the owner or operator demonstrates that such surface impoundment is located, designed and operated so as to assure that there will be no migration of any hazardous constituent into ground water or surface water at any future time. The Administrator or the State shall take into account locational criteria established under section 3004(o)(7).

(5) The owner or operator of any surface impoundment potentially subject to paragraph (1) who has reason to believe that on the basis of paragraph (2), (3), or (4) such surface impoundment is not required to comply with the requirements of paragraph (1), shall apply to the Administrator (or the State, in the case of a State with an authorized program) not later than twenty-four months after the date of enactment of the Hazardous and Solid Waste Amendments of 1984 for a determination of the applicability of paragraph (1) (in the case of paragraph (2) or (3)) or for a modification of

the requirements of paragraph (1) (in the case of paragraph (4)), with respect to such surface impoundment. Such owner or operator shall provide, with such application, evidence pertinent to such decision, including:

(A) an application for a final determination regarding the issuance of a permit under subsection (c) of this section for such facility, if not previously submitted;

(B) evidence as to compliance with all applicable ground water monitoring requirements and the information and analysis from such monitoring;

(C) all reasonably ascertainable evidence as to whether such surface impoundment is leaking; and

(D) in the case of applications under paragraph (2) or (3), a certification by a registered professional engineer with academic training and experience in ground water hydrology that—

(i) under paragraph (2), the liner of such surface impoundment is designed, constructed, and operated in accordance with applicable requirements, such surface impoundment is more than one-quarter mile from an under ground source of drinking water and there is no evidence such liner is leaking; or

(ii) under paragraph (3), based on analysis of those toxic pollutants and hazardous constituents that are likely to be present in the untreated waste stream, such impoundment satisfies the conditions of paragraph (3).

In the case of any surface impoundment for which the owner or operator fails to apply under this paragraph within the time provided by this paragraph or paragraph (6), such surface impoundment shall comply with paragraph (1) notwithstanding paragraph (2), (3), or (4). Within twelve months after receipt of such application and evidence and not later than thirty-six months after such date of enactment, and after notice and opportunity to comment, the Administrator (or, if appropriate, the State) shall advise such owner or operator on the applicability of paragraph (1) to such surface impoundment or as to whether and how the requirements of paragraph (1) shall be modified and applied to such surface impoundment.

(6) (A) In any case in which a surface impoundment becomes subject to paragraph (1) after the date of enactment of the Hazardous and Solid Waste Amendments of 1984 due to the promulgation of additional listings or characteristics for the identification of hazardous waste under section 3001, the period for compliance in paragraph (1) shall be four years after the date of such promulgation, the period for demonstrations under paragraph (4) and for submission of evidence under paragraph (5) shall be not later than twenty-four months after the date of such promulgation, and the period for the Administrator (or if appropriate, the State) to advise such owners or operators under paragraph (5) shall be not later than thirty-six months after the date of promulgation.

(B) In any case in which a surface impoundment is initially determined to be excluded from the requirements of paragraph (1) but due to a change in condition (including the existence of a leak) no longer satisfies the provisions of paragraph (2), (3), or (4) and therefore becomes subject to paragraph (1), the period for compliance in paragraph (1) shall be two years after the date of discovery of such change of condition, or in the case of a surface impoundment excluded under paragraph (3) three year after such date of discovery.

(7) (A) The Administrator shall study and report to the Congress on the number, range of size, construction, likelihood of hazardous constituents migrating into ground water, and potential threat to human health and the environment of existing surface impoundments excluded by paragraph (3) from the requirements of paragraph (1). Such report shall address the need, feasibility, and estimated costs of subjecting such existing surface impoundments to the requirements of paragraph (1).

(B) In the case of any existing surface impoundment or class of surface impoundments from which the Administrator (or the State, in the case of a State with an authorized program) determines hazardous constituents are likely to migrate into ground water, the Administrator (or if appropriate, the State) is authorized to impose such requirements as may be necessary to protect human health and the environment, including the requirements of section 3004(o) which would apply to such impoundments if they were new.

(C) In the case of any surface impoundment excluded by paragraph (3) from the requirements of paragraph (1) which is subsequently determined to be leaking, the Administrator (or, if appropriate, the State) shall require compliance with paragraph (1), unless the administrator (or, if appropriate, the State) determines that such compliance is not necessary to protect human health and the environment.

(8) In the case of any surface impoundment in which the liners and leak detection system have been installed pursuant to the requirements of paragraph (1) and in good faith compliance with section 3004(o) and the Administrator's regulations and guidance documents governing liners and leak detection systems, no liner or leak detection system which is different from that which was so installed pursuant to paragraph (1) shall be required for such unit by the Administrator when issuing the first permit under this section to such facility. Nothing in this paragraph shall preclude the Administrator from requiring installation of a new liner when the Administrator has reason to believe that any liner installed pursuant to the requirements of this subsection is leaking.

(9) In the case of any surface impoundment which has been excluded by paragraph (2) on the basis of a liner meeting the definition under paragraph (12)(A)(ii), at the closure of such impoundment the Administrator shall require the owner or operator of such impoundment to remove or decontaminate all waste residues, all contaminated liner material, and contaminated soil to the extent practicable. If all contaminated soil is not removed or decontaminated, the owner or operator of such impoundment shall be required to comply with appropriate post-closure requirements, including but not limited to ground water monitoring and corrective action.

(10) Any incremental cost attributable to the requirements of this subsection or section 3004(o) shall not be considered by the Administrator (or the State, in the case of a State with an authorized program under section 402 of the Clean Water Act)—

(A) in establishing effluent limitations and standards under section 301, 304, 306, 307, or 402 of the Clean Water Act based on effluent limitations guidelines and standards promulgated any time before twelve months after the date of enactment of the Hazardous and Solid Waste Amendments of 1984; or

(B) in establishing any other effluent limitations to carry out the provisions of section 301, 307, or 402 of the Clean Water Act on or before October 1, 1986.

(11) (A) If the Administrator allows a hazardous waste which is prohibited from one or more methods of land disposal under subsection (d), (e), or (g) of section 3004 (or under regulations promulgated by the Administrator under such subsections) to be placed in a surface impoundment (which is operating pursuant to interim status) for storage or treatment, such impoundment shall meet the requirements that are applicable to new surface impoundments under section 3004(o)(1), unless such impoundment meets the requirements of paragraph (2) or (4).

(B) In the case of any hazardous waste which is prohibited from one or more methods of land disposal under subsection (d), (e), or (g) of section 3004 (or under regulations promulgated by the Administrator under such subsection) the placement or maintenance of such hazardous waste in a surface impoundment for treatment is prohibited as of the effective date of such prohibition unless the treatment residues which are hazardous are, at a minimum, removed for subsequent management within one year of the entry of the waste into the surface impoundment.

(12) (A) For the purposes of paragraph (2)(A) of this subsection, the term "liner" means—

(i) a liner designed, constructed, installed, and operated to prevent hazardous waste from passing into the liner at any time during the active life of the facility; or

(ii) a liner designed, constructed, installed, and operated to prevent hazardous waste from migrating beyond the liner to adjacent subsurface soil, ground water, or surface water at any time during the active life of the facility.

(B) For the purposes of this subsection, the term "aggressive biological treatment facility" means a system of surface impoundments in which the initial impoundment of the secondary treatment segment of the facility utilizes intense mechanical aeration to enhance biological activity to degrade waste water pollutants and

(i) the hydraulic retention time in such initial impoundment is no longer than 5 days under normal operating conditions, on an annual average basis;

(ii) the hydraulic retention time in such initial impoundment is no longer than thirty days under normal operating conditions, on an annual average basis:*Provided*,That the sludge in such impoundment does not constitute a hazardous waste as identified by the extraction procedure toxicity characteristic in effect on the date of enactment of the Hazardous and Solid Waste Amendments of 1984; or

(iii) such system utilizes activated sludge treatment in the first portion of secondary treatment.

(C) For the purposes of this subsection, the term "underground source or drinking water" has the same meaning as provided in regulations under the Safe Drinking Water Act (title XIV of the Public Health Service Act).

(13) The Administrator may modify the requirements of paragraph (1) in the case of a surface impoundment for which the owner or operator, prior to October 1, 1984, has entered into, and is in compliance with, a consent order, decree, or agreement with the Administrator or a State with an authorized program mandating corrective action with respect to such surface impoundment that provides a degree of protection of human health and the environment which is at a minimum equivalent to that provided by paragraph (1).

[§3005(j) added by PL 98–616]

§6926. Authorized State Hazardous Waste Programs [Sec. 3006]

(a) Federal Guidelines.—Not later than eighteen months after the date of enactment of this Act, the Administrator, after consultation with State authorities, shall promulgate guidelines to assist States in the development of State hazardous waste programs.

(b) Authorization of State Program.—Any State which seeks to administer and enforce a hazardous waste program pursuant to this subtitle may develop and, after notice and opportunity for public hearing, submit to the Administrator an application, in such form as he shall require, for authorization of such program. Within ninety days following submission of an application under this subsection, the Administrator shall issue a notice as to whether or not he expects such program to be authorized, and within ninety days following such notice (and after opportunity for public hearing) he shall publish his findings as to whether or not the conditions listed in items (1), (2), and (3) below have been met. Such State is authorized to carry out such program in lieu of the Federal program under this subtitle in such State and to issue and enforce permits for the storage, treatment, or disposal of hazardous waste (and to enforce permits deemed to have been issued under section 3012(d)(1) unless, within ninety days following submission of the application the Administrator notifies such State that such program may not be authorized and, within ninety days following such notice and after opportunity for public hearing, he finds that (1) such State program is not equivalent to the Federal program under this subtitle, (2) such program is not consistent with the Federal or State programs applicable in other States, or (3) such program does not provide adequate enforcement of compliance with the requirements of this subtitle. In authorizing a State program, the Administrator may base his findings on the Federal program in effect one year prior to submission of a State's application or in effect on January 26, 1983, whichever is later.

[§3006(b) amended by PL 98–616]

(c) Interim Authorization. —

(1) Any State which has in existence a hazardous waste program pursuant to State law before the date ninety days after the date of promulgation of regulations under sections 3002, 3003, 3004, and 3005, may submit to the Administrator evidence of such existing program and may request a temporary authorization to carry out such program under this subtitle. The Administrator shall, if the evidence submitted shows the existing State program to be substantially equivalent to the Federal program under this subtitle, grant an interim authorization to the State to carry out such program in lieu of the Federal program pursuant to this subtitle for a period ending no later than January 31, 1986.

[§3006(c)(1) designated and amended by PL 98–616]

(2) The Administrator shall, by rule, establish a date for the expiration of interim authorization under this subsection.

[§3006(c)(2) added by PL 98–616]

(3) Pending interim or final authorization of a State program for any State which reflects the amendments made by the Hazardous and Solid Waste Amendments of 1984, the State may enter into an agreement with the Administrator under which the State may assist in the administration of the requirements and prohibitions which take effect pursuant to such Amendments.

[§3006(c)(3) added by PL 98–616]

(4) In the case of a State permit program for any State which is authorized under subsection (b) or under this subsection, until such program is amended to reflect the amendments made by the Hazardous and Solid Waste Amendments of 1984 and such program amendments receive interim or final authorization, the Administrator shall have the authority in such State to issue or deny permits or those portions of permits affected by the requirements and prohibitions established by the Hazardous and Solid Waste Amendments of 1984. The Administrator shall coordinate with States the procedures for issuing such permits.

[§3006(c)(4) added by PL 98–616]

(d) Effect of State Permit. — Any action taken by a State under a hazardous waste program authorized under this section shall have the same force and effect as action taken by the Administrator under this subtitle.

(e) Withdrawal of Authorization. — Whenever the Administrator determines after public hearing that a State is not administering and enforcing a program authorized under this section in accordance with requirements of this section, he shall so notify the State and, if appropriate corrective action is not taken within a reasonable time, not to exceed ninety days, the Administrator shall withdraw authorization of such program and establish a Federal program pursuant to this subtitle. The Administrator shall not withdraw authorization of any such program unless he shall first have notified the State, and made public, in writing, the reasons for such withdrawal.

(f) Availability of Information. — No State program may be authorized by the Administrator under this section
unless —

(1) such program provides for the public availability of information obtained by the State regarding facilities and sites for the treatment, storage, and disposal of hazardous waste; and

(2) such information is available to the public in substantially the same manner, and to the same degree, as would be the case if the Administrator was carrying out the provisions of this subtitle in such State.

[§3006(f) added by PL 98–616]

(g) Amendments Made by 1984 Act.

(1) Any requirement or prohibition which is applicable to the generation, transportation, treatment, storage, or disposal of hazardous waste and which is imposed under this subtitle pursuant to the amendments made by the Hazardous and Solid Waste Amendments of 1984 shall take effect in each State having an interim or finally authorized State program on the same date as such requirement takes effect in other States. The Administrator shall carry out such requirement directly in each such State unless the State program is finally authorized (or is granted interim authorization as provided in paragraph (2)) with respect to such requirement.

(2) Any State which, before the date of the enactment of the Hazardous and Solid Waste Amendments of 1984 has an existing hazardous waste program which has been granted interim or final authorization under this section may submit to the Administrator evidence that such existing program contains (or has been amended to include) any requirement which is substantially equivalent to a requirement referred to in paragraph (1) and may request interim authorization to carry out that requirement under this subtitle. The Administrator shall, if the evidence submitted shows the State requirement to be substantially equivalent to the requirement referred to in paragraph (1), grant an interim authorization to the State to carry out such requirement in lieu of direct administration in the State by the Administrator of such requirement.

[§3006(g) added by PL 98–616]

(h) State Programs for Used Oil. —In the case of used oil which is not listed or identified under this subtitle as a hazardous waste but which is regulated under section 3014, the provisions of this section regarding State programs shall apply in the same manner and to the same extent as such provisions apply to hazardous waste identified or listed under this subtitle.

[§3006(h) added by PL 99–499]

§6927. Inspections [Sec. 3007]

(a) Access Entry. —For purposes of developing or assisting in the development of any regulation or enforcing the provisions of this title, any person who generates, stores, treats, transports, disposes of, or otherwise handles or has handled hazardous wastes shall, upon request of any officer, employee or representative of the Environmental Protection Agency, duly designated by the Administrator, or upon request of any duly designated officer, employee or representative of a State having an authorized hazardous waste program, furnish information relating to such wastes and permit such person at all reasonable times to have access to, and to copy all records relating to such wastes. For the purposes of developing or assisting in the development of any regulation or enforcing the provisions of this title, such officers, employees or representatives are authorized—

(1) to enter at reasonable times any establishment or other place where hazardous wastes are or have been generated, stored, treated, disposed of, or transported from;

(2) to inspect and obtain samples from any person of any such wastes and samples of any containers or labeling for such wastes.

Each such inspection shall be commenced and completed with reasonable promptness. If the officer, employee or representative obtains any samples, prior to leaving the premises, he shall give to the owner, operator, or agent in charge a receipt describing the sample obtained and if requested a portion of each such sample equal in volume or weight to the portion retained. If any analysis is made of such samples, a copy of the results of such analysis shall be furnished promptly to the owner, operator, or agent in charge.

[§3007(a) amended by PL 96–482]

(b) Availability to Public. —

(1) Any records, reports, or information (including records, reports, or information obtained by representatives of the Environmental Protection Agency) obtained from any person under this section shall be available to the public, except that upon a showing satisfactory to the Administrator (or the State, as the case may be) by any person that records, reports, or information, (including records, reports, or information obtained by representatives of the Environmental Protection Agency) or particular part thereof, to which the Administrator (or the State, as the case may be) or any officer, employee or representative thereof has access under this section if made public, would divulge information (including records, reports, or information obtained by representatives of the Environmental Protection Agency) entitled to protection under section 1905 of title 18 of the United States Code, such information or particular portion thereof shall be considered confidential in accordance with the purposes of that section, except that such record, report, document, or information may be disclosed to other officers, employees, or authorized representatives of the United States concerned with carrying out this Act, or when relevant in any proceeding under this Act.

(2) Any person not subject to the provisions of section 1905 of title 18 of the United States Code who knowingly and willfully divulges or discloses any information (including records, reports, or information obtained by representatives of the Environmental Protection Agency) entitled to protection under this subsection shall, upon conviction, be subject to a fine of not more than $5,000 or to imprisonment not to exceed one year, or both.

(3) In submitting data under this Act, a person required to provide such data may—

(A) designate the data which such person believes is entitled to protection under this subsection, and

(B) submit such designated data separately from other data submitted under this Act.

A designation under this paragraph shall be made in writing and in such manner as the Administrator may prescribe.

(4) Notwithstanding any limitation contained in this section or any other provision of law, all information (including records, reports, or information obtained by representatives of the Environmental Protection Agency) reported to, or otherwise obtained by, the Administrator (or any representative of the Administrator) under this Act shall be made available, upon written request of any duly authorized committee of the Congress, to such committee (including records, reports, or information obtained by representatives of the Environmental Protection Agency).

(c) Federal Facility Inspections.—The Administrator shall undertake on an annual basis a thorough inspection of each facility for the treatment, storage, or disposal of hazardous waste which is owned or operated by a department, agency, or instrumentality of the United States to enforce its compliance with this subtitle and the regulations promulgated thereunder. The records of such inspections shall be available to the public as provided in subsection (b). Any State with an authorized hazardous waste program also may conduct an inspection of any such facility for purposes of enforcing the facility's compliance with the State hazardous waste program.

The department, agency, or instrumentality owning or operating each such facility shall reimburse the Environmental Protection Agency for the costs of the inspection of the facility. With respect to the first inspection of each such facility occurring after the date of the enactment of the Federal Facility Compliance Act of 1992, the

Administrator shall conduct a comprehensive ground water monitoring evaluation at the facility, unless such an evaluation was conducted during the 12-month period preceding such date of enactment.

[§3007(c) added by PL 98–616; amended by PL 102–386]

(d) State-Operated Facilities.—The Administrator shall annually undertake a thorough inspection of every facility for the treatment, storage, or disposal of hazardous waste which is operated by a State or local government for which a permit is required under section 3005 of this title. The records of such inspection shall be available to the public as provided in subsection (b).

[§3007(d) added by PL 98–616]

(e) Mandatory Inspections.—

(1) The Administrator (or the State in the case of a State having an authorized hazardous waste program under this subtitle) shall commence a program to thoroughly inspect every facility for the treatment, storage, or disposal of hazardous waste for which a permit is required under section 3005 no less often than every two years as to its compliance with this subtitle (and the regulations promulgated under this subtitle). Such inspections shall commence not later than twelve months after the date of enactment of the Hazardous and Solid Waste Amendments of 1984. The Administrator shall, after notice and opportunity for public comment, promulgate regulations governing the minimum frequency and manner of such inspections, including the manner in which records of such inspections shall be maintained and the manner in which reports of such inspections shall be filed. The Administrator may distinguish between classes and categories of facilities commensurate with the risks posed by each class or category.

(2) Not later than six months after the date of enactment of the Hazardous and Solid Waste Amendments of 1984, the Administrator shall submit to the Congress a report on the potential for inspections of hazardous waste treatment, storage, or disposal facilities by nongovernmental inspectors as a supplement to inspections conducted by officers, employees, or representatives of the Environmental Protection Agency or States having authorized hazardous waste programs or operating under a cooperative agreement with the Administrator. Such report shall be prepared in cooperation with the States, insurance companies offering environmental impairment insurance, independent companies providing inspection services, and other such groups as appropriate. Such report shall contain recommendations on provisions and requirements for a program of private inspections to supplement governmental inspections.

[§3007(e) added by PL 98–616]

§6928. Federal Enforcement [Sec. 3008]

(a) Compliance Orders. —

(1) Except as provided in paragraph (2), whenever on the basis of any information the Administrator determines that any person has violated or is in violation of any requirement of this subtitle, the Administrator may issue an order assessing a civil penalty for any past or current violation, requiring compliance immediately or within a specified time period, or both, or the Administrator may commence a civil action in the United States district court in the district in which the violation occurred for appropriate relief, including a temporary or permanent injunction.

[§3008(a)(1) amended by PL 96–482; PL 98–616]

(2) In the case of a violation of any requirement of this subtitle where such violation occurs in a State which is authorized to carry out a hazardous waste program under section 3006, the Administrator shall give notice to the State in which such violation has occurred prior to issuing an order or commencing a civil action under this section.

[§3008(a)(2) amended by PL 96–482]

(3) Any order issued pursuant to this subsection may include a suspension or revocation of any permit issued by the Administrator or a State under this subtitle and shall state with reasonable specificity the nature of the violation. Any penalty assessed in the order shall not exceed $25,000 per day of noncompliance for each violation of a requirement of this subtitle. In assessing such a penalty, the Administrator shall take into account the seriousness of the violation and any good faith efforts to comply with applicable requirements.

[§3008(a)(3) revised by PL 98–616]

(b) Public Hearing. — Any order issued under this section shall become final unless, no later than thirty days after the order is served, the person or persons named therein request a public hearing. Upon such request the Administrator shall promptly conduct a public hearing. In connection with any proceeding under this section the Administrator may issue subpoenas for the attendance and testimony of witnesses and the production of relevant papers, books, and documents, and may promulgate rules for discovery procedures.

[§3008(b) amended by PL 96–482; PL 98–616]

(c) Violation Of Compliance Orders. —If a violator fails to take corrective action within the time specified in a compliance order, the Administrator may assess a civil penalty of not more than $25,000 for each day of continued noncompliance with the order and Administrator may suspend or revoke any permit issued to the violator (whether issued by the Administrator or the State).

[§3008(c) amended by PL 96–482; revised by PL 98–616]

(d) Criminal Penalties. — Any person who—

(1) knowingly transports or causes to be transported any hazardous waste identified or listed under this subtitle to a facility which does not have a permit under this subtitle, or pursuant to title I of the Marine Protection, Research, and Sanctuaries Act (86 Stat. 1052).

(2) knowingly treats, stores, or disposes of any hazardous waste identified or listed under this subtitle—

(A) without a permit under this subtitle or pursuant to title I of the Marine Protection, Research, and Sanctuaries Act (86 Stat. 1052); or

(B) in knowing violation of any material condition or requirement of such permit; or

(C) in knowing violation of any material condition or requirement of any applicable interim status regulations or standards;

(3) knowingly omits material information or makes any false material statement or representation in any application, label, manifest, record, report, permit, or other document filed, maintained, or used for purposes of compliance with regulations promulgated by the Administrator (or by a State in the case of an authorized State program) under this subtitle;

(4) knowingly generates, stores, treats, transports, disposes of, exports, or otherwise handles any hazardous waste or any used oil not identified or listed as a hazardous waste under this subtitle (whether such activity took place before or takes place after the date of the enactment of this paragraph) and who knowingly destroys, alters, conceals, or fails to file any record, application, manifest, report, or other document required to be maintained or filed for purposes of compliance with regulations promulgated by the Administrator (or by a State in the case of an authorized State program) under this subtitle;

[§3008(d)(4) amended by PL 99–499]

(5) knowingly transports without a manifest, or causes to be transported without a manifest, any hazardous waste or any used oil not identified or listed as a hazardous waste under this subtitle required by regulations promulgated under this subtitle (or by a State in the case of a State program authorized under this subtitle) to be accompanied by a manifest;

[§3008(d)(5) amended by PL 99–499]

(6) knowingly exports a hazardous waste identified or listed under this subtitle (A) without the consent of the receiving country or, (B) where there exists an international agreement between the United States and the government of the receiving country establishing notice, export, and enforcement procedures for the transportation, treatment, storage, and disposal of hazardous wastes, in a manner which is not in conformance with such agreement; or

[§3008(d)(6) amended by PL 99–499]

(7) knowingly stores, treats, transports, or causes to be transported, disposes of, or otherwise handles any used oil not identified or listed as a hazardous waste under subtitle C of the Solid Waste Disposal Act—

(A) in knowing violation of any material condition or requirement of a permit under this subtitle C; or

(B) in knowing violation of any material condition or requirement of any applicable regulations or standards under this Act; shall, upon conviction, be subject to a fine of not more than $50,000 for each day of violation, or imprisonment not to exceed two years (five years in the case of a violation of paragraph (1) or (2)), or both. If the conviction is for a violation committed after a first conviction of such person under this paragraph, the maximum punishment under the respective paragraph shall be doubled with respect to both fine and imprisonment.

[§3008(d) revised by PL 96–482; PL 98–616; §3008(d)(7) added by PL 99–499]

(e) Knowing Endangerment. — Any person who knowingly transports, treats, stores, disposes of, or exports any hazardous waste identified or listed under this subtitle or used oil not identified or listed as a hazardous waste under this subtitle in violation of paragraph (1), (2), (3), (4), (5), (6), or (7) of subsection (d) of this section who knows at that time that he thereby places another person in imminent danger of death or serious bodily injury, shall, upon conviction, be subject to a fine of not more than $250,000 or imprisonment for not more than fifteen years, or both. A defendant that is an organization shall, upon conviction of violating this subsection, be subject to a fine of not more than $1,000,000.

[§3008(e) added by PL 96–482; amended by PL 98–616; PL 99–499]

(f) Special Rules. — For the purposes of subsection (e)—

(1) A person's state of mind is knowing with respect to—

(A) is conduct, if he is aware of the nature of his conduct;

(B) an existing circumstance, if he is aware or believes that the circumstance exists; or

(C) a result of his conduct, if he is aware or believes that his conduct is substantially certain to cause danger of death or serious bodily injury.

(2) In determining whether a defendant who is a natural person knew that his conduct placed another person in imminent danger of death or serious bodily injury—

(A) the person is responsible only for actual awareness or actual belief that he possessed; and

(B) knowledge possessed by a person other than the defendant but not by the defendant himself may not be attributed to the defendant;*Provided,*That in proving the defendant's possession of actual knowledge, circumstantial evidence may be used, including evidence that the defendant took affirmative steps to shield himself from relevant information.

(3) It is an affirmative defense to a prosecution that the conduct charged was consented to by the person endangered and that the danger and conduct charged were reasonably foreseeable hazards of—

(A) an occupation, a business, or a profession; or

(B) medical treatment or medical or scientific experimentation conducted by professionally approved methods and such other person had been made aware of the risks involved prior to giving consent. The defendant may establish an affirmative defense under this subsection by a preponderance of the evidence.

(4) All general defenses, affirmative defenses, and bars to prosecution that may apply with respect to other Federal criminal offenses may apply under subsection (e) and shall be determined by the courts of the United States according to the principles of common law as they may be interpreted in the light of reason and experience. Concepts of justification and excuse applicable under this section may be developed in the light of reason and experience.

(5) The term "organization" means a legal entity, other than a government, established or organized for any purpose, and such term includes a corporation, company, association, firm, partnership, joint stock company, foundation, institution, trust, society, union, or any other association of persons.

(6) The term "serious bodily injury" means—

(A) bodily injury which involves a substantial risk of death;

(B) unconsciousness;

(C) extreme physical pain;

(D) protracted and obvious disfigurement; or

(E) protracted loss or impairment of the function of a bodily member, organ, or mental faculty.

(g) Civil Penalty. — Any person who violates any requirement of this subtitle shall be liable to the United States for a civil penalty in an amount not to exceed $25,000 for each such violation. Each day of such violation shall, for purposes of this subsection, constitute a separate violation.

[§3008(g) added by PL 96–482]

(h) Interim Status Corrective Action Orders. —

(1) Whenever on the basis of any information the Administrator determines that there is or has been a release of hazardous waste into the environment from a facility authorized to operate under section 3005(e) of this subtitle, the Administrator may issue an order requiring corrective action or such other response measure as he deems necessary to protect human health or the environment or the Administrator may commence a civil action in the United States district court in the district in which the facility is located for appropriate relief, including a temporary or permanent injunction.

(2) Any order issued under this subsection may include a suspension or revocation of authorization to operate under section 3005(e) of this subtitle, shall state with reasonable

specificity the nature of the required corrective action or other response measure, and shall specify a time for compliance. If any person named in an order fails to comply with the order, the Administrator may assess, and such person shall be liable to the United States for, a civil penalty in an amount not to exceed $25,000 for each day of noncompliance with the order.

[§3008(h) added by PL 98–616]

§6929. Retention of State Authority [Sec. 3009]

Upon the effective date of regulations under this subtitle no State or political subdivision may impose any requirements less stringent than those authorized under this subtitle respecting the same matter as governed by such regulations, except that if application of a regulation with respect to any matter under this subtitle is postponed or enjoined by the action of any court, no State or political subdivision shall be prohibited from acting with respect to the same aspect of such matter until such time as such regulation takes effect. Nothing in this title shall be construed to prohibit any State or political subdivision thereof from imposing any requirements, including those for site selection, which are more stringent than those imposed by such regulations. Nothing in this title (or in any regulation adopted under this title) shall be construed to prohibit any State from requiring that the State be provided with a copy of each manifest used in connection with hazardous waste which is generated within that State or transported to a treatment, storage, or disposal facility within that State.

[§3009 amended by PL 96–482; PL 98–616]

§6930. Effective Date [Sec. 3010]

(a) Preliminary Notification. — Not later than ninety days after promulgation of regulations under section 3001 identifying by its characteristics or listing any substance as hazardous waste subject to this subtitle, any person generating or transporting such substance or owning or operating a facility for treatment, storage, or disposal of such substance shall file with the Administrator (or with States having authorized hazardous waste permit programs under section 3006) a notification stating the location and general description of such activity and the identified or listed hazardous wastes handled by such person.

Not later than fifteen months after the date of enactment of the Hazardous and Solid Waste Amendments of 1984—

(1) The owner or operator of any facility which produces a fuel (A) from any hazardous waste identified or listed under section 3001, (B) from such hazardous waste identified or listed under section 3001 and any other material, (C) from used oil, or (D) from used oil and any other material;

(2) the owner or operator of any facility (other than a single- or two-family residence) which burns for purposes of energy recovery any fuel produced as provided in paragraph (1) or any fuel which otherwise contains used oil or any hazardous waste identified or listed under section 3001; and

(3) any person who distributes or markets any fuel which is produced as provided in paragraph (1) or any fuel which otherwise contains used oil or any hazardous waste identified or listed under section 3001

shall file with the Administrator (and with the State in the case of a State with an authorized hazardous waste program) a notification stating the location and general description of the facility, together with a description of the identified or listed hazardous waste involved and, in the case of a facility referred to in paragraph (1) or (2), a description of the production or energy recovery activity carried out at the facility and such other information as the Administrator deems necessary. For purposes of the preceding provisions, the term "hazardous waste" listed under section 3001 also includes any commercial chemical product which is listed under section 3001 and which, in lieu of its original intended use, is (i) produced for use as (or as a component of) a fuel, (ii) distributed for use as a fuel, or (iii) burned as a fuel. Notification shall not be required under the second sentence of this subsection in the case of facilities (such as residential builders) where the Administrator determines that such notification is not necessary in order for the Administrator to obtain sufficient information respecting current practices of facilities using hazardous waste for energy recovery. Nothing in this subsection shall be construed to affect or impair the provisions of section 3001(b)(3). Nothing in this subsection shall affect regulatory determinations under section 3014. In revising any regulation under section 3001 identifying additional characteristics of hazardous waste or listing any additional substance as hazardous waste subject to this subtitle, the Administrator may require any person referred to in the preceding provisions to file with the Administrator (or with States having authorized hazardous waste permit programs under section 3006) the notification described in the preceding provisions. Not more than one such notification shall be required to be filed with respect to the same substance. No identified or listed hazardous waste subject to this subtitle may be transported, treated, stored, or disposed of unless notification has been given as required under this subsection.

[§3010(a) amended by PL 96–482; revised by PL 98–616]

(b) Effective Date of Regulation. — The regulations under this subtitle respecting requirements applicable to the generation, transportation, treatment, storage, or disposal of hazardous waste (including requirements respecting permits for such treatment, storage, or disposal) shall take effect on the date six months after the date of promulgation thereof (or six months after the date of revision in the case of any regulation which is revised after the date required for promulgation thereof. At the time a regulation is promulgated, the Administrator may provide for a shorter period prior to the effective date, or an immediate effective date for:

(1) a regulation with which the Administrator finds the regulated community does not need six months to come into compliance;

(2) a regulation which responds to an emergency situation; or

(3) other good cause found and published with the regulation.

[§3010(b) amended by PL 98–616]

§6931. Authorization of Assistance to States [Sec. 3011]

(a) Authorization. — There is authorized to be appropriated $25,000,000 for each of the fiscal years 1978 and 1979, $20,000,000 for fiscal year 1980, $35,000,000 for fiscal year 1981, $40,000,000 for the fiscal year 1982, $55,000,000 for the fiscal year 1985, $60,000,000 for the fiscal year 1986, $60,000,000 for the fiscal year 1987, and $60,000,000 for the fiscal year 1988 to be used to make grants to the States for purposes of assisting the States in the development and implementation of authorized State hazardous waste programs.

[§3011(a) amended by PL 96–482; PL 98–616]

(b) Allocation. — Amounts authorized to be appropriated under subsection (a) shall be allocated among the States on the basis of regulations promulgated by the Administrator, after consultation with the States, which take into account, the extent to which hazardous waste is generated, transported, treated, stored, and disposed of within such State, the extent of exposure of human beings and the environment within such State to such waste, and such other factors as the Administrator deems appropriate.

(c) Activities Included. — State hazardous waste programs for which grants may be made under subsection (a) may include (but shall not be limited to) planning for hazardous waste treatment, storage and disposal facilities, and the development and execution of programs to protect health and the environment from inactive facilities which may contain hazardous waste.

[§3011(c) added by PL 96–482]

§6933. Hazardous Waste Site Inventory [Sec. 3012]

(a) State Inventory Programs.—Each State shall, as expeditiously as practicable, undertake a continuing program to compile, publish, and submit to the Administrator an inventory describing the location of each site within such State at which hazardous waste has at any time been stored or disposed of. Such inventory shall contain—

(1) a description of the location of the sites at which any such storage or disposal has taken place before the date on which permits are required under section 3005 for such storage or disposal;

(2) such information relating to the amount, nature, and toxicity of the hazardous waste at each such site as may be practicable to obtain and as may be necessary to determine the extent of any health hazard which may be associated with such site;

(3) the name and address, or corporate headquarters of, the owner of each such site, determined as of the date of preparation of the inventory;

(4) an identification of the types or techniques of waste treatment or disposal which have been used at each such site; and

(5) information concerning the current status of the site, including information respecting whether or not hazardous waste is currently being treated or disposed of at such site (and if not, the date on which such activity ceased) and information respecting the nature of any other activity currently carried out at such site.

For purposes of assisting the States in compiling information under this section, the Administrator shall make available to each State undertaking a program under this section such information as is available to him concerning the items specified in paragraphs (1) through (5) with respect to the sites within such State, including such information as the Administrator is able to obtain from other agencies or departments of the United States and from surveys and studies carried out by any committee or subcommittee of the Congress. Any State may exercise the authority of section 3007 for purposes of this section in the same manner and to the same extent as provided in such section in the case of States having an authorized hazardous waste program, and any State may by order require any person to submit such information as may be necessary to compile the data referred to in paragraphs (1) through (5).

(b) Environmental Protection Agency Program.—If the Administrator determines that any State program under subsection (a) is not adequately providing information respecting the sites in such State referred to in subsection (a), the Administrator shall notify the State. If within ninety days following such notification, the State program has not been revised or amended in such manner as will adequately provide such information, the Administrator shall carry out the inventory program in such State. In any such case—

(1) the Administrator shall have the authorities provided with respect to State programs under subsection (a);

(2) the funds allocated under subsection (c) for grants to States under this section may be used by the Administrator for carrying out such program in such State; and

(3) no further expenditure may be made for grants to such State under this section until such time as the Administrator determines that such State is carrying out, or will carry out, an inventory program which meets the requirements of this section.

(c) Grants.—

(1) Upon receipt of an application submitted by any State to carry out a program under this section, the Administrator may make grants to the States for purposes of carrying out such a program. Grants under this section shall be allocated among the several States by the Administrator based upon such regulations as he prescribes to carry out the purposes of this section. The Administrator may make grants to any State which has conducted an inventory program which effectively carried out the purposes of this section before the date of the enactment of the Solid Waste Disposal Act Amendments of 1980 to reimburse such State for all, or any portion of, the costs incurred by such State in conducting such program.

(2) There are authorized to be appropriated to carry out this section $25,000,000 for each of the fiscal years 1985 through 1988.

[§3012(c)(2) amended by PL 98–616]

(d) No Impediment to Immediate Remedial Action.—Nothing in this section shall be construed to provide that the Administrator or any State should, pending completion of the inventory required under this section, postpone undertaking any enforcement or remedial action with respect to any site at which hazardous waste has been treated, stored, or disposed of.

[§3012 added by PL 96–482]

§6934. Monitoring, Analysis, and Testing [Sec. 3013]

(a) Authority of Administrators.—If the Administrator determines, upon receipt of any information, that—

(1) the presence of any hazardous waste at a facility or site at which hazardous waste is, or has been, stored, treated, or disposed of, or

(2) the release of any such waste from such facility or site may present a substantial hazard to human health or the environment, he may issue an order requiring the owner or operator of such facility or site to conduct such monitoring, testing, analysis, and reporting with respect to such facility or site, as the Administrator deems reasonable to ascertain the nature and extent of such hazard.

(b) Previous Owners and Operators.—In the case of any facility or site not in operation at the time a determination is made under subsection (a) with respect to the facility or site if the Administrator finds that the owner of such facility could not reasonably be expected to have actual knowledge of the presence of hazardous waste at such facility or site and of its potential for release, he may issue an order requiring the most recent previous owner or operator of such facility or site who could reasonably be expected to have such actual knowledge to carry out the actions referred to in subsection (a).

(c) Proposal.—An order under subsection (a) or (b) shall require the person to whom such order is issued to submit to the Administrator within 30 days from the issuance of such order a proposal for carrying out the required monitoring, testing, analysis, and reporting. The Administrator may, after providing such person with an opportunity to confer with the Administrator respecting such proposal, require such person to carry out such monitoring, testing, analysis, and reporting in accordance with such proposal, and such modifications in such proposal as the Administrator deems reasonable to ascertain the nature and extent of the hazard.

(d) Monitoring, Etc., Carried Out by Administrator.—

(1) If the Administrator determines that no owner or operator referred to in subsection (a) or (b) is able to conduct monitoring, testing, analysis, or reporting satisfactory to the Administrator, if the Administrator deems any such action carried out by an owner or operator to be unsatisfactory, or if the Administrator cannot initially determine that there is an owner or operator referred to in subsection (a) or (b) who is able to conduct such monitoring, testing, analysis, or reporting, he may—

(A) conduct monitoring, testing, or analysis (or any combination thereof) which he deems reasonable to ascertain the nature and extent of the hazard associated with the site concerned, or

(B) authorize a State or local authority or other person to carry out any such action,

and require, by order, the owner or operator referred to in subsection (a) or (b) to reimburse the Administrator or other authority or person for the costs of such activity.

(2) No order may be issued under this subsection requiring reimbursement of the costs of any action carried out by the Administrator which confirms the results of an order issued under subsection (a) or (b).

(3) For purposes of carrying out this subsection, the Administrator or any authority or other person authorized under paragraph (1), may exercise the authorities set forth in section 3007.

(e) Enforcement.—The Administrator may commence a civil action against any person who fails or refuses to comply with any order issued under this section. Such action shall be brought in the United States district court in which the defendant is located, resides, or is doing business. Such court shall have jurisdiction to require compliance with such order and to assess a civil penalty of not to exceed $5,000 for each day during which such failure or refusal occurs.

[§3013 added by PL 96–482]

§6935. Restrictions on Recycled Oil [Sec. 3014]

(a) In General—Not later than one year after the date of the enactment of this section, the Administrator shall promulgate regulations establishing such performance standards and other requirements as may be necessary to protect the public health and the environment from hazards associated with recycled oil. In developing such regulations, the Administrator shall conduct an analysis of the economic impact of the regulations on the oil recycling industry. The Administrator shall ensure that such regulations do not discourage the recovery or recycling of used oil, consistent with the protection of human health and the environment.

[Former §3012 added by PL 96–463; amended and redesignated as §3014(a) by PL 98–616]

(b) Identification or Listing Of Used Oil As Hazardous Waste.— Not later than twelve months after the date of enactment of the Hazardous and Solid Waste Amendments of 1984 the Administrator shall propose whether to list or identify used automobile and truck crankcase oil as hazardous waste under section 3001. Not later than twenty-four months after such date of enactment, the Administrator shall make a final determination whether to list or identify used automobile and truck crankcase oil and other used oil as hazardous wastes under section 3001.

[§3014(b) added by PL 98–616]

(c) Used Oil Which Is Recycled.—

(1) With respect to generators and transporters of used oil identified or listed as a hazardous waste under section 3001, the standards promulgated under section 3001(d), 3002, and 3003 of this subtitle shall not apply to such used oil if such used oil is recycled.

(2) (A) In the case of used oil which is exempt under paragraph (1), not later than twenty-four months after the date of enactment of the Hazardous and Solid Waste Amendments of 1984, the Administrator shall promulgate such standards under this subsection regarding the generation and transportation of used oil which is recycled as may be necessary to protect human health and the environment. In promulgating such regulations with respect to generators, the Administrator shall take into account the effect of such regulations on environmentally acceptable types of used oil recycling and the effect of such regulations on small quantity generators and generators which are small businesses (as defined by the Administrator).

(B) The regulations promulgated under this subsection shall provide that no generator of used oil which is exempt under paragraph (1) from the standards promulgated under section 3001(d), 3002, and 3003 shall be subject to any manifest requirement or any associated recordkeeping and reporting requirement with respect to such used oil if such generator—

(i) either—

(I) enters into an agreement or other arrangement (including an agreement or arrangement with an independent transporter or with an agent of the recycler) for delivery of such used oil to a recycling facility which has a permit under section 3005(c) (or for which a valid permit is deemed to be in effect under subsection (d)), or

(II) recycles such used oil at one or more facilities of the generator which has such a permit under section 3005 of this subtitle (or for which a valid permit is deemed to have been issued under subsection (d) of this section);

(ii) such used oil is not mixed by the generator with other types of hazardous wastes; and

(iii) the generator maintains such records relating to such used oil, including records of agreements or other arrangements for delivery of such used oil to any recycling facility referred to in clause (i)(I), as the Administrator deems necessary to protect human health and the environment.

(3) The regulations under this subsection regarding the transportation of used oil which is exempt from the standards promulgated under section 3001(d), 3002, and 3003 under paragraph (1) shall require the transporters of such used oil to deliver such used oil to a facility which has a valid permit under section 3005 of this subtitle or which is deemed to have a valid permit under subsection (d) of this section. The Administrator shall also establish other standards for such transporters as may be necessary to protect human health and the environment.

[§3014(c) added by PL 98–616]

(d) Permits.—

(1) The owner or operator of a facility which recycles used oil which is exempt under subsection (c)(1), shall be deemed to have a permit under this subsection for all such treatment or recycling (and any associated tank or container storage) if such owner and operator comply with standards promulgated by the Administrator under section 3004; except that the Administrator may require such owners and operators to obtain an individual permit under section 3005(c) if he determines that an individual permit is necessary to protect human health and the environment.

(2) Notwithstanding any other provision of law, any generator who recycles used oil which is exempt under subsection (c)(1) shall not be required to obtain a permit under section 3005(c) with respect to such used oil until the Administrator has promulgated standards under section 3004 regarding the recycling of such used oil.

§6936. Expansion During Interim Status [Sec. 3015]

(a) Waste Piles.—The owner or operator of a waste pile qualifying for the authorization to operate under section 3005(e) shall be subject to the same requirements for liners and leachate collection systems or equivalent protection provided in regulations promulgated by the Administrator under section 3004 before October 1, 1982, or revised under section 3004(o) (relating to minimum technological requirements), for new facilities receiving individual permits under subsection (c) of section 3005, with respect to each new unit, replacement of an existing unit, or lateral expansion of an existing unit that is within the waste management area identified in the permit application submitted under section 3005, and with respect to waste received beginning six months after the date of enactment of the Hazardous and Solid Waste Amendments of 1984.

(b) Landfills and Surface Impoundments.—

(1) The owner or operator of a landfill or surface impoundment qualifying for the authorization to operate under section 3005(e) shall be subject to the requirements of section 3004(o) (relating to minimum technological requirements), with respect to each new unit, replacement of an existing unit, or lateral expansion of an existing unit that is within the waste management area identified in the permit application submitted under this section, and with respect to waste received beginning 6 months after the date of enactment of the Hazardous and Solid Waste Amendments of 1984.

(2) The owner or operator of each unit referred to in paragraph (1) shall notify the Administrator (or the State, if appropriate) at least sixty days prior to receiving waste. The Administrator (or the State) shall require the filing, within six months of receipt of such notice, of an application for a final determination regarding

the issuance of a permit for each facility submitting such notice.

(3) In the case of any unit in which the liner and leachate collection system has been installed pursuant to the requirements of this section and in good faith compliance with the Administrator's regulations and guidance documents governing liners and leachate collection systems, no liner or leachate collection system which is different from that which was so installed pursuant to this section shall be required for such unit by the Administrator when issuing the first permit under section 3005 to such facility, except that the Administrator shall not be precluded from requiring installation of a new liner when the Administrator has reason to believe that any liner installed pursuant to the requirements of this section is leaking. The Administrator may, under section 3004, amend the requirements for liners and leachate collection systems required under this section as may be necessary to provide additional protection for human health and the environment.

[§3015 added by PL 98–616]

§6937. Inventory of Federal Agency Hazardous Waste Facilities [Sec. 3016]

(a) Each Federal agency shall undertake a continuing program to compile, publish, and submit to the Administrator (and to the State in the case of sites in States having an authorized hazardous waste program) an inventory of each site which the Federal agency owns or operates or has owned or operated at which hazardous waste is stored, treated, or disposed of or has been disposed of at any time. The inventory shall be submitted every two years beginning January 31, 1986. Such inventory shall be available to the public as provided in section 3007(b). Information previously submitted by a Federal agency under section 103 of the Comprehensive Environmental Response, Compensation, and Liability Act of 1980, or under section 3005 or 3010 of this Act, or under this section need not be resubmitted except that the agency shall update any previous submission to reflect the latest available data and information. The inventory shall include each of the following:

(1) A description of the location of each site at which any such treatment, storage, or disposal has taken place before the date on which permits are required under section 3005 for such storage, treatment, or disposal, and where hazardous waste has been disposed, a description of hydrogeology of the site and the location of withdrawal wells and surface water within one mile of the site.

(2) Such information relating to the amount, nature, and toxicity of the hazardous waste in each site as may be necessary to determine the extent of any health hazard which may be associated with any site.

(3) Information on the known nature and extent of environmental contamination at each site, including a description of the monitoring data obtained.

(4) Information concerning the current status of the site, including information respecting whether or not hazardous waste is currently being treated, stored, or disposed of at such site (and if not, the date on which such activity ceased) and information respecting the nature of any other activity currently carried out at such site.

(5) A list of sites at which hazardous waste has been disposed and environmental monitoring data has not been obtained, and the reasons for the lack of monitoring data at each site.

(6) A description of response actions undertaken or contemplated at contaminated sites.

(7) An identification of the types of techniques of waste treatment, storage, or disposal which have been used at each site.

(8) The name and address and responsible Federal agency for each site, determined as of the date of preparation of the inventory.

(b) Environmental Protection Agency Program. — If the Administrator determines that any Federal agency under subsection (a) is not adequately providing information respecting the sites referred to in subsection (a), the Administrator shall notify the chief official of such agency. If within ninety days following such notification, the Federal agency has not undertaken a program to adequately provide such information, the Administrator shall carry out the inventory program for such agency.

[§3016 added by PL 98–616]

§6938. Export of Hazardous Waste [Sec. 3017]

(a) In General.—Beginning twenty- four months after the date of enactment of the Hazardous and Solid Waste Amendments of 1984, no person shall export any hazardous waste identified or listed under this subtitle unless

(1) (A) such person has provided the notification required in subsection (c) of this section,

(B) the government of the receiving country has consented to accept such hazardous waste,

(C) a copy of the receiving country's written consent is attached to the manifest accompanying each waste shipment, and

(D) the shipment conforms with the terms of the consent of the government of the receiving country required pursuant to subsection (e), or

(2) the United States and the government of the receiving country have entered into an agreement as provided for in subsection (f) and the shipment conforms with the terms of such agreement.

(b) Regulations.—Not later than twelve months after the date of enactment of the Hazardous and Solid Waste Amendments of 1984, the Administrator shall promulgate the regulations necessary to implement this section. Such regulations shall become effective one hundred and eighty days after promulgation.

(c) Notification.—Any person who intends to export a hazardous waste identified or listed under this subtitle beginning twelve months after the date of enactment of the Hazardous and Solid Waste Amendments of 1984, shall, before such hazardous waste is scheduled to leave the United States, provide notification to the Administrator. Such notification shall contain the following information:

(1) the name and address of the exporter;

(2) the types and estimated quantities of hazardous waste to be exported;

(3) the estimated frequency or rate at which such waste is to be exported; and the period of time over which such waste is to be exported;

(4) the ports of entry;

(5) a description of the manner in which such hazardous waste will be transported to and treated, stored, or disposed in the receiving country; and

(6) the name and address of the ultimate treatment, storage or disposal facility.

(d) Procedures for Requesting Consent of the Receiving Country.—Within thirty days of the Administrator's receipt of a complete notification under this section, the Secretary of State, acting on behalf of the Administrator, shall—

(1) forward a copy of the notification to the government of the receiving country;

(2) advise the government that United States law prohibits the export of hazardous waste unless the receiving country consents to accept the hazardous waste;

(3) request the government to provide the Secretary with a written consent or objection to the terms of the notification; and

(4) forward to the government of the receiving country a description of the Federal regulations which would apply to the treatment, storage, and disposal of the hazardous waste in the United States.

(e) Conveyance of Written Consent to Exporter.—Within thirty days of receipt by the Secretary of State of the receiving country's written consent or objection (or any subsequent communication withdrawing a prior consent or objection), the Administrator shall forward such a consent, objection, or other communication to the exporter.

(f) International Agreements.—Where there exists an international agreement between the United States and the government of the receiving country establishing notice, export, and enforcement procedures for the transportation, treatment, storage, and disposal of hazardous wastes, only the requirements of subsections (a)(2) and (g) shall apply.

(g) Reports.—After the date of enactment of the Hazardous and Solid Waste Amendments of 1984, any person who exports any hazardous waste identified or listed under section 3001 of this subtitle shall file with the Administrator no later than March 1 of each year, a report summarizing the types, quantities, frequency, and ultimate destination of all such hazardous waste exported during the previous calendar year.

(h) Other Standards.—Nothing in this section shall preclude the Administrator from establishing other standards for the export of hazardous wastes under section 3002 or section 3003 of this subtitle.

[§3017 added by PL 98–616]

§6939. Domestic Sewage [Sec. 3018]

(a) Report.—The Administrator shall, not later than 15 months after the date of enactment of the Hazardous and Solid Waste Amendments of 1984, submit a report to the Congress concerning those substances identified or listed under section 3001 which are not regulated under this subtitle by reason of the exclusion for mixtures of domestic sewage and other wastes that pass through a sewer system to a publicly owned treatment works. Such report shall include the types, size and number of generators which dispose of such substances in this manner, the types and quantities disposed of in this manner, and the identification of significant generators, wastes, and waste constituents not regulated under existing Federal law or regulated in a manner sufficient to protect human health and the environment.

(b) Revisions of Regulations.—Within eighteen months after submitting the report specified in subsection (a), the Administrator shall revise existing regulations and promulgate such additional regulations pursuant to this subtitle (or any other authority of the Administrator, including section 307 of the Federal Water Pollution Control Act) as are necessary to assure that substances identified or listed under section 3001 which pass through a sewer system to a publicly owned treatment works are adequately controlled to protect human health and the environment.

(c) Report on Wastewater Lagoons.—The Administrator shall, within thirty-six months after the date of the enactment of the Hazardous and Solid Waste Amendments of 1984, submit a report to Congress concerning wastewater lagoons at publicly owned treatment works and their effect on groundwater quality. Such report shall include—

(1) the number and size of such lagoons;

(2) the types and quantities of waste contained in such lagoons;

(3) the extent to which such waste has been or may be released from such lagoons and contaminate ground water; and

(4) available alternatives for preventing or controlling such releases.

The Administrator may utilize the authority of sections 3007 and 3013 for the purpose of completing such report.

(d) Application of section 3010 and section 3007.—The provisions of sections 3007 and 3010 shall apply to solid or dissolved materials in domestic sewage to the same extent and in the same manner as such provisions apply to hazardous waste.

[§3018 added by PL 98–616]

§6939a. Exposure Information and Health Assessments [Sec. 3019]

(a) Exposure Information.—Beginning on the date nine months after the enactment of the Hazardous and Solid Waste Amendments of 1984, each application for a final determination regarding a permit under section 3005(c) for a landfill or surface impoundment shall be accompanied by information reasonably ascertainable by the owner or operator on the potential for the public to be exposed to hazardous wastes or hazardous constituents through releases related to the unit. At a minimum, such information must address:

(1) reasonably foreseeable potential releases from both normal operations and accidents at the unit, including releases associated with transportation to or from the unit;

(2) the potential pathways of human exposure to hazardous wastes or constituents resulting from the releases described under paragraph (1); and

(3) the potential magnitude and nature of the human exposure resulting from such releases.

The owner or operator of a landfill or surface impoundment for which an application for such a final determination under section 3005(c) has been submitted prior to the date of enactment of the Hazardous and Solid Waste Amendments of 1984 shall submit the information required by this subsection to the Administrator (or the State, in the case of a State with an authorized program) no later than the date nine months after such date of enactment.

(b) Health Assessments.—

(1) The Administrator (or the State, in the case of a State with an authorized program) shall make the information required by subsection (a), together with other relevant information, available to the Agency for Toxic Substances and Disease Registry established by section 104(i) of the Comprehensive Environmental Response, Compensation and Liability Act of 1980.

(2) Whenever in the judgment of the Administrator, or the State (in the case of a State with an authorized program), a landfill or a surface impoundment poses a substantial potential risk to human health, due to the existence of releases of hazardous constituents, the magnitude of contamination with hazardous constituents which may be the result of a release, or the magnitude of the population exposed to such release or contamination, the Administrator or the State (with the concurrence of the Administrator) may request the Administrator of the Agency for Toxic Substances and Disease Registry to conduct a health assessment in connection with such facility and take other appropriate action with respect to such risks as authorized by section 104(b) and (i) of the Comprehensive Environmental Response, Compensation and Liability Act of 1980. If funds are provided in connection with such

request the Administrator of such Agency shall conduct such health assessment.

(c) Members of the Public.—Any member of the public may submit evidence of releases of or exposure to hazardous constituents from such a facility, or as to the risks or health effects associated with such releases or exposure, to the Administrator of the Agency for Toxic Substances and Disease Registry, the Administrator, or the State (in the case of a State with an authorized program).

(d) Priority.—In determining the order in which to conduct health assessments under this subsection, the Administrator of the Agency for Toxic Substances and Disease Registry shall give priority to those facilities or sites at which there is documented evidence of release of hazardous constituents, at which the potential risk to human health appears highest, and for which in the judgment of the Administrator of such Agency existing health assessment data is inadequate to assess the potential risk to human health as provided in subsection (f).

(e) Periodic Reports.—The Administrator of such Agency shall issue periodic reports which include the results of all the assessments carried out under this section. Such assessments or other activities shall be reported after appropriate peer review.

(f) Definition.—For the purposes of this section, the term "health assessments" shall include preliminary assessments of the potential risk to human health posed by individual sites and facilities subject to this section, based on such factors as the nature and extent of contamination, the existence of potential for pathways of human exposure (including ground or surface water contamination, air emissions, and food chain contamination), the size and potential susceptibility of the community within the likely pathways of exposure, the comparison of expected human exposure levels to the short-term and long-term health effects associated with identified contaminants and any available recommended exposure or tolerance limits for such contaminants, and the comparison of existing morbidity and mortality data on diseases that may be associated with the observed levels of exposure. The assessment shall include an evaluation of the risks to the potentially affected population from all sources of such contaminants, including known point or nonpoint sources other than the site or facility in question. A purpose of such preliminary assessments shall be to help determine whether full-scale health or epidemiological studies and medical evaluations of exposed populations shall be undertaken.

(g) Cost Recovery.—In any case in which a health assessment performed under this section discloses the exposure of a population to the release of a hazardous substance, the costs of such health assessment may be recovered as a cost of response under section 107 of the Comprehensive Environmental Response, Compensation, and Liability Act of 1980 from persons causing or contributing to such release of such hazardous substance or, in the case of multiple releases contributing to such exposure, to all such release.

[§3019 added by PL 98–616]

§6939b. Interim Control of Hazardous Waste Injection [Sec. 3020]

[Former §7010 added by PL 98–616; redesignated as §3020 by PL 99–339]

(a) Underground Source of Drinking Water. — No hazardous waste may be disposed of by underground injection—

(1) into a formation which contains (within one-quarter mile of the well used for such underground injection) an underground source of drinking water; or

(2) above such a formation.

The prohibitions established under this section shall take effect 6 months after the enactment of the Hazardous and Solid Waste Amendments of 1984 except in the case of any State in which identical or more stringent prohibitions are in effect before such date under the Safe Drinking Water Act.

(b) Actions Under CERCLA.—Subsection (a) shall not apply to the injection of contaminated ground water into the aquifer from which it was withdrawn, if—

(1) such injection is—

(A) a response action taken under section 104 or 106 of the Comprehensive Environmental Response, Compensation and Liability Act of 1980, or

(B) part of corrective action required under this title intended to clean up such contamination;

(2) such contaminated ground water is treated to substantially reduce hazardous constituents prior to such injection; and

(3) such response action or corrective action will, upon completion, be sufficient to protect human health and the environment.

(c) Enforcement.—In addition to enforcement under the provisions of this Act, the prohibitions established under paragraphs (1) and (2) of subsection (a) shall be enforceable under the Safe Drinking Water Act in any State—

[Former §7010(c) amended and redesignated as §3020(c) by PL 99–339]

(1) which has adopted identical or more stringent prohibitions under part C of the Safe Drinking Water Act and which has assumed primary enforcement responsibility under that Act for enforcement of such prohibitions; or

(2) in which the Administrator has adopted identical or more stringent prohibitions under the Safe Drinking Water Act and is exercising primary enforcement responsibility under that Act for enforcement of such prohibitions.

(d) The terms "primary enforcement responsibility", "underground source of drinking water", "formation" and "well" have the same meanings as provided in regulations of the Administrator under the Safe Drinking Water Act. The term "Safe Drinking Water Act" means title XIV of the Public Health Service Act.

§6939c. Mixed Waste Inventory Reports and Plan. [Sec. 3021]

(a) Mixed Waste Inventory Reports.—

(1) Requirement.—Not later than 180 days after the date of the enactment of the Federal Facility Compliance Act of 1992, the Secretary of Energy shall submit to the Administrator and to the Governor of each State in which the Department of Energy stores or generates mixed wastes the following reports:

(A) A report containing a national inventory of all such mixed wastes, regardless of the time they were generated, on a State-by-State basis.

(B) A report containing a national inventory of mixed waste treatment capacities and technologies.

(2) Inventory of wastes.— The report required by paragraph (1)(A) shall include the following:

(A) A description of each type of mixed waste at each Department of Energy facility in each State, including, at a minimum, the name of the waste stream.

(B) The amount of each type of mixed waste currently stored at each Department of Energy facility in each State, set forth separately by mixed waste that is subject to the land disposal prohibition requirements of section 3004 and mixed waste that is not subject to such prohibition requirements.

(C) An estimate of the amount of each type of mixed waste the Department expects to generate in the next 5 years at each Department of Energy facility in each State.

(D) A description of any waste minimization actions the Department has implemented at each Department of Energy facility in each State for each mixed waste stream.

(E) The EPA hazardous waste code for each type of mixed waste containing waste that has been characterized at each Department of Energy facility in each State.

(F) An inventory of each type of waste that has not been characterized by sampling and analysis at each Department of Energy facility in each State.

(G) The basis for the Department's determination of the applicable hazardous waste code for each type of mixed waste at each Department of Energy facility and a description of whether the determination is based on sampling and analysis conducted on the waste or on the basis of process knowledge.

(H) A description of the source of each type of mixed waste at each Department of Energy facility in each State.

(I) The land disposal prohibition treatment technology or technologies specified for the hazardous waste component of each type of mixed waste at each Department of Energy facility in each State.

(J) A statement of whether and how the radionuclide content of the waste alters or affects use of the technologies described in subparagraph (I).

(3) Inventory of treatment capacities and technologies.—The report required by paragraph (1)(B) shall include the following:

(A) An estimate of the available treatment capacity for each waste described in the report required by paragraph (1)(A) for which treatment technologies exist.

(B) A description, including the capacity, number and location, of each treatment unit considered in calculating the estimate under subparagraph (A).

(C) A description, including the capacity, number and location, of any existing treatment unit that was not considered in calculating the estimate under subparagraph (A) but that could, alone or in conjunction with other treatment units, be used to treat any of the wastes described in the report required by paragraph (1)(A) to meet the requirements of regulations promulgated pursuant to section 3004(m).

(D) For each unit listed in subparagraph (C), a statement of the reasons why the unit was not included in calculating the estimate under subparagraph (A).

(E) A description, including the capacity, number, location, and estimated date of availability, of each treatment unit currently proposed to increase the treatment capacities estimated under subparagraph (A).

(F) For each waste described in the report required by paragraph (1)(A) for which the Department has determined no treatment technology exists, information sufficient to support such determination and a description of the technological approaches the Department anticipates will need to be developed to treat the waste.

(4) Comments and revisions.—Not later than 90 days after the date of the submission of the reports by the Secretary of Energy under paragraph (1), the Administrator and each State which received the reports shall submit any comments they may have concerning the reports to the Department of Energy. The Secretary of Energy shall consider and publish the comments prior to publication of the final report.

(5) Requests for additional information.—Nothing in this subsection limits or restricts the authority of States or the Administrator to request additional information from the Secretary of Energy.

(b) Plan for Development of Treatment Capacities and Technologies.—

(1) Plan requirement.—

(A) (i) For each facility at which the Department of Energy generates or stores mixed wastes, except any facility subject to a permit, agreement, or order described in clause (ii), the Secretary of Energy shall develop and submit, as provided in paragraph (2), a plan for developing treatment capacities and technologies to treat all of the facility's mixed wastes, regardless of the time they were generated, to the standards promulgated pursuant to section 3004(m).

(ii) Clause (i) shall not apply with respect to any facility subject to any permit establishing a schedule for treatment of such wastes, or any existing agreement or administrative or judicial order governing the treatment of such wastes, to which the State is a party.

(B) Each plan shall contain the following:

(i) For mixed wastes for which treatment technologies exist, a schedule for submitting all applicable permit applications, entering into contracts, initiating construction, conducting systems testing, commencing operations, and processing backlogged and currently generated mixed wastes.

(ii) For mixed wastes for which no treatment technologies exist, a schedule for identifying and developing such technologies, identifying the funding requirements for the identification and development of such technologies, submitting treatability study exemptions, and submitting research and development permit applications.

(iii) For all cases where the Department proposes radionuclide separation of mixed wastes, or materials derived from mixed wastes, it shall provide an estimate of the volume of waste generated by each case of radionuclide separation, the volume of waste that would exist or be generated without radionuclide separation, the estimated costs of waste treatment and disposal if radionuclide separation is used compared to the estimated costs if it is not used, and the assumptions underlying such waste volume and cost estimates.

(C) A plan required under this subsection may provide for centralized, regional, or onsite treatment of mixed wastes, or any combination thereof.

(2) Review and approval of plan.—

(A) For each facility that is located in a State (i) with authority under State law to prohibit land disposal of mixed waste until the waste has been treated and (ii) with both authority under State law to regulate the hazardous components of mixed waste and authorization from the Environmental Protection Agency under section 3006 to regulate the hazardous components of mixed waste, the Secretary of Energy shall submit the plan required under paragraph (1) to the appropriate State regulatory officials for their review and approval, modification, or disapproval. In reviewing the plan, the State shall consider the need for regional treatment facilities. The State shall consult with the Administrator and any other State in which a facility affected by the plan is located and consider public comments in making its determination on the plan. The State shall approve, approve with modifications, or disapprove the plan within 6 months after receipt of the plan.

(B) For each facility located in a State that does not have the authority described in subparagraph (A), the Secretary shall submit the plan required under paragraph (1) to the Administrator of the Environmental Protection Agency for review and approval, modification, or disapproval. A copy of the plan also shall be provided by the Secretary to the State in which such facility is located. In reviewing the plan, the Administrator shall consider the need for regional treatment facilities. The Administrator shall consult with the State or States in which any facility affected by the plan is located and consider public comments in making a determination on the plan. The Administrator shall approve, approve with modifications, or disapprove the plan within 6 months after receipt of the plan.

(C) Upon the approval of a plan under this paragraph by the Administrator or a State, the Administrator shall issue an order under section 3008(a), or the State shall issue an order under appropriate State authority, requiring compliance with the approved plan.

(3) Public participation.—Upon submission of a plan by the Secretary of Energy to the Administrator or a State, and before approval of the plan by the Administrator or a State, the Administrator or State shall publish a notice of the availability of the submitted plan and make such submitted plan available to the public on request.

(4) Revisions of plan.—If any revisions of an approved plan are proposed by the Secretary of Energy or required by the Administrator or a State, the provisions of paragraphs (2) and (3) shall apply to the revisions in the same manner as they apply to the original plan.

(5) Waiver of plan requirement.—

(A) A State may waive the requirement for the Secretary of Energy to develop and submit a plan under this subsection for a facility located in the State if the State (i) enters into an agreement with the Secretary of Energy that addresses compliance at that facility with section 3004(j) with respect to mixed waste, and (ii) issues an order requiring compliance with such agreement and which is in effect.

(B) Any violation of an agreement or order referred to in subparagraph (A) is subject to the waiver of sovereign immunity contained in section 6001(a).

(c) Schedule and Progress Reports.—

(1) Schedule.—Not later than 6 months after the date of the enactment of the Federal Facility Compliance Act of 1992, the Secretary of Energy shall publish in the Federal Register a schedule for submitting the plans required under subsection (b).

(2) Progress reports.—

(A) Not later than the deadlines specified in subparagraph (B), the Secretary of Energy shall submit to the Committee on Environment and Public Works of the Senate and the Committee on Energy and Commerce of the House of Representatives a progress report containing the following:

(i) An identification, by facility, of the plans that have been submitted to States or the Administrator of the Environmental Protection Agency pursuant to subsection (b).

(ii) The status of State and Environmental Protection Agency review and approval of each such plan.

(iii) The number of orders requiring compliance with such plans that are in effect.

(iv) For the first 2 reports required under this paragraph, an identification of the plans required under such subsection (b) that the Secretary expects to submit in the 12-month period following submission of the report.

(B) The Secretary of Energy shall submit a report under subparagraph (A) not later than 12 months after the date of the enactment of the Federal Facility Compliance Act of 1992, 24 months after such date, and 36 months after such date. .

[§3021 added by PL 102–386]

[Editor's Note: Section 105(c) of the "Federal Facility Compliance Act of 1992," PL 102–386 did not amend this Act directly, but contained provisions applicable to §3021. The text of the material follows.]

[Sec. 105]

(c) GAO Report.—

(1) Requirement.—Not later than 18 months after the date of the enactment of this Act, the Comptroller General shall submit to Congress a report on the Department of Energy's progress in complying with section 3021(b) of the Solid Waste Disposal Act.

(2) Matters to be included.—The report required under paragraph (1) shall contain, at a minimum, the following:

(A) The Department of Energy's progress in submitting to the States or the Administrator of the Environmental Protection Agency a plan for each facility for which a plan is required under section 3021(b) of the Solid Waste Disposal Act and the status of State or Environmental Protection Agency review and approval of each such plan.

(B) The Department of Energy's progress in entering into orders requiring compliance with any such plans that have been approved.

(C) An evaluation of the completeness and adequacy of each such plan as of the date of submission of the report required under paragraph (1).

(D) An identification of any recurring problems among the Department of Energy's submitted plans.

(E) A description of treatment technologies and capacity that have been developed by the Department of Energy since the date of the enactment of this Act and a list of the wastes that are expected to be treated by such technologies and the facilities at which the wastes are generated or stored.

(F) The progress made by the Department of Energy in characterizing its mixed waste streams at each such facility by sampling and analysis.

(G) An identification and analysis of additional actions that the Department of Energy must take to—

(i) complete submission of all plans required under such section 3021(b) for all such facilities;

(ii) obtain the adoption of orders requiring compliance with all such plans; and

(iii) develop mixed waste treatment capacity and technologies.

§6939d. Public Vessels. [Sec. 3022]

(a) Waste Generated on Public Vessels.—Any hazardous waste generated on a public vessel shall not be subject to the storage, manifest, inspection, or recordkeeping requirements of this Act until such waste is transferred to a shore facility, unless—

(1) the waste is stored on the public vessel for more than 90 days after the public vessel is placed in reserve or is otherwise no longer in service; or

(2) the waste is transferred to another public vessel within the territorial waters of the United States and is stored on such vessel or another public vessel for more than 90 days after the date of transfer.

(b) Computation of Storage Period.—For purposes of subsection (a), the 90-day period begins on the earlier of—

(1) the date on which the public vessel on which the waste was generated is placed in reserve or is otherwise no longer in service; or

(2) the date on which the waste is transferred from the public vessel on which the waste was generated to another public vessel within the territorial waters of the United States;

and continues, without interruption, as long as the waste is stored on the original public vessel (if in reserve or not in service) or another public vessel.

(c) Definitions.—For purposes of this section:

(1) The term "public vessel" means a vessel owned or bareboat chartered and operated by the United States, or by a foreign nation, except when the vessel is engaged in commerce.

(2) The terms "in reserve" and "in service" have the meanings applicable to those terms under section 7293 and sections 7304 through 7308 of title 10, United States Code, and regulations prescribed under those sections.

(d) Relationship to Other Law.—Nothing in this section shall be construed as altering or otherwise affecting the provisions of section 7311 of title 10, United States Code. .

[§3022 added by PL 102–386]

§6939d. Federally Owned Treatment Works. [Sec. 3023]

(a) In General.—For purposes of section 1004(27), the phrase "but does not include solid or dissolved material in domestic sewage" shall apply to any solid or dissolved material introduced by a source into a federally owned treatment works if—

(1) such solid or dissolved material is subject to a pretreatment standard under section 307 of the Federal Water Pollution Control Act (33 U.S.C. 1317), and the source is in compliance with such standard;

(2) for a solid or dissolved material for which a pretreatment standard has not been promulgated pursuant to section 307 of the Federal Water Pollution Control Act (33 U.S.C. 1317), the Administrator has promulgated a schedule for establishing such a pretreatment standard which would be applicable to such solid or dissolved material not later than 7 years after the date of enactment of this section, such standard is promulgated on or before the date established in the schedule, and after the effec-

tive date of such standard the source is in compliance with such standard;

(3) such solid or dissolved material is not covered by paragraph (1) or (2) and is not prohibited from land disposal under subsections (d), (e), (f), or (g) of section 3004 because such material has been treated in accordance with section 3004(m); or

(4) notwithstanding paragraphs (1), (2), or (3), such solid or dissolved material is generated by a household or person which generates less than 100 kilograms of hazardous waste per month unless such solid or dissolved material would otherwise be an acutely hazardous waste and subject to standards, regulations, or other requirements under this Act notwithstanding the quantity generated.

(b) Prohibition.—It is unlawful to introduce into a federally owned treatment works any pollutant that is a hazardous waste.

(c) Enforcement.—

(1) Actions taken to enforce this section shall not require closure of a treatment works if the hazardous waste is removed or decontaminated and such removal or decontamination is adequate, in the discretion of the Administrator or, in the case of an authorized State, of the State, to protect human health and the environment.

(2) Nothing in this subsection shall be construed to prevent the Administrator or an authorized State from ordering the closure of a treatment works if the Administrator or State determines such closure is necessary for protection of human health and the environment.

(3) Nothing in this subsection shall be construed to affect any other enforcement authorities available to the Administrator or a State under this subtitle.

(d) Definition.—For purposes of this section, the term "federally owned treatment works" means a facility that is owned and operated by a department, agency, or instrumentality of the Federal Government treating wastewater, a majority of which is domestic sewage, prior to discharge in accordance with a permit issued under section 402 of the Federal Water Pollution Control Act.

(e) Savings Clause.—Nothing in this section shall be construed as affecting any agreement, permit, or administrative or judicial order, or any condition or requirement contained in such an agreement, permit, or order, that is in existence on the date of the enactment of this section and that requires corrective action or closure at a federally owned treatment works or solid waste management unit or facility related to such a treatment works.

[§3023 added by PL 102–386]

SUBTITLE D—STATE OR REGIONAL SOLID WASTE PLANS

§6941. Objectives of Subtitle [Sec. 4001]

The objectives of this subtitle are to assist in developing and encouraging methods for the disposal of solid waste which are environmentally sound and which maximize the utilization of valuable resources including energy and materials which are recoverable from solid waste and to encourage resource conservation. Such objectives are to be accomplished through Federal technical and financial assistance to States or regional authorities for comprehensive planning pursuant to Federal guidelines designed to foster cooperation among Federal, State, and local governments and private industry. In developing such comprehensive plans, it is the intention of this Act that in determining the size of the waste- to-energy facility, adequate provision shall be given to the present and reasonably anticipated future needs, including those needs created by thorough implementation of section 6002(h), of the recycling and resource recovery interest within the area encompassed by the planning process.

[§4001 amended by PL 96–482; PL 98–616]

§6942. Federal Guidelines for Plans [Sec. 4002]

(a) Guidelines for Identification of Regions.—For purposes of encouraging and facilitating the development of regional planning for solid waste management, the Administrator, within one hundred and eighty days after the date of enactment of this section and after consultation with appropriate Federal, State, and local authorities, shall by regulation publish guidelines for the identification of those areas which have common solid waste management problems and are appropriate units for planning regional solid waste management services. Such guidelines shall consider—

(1) the size and location of areas which should be included,

(2) the volume of solid waste which should be included, and

(3) the available means of coordinating regional planning with other related regional planning and for coordination of such regional planning into the State plan.

(b) Guidelines for State Plans.—Not later than eighteen months after the date of enactment of this section and after notice and hearing, the Administrator shall, after consultation with appropriate Federal, State, and local authorities, promulgate regulations containing guidelines to assist in the development and implementation of State solid waste management plans (hereinafter in this title referred to as "State plans"). The guidelines shall contain methods for achieving the objectives specified in section 4001. Such guidelines shall be reviewed from time to time, but not less frequently than every three years, and revised as may be appropriate.

(c) Considerations for State Plan Guidelines.—The guidelines promulgated under subsection (b) shall consider—

(1) the varying regional, geologic, hydrologic, climatic, and other circumstances under which different solid waste practices are required in order to insure the reasonable protection of the quality of the ground and surface waters from leachate contamination, the reasonable protection of the quality of the surface waters from surface runoff contamination, and the reasonable protection of ambient air quality;

(2) characteristics and conditions of collection, storage, processing, and disposal operating methods, techniques and practices, and location of facilities where such operating methods, techniques, and practices are conducted, taking into account the nature of the material to be disposed:

(3) methods for closing or upgrading open dumps for purposes of eliminating potential health hazards;

(4) population density, distribution, and projected growth;

(5) geographic, geologic climatic, and hydrologic characteristics;

(6) the type and location of transportation;

(7) the profile of industries;

(8) the constituents and generation rates of waste;

(9) the political, economic, organizational, financial, and management problems affecting comprehensive solid waste management;

(10) types of resource recovery facilities and resource conservation systems which are appropriate; and

(11) available new and additional markets for recovered material and energy and energy resources recovered from solid waste as well as methods for conserving such materials and energy.

[§4002(c)(11) amended by PL 96–482]

[Amended by PL 96–463]

§6943. Requirements for Approval of Plans
[Sec. 4003]

(a) Minimum Requirements.—In order to be approved under section 4007, each State plan must comply with the following minimum requirements—

[Editor's Note: PL 96–463 and PL 96–482 both designated 4003(a) and added identical amendments.]

(1) The plan shall identify (in accordance with section 4006(b)) (A) the responsibilities of State, local, and regional authorities in the implementation of the State plan, (B) the distribution of Federal funds to the authorities responsible for development and implementation of the State plan, and (C) the means for coordinating regional planning and implementation under the State plan.

(2) The plan shall, in accordance with section 4004(b) and 4005(a), prohibit the establishment of new open dumps within the State, and contain requirements that all solid waste (including solid waste-originating in other States, but not including hazardous waste) shall be (A) utilized for resource recovery or (B) disposed of in sanitary landfills (within the meaning of section 4004(a)) or otherwise disposed of in an environmentally sound manner.

[§4003(a)(2) amended by PL 96–482]

(3) The plan shall provide for the closing or upgrading of all existing open dumps within the State pursuant to the requirements of section 4005.

(4) The plan shall provide for the establishment of such State regulatory powers as may be necessary to implement the plan.

(5) The plan shall provide that no state or local government within the State shall be prohibited under State or local law from negotiating and entering into long- term contracts for the supply of solid waste to resource recovery facilities, from entering into long-term contracts for the operation of such facilities, or from securing long-term markets for material and energy recovered from such facilities or for conserving materials or energy by reducing the volume of waste.

[§4003(a)(5) amended by PL 96–482]

(6) The plan shall provide for such resource conservation or recovery and for the disposal

of solid waste in sanitary landfills or any combination of practices so as may be necessary to use or dispose of such waste in a manner that is environmentally sound.

(b) Discretionary Plan Provisions Relating to Recycled Oil.—Any State plan submitted under this subtitle may include, at the option of the State, provisions to carry out each of the following:

(1) Encouragement, to the maximum extent feasible and consistent with the protection of the public health and the environment, of the use of recycled oil in all appropriate areas of State and local government.

(2) Encouragement of persons contracting with the State to use recycled oil to the maximum extent feasible, consistent with protection of the public health and the environment.

(3) Informing the public of the uses of recycled oil.

(4) Establishment and implementation of a program (including any necessary licensing of persons and including the use, where appropriate, of manifests) to assure that used oil is collected, transported, treated, stored, reused, and disposed of, in a manner which does not present a hazard to the public health or the environment.

Any plan submitted under this title before the date of the enactment of the Used Oil Recycling Act of 1980 may be amended, at the option of the State, at any time after such date to include any provision referred to in this subsection.

[§4003(b) added by PL 96–463]

(c) Energy and Materials Conservation and Recovery Feasibility Planning and Assistance.—

(1) A State which has a plan approved under this subtitle or which has submitted a plan for such approval shall be eligible for assistance under section 4008(a)(3) if the Administrator determines that under such plan the State will—

(A) analyze and determine the economic and technical feasibility of facilities and programs to conserve resources which contribute to the waste stream or to recover energy and materials from municipal waste;

(B) analyze the legal, institutional, and economic impediments to the development of systems and facilities for conservation of energy or materials which contribute to the waste stream or for the recovery of energy and materials from municipal waste and make recommendations to appropriate governmental authorities for overcoming such impediments;

(C) assist municipalities within the State in developing plans, programs, and projects to conserve resources or recover energy and materials from municipal waste; and

(D) coordinate the resource conservation and recovery planning under subparagraph (C).

(2) The analysis referred to in paragraph (1)(A) shall include—

(A) the evaluation of, and establishment of priorities among, market opportunities for industrial and commercial users of all types (including public utilities and industrial parks) to utilize energy and materials recovered from municipal waste;

(B) comparisons of the relative costs of energy recovered from municipal waste in relation to the costs of energy derived from fossil fuels and other sources;

(C) studies of the transportation and storage problems and other problems associated with the development of energy and materials recovery technology, including curbside source separation;

(D) the evaluation and establishment of priorities among ways of conserving energy and materials which contribute to the waste stream;

(E) comparison of the relative total costs between conserving resources and disposing of or recovering such waste; and

(F) studies of impediments to resource conservation or recovery, including business practices, transportation requirements, or storage difficulties.

Such studies and analyses shall also include studies of other sources of solid waste from which energy and materials may be recovered or minimized.

[Former §4003(b) added by PL 96–482; redesignated as (c) by PL 98–616]

(d) Size of Waste-To-Energy Facilities.—Notwithstanding any of the above requirements, it is the intention of this Act and the planning process developed pursuant to this Act that in determining the size of the waste-to-energy facility, adequate provision shall be given to the present and reasonably anticipated future needs of the recycling and resource recovery interest within the area encompassed by the planning process.

[§4003(d) added by PL 98–616]

§6944. Criteria for Sanitary Landfills; Sanitary Landfills Required for All Disposal [Sec. 4004]

(a) Criteria for Sanitary Landfills.—Not later than one year after the date of enactment of this section, after consultation with the States, and after notice and public hearings, the Administrator shall promulgate regulations containing criteria for determining which facilities shall be classified as sanitary landfills and which shall be classified as open dumps within the meaning of this Act. At a minimum, such criteria shall provide that a facility may be classified as a sanitary landfill and not an open dump only if there is no reasonable probability of adverse effects on health or the environment from disposal of solid waste at such facility. Such regulations may provide for the classification of the types of sanitary landfills.

(b) Disposal Required to be in Sanitary Landfills, etc.—For purposes of complying with section 4003(2) each State plan shall prohibit the establishment of open dumps and contain a requirement that disposal of all solid waste within the State shall be in compliance with such section 4003(2).

(c) Effective Date.—The prohibition contained in subsection (b) shall take effect on the date six months after the date of promulgation of regulations under subsection (a) or on the date of approval of the State plan, whichever is later.

[§4004(c) amended by PL 98–616]

§6945. Upgrading of Open Dumps [Sec. 4005]

(a) Closing or Upgrading of Existing Open Dumps.—Upon promulgation of criteria under section 1008(a)(3), any solid waste management practice or disposal of solid waste or hazardous waste which constitutes the open dumping of solid waste or hazardous waste is prohibited, except in the case of any practice or disposal of solid waste under a timetable or schedule for compliance established under this section. The prohibition contained in the preceding sentence shall be enforceable under section 7002 against persons engaged in the act of open dumping. For purposes of complying with section 4003(2) and 4003(3), each State plan shall contain a requirement that all existing disposal facilities or sites for solid waste in such State which are open dumps listed in the inventory under subsection (b) shall comply with such measures as may be promulgated by the Administrator to eliminate health hazards and minimize potential health hazards. Each such plan shall establish, for any entity which demonstrates that it has considered other public or private alternatives for solid waste management to comply with the prohibition on open dumping and is unable to utilize such alternatives to so comply, a timetable or schedule for compliance for such practice or disposal of solid waste which specifies a schedule of remedial measures, including an enforceable sequence of actions or operations, leading to compliance with the prohibition on open dumping solid waste within a reasonable time (not to exceed 5 years from the date of publication of criteria under section 1008(a)(3)).

[Former §4005(c) redesignated as (a) and amended by PL 96–482; PL 98–616]

(b) Inventory.—To assist the States in complying with section 4003(3), not later than one year after promulgation of regulations under section 4004, the Administrator, with the cooperation of the Bureau of the Census shall publish an inventory of all disposal facilities or sites in the United States which are open dumps within the meaning of this Act.

[§4005(b) amended by PL 96–482]

(c) Control of Hazardous Disposal.—

(1) (A) Not later than 36 months after the date of enactment of the Hazardous and Solid Waste Amendments of 1984, each State shall adopt and implement a permit program or other system of prior approval and conditions to assure that each solid waste management facility within such State which may receive hazardous household waste or hazardous waste due to the provision of section 3001(d) for small quantity generators (otherwise not subject to the requirement for a permit under section 3005) will comply with the applicable criteria promulgated under section 4004(a) and section1008(a)(3).

(B) Not later than eighteen months after the promulgation of revised criteria under subsection 4004(a) (as required by section 4010(c)), each State shall adopt and implement a permit program or other system or prior approval and conditions, to assure that each solid waste management facility within such State which may receive hazardous household waste or hazardous waste due to the provision of section 3001(d) for small quantity generators (otherwise not subject to the requirement for a permit under section 3005) will comply with the criteria revised under section 4004(a).

(C) The Administrator shall determine whether each State has developed an adequate program under this paragraph. The Administrator may make such a determination in conjunction with approval, disapproval or partial approval of a State plan under section 4007.

(2) (A) In any State that the Administrator determines has not adopted an adequate program for such facilities under paragraph (1)(B) by the date provided in such paragraph, the Administrator may use the authorities available under sections 3007 and 3008 of this title to enforce the prohibition contained in subsection (a) of this section with respect to such facilities.

(B) For purposes of this paragraph, the term "requirement of this subtitle" in section 3008 shall be deemed to include criteria promulgated by the Administrator under sections 1008(a)(3) and 4004(a) of this title, and the term "hazardous wastes in section 3007 shall be deemed to include solid waste at facilities that may handle hazardous household wastes or hazardous wastes from small quantity generators.

[§4005(c) added by PL 98–616]

§6946. Procedure for Development and Implementation of State Plan [Sec. 4006]

(a) Identification of Regions.—Within one hundred and eighty days after publication of guidelines under section 4002(a) (relating to identification of regions), the Governor of each State, after consultation with local elected officials, shall promulgate regulations based on such guidelines identifying the boundaries of each area within the State which, as a result of urban concentrations, geographic conditions, markets, and other factors, is appropriate for carrying out regional solid waste management. Such regulations may be modified from time to time (identifying additional or different regions) pursuant to such guidelines.

(b) Identification of State and Local Agencies and Responsibilities.—

(1) Within one hundred and eighty days after the Governor promulgates regulations under subsection (a), for purposes of facilitating the development and implementation of a State plan which will meet the minimum requirements of section 4003, the State, together with appropriate elected officials of general purpose units of local government, shall jointly (A) identify an agency to develop the State plan and identify one or more agencies to implement such plan, and (B) identify which solid waste management activities will, under such State plan, be planned for and carried out by the State and which such management activities will, under such State plan, be planned for and carried out by a regional or local authority or a combination of regional or local and State authorities. If a multi- functional regional agency authorized by State law to conduct solid waste planning and management (the members of which are appointed by the Governor) is in existence on the date of enactment of this Act, the Governor shall identify such authority for purposes of carrying out within such region clause (A) of this paragraph. Where feasible, designation of the agency for the affected area designated under section 208 of the Federal Water Pollution Control Act (86 Stat. 839) shall be considered. A state agency identified under this paragraph shall be established or designated by the Governor of such State. Local or regional agencies identified under this paragraph shall be composed of individuals at least a majority of whom are elected local officials.

[§4006(b)(1)(B) amended by PL 96–482]

(2) If planning and implementation agencies are not identified and designated or established as required under paragraph (1) for any affected area, the governor shall, before the date two hundred and seventy days after promulgation of regulations under subsection (a), establish or designate a State agency to develop and implement the State plan for such area.

(c) Interstate Regions.—

(1) In the case of any region which, pursuant to the guidelines published by the Administrator under section 4002(a) (relating to identification of regions), would be located in two or more States, the Governors of the respective States, after consultation with local elected officials, shall consult, cooperate, and enter into agreements identifying the boundaries of such region pursuant to subsection (a).

(2) Within one hundred and eighty days after an interstate region is identified by agreement under paragraph (1), appropriate elected officials of general purpose units of local government within such region shall jointly establish or designate an agency to develop a plan for such region. If no such agency is established or designated within such period by such officials, the Governors of the respective States may, by agreement, establish or designate for such purpose a single representative organization including elected officials of general purpose units of local government within such region.

(3) Implementation of interstate regional solid waste management plans shall be conducted by units of local government for any portion of a region within their jurisdiction, or by multi-jurisdictional agencies or authorities designated in accordance with State law, including those designated by agreement by such units of local government for such purpose. If no such unit, agency, or authority is so designated, the respective Governors shall designate or establish a single interstate agency to implement such plan.

(4) For purposes of this subtitle, so much of an interstate regional plan as is carried out within a particular State shall be deemed part of the State plan for such State.

§6947. Approval of State Plan; Federal Assistance [Sec. 4007]

(a) Plan Approval.—The Administrator shall, within six months after a State plan has been submitted for approval, approve or disapprove the plan. The Administrator shall approve a plan if he determines that—

(1) it meets the requirements of paragraphs (1), (2), (3), and (5) of section 4003; and

(2) it contains provision for revision of such plan, after notice and public hearing, whenever the Administrator, by regulation, determines—

(A) that revised regulations respecting minimum requirements have been promulgated under paragraphs (1), (2), (3), and (5) of section 4003 with which the State plan is not in compliance;

(B) that information has become available which demonstrates the inadequacy of the plan to effectuate the purposes of this subtitle; or

(C) that such revision is otherwise necessary. The Administrator shall review approved plans from time to time and if he determines that revision or corrections are necessary to bring such plan into compliance with the minimum requirements promulgated under section 4003 (including new or revised requirements), he shall, after notice and opportunity for public hearing, withdraw his approval of such plan. Such withdrawal of approval shall cease to be effective upon the Administrator's determination that such complies with such minimum requirements.

(b) Eligibility of States for Federal Financial Assistance.—

(1) The Administrator shall approve a State application for financial assistance under this subtitle, and make grants to such State, if such State and local and regional authorities within such State have complied with the requirements of section 4006 within the period required under such section and if such State has a State plan which has been approved by the Administrator under this subtitle.

(2) The Administrator shall approve a State application for financial assistance under this subtitle, and make grants to such State, for fiscal years 1978 and 1979 if the Administrator determines that the State plan continues to be eligible for approval under subsection (a) and is being implemented by the State.

(3) Upon withdrawal of approval of a State plan under subsection (a), the Administrator shall withhold Federal financial and technical assistance under this subtitle (other than such technical assistance as may be necessary to assist in obtaining the reinstatement of approval) until such time as such approval is reinstated.

(c) Existing Activities.—Nothing in this subtitle shall be construed to prevent or affect any activities respecting solid waste planning or management which are carried out by State, regional, or local authorities unless such activities are inconsistent with a State plan approved by the Administrator under this subtitle.

§6948. Federal Assistance [Sec. 4008]

(a) Authorization of Federal Financial Assistance.—

(1) There are authorized to be appropriated $30,000,000 for fiscal year 1978, $40,000,000 for fiscal year 1979, $20,000,000 for fiscal year 1980, $15,000,000 for fiscal year 1981, $20,000,000 for the fiscal year 1982, and $10,000,000 for each of the fiscal years 1985 through 1988 for purposes of financial assistance to States and local, regional, and interstate authorities for the development and implementation of plans approved by the Administrator under this subtitle (other than the provisions of such plans referred to in section 4003(b), relating to feasibility planning for municipal waste energy and materials conservation and recovery).

[§4008(a)(1) amended by PL 96–842; PL 98–616]

(2) (A) The Administrator is authorized to provide financial assistance to States, counties, municipalities, and intermunicipal agencies and State and local public solid waste man-

agement authorities for implementation of programs to provide solid waste management, resource recovery, and resource conservation services and hazardous waste management. Such assistance shall include assistance for facility planning and feasibility studies; expert consultation; surveys and analyses of market needs; marketing of recovered resources; technology assessments; legal expenses; construction feasibility studies; source separation projects; and fiscal or economic investigations or studies; but such assistance shall not include any other element of construction, or any acquisition of land or interest in land, or any subsidy for the price of recovered resources. Agencies assisted under this subsection shall consider existing solid waste management and hazardous waste management services and facilities as well as facilities proposed for construction.

(B) An applicant for financial assistance under this paragraph must agree to comply with respect to the project or program assisted with the applicable requirements of section 4005 and Subtitle C of this Act and apply applicable solid waste management practices, methods, and levels of control consistent with any guidelines published pursuant to section 1008 of this Act. Assistance under this paragraph shall be available only for programs certified by the State to be consistent with any applicable State or areawide solid waste management plan or program. Applicants for technical and financial assistance under this section shall not preclude or foreclose consideration of programs for the recovery of recyclable materials through source separation or other resource recovery techniques.

[§4008(a)(2)(B) amended by PL 96–482]

(C) There are authorized to be appropriated $15,000,000 for each of the fiscal years 1978 and 1979 for purposes of this section. There are authorized to be appropriated $10,000,000 for fiscal year 1980, $10,000,000 for fiscal year 1981, $10,000,000 for fiscal year 1982, and $10,000,000 for each of the fiscal years 1985 through 1988 for purposes of this paragraph.

[§4008(a)(2)(C) amended by PL 96–482; PL 98–616]

(D) There are authorized —

(i) to be made available $15,000,000 out of funds appropriated for fiscal year 1985, and

(ii) to be appropriated for each of the fiscal years 1986 though 1988, $20,000,000

for grants to States (and where appropriate to regional, local, and interstate agencies) to implement programs requiring compliance by solid waste management facilities with the criteria promulgated under section 4004(a) and section 1008(a)(3) and with the provisions of section 4005. To the extent practicable, such programs shall require such compliance not later than thirty-six months after the date of the enactment of the Hazardous and Solid Waste Amendments of 1984.

[§4008(a)(2)(D) added by PL 98–616]

(3) (A) There is authorized to be appropriated for the fiscal year beginning October 1, 1981, and for each fiscal year thereafter before October 1, 1986, $4,000,000 for purposes of making grants to States to carry out section 4003(b). No amount may be appropriated for such purposes for the fiscal year beginning on October 1, 1986, or for any fiscal year thereafter.

(B) Assistance provided by the Administrator under this paragraph shall be used only for the purposes specified in section 4003(b). Such assistance may not be used for purposes of land acquisition, final facility design, equipment purchase, construction, startup or operation activities.

(C) Where appropriate, any State receiving assistance under this paragraph may make all or any part of such assistance available to municipalities within the State to carry out the activities specified in section 4003(b)(1)(A) and (B).

[§4008(a)(3) added by PL 96–482]

(b) State Allotment. — The sums appropriated in any fiscal year under subsection (a)(1) shall be allotted by the Administrator among all States, in the ratio that the population in each State bears to the population in all of the States, except that no State shall receive less than one-half of 1 per centum of the sums so allotted in any fiscal year. No State shall receive any grant under this section during any fiscal year when its expenditures of non-Federal funds for other than nonrecurrent expenditures for solid waste management control programs will be less than its expenditures were for such programs during fiscal year 1975, except that such funds may be reduced by an amount equal to their proportionate share of any general reduction of State spending ordered by the Governor or legislature of such State. No State shall receive any grant for solid waste management programs unless the Administrator is satisfied that such grant will be so used as to supplement and, to the extent practicable, increase the level of State, local, regional, or other non-Federal funds that would in the absence of such grant be made available for the maintenance of such programs.

(c) Distribution of Federal Financial Assistance Within the State.—The Federal assistance allotted to the States under subsection (b) shall be allocated by the State receiving such funds to State, local, regional, and interstate authorities carrying out planning and implementation of the State plan. Such allocation shall be based upon the responsibilities of the respective parties as determined pursuant to section 4006(b).

(d) Technical Assistance.—

(1) The Administrator may provide technical assistance to State and local governments for purposes of developing and implementing State plans. Technical assistance respecting resource recovery and conservation may be provided through resource recovery and conservation panels, established in the Environmental Protection Agency under subtitle B, to assist the State and local governments with respect to particular resource recovery and conservation projects under consideration and to evaluate their effect on the State plan.

[§4008(d)(1) designated by PL 96–463 and PL 96–482]

(2) In carrying out this subsection, the Administrator may, upon request, provide technical assistance to States to assist in the removal or modification of legal, institutional, economic, and other impediments to the recycling of used oil. Such impediments may include laws, regulations, and policies, including State procurement policies, which are not favorable to the recycling of used oil.

[§4008(d)(2) added by PL 96–463]

(3) In carrying out this subsection, the Administrator is authorized to provide technical assistance to States, municipalities, regional authorities, and intermunicipal agencies upon request, to assist in the removal or modification of legal, institutional, and economic impediments which have the effect of impeding the development of systems and facilities to recover energy and materials from municipal waste or to conserve energy or materials which contribute to the waste stream. Such impediments may include—

(A) laws, regulations, and policies, including State and local procurement policies, which are not favorable to resource conservation and recovery policies, systems, and facilities;

(B) impediments to the financing of facilities to conserve or recover energy and materials from municipal waste through the exercise of State and local authority to issue revenue bonds and the use of State and local credit assistance; and

(C) impediments to institutional arrangements necessary to undertake projects for the conservation or recovery of energy and materials from municipal waste, including the creation of special districts, authorities, or corporations where necessary having the power to secure the supply of waste of a project, to conserve resources, to implement the project, and to undertake related activities.

[Former §4008(d)(2) added by PL 96–482; redesignated as (3) by PL 98–616]

(e) Special Communities.—

(1) The Administrator, in cooperation with State and local officials, shall identify local governments within the United States (A) having a solid waste disposal facility (i)which is owned by the unit of local government, (ii) for which an order has been issued by the State to cease receiving solid waste for treatment, storage, or disposal, and (iii) which is subject to a State-approved end-use recreation plan, and (B) which are located over an aquifer which is the source of drinking water for any person or public water system which has serious environmental problems resulting from the disposal of such solid waste, including methane migration.

(2) There is authorized to be appropriated to the Administrator $2,500,000 for the fiscal year 1980 and $1,500,000 for each of the fiscal years 1981 and 1982 to make grants to be used for the containment and stabilization of solid waste located at the disposal sites referred to in paragraph (1). Not more than one community in any State shall be eligible for grants under this paragraph and not more than one project in any State shall be eligible for such grants. No unit of local government shall be eligible for grants under this paragraph with respect to any site which exceeds 65 acres in size.

[§4008(e) revised by PL 96–482]

(f) Assistance to States for Discretionary Program for Recycled Oil.—

(1) The Administrator may make grants to States, which have a State plan approved under section 4007, or which have submitted a

State plan for approval under such section, if such plan includes the discretionary provisions described in section 4003(b). Grants under this subsection shall be for purposes of assisting the State in carrying out such discretionary provisions. No grant under this subsection may be used for construction or for the acquisition of land or equipment.

(2) Grants under this subsection shall be allotted among the States in the same manner as provided in the first sentence of subsection (b).

(3) No grant may be made under this subsection unless an application therefor is submitted to, and approved by, the Administrator. The application shall be in such form, be submitted in such manner, and contain such information as the Administrator may require.

(4) For purposes of making grants under this subsection, there are authorized to be appropriated $5,000,000 for fiscal year 1982, $5,000,000 for fiscal year 1983, and $5,000,000 for each of the fiscal years 1985 through 1988.

[§4008(f) added by PL 96–463; (f)(4) amended by PL 98–616]

(g) Assistance to Municipalities for Energy and Materials Conservation and Recovery Planning Activities.—

(1) The Administrator is authorized to make grants to municipalities, regional authorities, and intermunicipal agencies to carry out activities described in subparagraphs (A) and (B) of section 4003(b)(1). Such grants may be made only pursuant to an application submitted to the Administrator by the municipality which application has been approved by the State and determined by the State to be consistent with any State plan approved or submitted under this subtitle or any other appropriate planning carried out by the State.

(2) There is authorized to be appropriated for the fiscal year beginning October 1, 1981, and for each fiscal year thereafter before October 1, 1986, $8,000,000 for purposes of making grants to municipalities under this subsection. No amount may be appropriated for such purposes for the fiscal year beginning on October 1, 1986, or for any fiscal year thereafter.

(3) Assistance provided by the Administrator under this subsection shall be used only for the purposes specified in paragraph (1). Such assistance may not be used for purposes of land acquisition, final facility design, equipment purchase, construction, startup or operation activities.

[Former §4008(f) added by PL 96–482; redesignated as (g) by PL 98–616]

§6949. Rural Communities Assistance [Sec. 4009]

(a) In General.—The Administrator shall make grants to States to provide assistance to municipalities with a population of five thousand or less, or counties with a population of ten thousand or less or less than twenty persons per square mile and not within a metropolitan area, for solid waste management facilities (including equipment) necessary to meet the requirements of section 4005 of this Act or restrictions on open burning or other requirements arising under the Clean Air Act or the Federal Water Pollution Control Act. Such assistance shall only be available—

(1) to any municipality or county which could not feasibly be included in a solid waste management system or facility serving an urbanized, multijurisdictional area because of its distance from such systems;

(2) where existing or planned solid waste management services or facilities are unavailable or insufficient to comply with the requirements of section 4005 of this Act; and

(3) for systems which are certified by the State to be consistent with any plans or programs established under any State or areawide planning process.

(b) Allotment.—The Administrator shall allot the sums appropriated to carry out this section in any fiscal year among the States in accordance with regulations promulgated by him on the basis of the average of the ratio which the population of rural areas of each State bears to the total population of rural reas of all the States, the ratio which the population of counties in each State having less than twenty persons per square mile bears to the total population of such counties in all the States, and the ratio which the population of such low-density counties in each State having 33 per centum or more of all families with incomes not in excess of 125 per centum of the poverty level bears to the total population of such counties in all the States.

(c) Limit.—The amount of any grant under this section shall not exceed 75 per centum of the costs of the project. No assistance under this section shall be available for the acquisition of land or interests in land.

(d) Appropriations.—There are authorized to be appropriated $25,000,000 for each of the fiscal years 1978 and 1979 to carry out this section. There are authorized to be appropriated

$10,000,000 for the fiscal year 1980 and $15,000,000 for each of the fiscal years 1981 and 1982 to carry out this section.

[§4009(d) amended by PL 96–482]

§6949a. Adequacy of Certain Guidelines and Criteria [Sec. 4010]

(a) Study.—The Administrator shall conduct a study of the extent to which the guidelines and criteria under this Act (other than guidelines and criteria for facilities to which subtitle C applies) which are applicable to solid waste management and disposal facilities, including, but not limited to landfills and surface impoundments, are adequate to protect human health and the environment from ground water contamination. Such study shall include a detailed assessment of the degree to which the criteria under section 1008(a) and the criteria under section 4004 regarding monitoring, prevention of contamination, and remedial action are adequate to protect ground water and shall also include recommendation with respect to any additional enforcement authorities which the Administrator, in consultation with the Attorney General, deems necessary for such purposes.

(b) Report.—Not later than thirty-six months after the date of enactment of the Hazardous and Solid Waste Amendments of 1984, the Administrator shall submit a report to the Congress setting forth the results of the study required under this section, together with any recommendations made by the Administrator on the basis of such study.

(c) Revisions of Guidelines and Criteria.—Not later than March 31, 1988, the Administrator shall promulgate revisions of the criteria promulgated under paragraph (1) of section 4004(a) and under section 1008(a)(3) for facilities that may receive hazardous household wastes or hazardous wastes from small quantity generators under section 3001(d). The criteria shall be those necessary to protect human health and the environment and may take into account the practicable capability of such facilities. At a minimum such revisions for facilities potentially receiving such wastes should require ground water monitoring as necessary to detect contamination, establish criteria for the acceptable location of new or existing facilities, and provide for corrective action as appropriate.

[§4010 added by PL 98–616]

SUBTITLE E—DUTIES OF THE SECRETARY OF COMMERCE IN RESOURCE AND RECOVERY

§6951. Functions [Sec. 5001]

The Secretary of Commerce shall encourage greater commercialization of proven resource recovery technology by providing—

(1) accurate specifications for recovered materials;

(2) stimulation of development of markets for recovered materials;

(3) promotion of proven technology; and

(4) a forum for the exchange of technical and economic data relating to resource recovery facilities.

§6952. Development of Specifications for Secondary Materials [Sec. 5002]

The Secretary of Commerce, acting through the National Bureau of Standards, and in conjunction with national standards-setting organizations in resource recovery, shall, after public hearings, and not later than two years after September 1, 1979, publish guidelines for the development of specifications for the classification of materials recovered from waste which were destined for disposal. The specifications shall pertain to the physical and chemical properties and characteristics of such materials with regard to their use in replacing virgin materials in various industrial, commercial, and governmental uses. In establishing such guidelines the Secretary shall also, to the extent feasible, provide such information as may be necessary to assist Federal agencies with procurement of items containing recovered materials. The Secretary shall continue to cooperate with national standards-setting organizations, as may be necessary, to encourage the publication, promulgation and updating of standards for recovered materials and for the use of recovered materials in various industrial, commercial, and governmental uses.

[§5002 amended by PL 96–482]

§6953. Development of Markets for Recovered Materials [Sec. 5003]

The Secretary of Commerce shall within two years after September 1, 1979, take such actions as may be necessary to—

(1) identify the geographical location of existing or potential markets for recovered materials;

(2) identify the economic and technical barriers to the use of recovered materials; and

(3) encourage the development of new uses for recovered materials.

[§5003 amended by PL 96–482]

§6954. Technology Promotion [Sec. 5004]

The Secretary of Commerce is authorized to evaluate the commercial feasibility of resource recovery facilities and to publish the results of such evaluation, and to develop a data base for purposes of assisting persons in choosing such a system.

§6955. Nondiscrimination Requirement [Sec. 5005]

In establishing any policies which may affect the development of new markets for recovered materials and in making any determination concerning whether or not to impose monitoring or other controls on any marketing or transfer of recovered materials, the Secretary of Commerce may consider whether to establish the same or similar policies or impose the same or similar monitoring or other controls on virgin materials.

[§5005 added by PL 96–482]

§6956. Authorization of Appropriations [Sec. 5006]

There are authorized to be appropriated to the Secretary of Commerce $5,000, 000 for each of fiscal years 1980, 1981 and 1982 and $1,500,000 for each of the fiscal years 1985 through 1988 to carry out the purposes of this subtitle.

[§5006 added by PL 96–482; amended by PL 98–616]

SUBTITLE F—FEDERAL RESPONSIBILITIES

§6961. Application of Federal, State, and Local Law to Federal Facilities [Sec. 6001]

(a) In General—Each department, agency, and instrumentality of the executive, legislative, and judicial branches of the Federal Government (1) having jurisdiction over any solid waste management facility or disposal site, or (2) engaged in any activity resulting, or which may result, in the disposal or management of solid waste or hazardous waste shall be subject to, and complying with, all Federal, State, interstate, and local requirements, both substantive and procedural (including any requirement for permits or reporting or any provisions for injunctive relief and such sanctions as may be imposed by a court to enforce such relief), respecting control and abatement of solid waste or hazardous waste disposal and management in the same manner, and to the same extent, as any person is subject to such requirements, including the payment of reasonable service charges. The Federal, State, interstate, and local substantive and procedural requirements referred to in this subsection include, but are not limited to, all administrative orders and all civil and administrative penalties and fines, regardless of whether such penalties or fines are punitive or coercive in nature or are imposed for isolated, intermittent, or continuing violations. The United States hereby expressly waives any immunity otherwise applicable to the United States with respect to any such substantive or procedural requirement (including, but not limited to, any injunctive relief, administrative order or civil or administrative penalty or fine referred to in the preceding sentence, or reasonable service charge). The reasonable service charges referred to in this subsection include, but are not limited to, fees or charges assessed in connection with the processing and issuance of permits, renewal of permits, amendments to permits, review of plans, studies, and other documents, and inspection and monitoring of facilities, as well as any other nondiscriminatory charges that are assessed in connection with a Federal, State, interstate, or local solid waste or hazardous waste regulatory program. Neither the United States, nor any agent, employee, or officer thereof, shall be immune or exempt from any process or sanction of any State or Federal Court with respect to the enforcement of any such injunctive relief. No agent, employee, or officer of the United States shall be personally liable for any civil penalty under any Federal, State, interstate, or local solid or hazardous waste law with respect to any act or omission within the scope of the official duties of the agent, employee, or officer. An agent, employee, or officer of the United States shall be subject to any criminal sanction (including, but not limited to, any fine or imprisonment) under any Federal or State solid or hazardous waste law, but no department, agency, or instrumentality of the executive, legislative, or judicial branch of the Federal Government shall be subject to any such sanction. The President may exempt any solid waste management facility of any department, agency, or instrumentality in the executive branch from compliance with such a requirement if he determines it to be in the paramount interest of the United States to do so. No such exemption shall be granted due to lack of appropriation unless the President shall have specifically requested such appropriation as a part of the budgetary process and the Congress shall have failed to make available such requested appropriation. Any exemption shall be for a period not in excess of one year, but additional exemptions may be granted for periods not to exceed one year upon the President's making a new determination. The President shall report each January to the Congress all exemptions from the requirements of this section granted during the preceding calendar year, together with his reason for granting each such exemption.

[§6001(a) designated and amended by PL 102–386]

(b) Administrative Enforcement Actions.—

(1) The Administrator may commence an administrative enforcement action against any department, agency, or instrumentality of the executive, legislative, or judicial branch of the Federal Government pursuant to the enforcement authorities contained in this Act. The Administrator shall initiate an administrative enforcement action against such a department, agency, or instrumentality in the same manner and under the same circumstances as an action would be initiated against another person. Any voluntary resolution or settlement of such an action shall be set forth in a consent order.

(2) No administrative order issued to such a department, agency, or instrumentality shall become final until such department, agency, or instrumentality has had the opportunity to confer with the Administrator.

[§6001(b) added by PL 102–386]

(c) Limitation on State Use of Funds Collected from Federal Government.—Unless a State law in effect on the date of the enactment of the Federal Facility Compliance Act of 1992 or a State constitution requires the funds to be used in a different manner, all funds collected by a State from the Federal Government from penalties and fines imposed for violation of any substantive or procedural requirement referred to in subsection (a) shall be used by the State only for projects designed to improve or protect the environment or to defray the costs of environmental protection or enforcement.

[§6001(c) added by PL 102–386]

[Editor's Note: Subsections (a) and (b) of §102 of PL 102–386 amended §6001 of this Act and those provisions have been incorporated therein. Subsection (c) of §102, did not amend this Act directly, but contained provisions applicable to the effective date of §6001. The text of the material follows.]

[Sec. 102]

(c) Effective Dates.—

(1) In general.—Except as otherwise provided in paragraphs (2) and (3), the amendments made by subsection (a) shall take effect upon the date of the enactment of this Act.

(2) Delayed effective date for certain mixed waste.—Until the date that is 3 years after the date of the enactment of this Act, the waiver of sovereign immunity contained in section 6001(a) of the Solid Waste Disposal Act with respect to civil, criminal, and administrative penalties and fines (as added by the amendments made by subsection (a)) shall not apply to departments, agencies, and instrumentalities of the executive branch of the Federal Government for violations of section 3004(j) of the Solid Waste Disposal Act involving storage of mixed waste that is not subject to an existing agreement, permit, or administrative or judicial order, so long as such waste is managed in compliance with all other applicable requirements.

(3) Effective date for certain mixed waste.—

(A) Except as provided in subparagraph (B), after the date that is 3 years after the date of the enactment of this Act, the waiver of sovereign immunity contained in section 6001(a) of the Solid Waste Disposal Act with respect to civil, criminal, and administrative penalties and fines (as added by the amendments made by subsection (a)) shall apply to departments, agencies, and instrumentalities of the executive branch of the Federal Government for violations of section 3004(j) of the Solid Waste Disposal Act involving storage of mixed waste.

(B) With respect to the Department of Energy, the waiver of sovereign immunity referred to in subparagraph (A) shall not apply after the date that is 3 years after the date of the enactment of this Act for violations of section 3004(j) of such Act involving storage of mixed waste, so long as the Department of Energy is in compliance with both—

(i) a plan that has been submitted and approved pursuant to section 3021(b) of the Solid Waste Disposal Act and which is in effect; and

(ii) an order requiring compliance with such plan which has been issued pursuant to such section 3021(b) and which is in effect.

(4) Application of waiver to agreements and orders.—The waiver of sovereign immunity contained in section 6001(a) of the Solid Waste Disposal Act (as added by the amendments made by subsection (a)) shall take effect on the date of the enactment of this Act with respect to any agreement, permit, or administrative or judicial order existing on such date of enactment (and any subsequent modifications to such an agreement, permit, or order), including, without limitation, any provision of an agreement, permit, or order that

addresses compliance with section 3004(j) of such Act with respect to mixed waste.

(5) Agreement or order.—Except as provided in paragraph (4), nothing in this Act shall be construed to alter, modify, or change in any manner any agreement, permit, or administrative or judicial order, including, without limitation, any provision of an agreement, permit, or order—

(i) that addresses compliance with section 3004(j) of the Solid Waste Disposal Act with respect to mixed waste;

(ii) that is in effect on the date of enactment of this Act; and

(iii) to which a department, agency, or instrumentality of the executive branch of the Federal Government is a party.

§6962. Federal Procurement [Sec. 6002]

(a) Application of section.—Except as provided in subsection (b), a procuring agency shall comply with the requirements set forth in this section and any regulations issued under this section, with respect to any purchase or acquisition of a procurement item where the purchase price of the item exceeds $10,000 or where the quantity of such items or of functionally equivalent items purchased or acquired in the course of the preceding fiscal year was $10,000 or more.

(b) Procurement Subject to Other Law.—Any procurement, by any procuring agency, which is subject to regulations of the Administrator under section 6004 (as promulgated before the date of enactment of this section under comparable provisions of prior law) shall not be subject to the requirements of this section to the extent that such requirements are inconsistent with such regulations.

(c) Requirements.—

(1) After the date specified in applicable guidelines prepared pursuant to subsection (e) of this section, each procuring agency which procures any items designated in such guidelines shall procure such items composed of the highest percentage of recovered materials practicable and in the case of paper, the highest percentage of the post consumer recovered materials referred to in subsection (h)(1) practicable) consistent with maintaining a satisfactory level of competition, considering such guidelines. The decision not to procure such items shall be based on a determination that such procurement items—

[§6002(c)(1) amended by PL 96–482; PL 98–616]

(A) are not reasonably available within a reasonable period of time;

(B) fail to meet the performance standards set forth in the applicable specifications or fail to meet the reasonable performance standards of the procuring agencies; or

(C) are only available at an unreasonable price. Any determination under subparagraph (B) shall be made on the basis of the guidelines of the Bureau of Standards in any case in which such material is covered by such guidelines.

(2) Agencies that generate heat, mechanical, or electrical energy from fossil fuel in systems that have the technical capability of using energy or fuels derived from solid waste as a primary or supplementary fuel shall use such capability to the maximum extent practicable.

(3) After the date specified in any applicable guidelines prepared pursuant to subsection (e) of this section contracting, officers shall require that vendors:

(A) certify that the percentage of recovered materials to be used in the performance of the contract will be at least the amount required by applicable specifications or other contractual requirements and

(B) estimate the percentage of the total material utilized for the performance of the contract which is recovered materials.

[§6002(c)(3) amended by PL 96–482]

(d) Specifications.—All Federal agencies that have the responsibility for drafting or reviewing specifications for procurement items procured by Federal agencies shall—

(1) as expeditiously as possible but in any event no later than eighteen months after the date of enactment of the Hazardous and Solid Waste Amendments of 1984, eliminate from such specifications—

[§6002(d)(1) amended by PL 98–616]

(A) any exclusion of recovered materials and

(B) any requirement that items be manufactured from virgin materials; and

(2) within one year after the date of publication of applicable guidelines under subsection (e), or as otherwise specified in such guidelines, assure that such specifications require the use of recovered materials to the maximum extent possible without jeopardizing the intended end use of the item.

[§6002(d) revised by PL 96–482]

(e) Guidelines.—The Administrator, after consultation with the Administrator of General Services, the Secretary of Commerce (acting through the Bureau of Standards), and the Public Printer, shall prepare, and from time to time revise, guidelines for the use of procuring agencies in complying with the requirements of this section. Such guidelines shall—

(1) designate those items which are or can be produced with recovered materials and whose procurement by procuring agencies will carry out the objectives of this section, and in the case of paper, provide for maximizing the use of post consumer recovered materials referred to in subsection (h)(1); and

(2) set forth recommended practices with respect to the procurement of recovered materials and items containing such materials and with respect to certification by vendors of the percentage of recovered materials used,

and shall provide information as to the availability, relative price, and performance of such materials and items and where appropriate shall recommend the level of recovered material to be contained in the procured product. The Administrator shall prepare final guidelines for paper within one hundred and eighty days after the enactment of the Hazardous and Solid Waste Amendments of 1984, and for three additional product categories (including tires) by October 1, 1985. In making the designation under paragraph (1), the Administrator shall consider, but is not limited in his considerations, to—

(A) the availability of such items;

(B) the impact of the procurement of such items by procuring agencies on the volume of solid waste which must be treated, stored or disposed of;

(C) the economic and technological feasibility of producing and using such items; and

(D) other uses for such recovered materials.

[§6002(e) revised by PL 96–482; amended by PL 98–616]

(f) Procurement of Services.—A procuring agency shall, to the maximum extent practicable, manage or arrange for the procurement of solid waste management services in a manner which maximizes energy and resource recovery.

(g) Executive Office. —The Office of Procurement Policy in the Executive Office of the President, in cooperation with the Administrator, shall implement the requirements of this section. It shall be the responsibility of the Office of Procurement Policy to coordinate this policy with other policies for Federal procurement, in such a way as to maximize the use of recovered resources, and to, every two years beginning in 1984, report to the Congress on actions taken by Federal agencies and the progress made in the implementation of this section, including agency compliance with subsection (d).

[§6002(g) amended by PL 97–375; PL 98–616]

(h) Definition. — As used in this section, in the case of paper products, the term "recovered materials" includes—

(1) postconsumer materials such as—

(A) paper, paperboard, and fibrous wastes from retail stores, office buildings, homes, and so forth, after they have passed through their end-usage as a consumer item, including: used corrugated boxes; old newspapers; old magazines; mixed waste paper; tabulating cards; and used cordage; and

(B) all paper, paperboard, and fibrous wastes that enter and are collected from municipal solid waste, and

(2) manufacturing, forest residues, and other wastes such as—

(A) dry paper and paperboard waste generated after completion of the papermaking process (that is, those manufacturing operations up to and including the cutting and trimming of the paper machine reel into smaller rolls or rough sheets) including: envelope cuttings, bindery trimmings, and other paper and paperboard waste, resulting from printing, cutting, forming and other converting operations; bag, box, and carton manufacturing wastes; and butt rolls, mill wrappers, and rejected unused stock; and

(B) finished paper and paperboard from obsolete inventories of paper and paperboard manufacturers, merchants, wholesalers, dealers, printers, converters, or others;

(C) fibrous byproducts of harvesting, manufacturing, extractive, or wood-cutting processes, flax, straw, linters, bagasse, slash, and other forest residues;

(D) wastes generated by the conversion of goods made from fibrous material (that is, waste rope from cordage manufacture, textile mill waste, and cuttings); and

(E) fibers recovered from waste water which otherwise would enter the waste stream.

[§6002(h) added by PL 98–616]

(i) Procurement Program. —

(1) Within one year after the date of publication of applicable guidelines under subsection (e), each procuring agency shall develop an

affirmative procurement program which will assure that items composed of recovered materials will be purchased to the maximum extent practicable and which is consistent with applicable provisions of Federal procurement law.

(2) Each affirmative procurement program required under this subsection shall, at a minimum, contain—

(A) a recovered materials preference program;

(B) an agency promotion program to promote the preference program adopted under subparagraph (A);

(C) a program for requiring estimates of the total percentage of recovered material utilized in the performance of a contract; certification of minimum recovered material content actually utilized, where appropriate; and reasonable verification procedures for estimates and certifications; and

(D) annual review and monitoring of the effectiveness of an agency's affirmative procurement program.

In the case of paper, the recovered materials preference program required under subparagraph (A) shall provide for the maximum use of the post consumer recovered materials referred to in subsection (h)(1).

(3) In developing the preference program, the following options shall be considered for adoption:

(A) Case-by-Case Policy Development: Subject to the limitations of subsection (c)(1) (A) through (C), a policy of awarding contracts to the vendor offering an item composed of the highest percentage of recovered materials practicable (and in the case of paper, the highest percentage of the post consumer recovered materials referred to in subsection (h)(1)). Subject to such limitations, agencies may make an award to a vendor offering items with less than the maximum recovered materials content.

(B) Minimum Content Standards: Minimum recovered materials content specifications which are set in such a way as to assure that the recovered materials content (and in the case of paper, the content of post consumer materials referred to in subsection (h)(1)) required is the maximum available without jeopardizing the intended end use of the item, or violating the limitations of subsection (c)(1) (A) through (C).

Procuring agencies shall adopt one of the options set forth in subparagraphs (A) and (B) or a substantially equivalent alternative, for inclusion in the affirmative procurement program.

[§6002(i) added by PL 98–616]

[Editor's Note: §603 of PL 102–393 added the following provision pertaining to recycled toner cartridges.]

§6962j. Preference for recycled toner cartridges [Sec. 603]

(a) Notwithstanding any other provision of law, a Federal agency in conducting a procurement for toner cartridges for use in laser printers, photocopiers or microphotographic printers shall purchase recycled cartridges, unless the contracting or purchasing officer determines in writing that—

(1) adequate market research establishes that recycled cartridges for the type of equipment used by the agency do not exist,

(2) the price or life cycle cost offered for the recycled cartridge is higher than the original equipment manufacturer's new cartridge, or

(3) recycled cartridges are not available in quantities needed within the timeframes required.

(b) Nothing in this section shall prohibit the purchase of one newly manufactured cartridge (or a number equal to those normally supplied at the time of initial purchase) as part of an initial printer or copier acquisition.

(c) For purposes of this section, "recycled cartridge" means a laser printer, photocopier, or microphotographic toner cartridge which has been remanufactured in the United States by a small-business concern which has been certified by an independent laboratory to meet generally accepted industry standards. In the absence of an independent laboratory certification, a contracting officer may in his discretion rely on the agency's past experience with the offered recycled cartridge as evidence that the offered product meets generally accepted industry standards.

(d) For purposes of this section, "small-business concern" has the meaning given such term in the Small Business Act (15 U.S.C. 632(a)).

(e) For purposes of this section, "independent laboratory" means an independently owned engineering and product testing firm, whose primary business activity is not limited to the testing and certification of recycled cartridges.

§6963. Cooperation With the Environmental Protection Agency [Sec. 6003]

(a) General Rule.—All Federal agencies shall assist the Administrator in carrying out his functions under this Act and shall promptly make available all requested information concerning past or present Agency waste management practices and past or present Agency owned, leased, or operated solid or hazardous waste facilities. This information shall be provided in such format as may be determined by the Administrator.

(b) Information Relating to Energy and Materials Conservation and Recovery. — The Administrator shall collect, maintain, and disseminate information concerning the market potential of energy and materials recovered from solid waste, including materials obtained through source separation, and information concerning the savings potential of conserving resources contributing to the waste stream. The Administrator shall identify the regions in which the increased substitution of such energy for energy derived from fossil fuels and other sources is most likely to be feasible, and provide information on the technical and economic aspects of developing integrated resource conservation or recovery systems which provide for the recovery of source-separated materials to be recycled or the conservation of resources. The Administrator shall utilize the authorities of subsection (a) in carrying out this subsection.

[§6003 revised by PL 96–482]

§6964. Applicability of Solid Waste Disposal Guidelines to Executive Agencies [Sec. 6004]

(a) Compliance.—

(1) If—

(A) an Executive agency (as defined in section 105 of title 5, United States Code or any unit of the legislative branch of the Federal Government has jurisdiction over any real property or facility the operation or administration of which involves such agency in solid waste management activities, or

[§6004(a)(1)(A) amended by PL 96–482]

(B) such an agency enters into a contract with any person for the operation by such person of any Federal property or facility, and the performance of such contract involves such person in solid waste management activities. then such agency shall insure compliance with the guidelines recommended under section 1008 and the purposes of this Act in operation or administration of such property or facility, or the performance of such contract, as the case may be.

(2) Each Executive agency or any unit of the legislative branch of the Federal Government which conducts any activity—

[§6004(a)(2) amended by PL 96–482]

(A) which generates solid waste, and

(B) which, if conducted by a person other than such agency, would require a permit or license from such agency in order to dispose of such solid waste, shall insure compliance with such guidelines and the purposes of this Act in conducting such activity.

(3) Each Executive agency which permits the use of Federal property for purposes of disposal of solid waste shall insure compliance with such guidelines and the purposes of this Act in the disposal of such waste.

(4) The President or the Committee on House Administration of the House of Representatives and the Committee on Rules and Administration of the Senate with regard to any unit of the legislative branch of the Federal Government shall prescribe regulations to carry out this subsection.

[§6004(a)(4) amended by PL 96–482]

(b) Licenses and Permits. — Each Executive agency which issues any license or permit for disposal of solid waste shall, prior to the issuance of such license or permit, consult with the Administrator to insure compliance with guidelines recommended under section 1008 and the purposes of this Act.

SUBTITLE G—MISCELLANEOUS PROVISIONS

§6971. Employee Protection [Sec. 7001]

(a) General.—No person shall fire, or in any other way discriminate against, or cause to be fired or discriminated against, any employee or any authorized representative of employees by reason of the fact that such employee or representative has filed, instituted, or caused to be filed or instituted any proceeding under this Act or under any applicable implementation plan, or has testified or is about to testify in any proceeding resulting from the administration or enforcement of the provisions of this Act or of any applicable implementation plan.

(b) Remedy.—Any employee or a representative of employees who believes that he has been fired or otherwise discriminated against by any person in violation of subsection (a) of this section may, within thirty days after such alleged violation occurs, apply to the Secretary of Labor for a review of such firing or alleged discrimination. A copy of the application shall be sent to such person who shall be the respondent. Upon receipt of such application, the Secretary of Labor shall cause such investigation to be made as he deems appropriate. Such investigation shall provide an opportunity for a public hearing at the request of any party to such review to enable the parties to present information relating to such alleged violation. The parties shall be given written notice of the time and place of the hearing at least five days prior to the hearing. Any such hearing shall be of record and shall be subject to section 554 of title 5 of the United States Code. Upon receiving the report of such investigation, the Secretary of Labor shall make findings of fact. If he finds that such violation did occur, he shall issue a decision, incorporating an order therein and his findings, requiring the party committing such violation to take such affirmative action to abate the violation as the Secretary of Labor deems appropriate, including, but not limited to, the rehiring or reinstatement of the employee or representative of employees to his former position with compensation. If he finds that there was no such violation, he shall issue an order denying the application. Such order issued by the Secretary of Labor under this subparagraph shall be subject to judicial review in the same manner as orders and decisions of the Administrator subject to judicial review under this Act.

(c) Costs.—Whenever an order is issued under this section to abate such violation, at the request of the applicant, a sum equal to the aggregate amount of all costs and expenses (including the attorney's fees) as determined by the Secretary of Labor, to have been reasonably incurred by the applicant for, or in connection with, the institution and prosecution of such proceedings, shall be assessed against the person committing such violation.

(d) Exception.—This section shall have no application to any employee who, acting without direction from his employer (or his agent) deliberately violates any requirement of this Act.

(e) Employment Shifts and Loss.—The Administrator shall conduct continuing evaluations of potential loss or shifts of employment which may result from the administration or enforcement of the provisions of this Act and applicable implementation plans, including, where appropriate, investigating threatened plant closures or reductions in employment allegedly resulting from such administration or enforcement. Any employee who is discharged, or laid off, threatened with discharge or layoff, or otherwise discriminated against by any person because of the alleged results of such administration or enforcement, or any representative of such employee, may request the Administrator to conduct a full investigation of the matter. The Administrator shall thereupon investigate the matter and, at the request of any party, shall hold public hearings on not less than five days' notice, and shall at such hearings require the parties, including the employer involved, to present information relating to the actual or potential effect of such administration or enforcement on employment and on any alleged discharge, layoff, or other discrimination and the detailed reasons or justification therefor. Any such hearing shall be of record and shall be subject to section 554 of title 5 of the United States Code. Upon receiving the report of such investigation, the Administrator shall make findings of fact as to the effect of such administration or enforcement on employment and on the alleged discharge, layoff, or discrimination and shall make such recommendations as he deems appropriate. Such report, findings, and recommendations shall be available to the public. Nothing in this subsection shall be construed to require or authorize the Administrator or any State to modify or withdraw any standard, limitation, or any other requirement of this Act or any applicable implementation plan.

(f) Occupational Safety and Health.—In order to assist the Secretary of Labor and the Director of the National Institute for Occupational Safety and Health in carrying out their duties under the Occupational Safety and Health Act of 1970, the Administrator shall—

(1) provide the following information, as such information becomes available, to the Secretary and the Director:

(A) the identity of any hazardous waste generation, treatment, storage, disposal facility or site where cleanup is planned or underway;

(B) information identifying the hazards to which persons working at a hazardous waste generation, treatment, storage, disposal facility or site or otherwise handling hazardous waste may be exposed, the nature and extent of the exposure, and methods to protect workers from such hazards; and

(C) incidents of worker injury or harm at a hazardous waste generation, treatment, storage or disposal facility or site; and

(2) notify the Secretary and the Director of the Administrator's receipt of notifications under section 3010 or reports under sections 3002, 3003, and 3004 of this title and make such notifications and reports available to the Secretary and the Director.

[§7001(f) added by PL 96–482]

§6972. Citizen Suits [Sec. 7002]

(a) In General.—Except as provided in subsection (b) or (c) of this section, any person may commence a civil action on his own behalf—

(1) (A) against any person (including (a) the United States, and (b) any other governmental instrumentality or agency, to the extent permitted by the eleventh amendment to the Constitution) who is alleged to be in violation of any permit, standard, regulation, condition, requirement, prohibition, or order which has become effective pursuant to this Act; or

(B) against any person, including the United States and any other governmental instrumentality or agency, to the extent permitted by the eleventh amendment to the Constitution, and including any past or present generator, past or present transporter, or past or present owner or operator of a treatment, storage, or disposal facility, who has contributed or who is contributing to the past or present handling, storage, treatment, transportation, or disposal of any solid or hazardous waste which may present an imminent and substantial endangerment to health or the environment; or

(2) against the Administrator where there is alleged a failure of the Administrator to perform any act or duty under this Act which is not discretionary with the Administrator.

Any action under paragraph (a)(1) of this subsection shall be brought in the district court for the district in which the alleged violation occurred or the alleged endangerment may occur. Any action brought under paragraph (a)(2) of this subsection may be brought in the district court for the district in which the alleged violation occurred or in the District Court of the District of Columbia. The district court shall have jurisdiction, without regard to the amount in controversy or the citizenship of the parties, to enforce the permit, standard, regulation, condition, requirement, prohibition, or order, referred to in paragraph (1)(A), to restrain any person who has contributed or who is contributing to the past or present handling, storage, treatment, transportation, or disposal of any solid or hazardous waste referred to in paragraph (1)(B), to order such person to take such other action as may be necessary, or both, or to order the Administrator to perform the act or duty referred to in paragraph (2), as the case may be, and to apply any appropriate civil penalties under section 3008(a) and (g).

[§7002(a) amended by PL 98–616]

(b) Actions Prohibited.—

(1) No action may be commenced under subsection (a)(1)(A) of this section—

(A) prior to 60 days after the plaintiff has given notice of the violation to—

(i) the Administrator;

(ii) the State in which the alleged violation occurs; and

(iii) to any alleged violator of such permit, standard, regulation, condition, requirement, prohibition, or order, except that such action may be brought immediately after such notification in the case of an action under this section respecting a violation of subtitle C of this Act; or

(B) if the Administrator or State has commenced and is diligently prosecuting a civil or criminal action in a court of the United States or a State to require compliance with such permit, standard, regulation, condition, requirement, prohibition, or order.

In any action under subsection (a)(1)(A) in a court of the United States, any person may intervene as a matter of right.

(2) (A) No action may be commenced under subsection (a)(1)(B) of this section prior to ninety days after the plaintiff has given notice of the endangerment to—

(i) the Administrator;

(ii) the State in which the alleged endangerment may occur;

(iii) any person alleged to have contributed or to be contributing to the past or present handling, storage, treatment, transportation, or disposal of any solid or hazardous waste referred to in subsection (a)(1)(B),

except that such action may be brought immediately after such notification in the case of an action under this section respecting a violation of subtitle C of this Act.

(B) No action may be commenced under subsection (a)(1)(B) of this section if the Administrator, in order to restrain or abate acts or conditions which may have contributed or are contributing to the activities which may present the alleged endangerment—

(i) has commenced and is diligently prosecuting an action under section 7003 of this Act or under section 106 of the Comprehensive Environmental Response, Compensation and Liability Act of 1980,

(ii) is actually engaging in a removal action under section 104 of the Comprehensive Environmental Response, Compensation and Liability Act of 1980;

(iii) has incurred costs to initiate a Remedial Investigation and Feasibility Study under section 104 of the Comprehensive Environmental Response, Compensation and Liability Act of 1980 and is diligently proceeding with a remedial action under that Act; or

(iv) has obtained a court order (including a consent decree) or issued an administrative order under section 106 of the Comprehensive Environmental Response, Compensation and Liability Act of 1980 or section 70031 of this Act pursuant to which a responsible party is diligently conducting a removal action, Remedial Investigation and Feasibility Study (RIFS), or proceeding with a remedial action.

In the case of an administrative order referred to in clause (iv), actions under subsection (a)(1)(B) are prohibited only as to the scope and duration of the administrative order referred to in clause (iv).

(C) No action may be commenced under subsection (a)(1)(B) of this section if the State, in order to restrain or abate acts or conditions which may have contributed or are contributing to the activities which may present the alleged endangerment—

(i) has commenced and is diligently prosecuting an action under subsection (a)(1)(B);

(ii) is actually engaging in a removal action under section 104 of the Comprehensive Environmental Response, Compensation and Liability Act of 1980; or

(iii) has incurred costs to initiate a Remedial Investigation and Feasibility Study under section 104 of the Comprehensive Environmental Response, Compensation and Liability Act of 1980 and is diligently proceeding with a remedial action under that Act.

(D) No action may be commenced under subsection (a)(1)(B) by any person (other than a State or local government) with respect to the siting of a hazardous waste treatment, storage, or a disposal facility, nor to restrain or enjoin the issuance of a permit for such facility.

(E) In any action under subsection (a)(1)(B) in a court of the United States, any person may intervene as a matter of right when the applicant claims an interest relating to the subject of the action and he is so situated that the disposition of the action may, as a practical matter, impair or impede his ability to protect that interest, unless the Administrator or the State shows that the applicant's interest is adequately represented by existing parties.

(F) Whenever any action is brought under subsection (a)(1)(B) in a court of the United States, the plaintiff shall serve a copy of the complaint on the Attorney General of the United States and with the Administrator.

[§7002(b) revised by PL 98–616]

(c) Notice.—No action may be commenced under paragraph (a)(2) of this section prior to sixty days after the plaintiff has given notice to the Administrator that he will commence such action, except that such action may be brought immediately after such notification in the case of an action under this section respecting a violation of subtitle C of this Act. Notice under this subsection shall be given in such manner as the Administrator shall prescribe by regulation. Any action respecting a violation under this Act may be brought under this section only in the judicial district in which such alleged violation occurs.

[§7002(c) amended by PL 98–616]

(d) Intervention.—In any action under this section the Administrator, if not a party, may intervene as a matter of right.

(e) Costs.—The court, in issuing any final order in any action brought pursuant to this section, or section 7006 may award costs of litigation (including reasonable attorney and expert witness fees) to the prevailing or substantially prevailing party, whenever the court determines such an award is appropriate. The court may, if a temporary restraining order or preliminary injunction is sought, require the filing of a bond or equivalent security in accordance with the Federal Rules of Civil Procedure.

(f) Other Rights Preserved.—Nothing in this section shall restrict any right which any person (or class of persons) may have under any statute or common law to seek enforcement of any standard or requirement relating to the management of solid waste hazardous waste, or to seek any other relief (including relief against the Administrator or a State agency).

(g) Transporters.—A transporter shall not be deemed to have contributed or to be contributing to the handling, storage, treatment, or disposal, referred to in subsection (a)(1)(B) taking place after such solid waste or hazardous waste has left the possession or control of such transporter, if the transportation of such waste was under a sole contractual arrangement arising from a published tariff and acceptance for carriage by common carrier by rail and such transporter has exercised due care in the past or present handling, storage, treatment, transportation and disposal of such waste.

[§7002(g) added by PL 98–616]

§6973. Imminent Hazard [Sec. 7003]

(a) Authority of Administrator.—Notwithstanding any other provision of this Act, upon receipt of evidence that the past or present handling, storage, treatment, transportation or disposal of any solid waste or hazardous waste may present an imminent and substantial endangerment to health or the environment, the Administrator may bring suit on behalf of the United States in the appropriate district court against any person (including any past or present generator, past or present transporter, or past or present owner or operator of a treatment, storage or disposal facility) who has contributed or who is contributing to such handling, storage, treatment, transportation or disposal to restrain such person from such handling, storage, treatment, transportation, or disposal, to order such person to take such other action as may be necessary, or both. A transporter shall not be deemed to have contributed or to be contributing to such handling, storage, treatment, or disposal taking place after such solid waste or hazardous waste has left the possession or control of such transporter if the transportation of such waste was under a sole contractural arrangement arising from a published tariff and acceptance for carriage by common carrier by rail and such transporter has exercised due care in the past or present handling, storage, treatment, transportation and disposal of such waste. The Administrator shall provide notice to the affected State of any such suit. The Administrator may also, after notice to the affected State, take other action under this section including, but not limited to, issuing such orders as may be necessary to protect public health and the environment.

[§7003(a) designated and amended by PL 96–482; amended by PL 98–616]

(b) Violations.—Any person who willfully violates, or fails or refuses to comply with, any order of the Administrator under subsection (a) may, in an action brought in the appropriate United States district court to enforce such order, be fined not more than $5,000 for each day in which such violation occurs or such failure to comply continues.

[§7003(b) added by PL 96–482]

(c) Immediate Notice.—Upon receipt of information that there is hazardous waste at any site which has presented an imminent and substantial endangerment to human health or the environment, the Administrator shall provide immediate notice to the appropriate local government agencies. In addition, the Administrator shall require notice of such endangerment to be promptly posted at the site where the waste is located.

[§7003(c) added by PL 98–616]

(d) Public Participation in Settlements.—Whenever the United States or the Administrator proposes to covenant not to sue or to forbear from suit or to settle any claim arising under this section, notice, and opportunity for a public meeting in the affected area, and a reasonable opportunity to comment on the proposed settlement prior to its final entry shall be afforded to the public. The decision of the United States or the Administrator to enter into or not to enter into such Consent Decree, covenant or agreement shall not constitute a final agency action subject to judicial review under this Act or the Administrative Procedure Act.

[§7003(d) added by PL 98–616]

§6974. Petition for Regulations; Public Participation [Sec. 7004]

(a) Petition.—Any person may petition the Administrator for the promulgation, amendment, or repeal of any regulation under this Act. Within a reasonable time following receipt of such petition, the Administrator shall take action with respect to such petition and shall publish notice of such action in the Federal Register together with the reasons therefor.

(b) (1) Public Participation.—Public participation in the development, revision, implementation, and enforcement of any regulation, guideline, information, or program under this Act shall be provided for, encouraged, and assisted by the Administrator and the States. The Administrator, in cooperation with the States, shall develop and publish minimum guidelines for public participation in such processes.

[§7004(b)(1) designated by PL 96–482]

(2) Before the issuing of a permit to any person with any respect to any facility for the treatment, storage, or disposal of hazardous wastes under section 3005, the administrator shall—

(A) cause to be published in major local newspapers of general circulation and broadcast over local radio stations notice of the agency's intention to issue such permit, and

(B) transmit in writing notice of the agency's intention to issue such permit to each unit of local government having jurisdiction over the area in which such facility if proposed to be located and to each State agency having any authority under State law with respect to the construction or operation of such facility.

If within 45 days the Administrator receives written notice of opposition to the agency's intention to issue such permit and a request for a hearing, or if the Administrator determines on his own initiative, he shall hold an informal public hearing (including an opportunity for presentation of written and oral views) on whether he should issue a permit for the proposed facility. Whenever possible the Administrator shall schedule such hearing at a location convenient to the nearest population center to such proposed facility and give notice in the aforementioned manner of the date, time, and subject matter of such hearing. No State program which provides for the issuance of permits referred to in this paragraph may be authorized by the Administrator under section 3006 unless such program provides for the notice and hearing required by the paragraph.

[§7004(b)(2) added by PL 96–482]

§6975. Separability [Sec. 7005]

If any provision of this Act, or the application of any provision of this Act to any person or circumstance, is held invalid, the application of such provision to other persons or circumstances, and the remainder of this Act, shall not be affected thereby.

§6976. Judicial Review [Sec. 7006]

(a) Review of Final Regulations and Certain Petitions—Any judicial review of final regulations promulgated pursuant to this Act and the Administrator's denial of any petition for the promulgation, amendment, or repeal of any regulation under this Act shall be in accordance with sections 701 through 706 of title 5 of the United States Code, except that—

(1) a petition for review of action of the Administrator in promulgating any regulation, or requirement under this Act or denying any petition for the promulgation, amendment or repeal of any regulation under this Act may be filed only in the United States Court of Appeals for the District of Columbia, and such petition shall be filed with ninety days from the date of such promulgation or denial or after such date if such petition for review is based solely on grounds arising after such ninetieth day; action of the Administrator with respect to which review could have been obtained under this subsection shall not be subject to judicial review in civil or criminal proceedings for enforcement; and

[§7006(a) designated and (a)(1) amended by PL 96–482]

(2) in any judicial proceeding brought under this section in which review is sought of a determination under this Act required to be made on the record after notice and opportunity for hearing, if a party seeking review under this Act applies to the court for leave to adduce additional evidence, and shows to the satisfaction of the court that the information is material and that there were reasonable grounds for the failure to adduce such evidence in the proceeding before the Administrator, the court may order such additional evidence (and evidence in rebuttal thereof to be taken before the Administrator, and to be adduced upon the hearing in such manner and upon such terms and conditions as the court may deem proper; the Administrator may modify his findings as to the facts, or make new findings, by reason of the additional evidence so taken, and he shall file with the court such modified or new findings and his recommendation, if any for the modification or setting aside of his original order, with the return of such additional evidence.

[§7006(a)(2) amended by PL 96–482]

(b) Review of Certain Actions Under sections 3005 and 3006. —Review of the Administrator's action (1) in issuing, denying, modifying or revoking any permit under section 3005, or (2) in granting, denying, or withdrawing authorization or interim authorization under section 3006, may be had by any interested person in the Circuit Court of Appeals of the United States for the Federal judicial district in which such person resides or transacts such business upon application by such person. Any such application shall be made within ninety days from the date of such issuance, denial, modification, revocation, grant, or withdrawal, or after such date only if such application is based solely on grounds which arose after such ninetieth day. Action of the Administrator with respect to which review could have been obtained under this subsection shall not be subject to judicial review in civil or criminal proceedings for enforcement. Such review shall be in accordance with sections 701 through 706 of title 5 of the United States Code.

[§7006(b) added by PL 96–482; amended by PL 98–616]

§6977. Grants or Contracts for Training Projects [Sec. 7007]

(a) General Authority.—The Administrator is authorized to make grants to, and contracts with any eligible organization. For purposes of this section the term "eligible organization" means a State or interstate agency, a municipality, educational institution, and any other organization which is capable of effectively carrying out a project which may be funded by grant under subsection (b) of this section.

(b) Purposes.—

(1) Subject to the provisions of paragraph (2), grants or contracts may be made to pay all or a part of the costs, as may be determined by the Administrator, of any project operated or to be operated by an eligible organization, which is designed—

(A) to develop, expand, or carry out a program (which may combine training, education, and employment) for training persons for occupations involving the management, supervision, design, operation, or maintenance of solid waste management and resource recovery equipment and facilities; or

(B) to train instructors and supervisory personnel to train or supervise persons in occupations involving the design, operation, and maintenance of solid waste management and resource recovery equipment and facilities.

(2) A grant or contract authorized by paragraph (1) of this subsection may be made only upon application to the Administrator at such time or times and containing such information as he may prescribe, except that no such application shall be approved unless it provides for the same procedures and reports (and access to such reports and to other records) as required by section 207(b)(4) and (5) (as in effect before the date of the enactment of Resource Conservation and Recovery Act of 1976) with respect to applications made under such section (as in effect before the date of the enactment of Resource Conservation and Recovery Act of 1976).

(c) Study.—The Administrator shall make a complete investigation and study to determine—

(1) the need for additional trained State and local personnel to carry out plans assisted under this Act and other solid waste and resource recovery programs;

(2) means of using existing training programs to train such personnel; and

(3) the extent and nature of obstacles to employment and occupational advancement in the solid waste management and resource recovery field which may limit either available manpower or the advancement of personnel in such field. He shall report the results of such investigation and study, including his recommendations to the President and the Congress.

§6978. Payments [Sec. 7008]

(a) General Rule.—Payments of grants under this Act may be made (after necessary adjustment on account of previously made underpayments or overpayments) in advance or by way of reimbursement, and in such installments and on such conditions as the Administrator may determine.

(b) Prohibition.—No grant may be made under this Act to any private profitmaking organization.

§6979. Labor Standards [Sec. 7009]

No grant for a project of construction under this Act shall be made unless the Administrator finds that the application contains or is supported by reasonable assurance that all laborers and mechanics employed by contractors or subcontractors on projects of the type covered by the Davis-Bacon Act, as amended (40 U.S.C. 276a–276a–5), will be paid wages at rates not less than those prevailing on similar work in the locality as determined by the Secretary of Labor in accordance with that Act; and the Secretary of Labor shall have with respect to the labor standards specified in this section the authority and functions set forth in Reorganization Plan Numbered 14 of 1950 (15 F.R. 3176; 5 U.S.C. 133z–5) and section 2 of the Act of June 13, 1934, as amended (40 U.S.C. 276c).

[§7009 amended by PL 96–482]

§6979b. Law Enforcement Authority [Sec. 7010]

The Attorney General of the United States shall, at the request of the Administrator and on the basis of a showing of need, deputize qualified employees of the Environmental Protection Agency to serve as special deputy United States marshals in criminal investigations with respect to violations of the criminal provisions of this Act.

[Former §7012 added by PL 98–616; redesignated as §7010 by PL 99–339]

SUBTITLE H—RESEARCH, DEVELOPMENT, DEMONSTRATION, AND INFORMATION

§6981. Research, Demonstrations, Training, and Other Activities [Sec. 8001]

(a) General Authority.—The Administrator, alone or after consultation with the Administrator of the Federal Energy Administration, the Administrator of the Energy Research and Development Administration, or the Chairman of the Federal Power Commission, shall conduct, and encourage, cooperate with, and render financial and other assistance to appropriate public (whether Federal, State, interstate, or local) authorities, agencies, and institutions, private agencies and institutions, and individuals in the conduct of, and promote the coordination of, research, investigations, experiments, training, demonstrations, surveys, public education programs, and studies relating to—

(1) any adverse health and welfare effects of the release into the environment of material present in solid waste, and methods to eliminate such effects;

(2) the operation and financing of solid waste management programs;

(3) the planning, implementation, and operation of resource recovery and resource conservation systems and hazardous waste management systems, including the marketing of recovered resources;

(4) the production of usable forms of recovered resources, including fuel, from solid waste;

(5) the reduction of the amount of such waste and unsalvageable waste materials;

(6) the development and application of new and improved methods of collecting and disposing of solid waste and processing and recovering materials and energy from solid wastes;

(7) the identification of solid waste components and potential materials and energy recoverable from such waste components;

(8) small scale and low technology solid waste management systems, including but limited to, resource recovery source separation systems;

(9) methods to improve the performance characteristics of resources recovered from solid waste and the relationship of such performance characteristics to available and potentially available markets for such resources;

(10) improvements in land disposal practices for solid waste (including sludge) which may reduce the adverse environmental effects of such disposal and other aspects of solid waste disposal on land, including means for reducing the harmful environmental effects of earlier and existing landfills, means for restoring areas damaged by such earlier or existing landfills, means for rendering landfills safe for purposes of construction and other uses, and techniques of recovering materials and energy from landfills;

(11) methods for the sound disposal of, or recovery of resources, including energy, from, sludge (including sludge from pollution control and treatment facilities, coal slurry pipelines, and other sources);

(12) methods of hazardous waste management, including methods of rendering such waste environmentally safe; and

(13) any adverse effects on air quality (particularly with regard to the emission of heavy metals) which result from solid waste which is burned (either alone or in conjunction with other substances) for purposes of treatment, disposal or energy recovery.

(b) Management Program.—

(1) (A) In carrying out his functions pursuant to this Act and any other Federal legislation respecting solid waste or discarded material research, development, and demonstrations, the Administrator shall establish a management program or system to insure the coordination of all such activities and to facilitate and accelerate the process of development of sound new technology (or other discoveries) from the research phase, through development, and into the demonstration phase.

(B) The Administrator shall (i) assist, on the basis of any research projects which are developed with assistance under this Act or without Federal assistance, the construction of pilot plant facilities for the purpose of investigating or testing the technological feasibility of any promising new fuel, energy, or resource recovery or resource conservation method or technology; and (ii) demonstrate each such method and technology that appears justified by an evaluation at such pilot plant stage or at a pilot plant stage developed without Federal assistance. Each such demonstration shall incorporate new or innovative technical advances or shall apply such advances to different circumstances and conditions, for the purpose of evaluating design concepts or to test the performance, efficiency, and economic feasibility of a particular method or technology under actual operating conditions. Each such demonstration shall be so planned and designed that, if successful, it can be expanded or utilized directly as a full-scale operational fuel, energy, or resource recovery or resource conservation facility.

(2) Any energy-related research, development, or demonstration project for the conversion including bio-conversion, of solid waste carried out by the Environmental Protection Agency or by the Energy Research and Development Administration pursuant to this or any other Act shall be administered in accordance with the May 7, 1976, Interagency Agreement between the Environmental Protection Agency and the Energy Research and Development Administration on the Development of Energy from Solid Wastes and specifically, that in accordance with this agreement, (A) for those energy-related projects of mutual interest, planning will be conducted jointly by the Environmental Protection Agency and the Energy Research and Development Administration, following which project responsibility will be assigned to one agency; (B) energy-related portions of projects for recovery of synthetic fuels or other forms of energy from solid waste shall be the responsibility of the Energy Research and Development Administration; (C) the Environmental Protection Agency shall retain responsibility for the environmental, economic, and institutional aspects of solid waste projects and for assurance that such projects are consistent with any applicable suggested guidelines published pursuant to section 1008, and any applicable State or regional solid waste management plan; and (D) any activities undertaken under provisions of sections 8002 and 8003 as related to energy; as related to energy or synthetic fuels recovery from waste; or as related to energy conservation shall be accomplished through coordination and consultation with the Energy Research and Development Administration.

(c) Authorities.—

(1) In carrying out subsection (a) of this section respecting solid waste research, studies, development, and demonstration, except as otherwise specifically provided in section 8004(d), the Administrator may make grants to or enter into contracts (including contracts for construction) with, public agencies and authorities or private persons.

(2) Contracts for research, development, or demonstrations or for both (including contracts for construction) shall be made in accordance with and subject to the limitations provided with respect to research contracts of the military departments in title 10, United States Code, section 2353, except that the determination, approval, and certification required thereby shall be made by the Administrator.

(3) Any invention made or conceived in the course of, or under, any contract under this Act shall be subject to section 9 of the Federal Nonnuclear Energy Research and Development Act of 1974 to the same extent and in the same manner as inventions made or conceived in the course of contracts under such Act, except that in applying such section, the Environmental Protection Agency shall be substituted for the Energy Research and Development Administration and the words "solid waste" shall be substituted for the word "energy" where appropriate.

(4) For carrying out the purpose of this Act the Administrator may detail personnel of the Environmental Protection Agency to agencies eligible for assistance under this section.

§6982. Special Studies; Plans for Research, Development, and Demonstrations [Sec. 8002]

(a) Glass and Plastic. — The Administrator shall undertake a study and publish a report on resource recovery from glass and plastic waste, including a scientific, technological, and economic investigation of potential solutions to implement such recovery.

(b) Composition of Waste Stream. — The Administrator shall undertake a systematic study of the composition of the solid waste stream and of anticipated future changes in the composition of such stream and shall publish a report containing the results of such study and quantitatively evaluating the potential utility of such components.

(c) Priorities Study.—For purposes of determining priorities for research on recovery of materials and energy from solid waste and developing materials and energy recovery research, development, and demonstration strategies, the Administrator shall review, and make a study of, the various existing and promising techniques of energy recovery from solid waste (including, but not limited to, waterwall furnace incinerators, dry shredded fuel systems, pyrolysis, densified refuse-derived fuel systems, anerobic digestion, and fuel and feedstock preparation systems). In carrying out such study the Administrator shall investigate with respect to each such technique—

(1) the degree of public need for the potential results of such research development, or demonstration,

(2) the potential for research, development, and demonstration without Federal action, including the degree of restraint on such potential posed by the risks involved, and

(3) the magnitude of effort and period of time necessary to develop the technology to the point where Federal assistance can be ended.

(d) Small-Scale and Low Technology Study.— The Administrator shall undertake a comprehensive study and analysis of, and publish a report on, systems of small-scale and low technology solid waste management, including household resource recovery and resource recovery systems which have special application to multiple dwelling units and high density housing and office complexes. Such study and analysis shall include an investigation of the degree to which such systems could contribute to energy conservation.

(e) Front-End Source Separation. — The Administrator shall undertake research and studies concerning the compatibility of front-end source separation systems with high technology resource recovery systems and shall publish a report containing the results of such research and studies.

(f) Mining Waste. — The Administrator, in consultation with the Secretary of the Interior, shall conduct a detailed and comprehensive study on the adverse effects of solid wastes from active and abandoned surface and underground mines on the environment, including, but not limited to, the effects of such wastes on humans, water, air, health, welfare, and natural resources, and on the adequacy of means and measures currently employed by the mining industry, Government agencies, and others to dispose of and utilize such solid wastes and to prevent or substantially mitigate such adverse effects. Such study shall include an analysis of—

(1) the sources and volume of discarded material generated per year from mining;

(2) present disposal practices;

(3) potential dangers to human health and the environment from surface runoff of leachate and air pollution by dust;

(4) alternatives to current disposal methods;

(5) the cost of those alternatives in terms of the impact on mine product costs; and

(6) potential for use of discarded material as a secondary source of the mine product.

Not later than thirty-six months after the date of the enactment of the Solid Waste Disposal Act Amendments of 1980 the Administrator shall publish a report of such study and shall include appropriate findings and recommendations for Federal and non-Federal actions concerning such effects. Such report shall be submitted to the Committee on Environment and Public Works of the United States Senate and the Committee on Interstate and Foreign Commerce of the United States House of Representatives.

(g) Sludge. — The Administrator shall undertake a comprehensive study and publish a report on sludge. Such study shall include an analysis of—

(1) what types of solid waste (including but not limited to sewage and pollution treatment residues and other residues from industrial operations such as extraction of oil from shale, liquefaction and gasification of coal and coal slurry pipeline operations) shall be classified as sludge;

(2) the effects of air and water pollution legislation on the creation of large volumes of sludge;

(3) the amounts of sludge originating in each State and in each industry producing sludge;

(4) methods of disposal of such sludge, including the cost, efficiency and effectiveness of such methods;

(5) alternative methods for the use of sludge, including agricultural applications of sludge and energy recovery from sludge; and

(6) methods to reclaim areas which have been used for the disposal of sludge or which have been damaged by sludge.

(h) Tires. — The Administrator shall undertake a study and publish a report respecting discarded motor vehicle tires which shall include an analysis of the problems involved in the collection, recovery of resources including energy, and use of such tires.

(i) Resource Recovery Facilities. — The Administrator shall conduct research and report on the economics of, and impediments, to the effective functioning of resource recovery facilities.

(j) Resource Conservation Committee.

(1) The Administrator shall serve as Chairman of a Committee composed of himself, the Secretary of Commerce, the Secretary of Labor, the

Chairman of the Council on Environmental Quality, the Secretary of Treasury, the Secretary of the Interior, the Secretary of Energy, the Chairman of the Council of Economic Advisors, and a representative of the Office of Management and Budget, which shall conduct a full and complete investigation and study of all aspects of the economic, social and environmental consequences of resource conservation with respect to—

(A) the appropriateness of recommended incentives and disincentives to foster resource conservation;

(B) the effect of existing public policies (including subsidies and economic incentives and disincentives, percentage depletion allowances, capital gains treatment and other tax incentives and disincentives) upon resource conservation, and the likely effect of the modification or elimination of such incentives and disincentives upon resource conservation;

(C) the appropriateness and feasibility of restricting the manufacture or use of categories of consumer products as a resource conservation strategy;

(D) the appropriateness and feasibility of employing as a resource conservation strategy the imposition of solid waste management charges on consumer products, which charges would reflect the costs of solid waste management services, litter pickup, the value of recoverable components of such product, final disposal, and any social value associated with the nonrecycling or uncontrolled disposal of such product; and

(E) the need for further research, development, and demonstration in the area of resource conservation.

(2) The study required in paragraph (1)(D) may include pilot scale projects, and shall consider and evaluate alternative strategies with respect to—

(A) the product categories on which such charges would be imposed;

(B) the appropriate state in the production of such consumer product at which to levy such charge;

(C) appropriate criteria for establishing such charges for each consumer product category;

(D) methods for the adjustment of such charges to reflect actions such as recycling which would reduce the overall quantities of solid waste requiring disposal; and

(E) procedures for amending, modifying, or revising such charges to reflect changing conditions.

(3) The design for the study required in paragraph (1)(D) of this subsection shall include timetables for the completion of the study. A preliminary report putting forth the study design shall be sent to the President and the Congress within six months following enactment of this section and followup reports shall be sent six months thereafter. Each recommendation resulting from the study shall include at least two alternatives to the proposed recommendation.

(4) The results of such investigation and study, including recommendations, shall be reported to the President and the Congress not later than two years after enactment of this subsection.

(5) There are authorized to be appropriated not to exceed $2,000,000 to carry out this subsection.

(k) Airport Landfills. — The Administrator shall undertake a comprehensive study and analysis of and publish a report on systems to alleviate the hazards to aviation from birds congregating and feeding on landfills in the vicinity of airports.

(l) Completion of Research and Studies. — The Administrator shall complete the research and studies, and submit the reports, required under subsections (b), (c), (d), (e), (f), (g), and (k) not later than October 1, 1978. The Administrator shall complete the research and studies, and submit the reports, required under subsections (a), (h), and (i) not later than October 1, 1979. Upon completion, each study specified in subsections (a) through (k) of this section, the Administrator shall prepare a plan for research, development, and demonstration respecting the findings of the study and shall submit any legislative recommendations resulting from such study to appropriate committees of Congress.

(m) Drilling Fluids, Produced Waters, and Other Wastes Associated with the Exploration, Development, or Production of Crude Oil or Natural Gas or Geothermal Energy.—

(1) The Administrator shall conduct a detailed and comprehensive study and submit a report on the adverse effects, if any, of drilling fluids, produced waters, and other wastes associated with the exploration, development, or production of crude oil or natural gas or geothermal energy on human health and the environment, including, but not limited to the effects of such

wastes on humans, water, air, health, welfare, and natural resources and on the adequacy of means and measures currently employed by the oil and gas and geothermal drilling and production industry, Government agencies, and others to dispose of and utilize such wastes and to prevent or substantially mitigate such adverse effects. Such study shall include an analysis of—

(A) the sources and volume of discarded material generated per year from such wastes;

(B) present disposal practices;

(C) potential danger to human health and the environment from the surface runoff or leachate;

(D) documented cases which prove or have caused danger to human health and the environment from surface runoff or leachate;

(E) alternatives to current disposal methods;

(F) the cost of such alternatives; and

(G) the impact of those alternatives on the exploration for, and development and production of, crude oil and natural gas or geothermal energy.

In furtherance of this study, the Administrator shall, as he deems appropriate, review studies and other actions of other Federal agencies concerning such wastes with a view toward avoiding duplication of effort and the need to expedite such study. The Administrator shall publish a report of such study and shall include appropriate findings and recommendations for Federal and non-Federal actions concerning such effects.

(2) The Administrator shall complete the research and study and submit the report required under paragraph (1) not later than twenty-four months from the date of enactment of the Solid Waste Disposal Act Amendments of 1980. Upon completion of the study, the Administrator shall prepare a summary of the findings of the study, a plan for research, development, and demonstration respecting the findings of the study, and shall submit the findings and the study, along with any recommendations resulting from such study, to the Committee on Environment and Public Works of the United States Senate and the Committee on Interstate and Foreign Commerce of the United States House of Representatives.

(3) There are authorized to be appropriated not to exceed $1,000,000 to carry out the provisions of this subsection.

[§8002(m) added by PL 96–482]

(n) Materials Generated from the Combustion of Coal and Other Fossil Fuels.—The Administrator shall conduct a detailed and comprehensive study and submit a report on the adverse effects on human health and the environment, if any, of the disposal and utilization of fly ash waste, bottom ash waste, slag waste, flue gas emission control waste, and other byproduct materials generated primarily from the combustion of coal or other fossil fuels. Such study shall include an analysis of—

(1) the source and volumes of such material generated per year;

(2) present disposal and utilization practices;

(3) potential danger, if any, to human health and the environment from the disposal and reuse of such materials;

(4) documented cases in which danger to human health or the environment from surface runoff or leachate has been proved;

(5) alternatives to current disposal methods;

(6) the costs of such alternatives;

(7) the impact of those alternatives on the use of coal and other natural resources; and

(8) the current and potential utilization of such materials. In furtherance of this study, the Administrator shall, as he deems appropriate, review studies and other actions of other Federal and State agencies concerning such material and invite participation by other concerned parties, including industry and other Federal and State agencies, with a view toward avoiding duplication of effort. The Administrator shall publish a report on such study, which shall include appropriate findings, not later than twenty-four months after the enactment of the Solid Waste Disposal Act Amendments of 1980. Such study and findings shall be submitted to the Committee on Environment and Public Works of the United States Senate and the Committee on Interstate and Foreign Commerce of the United States House of Representatives.

[§8002(n) added by PL 96–482]

(o) Cement Kiln Dust Waste.—The Administrator shall conduct a detailed and comprehensive study of the adverse effects on human health and the environment, if any, of the disposal of cement kiln dust waste. Such study shall include an analysis of—

(1) the source and volumes of such materials generated per year;

(2) present disposal practices;

(3) potential danger, if any, to human health and the environment from the disposal of such materials;

(4) documented cases in which danger to human health or the environment has been proved;

(5) alternatives to current disposal methods;

(6) the costs of such alternatives;

(7) the impact of those alternatives on the use of natural resources; and

(8) the current and potential utilization of such materials.

In furtherance of this study the Administrator shall, as he deems appropriate, review studies and other actions of other Federal and State agencies concerning such waste or materials and invite participation by other concerned parties, including industry and other Federal and State agencies, with a view toward avoiding duplication of effort. The Administrator shall publish a report of such study, which shall include appropriate findings, not later than thirty-six months after the date of enactment of the Solid Waste Disposal Act Amendments of 1980. Such report shall be submitted to the Committee on Environment and Public Works of the United States Senate and the Committee on Interstate and Foreign Commerce of the United States House of Representatives.

[§8002(o) added by PL 96–482]

(p) Materials Generated from the Extraction, Beneficiation, and Processing of Ores and Minerals, Including Phosphate Rock and Overburden from Uranium Mining.—The Administrator shall conduct a detailed and comprehensive study on the adverse effects on human health and the environment, if any, of the disposal and utilization of solid waste from the extraction, beneficiation, and processing of ores and minerals, including phosphate rock and overburden from uranium mining. Such study shall be conducted in conjunction with the study of mining wastes required by subsection (f) of this section and shall include an analysis of—

(1) the source and volumes of such materials generated per year;

(2) present disposal and utilization practices;

(3) potential danger, if any, to human health and the environment from the disposal and reuse of such materials;

(4) documented cases in which danger to human health or the environment has been proved;

(5) alternativess to current disposal methods;

(6) the costs of such alternatives;

(7) the impact of those alternatives on the use of phosphate rock and uranium ore, and other natural resources; and

(8) the current and potential utilization of such materials. In furtherance of this study, the Administrator shall, as he deems appropriate, review studies and other actions of other Federal and State agencies concerning such waste or materials and invite participation by other concerned parties, including industry and other Federal and State agencies, with a view toward avoiding duplication of effort. The Administrator shall publish a report on such study, which shall include appropriate findings, not later than twenty-four months after the enactment of the Solid Waste Disposal Act amendments of 1980. Such study and findings shall be submitted to the Committee on Environment and Public Works of the United States Senate and the Committee on Interstate and Foreign Commerce of the United States House of Representatives.

[§8002(p) added by PL 96–482]

(q) Authorization of Appropriations.—There are authorized to be appropriated not to exceed $8,000,000 for the fiscal years 1978 and 1979 to carry out this section other than subsection (j).

(r) Minimization of Hazardous Waste.—The Administrator shall compile, and not later than October 1, 1986, submit to the Congress, a report on the feasibility and desirability of establishing standards of performance or of taking other additional actions under this Act to require the generators of hazardous waste to reduce the volume or quantity and toxicity of the hazardous waste they generate, and of establishing with respect to hazardous wastes required management practices or other requirements to assure such wastes are managed in ways that minimize present and future risks to human health and the environment. Such report shall include any recommendations for legislative changes which the Administrator determines are feasible and desirable to implement the national policy established by section 1003.

[§8002(r) added by PL 98–616]

(s) Extending Landfill Life and Reusing Landfilled Areas.—The Administrator shall conduct detailed, comprehensive studies of methods to extend the useful life of sanitary landfills and to better use sites in which filled or closed landfills are located. Such studies shall address—

(1) methods to reduce the volume of materials before placement in landfills;

(2) more efficient systems for depositing waste in landfills;

(3) methods to enhance the rate of decomposition of solid waste in landfills, in a safe and environmentally acceptable manner;

(4) methane production from closed landfill units;

(5) innovative uses of closed landfill sites, including use for energy production such a solar or wind energy and use for metals recovery;

(6) potential for use of sewage treatment sludge in reclaiming landfilled areas; and

(7) methods to coordinate use of a landfill owned by one municipality by nearby municipalities, and to establish equitable rates for such use, taking into account the need to provide future landfill capacity to replace that so used.

The Administrator is authorized to conduct demonstrations in the areas of study provided in this subsection. The Administrator shall periodically report on the results of such studies, with the first such report not later than October 1, 1986. In carrying out this subsection, the Administrator need not duplicate other studies which have been completed and may rely upon information which has previously been compiled.

[§8002(s) added by PL 98–616]

§6983. Coordination, Collection, and Dissemination of Information [Sec. 8003]

(a) Information.—The Administrator shall develop, collect, evaluate, and coordinate information on—

(1) methods and costs of the collection of solid waste;

(2) solid waste management practices, including data on the different management methods and the cost, operation, and maintenance of such methods;

(3) the amounts and percentages of resources (including energy) that can be recovered from solid waste by use of various solid waste management practices and various technologies;

(4) methods available to reduce the amount of solid waste that is generated;

(5) existing and developing technologies for the recovery of energy or materials from solid waste and the costs, reliability, and risks associated with such technologies;

(6) hazardous solid waste, including incidents of damage resulting from the disposal of hazardous solid wastes; inherently and potentially hazardous solid wastes; methods of neutralizing or properly disposing of hazardous solid wastes; facilities that properly dispose of hazardous wastes;

(7) methods of financing resource recovery facilities or, sanitary landfills, or hazardous solid waste treatment facilities, whichever is appropriate for the entity developing such facility or landfill (taking into account the amount of solid waste reasonably expected to be available to such entity);

(8) the availability of markets for the purchase of resources, either materials or energy, recovered from solid waste; and

(9) research and development projects respecting solid waste management.

(b) Library.—

(1) The Administrator shall establish and maintain a central reference library for (A) the materials collected pursuant to subsection (a) of this section and (B) the actual performance and cost effectiveness records and other data and information with respect to—

(i) the various methods of energy and resource recovery from solid waste,

(ii) the various systems and means of resource conservation,

(iii) the various systems and technologies for collection, transport, storage, treatment, and final disposition of solid waste, and

(iv) other aspects of solid waste and hazardous solid waste management.

Such central reference library shall also contain, but not be limited to, the model codes and model accounting systems developed under this section, the information collected under subsection (d), and, subject to any applicable requirements of confidentiality, information respecting any aspect of solid waste provided by officers and employees of the Environmental Protection Agency which has been acquired by them in the conduct of their functions under this Act and which may be of value to Federal, State, and local authorities and other persons.

(2) Information in the central reference library shall, to the extent practicable, be collated, analyzed, verified, and published and shall be made available to State and local governments and other persons at reasonable times and subject to such reasonable charges as may be nec-

essary to defray expenses of making such information available.

(c) Model Accounting System.—In order to assist State and local governments in determining the cost and revenues associated with the collection and disposal of solid waste and with resource recovery operations, the Administrator shall develop and publish a recommended model cost and revenue accounting system applicable to the solid waste management functions of State and local governments. Such system shall be in accordance with generally accepted accounting principles. The Administrator shall periodically, but not less frequently than once every five years, review such accounting system and revise it as necessary.

(d) Model Codes.—The Administrator is authorized, in cooperation with appropriate State and local agencies, to recommend model codes, ordinances, and statutes, providing for sound solid waste management.

(e) Information Programs.—

(1) The Administrator shall implement a program for the rapid dissemination of information on solid waste management, hazardous waste management, resource conservation, and methods of resource recovery from solid waste, including the results of any relevant research, investigations, experiments, surveys, studies, or other information which may be useful in the implementation of new or improved solid waste management practices and methods and information on any other technical, managerial, financial, or market aspect of resource conservation and recovery facilities.

(2) The Administrator shall develop and implement educational programs to promote citizen understanding of the need for environmentally sound solid waste management practices.

(f) Coordination.—In collecting and disseminating information under this section, the Administrator shall coordinate his actions and cooperate to the maximum extent possible with State and local authorities.

(g) Special Restriction.—Upon request, the full range of alternative technologies, programs or processes deemed feasible to meet the resource recovery or resource conservation needs of a jurisdiction shall be described in such a manner as to provide a sufficient evaluative basis from which the jurisdiction can make its decisions, but no officer or employee of the Environmental Protection Agency shall, in an official capacity, lobby for or otherwise represent an agency position in favor of resource recovery or resource conservation, as a policy alternative for adoption into ordinances, codes, regulations, or law by any State or political subdivision thereof.

§6984. Full-Scale Demonstration Facilities [Sec. 8004]

(a) Authority.—The Administrator may enter into contracts with public agencies or authorities or private persons for the construction and operation of a full- scale demonstration facility under this Act, or provide financial assistance in the form of grants to a full-scale demonstration facility under this Act only if the Administrator finds that—

(1) such facility or proposed facility will demonstrate at full scale a new or significantly improved technology or process, a practical and significant improvement in solid waste management practice, or the technological feasibility and cost effectiveness of an existing, but unproven technology, process, or practice, and will not duplicate any other Federal, State, local, or commercial facility which has been constructed or with respect to which construction has begun (determined as of the date action is taken by the Administrator under this Act),

(2) such contract or assistance meets the requirements of section 8001 and meets other applicable requirements of the Act,

(3) such facility will be able to comply with the guidelines published under section 1008 and with other laws and regulations for the protection of health and the environment,

(4) in the case of a contract for construction or operation, such facility is not likely to be constructed or operated by State, local, or private persons or in the case of an application for financial assistance, such facility is not likely to receive adequate financial assistance from other sources, and

(5) any Federal interest in, or assistance to, such facility will be disposed of or terminated, with appropriate compensation, within such period of time as may be necessary to carry out the basic objectives of this Act.

(b) Time Limitation.—No obligation may be made by the Administrator for financial assistance under this subtitle for any full-scale demonstration facility after the date ten years after the enactment of this section. No expenditure of funds for any such full-scale demonstration facility under this subtitle may be made by the

Administrator after the date fourteen years after such date of enactment.

(c) Cost Sharing.—

(1) Wherever practicable, in constructing, operating, or providing financial assistance under this subtitle to a full-scale demonstration facility, the Administrator shall endeavor to enter into agreements and make other arrangements for maximum practicable cost sharing with other Federal, State, and local agencies, private persons, or any combination thereof.

[§8004(c)(1) designated by PL 98–616]

(2) The Administrator shall enter into arrangements, wherever practicable and desirable, to provide monitoring of full- scale solid waste facilities (whether or not constructed or operated under this Act) for purposes of obtaining information concerning the performance, and other aspects, of such facilities. Where the Administrator provides only monitoring and evaluation instruments or personnel (or both) or funds for such instruments or personnel and provides no other financial assistance to a facility, notwithstanding section 8001(c)(3), title to any invention made or conceived of in the course of developing, constructing, or operating such facility shall not be required to vest in the United States and patents respecting such invention shall not be required to be issued to the United States.

(d) Prohibition.—After the date of enactment of this section, the Administrator shall not construct or operate any full- scale facility (except by contract with public agencies or authorities or private persons).

§6985. Special Study and Demonstration Projects on Recovery of Useful Energy and Materials [Sec. 8005]

(a) Studies.—The Administrator shall conduct studies and develop recommendations for administrative or legislative action on—

(1) means of recovering materials and energy from solid waste, recommended uses of such materials and energy for national or international welfare, including identification of potential markets for such recovered resources, the impact of distribution of such resources on existing markets, and potentials for energy conservation through resource conservation and resource recovery;

(2) actions to reduce waste generation which have been taken voluntarily or in response to governmental action, and those which practically could be taken in the future, and the economic, social, and environmental consequences of such actions;

(3) methods of collection, separation, and containerization which will encourage efficient utilization of facilities and contribute to more effective programs of reduction, reuse, or disposal of wastes;

(4) the use of Federal procurement to develop market demand for recovered resources;

(5) recommended incentives (including Federal grants, loans, and other assistance) and disincentives to accelerate the reclamation or recycling of materials from solid wastes, with special emphasis on motor vehicle hulks;

(6) the effect of existing public policies, including subsidies and economic incentives and disincentives, percentage depletion allowances, capital gains treatment and other tax incentives and disincentives, upon the recycling and reuse of materials, and the likely effect of the modification or elimination of such incentives and disincentives upon the reuse, recycling and conservation of such materials;

(7) the necessity and method of imposing disposal or other charges on packaging, containers, vehicles, and other manufactured goods, which charges would reflect the cost of final disposal, the value of recoverable components of the item, and any social costs associated with nonrecycling or uncontrolled disposal of such items; and

(8) the legal constraints and institutional barriers to the acquisition of land needed for solid waste management, including land for facilities and disposal sites;

(9) in consultation with the Secretary of Agriculture, agricultural waste management problems and practices, the extent of reuse and recovery of resources in such wastes, the prospects for improvement, Federal, State, and local regulations governing such practices, and the economic, social, and environmental consequences of such practices; and

(10) in consultation with the Secretary of the Interior, mining waste management problems, and practices, including an assessment of existing authorities, technologies, and economics, and the environmental and public health consequences of such practices.

(b) Demonstration.—The Administrator is also authorized to carry out demonstration projects to test and demonstrate methods and techniques developed pursuant to subsection (a).

(c) Application of Other Sections.—Section 8001(b) and (c) shall be applicable to investigations, studies, and projects carried out under this section.

§6986. Grants for Resource Recovery Systems and Improved Solid Waste Disposal Facilities [Sec. 8006]

(a) Authority.—The Administrator is authorized to make grants pursuant to this section to any State, municipal, or interstate or intermunicipal agency for the demonstration of resource recovery systems or for the construction of new or improved solid waste disposal facilities.

(b) Conditions.—

(1) Any grant under this section for the demonstration of a resource recovery system may be made only if it (A) is consistent with any plans which meet the requirements of subtitle D of this Act; (B) is consistent with the guidelines recommended pursuant to section 1008 of this Act; (C) is designed to provide area-wide resource recovery systems consistent with the purposes of this Act, as determined by the Administrator, pursuant to regulations promulgated under subsection (d) of this section; and (D) provides an equitable system for distributing the costs associated with the construction, operation, and maintenance of any resource recovery system among the users of such system.

(2) The Federal share for any project to which paragraph (1) applies shall not be more than 75 percent.

(c) Limitations.—

(1) A grant under this section for the construction of a new or improved solid waste disposal facility may be made only if—

(A) a State or interstate plan for solid waste disposal has been adopted which applies to the area involved, and the facility to be constructed (i) is consistent with such plan, (ii) is included in a comprehensive plan for the area involved which is satisfactory to the Administrator for the purpose of this Act, and (iii) is consistent with the guidelines recommended under section 1008, and

(B) the project advances the state of the art by applying new and improved techniques in reducing the environmental impact of solid waste disposal, in achieving recovery of energy or resources, or in recycling useful materials.

(2) The Federal share for any project to which paragraph (l) applies shall be not more than 50 percent in the case of a project serving an area which includes only one municipality, and not more than 75 percent in any other case.

(d) Regulations.—

(1) The Administrator shall promulgate regulations establishing a procedure for awarding grants under this section which—

(A) provides that projects will be carried out in communities of varying sizes, under such conditions as will assist in solving the community waste problems of urban-industrial centers, metropolitan regions, and rural areas, under representative geographic and environmental conditions; and

(B) provides deadlines for submission of, and action on, grant requests.

(2) In taking action on applications for grants under this section, consideration shall be given by the Administrator (A) to the public benefits to be derived by the construction and the propriety of Federal aid in making such grant; (B) to the extent applicable, to the economic and commercial viability of the project (including contractual arrangements with the private sector to market any resources recovered); (C) to the potential of such project for general application to community solid waste disposal problems; and (D) to the use by the applicant of comprehensive regional or metropolitan area planning.

(e) Additional Limitations.—A grant under this section—

(1) may be made only in the amount of the Federal share of (A) the estimated total design and construction costs, plus (B) in the case of a grant to which subsection (b)(1) applies, the first-year operation and maintenance costs;

(2) may not be provided for land acquisition or (except as otherwise provided in paragraph (1)(B)) for operating or maintenance costs;

(3) may not be made until the applicant has made provision satisfactory to the Administrator for proper and efficient operation and maintenance of the project (subject to paragraph (1)(B)); and

(4) may be made subject to such conditions and requirements, in addition to those provided in this section, as the Administrator may require to properly carry out his functions pursuant to this Act.

For purposes of paragraph (1), the non- Federal share may be in any form, including, but not limited to, lands or interests therein needed for the project or personal property or services, the value of which shall be determined by the Administrator.

(f) Single State.—

(1) Not more than 15 percent of the total of funds authorized to be appropriated for any fiscal year to carry out this section shall be granted under this section for projects in any one State.

(2) The Administrator shall prescribe by regulation the manner in which this subsection shall apply to a grant under this section for a project in an area which includes all or part of more than one State.

§6987. Authorization of Appropriations [Sec. 8007]

There are authorized to be appropriated not to exceed $35,000,000 for the fiscal year 1978 to carry out the purposes of this subtitle (except for section 8002).

SUBTITLE I—REGULATION OF UNDERGROUND STORAGE TANKS

§6991. Definitions and Exemptions [Sec. 9001]

[§9001 added by PL 98–616]

For the purposes of this subtitle—

(1) The term "underground storage tank" means any one or combination of tanks (including underground pipes connected thereto) which is used to contain an accumulation of regulated substances, and the volume of which (including the volume of the underground pipes connected thereto) is 10 per centum or more beneath the surface of the ground. Such term does not include any—

(A) farm or residential tank of 1,100 gallons or less capacity used for storing motor fuel for noncommercial purposes,

(B) tank used for storing heating oil for consumptive use on the premises where stored,

(C) septic tank,

(D) pipeline facility (including gathering lines)—

(i) which is regulated under the Natural Gas Pipeline Safety Act of 1968 (49 U.S.C. App. 1671 et seq.),

(ii) which is regulated under the Hazardous Liquid Pipeline Safety Act of 1979 (49 U.S.C. App. 2001 et seq.), or

(iii) which is an intrastate pipeline facility regulated under State laws as provided in the provisions of law referred to in clause (i) or (ii) of this subparagraph,

and which is determined by the Secretary to be connected to a pipeline or to be operated or intended to be capable of operating at pipeline pressure or as an integral part of a pipeline,

[§9001(1)(D) amended by PL 102–508]

(E) surface impoundment, pit, pond, or lagoon,

(F) storm water or waste water collection system,

(G) flow-through process tank,

(H) liquid trap or associated gathering lines directly related to oil or gas production and gathering operations, or

(I) storage tank situated in an underground area (such as a basement, cellar, mineworking, drift, shaft, or tunnel) if the storage tank is situated upon or above the surface of the floor.

The term "underground storage tank" shall not include any pipes connected to any tank which is described in subparagraphs (A) through (I).

(2) The term "regulated substance" means—

(A) any substance defined in section 101(14) of the Comprehensive Environmental Response, Compensation, and Liability Act of 1980 (but not including any substance regulated as a hazardous waste under subtitle C), and

(B) petroleum.

[§9001(2)(B) revised by PL 99–499]

(3) The term "owner" means—

(A) in the case of an underground storage tank in use on the date of enactment of the Hazardous and Solid Waste Amendments of 1984, or brought into use after that date, any person who owns an underground storage tank used for the storage, use, or dispensing of regulated sustances, and

(B) in the case of any underground storage tank in use before the date of enactment of the Hazardous and Solid Waste Amendments of 1984, but no longer in use on the date of enactment of such Amendments, any person who owned such tank immediately before the discontinuation of its use.

(4) The term "operator" means any person in control of, or having responsibility for, the daily operation of the underground storage tank.

(5) The term "release" means any spilling, leaking, emitting, discharging, escaping, leaching, or disposing from an underground storage tank into ground water, surface water or subsurface soils.

(6) The term "person" has the same meaning as provided in section 1004(15), except that such term includes a consortium, a joint venture, and a commercial entity, and the United States Government.

(7) The term "nonoperational storage tank" means any underground storage tank in which regulated substances will not be deposited or from which regulated substances will not be dispensed after the date of the enactment of the Hazardous and Solid Waste Amendments of 1984.

(8) The term "petroleum" means petroleum, including crude oil or any fraction thereof which is liquid at standard conditions of temperature and pressure (60 degrees Fahrenheit and 14.7 pounds per square inch absolute).

[§9001(8) added by PL 99–499]

§6991a. Notification [Sec. 9002]

[§9002 added by PL 98–616]

(a) Underground Storage Tanks.—

(1) Within 18 months after the date of enactment of the Hazardous and Solid Waste Amendments of 1984, each owner of an underground storage tank shall notify the State or local agency or department designated pursuant to subsection (b)(1) of the existence of such tank, specifying the age, size, type, location, and uses of such tank.

(2) (A) For each underground storage tank taken out of operation after January 1, 1974, the owner of such tank shall, within eighteen months after the date of enactment of the Hazardous and Solid Waste Amendments of 1984, notify the State or local agency, or department designated pursuant to subsection (b)(1) of the existence of such tanks (unless the owner knows the tank subsequently was removed from the ground). The owner of a tank taken out of operation on or before January 1, 1974, shall not be required to notify the State or local agency under this subsection.

(B) Notice under subparagraph (A) shall specify, to the extent known to the owner—

(i) the date the tank was taken out of operation,

(ii) the age of the tank on the date taken out of operation,

(iii) the size, type and location of the tank, and

(iv) the type and quantity of substances left stored in such tank on the date taken out of operation.

(3) Any owner which brings into use an underground storage tank after the initial notification period specified under paragraph (1), shall notify the designated State or local agency or department within thirty days of the existence of such tank, specifying the age, size, type, location and uses of such tank.

(4) Paragraphs (1) through (3) of this subsection shall not apply to tanks for which notice was given pursuant to section 103(c) of the Comprehensive Environmental Response, Compensation, and Liability Act of 1980.

(5) Beginning thirty days after the Administrator prescribes the form of notice pursuant to subsection (b)(2) and for eighteen months thereafter, any person who deposits regulated substances in an underground storage tank shall reasonably notify the owner or operator of such tank of the owner's notification requirements pursuant to this subsection.

(6) Beginning thirty days after the Administrator issues new tank performance standards pursuant to section 9003(e) of this subtitle, any person who sells a tank intended to be used as an underground storage tank shall notify the purchaser of such tank of the owner's notification requirements pursuant to this subsection.

(b) Agency Designation.—

(1) Within one hundred and eighty days after the enactment of the Hazardous and Solid Waste Amendments of 1984, the Governors of each State shall designate the appropriate State agency or department or local agencies or departments to receive the notifications under subsection (a) (1), (2), or (3).

(2) Within twelve months after the date of enactment of the Hazardous and Solid Waste Amendments of 1984, the Administrator, in consultation with State and local officials designated pursuant to subsection (b)(1), and after notice and opportunity for public comment, shall prescribe the form of the notice and the information to be included in the notifications under subsection (a) (1), (2), or (3). In prescribing the form of such notice, the Administrator shall take into account the effect on small businesses and other owners and operators.

(c) State Inventories. — Each State shall make 2 separate inventories of all underground storage tanks in such State containing regulated substances. One inventory shall be made with respect to petroleum and one with respect to other regulated substances. In making such inventories, the State shall utilize and aggregate the data in the notification forms submitted pursuant to subsections (a) and (b) of this section. Each State shall submit such aggregated data to the Administrator not later than 270 days after the enactment of the Superfund Amendments and Reauthorization Act of 1986.

[§9002(c) added by PL 99–499]

§6991b. Release Detection, Prevention, and Correction Regulations [Sec. 9003]

[§9003 added by PL 98–616]

(a) Regulations.—The Administrator, after notice and opportunity for public comment, and at least three months before the effective dates specified in subsection (f), shall promulgate release detection, prevention, and correction regulations applicable to all owners and operators of underground storage tanks, as may be necessary to protect human health and the environment.

(b) Distinctions in Regulations.—In promulgating regulations under this section, the Administrator may distinguish between types, classes, and ages of underground storage tanks. In making such distinctions, the Administrator may take into consideration factors, including, but not limited to: location of the tanks, soil and climate conditions, uses of the tanks, history of maintenance, age of the tanks, current industry recommended practices, national consensus codes, hydrogeology, water table, size of the tanks, quantity of regulated substances periodically deposited in or dispensed from the tank, the technical capability of the owners and operators, and the compatibility of the regulated substance and the materials of which the tank is fabricated.

(c) Requirements.—The regulations promulgated pursuant to this section shall include, but need not be limited to, the following requirements respecting all underground storage tanks—

(1) requirements for maintaining a leak detection system, an inventory control system together with tank testing, or a comparable system or method designed to identity releases in a manner consistent with the protection of human health and the environment;

(2) requirements for maintaining records of any monitoring or leak detection system or inventory control system or tank testing or comparable system;

(3) requirements for reporting of releases and corrective action taken in response to a release from an underground storage tank;

(4) requirements for taking corrective action in response to a release from an underground storage tank;

[§9003(c)(4) amended by PL 99–499]

(5) requirements for the closure of tanks to prevent future releases of regulated substances into the environment; and

[§9003(c)(5) amended by PL 99–499]

(6) requirements for maintaining evidence of financial responsibility for taking corrective action and compensating third parties for bodily injury and property damage caused by sudden and nonsudden accidental releases arising from operating an underground storage tank.

[§9003(c)(6) added by PL 99–499]

(d) Financial Responsibility.—

(1) Financial responsibility required by this subsection may be established in accordance with regulations promulgated by the Administrator by any one, or any combination, of the following: insurance, guarantee, surety bond, letter of credit, qualification as a self-insurer or any other method satisfactory to the Administrator. In promulgating requirements under this subsection, the Administrator is authorized to specify policy or other contractual terms, conditions, or defenses which are necessary or are unacceptable in establishing such evidence of financial responsibility in order to effectuate the purposes of this subtitle.

[Former §9003(d)(2) amended and redesignated as (1) by PL 99–499]

(2) In any case where the owner or operator is in bankruptcy, reorganization, or arrangement pursuant to the Federal Bankruptcy Code or where with reasonable diligence jurisdiction in any State court of the Federal Courts cannot be obtained over an owner or operator likely to be solvent at the time of judgment, any claim arising from conduct for which evidence of financial responsibility must be provided under this subsection may be asserted directly against the guarantor providing such evidence of financial responsibility. In the case of any action pursuant to this paragraph such guarantor shall be entitled to invoke all rights and defenses which would have been available to the owner or operator if any action had been brought against the owner or operator by the claimant and which would have been available to the guarantor if an action had been brought against the guarantor by the owner or operator.

(3) The total liability of any guarantor shall be limited to the aggregate amount which the guarantor has provided as evidence of financial responsibility to the owner or operator under this section. Nothing in this subsection shall be construed to limit any other State or Federal statutory, contractual or common law liability of a guarantor to its owner or operator including, but not limited to, the liability of such guarantor for bad faith either in negotiating or in failing to negotiate the settlement of any claim. Nothing in this subsection shall be construed to diminish the liability of any person under section 107 or 111 of the Comprehensive Environmental Response, Compensation and Liability Act of 1980 or other applicable law.

(4) For the purpose of this subsection, the term "guarantor" means any person, other than the owner or operator, who provides evidence of financial responsibility for an owner or operator under this subsection.

(5) (A) The Administrator, in promulgating financial responsibility regulations under this section, may establish an amount of coverage for particular classes or categories of underground storage tanks containing petroleum which shall satisfy such regulations and which shall not be less than $1,000,000 for each occurrence with an appropriate aggregate requirement.

(B) The Administrator may set amounts lower than the amounts required by subparagraph (A) of this paragraph for underground storage tanks containing petroleum which are at facilities not engaged in petroleum production, refining, or marketing and which are not used to handle substantial quantities of petroleum.

(C) In establishing classes and categories for purposes of this paragraph, the Administrator may consider the following factors:

(i) The size, type, location, storage, and handling capacity of underground storage tanks in the class or category and the volume of petroleum handled by such tanks.

(ii) The likelihood of release and the potential extent of damage from any release from underground storage tanks in the class or category.

(iii) The economic impact of the limits on the owners and operators of each such class or category, particularly relating to the small business segment of the petroleum marketing industry.

(iv) The availability of methods of financial responsibility in amounts greater than the amount established by this paragraph.

(v) Such other factors as the Administrator deems pertinent.

(D) The Administrator may suspend enforcement of the financial responsibility requirements for a particular class or category of underground storage tanks or in a particular State, if the Administrator makes a determination that methods of financial responsibility satisfying the requirements of this subsection are not generally available for underground storage tanks in that class or category, and —

(i) steps are being taken to form a risk retention group for such class of tanks; or

(ii) such State is taking steps to establish a fund pursuant to section 9004(c)(1) of this Act to be submitted as evidence of financial responsibility. A suspension by the Administrator pursuant to this paragraph shall extend for a period not to exceed 180 days. A determination to suspend may be made with respect to the same class or category or for the same State at the end of such period, but only if substantial progress has been made in establishing a risk retention group, or the owners or operators in the class or category demonstrate, and the Administrator finds, that the formation of such a group is not possible and that the State is unable or unwilling to establish such a fund pursuant to clause (ii).

[§9003(d)(5) added by PL 99–499]

(e) New Tank Performance Standards.—The Administrator shall, not later than three months prior to the effective date specified in subsection (f), issue performance standards for underground storage tanks brought into use on or after the effective date of such standards. The performance standards for new underground storage tanks shall include, but need not be limited to, design, construction, installation, release detection, and compatibility standards.

(f) Effective Dates.—

(1) Regulations issued pursuant to subsection (c) and (d) of this section, and standards issued pursuant to subsection (e) of this section, for underground storage tanks containing regulated substances defined in section 9001(2)(B) (petroleum, including crude oil or any fraction thereof which is liquid at standard conditions of temperature and pressure) shall be effective not later than thirty months after the date of

enactment of the Hazardous and Solid Waste Amendments of 1984.

(2) Standards issued pursuant to subsection (e) of this section (entitled "New Tank Performance Standards") for underground storage tanks containing regulated substances defined in section 9001(2)(A) shall be effective not later than thirty-six months after the date of enactment of the Hazardous and Solid Waste Amendments of 1984.

(3) Regulations issued pursuant to subsection (c) of this section (entitled "Requirements") and standards issued pursuant to subsection (d) of this section (entitled "Financial Responsibility") for underground storage tanks containing regulated substances defined in section 9001(2)(A) shall be effective not later than forty-eight months after the date of enactment of the Hazardous and Solid Waste Amendments of 1984.

(g) Interim Prohibition.—

(1) Until the effective date of the standards promulgated by the Administrator under subsection (e) and after one hundred and eighty days after the date of the enactment of the Hazardous and Solid Waste Amendments of 1984, no person may install an underground storage tank for the purpose of storing regulated substances unless such tank (whether of single or double wall construction)—

(A) will prevent releases due to corrosion or structural failure for the operational life of the tank;

(B) is cathodically protected against corrosion, constructed of noncorrosive material, steel clad with a noncorrosive material, or designed in a manner to prevent the release or threatened release of any stored substance; and

(C) the material used in the construction or lining of the tank is compatible with the substance to be stored.

(2) Notwithstanding paragraph (1), if soil tests conducted in accordance with ASTM Standard G57–78, or another standard approved by the Administrator, show that soil resistivity in an installation location is 12,000 ohm/cm or more (unless a more stringent standard is prescribed by the Administrator by rule), a storage tank without corrosion protection may be installed in that location during the period referred to in paragraph (1).

(h) EPA Response Program for Petroleum. —

(1) Before regulations — Before the effective date of regulations under subsection (c), the Administrator (or a State pursuant to paragraph (7)) is authorized to—

(A) require the owner or operator of an underground storage tank to undertake corrective action with respect to any release of petroleum when the Administrator (or the State) determines that such corrective action will be done properly and promptly by the owner or operator of the underground storage tank from which the release occurs; or

(B) undertake corrective action with respect to any release of petroleum into the environment from an underground storage tank if such action is necessary, in the judgment of the Administrator (or the State), to protect human health and the environment.

The corrective action undertaken or required under this paragraph shall be such as may be necessary to protect human health and the environment. The Administrator shall use funds in the Leaking Underground Storage Tank Trust Fund for payment of costs incurred for corrective action under subparagraph (B), enforcement action under subparagraph (A), and cost recovery under paragraph (6) of this subsection. Subject to the priority requirements of paragraph (3), the Administrator (or the State) shall give priority in undertaking such actions under subparagraph (B) to cases where the Administrator (or the State) cannot identify a solvent owner or operator or the tank who will undertake action properly.

(2) After regulations.—Following the effective date of regulations under subsection (c), all actions or orders of the Administrator (or a State pursuant to paragraph (7)) described in paragraph (1) of this subsection shall be in conformity with such regulations. Following such effective date, the Administrator (or the State) may undertake corrective action with respect to any release of petroleum into the environment from an underground storage tank only if such action is necessary, in the judgment of the Administrator (or the State), to protect human health and the environment and one or more of the following situations exists.

(A) No person can be found, within 90 days or such shorter period as may be necessary to protect human health and the environment, who is—

(i) an owner or operator of the tank concerned,

(ii) subject to such corrective action regulations, and

(iii) capable of carrying out such corrective action properly.

(B) A situation exists which requires prompt action by the Administrator (or the State) under this paragraph to protect human health and the environment.

(C) Corrective action costs at a facility exceed the amount of coverage required by the Administrator pursuant to the provisions of subsections (c) and (d)(5) of this section and, considering the class or category of underground storage tank from which the release occurred, expenditures from the Leaking Underground Storage Tank Trust Fund are necessary to assure an effective corrective action.

(D) The owner or operator of the tank has failed or refused to comply with an order of the Administrator under this subsection or section 9006 or with the order of a State under this subsection to comply with the corrective action regulations.

(3) Priority of corrective actions.—The Administrator (or a State pursuant to paragraph (7)) shall give priority in undertaking corrective actions under this subsection, and in issuing orders requiring owners or operators to undertake such actions, to releases of petroleum from underground storage tanks which pose the greatest threat to human health and the environment.

(4) Corrective action orders.—The Administrator is authorized to issue orders to the owner or operator of an underground storage tank to carry out subparagraph (A) of paragraph (1) or to carryout regulations issued under subsection (c)(4). A State acting pursuant to paragraph (7) of the subsection is authorized to carry out subparagraph (A) of paragraph (1) only until the State's program is approved by the Administrator under section 9004 of this subtitle. Such orders shall be issued and enforced in the same manner and subject to the same requirements as orders under section 9006.

(5) Allowable corrective actions.—The corrective actions undertaken by the Administrator (or a State pursuant to paragraph (7)) under paragraph (1) or (2) may include temporary or permanent relocation of residents and alternative household water supplies. In connection with the performance of any corrective action under paragraph (1) or (2), the Administrator may undertake an exposure assessment as defined in paragraph (10) of this subsection or provide for such an assessment in a cooperative agreement with a State pursuant to paragraph (7) of this subsection. The costs of any such assessment may be treated as corrective action for purposes of paragraph (6), relating to cost recovery.

(6) Recovery of costs.—

(A) In general. — Whenever costs have been incurred by the Administrator, or by a State pursuant to paragraph (7), for undertaking corrective action or enforcement action with respect to the release of petroleum from an underground storage tank, the owner or operator of such tank shall be liable to the Administrator or the State for such costs. The liability under this paragraph shall be construed to be the standard of liability which obtains under section 311 of the Federal Water Pollution Control Act.

(B) Recovery. — In determining the equities for seeking the recovery of costs under subparagraph (A), the Administrator (or a State pursuant to paragraph (7) of this subsection) may consider the amount of financial responsibility required to be maintained under subsections (c) and (d)(5) of this section and the factors considered in establishing such amount under subsection (d)(5).

(C) Effect on liability. —

(i) No transfers of liability. — No indemnification, hold harmless, or similar agreement or conveyance shall be effective to transfer from the owner or operator ofany underground storage tank or from any person who may be liable for a release or threat of release under this subsection, to any other person the liability imposed under this subsection. Nothing in this subsection shall bar any agreement to insure, hold harmless, or indemnify a party to such agreement for any liability under this section.

(ii) No bar to cause of action. — Nothing in this subsection, including the provisions of clause (i) of this subparagraph, shall bar a cause of action that an owner or operator or any other person subject to liability under this section, or a guarantor, has or would have, by reason of subrogation or otherwise against any person.

(D) Facility. — For purposes of this paragraph, the term "facility" means, with respect to any owner or operator, all underground storage tanks used for the storage of petroleum which are owned or operated by such owner or operator and located on a single parcel of property (or on any contiguous or adjacent property).

(7) State authorities.—

(A) General. — A State may exercise the authorities in paragraphs (1) and (2) of this subsection, subject to the terms and conditions of paragraphs (3), (5), (9), (10), and (11), and including the authorities of paragraphs (4), (6), and (8) of this subsection if—

(i) the Administrator determines that the State has the capabilities to carry out effective corrective actions and enforcement activities; and

(ii) the Administrator enters into a cooperative agreement with the State setting out the actions to be undertaken by the State.

The Administrator may provide funds from the Leaking Underground Storage Tank Trust Fund for the reasonable costs of the State's actions under the cooperative agreement.

(B) Cost share. — Following the effective date of the regulations under subsection (c) of this section, the State shall pay 10 per centum of the cost of corrective actions undertaken either by the Administrator or by the State under a cooperative agreement, except that the Administrator may take corrective action at a facility where immediate action is necessary to respond to an imminent and substantial endangerment to human health or the environment if the State fails to pay the cost share.

(8) Emergency procurement powers. — Notwithstanding any other provision of law, the Administrator may authorize the use of such emergency procurement powers as he deems necessary.

(9) Definition of owner. — As used in this subsection, the term "owner" does not include any person who, without participating in the management of an underground storage tank and otherwise not engaged in petroleum production, refining, and marketing, holds indicia of ownership primarily to protect the owner's security interest in the tank.

(10) Definition of exposure assessment. —As used in this subsection, the term "exposure assessment" means an assessment to determine the extent of exposure of, or potential for exposure of, individuals to petroleum from a release from an underground storage tank based on such factors as the nature and extent of contamination and the existence of or potential for pathways of human exposure (including ground or surface water contamination, air emissions, and food chain contamination), the size of the community within the likely pathways of exposure, and the comparison of expected human exposure levels to the short-term and long- term health effects associated with identified contaminants and any available recommended exposure or tolerance limits for such contaminants. Such assessment shall not delay corrective action to abate immediate hazards or reduce exposure.

(11) Facilities without financial responsibility.—At any facility where the owner or operator has failed to maintain evidence of financial responsibility in amounts at least equal to the amounts established by subsection (d)(5)(A) of this section (or a lesser amount if such amount is applicable to such facility as a result of subsection (d)(5)(B) of this section) for whatever reason the Administrator shall expend no monies from the Leaking Underground Storage Tank Trust Fund to clean up releases at such facility pursuant to the provisions of paragraph (1) or (2) of this subsection. At such facilities the Administrator shall use the authorities provided in subparagraph (A) of paragraph (1) and paragraph (4) of this subsection and section 9006 of this subtitle to order corrective action to clean up such releases. States acting pursuant to paragraph (7) of this subsection shall use the authorities provided in subparagraph (A) of paragraph (1) and paragraph (4) of this subsection to order corrective action to clean up such releases. Notwithstanding the provisions of this paragraph, the Administrator may use monies from the fund to take the corrective actions authorized by paragraph (5) of this subsection to protect human health at such facilities and shall seek full recovery of the costs of all such actions pursuant to the provisions of paragraph (6)(A) of this subsection and without consideration of the factors in paragraph (6)(B) of this subsection. Nothing in this paragraph shall prevent the Administrator (or a State pursuant to paragraph (7) of this subsection) from taking corrective action at a facility where there is no solvent owner or operator or where immediate action is necessary to respond to an imminent and substantial endangerment of human health or the environment.

[§9003(h) added by PL 99–499]

§6991c. Approval of State Programs [Sec. 9004]

(a) Elements of State Program.—Beginning 30 months after the date of enactment of the Hazardous and Solid Waste Amendments of 1984, any State may, submit an underground storage tank release detection, prevention, and correction program for review and approval by the

Administrator. The program may cover tanks used to store regulated substances referred to in 9001(2) (A) or (B) or both. A State program may be approved by the Administrator under this section only if the State demonstrates that the State program includes the following requirements and standards and provides for adequate enforcement of compliance with such requirements and standards—

(1) requirements for maintaining a leak detection system, an inventory control system together with tank testing, or a comparable system or method designed to identify releases in a manner consistent with the protection of human health and the environment;

(2) requirements for maintaining records of any monitoring or leak detection system or inventory control system or tank testing system;

(3) requirements for reporting of any releases and corrective action taken in response to a release from an underground storage tank;

(4) requirements for taking corrective action in response to a release from an underground storage tank;

(5) requirements for the closure of tanks to prevent future releases of regulated substances into the environment;

(6) requirements for maintaining evidence of financial responsibility for taking corrective action and compensating third parties for bodily injury and property damage caused by sudden and nonsudden accidental releases arising from operating an underground storage tank;

(7) standards of performance for new underground storage tanks; and

(8) requirements—

(A) for notifying the appropriate State agency or department (or local agency or department) designated according to section 9002(b)(1) of the existence of any operational or non-operational underground storage tank; and

(B) for providing the information required on the form issued pursuant to section 9002(b)(2).

(b) Federal Standards.—

(1) A State program submitted under this section may be approved only if the requirements under paragraphs (1) through (7) of subsection (a) are no less stringent than the corresponding requirements standards promulgated by the Administrator pursuant to section 9003(a).

(2) (A) A State program may be approved without regard to whether or not the requirements referred to in paragraphs (1), (2), (3), and (5) of subsection (a) are less stringent than the corresponding standards under section 9003(a) during the one-year period commencing on the date of promulgation of regulations under section 9003(a) if State regulatory action but no State legislative action is required in order to adopt a State program.

(B) If such State legislative action is required, the State program may be approved without regard to whether or not the requirements referred to in paragraphs (1), (2), (3), and (5) of subsection (a) are less stringent than the corresponding standards under section 9003(a) during the two-year period commencing on the date of promulgation of regulations under section 9003(a) (and during an additional one-year period after such legislative action if regulations are required to be promulgated by the State pursuant to such legislative action).

(c) Financial Responsibility.—

(1) Corrective action and compensation programs administered by State or local agencies or departments may be submitted for approval under subsection (a)(6) as evidence of financial responsibility.

[§9004(c)(1) amended by PL 99–499]

(2) Financial responsibility required by this subsection may be established in accordance with regulations promulgated by the Administrator by any one, or any combination, of the following: insurance, guarantee, surety bond, letter of credit, qualification as a self-insurer or any other method satisfactory to the Administrator. In promulgating requirements under this subsection, the Administrator is authorized to specify policy or other contractual terms, including the amount of coverage required for various classes and categories of underground storage tanks pursuant to section 9003(d)(5), conditions, or defenses which are necessary or are unacceptable in establishing such evidence of financial responsibility in order to effectuate the purposes of this subtitle.

[§9004(c)(2) amended by PL 99–499]

(3) In any case where the owner or operator is in bankruptcy, reorganization, or arrangement pursuant to the Federal Bankruptcy Code or where with reasonable diligence jurisdiction in any State court of the Federal courts cannot be obtained over an owner or operator likely to be solvent at the time of judgment, any claim aris-

ing from conduct for which evidence of financial responsibility must be provided under this subsection may be asserted directly against the guarantor providing such evidence of financial responsibility. In the case of any action pursuant to this paragraph such guarantor shall be entitled to invoke all rights and defenses which would have been available to the owner or operator if any action had been brought against the owner or operator by the claimant and which would have been available to the guarantor if an action had been brought against the guarantor by the owner or operator.

(4) The total liability of any guarantor shall be limited to the aggregate amount which the guarantor has provided as evidence of financial responsibility to the owner or operator under this section. Nothing in this subsection shall be construed to limit any other State or Federal statutory, contractual or common law liability of a guarantor to its owner or operator including, but not limited to, the liability of such guarantor for bad faith either in negotiating or in failing to negotiate the settlement of any claim. Nothing in this subsection shall be construed to diminish the liability of any person under section 107 or 111 of the Comprehensive Environmental Response, Compensation and Liability Act of 1980 or other applicable law.

(5) For the purpose of this subsection, the term "guarantor" means any person, other than the owner or operator, who provides evidence of financial responsibility for an owner or operator under this subsection.

(d) EPA Determination. —

(1) Within one hundred and eighty days of the date of receipt of a proposed State program, the Administrator shall, after notice and opportunity for public comment, make a determination whether the State's program complies with the provisions of this section and provides for adequate enforcement of compliance with the requirements and standards pursuant to this section.

(2) If the Administrator determines that a State program complies with the provisions of this section and provides for adequate enforcement of compliance with the requirements and standards adopted pursuant to this section, he shall approve the State program in lieu of the Federal program and the State shall have primary enforcement responsibility with respect to requirements of its program.

(e) Withdrawal of Authorization. — Whenever the Administrator determines after public hearing that a State is not administering and enforcing a program authorized under this subtitle in accordance with the provisions of this section, he shall so notify the State. If appropriate action is not taken within a reasonable time, not to exceed one hundred and twenty days after such notification, the Administrator shall withdraw approval of such program and reestablish the Federal programs pursuant to this subtitle.

[§9004 added by PL 98–616]

§6991d. Inspections, Monitoring, Testing and Corrective Action [Sec. 9005]

(a) Furnishing Information. — For the purposes of developing or assisting in the development of any regulation, conducting any study, taking any corrective action or enforcing the provisions of this subtitle, any owner or operator of an underground storage tank (or any tank subject to study under section 9009 that is used for storing regulated substances) shall, upon request of any officer, employee or representative of the Environmental Protection Agency, duly designated by the Administrator, or upon request of any duly designated officer, employee, or representative of a State acting pursuant to subsection (h)(7) of section 9003 or with an approved program, furnish information relating to such tanks, their associated equipment, their contents, conduct monitoring or testing, permit such officer at all reasonable times to have access to, and to copy all records relating to such tanks and permit such officer to have access for corrective action. For the purposes of developing or assisting in the development of any regulation, conducting any study, taking corrective action, or enforcing the provisions of this subtitle, such officers, employees, or representatives are authorized—

(1) to enter at reasonable times any establishment or other place where an underground storage tank is located;

(2) to inspect and obtain samples from any person of any regulated substances contained in such tank;

(3) to conduct monitoring or testing of the tanks, associated equipment, contents, or surrounding soils, air, surface water or ground water; and

Each such inspection shall be commenced and completed with reasonable promptness.

(4) to take corrective action.

[§9005(a) amended by PL 99–499]

(b) Confidentiality. —

(1) Any records, reports, or information obtained from any persons under this section shall be available to the public except that upon a showing satisfactory to the Administrator (or the State, as the case may be) by any person that records, reports, or information, or a particular part thereof, to which the Administrator (or the State, as the case may be) or any officer, employee, or representative thereof has access under this section if made public, would divulge information entitled to protection under section 1905 of title 18 of the United States Code, such information or particular portion thereof shall be considered confidential in accordance with the purposes of that section, except that such record, report, document, or information may be disclosed to other officers, employees, or authorized representatives of the United States concerned with carrying out this Act, or when relevant in any proceeding under this Act.

(2) Any person not subject to the provisions of section 1905 of title 18 of the United States Code who knowingly and willfully divulges or discloses any information entitled to protection under this subsection shall, upon conviction, be subject to a fine of not more than $5,000 or to imprisonment not to exceed one year, or both.

(3) In submitting data under this subtitle, a person required to provide such data may—

(A) designate the data which such person believes is entitled to protection under this subsection, and

(B) submit such designated data separately from other data submitted under this subtitle. A designation under this paragraph shall be made in writing and in such manner as the Administrator may prescribe.

(4) Notwithstanding any limitation contained in this section or any other provision of law, all information reported to, or otherwise obtained, by the Administrator (or any representative of the Administrator) under this Act shall be made available, upon written request of any duly authorized committee of the Congress, to such committee (including records, reports, or information obtained by representatives of the Environmental Protection Agency).

[§9005 added by PL 98–616]

§6991e. Federal Enforcement [Sec. 9006]

(a) Compliance Orders. —

(1) Except as provided in paragraph (2), whenever on the basis of any information, the Administrator determines that any person is in violation of any requirement of this subtitle, the Administrator may issue an order requiring compliance within a reasonable specified time period or the Administrator may commence a civil action in the United States district court in which the violation occurred for appropriate relief, including a temporary or permanent injunction.

(2) In the case of a violation of any requirement of this subtitle where such violation occurs in a State with a program approved under section 9004, the Administrator shall give notice to the State in which such violation has occurred prior to issuing an order or commencing a civil action under this section.

(3) If a violator fails to comply with an order under this subsection within the time specified in the order, he shall be liable for a civil penalty of not more than $25,000 for each day of continued noncompliance.

(b) Procedure. — Any order issued under this section shall become final unless, no later than thirty days after the order is served, the person or persons named therein request a public hearing. Upon such request the Administrator shall promptly conduct a public hearing. In connection with any proceeding under this section the Administrator may issue subpoenas for the attendance and testimony of witnesses and the production of relevant papers, books, and documents, and may promulgate rules for discovery procedures.

(c) Contents of Order. — Any order issued under this section shall state with reasonable specificity the nature of the violation, specify a reasonable time for compliance, and assess a penalty, if any, which the Administrator determines is reasonable taking into account the seriousness of the violation and any good faith efforts to comply with the applicable requirements.

(d) Civil Penalties. —

(1) Any owner who knowingly fails to notify or submits false information pursuant to section 9002(a) shall be subject to a civil penalty not to exceed $10,000 for each tank for which notification is not given or false information is submitted.

(2) Any owner or operator of an underground storage tank who fails to comply with—

(A) any requirement or standard promulgated by the Administrator under section 9003;

(B) any requirement or standard of a State program approved pursuant to section 9004; or

(C) the provisions of section 9003(g) (entitled "Interim Prohibition") shall be subject to a civil penalty not to exceed $10,000 for each tank for each day of violation.

[§9006 added by PL 98–616]

§6991f. Federal Facilities [Sec. 9007]

(a) Application of Subtitle. — Each department, agency, and instrumentality of the executive, legislative, and judicial branches of the Federal Government having jurisdiction over any underground storage tank shall be subject to and comply with all Federal, State, interstate, and local requirements, applicable to such tank, both substantive and procedural, in the same manner, and to the same extent, as any other person is subject to such requirements, including payment of reasonable service charges. Neither the United States, nor any agent, employee, or officer thereof, shall be immune or exempt from any process or sanction of any State or Federal court with respect to the enforcement of any such injunctive relief.

(b) Presidential Exemption. — The President may exempt any underground storage tanks of any department, agency, or instrumentality in the executive branch from compliance with such a requirement if he determines it to be in the paramount interest of the United States to do so. No such exemption shall be granted due to lack of appropriation unless the President shall have specifically requested such appropriation as a part of the budgetary process and the Congress shall have failed to make available such requested appropriations. Any exemption shall be for a period not in excess of one year, but additional exemptions may be granted for periods not to exceed one year upon the President's making a new determination. The President shall report each January to the Congress all exemptions from the requirements of this section granted during the preceding calendar year, together with his reason for granting each such exemption.

[§9007 added by PL 98–616]

§6991g. State Authority [Sec. 9008]

Nothing in this subtitle shall preclude or deny any right of any State or political subdivision thereof to adopt or enforce any regulation, requirement, or standard of performance respecting underground storage tanks that is more stringent than a regulation, requirement, or standard of performance in effect under this subtitle or to impose any additional liability with respect to the release of regulated substances within such State or political subdivision.

[§9008 added by PL 98–616; amended by PL 99–499]

§6991h. Study of Underground Storage Tanks [Sec. 9009]

(a) Petroleum Tanks. — Not later than twelve months after the date of enactment of the Hazardous and Solid Waste Amendments of 1984, the Administrator shall complete a study of underground storage tanks used for the storage of regulated substances defined in section 9001(2)(B) 42 U.S.C. 6997(2)(B).

(b) Other Tanks. — Not later than thirty-six months after the date of enactment of the Hazardous and Solid Waste Amendments of 1984, the Administrator shall complete a study of all other underground storage tanks.

(c) Elements of Studies. — The studies under subsections (a) and (b) shall include an assessment of the ages, types (including methods of manufacture, coatings, protection systems, the compatibility of the construction materials and the installation methods) and locations (including the climate of the locations) of such tanks; soil conditions water tables, and the hydrogeology of tank locations; the relationship between the foregoing factors and the likelihood of releases from underground storage tanks; the effectiveness and costs of inventory systems, tank testing, and leak detection systems; and such other factors as the Administrator deems appropriate.

(d) Farm and Heating Oil Tanks. — Not later than thirty-six months after the date of enactment of the Hazardous and Solid Waste Amendments of 1984, the Administrator shall conduct a study regarding the tanks referred to in section 9001(1)(A) and (B). Such study shall include estimates of the number and location of such tanks and an analysis of the extent to which there may be releases or threatened releases from such tanks into the environment.

(e) Reports. — Upon completion of the studies authorized by this section, the Administrator shall submit reports to the President and to the Congress containing the results of the studies and recommendations respecting whether or not such tanks should be subject to the preceding provisions of this subtitle.

(f) Reimbursement. —

(1) If any owner or operator (excepting an agency, department, or instrumentality of the United States Government, a State or a political subdivision thereof) shall incur costs, including the loss of business opportunity, due to the closure or interruption of operation of an underground storage tank solely for the purpose of conducting studies authorized by this section, the Administrator shall provide such person fair and equitable reimbursement for such costs.

(2) All claims for reimbursement shall be filed with the Administrator not later than ninety days after the closure or interruption which gives rise to the claim.

(3) Reimbursements made under this section shall be from funds appropriated by the Congress pursuant to the authorization contained in section 207(g).

(4) For purposes of judicial review, a determination by the Administrator under this subsection shall be considered final agency action.

[§9009 added by PL 98–616]

§6991i. Authorization of Appropriations [Sec. 9010]

For authorization of appropriations to carry out this subtitle, see section 2007(g).

[§9010 added by PL 98–616]

SUBTITLE J — DEMONSTRATION MEDICAL WASTE TRACKING PROGRAM

[Subtitle J added by PL 100–582]

§6992. Scope of Demonstration Program for Medical Waste [Sec. 11001]

(a) Covered States. — The States within the demonstration program established under this subtitle for tracking medical wastes shall be New York, New Jersey, Connecticut, the States contiguous to the Great Lakes and any State included in the program through the petition procedure described in subsection (c), except for any of such States in which the Governor notifies the Administrator under subsection (b) that such State shall not be covered by the program.

(b) Opt Out. —

(1) If the Governor of any State covered under subsection (a) which is not contiguous to the Atlantic Ocean notifies the Administrator that such State elects not to participate in the demonstration program, the Administrator shall remove such State from the program.

(2) If the Governor of any other State covered under subsection (a) notifies the Administrator that such State has implemented a medical waste tracking program that is no less stringent than the demonstration program under this subtitle and that such State elects not to participate in the demonstration program, the Administrator shall, if the Administrator determines that such State program is no less stringent than the demonstration program under this subtitle, remove such State from the demonstration program.

(3) Notifications under paragraphs (1) or (2) shall be submitted to the Administrator no later than 30 days after the promulgation of regulations implementing the demonstration program under this subtitle.

(c) Petition In. — The Governor of any State may petition the Administrator to be included in the demonstration program and the Administrator may, in his discretion, include any such State. Such petition may not be made later than 30 days after promulgation of regulations establishing the demonstration program under this subtitle, and the Administrator shall determine whether to include the State within 30 days after receipt of the State's petition.

(d) Expiration of Demonstration Program. — The demonstration program shall expire on the date 24 months after the effective date of the regulations under this subtitle.

§6992a. Listing of Medical Wastes [Sec. 11002]

(a) List. — Not later than 6 months after the enactment of this subtitle, the Administrator shall promulgate regulations listing the types of medical waste to be tracked under the demonstration program. Except as provided in subsection (b), such list shall include, but need not be limited to, each of the following types of solid waste:

(1) Cultures and stocks of infectious agents and associated biologicals, including cultures from medical and pathological laboratories, cultures and stocks of infectious agents from research and industrial laboratories, wastes from the production of biologicals, discarded live and attenuated vaccines, and culture dishes and devices used to transfer, inoculate, and mix cultures.

(2) Pathological wastes, including tissues, organs, and body parts that are removed during surgery or autopsy.

(3) Waste human blood and products of blood, including serum, plasma, and other blood components.

(4) Sharps that have been used in patient care or in medical, research or industrial laboratories, including hypodermic needles, syringes, pasteur pipettes, broken glass, and scalpel blades.

(5) Contaminated animal carcasses, body parts, and bedding of animals that were exposed to infectious agents during research, production of biologicals, or testing of pharmaceuticals.

(6) Wastes from surgery or autopsy that were in contact with infectious agents, including solid dressings, sponges, drapes, lavage tubes, drainage sets, underpads, and surgical gloves.

(7) Laboratory wastes from medical, pathological, pharmaceutical, or other research, commercial, or industrial laboratories that were in contact with infectious agents, including slides and cover slips, disposable gloves, laboratory coats, and aprons.

(8) Dialysis wastes that were in contact with the blood of patients undergoing hemodialysis, including contaminated disposable equipment and supplies such as tubing, filters, disposable sheets, towels, gloves, aprons, and laboratory coats.

(9) Discarded medical equipment and parts that were in contact with infectious agents.

(10) Biological waste and discarded materials contaminated with blood, excretion, exudates or secretion from human beings or animals who are isolated to protect others from communicable diseases.

(11) Such other waste material that results from the administration of medical care to a patient by a health care provider and is found by the Administrator to pose a threat to human health or the environment.

(b) Exclusions From List. — The Administrator may exclude from the list under this section any categories or items described in paragraphs (6) through (10) of subsection (a) which he determines do not pose a substantial present or potential hazard to human health or the environment when improperly treated, stored, transported disposed of, or otherwise managed.

§6992b. Tracking of Medical Waste [Sec. 11003]

(a) Demonstration Program. — Not later than 6 months after the enactment of this subtitle, the Administrator shall promulgate regulations establishing a program for the tracking of the medical waste listed in section 11002 which is generated in a State subject to the demonstration program. The program shall (l) provide for tracking of the transportation of the waste from the generator to the disposal facility, except that waste that is incinerated need not be tracked after incineration, (2) include a system for providing the generator of the waste with assurance that the waste is received by the disposal facility, (3) use a uniform form for tracking in each of the demonstration States, and (4) include the following requirements:

(A) A requirement for segregation of the waste at the point of generation where practicable.

(B) A requirement of placement of the waste in containers that will protect waste handlers and the public from exposure.

(C) A requirement for appropriate labeling of containers of the waste.

(b) Small Quantities. — In the program under subsection (a), the Administrator may establish an exemption for generators of small quantities of medical waste listed under section 11002, except that the Administrator may not exempt from the program any person who, or facility that, generates 50 pounds or more of such waste in any calendar month.

(c) On-Site Incinerators. — Concurrently with the promulgation of regulations under section (a), the Administrator shall promulgate a recordkeeping and reporting requirement for any generator in a demonstration State of medical waste listed in section 11002 that (1) incinerates medical waste listed in section 11002 on site and (2) does not track such waste under the regulations promulgated under subsection (a). Such requirement shall require the generator to report to the Administrator on the volume and types of medical waste listed in section 11002 that the generator incinerated on site during the 6 months following the effective date of the requirements of this subsection.

(d) Type of Medical and Types of Generators.— For each of the requirements of this section, the regulations may vary for different types of medical waste and for different types of medical waste generators.

§6992c. Inspections [Sec. 11004]

(a) Requirements for Access. — For purposes of developing or assisting in the development of any regulation or report under this subtitle or enforcing any provision of this subtitle, any person who generates, stores, treats, transports, disposes of, or otherwise handles or has handled medical waste shall, upon request of any officer, employee, or representative of the Environmental Protection Agency duly designated by the Administrator, furnish information relating to such waste, including any tracking forms required to be maintained under section 11003, conduct monitoring or testing, and permit such person at all reasonable times to have access to, and to copy, all records relating to such waste. For such purposes, such officers, employees, or representatives are authorized to—

(1) enter at reasonable times any establishment or other place where medical wastes are or have been generated, stored, treated, disposed of, or transported from;

(2) conduct monitoring or testing; and

(3) inspect and obtain samples from any person of any such wastes and samples of any containers or labeling for such wastes.

(b) Procedures. — Each inspection under this section shall be commenced and completed with reasonable promptness. If the officer, employee, or representative obtains any samples, prior to leaving the premises he shall give to the owner, operator, or agent in charge a receipt describing the sample obtained and, if requested, a portion of each such sample equal in volume or weight to the portion retained if giving such an equal portion is feasible. If any analysis is made of such samples, a copy of the results of such analysis shall be furnished promptly to the owner, operator, or agent in charge of the premises concerned.

(c) Availability to Public. — The provisions of section 3007(b) of this Act shall apply to records, reports, and information obtained under this section in the same manner and to the same extent as such provisions apply to records, reports, and information obtained under section 3007.

§6992d. Enforcement [Sec. 11005]

(a) Compliance Orders. —

(1) Violations. — Whenever on the basis of any information the Administrator determines that any person has violated, or is in violation of, any requirement or prohibition in effect under this subtitle (including any requirement or prohibition in effect under regulations under this subtitle) (A) the Administrator may issue an order (i) assessing a civil penalty for any past or current violation, (ii) requiring compliance immediately or within a specified time period, or (iii) both, or (B) the Administrator may commence a civil action in the United States district court in the district in which the violation occurred for appropriate relief, including a temporary or permanent injunction. Any order issued pursuant to this subsection shall state with reasonable specificity the nature of the violation.

(2) Orders Assessing Penalties. — Any penalty assessed in an order under this subsection shall not exceed $25,000 per day of noncompliance for each violation of a requirement or prohibition in effect under this subtitle. In assessing such a penalty, the Administrator shall take into account the seriousness of the violation and any good faith efforts to comply with applicable requirements.

(3) Public Hearing. — Any order issued under this subsection shall become final unless, not later than 30 days after issuance of the order, the persons named therein request a public hearing. Upon such request, the Administrator shall promptly conduct a public hearing. In connection with any proceeding under this section, the Administrator may issue subpoenas for the production of relevant papers, books, and documents, and may promulgate rules for discovery procedures.

(4) Violation of Compliance Orders. — In the case of an order under this subsection requiring compliance with any requirement of or regulation under this subtitle, if a violator fails to take corrective action within the time specified in an order, the Administrator may assess a civil penalty of not more than $25,000 for each day of continued noncompliance with the order.

(b) Criminal Penalties. — Any person who—

(1) knowingly violates the requirements of or regulations under this subtitle;

(2) knowingly omits material information or makes any false material statement or representation in any label, record, report, or other document filed, maintained, or used for purposes of compliance with this subtitle or regulations thereunder; or

(3) knowingly generates, stores, treats, transports, disposes of, or otherwise handles any medical waste (whether such activity took place before or takes place after the date of the enactment of this paragraph) and who knowingly destroys, alters, conceals, or fails to file any record, report, or other document required to be maintained or filed for purposes of compliance with this subtitle or regulations thereunder

shall, upon conviction, be subject to a fine or not more than $50,000 for each day of violation, or imprisonment not to exceed 2 years (5 years in the case of a violation of paragraph (1)). If the conviction is for a violation committed after a first conviction of such person under this paragraph, the maximum punishment under the respective paragraph shall be doubled with respect to both fine and imprisonment.

(c) Knowing Endangerment. — Any person who knowingly violates any provision of subsection (b) who knows at that time that he thereby places another person in imminent danger of death or serious bodily injury, shall upon conviction be subject to a fine of not more than $250,000 or imprisonment for not more than 15 years, or both. A defendant that is an organization shall, upon conviction under this subsection, be subject to a fine of not more than $1,000,000. The terms of this paragraph shall be interpreted in accordance with the rules provided under section 3008(f) of this Act.

(d) Civil Penalties. — Any person who violates any requirement of or regulation under this subtitle shall be liable to the United States for a civil penalty in an amount not to exceed $25,000 for each such violation. Each day of such violation shall, for purposes of this section constitute a separate violation.

(e) Civil Penalty Policy. — Civil penalties assessed by the United States or by the States under this subtitle shall be assessed in accordance with the Administrator's "RCRA Civil Penalty Policy", as such policy may be amended from time to time.

§6992e. Federal Facilities [Sec. 11006]

(a) In General. — Each department, agency, and instrumentality of the executive, legislative, and judicial branches of the Federal Government in a demonstration State (l) having jurisdiction over any solid waste management facility or disposal site at which medical waste is disposed of or otherwise handled, or (2) engaged in any activity resulting, or which may result, in the disposal, management, or handling of medical waste shall be subject to, and comply with all Federal, State, interstate, and local requirements, both substantive and procedural (including any requirement for permits or reporting or any provisions for injunctive relief and such sanctions as may be imposed by a court to enforce such relief), respecting control and abatement of medical waste disposal and management in the same manner, and to the same extent, as any person is subject to such requirements, including the payment of reasonable service charges. The Federal, State, interstate, and local substantive and procedural requirements referred to in this subsection include, but are not limited to, all administrative orders, civil, criminal, and administrative penalties, and other sanctions, including injunctive relief, fines, and imprisonment. Neither the United States, nor any agent, employee, or officer thereof, shall be immune or exempt from any process or sanction of any State or Federal court with respect to the enforcement of any such order, penalty, or other sanction. For purposes of enforcing any such substantive or procedural requirement (including, but not limited to, any injunctive relief, administrative order, or civil, criminal, administrative penalty, or other sanction), against any such department, agency, or instrumentality, the United States hereby expressly waives any immunity otherwise applicable to the United States. The President may exempt any department, agency, or instrumentality in the executive branch from compliance with such a requirement if he determines it to be in the paramount interest of the United States to do so. No such exemption shall be granted due to lack of appropriation unless the President shall have specifically requested such appropriation as a part of the budgetary process and the Congress shall have failed to make available such requested appropriation. Any exemption shall be for a period not in excess of one year, but additional exemptions may be granted for periods not to exceed one year upon the President's making a new determination. The President shall report each January to the Congress all exemptions from the requirements of this section granted during the preceding calendar year, together with his reason for granting each such exemption.

(b) Definition of Person. — For purposes of this Act, the term "person" shall be treated as including each department, agency, and instrumentality of the United States.

§6992f. Relationship to State Law [Sec. 11007]

(a) State Inspections and Enforcement. —A State may conduct inspections under 11004 and take enforcement actions under section 11105 against any person, including any person who has imported medical waste into a State in violation of the requirements of, or regulations under, this subtitle, to the same extent as the Administrator. At the time a State initiates an enforcement action under section 11005 against any person, the State shall notify the Administrator in writing.

(b) Retention of State Authority. — Nothing in this subtitle shall —

(1) preempt any State or local law; or

(2) except as provided in subsection (c), otherwise affect any State or local law or the author-

ity of any State or local government to adopt or enforce any State or local law.

(c) State Forms. — Any State or local law which requires submission of a tracking form from any person subject to this subtitle shall require that the form be identical in content and format to the form required under section 11003, except that a State may require the submission of other tracking information which is supplemental to the information required on the form required under section 11003 through additional sheets or such other means as the State deems appropriate.

§6992g. Report to Congress [Sec. 11008]

(a) Final Report. — Not later than 3 months after the expiration of the demonstration program, the Administrator shall report to Congress on the following topics:

(1) The types, number, and size of generators of medical waste (including small quantity generators) in the United States, the types and amounts of medical waste generated, and the on-site and off-site methods currently used to handle, store, transport, treat, and dispose of the medical waste, including the extent to which such waste is disposed of in sewer systems.

(2) The present or potential threat to human health and the environment posed by medical waste or the incineration thereof.

(3) The present and potential costs (A) to local economies, persons, and the environment from the improper handling, storage, transportation, treatment or disposal of medical waste and (B) to generators, transporters, and treatment, storage, and disposal facilities from regulations establishing requirements for tracking, handling, storage, transportation, treatment, and disposal of medical waste.

(4) (A) The success of the demonstration program established under this subtitle in tracking medical waste,

(B) changes in incineration and storage practices attributable to the demonstration program, and

(C) other available and potentially available methods for tracking medical waste and their advantages and disadvantages, including the advantages and disadvantages of extending tracking requirements to (i) rural areas and (ii) small quantity generators.

(5) Available and potentially available methods for handling, storing, transporting, and disposing of medical waste and their advantages and disadvantages.

(6) Available and potentially available methods for treating medical waste, including the methods of incineration, sterilization, chemical treatment, and grinding, and their advantages, including their ability to render medical waste noninfectious or less infectious, and unrecognizable and otherwise protect human health and the environment, and disadvantages.

(7) Factors affecting the effectiveness of the treatment methods identified in subsection (a)(5), including quality control and quality assurance procedures, maintenance procedures, and operator training.

(8) Existing State and local controls on the handling, storage, transportation, treatment, and disposal of medical waste, including the enforcement and regulatory supervision thereof.

(9) The appropriateness of using any existing State requirements or the requirements contained in subtitle C as nationwide requirements to monitor and control medical waste.

(10) The appropriateness of the penalties provided in section 11006 for insuring compliance with the requirements of this subtitle, including a review of the level of penalties imposed under this subtitle.

(11) (A) The effect of excluding households and small quantity generators from any regulations governing the handling, storage, transportation, treatment, and disposal of medical waste, and

(B) potential guidelines for the handling, storage, treatment, and disposal of medical waste by households and small quantity generators.

(12) Available and potentially available methods for the reuse or reduction of the volume of medical waste generated.

(b) Interim Reports. — The Administrator shall submit two interim reports to Congress on the topics listed in subsection (a). The interim reports shall contain the information on the topics available to the Administrator at the time of submission. One interim report shall be due 9 months after enactment of this subtitle and one shall be due 12 months after the effective date of regulations under this subtitle.

(c) Consultation. — In preparing the reports under this section, the Administrator shall consult with appropriate State and local agencies.

§6992h. Health Impacts Reports [Sec. 11009]

Within 24 months after the enactment of this section, the Administrator of the Agency for Toxic Substances and Disease Registry shall prepare for Congress a report on the health effects of medical waste, including each of the following—

(1) A description of the potential for infection or injury from the segregation, handling, storage, treatment, or disposal of medical wastes.

(2) An estimate of the number of people injured or infected annually by sharps, and the nature and seriousness of those injuries or infections.

(3) An estimate of the number of people infected annually by other means related to waste segregation, handling, storage, treatment, or disposal, and the nature and seriousness of those infections.

(4) For diseases possibly spread by medical waste, including Acquired Immune Deficiency Syndrome and hepatitis B, an estimate of what percentage of the total number of cases nationally may be traceable to medical wastes.

§6992i. General Provisions [Sec. 11010]

(a) Consultation.—

(1) In promulgating regulations under this subtitle, the Administrator shall consult with the affected States and may consult with other interested parties.

(2) The Administrator shall also consult with the International Joint Commission to determine how to monitor the disposal of medical waste emanating from Canada.

(b) Public Comment.— In the case of the regulations required by this subtitle to be promulgated within 9 months after the enactment of this subtitle, the Administrator may promulgate such regulations in interim final form without prior opportunity for public comment, but the Administrator shall provide an opportunity for public comment on the interim final rule. The promulgation of such regulations shall not be subject to the Paperwork Reduction Act of 1980.

(c) Relationship to Subtitle C.—Nothing in this subtitle shall affect the authority of the Administrator to regulate medical waste, including medical waste listed under section 11002, under subtitle C of this Act.

§6992j. Effective Date [Sec. 11011]

The regulations promulgated under this subtitle shall take effect within 90 days after promulgation, except that, at the time of promulgation, the Administrator may provide for a shorter period to the effective date if he finds the regulated community does not need 90 days to come into compliance.

§6992k. Authorization of Appropriations [Sec. 11012]

There are authorized to be appropriated to the Administrator such sums as may be necessary for each of the fiscal years 1989 through 1991 for purposes of carrying out activities under this subtitle.

[Editor's Note: This ends §2 of RCRA and its rewriting of the Solid Waste Disposal Act. Now begins §3 of RCRA.]

Solid Waste Cleanup on Federal Lands in Alaska [Sec. 3]

[Repealed by PL 96–482]

§6981. Llangollen Landfill, Del., Leachate Control Research Program [Sec. 4]

(a) In order to demonstrate effective means of dealing with contamination of public water supplies by leachate from abandoned or other landfills, the Administrator of the Environmental Protection Agency is authorized to provide technical and financial assistance for a research program to control leachate from the Llangollen Landfill in New Castle County, Delaware.

(b) The research program authorized by this section shall be designed by the New Castle County areawide waste treatment management program, in cooperation with the Environmental Protection Agency, to develop methods for controlling leachate contamination from abandoned and other landfills that may be applied at the Llangollen Landfill and at other landfills throughout the Nation. Such research program shall investigate all alternative solutions or corrective actions, including—

(1) hydrogeologic isolation of the landfill combined with the collection and treatment of leachate;

(2) excavation of the refuse, followed by some type of incineration;

(3) excavation and transportation of the refuse to another landfill; and

(4) collection and treatment of contaminated leachate or ground water.

Such research progarm shall consider the economic, social, and environmental consequences of each such alternative.

(c) The Administrator of the Environmental Protection Agency shall make available personnel of the Agency, including those of the Solid and

Hazardous Waste Research Laboratory (Cincinnati, Ohio), and shall arrange for other Federal personnel to be made available, to provide technical assistance and aid in such research. The Administrator may provide up to $250,000, of the sums appropriated under the Solid Waste Disposal Act, to the New Castle County areawide waste treatment management program to conduct such research, including obtaining consultant services.

(d) In order to prevent further damage to public water supplies during the period of this study, the Administrator of the Environmental Protection Agency shall provide up to $200,000 in each of fiscal years 1977 and 1978, of the sums appropriated under the Solid Waste Disposal Act for the operating costs of a counter-pumping program to contain the leachate from the Llangollen Landfill.

42 U.S.C. §6981

ADDITIONAL PROVISIONS

[Editor's Note: §32(b), (c), (d), (e), (f), and (g) of PL 96–482 amended the Solid Waste Disposal Act directly. Those provisions have been incorporated into the Act. The remaining provisions of §32 and of §33, which are relevant to this Act, follow.]

§6941a. Energy and Materials Conservation and Recovery [Sec. 32]

(a) The Congress finds that—

(1) significant savings could be realized by conserving materials in order to reduce the volume or quantity of material which ultimately becomes waste;

(2) solid waste contains valuable energy and material resources which can be recovered and used thereby conserving increasingly scarce and expensive fossil fuels and virgin materials;

(3) the recovery of energy and materials from municipal waste, and the conservation of energy and materials contributing to such waste streams, can have the effect of reducing the volume of the municipal waste stream and the burden of disposing of increasing volumes of solid waste;

(4) the technology to conserve resources exists and is commercially feasible to apply;

(5) the technology to recover energy and materials from solid waste is of demonstrated commercial feasibility; and

(6) various communities throughout the nation have different needs and different potentials for conserving resources and for utilizing techniques for the recovery of energy and materials from waste, and Federal assistance in planning and implementing such energy and materials conservation and recovery programs should be available to all such communities on an equitable basis in relation to their needs and potential.

[§32 added by PL 96–482]

§6981. National Advisory Commission on Resource Conservation and Recovery [Sec. 33]

(a) (1) There is hereby established in the executive branch of the United States the National Advisory Commission on Resource Conservation and Recovery, hereinafter in this section referred to as the "Commission."

(2) The Commission shall be composed of nine members to be appointed by the President. Such members shall be qualified by reason of their education, training, or experience to represent the view of consumer groups, industry associations, and environmental and other groups concerned with resource conservation and recovery and at least two shall be elected or appointed State or local officials. Members shall be appointed for the life of the Commission.

(3) A vacancy in the Commission shall be filled in the manner in which the original appointment was made.

(4) Five members of the Commission shall constitute a quorum for transacting business of the Commission except that a lesser number may hold hearings and conduct information-gathering meetings.

(5) The Chairperson of the Commission shall be designated by the President from among the members.

(6) Upon the expiration of the two-year period beginning on (A) the date when all initial members of the Commission have been appointed or when (B) the date when initial funds become available to carry out this section, whichever is later, the Commission shall transmit to the President, and to each House of the Congress, a final report containing a detailed statement of the findings and conclusions of the Commission, together with such recommendations as it deems advisable.

(7) The Commission shall submit an interim report on February 15, 1982, and the Commission may also submit, for legislative and administrative actions relating to the Solid Waste Disposal Act, other interim reports prior to the submission of its final report.

(8) The Commission shall cease to exist 30 days after submission of its final report.

(b) The Commission shall—

(1) after consultation with the appropriate Federal agencies, review budgetary priorities relating to resource conservation and recovery, determine to what extent program goals relating to resource conservation and recovery are being realized, and make recommendations concerning the appropriate program balance and priorities;

(2) review any existing or proposed resource conservation and recovery guidelines or regulations;

(3) determine the economic development or savings potential of resource conservation and recovery, including the availability of markets for recovered energy and materials, for economic materials savings through conservation, and make recommendations concerning the utilization of such potential;

(4) identify, and make recommendations addressing, institutional obstacles impeding the development of resource conservation and resource recovery; and

(5) evaluate the status of resource conservation and recovery technology and systems including both materials and energy recovery technologies, recy-

cling methods, and other innovative methods for both conserving energy and materials extractable from solid waste.

The review referred to in paragraph (1) should include but not be limited to an assessment of the effectiveness of the technical assistance panels, the public participation program and other program activities under the Solid Waste Disposal Act.

(c) (1) Members of the Commission while serving on business of the Commission, shall be compensated at a rate not to exceed the rate specified at the time of such service for grade GS–16 of the General Schedule for each day they are engaged in the actual performance of Commission duties, including travel time; and while so serving away from their homes or regular places of business, all members of the Commission may be allowed travel expenses, including per diem in lieu of subsistence, as authorized by section 5703 of title 5, United States Code, for persons in Government service employed intermittently.

(2) Subject to such rules as may be adopted by the Commission, the Chairperson, without regard to the provisions of title 5, United States Code, governing appointments in the competitive service and without regard to the provisions of chapter 51 and subchapter III of chapter 53 of such title relating to classification and General Schedule pay rates, shall have the power to—

(A) appoint a Director, who shall be paid at a rate not to exceed the rate of basic pay for level I, GS–16 of the General Schedule; and

(B) appoint and fix the compensation of not more than 5 additional staff personnel.

(3) This Commission is authorized to procure temporary and intermittent services of experts and consultants as are necessary to the extent authorized by section 3109 of title 5, United States Code, but at rates not to exceed the rate specified at the time of such service for grade GS–16 in section 5332 of such title. Experts and consultants may be employed without compensation if they agree to do so in advance.

(4) Upon request of the Commission, the head of any Federal agency is authorized to detail on a reimbursable or nonreimbursable basis any of the personnel of such agency to the Commission to assist the Commission in carrying out its duties under this section.

(5) The Commission is exempt from the requirements of sections 4301 through 4308of title 5, United States Code.

(6) The Commission is authorized to enter into contracts with Federal and State agencies, private firms, institutions, and individuals for the conduct of research or surveys, the preparation of reports, and other activities necessary to the discharge of its duties and responsibilities.

(7) In order to expedite matters pertaining to the planning for, and work of, the Commission, the Commission is authorized to make purchases and contracts without regard to section 252 of title 41 of the United States Code, pertaining to advertising and competitive bidding, and may arrange for the printing of any material pertaining to the work of the Commission without regard to the Government Printing and Binding Regulations and any related laws or regulations.

(8) The Commission may use the United States mail in the same manner and under the same conditions as other departments and agencies of the United States.

(9) The Commission may secure directly from any department or agency of the United States information necessary to enable it to carry out its duties and functions. Upon request of the Chairperson, the head of any such Federal agency shall furnish such information to the Commission subject to applicable law.

(10) Financial and administrative services (including those related to budget and accounting, financial reporting, personnel, and procurement) shall be provided to the Commission by the General Services Administration for which payment shall be made in advance, or by reimbursement, from funds of the Commission, in such amounts as may be agreed upon by the Chairperson of the Commission and the Administrator of General Services.

(d) In carrying out its duties under this section the Commission, or any duly authorized committee thereof, is authorized to hold such hearings and take testimony, with respect to matters to which it has a responsibility under this section as the Commission may deem advisable. The Chairperson of the Commission or any member authorized by him may administer oaths or affirmations to witnesses appearing before the Commission or before any committee thereof.

(e) From the amounts authorized to be appropriated under the Solid Waste Disposal Act for the fiscal years 1981 and 1982, not more than $1,000,000 may be used to carry out the provisions of this section.

[§33 added by PL 96–482]

[Editor's Note: Sections 701, 703, and 704 of PL 98–616 do not amend this Act, but contain provisions pertaining to a report to Congress on injection wells, the relationship of the 1984 amendments to other laws, and the establishment of a commission to study ground water contamination from hazardous waste. The text of the relevant sections follows.]

Additional Provisions

TITLE VII–OTHER PROVISIONS

Report to Congress on Injection of Hazardous Waste [Sec. 701]

(a) The Administrator, in cooperation with the States, shall compile and, not later than six months after the date of enactment of the Hazardous and Solid Waste Amendments of 1984, submit to the Committee on Environment and Public Works of the United States Senate and the Committee on Energy and Commerce of the United States House of Representatives, an inventory of all wells in the United States which inject hazardous wastes. The inventory shall include the following information:

(1) the location and depth of each well;

(2) engineering and construction details of each, including the thickness and composition of its casing, the width and content of the annulus, and pump pressure and capacity;

(3) the hydrogeological characteristics of the overlying and underlying strata, as well as that into which the waste is injected;

(4) the location and size of all drinking water aquifers penetrated by the well, or within a one-mile radius of the well or within two hundred feet below the well injection point;

(5) the location, capacity, and population served by each well providing drinking or irrigation water which is within a five-mile radius of the injection well;

(6) the nature and volume of the waste injected during the one-year period immediately preceding the date of the report;

(7) the dates and nature of the inspections of the injection well conducted by independent third parties or agents of State, Federal, or local government;

(8) the name and address of all owners and operators of the well and any disposal facility associated with it;

(9) the identification of all wells at which enforcement actions have been initiated under this Act (by reason of well failure, operator error, ground water contamination or for other reasons) and an identification of the wastes involved in such enforcement actions; and

(10) such other information as the Administrator may, in his discretion, deem necessary to define the scope and nature of hazardous waste disposal in the United States through underground injection.

(b) In fulfilling the requirements of paragraphs (3) through (5) of subsection (a), the Administrator need only submit such information as can be obtained from currently existing State records and from site visits to at least twenty facilities containing wells which inject hazardous waste.

(c) The States shall make available to the Administrator such information as he deems necessary to accomplish the objectives of this section.

Uranium Mill Tailings [Sec. 703]

Nothing in the Hazardous and Solid Waste Amendments of 1984 shall be construed to affect, modify, or amend the Uranium Mill Tailings Radiation Control Act of 1978.

National Ground Water Commission [Sec. 704]

(a) There is established a commission to be known as the National Ground Water Commission (hereinafter in this section referred to as the "Commission").

(b) The duties of the Commission are to:

(1) Assess generally the amount, location, and quality of the Nation's ground water resources.

(2) Identify generally the sources, extent, and types of ground water contamination.

(3) Assess the scope and nature of the relationship between ground water contamination and ground water withdrawal and develop projections of available, usable ground water in future years on a nationwide basis.

(4) Assess the relationship between surface water pollution and ground water pollution.

(5) Assess the need for a policy to protect ground water from degradation caused by contamination.

(6) Assess generally the extent of overdrafting of ground water resources, and the adequacy of existing mechanisms for preventing such overdrafting.

(7) Assess generally the engineering and technological capability to recharge aquifers.

(8) Assess the adequacy of the present understanding of ground water recharge zones and sole source aquifers and assess the adequacy of knowledge regarding the interrelationship of designated aquifers and recharge zones.

(9) Assess the role of land-use patterns as these relate to protecting ground water from contamination.

(10) Assess methods for remedial abatement of ground water contamination as well as the costs and benefits of cleaning up polluted ground water and compare cleanup costs to the costs of substitute water supply methods.

(12) Investigate policies and actions taken by foreign governments to protect ground water from contamination.

Assess the use and effectiveness of existing interstate compacts to address ground water protection from contamination.

(13) Analyze existing legal rights and remedies regarding contamination of ground water.

(14) Assess the adequacy of existing standards for ground water quality under State and Federal law.

(15) Assess monitoring methodologies of the States and the Federal Government to achieve the level of protection of the resource as required by State and Federal law.

(16) Assess the relationship between ground water flow systems (and associated recharge areas) and the control of sources of contamination.

(17) Assess the role of underground injection practices as a means of disposing of waste fluids while protecting ground water from contamination.

(18) Assess methods for abatement and containment of ground water contamination and for aquifer restoration including the costs and benefits of alternatives to abatement and containment.

(19) Assess State and Federal ground water law and mechanisms with which to manage the quality of the ground water resource.

(20) Assess the adequacy of existing ground water research and determine future ground water research needs.

(21) Assess the roles of State, local, and Federal Governments in managing ground water quality.

(c) (1) The Commission shall be composed of nineteen members as follows:

(A) six appointed by the Speaker of the United States House of Representatives from among the Members of the House of Representatives, two of whom shall be members of the Committee on Energy and Commerce, two of whom shall be members of the Committee on Public Works and Transportation, and two of whom shall be members of the Committee on Interior and Insular Affairs;

(B) four appointed by the majority leaders of the United States Senate from among the Members of the United States Senate;

(C) eight appointed by the President as follows:

(i) four from among a list of nominations submitted to the President by the National Governors Association, two of whom shall be representatives of ground water appropriation States and two of whom shall be representatives of ground water riparian States;

(ii) one from among a list of nominations submitted to the President by the National League of Cities and the United States Conference of Mayors;

(iii) one from among a list of nominations submitted to the President by the National Academy of Science;

(iv) one from among a list of nominations submitted to the President by groups, organizations, or associations of industries the activities of which may affect ground water; and

(v) one from among a list of nominations submitted to the President from groups, organizations, or associations of citizens which are representative of persons concerned with pollution and environmental issues and which have participated, at the State or Federal level, in studies, administrative proceedings, or litigation (or any combination thereof) relating to ground water; and

(D) the Director of the Office of Technology Assessment. A vacancy in the Commission shall be filled in the manner in which the original appointment was made. Appointments may be made under this subsection without regard to section 5311(b) of title 5, United States Code. Not more than three of the six members appointed under subparagraph (A) and not more than two of the four members appointed under subparagraph (B) may be of the same political party. No member appointed under paragraph (C) may be an officer or employee of the Federal Government.

(2) If any member of the Commission who was appointed to the Commission as a Member of the Congress leaves that office, or if any member of the Commission who was appointed from persons who are not officers or employees of any government becomes an officer or employee of a government, he may continue as a member of the Commission for not longer than the ninety-day period beginning on the date he leaves that office or becomes such an officer or employee, as the case may be.

(3) Members shall be appointed for the life of the Commission

(4) (A) Except as provided in subparagraph (B), members of the Commission shall each be entitled (subject to appropriations provided in advance) to receive the daily equivalent of the maximum annual rate of basic pay in effect for grade GS–18 of the General Schedule for each day (including travel time) during which they are engaged in the actual performance of duties vested in the Commission. While away from their homes or regular places of business in the performance of services for the Commission, members of the Commission shall be allowed travel expenses, including per diem in lieu of subsistence, in the same manner as persons employed intermittently in Government service are allowed expenses under section 5703 of title 5 of the United States Code.

(B) Members of the Commission who are Members of the Congress shall receive no additional pay, allowances, or benefit by reason of their service on the Commission.

(5) Five members of the Commission shall constitute a quorum but two may hold hearings.

(6) The Chairman of the Commission shall be appointed by the Speaker of the House of Representatives from among members appointed under paragraph (1)(A) of this subsection and the Vice Chairman of the Commission shall be appointed by the majority leader of the Senate from among members appointed under paragraph (1)(B) of this subsection. The Chairman and the Vice Chairman of the Commission hall serve for the life of the Commission unless they cease to be members of the Commission before the termination of the Commission.

(7) The Commission shall meet at the call of the Chairman or a majority of its members.

(d) (1) The Commission shall have a Director who shall be appointed by the Chairman, without regard to section 5311(b) of title 5, United States Code.

(2) The Chairman may appoint and fix the pay of such additional personnel as the Chairman considers appropriate.

(3) With the approval of the Commission, the Chairman may procure temporary and intermittent services under section 3109(b) of title 5 of the United States Code.

(4) The Commission shall request, and the Chief of Engineers and the Director of the Geological Survey are each authorized to detail, on a reimbursable basis, any of the personnel of their respective agencies to the Commission to assist it in carrying out its duties under this section. Upon request of the Commission, the head of any other Federal agency is authorized to detail, on a reimbursable basis, any of the personnel of such agency to the Commission to assist it in carrying out its duties under this section.

(e) (1) The Commission may, for the purpose of carrying out this section, hold such hearings, sit and act at such times and places, take such testimony, and receive such evidence, as the Commission considers appropriate.

(2) Any member or agent of the Commission may, if so authorized by the Commission, take any action which the Commission is authorized to take by this section.

(3) The Commission may use the United States mails in the same manner and under the same conditions as other departments and agencies of the United States.

(4) The Administrator of General Services shall provide to the Commission on a reimbursable basis such administrative support services as the Commission may request.

(5) The Commission may secure directly from any department or agency of the United States information necessary to enable it to carry out this section. Upon request of the Chairman of the Commission, the head of such department or agency shall furnish such information to the Commission.

(f) (1) The Commission shall transmit to the President and to each House of the Congress a report not later than October 30, 1986. The report shall contain a detailed statement of the findings and conclusions of the Commission with respect to each item listed in subsection (b), together with its recommendations for such legislation; and administrative actions, as it considers appropriate.

(2) Not later than one year after the enactment of the Hazardous and Solid Waste Amendments of 1984, the Commission shall complete a preliminary study concerning ground water contamination from hazardous and other solid waste and submit to the President and to the Congress a report containing the findings and conclusions of such preliminary study. The study shall be continued thereafter, and final findings and conclusions shall be incorporated as a separate chapter in the report required under paragraph (1). The preliminary study shall include an analysis of the extent of ground water contamination caused by hazardous and other solid waste, the regions and major water supplies most significantly affected by such contamination, and any recommendations of the Commission for preventive or remedial measures to protect human health and the environment from the effects of such contamination.

(g) The Commission shall cease to exist on January 1, 1987.

(h) Nothing in this section and no recommendation of the Commission shall affect any rights to quantities of water established under State law, interstate compact, or Supreme Court decree.

(i) There is authorized to be appropriated for the fiscal years 1985 through 1987 not to exceed $7,000,000 to carry out this section.

[Editor's Note: Sections 109 and 110 of PL 102–386 did not amend this Act directly, but contained provisions relative to it. The text of the material follows.]

§6908. Small Town Environmental Planning. [Sec. 109]

(a) Establishment.—The Administrator of the Environmental Protection Agency (hereafter referred to as the "Administrator") shall establish a program to

Additional Provisions

assist small communities in planning and financing environmental facilities. The program shall be known as the "Small Town Environmental Planning Program".

(b) Small Town Environmental Planning Task Force.—

(1) The Administrator shall establish a Small Town Environmental Planning Task Force which shall be composed of representatives of small towns from different areas of the United States, Federal and State governmental agencies, and public interest groups. The Administrator shall terminate the Task Force not later than 2 years after the establishment of the Task Force.

(2) The Task Force shall—

(A) identify regulations developed pursuant to Federal environmental laws which pose significant compliance problems for small towns;

(B) identify means to improve the working relationship between the Environmental Protection Agency (hereafter referred to as the Agency) and small towns;

(C) review proposed regulations for the protection of the environmental and public health and suggest revisions that could improve the ability of small towns to comply with such regulations;

(D) identify means to promote regionalization of environmental treatment systems and infrastructure serving small towns to improve the economic condition of such systems and infrastructure; and

(E) provide such other assistance to the Administrator as the Administrator deems appropriate.

(c) Identification of Environmental Requirements.—

(1) Not later than 6 months after the date of the enactment of this Act, the Administrator shall publish a list of requirements under Federal environmental and public health statutes (and the regulations developed pursuant to such statutes) applicable to small towns. Not less than annually, the Administrator shall make such additions and deletions to and from the list as the Administrator deems appropriate.

(2) The Administrator shall, as part of the Small Town Environmental Planning Program under this section, implement a program to notify small communities of the regulations identified under paragraph (1) and of future regulations and requirements through methods that the Administrator determines to be effective to provide information to the greatest number of small communities, including any of the following:

(A) Newspapers and other periodicals.

(B) Other news media.

(C) Trade, municipal, and other associations that the Administrator determines to be appropriate.

(D) Direct mail.

(d) Small Town Ombudsman.—The Administrator shall establish and staff an Office of the Small Town Ombudsman. The Office shall provide assistance to small towns in connection with the Small Town Environmental Planning Program and other business with the Agency. Each regional office shall identify a small town contact. The Small Town Ombudsman and the regional contacts also may assist larger communities, but only if first priority is given to providing assistance to small towns.

(e) Multi-Media Permits.—

(1) The Administrator shall conduct a study of establishing a multi-media permitting program for small towns. Such evaluation shall include an analysis of—

(A) environmental benefits and liabilities of a multi-media permitting program;

(B) the potential of using such a program to coordinate a small town's environmental and public health activities; and

(C) the legal barriers, if any, to the establishment of such a program.

(2) Within 3 years after the date of enactment of this Act, the Administrator shall report to Congress on the results of the evaluation performed in accordance with paragraph (1). Included in this report shall be a description of the activities conducted pursuant to subsections (a) through (d).

(f) Definition.—For purposes of this section, the term "small town" means an incorporated or unincorporated community (as defined by the Administrator) with a population of less than 2,500 individuals.

(g) Authorization.—There is authorized to be appropriated the sum of $500,000 to implement this section.

§6965. Chief Financial Officer Report. [Sec. 110]

The Chief Financial Officer of each affected agency shall submit to Congress an annual report containing, to the extent practicable, a detailed description of the compliance activities undertaken by the agency for mixed waste streams, and an accounting of the fines and penalties imposed on the agency for violations involving mixed waste.

4

Comprehensive Environmental Response, Compensation, and Liability Act Of 1980

INTRODUCTION

Hazardous waste, largely a byproduct of the synthetic organic chemical revolution of post-World War II America, followed air and water pollution control in gaining the attention of the public and environmental regulators. Although Congress gave the Environmental Protection Agency (EPA) authority to regulate hazardous waste in 1976, the chemical contamination of homes in the Love Canal area of Niagara Falls, N.Y., in 1978 was the event that stirred the national consciousness, spurring EPA to accelerate rules to carry out that task.

In 1980, Congress passed Public Law 96-510, the "superfund law" or, more properly, the Comprehensive Environmental Response, Compensation, and Liability Act, which authorized $1.6 billion to finance the cleanup of Love Canal and other abandoned dumpsites. The Act, a logical complement to the provisions in the Resource Conservation and Recovery Act for the safe treatment and disposal of wastes, allows EPA to recover cleanup costs. It established the Post-Closure Liability Trust Fund, which is financed by a tax on the receipt of hazardous waste at a qualified hazardous waste disposal facility. The cleanup fund established by the Act, formally called the Hazardous Substance Response Trust Fund, is financed by a tax on crude oil (delivered to a refinery or imported into the United States) and chemicals feedstocks.

The concept of a "superfund" to pay for cleaning up abandoned hazardous waste sites originated with a proposal by the large oil companies to finance a fund to pay for the cleanup of oil spills from their supertankers. The spills had aroused outrage and caused tremendous environmental damage worldwide. In return for their contributions to the cleanup fund, the oil companies wanted to be released from liability for damages. "It was to be a superfund to clean up spills from supertankers," a Senate aide recalled. Although that idea was never taken up, in December 1980, Congress responded to the public's demand for hazardous waste cleanup with the passage of the "superfund."

In the spring of 1983, congressional charges of mismanagement of the hazardous waste program and allegations of conflict of interest became the center of a controversy that resulted in the resignations or firings of more than 20 top EPA officials, including Administrator Anne Gorsuch Burford. Democrats contended the issue demonstrated the Administration's indifference to environmental concerns. In the midst of the controversy, public concern about hazardous waste was heightened when high levels of dioxin were found at Times Beach, Mo., forcing a government buyout of the town and the relocation of 2,400 families.

Burford's immediate successor, William D. Ruckelshaus, changed EPA's superfund policies to speed cleanup. Yet it was the judgment of many, including many in Congress, that EPA had been given a powerful tool in CERCLA, but because there had been so few completed cleanups, something was not working the way they had envisioned in 1980. Congressional efforts to strengthen the law culminated in the signing of the Superfund Amendments and Reauthorization Act of 1986 (P.L. 99-499), which increased the amount of money in the fund from the original $1.6 billion to $8.5 billion over five years.

SARA preserves the 1980 Act's basic concept of liability. The message remains: liability was and remains strict, joint and several. On the House floor just before the House passed SARA in October 1986, Rep. John D. Dingell (D-Mich) said, "Nothing in this legislation is intended to change the application of the uniform federal rule of joint and several liability enunciated in the Chem-Dyne case and followed by a number of other federal courts." The case referred to is one of the basic judicial articulations of the strict, joint and several liability issue as applied to superfund cases (*U.S. v. Chem-Dyne*, 572 F. Supp. 802, 19 ER Cases 1953 (S.D. Ohio 1983)).

That is perhaps the government's most powerful tool. All it has to do is establish a link to a superfund site and it can seek to recover cleanup costs from a potentially responsible party (PRP). However, because litigation can be a protracted process in even the best of situations, Congress also decided it had to improve the settlement procedures. As a way of enticing parties to enter voluntary settlements, Congress gave settlors protection against contribution actions by nonsettling parties and also insulated them against being sued by the federal government in a "covenant not to sue." The amendments also codified an "innocent landowner" defense to liability.

EPA's control over settlement negotiations with PRPs was strengthened by SARA. Only information placed in the administrative record may be used to challenge the agency's choice of remedy at a superfund site.

In addition, the agency was given authority to use mixed funding—use of money from the fund to supplement contributions from settling PRPs. The first preauthorized mixed funding agreements came in the summer of 1987 at the Motco site in Texas and the Harvey and Knotts site in Delaware. Congress also established a unique concept in the "non-binding allocation to responsibility (NBAR)," under which EPA may decide to make a preliminary allocation of responsibility among parties as a way of achieving a quick settlement. Such settlements arrived at through the NBAR process, according to the amendments, "shall not be admissible as evidence in any proceeding, and no Court shall have jurisdiction to review the non-binding permanent allocation of responsibility."

There is a new statutory authorization of *de minimis* settlements by parties who may be able to "buy" their way out of the cleanup process because of their limited involvement. The idea is to facilitate the settlement process and also to use the revenues gained from the *de minimis* parties to entice other PRPs to settle. As part of its effort to make administrative improvements to superfund, EPA in the summer of 1993 issued a revised guidance on settling with *de minimis* parties—those who contributed on a very small amount of waste to a site. In addition, the agency issued guidance for settling with *de micromis* parties—those who contributed extremely small quantities of waste to a site. The agency reported in November 1993 that it has entered into 125 *de minimis* settlements involving more than 6,100 parties.

SARA also established a strong preference for permanent remedies at superfund sites and set schedules for beginning cleanup work and studies.

The 101st Congress, in lieu of taking on the often contentious issues surrounding superfund reauthorization, approved a simple three-year extension of the cleanup program and a four-year extension of superfund tax authority.

In October 1992, at the end of the 102nd Congress, CERCLA was amended by the Community Environmental Response Facilitation Act. CERCLA Section 120(h) was amended to require the identification of uncontaminated parcels of land on federal facilities that are slated to be closed. The purpose of the amendment was to facilitate the transfer and redevelopment of government property that is deemed to be unpolluted.

Among the more frequently mentioned reforms were increasing state involvement in the superfund process, improving the "fairness" of the settlement process by possibly exempting some small parties, lenders, some trustees, recyclers, and municipal solid waste generators from liability, requiring the development of national cleanup standards, increasing the use of mixed funding, and adding consideration of future land use to cleanup decisions.

A report by The RAND Corp. estimated that some smaller companies that are found liable at superfund sites pay more for legal and administrative costs than they do for actual cleanups. For insurance companies, these "transaction costs" are 69 percent of the total. Overall, according to the research group's study, the average transaction costs associated with superfund liability are between 25 percent and 35 percent of the total superfund costs for liable parties from the private sector.

Although most observers said they saw no real chance that basic liability scheme of CERCLA would be changed, they conceded that some changes are possible. Among the changes discussed was elimination of retroactive liability.

One proposal that has generated considerable controversy was put forward by the Treasury Department, which has advocated doing away with the strict, joint and several liability scheme altogether and replacing it with apportioned liability. The trust fund would be used to pay for so-called orphan cleanup shares. Treasury's proposal has won support from business, local governments, and insurance companies, among others, but has little backing from key legislators, who asked the Administration of President Bill Clinton to reject it out of hand as "seriously flawed on the merits."

The Clinton Administration is expected to be a major factor in the reauthorization of CERCLA, and has promised to produce recommendations. By the end of 1993, the Superfund Evaluation Committee of the National Advisory Council on Environmental Policy and Technology, which advises EPA, completed its examination of the superfund program and was preparing a series of proposals for the agency to consider.

Congressional committees have called the administration inconsistent on reform, however, despite the NACEPT effort and despite Clinton's singling out of superfund as a prime example of a government program that does not work. Rep. Al Swift (D-Wash), chairman of the House Energy and Commerce Subcommittee on Transportation and Hazardous Materials, said the success of reauthorization efforts in 1994 would depend upon the commitment of the Administration.

Late in 1993, a report by the staff of the House Public Works and Transportation Subcommittee on Investigations and Oversight recommended that CERCLA be changed to provide for arbitration and mediation to resolve cost-allocation disputes among responsible parties.

It also recommended that the law be changed to provide relief from liability for municipal waste generators and transporters, to delegation of cleanup authority to states on a site-by-site basis, to expand the technical assistance grants program, and to provide a substantial increase in research funds to help

EPA establish national cleanup standards. The staff's report also proposed the future land use be considered in the selection of a cleanup remedy for a site.

In December, the National Commission on Superfund, also known as the Keystone Commission, a broad-based coalition convened by the Colorado-based Keystone Center, recommended that CERCLA be reformed to include a binding system of allocating liability and that national health-based standards be used for cleanups, with a "limited number of site-specific variables" that would permit restricted land use in some cases. The commission also urged improvements in the development and use of innovative cleanup technologies, correction of environmental injustices, and changes to the process by which priorities are set for cleanup actions.

After months of interdepartmental wrangling, during which it recieved considerable criticism for delaying the reauthorization process, the Clinton Administration in early February 1994 finally produced its recommendations for superfund reform. Consistent in many respects with the recommendations of the Keystone Commission, the Administration's proposals included significant changes to the current liability scheme, a cap on liability for municipalities that generated or transported waste to a superfund site, non-binding allocation of liability, a tax on the insurance industry to help pay for cleanups, and risk-based national cleanup standards.

Legislation based on the Administration's proposals was introduced in the House (HR 3800) by Rep. Al Swift (D-Wash) and in the Senate (S 1834) by Sen. Max S. Baucus (D-Mont). Although many observers were initially sanguine that reform would be possible in the 103rd Congress, it soon became obvious that continued wrangling over contentious issues could delay or even doom reauthorization in 1994. At best, the Administration's plan was called "a good beginning."

In May 1994, the House Energy and Commerce Committee approved HR 3800. As approved, the legislation eliminates retroactive liability. It would require that a national risk goal be set for cleanups. The goal would be developed through a negotiated rule-making process. The bill also would extend coverage of the law for liability purposes to "pollutants and contaminants." Limitations would be set for the transportation or generation of sewage sludge. Municipalities' liability stemming from the ownership of sewage lines would similarly be limited.

In mid-June 1994, the Senate Environment and Public Works Subcommittee on Superfund, Recycling, and Solid Waste Management approved S 1834. The bill, which retains many of the Administration's proposals, is similar to the version approved in the House committee; however, significant differences remain between the two versions.

In the Senate bill, the Environmental Protection Agency would have the authority to develop a national risk goal for cleanups and a risk protocol unilaterally. Unlike the House version, it would not expand coverage to include "pollutants and contaminants," and it would not include limitations on liability for sewage sludge or municipal sewage lines. The measure also would loosen some cleanup requirements. For example, ground water that is contaminated by sources other than "facilities for which remedial actions will be taken" and ground water that contains more than 10,000 milligrams of total dissolved solids per liter would not be considered drinking water for superfund cleanup purposes.

Both versions included the insurance industry tax, although some differences remained in its application.

As Congress approached the Independence Day recess, however, many sources said the remaining hurdles facing the legislations made its chances for passage in the 103rd Congress uncertain.

FINDING LIST

COMPREHENSIVE ENVIRONMENTAL RESPONSE, COMPENSATION, AND LIABILITY ACT OF 1980

Public Law 96–510, effective Dec. 11, 1980, 94 Stat. 2767.

42 U.S.C. §§9601 et seq.

Amended by PL 96–561, Dec. 22, 1980; PL 97–272, Sept. 30, 1982; PL 98–45, July 12, 1983; PL 98–80, Aug. 23, 1983; PL 98–369, July 18, 1984; PL 98–371, July 18, 1984; PL 98–396, Aug. 22, 1984; PL 99–499, Oct. 17, 1986; PL 99–509, Oct. 21, 1986; PL 100–202, Dec. 22, 1987; PL 100–647, Nov. 10, 1988; PL 100–707, Nov. 23, 1988; PL 101–144, Nov. 9, 1989; PL 101–221, Dec. 12, 1989; PL 101–239, Dec. 19, 1989; PL 101–380, Aug. 18, 1990; PL 101–508, Nov. 5, 1990; PL 101–584, Nov. 15, 1990; PL 102–426, Oct. 19, 1992; PL 102–484, Oct. 23, 1992; PL 102–531, Oct. 27, 1992

[Editor's Note: Title III of the Superfund Amendments and Reauthorization Act (PL 99–499), separately entitled the Emergency Planning and Community Right-to-Know Act, is published in Chapter 8.]

TITLE I — HAZARDOUS SUBSTANCES RELEASES, LIABILITY, COMPENSATION

§9601. Definitions [Sec. 101]

For purpose of this title —

[§101 amended by PL 99–499]

(1) The term "act of God" means an unanticipated grave natural disaster or other natural phenomenon of an exceptional, inevitable, and irresistible character, the effects of which could not have been prevented or avoided by the exercise of due care or foresight.

(2) The term "Administrator" means the Administrator of the United States Environmental Protection Agency.

(3) The term "barrel" means forty-two United States gallons at sixty degrees Fahrenheit.

(4) The term "claim" means a demand in writing for a sum certain.

(5) The term "claimant" means any person who presents a claim for compensation under this Act.

(6) The term "damages" means damages for injury or loss of natural resources as set forth in section 107(a) or 111(b) of this Act.

(7) The term "drinking water supply" means any raw or finished water source that is or may be used by a public water system (as defined in the Safe Drinking Water Act) or as drinking water by one or more individuals.

(8) The term "environment" means (A) the navigable waters, the waters of the contiguous zone, and the ocean waters of which the natural resources are under the exclusive management authority of the United States under the Magnuson Fishery Conservation and Management Act of 1976, and (B) any other surface water, ground water, drinking water supply, land surface or subsurface strata, or ambient air within the United States or under the jurisdiction of the United States.

[§101(8) amended by PL 96–561]

(9) The term "facility" means (A) any building, structure, installation, equipment, pipe or pipeline (including any pipe into a sewer or publicly owned treatment works), well, pit, pond, lagoon, impoundment, ditch, landfill, storage container, motor vehicle, rolling stock, or aircraft, or (B) any site or area where a hazardous substance has been deposited, stored, disposed of, or placed, or otherwise come to be located; but does not include any consumer product in consumer use or any vessel.

(10) The term "federally permitted release" means (A) discharges in compliance with a permit under section 402 of the Federal Water Pollution Control Act, (B) discharges resulting from circumstances identified and reviewed and made part of the public record with respect to a permit issued or modified under section 402 of the Federal Water Pollution Control Act and subject to a condition of such permit, (C) continuous or anticipated intermittent discharges from a point source, identified in a permit or permit application under section 402 of the Federal Water Pollution Control Act, which are caused by events occurring within the scope of relevant operating or treatment systems, (D) discharges in compliance with a legally enforceable permit under section 404 of the Federal Water Pollution Control Act, (E) releases in compliance with a legally enforceable final permit issued pursuant to section 3005(a) through (d) of the Solid Waste Disposal Act from a hazardous waste treatment, storage, or disposal facility when such permit specifically identifies the hazardous substances and makes such substances subject to a standard of practice, control procedure or bioassay limitation or condition, or other control on the hazardous substances in such releases, (F) any release in compliance with a legally enforceable permit issued under section 102 of section 103 of the Marine Protection, Research, and Sanctuaries Act of 1972, (G) any injection of fluids authorized under Federal underground injection control programs or State programs submitted for

Federal approval (and not disapproved by the Administrator of the Environmental Protection Agency) pursuant to part C of the Safe Drinking Water Act, (H) any emission into the air subject to a permit or control regulation under section 111, section 112, title I part C, title I part D, or State implementation plans submitted in accordance with section 110 of the Clean Air Act (and not disapproved by the Administrator of the Environmental Protection Agency), including any schedule or waiver granted, promulgated, or approved under these sections, (I) any injection of fluids or other materials authorized under applicable State law (i) for the purpose of stimulating or treating wells for the production of crude oil, natural gas, or water, (ii) for the purpose of secondary, tertiary, or other enhanced recovery of crude oil or natural gas, or (iii) which are brought to the surface in conjunction with the production of crude oil or natural gas and which are reinjected, (J) the introduction of any pollutant into a publicly owned treatment works when such pollutant is specified in and in compliance with applicable pretreatment standards of section 307(b) or (c) of the Clean Water Act and enforceable requirements in a pretreatment program submitted by a State or municipality for Federal approval under section 402 of such Act, and (K) any release of source, special nuclear, or byproduct material, as those terms are defined in the Atomic Energy Act of 1954, in compliance with a legally enforceable license, permit regulation, or order issued pursuant to the Atomic Energy Act of 1954.

(11) The term "Fund" or "Trust Fund" means the Hazardous Substance Superfund established by section 9507 of the Internal Revenue Code of 1986.

[§101(11) revised by PL 99–499]

(12) The term "ground water" means water in a saturated zone or stratum beneath the surface of land or water.

(13) The term "guarantor" means any person, other than the owner or operator, who provides evidence of financial responsibility for an owner or operator under this Act.

(14) The term "hazardous substance" means (A) any substance designated pursuant to section 311(b)(2)(A) of the Federal Water Pollution Control Act, (B) any element, compound, mixture, solution, or substance designated pursuant to section 102 of this Act, (C) any hazardous waste having the characteristics identified under or listed pursuant to section 3001 of the Solid Waste Disposal Act (but not including any waste the regulation of which under the Solid Waste Disposal Act has been suspended by Act of Congress), (D) any toxic pollutant listed under section 307(a) of the Federal Water Pollution Control Act, (E) any hazardous air pollutant listed under section 112 of the Clean Air Act, and (F) any imminently hazardous chemical substance or mixture with respect to which the Administrator has taken action pursuant to section 7 of the Toxic Substances Control Act. The term does not include petroleum, including crude oil or any fraction thereof which is not otherwise specifically listed or designated as a hazardous substance under subparagraphs (A) through (F) of this paragraph, and the term does not include natural gas, natural gas liquids, liquefied natural gas, or synthetic gas usable for fuel (or mixtures of natural gas and such synthetic gas).

(15) The term "navigable waters" or "navigable waters of the United States" means the waters of the United States, including the territorial seas.

(16) The term "natural resources" means land, fish, wildlife, biota, air, water, ground water, drinking water supplies, and other such resources belonging to, managed by, held in trust by, appertaining to, or otherwise controlled by the United States (including the resources of the fishery conservation zone established by the Magnuson Fishery Conservation and Management Act of 1976), any State or local government, any foreign government, any Indian Tribe, or, if such resources are subject to a trust restriction on alienation, any member of an Indian Tribe.

[§101(16) amended by PL 96–561; PL 99–499]

(17) The term "offshore facility" means any facility of any kind located in, on, or under, any of the navigable waters of the United States, and any facility of any kind which is subject to the jurisdiction of the United States and is located in, on, or under any other waters, other than a vessel or a public vessel.

(18) The term "onshore facility" means any facility (including, but not limited to, motor vehicles and rolling stock) of any kind located in, on, or under, any land or nonnavigable waters within the United States.

(19) The term "otherwise subject to the jurisdiction of the United States" means subject to the jurisdiction of the United States by virtue of United States citizenship, United States vessel documentation or numbering, or as provided by international agreement to which the United States is a party.

(20) (A) The term "owner or operator" means (i) in the case of a vessel, any person owning, operating, or chartering by demise, such vessel, (ii) in the case of an onshore facility or an offshore facility, any person owning or operating such facility, and (iii) in the case of any facility, title or control of which was conveyed due to bankruptcy, foreclosure, tax delinquency, abandonment, or similar means to a unit of State or local government, any person who owned, operated, or otherwise controlled activities at such facility immediately beforehand. Such term does not include a person, who, without participating in the management of a vessel or facility, holds indicia of ownership primarily to protect his security interest in the vessel or facility.

[§101(20)(A) amended by PL 99–499]

(B) In the case of a hazardous substance which has been accepted for transportation by a common or contract carrier and except as provided in section 107(a)(3) or (4) of this Act, (i) the term "owner or operator" shall mean such common carrier or other bona fide for hire carrier acting as an independent contractor during such transportation, (ii) the shipper of such hazardous substance shall not be considered to have caused or contributed to any release during such transportation which resulted solely from circumstances or conditions beyond his control.

[§101(20)(B) amended by PL 99–499]

(C) In the case of a hazardous substance which has been delivered by a common or contract carrier to a disposal or treatment facility and except as provided in section 107(a)(3) or (4)(i) the term "owner or operator" shall not include such common or contract carrier, and (ii) such common or contract carrier shall not be considered to have caused or contributed to any release at such disposal or treatment facility resulting from circumstances or conditions beyond its control.

[§101(20)(C) amended by PL 99–499]

(D) The term "owner or operator" does not include a unit of State or local government which acquired ownership or control involuntarily through bankruptcy, tax delinquency, abandonment, or other circumstances in which the government involuntarily acquires title by virtue of its function as sovereign. The exclusion provided under this paragraph shall not apply to any State or local government which has caused or contributed to the release or threatened release of a hazardous substance from the facility, and such a State or local government shall be subject to the provisions of this Act in the same manner and to the same extent, both procedurally and substantively, as any nongovernmental entity, including liability under section 107.

[§101(20)(D) added by PL 99–499]

(21) The term "person" means an individual, firm, corporation, association, partnership, consortium, joint venture, commercial entity, United States Government, State, municipality, commission, political subdivision of a State, or any interstate body.

(22) The term "release" means any spilling, leaking, pumping, pouring, emitting, emptying, discharging, injecting, escaping, leaching, dumping, or disposing into the environment (including the abandonment or discarding of barrels, containers, and other closed receptacles containing any hazardous substance or pollutant or contaminant), but excludes (A) any release which results in exposure to persons solely within a workplace, with respect to a claim which such persons may assert against the employer of such persons, (B) emissions from the engine exhaust of a motor vehicle, rolling stock, aircraft, vessel, or pipeline pumping station engine, (C) release of source, byproduct, or special nuclear material from a nuclear incident, as those terms are defined in the Atomic Energy Act of 1954, if such release is subject to requirements with respect to financial protection established by the Nuclear Regulatory Commission under section 170 of such Act, or, for the purposes of section 104 of this title or any other response action, any release of source byproduct, or special nuclear material from any processing site designated under section 102(a)(1) or 302(a) of the Uranium Mill Tailings Radiation Control Act of 1978, and (D) the normal application of fertilizer.

[§101(22) amended by PL 99–499]

(23) The terms "remove" or "removal" means the cleanup or removal of released hazardous substances from the environment, such actions as may be necessary taken in the event of the threat of release of hazardous substances into the environment, such actions as may be necessary to monitor, assess, and evaluate the release or threat of release of hazardous substances, the disposal of removed material, or the taking of such other actions as may be necessary to prevent, minimize or mitigate damage to the public health or welfare or to the environment, which may otherwise result from a release or threat of release. The term includes, in addition, without

being limited to, security fencing or other measures to limit access, provision of alternative water supplies, temporary evacuation and housing of threatened individuals not otherwise provided for, action taken under section 104(b) of this Act, and any emergency assistance which may be provided under the Disaster Relief and Emergency Assistance Act.

[§101(23) amended by PL 100–707]

(24) The terms "remedy" or "remedial action" means those actions consistent with permanent remedy taken instead of or in addition to removal actions in the event of a release or threatened release of a hazardous substance into the environment, to prevent or minimize the release of hazardous substances so that they do not migrate to cause substantial danger to present or future public health or welfare or the environment. The term includes, but is not limited to, such actions at the location of the release as storage, confinement, perimeter protection using dikes, trenches, or ditches, clay cover, neutralization, cleanup of released hazardous substances and associated contaminated materials, recycling or reuse, diversion, destruction, segregation of reactive wastes, dredging or excavations, repair or replacement of leaking containers, collection of leachate and runoff, onsite treatment or incineration, provision of alternative water supplies, and any monitoring reasonably required to assure that such actions protect the public health and welfare and the environment. The term includes the costs of permanent relocation of residents and businesses and community facilities where the President determines that, alone or in combination with other measures, such relocation is more cost effective than and environmentally preferable to the transportation, storage, treatment, destruction, or secure disposition offsite of hazardous substances, or may otherwise be necessary to protect the public health or welfare; the term includes offsite transport and offsite storage, treatment, destruction, or secure disposition of hazardous substances and associated contaminated materials.

[§101(24) amended by PL 99–499]

(25) The terms "respond" or "response" means remove, removal, remedy, and remedial action, all such terms (including the terms "removal" and "remedial action") include enforcement activities related thereto.

[§101(25) amended by PL 99–499]

(26) The terms "transport" or "transportation" means the movement of a hazardous substance by any mode, including pipeline (as defined in the Pipeline Safety Act), and in the case of a hazardous substance which has been accepted for transportation by a common or contract carrier, the term "transport" or "transportation" shall include any stoppage in transit which is temporary, incidental to the transportation movement, and at the ordinary operating convenience of a common or contract carrier, and any such stoppage shall be considered as a continuity of movement and not as the storage of a hazardous substance.

(27) The terms "United States" and "State" include the several States of the United States, the District of Columbia, the Commonwealth of Puerto Rico, Guam, American Samoa, the United States Virgin Islands, the Commonwealth of the Northern Marianas, and any other territory or possession over which the United States has jurisdiction.

(28) The term "vessel" means every description of watercraft or other artificial contrivance used, or capable of being used, as a means of transportation on water.

(29) The terms "disposal", "hazardous waste", and "treatment" shall have the meaning provided in section 1004 of the Solid Waste Disposal Act.

(30) The terms "territorial sea" and "contiguous zone" shall have the meaning provided in section 502 of the Federal Water Pollution Control Act.

(31) The term "national contingency plan" means the national contingency plan published under section 311(c) of the Federal Water Pollution Control Act or revised pursuant to section 105 of this Act.

(32) The term "liable" or "liability" under this title shall be construed to be the standard of liability which obtains under section 311 of the Federal Water Pollution Control Act.

(33) The term "pollutant or contaminant" shall include, but not be limited to, any element, substance, compound, or mixture, including disease-causing agents, which after release into the environment and upon exposure, ingestion, inhalation, or assimilation into any organism, either directly from the environment or indirectly by ingestion through food chains, will or may reasonably be anticipated to cause death, disease, behavioral abnormalities, cancer, genetic mutation, physiological malfunctions (including malfunctions in reproduction) or physical deformations, in such organisms or their offspring; except that the term "pollutant

or contaminant" shall not include petroleum, including crude oil or any fraction thereof which is not otherwise specifically listed or designated as a hazardous substance under subparagraphs (A) through (F) of paragraph (14) and shall not include natural gas, liquefied natural gas, or synthetic gas of pipeline quality (or mixtures of natural gas and such synthetic gas).

[§101(33) added by PL 99–499]

(34) The term "alternative water supplies" includes, but is not limited to, drinking water and household water supplies.

[§101(34) added by PL 99–499]

(35) (A) The term "contractual relationship", for the purpose of section 107(b)(3) , includes, but is not limited to, land contracts, deeds or other instruments transferring title or possession, unless the real property on which the facility concerned is located was acquired by the defendant after the disposal or placement of the hazardous substance on, in, or at the facility, and one or more of the circumstances described in clause (i), (ii), or (iii) is also established by the defendant by a preponderance of the evidence:

(i) At the time the defendant acquired the facility the defendant did not know and had no reason to know that any hazardous substance which is the subject of the release or threatened release was disposed of on, in, or at the facility.

(ii) The defendant is a government entity which acquired the facility by escheat, or through any other involuntary transfer or acquisition, or through the exercise of eminent domain authority by purchase or condemnation.

(iii) The defendant acquired the facility by inheritance or bequest. In addition to establishing the foregoing, the defendant must establish that he has satisfied the requirements of section 107(b)(3)(a) and (b).

(B) To establish that the defendant had no reason to know, as provided in clause (i) of subparagraph (A) of this paragraph, the defendant must have undertaken, at the time of acquisition, all appropriate inquiry into the previous ownership and uses of the property consistent with good commercial or customary practice in an effort to minimize liability. For purposes of the preceding sentence the court shall take into account any specialized knowledge or experience on the part of the defendant, the relationship of the purchase price to the value of the property if uncontaminated, commonly known or reasonably ascertainable information about the property, the obviousness of the presence or likely presence of contamination at the property, and the ability to detect such contamination by appropriate inspection.

(C) Nothing in this paragraph or in section 107(b)(3) shall diminish the liability of any previous owner or operator of such facility who would otherwise be liable under this Act. Notwithstanding this paragraph, if the defendant obtained actual knowledge of the release or threatened release of a hazardous substance at such facility when the defendant owned the real property and then subsequently transferred ownership of the property to another person without disclosing such knowledge, such defendant shall be treated as liable under section 107(a)(1) and no defense under section 107(b)(3) shall be available to such defendant.

(D) Nothing in this paragraph shall affect the liability under this Act of a defendant who, by any act or omission, caused or contributed to the release or threatened release of a hazardous substance which is the subject of the action relating to the facility.

[§101(35) added by PL 99–499]

(36) The term "Indian tribe" means any Indian tribe, band, nation, or other organized group or community, including any Alaska Native village but not including any Alaska Native regional or village corporation, which is recognized as eligible for the special programs and services provided by the United States to Indians because of their status as Indians.

[§101(36) added by PL 99–499]

(37) (A) The term "service station dealer" means any person—

(i) who owns or operates a motor vehicle service station, filling station, garage, or similar retail establishment engaged in the business of selling, repairing, or servicing motor vehicles, where a significant percentage of the gross revenue of the establishment is derived from the fueling, repairing, or servicing of motor vehicles, and

(ii) who accepts for collection, accumulation, and delivery to an oil recycling facility, recycled oil that (I) has been removed from the engine of a light duty motor vehicle or household appliances by the owner of such vehicle or appliances, and (II) is presented, by such owner, to such person for collection, accumulation, and delivery to an oil recycling facility.

(B) For purposes of section 114(c) , the term "service station dealer" shall, notwithstanding the provisions of subparagraph (A), include any government agency that establishes a facility solely for the purpose of accepting recycled oil that satisfies the criteria set forth in subclauses (I) and (II) of subparagraph (A)(ii), and, with respect to recycled oil that satisfies the criteria set forth in subclauses (I) and (II), owners or operators of refuse collection services who are compelled by State law to collect, accumulate, and deliver such oil to an oil recycling facility.

(C) The President shall promulgate regulations regarding the determination of what constitutes a significant percentage of the gross revenues of an establishment for purposes of this paragraph.

[§101(37) added by PL 99–499]

(38) The term "incineration vessel" means any vessel which carries hazardous substances for the purpose of incineration of such substances, so long as such sub- stances or residues of such substances are on board.

[§101(38) added by PL 99–499]

§9602. Reportable Quantities and Additional Designations [Sec. 102]

(a) The Administrator shall promulgate and revise as may be appropriate. regulations designating as hazardous substances in addition to those referred to in section 101(14) of this title, such elements, compounds, mixtures, solutions, and substances which, when released into the environment may present substantial danger to the public health or welfare or the environment, and shall promulgate regulations establishing that quantity of any hazardous substance the release of which shall be reported pursuant to section 103 of this title. The Administrator may determine that one single quantity shall be the reportable quantity for any hazardous substance, regardless of the medium into which the hazardous substance is released. For all hazardous substances for which proposed regulations establishing reportable quantities were published in the Federal Register under this subsection on or before March 1, 1986, the Administrator shall promulgate under this subsection final regulations establishing reportable quantities not later than December 31, 1986. For all hazardous substances for which proposed regulations establishing reportable quantities were not published in the Federal Register under this subsection on or before March 1, 1986, the Administrator shall publish under this subsection proposed regulations establishing reportable quantities not later than December 31, 1986, and promulgate final regulations under this subsection establishing reportable quantities not later than April 30, 1988.

[§102(a) amended by PL 99–499]

(b) Unless and until superseded by regulations establishing a reportable quantity under subsection (a) of this section for any hazardous substance as defined in section 101(14) of this title, (1) a quantity of one pound, or (2) for those hazardous substances for which reportable quantities have been established pursuant to section 311(b)(4) of the Federal Water Pollution Control Act, such reportable quantity, shall be deemed that quantity, the release of which requires notification pursuant to section 103(a) or (b) of this title.

§9603. Notices, Penalties [Sec. 103]

(a) Any person in charge of a vessel or an offshore or an onshore facility shall, as soon as he has knowledge of any release (other than a federally permitted release) of a hazardous substance from such vessel or facility in quantities equal to or greater than those determined pursuant to section 102 of this title, immediately notify the National Response Center established under the Clean Water Act of such release. The National Response Center shall convey the notification expeditiously to all appropriate Government agencies, including the Governor of any affected State.

(b) Any person—

(1) in charge of a vessel from which a hazardous substance is released, other than a federally permitted release, into or upon the navigable waters of the United States, adjoining shorelines, or into or upon the waters of the contiguous zone, or

(2) in charge of a vessel from which a hazardous substance is released, other than a federally permitted release, which may affect natural resources belonging to, appertaining to, or under the exclusive management authority of the United States (including resources under the Magnuson Fishery Conservation and Management Act of 1976), and who is otherwise subject to the jurisdiction of the United States at the time of the release, or

[§103(b)(2) amended by PL 96–561]

(3) in charge of a facility from which a hazardous substance is released, other than a federally permitted release, in a quantity equal to or greater than that determined pursuant to sec-

tion 102 of this title who fails to notify immediately the appropriate agency of the United States Government as soon as he has knowledge of such release or who submits in such a notification any information which he knows to be false or misleading shall, upon conviction, be fined in accordance with the applicable provisions of title 18 of the United States Code or imprisoned for not more than 3 years (or not more than 5 years in the case of a second or subsequent conviction), or both. Notification received pursuant to this subsection or information obtained by the exploitation of such notification shall not be used against any such person in any criminal case, except a prosecution for perjury or for giving a false statement.

[§103(b)(3) amended by PL 99–499]

(c) Within one hundred and eighty days after the enactment of this Act, any person who owns or operates or who at the time of disposal owned or operated, or who accepted hazardous substances for transport and selected, a facility at which hazardous substances (as defined in section 101(14)(C) of this title) are or have been stored, treated, or disposed of shall, unless such facility has a permit issued under, or has been accorded interim status under, subtitle C of the Solid Waste Disposal Act, notify the Administrator of the Environmental Protection Agency of the existence of such facility, specifying the amount and type of any hazardous substance to be found there, and any known, suspected, or likely releases of such substances from such facility. The Administrator may prescribe in greater detail the manner and form of the notice and the information included. The Administrator shall notify the affected State agency, or any department designated by the Governor to receive such notice, of the existence of such facility. Any person who knowingly fails to notify the Administrator of the existence of any such facility shall, upon conviction, be fined not more than $10,000, or imprisoned for not more than one year, or both. In addition, any such person who knowingly fails to provide the notice required by this subsection shall not be entitled to any limitation of liability or to any defenses to liability set out in section 107 of this Act:*Provided, however,*That notification under this subsection is not required for any facility which would be reportable hereunder solely as a result of any stoppage in transit which is temporary, incidental to the transportation movement, or at the ordinary operating convenience of a common or contract carrier, and such stoppage shall be considered as a continuity of movement and not as the storage of a hazardous substance. Notification received pursuant to this subsection or information obtained by the exploitation of such notification shall not be used against any such person in any criminal case, except a prosecution for perjury or for giving a false statement.

(d) (1) The Administrator of the Environmental Protection Agency is authorized to promulgate rules and regulations specifying, with respect to—

(A) the location, title, or condition of a facility, and

(B) the identity, characteristics, quantity, origin, or condition (including containerization and previous treatment) of any hazardous substances contained or deposited in a facility; the records which shall be retained by any person required to provide the notification of a facility set out in subsection (c) of this section. Such specification shall be in accordance with the provisions of this subsection.

(2) Beginning with the date of enactment of this Act, for fifty years thereafter or for fifty years after the date of establishment of a record (whichever is later), or at any such earlier time as a waiver if obtained under paragraph (3) of this subsection, it shall be unlawful for any such person knowingly to destroy, mutilate, erase, dispose of, conceal, or otherwise render unavailable or unreadable or falsify any records identified in paragraph (l) of this subsection. Any person who violates this paragraph shall, upon conviction, be fined in accordance with the applicable provisions of title 18 of the United States Code or imprisoned for not more than 3 years (or not more than 5 years in the case of a second or subsequent conviction), or both.

[§103(d)(2) amended by PL 99–499]

(3) At any time prior to the date which occurs fifty years after the date of enactment of this Act, any person identified under paragraph (1) of this subsection may apply to the Administrator of the Environmental Protection Agency for a waiver of the provisions of the first sentence of paragraph (2) of this subsection. The Administrator is authorized to grant such waiver if, in his discretion, such waiver would not unreasonably interfere with the attainment of the purposes and provisions of this Act. The Administrator shall promulgate rules and regulations regarding such a waiver so as to inform parties of the proper application procedure and conditions for approval of such a waiver.

(4) Notwithstanding the provisions of this subsection, the Administrator of the Environmental Protection Agency may in his discretion require any such person to retain any record identified pursuant to paragraph (1) of this subsection for such a time period in excess of the period specified in paragraph (2) of this subsection as the Administrator determines to be necessary to protect the public health or welfare.

(e) This section shall not apply to the application of a pesticide product registered under the Federal Insecticide, Fungicide, and Rodenticide Act or to the handling and storage of such a pesticide product by an agricultural producer.

(f) No notification shall be required under subsection (a) or (b) of this section for any release of a hazardous substance—

(1) which is required to be reported (or specifically exempted from a requirement for reporting) under subtitle C of the Solid Waste Disposal Act or regulations thereunder and which has been reported to the National Response Center, or

(2) which is a continuous release, stable in quantity and rate, and is—

(A) from a facility for which notification has been given under subsection (c) of this section, or

(B) a release of which notification has been given under subsections (a) and (b) of this section for a period sufficient to establish the continuity, quantity, and regularity of such release: *Provided,* That notification in accordance with subsections (a) and (b) of this paragraph shall be given for releases subject to this paragraph annually, or at such time as there is any statistically significant increase in the quantity of any hazardous substance or constituent thereof released, above that previously reported or occurring.

§9604. Response Authorities [Sec. 104]

(a) (1) Whenever (A) any hazardous substance is released or there is a substantial threat of such a release into the environment, or (B) there is a release or substantial threat of release into the environment of any pollutant or contaminant which may present an imminent and substantial danger to the public health or welfare, the President is authorized to act, consistent with the national contingency plan, to remove or arrange for the removal of, and provide for remedial action relating to such hazardous substance, pollutant, or contaminant at any time (including its removal from any contaminated natural resource), or take any other response measure consistent with the national contingency plan which the President deems necessary to protect the public health or welfare or the environment. When the President determines that such action will be done properly and promptly by the owner or operator of the facility or vessel or by any other responsible party, the President may allow such person to carry out the action, conduct the remedial investigation, or conduct the feasibility study in accordance with section 122 . No remedial investigation or feasibility study (RI/FS) shall be authorized except on a determination by the President that the party is qualified to conduct the RI/FS and only if the President contracts with or arranges for a qualified person to assist the President in overseeing and reviewing the conduct of such RI/FS and if the responsible party agrees to reimburse the Fund for any cost incurred by the President under, or in connection with, the oversight contract or arrangement. In no event shall a potentially responsible party be subject to a lesser standard of liability, receive preferential treatment, or in any other way, whether direct or indirect, benefit from any such arrangements as a response action contractor, or as a person hired or retained by such a response action contractor, with respect to the release or facility in question. The President shall give primary attention to those releases which the President deems may present a public health threat.

[§104(a)(1) amended by PL 99–499]

(2) Removal Action. — Any removal action undertaken by the President under this subsection (or by any other person referred to in section 122) should, to the extent the President deems practicable, contribute to the efficient performance of any long term remedial action with respect to the release or threatened release concerned.

[§104(a)(2) revised by PL 99–499]

(3) Limitations on Response. — The President shall not provide for a removal or remedial action under this section in response to a release or threat of release—

(A) of a naturally occurring substance in its unaltered form, or altered solely through naturally occurring processes or phenomena, from a location where it is naturally found;

(B) from products which are part of the structure of, and result in exposure within, residential buildings or business or community structures; or

(C) into public or private drinking water supplies due to deterioration of the system through ordinary use.

[§104(a)(3) added by PL 99–499]

(4) Exception to Limitations. — Notwithstanding paragraph (3) of this subsection, to the extent authorized by this section, the President may respond to any release or threat of release if in the President's discretion, it constitutes a public health or environmental emergency and no other person with the authority and capability to respond to the emergency will do so in a timely manner.

[§104(a)(4) added by PL 99–499]

(b) (1) Information: Studies And Investigations. —Whenever the President is authorized to act pursuant to subsection (a) of this section, or whenever the President has reason to believe that a release has occurred or is about to occur, or that illness disease, or complaints thereof may be attributable to exposure to a hazardous substance, pollutant, or contaminant and that a release may have occurred or be occurring, he may undertake such investigations, monitoring, surveys, testing, and other information gathering as he may deem necessary or appropriate to identify the existence and extent of the release or threat thereof, the source and nature of the hazardous substances, pollutants or contaminants involved, and the extent of danger to the public health or welfare or to the environment. In addition, the President may undertake such planning, legal, fiscal, economic, engineering, architectural, and other studies or investigations as he may deem necessary or appropriate to plan and direct response actions, to recover the costs thereof, and to enforce the provisions of this Act.

[§104(b)(1) designated by PL 99–499]

(2) Coordination of investigations. — The President shall promptly notify the appropriate Federal and State natural resource trustees of potential damages to natural resources resulting from releases under investigation pursuant to this section and shall seek to coordinate the assessments, investigations, and planning under this section with such Federal and State trustees.

[§104(b)(2) added by PL 99–499]

(c) (1) Unless (A) the President finds that (i) continued response actions are immediately required to prevent, limit, or mitigate an emergency, (ii) there is an immediate risk to public health or welfare or the environment, and (iii) such assistance will not otherwise be provided on a timely basis, or (B) the President has determined the appropriate remedial actions pursuant to paragraph (2) of this subsection and the State or States in which the source of the release is located have complied with the requirements of paragraph (3) of this subsection, or (C) continued response action is otherwise appropriate and consistent with the remedial action to be taken, obligations from the Fund, other than those authorized by subsection (b) of this section, shall not continue after $2,000,000 has been obligated for response actions or 12 months has elapsed from the date of initial response to a release or threatened release of hazardous substances.

[§104(c)(1) amended by PL 99–499]

(2) The President shall consult with the affected State or States before determining any appropriate remedial action to be taken pursuant to the authority granted under subsection (a) of this section.

(3) The President shall not provide any remedial actions pursuant to this section unless the State in which the release occurs first enters into a contract or cooperative agreement with the President providing assurances deemed adequate by the President that (A) the State will assure all future maintenance of the removal and remedial actions provided for the expected life of such actions as determined by the President; (B) the State will assure the availability of a hazardous waste disposal facility acceptable to the President and in compliance with the requirements of subtitle C of the Solid Waste Disposal Act for any necessary offsite storage, destruction, treatment, or secure disposition of the hazardous substances; and (C) the State will pay or assure payment of (i) 10 per centum of the costs of the remedial action, including all future maintenance, or (ii) 50 percent (or such greater amount as the President may determine appropriate, taking into account the degree of responsibility of the State or political subdivision for the release) of any sums expended in response to a release at a facility, that was operated by the State or a political subdivision thereof, either directly or through a contractual relationship or otherwise, at the time of any disposal of hazardous substances therein. For the purpose of clause (ii) of this subparagraph, the term "facility" does not include navigable waters or the beds underlying those waters. The President shall grant the State a credit against the share of the costs for which it is responsible under this paragraph for any doc-

umented direct out-of-pocket non-Federal funds expended or obligated by the State or a political subdivision thereof after January 1, 1978, and before the date of enactment of this Act for cost-eligible response actions and claims for damages compensable under section 111 of this title relating to the specific release in question: *Provided, however,* That in no event shall the amount of the credit granted exceed the total response costs relating to the release. In the case of remedial action to be taken on land or water held by an Indian tribe, held by the United States in trust for Indians, held by a member of an Indian tribe (if such land or water is subject to a trust restriction on alienation), or otherwise within the borders of an Indian reservation, the requirements of this paragraph for assurances regarding future maintenance and cost-sharing shall not apply, and the President shall provide the assurance required by this paragraph regarding the availability of a hazardous waste disposal facility.

[§104(c)(3) amended by PL 99–499]

(4) Selection of Remedial Action. — The President shall select remedial actions to carry out this section in accordance with section 121 of this Act (relating to cleanup standards).

[§104(c)(4) revised by PL 99–499]

(5) State Credits.—

(A) Granting of credit. — The President shall grant a State a credit against the share of the costs, for which it is responsible under paragraph (3) with respect to a facility listed on the National Priorities List under the National Contingency Plan, for amounts expended by a State for remedial action at such facility pursuant to a contract or cooperative agreement with the President. The credit under this paragraph shall be limited to those State expenses which the President determines to be reasonable, documented, direct out-of-pocket expenditures of non-Federal funds.

(B) Expenses before listing or agreement. — The credit under this paragraph shall include expenses for remedial action at a facility incurred before the listing of the facility on the National Priorities List or before a contract or cooperative agreement is entered into under subsection (d) for the facility if—

(i) after such expenses are incurred the facility is listed on such list and a contract or cooperative agreement is entered into for the facility, and

(ii) the President determines that such expenses would have been credited to the State under subparagraph (A) had the expenditures been made after listing of the facility on such list and after the date on which such contract or cooperative agreement is entered into.

(C) Response actions between 1978 and 1980. — The credit under this paragraph shall include funds expended or obligated by the State or a political subdivision thereof after January 1, 1978, and before December 11, 1980, for cost-eligible response actions and claims for damages compensable under section 111 .

(D) State expenses after December 11, 1980, in excess of 10 percent of costs. — The credit under this paragraph shall include 90 percent of State expenses incurred at a facility owned, but not operated, by such State or by a political subdivision thereof. Such credit applies only to expenses incurred pursuant to a contract or cooperative agreement under subsection (d) and only to expenses incurred after December 11, 1980, but before the date of the enactment of this paragraph.

(E) Item-by-item approval. — In the case of expenditures made after the date of the enactment of this paragraph, the President may require prior approval of each item of expenditure as a condition of granting a credit under this paragraph.

(F) Use of credits. — Credits granted under this paragraph for funds expended with respect to a facility may be used by the State to reduce all or part of the share of costs otherwise required to be paid by the State under paragraph (3) in connection with remedial actions at such facility. If the amount of funds for which credit is allowed under this paragraph exceeds such share of costs for such facility, the State may use the amount of such excess to reduce all or part of the share of such costs at other facilities in that State. A credit shall not entitle the State to any direct payment.

[§104(c)(5) added by PL 99–499]

(6) Operation and Maintenance. — For the purposes of paragraph (3) of this subsection, in the case of ground or surface water contamination, completed remedial action includes the completion of treatment or other measures, whether taken onsite or offsite, necessary to restore ground and surface water quality to a level that assures protection of human health and the environment. With respect to such

measures, the operation of such measures for a period of up to 10 years after the construction or installation and commencement of operation shall be considered remedial action. Activities required to maintain the effectiveness of such measures following such period or the completion of remedial action, whichever is earlier, shall be considered operation or maintenance.

[§104(c)(6) added by PL 99–499]

(7) Limitation on Source of Funds for O & M. — During any period after the availability of funds received by the Hazardous Substance Superfund established under subchapter A of chapter 98 of the Internal Revenue Code of 1954 from tax revenues or appropriations from general revenues, the Federal share of the payment of the cost of operation or maintenance pursuant to paragraph (3)(C)(i) or paragraph (6) of this subsection (relating to operation and maintenance) shall be from funds received by the Hazardous Substance Superfund from amounts recovered on behalf of such fund under this Act.

[§104(c)(7) added by PL 99–499]

(8) Recontracting. — The President is authorized to undertake or continue whatever interim remedial actions the President determines to be appropriate to reduce risks to public health or the environment where the performance of a complete remedial action requires recontracting because of the discovery of sources, types, or quantities of hazardous substances not known at the time of entry into the original contract. The total cost of interim actions undertaken at a facility pursuant to this paragraph shall not exceed $2,000,000.

[§104(c)(8) added by PL 99–499]

(9) Siting. — Effective 3 years after the enactment of the Superfund Amendments and Reauthorization Act of 1986, the President shall not provide any remedial actions pursuant to this section unless the State in which the release occurs first enters into a contract or cooperative agreement with the President providing assurances deemed adequate by the President that the State will assure the availability of hazardous waste treatment or disposal facilities which—

(A) have adequate capacity for the destruction, treatment, or secure disposition of all hazardous wastes that are reasonably expected to be generated within the State during the 20–year period following the date of such contract or cooperative agreement and to be disposed of, treated, or destroyed,

(B) are within the State or outside the State in accordance with an interstate agreement or regional agreement or authority,

(C) are acceptable to the President, and

(D) are in compliance with the requirements of subtitle C of the Solid Waste Disposal Act.

[§104(c)(9) added by PL 99–499]

(d) (1) Cooperative Agreements. —

(A) State applications. — A State or political subdivision thereof or Indian tribe may apply to the President to carry out actions authorized in this section. If the President determines that the State or political subdivision or Indian tribe has the capability to carry out any or all of such actions in accordance with the criteria and priorities established pursuant to section 105(a)(8) and to carry out related enforcement actions, the President may enter into a contract or cooperative agreement with the State or political subdivision or Indian tribe to carry out such actions. The President shall make a determination regarding such an application within 90 days after the President receives the application.

(B) Terms and conditions. — A contract or cooperative agreement under this paragraph shall be subject to such terms and conditions as the President may prescribe. The contract or cooperative agreement may cover a specific facility or specific facilities.

(C) Reimbursements. — Any State which expended funds during the period beginning September 30, 1985, and ending on the date of the enactment of this subparagraph for response actions at any site included on the National Priorities List and subject to a cooperative agreement under this Act shall be reimbursed for the share of costs of such actions for which the Federal Government is responsible under this Act.

[§104(d)(1) revised by PL 99–499]

(2) If the President enters into a cost-sharing agreement pursuant to subsection (c) of this section or a contract or cooperative agreement pursuant to this subsection, and the State or political subdivision thereof fails to comply with any requirements of the contract, the President may, after providing sixty days notice, seek in the appropriate Federal district court to enforce the contract or to recover any funds advanced or any costs incurred because of the breach of the contract by the State or political subdivision.

(3) Where a State or a political subdivision thereof is acting in behalf of the President, the President is authorized to provide technical and legal assistance in the administration and enforcement of any contract or subcontract in connection with response actions assisted under this title, and to intervene in any civil action involving the enforcement of such contract or subcontract.

(4) Where two or more noncontiguous facilities are reasonably related on the basis of geography, or on the basis of the threat, or potential threat to the public health or welfare or the environment, the President may, in his discretion, treat these related facilities as one for purposes of this section.

(e) Information Gathering And Access.—

(1) Action Authorized. — Any officer, employee, or representative of the President, duly designated by the President, is authorized to take action under paragraph (2), (3), or (4) (or any combination thereof) at a vessel, facility, establishment, place, property, or location or, in the case of paragraph (3) or (4), at any vessel, facility, establishment, place, property, or location which is adjacent to the vessel, facility, establishment, place, property, or location referred to in such paragraph (3) or (4). Any duly designated officer, employee, or representative of a State or political subdivision under a contract or cooperative agreement under subsection (d)(1) is also authorized to take such action. The authority of paragraphs (3) and (4) may be exercised only if there is a reasonable basis to believe there may be a release or threat of release of a hazardous substance or pollutant or contaminant. The authority of. this subsection may be exercised only for the purposes of determining the need for response, or choosing or taking any response action under this title, or otherwise enforcing the provisions of this title.

[§104(e)(1) revised by PL 99–499]

(2) Access To Information. — Any officer, employee, or representative described in paragraph (1) may require any person who has or may have information relevant to any of the following to furnish, upon reasonable notice, information or documents relating to such matter:

(A) The identification, nature, and quantity of materials which have been or are generated, treated, stored, or disposed of at a vessel or facility or transported to a vessel or facility.

(B) The nature or extent of a release or threatened release of a hazardous substance or pollutant or contaminant at or from a vessel or facility.

(C) Information relating to the ability of a person to pay for or to perform a cleanup. In addition, upon reasonable notice, such person either (i) shall grant any such officer, employee, or representative access at all reasonable times to any vessel, facility, establishment, place, property, or location to inspect and copy all documents or records relating to such matters or (ii) shall copy and furnish to the officer, employee, or representative all such documents or records, at the option and expense of such person.

[§104(e)(2) added by PL 99–499]

(3) Entry. — Any officer, employee, or representative described in paragraph (1) is authorized to enter at reasonable times any of the following:

[§104(e)(3) added by PL 99–499]

(A) Any vessel, facility, establishment, or other place or property where any hazardous substance or pollutant or contaminant may be or has been generated, stored, treated, disposed of, or transported from.

(B) Any vessel, facility, establishment, or other place or property from which or to which a hazardous substance or pollutant or contaminant has been or may have been released.

(C) Any vessel, facility, establishment, or other place or property where such release is or may be threatened.

(D) Any vessel, facility, establishment, or other place or property where entry is needed to determine the need for response or the appropriate response or to effectuate a response action under this title.

(4) Inspection And Samples.—

(A) Authority. — Any officer, employee or representative described in paragraph (1) is authorized to inspect and obtain samples from any vessel, facility, establishment, or other place or property referred to in paragraph (3) or from any location of any suspected hazardous substance or pollutant or contaminant. Any such officer, employee, or representative is authorized to inspect and obtain samples of any containers or labeling for suspected hazardous substances or pollutants or contaminants. Each such inspection shall be completed with reasonable promptness.

(B) Samples. — If the officer, employee, or representative obtains any samples, before leaving the premises he shall give to the owner, operator, tenant, or other person in charge of the place from which the samples were obtained a receipt describing the sample obtained and, if requested, a portion of each such sample. A copy of the results of any analysis made of such samples shall be furnished promptly to the owner, operator, tenant, or other person in charge, if such person can be located.

[§104(e)(4) added by PL 99–499]

(5) Compliance Orders.—

(A) Issuance. — If consent is not granted regarding any request made by an officer, employee, or representative under paragraph (2), (3), or (4), the President may issue an order directing compliance with the request. The order may be issued after such notice and opportunity for consultation as is reasonably appropriate under the circumstances.

(B) Compliance. — The President may ask the Attorney General to commence a civil action to compel compliance with a request or order referred to in subparagraph (A). Where there is a reasonable basis to believe there may be a release or threat of a release of a hazardous substance or pollutant or contaminant, the court shall take the following actions:

(i) In the case of interference with entry or inspection, the court shall enjoin such interference or direct compliance with orders to prohibit interference with entry or inspection unless under the circumstances of the case the demand for entry or inspection is arbitrary and capricious, an abuse of discretion, or otherwise not in accordance with law.

(ii) In the case of information or document requests or orders, the court shall enjoin interference with such information or document requests or orders or direct compliance with the requests or orders to provide such information or documents unless under the circumstances of the case the demand for information or documents is arbitrary and capricious, an abuse of discretion, or otherwise not in accordance with law.

The court may assess a civil penalty not to exceed $25,000 for each day of noncompliance against any person who unreasonably fails to comply with the provisions of paragraph (2), (3), or (4) or an order issued pursuant to subparagraph (A) of this paragraph.

[§104(e)(5) added by PL 99–499]

(6) Other Authority. — Nothing in this subsection shall preclude the President from securing access or obtaining information in any other lawful manner.

[§104(e)(6) added by PL 99–499]

(7) Confidentiality Of Information.—

(A) Any records, reports, or information obtained from any person under this section (including records, reports, or information obtained by representatives of the President) shall be available to the public, except that upon a showing satisfactory to the President (or the State, as the case may be) by any person that records, reports, or information, or particular part thereof (other than health or safety effects data), to which the President (or the State, as the case may be) or any officer, employee, or representative has access under this section if made public would divulge information entitled to protection under section 1905 of title 18 of the United States Code, such information or particular portion thereof shall be considered confidential in accordance with the purposes of that section, except that such record, report, document or information may be disclosed to other officers, employees, or authorized representatives of the United States concerned with carrying out this Act, or when relevant in any proceeding under this Act.

(B) Any person not subject to the provisions of section 1905 of title 18 of the United States Code who knowingly and willfully divulges or discloses any information entitled to protection under this subsection shall, upon conviction, be subject to a fine of not more than $5,000 or to imprisonment not to exceed one year, or both.

(C) In submitting data under this Act, a person required to provide such data may (i) designate the data which such person believes is entitled to protection under this subsection and (ii) submit such designated data separately from other data submitted under this Act. A designation under this paragraph shall be made in writing and in such manner as the President may prescribe by regulation.

(D) Notwithstanding any limitation contained in this section or any other provision of law, all information reported to or otherwise obtained by the President (or any representative of the President) under this Act shall be made available, upon written request of any duly authorized committee of the Congress, to such committee.

(E) No person required to provide information under this Act may claim that the information is entitled to protection under this paragraph unless such person shows each of the following:

(i) Such person has not disclosed the information to any other person, other than a member of a local emergency planning committee established under title III of the Amendments and Reauthorization Act of 1986, an officer or employee of the United States or a State or local government, an employee of such person, or a person who is bound by a confidentiality agreement, and such person has taken reasonable measures to protect the confidentiality of such information and intends to continue to take such measures.

(ii) The information is not required to be disclosed, or otherwise made available, to the public under any other Federal or State law.

(iii) Disclosure of the information is likely to cause substantial harm to the competitive position of such person.

(iv) The specific chemical identity, if sought to be protected, is not readily discoverable through reverse engineering.

(F) The following information with respect to any hazardous substance at the facility or vessel shall not be entitled to protection under this paragraph:

(i) The trade name, common name, or generic class or category of the hazardous substance.

(ii) The physical properties of the substance, including its boiling point, melting point, flash point, specific gravity, vapor density, solubility in water, and vapor pressure at 20 degrees celsius.

(iii) The hazards to health and the environment posed by the substance, including physical hazards (such as explosion) and potential acute and chronic health hazards.

(iv) The potential routes of human exposure to the substance at the facility, establishment, place, or property being investigated, entered, or inspected under this subsection.

(v) The location of disposal of any waste stream.

(vi) Any monitoring data or analysis of monitoring data pertaining to disposal activities.

(vii) Any hydrogeologic or geologic data.

(viii) Any groundwater monitoring data.

[Former §104(e)(2) amended and redesignated as (7) by PL 99–499]

(f) In awarding contracts to any person engaged in response actions, the President or the State, in any case where it is awarding contracts pursuant to a contract entered into under subsection (d) of this section, shall require compliance with Federal health and safety standards established under section 301(f) of this Act by contractors and subcontractors as a condition of such contracts.

(g) (1) All laborers and mechanics employed by contractors or subcontractors in the performance of construction, repair, or alteration work funded in whole or in part under this section shall be paid wages at rates not less than those prevailing on projects of a character similar in the locality as determined by the Secretary of Labor in accordance with the Davis-Bacon Act. The President shall not approve any such funding without first obtaining adequate assurance that required labor standards will be maintained upon the construction work.

(2) The Secretary of Labor shall have, with respect to the labor standards specified in paragraph (1), the authority and functions set forth in Reorganization Plan Numbered 14 of 1950 (15 F.R. 3176: 64 Stat. 1267) and section 276c of title 40 of the United States Code.

(h) Notwithstanding any other provision of law, subject to the provisions of section 111 of this Act, the President may authorize the use of such emergency procurement powers as he deems necessary to effect the purpose of this Act. Upon determination that such procedures are necessary, the President shall promulgate regulations prescribing the circumstances under which such authority shall be used and the procedures governing the use of such authority.

(i)(1) There is hereby established within the Public Health Service an agency, to be known as the Agency for Toxic Substances and Disease Registry, which shall report directly to the Surgeon General of the United States. The Administrator of said Agency shall, with the cooperation of the Administrator of the Environmental Protection Agency, the Commissioner of the Food and Drug Administration, the Directors of the National Institute of Medicine, National Institute of Environmental Health Sciences, National Institute of Occupational Safety and Health, Centers for Disease Control and Prevention, the Administrator of the Occupational Safety and Health Administration, the Administrator of the Social Security Administration, the Secretary of Transportation, and appropriate State and local health officials, effectuate and implement the health related authorities of this Act. In addition, said Administrator shall—

[§104(i)(1) amended by PL 102–531]

(A) in cooperation with the States, establish and maintain a national registry of serious diseases and illnesses and a national registry of persons exposed to toxic substances;

(B) establish and maintain inventory of literature, research, and studies on the health effects of toxic substances;

(C) in cooperation with the States, and other agencies of the Federal Government, establish and maintain a complete listing of areas closed to the public or otherwise restricted in use because of toxic substance contamination;

(D) in cases of public health emergencies caused or believed to be caused by exposure to toxic substances, provide medical care and testing to exposed individuals, including but not limited to tissue sampling, chromosomal testing where appropriate, epidemiological studies, or any other assistance appropriate under the circumstances; and

(E) either independently or as part of other health status survey, conduct periodic survey and screening programs to determine relationships between exposure to toxic substances and illness. In cases of public health emergencies, exposed persons shall be eligible for admission to hospitals and other facilities and services operated or provided by the Public Health Service.

[New §104(i)(1) designated and former (1)–(5) redesignated as (A)-(E) by PL 99–499]

(2)(A) Within 6 months after the enactment of the Superfund Amendments and Reauthorization Act of 1986, the Administrator of the Agency for Toxic Substances and Disease Registry (ATSDR) and the Administrator of the Environmental Protection Agency (EPA) shall prepare a list, in order of priority, of at least 100 hazardous substances which are most commonly found at facilities on the National Priorities List and which, in their sole discretion, they determine are posing the most significant potential threat to human health due to their known or suspected toxicity to humans and the potential for human exposure to such substances at facilities on the National Priorities List or at facilities to which a response to a release or a threatened release under this section is under consideration.

(B) Within 24 months after the enactment of the Superfund Amendments and Reauthorization Act of 1986, the Administrator of ATSDR and the Administrator of EPA shall revise the list prepared under subparagraph (A). Such revision shall include, in order of priority, the addition of 100 or more such hazardous substances. In each of the 3 consecutive 12–month periods that follow, the Administrator of ATSDR and the Administrator of EPA shall revise, in the same manner as provided in the 2 preceding sentences, such list to include not fewer than 25 additional hazardous substances per revision. The Administrator of ATSDR and the Administrator of EPA shall not less often than once every year thereafter revise such list to include additional hazardous substances in accordance with the criteria in subparagraph (A).

[§104(i)(2) added by PL 99–499]

(3) Based on all available information, including information maintained under paragraph (1)(B) and data developed and collected on the health effects of hazardous substances under this paragraph, the Administrator of ATSDR shall prepare toxicological profiles of each of the substances listed pursuant to paragraph (2). The toxicological profiles shall be prepared in accordance with guidelines developed by the Administrator of ATSDR and the Administrator of EPA. Such profiles shall include, but not be limited to each of the following:

(A) An examination, summary, and interpretation of available toxicological information and epidemiologic evaluations on a hazardous substance in order to ascertain the levels of significant human exposure for the substance and the associated acute, subacute, and chronic health effects.

(B) A determination of whether adequate information on the health effects of each substance is available or in the process of development to determine levels of exposure which present a significant risk to human health of acute, subacute, and chronic health effects.

(C) Where appropriate, an identification of toxicological testing needed to identify the types or levels of exposure that may present significant risk of adverse health effects in humans. Any toxicological profile or revision thereof shall reflect the Administrator of ATSDR'S assessment of all relevant toxicological testing which has been peer reviewed. The profiles required to be prepared under this paragraph for those hazardous substances listed under subparagraph (A) of paragraph (2) shall be completed, at a rate of no fewer than 25 per year, within 4 years after the enactment of the Superfund Amendments and Reauthorization Act of 1986. A profile required on a substance listed pursuant to subparagraph (B) of paragraph (2) shall be completed within 3 years after addition to the list. The profiles prepared under this paragraph shall be of those substances highest on the list of priorities under paragraph (2) for which profiles have not previously been prepared. Profiles required under this paragraph shall be revised and republished as necessary, but no less often than once every 3 years. Such profiles shall be provided to the States and made available to other interested parties.

[§104(i)(3) added by PL 99–499]

(4) The Administrator of the ATSDR shall provide consultations upon request on health issues relating to exposure to hazardous or toxic substances, on the basis of available information, to the Administrator of EPA, State officials, and local officials. Such consultations to individuals may be provided by States under cooperative agreements established under this Act.

[§104(i)(4) added by PL 99–499]

(5) (A) For each hazardous substance listed pursuant to paragraph(2), the Administrator of ATSDR (in consultation with the Administrator of EPA and other agencies and programs of the Public Health Service) shall assess whether adequate information on the health effects of such substance is available. For any such substance for which adequate information is not available (or under development), the Administrator of ATSDR, in cooperation with the Director of the National Toxicology Program, shall assure the initiation of a program of research designed to determine the health effects (and techniques for development of methods to determine such health effects) of such substance. Where feasible, such program shall seek to develop methods to determine the health effects of such substance in combination with other substances with which it is commonly found. Before assuring the initiation of such program, the Administrator of ATSDR shall consider recommendations of the Interagency Testing Committee established under section 4(e) of the Toxic Substances Control Act on the types of research that should be done. Such program shall include, to the extent necessary to supplement existing information, but shall not be limited to—

(i) laboratory and other studies to determine short, intermediate, and long-term effects;

(ii) laboratory and other studies to determine organ-specific, site-specific, and system-specific acute and chronic toxicity;

(iii) laboratory and other studies to determine the manner in which such substances are metabolized or to otherwise develop an understanding of the biokinetics of such substances; and

(iv) where there is a possibility of obtaining human data, the collection of such information.

(B) In assessing the need to perform laboratory and other studies, as required by subparagraph (A), the Administrator of ATSDR shall consider—

(i) the availability and quality of existing test data concerning the substance on the suspected health effect in question;

(ii) the extent to which testing already in progress will, in a timely fashion, provide data that will be adequate to support the preparation of toxicological profiles as required by paragraph (3); and

(iii) such other scientific and technical factors as the Administrator of ATSDR may determine are necessary for the effective implementation of this subsection.

(C) In the development and implementation of any research program under this paragraph, the Administrator of ATSDR and the Administrator of EPA shall coordinate such research program implemented under this paragraph with the National Toxicology Program and with programs of toxicological testing established under the Toxic Substances Control Act and the Federal Insecticide, Fungicide and Rodenticide Act. The purpose of such coordination shall be to avoid duplication of effort and to assure that the hazardous substances listed pursuant to this subsection are tested thoroughly at the earliest practicable date. Where appropriate, consistent with such purpose, a research program under this paragraph may be carried out using such programs of toxicological testing.

(D) It is the sense of the Congress that the costs of research programs under this paragraph be borne by the manufacturers and processors of the hazardous substance in question, as required in programs of toxicological testing under the Toxic Substances Control Act. Within 1 year after the enactment of the Superfund Amendments and Reauthorization Act of 1986, the Administrator of EPA shall promulgate regulations which provide, where appropriate, for payment of such costs by manufacturers and processors under the Toxic Substances Control Act, and registrants under the Federal Insecticide, Fungicide, and Rodenticide Act, and recovery of such costs from responsible parties under this Act.

[§104(i)(5) added by PL 99–499]

(6) (A) The Administrator of ATSDR shall perform a health assessment for each facility on the National Priorities List established under section 105 . Such health assessment shall be completed not later than December 10, 1988, for each facility proposed for inclusion on such list prior to the date of the enactment of the Superfund Amendments and Reauthorization Act of 1986 or not later than one year after the date of proposal for inclusion on such list for each facility proposed for inclusion on such list after such date of enactment.

(B) The Administrator of ATSDR may perform health assessments for releases or facilities where individual persons or licensed physicians provide information that individuals have been exposed to a hazardous substance, for which the probable source of such exposure is a release. In addition to other methods (formal or informal) of providing such information, such individual persons or licensed physicians may submit a petition to the Administrator of ATSDR providing such information and requesting a health assessment. If such a petition is submitted and the Administrator of ATSDR does not initiate a health assessment, the Administrator of ATSDR shall provide a written explanation of why a health assessment is not appropriate.

(C) In determining the priority in which to conduct health assessments under this subsection, the Administrator of ATSDR, in consultation with the Administrator of EPA, shall give priority to those facilities at which there is documented evidence of the release of hazardous substances, at which the potential risk to human health appears highest, and for which in the judgment of the Administrator of ATSDR existing health assessment data are inadequate to assess the potential risk to human health as provided in subparagraph (F). In determining the priorities for conducting health assessments under this subsection, the Administrator of ATSDR shall consider the National Priorities List schedules and the needs of the Environmental Protection Agency and other Federal agencies pursuant to schedules for remedial investigation and feasibility studies.

(D) Where a health assessment is done at a site on the National Priorities List, the Administrator of ATSDR shall complete such assessment promptly and, to the maximum extent practicable, before the completion of the remedial investigation and feasibility study at the facility concerned.

(E) Any State or political subdivision carrying out a health assessment for a facility shall report the results of the assessment to the Administrator of ATSDR and the Administrator of EPA and shall include recommendations with respect to further activities which need to be carried out under this section. The Administrator of ATSDR shall state such recommendation in any report on the results of any assessment carried out directly by the Administrator of ATSDR for such facility and shall issue periodic reports which include the results of all the assessments carried out under this subsection.

(F) For the purposes of this subsection and section 111(c)(4) , the term 'health assessments' shall include preliminary assessments of the potential risk to human health posed by individual sites and facilities, based on such factors as the nature and extent of contamination, the existence of potential pathways of human exposure (including ground or surface water contamination, air emissions, and food chain contamination), the size and potential susceptibility of the community within the likely pathways of exposure, the comparison of expected human exposure levels to the short-term and long-term health effects associated with identified hazardous substances and any available recommended exposure or tolerance limits for such hazardous substances, and the comparison of existing morbidity and mortality data on diseases that may be associated with the observed levels of exposure. The Administrator of ATSDR shall use appropriate data, risk assessments, risk evaluations and studies available from the Administrator of EPA.

(G) The purpose of health assessments under this subsection shall be to assist in determining whether actions under paragraph (II) of this subsection should be taken to reduce human exposure to hazardous substances from a facility and whether additional information on human exposure and associated health risks is needed and should be acquired by conducting epidemiological studies under paragraph (7), establishing a registry under paragraph (8), establishing a health surveillance program under paragraph (9), or through other means. In using the results of health assessments for determining additional actions to be taken under this section, the Administrator of ATSDR may consider additional information on the risks to the potentially affected population from all sources of such hazardous substances including known point or nonpoint sources other than those from the facility in question.

(H) At the completion of each health assessment, the Administrator of ATSDR shall provide the Administrator of EPA and each affected State with the results of such assessment, together with any recommendations for further actions under this subsection or otherwise under this Act. In addition, if the health assessment indicates that the release or threatened release concerned máy pose a serious threat to human health or the environment, the Administrator of ATSDR shall so notify the Administrator of EPA who shall promptly evaluate such release or threatened release in accordance with the hazard ranking system referred to in section 105(a)(8)(A) to determine whether the site shall be placed on the National Priorities List or, if the site is already on the list, the Administrator of ATSDR may recommend to the Administrator of EPA that the site be accorded a higher priority.

[§104(i)(6) added by PL 99–499]

(7) (A) Whenever in the judgment of the Administrator of ATSDR it is appropriate on the basis of the results of a health assessment, the Administrator of ATSDR shall conduct a pilot study of health effects for selected groups of exposed individuals in order to determine the desirability of conducting full scale epidemiological or other health studies of the entire exposed population.

(B) Whenever in the judgment of the Administrator of ATSDR it is appropriate on the basis of the results of such pilot study or other study or health assessment, the Administrator of ATSDR shall conduct such full scale epidemiological or other health studies as may be necessary to determine the health effects on the population exposed to hazardous substances from a release or threatened release. If a significant excess of disease in a population is identified, the letter of transmittal of such study shall include an assessment of other risk factors, other than a release, that may, in the judgment of the peer review group, be associated with such disease, if such risk factors were not taken into account in the design or conduct of the study.

[§104(i)(7) added by PL 99–499]

(8) In any case in which the results of a health assessment indicate a potential significant risk to human health, the Administrator of ATSDR, shall consider whether the establishment of a registry of exposed persons would contribute to accomplishing the purposes of this subsection, taking into account circumstances bearing on the usefulness of such a registry, including the seriousness or unique character of identified diseases or the likelihood of population migration from the affected area.

[§104(i)(8) added by PL 99–499]

(9) Where the Administrator of ATSDR has determined that there is a significant increased risk of adverse health effects in humans from exposure to hazardous substances based on the results of a health assessment conducted under paragraph (6), an epidemiologic study conducted under paragraph (7), or an exposure registry that has been established under paragraph (8), and the Administrator of ATSDR has determined that such exposure is the result of a release from a facility, the Administrator of ATSDR shall initiate a health surveillance program for such population. This program shall include but not be limited to—

(A) periodic medical testing where appropriate of population subgroups to screen for diseases for which the population or subgroup is at significant increased risk; and

(B) a mechanism to refer for treatment those individuals within such population who are screened positive for such diseases.

[§104(i)(9) added by PL 99–499]

(10) Two years after the date of the enactment of the Superfund Amendments and Reauthori-

zation Act of 1986, and every 2 years thereafter, the Administrator of ATSDR shall prepare and submit to the Administrator of EPA and to the Congress a report on the results of the activities of ATSDR regarding—

(A) health assessments and pilot health effects studies conducted;

(B) epidemiologic studies conducted;

(C) hazardous substances which have been listed under paragraph (2), toxicological profiles which have been developed, and toxicologic testing which has been conducted or which is being conducted under this subsection;

(D) registries established under paragraph (8); and

(E) an overall assessment, based on the results of activities conducted by the Administrator of ATSDR, of the linkage between human exposure to individual or combinations of hazardous substances due to releases from facilities covered by this Act or the Solid Waste Disposal Act and any increased incidence or prevalence of adverse health effects in humans.

[§104(i)(10) added by PL 99–499]

(11) If a health assessment or other study carried out under this subsection contains a finding that the exposure concerned presents a significant risk to human health, the President shall take such steps as may be necessary to reduce such exposure and eliminate or substantially mitigate the significant risk to human health. Such steps may include the use of any authority under this Act, including but not limited to—

(A) provision of alternative water supplies, and

(B) permanent or temporary relocation of individuals. In any case in which information is insufficient, in the judgment of the Administrator of ATSDR or the President to determine a significant human exposure level with respect to a hazardous substance, the President may take such steps as may be necessary to reduce the exposure of any person to such hazardous substance to such level as the President deems necessary to protect human health.

[§104(i)(11) added by PL 99–499]

(12) In any case which is the subject of a petition, a health assessment or study, or a research program under this subsection, nothing in this subsection shall be construed to delay or otherwise affect or impair the authority of the President, the Administrator of ATSDR or the Administrator of EPA to exercise any authority vested in the President, the Administrator of ATSDR or the Administrator of EPA under any other provision of law (including, but not limited to, the imminent hazard authority of section 7003 of the Solid Waste Disposal Act) or the response and abatement authorities of this Act.

[§104(i)(12) added by PL 99–499]

(13) All studies and results of research conducted under this subsection (other than health assessments) shall be reported or adopted only after appropriate peer review. Such peer review shall be completed, to the maximum extent practicable, within a period of 60 days. In the case of research conducted under the National Toxicology Program, such peer review may be conducted by the Board of Scientific Counselors. In the case of other research, such peer review shall be conducted by panels consisting of no less than three nor more than seven members, who shall be disinterested scientific experts selected for such purpose by the Administrator of ATSDR or the Administrator of EPA, as appropriate, on the basis of their reputation for scientific objectivity and the lack of institutional ties with any person involved in the conduct of the study or research under review. Support services for such panels shall be provided by the Agency for Toxic Substances and Disease Registry, or by the Environmental Protection Agency, as appropriate.

[§104(i)(13) added by PL 99–499]

(14) In the implementation of this subsection and other health-related authorities of this Act, the Administrator of ATSDR shall assemble, develop as necessary and distribute to the States, and upon request to medical colleges, physicians, and other health professionals, appropriate educational materials (including short courses) on the medical surveillance, screening, and methods of diagnosis and treatment of injury or disease related to exposure to hazardous substances (giving priority to those listed in paragraph (2)), through such means as the Administrator of ATSDR deems appropriate.

[§104(i)(14) added by PL 99–499]

(15) The activities of the Administrator of ATSDR described in this subsection and section 111(c)(4) shall be carried out by the Administrator of ATSDR, either directly or through cooperative agreements with States

(or political subdivisions thereof) which the Administrator of ATSDR determines are capable of carrying out such activities. Such activities shall include provision of consultations on health information, the conduct of health assessments, including those required under section 3019(b) of the Solid Waste Disposal Act, health studies, registries, and health surveillance.

[§104(i)(15) added by PL 99–499]

(16) The President shall provide adequate personnel for ATSDR, which shall not be fewer than 100 employees. For purposes of determining the number of employees under this subsection, an employee employed by ATSDR on a part-time career employment basis shall be counted as a fraction which is determined by dividing 40 hours into the average number of hours of such employee's regularly scheduled workweek.

[§104(i)(16) added by PL 99–499]

(17) In accordance with section 120 (relating to Federal facilities), the Administrator of ATSDR shall have the same authorities under this section with respect to facilities owned or operated by a department, agency, or instrumentality of the United States as the Administrator of ATSDR has with respect to any nongovernmental entity.

[§104(i)(17) added by PL 99–499]

(18) If the Administrator of ATSDR determines that it is appropriate for purposes of this section to treat a pollutant or contaminant as a hazardous substance, such pollutant or contaminant shall be treated as a hazardous substance for such purpose.

[§104(i)(18) added by PL 99–499]

(j) Acquisition of Property.—

(1) Authority. — The President is authorized to acquire, by purchase, lease, condemnation, donation, or otherwise, any real property or any interest in real property that the President in his discretion determines is needed to conduct a remedial action under this Act. There shall be no cause of action to compel the President to acquire any interest in real property under this Act.

(2) State assurance. — The President may use the authority of paragraph (1) for a remedial action only if, before an interest in real estate is acquired under this subsection, the State in which the interest to be acquired is located assures the President, through a contract or cooperative agreement or otherwise, that the State will accept transfer of the interest following completion of the remedial action.

(3) Exemption. — No Federal, State, or local government agency shall be liable under this Act solely as a result of acquiring an interest in real estate under this subsection.

[§104(j) added by PL 99–499]

§9605. National Contingency Plan [Sec. 105]

(a) Revision And Republication.— Within one hundred and eighty days after the enactment of this Act, the President shall, after notice and opportunity for public comments, revise and republish the national contingency plan for the removal of oil and hazardous substances, originally prepared and published pursuant to section 311 of the Federal Water Pollution Control Act, to reflect and effectuate the responsibilities and powers created by this Act, in addition to those matters specified in section 311(c)(2). Such revision shall include a section of the plan to be known as the national hazardous substance response plan which shall establish procedures and standards for responding to releases of hazardous substances, pollutants, and contaminants, which shall include at a minimum:

(1) methods for discovering and investigating facilities at which hazardous substances have been disposed of or otherwise come to be located;

(2) methods for evaluating, including analyses of relative cost, and remedying any releases or threats of releases from facilities which pose substantial danger to the public health or the environment;

(3) methods and criteria for determining the appropriate extent of removal, remedy, and other measures authorized by this Act;

(4) appropriate roles and responsibilities for the Federal, State, and local governments and for interstate and nongovernmental entities in effectuating the plan;

(5) provision for identification, procurement, maintenance, and storage of response equipment and supplies;

(6) a method for and assignment of responsibility for reporting the existence of such facilities which may be located on federally owned or controlled properties and any releases of hazardous substances from such facilities;

(7) means of assuring that remedial action measures are cost-effective over the period of potential exposure to the hazardous substances or contaminated materials;

(8) (A) criteria for determining priorities among releases or threatened releases throughout the United States for the purpose of taking remedial action and, to the extent practicable taking into account the potential urgency of such action, for the purpose of taking removal action. Criteria and priorities under this paragraph shall be based upon relative risk or danger to public health or welfare or the environment, in the judgment of the President, taking into account to the extent possible the population at risk, the hazard potential of the hazardous substances at such facilities, the potential for contamination of drinking water supplies, the potential for direct human contact, the potential for destruction of sensitive ecosystems, the damage to natural resources which may affect the human food chain and which is associated with any release or threatened release, the contamination or potential contamination of the ambient air which is associated with the release or threatened release, State preparedness to assume State costs and responsibilities, and other appropriate factors;

[§105(a)(8)(A) amended by PL 99–499]

(B) based upon the criteria set forth in subparagraph (A) of this paragraph, the President shall list as part of the plan national priorities among the known releases or threatened releases throughout the United States and shall revise the list no less often than annually. Within one year after the date of enactment of this Act, and annually thereafter, each State shall establish and submit for consideration by the President priorities for remedial action among known releases and potential releases in that State based upon the criteria set forth in subparagraph (A) of this paragraph. In assembling or revising the national list, the President shall consider any priorities established by the States. To the extent practicable, the highest priority facilities shall be designated individually and shall be referred to as the "top priority among known response targets", and, to the extent practicable, shall include among the one hundred highest priority facilities one such facility from each State which shall be the facility designated by the State as presenting the greatest danger to public health or welfare or the environment among the known facilities in such State. A State shall be allowed to designate its highest priority facility only once. Other priority facilities or incidents may be listed singly or grouped for response priority purposes;

[§105(a)(8)(B) amended by PL 99–499]

(9) specified roles for private organizations and entities in preparation for response and in responding to releases of hazardous substances, including identification of appropriate qualifications and capacity therefor and including consideration of minority firms in accordance with subsection (f); and

[§105(a)(9) amended by PL 99–499]

(10) standards and testing procedures by which alternative or innovative treatment technologies can be determined to be appropriate for utilization in response actions authorized by this Act.

[§105(a)(10) added by PL 99–499]

The plan shall specify procedures, techniques, materials, equipment, and methods to be employed in identifying, removing, or remedying releases of hazardous substances comparable to those required under section 311(c)(2)(F) and (G) and (j)(1) of the Federal Water Pollution Control Act. Following publication of the revised national contingency plan, the response to and actions to minimize damage from hazardous substances releases shall, to the greatest extent possible be in accordance with the provisions of the plan, The President may, from time to time, revise and republish the national contingency plan.

(b) Revision Of Plan. — Not later than 18 months after the enactment of the Superfund Amendments and Reauthorization Act of 1986, the President shall revise the National Contingency Plan to reflect the requirements of such amendments. The portion of such Plan known as "the National Hazardous Substance Response Plan" shall be revised to provide procedures and standards for remedial actions undertaken pursuant to this Act which are consistent with amendments made by the Superfund Amendments and Reauthorization Act of 1986 relating to the selection of remedial action.

[§105(b) added by PL 99–499]

(c) Hazard Ranking System.—

(1) Revision. — Not later than 18 months after the enactment of the Superfund Amendments and Reauthorization Act of 1986 and after publication of notice and opportunity for submission of comments in accordance with section 553 of title 5, United States Code, the President shall by rule promulgate amendments to the hazard ranking system in effect on September 1, 1984. Such amendments shall assure, to the maximum extent feasible, that the hazard ranking system accurately assesses the relative

degree of risk to human health and the environment posed by sites and facilities subject to review. The President shall establish an effective date for the amended hazard ranking system which is not later than 24 months after enactment of the Superfund Amendments and Reauthorization Act of 1986. Such amended hazard ranking system shall be applied to any site or facility to be newly listed on the National Priorities List after the effective date established by the President. Until such effective date of the regulations, the hazard ranking system in effect on September 1, 1984, shall continue in full force and effect.

(2) Health Assessment Of Water Contamination Risks. — In carrying out this subsection, the President shall ensure that the human health risks associated with the contamination or potential contamination (either directly or as a result of the runoff of any hazardous substance or pollutant or contaminant from sites or facilities) of surface water are appropriately assessed where such surface water is, or can be, used for recreation or potable water consumption. In making the assessment required pursuant to the preceding sentence, the President shall take into account the potential migration of any hazardous substance or pollutant or contaminant through such surface water to downstream sources of drinking water.

(3) Reevaluation Not Required. — The President shall not be required to reevaluate, after the date of the enactment of the Superfund Amendments and Reauthorization Act of 1986, the hazard ranking of any facility which was evaluated in accordance with the criteria under this section before the effective date of the amendments to the hazard ranking system under this subsection and which was assigned a national priority under the National Contingency Plan.

(4) New Information. — Nothing in paragraph (3) shall preclude the President from taking new information into account in undertaking response actions under this Act.

[§105(c) added by PL 99–499]

(d) Petition For Assessment Of Release. — Any person who is, or may be, affected by release or threatened release of a hazardous substance or pollutant or contaminant, may petition the President to conduct a preliminary assessment of the hazards to public health and the environment which are associated with such release or threatened release. If the President has not previously conducted a preliminary assessment of such release, the President shall, within 12 months after the receipt of any such petition, complete such assessment or provide an explanation of why the assessment is not appropriate. If the preliminary assessment indicates that the release or threatened release concerned may pose a threat to human health or the environment, the President shall promptly evaluate such release or threatened release in accordance with the hazard ranking system referred to in paragraph (8)(A) of subsection (a) to determine the national priority of such release or threatened release.

[§105(d) added by PL 99–499]

(e) Releases From Earlier Sites. — Whenever there has been, after January 1, 1985, a significant release of hazardous substances or pollutants or contaminants from a site which is listed by the President as a "Site Cleaned Up To Date" on the National Priorities List (revised edition, December 1984) the site shall be restored to the National Priorities List, without application of the hazard ranking system.

[§105(e) added by PL 99–499]

(f) Minority Contractors. — In awarding contracts under this Act, the President shall consider the availability of qualified minority firms. The President shall describe, as part of any annual report submitted to the Congress under this Act, the participation of minority firms in contracts carried out under this Act. Such report shall contain a brief description of the contracts which have been awarded to minority firms under this Act and of the efforts made by the President to encourage the participation of such firms in programs carried out under this Act.

[§105(f) added by PL 99–499]

(g) Special Study Wastes.—

(1) Application. This subsection applies to facilities —

(A) which as of the date of enactment of the Superfund Amendments and Reauthorization Act of 1986 'where not included on, or proposed for inclusion on, the National Priorities List; and

(B) at which special study wastes described in paragraph (2), (3)(A)(ii) or (3)(A)(iii) of section 3001(b) of the Solid Waste Disposal Act are present in significant quantities, including any such facility from which there has been a release of a special study waste.

(2) Considerations In Adding Facilities To NPL. — Pending revision of the hazard ranking system under subsection (c), the President

shall consider each of the following factors in adding facilities covered by this section to the National Priorities List:

(A) The extent to which hazard ranking system score for the facility is affected by the presence of any special study waste at, or any release from, such facility.

(B) Available information as to the quantity, toxicity, and concentration of hazardous substances that are constituents of any special study waste at, or released from such facility, the extent of or potential for release of such hazardous constituents, the exposure or potential exposure to human population and the environment, and the degree of hazard to human health or the environment posed by the release of such hazardous constituents at such facility. This subparagraph refers only to available information on actual concentrations of hazardous substances and not on the total quantity of special study waste at such facility.

(3) Savings Provisions. Nothing in this subsection shall be construed to limit the authority of the President to remove any facility which as of the date of enactment of the Superfund Amendments and Reauthorization Act of 1986 is included on the National Priorities List from such List, or not to list any facility which as of such date is proposed for inclusion on such list.

(4) Information Gathering And Analysis. Nothing in this Act shall be construed to preclude the expenditure of monies from the Fund for gathering and analysis of information which will enable the President to consider the specific factors required by paragraph (2).

[§105(g) added by PL 99–499]

§9606. Abatement Action [Sec. 106]

(a) In addition to any other action taken by a State or local government, when the President determines that there may be an imminent and substantial endangerment to the public health or welfare or the environment because of an actual or threatened release of a hazardous substance from a facility, he may require the Attorney General of the United States to secure such relief as may be necessary to abate such danger or threat, and the district court of the United States in the district in which the threat occurs shall have jurisdiction to grant such relief as the public interest and the equities of the case may require. The President may also, after notice to the affected State, take other action under this section including, but not limited to, issuing such orders as may be necessary to protect public health and welfare and the environment.

(b) (1) Any person who, without sufficient cause, willfully violates, or fails or refuses to comply with, any order of the President under subsection (a) may, in an action brought in the appropriate United States district court to enforce such order, be fined not more than $25,000 for each day in which such violation occurs or such failure to comply continues.

[§106(b)(1) designated and amended by PL 99–499]

(2) (A) Any person who receives and complies with the terms of any order issued under subsection (a) may, within 60 days after completion of the required action, petition the President for reimbursement from the Fund for the reasonable costs of such action, plus interest. Any interest payable under this paragraph shall accrue on the amounts expended from the date of expenditure at the same rate as specified for interest on investments of the Hazardous Substance Superfund established under subchapter A of chapter 98 of the Internal Revenue Code of 1954.

(B) If the President refuses to grant all or part of a petition made under this paragraph, the petitioner may within 30 days of receipt of such refusal file an action against the President in the appropriate United States district court seeking reimbursement from the Fund.

(C) Except as provided in subparagraph (D), to obtain reimbursement, the petitioner shall establish by a preponderance of the evidence that it is not liable for response costs under section 107(a) and that costs for which it seeks reimbursement are reasonable in light of the action required by the relevant order.

(D) A petitioner who is liable for response costs under section 107(a) may also recover its reasonable costs of response to the extent that it can demonstrate, on the administrative record, that the President's decision in selecting the response action ordered was arbitrary and capricious or was otherwise not in accordance with law. Reimbursement awarded under this subparagraph shall include all reasonable response costs incurred by the petitioner pursuant to the portions of the order found to be arbitrary and capricious or otherwise not in accordance with law.

(E) Reimbursement awarded by a court under subparagraph (C) or (D) may include appropriate costs, fees, and other expenses in accordance with subsections (a) and (d) of section 2412 of title 28 of the United States Code.

[§106(b)(2) added by PL 99–499]

(c) Within one hundred and eighty days after enactment of this Act, this Act, the Administrator of the Environmental Protection Agency shall, after consultation with the Attorney General, establish and publish guidelines for using the imminent hazard, enforcement, and emergency response authorities of this section and other existing statutes administered by the Administrator of the Environmental Protection Agency to effectuate the responsibilities and powers created by this Act. Such guidelines shall to the extent practicable be consistent with the national hazardous substance response plan, and shall include, at a minimum, the assignment of responsibility for coordinating response actions with the issuance of administrative orders, enforcement of standards and permits, the gathering of information, and other imminent hazard and emergency powers authorized by (1) sections 311(c)(2), 308,309, and 504(a) of the Federal Water Pollution Control Act, (2) sections 3007, 3008, 3013, and 7003 of the Solid Waste Disposal Act, (3) sections 1445 and 1431 of the Safe Drinking Water Act, (4) sections 113, 114, and 303 of the Clean Air Act, and (5) section 7 of the Toxic Substances Control Act.

§9607. Liability [Sec. 107]

(a) Notwithstanding any other provision or rule of law, and subject only to the defenses set forth in subsection (b) of this section—

(1) the owner and operator of a vessel or a facility,

[§107(a)(1) amended by PL 99–499]

(2) any person who at the time of disposal of any hazardous substance owned or operated any facility at which such hazardous substances were disposed of,

(3) any person who by contract, agreement, or otherwise arranged for disposal or treatment, or arranged with a transporter for transport for disposal or treatment, of hazardous substances owned or possessed by such person, by any other party or entity, at any facility or incineration vessel owned or operated by another party or entity and containing such hazardous substances, and

[§107(a)(3) amended by PL 99–499]

(4) any person who accepts or accepted any hazardous substances for transport to disposal or treatment facilities, incineration vessels or sites selected by such person, from which there is a release, or a threatened release which causes the incurrence of response coats, of a hazardous substance, shall be liable for —

(A) all costs of removal or remedial action incurred by the United States Government or a State or an Indian tribe not inconsistent with the national contingency plan;

(B) any other necessary costs of response incurred by any other person consistent with the national contingency plan;

(C) damages for injury to, destruction of, or loss of natural resources, including the reasonable costs of assessing such injury, destruction, or loss resulting from such a release; and

(D) the costs of any health assessment or health effects study carried out under section 104(i) .

The amounts recoverable in an action under this section shall include interest on the amounts recoverable under subparagraphs (A) through (D). Such interest shall accrue from the later of (i) the date payment of a specified amount is demanded in writing, or (ii) the date of the expenditure concerned. The rate of interest on the outstanding unpaid balance of the amounts recoverable under this section shall be the same rate as is specified for interest on investments of the Hazardous Substance Superfund established under subchapter A of chapter 98 of the Internal Revenue Code of 1954. For purposes of applying such amendments to interest under this subsection, the term 'comparable maturity' shall be determined with reference to the date on which interest accruing under this subsection commences.

[§107 (a)(4), (A) — (C) amended and (D) added by PL 99–499]

(b) There shall be no liability under subsection (a) of this section for a person otherwise liable who can establish by a preponderance of the evidence that the release or threat of release of a hazardous substance and the damages resulting therefrom were caused solely by—

(1) an act of God;

(2) an act of war;

(3) an act or omission of a third party other than an employee or agent of the defendant, or than one whose act or omission occurs in connection with a contractual relationship, existing directly or indirectly, with the defendant (except where the sole contractual arrangement arises from a published tariff and acceptance for carriage by a common carrier by rail), if the defendant establishes by a preponder-

ance of the evidence that (a) he exercised due care with respect to the hazardous substance concerned, taking into consideration the characteristics of such hazardous substance, in light of all relevant facts and circumstances, and (b) he took precautions against foreseeable acts or omissions of any such third party and the consequences that could foreseeably result from such acts or omissions; or

(4) any combination of the foregoing paragraphs.

(c) (1) Except as provided in paragraph (2) of this subsection, the liability under this section of an owner or operator or other responsible person for each release of a hazardous substance or incident involving release of a hazardous substance shall not exceed—

(A) for any vessel, other than an incineration vessel, which carries any hazardous substance as cargo or residue, $300 per gross ton, or $5,000,000, whichever is greater:

[§107(c)(1)(A) amended by PL 99–499]

(B) for any other vessel, other than an incineration vessel, $300 per gross ton, or $500,000, whichever is greater;

[§107(c)(1)(B) amended by PL 99–499]

(C) for any motor vehicle, aircraft, pipeline (as defined in the Hazardous Liquid Pipeline Safety Act of 1979) or rolling stock, $50,000,000 or such lesser amount as the President shall establish by regulation, but in no event less than $5,000,000 (or, for releases of hazardous substances as defined in section 101(14)(A) of this title into the navigable waters, $8,000,000). Such regulations shall take into account the size, type, location, storage, and handling capacity and other matters relating to the likelihood of release in each such class and to the economic impact of such limits on each such class; or

(D) for any incineration vessel or any facility other than those specified in subparagraph (C) of this paragraph, the total of all costs of response plus $50,000,000 for any damages under this title.

[§107(c)(1)(D) amended by PL 99–499]

(2) Notwithstanding the limitations in paragraph (1) of this subsection, the liability of an owner or operator or other responsible person under this section shall be the full and total costs of response and damages, if (A)(i) the release or threat of release of a hazardous substance was the result of willful misconduct or willful negligence within the privity or knowledge of such person, or (ii) the primary cause of the release was a violation (within the privity or knowledge of such person) of applicable safety, construction, or operating standards or regulations; or (B) such person fails or refuses to provide all reasonable cooperation and assistance requested by a responsible public official in connection with response activities under the national contingency plan with respect to regulated carriers subject to the provisions of title 49 of the United States Code or vessels subject to the provisions of title 33 or 46 of the United States Code, subparagraph (A)(ii) of this paragraph shall be deemed to refer to Federal standards or regulations.

(3) If any person who is liable for a release or threat of release of a hazardous substance fails without sufficient cause to properly provide removal or remedial action upon order of the President pursuant to section 104 or 106 of this Act, such person may be liable to the United States for punitive damages in an amount at least equal to, and not more than three times, the amount of any costs incurred by the Fund as a result of such failure to take proper action. The President is authorized to commence a civil action against any such person to recover the punitive damages, which shall be in addition to any costs recovered from such person pursuant to section 112(c) of this Act. Any moneys received by the United States pursuant to this subsection shall be deposited in the Fund.

(d) Rendering Care Or Advice. —

(1) In General. — Except as provided in paragraph (2), no person shall be liable under this title for costs or damages as a result of actions taken or omitted in the course of rendering care, assistance, or advice in accordance with the National Contingency Plan ('NCP') or at the direction of an onscene coordinator appointed under such plan, with respect to an incident creating a danger to public health or welfare or the environment as a result of any releases of a hazardous substance or the threat thereof. This paragraph shall not preclude liability for costs or damages as the result of negligence on the part of such person.

(2) State And Local Governments. — No State or local government shall be liable under this title for costs or damages as a result of actions taken in response to an emergency created by the release or threatened release of a hazardous substance generated by or from a facility owned by another person. This paragraph shall not preclude liability for costs or damages as a result of gross negligence or inten-

tional misconduct by the State or local government. For the purpose of the preceding sentence, reckless, willful, or wanton misconduct shall constitute gross negligence.

(3) Savings Provision. — This subsection shall not alter the liability of any person covered by the provisions of paragraph (1), (2), (3), or (4) of subsection (a) of this section with respect to the release or threatened release concerned.

[§107(d) revised by PL 99–499]

(e) (1) No indemnification, hold harmless, or similar agreement or conveyance shall be effective to transfer from the owner or operator of any vessel or facility or from any person who may be liable for a release or threat of release under this section, to any other person the liability imposed under this section. Nothing in this subsection shall bar any agreement to insure, hold harmless, or indemnify a party to such agreement for any liability under this section.

(2) Nothing in this title, including the provisions of paragraph (1) of this subsection, shall bar a cause of action that an owner or operator or any other person subject to liability under this section, or a guarantor, has or would have, by reason of subrogation or otherwise against any person.

(f) (1) Natural Resources Liability.— In the case of an injury to, destruction of, or loss of natural resources under subparagraph (C) of subsection (a) liability shall be to the United States Government and to any State for natural resources within the State or belonging to, managed by, controlled by, or appertaining to such State and to any Indian tribe for natural resources belonging to, managed by, controlled by, or appertaining to such tribe, or held in trust for the benefit of such tribe, or belonging to a member of such tribe if such resources are subject to a trust restriction on alienation. *Provided, however,* That no liability to the United States or State or Indian tribe shall be imposed under subparagraph (C) of subsection (a), where the party sought to be charged has demonstrated that the damages to natural resources complained of were specifically identified as an irreversible and irretrievable commitment of natural resources in an environmental impact statement, or other comparable environment analysis, and the decision to grant a permit or license authorizes such commitment of natural resources, and the facility or project was otherwise operating within the terms of its permit or license, so long as, in the case of damages to an Indian tribe occurring pursuant to a Federal permit or license, the issuance of that permit or license was not inconsistent with the fiduciary duty of the United States with respect to such Indian tribe. The President, or the authorized representative of any State, shall act on behalf of the public as trustee of such natural resources to recover for such damages.

[Editor's Note: §107(f)(1) was amended by two provisions of PL 99–499. The text of both amendments follow. The following is the text of the third sentence of §107(f)(1) as amended by Section 107(d)(2) of PL 99–499:

Sums recovered by the United States Government as trustee under this subsection shall be retained by the trustee, without further appropriations, for use only to restore, replace, or acquire the equivalent of such natural resources. Sums recovered by a State as trustee under this subsection shall be available for use only to restore, replace, or acquire the equivalent of such natural resources by the State. The measure of damages in any action under subparagraph (C) of subsection (a) shall not be limited by the sums which can be used to restore or replace such resources. There shall be no double recovery under this Act for natural resource damages, including the costs of damage assessment or restoration, rehabilitation, or acquisition for the same release and natural resource.

Following is the text of the third sentence of 107(f)(1) as amended by Section 207(c)(2)(D) of PL 99–499:

Sums recovered shall be available for use to restore, rehabilitate or acquire the equivalent of such natural resources by the appropriate agencies of the Federal Government or the State government or the Indian tribe, but the measure of such damages shall not be limited by the sums which can be used to restore or replace such resources.]

There shall be no recovery under the authority of subparagraph (C) of subsection (a) where such damages and the release of a hazardous substance from which such damagesa and the release of a hazardous substance damage from which such resulted have occurred wholly before the enactment of this Act.

[§107(f)(1) amended by PL 99–499]

(2) Designation Of Federal And State Officials. —

(A) Federal. — The President shall designate in the National Contingency Plan published under section 105 of this Act the Federal officials who shall act on behalf of the public as trustees for natural resources under this Act and section 311 of the Federal Water Pollution Control Act. Such officials shall assess damages for injury to, destruction of, or loss of natural resources for purposes of this Act and such section 311 for those resources under their trusteeship and may, upon request of and reimbursement from a State and at the Federal officials' discretion, assess damages for those natural resources under the State's trusteeship.

(B) State. — The Governor of each State shall designate State officials who may act on behalf of the public as trustees for natural resources under this Actand section 311 of the Federal Water Pollution Control Act and shall notify the President of such designations. Such State officials shall assess damages to natural resources for the purposes of this Act and such section 311 for those natural resources under their trusteeship.

(C) Rebuttable Presumption. — Any determination or assessment of damages to natural resources for the purposes of this Act and section 311 of the Federal Water Pollution Control Act made by a Federal or State trustee in accordance with the regulations promulgated under section 301(c) of this Act shall have the force and effect of a rebuttable presumption on behalf of the trustee in any administrative or judicial proceeding under this Act or section 311 of the Federal Water Pollution Control Act.

[§107(f)(2) added by PL 99–499]

(g) Federal Agencies. — For provisions relating to Federal agencies, see section 120 of this Act.

[§107(g) revised by PL 99–499]

(h) The owner or operator of a vessel shall be liable in accordance with this section, under maritime tort law, and as provided under section 114 of this Act notwithstanding any provision of the Act of March 3, 1851 (46 U.S.C. 183ff) or the absence of any physical damage to the proprietary interest of the claimant.

[§107(h) amended by PL 99–499]

(i) No person (including the United States or any State or Indian tribe may recover under the authority of this section for any response costs or damages resulting from the application of a pesticide product registered under the Federal Insecticide, Fungicide, and Rodenticide Act. Nothing in this paragraph shall affect or modify in any way the obligations or liability of any person under any other provision of State or Federal law, including common law, for damages, injury, or loss resulting from a release of any hazardous substance or for removal or remedial action or the costs of removal or remedial action of such hazardous substance.

[§107(i) amended by PL 99–499]

(j) Recovery by any person (including the United States or any State or Indian tribe) for response costs or damages resulting from a federally permitted release shall be pursuant to existing law in lieu of this section. Nothing in this paragraph shall affect or modify in any way the obligations or liability of any person under any other provision of State or Federal law, including common law, for damages, injury, or loss resulting from a release of any hazardous substance or for removal or remedial action or the costs of removal or remedial action of such hazardous substance. In addition, costs of response incurred by the Federal Government in connection with a discharge specified in section 101(10)(B) or (C) shall be recoverable in an action brought under section 309(b) of the Clean Water Act.

(k) (1) The liability established by this section or any other law for the owner or operator of a hazardous waste disposal facility which has received a permit under subtitle C of the Solid Waste Disposal Act, shall be transferred to and assumed by the Post-closure Liability Fund established by section 232 of this Act when—

(A) such facility and the owner and operator thereof has complied with the requirements of subtitle C of the Solid Waste Disposal Act and regulations issued thereunder, which may affect the performance of such facility after closure; and

(B) such facility has been closed in accordance with such regulations and the conditions of such permit, and such facility and the surrounding area have been monitored as required by such regulations and permit conditions for a period not to exceed five years after closure to demonstrate that there is no substantial likelihood that any migration offsite or release from confinement of any hazardous substance or other risk to public health or welfare will occur.

(2) Such transfer of liability shall be effective ninety days after the owner or operator of such facility notifies the Administrator of the Environmental Protection Agency (and the State where it has an authorized program under section 3006(b) of the Solid Waste Disposal Act) that the conditions imposed by this subsection have been satisfied. If within such ninety-day period the Administrator of the Environmental Protection Agency or such State determines that any such facility has not complied with all

the conditions imposed by this subsection or that insufficient information has been provided to demonstrate such compliance, the Administrator or such State shall so notify the owner and operator of such facility and the administrator of the Fund established by section 232 of this Act, and the owner and operator of such facility shall continue to be liable with respect to such facility under this section and other law until such time as the Administrator and such State determines that such facility has complied with all conditions imposed by this subsection. A determination by the Administrator or such State that a facility has not complied with all conditions imposed by this subsection or that insufficient information has been supplied to demonstrate compliance, shall be a final administrative action for purposes of judicial review. A request for additional information shall state in specific terms the data required.

(3) In addition to the assumption of liability of owners and operators under paragraph (1) of this subsection, the Post-closure Liability Fund established by section 232 of this Act may be used to pay costs of monitoring and care and maintenance of a site incurred by other persons after the period of monitoring required by regulations under subtitle C of the Solid Waste Disposal Act for hazardous waste disposal facilities meeting the conditions of paragraph (1) of this subsection.

(4) (A) Not later than one year after the date of enactment of this Act, the Secretary of the Treasury shall conduct a study and shall submit a report thereon to the Congress on the feasibility of establishing or qualifying an optional system of private insurance for postclosure financial responsibility for hazardous waste disposal facilities to which this subsection applies. Such study shall include a specification of adequate and realistic minimum standards to assure that any such privately placed insurance will carry out the purposes of this subsection in a reliable, enforceable, and practical manner. Such a study shall include an examination of the public and private incentives, programs, and actions necessary to make privately placed insurance a practical and effective option to the financing system for the Postclosure Liability Fund provided in title II of this Act.

(B) Not later than eighteen months after the date of enactment of this Act and after a public hearing, the President shall by rule determine whether or not it is feasible to establish or qualify an optional system of private insurance for postclosure financial responsibility for hazardous waste disposal facilities to which this subsection applies. If the President determines the establishment or qualification of such a system would be infeasible, he shall promptly publish an explanation of the reasons for such a determination. If the President determines the establishment or qualification of such a system would be feasible, he shall promptly publish notice of such determination. Not later than six months after an affirmative determination under the preceding sentence and after a public hearing, the President shall by rule promulgate adequate and realistic minimum standards which must be met by any such privately placed insurance, taking into account the purposes of this Act and this subsection. Such rules shall also specify reasonably expeditious procedures by which privately placed insurance plans can qualify as meeting such minimum standards.

(C) In the event any privately placed insurance plan qualifies under subparagraph (B), any person enrolled in, and complying with the terms of, such plan shall be excluded from the provisions of paragraphs (1), (2), and (3) of this subsection and exempt from the requirements to pay any tax or fee to the Post-closure Liability Fund under title II of this Act.

(D) The President may issue such rules and take such other actions as are necessary to effectuate the purposes of this paragraph.

(5) Suspension of liability transfer. — Notwithstanding paragraphs (l), (2), (3), and (4) of this subsection and subsection (j) of section 111 of this Act, no liability shall be transferred to or assumed by the Post-Closure Liability Trust Fund established by section 232 of this Act prior to completion of the study required under paragraph (6) of this subsection, transmission of a report of such study to both Houses of Congress, and authorization of such a transfer or assumption by Act of Congress following receipt of such study and report.

[§107(k)(5) added by PL 99–499]

(6) Study of Options For Post-Closure Program.—

(A) Study. — The Comptroller General shall conduct a study of options for a program for the management of the liabilities associated with hazardous waste treatment, storage, and disposal sites after their closure which complements the policies set forth in the

Hazardous and Solid Waste Amendments of 1984 and assures the protection of human health and the environment.

(B) Program elements. — The program referred to in subparagraph (A) shall be designed to assure each of the following:

(i) Incentives are created and maintained for the safe management and disposal of hazardous wastes so as to assure protection of human health and the environment.

(ii) Members of the public will have reasonable confidence that hazardous wastes will be managed and disposed of safely and that resources will be available to address any problems that may arise and to cover costs of long-term monitoring, care, and maintenance of such sites.

(iii) Persons who are or seek to become owners and operators of hazardous waste disposal facilities will be able to manage their potential future liabilities and to attract the investment capital necessary to build, operate, and close such facilities in a manner which assures protection of human health and the environment.

(C) Assessments. — The study under this paragraph shall include assessments of treatment, storage, and disposal facilities which have been or are likely to be issued a permit under section 3005 of the Solid Waste Disposal Act and the likelihood of future insolvency on the part of owners and operators of such facilities. Separate assessments shall be made for different classes of facilities and for different classes of land disposal facilities and shall include but not be limited to—

(i) the current and future financial capabilities of facility owners and operators;

(ii) the current and future costs associated with facilities, including the costs of routine monitoring and maintenance, compliance monitoring, corrective action, natural resource damages, and liability for damages to third parties; and

(iii) the availability of mechanisms by which owners and operators of such facilities can assure that current and future costs, including post-closure costs, will be financed.

(D) Procedures. — In carrying out the responsibilities of this paragraph, the Comptroller General shall consult with the Administrator, the Secretary of Commerce, the Secretary of the Treasury, and the heads of other appropriate Federal agencies.

(E) Consideration of options. — In conducting the study under this paragraph, the Comptroller General shall consider various mechanisms and combinations of mechanisms to complement the policies set forth in the Hazardous and Solid Waste Amendments of 1984 to serve the purposes set forth in subparagraph (B) and to assure that the current and future costs associated with hazardous waste facilities, including post-closure costs, will be adequately financed and, to the greatest extent possible, borne by the owners and operators of such facilities. Mechanisms to be considered include, but are not limited to —

(i) revisions to closure, post-closure, and financial responsibility requirements under subtitles C and I of the Solid Waste Disposal Act;

(ii) voluntary risk pooling by owners and operators;

(iii) legislation to require risk pooling by owners and operators;

(iv) modification of the Post-Closure Liability Trust Fund previously established by section 232 of this Act, and the conditions for transfer of liability under this subsection, including limiting the transfer of some or all liability under this subsection only in the case of insolvency of owners and operators;

(v) private insurance;

(vi) insurance provided by the Federal Government;

(vii) coinsurance, reinsurance, or pooled-risk insurance, whether provided by the private sector or provided or assisted by the Federal Government; and

(viii) creation of a new program to be administered by a new or existing Federal agency or by a federally chartered corporation.

(F) Recommendations. — The Comptroller General shall consider options for funding any program under this section and shall, to the extent necessary, make recommendations to the appropriate committees of Congress for additional authority to implement such program.

[§107(k)(6) added by PL 99–499]

(l) Federal Lien. —

(1) In general. — All costs and damages for which a person is liable to the United States under subsection (a) of this section (other than the owner or operator of a vessel under paragraph (1) of subsection (a)) shall constitute a

lien in favor of the United States upon all real property and rights to such property which —

(A) belong to such person; and

(B) are subject to or affected by a removal or remedial action.

(2) Duration. — The lien imposed by this subsection shall arise at the later of the following:

(A) The time costs are first incurred by the United States with respect to a response action under this Act.

(B) The time that the person referred to in paragraph (1) is provided (by certified or registered mail) written notice of potential liability.

Such lien shall continue until the liability for the costs (or a judgment against the person arising out of such liability) is satisfied or becomes unenforceable through operation of the statute of limitations provided in section 113.

(3) Notice and validity. — The lien imposed by this subsection shall be subject to the rights of any purchaser, holder of a security interest, or judgment lien creditor whose interest is perfected under applicable State law before notice of the lien has been filed in the appropriate office within the State (or county or other governmental subdivision), as designated by State law, in which the real property subject to the lien is located. Any such purchaser, holder of a security interest, or judgment lien creditor shall be afforded the same protections against the lien imposed by this subsection as are afforded under State law against a judgment lien which arises out of an unsecured obligation and which arises as of the time of the filing of the notice of the lien imposed by this subsection. If the State has not by law designated one office for the receipt of such notices of liens, the notice shall be filed in the office of the clerk of the United States district court for the district in which the real property is located. For purposes of this subsection, the terms 'purchaser' and 'security interest' shall have the definitions provided under section 6323(h) of the Internal Revenue Code of 1954.

(4) Action in rem. — The costs constituting the lien may be recovered in an action in rem in the United States district court for the district in which the removal or remedial action is occurring or has occurred. Nothing in this subsection shall affect the right of the United States to bring an action against any person to recover all costs and damages for which such person is liable under subsection (a) of this section.

[§107(1) added by PL 99–499]

(m) Maritime Lien. — All costs and damages for which the owner or operator of a vessel is liable under subsection (a)(1) with respect to a release or threatened release from such vessel shall constitute a maritime lien in favor of the United States on such vessel. Such costs may be recovered in an action in rem in the district court of the United States for the district in which the vessel may be found. Nothing in this subsection shall affect the right of the United States to bring an action against the owner or operator of such vessel in any court of competent jurisdiction to recover such costs.

[§107(m) added by PL 99–499]

§9608. Financial Responsibility [Sec. 108]

(a) (1) The owner or operator of each vessel (except a non-self-propelled barge that does not carry hazardous substances as cargo) over three hundred gross tons that uses any port or place in the United States or the navigable waters or any offshore facility, shall establish and maintain, in accordance with regulations promulgated by the President, evidence of financial responsibility of $300 per gross ton (or for a vessel carrying hazardous substances as cargo, or $5,000,000, whichever is greater to cover the liability prescribed under paragraph (1) of section 107(a) of this Act. Financial responsibility may be established by any one, or any combination, of the following: insurance, guarantee, surety bond, or qualification as a self-insurer. Any bond fined shall be issued by a bonding company authorized to do business in the United States. In cases where an owner or operator owns, operates, or charters more than one vessel subject to this subsection, evidence of financial responsibility need be established only to meet the maximum liability applicable to the larger of such vessels.

(2) The Secretary of the Treasury shall withhold or revoke the clearance required by section 4197 of the Revised Statutes of the United States of any vessel subject to this subsection that does not have certification furnished by the President that the financial responsibility provisions of paragraph (1) of this subsection have been complied with.

(3) The Secretary of Transportation, in accordance with regulations issued by him, shall (A) deny entry to any port or place in the United States or navigable waters to, and (B) detain at

the port or place in the United States from which it is about to depart for any other port or place in the United States, any vessel subject to this subsection that, upon request, does not produce certification furnished by the President that the financial responsibility provisions of paragraph (1) of this subsection have been complied with.

(4) In addition to the financial responsibility provisions of paragraph (1) of this subsection, the President shall require additional evidence of financial responsibility for incineration vessels in such amounts, and to cover such liabilities recognized by law, as the President deems appropriate, taking into account the potential risks posed by incineration and transport for incineration, and any other factors deemed relevant.

[§108(a)(4) added by PL 99–499]

(b) (1) Beginning not earlier than five years after the date of enactment of this Act, the President shall promulgate requirements (for facilities in addition to those under subtitle C of the Solid Waste Disposal Act and other Federal law) that classes of facilities establish and maintain evidence of financial responsibility consistent with the degree and duration of risk associated with the production, transportation, treatment, storage, or disposal of hazardous substances. Not later than three years after the date of enactment of the Act, the President shall identify those classes for which requirements will be first developed and publish notice of such identification in the Federal Register. Priority in the development of such requirements shall be accorded to those classes of facilities, owners, and operators which the President determines present the highest level of risk of injury.

(2) The level of financial responsibility shall be initially established, and, when necessary, adjusted to protect against the level of risk which the President in his discretion believes is appropriate based on the payment experience of the Fund, commercial insurers, courts settlements and judgments, and voluntary claims satisfaction. To the maximum extent practicable, the President shall cooperate with and seek the advice of the commercial insurance industry in developing financial responsibility requirements. Financial responsibility may be established by any one, or any combination, of the following: insurance, guarantee, surety bond, letter of credit, or qualification as a self-insurer. In promulgating requirements under this section, the President is authorized to specify policy or other contractual terms, conditions, or defenses which are necessary, or which are unacceptable, in establishing such evidence of financial responsibility in order to effectuate the purposes of this Act.

[§108(b)(2) amended by PL 99–499]

(3) Regulations promulgated under this subsection shall incrementally impose financial responsibility requirements as quickly as can reasonably be achieved but in no event more than 4 years after the date of promulgation. Where possible, the level of financial responsibility which the President believes appropriate as a final requirement shall be achieved through incremental, annual increases in the requirements.

[§108(b)(3) amended by PL 99–499]

(4) Where a facility is owned or operated by more than one person, evidence of financial responsibility covering the facility may be established and maintained by one of the owners or operators, or, in consolidated form, by or on behalf of two or more owners or operators. When evidence of financial responsibility is established in a consolidated form, the proportional share of each participant shall be shown. The evidence shall be accompanied by a statement authorizing the applicant to act for and in behalf of each participant in submitting and maintaining the evidence of financial responsibility.

(5) The requirements for evidence of financial responsibility for motor carriers covered by this Act shall be determined under section 30 of the Motor Carrier Act of 1980, Public Law 96–296.

(c) Direct Action.—

(1) Releases from Vessels. — In the case of a release or threatened release from a vessel, any claim authorized by section 107 or 111 may be asserted directly against any guarantor providing evidence of financial responsibility for such vessel under subsection (a). In defending such a claim, the guarantor may invoke all rights and defenses which would be available to the owner or operator under this title. The guarantor may also invoke the defense that the incident was caused by the willful misconduct of the owner or operator, but the guarantor may not invoke any other defense that the guarantor might have been entitled to invoke in a proceeding brought by the owner or operator against him.

(2) Releases from facilities. — In the case of a release or threatened release from a facility, any claim authorized by section 107 or 111 may

be asserted directly against any guarantor providing evidence of financial responsibility for such facility under subsection (b), if the person liable under section 107 is in bankruptcy, reorganization, or arrangement pursuant to the Federal Bankruptcy Code, or if, with reasonable diligence, jurisdiction in the Federal courts cannot be obtained over a person liable under section 107 who is likely to be solvent at the time of judgment. In the case of any action pursuant to this paragraph, the guarantor shall be entitled to invoke all rights and defenses which would have been available to the person liable under section 107 if any action had been brought against such person by the claimant and all rights and defenses which would have been available to the guarantor if an action had been brought against the guarantor by such person.

[§108(c) revised by PL 99–499]

(d) Limitations of Guarantor Liability. —

(1) Total liability. — The total liability of any guarantor in a direct action suit brought under this section shall be limited to the aggregate amount of the monetary limits of the policy of insurance, guarantee, surety bond, letter of credit, or similar instrument obtained from the guarantor by the person subject to liability under section 107 for the purpose of satisfying the requirement for evidence of financial responsibility.

(2) Other liability. — Nothing in this subsection shall be construed to limit any other State or Federal statutory, contractual, or common law liability of a guarantor, including, but not limited to, the liability of such guarantor for bad faith either in negotiating or in failing to negotiate the settlement of any claim. Nothing in this subsection shall be construed, interpreted, or applied to diminish the liability of any person under section 107 of this Act or other applicable law.

[§108(d) revised by PL 99–499]

§9609. Civil Penalties and Awards. [Sec. 109]

[§109 revised by PL 99–499]

(a) Class I Administrative Penalty. —

(1) Violations. — A civil penalty of not more than $25,000 per violation may be assessed by the President in the case of any of the following —

(A) A violation of the requirements of section 103(a) or (b) (relating to notice).

(B) A violation of the requirements of section 103(d)(2) (relating to destruction of records, etc.).

(C) A violation of the requirements of section 108 (relating to financial responsibility, etc.), the regulations issued under section 108 , or with any denial or detention order under section 108 .

(D) A violation of an order under section 122(d)(3) (relating to settlement agreements for action under section 104(b)).

(E) Any failure or refusal referred to in section 122(1) (relating to violations of administrative orders, consent decrees, or agreements under section 120).

(2) Notice and hearings. — No civil penalty may be assessed under this subsection unless the person accused of the violation is given notice and opportunity for a hearing with respect to the violation.

(3) Determining Amount. — In determining the amount of any penalty assessed pursuant to this subsection, the President shall take into account the nature, circumstances, extent and gravity of the violation or violations and, with respect to the violator, ability to pay, any prior history of such violations, the degree of culpability, economic benefit or savings (if any) resulting from the violation, and such other matters as justice may require.

(4) Review. — Any person against whom a civil penalty is assessed under this subsection may obtain review thereof in the appropriate district court of the United States by filing a notice of appeal in such court within 30 days from the date of such order and by simultaneously sending a copy of such notice by certified mail to the President. The President shall promptly file in such court a certified copy of the record upon which such violation was found or such penalty imposed. If any person fails to pay an assessment of a civil penalty after it has become a final and unappealable order or after the appropriate court has entered final judgment in favor of the United States, the President may request the Attorney General of the United States to institute a civil action in an appropriate district court of the United States to collect the penalty, and such court shall have jurisdiction to hear and decide any such action. In hearing such action, the court shall have authority to review the violation and the assessment of the civil penalty on the record.

(5) Subpoenas. — The President may issue subpoenas for the attendance and testimony of witnesses and the production of relevant papers, books, or documents in connection with hearings under this subsection. In case of contumacy or refusal to obey a subpoena issued pursuant to this paragraph and served upon any person, the district court of the United States for any district in which such person is found, resides, or transacts business, upon application by the United States and after notice to such person, shall have jurisdiction to issue an order requiring such person to appear and give testimony before the administrative law judge or to appear and produce documents before the administrative law judge, or both, and any failure to obey such order of the court may be punished by such court as a contempt thereof.

(b) Class II Administrative Penalty. — A civil penalty of not more than $25,000 per day for each day during which the violation continues may be assessed by the President in the case of any of the following—

(1) A violation of the notice requirements of section 103(a) or (b).

(2) A violation of section 103(d)(2) (relating to destruction of records, etc.).

(3) A violation of the requirements of section 108 (relating to financial responsibility, etc.), the regulations issued under section 108, or with any denial or detention order under section 108.

(4) A violation of an order under section 122(d)(3) (relating to settlement agreements for action under section 104(b)).

(5) Any failure or refusal referred to in section 122(1) (relating to violations of administrative orders, consent decrees, or agreements under section 120).

In the case of a second or subsequent violation the amount of such penalty may be not more than $75,000 for each day during which the violation continues. Any civil penalty under this subsection shall be assessed and collected in the same manner, and subject to the same provisions, as in the case of civil penalties assessed and collected after notice and opportunity for hearing on the record in accordance with section 554 of title 5 of the United States Code. In any proceeding for the assessment of a civil penalty under this subsection the President may issue subpoenas for the attendance and testimony of witnesses and the production of relevant papers, books, and documents and may promulgate rules for discovery procedures. Any person who requested a hearing with respect to a civil penalty under this subsection and who is aggrieved by an order assessing the civil penalty may file a petition for judicial review of such order with the United States Court of Appeals for the District of Columbia Circuit or for any other circuit in which such person resides or transacts business. Such a petition may only be filed within the 30–day period beginning on the date the order making such assessment was issued.

(c) Judicial Assessment. — The President may bring an action in the United States district court for the appropriate district to assess and collect a penalty of not more than $25,000 per day for each day during which the violation (or failure or refusal) continues in the case of any of the following—

(1) A violation of the notice requirements of section 103(a) or (b).

(2) A violation of section 103(d)(2) (relating to destruction of records, etc.).

(3) A violation of the requirements of section 108 (relating to financial responsibility, etc.), the regulations issued under section 108, or with any denial or detention order under section 108.

(4) A violation of an order under section 122(d)(3) (relating to settlement agreements for action under section 104(b)).

(5) Any failure or refusal referred to in section 122(1) (relating to violations of administrative orders, consent decrees, or agreements under section 120).

In the case of a second or subsequent violation (or failure or refusal), the amount of such penalty may be not more than $75,000 for each day during which the violation (or failure or refusal) continues. For additional provisions providing for judicial assessment of civil penalties for failure to comply with a request or order under section 104(e) (relating to information gathering and access authorities), see section 104(e).

(d) Awards. — The President may pay award of up to $10,000 to any individual who provides information leading to the arrest and conviction of any person for a violation subject to a criminal penalty under this Act, including any violation of section 103 and any other violation referred to in this section. The President shall, by regulation, prescribe criteria for such an award and may pay any award under this subsection from the Fund, as provided in section 111.

(e) Procurement Procedures. — Notwithstanding any other provision of law, any executive agency may use competitive procedures or procedures other than competitive procedures to procure the services of experts for use in preparing or prosecuting a civil or criminal action under this Act, whether or not the expert is expected to testify at trial. The executive agency need not provide any written justification for the use of procedures other than competitive procedures when procuring such expert services under this Act and need not furnish for publication in the Commerce Business Daily or otherwise any notice of solicitation or synopsis with respect to such procurement.

(f) Savings Clause. — Action taken by the President pursuant to this section shall not affect or limit the President's authority to enforce any provisions of this Act.

§9610. Employee Protection [Sec. 110]

(a) No person shall fire or in any other way discriminate against, or cause to be fired or discriminated against, any employee or any authorized representative of employees by reason of the fact that such employee or representative has provided information to a State or to the Federal Government, filed, instituted, or caused to be filed or instituted any proceeding under this Act, or has testified or is about to testify in any proceeding resulting from the administration or enforcement of the provisions of this Act.

(b) Any employee or a representative of employees who believes that he has been fired or otherwise discriminated against by any person in violation of subsection (a) of this section may, within thirty days after such alleged violation occurs, apply to the Secretary of Labor for a review of such firing or alleged discrimination. A copy of the application shall be sent to such person, who shall be the respondent. Upon receipt of such application, the Secretary of Labor shall cause such investigation to be made as he deems appropriate. Such investigation shall provide an opportunity for a public hearing at the request of any party to such review to enable the parties to present information relating to such alleged violation. The parties shall be given written notice of the time and place of the hearing at least five days prior to the hearing. Any such hearing shall be of record and shall be subject to section 554 of title 5, United States Code. Upon receiving the report of such investigation, the Secretary of Labor shall make findings of fact. If he finds that such violation did occur, he shall issue a decision, incorporating an order therein and his findings, requiring the party committing such violation to take such affirmative action to abate the violation as the Secretary of Labor deems appropriate, including, but not limited to, the rehiring or reinstatement of the employee or representative of employees to his former position with compensation. If he finds that there was no such violation, he shall issue an order denying the application. Such order issued by the Secretary of Labor under this subparagraph shall be subject to judicial review in the same manner as orders and decisions are subject to judicial review under this Act.

(c) Whenever an order is issued under this section to abate such violation, at the request of the applicant a sum equal to the aggregate amount of all costs and expenses (including the attorney's fees) determined by the Secretary of Labor to have been reasonably incurred by the applicant for, or in connection with, the institution and prosecution of such proceedings, shall be assessed against the person committing such violation.

(d) This section shall have no application to any employee who acting without discretion from his employer (or his agent) deliberately violates any requirement of this Act.

(e) The President shall conduct continuing evaluations of potential loss of shifts of employment which may result from the administration or enforcement of the provisions of this Act, including, where appropriate, investigating threatened plant closures or reductions in employment allegedly resulting from such administration or enforcement. Any employee who is discharged, or laid off, threatened with discharge or layoff, or otherwise discriminated against by any person because of the alleged results of such administration or enforcement, or any representative of such employee, may request the President to conduct a full investigation of the matter and, at the request of any party, shall hold public hearings, require the parties, including the employer involved, to present information relating to the actual or potential effect of such administration or enforcement on employment and any alleged discharge, layoff, or other discrimination, and the detailed reasons or justification therefore. Any such hearing shall be of record and shall be subject to section 554 of title 5, United States Code. Upon receiving the report of such investigation, the President shall make findings of fact as to the effect of such administration or enforcement on employment and on the alleged discharge, layoff, or discrimination and shall make such recommendations as he deems appropriate. Such report, findings, and recommendations shall be available to the public. Nothing in this subsection shall be construed to require or authorize the President or any State to modify or withdraw any action, standard, limitation, or any other requirement of this Act.

§9611. Uses of Fund [Sec. 111]

(a) In General. — For the purposes specified in this section there is authorized to be appropriated from the Hazardous Substance Superfund established under subchapter A of chapter 98 of the Internal Revenue Code of 1986 not more than $8,500,000,000 for the 5-year period beginning on the date of enactment of the Superfund Amendments and Reauthorization Act of 1986, and not more than $5,100,000,000 for the period commencing October 1, 1991, and ending September 30, 1994, and such sums shall remain available until expended. The preceding sentence constitutes a specific authorization for the funds appropriated under title II of Public Law 99–160 (relating to payment to the Hazardous Substances Trust Fund). The President shall use the money in the Fund for the following purposes:

[§111(a) revised by PL 99–499; amended by PL 101–508]

(1) Payment of governmental response costs incurred pursuant to section 104 of this title, including costs incurred pursuant to the Intervention on the High Seas Act.

(2) Payment of any claim for necessary response costs incurred by any other person as a result of carrying out the national contingency plan established under section 311(c) of the Clean Water Act and amended by section 105 of this title:*Provided, however,* That such costs must be approved under said plan and certified by the responsible Federal official.

(3) Payment of any claim authorized by subsection (b) of this section and finally decided pursuant to section 112 of this title, including those costs set out in subsection 112(c)(3) of this title.

(4) Payment of costs specified under subsection (c) of this section.

(5) Grants for technical assistance. — The cost of grants under section 117(e) (relating to public participation grants for technical assistance).

[§111(a)(5) added by PL 99–499]

(6) Lead contaminated soil. — Payment of not to exceed $15,000,000 for the costs of a pilot program for removal, decontamination, or other action with respect to lead-contaminated soil in one to three different metropolitan areas.

The President shall not pay for any administrative costs or expenses out of the Fund unless such costs and expenses are reasonably necessary for and incidental to the implementation of this title.

[§111(a)(6) added by PL 99–499]

(b) (1) In General. — Claims asserted and compensable but unsatisfied under provisions of section 311 of the Clean Water Act, which are modified by section 304 of this Act may be asserted against the Fund under this title; and other claims resulting from a release or threat of release of a hazardous substance from a vessel or a facility may be asserted against the Fund under this title for injury to, or destruction or loss of, natural resources, including cost for damage assessment: *Provided, however,* That any such claim may be asserted only by the President, as trustee, for natural resources over which the United States has sovereign rights, or natural resources within the territory or the fishery conservation zone of the United States to the extent they are managed or protected by the United States, or by any State for natural resources within the boundary of that State belonging to, managed by, controlled by, or appertaining to the State, or by any Indian tribe or by the United States acting on behalf of any Indian tribe for natural resources belonging to, managed by, controlled by, or appertaining to such tribe, or held in trust for the benefit of such tribe, or belonging to a member of such tribe if such resources are subject to a trust restriction on alienation.

[§111(b)(1) amended by PL 99–499]

(2) Limitation on payment of natural resource claims.—

(A) General Requirements. — No natural resource claim may be paid from the Fund unless the President determines that the claimant has exhausted all administrative and judicial remedies to recover the amount of such claim from persons who may be liable under section 107 .

(B) Definition. — As used in this paragraph, the term 'natural resource claim' means any claim for injury to, or destruction or loss of, natural resources. The term does not include any claim for the costs of natural resource damage assessment.

[§111(b)(2) added by PL 99–499]

(c) Uses of the Fund under subsection (a) of this section include—

(1) The costs of assessing both short- term and long-term injury to, destruction of, or loss of any natural resources resulting from a release of a hazardous substance.

[§111(c)(1) amended by PL 99–499]

(2) The costs of Federal or State or Indian tribe efforts in the restoration, rehabilitation, or replacement or acquiring the equivalent of any natural resources injured, destroyed, or lost as a result of a release of a hazardous substance.

[§111(c)(2) amended by PL 99–499]

(3) Subject to such amounts as are provided in appropriation Acts, the costs of a program to identify, investigate, and take enforcement and abatement action against releases of hazardous substances.

[§111(c)(3) amended by PL 99–499]

(4) Any costs incurred in accordance with subsection (m) of this section (relating to ATSDR) and section 104(i) , including the costs of epidemiologic and laboratory studies, health assessments, preparation of toxicologic profiles, development and maintenance of a registry of persons exposed to hazardous substances to allow long-term health effect studies, and diagnostic services not otherwise available to determine whether persons in populations exposed to hazardous substances in connection with a release or a suspected release are suffering from long- latency diseases.

[§111(c)(4) amended by PL 99–499]

(5) Subject to such amounts as are provided in appropriation Acts, the costs of providing equipment and similar overhead related to the purposes of this Act and section 311 of the Clean Water Act, and needed to supplement equipment and services available through contractors or other non-Federal entities, and of establishing and maintaining damage assessment capability, for any Federal agency involved in strike forces, emergency task forces, or other response teams under the national contingency plan.

[§111(c)(5) amended by PL 99–499]

(6) Subject to such amounts as are provided in appropriation Acts, the costs of a program to protect the health and safety of employees involved in response to hazardous substance releases. Such program shall be developed jointly by the Environmental Protection Agency, the Occupational Safety and Health Administration, and the National Institute for Occupational Safety and Health and shall include, but not be limited to, measures for identifying and assessing hazards to which persons engaged in removal, remedy, or other response to hazardous substances may be exposed, methods to protect workers from such hazards, and necessary regulatory and enforcement measures to assure adequate protection of such employees.

[§111(c)(6) amended by PL 99–499]

(7) Evaluation costs under petition provisions of section 105(d) . — Costs incurred by the President in evaluating facilities pursuant to petitions under section 105(d) (relating to petitions for assessment of release).

[§111(c)(7) added by PL 99–499]

(8) Contract costs under section 104(a)(1) . — The costs of contracts or arrangements entered into under section 104(a)(1) to oversee and review the conduct of remedial investigations and feasibility studies undertaken by persons other than the President and the costs of appropriate Federal and State oversight of remedial activities at National Priorities List sites resulting from consent orders or settlement agreements.

[§111(c)(8) added by PL 99–499]

(9) Acquisition costs under section 104(j) . — The costs incurred by the President in acquiring real estate or interests in real estate under section 104(j) (relating to acquisition of property).

[§111(c)(9) added by PL 99–499]

(10) Research, development, and demonstration costs under section 311. — The cost of carrying out section 311 (relating to research, development, and demonstration), except that the amounts available for such purposes shall not exceed the amounts specified in subsection (n) of this section.

[§111(c)(10) added by PL 99–499]

(11) Local government reimbursement. — Reimbursements to local governments under section 123 , except that during the 8–fiscal year period beginning October 1, 1986, not more than 0.1 percent of the total amount appropriated from the Fund may be used for such reimbursements.

[§111(c)(11) added by PL 99–499; amended by PL 101–508]

(12) Worker training and education grants. — The costs of grants under section 126(g) of the Superfund Amendments and Reauthorization Act of 1986 for training and education of workers to the extent that such costs do not exceed

$20,000,000 for each of the fiscal years 1987, 1988, 1989, 1990, 1991, 1992, 1993, and 1994.

[§111(c)(12) added by PL 99–499; amended by PL 101–144; PL 101–508]

(13) Awards under section 109 . — The costs of any awards granted under section 109(d)

(14) Lead poisoning study. — The cost of carrying out the study under subsection (f) of section 118 of the Superfund Amendments and Reauthorization Act of 1986 (relating to lead poisoning in children).

(d) (1) No money in the Fund may be used under subsection (c)(1) and (2) of this section, nor for the payment of any claim under subsection (b) of this section, where the injury, destruction, or loss of naturalresources and the release of a hazardous substance from which such damages resulted have occurred wholly before the enactment of this Act.

(2) No money in the Fund may be used for the payment of any claim under subsection (b) of this section where such expenses are associated with injury or loss resulting from long-term exposure to ambient concentrations of air pollutants from multiple or diffuse sources.

(e) (1) Claims against or presented to the Fund shall not be valid or paid in excess of the total money in the Fund at any one time. Such claims become valid only when additional money is collected, appropriated, or otherwise added to the Fund. Should the total claims outstanding at any time exceed the current balance of the Fund, the President shall pay such claims, to the extent authorized under this section, in full in the order in which they were finally determined.

(2) In any fiscal year, 85 percent of the money credited to the Fund under title II of this Act shall be available only for the purposes specified in paragraphs (1), (2), and (4) of subsection (a) of this section. No money in the Fund may be used for the payment of any claim under subsection (a)(3) or subsection (b) of this section in any fiscal year for which the President determines that all of the Fund is needed for response to threats to public health from releases or threatened releases of hazardous substances.

[§111(e)(2) amended by PL 99–499]

(3) No money in the Fund shall be available for remedial action, other than actions specified in subsection (c) of this section, with respect to federally owned facilities; except that money in the Fund shall be available for the provision of alternative water supplies (including the reimbursement of costs incurred by a municipality) in any case involving groundwater contamination outside the boundaries of a federally owned facility in which the federally owned facility is not the only potentially responsible party.

[§111(e)(3) amended by PL 99–499]

(4) Paragraphs (1) and (4) of subsection (a) of this section shall in the aggregate be subject to such amounts as are provided in appropriation Acts.

(f) The President is authorized to promulgate regulations designating one or more Federal officials who may obligate money in the Fund in accordance with this section or portions thereof. The President is also authorized to delegate authority to obligate money in the Fund or to settle claims to officials of a State or Indian tribe operating under a contract or cooperative agreement with the Federal Government pursuant to section 104(d) of this title.

[§111(f) amended by PL 99–499]

(g) The President shall provide for the promulgation of rules and regulations with respect to the notice to be provided to potential injured parties by an owner and operator of any vessel, or facility from which a hazardous substance has been released. Such rules and regulations shall consider the scope and form of the notice which would be appropriate to carry out the purposes of this title. Upon promulgation of such rules and regulations, the owner and operator of any vessel or facility from which a hazardous substance has been released shall provide notice in accordance with such rules and regulations. With respect to releases from public vessels, the President shall provide such notification as is appropriate to potential injured parties. Until the promulgation of such rules and regulations, the owner and operator of any vessel or facility from which a hazardous substance has been released shall provide reasonable notice to potential injured parties by publication in local newspapers serving the affected area.

(h) [Repealed]

[§111(h) repealed by PL 99–499]

(i) Except in a situation requiring action to avoid an irreversible loss of natural resources or to prevent or reduce any continuing danger to natural resources or similar need for emergency action, funds may not be used under this Act for the restoration, rehabilitation, or replacement or acquisition of the equivalent of any natural resources until a plan for the use of such funds for such purposes has been developed and adopted by affected Federal agencies and the Governor or Governors of any State and by the governing body of any Indian tribe having sustained damage to natural resources belonging to, managed by, controlled by, or appertaining to such tribe, or held in trust for the benefit of such tribe, or belonging to a member of such tribe if such resources are subject to a trust restriction on alienation, having sustained damage to natural resources within its borders, belonging to, managed by or appertaining to such State and by the governing body of any Indian tribe having sustained damage to natural resources belonging to, managed by, controlled by, or appertaining to such tribe, or held in trust for the benefit of such tribe, or belonging to a member of such tribe if such resources are subject to a trust restriction on alienation, after adequate public notice and opportunity for hearing and consideration of all public comment.

[§111(i) amended by PL 99–499]

(j) The President shall use the money in the Post-closure Liability Fund for any of the purposes specified in subsection (a) of this section with respect to a hazardous waste disposal facility for which liability has transferred to such fund under section 107(k) of this Act, and, in addition, for payment of any claim or appropriate request for costs of response, damages, or other compensation for injury or loss under section 107 of this Act or any other State or Federal law, resulting from a release of a hazardous substance from such a facility.

(k) Inspector General. — In each fiscal year, the Inspector General of each department, agency, or instrumentality of the United States which is carrying out any authority of this Act shall conduct an annual audit of all payments, obligations, reimbursements, or other uses of the Fund in the prior fiscal year, to assure that the Fund is being properly administered and that claims are being appropriately and expeditiously considered. The audit shall include an examination of a sample of agreements with States (in accordance with the provisions of the Single Audit Act) carrying out response actions under this title and an examination of remedial investigations and feasibility studies prepared for remedial actions. The Inspector General shall submit to the Congress an annual report regarding the audit report required under this subsection. The report shall contain such recommendations as the Inspector General deems appropriate. Each department, agency, or instrumentality of the United States shall cooperate with its inspector general in carrying out this subsection.

[§111(k) revised by PL 99–499]

(l) To the extent that the provisions of this Act permit, a foreign claimant may assert a claim to the same extent that a United States claimant may assert a claim if —

(1) the release of a hazardous substance occurred (A) in the navigable waters or (B) in or on the territorial sea or adjacent shoreline of a foreign country of which the claimant is a resident;

(2) the claimant is not otherwise compensated for his loss;

(3) the hazardous substance was released from a facility or from a vessel located adjacent to or within the navigable waters or was discharged in connection with activities conducted under the Outer Continental Shelf Lands Act, as amended (43 U.S.C. 1331 et seq.) or the Deepwater Port Act of 1974, as amended (33 U.S.C. 1501 et seq.); and

(4) recovery is authorized by a treaty or an executive agreement between the United States and foreign country involved, or if the Secretary of State, in consultation with the Attorney General and other appropriate officials, certifies that such country provides a comparable remedy for United States claimants.

(m) Agency for Toxic Substances and Disease Registry. — There shall be directly available to the Agency for Toxic Substances and Disease Registry to be used for the purpose of carrying out activities described in subsection (c)(4) and section 104(i) not less than $50,000,000 per fiscal year for each of fiscal years 1987 and 1988, not less than $55,000,000 for fiscal year 1989, and not less than $60,000,000 per fiscal year for each of fiscal years 1990, 1991, 1992, 1993, and 1994. Any funds so made available which are not obligated by the end of the fiscal year in which made available shall be returned to the Fund.

[§111(m) added by PL 99–499; amended by PL 101–508]

(n) Limitations on Research, Development, and Demonstration Program.—

(1) Section 311(b). — For each of the fiscal years 1987, 1988, 1989, 1990, 1991, 1992, 1993, and 1994, not more than $20,000,000 of the amounts available in the Fund may be used for the purposes of carrying out the applied research, development, and demonstration program for alternative or innovative technologies and

training program authorized under section 311(b) (relating to research, development, and demonstration) other than basic research. Such amounts shall remain available until expended.

(2) Section 311(a). — From the amounts available in the Fund, not more than the following amounts may be used for the purposes of section 311(a) (relating to hazardous substance research, demonstration, and training activities):

(A) For the fiscal year 1987, $3,000,000.

(B) For the fiscal year 1988, $10,000,000.

(C) For the fiscal year 1989, $20,000,000.

(D) For the fiscal year 1990, $30,000,000.

(E) For each of the fiscal years 1991, 1992, 1993, and 1994, $35,000,000.

No more than 10 percent of such (amounts) shall be used for training under section 311(a) in any fiscal year.

(3) Section 311(d). — For each of the fiscal years 1987, 1988, 1989, 1990, 1991, 1992, 1993, and 1994, not more than $5,000,000 of the amounts available in the Fund may be used for the purposes of section 311(d) (relating to university hazardous substance research centers).

[§111(n) added by PL 99–499; amended by PL 101–508]

(o) Notification Procedures for Limitations on Certain Payments. — Not later than 90 days after the enactment of this subsection, the President shall develop and implement procedures to adequately notify, as soon as practicable after a site is included on the National Priorities List, concerned local and State officials and other concerned persons of the limitations, set forth in subsection (a)(2) of this section, on the payment of claims for necessary response costs incurred with respect to such site.

[§111(o) added by PL 99–499]

(p) General Revenue Share of Superfund.—

(1) In general. — The following sums are authorized to be appropriated, out of any money in the Treasury not otherwise appropriated, to the Hazardous Substance Superfund:

(A) For fiscal year 1987, $212,500,000.

(B) For fiscal year 1988, $212,500,000.

(C) For fiscal year 1989, $212,500,000.

(D) For fiscal year 1990, $212,500,000.

(E) For fiscal year 1991, $212,500,000.

(F) For fiscal year 1992, $212,500,000.

(G) For fiscal year 1983, $212,500,000.

(H) For fiscal year 1994, $212,500,000.

In addition there is authorized to be appropriated to the Hazardous Substance Superfund for each fiscal year an amount equal to so much of the aggregate amount authorized to be appropriated under this subsection (and paragraph (2) of section 221(b) of the Hazardous Substance Response Revenue Act of 1980) as has not been appropriated before the beginning of the fiscal year involved.

(2) Computation. — The amounts authorized to be appropriated under paragraph (1) of this subsection in a given fiscal year shall be available only to the extent that such amount exceeds the amount determined by the Secretary under section 9507(b)(2) of the Internal Revenue Code of 1986 for the prior fiscal year.

[§111(p) added by PL 99–499; amended by PL 101–508]

§9612. Claims Procedure [Sec. 112]

(a) Claims Against the Fund for Response Costs. — No claim may be asserted against the Fund pursuant to section 111(a) unless such claim is presented in the first instance to the owner, operator, or guarantor of the vessel or facility from which a hazardous substance has been released, if known to the claimant, and to any other person known to the claimant who may be liable under section 107 . In any case where the claim has not been satisfied within 60 days of presentation in accordance with this subsection, the claimant may present the claim to the Fund for payment. No claim against the Fund may be approved or certified during the pendency of an action by the claimant in court to recover costs which are the subject of the claim.

[§112(a) revised by PL 99–499]

(b) (1) Prescribing Forms and Procedures. — The President shall prescribe appropriate forms and procedures for claims filed hereunder, which shall include a provision requiring the claimant to make a sworn verification of the claim to the best of his knowledge. Any person who knowingly gives or causes to be given any false information as a part of any such claim shall, upon conviction, be fined in accordance with the applicable provisions of title 18 of the United States Code or imprisoned for not more than 3 years (or not more than 5 years in the case of a second or subsequent conviction), or both.

[§112(b)(1) amended by PL 99–499]

(2) Payment or Request for Hearing. —The President may, if satisfied that the information

developed during the processing of the claim warrants it, make and pay an award of the claim, except that no claim may be awarded to the extent that a judicial judgment has been made on the costs that are the subject of the claim. If the President declines to pay all or part of the claim, the claimant may, within 30 days after receiving notice of the President's decision, request an administrative hearing.

[§112(b)(2) revised by PL 99–499]

(3) Burden of Proof. — In any proceeding under this subsection, the claimant shall bear the burden of proving his claim.

[§112(b)(3) revised by PL 99–499]

(4) Decisions. — All administrative decisions made hereunder shall be in writing, with notification to all appropriate parties, and shall be rendered within 90 days of submission of a claim to an administrative law judge, unless all the parties to the claim agree in writing to an extension or unless the President, in his discretion, extends the time limit for a period not to exceed sixty days.

[§112(b)(4) revised by PL 99–499]

(5) Finality and Appeal. — All administrative decisions hereunder shall be final, and any party to the proceeding may appeal a decision within 30 days of notification of the award or decision. Any such appeal shall be made to the Federal district court for the district where the release or threat of release took place. In any such appeal, the decision shall be considered binding and conclusive, and shall not be overturned except for arbitrary or capricious abuse of discretion.

[§112(b)(5) added by PL 99–499]

(6) Payment. — Within 20 days after the expiration of the appeal period for any administrative decision concerning an award, or within 20 days after the final judicial determination of any appeal taken pursuant to this subsection, the President shall pay any such award from the Fund. The President shall determine the method, terms, and time of payment.

[§112(b)(6) added by PL 99–499]

(c) (1) Payment of any claim by the Fund under this section shall be subject to the United States Government acquiring by subrogation the rights of the claimant to recover those costs of removal or damages for which it has compensated the claimant from the person responsible or liable for such release.

(2) Any person, including the Fund, who pays compensation pursuant to this Act to any claimant for damages or costs resulting from a release of a hazardous substance shall be subrogated to all rights, claims, and causes of action for such damages and costs of removal that the claimant has under this Act or any other law.

(3) Upon request of the President, the Attorney General shall commence an action on behalf of the Fund to recover any compensation paid by the Fund to any claimant pursuant to this title, and, without regard to any limitation of liability, all interest, administrative and adjudicative costs, and attorney's fees incurred by the Fund by reason of the claim. Such an action may be commenced against any owner, operator, or guarantor, or against any other person who is liable, pursuant to any law, to the compensated claimant or to the Fund, for the damages or costs for which compensation was paid.

(d) Statute of limitations. —

(1) Claims for recovery of costs. — No claim may be presented under this section for recovery of the costs referred to in section 107(A) after the date 6 years after the date of completion of all response action.

(2) Claims for recovery of damages. — No claim may be presented under this section for recovery of the damages referred to in section 107(a) unless the claim is presented within 3 years after the later of the following:

(A) The date of the discovery of the loss and its connection with the release in question.

(B) The date on which final regulations are promulgated under section 301(c) .

(3) Minors and incompetents. — The time limitations contained herein shall not begin to run —

(A) against a minor until the earlier of the date when such minor reaches 18 years of age or the date on which a legal representative is duly appointed for the minor, or

(B) against an incompetent person until the earlier of the date on which such person's incompetency ends or the date on which a legal representative is duly appointed for such incompetent person.

[§112(d) revised by PL 99–499]

(e) Regardless of any State statutory or common law to the contrary, no person who asserts a claim against the Fund pursuant to this title shall be deemed or held to have waived any other claim not covered or assertable against the Fund under this title arising from the same incident, transaction, or set of circumstances, nor to have split a cause of action. Further, no person asserting a claim against the Fund pursuant to this title shall as a result of any determination of a question of fact or law made in connection with that claim be deemed or held to be collaterally estopped from raising such question in connection with any other claim not covered or assertable against the Fund under this title arising from the same incident, transaction, or set of circumstances.

(f) Double recovery prohibited. — Where the President has paid out of the Fund for any response costs or any costs specified under section 111(c)(1) or (2) , no other claim may be paid out of the Fund for the same costs.

[§112(f) added by PL 99–499]

§9613. Litigation, Jurisdiction and Venue
[Sec. 113]

(a) Review of any regulation promulgated under this Act may be had upon application by any interested person only in the Circuit Court of Appeals of the United States for the District of Columbia. Any such application shall be made within ninety days from the date of promulgation of such regulations. Any matter with respect to which review could have been obtained under this subsection shall not be subject to judicial review in any civil or criminal proceeding for enforcement or to obtain damages or recovery of response costs.

(b) Except as provided in subsections (a) and (h) of this section, the United States district courts shall have exclusive original jurisdiction over all controversies arising under this Act, without regard to the citizenship of the parties or the amount in controversy. Venue shall lie in any district in which the release or damages occurred, or in which the defendant resides, may be found, or has his principal office. For the purposes of this section, the Fund shall reside in the District of Columbia.

[§113(b) amended by PL 99–499]

(c) The provisions of subsections (a) and (b) of this section shall not apply to any controversy or other matter resulting from the assessment of collection of any tax, as provided by title II of this Act, or to the review of any regulation promulgated under the Internal Revenue Code of 1954.

(d) No provision of this Act shall be deemed or held to moot any litigation concerning any release of any hazardous substance, or any damages associated therewith, commenced prior to enactment of this Act.

(e) Nationwide service of process. — In any action by the United States under this Act, process may be served in any district where the defendant is found, resides, transacts business, or has appointed an agent for the service of process.

[§113(e) added by PL 99–499]

(f) Contribution. —

[§113(f) added by PL 99–499]

(1) Contribution. — Any person may seek contribution from any other person who is liable or potentially liable under section 107(a) , during or following any civil action under section 106 or under section 107(a) . Such claims shall be brought in accordance with this section and the Federal Rules of Civil Procedure, and shall be governed by Federal law. In resolving contribution claims, the court may allocate response costs among liable parties using such equitable factors as the court determines are appropriate. Nothing in this subsection shall diminish the right of any person to bring an action for contribution in the absence of a civil action under section 106 or section 107 .

[§113(f)(1) added by PL 99–499]

(2) Settlement. — A person who has resolved its liability to the United States or a State in an administrative or judicially approved settlement shall not be liable for claims for contribution regarding matters addressed in the settlement. Such settlement does not discharge any of the other potentially liable persons unless its terms so provide, but it reduces the potential liability of the others by the amount of the settlement.

(3) Persons not part to settlement. —

(A) If the United States or a State has obtained less than complete relief from a person who has resolved its liability to the United States or the State in an administrative or judicially approved settlement, the United States or the State may bring an action against any person who has not so resolved its liability.

(B) A person who has resolved its liability to the United States or a State for some or all of a response action or for some or all of the costs of such action in an administrative or judicially approved settlement may seek contribution from any person who is not party to a settlement referred to in paragraph (2).

(C) In any action under this paragraph, the rights of any person who has resolved its liability to the United States or a State shall be subordinate to the rights of the United States or the State. Any contribution action brought under this paragraph shall be governed by Federal law.

(g) Period in Which Action May Be Brought. —

(1) Actions for natural resource damages. — Except as provided in paragraphs (3) and (4), no action may be commenced for damages (as defined in section 101(6)) under this Act, unless that action is commenced within 3 years after the later of the following:

(A) The date of the discovery of the loss and its connection with the release in question.

(B) The date on which regulations are promulgated under section 301(c).

With respect to any facility listed on the National Priorities List (NPL), any Federal facility identified under section 120 (relating to Federal facilities), or any vessel or facility at which a remedial action under this Act is otherwise scheduled, an action for damages under this Act must be commenced within 3 years after the completion of the remedial action (excluding operation and maintenance activities) in lieu of the dates referred to in subparagraph (A) or (B). In no event may an action for damages under this Act with respect to such a vessel or facility be commenced (i) prior to 60 days after the Federal or State natural resource trustee provides to the President and the potentially responsible party a notice of intent to file suit, or (ii) before selection of the remedial action if the President is diligently proceeding with a remedial investigation and feasibility study under section 104(b) or section 120 (relating to Federal facilities). The limitation in the preceding sentence on commencing an action before giving notice or before selection of the remedial action does not apply to actions filed on or before the enactment of the Superfund Amendments and Reauthorization Act of 1986.

(2) Actions for recovery of costs. — An initial action for recovery of the costs referred to in section 107 must be commenced —

(A) for removal action, within 3 years after completion of the removal action, except that such cost recovery action must be brought within 6 years after a determination to grant a waiver under section 104(c)(1)(C) for continued response action; and

(B) for a remedial action, within 6 years after initiation of physical on-site construction of the remedial action, except that, if the remedial action is initiated within 3 years after the completion of the removal action, costs incurred in the removal action may be recovered in the cost recovery action brought under this subparagraph.

In any such action described in this subsection, the court shall enter a declaratory judgment on liability for response costs or damages that will be binding on any subsequent action or actions to recover further response costs or damages. A subsequent action or actions under section 107 for further response costs at the vessel or facility may be maintained at any time during the response action, but must be commenced no later than 3 years after the date of completion of all response action. Except as otherwise provided in this paragraph, an action may be commenced under section 107 for recovery of costs at any time after such costs have been incurred.

(3) Contribution. — No action for contribution for any response costs or damages may be commenced more than 3 years after—

(A) the date of judgment in any action under this Act for recovery of such costs or damages, or

(B) the date of an administrative order under section 122(g) (relating to de minimis settlements) or 122(h) (relating to cost recovery settlements) or entry of a judicially approved settlement with respect to such costs or damages.

(4) Subrogation. — No action based on rights subrogated pursuant to this section by reason of payment of a claim may be commenced under this title more than 3 years after the date of payment of such claim.

(5) Actions to recover indemnification payments. — Notwithstanding any other provision of this subsection, where a payment pursuant to an indemnification agreement with a response action contractor is made under section 119 , an action under section 107 for recovery of such indemnification payment from a potentially responsible party may be brought at any time before the expiration of 3 years from the date on which such payment is made.

(6) Minors and incompetents. — The time limitations contained herein shall not begin to run—

(A) against a minor until the earlier of the date when such minor reaches 18 years of age or the date on which a legal representative is duly appointed for such minor, or

(B) against an incompetent person until the earlier of the date on which such incompetent's incompetency ends or the date on which a legal representative is duly appointed for such incompetent.

(h) Timing of Review. — No Federal court shall have jurisdiction under Federal law other than under section 1332 of title 28 of the United States Code (relating to diversity of citizenship jurisdiction) or under State law which is applicable or relevant and appropriate under section 121 (relating to cleanup standards) to review any challenges to removal or remedial action selected under section 104 , or to review any order issued under section 106(a) , in any action except one of the following:

(1) An action under section 107 to recover response costs or damages or for contribution.

(2) An action to enforce an order issued under section 106(a) or to recover a penalty for violation of such order.

(3) An action for reimbursement under section 106(b)(2) .

(4) An action under section 310 (relating to citizens suits) alleging that the removal or remedial action taken under section 104 or secured under section 106 was in violation of any requirement of this Act. Such an action may not be brought with regard to a removal where a remedial action is to be undertaken at the site.

(5) An action under section 106 in which the United States has moved to compel a remedial action.

(i) Intervention. — In any action commenced under this Act or under the Solid Waste Disposal Act in a court of the United States, any person may intervene as a matter of right when such person claims an interest relating to the subject of the action and is so situated that the disposition of the action may, as a practical matter, impair or impede the person's ability to protect that interest, unless the President or the State shows that the person's interest is adequately represented by existing parties.

(j) Judicial Review.—

(1) Limitation. — In any judicial action under this Act, judicial review of any issues concerning the adequacy of any response action taken or ordered by the President shall be limited to the administrative record. Otherwise applicable principles of administrative law shall govern whether any supplemental materials may be considered by the court.

(2) Standard. — In considering objections raised in any judicial action under this Act, the court shall uphold the President's decision in selecting the response- action unless the objecting party can demonstrate, on the administrative record, that the decision was arbitrary and capricious or otherwise not in accordance with law.

(3) Remedy. — If the court finds that the selection of the response action was arbitrary and capricious or otherwise not in accordance with law, the court shall award (A) only the response costs or damages that are not inconsistent with the national contingency plan, and (B) such other relief as is consistent with the National Contingency Plan.

(4) Procedural errors. — In reviewing alleged procedural errors, the court may disallow costs or damages only if the errors were so serious and related to matters of such central relevance to the action that the action would have been significantly changed had such errors not been made.

(k) Administrative Record and Participation Procedures.—

(1) Administrative record. — The President shall establish an administrative record upon which the President shall base the selection of a response action. The administrative record shall be available to the public at or near the facility at issue. The President also may place duplicates of the administrative record at any other location.

(2) Participation procedures.—

(A) Removal action. — The President shall promulgate regulations in accordance with chapter 5 of title 5 of the United States Code establishing procedures for the appropriate participation of interested persons in the development of the administrative record on which the President will base the selection of removal actions and on which judicial review of removal actions will be based.

(B) Remedial action. — The President shall provide for the participation of interested persons, including potentially responsible parties, in the development of the administrative record on which the President will base the selection of remedial actions and on which judicial review of remedial actions will be based. The procedures developed under this subparagraph shall include, at a minimum, each of the following:

(i) Notice to potentially affected persons and the public, which shall be accompanied by a brief analysis of the plan and alternative plans that were considered.

(ii) A reasonable opportunity to comment and provide information regarding the plan.

(iii) An opportunity for a public meeting in the affected area, in accordance with section 117(a)(2) (relating to public participation).

(iv) A response to each of the significant comments, criticisms, and new data submitted in written or oral presentations.

(v) A statement of the basis and purpose of the selected action. For purposes of this subparagraph, the administrative record shall include all items developed and received under this subparagraph and all items described in the second sentence of section 117(d) . The President shall promulgate regulations in accordance with chapter 5 of title 5 of the United States Code to carry out the requirements of this subparagraph.

(C) Interim record. — Until such regulations under subparagraphs (A) and (B) are promulgated, the administrative record shall consist of all items developed and received pursuant to current procedures for selection of the response action, including procedures for the participation of interested parties and the public. The development of an administrative record and the selection of response action under this Act shall not include an adjudicatory hearing.

(D) Potentially responsible parties. — The President shall make reasonable efforts to identify and notify potentially responsible parties as early as possible before selection of a response action. Nothing in this paragraph shall be construed to be a defense to liability.

(l) Notice of Actions. — Whenever any action is brought under this Act in a court of the United States by a plaintiff other than the United States, the plaintiff shall provide a copy of the complaint to the Attorney General of the United States and to the Administrator of the Environmental Protection Agency.

§9614. Relationship to Other Law [Sec. 114]

(a) Nothing in this Act shall be construed or interpreted as preempting any State from imposing any additional liability or requirements with respect to the release of hazardous substances within such State.

(b) Any person who receives compensation for removal costs or damages or claims pursuit to this Act shall be precluded from recovering compensation for the same removal costs or damages or claims pursuant to any other State or Federal law. Any person who receives compensation for removal costs or damages or claims pursuant to any other Federal or State law shall be precluded from receiving compensation for the same removal costs or damages or claims as provided in this Act.

(c) Recycled Oil.—

(1) Service Station Dealers, Etc. — No person (including the United States or any State) may recover, under the authority of subsection (a)(3) or (a)(4) of section 107 , from a service station dealer for any response costs or damages resulting from a release or threatened release of recycled oil, or use the authority of section 106 against a service station dealer other than a person described in subsection (a)(1) or (a)(2) of section 107 , if such recycled oil—

(A) is not mixed with any other hazardous substance, and

(B) is stored, treated, transported, or otherwise managed in compliance with regulations or standards promulgated pursuant to section 3014 of the Solid Waste Disposal Act and other applicable authorities.

Nothing in this paragraph shall affect or modify in any way the obligations or liability of any person under any other provision of State or Federal law, including common law, for damages, injury, or loss resulting from a release or threatened release of any hazardous substance or for removal or remedial action or the costs of removal or remedial action.

(2) Presumption. — Solely for the purposes of this subsection, a service station dealer may presume that a small quantity of used oil is not mixed with other hazardous substances if it—

(A) has been removed from the engine of a light duty motor vehicle or household appliances by the owner of such vehicle or appliances, and

(B) is presented, by such owner, to the dealer for collection, accumulation, and delivery to an oil recycling facility.

(3) Definition. — For purposes of this subsection, the terms 'used oil' and 'recycled oil' have the same meanings as set forth in sections 1004(36) and 1004(37) of the Solid Waste Disposal Act and regulations promulgated pursuant to that Act.

(4) Effective Date. — The effective date of paragraphs (1) and (2) of this subsection shall be the effective date of regulations or standards promulgated under section 3014 of the Solid Waste Disposal Act that include, among other provisions, a requirement to conduct correc-

tive action to respond to any releases of recycled oil under subtitle C or subtitle I of such Act.

[§114(c) revised by PL 99–499]

(d) Except as provided in this title, no owner or operator of a vessel or facility who establishes and maintains evidence of financial responsibility in accordance with this title shall be required under any State or local law, rule, or regulation to establish or maintain any other evidence of financial responsibility in connection with liability for the release of a hazardous substance from such vessel or facility. Evidence of compliance with the financial responsibility requirements of this title shall be accepted by a State in lieu of any other requirement of financial responsibility imposed by such State in connection with liability for the release of a hazardous substance from such vessel or facility.

§9615. Authority to Delegate, Issue Regulations [Sec. 115]

The President is authorized to delegate and assign any duties or powers imposed upon or assigned to him and to promulgate any regulations necessary to carry out the provisions of this title.

§9616. Schedules [Sec. 116]

[§116 added by PL 99–499]

(a) Assessment And Listing Of Facilities. — It shall be a goal of this Act that, to the maximum extent practicable—

(1) not later than January 1, 1988, the President shall complete preliminary assessments of all facilities that are contained (as of the date of enactment of the Superfund Amendments and Reauthorization Act of 1986) on the Comprehensive Environmental Response, Compensation, and Liability Information System (CERCLIS) including in each assessment a statement as to whether a site inspection is necessary and by whom it should be carried out; and

(2) not later than January 1, 1989, the President shall assure the completion of site inspections at all facilities for which the President has stated a site inspection is necessary pursuant to paragraph (1).

(b) Evaluation. — Within 4 years after enactment of the Superfund Amendments and Reauthorization Act of 1986, each facility listed (as of the date of such enactment) in the CERCLIS shall be evaluated if the President determines that such evaluation is warranted on the basis of a site inspection or preliminary assessment. The evaluation shall be in accordance with the criteria established in section 105 under the National Contingency Plan for determining priorities among release for inclusion on the National Priorities List. In the case of a facility listed in the CERCLIS after the enactment of the Superfund Amendments and Reauthorization Act of 1986, the facility shall be evaluated within 4 years after the date of such listing if the President determines that such evaluation is warranted on the basis of a site inspection or preliminary assessment.

(c) Explanations. — If any of the goals established by subsection (a) or (b) are not achieved, the President shall publish an explanation of why such action could not be completed by the specified date.

(d) Commencement Of RI/FS. — The President shall assure that remedial investigations and feasibility studies (RI/FS) are commenced for facilities listed on the National Priorities List, in addition to those commenced prior to the date of enactment of the Superfund Amendments and Reauthorization Act of 1986, in accordance with the following schedule:

(1) not fewer then 275 by the date 36 months after the date of enactment of the Superfund Amendments and Reauthorization Act of 1986, and

(2) if the requirement of paragraph (1) is not met, not fewer than an additional 175 by the date 4 years after such date of enactment, an additional 200 by the date 5 years after such date of enactment, and a total of 650 by the date 5 years after such date of enactment.

(e) Commencement Of Remedial Action. — The President shall assure that substantial and continuous physical on- site remedial action commences at facilities on the National Priorities List, in addition to those facilities on which remedial action has commenced prior to the date of enactment of the Superfund Amendments and Reauthorization Act of 1986, at a rate not fewer than:

(1) 175 facilities during the first 36–month period after enactment of this subsection; and

(2) 200 additional facilities during the following 24 months after such 36–month period.

§9617. Public Participation [Sec. 117]

[§117 added by PL 99–499]

(a) Proposed Plan. — Before adoption of any plan for remedial action to be undertaken by the President, by a State, or by any other person, under section 104, 106, 120, or 122 , the President or State, as appropriate, shall take both the following actions:

(1) Publish a notice and brief analysis of the proposed plan and make such plan available to the public.

(2) Provide a reasonable opportunity for submission of written and oral comments and an opportunity for a public meeting at or near the facility at issue regarding the proposed plan and regarding any proposed findings under section 121(d)(4) (relating to cleanup standards). The President or the State shall keep a transcript of the meeting and make such transcript available to the public.

The notice and analysis published under paragraph (1) shall include sufficient information as may be necessary to provide a reasonable explanation of the proposed plan and alternative proposal considered.

(b) Final Plan. — Notice of the final remedial action plan adopted shall be published and the plan shall be made available to the public before commencement of any remedial action. Such final plan shall be accompanied by a discussion of any significant changes (and the reasons for such changes) in the proposed plan and a response to each of the significant comments, criticisms, and new data submitted in written or oral presentations under subsection (a).

(c) Explanation Of Differences — After adoption of a final remedial action plan—

(1) if any remedial action is taken,

(2) if any enforcement action under section 106 is taken, or

(3) if any settlement or consent decree under section 106 or section 122 is entered into,and if such action, settlement, or decree differs in any significant respects from the final plan, the President or the State shall publish an explanation of the significant differences and the reasons such changes were made.

(d) Publication. — For the purposes of this section, publication shall include, at a minimum, publication in a major local newspaper of general circulation. In addition, each item developed, received, published, or made available to the public under this section shall be available for public inspection and copying at or near the facility at issue.

(e) Grants For Technical Assistance.—

(1) Authority. — Subject to such amounts as are provided in appropriations Acts and in accordance with rules promulgated by the President, the President may make grants available to any group of individuals which may be affected by a release or threatened release at any facility which is listed on the National Priorities List under the National Contingency Plan. Such grants may be used to obtain technical assistance in interpreting information with regard to the nature of the hazard, remedial investigation and feasibility study, record of decision, remedial design, selection and construction of remedial action, operation and maintenance, or removal action at such facility.

(2) Amount. — The amount of any grant under this subsection may not exceed $50,000 for a single grant recipient. The President may waive the $50,000 limitation in any case where such waiver is necessary to carry out the purposes of this subsection. Each grant recipient shall be required, as a condition of the grant, to contribute at least 20 percent of the total of costs of the technical assistance for which such grant is made. The President may waive the 20 percent contribution requirement if the grant recipient demonstrates financial need and such waiver is necessary to facilitate public participation in the selection of remedial action at the facility. Not more than one grant may be made under this subsection with respect to a single facility, but the grant may be renewed to facilitate public participation at all stages of remedial action.

§9618. High Priority for Drinking Water Supplies [Sec. 118]

[§118 added by PL 99–499]

For purposes of taking action under section 104 or 106 and listing facilities on the National Priorities List, the President shall give a high priority to facilities where the release of hazardous substances or pollutants or contaminants has resulted in the closing of drinking water wells or has contaminated a principal drinking water supply.

§9619. Response Action Contractors [Sec. 119]

[§119 added by PL 99–499]

(a) Liability of Response Action Contractors.—

(1) Response action contractors. — A person who is a response action contractor with respect to any release or threatened release of a hazardous substance or pollutant or contaminant from a vessel or facility shall not be liable under this title or under any other Federal law to any person for injuries, costs, damages, expenses, or other liability (including but not limited to claims for indemnification or contribution and claims by third parties for death,

personal injury, illness or loss of or damage to property or economic loss) which results from such release or threatened release.

(2) Negligence, etc. — Paragraph (1) shall not apply in the case of a release that is caused by conduct of the response action contractor which is negligent, grossly negligent, or which constitutes intentional misconduct.

(3) Effect on warranties; employer liability. — Nothing in this subsection shall affect the liability of any person under any warranty under Federal, State, or common law. Nothing in this subsection shall affect the liability of an employer who is a response action contractor to any employee of such employer under any provision of law, including any provision of any law relating to worker's compensation.

(4) Governmental employees. — A state employee or an employee of a political subdivision who provides services relating to response action while acting within the scope of his authority as a governmental employee shall have the same exemption from liability (subject to the other provisions of this section) as is provided to the response action contractor under this section.

(b) Savings Provisions.—

(1) Liability of other persons. — The defense provided by section 107(b)(3) shall not be available to any potentially responsible party with respect to any costs or damages caused by any act or omission of a response action contractor. Except as provided in subsection (a)(4) and the preceding sentence, nothing in this section shall affect the liability under this Act or under any other Federal or State law of any person, other than a response action contractor.

(2) Burden of plaintiff. — Nothing in this section shall affect the plaintiff's burden of establishing liability under this title.

(c) Indemnification.—

(1) In general. — The President may agree to hold harmless and indemnify any response action contractor meeting the requirements of this subsection against any liability (including the expenses of litigation or settlement) for negligence arising out of the contractor's performance in carrying out response action activities under this title, unless such liability was caused by conduct of the contractor which was grossly negligent or which constituted intentional misconduct.

(2) Applicability. — This subsection shall apply only with respect to a response action carried out under written agreement with—

(A) the President;

(B) any Federal agency;

(C) a State or political subdivision which has entered into a contract or cooperative agreement in accordance with section 104(d)(1) of this title; or

(D) any potentially responsible party carrying out any agreement under section 122 (relating to settlements) or section 106 (relating to abatement).

(3) Source of funding. — This subsection shall not be subject to section 1301 or 1341 of title 31 of the United States Code or section 3732 of the Revised Statutes (41 U.S.C. 11) or to section 3 of the Superfund Amendments and Reauthorization Act of 1986. For purposes of section 111, amounts expended pursuant to this subsection for indemnification of any response action contractor (except with respect to federally owned or operated facilities) shall be considered governmental response costs incurred pursuant to section 104. If sufficient funds are unavailable in the Hazardous Substance Superfund established under subchapter A of chapter 98 of the Internal Revenue Code of 1954 to make payments pursuant to such indemnification or if the Fund is repealed, there are authorized to be appropriated such amounts as may be necessary to make such payments.

(4) Requirements. — An indemnification agreement may be provided under this subsection only if the President determines that each of the following requirements are met:

(A) The liability covered by the indemnification agreement exceeds or is not covered by insurance available, at a fair and reasonable price, to the contractor at the time the contractor enters into the contract to provide response action, and adequate insurance to cover such liability is not generally available at the time the response action contract is entered into.

(B) The response action contractor has made diligent efforts to obtain insurance coverage from non-Federal sources to cover such liability.

(C) In the case of a response action contract covering more than one facility, the response action contractor agrees to continue to make such diligent efforts each time the contractor begins work under the contract at a new facility.

(5) Limitations.—

(A) Liability covered. — Indemnification under this subsection shall apply only to response action contractor liability which results from a release of any hazardous substance or pollutant or contaminant if such release arises out of response action activities.

(B) Deductibles and limits. — An indemnification agreement under this subsection shall include deductibles and shall place limits on the amount of indemnification to be made available.

(C) Contracts with potentially responsible parties.—

(i) Decision to indemnify. — In deciding whether to enter into an indemnification agreement with a response action contractor carrying out a written contract or agreement with any potentially responsible party, the President shall determine an amount which the potentially responsible party is able to indemnify the contractor. The President may enter into such an indemnification agreement only if the President determines that such amount of indemnification is inadequate to cover any reasonable potential liability of the contractor arising out of the contractor's negligence in performing the contract or agreement with such party. The President shall make the determinations in the preceding sentences (with respect to the amount and the adequacy of the amount) taking into account the total net assets and resources of potentially responsible parties with respect to the facility at the time of such determinations.

(ii) Conditions. — The President may pay a claim under an indemnification agreement referred to in clause (i) for the amount determined under clause (i) only if the contractor has exhausted all administrative, judicial, and common law claims for indemnification against all potentially responsible parties participating in the cleanup of the facility with respect to the liability of the contractor arising out of the contractor's negligence in performing the contract or agreement with such party. Such indemnification agreement shall require such contractor to pay any deductible established under subparagraph (B) before the contractor may recover any amount from the potentially responsible party or under the indemnification agreement.

(D) RCRA facilities. — No owner or operator of a facility regulated under the Solid Waste Disposal Act may be indemnified under this subsection with respect to such facility.

(E) Persons retained or hired. — A person retained or hired by a person described in subsection (e)(2)(B) shall be eligible for indemnification under this subsection only if the President specifically approves of the retaining or hiring of such person.

(6) Cost recovery. — For purposes of section 107, amounts expended pursuant to this subsection for indemnification of any person who is a response action contractor with respect to any release or threatened release shall be considered a cost of response incurred by the United States Government with respect to such release.

(7) Regulations. — The President shall promulgate regulations for carrying out the provisions of this subsection. Before promulgation of the regulations, the President shall develop guidelines to carry out this section. Development of such guidelines shall include reasonable opportunity for public comment.

(8) Study. — The Comptroller General shall conduct a study in the fiscal year ending September 30, 1989, on the application of this subsection, including whether indemnification agreements under this subsection are being used, the number of claims that have been filed under such agreements, and the need for this subsection. The Comptroller General shall report the findings of the study to Congress no later than September 30, 1989.

(d) Exception. — The exemption provided under subsection (a) and the authority of the President to offer indemnification under subsection (c) shall not apply to any person covered by the provisions of paragraph (1), (2), (3), or (4) of section 107(a) with respect to the release or threatened release concerned if such person would be covered by such provisions even if such person had not carried out any actions referred to in subsection of this section.

(e) Definitions. — For purposes of this section—

(1) Response action contract. — The term 'response action contract' means any written contract or agreement entered into by a response action contractor (as defined in paragraph (2)(A) of this subsection) with—

(A) the President;

(B) any Federal agency;

(C) a State or political subdivision which has entered into a contract or cooperative agreement in accordance with section 104(d)(1) of this Act; or

(D) any potentially responsible party carrying out an agreement under section 106 or 122; to provide any remedial action under this Act at a facility listed on the National Priorities List, or any removal under this Act, with respect to any release or threatened release of a hazardous substance or pollutant or contaminant from the facility or to provide any evaluation, planning, engineering, surveying and mapping, design, construction, equipment, or any ancillary services thereto for such facility.

(2) Response action contractor. — The term "response action contractor" means—

(A) any—

(i) person who enters into a response action contract with respect to any release or threatened release of a hazardous substance or pollutant or contaminant from a facility and is carrying out such contract; and

(ii) person, public or nonprofit private entity, conducting a field demonstration pursuant to section 311(b); and

(iii) Recipients of grants (including subgrantees) under section 126 for the training and education of workers who are or may be engaged in activities related to hazardous waste removal, containment, or emergency response under this Act; and

[§119(e)(2)(A)(iii) added by PL 100–202]

(B) any person who is retained or hired by a person described in subparagraph (A) to provide any services relating to a response action; and

[§119(e)(2)(B) amended by PL 101–584]

(C) any surety who after October 16, 1990, and before January 1, 1996, provides a bid, performance or payment bond to a response action contractor, and begins activities to meet its obligations under such bond, but only in connection with such activities or obligations.

[§119(e)(2)(C) added by PL 101–584;amended by PL 102–484]

(3) Insurance. — The term 'insurance' means liability insurance which is fair and reasonably priced, as determined by the President, and which is made available at the time the contractor enters into the response action contract to provide response action.

(f) Competition. — Response action contractors and subcontractors for program management, construction management, architectural and engineering, surveying and mapping, and related services shall be selected in accordance with title IX of the Federal Property and Administrative Services Act of 1949. The Federal selection procedures shall apply to appropriate contracts negotiated by all Federal governmental agencies involved in carrying out this Act. Such procedures shall be followed by response action contractors and subcontractors.

[§119(g) added by PL 101–584]

(g) Surety Bonds. —

(1) If under the Act of August 24, 1935 (40 U.S.C. 270a–270d), commonly referred to as the "Miller Act", surety bonds are required for any direct Federal procurement of any response action contract and are not waived pursuant to the Act of April 29, 1941 (40 U.S.C. 270e–270f), they shall be issued in accordance with such Act of August 24, 1935.

[§119(g)(1) amended by PL 102–484]

(2) If under applicable Federal law surety bonds are required for any direct Federal procurement of any response action contract, no right of action shall accrue on the performance bond issued on such response action contract to or for the use of any person other than the obligee named in the bond.

(3) If under applicable Federal law surety bonds are required for any direct Federal procurement of any response action contract, unless otherwise provided for by the procuring agency in the bond, in the event of a default, the surety's liability on a performance bond shall be only for the cost of completion of the contract work in accordance with the plans and specifications less the balance of funds remaining to be paid under the contract, up to the penal sum of the bond. The surety shall in no event be liable on bonds to indemnify or compensate the obligee for loss or liability arising from personal injury or property damage whether or not caused by a breach of the bonded contract.

(4) Nothing in this subsection shall be construed as preempting, limiting, superseding, affecting, applying to, or modifying any State laws, regulations, requirements, rules, practices or procedures. Nothing in this subsection shall be construed as affecting, applying to, modifying, limiting, superseding, or preempting any rights, authorities, liabilities, demands, actions, causes of action, losses, judgments, claims, statutes of limitation, or obligations

under Federal or State law, which do not arise on or under the bond.

(5) This subsection shall not apply to bonds executed before October 17, 1990, or after December 31, 1995.

[§119(g)(5) amended by PL 102–484]

§9620. Federal Facilities [Sec. 120]

[§120 added by PL 99–499]

(a) Application of Act to Federal Government.—

(1) In general. — Each department, agency, and instrumentality of the United States (including the executive, legislative, and judicial branches of government) shall be subject to, and comply with, this Act in the same manner and to the same extent, both procedurally and substantively, as any nongovernmental entity, including liability under section 107 of this Act. Nothing in this section shall be construed to affect the liability of any person or entity under sections 106 and 107.

(2) Application of requirements to federal facilities. — All guidelines, rules, regulations, and criteria which are applicable to preliminary assessments carried out under this Act for facilities at which hazardous substances are located, applicable to evaluations of such facilities under the National Contingency Plan, applicable to inclusion on the National Priorities List, or applicable to remedial actions at such facilities shall also be applicable to facilities which are owned or operated by a department, agency, or instrumentality of the United States in the same manner and to the extent as such guidelines, rules, regulations, and criteria are applicable to other facilities. No department, agency, or instrumentality of the United States may adopt or utilize any such guidelines, rules, regulations, or criteria which are inconsistent with the guidelines, rules, regulations, and criteria established by the Administrator under this Act.

(3) Exceptions. — This subsection shall not apply to the extent otherwise provided in this section with respect to applicable time periods. This subsection shall also not apply to any requirements relating to bonding, insurance, or financial responsibility. Nothing in this Act shall be construed to require a State to comply with section 104(c)(3) in the case of a facility which is owned or operated by any department, agency, or instrumentality of the United States.

(4) State laws. — State laws concerning removal and remedial action, including State laws regarding enforcement, shall apply to removal and remedial action at facilities owned or operated by a department, agency, or instrumentality of the United States when such facilities are not included on the National Priorities List. The preceding sentence shall not apply to the extent a State law would apply any standard or requirement to such facilities which is more stringent than the standards and requirements applicable to facilities which are not owned or operated by any such department, agency, or instrumentality.

(b) Notice. — Each department, agency, and instrumentality of the United States shall add to the inventory of Federal agency hazardous waste facilities required to be submitted under section 3016 of the Solid Waste Disposal Act (in addition to the information required under section 3016(a)(3) of such Act) information on contamination from each facility owned or operated by the department, agency, or instrumentality if such contamination affects contiguous or adjacent property owned by the department, agency, or instrumentality or by any other person, including a description of the monitoring data obtained.

(c) Federal Agency Hazardous Waste Compliance Docket. — The Administrator shall establish a special Federal Agency Hazardous Waste Compliance Docket (hereinafter in this section referred to as the "docket") which shall contain each of the following:

(1) All information submitted under section 3016 of the Solid Waste Disposal Act and subsection (b) of this section regarding any Federal facility and notice of each subsequent action taken under this Act with respect to the facility.

(2) Information submitted by each department, agency, or instrumentality of the United States under section 3005 or 3010 of such Act.

(3) Information submitted by the department, agency, or instrumentality under section 103. of this Act.

The docket shall be available for public inspection at reasonable times. Six months after establishment of the docket and every 6 months thereafter, the Administrator shall publish in the Federal Register a list of the Federal facilities which have been included in the docket during the immediately preceding 6-month period. Such publication shall also indicate where in the appropriate regional office of the Environmental Protection Agency additional information may be obtained with respect to any facility on the docket. The Administrator shall establish a program to provide information to the public with respect to facilities which are included in the docket under this subsection.

(d) Assessment and Evaluation. — Not later than 18 months after the enactment of the Superfund Amendments and Reauthorization Act of 1986, the Administrator shall take steps to assure that a preliminary assessment is conducted for each facility on the docket. Following such preliminary assessment, the Administrator shall, where appropriate—

(1) evaluate such facilities in accordance with the criteria established in accordance with section 105 under the National Contingency Plan for determining priorities among releases; and

(2) include such facilities on the National Priorities List maintained under such plan if the facility meets such criteria. Such criteria shall be applied in the same manner as the criteria are applied to facilities which are owned or operated by other persons. Evaluation and listing under this subsection shall be completed not later than 30 months after such date of enactment. Upon the receipt of a petition from the Governor of any State, the Administrator shall make such an evaluation of any facility included in the docket.

(e) Required Action by Department. —

(1) RI/FS. — Not later than 6 months after the inclusion of any facility on the National Priorities List, the department, agency, or instrumentality which owns or operates such facility shall, in consultation with the Administrator and appropriate State authorities, commence a remedial investigation and feasibility study for such facility. In the case of any facility which is listed on such list before the date of the enactment of this section, the department, agency, or instrumentality which owns or operates such facility shall, in consultation with the Administrator and appropriate State authorities, commence such an investigation and study for such facility within one year after such date of enactment. The Administrator and appropriate State authorities shall publish a timetable and deadlines for expeditious completion of such investigation and study.

(2) Commencement of Remedial Action; Interagency Agreement. — The Administrator shall review the results of each investigation and study conducted as provided in paragraph (1). Within 180 days thereafter, the head of the department, agency, or instrumentality concerned shall enter into an interagency agreement with the Administrator for the expeditious completion by such department, agency, or instrumentality of all necessary remedial action at such facility. Substantial continuous physical onsite remedial action shall be commenced at each facility not later than 15 months after completion of the investigation and study. All such interagency agreements, including review of alternative remedial action plans and selection of remedial action, shall comply with the public participation requirements of section 117.

(3) Completion of Remedial Actions. —Remedial actions at facilities subject to interagency agreements under this section shall be completed as expeditiously as practicable. Each agency shall include in its annual budget submissions to the Congress a review of alternative agency funding which could be used to provide for the costs of remedial action. The budget submission shall also include a statement of the hazard posed by the facility to human health, welfare, and the environment and identify the specific consequences of failure to begin and complete remedial action.

(4) Contents of Agreement. — Each interagency agreement under this subsection shall include, but shall not be limited to, each of the following:

(A) A review of alternative remedial actions and selection of a remedial action by the head of the relevant department, agency, or instrumentality and the Administrator or, if unable to reach agreement on selection of a remedial action, selection by the Administrator.

(B) A schedule for the the completion of each such remedial action.

(C) Arrangements for long-term operation and maintenance of the facility.

(5) Annual Report. — Each department, agency, or instrumentality responsible for compliance with this section shall furnish an annual report to the Congress concerning its progress in implementing the requirements of this section. Such reports shall include, but shall not be limited to, each of the following items:

(A) A report on the progress in reaching interagency agreements under its section.

(B) The specific cost estimates and budgetary proposals involved in each interagency agreement.

(C) A brief summary of the public comments regarding each proposed interagency agreement.

(D) A description of the instances in which no agreement was reached.

(E) A report on progress in conducting investigations and studies under paragraph (1).

(F) A report on progress in conducting remedial actions.

(G) A report on progress in conducting remedial action at facilities which are not listed on the National Priorities List. With respect to instances in which no agreement was reached within the required time period, the department, agency, or instrumentality filing the report under this paragraph shall include in such report an explanation of the reasons why no agreement was reached. The annual report required by this paragraph shall also contain a detailed description on a State-by-State basis of the status of each facility subject to this section, including a description of the hazard presented by each facility, plans and schedules for initiating and completing response action, enforcement status (where appropriate), and an explanation of any postponements or failure to complete response action. Such reports shall also be submitted to the affected States.

(6) Settlements with other parties. — If the Administrator, in consultation with the head of the relevant department, agency, or instrumentality of the United States, determines that remedial investigations and feasibility studies or remedial action will be done properly at the Federal facility by another potentially responsible party within the deadlines provided in paragraphs (1) (2), and (3) of this subsection, the Administrator may enter into an agreement with such party under section 122 (relating to settlements). Following approval by the Attorney General of any such agreement relating to a remedial action, the agreement shall be entered in the appropriate United States district court as a consent decree under section 106 of this Act.

(f) State and Local Participation. — The Administrator and each department, agency, or instrumentality responsible for compliance with this section shall afford to relevant State and local officials the opportunity to participate in the planning and selection of the remedial action, including but not limited to the review of all applicable data as it becomes available and the development of studies, reports, and action plans. In the case of State officials, the opportunity to participate shall be provided in accordance with section 121.

(g) Transfer of Authorities. — Except for authorities which are delegated by the Administrator to an officer or employee of the Environmental Protection Agency, no authority vested in the Administrator under this section may be transferred, by executive order of the President or otherwise, to any other officer or employee of the United States or to any other person.

(h) Property Transferred by Federal Agencies. —

(1) Notice. — After the last day of the 6–month period beginning on the effective date of regulations under paragraph (2) of this subsection, whenever any department, agency, or instrumentality of the United States enters into any contract for the sale or other transfer of real property which is owned by the United States and on which any hazardous substance was stored for one year or more, known to have been released, or disposed of, the head of such department, agency, or instrumentality shall include in such contract notice of the type and quantity of such hazardous substance and notice of the time at which such storage, release, or disposal took place, to the extent such information is available on the basis of a complete search of agency files.

(2) Form of notice; regulations. — Notice under this subsection shall be provided in such form and manner as may be provided in regulations promulgated by the Administrator. As promptly as practicable after the enactment of this subsection but not later than 18 months after the date of such enactment, and after consultation with the Administrator of the General Services Administration, the Administrator shall promulgate regulations regarding the notice required to be provided under this subsection.

(3) Contents of certain deeds. — After the last day of the 6-month period beginning on the effective date of regulations under paragraph (2) of this subsection, in the case of any real property owned by the United States on which any hazardous substance was stored for one year or more, known to have been released, or disposed of, each deed entered into for the transfer of such property by the United States to any other person or entity shall contain —

(A) to the extent such information is available on the basis of a complete search of agency files —

(i) a notice of the type and quantity of such hazardous substances,

(ii) notice of the time at which such storage, release, or disposal took place, and

(iii) a description of the remedial action taken, if any;

(B) a covenant warranting that—

(i) all remedial action necessary to protect human health and the environment with respect to any such substance remaining on the property has been taken before the date of such transfer, and

(ii) any additional remedial action found to be necessary after the date of such transfer shall be conducted by the United States. The requirements of subparagraph (B) shall not apply in any case in which the person or entity to whom the property is transferred is a potentially responsible party with respect to such real property; and

(C) a clause granting the United States access to the property in any case in which remedial action or corrective action is found to be necessary after the date of such transfer.

For purposes of subparagraph (B)(i), all remedial action described in such subparagraph has been taken if the construction and installation of an approved remedial design has been completed, and the remedy has been demonstrated to the Administrator to be operating properly and successfully. The carrying out of long-term pumping and treating, or operation and maintenance, after the remedy has been demonstrated to the Administrator to be operating properly and successfully does not preclude the transfer of the property.

[§120(h)(3) amended by PL 102–426]

(4) Identification of uncontaminated property.—

(A) In the case of real property to which this paragraph applies (as set forth in subparagraph (E)), the head of the department, agency, or instrumentality of the United States with jurisdiction over the property shall identify the real property on which no hazardous substances and no petroleum products or their derivatives were stored for one year or more, known to have been released, or disposed of. Such identification shall be based on an investigation of the real property to determine or discover the obviousness of the presence or likely presence of a release or threatened release of any hazardous substance or any petroleum product or its derivatives, including aviation fuel and motor oil, on the real property. The identification shall consist, at a minimum, of a review of each of the following sources of information concerning the current and previous uses of the real property:

(i) A detailed search of Federal Government records pertaining to the property.

(ii) Recorded chain of title documents regarding the real property.

(iii) Aerial photographs that may reflect prior uses of the real property and that are reasonably obtainable through State or local government agencies.

(iv) A visual inspection of the real property and any buildings, structures, equipment, pipe, pipeline, or other improvements on the real property, and a visual inspection of properties immediately adjacent to the real property.

(v) A physical inspection of property adjacent to the real property, to the extent permitted by owners or operators of such property.

(vi) Reasonably obtainable Federal, State, and local government records of each adjacent facility where there has been a release of any hazardous substance or any petroleum product or its derivatives, including aviation fuel and motor oil, and which is likely to cause or contribute to a release or threatened release of any hazardous substance or any petroleum product or its derivatives, including aviation fuel and motor oil, on the real property.

(vii) Interviews with current or former employees involved in operations on the real property.

Such identification shall also be based on sampling, if appropriate under the circumstances. The results of the identification shall be provided immediately to the Administrator and State and local government officials and made available to the public.

(B) The identification required under subparagraph (A) is not complete until concurrence in the results of the identification is obtained, in the case of real property that is part of a facility on the National Priorities List, from the Administrator, or, in the case of real property that is not part of a facility on the National Priorities List, from the appropriate State official. In the case of a concurrence which is required from a State official, the concurrence is deemed to be obtained if, within 90 days after receiving a request for the concurrence, the State official has not acted (by either concurring or declining to concur) on the request for concurrence.

(C) (i) Except as provided in clauses (ii), (iii), and (iv), the identification and concurrence required under subparagraphs (A) and (B), respectively, shall be made at least 6 months before the termination of operations on the real property.

(ii) In the case of real property described in subparagraph (E)(i)(II) on which operations have been closed or realigned or scheduled for closure or realignment pursuant to a base closure law described in subparagraph (E)(ii)(I) or (E)(ii)(II) by the date of the enactment of the Community Environmental Response Facilitation Act, the identification and concurrence required under subparagraphs (A) and (B), respectively, shall be made not later than 18 months after such date of enactment.

(iii) In the case of real property described in subparagraph (E)(i)(II) on which operations are closed or realigned or become scheduled for closure or realignment pursuant to the base closure law described in subparagraph (E)(ii)(II) after the date of the enactment of the Community Environmental Response Facilitation Act, the identification and concurrence required under subparagraphs (A) and (B), respectively, shall be made not later than 18 months after the date by which a joint resolution disapproving the closure or realignment of the real property under section 2904(b) of such base closure law must be enacted, and such a joint resolution has not been enacted.

(iv) In the case of real property described in subparagraphs (E)(i)(II) on which operations are closed or realigned pursuant to a base closure law described in subparagraph (E)(ii)(III) or (E)(ii)(IV), the identification and concurrence required under subparagraphs (A) and (B), respectively, shall be made not later than 18 months after the date on which the real property is selected for closure or realignment pursuant to such a base closure law.

(D) In the case of the sale or other transfer of any parcel of real property identified under subparagraph (A), the deed entered into for the sale or transfer of such property by the United States to any other person or entity shall contain—

(i) a covenant warranting that any response action or corrective action found to be necessary after the date of such sale or transfer shall be conducted by the United States; and

(ii) a clause granting the United States access to the property in any case in which a response action or corrective action is found to be necessary after such date at such property, or such access is necessary to carry out a response action or corrective action on adjoining property.

(E)(i) This paragraph applies to—

(I) real property owned by the United States and on which the United States plans to terminate Federal Government operations, other than real property described in subclause (II); and

(II) real property that is or has been used as a military installation and on which the United States plans to close or realign military operations pursuant to a base closure law.

(ii) For purposes of this paragraph, the term "base closure law" includes the following:

(I) Title II of the Defense Authorization Amendments and Base Closure and Realignment Act (Public Law 100–526; 10 U.S.C. 2687 note).

(II) The Defense Base Closure and Realignment Act of 1990 (part A of title XXIX of Public Law 101–510; 10 U.S.C. 2687 note).

(III) Section 2687 of title 10, United States Code.

(IV) Any provision of law authorizing the closure or realignment of a military installation enacted on or after the date of enactment of the Community Environmental Response Facilitation Act.

(F) Nothing in this paragraph shall affect, preclude, or otherwise impair the termination of Federal Government operations on real property owned by the United States.

[§120(h)(4) added by PL 102–426]

(5) Notification of states regarding certain leases.—In the case of real property owned by the United States, on which any hazardous substance or any petroleum product or its derivatives (including aviation fuel and motor oil) was stored for one year or more, known to have been released, or disposed of, and on which the United States plans to terminate Federal Government operations, the head of the department, agency, or instrumentality of the United States with jurisdiction over the property shall notify the State in which the property is located of any lease entered into by the United States that will encumber the property beyond the date of termination of opera-

tions on the property. Such notification shall be made before entering into the lease and shall include the length of the lease, the name of person to whom the property is leased, and a description of the uses that will be allowed under the lease of the property and buildings and other structures on the property.

[§120(h)(5) added by PL 102–426]

(i) Obligations Under Solid Waste Disposal Act. — Nothing in this section shall affect or impair the obligation of any department, agency, or instrumentality of the United States to comply with any requirement of the Solid Waste Disposal Act (including corrective action requirements).

(j) National Security. —

(1) Site specific presidential orders. — The President may issue such orders regarding response actions at any specified site or facility of the Department of Energy or the Department of Defense as may be necessary to protect the national security interests of the United States at that site or facility. Such orders may include, where necessary to protect such interests, an exemption from any requirement contained in this title or under title 111 of the Superfund Amendments and Reauthorization Act of 1986 with respect to the site or facility concerned. The President shall notify the Congress within 30 days of the issuance of an order under this paragraph providing for any such exemption. Such notification shall include a statement of the reasons for the granting of the exemption. An exemption under this paragraph shall be for a specified period which may not exceed one year. Additional exemptions may be granted, each upon the President's issuance of a new order under this paragraph for the site or facility concerned. Each such additional exemption shall be for a specified period which may not exceed one year. It is the intention of the Congress that whenever an exemption is issued under this paragraph the response action shall proceed as expeditiously as practicable. The Congress shall be notified periodically of the progress of any response action with respect to which an exemption has been issued under this paragraph. No exemption shall be granted under this paragraph due to lack of appropriation unless the President shall have specifically requested such appropriation as a part of the budgetary process and the Congress shall have failed to make available such requested appropriation.

(2) Classified information. — Notwithstanding any other provision of law, all requirements of the Atomic Energy Act and all Executive orders concerning the handling of restricted data and national security in formation, including 'need to know' requirements, shall be applicable to any grant of access to classified information under the provisions of this Act or under title III of the Superfund Amendments and Reauthorization Act of 1986.

[Editor's Note: Section 120(b) of PL 99–499 provides: (b) Limited Grandfather.— Section 120 of CERCLA shall not apply to any response action or remedial action for which a plan is under development by the Department of Energy on the date of enactment of this Act with respect to facilities — (1) owned or operated by the United States and subject to the jurisdiction of such Department; (2) located in St. Charles and St. Louis counties, Missouri, or the City of St. Louis, Missouri, and (3) published in the National Priorities List. In preparing such plans, the Secretary of Energy shall consult with the Administrator of the Environmental Protection Agency.]

§9621. Cleanup Standards [Sec. 121]

[§121 added by PL 99–499]

(a) Selection of Remedial Action.—The President shall select appropriate remedial actions determined to be necessary to be carried out under section 104 or secured under section 106 which are in accordance with this section and, to the extent practicable, the national contingency plan, and which provide for cost- effective response. In evaluating the cost effectiveness of proposed alternative remedial actions, the President shall take into account the total short- and long-term costs of such actions, including the costs of operation and maintenance for the entire period during which such activities will be required.

(b) General Rules.—

(1) Remedial actions in which treatment which permanently and significantly reduces the volume, toxicity or mobility of the hazardous substances, pollutants, and contaminants is a principal element, are to be preferred over remedial actions not involving such treatment. The offsite transport and disposal of hazardous substances or contaminated materials without such treatment should be the least favored alternative remedial action where practicable treatment technologies are available. The President shall conduct an assessment of permanent solutions and alternative treatment technologies or resource recovery

technologies that, in whole or in part, will result in a permanent and significant decrease in the toxicity, mobility, or volume of the hazardous substance, pollutant, or contaminant. In making such assessment, the President shall specifically address the long-term effectiveness of various alternatives. In assessing alternative remedial actions, the President shall, at a minimum, take into account:

(A) the long-term uncertainties associated with land disposal;

(B) the goals, objectives, and requirements of the Solid Waste Disposal Act;

(C) the persistence, toxicity, mobility, and propensity to bioaccumulate of such hazardous substances and their constituents;

(D) short- and long-term potential for adverse health effects from human exposure;

(E) long-term maintenance costs;

(F) the potential for future remedial action costs if the alternative remedial action in question were to fail; and

(G) the potential threat to human health and the environment associated with excavation, transportation, and redisposal, or containment.

The President shall select a remedial action that is protective of human health and the environment, that is cost effective, and that utilizes permanent solutions and alternative treatment technologies or resource recovery technologies to the maximum extent practicable. If the President selects a remedial action not appropriate for a preference under this subsection, the President shall publish an explanation as to why a remedial action involving such reductions was not selected.

(2) The President may select an alternative remedial action meeting the objectives of this subsection whether or not such action has been achieved in practice at any other facility or site that has similar characteristics. In making such a selection, the President may take into account the degree of support for such remedial action by parties interested in such site.

(c) Review.—If the President selects a remedial action that results in any hazardous substances, pollutants, or contaminants remaining at the site, the President shall review such remedial action no less often than each 5 years after the initiation of such remedial action to assure that human health and the environment are being protected by the remedial action being implemented. In addition, if upon such review it is the judgment of the President that action is appropriate at such site in accordance with section 104 or 106, the President shall take or require such action. The President shall report to the Congress a list of facilities for which such review is required, the results of all such reviews, and any actions taken as a result of such reviews.

(d) Degree of Cleanup.—

(1) Remedial actions selected under this section or otherwise required or agreed to by the President under this Act shall attain a degree of cleanup of hazardous substances, pollutants, and contaminants released into the environment and of control of further release at a minimum which assures protection of human health and the environment. Such remedial actions shall be relevant and appropriate under the circumstances presented by the release or threatened release of such substance, pollutant or contaminant.

(2) (A) With respect to any hazardous substance, pollutant, or contaminant that will remain onsite, if—

(i) any standard, requirement, criteria, or limitation under any Federal environmental law, including, but not limited to, the Toxic Substances Control Act, the Safe Drinking Water Act, the Clean Air Act, the Clean Water Act, the Marine Protection, Research and Sanctuaries Act, or the Solid Waste Disposal Act; or

(ii) any promulgated standard, requirement, criteria, or limitation under a State environmental or facility siting law that is more stringent than any Federal standard, requirement, criteria, or limitation, including each such State standard, requirement, criteria, or limitation contained in a program approved, authorized or delegated by the Administrator under a statute cited in subparagraph (A), and that has been identified to the President by the State in a timely manner,is legally applicable to the hazardous substance or pollutant or contaminant concerned or is relevant and appropriate under the circumstances of the release or threatened release of such hazardous substance or pollutant or contaminant, the remedial action selected under section 104 or secured under section 106 shall require, at the completion of the remedial action, a levelor standard of control for such hazardous substance or pollutant or contaminant which at least attains such legally applicable or relevant and appropriate standard, requirement, criteria, or limitation. Such remedial action shall require a level or standard of control which at least attains Maximum Contaminant Level Goals established under the Safe Drinking Water Act and water quality criteria established under section 304 or 303 of the Clean Water Act, where such goals or criteria are relevant and appropriate under the circumstances of the release or threatened release.

(B) (i) In determining whether or not any water quality criteria under the Clean Water Act is relevant and appropriate under the circumstances of the release or threatened release, the President shall consider the designated or potential use of the surface or groundwater, the environmental media affected, the purposes for which such criteria were developed, and the latest information available.

(ii) For the purposes of this section, a process for establishing alternate concentration limits to those otherwise applicable for hazardous constituents in groundwater under subparagraph (A) may not be used to establish applicable standards under this paragraph if the process assumes a point of human exposure beyond the boundary of the facility, as defined at the conclusion of the remedial investigation and feasibility study, except where—

(I) there are known and projected points of entry of such groundwater into surface water; and

(II) on the basis of measurements or projections, there is or will be no statistically significant increase of such constituents from such groundwater in such surface water at the point of entry or at any point where there is reason to believe accumulation of constituents may occur downstream; and

(III) the remedial action includes enforceable measures that will preclude human exposure to the contaminated groundwater at any point between the facility boundary and all known and projected points of entry of such groundwater into surface water then the assumed point of human exposure may be at such known and projected points of entry.

(C) (i) Clause (ii) of this subparagraph shall be applicable only in cases where, due to the President's selection, in compliance with subsection (b)(1), of a proposed remedial action which does not permanently and significantly reduce the volume, toxicity, or mobility of hazardous substances, pollutants, or contaminants, the proposed disposition of waste generally by or associated with the remedial action selected by the President is land disposal in a State referred to in clause (ii).

(ii) Except as provided in clauses (iii) and (iv), a State standard, requirement, criteria, or limitation (including any State siting standard or requirement) which could effectively result in the statewide prohibition of land disposal of hazardous substances, pollutants, or contaminants shall not apply.

(iii) Any State standard, requirement, criteria, or limitation referred to in clause (ii) shall apply where each of the following conditions is met:

(I) The State standard, requirement, criteria, or limitation is of general applicability and was adopted by formal means.

(II) The State standard, requirement, criteria, or limitation was adopted on the basis of hydrologic, geologic, or other relevant considerations and was not adopted for the purpose of precluding onsite remedial actions or other land disposal for reasons unrelated to protection of human health and the environment.

(III) The State arranges for, and assures payment of the incremental costs of utilizing, a facility for disposition of the hazardous substances, pollutants, or contaminants concerned.

(iv) Where the remedial action selected by the President does not conform to a State standard and the State has initiated a law suit against the Environmental Protection Agency prior to May 1, 1986, to seek to have the remedial action conform to such standard, the President shall conform the remedial action to the State standard. The State shall assure the availability of an off-site facility for such remedial action.

(3) In the case of any removal or remedial action involving the transfer of any hazardous substance or pollutant or contaminant offsite, such hazardous substance or pollutant or contaminant shall only be transferred to a facility which is operating with section 3004 and 3005 of the Solid Waste Disposal Act (or, where applicable, in compliance with the Toxic Substances Control Act or other applicable Federal law) and all applicable State requirements. Such substance or pollutant or contaminant may be transferred to a land disposal facility

only if the President determines that both of the following requirements are met:

(A) The unit to which the hazardous substance or pollutant or contaminant is transferred is not releasing any hazardous waste, or constituent thereof, into the groundwater or surface water or soil.

(B) All such releases from other units at the facility are being controlled by a corrective action program approved by the Administrator under subtitle C of the Solid Waste Disposal Act. The president shall notify the owner or operator of such facility of determinations under this paragraph.

(4) The President may select a remedial action meeting the requirements of paragraph (1) that does not attain a level or standard of control at least equivalent to a legally applicable or relevant and appropriate standard, requirement, criteria, or limitation as required by paragraph (2) (including subparagraph (B) thereof), if the President finds that—

(A) the remedial action selected is only part of a total remedial action that will attain such level or standard of control when completed;

(B) compliance with such requirement at that facility will result in greater risk to human health and the environment than alternative options;

(C) compliance with such requirements is technically impracticable from an engineering perspective;

(D) the remedial action selected will attain a standard of performance that is equivalent to that required under the otherwise applicable standard, requirement, criteria, or limitation, through use of another method or approach;

(E) with respect to a State standard, requirement, criteria, or limitation, the State has not consistently applied (or demonstrated the intention to consistently apply) the standard, requirement, criteria, or limitation in similar circumstances at other remedial actions within the State; or

(F) in the case of a remedial action to be undertaken solely under section 104 using the Fund, selection of a remedial action that attains such level or standard of control will not provide a balance between the need for protection of public health and welfare and the environment at the facility under consideration, and the availability of amounts from the Fund to respond the other sites which present or may present a threat to public health or welfare or the environment, taking into consideration the relative immediacy of such threats.

The President shall publish such findings, together with an explanation and appropriate documentation.

(e) Permits and Enforcement.—

(1) No Federal, State, or local permit shall be required for the portion of any removal or remedial action conducted entirely on-site, where such remedial action is selected and carried out in compliance with this section.

(2) A State may enforce any Federal or State standard, requirement, criteria, or limitation to which the remedial action is required to conform under this Act in the United States district court for the district in which the facility is located. Any consent decree shall require the parties to attempt expeditiously to resolve disagreements concerning implementation of the remedial action informally with the appropriate Federal and State agencies. Where the parties agree, the consent decree may provide for administrative enforcement. Each consent decree shall also contain stipulated penalties for violations of the decree in an amount not to exceed $25,000 per day, which may be enforced by either the President or the State. Such stipulated penalties shall not be construed to impair or affect the authority of the court to order compliance with the specific terms of any such decree.

(f) State Involvement.—

(1) The President shall promulgate regulations providing for substantial and meaningful involvement by each State in initiation, development, and selection of remedial actions to be undertaken in that State. The regulations, at a minimum, shall include each of the following:

(A) State involvement in decisions whether to perform a preliminary assessment and site inspection.

(B) Allocation of responsibility for hazard ranking system scoring.

(C) State concurrence in deleting sites from the National Priorities List.

(D) State participation in the long-term planning process for all remedial sites within the State.

(E) A reasonable opportunity for States to review and comment on each of the following:

(i) The remedial investigation and feasibility study and all data and technical documents leading to its issuance.

(ii) The planned remedial action identified in the remedial investigation and feasibility study.

(iii) The engineering design following selection of the final remedial action.

(iv) Other technical data and reports relating to implementation of the remedy.

(v) Any proposed finding or decision by the President to exercise the authority of subsection (d)(4).

(F) Notice to the State of negotiations with potentially responsible parties regarding the scope of any response action at a facility in the State and an opportunity to participate in such negotiations and, subject to paragraph (2), be a party to any settlement.

(G) Notice to the State and an opportunity to comment or the President's proposed plan for remedial action as well as on alternative plans under consideration. The President's proposed decision regarding the selection of remedial action shall be accompanied by a response to the comments submitted by the State, including an explanation regarding any decision under subsection (d)(4) on compliance with promulgated State standards. A copy of such response shall also be provided to the State.

(H) Prompt notice and explanation of each proposed action to the State in which the facility is located. Prior to the promulgation of such regulations, the President shall provide notice to the State of negotiations with potentially responsible parties regarding the scope of any response action at a facility in the State, and such State may participate in such negotiations and, subject to paragraph (2), any settlements.

(2) (A) This paragraph shall apply to remedial actions secured under section 106. At least 30 days prior to the entering of any consent decree, if the President proposes to select a remedial action that does not attain a legally applicable or relevant and appropriate standard, requirement, criteria, or limitation, under the authority of subsection (d)(4), the President shall provide an opportunity for the State to concur or not concur in such selection. If the State concurs, the State may become a signatory to the consent decree.

(B) If the State does not concur in such selection, and the State desires to have the remedial action conform to such standard, requirement, criteria, or limitation, the State shall intervene in the action under section 106 before entry of the consent decree, to seek to have the remedial action so conform. Such intervention shall be a matter of right. The remedial action shall conform to such standard, requirement, criteria, or limitation if the State establishes, on the administrative record, that the finding of the President was not supported by substantial evidence. If the court determines that the remedial action shall conform to such standard, requirement, criteria, or limitation, the remedial action shall be so modified and the State may become a signatory to the decree. If the court determines that the remedial action need not conform to such standard, requirement, criteria, or limitation, and the State pays or assures the payment of the additional costs attributable to meeting such standard, requirement, criteria, or limitation, the remedial action shall be so modified and the State shall become a signatory to the decree.

(C) The President may conclude settlement negotiations with potentially responsible parties without State concurrence.

(3) (A) This paragraph shall apply to remedial actions at facilities owned or operated by a department, agency, or instrumentality of the United States. At least 30 days prior to the publication of the President's final remedial action plan, if the President proposes to select a remedial action that does not attain a legally applicable or relevant and appropriate standard, requirement, criteria, or limitation, under the authority of subsection (d)(4), the President shall provide an opportunity for the State to concur or not concur in such selection. If the State concurs, or does not act within 30 days, the remedial action may proceed.

(B) If the State does not concur in such selection as provided in subparagraph (A), and desires to have the remedial action conform to such standard, requirement, criteria, or limitation, the State may maintain an action as follows:

(i) If the President has notified the State of selection of such a remedial action, the State may bring an action within 30 days of such notification for the sole purpose of determining whether the finding of the President is supported by substantial evidence. Such action shall be brought in the United States district court for the district in which the facility is located.

(ii) If the State establishes, on the administrative record, that the President's finding is not supported by substantial evidence, the remedial action shall be modified to conform to such standard, requirement, criteria, or limitation.

(iii) If the State fails to establish that the President's finding was not supported by substantial evidence and if the State pays, within 60 days of judgment, the additional costs attributable to meeting such standard, requirement, criteria, or limitation, the remedial action shall be selected to meet such standard, requirement, criteria, or limitation. If the State fails to pay within 60 days, the remedial action selected by the President shall proceed through completion.

(C) Nothing in this section precludes, and the court shall not enjoin, the Federal agency from taking any remedial action unrelated to or not inconsistent with such standard, requirement, criteria, or limitation.

[Editor's Note: Section 121(b) of PL 99–499 gives provisions on the effective date for section 121. The text follows.]

(b) Effective Date.—With respect to section 121 of CERCLA, as added by this section—

(1) The requirements of section 121 of CERCLA shall not apply to any remedial action for which the Record of Decision (hereinafter in this section referred to as the "ROD") was signed, or the consent decree was lodged, before date of enactment.

(2) If the ROD was signed, or the consent decree lodged, within the 30–day period immediately following enactment of the Act, the Administrator shall certify in writing that the portion of the remedial action covered by the ROD or consent decree complies to the maximum extent practicable with section 121 of CERCLA. Any ROD signed before enactment of this Act and reopened after enactment of this Act to modify or supplement the selection of remedy shall be subject to the requirements of section 121 of CERCLA.

§9622. Settlements. [Sec. 122]

[§122 added by PL 99–499]

(a) Authority To Enter Into Agreements.—The President, in his discretion, may enter into an agreement with any person (including the owner or operator of the facility from which a release or substantial threat of release emanates, or any other potentially responsible person), to perform any response action (including any action described in section 104(b)) if the President determines that such action will be done properly by such person. Whenever practicable and in the public interest, as determined by the President, the President shall act to facilitate agreements under this section that are in the public interest and consistent with the National Contingency Plan in order to expedite effective remedial actions and minimize litigation. If the President decides not to use the procedures in this section, the President shall notify in writing potentially responsible parties at the facility of such decision and the reasons why use of the procedures is inappropriate. A decision of the President to use or not to use the procedures in this section is not subject to judicial review.

(b) Agreements With Potentially Responsible Parties.—

(1) Mixed funding.—An agreement under this section may provide that the President will reimburse the parties to the agreement from the Fund, with interest, for certain costs of actions under the agreement that the parties have agreed to perform but which the President has agreed to finance. In any case in which the President provides such reimbursement, the President shall make all reasonable efforts to recover the amount of such reimbursement under section 107 or under other relevant authorities.

(2) Reviewability.—The President's decisions regarding the availability of fund financing under this subsection shall not be subject to judicial review under subsection (d).

(3) Retention of funds.—If, as part of any agreement, the President will be carrying out any action and the parties will be paying amounts to the President, the President may, notwithstanding any other provision of law, retain and use such amounts for purposes of carrying out the agreement.

(4) Future Obligation of fund.—In the case of a completed remedial action pursuant to an agreement described in paragraph (1), the Fund shall be subject to an obligation for subsequent remedial actions at the same facility but only to the extent that such subsequent actions are necessary by reason of the failure of the original remedial action. Such obligation shall be in a proportion equal to, but not exceeding, the proportion contributed by the Fund for the original remedial action. The Fund's obligation for such future remedial action may be met through Fund expenditures or through payment, following settlement or enforcement action, by parties who were not signatories to the original agreement.

(c) Effect of Agreement.—

(1) Liability.—Whenever the President has entered into an agreement under this section,

the liability to the United States under this Act of each party to the agreement, including any future liability to the United States, arising from the release or threatened release that is the subject of the agreement shall be limited as provided in the agreement pursuant to a covenant not to sue in accordance with subsection (f). A covenant not to sue may provide that future liability to the United States of a settling potentially responsible party under the agreement may be limited to the same proportion as that established in the original settlement agreement. Nothing in this section shall limit or otherwise affect the authority of any court to review in the consent decree process under subsection (d) any covenant not to sue contained in an agreement under this section. In determining the extent to which the liability of parties to an agreement shall be limited pursuant to a covenant not to sue, the President shall be guided by the principle that a more complete covenant not to sue shall be provided for a more permanent remedy undertaken by such parties.

(2) Actions against other persons.—If an agreement has been entered into under this section, the President may take any action under section 106 against any person who is not a party to the agreement, once the period for submitting a proposal under subsection (e)(2)(B) has expired. Nothing in this section shall be construed to affect either of the following:

(A) The liability of any person under section 106 or 107 with respect to any costs or damages which are not included in the agreement.

(B) The authority of the President to maintain an action under this Act against any person who is not a party to the agreement.

(d) Enforcement.—

(1) Cleanup agreements.—

(A) Consent decree.—Whenever the President enters into an agreement under this section with any potentially responsible party with respect to remedial action under section 106, following approval of the agreement by the Attorney General, except as otherwise provided in the case of certain administrative settlements referred to in subsection (g), the agreement shall be entered in the appropriate United States district court as a consent decree. The President need not make any finding regarding an imminent and substantial endangerment to the public health or the environment in connection with any such agreement or consent decree.

(B) Effect.— The entry of any consent decree under this subsection shall not be construed to be an acknowledgment by the parties that the release or threatened release concerned constitutes an imminent and substantial endangerment to the public health or welfare or the environment. Except as otherwise provided in the Federal Rules of Evidence, the participation by any party in the process under this section shall not be considered an admission of liability for any purpose, and the fact of such participation shall not be admissible in any judicial or administrative proceeding, including a subsequent proceeding under this section.

(C) Structure.— The President may fashion a consent decree so that the entering of such decree and compliance with such decree or with any determination or agreement made pursuant to this section shall not be considered an admission of liability for any purpose.

(2) Public participation.—

(A) Filing of proposed judgment.— At least 30 days before a final judgment is entered under paragraph (1), the proposed judgment shall be filed with the court.

(B) Opportunity for comment.— The Attorney General shall provide an opportunity to persons who are not named as parties to the action to comment on the proposed judgment before its entry by the court as a final judgment. The Attorney General shall consider, and file with the court, any written comments, views, or allegations relating to the proposed judgment. The Attorney General may withdraw or withhold its consent to the proposed judgment. The Attorney General may withdraw or withhold its consent to the proposed judgment if the comments, views, and allegations concerning the judgment disclose facts or considerations which indicate that the proposed judgment is inappropriate, improper, or inadequate.

(3) 104(b) Agreements.— Whenever the President enters into an agreement under this section with any potentially responsible party with respect to action under section 104(b), the President shall issue an order or enter into a decree setting forth the obligations of such party. The United States district court for the district in which the release or threatened release occurs may enforce such order or decree.

(e) Special notice procedures.—

(1) Notice.— Whenever the President determines that a period of negotiation under this subsection would facilitate an agreement with potentially responsible parties for taking response action (including any action described in section 104(b)) and would expedite remedial action, the President shall so notify all such parties and shall provide them with information concerning each of the following:

(A) The names and addresses of potentially responsible parties (including owners and operators and other persons referred to in section 107(a)), to the extent such information is available.

(B) To the extent such information is available, the volume and nature of substances contributed by each potentially responsible party identified at the facility.

(C) A ranking by volume of the substances at the facility, to the extent such information is available. The President shall make the information referred to in this paragraph available in advance of notice under this paragraph upon the request of a potentially responsible party in accordance with procedures provided by the President. The provisions of subsection (e) of section 104 regarding protection of confidential information apply to information provided under this paragraph. Disclosure of information generated by the President under this section to persons other than the Congress, or any duly authorized Committee thereof, is subject to other privileges or protections provided by law, including (but not limited to) those applicable to attorney work product. Nothing contained in this paragraph or in other provisions of this Act shall be construed, interpreted, or applied to diminish the required disclosure of information under other provisions of this or other Federal or State laws.

(2) Negotiation.—

(A) Moratorium.— Except as provided in this subsection, the President may not commence action under section 104(a) or take any action under section 106 for 120 days after providing notice and information under this subsection with respect to such action. Except as provided in this subsection, the President may not commence a remedial investigation and feasibility study under section 104(b) for 90 days after providing notice and information under this subsection with respect to such action. The President may commence any additional studies or investigations authorized under section 104(b), including remedial design, during the negotiation period.

(B) Proposals.— Persons receiving notice and information under paragraph (l) of this subsection with respect to action under section 106 shall have 60 days from the date of receipt of such notice to make a proposal to the President for undertaking or financing the action under section 106. Persons receiving notice and information under paragraph (1) of this subsection with respect to action under section 104(b) shall have 60 days from the date of receipt of such notice to make proposal to the President for undertaking or financing the action under section 104(b).

(C) Additional parties.— If an additional potentially responsible party is identified during the negotiation period or after an agreement has been entered into under this subsection concerning a release or threatened release, the President may bring the additional party into the negotiation or enter into a separate agreement with such party.

(3) Preliminary allocation of responsibility.—

(A) In general.— The President shall develop guidelines for preparing nonbinding preliminary allocations of responsibility. In developing these guidelines the President may include such factors as the President considers relevant, such as: volume, toxicity, mobility, strength of evidence, ability to pay, litigative risks, public interest considerations, precedential value, and inequities and aggravating factors. When it would expedite settlements under this section and remedial action, the President may, after completion of the remedial investigation and feasibility study, provide a nonbinding preliminary allocation of responsibility which allocates percentages of the total cost of response among potentially responsible parties at the facility.

(B) Collection of information.— To collect information necessary or appropriate for performing the allocation under subparagraph (A) or for otherwise implementing this section, the President may by subpoena require the attendance and testimony of witnesses and the production of reports, papers, documents, answers to questions, and other information that the President deems necessary. Witnesses shall be paid the same fees and mileage that are paid witnesses in the courts of the United States. In the event of contumacy or failure or refusal of any person to obey any such subpoena, any district court of the United States in which venue is proper shall have jurisdiction to order any such person to comply with such subpoena. Any failure to obey such an order of the court is punishable by the court as a contempt thereof.

(C) Effect.— The nonbinding preliminary allocation of responsibility shall not be admissible as evidence in any proceeding, and no court shall have jurisdiction to review the nonbinding preliminary allocation of responsibility. The nonbinding preliminary allocation of responsibility, shall not constitute an apportionment or other statement on the divisibility of harm or causation.

(D) Costs.— The costs incurred by the President in producing the nonbinding preliminary allocation of responsibility shall be reimbursed by the potentially responsible parties whose offer is accepted by the President. Where an offer under this section is not accepted, such costs shall be considered costs of response.

(E) Decision To Reject Offer. — Where the President, in his discretion, has provided a nonbinding preliminary allocation of responsibility and the potentially responsible parties have made a substantial offer providing for response to the President which he rejects, the reasons for the rejection shall be provided in a written explanation. The President's decision to reject such an offer shall not be subject to judicial review.

(4) Failure To Propose. — If the President determines that a good faith proposal for undertaking or financing action under section 106 has not been submitted within 60 days of the provision of notice pursuant to this subsection, the President may thereafter commence action under section 104(a) or take an action against any person under section 106 of this Act. If the President determines that a good faith proposal for undertaking or financing action under section 104(b) has not been submitted within 60 days after the provision of notice pursuant to this subsection, the President may thereafter commence action under section 104(b).

(5) Significant Threats. — Nothing in this subsection shall limit the President's authority to undertake response or enforcement action regarding a significant threat to public health or the environment within the negotiation period established by this subsection.

(6) Inconsistent Response Action. — When either the President, or a potentially responsible party pursuant to an administrative order or consent decree under this Act, has initiated a remedial investigation and feasibility study for a particular facility under this Act, no potentially responsible party may undertake any remedial action at the facility unless such remedial action has been authorized by the President.

(f) Covenant Not To Sue.—

(1) Discretionary Covenants. — The President may, in his discretion, provide any person with a covenant not to sue concerning any liability to the United States under this Act, including future liability, resulting from a release or threatened release of a hazardous substance addressed by a remedial action, whether that action is onsite or offsite, if each of the following conditions is met:

(A) The covenant not to sue is in the public interest.

(B) The covenant not to sue would expedite response action consistent with the National Contingency Plan under section 105 of this Act.

(C) The person is in full compliance with a consent decree under section 106 (including a consent decree entered into in accordance with this section) for response to the release or threatened release concerned.

(D) The response action has been approved by the President.

(2) Special Covenants Not To Sue. — In the case of any person to whom the President is authorized under paragraph (1) of this subsection to provide a covenant not to sue, for the portion of remedial action—

(A) which involves the transport and secure disposition offsite of hazardous substances in a facility meeting the requirements of section 3004(c), (d), (e), (f), (g), (m), (o), (p), (u), and (v) and 3005(c) of the Solid Waste Disposal Act, where the President has rejected a proposed remedial action that is consistent with the National Contingency Plan that does not include such offsite disposition and has thereafter required offsite disposition; or

(B) which involves the treatment of hazardous substances so as to destroy, eliminate, or permanently immobilize the hazardous constituents of such substances, such that, in the judgment of the President, the substance no longer present any current or currently foreseeable future significant risk to public health, welfare or the environment, no byproduct of the treatment or destruction process presents any significant hazard to public health, welfare or the environment, and all byproducts are themselves treated, destroyed, or contained in a manner which assures that such byproducts do not present any current or currently foreseeable future significant risk to public health, welfare or the environment, the President shall provide such person with a covenant not to sue with respect to future liability to the United States under this Act for a future release or threatened release of hazardous substances from such facility, and a person provided such covenant not to sue shall not be liable to the United States under section 106 or 107 with respect to such release or threatened release at a future time.

(3) Requirement That Remedial Action Be Completed. — A covenant not to sue concerning future liability to the United States shall not take effect until the President certifies that remedial action has been completed in accordance with the requirements of this Act at the facility that is the subject of such covenant.

(4) Factors. — In assessing the appropriateness of a covenant not to sue under paragraph (1) and any condition to be included in a covenant not to sue under paragraph (1) or (2), the President shall consider whether the covenant or condition is in the public interest on the basis of such factors as the following:

(A) The effectiveness and reliability of the remedy, in light of the other alternative remedies considered for the facility concerned.

(B) The nature of the risks remaining at the facility.

(C) The extent to which performance standards are included in the order or decree.

(D) The extent to which the response action provides a complete remedy for the facility, including a reduction in the hazardous nature of the substances at the facility.

(E) The extent to which the technology used in the response action is demonstrated to be effective.

(F) Whether the Fund or other sources of funding would be available for any additional remedial actions that might eventually be necessary at the facility.

(G) Whether the remedial action will be carried out, in whole or in significant part, by the responsible parties themselves.

(5) Satisfactory Performance. — Any covenant not to sue under this subsection shall be subject to the satisfactory performance by such party of its obligations under the agreement concerned.

(6) Additional Condition For Future Liability. —

(A) Except for the portion of the remedial action which is subject to a covenant not to sue under paragraph (2) or under subsection (g) (relating to de minimis settlements), a covenant not to sue a person concerning future liability to the United States shall include an exception to the covenant that allows the President to sue such person concerning future liability resulting from the release or threatened release that is the subject of the covenant where such liability arises out of conditions which are unknown at the time the President certifies under paragraph (3) that remedial action has been completed at the facility concerned.

(B) In extraordinary circumstances, the President may determine, after assessment of relevant factors such as those referred to in paragraph (4) and volume, toxicity, mobility, strength of evidence, ability to pay, litigative risks, public interest considerations, precedential value, and the inequities and aggravating factors, not to include the exception referred to in subparagraph (A) if other terms, conditions, or requirements of the agreement containing the covenant not to sue are sufficient to provide all reasonable assurances that public health and the environment will be protected from any future release at or from the facility.

(C) The President is authorized to include any provisions allowing future enforcement action under section 106 or 107 that in the discretion of the President are necessary and appropriate to assure protection of public health, welfare, and the environment.

(g) De Minimis Settlements. —

(1) Expedited Final Settlement. — Whenever practicable and in the public interest, as determined by the President, the President shall as promptly as possible reach a final settlement with a potentially responsible party in an administrative or civil action under section 106 or 107 if such settlement involves only a minor portion of the response costs at the facility concerned and, in the judgment of the President, the conditions in either of the following subparagraph (A) or (B) are met:

(A) Both of the following are minimal in comparison to other hazardous substances at the facility:

(i) The amount of the hazardous substances contributed by that party to the facility.

(ii) The toxic or other hazardous effects of the substances contributed by that party to the facility.

(B) The potentially responsible party—

(i) is the owner of the real property on or in which the facility is located;

(ii) did not conduct or permit the generation, transportation, storage, treatment, or disposal of any hazardous substance at the facility; and

(iii) did not contribute to the release or threat of release of a hazardous substance at the facility through any action or omission.

This subparagraph (B) does not apply if the potentially responsible party purchased the real property with actual or constructive knowledge that the property was used for the generation, transportation, storage, treatment, or disposal of any hazardous substance.

(2) Covenant Not To Sue. — The President may provide a covenant not to sue with respect to the facility concerned to any party who has entered into a settlement under this subsection unless such a covenant would be inconsistent with the public interest as determined under subsection (f).

(3) Expedited Agreement. — The President shall reach any such settlement or grant any such covenant not to sue as soon as possible after the President has available the information necessary to reach such a settlement or grant such a covenant.

(4) Consent Decree or Administrative Order. — A settlement under this subsection shall be entered as a consent decree or embodied in an administrative order setting forth the terms of the settlement. In the case of any facility where the total response costs exceed $500,000 (excluding interest), if the settlement is embodied as an administrative order, the order may be issued only with the prior written approval of the Attorney General. If the Attorney General or his designee has not approved or disapproved the order within 30 days of this referral, the order shall be deemed to be approved unless the Attorney General and the Administrator have agreed to extend the time. The district court for the district in which the release or threatened release occurs may enforce any such administrative order.

(5) Effect of Agreement. — A party who has resolved its liability to the United States under this subsection shall not be liable for claims for contribution regarding matters addressed in the settlement. Such settlement does not discharge any of the other potentially responsible parties unless its terms so provide, but it reduces the potential liability of the others by the amount of the settlement.

(6) Settlements With Other Potentially Responsible Parties. — Nothing in this subsection shall be construed to affect the authority of the President to reach settlements with other potentially responsible parties under this Act.

(h) Cost Recovery Settlement Authority.—

(1) Authority To Settle. — The head of any department or agency with authority to undertake a response action under this Act pursuant to the national contingency plan may consider, compromise, and settle a claim under section 107 for costs incurred by the United States Government if the claim has not been referred to the Department of Justice for further action. In the case of any facility where the total response costs exceed $500,000 (excluding interest), any claim referred to in the preceding sentence may be compromised and settled only with the prior written approval of the Attorney General.

(2) Use of Arbitration. — Arbitration in accordance with regulations promulgated under this subsection may be used as a method of settling claims of the United States where the total response costs for the facility concerned do not exceed $500,000 (excluding interest). After consultation with the Attorney General, the department or agency head may establish and publish regulations for the use of arbitration or settlement under this subsection.

(3) Recovery of Claims. — If any person fails to pay a claim that has been settled under this subsection, the department or agency head shall request the Attorney General to bring a civil action in an appropriate district court to recover the amount of such claim, plus costs, attorneys' fees, and interest from the date of the settlement. In such an action, the terms of the settlement shall not be subject to review.

(4) Claims for Contribution. — A person who has resolved its liability to the United States under this subsection shall not be liable for claims for contribution regarding matters addressed in the settlement. Such settlement shall not discharge any of the other potentially liable persons unless its terms so provide, but it reduces the potential liability of the others by the amount of the settlement.

(i) Settlement Procedures. —

(1) Publication in Federal Register. — At least 30 days before any settlement (including any settlement arrived at through arbitration) may become final under subsection (h), or under subsection (g) in the case of a settlement embodied in any administrative order, the head of the department or agency which has jurisdiction over the proposed settlement shall publish in the Federal Register notice of the proposed settlement. The notice shall identify the facility concerned and the parties to the proposed settlement.

(2) Comment Period. — For a 30-day period beginning on the date of publication of notice under paragraph (l) of a proposed settlement, the head of the department or agency which has jurisdiction over the proposed settlement shall provide an opportunity for persons who are not parties to the proposed settlement to file written comments relating to the proposed settlement.

(3) Consideration of Comments. — The head of the department or agency shall consider any comments filed under paragraph (2) in determining whether or not to consent to the proposed settlement and may withdraw or withhold consent to the proposed settlement if such comments disclose facts or considerations which indicate the proposed settlement is inappropriate, improper, or inadequate.

(j) Natural Resources.—

(1) Notification of Trustee. — Where a release or threatened release of any hazardous substance that is the subject of negotiations under this section may have resulted in damages to natural resources under the trusteeship of the United States, the President shall notify the Federal natural resource trustee of the negotiations and shall encourage the participation of such trustee in the negotiations.

(2) Covenant Not To Sue. — An agreement under this section may contain a covenant not to sue under section 107(a)(4)(C) for damages to natural resources under the trusteeship of the United States resulting from the release or threatened release of hazardous substances that is the subject of the agreement, but only if the Federal natural resource trustee has agreed in writing to such covenant. The Federal natural resource trustee may agree to such covenant if the potentially responsible party agrees to undertake appropriate actions necessary to protect and restore the natural resources damaged by such release or threatened release of hazardous substances.

(k) Section Not Applicable To Vessels.— The provisions of this section shall not apply to releases from a vessel.

(l) Civil Penalties. — A potentially responsible party which is a party to an administrative order or consent decree entered pursuant to an agreement under this section or section 120 (relating to Federal facilities) or which is a party to an agreement under section 120 and which fails or refuses to comply with any term or condition of the order, decree or agreement shall be subject to a civil penalty in accordance with section 109.

(m) Applicability Of General Principles Of Law. — In the case of consent decrees and other settlements under this section (including covenants not to sue), no provision of this Act shall be construed to preclude or otherwise affect the applicability of general principles of law regarding the setting aside or modification of consent decrees or other settlements.

§9623. Reimbursement to Local Governments [Sec. 123]

[§123 added by PL 99–499]

(a) Application. — Any general purpose unit of local government for a political subdivision which is affected by a release or threatened release at any facility may apply to the President for reimbursement under this section.

(b) Reimbursement.—

(1) Temporary Emergency Measures. —The President is authorized to reimburse local community authorities for expenses incurred (before or after the enactment of the Superfund Amendments and Reauthorization Act of 1986) in carrying out temporary emergency measures necessary to prevent or mitigate injury to human health or the environment associated with the release or threatened release of any hazardous substance or pollutant or contaminant. Such measures may include, where appropriate, security fencing to limit access, response to fires and explosions, and other measures which require immediate response at the local level.

(2) Local Funds Not Supplanted. — Reimbursement under this section shall not supplant local funds normally provided for response.

(c) Amount. — The amount of any reimbursement to any local authority under subsection (b)(1) may not exceed $25,000 for a single response. The reimbursement under this section with respect to a single facility shall be limited to the units of local government having jurisdiction over the political subdivision in which the facility is located.

(d) Procedure. — Reimbursements authorized pursuant to this section shall be in accordance with rules promulgated by the Administrator within one year after the enactment of the Superfund Amendments and Reauthorization Act of 1986.

§9624. Methane Recovery [Sec. 124]

[§124 added by PL 99–499]

(a) In General. — In the case of a facility at which equipment for the recovery or processing (including recirculation of condensate) of methane has been installed, for purposes of this Act:

(1) The owner or operator of such equipment shall not be considered an 'owner or operator', as defined in section 101(20), with respect to such facility.

(2) The owner or operator of such equipment shall not be considered to have arranged for disposal or treatment of any hazardous substance at such facility pursuant to section 107 of this Act.

(3) The owner or operator of such equipment shall not be subject to any action under section 106 with respect to such facility.

(b) Exceptions. — Subsection (a) does not apply with respect to a release or threatened release of a hazardous substance from a facility described in subsection (a) if either of the following circumstances exist:

(1) The release or threatened release was primarily caused by activities of the owner or operator of the equipment described in subsection (a).

(2) The owner or operator of such equipment would be covered by paragraph (1), (2), (3), or (4) of subsection (a) of section 107 with respect to such release or threatened release if he were not the owner or operator of such equipment. In the case of any release or threatened release referred to in paragraph (1), the owner or operator of the equipment described in subsection (1) shall be liable under this Act only for costs or damages primarily caused by the activities of such owner or operator.

[Editor's Note: Section 124(b) of PL 99–499 provides language about methane recovery under the Solid Waste Disposal Act. For the complete text of that Act, see Chapter 3. The relevant provisions follow.]

(b) Regulation Under The Solid Waste Disposal Act. — Unless the Administrator of the Environmental Protection Agency promulgates regulations under subtitle C of the Solid Waste Disposal Act addressing the extraction of wastes from landfills as part of the process of recovering methane from such landfills, the owner and operator of equipment used to recover methane from a landfill shall not be deemed to be managing, generating, transporting, treating, storing, or disposing of hazardous or liquid wastes within the meaning of that subtitle. If the aqueous or hydrocarbon phase of the condensate or any other waste material removed from the gas recovered from the landfill meets any of the characteristics identified under section 3001 of subtitle C of the Solid Waste Disposal Act, the preceding sentence shall not apply and such condensate phase or other waste material shall be deemed a hazardous waste under that subtitle, and shall be regulated accordingly.

§9625. Section 3001(b)(A)(i) Waste [Sec. 125]

[§125 added by PL 99–499]

(a) Revision Of Hazard Ranking System. — This section shall apply only to facilities which are not included or proposed for inclusion on the National Priorities List and which contain substantial volumes of waste described in section 3001(b)(3)(A)(i) of the Solid Waste Disposal Act. As expeditiously as practicable, the President shall revise the hazard ranking system in effect under the National Contingency Plan with respect to such facilities in a manner which assures appropriate consideration of each of the following site-specific characteristics of such facilities:

(1) The quantity, toxicity, and concentrations of hazardous constituents which are present in such waste and a comparison thereof with other wastes.

(2) The extent of, and potential for, release of such hazardous constituents into the environment.

(3) The degree of risk to human health and the environment posed by such constituents.

(b) Inclusion Prohibited. — Until the hazard ranking system is revised as required by this section, the President may not include on the National Priorities List any facility which contains substantial volumes of waste described in section 3001(b)(3)(A)(i) of the Solid Waste Disposal Act on the basis of an evaluation made principally on the volume of such waste and not on the concentrations of the hazardous constituents of such waste. Nothing in this section shall be construed to affect the President's authority to include any such facility on the National Priorities List based on the presence of other substances at such facility or to exercise any other authority of this Act with respect to such other substances.

§9626. Indian Tribes [Sec. 126]

[§126 added by PL 99–499]

(a) Treatment Generally. — The governing body of an Indian Tribe shall be afforded substantially the same treatment as a State with respect to the provisions of section 103(a) (regarding notification of releases), section 104(c)(2) (regarding consultation on remedial actions), section 104(e) (regarding access to information), section 104(i) (regarding health authorities) and section 105 (regarding roles and responsibilities under the national contingency plan and submittal of priorities for remedial action, but not including the provision regarding the inclusion of at least one facility per State on the National Priorities List).

(b) Community Relocation. — Should the President determine that proper remedial action is the permanent relocation of tribal members away from a contaminated site because it is cost effective and necessary to protect their health and welfare, such finding must be concurred in by the affected tribal government before relocation shall occur. The President, in cooperation with the Secretary of the Interior, shall also assure that all benefits of the relocation program are provided to the affected tribe and that alternative land of equivalent value is available and satisfactory to the tribe. Any lands acquired for relocation of tribal members shall be held in trust by the United States for the benefit of the tribe.

(c) Study. — The President shall conduct a survey, in consultation with the Indian tribes, to determine the extent of hazardous waste sites on Indian lands. Such survey shall be included within a report which shall make recommendations on the program needs of tribes under this Act, with particular emphasis on how tribal participation in the administration of such programs can be maximized. Such report shall be submitted to Congress along with the President's budget request for fiscal year 1988.

(d) Limitation. — Notwithstanding any other provision of this Act, no action under this Act by an Indian tribe shall be barred until the later of the following:

(1) The applicable period of limitations has expired.

(2) 2 years after the United States, in its capacity as trustee for the tribe, gives written notice to the governing body of the tribe that it will not present a claim or commence an action on behalf of the tribe or fails to present a claim or commence an action within the time limitations specified in this Act.

SUBTITLE B—ESTABLISHMENT OF HAZARDOUS SUBSTANCE RESPONSE TRUST FUND [Repealed]

[Editor's Note: §517 of PL 99–499 repealed Subtitle B of the Hazardous Substance Response Revenue Act of 1980 and added a new section (26 U.S.C. 9507) in Subchapter A of chapter 98 of the Internal Revenue Code of 1986 establishing the Hazardous Substance Superfund.]

SUBTITLE C—POST-CLOSURE TAX AND TRUST FUND [Repealed]

[Editor's Note: §514 of PL 99–499 repealed Subtitle C of the Hazardous Substance Response Revenue Act of 1980.]

TITLE III—MISCELLANEOUS PROVISIONS

§9651. Reports and Studies [Sec. 301]

(a) (1) The President shall submit to the Congress, within four years after enactment of this Act, a comprehensive report on experience with the implementation of this Act, including, but not limited to—

(A) the extent to which the Act and Fund are effective in enabling Government to respond to and mitigate the effects of releases of hazardous substances;

(B) a summary of past receipts and disbursements from the Fund;

(C) a projection of any future funding needs remaining after the expiration of authority to collect taxes, and of the threat to public health, welfare, and the environment posed by the projected releases which create any such needs;

(D) the record and experience of the Fund in recovering Fund disbursements from liable parties;

(E) the record of State participation in the system of response, liability, and compensation established by this Act;

(F) the impact of the taxes imposed by title II of this Act on the Nation's balance of trade with other countries;

(G) an assessment of the feasibility and desirability of a schedule of taxes which would take into account one or more of the following: the likelihood of a release of a hazardous substance, the degree of hazard and risk of harm to public health, welfare, and the environment resulting from any such release, incentives to proper handling, recycling, incineration, and neutralization of hazardous wastes, and disincentives to improper or illegal handling or disposal of hazardous materials, administrative and reporting burdens on Government and industry, and the extent to which the tax burden falls on the substances and parties which create the problems addressed by this Act. In preparing the report, the President shall consult with appropriate Federal, State, and local agencies, affected industries and claimants, and such other interested parties as he may find useful. Based upon the analyses and consultation required by this subsection, the President shall also include in the report any recommendations for legislative changes he may deem necessary for the better effectuation of the purposes of this Act, including but not limited to recommendations concerning authorization levels, taxes, State participation, liability and liability limits, and financial responsibility provisions for the Response Trust Fund and the Post-closure Liability Trust Fund;

(H) an exemption from or an increase in the substances or the amount of taxes imposed by section 4661 of the Internal Revenue Code of 1954 for copper, lead, and zinc oxide, and for feedstocks when used in the manufacture and production of fertilizers, based upon the expenditure experience of the Response Trust Fund;

(I) the economic impact of taxing coal-derived substances and recycled metals.

(2) The Administrator of the Environmental Protection Agency (in consultation with the Secretary of the Treasury) shall submit to the Congress (i) within four years after enactment of this Act, a report identifying additional wastes designated by rule as hazardous after the effective date of this Act and pursuant to section 3001 of the Solid Waste Disposal Act and recommendations on appropriate tax rates for such wastes for the Post-closure Liability Trust Fund. The report shall, in addition, recommend a tax rate, considering the quantity and potential danger to human health and the environment posed by the disposal of any wastes which the Administrator, pursuant to subsection 3001(b)(2)(B) and subsection 3001(b)(3)(A) of the Solid Waste Disposal Act of 1980, has determined should be subject to regulation under subtitle C of such Act, (ii) within three years after enactment of this Act, a report on the necessity for and the adequacy of the revenue raised, in relation to estimated future requirements, of the Post-closure Liability Trust Fund.

(b) The President shall conduct a study to determine (1) whether adequate private insurance protection is available on reasonable terms and conditions to the owners and operators of vessels and facilities subject to liability under section 107 of this Act, and (2) whether the market for such insurance is sufficiently competitive to assure purchasers of features such as a reasonable range of deductibles, coinsurance provisions, and exclusions. The President shall submit the results of his study, together with his recommendations, within two years of the date of enactment of this Act, and shall submit an interim report on his study within one year of the date of enactment of this Act.

(c) (1) The President, acting through Federal officials designated by the National Contingency Plan published under section 105 of this Act, shall study and, not later than two years after the enactment of this Act, shall promulgate regulations for the assessment of damages for injury to, destruction of, or loss of natural resources resulting from a release of oil or a hazardous substance for the purposes of this Act and section 311 (f) (4) and (5) of the Federal Water Pollution Control Act. Notwithstanding the failure of the President to promulgate the regulations required under this subsection on the required date, the President shall promulgate such regulations not later than 6 months after the enactment of the Superfund Amendments and Reauthorization Act of 1986.

[§301(c)(1) amended by PL 99–499]

(2) Such regulations shall specify (A) standard procedures for simplified assessments requiring minimal field observation, including establishing measures of damages based on units of discharge or release or units of affected area, and (B) alternative protocols for conducting assessments in individual cases to determine the type and extent of short- and long- term injury destruction, or loss. Such regulations shall identify the best available procedures to determine such damages, including both direct and indirect injury, destruction, or loss and shall take into consideration factors including, but not limited to, replacement value, use value, and ability of the ecosystem or resource to recover.

(3) Such regulations shall be reviewed and revised as appropriate every two years.

(d) The Administrator of the Environmental Protection Agency shall, in consultation with other Federal agencies and appropriate representatives of State and local governments and nongovernmental agencies, conduct a study and report to the Congress within two years of the date of enactment of this Act on the issues, alternatives, and policy considerations involved in the selection of locations for hazardous waste treatment, storage, and disposal facilities. This study shall include—

(A) an assessment of current and projected treatment, storage, and disposal capacity needs and shortfalls for hazardous waste by management category on a State-by-State basis;

(B) an evaluation of the appropriateness of a regional approach to siting and designing hazardous waste management facilities and the identification of hazardous waste management regions, interstate or intrastate, or both, with similar hazardous waste management needs;

(C) solicitation and analysis of proposals for the construction and operation of hazardous waste management facilities by nongovernmental entities, except that no proposal solicited under terms of this subsection shall be analyzed if it involves cost to the United States Government or fails to comply with the requirements of subtitle C of the Solid Waste Disposal Act and other applicable provisions of law;

(D) recommendations on the appropriate balance between public and private sector involvement in the siting, design, and operation of new hazardous waste management facilities;

(E) documentation of the major reasons for public opposition to new hazardous waste management facilities; and

(F) an evaluation of the various options for overcoming obstacles to siting new facilities, including needed legislation for implementing the most suitable option or options.

(e) (1) In order to determine the adequacy of existing common law and statutory remedies in providing legal redress for harm to man and the environment caused by the release of hazardous substances into the environment, there shall be submitted to the Congress a study within twelve months of enactment of this Act.

(2) This study shall be conducted with the assistance of the American Bar Association, the American Law Institute, the Association of American Trial Lawyers, and the National Association of State Attorneys General with the President of each entity selecting three members from each organization to conduct the study. The study chairman and one reporter shall be elected from among the twelve members of the study group.

(3) As part of their review of the adequacy of existing common law and statutory remedies, the study group shall evaluate the following:

(A) the nature, adequacy, and availability of existing remedies under present law in compensating for harm to man from the release of hazardous substances;

(B) the nature of barriers to recovery (particularly with respect to burdens of going forward and of proof and relevancy) and the role such barriers play in the legal system;

(C) the scope of the evidentiary burdens placed on the plaintiff in proving harm from the release of hazardous substances, particularly in light of the scientific uncertainty over causation with respect to—

(i) carcinogens, mutagens, and teratogens, and

(ii) the human health effects of exposure to low doses of hazardous substances over long periods of time;

(D) the nature and adequacy of existing remedies under present law in providing compensation for damages to natural resources from the release of hazardous substances;

(E) the scope of liability under existing law and the consequences, particularly with respect to obtaining insurance, of any changes in such liability;

(F) barriers to recovery posed by existing statutes of limitations.

(4) The report shall be submitted to the Congress with appropriate recommendations. Such recommendations shall explicitly address—

(A) the need for revisions in existing statutory or common law, and

(B) whether such revisions should take the form of Federal statutes or the development of a model code which is recommended for adoption by the States.

(5) The Fund shall pay administrative expenses incurred for the study. No expenses shall be available to pay compensation, except expenses on a per diem basis for the one reporter, but in no case shall the total expenses of the study exceed $300,000.

(f) The President, acting through the Administrator of the Environmental Protection Agency, the Secretary of Transportation, the Administrator of the Occupational Safety and Health Administration, and the Director of the National Institute for Occupational Safety and Health shall study and, not later than two years after the enactment of this Act, shall modify the national contingency plan to provide for the protection of the health and safety of employees involved in response actions.

(g) Insurability Study.—

(1) Study by comptroller general. — The Comptroller General of the United States, in consultation with the persons described in paragraph (2), shall undertake a study to determine the insurability, and effects on the standard of care, of the liability of each of the following:

(A) Persons who generate hazardous substances; liability for costs and damages under this Act.

(B) Persons who own or operate facilities; liability for costs and damages under this Act.

(C) Persons liable for injury to persons or property caused by the release of hazardous substances into the environment.

(2) Consultation. — In conducting the study under this subsection, the Comptroller General shall consult with the following:

(A) Representatives of the Administrator.

(B) Representatives of persons described in subparagraphs (A) through (C) of the preceding paragraph.

(C) Representatives (i) of groups or organizations comprised generally of persons adversely affected by releases or threatened releases of hazardous substances and (ii) of groups organized for protecting the interests of consumers.

(D) Representatives of property and casualty insurers.

(E) Representatives of reinsurers.

(F) Persons responsible for the regulation of insurance at the State level.

(3) Items evaluated. — The study under this section shall include, among other matters, an evaluation of the following:

(A) Current economic conditions in, and the future outlook for, the commercial market for insurance and reinsurance.

(B) Current trends in statutory and common law remedies.

(C) The impact of possible changes in traditional standards of liability, proof, evidence, and damages on existing statutory and common law remedies.

(D) The effect of the standard of liability and extent of the persons upon whom it is imposed under this Act on the protection of human health and the environment and on the availability, underwriting, and pricing of insurance coverage.

(E) Current trends, if any, in the judicial interpretation and construction of applicable insurance contracts, together with the degree to which amendments in the language of such contracts and the description of the risks assumed, could affect such trends.

(F) The frequency and severity of a representative sample of claims closed during the calendar year immediately preceding the enactment of this subsection.

(G) Impediments to the acquisition of insurance or other means of obtaining liability coverage other than those referred to in the preceding subparagraphs.

(H) The effects of the standards of liability and financial responsibility requirements imposed pursuant to this Act on the cost of, and incentives for, developing and demonstrating alternative and innovative treatment technologies, as well as waste generation minimization.

(4) Submission. — The Comptroller General shall submit a report on the results of the study to Congress with appropriate recommendations within 12 months after the enactment of this subsection.

[§301(g) added by PL 99–499]

(h) Report and Oversight Requirements.—

(1) Annual report by EPA. — On January 1 of each year the Administrator of the Environmental Protection Agency shall submit an annual report to Congress of such Agency on the progress achieved in implementing this Act during the preceding fiscal year. In addition such report shall specifically include each of the following:

(A) A detailed description of each feasibility study carried out at a facility under title I of this Act.

(B) The status and estimated date of completion of each such study.

(C) Notice of each study which will not meet a previously published schedule for completion and the new estimated date for completion.

(D) An evaluation of newly developed feasible and achievable permanent treatment technologies.

(E) Progress made in reducing the number of facilities subject to review under section 121(c).

(F) A report on the status of all remedial and enforcement actions undertaken during the prior fiscal year, including a comparison to remedial and enforcement actions undertaken in prior fiscal years.

(G) An estimate of the amount of resources, including the number of work years or personnel, which would be necessary for each department, agency, or instrumentality which is carrying out any activities of this Act to complete the implementation of all duties vested in the department, agency, or instrumentality under this Act.

(2) Review by inspector general. — Consistent with the authorities of the Inspector General Act of 1978 the Inspector General of the Environmental Protection Agency shall review any report submitted under paragraph (1) related to EPA's activities for reasonableness and accuracy and submit to Congress, as a part of such report a report on the results of such review.

(3) Congressional oversight. — After receiving the reports under paragraphs (1) and (2) of this subsection in any calendar year, the appropriate authorizing committees of Congress shall conduct oversight hearings to ensure that this Act is being implemented according to the purposes of this Act and congressional intent in enacting this Act.

[§301(h) added by PL 99–499]

§9652. Effective Dates, Savings Provision [Sec. 302]

(a) Unless otherwise provided, all provisions of this Act shall be effective on the date of enactment of this Act.

(b) Any regulation issued pursuant to any provisions of section 311 of the Clean Water Act which is repealed or superseded by this Act and which is in effect on the date immediately preceding the effective date of this Act shall be deemed to be a regulation issued pursuant to the authority of this Act and shall remain in full force and effect unless or until superseded by new regulations issued thereunder.

(c) Any regulation—

(1) respecting financial responsibility,

(2) issued pursuant to any provision of law repealed or superseded by this Act, and

(3) in effect on the date immediately preceding the effective date of this Act shall be deemed to be a regulation issued pursuant to the authority of this Act and shall remain in full force and effect unless or until superseded by new regulations issued thereunder.

(d) Nothing in this Act shall affect or modify in any way the obligations or liabilities of any person under other Federal or State law, including common law, with respect to releases of hazardous substances or other pollutants or contaminants. The provisions of this Act shall not be considered, interpreted, or construed in any way as reflecting a determination, in part or whole, of policy regarding the inapplicability of strict liability, or strict liability doctrines, to activities relating to hazardous substances, pollutants, or contaminants or other such activities.

§9653. Expiration, Sunset Provision [Repealed] [Sec. 303]

[Editor's Note: §303 was repealed by PL 99–499. The section had provided that the authority to collect taxes under CERCLA would terminate on Sept. 30, 1985, or when amounts received in the U.S. Treasury under 26 U.S.C. 4611 and 4661 totaled $1,380,000,000.]

§9654. Conforming Amendments [Sec. 304]

(a) Subsection (b) of section 504 of the Federal Water Pollution Control Act is hereby repealed.

(b) One-half of the unobligated balance remaining before the date of the enactment of this Act under subsection (k) of section 311 of the Federal Water Pollution Control Act and all sums appropriated under section 504(b) of the Federal Water Pollution Control Act shall be transferred to the Fund established under title II of this Act.

(c) In any case in which any provision of section 311 of the Federal Water Pollution Control Act is determined to be in conflict with any provisions of this Act, the provisions of this Act shall apply.

§9655. Legislative Veto [Sec. 305]

(a) Notwithstanding any other provision of law, simultaneously with promulgation or repromulgation of any rule or regulation under authority of title I of this Act, the head of the department, agency, or instrumentality promulgating such rule or regulation shall transmit a copy thereof to the Secretary of the Senate and the Clerk of the House of Representatives. Except as provided in subsection (b) of this section, the rule or regulation shall not become effective, if—

(1) within ninety calendar days of continuous session of Congress after the date of promulgation, both Houses of Congress adopt a concurrent resolution, the matter after the resolving clause of which is as follows: "That Congress disapproves the rule or regulation promulgated by the________________ dealing with the matter of________________, which rule or regulation was transmitted to Congress on________________", the blank spaces therein being appropriately filled; or

(2) within sixty calendar days of continuous session of Congress after the date of promulgation, one House of Congress adopts such a concurrent resolution and transmits such resolution to the other House, and such resolution is not disapproved by such other House within thirty calendar days of continuous session of Congress after such transmittal.

(b) If, at the end of sixty calendar days of continuous session of Congress after the date of promulgation of a rule or regulation, no committee of either House of Congress has reported or been discharged from further consideration of a concurrent resolution disapproving the rule or regulation and neither House has adopted such a resolution, the rule or regulation may go into effect immediately. If, within such sixty calendar days, such a committee has reported or been discharged from further consideration of such a resolution, or either House has adopted such a resolution, the rule or regulation may go into effect not sooner than ninety calendar days of continuous session of Congress after such rule is prescribed unless disapproved as provided in subsection (a) of this section.

(c) For purposes of subsections (a) and (b) of this section—

(1) continuity of session is broken only by an adjournment of Congress sine die; and

(2) the days on which either House is not in session because of an adjournment of more than three days to a day certain are excluded in the computation of thirty, sixty, and ninety calendar days of continuous session of Congress.

(d) Congressional inaction on, or rejection of, a resolution of disapproval shall not be deemed an expression of approval of such rule or regulation.

§9656. Transportation [Sec. 306]

(a) hazardous substance which is listed or designated as provided in section 101(14) of this Act shall, within 30 days after the enactment of the Superfund Amendments and Reauthorization Act of 1986 or at the time of such listing or designation, whichever is later, be listed and regulated as a hazardous material under the Hazardous Materials Transportation Act.

[§306(a) amended by PL 99–499]

(b) A common or contract carrier shall be liable under other law in lieu of section 107 of this Act for damages or remedial action resulting for the release of a hazardous substance during the course of transportation which commenced prior to the effective date of the listing and regulation of such substance as a hazardous material under the Hazardous Materials Transportation Act, or for substances listed pursuant to subsection (a) of this section, prior to the effective date of such listing: *Provided, however,* That this subsection shall not apply where such a carrier can demonstrate that he did not have actual knowledge of the identity or nature of the substance released.

[§306(b) amended by PL 99–499]

(c) Section 11901 of title 49, United States Code, is amended by—

(1) redesignating subsection (h) as subsection (i);

(2) by inserting "and subsection (h)" after "subsection (g)" in subsection (i)(2) as so redesignated by paragraph (1) of this subsection; and

(3) by inserting the following new subsection (h): "(h) A person subject to the jurisdiction of the Commission under subchapter II of chapter 105 of this title, or an officer, agent, or employee of that person, and who is required to comply with section 10921 of this title but does not so comply with respect to the transportation of hazardous wastes as defined by the Environmental Protection Agency pursuant to section 3001 of the Solid Waste Disposal Act (but not including any waste the regulation of which under the Solid Waste Disposal Act has been suspended by Congress) shall, in any action brought by the Commission, be liable to the United States for a civil penalty not to exceed $20,000 for each violation.".

Assistant Administrator for Solid Waste
[Sec. 307]

(a) Section 2001 of the Solid Waste Disposal Act is amended by striking out 'a Deputy Assistant' and inserting in lieu thereof 'an Assistant'.

(b) The Assistant Administrator of the Environmental Protection Agency appointed to head the Office of Solid Waste shall be in addition to the five Assistant Administrators of the Environmental Protection Agency provided for in section 1(d) of Reorganization Plan Numbered 3 of 1970 and the additional Assistant Administrator provided by the Toxic Substances Control Act, shall be appointed by the President by and with the advice and consent of the Senate.

[§307(b) amended by PL 98–80]

(c) The amendment made by subsection (a) shall become effective ninety days after the date of the enactment of this Act.

§9657. Separability [Sec. 308]

If any provision of this Act, or the application of any provision of this Act to any person or circumstance, is held invalid, the application of such provision to other persons or circumstances and the remainder of this Act shall not be affected thereby. If an administrative settlement under section 122 has the effect of limiting any person's right to obtain contribution from any party to such settlement, and if the effect of such limitation would constitute a taking without just compensation in violation of the fifth amendment of the Constitution of the United States, such person shall not be entitled, under other laws of the United States, to recover compensation from the United States for such taking, but in any such case, such limitation on the right to obtain contribution shall be treated as having no force and effect.

[§308 amended by PL 99–499]

§9658. Actions Under State Law for Damages from Exposure to Hazardous Substances.
[Sec. 309]

[§309 added by PL 99–499]

(a) State Statutes Of Limitations For Hazardous Substance Cases.—

(1) Exception To State Statutes.— In the case of any action brought under State law for personal injury, or property damages, which are caused or contributed to by exposure to any hazardous substance, or pollutant or contaminant, released into the environment from a facility, if the applicable limitations period for such action (as specified in the State statute of limitations or under common law) provides a commencement date which is earlier than the federally required commencement date, such period shall commence at the federally required commencement date in lieu of the date specified in such State statute.

(2) State Law Generally Applicable.— Except as provided in paragraph (1), the statute of limitations established under State law shall apply in all actions brought under State law for personal injury, or property damages, which are caused or contributed to by exposure to any hazardous substance, or pollutant or contaminant, released into the environment from a facility.

(3) Actions Under Section 107.— Nothing in this section shall apply with respect to any cause of action brought under section 107 of this Act.

(b) Definitions.— As used in this section —

(1) Title I Terms.— The terms used in this section shall have the same meaning as when used in title I of this Act.

(2) Applicable Limitations Period.— The term 'applicable limitations period' means the period specified in a statute of limitations during which a civil action referred to in subsection (a)(1) may be brought.

(3) Commencement Date.— The term 'commencement date' means the date specified in a statute of limitations as the beginning of the applicable limitations period.

(4) Federally Required Commencement Date.—

(A) In General.— Except as provided in subparagraph (B), the term 'federally required commencement date' means the date plaintiff knew (or reasonably should have known) that the personal injury or property damages referred to in subsection (a)(1) were caused or contributed to by the hazardous substance or pollutant or contaminant concerned.

(B) Special Rules.—In the case of a minor or incompetent plaintiff, the term 'federally required commencement date' means the later of the date referred to in subparagraph (A) or the following:

(i) In the case of a minor, the date on which the minor reaches the age of majority, as determined by State law, or has a legal representative appointed.

(ii) In the case of an incompetent individual, the date on which such individual becomes competent or has had a legal representative appointed.

§9659. Citizens Suits [Sec. 310]

[§310 added by PL 99–499]

(a) Authority To Bring Civil Actions.—Except as provided in subsections (d) and (e) of this section and in section 113(h) (relating to timing of judicial review), any person may commence a civil action on his own behalf—

(1) against any person (including the United States and any other governmental instrumen-

tality or agency, to the extent permitted by the eleventh amendment to the Constitution) who is alleged to be in violation of any standard, regulation, condition, requirement, or order which has become effective pursuant to this Act (including any provision of an agreement under section 120, relating to Federal facilities); or

(2) against the President or any other officer of the United States (including the Administrator of the Environmental Protection Agency and the Administrator of the ATSDR) where there is alleged a failure of the President or of such other officer to perform any act or duty under this Act, including an act or duty under section 120 (relating to Federal facilities), which is not discretionary with the President or such other officer. Paragraph (2) shall not apply to any act or duty under the provisions of section 311 (relating to research, development, and demonstration).

(b) Venue.—

(1) Actions Under Subsection (a)(1).— Any action under subsection (a) (1) shall be brought in the district court for the district in which the alleged violation occurred.

(2) Actions Under Subsection (a)(2).— Any action brought under subsection (a)(2) may be brought in the United States District Court for the District of Columbia.

(c) Relief.— The district court shall have jurisdiction in actions brought under subsection (a)(1) to enforce the standard, regulation, condition, requirement, or order concerned (including any provision of an agreement under section 120), to order such actions as may be necessary to correct the violation, and to impose any civil penalty provided for the violation. The district court shall have jurisdiction in actions brought under subsection (a) (2) to order the President or other officer to perform the act or duty concerned.

(d) Rules Applicable To Subsection (a)(1) Actions.—

(1) Notice. — No action may be commenced under subsection (a) (1) of this section before 60 days after the plaintiff has given notice of the violation to each of the following:

(A) The President.

(B) The State in which the alleged violation occurs.

(C) Any alleged violator of the standard, regulation, condition, requirement, or order concerned (including any provision of an agreement under section 120). Notice under this paragraph shall be given in such manner as the President shall prescribe by regulation.

(2) Diligent Prosecution. — No action may be commenced under paragraph (l) of subsection (a) if the President has commenced and is diligently prosecuting an action under this Act, or under the Solid Waste Disposal Act to require compliance with the standard, regulation, condition, requirement, or order concerned (including any provision of an agreement under section 120).

(e) Rules Applicable to Subsection (a)(2) Actions. — No action may be commenced under paragraph (2) of subsection (a) before the 60th day following the date on which the plaintiff gives notice to the Administrator or other department, agency, or instrumentality that the plaintiff will commence such action. Notice under this subsection shall be given in such manner as the President shall prescribe by regulation.

(f) Costs. — The court, in issuing any final order in any action brought pursuant to this section, may award costs of litigation (including reasonable attorney and expert witness fees) to the prevailing or the substantially prevailing party whenever the court determines such an award is appropriate. The court may, if a temporary restraining order or preliminary injunction is sought, require the filing of a bond or equivalent security in accordance with the Federal Rules of Civil Procedure.

(g) Intervention. — In any action under this section, the United States or the State, or both, if not a party may intervene as a matter of right. For other provisions regarding intervention, see section 113.

(h) Other Rights. — This Act does not affect or otherwise impair the rights of any person under Federal, State, or common law, except with respect to the timing of review as provided in section 113(h) or as otherwise provided in section 309 (relating to actions under State law).

(i) Definitions. — The terms used in this section shall have the same meanings as when used in title I.

§9660. Research, Development, and Demonstration [Sec. 311]

[§311 added by PL 99–499]

(a) Hazardous Substance Research and Training.—

(1) Authorities of secretary. — The Secretary of Health and Human Services (hereinafter in this subsection referred to as the Secretary), in

consultation with the Administrator, shall establish and support a basic research and training program (through grants, cooperative agreements, and contracts) consisting of the following:

(A) Basic research (including epidemiologic and ecologic studies) which may include each of the following:

(i) Advanced techniques for the detection, assessment, and evaluation of the effects on human health of hazardous substances.

(ii) Methods to assess the risks to human health presented by hazardous substances.

(iii) Methods and technologies to detect hazardous substances in the environment and basic biological, chemical, and physical methods to reduce the amount and toxicity of hazardous substances.

(B) Training, which may include each of the following:

(i) Short courses and continuing education for State and local health and environment agency personnel and other personnel engaged in the handling of hazardous substances, in the management of facilities at which hazardous substances are located, and in the evaluation of the hazards to human health presented by such facilities.

(ii) Graduate or advanced training in environmental and occupational health and safety and in the public health and engineering aspects of hazardous waste control.

(iii) Graduate training in the geosciences, including hydrogeology, geological engineering, geophysics, geochemistry, and related fields necessary to meet professional personnel needs in the public and private sectors and to effectuate the purposes of this Act.

(2) Director of NIEHS.— The Director of the National Institute for Environmental Health Sciences shall cooperate fully with the relevant Federal agencies referred to in subparagraph (A) of a paragraph (5) in carrying out the purposes of this section.

(3) Recipients of grants. etc.— A grant, cooperative agreement, or contract may be made or entered into under paragraph (1) with an accredited institution of higher education. The institution may carry out the research or training under the grant, cooperative agreement, or contract through contracts, including contracts with any of the following:

(A) Generators of hazardous wastes.

(B) Persons involved in the detection, assessment, evaluation, and treatment of hazardous substances.

(C) Owners and operators of facilities at which hazardous substances are located.

(D) State and local governments.

(4) Procedures.— In making grants and entering into cooperative agreements and contracts under this subsection, the Secretary shall act through the Director of the National Institute for Environmental Health Sciences. In considering the allocation of funds for training purposes, the Director shall ensure that at least one grant, cooperative agreement, or contract shall be awarded for training described in each of clauses (i), (ii), (iii) of paragraph (1)(B). Where applicable, the Director may choose to operate training activities in cooperation with the Director of the National Institute for Occupational Safety and Health. The procedures applicable to grants and contacts under title IV of the Public Health Service Act shall be followed under this subsection.

(5) Advisory council.— To assist in the implementation of this subsection and to aid in the coordination of research and demonstration and training activities funded from the Fund under this section, the Secretary shall appoint an advisory council (hereinafter in this subsection) which shall consist of representatives of the following:

(A) The relevant Federal agencies.

(B) The chemical industry.

(C) The toxic waste management industry.

(D) Institutions of higher education.

(E) State and local health and environmental agencies.

(F) The general public.

(6) Planning.— Within nine months after the date of the enactment of this subsection, the Secretary, acting through the Director of the National Institute for Environmental Health Sciences, shall issue a plan for the implementation of paragraph (1). The plan shall include priorities for actions under paragraph (1) and include research and training relevant to scientific and technological issues resulting from site specific hazardous substance response experience. The Secretary shall, to the maximum extent practicable, take appropriate steps to coordinate program activities under this plan with the activities of other Federal agencies in order to avoid duplication of effort. The plan shall be consistent with the need for the

development of new technologies for meeting the goals of response actions in accordance with the provisions of this Act. The Advisory Council shall be provided an opportunity to review and comment on the plan and priorities and assist appropriate coordination among the relevant Federal agencies referred to in subparagraph (A) of paragraph (5).

(b) Alternative or innovative treatment technology research and demonstration program.—

(1) Establishment.— The Administrator is authorized and directed to carry out a program of research, evaluation, testing, development, and demonstration of alternative or innovative treatment technologies (hereinafter in this subsection referred to as the "program") which may be utilized in response actions to achieve more permanent protection of human health and welfare and the environment.

(2) Administration. — The program shall be administered by the Administrator, acting through an office of technology demonstration and shall be coordinated with programs carried out by the Office of Solid Waste and Emergency Response and the Office of Research and Development.

(3) Contracts and Grants. — In carrying out the program, the Administrator is authorized to enter into contracts and cooperative agreements with, and make grants to, persons, public entities, and non-profit private entities which are exempt from tax under section 501(c)(3) of the Internal Revenue Code of 1954. The Administrator shall, to the maximum extent possible, enter into appropriate cost sharing arrangements under this subsection.

(4) Use of Sites. — In carrying out the program, the Administrator may arrange for the use of sites at which a response may be undertaken under section 104 for the purposes of carrying out research, testing, evaluation, development, and demonstration projects. Each such project shall be carried out under such terms and conditions as the Administrator shall require to assure the protection of human health and the environment and to assure adequate control by the Administrator of the research, testing, evaluation, development, and demonstration activities at the site.

(5) Demonstration Assistance. —

(A) Program Components. — The demonstration assistance program shall include the following:

(i) The publication of a solicitation and the evaluation of applications for demonstration projects utilizing alternative or innovative technologies.

(ii) The selection of sites which are suitable for the testing and evaluation of innovative technologies.

(iii) The development of detailed plans for innovative technology demonstration projects.

(iv) The supervision of such demonstration projects and the providing of quality assurance for data obtained.

(v) The evaluation of the results of alternative innovative technology demonstration projects and the determination of whether or not the technologies used are effective and feasible.

(B) Solicitation. — Within 90 days after the date of the enactment of this section, and no less often than once every 12 months thereafter, the Administrator shall publish a solicitation for innovative or alternative technologies at a stage of development suitable for full-scale demonstrations at sites at which a response action may be undertaken under section 104. The purpose of any such project shall be to demonstrate the use of an alternative or innovative treatment technology with respect to hazardous substances or pollutants or contaminants which are located at the site or which are to be removed from the site. The solicitation notice shall prescribe information to be included in the application, including technical and economic data derived from the applicant's own research and development efforts, and other information sufficient to permit the Administrator to assess the technology's potential and the types of remedial action to which it may be applicable.

(C) Applications. — Any person and any public or private nonprofit entity may submit an application to the Administrator in response to the solicitation. The application shall contain a proposed demonstration plan setting forth how and when the project is to be carried out and such other information as the Administrator may require.

(D) Project Selection. — In selecting technologies to be demonstrated, the Administrator shall fully review the applications submitted and shall consider at least the criteria specified in paragraph (7). The Administrator shall select or refuse to select a project for demonstration under this subsection within

90 days of receiving the completed application for such project. In the case of a refusal to select the project, the Administrator shall notify the applicant within such 90–day period of the reasons for his refusal.

(E) Site Selection. — The Administrator shall propose 10 sites at which a response may be undertaken under section 104 to be the location of any demonstration project under this subsection within 60 days after the close of the public comment period. After an opportunity for notice and public comment, the Administrator shall select such sites and projects. In selecting any such site, the Administrator shall take into account the applicant's technical data and preferences either for onsite operation or for utilizing the site as a source of hazardous substances or pollutants or contaminants to be treated offsite.

(F) Demonstration Plan. — Within 60 days after the selection of the site under this paragraph to be the location of a demonstration project, the Administrator shall establish a final demonstration plan for the project, based upon the demonstration plan contained in the application for the project. Such plan shall clearly set forth how and when the demonstration project will be carried out.

(G) Supervision and Testing. — Each demonstration project under this subsection shall be performed by the applicant, or by a person satisfactory to the applicant, under the supervision of the Administrator. The Administrator shall enter into a written agreement with each applicant granting the Administrator the responsibility and authority for testing procedures, quality control, monitoring, and other measurements necessary to determine and evaluate the results of the demonstration project. The Administrator may pay the costs of testing, monitoring, quality control, and other measurements required by the Administrator to determine and evaluate the results of the demonstration project, and the limitations established by subparagraph (J) shall not apply to such costs.

(H) Project Completion. — Each demonstration project under this subsection shall be completed within such time as is established in the demonstration plan.

(I) Extensions. — The Administrator may extend any deadline established under this paragraph by mutual agreement with the applicant concerned.

(J) Funding Restrictions. — The Administrator shall not provide any Federal assistance for any part of a full-scale field demonstration project under this subsection to any applicant unless such applicant can demonstrate that it cannot obtain appropriate private financing on reasonable terms and conditions sufficient to carry out such demonstration project without such Federal assistance. The total Federal funds for any full-scale field demonstration project under this subsection shall not exceed 50 percent of the total cost of such project estimated at the time of the award of such assistance. The Administrator shall not expend more than $ 10,000,000 for assistance under the program in any fiscal year and shall not expend more than $3,000,000 for any single project.

(6) Field Demonstrations. — In carrying out the program, the Administrator shall initiate or cause to be initiated at least 10 field demonstration projects of alternative or innovative treatment technologies at sites at which a response may be undertaken under section 104, in fiscal year 1987 and each of the succeeding three fiscal years. If the Administrator determines that 10 field demonstration projects under this subsection cannot be initiated consistent with the criteria set forth in paragraph (7) in any of such fiscal years, the Administrator shall transmit to the appropriate committees of Congress a report explaining the reasons for his inability to conduct such demonstration projects.

(7) Criteria. — In selecting technologies to be demonstrated under this subsection, the Administrator shall, consistent with the protection of human health and the environment, consider each of the following criteria:

(A) The potential for contributing to solutions to those waste problems which pose the greatest threat to human health, which cannot be adequately controlled under present technologies, or which otherwise pose significant management difficulties.

(B) The availability of technologies which have been sufficiently developed for field demonstration and which are likely to be cost-effective and reliable.

(C) The availability and suitability of sites for demonstrating such technologies, taking into account the physical, biological, chemical, and geological characteristics of the sites, the extent and type of contamination found at the site, and the capability to conduct demonstration projects in such a manner as to assure the protection of human health and the environment.

(D) The likelihood that the data to be generated from the demonstration project at the site will be applicable to other sites.

(8) Technology Transfer. — In carrying out the program, the Administrator shall conduct a technology transfer program including the development, collection, evaluation, coordination, and dissemination of information relating to the utilization of alternative or innovative treatment technologies for response actions. The Administrator shall establish and maintain a central reference library for such information. The information maintained by the Administrator shall be made available to the public, subject to the provisions of section 552 of title 5 of the United States Code and section 1905 of title 18 of the United States Code, and to other Government agencies in a manner that will facilitate its dissemination: except, that upon a showing satisfactory to the Administrator by any person that any information or portion thereof obtained under this subsection by the Administrator directly or indirectly from such person, would, if made public, divulge —

(A) trade secrets; or

(B) other proprietary information of such person, the Administrator shall not disclose such information and disclosure thereof shall be punishable under section 1905 of title 18 of the United States Code. This subsection is not authority to withhold information from Congress or any committee of Congress upon the request of the chairman of such committee.

(9) Training. — The Administrator is authorized and directed to carry out, through the Office of Technology Demonstration, a program of training and an evaluation of training needs for each of the following:

(A) Training in the procedures for the handling and removal of hazardous substances for employees who handle hazardous substances.

(B) Training in the management of facilities at which hazardous substances are located and in the evaluation of the hazards to human health presented by such facilities for State and local health and environment agency personnel.

(10) Definition. — For purposes of this subsection, the term 'alternative or innovative treatment technologies' means those technologies, including proprietary or patented methods, which permanently alter the composition of hazardous waste through chemical, biological, or physical means so as to significantly reduce the toxicity, mobility, or volume (or any combination thereof) of the hazardous waste or contaminated materials being treated. The term also includes technologies that characterize or assess the extent of contamination, the chemical and physical character of the contaminants, and the stresses imposed by the contaminants on complex ecosystems at sites.

(c) Hazardous Substance Research. — The Administrator may conduct and support, through grants, cooperative agreements, and contracts, research with respect to the detection, assessment, and evaluation of the effects on and risks to human health of hazardous substances and detection of hazardous substances in the environment. The Administrator shall coordinate such research with the Secretary of Health and Human Services, acting through the advisory council established under this section, in order to avoid duplication of effort.

(d) University Hazardous Substance Research Centers.—

(1) Grant program. — The Administrator shall make grants to institutions of higher learning to establish and operate not fewer than 5 hazardous substance research centers in the United States. In carrying out the program under this subsection, the Administrator should seek to have established and operated 10 hazardous substance research centers in the United States.

(2) Responsibilities of centers. — The responsibilities of each hazardous substance research center established under this subsection shall include, but not be limited to, the conduct of research and training relating to the manufacture, use, transportation, disposal and management of hazardous substances and publication and dissemination of the results of such research.

(3) Applications. — Any institution of higher learning interested in receiving a grant under this subsection shall submit to the Administrator an application in such form and containing such information as the Administrator may require by regulation.

(4) Selection criteria. — The Administrator shall select recipients of grants under this subsection on the basis of the following criteria:

(A) The hazardous substance research center shall be located in a State which is representative of the needs of the region in which such State is located for improved hazardous waste management.

(B) The grant recipient shall be located in an area which has experienced problems with hazardous substance management.

(C) There is available to the grant recipient for carrying out this subsection demonstrated research resources.

(D) The capability of the grant recipient to provide leadership in making national and regional contributions to the solution of both long-range and immediate hazardous substance management problems.

(E) The grant recipient shall make a commitment to support ongoing hazardous substance research programs with budgeted institutional funds of at least $100,000 per year.

(F) The grant recipient shall have an interdisciplinary staff with demonstrated expertise in hazardous substance management and research.

(G) The grant recipient shall have a demonstrated ability to disseminate results of hazardous substance research and educational programs through an interdisciplinary continuing education program.

(H) The projects which the grant recipient proposes to carry out under the grant are necessary and appropriate.

(5) Maintenance of effort. — No grant may be made under this subsection in any fiscal year unless the recipient of such grant enters into such agreements with the Administrator as the Administrator may require to ensure that such recipient will maintain its aggregate expenditures from all other sources for establishing and operating a regional hazardous substance research center and related research activities at or above the average level of such expenditures in its 2 fiscal years preceding the date of the enactment of this subsection.

(6) Federal share. — The Federal share of a grant under this subsection shall not exceed 80 percent of the costs of establishing and operating the regional hazardous substance research center and related research activities carried out by the grant recipient.

(7) Limitation on use of funds. — No funds made available to carry out this subsection shall be used for acquisition of real property (including buildings) or construction of any building.

(8) Administration through the office of the administrator. — Administrative responsibility for carrying out this subsection shall be in the Office of the Administrator.

(9) Equitable distribution of funds. — The Administrator shall allocate funds made available to carry out this subsection equitably among the regions of the United States.

(10) Technology transfer activities. — Not less than five percent of the funds made available to carry out this subsection for any fiscal year shall be available to carry out technology transfer activities.

(e) Report to Congress. — At the time of the submission of the annual budget request to Congress, the Administrator shall submit to the appropriate committees of the House of Representatives and the Senate and to the advisory council established under subsection (a), a report on the progress of the research, development, and demonstration program authorized by subsection (b), including an evaluation of each demonstration project completed in the preceding fiscal year, findings with respect to the efficacy of such demonstrated technologies in achieving permanent and significant reductions in risk from hazardous wastes, the costs of such demonstration projects, and the potential applicability of, and projected costs for, such technologies at other hazardous substance sites.

(f) Saving Provision. — Nothing in this section shall be construed to affect the provisions of the Solid Waste Disposal Act.

(g) Small Business Participation. — The Administrator shall ensure, to the maximum extent practicable, an adequate opportunity for small business participation in the program established by subsection (b).

[Editor's Note: Section 213(a)(2) of PL 99–499 added a new §312 to CERCLA Regarding Love Canal. §213(a)(2) gave the following explanation of the need for special provisions: (2) Because Love Canal came to the Nation's attention prior to the passage of CERCLA and because the fund under CERCLA was not available to compensate for all of the hardships endured by the citizens in the area, Congress has determined that special provisions are required. These provisions do not affect the lawfulness, implementation, or selection of any other response actions at Love Canal or at any other facilities.]

§9661. Love Canal Property Acquisition
[Sec. 312]

[§312 added by PL 99–499]

(a) Acquisition of Property in Emergency Declaration Area. — The Administrator of the Environmental Protection Agency (hereinafter referred to as the "Administrator") may make grants not to exceed $2,500,000 to the State of New York (or to any duly constituted public agency or authority thereof) for purposes of acquisition of private property in the Love Canal Emergency Declaration Area. Such acquisition shall include (but shall not be limited to) all private property within the Emergency Declaration Area, including non-owner occupied residential properties, commercial, industrial, public, religious, non-profit, and vacant properties.

(b) Procedures for Acquisition. — No property shall be acquired pursuant to this section unless the property owner voluntarily agrees to such acquisition. Compensation for any property acquired pursuant to this section shall be based upon the fair market value of the property as it existed prior to the emergency declaration. Valuation procedures for property acquired with funds provided under this section shall be in accordance with those set forth in the agreement entered into between the New York State Disaster Preparedness Commission and the Love Canal Revitalization Agency on October 9, 1980.

(c) State Ownership. — The Administrator shall not provide any funds under this section for the acquisition of any properties pursuant to this section unless a public agency or authority of the State of New York first enters into a cooperative agreement with the Administrator providing assurances deemed adequate by the Administrator that the State or an agency created under the laws of the State shall take title to the properties to be so acquired.

(d) Maintenance of Property. — The Administrator shall enter into a cooperative agreement with an appropriate public agency or authority of the State of New York under which the Administrator shall maintain or arrange for the maintenance of all properties within the Emergency Declaration Area that have been acquired by any public agency or authority of the State. Ninety (90) percent of the costs of such maintenance shall be paid by the Administrator. The remaining portion of such costs shall be paid by the State (unless a credit is available under section 104(c)). The Administrator is authorized, in his discretion, to provide technical assistance to any public agency or authority of the State of New York in order to implement the recommendations of the habitability and land-use study in order to put the land within the Emergency Declaration Area to its best use.

(e) Habitability and Land Use Study. —The Administrator shall conduct or cause to be conducted a habitability and land-use study. The study shall—

(1) assess the risks associated with inhabiting of the Love Canal Emergency Declaration Area;

(2) compare the level of hazardous waste contamination in that Area to that present in other comparable communities; and

(3) assess the potential uses of the land within the Emergency Declaration Area, including but not limited to residential, industrial, commercial and recreational, and the risks associated with such potential uses.

The Administrator shall publish the findings of such study and shall work with the State of New York to develop recommendations based upon the results of such study.

(f) Funding. — For purposes of section 111 and 221(c) of this Act, the expenditures authorized by this section shall be treated as a cost specified in section 111(c).

(g) Response. — The provisions of this section shall not affect the implementation of other response actions within the Emergency Declaration Area that the Administrator has determined (before enactment of this section) to be necessary to protect the public health or welfare or the environment.

(h) Definitions. — For purposes of this section:

(i) Emergency declaration area. — The terms 'Emergency Declaration Area' and 'Love Canal Emergency Declaration Area' mean the Emergency Declaration Area as defined in section 950, paragraph (2) of the General Municipal Law of the State of New York, Chapter 259, Laws of 1980, as in effect on the date of the enactment of this section.

(2) Private property — As used in subsection (a), the term 'private property, means all property which is not owned by a department, agency, or instrumentality of—

(A) the United States, or

(B) the State of New York (or any public agency or authority thereof).

§9662. Limitation on Contract and Borrowing Authority [Sec. 313]

Any authority provided by this Act, including any amendment made by this Act, to enter into contracts to obligate the United States or to incur indebtedness for the repayment of which the United States is liable shall be effective only to such extent or in such amounts as are provided in appropriation Acts.

TITLE IV — POLLUTION INSURANCE

[Added by PL 99–499]

§9671. Definitions [Sec. 401]

As used in this title—

(1) Insurance. — The term 'insurance' means primary insurance, excess insurance, reinsurance, surplus lines insurance, and any other arrangement for shifting and distributing risk which is determined to be insurance under applicable State or Federal law.

(2) Pollution liability. — The term 'pollution liability' means liability for injuries arising from the release of hazardous substances or pollutants or contaminants.

(3) Risk retention group. — The term 'risk retention group' means any corporation or other limited liability association taxable as a corporation, or as an insurance company, formed under the laws of any State—

(A) whose primary activity consists of assuming and spreading all, or any portion, of the pollution liability of its group members;

(B) which is organized for the primary purpose of conducting the activity described under subparagraph (A);

(C) which is chartered or licensed as an insurance company and authorized to engage in the business of insurance under the laws of any State; and

(D) which does not exclude any person from membership in the group solely to provide for members of such a group a competitive advantage over such a person.

(4) Purchasing group. — The term 'purchasing group' means any group of persons which has as one of its purposes the purchase of pollution liability insurance on a group basis.

(5) State. — The term 'State' means any State of the United States, the District of Columbia, the Commonwealth of Puerto Rico, Guam, American Samoa, the Virgin Islands, the Commonwealth of the Northern Marianas, and any other territory or possession over which the United States has jurisdiction.

§9672. State Laws; Scope of Title [Sec. 402]

(a) State Laws. — Nothing in this title shall be construed to affect either the tort law or the law governing the interpretation of insurance contracts of any State. The definitions of pollution liability and pollution liability insurance under any State law shall not be applied for the purposes of this title, including recognition or qualification of risk retention groups or purchasing groups.

(b) Scope of Title. — The authority to offer or to provide insurance under this title shall be limited to coverage of pollution liability risks and this title does not authorize a risk retention group or purchasing group to provide coverage of any other line of insurance.

§9673. Risk Retention Groups [Sec. 403]

(a) Exemption. — Except as provided in this section, a risk retention group shall be exempt from the following:

(1) A State law, rule, or order which makes unlawful, or regulates, directly or indirectly, the operation of a risk retention group.

(2) A State law, rule, or order which requires or permits a risk retention group to participate in any insurance insolvency guaranty association to which an insurer licensed in the State is required to belong.

(3) A State law, rule, or order which requires any insurance policy issued to a risk retention group or any member of the group to be countersigned by an insurance agent or broker residing in the State.

(4) A State law, rule, or order which otherwise discriminates against a risk retention group or any of its members.

(b) Exceptions.—

(1) State laws generally applicable.— Nothing in subsection (a) shall be construed to affect the applicability of State laws generally applicable to persons or corporations. The State in which a risk retention group is chartered may regulate the formation and operation of the group.

(2) State regulations not subject to exemption. — Subsection (a) shall not apply to any State law which requires a risk retention group to do any of the following:

(A) Comply with the unfair claim settlement practices law of the State.

(B) Pay, on a nondiscriminatory basis, applicable premium and other taxes which are levied on admitted insurers and surplus line insurers, brokers, or policyholders under the laws of the State.

(C) Participate, on a nondiscriminatory basis, in any mechanism established or authorized under the law of the State for the equitable apportionment among insurers of pollution liability insurance losses and expenses incurred on policies written through such mechanism.

(D) Submit to the appropriate authority reports and other information required of licensed insurers under the laws of a State relating solely to pollution liability insurance losses and expenses.

(E) Register with and designate the State insurance commissioner as its agent solely for the purpose of receiving service of legal documents or process.

(F) Furnish, upon request, such commissioner a copy of any financial report submitted by the risk retention group to the commissioner of the chartering or licensing jurisdiction.

(G) Submit to an examination by the State insurance commissioner in any State in which the group is doing business to determine the group's financial condition, if—

(i) the commissioner has reason to believe the risk retention group is in a financially impaired condition; and

(ii) the commissioner of the jurisdiction in which the group is chartered has not begun or has refused to initiate an examination of the group.

(H) Comply with a lawful order issued in a delinquency proceeding commenced by the State insurance commissioner if the commissioner of the jurisdiction in which the group is chartered has failed to initiate such a proceeding after notice of a finding of financial impairment under subparagraph (G).

(c) Application of Exemptions. — The exemptions specified in subsection (a) apply to—

(1) pollution liability insurance coverage provided by a risk retention group for—

(A) such group; or

(B) any person who is a member of such group;

(2) the sale of pollution liability insurance coverage for a risk retention group; and

(3) the provision of insurance related services or management services for a risk retention group or any member of such a group.

(d) Agents or Brokers — A State may require that a person acting, or offering to act, as an agent or broker for a risk retention group obtain a license from that State, except that a State may not impose any qualification or requirement which discriminates against a nonresident agent or broker.

42 U.S.C. §9674

§9674. Purchasing Groups [Sec. 404]

(a) Exemption. — Except as provided in this section, a purchasing group is exempt from the following:

(1) A State law, rule, or order which prohibits the establishment of a purchasing group.

(2) A State law, rule, or order which makes it unlawful for an insurer to provide or offer to provide insurance on a basis providing, to a purchasing group or its member, advantages, based on their loss and expense experience, not afforded to other persons with respect to rates, policy forms, coverages, or other matters.

(3) A State law, rule, or order which prohibits a purchasing group or its members from purchasing insurance on the group basis described in paragraph (2) of this subsection.

(4) A State law, rule, or order which prohibits a purchasing group from obtaining insurance on a group basis because the group has not been in existence for a minimum period of time or because any member has not belonged to the group for a minimum period of time.

(5) A State law, rule, or order which requires that a purchasing group must have a minimum number of members, common ownership or affiliation, or a certain legal form.

(6) A State law, rule, or order which requires that a certain percentage of a purchasing group must obtain insurance on a group basis.

(7) A State law, rule, or order which requires that any insurance policy issued to a purchasing group or any members of the group be countersigned by an insurance agent or broker residing in that State.

(8) A State law, rule, or order which otherwise discriminate against a purchasing group or any of its members.

(b) Application of Exemptions. — The exemptions specified in subsection (a) apply to the following:

(1) Pollution liability insurance, and comprehensive general liability insurance which includes this coverage, provided to —

(A) a purchasing group; or

(B) any person who is a member of a purchasing group.

(2) The sale of any one of the following to a purchasing group or a member of the group:

(A) Pollution liability insurance and comprehensive general liability coverage.

(B) Insurance related services.

(C) Management services.

(c) Agents or Brokers. — A State may require that a person acting, or offering to act, as an agent or broker for a purchasing group obtain a license from that State, except that a State may not impose any qualification or requirement which discriminates against a nonresident agent or broker.

§9675. Applicability of Securities Laws
[Sec. 405]

(a) Ownership Interests. — The ownership interests of members of a risk retention group shall be considered to be —

(1) exempted securities for purposes of section 5 of the Securities Act of 1933 and for purposes of section 12 of the Securities Exchange Act of 1934; and

(2) securities for purposes of the provisions of section 17 of the Securities Act of 1933 and the provisions of section 10 of the Securities Exchange Act of 1934.

(b) Investment Company Act. — A risk retention group shall not be considered to be an investment company for purposes of the Investment Company Act of 1940 (15 U.S.C. 80a–1 et seq.).

(c) Blue Sky Law. — The ownership interests of members in a risk retention group shall not be considered securities for purposes of any State blue sky law.

ADDITIONAL PROVISIONS

[Editor's Note: Section 118 of PL 99–499 did not amend this act directly, but concerns remedial actions for certain states, submission of reports, and establishment of research and demonstration centers. The text of the relevant provisions follows.]

Removal and Temporary Storage of Containers of Radon [Sec. 118]

(b) Contaminated Soil. — Not later than 90 days after the enactment of this Act, the Administrator shall make a grant of $7,500,000 to the State of New Jersey for transportation from residential areas in the State of New Jersey and temporary storage of approximately 14,000 containers of radon contaminated soil which is the subject of a remedial action for which a remedial investigation and feasibility study has been initiated before such date. Such containers shall be transported to and temporarily stored at any site in the State of New Jersey designated by the Governor of such State. For purposes of section 111(a) of CERCLA, the grant under this subsection for transportation and storage of such containers shall be treated as payment of governmental response cost incurred pursuant to section 104 of CERCLA.

(c) Unconsolidated Quarternary Aquifer. — Notwithstanding any other provision of law, no person may —

(1) locate or authorize the location of a landfill, surface impoundment, waste pile, injection well, or land treatment facility over the Unconsolidated Quarternary Aquifer, or the recharge zone or streamflow source zone of such aquifer, in the Rockaway River Basin, New Jersey (as such aquifer and zones are described in the Federal Register, January 24, 1984, pages 2946–2948); or

(2) place or authorize the placement of solid waste in a landfill, surface impoundment, waste pile, injection well, or land treatment facility over such aquifer or zone. This subsection may be enforced under sections 309(a) and (b) of the Federal Water Pollution Control Act. For purposes of section 309(c) of such Act, a violation of this subsection shall be considered a violation of section 301 of such Act.

(d) Study of Shortages of Skilled Personnel. — The Comptroller General shall study the problem of shortages of skilled personnel in the Environmental Protection Agency to carry out response actions under CERCLA. In particular the Comptroller General shall study —

(1) the types of skilled personnel needed for response actions for which there are shortages in the Environmental Protection Agency,

(2) the extent of such shortages,

(3) paloy differential between the public and private sectors for the skilled positions involved it, response actions,

(4) the extent to which skilled personnel of Federal and State governments involved in response actions are leaving their positions for employment in the private sector,

(5) the success of programs of the Department of Defense and the Office of Personnel Management in retaining skilled personnel, and

(6) the types of training required to improve the skills of employees carrying out response actions. The Comptroller General shall complete the study required by this subsection and submit a report on the results thereof to Congress not later than July 1, 1987.

(e) State Requirements Not Applicable to Certain Transfers. — No State or local requirement shall apply to the transfer and disposal of any hazardous substance or pollutant or contaminant from a facility at which a release or threatened release has occurred to a facility for which a final permit under section 3005(a) of the Solid Waste Disposal Act is in effect if the following conditions apply —

(1) Such permit was issued after January 1, 1983, and before November 1, 1984.

(2) The transfer and disposal is carried out pursuant to a cooperative agreement between the Administrator and the State.

(3) The facility at which the release or threatened release has occurred is identified as the McColl Site in Fullerton, California. The terms used in this section shall have the same meaning as when used in title I of CERCLA.

(f) Study of Lead Poisoning in Children. — (1) The Administrator of the Agency for Toxic Substances and Disease Registry shall, in consultation with the Administrator of the Environmental Protection Agency and other officials as appropriate, not later than March 1, 1987, submit to the Congress, a report on the nature and extent of lead poisoning in children from environmental sources. Such report shall include, at a minimum, the following information —

(A) an estimate of the total number of children, arrayed according to Standard Metropolitan Statistical Area or other appropriate geographic unit, exposed to environmental sources of lead at concentrations sufficient to cause adverse health effects;

(B) an estimate of the total number of children exposed to environmental sources of lead arrayed according to source or source types;

(C) a statement of the long-term consequences for public health of unabated exposures to environmental sources of lead and including but not limited to,

diminution in intelligence, increases in morbidity and mortality; and

(D) methods and alternatives available for reducing exposures of children to environmental sources of lead.

(2) Such report shall also score and evaluate specific sites at which children are known to be exposed to environmental sources of lead due to releases, utilizing the Hazard Ranking system of the National Priorities List.

(3) The costs of preparing and submitting the report required by this section shall be borne by the Hazardous Substance Superfund established under subchapter A of chapter 98 of Internal Revenue Code of 1954.

(g) Federally Licensed Dam. — For purposes of CERCLA in the case of the Milltown Dam in the State of Montana licensed under part I of the Federal Power Act and designated as FERC license number 2543–004, if a hazardous substance, pollutant, or contaminant —

(1) has been released into the environment upstream of the dam, and

(2) has subsequently come to be located in the reservoir created by such dam notwithstanding section 101(20) of such Act, the term "owner or operator" does not include the owner or operator of the dam unless such owner or operator is a person who would otherwise be liable for such release or threatened release under section 107 of such Act.

(h) Community Relocation at Times Beach Site. — For purposes of any Missouri dioxin site at which a temporary or permanent relocation decision has been made, or is under active consideration, by the Administrator as of the enactment of this Act, the terms "remove" and "removal" as used in CERCLA shall be deemed to include the costs of permanent relocation of residents where it is determined that such permanent relocation is cost effective or may be necessary to protect health or welfare. In the case of a business located in an area of evacuation or relocation at such facility, such terms may also include the payment of those installments of principal and interest on business debt which accrue between the date of evacuation or temporary relocation and 30 days following the date that permanent relocation is actually accomplished or, if permanent relocation is formally rejected as the appropriate response, the date on which evacuation or temporary relocation ceases. In the case of an individual unemployed as a result of such evacuation or relocation, such terms may also include the provision of assistance identical to that authorized by sections 407, 408, and 409 of the Disaster Relief Act of 1974; except that the costs of such assistance shall be paid from the Trust Fund established under amendments made to the Internal Revenue Code of 1954 by this Act. Section 104(c)(1) of CERCLA shall not apply to obligations from the Fund for permanent relocation under this paragraph.

(i) Limited Waivers in State of Illinois.—

(1) Mobile incinerators. — In the case of remedial actions specifically involving mobile incinerator units in the State of Illinois, if such remedial actions are undertaken by the State under the authority of a State Superfund law or equivalent authority, the State may, with the approval of the Administrator, waive any permit requirement under subtitle C of the Solid Waste Disposal Act which would be otherwise applicable to such action to the extent that the following conditions are met:

(A) No transfer. — The incinerator does not involve the transfer of a hazardous substance or pollutant or contaminant from the facility in which the release or threatened release occurs to an offsite facility.

(B) Remedial action. — The remedial action provides each of the following:

(i) Changes in the character or composition of the hazardous substance or pollutant or contaminant concerned so that it no longer presents a risk to public health.

(ii) Protection against accidental emissions during operation.

(iii) Protection of public health considering the multimedia impacts of the treatment process.

(C) Public participation. — The State provides procedures for public participation regarding the response action which are at least equivalent to the level of public participation procedures applicable under CERCLA and under the Solid Waste Disposal Act.

(2) Effect of waiver. — The waiver of any permit requirement under this subsection shall not be construed to waive any standard or level of control which—

(A) is applicable to any hazardous substance or pollutant or contaminant involved in the remedial action; and

(B) would otherwise be contained in the permit. Such waiver of any permit requirement under subtitle C of the Solid Waste Disposal Act shall only apply to the extent that the facility or remedial action involves the onsite treatment with a mobile incineration of waste present at such site. The waiver shall not apply to any other regulated or potentially regulated activity, including the use of the mobile incineration unit for actions not authorized by the State.

(3) Expiration of Authority. — The authority of this subsection shall terminate at the end of 3 years, unless the State demonstrates, to the satisfaction of the Administrator, that the operation of mobile incinerators in the State has sufficiently protected public health and the environment and is consistent with the criteria required for a permit under subtitle C of the Solid Waste Disposal Act.

(j) Study of Joint Use of Trucks.—

(1) Study. — The Administrator, in consultation with the Secretary of Transportation, shall conduct a study of problems associated with the use of any vehicle for purposes other than the transportation of hazardous substances when that vehicle is used at other times for the transportation of hazardous substances. At a minimum, the Administrator shall consider—

(A) whether such joint use of vehicles should be prohibited, and

(B) whether, if such joint use is permitted, special safeguards should be taken to minimize threats to public health and the environment.

(2) Report. — The Administrator shall submit a report, along with recommendations, to Congress on the results of the study conducted under paragraph (1) not later than 180 days after the date of the enactment of this Act.

(k) Radon Assessment and Mitigation.—

(1) National assessment of radon gas. —No later than one year after the enactment of this Act, the Administrator shall submit to the Congress a report which shall, to the extent possible—

(A) identify the locations in the United States where radon is found in structures where people normally live or work, including educational institutions;

(B) assess the levels of radon gas that are present in such structures;

(C) determine the level of radon gas and radon daughters which poses a threat to human health and assess for each location identified under subparagraph (A) the extent of the threat to human health;

(D) determine methods of reducing or eliminating the threat to human health of radon gas and radon daughters; and

(E) include guidance and public information materials based on the findings or research of mitigating radon.

(2) Radon mitigation demonstration program.—

(A) Demonstration program. — The Administrator shall conduct a demonstration program to test methods and technologies of reducing or eliminating radon gas and radon daughters where it poses a threat to human health. The Administrator shall take into consideration any demonstration program underway in the Reading Prong of Pennsylvania, New Jersey, and New York and at other sites prior to enactment. The demonstration program under this section shall be conducted in the Reading Prong, and at such other sites as the Administrator considers appropriate.

(B) Annual reports. — The Administrator shall submit annual reports not later than February 1 of each year (beginning February 1, 1987) on the status of the demonstration program carried out under this subsection and on any such demonstration program initiated prior to enactment.

(C) Liability. — Liability, if any, for persons undertaking activities pursuant to the radon mitigation demonstration program authorized under this subsection shall be determined under principles of existing law.

(3) Construction of section. — Nothing in this subsection shall be construed to authorize the Administrator to carry out any regulatory program or any activity other than research, development, and related reporting, information dissemination, and coordination activities specified in this subsection. Nothing in paragraph (1) or (2) shall be construed to limit the authority of the Administrator or of any other agency or instrumentality of the United States under any other-authority of law.

(l) Gulf Coast Hazardous Substance Research, Development, and Demonstration Center. —

(1) Establishment of hazardous substance research, development, and demonstration center. — The Administrator shall establish a hazardous substance research, development, and demonstration center (hereinafter in this subsection referred to as the "Center") for the purpose of conducting research to aid in more effective hazardous substance response and waste management throughout the Gulf Coast.

(2) Purposes of the center. — The Center shall carry out a program of research, evaluation, testing, development, and demonstration of alternative or innovative technologies which may be utilized in response actions or in normal handling of hazardous wastes to achieve better protection of human health and the environment.

(3) Operation of center. —

(A) For purposes of operating the Center, the Administrator is authorized to enter into contracts and cooperative agreements with, and make grants to, a university related institute involved with the improvement of waste management. Such institute shall be located in Jefferson County, Texas.

Additional Provisions

(B) The Center shall be authorized to make grants, accept contributions, and enter into agreements with universities located in the States of Texas, Louisiana, Mississippi, Alabama, and Florida in order to carry out the purposes of the Center.

(4) Authorization of appropriations. — There are authorized to be appropriated to the Administrator for purposes of carrying out this subsection for fiscal years beginning after September 30, 1986, not more than $5,000,000.

(m) Radon Protection at Current National Priorities List Sites. — It is the sense of the Congress that the President, in selecting response action for facilities included on the National Priorities List published under section 105 of the Comprehensive Environmental Response, Compensation, and Liability Act of 1980 because of the presence of radon, is not required by statute or regulations to use fully demonstrated methods, particularly those involving the offsite transport and disposition of contaminated material, but may use innovative or alternative methods which protect human health and the environment in a more cost-effective manner.

(n) Spill Control Technology.—

(1) Establishment of program. — Within 180 days of enactment of this subsection, the Secretary of the United States Department of Energy is directed to carry out a program of testing and evaluation of technologies which may be utilized in responding to liquefied gaseous and other hazardous substance spills at the Liquefied Gaseous Fuels Spill Test Facility that threaten public health or the environment.

(2) Technology transfer. — In carrying out the program established under this subsection, the Secretary shall conduct a technology transfer program that, at a minimum—

(A) documents and archives spill control technology;

(B) investigates and analyzes significant hazardous spill incidents;

(C) develops and provides generic emergency action plans;

(D) documents and archives spill test results;

(E) develops emergency action plans to respond to spills;

(F) conducts training of spill response personnel; and

(G) establishes safety standards for personnel engaged in spill response activities.

(3) Contracts and grants. — The Secretary is directed to enter into contracts and grants with a nonprofit organization in Albany County, Wyoming, that is capable of providing the necessary technical support and which is involved in environmental activities related to such hazardous substance related emergencies.

(4) Use of site. — The Secretary shall arrange for the use of the Liquefied Gaseous Fuels Spill Test Facility to carry out the provisions of this subsection.

(o) Pacific Northwest Hazardous Substance Research, Development, and Demonstration Center.—

(1) Establishment. — The Administrator shall establish a hazardous substance research, development, and demonstration center (hereinafter in this subsection referred to as the "Center") for the purpose of conducting research to aid in more effective hazardous substance response in the Pacific Northwest.

(2) Purposes of center. — The Center shall carry out a program of research, evaluation, testing, development, and demonstration of alternative or innovative technologies which may be utilized in response actions to achieve more permanent protection of human health and welfare and the environment.

(3) Operation of center.—

(A) Nonprofit entity. — For the purposes of operating the Center, the Administrator is authorized to enter into contracts and cooperative agreements with, and make grants to, a nonprofit private entity as defined in section 201(i) of Public Law 96–517 which entity shall agree to provide the basic technical and management personnel. Such nonprofit private entity shall also agree to provide at least two permanent research facilities, one of which shall be located in Benton County, Washington, and one of which shall be located in Clallam County, Washington.

(B) Authorities. — The Center shall be authorized to make grants, accept contributions, and enter into agreements with universities located in the States of Washington, Oregon, Idaho, and Montana in order to carry out the purposes of the Center.

(4) Hazardous waste research at the Hanford site.—

(A) Interagency agreements. — The Administrator and the Secretary of Energy are authorized to enter into interagency agreements with one another for the purpose of providing for research, evaluation, testing, development, and demonstration into alternative or innovative technologies to characterize and assess the nature and extent of hazardous waste (including radioactive mixed waste) contamination at the Hanford site, in the State of Washington.

(B) Funding. — There is authorized to be appropriated to the Secretary of Energy for purposes of carrying out this paragraph for fiscal years beginning after September 30, 1986, not more than $5,000,000. All sums appropriated under this subparagraph shall be provided to the Administrator by the Secretary of Energy, pursuant to the interagency agreement entered into under subparagraph (A), for the purpose of the Administrator entering into contracts and cooperative agreements with, and making grants to, the Center in order to carry out the research, evaluation, testing, development, and demonstration described in paragraph (1).

(5) Authorization of appropriations. — There is authorized to be appropriated to the Administrator for purposes of carrying out this subsection (other than paragraph (4)) for fiscal years beginning after September 30, 1986, not more than $5,000,000.

(p) Silver Creek Tailings. — Effective with the date of enactment of this Act, the facility listed in Group 7 in EPA National Priorities List Update #4 (50 Federal Register 37956, September 18, 1985), the site in Park City, Utah, which is located on tailings from noncoal mining operations, shall be deemed removed from the list of sites recommended for inclusion on the National Priorities List, unless the President determines upon site specific data not used in the proposed listing of such facility, that the facility meets requirements of the Hazard Ranking System or any revised Hazard Ranking System.

5

The Safe Drinking Water Act

INTRODUCTION

The Safe Drinking Water Act was passed by Congress in 1974, despite opposition from the Ford Administration and from the National Governors' Conference.

Although the Senate had approved drinking water legislation in 1973, progress in the House of Representatives bogged down amid widespread misunderstanding about the House bill's provisions, particularly concerning the enforcement authority of the Environmental Protection Agency. Late in the year, however, reports of two studies were crucial in arousing public opinion and swaying the House from its months of delay.

On November 7, 1973, the Environmental Defense Fund, releasing preliminary findings of a study of drinking water in New Orleans, said there was a "significant relationship" between cancer mortality in the study group and drinking water from the Mississippi River. The next day, EPA announced that its own study of New Orleans drinking water had detected 66 potentially carcinogenic organic chemicals, and that New Orleans was not an isolated case. On November 19, 1973, the House approved the legislation (HR 13002) without significant opposition on the floor. A House aide said at the time that a vote against the bill would have been seen as "pro-cancer."

The House-passed measure included provisions that required EPA to set mandatory drinking water standards and controls on underground injection of hazardous waste. Under the House scheme, the states would have primary responsibility for enforcing the law's provisions. The Senate's version contained provisions for citizen suits and strong enforcement by EPA, but lacked the underground injection provisions of the House bill. On November 26, 1974, the Senate gave its approval to the House legislation, adding the citizen suit and civil penalties provisions from its own bill. On December 3, 1974, the House approved the Senate amendments by unanimous consent. Despite earlier fears that he might veto it, President Ford signed the measure.

Authorization of appropriations for the original law expired at the end of fiscal 1982, but reauthorization was not easy. An early effort in the Senate (S 1866) went nowhere before the 97th Congress adjourned. In the 98th Congress, legislation (HR 5959) was passed by the House, but a measure in the Senate (S 2649) never came up for a floor vote.

Final action came on the drinking water reauthorization in the 99th Congress, with the Senate passing legislation (S 124) in 1985 that eventually became the Safe Drinking Water Act Amendments of 1986. In its report on S 124 (SRep 99-56), the Senate Environment and Public Works Committee wrote that the amendments were crafted to "rectify major deficiencies" in the drinking water programs.

Under the amended law, EPA is required to list, every three years, contaminants that must be regulated to protect the public's health. Two years after listing, standards—in the form of maximum contaminant levels (national primary drinking water regulations) or maximum contaminant level goals (formerly called recommended maximum contaminant levels)—must be proposed. Within a year of their proposal, these standards must be issued in final form. The law specifies a schedule for setting standards for the substances listed in the conference report on the amendments.

To address the problem noted in the Senate report concerning viral and bacterial contamination, Congress specified in the amendments that EPA must establish criteria for when water utilities must filter surface water that is used for drinking water. The amendments also required the agency to issue national primary drinking water regulations regarding disinfection of drinking water. In June 1989, EPA issued regulations requiring 10,000 water supply systems across the United States to install or improve the bacterial filtration systems. Implementation was estimated to cost $3 billion.

Two incidents in 1993 could cause even further action to provide additional protection, at even greater cost, for microorganisms such as cryptosporidium. In mid-1993, the organism was found in Milwaukee's drinking water, causing thousands of people who drank the water to become ill, some seriously. Then in December 1993, a similar scare was raised in the Washington, D.C., area when high turbidity levels were detected at a filtration plant run by the U.S. Army Corps of Engineers following heavy rains—a situation similar to that preceding the Milwaukee incident—led federal officials to declare a drinking water emergency in the nation's capital. The Natural Resources Defense Council called on Congress to strengthen the law's health standards for dealing with contaminants such as cryptosporidium.

In August 1989, EPA's Steering Committee approved a development plan for a rule-making on drinking water disinfectants and the byproducts of disinfection. A negotiated rule-making committee was constituted, and it finished its deliberations in July 1993. On February 10, 1994, EPA issued the first of three proposals in a regulatory package on disinfectants and disinfection by-products. This first proposal (59 FR 6332) requires public drinking water systems serving more than 10,000 people to provide EPA with monitoring data and other information.

Final SDWA rules to limit exposure to lead and copper in drinking water were expected by November 1990 but were not issued until June 1991 (56 FR 26460). The rules establish a maximum contaminant level goal of zero for lead and 1.3 milligram per liter for copper. The rules also required drinking water systems to monitor water at the tap and to institute control measures if lead exceeded an action level of 15 parts of lead per billion parts of water. These measures include corrosion control, source water treatment, replacement of lead service lines, and public education. The agency said its new standard corresponds to a level of 5 ppb of lead in drinking water, 10 times more stringent that the previous standard of 50 ppb.

The agency missed an October 1, 1993, deadline for issuing a standard for radionuclides in drinking water, but on February 11, 1994, an agreement was reached with Bull Run Coalition, an Oregon-based activist group that had sued EPA for not meeting the compliance schedules in the Act, on a new schedule for a series of rule-makings. The agreement would affect publication of rules on trihalomethanes, fluoride, sulfate, and radionuclides.

Concerns about lead in drinking water also resulted in the Lead Contamination Control Act of 1988 (HR 4939), a measure that amended the SDWA to require the recall of lead-lined water coolers. Lead levels in drinking water received widespread public attention in early summer 1988, after a government study revealed that 8 out of 12 water coolers tested contained lead liners.

Lead from coolers was leaching into the drinking water at levels greater than the current 50 ppb standard. Members of Congress criticized EPA, asserting that the agency was moving too slowly on lead problems.

With the SDWA due for reauthorization in 1994, the Clinton Administration sent Congress a set of recommendations in September 1993. It asked for $600 million in fiscal 1994 for a safe drinking water revolving loan fund, patterned after the Clean Water Act's state revolving fund, to help local drinking water systems meet the ever-increasing costs of compliance with the act. Across the nation, states had raised a cry about the compliance costs, and some had said they could no longer afford to run their programs and would seek to turn them back to the federal government. A second proposal would create a users fee, modeled after the Clean Air Act permit fees, for states that need funds to oversee drinking water quality. The administration also told Congress that states should have the flexibility to consolidate small, uneconomical systems, bringing them into larger systems where they could share resources. Other proposals included changing the SDWA requirement that EPA set standards for 25 contaminants per year, giving water systems more time to comply with federal standards, and adding stronger enforcement provisions to the Act.

In October 1993, Sen. Max S. Baucus (D-Mont) introduced S 1547 (the Safe Drinking Water Act Amendments of 1993). His proposal, which took the Administration's recommendations into account, was approved by the Senate Environment and Public Works Committee in March 1994. The version approved by the committee was reintroduced by Baucus April 14 as S 2019. It incorporated "manager's amendments" offered by Baucus and took into account changes offered by the committee's ranking Republican, Sen. John Chafee (R-RI).

Baucus, however, decided to hold up floor action on the bill until consensus could be reached on the issue of risk analysis in the process of setting standards for drinking water contaminants.

In the meantime, a movement among a large number of lawmakers had been gathering momentum. In summary, their concerns had been dubbed the "unholy trinity" by some environmental groups-risk assessment, "taking" of private property by regulatory restrictions on use, and "unfunded mandates." This last concern refers to the imposition of requirements by the federal government on state and local governments without provision of the funding needed to carry out those requirements. Seeing the Safe Drinking Water Act reauthorization legislation as the environmental measure most likely to be approved in the 103rd Congress, proponents of the "unholy trinity" wanted to use it as a test vehicle.

In early May, the Senate finally began its consideration of the legislation after Baucus with an agreement among key senators that would allow the EPA administrator to set standards for carcinogens that are less stringent than what is "technically feasible" as long as there are considerable cost savings and no significant increase in individual lifetime cancer risks. For non-carcinogens, EPA standards could also be less stringent than feasible as long as there are cost savings and a "reasonable certainty of no harm." The change, Baucus said, "preserves our fundamental health protections while avoiding unnecessary costs." Those "unnecessary costs," he said, were the chief failing of the existing law, which does not "take into account the economic burden on those who operate small [drinking water] systems."

In action on the "unholy trinity," the Senate approved an amendment on risk assessment, offered by Sen. J. Bennett Johnston (D-La), that would require EPA to describe and quantify the risks addressed by its regulations, compare those risks to other risks, estimate the cost of the regulation, and certify that the benefits of regulation justify the costs. The Senate also approved "takings" amendment offered by Sen. Dale Bumpers (D-Ark) that would require federal agencies to analyze the effects of a proposed rule on property value. A third amendment, on unfunded mandates, was tabled. That amendment was offered by Sen. Gregg Judd (R-NH).

Clearly the most surprising amendment approved by the Senate, however, was offered by Sen. John Glenn (D-Ohio). The amendment, essentially free-standing legislation, would elevate EPA to the president's Cabinet. It was substantially similar to S 171, the EPA Cabinet bill approved by the Senate in the spring of 1993.

Among its other provisions, S 2019 would establish a state loan fund that would allow local communities to borrow a total of $6.6 billion through fiscal 2000 to operate and upgrade their drinking water systems. It also would replace the current requirement that EPA regulate 25 contaminants every three years with a requirement that the agency list possible new contaminants, study their relative danger, and then decide whether to regulate them based on risk and frequency of occurrence.

House legislation probably will be "as clean as possible," according to one congressional aide, who decried the "extraneous and non-germane" amendments tacked on to the Senate bill. The primary vehicles on which House negotiators are focusing in an attempt to come with consensus legislation are HR 4314, introduced by Reps. Blanche Lambert (D-Ark), Gerry E. Studds (D-Mass), and Michael L. Synar (D-Okla), and HR 3392, introduced by Reps. Thomas J. Bliley (R-Va) and Jim Slattery (D-Kan). If the House does approve a measure, it seems unlikely that some of the more controversial amendments added to S 2019 will survive the conference committee.

FINDING LIST

SAFE DRINKING WATER ACT

Public Law 93–523, effective Dec. 16, 1974, 88 Stat. 1660.

42 U.S.C. §§300f et seq.

Amended by PL 94–317, June 23, 1976; PL 94–484, Oct. 12, 1976; PL 95–190, Nov. 16, 1977; PL 96–63, Sept. 6, 1979; PL 96–502, Dec. 5, 1980; PL 98–620, Nov. 11, 1984; PL 99–339, June 19, 1986; PL 100–572, Oct. 31, 1988.

Short Title. [Sec. 1]

This Act may be cited as the "Safe Drinking Water Act." [Sec. 1]

Public Water Systems [Sec. 2]

(a) The Public Health Service Act is amended by inserting after title XIII the following new title:

TITLE XIV — SAFETY OF PUBLIC WATER SYSTEMS

PART A—DEFINITIONS

§300f. Definitions. [Sec. 1401]

For purposes of this title:

(1) The term 'primary drinking water regulation' means a regulation which —

(A) applies to public water systems;

(B) specifies contaminants which, in the judgment of the Administrator, may have any adverse effect on the health of persons:

(C) specifies for each such contaminant either —

(i) a maximum contaminant level, if, in the judgment of the Administrator, 'it is economically and technologically feasible to ascertain the level of such contaminant in water in public water systems, or

(ii) if, in the judgment of the Administrator, it is not economically or technologically feasible to so ascertain the level of such contaminant, each treatment technique known to the Administrator which leads to a reduction in the level of such contaminant sufficient to satisfy the requirements of section 1412 ; and

(D) contains criteria and procedures to assure a supply of drinking water which dependably complies with such maximum contaminant levels; including quality control and testing procedures to insure compliance with such levels and to insure proper operation and maintenance of the system, and requirements as to (i) the minimum quality of water which may be taken into the system and siting for new facilities for public systems.

(2) The term 'secondary drinking water regulation' means a regulation which applies to public water systems and which specifies the maximum contaminant levels which, in the judgment of the Administrator, are requisite to protect the public welfare. Such regulations may apply to any contaminant in drinking water (A) which may adversely affect the odor or appearance of such water and consequently may cause a substantial number of the persons served by the public water system providing such water to discontinue its use, or (B) which may otherwise adversely affect the public welfare. Such regulations may vary according to geographic and other circumstances.

(3) The term 'maximum contaminant level' means the maximum permissible level of a contaminant in water which is delivered to any user of a public water system.

(4) The term 'public water system' means a system for the provision to the public of piped water for human consumption, if such system has at least fifteen service connections or regularly serves at least twenty-five individuals. Such term includes (A) any collection, treatment, storage, and distribution facilities under control of the operator of such system and used primarily in connection with such system, and (B) any collection or pretreatment storage facilities not under such control which are used primarily in connection with such system.

(5) The term 'supplier of water' means any person who owns or operates a public water system.

(6) The term 'contaminant' means any physical, chemical, biological, or radiological substance or matter in water.

(7) The term 'Administrator' means the Administrator of the Environmental Protection Agency.

(8) The term 'Agency' means the Environmental Protection Agency.

(9) The term 'Council' means the National Drinking Water Advisory Council established under section 1446 .

(10) The term 'municipality' means a city, town, or other public body created by or pursuant to State law, or an Indian Tribe.

[§1401(10) amended by PL 99–339]

(11) The term 'Federal agency' means any department agency, or instrumentality of the United States.

(12) The term 'person' means an individual, corporation, company, association, partnership, State, municipality, or Federal agency (and

includes officers, employees, and agents of any corporation, company, association, State, municipality, or Federal agency).

[§1401(12)9 amended by PL 95–190]

(13) The term 'State' includes, in addition to the several States, only the District of Columbia, Guam, and Commonwealth of Puerto Rico, the Northern Mariana Islands, the Virgin Islands, American Samoa, and the Trust Territory of the Pacific Islands.

[§1401(13) added by PL 94–317; amended by PL 94–484]

(14) The term 'Indian Tribe' means any Indian tribe having a Federally recognized governing body carrying out substantial governmental duties and powers over any area.

[§1401(14) added by PL 99–339]

PART B — PUBLIC WATER SYSTEMS

§300g. Coverage. [Sec. 1411]

Subject to sections 1415 and 1416 , national primary drinking water regulations under this part shall apply to each public water system in each State; except that such regulations shall not apply to a public water system —

(1) which consists only of distribution and storage facilities (and does not have any collection and treatment facilities);

(2) which obtains all of its water from, but is not owned or operated by, a public water system to which such regulations apply;

(3) which does not sell water to any person; and

(4) which is not a carrier which conveys passengers in interstate commerce.

§300g–1. National Drinking Water Regulations. [Sec. 1412]

(a) (1) Effective on the enactment of the Safe Drinking Water Act Amendments of 1986, each national interim or revised primary drinking water regulation promulgated under this section before such enactment shall be deemed to be a national primary drinking water regulation under subsection (b). No such regulation shall be required to comply with the standards set forth in subsection (b)(4) unless such regulation is amended to establish a different maximum contaminant level after the enactment of such amendments.

(2) After the enactment of the Safe Drinking Water Act Amendments of 1986 each recommended maximum contaminant level published before the enactment of such amendment shall be treated as a maximum contaminant level goal.

(3) Whenever a national primary drinking water regulation is proposed under paragraph (1), (2), or (3) of subsection (b) for any contaiminant, the maximum contaminant level goal for such contaminant shall be proposed simultaneously. Whenever a national primary drinking water regulation is promulgated under paragraph (1), (2), or (3) of subsection (b) for any contaminant, the maximum contaminant level goal for such contaminant shall be published simultaneously.

(4) Paragraph (3) shall not apply to any recommended maximum contaminant level published before the enactment of the Safe Drinking Water Act Amendments of 1986.

[§1412(a) revised by PL 99–339]

(b) (1) In the case of those contaminants listed in the Advance Notice of Proposed Rulemaking published in volume 47, Federal Register, page 9352, and in volume 48, Federal Register, page 45502, the Administrator shall publish maximum contaminant level goals and promulgate national primary drinking water regulations—

(A) not later than 12 months after the enactment of the Safe Drinking Water Act Amendments of 1986 for not less than 9 of those listed contaminants;

(B) not later than 24 months after such enactment for not less than 40 of those listed contaminants; and

(C) not later than 36 months after such enactment for the remainder of such listed contaminants.

[§1412(b)(1) revised by PL 99–339]

(2) (A) If the Administrator identifies a drinking water contaminant the regulation of which, in the judgment of the Administrator, is more likely to be protective of public health (taking into account the schedule for regulation under paragraph (1)) than a contaminant referred to in paragraph (1), the Administrator may publish a maximum contaminant level goal and promulgate a national primary drinking water regulation for such identified contaminant in lieu of regulating the contaminant referred to in such paragraph. There may be no more than 7 contaminants in paragraph (1) for which substitutions may be made. Regulation of a contaminant identified under this paragraph shall be in accordance with the schedule applicable to the contaminant for which the substitution is made.

(B) If the Administrator identifies one or more contaminants for substitution under this paragraph, the Administrator shall publish in the Federal Register not later than one year after the enactment of the Safe Drinking Water Act Amendments of 1986 a list of contaminants proposed for substitution, the contaminants referred to in paragraph (1) for which substitutions are to be made, and the basis for the judgment that regulation of such proposed substitute contaminants is more likely to be protective of public health (taking into account the schedule for regulation under such paragraph). Following a period of 60 days for public comment, the Administrator shall publish in the Federal Register a final list of contaminants to be substituted and contaminants referred to in paragraph (1) for which substitutions are to be made, together with responses to significant comments.

(C) Any contaminant referred to in paragraph (1) for which a substitution is made, pursuant to subparagraph (A) of this paragraph, shall be included on the priority list to be published by the Administrator not later than January 1, 1988, pursuant to paragraph (3)(A).

(D) The Administrator's decision to regulate a contaminant identified pursuant to this paragraph in lieu of a contaminant referred to in paragraph (1) shall not be subject to judicial review.

[§1412(b)(2) revised by PL 99–339]

(3) (A) The Administrator shall publish maximum contaminant level goals and promulgate national primary drinking water regulations for each contaminant (other than a contaminant referred to in paragraph (1) or (2) for which a national primary drinking water regulation was promulgated) which, in the judgment of the Administrator, may have any adverse effect on the health of persons and which is known or anticipated to occur in public water systems. Not later than January 1, 1988, and at 3 year intervals thereafter, the Administrator shall publish a list of contaminants which are known or anticipated to occur in public water systems and which may require regulation under this Act.

(B) For the purpose of establishing the list under subparagraph (A), the Administrator shall form an advisory working group including members from the National Toxicology Program and the Environmental Protection Agency's Offices of Drinking Water, Pesticides Toxic Substances, Ground Water, Solid Waste and Emergency Response and any others the Administrator deems appropriate. The Administrator's consideration of priorities shall include, but not be limited to, substances referred to in section 101(14) of the Comprehensive Environmental Response, Compensation, and Liability Act of 1980, and substances registered as pesticides under the Federal Insecticide, Fungicide, and Rodenticide Act.

(C) Not later than 24 months after the listing of contaminants under subparagraph (A), the Administrator shall publish proposed maximum contaminant level goals and national primary drinking water regulations for not less than 25 contaminants from the list established under subparagraph (A).

(D) Not later than 36 months after the listing of contaminants under subparagraph (A), the Administrator shall publish a maximum contaminant goal and promulgate a national primary drinking water regulation for those contaminants for which proposed maximum contaminant level goals and proposed national primary drinking water regulations were published under subparagraph (C).

[§1412(b)(3) revised by PL 99–339]

(4) Each maximum contaminant level goal established under this subsection shall be set at the level at which no known or anticipated adverse effects on the health of person occur and which allows an adequate margin of safety. Each national primary drinking water regulation for a contaminant for which a maximum contaminant level goal is established under this subsection shall specify a maximum level for such contaminant which is as close to the maximum contaminant level goal as is feasible.

[§1412(b)(4) added by PL 99–339]

(5) For the purposes of this subsection, the term 'feasible' means feasible with the use of the best technology, treatment techniques and other means which the Administrator finds, after examination for efficacy under field conditions and not solely under laboratory conditions, are available (taking cost into consideration). For the purpose of paragraph (4), granular activated carbon is feasible for the control of synthetic organic chemicals, and any technology, treatment technique, or other means found to be the best available for the control of synthetic organic chemicals must be at least as effective in controlling synthetic

organic chemicals as granular activated carbon.

[§1412(b)(5) added by PL 99–339]

(6) Each national primary drinking water regulation which establishes a maximum contaminant level shall list the technology, treatment techniques, and other means which the Administrator finds to be feasible for purposes of meeting such maximum contaminant level, but a regulation under this paragraph shall not require that any specified technology, treatment technique, or other means be used for purposes of meeting such maximum contaminant level.

[§1412(b)(6) added by PL 99–339]

(7) (A) The Administrator is authorized to promulgate a national primary drinking water regulation that requires the use of a treatment technique in lieu of establishing a maximum contaminant level, if the Administrator makes a finding that it is not economically or technologically feasible to ascertain in the level of the contaminant. In such case, the Administrator shall identify those treatment techniques which, in the Administrator's judgment, would prevent known or anticipated adverse effects on the health of persons to the extent feasible. Such regulations shall specify each treatment technique known to the Administrator which meets the requirements of this paragraph, but the Administrator may grant a variance from any specified treatment technique in accordance with section 1415(a)(3) .

(B) Any scheduled referred to in this subsection for the promulgation of a national primary drinking water regulation for any contaminant shall apply in the same manner if the regulation requires a treatment technique in lieu of establishing a maximum contaminant level.

(C) (i) Not later than 18 months after the enactment of the Safe Drinking Water Act Amendments of 1986, the Administrator shall propose and promulgate national primary drinking water regulations specifying criteria under which filtration (including coagulation and sedimentation as appropriate) is required as a treatment technique for public water systems supplied by surface water sources. In promulgating such rules, the Administrator shall consider the quality of source waters, protection afforded by watershed management, treatment practices (such as disinfection and length of water storage) and other factors relevant to protection of health.

(ii) In lieu of the provisions of section 1415 the Administrator shall specify procedures by which the State determines which public water systems within its jurisdiction shall adopt filtration under the criteria of clause (i). The State may require the public water system to provide studies or other information to assist in this determination. The procedures shall provide notice and opportunity for public hearing on this determination. If the State determines that filtration is required, the State shall prescribe a schedule for compliance by the public water system with the filtration requirement. A schedule shall require compliance within 18 months of a determination made under clause (iii).

(iii) Within 18 months from the time that the Administrator establishes the criteria and procedures under this subparagraph, a State with primary enforcement responsibility shall adopt any necessary regulations to implement this subparagraph. Within 12 months of adoption of such regulations the State shall make determinations regarding filtration for all the public water systems within its jurisdiction supplied by surface waters.

(iv) If a State does not have primary enforcement responsibility for public water systems, the Administrator shall have the same authority to make the determination in clause (ii) in such State as the State would have under that clause. Any filtration requirement or schedule under this subparagraph shall be treated as if it were a requirement of a national primary drinking water regulation.

[§1412(b)(7) added by PL 99–339]

(8) Not later than 36 months after the enactment of the Safe Drinking Water Act Amendments of 1986, the Administrator shall propose and promulgate national primary drinking water regulations requiring disinfection as a treatment technique for all public water systems. The Administrator shall simultaneously promulgate a rule specifying criteria that will be used by the Administrator (or delegated State authorities) to grant variances from this requirement according to the provisions of sections 1415(a)(1)(B) and 1415(a)(3) . In implementing section 1442(g) the Administrator or the delegated State authority shall, where appropriate, give special consideration to pro-

viding technical assistance to small public water systems in complying with the regulations promulgated under this paragraph.

[§1412(b)(8) added by PL 99–339]

(9) National primary drinking water regulations shall be amended whenever changes in technology, treatment techniques, and other means permit greater protection of the health of persons, but in any event such regulations shall be reviewed at least once every 3 years. Such review shall include an analysis of innovations or changes in technology, treatment techniques or other activities that have occurred over the previous 3–year period and that may provide for greater protection of the health of persons. The findings of such review shall be published in the Federal Register. If, after opportunity for public comment, the Administrator concludes that the technology, treatment techniques, or other means resulting from such innovations or changes are not feasible within the meaning of paragraph (5), an explanation of such conclusion shall be published in the Federal Register.

[Former §1412(b)(4) amended and redesignated as (9) by PL 99–339]

(10) National primary drinking water regulations promulgated under this subsection (and amendments thereto) shall take effect eighteen months after the date of their promulgation. Regulations under subsection (a) shall be superseded by regulations under this subsection to the extent provided by the regulations under this subsection.

[Former §1412(b)(5) amended and redesignated as (10) by PL 99–339]

(11) No national primary drinking water regulation may require addition of any substance for preventive health care purposes unrelated to contamination of drinking water.

[Former §1412(b)(6) redesignated as (11) by PL 99–339]

(c) The Administrator shall publish proposed national secondary drinking water regulations within 270 days after the date of enactment of this title. Within 90 days after publication of any such regulation, he shall promulgate such regulation with such modifications as he deems appropriate. Regulations under this subsection may be amended from time to time.

(d) Regulation under this section shall be prescribed in accordance with section 553 of title 5, United States Code (relating to rulemaking), except that the Administrator shall provide opportunity for public hearing prior to promulgation of such regulations. In proposing and promulgating regulations under this section, the Administrator shall consult with the Secretary and the National Drinking Water Advisory Council.

(e) The Administrator shall request comments from the Science Advisory Board (established under the Environmental Research, Development, and Demonstration Act of 1978) prior to proposal of a maximum contaminant level goal and national primary drinking water regulation. The Board shall respond, as it deems appropriate, within the time period applicable for promulgation of the national primary drinking water standard concerned. This subsection shall, under no circumstances, be used to delay final promulgation of any national primary drinking water standard.

[§1412(e) revised by PL 99–339]

§300g–2. State Primary Enforcement Responsibility. [Sec. 1413]

(a) For purposes of this title, a State has primary enforcement responsibility for public water systems during any period for which the Administrator determines (pursuant to regulations prescribed under subsection (b) that such State —

(1) has adopted drinking water regulations which are no less stringent than the national primary drinking water regulations in effect under sections 1412(a) and 1412(b);

[§1413(a)(1) revised by PL 99–339]

(2) has adopted and is implementing adequate procedures for the enforcement of such State regulations, including conducting such monitoring and making such inspections as the Administrator may require by regulation;

(3) will keep such records and make such reports with respect to its activities under paragraphs (1) and (2) as the Administrator may require by regulation;

(4) if it permits variances or exemptions, or both, from the requirements of its drinking water regulations which meet the requirements of paragraph (1), permits such variances and exemptions under conditions and in a manner which is not less stringent than the conditions under, and the manner in, which variances and exemptions may be granted under sections 1415 and 1416 ; and

(5) has adopted and can implement an adequate plan for the provision of safe drinking water under emergency circumstances.

(b) (1) The Administrator shall, by regulation (proposed within 180 days of the date of the enactment of this title), prescribe the manner in which a State may apply to the Administrator for a determination that the requirements of paragraphs (1), (2), (3), and (4) of subsection (a) are satisfied with respect to the State, the manner in which the determination is made, the period for which the determination will be effective, and the manner in which the Administrator may determine that such requirements are no longer met. Such regulations shall require that before a determination of the Administrator that such requirements are met are no longer met with respect to a State may become effective, the Administrator shall notify such State of the determination and the reasons therefor and shall provide an opportunity for public hearing on the determination. Such regulations shall be promulgated (with such modifications as the Administrator deems appropriate) within 90 days of the publication of the proposed regulations in the Federal Register. The Administrator shall promptly notify in writing the chief executive officer of each State of the promulgation of regulations under this paragraph. Such notice shall contain a copy of the regulations and shall specify a State's authority under this title when it is determined to have primary enforcement responsibility for public water systems.

(2) When an application is submitted in accordance with the Administrator's regulations under paragraph (1), the Administrator shall within 90 days of the date on which such application is submitted (A) make the determination applied for, or (B) deny the application and notify the applicant in writing of the reasons for his denial.

§300g–3. Enforcement of Drinking Water Regulations. [Sec. 1414]

[§1414 head amended by PL 99–339]

(a) (1) (A) Whenever the Administrator finds during a period during which a State has primary enforcement responsibility for public water systems (within the meaning of section 1413(a)) that any public water system —

(i) for which a variance under section 1415 or an exemption under section 1416 is not in effect, does not comply with any national primary drinking water regulation in effect under section 1412, or

(ii) for which a variance under section 1415 or an exemption under section 1416 is in effect, does not comply with any schedule, or other requirement imposed pursuant thereto, he shall so notify the State and such public water system and provide such advice and technical assistance to such State and public water system as may be appropriate to bring the system into compliance with such regulation or requirement by the earliest feasible time.

[§1414(a)(1)(A) revised by PL 99–339]

(B) If, beyond the thirtieth day after the Administrator's notification under subparagraph (A), the State has not commenced appropriate enforcement action, the Administrator shall issue an order under subsection (g) requiring the public water system to comply with such regulation or requirement or the Administrator shall commence a civil action under subsection (b).

[§1414(a)(1)(B) revised by PL 99–339]

(2) Whenever, on the basis of information available to him, the Administrator finds during a period during which a State does not have primary enforcement responsibility or public water systems that a public water system in such State —

(A) for which a variance under section 1415(a)(2) or an exemption under section 1416(f) is not in effect, does not comply with any national primary drinking water regulation in effect under section 1412 , or

(B) for which a variance under section 1415(a)(2) or an exemption under section 1416(f) is in effect, does not comply with any schedule or other requirement imposed pursuant thereto, the Administrator shall issue an order under subsection (g) requiring the public water system to comply with such regulation or requirement or the Administrator shall commence a civil action under subsection (b).

[§1414(a)(2) amended by PL 99–339]

(b) The Administrator may bring a civil action in the appropriate United States district court to require compliance with a national primary drinking water regulation, with an order issued under subsection (g), or with any schedule or other requirement imposed pursuant to a variance or exemption granted under section 1415 or 1416 if —

(1) authorized under paragraph (1) or (2) of subsection (a), or

(2) if requested by (A) the chief executive officer of the State in which is located the public water system which is not in compliance with such regulation or requirement, or (B) the

agency of such State which has jurisdiction over compliance by public water systems in the State with national primary drinking water regulations or State drinking water regulations. The court may enter, in an action brought under this subsection, such judgment as protection of public health may require, taking into consideration the time necessary to comply and the availability of alternative water supplies; and, if the court determines that there has been a violation of the regulation or schedule or other requirement with respect which the action was brought, the court may, taking into account the seriousness of the violation, the population at risk, and other appropriate factors, impose on the violator a civil penalty of not to exceed $25,000 for each day in which such violation occurs.

[§1414(b) amended by PL 99–339]

(c) Each owner or operator of a public water system shall give notice to the persons served by it—

(1) of any failure on the part of the public water system to —

(A) comply with an applicable maximum contaminant level or treatment technique requirement of, or a testing procedure prescribed by, a national primary drinking water regulation, or

(B) perform monitoring required by section 1445(a), and

(2) if the public water system is subject to a variance granted under section 1415(a)(1)(A) or 1415(a)(2) for an inability to meet a maximum contaminant level requirement or is subject to an exemption granted under section 1416, of —

(A) the existence of such variance or exemption, and

(B) any failure to comply with the requirements of any schedule prescribed pursuant to the variance or exemption. The Administrator shall by regulation prescribe the form, manner, and frequency for giving notice under this subsection. Within 15 months after the enactment of the Safe Drinking Water Act Amendments of 1986, the Administrator shall amend such regulations to provide for different types and frequencies of notice based on the differences between violations which are intermittent or infrequent and violations which are continuous or frequent. Such regulations shall also take into account the seriousness of any potential adverse health effects which may be involved. Notice of any violation of a maximum contaminant level or any other violation designated by the Administrator as posing a serious potential adverse health effect shall be given as soon as possible, but in no case later than 14 days after the violation. Notice of a continuous violation of a regulation other than a maximum contaminant level shall be given no less frequently than every 3 months. Notice of violations judged to be less serious shall be given no less frequently than annually. The Administrator shall specify the types of notice to be used to provide information as promptly and effectively as possible taking into account both the seriousness of any potential adverse health effects and the likelihood of reaching all affected persons. Notification of violations shall include notice by general circulation newspaper serving the area and, whenever appropriate, shall also include a press release to electronic media and individual mailings. Notice under this subsection shall provide a clear and readily understandable explanation of the violation, any potential adverse health effects, the steps that the system is taking to correct such violation, and the necessity for seeking alternative water supplies, if any, until the violation is corrected. Until such amended regulations are promulgated, the regulations in effect on the date of the enactment of the Safe Drinking Water Act Amendments of 1986 shall remain in effect. The Administrator may also require the owner or operator of a public water system to give notice to the persons served by it of contaminant levels of any unregulated contaminant required to be monitored under section 1445(a). Any person who violates this subsection or regulations issued under this subsection shall be subject to a civil penalty of not to exceed $25,000.

[§1414(c) amended by PL 95–190; PL 99–339]

(d) Whenever, on the basis of information available to him, the Administrator finds that within a reasonable time after national secondary drinking water regulations have been promulgated, one or more public water systems in a State do not comply with such secondary regulations, and that such noncompliance appears to result from a failure of such State to take reasonable action to assure that public water systems throughout such State meet such secondary regulations, he shall so notify the State.

(e) Nothing in this title shall diminish any authority of a State or political subdivision to adopt or enforce any law or regulation respecting drinking water regulations or public water systems, but no such law or regulation shall relieve any person of any requirement otherwise applicable under this title.

(f) If the Administrator makes a finding of noncompliance (described in subparagraph (A) or (B) of subsection (a)(1)) with respect to a public water system in a State which has primary enforcement responsibility, the Administrator may, for the purpose of assisting that State in carrying out such responsibility and upon the petition of such State or public water system or persons served by such system, hold, after appropriate notice, public hearings for the purpose of gathering information from technical or other experts, Federal, State, or other public officials, representatives of such public water system, persons served by such system, and other interested persons on —

(1) the ways in which such systems can within the earliest feasible time be brought into compliance with the regulation or requirement with respect to which such finding was made, and

(2) the means for the maximum feasible protection of the public health during any period in which such system is not in compliance with a national primary drinking water regulation or requirement applicable to a variance or exemption.

On the basis of such hearings the Administrator shall issue recommendations which shall be sent to such State and public water system and shall be made available to the public and communications media.

(g) (1) In any case in which the Administrator is authorized to bring a civil action under this section or under section 1445 with respect to any regulation, schedule, or other requirement, the Administrator also may issue an order to require compliance with such regulation, schedule, or other requirement.

(2) An order issued under this subsection shall not take effect until after notice and opportunity for public hearing and, in the case of a State having primary enforcement responsibility for public water systems in that State, until after the Administrator has provided the State with an opportunity to confer with the Administrator regarding the proposed order. A copy of any order proposed to be issued under this subsection shall be sent to the appropriate State agency of the State involved if the State has primary enforcement responsibility for public water systems in that State. Any order issued under this subsection shall state with reasonable specificity the nature of the violation. In any case in which an order under this subsection is issued to a corporation, a copy of such order that be issued to appropriate corporate officers.

(3) (A) Any person who violates, or fails or refuses to comply with, an order under this subsection shall be liable to the United States for a civil penalty of not more than $25,000 per day of violation.

(B) Whenever any civil penalty sought by the Administrator under this paragraph does not exceed a total of $5,000, the penalty shall be assessed by the Administrator after notice and opportunity for a hearing on the record in accordance with section 554 of title 5 of the United States Code.

(C) Whenever any civil penalty sought by the Administrator under this paragraph exceeds $5,000, the penalty shall be assessed by a civil action brought by the Administrator in the appropriate United States district court (as determined under the provisions of title 28 of the United States Code).

(D) If any person fails to pay an assessment of a civil penalty after it has become a final and unappealable order, or after the appropriate court of appeals has entered final judgment in favor of the Administrator, the Attorney General shall recover the amount for which such person is liable in any appropriate district court of the United States. In any such action, the validity and appropriateness of the final order imposing the civil penalty shall not be subject to review.

[§1414(g) added by PL 99–339]

§300g–4. Variances. [Sec. 1415]

(a) Notwithstanding any other provision of this part, variances from national primary drinking water regulations may be granted as follows:

(1) (A) A State which has primary enforcement responsibility for public water systems may grant one or more variances from an applicable national primary drinking water regulation to one or more public water systems within its jurisdiction which, because of characteristics of the raw water sources which are reasonably available to the systems, cannot meet the requirements respecting the maximum contaminant levels of such drinking water regulation. A variance may only be issued to system after the system's application of the best technology, treatment techniques, or other means, which the

Administrator finds are available (taking costs into consideration). The Administrator shall propose and promulgate his finding of the best available technology, treatment techniques or other means available for each contaminant for purposes of this subsection at the time he proposes and promulgates a maximum contaminant level for each such contaminant. The Administrator's finding of best available technology, treatment techniques or other means for purposes of this subsection may vary depending on the number of persons served by the system or for other physical conditions related to engineering feasibility and costs of compliance with maximum contaminant levels as considered appropriate by the Administrator. Before a State may grant a variance under this subparagraph, the State must find that the variance will not result in an unreasonable risk to health. If a State grants a public water system a variance under this subparagraph, the State shall prescribe at the time the variance is granted, a schedule for —

(i) compliance (including increments of progress) by the public water system with each contaminant level requirement with respect to which the variance was granted, and

(ii) implementation by the public water system of such additional control measures as the State may require for each contaminant, subject to such contaminant level requirement, during the period ending on the date compliance with such requirement is required. Before a schedule prescribed by a State pursuant to this subparagraph may take effect, the State shall provide notice and opportunity for a public hearing on the schedule. A notice given pursuant to the preceding sentence may cover the prescribing of more than one such schedule and a hearing held pursuant to such notice shall include each of the schedules covered by the notice. A schedule prescribed pursuant to this subparagraph for a public water system granted a variance shall require compliance by the system with each contaminant level requirement with respect to which the variance was granted as expeditiously as practicable (as the State may reasonably determine).

[§1415(a)(1)(A) amended by PL 99–339]

(B) A State which has primary enforcement responsibility for public water systems may grant to one or more public water systems within its jurisdiction one or more variances from any provision of a national primary drinking water regulation which requires the use of a specified treatment technique with respect to a contaminant if the public water system applying for the variance demonstrates to the satisfaction of the State that such treatment technique is not necessary to protect the health of persons because of the nature of the raw water source of such system. A variance granted under this subparagraph shall be conditioned on such monitoring and other requirements as the Administrator may prescribe.

(C) Before a variance proposed to be granted by a State under subparagraph (A) or (B) may take effect, such State shall provide notice and opportunity for public hearing on the proposed variance. A notice given pursuant to the preceding sentence may cover the granting of more than one variance and a hearing held pursuant to such notice shall include each of the variances covered by the notice. The State shall promptly notify the Administrator of all variances granted by it. Such notification shall contain the reason for the variance (and in the case of a variance under subparagraph (A), the basis for the finding required by that subparagraph before the granting of the variance) and documentation of the need for the variance.

(D) Each public water system's variance granted by a State under subparagraph (A) shall be conditioned by the State upon compliance by the public water system with the schedule prescribed by the State pursuant to that subparagraph. The requirements of each schedule prescribed by a State pursuant to that subparagraph shall be enforceable by the State under its laws. Any requirement of a schedule on which a variance granted under that subparagraph is conditioned may be enforced under section 1414 as if such requirement was part of a national primary drinking water regulation.

(E) Each schedule prescribed by a State pursuant to subparagraph (A) shall be deemed approved by the Administrator unless the variance for which it was prescribed is revoked by the Administrator under subparagraph (G) or the schedule is revised by the Administrator under such subparagraph.

(F) Not later than 18 months after the effective date of the interim national primary drinking water regulations the Administrator shall complete a comprehensive review of the variances granted under subparagraph (A) (and schedules prescribed pursuant thereto) and under subparagraph (B) by the States during the one-year period beginning on such effective date. The Administrator shall conduct such subsequent reviews of variances and schedules as he deems necessary to carry out the purposes of this title, but each subsequent review shall be completed within each 3–year period following the completion of the first review under this subparagraph. Before conducting any review under this subparagraph, the Administrator shall publish notice of the proposed review in the Federal Register. Such notice shall (i) provide information respecting the locaton of data and other information respecting the variances to be reviewed (including data and other information concerning new scientific matters bearing on such variances), and (ii) advise of the opportunity to submit comments on the variances reviewed and on the need for continuing them. Upon completion of any such review, the Administrator shall publish in the Federal Register the results of his review together with findings responsive to comments submitted in connection with such review.

(G) (i) If the Administrator finds that a State has, in a substantial number of instances, abused its discretion in granting variances under subparagraph (A) or (B) or that in a substantial number of cases the State has failed to prescribe schedules in accordance with subparagraph (A), the Administrator shall notify the State of his findings. In determining if a State has abused its discretion in granting variances in a substantial number of instances, the Administrator shall consider the number of persons who are affected by the variances and if the requirements applicable to the granting of the variances were complied with. A notice under this clause shall—

(I) identify each public water system with respect to which the finding was made

(II) specify the reasons for the finding, and

(III) as appropriate, propose revocations of specific variances or propose revised schedules or other requirements for specific public water systems granted variances, or both.

(ii) The Administrator shall provide reasonable notice and public hearing on the provisions of each notice given pursuant to clause (i) of this subparagraph. After a hearing on a notice pursuant to such clause, the Administrator shall (I) rescind the finding for which the notice was given and promptly notify the State of such rescission, or (II) promulgate (with such modifications as he deems appropriate) such variance revocations and revised schedules or other requirements proposed in such notice as he deems appropriate. Not later than 180 days after the date a notice is given pursuant to clause (i) of this subparagraph, the Administrator shall complete the hearing on the notice and take the action required by the preceding sentence.

(iii) If a State is notified under clause (i) of this subparagraph of a finding of the Administrator made with respect to a variance granted a public water system within that State or to a schedule or other requirement for a variance and if, before a revocation of such variance or a revision of such schedule or other requirement promulgated by the Administrator takes effect, the State takes corrective action with respect to such variance or schedule or other requirement which the Administrator determines makes his finding inapplicable to such variance or schedule or other requirement, the Administrator shall rescind the application of his finding to that variance or schedule or other requirement. No variance revocation or revised schedule or other requirement may take effect before the expiration of 90 days following the date of the notice in which the revocation or revised schedule or other requirement was proposed.

(2) If a State does not have primary enforcement responsibility for public water systems, the Administrator shall have the same authority to grant variances in such State as the State would have under paragraph (1) if it had primary enforcement responsibility.

(3) The Administrator may grant a variance from any treatment technique requirement of a national primary drinking water regulation upon a showing by any person that an alternative treatment technique not included in such requirement is a least as efficient in lowering the level of the contaminant with respect to which such requirement was prescribed. A variance under this paragraph shall be conditioned on the use of the alternative treatment technique which is the basis of the variance.

(b) Any schedule or other requirement on which a variance granted under paragraph (1)(B) or (2) of subsection (a) is conditioned may be enforced under section 1414 as if such schedule or other requirement was part of a national primary drinking water regulation.

(c) If an application for a variance under subsection (a) is made, the State receiving the application or the Administrator, as the case may be, shall act upon such application within a reasonable period (as determined under regulations prescribed by the Administrator) after the date of its submission.

(d) For purposes of this section, the term 'treatment technique requirement' means requirement in a national primary drinking water regulation which specifies for a contaminant (in accordance with section 1401(1)(C)(ii) each treatment technique known to the Administrator which leads to a reduction in the level of such contaminant sufficient to satisfy the requirements of section 1412(b)(3) .

§300g–5. Exemptions. [Sec. 1416]

(a) A State which has primary enforcement responsibility may exempt any public water system within the State's jurisdiction from any requirement respecting a maximum contaminant level or any treatment technique requirement, or from both, of an applicable national primary drinking water regulation upon a finding that —

(1) due to compelling factors (which may include economic factors), the public water system is unable to comply with such contaminant level or treatment technique requirement,

(2) the public water system was in operation on the effective date of such contaminant level or treatment technique requirement, or, for a system that was not in operation by that date, only if no reasonable alternative source of drinking water is available to such new system, and

[§1416(a)(2) amended by PL 96–502]

(3) the granting of the exemption will not result in an unreasonable risk to health.

(b) (1) If a State grants a public water system an exemption under subsection (a), the State shall prescribe, at the time the exemption is granted, a schedule for —

(A) compliance (including increments of progress) by the public water system with each contaminant level requirement and treatment technique requirement with respect to which the exemption was granted, and

(B) implementation by the public water system of such control measures as the State may require for each contaminant, subject to such contaminant level requirement or treatment technique requirement, during the period ending on the date compliance with such requirement is required.

Before a schedule prescribed by a State pursuant to this subsection may take effect, the State shall provide notice and opportunity for a public hearing on the schedule. A notice given pursuant to the preceding sentence may cover the prescribing of more than one such schedule and a hearing held pursuant to such notice shall included each of the schedules covered by the notice.

[§1416(b)(1) amended by PL 95–190; PL 99–339]

(2) (A) A schedule prescribed pursuant to this subsection for a public water system granted an exemption under subsection (A) shall require compliance by the system with each contaminant level and treatment technique requirement with respect to which the exemption was granted as expeditiously as practicable (as the State may reasonably determine) but (except as provided in subparagraph (B)) —

(i) in the case of an exemption granted with respect to a contaminant level or treatment technique requirement prescribed by the national primary drinking water regulations promulgated under section 1412(a) , not later than 12 months after enactment of the Safe Drinking Water Act Amendments of 1986; and

[§1416(b)(2)(A)(i) amended by PL 96–502; PL 99–339]

(ii) in the case of an exemption granted with respect to a contaminant level or treatment technique requirement prescribed by national primary drinking water regulations, other than a regulation referred to in section 1412(a) , 12 months after the date of the issuance of the exemption.

(B) The final date for compliance provided in any schedule in the case of any exemption may be extended by the State (in the case of a State which has primary enforcement responsibility) or by the Administrator (in any other case) for a period not to exceed 3 years after the date of the issuance of the exemption if the public water system establishes that —

(i) the system cannot meet the standard without capital improvements which cannot be completed within the period of such exemption;

(ii) in the case of a system which needs financial assistance for the necessary improvements, the system has entered into an agreement to obtain such financial assistance; or

(iii) the system has entered into an enforceable agreement to become a part of a regional public water system; and the system is taking all practicable steps to meet the standard.

[§1416(b)(2)(B) amended by PL 96–502; revised by PL 99–339]

(C) In the case of a system which does not serve more than 500 service connections and which needs financial assistance for the necessary improvements, an exemption granted under clause (i) or (ii) of subparagraph (B) may be renewed for one or more additional 2–year periods if the system establishes that it is taking all practicable steps to meet the requirements of subparagraph (B).

[§1416(b)(2)(C) added by PL 99–339]

(3) Each public water system's exemption granted by a State under subsection (a) shall be conditioned by the State upon compliance by the public water system with the schedule prescribed by the State pursuant to this subsection. The requirements of each schedule prescribed by a State pursuant to this subsection shall be enforceable by the State under its laws. Any requirement of a schedule on which an exemption granted under this section is conditioned may be enforced under section 1414 as if such requirement was part of a national primary drinking water regulation.

(4) Each schedule prescribed by a State pursuant to this subsection shall be deemed approved by the Administrator unless the exemption for which it was prescribed is revoked by the Administrator under subsection (d)(2) or the schedule is revised by the Administrator under such subsection.

(c) Each State which grants an exemption under subsection (a) shall promptly notify the Administrator of the granting of such exemption. Such notification shall contain the reasons for the exemption (including the basis of the finding required by subsection (a)(3) before the exemption may be granted) and document the need for the exemption.

(d) (1) Not later than 18 months after the effective date of the interim national primary drinking water regulations the Administrator shall complete a comprehensive review of the exemptions granted (and schedules prescribed pursuant thereto) by the States during the one-year period beginning on such effective date. The Administrator shall conduct such subsequent reviews of exemptions and schedules as he deems necessary to carry out the purposes of this title, but each subsequent review shall be completed within each 3–year period following the completion of the first review under this subparagraph. Before conducting any review under this subparagraph, the Administrator shall publish notice of the proposed review in the Federal Register. Such notice shall (A) provide information respecting the location of data and other information respecting the exemptions to be reviewed (including data and other information concerning new scientific matters bearing on such exemptions), and (B) advise of the opportunity to submit comments on the exemptions reviewed and on the need for continuing them. Upon completion of any such review, the Administrator shall publish in the Federal Register the results of his review together with findings responsive to comments submitted in connection with such review.

(2) (A) If the Administrator finds that a State has, in a substantial number of instances, abused its discretion in granting exemptions under subsection (a) or failed to prescribe schedules in accordance with subsection (b), the Administrator shall notify the State of his finding. In determining if a State has abused its discretion in granting exemptions in a substantial number of instances, the Administrator shall consider the number of persons who are affected by the exemptions and if the requirements applicable to the granting of the exemptions were complied with. A notice under this subparagraph shall —

(i) identify each exempt public water system with respect to which the finding was made,

(ii) specify the reasons for the finding, and

(iii) as appropriate, propose revocations of specific exemptions or propose revised schedules for specific exempt public water systems, or both.

(B) The Administrator shall provide reasonable notice and public hearing on the provisions of each notice given pursuant to subparagraph (A). After a hearing on a notice pursuant to subparagraph (A), the Administrator shall (i) rescind the finding for which the notice was given and promptly notify the State of such rescission, or (ii) promulgate (with such modifications as he deems appropriate) such exemption revocations and revised schedules proposed in such notice as he deems appropriate. Not later than 180 days after the date a notice is given pursuant to subparagraph (A), the Administrator shall complete the hearing on the notice and take the action required by the preceding sentence.

(C) If a State is notified under subparagraph (A) of a finding of the Administrator made with respect to an exemption granted a public water system within that State or to a schedule prescribed pursuant to such an exemption and if before a revocation of such exemption or a revision of such schedule promulgated by the Administrator takes effect the State takes corrective action with respect to such exemption or schedule which the Administrator determines makes his finding inapplicable to such exemption or schedule, the Administrator shall rescind the application of his finding to that exemption or schedule. No exemption revocation or revised schedule may take effect before the expiration of 90 days following the date of the notice in which the revocation or revised schedule was proposed.

(e) For purposes of this section, the term 'treatment technique requirement' means a requirement in a national primary drinking water regulation which specifies for a contaminant (in accordance with section 1401(1)(C)(ii)) each treatment technique known to the Administrator which leads to a reduction in the level of such contaminant sufficient to satisfy the requirements of section 1412(b) .

[§1416(e) amended by PL 99–339]

(f) If a State does not have primary enforcement responsibility for public water systems, the Administrator shall have the same authority to exempt public water systems in such state from maximum contaminant level requirements and treatment technique requirements under the same conditions and in the same manner as the State would be authorized to grant exemptions under this section if it had primary enforcement responsibility.

(g) If an application for an exemption under this section is made, the State receiving the application or the Administrator, as the case may be, shall act upon such application within a reasonable period (as determined under regulations prescribed by the Administrator) after the date of its submission.

§300g–6. Prohibition On Use of Lead Pipes, Solder, and Flux. [Sec. 1417]

(a) In General. —

(1) Prohibition. — Any pipe, solder, or flux, which is used after the enactment of the Safe Drinking Water Act Amendments of 1986, in the installation or repair of —

(A) any public water system, or

(B) any plumbing in a residential or nonresidential facility providing water for human consumption which is connected to a public water system,shall be lead free (within the meaning of subsection (d)). This paragraph shall not apply to leaded joints necessary for the repair of cast iron pipes.

(2) Public Notice Requirements.—

(A) In General. — Each public water system shall identify and provide notice to persons that may be affected by lead contamination of their drinking water where such contaminants results from either or both of the following:

(i) The lead content in the construction materials of the public water distribution system.

(ii) Corrosivity of the water supply sufficient to cause leaching of lead. The notice shall be provided in such manner and form as may be reasonably required by the Administrator. Notice under this paragraph shall be provided notwithstanding the absence of a violation of any national drinking water standard.

(B) Contents Of Notice. — Notice under this paragraph shall provide a clear and readily understandable explanation of —

(i) the potential sources of lead in the drinking water,

(ii) potential adverse health effects,

(iii) reasonably available methods of mitigating known or potential lead content in drinking water,

(iv) any steps the system is taking to mitigate lead content in drinking water, and

(v) the necessity for seeking alternative water supplies, if any.

(b) State Enforcement. —

(1) Enforcement Of Prohibition. — The requirements of subsection (a)(1) shall be enforced in all States effective 24 months after the enactment of this section. States shall enforce such requirements through State or local plumbing codes, or such other means of enforcement as the State may determine to be appropriate.

(2) Enforcement Of Public Notice Requirements.— The requirements of subsection (a)(2) shall apply in all States effective 24 months after the enactment of this section.

(c) Penalties. — If the Administrator determines that a State is not enforcing the requirements of subsection (a) as required pursuant to subsection (b), the Administrator may withhold up to 5 percent of Federal funds available to that State for State program grants under section 1443(a) .

(d) Definition Of Lead Free. — For purposes of this section, the term 'lead free'—

(1) when used with respect to solders and flux refers to solders and flux containing not more than 0.2 percent lead, and

(2) when used with respect to pipes and pipe fittings refers to pipes and pipe fittings containing not more than 8.0 percent lead.

PART C — PROTECTION OF UNDERGROUND SOURCES OF DRINKING WATER.

§300h. Regulations for State Programs.
[Sec. 1421]

(a) (1) The Administrator shall publish proposed regulations for State underground injection control programs within 180 days after the date of enactment of this title. Within 180 days after publication of such proposed regulations, he shall promulgate such regulations, with such modifications as he deems appropriate. Any regulation under this subsection may be amended from time to time.

(2) Any regulation under this section shall be proposed and promulgated in accordance with section 553 of title 5, United States Code (relating to rulemaking), except that the Administrator shall provide opportunity for public hearing prior to promulgation of such regulations. In proposing and promulgating regulations under this section, the Administrator shall consult with the Secretary, the National Drinking Water Advisory Council, and other appropriate Federal entities and with interested State entities.

(b) (1) Regulations under subsection (a) for State underground injection programs shall contain minimum requirements for effective programs to prevent underground injection which endangers drinking water sources within the meaning of subsection (d)(2). Such regulations shall require that a State program, in order to be approved under section 1422 —

(A) shall prohibit, effective on the date on which the applicable underground injection control program takes effect, any underground injection in such State which is not authorized by a permit issued by the State (except that the regulations may permit a State to authorize underground injection by rule);

[§1421(b)(1)(A) amended by PL 96–502]

(B) shall require (i) in the case of a program which provides for authorization of underground injection by permit, that the applicant for the permit to inject must satisfy the State that the underground injection will not endanger drinking water sources, and (ii) in the case of program which provides for such an authorization by rule, that no rule may be promulgated which authorizes any underground injection which endangers drinking water sources;

(C) shall include inspection, monitoring, recordkeeping, and reporting requirements; and

(D) shall apply (i) as prescribed by section 1447(6), to underground injections by Federal agencies, and (ii) to underground injections by any other person whether or not occurring on property owned or leased by the United States.

(2) Regulations of the Administrator under this section for State underground injection control programs may not prescribe requirements which interfere with or impede —

(A) the underground injection of brine or other fluids which are brought to the surface in connection with oil or natural gas production or natural gas storage operations, or

[§1421(b)(2)(A) amended by PL 99–339]

(B) any underground injection for the secondary or tertiary recovery of oil or natural gas, unless such requirements are essential to assure that underground sources of drinking water will not be endangered by such injection.

(3) (A) The regulations of the Administrator under this section shall permit or provide for consideration of varying geologic, hydrological, or historical conditions in different States and in different areas within a State.

(B) (i) In prescribing regulations under this section the Administrator shall, to the extent feasible, avoid promulgation of requirements which would unnecessarily disrupt State underground injection control programs which are in effect and being enforced in a substantial number of States.

(ii) For the purpose of this subparagraph, a regulation prescribed by the Administrator under this section shall be deemed to disrupt a State underground injection control program only if it would be infeasible to comply with both such regulation and the State underground injection control program.

(iii) For the purpose of this subparagraph, a regulation prescribed by the Administrator under this section shall be deemed unnecessary only if, without such regulation, underground source of drinking water will not be endangered by any underground injection.

(C) Nothing in this section shall be construed to alter or affect the duty to assure that underground sources of drinking water will not be endangered by any underground injection.

[§1421(b)(3) added by PL 95–190]

(c) (1) The Administrator may, upon application of the Governor of a State which authorizes underground injection by means of permits, authorize such State to issue (without regard to subsection (b)(1)(B)(i)) temporary permits for underground injection which maybe effective until the expiration of four years after the date of enactment of this title, if —

(A) the Administrator finds that the State has demonstrated that it is unable and could not reasonably have been able to process all permit applications within the time available;

(B) the Administrator determines the adverse effect on the environment of such temporary permits is not unwarranted;

(C) such temporary permits will be issued only with respect to injection wells in operation on the date on which such State's permit program approved under this part first takes effect and for which there was inadequate time to process its permit application; and

(D) the Administrator determines the temporary permits require the use of adequate safeguards established by rules adopted by him.

(2) The Administrator may, upon application of the Governor or a State which authorizes underground injection by means of permits, authorize such State to issue (without regard to subsection (b)(1)(B)(i)), but after reasonable notice and hearing, one or more temporary permits each of a which is applicable to a particular injection well and to the underground injection of a particular fluid and which may be effective until the expiration of four year after the date of enactment of this title, if the State finds, on the record of such hearing —

(A) that technology (or other means) to permit safe injection of the fluid in accordance with the applicable underground injection control program is not generally available (taking costs into consideration);

(B) that injection of the fluid would be less harmful to health than the use of other available means of disposing of waste or producing the desired product; and

(C) that available technology or other means have been employed (and will be employed) to reduce the volume and toxicity of the fluid and to minimize the potentially adverse effect of the injection on the public health.

(d) For purposes of this part;

(1) The term 'underground injection' means the subsurface emplacement of fluids by well injection. Such term does not include the underground injection of natural gas for purposes of storage.

[§1421(d)(1) amended by PL 96–502]

(2) Underground injection endangers drinking water sou1rces if such injection may result in the presence in underground water which supplies or can reasonably be expected to supply any public water system of any contaminant, and if the presence of such contaminant may result in such system's not complying with any national primary drinking water regulation or may otherwise adversely affect the health of persons.

§300h–1. State Primary Enforcement Responsibility. [Sec. 1422]

(a) Within 180 days after the date of enactment of this title, the Administrator shall list in the Federal Register each State for which in his judgment a State underground injection control program may be necessary to assure that underground injection will not endanger drinking water sources. Such list may be amended from time to time.

(b) (1) (A) Each State listed under subsection (a) shall within 270 days after the date of promulgation of any regulation under section 1421 (or, if later, within 270 days after such State is first listed under subsection (a)) submit to the Administrator an application which contains a showing satisfactory to the Administrator that the State—

(i) has adopted after reasonable notice and public hearings, and will implement, an underground injection control program which meets the requirements of regulations in effect under section 1421 ; and

(ii) will keep such records and make such report with respect to its activities under its underground injection control program as the Administrator may require by regulation.

The Administrator may, for good cause, extend the date for submission of an application by any State under this subparagraph for a period not to exceed an additional 270 days.

[§1422(b)(1)(A) amended by PL 95–190]

(B) Within 270 days of any amendment of a regulation under section 1421 revising or adding any requirement respecting State underground injection control programs, each State listed under subsection (a) shall submit (in such form and manner as the Administrator may require) a notice to the Administrator containing a showing satisfactory to him that the State underground injection control program meets the revised or added requirement.

(2) Within ninety days after the State's application under paragraph (1)(A) or notice under paragraph (1)(B) and after reasonable opportunity for presentation of views, the Administrator shall by rule either approve, disapprove, or approve in part and disapprove in part, the State's underground injection control program.

(3) If the Administrator approves the State's program under paragraph (2), the State shall have primary enforcement responsibility for underground water sources until such time as the Administrator determines, by rule, that such State no longer meets the requirements of clause (i) or (ii) of paragraph (1)(A) of this subsection.

(4) Before promulgating any rule under paragraph (2) or (3) of this subsection, the Administrator shall provide opportunity for public hearing respecting such rule,

(c) If the Administrator disapproves a State's program (or part thereof) under subsection (b)(2), if the Administrator determines under subsection (b)(3) that a State no longer meets the requirements of clause (i) or (ii) of subsection (b)(1)(A), or if a State fails to submit an application or notice before the date of expiration of the period specified in subsection (b)(1), the Administrator shall by regulation within 90 days after the date of such disapproval, determination, or expiration (as the case may be) prescribe (and may from time to time by regulation revise) a program applicable to such State meeting the requirements of section 1421(b) . Such program may not include requirements which interfere with or impede—

(1) the underground injection of brine or other fluids which are brought to the surface in connection with oil or natural gas production or natural gas storage operations, or

[§1422(c)(1) amended by PL 99–339]

(2) any underground injection for the secondary or tertiary recovery of oil or natural gas, unless such requirements are essential to assure that underground sources of drinking water will not be endangered by such injection. Such program shall apply in such State to the extent that a program adopted by such State which the Administrator determines meets such requirements is not in effect. Before promulgating any regulation under this section, the Administrator shall provide opportunity for public hearing respecting such regulation.

(d) For purposes of this title, the term 'applicable underground injection control program' with respect to a State means the program (or most recent amendment thereof) (1) which has been adopted by the State and which has been approved under subsection (b), or (2) which has been prescribed by the Administrator under subsection (c).

(e) An Indian Tribe may assume primary enforcement responsibility for underground injection control under this section consistent with such regulations as the Administrator has prescribed pursuant to Part C and section 1451 of this Act. The area over which such Indian Tribe exercises governmental jurisdiction need not have been listed under subsection (a) of this section, and such Tribe need not submit an application to assume primary enforcement responsibility within the 270–day deadline noted in subsection (b)(1)(A) of this section. Until an Indian Tribe assumes primary enforcement responsibility, the currently applicable underground injection control program shall continue to apply. If an applicable underground injection control program does not exist for an Indian Tribe, the Administrator shall prescribe such a program pursuant to subsection (c) of this section, and consistent with section 1421(b) , within 270 days after the enactment of the Safe Drinking Water Act Amendments of 1986, unless an Indian Tribe first obtains approval to assume primary enforcement responsibility for underground injection control.

[§1422(e) added by PL 99–339]

§300h–2. Enforcement of Program. [Sec. 1423]

[§1423 head amended by PL 99–339]

(a) (1) Whenever the Administrator finds during a period during which a State has primary enforcement responsibility for underground water sources (within the meaning of section 1422(b)(3) or section 1425(c)) that any person who is subject to a requirement of an applicable underground injection control program in such State is violating such requirement, he shall so notify the State and the person violating such requirement. If beyond the thirtieth day after the Administrator's notification the State has not commenced appropriate enforcement action, the Administrator shall issue an order under subsection (c) requiring the person to comply with such requirement or the Administrator shall commence a civil action under subsection (b).

[§1423(a)(1) amended by PL 96–502; revised by PL 99–339]

(2) Whenever the Administrator finds during a period during which a State does not have primary enforcement responsibility for underground water sources that any person subject to any requirement of any applicable underground injection control program in such State is violating such requirement, the Administrator shall issue an order under subsection (c) requiring the person to comply with such requirement or the Administrator shall commence civil action under subsection (b).

[§1423(a)(2) amended by PL 99–339]

(b) Civil and Criminal Actions. — Civil actions referred to in paragraphs (1) and (2) of subsection (a) shall be brought in the appropriate United States district court. Such court shall have jurisdiction to require compliance with any requirement of an applicable underground injection program or with an order issued under subsection (c). The court may enter such judgment as protection of public health may require. Any person who violates any requirement of an applicable underground injection control program or an order requiring compliance under subsection (c)—

(1) shall be subject to a civil penalty of not more than $25,000 for each day of such violation, and

(2) if such violation is willful, such person may, in addition to or in lieu of the civil penalty authorized by paragraph (1), be imprisoned for not more than 3 years, or fined in accordance with title 18 of the United States Code, or both.

[§1423(b) revised by PL 99–339]

(c) Administrative Orders. —

(1) In any case in which the Administrator is authorized to bring a civil action under this section with respect to any regulation or other requirement of this part other than those relating to —

(A) the underground injection of brine or other fluids which are brought to the surface in connection with oil or natural gas production, or

(B) any underground injection for the secondary or tertiary recovery of oil or natural gas,the Administrator may also issue an order under this subsection either assessing a civil penalty of not more than $10,000 for each day of violation for any past or current violation, up to a maximum administrative penalty of $125,000, or requiring compliance with such regulation or other requirement, or both.

(2) In any case in which the Administrator is authorized to bring a civil action under this section with respect to any regulation, or other requirement of this part relating to —

(A) the underground injection of brine or other fluids which are brought to the surface in connection with oil or natural gas production, or

(B) any underground injection for the secondary or tertiary recovery of oil or natural gas,the Administrator may also issue an order under this subsection either assessing a civil penalty of not more than $5,000 for each day of violation for any past or current violation, up to a maximum administrative penalty of $125,000, or requiring compliance with such regulation or other requirement, or both.

(3) (A) An order under this subsection shall be issued by the Administrator after opportunity (provided in accordance with this subparagraph) for a hearing. Before issuing the order, the Administrator shall give to the person to whom it is directed written notice of the Administrator's proposal to issue such order and the opportunity to request, within 30 days of the date the notice is received by such person, a hearing on the order. Such hearing shall not be subject to section 554 or 556 of title 5, United States Code, but shall provide a reasonable opportunity to be heard and to present evidence.

(B) The Administrator shall provide public notice of, and reasonable opportunity to comment on, any proposed order.

(C) Any citizen who comments on any proposed order under subparagraph (B) shall be given notice of any hearing under this subsection and of any order. In any hearing held under subparagraph (A), such citizen shall have a reasonable opportunity to be heard and to present evidence.

(D) Any order issued under this subsection shall become effective 30 days following its issuance unless an appeal is taken pursuant to paragraph (6).

(4) (A) Any order issued under this subsection shall state with reasonable specificity the nature of the violation and may specify a reasonable time for compliance.

(B) In assessing any civil penalty under this subsection, the Administrator shall take into account appropriate factors, including (i) the seriousness of the violation; (ii) the economic benefit (if any) resulting from the violation; (iii) any history of such violations; (iv) any good-faith efforts to comply with the applicable requirements; (v) the economic impact of the penalty on the violator; and (vi) such other matters as justice may require.

(5) Any violation with respect to which the Administrator has commenced and is diligently prosecuting an action, or has issued an order under this subsection assessing a penalty, shall not be subject to an action under subsection (b) of this section or section 1424(c) or 1449 , except that the foregoing limitation on civil actions under section 1449 of this Act shall not apply with respect to any violation for which—

(A) a civil action under section 1449(a)(1) has been filed prior to commencement of an action under this subsection, or

(B) a notice of violation under section 1449(b)(1) has been given before commencement of an action under this subsection and an action under section 1449(a)(1) of this Act is filed before 120 days after such notice is given.

(6) Any person against whom an order is issued or who commented on a proposed order pursuant to paragraph (3) may file an appeal of such order with the United States District Court for the District of Columbia or the district in which the violation is alleged to have occurred. Such an appeal may only be filed within the 30–day period beginning on the date the order is issued. Appellant shall simultaneously send a copy of the appeal by certified mail to the Administrator and to the Attorney General. The Administrator shall promptly file in such court a certified copy of the record on which such order was imposed. The district court shall not set aside or remand such order unless there is not substantial evidence on the record, taken as a whole, to support the finding of a violation or, unless the Administrator's assessment of penalty or requirement for compliance constitutes an abuse of discretion. The district court shall not impose additional civil penalities for the same violation unless the Administrator's assessment of a penalty constitutes an abuse of discretion. Notwithstanding section 1448(a)(2) , any order issued under paragraph (3) shall be subject to judicial review exclusively under this paragraph.

(7) If any person fails to pay an assessment of a civil penalty —

(A) after the order becomes effective under paragraph (3), or

(B) after a court, in an action brought under paragraph (6), has entered a final judgment in favor of the Administrator, the Administrator may request the Attorney General to bring a civil action in an appropriate district court to recover the amount assessed (plus costs, attorneys' fees, and interest at currently prevailing rates from the date the order is effective or the date of such final judgment, as the case may be). In such an action, the validity, amount, and appropriateness of such penalty shall not be subject to review.

(8) The Administrator may, in connection with administrative proceedings under this subsection, issue subpoenas compelling the attendance and testimony of witnesses and subpoenas duces tecum, and may request the Attorney General to bring an action to enforce any subpoena under this section. The district courts shall have jurisdiction to enforce such subpoenas and impose sanction.

[New §1423(c) added by PL 99–339]

(d) Nothing in this title shall diminish any authority of a State or political subdivision to adopt or enforce any law or regulation respecting underground injection but no such law or regulation shall relieve any person of any requirement otherwise applicable under this title.

[Former §1423(c) redesignated as (d) by PL 99–339]

§300h–3. Interim Regulation of Underground Injections. [Sec. 1424]

(a)(1) Any person may petition the Administrator to have an area of a State (or States) designated as an area in which no new underground injection well may be operated during the period beginning on the date of the designation and ending on the date on which the applicable underground injection control program covering such area takes effect unless a permit for the operation of such well has been issued by the Administrator under subsection (b). The Administrator may so designate an area within a State if he finds that the area has one aquifer which is the sole or principal drinking water source for the area and which, if contaminated, would create a significant hazard to public health.

(2) Upon receipt of a petition under paragraph (1) of this subsection, the Administrator shall publish it in the Federal Register and shall provide an opportunity to interested persons to submit written data, views, or arguments thereon. Not later than the 30th day following the date of the publication of a petition under this paragraph in the Federal Register, the Administrator shall either make the designation for which the petition is submitted or deny the petition.

(b) (1) During the period beginning on the date an area is designated under subsection (a) and ending on the date the applicable underground injection control program covering such area takes effect, no new underground injection well may be operated in such area unless the Administrator has issued a permit for such operation.

(2) Any person may petition the Administrator for the issuance of a permit for the operation of such a well in such an area. A petition submitted under this paragraph shall be submitted in such manner and contain such information as the Administrator may require by regulation. Upon receipt of such a petition, the Administrator shall publish it in the Federal Register. The Administrator shall give notice of any proceeding on a petition and shall provide opportunity for agency hearing. The Administrator shall act upon such petition on the record of any hearing held pursuant to the preceding sentence respecting such petition. Within 120 days of the publication in the Federal Register of a petition submitted under this paragraph, the Administrator shall either issue the permit for which the petition was submitted or shall deny its issuance.

(3) The Administrator may issue a permit for the operation of a new underground injection well in an area designated under subsection (a) only if he finds that the operation of such well will not cause contamination of the aquifer of such area so as to create a significant hazard to public health. The Administrator may condition the issuance of such a permit upon the use of such control measures in connection with the operation of such well, for which the permit is to be issued, as he deems necessary to assure that the operation of the well will not contaminate the aquifer of the designated area in which the well is located so as to create a significant hazard to public health.

(c) Any person who operates a new underground injection well in violation of subsection (b), (1) shall be subject to a civil penalty of not more than $5,000 for each day in which such violation occurs, or (2) if such violation is willful, such person may, in lieu of the civil penalty authorized by clause (1) be fined not more than $10,000 for each day in which such violation occurs. If the Administrator has reason to believe that any person is violating or will violate subsection (b), he may petition the United States district court to issue a temporary restraining order or injunction (including a mandatory injunction) to enforce such subsection.

(d) For purposes of this section, the term 'new underground injection well' means an underground injection well whose operation was not approved by appropriate State and Federal agencies before the date of the enactment of this title.

(e) If the Administrator determines, on his own initiative or upon petition, that an area has an aquifer which is the sole or principal drinking water source for the area and which, if contaminated, would create a significant hazard to public health, he shall publish notice of that determination in the Federal Register. After the publication of any such notice, no commitment for Federal financial assistance (through a grant, contract, loan guarantee, or otherwise) may be entered into for any project which the Administrator determines may contaminate such aquifer through a recharge zone so as to create a significant hazard to public health, but a commitment for Federal financial assistance may, if authorized under another provision of law, be entered into to plan or design the project to assure that it will not so contaminate the aquifer.

§300h–4. Optional Demonstration by States Relating to Oil or Natural Gas. [Sec. 1425]

[§1425 added by PL 96–502]

(a) For purposes of the Administrator's approval or disapproval under section 1422 of that portion of any State underground injection control program which relates to—

(1) the underground injection of brine or other fluids which are brought to the surface in connection with oil or natural gas production or natural gas storage operations, or

[§1425(a)(1) amended by PL 99–339]

(2) any underground injection for the secondary or tertiary recovery of oil or natural gas. In lieu of the showing required under subparagraph (A) of section 1422(b)(1) the State may demonstrate that such portion of the State program meets the requirements of subparagraphs (A) through (D) of section 1421(b)(1) and represents an effective program (including adequate recordkeeping and reporting) to prevent underground injection which endangers drinking water sources.

(b) If the Administrator revises or amends any requirement of a regulation under section 1421 relating to any aspect of the underground injection referred to in subsection (a), in the case of that portion of a State underground injection control program for which the demonstration referred to in subsection (a) has been made, in lieu of the showing required under section 1422(b)(1)(B) the State may demonstrate that, with respect to that aspect of such underground injection, the State program meets the requirements of subparagraphs (A) through (D) of section 1421(b)(1) and represents an effective program (including adequate recordkeeping and reporting) to prevent underground injection which endangers drinking water sources.

(c) (1) Section 1422(b)(3) shall not apply to that portion of any State underground injection control program approved by the Administrator pursuant to a demonstration under subsection of this section (and under subsection (b) of this section where applicable).

(2) If pursuant to such a demonstration, the Administrator approves such portion of the State program, the State shall have primary enforcement responsibility with respect to that portion until such time as the Administrator determines, by rule, that such demonstration is no longer valid. Following such a determination, the Administrator may exercise the authority of subsection (c) of section 1422 in the same manner as provided in such subsection with respect to a determination described in such subsection.

(3) Before promulgating any rule under paragraph (2), the Administrator shall provide opportunity for public hearing respecting such rule.

§300h–5. Regulation of State Programs. [Sec. 1426]

[§1426 added by PL 99–339]

(a) Monitoring Methods. — Not later than 18 months after enactment of the Safe Drinking Water Act Amendments of 1986, the Administrator shall modify regulations issued under this Act for Class I injection wells to identify monitoring methods, in addition to those in effect on November 1, 1985, including groundwater monitoring. In accordance with such regulations, the Administrator, or delegated State authority, shall determine the applicability of such monitoring methods, wherever appropriate, at locations and in such a manner as to provide the earliest possible detection of fluid migration into, or in the direction of, underground sources of drinking water from such wells, based on its assessment of the potential for fluid migration from the injection zone that may be harmful to human health or the environment. For purposes of this subsection, a class I injection well is defined in accordance with 40 CFR 146.05 as in effect on November 1, 1985.

(b) Report. — The Administrator shall submit a report to Congress, no later than September 1987, summarizing the results of State surveys required by the Administrator under this section. The report shall include each of the following items of information:

(1) The numbers and categories of class V wells which discharge nonhazardous waste into or above an underground source of drinking water.

(2) The primary contamination problems associated with different categories of these disposal wells.

(3) Recommendations for minimum design, construction, installation, and siting requirements that should be applied to protect underground sources of drinking water from such contamination wherever necessary.

§300h–6. Sole Source Aquifer Demonstration Program. [Sec. 1427]

[§1427 added by PL 99–339]

(a) Purpose. — The purpose of this section is to establish procedures for development, implementation, and assessment of demonstration program designed to protect critical aquifer protection areas located within areas designated as sole or principal source aquifers under section 1424(e) of this Act.

(b) Definition. — Four purposes of this section, the term 'critical aquifer protection area' means either of the following:

(1) All or part of an area located within an area for which an application or designation as a sole or principal source aquifer pursuant to section 1424(e) , has been submitted and approved by the Administrator not later than 24 months after the enactment of the Safe Drinking Water Act Amendments of 1986 and which satisfies the criteria established by the Administrator under subsection (d).

(2) All or part of an area which is within an aquifer designated as a sole source aquifer as of the enactment of the Safe Drinking Water Act Amendments of 1986 and for which an areawide ground water quality protection plan has been approved under section 208 of the Clean Water Act prior to such enactment.

(c) Application. — Any State, municipal or local government or political subdivision thereof or any planning entity (including any interstate regional planning entity) that identifies a critical aquifer protection area over which it has authority or jurisdiction may apply to the Administrator for the selection of such area for a demonstration program under this section. Any applicant shall consult with other government or planning entities with authority or jurisdiction in such area prior to application. Applicants, other than the Governor, shall submit the application for a demonstration program jointly with the Governor.

(d) Criteria. — Not later than 1 year after the enactment of the Safe Drinking Water Act Amendments of 1986, the Administrator shall, by rule, establish criteria for identifying critical aquifer protection areas under this section. In establishing such criteria, the Administrator shall consider each of the following:

(1) The vulnerability of the aquifer to contamination due to hydrogeologic characteristics.

(2) The number of persons or the proportion of population using the ground water as a drinking water source.

(3) The economic, social and environmental benefits that would result to the area from maintenance of ground water of high quality.

(4) The economic, social and environmental costs that would result from degradation of the quality of the ground water.

(e) Contents of Application. — An application submitted to the Administrator by any applicant for a demonstration program under this section shall meet each of the following requirements:

(1) The application shall propose boundaries for the critical aquifer protection area within its jurisdiction.

(2) The application shall designate or, if necessary, establish a planning entity (which shall be a public agency and which shall include representation of elected local and State governmental officials) to develop a comprehensive management plan (hereinafter in this section referred to as the 'plan') for the critical protection area. Where a local government planning agency exists with adequate authority to carry out this section with respect to any proposed critical protection area, such agency shall be designated as the planning entity.

(3) The application shall establish procedures for public participation in the development of the plan, for review, approval, and adoption of the plan, and for assistance to municipalities and other public agencies with authority under State law to implement the plan.

(4) The application shall include a hydrogeologic assessment of surface and ground water resources within the critical protection area.

(5) The application shall include a comprehensive management plan for the proposed protection area.

(6) The application shall include the measures and schedule proposed for implementation of such plan.

(f) Comprehensive Plan. —

(1) The objective of a comprehensive management plan submitted by an applicant under this section shall be to maintain the quality of the ground water in the critical protection area in a manner reasonably expected to protect human health, the environment and ground water resources. In order to achieve such objective, the plan may be designed to maintain, to the maximum extent possible, the natural vegetative and hydrogeological conditions. Each of the following elements shall be included in such a protection plan:

(A) A map showing the detailed boundary of the critical protection area.

(B) An identification of existing and potential point and nonpoint sources of ground water degradation.

(C) An assessment of the relationship between activities on the land surface and ground water quality.

(D) Specific actions and management practices to be implemented in the critical protection area to prevent adverse impacts on ground water quality.

(E) Identification of authority adequate to implement the plan, estimates of program costs, and sources of State matching funds.

(2) Such plan may also include the following:

(A) A determination of the quality of the existing ground water recharged through the special protection area and the natural recharge capabilities of the special protection area watershed.

(B) Requirements designed to maintain existing underground drinking water quality or improve underground drinking water quality if prevailing conditions fail to meet drinking water standards, pursuant to this Act and State law.

(C) Limits on Federal, State, and local government, financially assisted activities and projects which may contribute to degradation of such ground water or any loss of natural surface and subsurface infiltration of purification capability of the special protection watershed.

(D) A comprehensive statement of land use management including emergency contingency planning as it pertains to the maintenance of the quality of underground sources of drinking water or to the improvement of such sources if necessary to meet drinking water standards pursuant to this Act and State law.

(E) Actions in the special protection area which would avoid adverse impacts on water quality, recharge capabilities, or both.

(F) Consideration of specific techniques which may include clustering, transfer of development rights, and other innovative measures sufficient to achieve the objectives of this section.

(G) Consideration of the establishment of a State institution to facilitate and assist funding a development transfer credit system.

(H) A program for State and local implementation of the plan described in this subsection in a manner that will insure the continued, uniform, consistent protection of the critical protection area in accord with the purposes of this section.

(I) Pollution abatement measures, if appropriate.

(g) Plans Under Section 208 of the Clean Water Act. — A plan approved before the enactment of the Safe Drinking Water Act Amendments of 1986 under section 208 of the Clean Water Act to protect a sole source aquifer designated under section 1424(e) of this Act shall be considered a comprehensive management plan for the purposes of this section.

(h) Consultation and Hearings. — During the development of a comprehensive management plan under this section, the planning entity shall consult with, and consider the comments of, appropriate officials of any municipality and State or Federal agency which has jurisdiction over lands and waters within the special protection area, other concerned organizations and technical and citizen advisory committees. The planning entity shall conduct public hearings at places within the special protection area for the purpose of providing the opportunity to comment on any aspect of the plan.

(i) Approval or Disapproval. — Within 120 days after receipt of an application under this section, the Administrator shall approve or disapprove the application. The approval or disapproval shall be based on a determination that the critical protection area satisfies the criteria established under subsection (d) and that a demonstration program for the area would provide protection for ground water quality consistent with the objectives stated in subsection (f). The Administrator shall provide to the Governor a written explanation of the reasons for the disapproval of any such application. Any petitioner may modify and resubmit any application which is not approved. Upon approval of an application, the Administrator may enter into a cooperative agreement with the applicant to establish a demonstration program under this section.

(j) Grants and Reimbursement. — Upon entering a cooperative agreement under subsection (i), the Administrator may provide to the applicant, on a matching basis, a grant of 50 per centum of the costs of implementing the plan established under this section. The Administrator may also reimburse the applicant of an approved plan up to 50 per centum of the costs of developing such plan, except for plans approved under section 208 of the Clean Water Act. The total amount of grants under this section for any one aquifer, designated under section 1424(e) , shall not exceed $4,000,000 in any one fiscal year.

(k) Activities Funded Under Other Law. — No funds authorized under this subsection may be used to fund activities funded under other sections of this Act or the Clean Water Act, the Solid Waste Disposal Act, the Comprehensive Environmental Response, Compensation, and Liability Act of 1980 or other environmental laws.

(l) Report. — Not later than December 31, 1989, each State shall submit to the Administrator a report assessing the impact of the program on ground water quality and identifying those measures found to be effective in protecting ground water resources. No later than September 30, 1990, the Administrator shall submit to Congress a report summarizing the State reports, and assessing the accomplishments of the sole source aquifer demonstration program including an identification of protection methods found to be most effective and recommendations for their application to protect ground water resources from contamination whenever necessary.

(m) Savings Provision. — Nothing under this section shall be construed to amend, supersede or abrogate rights to quantities of water which have been established by interstate water compacts, Supreme Court decrees, or State water laws; or any requirement imposed or right provided under any Federal or State environmental or public health statute.

(n) Authorization. — There are authorized to be appropriated to carry out this section not more than the following amounts:

Fiscal year:	Amount
1987	$10,000,000
1988	$15,000,000
1989	$17,500,000
1990	$17,500,000
1991	$17,500,000

Matching grants under this section may also be used to implement or update any water quality management plan for a sole or principal source aquifer approved (before the date of the enactment of this section) by the Administrator under section 208 of the Federal Water Pollution Control Act.

§300h–7. State Programs to Establish Wellhead Protection Areas. [Sec. 1428]

[§1428 added by PL 99–339]

(a) State Programs. — The Governor or Governor's designee of each State shall, within 3 years of the date of enactment of the Safe Drinking Water Act Amendments of 1986, adopt and submit to the Administrator a State program to protect wellhead areas within their jurisdiction from contaminants which may have any adverse effect on the health of persons. Each State program under this section shall, at a minimum —

(1) specify the duties of State agencies, local governmental entities, and public water supply systems with respect to the development and implementation of programs required by this section;

(2) for each wellhead, determine the wellhead protection area as defined in subsection (e) based on all reasonably available hydrogeologic information on ground water flow, recharge and discharge and other information the State deems necessary to adequately determine the wellhead protection area;

(3) identify within each wellhead protection area all potential anthropogenic sources of contaminants which may have any adverse effect on the health of persons;

(4) describe a program that contains, as appropriate, technical assistance, financial assistance, implementation of control measures, education, training, and demonstration projects to protect the water supply within wellhead protection areas from such contaminants;

(5) include contingency plans for the location and provision of alternate drinking water supplies for each public water system in the event of well or wellfield contamination by such contaminants; and

(6) include a requirement that consideration be given to all potential sources of such contaminants within the expected wellhead area of a new water well which serves a public water supply system.

(b) Public Participation. — To the maximum extent possible, each State shall establish procedures, including but not limited to the establishment of technical and citizens' advisory committees, to encourage the public to participate in developing the protection program for wellhead areas. Such procedures shall include notice and opportunity for public hearing on the State program before it is submitted to the Administrator.

(c) Disapproval. —

(1) In General. — If, in the judgment of the Administrator a State program (or portion thereof, including the definition of a wellhead protection area), is not adequate to protect

public water systems as required by this section, the Administrator shall disapprove such program (or portion thereof). A State program developed pursuant to subsection (a) shall be deemed to be adequate unless the Administrator determines, within 9 months of the receipt of a State program, that such program (or portion thereof) is inadequate for the purpose of protecting public water systems as required by this section from contaminants that may have any adverse effect on the health of persons. If the Administrator determines that a proposed State program (or any portion thereof) is inadequate, the Administrator shall submit a written statement of the reasons for such determination to the Governor of the State.

(2) Modification and Resubmission. — Within 6 months after receipt of the Administrator's written notice under paragraph (1) that any proposed State program (or portion thereof) is inadequate, the Governor or Governor's designee, shall modify the program based upon the recommendations of the Administrator and resubmit the modified program to the Administrator.

(d) Federal Assistance. — After the date 3 years after the enactment of this section, no State shall receive funds authorized to be appropriated under this section except for the purpose of implementing the program and requirements of paragraphs (4) and (6) of subsection (a).

(e) Definition of Wellhead Protection Area. — As used in this section, the term 'wellhead protection area' means the surface and subsurface area surrounding a water well or wellfield, supplying a public water system, through which contaminants are reasonably likely to move toward and reach such water well or wellfield. The extent of a wellhead protection area, within a State, necessary to provide protection from contaminants which may have any adverse effect on the health of persons is to be determined by the State in the program submitted under subsection (a). Not later than one year after the enactment of the Safe Drinking Water Act Amendments of 1986, the Administrator shall issue technical guidance which States may use in making such determination. Such guidance may reflect such factors as the radius of influence around a well or wellfield, the depth of drawdown of the water table by such well or wellfield at any given point, the time or rate of travel of various contaminants in various hydrologic conditions, distance from the well or wellfield, or other factors affecting the likelihood of contaminants reaching the well or wellfield, taking into account available engineering pump tests or comparable data, field reconnaissance, topographic information, and the geology of the formation in which the well or wellfield is located.

(f) Prohibitions.—

(1) Activities under other laws. — No funds authorized to be appropriate under this section may be used to support activities authorized by the Federal Water Pollution Control Act, the Solid Waste Disposal Act, the Comprehensive Environmental Response, Compensation, and Liability Act of 1980, or other sections of this Act.

(2) Individual sources. — No funds authorized to be appropriated under this section may be used to bring individual sources of contamination into compliance.

(g) Implementation — Each State shall make every reasonable effort to implement the State wellhead area protection program under this section within 2 years of submitting the program to the Administrator. Each State shall submit to the Administrator a biennial status report describing the State's progress in implementing the program. Such report shall include amendments to the State program for water wells sited during the biennial period.

(h) Federal Agencies. — Each department, agency, and instrumentality of the executive, legislative, and judicial branches of the Federal Government having jurisdiction over any potential source of contaminants identified by a State program pursuant to the provisions of subsection (a)(3) shall be subject to and comply with all requirements of the State program developed according to subsection (a)(4) applicable to such potential source of contaminants, both substantive and procedural, in the same manner and to the same extent, as any other person is subject to such requirements, including payment of reasonable charges and fees. The President may exempt any potential source under the jurisdiction of any department, agency, or instrumentality in the executive branch if the President determines it to be in the paramount interest of the United States to do so. No such exemption shall be granted due to the lack of an appropriation unless the President shall have specifically requested such appropriation as part of the budgetary process and the Congress shall have failed to make available such requested appropriations.

(i) Additional Requirement. —

(1) In General. — In addition to the provisions of subsection (a) of this section, States in which there are more than 2,500 active wells at which annular injection is used as of January 1, 1986, shall include in their State program a certification that a State program exists and is being adequately enforced that provides protection from contaminants which may have any adverse effect on the health of persons and which are associated with the annual injection or surface disposal of brines associated with oil and gas production.

(2) Definition. — For purposes of this subsection, the term 'annular injection' means the reinjection of brines associated with the production of oil or gas between the production and surface casings of a conventional oil or gas producing well.

(3) Review. — The Administrator shall conduct a review of each program certified under this subsection.

(4) Disapproval. — If a State fails to include the certification required by this subsection or if in the judgment of the Administrator the State program certified under this subsection is not being adequately enforced, the Administrator shall disapprove the State program submitted under subsection (a) of this section.

(j) Coordination With Other Laws. — Nothing in this section shall authorize or require any department, agency, or other instrumentality of the Federal Government or State or local government to apportion, allocate or otherwise regulate the withdrawal or beneficial use of ground or surface waters, so as to abrogate or modify any existing rights to water established pursuant to State or Federal law, including interstate compacts.

(k) Authorization of Appropriations. — Unless the State program is disapproved under this section, the Administrator shall make grants to the State for not less than 50 or more than 90 percent of the costs incurred by a State (as determined by the Administrator) in developing and implementing each State program under this section. For purposes of making such grants there is authorized to be appropriated not more than the following amounts:

Fiscal year:	**Amount**
1987	$20,000,000
1988	$20,000,000
1989	$35,500,000
1990	$35,500,000
1991	$35,500,000

PART D — EMERGENCY POWERS

§300i. Emergency Powers. [Sec. 1431]

(a) Notwithstanding any other provision of this title, the Administrator, upon receipt of information that a contaminant which is present in or is likely to enter a public water system or an underground source of drinking water may present an imminent and substantial endangerment to the health of persons, and that appropriate State and local authorities have not acted to protect the health of such persons, may take such actions as he may deem necessary in order to protect the health of such persons. To the extent he determines it to be practicable in light of such imminent endangerment, he shall consult with the State and local authorities in order to confirm the correctness of the information on which action proposed to be taken under this subsection is based and to ascertain the action which such authorities are or will be taking. The action which the Administrator may take may include (but shall not be limited to) (1) issuing such orders as may be necessary to protect the health of persons who are or may be users of such system (including travelers), including orders requiring the provision of alternative water supplies by persons who caused or contributed to the endangerment, and (2) commencing a civil action for appropriate relief, including a restraining order or permanent or temporary injunction.

[§1431(a) amended by PL 99–339]

(b) Any person who violates or fails or refuses to comply with any order issued by the Administrator under subsection (a)(1) may, in an action brought in the appropriate United States district court to enforce such order, be subject to a civil penalty of not to exceed $5,000 for each day in which such violation occurs or failure to comply continues.

[§1431(b) amended by PL 99–339]

§300i–1. Tampering with Public Water Systems. [Sec. 1432]

[§1432 added by PL 99–339]

(a) Tampering. — Any person who tampers with a public water system shall be imprisoned for not more than 5 years, or fined in accordance with title 18 of the United States Code, or both.

(b) Attempt or Threat. — Any person who attempts to tamper, or makes a threat to tamper, with a public drinking water system be imprisoned for not more than 3 years, or fined in accordance with title 18 of the United States Code, or both.

(c) Civil Penalty. — The Administrator may bring a civil action in the appropriate United States district court (as determined under the provisions of title 28 of the United States Code) against any person who tampers, attempts to tamper, or makes a threat to tamper with a public water system. The court may impose on such person a civil penalty of not more than $50,000 for such tampering or not more than $20,000 for such attempt or threat.

(d) Definition of "Tamper". — For purposes of this section, the term 'tamper' means —

(1) to introduce a contaminant into a public water system with the intention of harming persons; or

(2) to otherwise interfere with the operation of a public water system with the intention of harming persons.

PART E — GENERAL PROVISIONS

§300j. Assurance of Availability of Adequate Supplies of Chemicals Necessary for Treatment of Water. [Sec. 1441]

(a) If any person who uses chlorine, activated carbon, lime, ammonia, soda ash, potassium permanganate caustic soda, or other chemical or substance for the purpose of treating water in any public water system or in any public treatment works determines that the amount of such chemical or substance necessary to effectively treat such water is not reasonably available to him or will not be so available to him when required for the effective treatment of such water, such person may apply to the Administrator for a certification (hereinafter in this section referred to as a "certification of need") that the amount of such chemical or substance which such person requires to effectively treat such water is not reasonably available to him or will not be so available when required for the effective treatment of such water.

(b) (1) An application for a certification of need shall be in such form and submitted in such manner as the Administrator may require and shall (A) specify the persons the applicant determines are able to provide the chemical or substance with respect to which the application is submitted, (B) specify the persons from whom the applicant has sought such chemical or substance, and (C) contain such other information as the Administrator may require.

(2) Upon receipt of an application under this section, the Administrator shall (A) publish in the Federal Register a notice of the receipt of the application and a brief summary of it, notify in writing each person whom the President or his delegate (after consultation with the Administrator) determines could be made subject to an order required to be issued upon the issuance of the certification of need applied for in such application, and (C) provide an opportunity for the submission of written comments on such application. The requirements of the preceding sentence of this paragraph shall not apply when the Administrator for good cause finds (and incorporates the finding with a brief statement of reasons therefor in the order issued) that waiver of such requirements is necessary in order to protect the public health.

(3) Within 30 days after—

(A) the date a notice is published under paragraph (2) in the Federal Register with respect to an application submitted under this section for the issuance of a certification of need, or

(B) the date on which such application is received if as authorized by the second sentence of such paragraph no notice is published with respect to such application, the Administrator shall take action either to issue or deny the issuance of a certification of need.

(c) (1) If the Administrator finds that the amount of a chemical or substance necessary for an applicant under an application submitted under this section to effectively treat water in a public water system or in a public treatment works is not reasonably available to the applicant or will not be so available to him when required for the effective treatment of such water, the Administrator shall issue a certification of need. Not later than seven days following the issuance of such certification, the President or his delegate shall issue an order requiring the provision to such person of such amounts of such chemical or substance as the Administrator deems necessary in the certification of need issued for such person. Such order shall apply to such manufacturers, producers, processors, distributors, and repackagers of such chemical or substance as the President or his delegate deems necessary and appropriate, except that such order may not apply to any manufacturer, producer, or processor of such chemical or substance who manufactures, produces, or processes (as the case may be) such chemical or substance solely for its own use. Persons subject to an order issued under this section shall be given a reasonable opportunity to consult with the President or his delegate with respect to the implementation of the order.

(2) Orders which are to be issued under paragraph (1) to manufacturers, producers, and processors of a chemical or substance shall be equitably apportioned, as far as practicable, among all manufacturers, producers, and processors of such chemical or substance; and orders which are to be issued under paragraph (1) to distributors and repackagers of a chemical or substance shall be equitably apportioned, as far as practicable, among all distributors and repackagers of such chemical or substance. In apportioning orders issued under paragraph (1) to manufacturers, producers, processors, distributors, and repackagers of chlorine, the President or his delegate shall, in carrying out the requirements of the preceding sentence, consider.—

(A) the geographical relationships and established commercial relationships between such manufacturers, producers, processors, distributors, and repackagers and the persons for whom the orders are issued;

(B) in the case of orders to be issued to producers of chlorine, the (i) amount of chlorine historically supplied by each such producer to treat water in public water systems and public treatment works, and (ii) share of each such producer of the total annual production of chlorine in the United States; and

(C) such other factors as the President or his delegate may determine are relevant to the apportionment of orders in accordance with the requirements of the preceding sentence.

(3) Subject to subsection (f), any person for whom a certification of need has been issued under this subsection may upon the expiration of the order issued under paragraph (1) upon such certification apply under this section for additional certifications.

(d) There shall be available as a defense to any action brought for breach of contract in a Federal or State court arising out of delay or failure to provide, sell, or offer for sale or exchange a chemical or substance subject to an order issued pursuant to subsection (c)(1), that such delay or failure was caused solely by compliance with such order.

(e) (1) Whoever knowingly fails to comply with any order issued pursuant to subsection (c)(1) shall be fined not more than $5,000 for each such failure to comply.

(2) Whoever fails to comply with any order issued pursuant to subsection (c)(1) shall be subject to a civil penalty of not more than $2,500 for each such failure to comply.

(3) Whenever the Administrator or the President or his delegate has reason to believe that any person is violating or will violate any order issued pursuant to subsection (c)(1), he may petition a United States district court to issue a temporary restraining order or preliminary or permanent injunction (including a mandatory injunction) to enforce the provision of such order.

(f) No certification of need or order issued under this section may remain in effect for more than one year.

[§1441(f) amended by PL 95–190; PL 96–63; PL 99–339]

§300j–1. Research, Technical Assistance, Information, Training of Personnel. [Sec. 1442]

(a) (1) The Administrator may conduct research, studies, and demonstrations relating to the causes, diagnosis, treatment, control, and prevention of physical and mental diseases and other impairments of man resulting directly or indirectly from contaminants in water, or to the provision of a dependably safe supply of drinking water, including—

(A) improved methods (i) to identify and measure the existence of contaminants in drinking water (including methods which may be used by State and local health and water officials), and (ii) to identify the source of such contaminants;

(B) improved methods to identify and measure the health effects of contaminants in drinking water;

(C) new methods of treating raw water to prepare it for drinking so as to improve the efficiency of water treatments and to remove contaminants from water;

(D) improved methods of providing a dependably safe supply of drinking water, including improvements in water purification and distribution, and methods of assessing the health related hazards of drinking water; and

(E) improved methods of protecting underground water sources of public water systems from contaminantion.

(2) (A) The Administrator shall, to the maximum extent feasible, provide technical assistance to the States and municipalities in the establishment and administration of public water system supervision programs (as defined in section 1443(c)(1)).

[§1442(a)(2)(A) designated by PL 95–190]

(B) The Administrator is authorized to provide technical assistance and to make grants to States, or publicly owned water systems to assist in responding to and alleviating any emergency situation affecting public water systems (including sources of water for such systems) which the Administrator determines to present substantial danger to the public health. Grants provided under this subparagraph shall be used only to support those actions which (i) are necessary for preventing, limiting or mitigating danger to the public health in such emergency situation and (ii) would not, in the judgment of the Administrator, be taken without such emergency assistance. The Administrator may carry out the program authorized under this subparagraph as part of, and in accordance with the terms and conditions of, any other program of assistance for environmental emergencies which the Administrator is authorized to carry out under any other provision of law. No limitation on appropriations for any such other program shall apply to amounts appropriated under the subparagraph.

[§1442(a)(2)(B) added and amended by PL 95–190]

(3) (A) The Administrator shall conduct studies, and make periodic reports to Congress, on the costs of carrying out regulations prescribed under section 1412 .

[§1442(a)(3)(A) designated by PL 95–190]

(B) Not later than eighteen months after the date of enactment of this subparagraph, the Administrator shall submit a report to Congress which identifies and analyzes—

(i) the anticipated costs of compliance with interim and revised national primary drinking water regulations and the anticipated costs to States and units of local governments in implementing such regulations;

(ii) alternative methods of (including alternative treatment techniques for) compliance with such regulations;

(iii) methods of paying the costs of compliance by public water systems with national primary drinking water regulations, including user charges, State or local taxes or subsidies, Federal grants (including planning or construction grants, or both), loans, and loan guarantees, and other methods of assisting in paying the costs of such compliance;

(iv) the advantages and disadvantages of each of the methods referred to in clauses (ii) and (iii);

(v) the sources of revenue presently available (and projected to be available) to public water systems to meet current and future expenses; and

(vi) the costs of drinking water paid by residential and industrial consumers in a sample of large, medium, and small public water systems and of individually owned wells, and the reasons for any differences in such costs. The report required by this subparagraph shall identify and analyze the items required in clauses (i) through (v) separately with respect to public water systems serving small communities.

The report required by this subparagraph shall include such recommendations as the Administrator deems appropriate.

[§1442(a)(3)(B) added by PL 95–190]

(4) The Administrator shall conduct a survey and study of—

(A) disposal of water (including residential waste) which may endanger underground water which supplies, or can reasonably be expected to supply, any public water systems, and

(B) means of control of such waste disposal. Not later than one year after the date of enactment of this title, he shall transmit to the Congress the results of such survey and study, together with such recommendations as he deems appropriate.

(5) The Administrator shall carry out a study of methods of underground injection which do not result in the degradation of underground drinking water sources.

(6) The Administrator shall carry out a study of methods of preventing, detecting, and dealing with surface spills of contaminants which may degrade underground water sources for public water systems.

(7) The Administrator shall carry out a study of virus contamination of drinking water sources and means of control of such contamination.

(8) The Administrator shall carry out a study of the nature and extent of the impact on underground water which supplies or can reasonably be expected to supply public water systems of (A) abandoned injection or extraction wells; (B) intensive application of pesticides and fertilizers in underground water

recharge areas; and (C) ponds, pools, lagoons, pits, or other surface disposal of contaminants in underground water recharge areas.

(9) The Administrator shall conduct a comprehensive study of public water supplies and drinking water sources to determine the nature, extent, sources of and means of control of contamination by chemicals or other substances suspected of being carcinogenic. Not later than six months after the date of enactment of this title, he shall transmit to the Congress the initial results of such study, together with such recommendations for further review and corrective action as he deems appropriate.

(10) The Administrator shall carry out a study of the reaction of chlorine and humic acids and the effects of the contaminants which result from such reaction on public health and on the safety of drinking water, including any carcinogenic effect.

[§1442(a)(10), added by PL 95–190]

(11) The Administrator shall carry out a study of polychlorinated biphenyl contamination of actual or potential sources of drinking water, contamination of such sources by other substances known or suspected to be harmful to public health, the effects of such contamination, and means of removing, treating, or otherwise controlling such contamination. To assist in carrying out this paragraph, the Administrator is authorized to make grants to public agencies and private nonprofit institutions.

[§1442(a)(11) added by PL 95–190]

(b) In carrying out this title, the Administrator is authorized to —

(1) collect and make available information pertaining to research, investigations, and demonstrations with respect to providing a dependably safe supply of drinking water together with appropriate recommendations in connection therewith;

(2) make available research facilities of the Agency to appropriate public authorities, institutions, and individuals engaged in studies and research relating to the purposes of this title;

(3) make grants to, and enter into contracts with, any public agency, educational institution, and any other organization, in accordance with procedures prescribed by the Administrator, under which he may pay all or a part of the costs (as may be determined by the Administrator) of any project or activity which is designed—

(A) to develop, expand, or carry out a program (which may combine training education and employment) for training persons for occupations involving the public health aspects of providing safe drinking water;

(B) to train inspectors and supervisory personnel to train or supervise persons in occupations involving the public health aspects of providing safe drinking water; or

(C) to develop and expand the capability of programs of States and municipalities to carry out the purposes of this title (other than by carrying out State programs of public water system supervision or underground water source protection (as defined in section 1443(c)).

[§1442(b)(3)(C) amended by PL 95–190]

(c) Not later than eighteen months after the date of enactment of this subsection, the Administrator shall submit a report to Congress on the present and projected future availability of an adequate and dependable supply of safe drinking water to meet present and projected future need. Such report shall include an analysis of the future demand for drinking water and other competing uses of water, the availability and use of methods to conserve water or reduce demand, the adequacy of present measures to assure adequate and dependable supplies of safe drinking water, and the problems (financial, legal, or other) which need to be resolved in order to assure the availability of such supplies for the future. Existing information and data compiled by the National Water Commission and others shall be utilized to the extent possible.

(d) The Administrator shall—

(1) provide training for, and make grants for training (including postgraduate training) of (A) personnel of State agencies which have primary enforcement responsibility and of agencies or units of local government to which enforcement responsibilities have been delegated by the State, and (B) personnel who manage or operate public water systems, and

(2) make grants for postgraduate training of individuals (including grants to educational institutions for traineeships) for purposes of qualifying such individuals to work as personnel referred to in paragraph (1). Reasonable fees may be charged for training provided under paragraph (1)(B) to persons other than personnel of State or local agencies but such training shall be provided to personnel of State or local agencies without charge.

[§1442(d) added by PL 95–190]

(e) [Repealed]

[§1442(e) added by PL 96–502; repealed by PL 99–339]

(f) There are authorized to be appropriated to carry out the provisions of this section other than subsections (a)(2)(B) and provisions relating to research $15,000,000 for the fiscal year ending June 30, 1975; $25,000,000 for the fiscal year ending June 30, 1976; $35,000,000 for the fiscal year ending June 30, 1977; $17,000,000 for each of the fiscal years 1978 and 1979; $21,405,000 for the fiscal year ending September 30, 1980; $30,000,000 for the fiscal year ending September 30, 1981; and $35,000,000 for the fiscal year ending September 30, 1982. There are authorized to be appropriated to carry out subsection (a)(2)(B) $8,000,000 for each of the fiscal years 1978 through 1982. There are authorized to be appropriated to carry out subsection (a)(2)(B) not more than the following amounts:

Fiscal year:	Amount
1987	$7,650,000
1988	$7,650,000
1989	$8,050,000
1990	$8,050,000
1991	$8,050,000

There are authorized to be appropriated to carry out the provisions of this section (other than subsection (g), subsection (a)(2)(B), and provisions relating to research), not more than the following amounts:

Fiscal year:	Amount
1987	$35,600,000
1988	$35,600,000
1989	$38,020,000
1990	$38,020,000
1991	$38,020,000

[Former §1442(c) redesignated as (e) by PL 95–190; amended by PL 96–63; redesignated as (f) by PL 96–502; amended by PL 99–339]

(g) The Administrator is authorized to provide technical assistance to small public water systems to enable such systems to achieve and maintain compliance with national drinking water regulations. Such assistance may include 'circuit-rider' programs, training, and preliminary engineering studies. There are authorized to be appropriated to carry out this subsection $10,000,000 for each of the fiscal years 1987 through 1991. Not less than the greater of —

(1) 3 percent of the amounts appropriated under this subsection, or

(2) $280,000 shall be utilized for technical assistance to public water systems owned or operated by Indian tribes.

[§1442(g) added and amended by PL 99–339]

§300j–2. Grants for State Programs. [Sec. 1443]

(a) (1) From allotments made pursuant to paragraph (4), the Administrator may make grants to States to carry out public water system supervision programs.

(2) No grant may be made under paragraph (1) unless an application therefor has been submitted to the Administrator in such form and manner as he may require. The Administrator may not approve an application of a State for its first grant under paragraph (1) unless he determines that the State—

(A) has established or will establish within one year from the date of such grant a public water system supervision program, and

(B) will, within that one year, assume primary enforcement responsibility for public water systems within the State. No grant may be made to a State under paragraph (1) for any period beginning more than one year after the date of the State's first grant unless the State has assumed and maintains primary enforcement responsibility for public water systems within the State. The prohibitions contained in the preceding two sentences shall not apply to such grants when made to Indian Tribes.

[§1443(a)(2) amended by PL 99–339]

(3) A grant under paragraph (1) shall be made to cover not more than 75 per centum of the grant recipient's costs (as determined under regulations of the Administrator) in carrying out, during the one-year period beginning on the date the grant is made, a public water system supervision program.

(4) In each fiscal year the Administrator shall, in accordance with regulations, allot the sums appropriated for such year under paragraph (5) among the States on the basis of population, geographical area, number of public water systems, and other relevant factors.

No State shall receive less than 1 per centum of the annual appropriation for grants under paragraph (1): *Provided,* That the Administrator may, by regulation, reduce such percentage in accordance with the criteria specified in this paragraph: *And provided further,* That such percentage shall not apply to grants allotted to Guam, American Samoa, or the Virgin Islands.

(5) The prohibition contained in the last sentence of paragraph (2) may be waived by the Administrator with respect to a grant to a State through fiscal year 1979 but such prohibition may only be waived if, in the judgment of the Administrator—

(A) the state is making a diligent effort to assume and maintain primary enforcement responsibility for public water systems within the state:

(B) the State has made significant progress toward assuming and maintaining such primary enforcement responsibility; and

(C) there is reason to believe the State will assume such primary enforcement responsibility by October 1, 1979.

The amount of any grant awarded for the fiscal years 1978 and 1979 pursuant to a waiver under this paragraph may not exceed 75 per centum of the allotment which the State would have received for such fiscal year if it had assumed and maintained such primary enforcement responsibility. The remaining 25 per centum of the amount allotted to such State for such fiscal year shall be retained by the Administrator, and the Administrator may award such amount to such State at such time as the State assumes such responsibility before the beginning of fiscal year 1980. At the beginning of each fiscal years 1979 and 1980 the amounts retained by the Administrator for any preceding fiscal year and not awarded by the beginning of fiscal year 1979 or 1980 to the states to which such amounts were originally allotted may be removed from the original allotment and reallotted for fiscal year 1979 or 1980 (as the case may be) to States which have assumed primary enforcement responsibility by the beginning of such fiscal year.

(6) The Administrator shall notify the State of the approval or disapproval of any application for a grant this section—

(A) within ninety days after receipt of such application, or

(B) not later than the first day of the fiscal year for which the grant application is made, whichever is later.

(7) For purposes of making grants under paragraph (1) there are authorized to be appropriated $15,000,000 for the fiscal year ending June 30, 1976, $25,000,000 for the fiscal year ending June 30, 1977, $35,000,000 for fiscal year 1978, $45,000,000 for fiscal year 1979; $29,450,000 for the fiscal year ending September 30, 1980, $32,000,000 for the fiscal year ending September 30, 1981, and $34,000,000 for the fiscal year ending September 30, 1982. For the purposes of making grants under paragraph (1) there are authorized to be appropriated not more than the following amounts:

Fiscal year:	Amount
1987	$37,200,000
1988	$37,200,000
1989	$40,150,000
1990	$40,150,000
1991	$40,150,000

[§1443(a)(7) amended by PL 96–63; PL 99–339]

(b) (1) From allotments made pursuant to paragraph (4), the Administrator may make grants to States to carry out underground water source protection programs.

(2) No grant may be made under paragraph (1) unless an application therefor has been submitted to the Administrator in such form and manner as he may require. No grant may be made to any State under paragraph (1) unless the State has assumed primary enforcement responsibility within two years after the date the Administrator promulgates regulations for State underground injection control programs under section 1421 . The prohibition contained in the preceding sentence shall not apply to such grants when made to Indian Tribes.

[§1443(b)(2) revised by PL 96–502; amended by PL 99–339]

(3) A grant under paragraph (1) shall be made to cover not more than 75 per centum of the grant recipient's costs (as determined under regulations of the Administrator) in carrying out, during the one-year period beginning on the date the grant is made, an underground water source protection program.

(4) In each fiscal year the Administrator shall, in accordance with regulations, allot the sums appropriated for each year under paragraph (5) among the States on the basis of population, geographical area, and other relevant factors;

(5) For purposes of making grants under paragraph (1) there are authorized to be appropriated $5,000,000 for the fiscal year ending June 30, 1976, $7,500,000 for the fiscal year ending June 30, 1977, $10,000,000 for each of the fiscal years 1978 and 1979, $7,795,000 for the fiscal

year ending September 30, 1980, $18,000,000 for the fiscal year ending September 30, 1981, and $21,000,000 for the fiscal year ending September 30, 1982. For the purpose of making grants under paragraph (1) there are authorized to be appropriated not more than the following amounts:

Fiscal year:	Amount
1987	$19,700,000
1988	$19,700,000
1989	$20,850,000
1990	$20,850,000
1991	$20,850,000

[§1443(b)(5) amended by PL 95–63; PL 99–339]

(c) For purposes of this section:

(1) The term 'public water system supervision program' means a program for the adoption and enforcement of drinking water regulations (with such variances and exemptions from such regulations under conditions and in a manner which is not less stringent than the conditions under, and the manner in, which variances and exemptions may be granted under sections 1415 and 1416) which are no less stringent than the national primary drinking water regulations under section 1412, and for keeping records and making reports required by section 1413(a)(3).

(2) The term 'underground water source protection program' means a program for the adoption and enforcement of a program which meets the requirements of regulations under section 1421 and for keeping records and making reports required by section 1422(b)(1)(A)(ii). Such term includes, where applicable, a program which meets the requirements of section 1425 .

[§1443(c)(2) amended by PL 96–502]

§300j–3. Special Study and Demonstration Project Grants; Guaranteed Loans. [Sec. 1444]

(a) The Administrator may make grants to any person for the purposes of—

(1) assisting in the development and demonstration (including construction) of any project which will demonstrate a new or improved method, approach, or technology for providing a dependably safe supply of drinking water to the public; and

(2) assisting in the development and demonstration (including construction) of any project which will investigate and demonstrate health implications involved in the reclamation, recycling, and reuse of waste waters for drinking and the processes and methods for the preparation of safe and acceptable drinking water.

(b) Grants made by the Administrator under this section shall be subject to the following limitations:

(1) Grants under this section shall not exceed 66 $^2/_3$ per centum of the total cost of construction of any facility and 75 per centum of any other costs, as determined by the Administrator.

(2) Grants under this section shall not be made for any project involving the construction or modification of any facilities for any public water system in a State unless such project has been approved by the State agency charged with the responsibility for safety of drinking water (or if there is no such agency in a State, by the State health authority).

(3) Grants under this section shall not be made for any project unless the Administrator determines, after consulting the National Drinking Water Advisory Council, that such project will serve a useful purpose relating to the development and demonstration of new or improved techniques, methods, or technologies for the provision of safe water to the public for drinking.

(4) Priority for grants under this section shall be given where there are known or potential public health hazards which require advanced technology for the removal of particles which are too small to be removed by ordinary treatment technology.

(c) For the purposes of making grants under subsections (a) and (b) of this section there are authorized to be appropriated $7,500,000 for the fiscal year ending June 30, 1975; and $7,500,000 for the fiscal year ending June 30, 1976; and $10,000,000 for the fiscal year ending June 30, 1977.

(d) The Administrator during the fiscal years ending June 30, 1975, and June 30, 1976, shall carry out a program of guaranteeing loans made by private lenders to small public water systems for the purpose of enabling such systems to meet national primary drinking water regulations prescribed under section 1412 . No such guarantee may be made with respect to a system unless (1) such system cannot reasonably obtain financial assistance necessary to comply with such regulations from any other source, and (2) the Administrator determines that any facilities constructed with a loan guaranteed under this subsection is not likely to be made obsolete by subsequent changes in primary regulations. The aggregate amount of indebtedness guaranteed with respect to any system may not exceed $50,000. The aggregate amount of indebtedness guaranteed under this subsection may not exceed $50,000,000. The Administrator shall prescribe regulations to carry out this subsection.

[§1444(d) amended by PL 99–339]

§300j–4. Record and Inspections. [Sec. 1445]

(a) (1) Every person who is a supplier of water, who is or may be otherwise subject to a primary drinking water regulation prescribed under section 1412 or to an applicable underground injection control program (as defined in section 1422(c)), who is or may be subject to the permit requirement of section 1424 or to an order issued under section 1441 , or who is a grantee, shall establish and maintain such records, make such reports, conduct such monitoring, and provide such information as the Administrator may reasonably require by regulation to assist him in establishing regulations under this title, in determining whether such person has acted or is acting in compliance with this title, in administering any program of financial assistance under this title in evaluating the health risks of unregulated contaminants, or in advising the public of such risks. In requiring a public water system to monitor under this subsection, the Administrator may take into consideration the system size and the contaminants likely to be found in the system's drinking water.

[§1445(a) amended by PL 95–190; (a)(1) designated and amended by PL 99–339]

(2) Not later than 18 months after enactment of the Safe Drinking Water Act Amendments of 1986, the Administrator shall promulgate regulations requiring every public water system to conduct a monitoring program for unregulated contaminants. The regulations shall require monitoring of drinking water supplied by the system and shall vary the frequency and schedule of monitoring requirements for systems based on the number of persons served by the system, the source of supply, and the contaminants likely to be found. Each system shall be required to monitor at least once every 5 years after the effective date of the Administrator's regulations unless the Administrator requires more frequent monitoring.

[§1445(a)(2) added by PL 99–339]

(3) Regulations under paragraph (2) shall list unregulated contaminants for which systems may be required to monitor, and shall include criteria by which the primary enforcement authority in each State could show cause for addition or deletion of contaminants from the designated list. The primary State enforcement authority may delete contaminants for an individual system, in accordance with these criteria, after obtaining approval of assessment of the contaminants potentially to be found in the system. The Administrator shall approve or disapprove such an assessment submitted by a State within 60 days. A State may add contaminants, in accordance with these criteria, without making an assessment, but in no event shall such additions increase Federal expenditures authorized by this section.

[§1445(a)(3) added by PL 99–339]

(4) Public water systems conducting monitoring of unregulated contaminants pursuant to this section shall provide the results of such monitoring to the primary enforcement authority.

[§1445(a)(4) added by PL 99–339]

(5) Notification of the availability of the results of the monitoring programs required under paragraph (2), and notification of the availability of the results of the monitoring program referred to in paragraph (6), shall be given to the persons served by the system and the Administrator.

[§1445(a)(5) added by PL 99–339]

(6) The Administrator may waive the monitoring requirement under paragraph (2) for a system which has conducted a monitoring program after January 1, 1983, if the Administrator determines the program to have been consistent with the regulations promulgated under this section.

[§1445(a)(6) added by PL 99–339]

(7) Any system supplying less than 150 service connections shall be treated as complying with this subsection if such system provides water samples for the opportunity for sampling according to rules established by the Administrator.

[§1445(a)(7) added by PL 99–339]

(8) There are authorized to be appropriated $30,000,000 in the fiscal year ending September 30, 1987 to remain available until expended to carry out the provisions of this subsection.

[§1445(a)(8) added by PL 99–339]

(b) (1) Except as provided in paragraph (2), the Administrator, or representatives of the Administrator duly designated by him, upon presenting appropriate credentials and a written notice to any supplier of water or other person subject to (A) a national primary drinking water regulation prescribed under section 1412(B), an applicable underground injection control program or (C) any requirement to monitor an unregulated contaminant pursuant to subsection (a), or person in charge of any of the property of such supplier or other person referred to in clause (A), (B), or (C), is authorized to enter any establishment, facility, or other property of such supplier or other person in order to determine whether such supplier or other person has acted or is acting in compliance with this title, including for this purpose, inspection, at reasonable times, of records, files, papers, processes, controls, and facilities, or in order to test any feature of a public water system, including its raw water source. The Administrator or the Comptroller General (or any representative designated by either) shall have access for the purpose of audit and examination to any records, reports, or information of a grantee which are required to be maintained under subsection (a) or which are pertinent to any financial assistance under this title.

[§1445(b)(1) amended by PL 95–190]

(2) No entry may be made under the first sentence of paragraph (1) in an establishment, facility, or other property of a supplier of water or other person subject to a national primary drinking water regulation if the establishment, facility, or other property is located in a State which has primary enforcement responsibility for public water systems unless, before written notice of such entry is made, the Administrator (or his representative) notifies the State agency charged with responsibility for safe drinking water of the reasons for such entry. The Administrator shall, upon a showing by the State agency that such an entry will be detrimental to the administration of the State's program of primary enforcement responsibility, take such showing into consideration in determining whether to make such entry. No State agency which receives notice under this paragraph of an entry proposed to be made under paragraph (1) may use the information contained in the notice to inform the person whose property is proposed to be entered of the proposed entry; and if a State agency so uses such information, notice to the agency under this paragraph is not required until such time as the Administrator determines the agency has provided him satisfactory assurances that it will no longer so use information contained in a notice under this paragraph.

(c) Whoever fails or refuses to comply with any requirement of subsection (a) or to allow the Administrator, the Comptroller General, or representatives of either, to enter and conduct any audit or inspection authorized by subsection (b) shall be subject to a civil penalty of not to exceed $25,000.

[§1445(c) amended by PL 99–339]

(d) (1) Subject to paragraph (2), upon a showing satisfactory to the Administrator by any person that any information required under this section from such person, if made public, would divulge trade secrets or secret processes of such person, the Administrator shall consider such information confidential in accordance with the purposes of section 1905 of title 18 of the United States Code. If the applicant fails to make a showing satisfactory to the Administrator, the Administrator shall give such applicant thirty days' notice before releasing the information to which the application relates (unless the public health or safety requires an earlier release of such information).

(2) Any information required under this section (A) may be disclosed to other officers, employees, or authorized representatives of the United States concerned with carrying out this title or to committees of the Congress, or when relevant in any proceeding under this title, and (B) shall be disclosed to the extent it deals with the level of contaminants in drinking water. For purposes of this subsection the term 'information required under this section' means any papers, books, documents, or information, or any particular part thereof, reported to or otherwise obtained by the Administrator under this section.

(e) For purposes of this section, (1) the term 'grantee' means any person who applies for or receives financial assistance, by grant, contract, or loan guarantee under this title, and (2) the term 'person' includes a Federal agency.

(f) Information Regarding Drinking Water Coolers.—The Administator may utilize the authorities of this section for purposes of part F. Any person who manufactures, imports, sells, or distributes drinking water coolers in interstate commerce shall be treated as a supplier of water for purposes of applying the provisions of this section in the case of persons subject to part F.

[§1445(f) added by PL 100–572]

§300j–5. National Drinking Water Advisory Council. [Sec. 1446]

(a) There is established a National Drinking Water Advisory Council which shall consist of fifteen members appointed by the Administrator after consultation with the Secretary. Five members shall be appointed from the general public: five members shall be appointed from appropriate State and local agencies concerned with water hygiene and public water supply; and five members shall be appointed from representatives of private organizations or groups demonstrating an active interest in the field of water hygiene and public water supply. Each member of the Council shall hold office for a term of three years, except that—

(1) any member appointed to fill a vacancy occurring prior to the expiration of the term for which his predecessor was appointed shall be appointed for the remainder of such term; and

(2) the terms of the members first taking office shall expire as follows: Five shall expire three years after the date of enactment of this title, five shall expire two years after such date, and five shall expire one year after such date, as designated by the Administrator at the time of appointment. The members of the Council shall be eligible for reappointment.

(b) The Council shall advise, consult with, and make recommendations to, the Administrator on matters relating to activities, functions, and policies of the Agency under this title.

(c) Members of the Council appointed under this section shall, while attending meetings or conferences of the Council or otherwise engaged in business of the Council, receive compensation and allowances at a rate to be fixed by the Administrator, but not exceeding the daily equivalent of the annual rate of basic pay in effect for grade GS–18 of the General Schedule for each day (including traveltime) during which they are engaged in the actual performance of duties vested in the Council. While away from their homes or regular places of business in the performance of services for the Council, members of the Council shall be allowed travel expenses, including per diem in lieu of subsistence, in the same manner as persons employed intermittently in the Government service are allowed expenses under sections 5703(b) of title 5 of the United States Code.

(d) Section 14(a) of the Federal Advisory Committee Act (relating to termination) shall not apply to the Council.

§300j–6. Federal Agencies. [Sec. 1447]

(a) Each Federal agency (1) having jurisdiction over any federally owned or maintained public water system or (2) engaged in any activity resulting, or which my result in, underground injection which endangers drinking water (within the meaning of section 1421(d)(2) shall be subject to and comply with, all Federal, State, and local requirements, administrative authorities, and process and sanctions respecting the provision of safe drinking water and respecting any underground injection program in the same manner, and to the same extent, as any nongovernmental entity. The preceding sentence shall apply (A) to any requirement whether substantive or procedural (including any recordkeeping or reporting requirement, any requirement respecting permits, and any other requirement whatsoever), (B) to the exercise of any Federal, State, or local administrative authority, and (C) to any process or sanction, whether enforced in Federal, State, or local courts or in any other manner. This subsection shall apply, not withstanding any immunity of such agencies, under any law or rule of law. No officer, agent, or employee of the United States shall be personally liable for any civil penalty under this title with respect to any act or omission within the scope of his official duties.

[§1447(a) amended by PL 95–190]

(b) The Administrator shall waive compliance with subsection (a) upon request of the Secretary of Defense and upon a determination by the President that the requested waiver is necessary in the interest of national security. The Administrator shall maintain a written record of the basis upon which such waiver was granted and make such record available for in camera examination when relevant in a judicial proceeding under this title. Upon the issuance of such a waiver, the Administator shall publish in the Federal Register a notice that the waiver was granted for national security purposes, unless, upon the request of the Secretary of Defense, the Administrator determines to omit such publication because the publication itself would be contrary to the interests of national security, in which event the Administrator shall submit notice to the Armed Services Committee of the Senate and House of Representatives.

(c)(1) Nothing in the Safe Drinking Water Amendments of 1977 shall be construed to alter or affect the status of American Indian lands or water rights nor to waive any sovereignty over Indian lands guaranteed by treaty or statute.

(2) For the purposes of this Act, the term 'Federal agency' shall not be construed to refer to or include any American Indian tribe, nor to

the Secretary of the Interior in his capacity as trustee of Indian lands.

§300j–7. Judicial Review. [Sec. 1448]

(a) A petition for review of—

(1) actions pertaining to the establishment of national primary drinking water regulations (including maximum contaminant level goals) may be filed only in the United States Court of Appeals for the District of Columbia circuit; and

[§1448(a)(1) revised by PL 99–339]

(2) any other action of the Administrator under this Act may be filed in the circuit in which the petitioner resides or transacts business which is directly affected by the action.

Any such petition shall be filed within the 45–day period beginning on the date of the promulgation of the regulation or issuance of the order with respect to which review is sought or on the date of the determination with respect to which review is sought, and may be filed after the expiration of such 45–day period if the petition is based solely on grounds arising after the expiration of such period. Action of the Administrator with respect to which review could have been obtained under this subsection shall not be subject to judicial review in any civil or criminal proceeding for enforcement or in any civil action to enjoin enforcement.

[§1448(a)(2) revised by PL 99–339]

(b) The United States district courts shall have jurisdiction of actions brought to review (1) the granting of, or the refusing to grant, a variance or exemption under section 1415 or 1416 or (2) the requirements of any schedule prescribed for a variance or exemption under such section or the failure to prescribe such a schedule. Such an action may only be brought upon a petition for review filed with the court within the 45–day period beginning on the date the action sought to be reviewed is taken or, in the case of a petition to review the refusal to grant a variance or exemption or the failure to prescribe a schedule, within the 45-day period beginning on the date action is required to be taken on the variance, exemption, or schedule, as the case may be. A petition for such review may be filed after the expiration of such period if the petition is based solely on grounds arising after the expiration of such period. Action with respect to which review could have been obtained under this subsection shall not be subject to judicial review in any civil or criminal proceeding for enforcement or in any civil action to enjoin enforcement.

(c) In any judicial proceeding in which review is sought of a determination under this title required to be made on the record after notice and opportunity for hearing, if any party applies to the court for leave to adduce additional evidence and shows to the satisfaction of the court that such additional evidence is material and that there were reasonable grounds for the failure to adduce such evidence in the proceeding before the Administrator, the court may order such additional evidence (and evidence in rebuttal thereof) to be taken before the Administrator, in such manner and upon such terms and conditions as to the court may deem proper. The Administrator may modify his findings as to the facts, or make new findings, by reason of the additional evidence so taken, and he shall file such modified or new findings, and his recommendation, if any, for the modification or setting aside of his original determination, with the return of such additional evidence.

§300j–8. Citizen's Civil Action. [Sec. 1449]

(a) Except as provided in subsection (b) of this section, any person may commence a civil action on his own behalf—

(1) against any person (including (A) the United States, and (B) any other governmental instrumentality or agency to the extent permitted by the eleventh amendment to the Constitution) who is alleged to be in violation of any requirement prescribed by or under this title, or

(2) against the Administrator where there is alleged a failure of the Administrator to perform any act or duty under this title which is not discretionary with the Administrator. No action may be brought under paragraph (1) against a public water system for a violation of a requirement prescribed by or under this title which occurred within the 27–month period beginning on the first day of the month in which this title is enacted. The United States district courts shall have jurisdiction, without regard to the amount in controversy or the citizenship of the parties, to enforce in an action brought under this subsection any requirement prescribed by or under this title or to order the Administrator to perform an act or duty described in paragraph (2), as the case may be.

(b) No civil action may be commenced—

(1) under subsection (a)(1) of this section respecting violation of a requirement prescribed by or under this title—

(A) prior to sixty days after the plaintiff has given notice of such violation (i) to the

Administrator, (ii) to any alleged violator of such requirement and (iii) to the State in which the violation occurs, or

(B) if the Administrator, the Attorney General, or the State has commenced and is diligently prosecuting a civil action in a court of the United States to require compliance with such requirement, but in any such action in a court of the United States any person may intervene as a matter of right; or

(2) under subsection (a)(2) of this section prior to sixty days after the plaintiff has given notice of such action to the Administrator. Notice required by this subsection shall be given in such manner as the Administrator shall prescribe by regulation. No person may commence a civil action under subsection (a) to require a State to prescribe a schedule under section 1415 or 1416 for a variance or exemption, unless such person shows to the satisfaction of the court that the State has in a substantial number of cases failed to prescribe such schedules.

(c) In any action under this section, the Administrator or the Attorney General, if not a party, may intervene as a matter of right.

(d) The court, in issuing any final order in any action brought under subsection (a) of this section, may award costs of litigation (including reasonable attorney and expert witness fees) to any party whenever the court determines such an award is appropriate. The court may, if a temporary restraining order or preliminary injunction is sought, require the filing of a bond or equivalent security in accordance with the Federal Rules of Civil Procedure.

(e) Nothing in this section shall restrict any right which any person (or class of persons) may have under any statute or common law to seek enforcement of any requirement prescribed by or under this title or to seek any other relief. Nothing in this section or in any other law of the United States shall be construed to prohibit, exclude, or restrict any State or local government from —

(1) bringing any action or obtaining any remedy or sanction in any State or local court, or

(2) bringing any administrative action or obtaining any administrative remedy or sanction,

against any agency of the United States under State or local law to enforce any requirement respecting the provision of safe drinking water or respecting any underground injection control program. Nothing in this section shall be construed to authorize judicial review of regulations or orders of the Administrator under this title, except as provided in section 1448. For provisions providing for application of certain requirements to such agencies in the same manner as to nongovernmental entities, see section 1447 .

[§1449(e) amended by PL 95–190]

§300j–9. General Provisions. [Sec. 1450]

(a) (1) The Administrator is authorized to prescribe such regulations as are necessary or appropriate to carry out his functions under this title.

(2) The Administrator may delegate any of his functions under this title (other than prescribing regulations) to any officer or employee of the Agency.

(b) The Administrator, with the consent of the head of any other agency of the United States, may utilize such officers and employees of such agency as he deems necessary to assist him in carrying out the purposes of this title.

(c) Upon the request of a State or interstate agency, the Administrator may assign personnel of the Agency to such State or interstate agency for the purposes of carrying out the provisions of this title.

(d) (1) The Administrator may make payments of grants under this title (after necessary adjustment on account of previously made underpayments or overpayments) in advance or by way of reimbursement, and in such installments and on such conditions as he may determine.

(2) Financial assistance may be made available in the form of grants only to individuals and nonprofit agencies or institutions. For purposes of this paragraph, the term 'nonprofit agency or institution' means an agency or institution no part of the net earnings of which inure, or may lawfully inure, to the benefit of any private shareholder or individual.

(e) The Administrator shall take such action as may be necessary to assure compliance with provisions of the Act of March 3, 1931 (known as the Davis-Bacon Act; 40 U.S.C. 276a–276a(5)). The Secretary of Labor shall have, with respect to the labor standards specified in this subsection, the authority and functions set forth in Reorganization Plan Numbered 14 of 1950 (15 F.R. 3176; 64 Stat. 1267) and section 2 of the Act of June 13, 1934 (40 U.S.C. 276c).

(f) The Administrator shall request the Attorney General to appear and represent him in any civil action instituted under this title to which the Administrator is a party. Unless, within a reasonable time, the Attorney General notifies the Administrator that he will appear in such action, attorneys appointed by the Administrator shall appear and represent him.

(g) The provisions of this title shall not be construed as affecting any authority of the Administrator under part G of title III of this Act.

(h) Not later than April 1 of each year, the Administrator shall submit to the Committee on Commerce of the Senate and the Committee on Interstate and Foreign Commerce of the House of Representatives a report respecting the activities of the Agency under this title and containing such recommendations for legislation as he considers necessary. The report of the Administrator under this subsection which is due not later than April 1, 1975, and each subsequent report of the Administrator under this subsection shall include a statement on the actual and anticipated cost to public water systems in each State of compliance with the requirements of this title. The Office of Management and Budget may review any report required by this subsection before its submission to such committees of Congress, but the Office may not revise any such report, require any revision in any such report, or delay its submission beyond the day prescribed for its submission, and may submit to such committees of Congress its comments respecting any such report.

(i) (1) No employer may discharge any employee or otherwise discriminate against any employee with respect to his compensation, terms, conditions, or privileges of employment because the employee (or any person acting pursuant to a request of the employee) has—

(A) commenced, caused to be commenced, or is about to commence or cause to be commenced a proceeding under this title or a proceeding for the administration or enforcement of drinking water regulations or underground injection control programs of a State,

(B) testified or is about to testify in any such proceeding, or

(C) assisted or participated or is about to assist or participate in any manner in such a proceeding or in any other action to carry out the purposes of this title.

(2) (A) Any employee who believes that he has been discharged or otherwise discriminated against by any person in violation of paragraph (1) may, within 30 days after such violation occurs, file (or have any person file on his behalf) a complaint with the Secretary of Labor (hereinafter in this subsection referred to as the "Secretary") alleging such discharge or discrimination. Upon receipt of such a complaint, the Secretary shall notify the person named in the complaint of the filing of the complaint.

(B) (i) Upon receipt of a complaint filed under subparagraph (A), the Secretary shall conduct an investigation of the violation alleged in the complaint. Within 30 days of the receipt of such complaint, the Secretary shall complete such investigation and shall notify in writing the complainant (any person acting in his behalf) and the person alleged to have committed such violation of the results of the investigation conducted pursuant to this subparagraph. Within 90 days of the receipt of such complaint the Secretary shall, unless the proceeding on the complaint is terminated by the Secretary on the basis of a settlement entered into by the Secretary and the person alleged to have committed such violation, issue an order either providing the relief prescribed by clause (ii) or denying the complaint. An order of the Secretary shall be made on the record after notice and opportunity for agency hearing. The Secretary may not enter into a settlement terminating a proceeding on a complaint without the participation and consent of the complainant.

(ii) If in response to a complaint filed under subparagraph (A) the Secretary determines that a violation of paragraph (1) has occurred, the Secretary shall order (1) the person who committed such violation to take the affirmative action to abate the violation,(II) such person to reinstate the complainant to his former position together with the compensation (including back pay), terms, conditions, and privileges of his employment, (III) compensatory damages, and (IV) where appropriate, exemplary damages. If such an order is issued, the Secretary, at the request of the complainant, shall assess against the person against whom the order is issued a sum equal to the aggregate amount of all costs and expenses (including attorneys' fees) reasonably incurred, as determined by the Secretary, by the complainant for, or in connection with, the bringing of the complaint upon which the order was issued.

(3) (A) Any person adversely affected or aggrieved by an order issued under para-

graph (2) may obtain review of the order in the United States Court of Appeals for the circuit in which the violation, with respect to which the order was issued, allegedly occurred. The petition for review must be filed within sixty days from the issuance of the Secretary's order. Review shall conform to chapter 7 of title 5 of the United States Code. The commencement of proceedings under this subparagraph shall not, unless ordered by the court, operate as a stay of the Secretary's order.

(B) An order of the Secretary with respect to which review could have been obtained under subparagraph (A) shall not be subject to judicial review in any criminal or other civil proceeding.

(4) Whenever a person has failed to comply with an order issued under paragraph (2)(B), the Secretary shall file a civil action in the United States District Court for the district in which the violation was found to occur to enforce such order. In actions brought under this paragraph, the district courts shall have jurisdiction to grant all appropriate relief including, but not limited to, injunctive relief, compensatory, and exemplary damages.

[§1450(i)(4) amended by PL 98–620]

(5) Any nondiscretionary duty imposed by this section is enforceable in mandamus proceeding brought under section 1361 of title 28 of the United States Code.

(6) Paragraph (1) shall not apply with respect to any employee who, acting without direction from his employer (or the employer's agent), deliberately causes a violation of any requirement of this title.

§300j–11. Indian Tribes. [Sec. 1451]

[§1451 added by PL 99–339]

(a) In General. — Subject to the provisions of subsection (b), the Administrator—

(1) is authorized to treat Indian Tribes as States under this title,

(2) may delegate to such Tribes primary enforcement responsibility for public water systems and for underground injection control, and

(3) may provide such Tribes grant and contract assistance to carry out functions provided by this title.

(b) EPA Regulations. —

(1) Specific Provisions. — The Administrator shall, within 18 months after the enactment of the Safe Drinking Water Act Amendments of 1986, promulgate final regulations specifying those provisions of this title for which it is appropriate to treat Indian Tribes as States. Such treatment shall be authorized only if:

(A) the Indian Tribe is recognized by the Secretary of the Interior and has a governing body carrying out substantial governmental duties and powers;

(B) the functions to be exercised by the Indian Tribe are within the area of the Tribal Government's jurisdiction; and

(C) the Indian Tribe is reasonably expected to be capable, in the Administrator's judgment, of carrying out the functions to be exercised in a manner consistent with the terms and purposes of this title and of all applicable regulations.

(2) Provisions where treatment as state inappropriate. — For any provision of this title where treatment of Indian Tribes as identical to States is inappropriate, administratively infeasible or otherwise inconsistent with the purposes of this title, the Administrator may include in the regulations promulgated under this section, other means for administering such provision in a manner that will achieve the purpose of the provision. Nothing in this section shall be construed to allow Indian Tribes to assume or maintain primary enforcement responsibility for public water systems or for underground injection control in a manner less protective of the health of persons than such responsibility may be assumed or maintained by a State. An Indian tribe shall not be required to exercise criminal enforcement jurisdiction for purposes of complying with the preceding sentence.

PART F — ADDITIONAL REQUIREMENTS TO REGULATE THE SAFETY OF DRINKING WATER.

§300j–21. [Sec. 1461]

Definitions as used in this part —

(1) Drinking Water Cooler — The term 'drinking water cooler' means any mechanical device affixed to drinking water supply plumbing which actively cools water for human consumption.

(2) Lead Free. — The term 'lead free' means, with respect to a drinking water cooler, that each part or component of the cooler which may come in contact with drinking water contains not more than 8 percent lead, except that no drinking water cooler which contains any solder, flux, or storage tank interior surface which

may come in contact with drinking water shall be considered lead free if the solder, flux, or storage tank interior surface contains more than 0.2 percent lead. The Administrator may establish more stringent requirements for treating any part or component of a drinking water cooler as lead free for purposes of this part whenever he determines that any such part may constitute an important source of lead in drinking water.

(3) Local Educational Agency. — The term 'local educational agency' means—

(A) any local educational agency as defined in section 198 of the Elementary and Secondary Education Act of 1965 (20 U.S.C. 3381),

(B) the owner of any private, nonprofit elementary or secondary school building, and

(C) the governing authority of any school operating under the defense dependent's education system provided for under the Defense Dependent's Education Act of 1978 (20 U.S.C. 921 and following).

(4) Repair — The term 'repair' means, with respect to a drinking water cooler, to take such corrective action as is necessary to ensure that water cooler is lead free.

(5) Replacement. — The term 'replacement', when used with respect to a drinking water cooler, means the permanent removal of the water cooler and the installation of a lead free water cooler.

(6) School — The term 'school' means any elementary school or secondary school as defined in section 198 of the Elementary and Secondary Education Act of 1965 (20 U.S.C. 2854) and any kindergarten or day care facility.

(7) Lead-Lined Tank. — The term 'lead-lined tank' means a water reservoir container in a drinking water cooler which container is constructed of lead or which has an interior surface which is notlead free.

§300j–22. Recall of Drinking Water Coolers with Lead-Lined Tanks. [Sec. 1462]

For purposes of the Consumer Product Safety Act, all drinking water coolers identified by the Administrator on the list under section 1463 as having a lead-lined tank shall be considered to be imminently hazardous consumer products within the meaning of section 12 of such Act (15 U.S.C. 2061). After notice and opportunity for comment, including a public hearing, the Consumer Product Safety Commission shall issue an order requiring the manufacturers and importers of such coolers to repair, replace, or recall and provide a refund for such coolers within 1 year after the enactment of the Lead Contamination Control Act of 1988. For purposes of enforcement, such order shall be treated as an order under section 15(d) of that Act (15 U.S.C. 2064(d)).

§300j–23. Drinking Water Coolers Containing Lead. [Sec. 1463]

(a) Publication Of Lists. — The Administrator shall, after notice and opportunity for public comment, identify each brand and model of drinking water cooler which is not lead free, including each brand and model of drinking water cooler which has a lead-free tank. For purposes of identifying the brand and model of drinking water coolers under this subsection, the Administrator shall use the best information available to the Environmental Protection Agency. Within 200 days after the enactment of this section, the Administrator shall publish a list of each brand and model of drinking water cooler identified under this subsection. Such list shall separately identify each brand and model of cooler which has a lead-lined tank. The Administrator shall continue to gather information regarding lead in drinking water coolers and shall revise and republish the list from time to time as may be appropriate as new information or analysis becomes available regarding lead contamination in drinking water coolers.

(b) Prohibition. — No person may sell in interstate commerce, or manufacture for sale in interstate commerce, any drinking water cooler listed under subsection (a) or any other drinking water cooler which is not lead free, including a lead- lined drinking water cooler.

(c) Criminal Penalty. — Any person who knowingly violates the prohibition contained in subsection (b) shall be imprisoned for not more than 5 years, or fined in accordance with title 18 of the United States Code, or both.

(d) Civil Penalty. — The Administrator may bring a civil action in the appropriate United States District Court (as determined under the provisions of title 28 of the United States Code) to impose a civil penalty on any person who violates subsection (b). In any such action the court may impose on such person a civil penalty of not more than $5,000 ($50,000 in the case of a second or subsequent violation).

§300j–24. Lead Contamination in School Drinking Water. [Sec. 1464]

(a) Distribution Of Drinking Water Cooler List. — Within 100 days after the enactment of this section, the Administrator shall distribute to the States a lists of each brand and model of drinking water cooler identified and listed by the Administrator under section 1463(a) .

(b) Guidance Document And Testing Protocol. — The Administrator shall publish a guidance document and a testing protocol to assist schools in determining the source and degree of lead contamination in school drinking water supplies and in remedying such contamination. The guidance document shall include guidelines for sample preservation. The guidance document shall also include guidance to assist States, schools, and the general public in ascertaining the levels of lead contamination in drinking water coolers and in taking appropriate action to reduce or eliminate such contamination. The guidance document shall contain a testing protocol for the identification of drinking water coolers which contribute to lead contamination in drinking water. Such document and protocol may be revised, republished and redistributed as the Administrator deems necessary. The Administrator shall distribute the guidance document and testing protocol to the State within 100 days after the enactment of this section.

(c) Dissemination To Schools Etc. — Each State shall provide for the dissemination to local educational agencies, private nonprofit elementary or secondary schools and to day care centers of the guidance document and testing protocol published under subsection (b), together with the list of drinking water coolers published under section 1463(a).

(d) Remedial Action Program. —

(1) Testing And Remedying Lead Contamination. — Within 9 months after the enactment of this section, each State shall establish a program, consistent with this section, to assist local educational agencies in testing for, and remedying, lead contamination in drinking water from coolers and from other sources of lead contamination at schools under the jurisdiction of such agencies.

(2) Public Availability. — Copy of the results of any testing under paragraph (1) shall be available in the administrative offices of the local educational agency for inspection by the public, including teachers, other school personnel, and parents. The local educational agency shall notify parent, teacher, and employee organizations of the availability of such testing results.

(3) Coolers. — In the case of drinking water coolers, such program shall include measures for the reduction or elimination of lead contamination from those water coolers which are not lead free and which are located in schools. Such measures shall be adequate to ensure that within 15 months after the enactment of this subsection all such water coolers in schools under the jurisdiction of such agencies are repaired, replaced, permanently removed, or rendered inoperable unless the cooler is tested and found (within the limits of testing accuracy) not to contribute lead to drinking water.

§300j–25. Federal Assistance For State Programs Regarding Lead Contamination In School Drinking Water. [Sec. 1465]

(a) School Drinking Water Programs. —The Administrator shall make grants to States to establish and carry out State programs under section 1464 to assist local educational agencies in testing for, and remedying, lead contamination in drinking water from drinking water coolers and from other sources of lead contamination at schools under the jurisdiction of such agencies. Such grants may be used by State to reimburse local educational agencies for expenses incurred after the enactment of this section for such testing and remedial action.

(b) Limits. — Each grant under this section shall be used as by the State for testing water coolers in accordance with section 1464 , for testing for lead contamination in other drinking water supplies under section 1464 , or for remedial action under State programs under section 1464 . Not more than 5 percent of the grant may be used for program administration.

(c) Authorization Of Appropriations. —There are authorized to be appropriated to carry out this section not more than $30,000,000 for fiscal year 1989, $30,000,000 for fiscal year 1990, and $30,000,000 for fiscal year 1991.

(b) Section 2(f) of the Public Health Service Act is amended by inserting "(1)" after "except that" and by inserting before the semicolon at the end thereof the following: ", and (2) as used in Title XIV such term includes Guam, American Samoa, and the Trust Territory of the Pacific Islands".

§300f. Rural Water Survey. [Sec. 3]

(a) The Administrator of the Environmental Protection Agency shall (after consultation with the Secretary of Agriculture and the several States) enter into arrangements with public or private entities as may be appropriate to conduct a survey of the quantity, quality, and availability of rural drinking water supplies. Such survey shall include, but not be limited to, the consideration of the number of residents in each rural area —

(1) presently being inadequately served by a public or private drinking water supply system, or by an individual home drinking water supply system;

(2) presently having limited or otherwise inadequate access to drinking water;

(3) who, due to the absence or inadequacy of a drinking water supply system, are exposed to an increased health hazard; and

(4) who have experienced incidents of chronic or acute illness, which may be attributed to the absence or inadequacy of a drinking water supply system.

(b) Such survey shall be completed within eighteen months of the date of enactment of this Act and a final report thereon submitted, not later than six months after the completion of such survey, to the President and to the Congress. Such report shall include recommendations for improving rural water supplies.

[§3(b) amended by PL 95–190]

(c) There are authorized to be appropriated to carry out the provisions of this section $1,000,000 for the fiscal year ending June 30, 1975; $2,000,000 for the fiscal year ending June 30, 1976; $1,000,000 for the fiscal year ending June 30, 1977; and $1,000,000 for each of fiscal years 1978 and 1979.

[§3(c) amended by PL 95–190]

§349. Bottled Drinking Water [Sec. 4]

Chapter IV of the Federal Food, Drug, and Cosmetic Act is amended by adding after section 409 the following new section:

Bottled Drinking Water Standards. [Sec. 410]

Whenever the Administrator of the Environmental Protection Agency prescribes interim or revised national primary drinking water regulations under section 1412 of the Public Health Service Act, the Secretary shall consult with the Administrator and within 180 days after the promulgation of such drinking water regulations either promulgate amendments to regulations under this chapter applicable to bottled drinking water or publish in the Federal Register his reasons for not making such amendments.

ADDITIONAL PROVISIONS

[Editor's Note: Several provisions of PL 95–190 did not amend the Safe Drinking Water Act directly but are relevant. Those provisions follow.]

[Sec. 2]

(e) Nothing in this Act shall be construed to authorize thc appropriation of any amount for research under title XIV of the Public Health Service Act (relating to safe drinking water).

[Sec. 3]

(e) (2) Nothing in this Act shall be construed to alter or affect the Administrator's authority or duty under title 14 of the Public Health Service Act to promulgate regulations or take other action with respect to any contaminant.

[Sec. 11]

(b) To the extent that the Administrator of the Environmental Protection Agency deems such action necessary to the discharge of his functions under title XIV of the Public Health Service Act (relating to safe drinking water) and under other provisions of law, he may appointment personnel to fill not more than thirty scientific, engineering, professional, legal, and administrative positions within the Environmental Protection Agency without regard to the civil service laws and may fix the compensation of such personnel not in excess of the maximum rate payable for GS–18 of the General Schedule under section 5332 of title 5, United States Code.

[Editor's Note: §304(b) and (e) of PL 99–339 contained requirements for surveys to be conducted by the EPA. Those provisions follow.]

[Sec. 304]

(b) Comparative Health Effects Assessment. — The Administrator of the Environmental Protection Agency shall conduct a comparative health effects assessment, using available data, to compare the public health effects (both positive and negative) associated with water treatment chemicals and their byproducts to the public health effects associated with contaminants found in public water supplies. Not later than 18 months after the date of the enactment of this Act, the Administrator shall submit a report to the Congress setting forth the results of such assessment.

[Sec. 304]

(e) Study. — The Administrator of the Environmental Protection Agency, in cooperation with the Director of the Indian Health Service, shall, within 12 months after the enactment of this Act, conduct a survey of drinking water on Indian reservations, identifying drinking water problems and the need, if any, for alternative drinking water supplies.

[Editor's Note: §4 of PL 100–572 relates to testing laboratories. Its provisions follow.]

Certification Of Testing Laboratories. [Sec. 4]

The Administrator of the Environmental Protection Agency shall assure that programs for the certification of testing laboratories which test drinking water supplies for lead contamination certify only those laboratories which provide reliable accurate testing. The Administrator (or thc State in the case of a State to which certification authority is delegated under this subsection) shall publish and make available to the public upon request the list of laboratories certified under this subsection.

6

Toxic Substances Control Act

INTRODUCTION

In 1976, after five years of effort dating from a 1971 report of the Council on Environmental Quality (CEQ), Congress enacted the Toxic Substances Control Act (TSCA) (P.L. 94-469) and passed to the Environmental Protection Agency a new system for identifying and evaluating environmental and health effects of existing chemicals and any new substances entering the U.S. market.

The law's intent was to complete the chain of federal environmental protection statutes enacted piecemeal between 1970, when EPA was created, and 1976. In contrast to laws designed to improve and protect the quality of water, air, and natural resources, TSCA was designed as a gap-filling law and empowered EPA to evaluate the safety of raw materials. It gave the agency broad authority to control chemical risks that could not be dealt with under other environmental statutes.

The term "toxic" in the title of the law is a misnomer, referring not only to threats of acute poisoning but also to long-term, chronic effects on people and the environment. Such effects include cancer, genetic damage, birth defects, or bioaccumulation in the food chain with deleterious effects.

Section 5 of TSCA requires any company planning to manufacture or import a new chemical to submit to EPA a premanufacture notice containing information on the identity, use, anticipated production or import volume, workplace hazards, and disposal characteristics of the substance. A "new" chemical is one not included in an inventory list of chemicals already in production, drawn up under authority of TSCA. EPA has 90 days to consider the notice and approve production. If the agency anticipates problems, it may require additional data before manufacture or import may begin. Also under Section 5, the agency may prohibit or control any "significant new use" of a chemical listed in the inventory.

EPA may move to ban production of any new or existing chemical under Section 6 of TSCA, or to control the conditions under which the substance may be made. In the years since enactment, several of the concerns that spawned TSCA have been subjected to extensive regulations under Sections 5 and 6, among them polychlorinated biphenyls, chlorofluorocarbons, and many new chemicals.

In July 1989, the agency issued its first "blockbuster" rule under Section 6, phasing out and banning major uses of asbestos throughout most of the decade of the 1990s. In December 1989, Charles Elkins, director of the Office of Toxic Substances at EPA, said the next major initiative under Section 6 probably would concern lead, including recycling and reductions of imports. He added that the agency would expand use of the statute throughout the 1990s, especially issuing Section 6 bans on a small scale "as a scalpel" to eliminate unreasonable risks; one such ban under consideration is on the use of acrylamide as a grouting agent.

In 1986 the agency began planning to bring new substances created through genetic engineering under the TSCA regulatory programs. A draft proposal has circulated, but opposition has come both from the biotechnology industry and from environmentalists such as Jeremy Rifkin. It was expected that Regulations would be proposed by the end of 1989, but they were not.

Under Section 8 of TSCA, EPA has broad powers to collect information about chemicals. Production, use, exposure, and risk data may be collected from producers and importers under Section 8(a), and under Section 8(d) the agency can require manufacturers and processors to report unpublished health and safety studies on listed chemicals. Companies are required to collect allegations of adverse reactions and keep records of them. And, under Section 8(e) firms must report to EPA any time they receive information that a substance may pose a significant risk to humans or the environment.

In recent years, the agency has begun to use the law's authorities for programs throughout the agency and in other federal agencies. In June 1988 the agency issued a final rule requiring testing of 24 substances that would be regulated as hazardous wastes under the Resource Conservation and Recovery Act. In November 1993, the agency proposed to require manufacturers and processors of five chemicals listed as air toxics under the Clean Air Act to perform health and environmental effects studies on the chemicals (58 FR 61654).

Despite the agency's slow start in using TSCA to control exposure to harmful substances, Congress has not amended the law substantially since it was enacted in 1976. Conforming amendments were included in revisions to RCRA in 1984, and new titles—on asbestos, radon, and lead-based paint—were added in 1986, 1988, and 1992 respectively.

The Asbestos Hazard Emergency Response Act, approved by Congress in October 1986 as Title II of TSCA, requires school systems to inspect for and abate asbestos hazards found in school buildings. The title was amended in 1988 to extend the deadline for schools to submit asbestos management plans to their state governors and to add a new section on worker protection.

Responding to increased concerns about the dangers of exposure to radon in buildings, Congress in October 1988 again amended TSCA by adding a Title III concerning indoor radon abatement. The law requires EPA to provide public updates on the health risks associated with exposure to radon, to develop model construction standards for use by builders to control radon levels, and to study radon levels in schools.

The 102nd Congress in October 1992 approved legislation (HR 5334) introduced by Rep. Henry B. Gonzalez (D-Texas) adding a fourth title to TSCA. Title X of P.L. 102-550 added the new TSCA Title IV, also known as the Lead-Based Paint Exposure Reduction Act. In enacting the new law, Congress noted that lead poisoning affects as many as 3 million children under the age of 6 and causes learning disabilities, hearing problems, reduced attention span, and behavioral problems.

The purposes of the new title include the elimination of lead-based paint hazards in housing "as expeditiously as possible," the prevention of childhood lead poisoning, and education of the public about the hazards and sources of lead-based paint poisoning and how to reduce and eliminate these hazards.

In the 103rd Congress, legislation (S 729) was approved in the Senate to amend TSCA to require lead-content labels for products that contain unsafe amounts of lead. Companion legislation was expected to be approved in the House by the end of the summer, but it remained unclear whether the measure would win full congressional approval before the end of the session.

An effort was begun to consider isuues that will have to be dealt with when Congress makes a concerted effort to reauthorize the Act in the 104th Congress, beginning in 1995.

FINDING LIST

TOXIC SUBSTANCES CONTROL ACT

Public Law 94–469, effective Oct. 11, 1976, 90 Stat. 2003.

15 U.S.C. §§2601 et seq.

Amended by PL 97–129, Dec. 29, 1981; PL 97–258, Sept. 13, 1982; PL 98–80, Aug. 23, 1983; PL 98–620, Nov. 11, 1984; PL 99–519, Oct. 22, 1986; PL 100–368, July 18, 1988; PL 100–418, Aug. 23, 1988; PL 100–551, Oct. 28, 1988; PL 101–637, Nov. 28, 1990; PL 101–508, Nov. 5, 1990; PL 102–550, Oct. 28, 1992.

TITLE I—CONTROL OF TOXIC SUBSTANCES

[Title I designated by PL 99–519, Oct. 22, 1986]

Short Title and Table of Contents. [Sec. 1]

[Omitted]

[§1 amended by PL 102-550, Oct. 28, 1992]

§2601. Findings, Policy, and Intent. [Sec. 2]

(a) Findings.—The Congress finds that—

(1) human beings and the environment are being exposed each year to a large number of chemical substances and mixtures;

(2) among the many chemical substances and mixtures which are constantly being developed and produced, there are some whose manufacture, processing, distribution in commerce, use, or disposal may present an unreasonable risk of injury to health or the environment; and

(3) the effective regulation of interstate commerce in such chemical substances and mixtures also necessitates the regulation of intrastate commerce in such chemical substances and mixtures.

(b) Policy.—It is the policy of the United States that—

(1) adequate data should be developed with respect to the effect of chemical substances and mixtures on health and the environment and that the development of such data should be the responsibility of those who manufacture and those who process such chemical substances and mixtures;

(2) adequate authority should exist to regulate chemical substances and mixtures which present an unreasonable risk of injury to health or the environment, and to take action with respect to chemical substances and mixtures which are imminent hazards; and

(3) authority over chemical substances and mixtures should be exercised in such a manner as not to impede unduly or create unnecessary economic barriers to technological innovation while fulfilling the primary purpose of this Act to assure that such innovation and commerce in such chemical substances and mixtures do not present an unreasonable risk of injury to health or the environment.

(c) Intent Of Congress.—It is the intent of Congress that the Administrator shall carry out this Act in a reasonable and prudent manner, and that the Administrator shall consider the environmental, economic, and social impact of any action the Administrator takes or proposes to take under this Act.

§2602. Definitions. [Sec. 3]

As used in this Act:

(1) the term "Administrator" means the Administrator of the Environmental Protection Agency.

(2) (A) Except as provided in subparagraph (B), the term "chemical substance" means any organic or inorganic substance of a particular molecular identity, including—

(i) any combination of such substances occurring in whole or in part as a result of a chemical reaction or occurring in nature, and

(ii) any element or uncombined radical.

(B) Such term does not include—

(i) any mixture,

(ii) any pesticide (as defined in the Federal Insecticide, Fungicide, and Rodenticide Act) when manufactured, processed, or distributed in commerce for use as a pesticide,

(iii) tobacco or any tobacco product,

(iv) any source material, special nuclear material, or byproduct material (as such terms are defined in the Atomic Energy Act of 1954 and regulations issued under such Act),

(v) any article the sale of which is subject to the tax imposed by section 4181 of the Internal Revenue Code of 1954 (determined without regard to any exemptions from such tax provided by section 4182 or 4221 or any other provision of such Code), and

(vi) any food, food additive, drug, cosmetic, or device (as such terms are defined in section 201 of the Federal Food, Drug, and Cosmetic Act) when manufactured, processed, or distributed in commerce for use as a food, food additive, drug, cosmetic, or device.

The term "food" as used in clause (vi) of this subparagraph includes poultry and poultry products (as defined in sections 4(e) and 4(f) of the Poultry Products Inspection Act), meat and meat food products (as defined in section 1(j) of the Federal Meat Inspection Act), and eggs and egg products (as defined in section 4 of the Egg Products Inspection Act).

(3) The term "commerce" means trade, traffic, transportation, or other commerce (A) between a place in a State and any place outside of such State, or (B) which affects trade, traffic, transportation, or commerce described in clause (A).

(4) The terms "distribute in commerce" and "distribution in commerce" when used to describe an action taken with respect to a chemical substance or mixture or article containing a substance or mixture mean to sell, or the sale of, the substance, mixture, or article in commerce; to introduce or deliver for introduction into commerce, or the introduction or delivery for introduction into commerce of, the substance, mixture, or article; or to hold, or the holding of, the substance, mixture, or article after its introduction into commerce.

(5) The term "environment" includes water, air, and land and the interrelationship which exists among and between water, air, and land and all living things.

(6) The term "health and safety study" means any study of any effect of a chemical substance or mixture on health or the environment or on both, including underlying data and epidemiological studies, studies of occupational exposure to a chemical substance or mixture, toxicological, clinical, and ecological studies of a chemical substance or mixture, and any test performed pursuant to this Act.

(7) The term "manufacture" means to import into the customs territory of the United States (as defined in general note 2 of the Harmonized Tarriff Schedule of the United States), produce, or manufacture.

[§3(7) amended by PL 100–418]

(8) The term "mixture" means any combination of two or more chemical substances if the combination does not occur in nature and is not, in whole or in part, the result of a chemical reaction; except that such term does include any combination which occurs, in whole or in part, as a result of a chemical reaction if none of the chemical substances comprising the combination is a new chemical substance and if the combination could have been manufactured for commercial purposes without a chemical reaction at the time the chemical substances comprising the combination were combined.

(9) The term "new chemical substance" means any chemical substance which is not included in the chemical substance list compiled and published under section 8(b).

(10) The term "process" means the preparation of a chemical substance or mixture, after its manufacture, for distribution in commerce—

(A) in the same form or physical state as, or in a different form or physical state from, that in which it was received by the person so preparing such substance or mixture, or

(B) as part of an article containing the chemical substance or mixture.

(11) The term "processor" means any person who processes a chemical substance or mixture.

(12) The term "standards for the development of test data" means a prescription of—

(A) the—

(i) health and environmental effects, and

(ii) information relating to toxicity, persistence, and other characteristics which affect health and the environment, for which test data for a chemical substance or mixture are to be developed and any analysis that is to be performed on such data, and

(B) to the extent necessary to assure that data respecting such effects and characteristics are reliable and adequate—

(i) the manner in which such data are to be developed,

(ii) the specification of any test protocol or methodology to be employed in the development of such data, and

(iii) such other requirements as are necessary to provide such assurance.

(13) The term "State" means any State of the United States, the District of Columbia, the Commonwealth of Puerto Rico, the Virgin Islands, Guam, the Canal Zone, American Samoa, the Northern Mariana Islands, or any other territory or possession of the United States.

(14) The term "United States", when used in the geographic sense, means all of the States.

§2603. Testing of Chemical Substances and Mixtures. [Sec. 4]

(a) Testing Requirements.—If the Administrator finds that—

(1) (A) (i) the manufacture, distribution in commerce, processing, use, or disposal of a chemical substance or mixture, or that any combination of such activities, may present

an unreasonable risk of injury to health or the environment.

(ii) there are insufficient data and experience upon which the effects of such manufacture, distribution in commerce, processing, use, or disposal of such substance or mixture or of any combination of such activities on health or the environment can reasonably be determined or predicted, and

(iii) testing of such substance or mixture with respect to such effects is necessary to develop such data; or

(B) (i) a chemical substance or mixture is or will be produced in substantial quantities, and (I) it enters or may reasonably be anticipated to enter the environment in substantial quantities or (II) there is or may be significant or substantial human exposure to such substance or mixture,

(ii) there are insufficient data and experience upon which the effects of the manufacture, distribution in commerce, processing, use, or disposal of such substance or mixture or of any combination of such activities on health or the environment can reasonably to determined or predicted, and

(iii) testing of such substance or mixture with respect to such effects is necessary to develop such data; and

(2) in the case of a mixture, the effects which the mixture's manufacture, distribution in commerce, processing, use, or disposal or any combination of such activities may have on health or the environment may not be reasonably and more efficiently determined or predicted by testing the chemical substances which comprise the mixture;

the Administrator shall by rule require that testing be conducted on such substance or mixture to develop data with respect to the health and environmental effects for which there is an insufficiency of data and experience and which are relevant to a determination that the manufacture, distribution in commerce, processing, use, or disposal of such substance or mixture, or that any combination of such activities, does or does not present an unreasonable risk of injury to health or the environment.

(b) (1) Testing Requirement Rule.—A rule under subsection (a) shall include—

(A) identification of the chemical substance or mixture for which testing is required under the rule,

(B) standards for the development of test data for such substance or mixture, and

(C) with respect to chemical substances which are not new chemical substances and to mixtures, a specification of the period (which period may not be of unreasonable duration) within which the persons required to conduct the testing shall submit to the Administrator data developed in accordance with the standards referred to in subparagraph (B).

In determining the standards and period to be included, pursuant to subparagraphs (B) and (C), in a rule under subsection (a), the Administrator's considerations shall include the relative costs of the various test protocols and methodologies which may be required under the rule and the reasonably foreseeable availability of the facilities and personnel needed to perform the testing required under the rule. Any such rule may require the submission to the Administrator of preliminary data during the period prescribed under subparagraph (C).

(2) (A) The health and environmental effects for which standards for the development of test data may be prescribed include carcinogenesis, mutagenesis, teratogenesis, behavioral disorders, cumulative or synergistic effects, and any other effect which may present an unreasonable risk of injury to health or the environment. The characteristics of chemical substances and mixtures for which such standards may be prescribed include persistence, acute toxicity, subacute toxicity, chronic toxicity, and any other characteristic which may present such a risk. The methodologies that may be prescribed in such standards include epidemiologic studies, serial or hierarchical tests, in vitro tests, and whole animal tests, except that before prescribing epidemiologic studies of employees, the Administrator shall consult with the Director of the National Institute for Occupational Safety and Health.

(B) From time to time, but not less than once each 12 months, the Administrator shall review the adequacy of the standards for development of data prescribed in rules under subsection (a) and shall, if necessary, institute proceedings to make appropriate revisions of such standards.

(3) (A) A rule under subsection (a) respecting a chemical substance or mixture shall require the persons described in subparagraph (b) to conduct tests and submit data to the Administrator on such substance or mixture, except

that the Administrator may permit two or more of such persons to designate one such person or a qualified third party to conduct such tests and submit such data on behalf of the persons making the designation.

(B) The following persons shall be required to conduct tests and submit data on a chemical substance or mixture subject to a rule under subsection (a):

(i) Each person who manufactures or intends to manufacture such substance or mixture if the Administrator makes a finding described in subsection (a)(1)(A)(ii) or (a)(1)(B)(ii) with respect to the manufacture of such substance or mixture.

(ii) Each person who processes or intends to process such substance or mixture if the Administrator makes a finding described in subsection (a)(1)(A)(ii) or (a)(1)(B)(ii) with respect to the processing of such substance or mixture.

(iii) Each person who manufactures or processes or intends to manufacture or process such substance or mixture if the Administrator makes a finding described in subsection (a)(1)(A)(ii) or (a)(1)(B)(ii) with respect to the distribution in commerce, use, or disposal of such substance or mixture.

(4) Any rule under subsection (a) requiring the testing of and submission of data for a particular chemical substance or mixture shall expire at the end of the reimbursement period (as defined in subsection (c)(3)(B)) which is applicable to test data for such substance or mixture unless the Administrator repeals the rule before such date; and a rule under subsection (a) requiring the testing of and submission of data for a category of chemical substances or mixtures shall expire with respect to a chemical substance or mixture included in the category at the end of the reimbursement period (as so defined) which is applicable to test data for such substance or mixture unless the Administrator before such date repeals the application of the rule to such substance or mixture or repeals the rule.

(5) Rules issued under subsection (a) (and any substantive amendment thereto or repeal thereof) shall be promulgated pursuant to section 553 of title 5, United States Code, except that (A) the Administrator shall give interested persons an opportunity for the oral presentation of data, views, or arguments, in addition to an opportunity to make written submissions; (B) a transcript shall be made of any oral presentation; and (C) the Administrator shall make and publish with the rule the findings described in paragraph (1)(A) or (1)(B) of subsection (a) and, in the case of a rule respecting a mixture, the finding described in paragraph (2) of such subsection.

(c) Exemption.—(1) Any person required by a rule under subsection (a) to conduct tests and submit data on a chemical substance or mixture may apply to the Administrator (in such form and manner as the Administrator shall prescribe) for an exemption from such requirement.

(2) If, upon receipt of an application under paragraph (1), the Administrator determines that—

(A) the chemical substance or mixture with respect to which such application was submitted is equivalent to a chemical substance or mixture for which data has been submitted to the Administrator in accordance with a rule under subsection (a) or for which data is being developed pursuant to such a rule, and

(B) submission of data by the applicant on such substance or mixture would be duplicative of data which has been submitted to the Administrator in accordance with such rule or which is being developed pursuant to such rule,

the Administrator shall exempt, in accordance with paragraph (3) or (4), the applicant from conducting tests and submitting data on such substance or mixture under the rule with respect to which such application was submitted.

Fair and equitable reimbursement.

(3) (A) If the exemption under paragraph (2) of any person from the requirement to conduct tests and submit test data on a chemical substance or mixture is granted on the basis of the existence of previously submitted test data and if such exemption is granted during the reimbursement period for such test data (as prescribed by subparagraph (B)), then (unless such person and the persons referred to in clauses (i) and (ii) agree on the amount and method of reimbursement) the Administrator shall order the person granted the exemption to provide fair and equitable reimbursement (in an amount determined under rules of the Administrator)—

(i) to the person who previously submitted such test data, for a portion of the costs incurred by such person in complying with the requirement to submit such data, and

(ii) to any other person who has been required under this subparagraph to contribute with respect to such costs, for a portion of the amount such person was required to contribute.

In promulgating rules for the determination of fair and equitable reimbursement to the persons described in clauses (i) and (ii) for costs incurred with respect to a chemical substance or mixture, the Administrator shall, after consultation with the Attorney General and the Federal Trade Commission, consider all relevant factors, including the effect on the competitive position of the person required to provide reimbursement in relation to the person to be reimbursed and the share of the market for such substance or mixture of the person required to provide reimbursement in relation to the share of such market of the persons to be reimbursed. An order under this subparagraph shall, for purposes of judicial review, be considered final agency action.

(B) For purposes of subparagraph (A), the reimbursement period for any test data for a chemical substance or mixture is a period—

(i) beginning on the data such data is submitted in accordance with a rule promulgated under subsection (a), and

(ii) ending—

(I) five years after the date referred to in clause (i), or

(II) at the expiration of a period which begins on the date referred to in clause (i) and which is equal to the period which the Administrator determines was necessary to develop such data, whichever is later.

(4) (A) If the exemption under paragraph (2) of any person from the requirement to conduct tests and submit test data on a chemical substance or mixture is granted on the basis of the fact that test data is being developed by one or more persons pursuant to a rule promulgated under subsection (a), then (unless such person and the persons referred to in clauses (i) and (ii) agree on the amount and method of reimbursement) the Administrator shall order the person granted the exemption to provide fair and equitable reimbursement (in an amount determined under rules of the Administrator)—

(i) to each such person who is developing such test data, for a portion of the costs incurred by each such person in complying with such rule, and

(ii) to any other person who has been required under this subparagraph to contribute with respect to the costs of complying with such rule, for a portion of the amount such person was required to contribute.

In promulgating rules for the determination of fair and equitable reimbursement to the persons described in clauses (i) and (ii) for costs incurred with respect to a chemical substance or mixture, the Administrator shall, after consultation with the Attorney General and the Federal Trade Commission, consider the factors described in the second sentence of paragraph (3)(A). An order under this subparagraph shall, for purposes of judicial review, be considered final agency action.

(B) If any exemption is granted under paragraph (2) on the basis of the fact that one or more persons are developing test data pursuant to a rule promulgated under subsection (a) and if after such exemption is granted the Administrator determines that no such person has complied with such rule, the Administrator shall (i) after providing written notice to the person who holds such exemption and an opportunity for a hearing, by order terminate such exemption, and (ii) notify in writing such person of the requirements of the rule with respect to which such exemption was granted.

(d) Notice.—Upon the receipt of any test data pursuant to a rule under subsection (a), the Administrator shall publish a notice of the receipt of such data in the Federal Register within 15 days of its receipt. Subject to section 14, each such notice shall (1) identify the chemical substance or mixture for which data have been received; (2) list the uses or intended uses of such substance or mixture and the information required by the applicable standards for the development of test data; and (3) describe the nature of the test data developed. Except as otherwise provided in section 14, such data shall be made available by the Administrator for examination by any person.

(e) Priority List.—

(1) (A) There is established a committee to make recommendations to the Administrator respecting the chemical substances and mixtures to which the Administrator should give priority consideration for the promulgation of a rule under subsection (a). In making such a recommendation with respect to any chemical substance or mixture, the committee shall consider all relevant factors, including—

(i) the quantities in which the substance or mixture is or will be manufactured,

(ii) the quantities in which the substance or mixture enters or will enter the environment,

(iii) the number of individuals who are or will be exposed to the substance or mixture in their places of employment and the duration of such exposure,

(iv) the extent to which human beings are or will be exposed to the substance or mixture,

(v) the extent to which the substance or mixture is closely related to a chemical substance or mixture which is known to present an unreasonable risk of injury to health or the environment,

(vi) the existence of data concerning the effects of the substance or mixture on health or the environment,

(vii) the extent to which testing of the substance or mixture may result in the development of data upon which the effects of the substance or mixture on health or the environment can reasonably be determined or predicted, and

(viii) the reasonably foreseeable availability of facilities and personnel for performing testing on the substance or mixture.

The recommendations of the committee shall be in the form of a list of chemical substances and mixtures which shall be set forth, either by individual substance or mixture or by groups of substances or mixtures, in the order in which the committee determines the Administrator should take action under subsection (a) with respect to the substances and mixtures. In establishing such list, the committee shall give priority attention to those chemical substances and mixtures which are known to cause or contribute to or which are suspected of causing or contributing to cancer, gene mutations, or birth defects. The committee shall designate chemical substances and mixtures on the list with respect to which the committee determines the Administrator should, within 12 months of the date on which such substances and mixtures are first designated, initiate a proceeding under subsection (a). The total number of chemical substances and mixtures on the list which are designated under the preceding sentence may not, at any time, exceed 50.

(B) As soon as practicable but not later than nine months after the effective date of this Act, the committee shall publish in the Federal Register and transmit to the Administrator the list and designations required by subparagraph (A) together with the reasons for the committee's inclusion of each chemical substance or mixture on the list. At least every six months after the date of the transmission to the Administrator of the list pursuant to the preceding sentence, the committee shall make such revisions in the list as it determines to be necessary and shall transmit them to the Administrator together with the committee's reasons for the revisions. Upon receipt of any such revision, the Administrator shall publish in the Federal Register the list with such revision, the reasons for such revision, and the designations made under subparagraph (A). The Administrator shall provide reasonable opportunity to any interested person to file with the Administrator written comments on the committee's list, any revision of such list by the committee, and designations made by the committee, and shall make such comments available to the public. Within the 12–month period beginning on the date of the first inclusion on the list of a chemical substance or mixture designated by the committee under subparagraph (A) the Administrator shall with respect to such chemical substance or mixture either initiate a rulemaking proceeding under subsection (a) or if such a proceeding is not initiated within such period, publish in the Federal Register the Administrator's reason for not initiating such a proceeding.

(2) (A) The committee established by paragraph (1)(A) shall consist of eight members as follows:

(i) One member appointed by the Administrator from the Environmental Protection Agency.

(ii) One member appointed by the Secretary of Labor from officers or employees of the Department of Labor engaged in the Secretary's activities under the Occupational Safety and Health Act of 1970.

(iii) One member appointed by the Chairman of the Council on Environmental Quality from the Council or its officers or employees.

(iv) One member appointed by the Director of the National Institute for Occupational Safety and Health from officers or employees of the Institute.

(v) One member appointed by the Director of the National Institute of Environmental Health Sciences from officers or employees of the Institute.

(vi) One member appointed by the Director of the National Cancer Institute from officers or employees of the Institute.

(vii) One member appointed by the Director of the National Science Foundation from officers or employees of the Foundation.

(viii) One member appointed by the Secretary of Commerce from officers or employees of the Department of Commerce.

(B) (i) An appointed member may designate an individual to serve on the committee on the member's behalf. Such a designation may be made only with the approval of the applicable appointing authority and only if the individual is from the entity from which the member was appointed.

(ii) No individual may serve as a member of the committee for more than four years in the aggregate. If any member of the committee leaves the entity from which the member was appointed, such member may not continue as a member of the committee, and the member's position shall be considered to be vacant. A vacancy in the committee shall be filled in the same manner in which the original appointment was made.

(iii) Initial appointments to the committee shall be made not later than the 60th day after the effective date of this Act. Not later than the 90th day after such date the members of the committee shall hold a meeting for the selection of a chairperson from among their number.

(C) (i) No member of the committee, or designee of such member, shall accept employment or compensation from any person subject to any requirement of this Act or of any rule promulgated or order issued thereunder, for a period of at least 12 months after termination of service on the committee.

(ii) No person, while serving as a member of the committee, or designee of such member, may own any stocks or bonds, or have any pecuniary interest, of substantial value in any person engaged in the manufacture, processing, or distribution in commerce of any chemical substance or mixture subject to any requirement of this Act or of any rule promulgated or order issued thereunder.

(iii) The Administrator, acting through attorneys of the Environmental Protection Agency, or the Attorney General may bring an action in the appropriate district court of the United States to restrain any violation of this subparagraph.

(D) The Administrator shall provide the committee such administrative support services as may be necessary to enable the committee to carry out its function under this subsection.

(f) Required Actions.—Upon the receipt of—

(1) any test data required to be submitted under this Act, or

(2) any other information available to the Administrator, which indicates to the Administrator that there may be a reasonable basis to conclude that a chemical substance or mixture presents or will present a significant risk of serious or widespread harm to human beings from cancer, gene mutations, or birth defects, the Administrator shall, within the 180–day period beginning on the date of the receipt of such data or information, initiate appropriate action under section 5, 6, or 7 to prevent or reduce to a sufficient extent such risk or publish in the Federal Register a finding that such risk is not unreasonable. For good cause shown the Administrator may extend such period for an additional period of not more than 90 days. The Administrator shall publish in the Federal Register notice of any such extension and the reasons therefor. A finding by the Administrator that a risk is not unreasonable shall be considered agency action for purposes of judicial review under chapter 7 of title 5, United States Code. This subsection shall not take effect until two years after the effective date of this Act.

(g) Petition for Standards for the Development of Test Data.— A person intending to manufacture or process a chemical substance for which notice is required under section 5(a) and who is not required under a rule under subsection (a) to conduct tests and submit data on such substance may petition the Administrator to prescribe standards for the development of test data for such substance. The Administrator shall by order either grant or deny any such petition within 60 days of its receipt. If the petition is granted, the Administrator shall prescribe such standards for such substance within 75 days of the date the petition is granted. If the petition is denied, the Administrator shall publish, subject to section 14, in the Federal Register the reasons for such denial.

§2604. Manufacturing and Processing Notices. [Sec. 5]

(a) In General.—

(1) Except as provided in subsection (h), no person may—

(A) manufacture a new chemical substance on or after the 30th day after the date on which the Administrator first publishes the list required by section 8(b), or

(B) manufacture or process any chemical substance for a use which the Administrator has determined, in accordance with paragraph (2), is a significant new use,

unless such person submits to the Administrator, at least 90 days before such manufacture or processing, a notice, in accordance with subsection (d), of such person's intention to manufacture or process such substance and such person complies with any applicable requirement of subsection (b).

(2) A determination by the Administrator that a use of a chemical substance is a significant new use with respect to which notification is required under paragraph (1) shall be made by a rule promulgated after a consideration of all relevant factors, including—

(A) the projected volume of manufacturing and processing of a chemical substance,

(B) the extent to which a use changes the type or form of exposure of human beings or the environment to a chemical substance,

(C) the extent to which a use increases the magnitude and duration of exposure of human beings or the environment to a chemical substance, and

(D) the reasonably anticipated manner and methods of manufacturing, processing, distribution in commerce, and disposal of a chemical substance.

(b) Submission of Test Data.—

(1) (A) If (i) a person is required by subsection (a)(1) to submit a notice to the Administrator before beginning the manufacture or processing of a chemical substance, and (ii) such person is required to submit test data for such substance pursuant to a rule promulgated under section 4 before the submission of such notice, such person shall submit to the Administrator such data in accordance with such rule at the time notice is submitted in accordance with subsection (a)(1).

(B) If—

(i) a person is required by subsection (a)(1) to submit a notice to the Administrator, and

(ii) such person has been granted an exemption under section 4(c) from the requirements of a rule promulgated under section 4 before the submission of such notice,

such person may not, before the expiration of the 90 day period which begins on the date of the submission in accordance with such rule of the test data the submission or development of which was the basis for the exemption, manufacture such substance if such person is subject to subsection (a)(1)(A) or manufacture or process such substance for a significant new use if the person is subject to subsection (a)(1)(B).

(2) (A) If a person—

(i) is required by subsection (a)(1) to submit a notice to the Administrator before beginning the manufacture or processing of a chemical substance listed under paragraph (4), and

(ii) is not required by a rule promulgated under section 4 before the submission of such notice submit test data for such substance,

such person shall submit to the Administrator data prescribed by subparagraph (B) at the time notice is submitted in accordance with subsection (a)(1).

(B) Data submitted pursuant to subparagraph (A) shall be data which the person submitting the data believes show that—

(i) in the case of a substance with respect to which notice is required under subsection (a)(1)(A) the manufacture, processing, distribution in commerce, use, and disposal of the chemical substance or any combination of such activities will not present an unreasonable risk of injury to health or the environment, or

(ii) in the case of a chemical substance with respect to which notice is required under subsection (a)(1)(B), the intended significant new use of the chemical substance will not present an unreasonable risk of injury to health or the environment.

(3) Data submitted under paragraph (1) or (2) shall be made available, subject to section 14, for examination by interested persons.

(4) (A) (i) The Administrator may, by rule, compile and keep current a list of chemical substances with respect to which the Administrator finds that the manufacture, processing, distribution in commerce, use, or disposal, or any combination of such activities, presents or may present an unreasonable risk of injury to health or the environment.

(ii) In making a finding under clause (i) that the manufacture, processing, distribution in commerce, use, or disposal of a chemical substance or any combination of such activities presents or may present an unreasonable risk of injury to health or the environment, the Administrator shall consider all relevant factors, including—

(I) the effects of the chemical substance on health and the magnitude of human exposure to such substance; and

(II) the effects of the chemical substance on the environment and the magnitude of environmental exposure to such substance.

(B) The Administrator shall, in prescribing a rule under subparagraph (A) which lists any chemical substance, identify those uses, if any, which the Administrator determines, by rule under subsection (a)(2), would constitute a significant new use of such substance.

(C) Any rule under subparagraph (A), and any substantive amendment or repeal of such a rule, shall be promulgated pursuant to the procedures specified in section 553 of title 5, United States Code, except that (i) the Administrator shall give interested persons an opportunity for the oral presentation of data, views, or arguments, in addition to an opportunity to make written submissions, (ii) a transcript shall be kept of any oral presentation, and (iii) the Administrator shall make and publish with the rule the finding described in subparagraph (A).

(c) Extension of Notice Period.—The Administrator may for good cause extend for additional periods (not to exceed in the aggregate 90 days) the period, prescribed by subsection (a) or (b) before which the manufacturing or processing of a chemical substance subject to such subsection may begin. Subject to section 14, such an extension and the reasons therefor shall be published in the Federal Register and shall constitute a final agency action subject to judicial review.

(d) Content of Notice; Publication in the Federal Register.—

(1) The notice required by subsection (a) shall include—

(A) insofar as known to the person submitting the notice or insofar as reasonably ascertainable, the information described in subparagraphs (A), (B), (C), (D), (F), and (G) of section 8(a)(2), and

(B) in such form and manner as the Administrator may prescribe, any test data in the possession or control of the person giving such notice which are related to the effect of any manufacture, processing, distribution in commerce, use, or disposal of such substance or any article containing such substance, or of any combination of such activities, on health or the environment, and

(C) a description of any other data concerning the environmental and health effects of such substance, insofar as known to the person making the notice or insofar as reasonably ascertainable.

Such a notice shall be made available, subject to section 14, for examination by interested persons.

(2) Subject to section 14, not later than five days (excluding Saturdays, Sundays and legal holidays) after the date of the receipt of a notice under subsection (a) or of data subsection (b), the Administrator shall publish in the Federal Register a notice which—

(A) identifies the chemical substance for which notice or data has been received;

(B) lists the uses or intended uses of such substance; and

(C) in the case of the receipt of data under subsection (b), describes the nature of the tests performed on such substance and any data which was developed pursuant to subsection (b) or a rule under section 4.

A notice under this paragraph respecting a chemical substance shall identify the chemical substance by generic class unless the Administrator determines that more specific identification is required in the public interest.

(3) At the beginning of each month the Administrator shall publish a list in the Federal Register of (A) each chemical substance for which notice has been received under subsection (a) and for which the notification period prescribed by subsection (a), (b), or (c) has not expired, and (B) each chemical substance for which such notification period has expired since the last publication in the Federal Register of such list.

(e) Regulation Pending Development of Information.—

(1) (A) If the Administrator determines that—

(i) the information available to the Administrator is insufficient to permit a reasoned evaluation of the health and environmental effects of a chemical substance with respect to which notice is required by subsection (a); and

(ii) (I) in the absence of sufficient information to permit the Administrator to make such an evaluation, the manufacture, processing, distribution in commerce, use, or disposal of such substance, or any combination of such activities, may present an unreasonable risk of injury to health or the environment, or

(II) such substance is or will be produced in substantial quantities, and such substance either enters or may reasonably be anticipated to enter the environment in substantial quantities or there is or may be significant or substantial human exposure to the substance,

the Administrator may issue a proposed order, to take effect on the expiration of the notification period applicable to the manufacturing or processing of such substance under subsection (a), (b), or (c), to prohibit or limit the manufacture, processing, distribution in commerce, use, or disposal of such substance or to prohibit or limit any combination of such activities.

(B) A proposed order may not be issued under subparagraph (A) respecting a chemical substance (i) later than 45 days before the expiration of the notification period applicable to the manufacture or processing of such substance under subsection (a), (b), or (c), and (ii) unless the Administrator has, on or before the issuance of the proposed order, notified, in writing, each manufacturer or processor, as the case may be, of such substance of the determination which underlies such order.

(C) If a manufacturer or processor of a chemical substance to be subject to a proposed order issued under subparagraph (A) files with the Administrator (within the 30–day period beginning on the date such manufacturer or processor received the notice required by subparagraph (B)(ii) objections specifying with particularity the provisions of the order deemed objectionable and stating the grounds therefore, the proposed order shall not take effect.

(2) (A) (i) Except as provided in clause (ii), if with respect to a chemical substance with respect to which notice is required by subsection (a), the Administrator makes the determination described in paragraph (1)(A) and if—

(I) the Administrator does not issue a proposed order under paragraph (1) respecting such substance, or

(II) the Administrator issues such an order respecting such substance but such order does not take effect because objections were filed under paragraph (1)(C) with respect to it,

the Administrator, through attorneys of the Environmental Protection Agency, shall apply to the United States District Court for the District of Columbia or the United States district court for the judicial district in which the manufacturer or processor, as the case may be, of such substance is found, resides, or transacts business for an injunction to prohibit or limit the manufacture, processing, distribution in commerce, use, or disposal of such substance (or to prohibit or limit any combination of such activities).

(ii) If the Administrator issues a proposed order under paragraph (1)(A) respecting a chemical substance but such order does not take effect because objections have been filed under paragraph (1)(C) with respect to it, the Administrator is not required to apply for an injunction under clause (i) respecting such substance if the Administrator determines, on the basis of such objections, that the determinations under paragraph (1)(A) may not be made.

(B) A district court of the United States which receives an application under subparagraph (A)(i) for an injunction respecting a chemical substance shall issue such injunction if the court finds that—

(i) the information available to the Administrator is insufficient to permit a reasoned evaluation of the health and environmental effects of a chemical substance with respect to which notice is required by subsection (a); and

(ii) (I) in the absence of sufficient information to permit the Administrator to make such an evaluation, the manufacture, processing, distribution in commerce, use, or disposal of such substance, or any combination of such activities, may present an unreasonable risk of injury to health or the environment or

(II) such substance is or will be produced in substantial quantities, and such substance either enters or may reasonably be anticipated to enter the environment in substantial quantities or there is or may be significant or substantial human exposure to the substance.

(C) Pending the completion of a proceeding for the issuance of an injunction under subparagraph (B) respecting a chemical substance, the court may, upon application of the

Administrator made through attorneys of the Environmental Protection Agency, issue a temporary restraining order or a preliminary injunction to prohibit the manufacture, processing, distribution in commerce, use, or disposal of such a substance (or any combination of such activities) if the court finds that the notification period applicable under subsection (a), (b), or (c) to the manufacturing or processing of such substance may expire before such proceeding can be completed.

(D) After the submission to the Administrator of test data sufficient to evaluate the health and environmental effects of a chemical substance subject to an injunction issued under subparagraph (B) and the evaluation of such data by the Administrator, the district court of the United States which issued such injunction shall, upon petition, dissolve the injunction unless the Administrator has initiated a proceeding for the issuance of a rule under section 6(a) respecting the substance. If such a proceeding has been initiated, such court shall continue the injunction in effect until the effective date of the rule promulgated in such proceeding or, if such proceeding is terminated without the promulgation of a rule, upon the termination of the proceeding, whichever occurs first.

(f) Protection Against Unreasonable Risks.—

(1) If the Administrator finds that there is a reasonable basis to conclude that the manufacture, processing, distribution in commerce, use, or disposal of a chemical substance with respect to which notice is required by subsection (a), or that any combination of such activities, presents or will present an unreasonable risk of injury to health or environment before a rule promulgated under section 6 can protect against such risk, the Administrator shall, before the expiration of the notification period applicable under subsection (a), (b), or (c) to the manufacturing or processing of such substance, take the action authorized by paragraph (2) or (3) to the extent necessary to protect against such risk.

(2) The Administrator may issue a proposed rule under section 6(a) to apply to a chemical substance with respect to which a finding was made under paragraph (1)—

(A) a requirement limiting the amount of such substance which may be manufactured, processed, or distributed in commerce,

(B) a requirement described in paragraph (2), (3), (4), (5), (6), or (7) of section 6(a), or

(C) any combination of the requirements referred to in subparagraph (B).

Such a proposed rule shall be effective upon its publication in the Federal Register. Section 6(d)(2)(B) shall apply with respect to such rule.

(3) (A) The Administrator may—

(i) issue a proposed order to prohibit the manufacture, processing, or distribution in commerce of a substance with respect to which a finding was made under paragraph (1), or

(ii) apply, through attorneys of the Environmental Protection Agency, to the United States District Court for the District of Columbia or the United States district court for the judicial district in which the manufacturer, or processor, as the case may be, of such substance, is found, resides, or transacts business for an injunction to prohibit the manufacture, processing, or distribution in commerce of such substance.

A proposed order issued under clause (i) respecting a chemical substance shall take effect on the expiration of the notification period applicable under subsection (a), (b), or (c) to the manufacture or processing of such substance.

(B) If the district court of the United States to which an application has been made under subparagraph (A)(ii) finds that there is a reasonable basis to conclude that the manufacture, processing, distribution in commerce, use, or disposal of the chemical substance with respect to which such application was made, or that any combination of such activities, presents or will present an unreasonable risk of injury to health or the environment before a rule promulgated under section 6 can protect against such risk, the court shall issue an injunction to prohibit the manufacture, processing, or distribution in commerce of such substance or to prohibit any combination of such activities.

(C) The provisions of subparagraphs (B) and (C) of subsection (e)(2) shall apply with respect to an order issued under clause (i) of subparagraph (A); and the provisions of subparagraph (C) of subsection (e)(2) shall apply with respect to an injunction issued under subparagraph (B).

(D) If the Administrator issues an order pursuant to subparagraph (A)(i) respecting a chemical substance and objections are filed in accordance with subsection (e)(1)(C), the Administrator shall seek an injunction under subparagraph (A)(ii) respecting such substance unless the Administrator determines, on the basis of such objections, that such substance does not or will not present an unreasonable risk of injury to health or the environment.

(g) Statement Of Reasons For Not Taking Action.—If the Administrator has not initiated any action under this section or section 6 or 7 to prohibit or limit the manufacture, processing, distribution in commerce, use, or disposal of a chemical substance, with respect to which notification or data is required by subsection (a)(1)(B) or (b), before the expiration of the notification period applicable to the manufacturing or processing of such substance, the Administrator shall publish a statement of the Administrator's reasons for not initiating such action. Such a statement shall be published in the Federal Register before the expiration of such period. Publication of such statement in accordance with the preceding sentence is not a prerequisite to the manufacturing or processing of the substance with respect to which the statement is to be published.

(h) Exemptions.—

(1) The Administrator may, upon application, exempt any person from any requirement of subsection (a) or (b) to permit such person to manufacture or process a chemical substance for test marketing purposes—

(A) upon a showing by such person satisfactory to the Administrator that the manufacture, processing, distribution in commerce, use, and disposal of such substance, and that any combination of such activities, for such purposes will not present any unreasonable risk of injury to health or the environment, and

(B) under such restrictions as the Administrator considers appropriate.

(2) (A) The Administrator may, upon application, exempt any person from the requirement of subsection (b)(2) to submit data for a chemical substance. If, upon receipt of an application under the preceding sentence, the Administrator determines that—

(i) the chemical substance with respect to which such application was submitted is equivalent to a chemical substance for which data has been submitted to the Administrator as required by subsection (b)(2), and

(ii) submission of data by the applicant on such substance would be duplicative of data which has been submitted to the Administrator in accordance with such subsection,

the Administrator shall exempt the applicant from the requirement to submit such data on such substance. No exemption which is granted under this subparagraph with respect to the submission of data for a chemical substance may take effect before the beginning of the reimbursement period applicable to such data.

(B) If the Administrator exempts any person, under subparagraph (A), from submitting data required under subsection (b)(2) for a chemical substance because of the existence of previously submitted data and if such exemption is granted during the reimbursement period for such data, then (unless such person and the persons referred to in clauses (i) and (ii) agree on the amount and method of reimbursement) the Administrator shall order the person granted the exemption to provide fair and equitable (in an amount determined under rules of the Administrator)—

(i) to the person who previously submitted the data on which the exemption was based, for a portion of the costs incurred by such person in complying with the requirement under subsection (b)(2) to submit such data, and

(ii) to any other person who has been required under this sub-paragraph to contribute with respect to such costs, for a portion of the amount such person was required to contribute.

In promulgating rules for the determination of fair and equitable reimbursement to the persons described in clauses (i) and (ii) for costs incurred with respect to a chemical substance, the Administrator shall, after consultation with the Attorney General and the Federal Trade Commission, consider all relevant factors, including the effect on the competitive position of the person required to provide reimbursement in relation to the persons to be reimbursed and the share of the market for such substance of the person required to provide reimbursement in relation to the share of such market of the persons to be reimbursed. For purposes of judicial review, an order under this subparagraph shall be considered final agency action.

(C) For purposes of this paragraph, the reimbursement period for any previously submitted data for a chemical substance is a period—

(i) beginning on the date of the termination of the prohibition, imposed under this section, on the manufacture or processing of such substance by the person who submitted such data to the Administrator, and

(ii) ending—

(I) five years after the date referred to in clause (i), or

(II) at the expiration of a period which begins on the date referred to in clause (i) and is equal to the period which the Administrator determines was necessary to develop such data,

whichever is later.

(3) The requirements of subsections (a) and (b) do not apply with respect to the manufacturing or processing of any chemical substance which is manufactured or processed, or proposed to be manufactured or processed, only in small quantities (as defined by the Administrator by rule) solely purposes of—

(A) scientific experimentation or analysis, or

(B) chemical research on, or analysis of such substance or another substance, including such research or analysis for the development of a product,

if all persons engaged in such experimentation, research, or analysis for a manufacturer or processor are notified (in such form and manner as the Administrator may prescribe) of any risk to health which the manufacturer, processor, or the Administrator has reason to believe may be associated with such chemical substance.

(4) The Administrator may, upon application and by rule, exempt the manufacturer of any new chemical substance from all or part of the requirements of this section if the Administrator determines that the manufacture, processing, distribution in commerce, use, or disposal of such chemical substance, or that any combination of such activities, will not present an unreasonable risk of injury to health or the environment. A rule promulgated under this paragraph (and any substantive amendment to, or repeal of, such a rule) shall be promulgated in accordance with paragraphs (2) and (3) of section 6(c).

(5) The Administrator may, upon application, make the requirements of subsections (a) and (b) inapplicable with respect to the manufacturing or processing of any chemical substance (A) which exists temporarily as a result of a chemical reaction in the manufacturing or processing of a mixture or another chemical substance, and (B) to which there is no, and will not be, human or environmental exposure.

(6) Immediately upon receipt of an application under paragraph (1) or (5) the Administrator shall publish in the Federal Register notice of the receipt of such application. The Administrator shall give interested persons an opportunity to comment upon any such application and shall, within 45 days of its receipt, either approve or deny the application. The Administrator shall publish in the Federal Register notice of the approval or denial of such an application.

(i) Definition.—For purposes of this section, the terms "manufacture" and "process" mean manufacturing or processing for commercial purposes.

§2605. Regulation of Hazardous Chemical Substances and Mixtures. [Sec. 6]

(a) Scope Of Regulation.—If the Administrator finds that there is a reasonable basis to conclude that the manufacture, processing, distribution in commerce, use, or disposal of a chemical substance or mixture, or that any combination of such activities, presents or will present an unreasonable risk of injury to health or the environment, the Administrator shall by rule apply one or more of the following requirements to such substance or mixture to the extent necessary to protect adequately against such risk using the least burdensome requirements:

(1) A requirement (A) prohibiting the manufacturing, processing, or distribution in commerce of such substance or mixture, or (B) limiting the amount of such substance or mixture which may be manufactured, processed, or distributed in commerce.

(2) A requirement—

(A) prohibiting the manufacture, processing, or distribution in commerce of such substance or mixture for (i) a particular use or (ii) a particular use in a concentration in excess of a level specified by the Administrator in the rule imposing the requirement, or

(B) limiting the amount of such substance or mixture which may be manufactured, processed, or distributed in commerce for (i) a particular use or (ii) a particular use in a concentration in excess of a level specified by the Administrator in the rule imposing the requirement.

(3) A requirement that such substance or mixture or any article containing such substance or

mixture be marked with or accompanied by clear and adequate warnings and instructions with respect to its use, distribution in commerce, or disposal or with respect to any combination of such activities. The form and content of such warnings and instructions shall be prescribed by the Administrator.

(4) A requirement that manufacturers and processors of such substance or mixture make and retain records of the processes used to manufacture or process such substance or mixture and monitor or conduct tests which are reasonable and necessary to assure compliance with the requirements of any rule applicable under this subsection.

(5) A requirement prohibiting or otherwise regulating any manner or method of commercial use of such substance or mixture.

(6) (A) A requirement prohibiting or otherwise regulating any manner or method of disposal of such substance or mixture, or of any article containing such substance or mixture, by its manufacturer or processor or by any other person who uses, or disposes of, it for commercial purposes.

(B) A requirement under subparagraph (A) may not require any person to take any action which would be in violation of any law or requirement of, or in effect for, a State or political subdivision, and shall require each person subject to it to notify each State and political subdivision in which a required disposal many occur of such disposal.

(7) A requirement directing manufacturers or processors of such substance or mixture (A) to give notice of such unreasonable risk of injury to distributors in commerce of such substance or mixture and, to the extent reasonably ascertainable, to other persons in possession of such substance or mixture or exposed to such substance or mixture, (B) to give public notice of such risk of injury, and (C) to replace or repurchase such substance or mixture as elected by the person to which the requirement is directed.

Any requirement (or combination of requirements) imposed under this subsection may be limited in application to specified geographic areas.

(b) Quality Control.—If the Administrator has a reasonable basis to conclude that a particular manufacturer or processor is manufacturing or processing a chemical substance or mixture in a manner which unintentionally causes the chemical substance or mixture to present or which will cause it to present an unreasonable risk of injury to health or the environment—

(1) the Administrator may by order require such manufacturer or processor to submit a description of the relevant quality control procedures followed in the manufacturing or processing of such chemical substance or mixture; and

(2) if the Administrator determines—

(A) that such quality control procedures are inadequate to prevent the chemical substance or mixture from presenting such risk of injury, the Administrator may order the manufacturer or processor to revise such quality control procedures to the extent necessary to remedy such inadequacy; or

(B) that the use of such quality control procedures has resulted in the distribution in commerce of chemical substances or mixtures which present an unreasonable risk of injury to health or the environment, the Administrator may order the manufacturer or processor to (i) give notice of such risk to processors or distributors in commerce of any such substance or mixture, or to both, and, to the extent reasonably ascertainable, to any other person in possession of or exposed to any such substance, (ii) to give public notice of such risk, and (iii) to provide such replacement or repurchase of any such substance or mixture as is necessary to adequately protect health or the environment.

A determination under subparagraph (A) or (B) of paragraph (2) shall be made on the record after opportunity for hearing in accordance with section 554 of title 5, United States Code. Any manufacturer or processor subject to a requirement to replace or repurchase a chemical substance or mixture may elect either to replace or repurchase the substance or mixture and shall take either such action in the manner prescribed by the Administrator.

(c) Promulgation of Subsection (a) Rules.—

(1) In promulgating any rule under subsection (a) with respect to a chemical substance or mixture, the Administrator shall consider and publish a statement with respect to—

(A) the effects of such substance or mixture on health and the magnitude of the exposure of human beings to such substance or mixture.

(B) the effects of such substance or mixture on the environment and the magnitude of the exposure of the environment to such substance or mixture,

(C) the benefits of such substance or mixture for various uses and the availability of substitutes for such uses, and

(D) the reasonably ascertainable economic consequences of the rule, after consideration of the effect on the national economy, small business, technological innovation, the environment, and public health.

If the Administrator determines that a risk of injury to health or the environment could be eliminated or reduced to a sufficient extent by actions taken under another Federal law (or laws) administered in whole or in part by the Administrator, the Administrator may not promulgate a rule under subsection (a) to protect against such risk of injury unless the Administrator finds, in the Administrator's discretion, that it is in the public interest to protect against such risk under this Act. In making such a finding the Administrator shall consider (i) all relevant aspects of the risk, as determined by the Administrator in the Administrator's discretion, (ii) a comparison of the estimated costs of complying with actions taken under this Act and under such law (or laws), and (iii) the relative efficiency of actions under this Act and under such law (or laws) to protect against such risk of injury.

(2) When prescribing a rule under subsection (a) the Administrator shall proceed in accordance with section 553 of title 5, United States Code (without regard to any reference in such section to sections 556 and 557 of such title), and shall also (A) publish a notice of proposed rulemaking stating with particularity the reason for the proposed rule; (B) allow interested persons to submit written data, views, and arguments, and make all such submissions publicly, available; (C) provide an opportunity for an informal hearing in accordance with paragraph (3); (D) promulgate, if appropriate, a final rule based on the matter in the rulemaking record (as defined in section 19(a)), and (E) make and publish with the rule the finding described in subsection (a).

(3) Informal hearings required by paragraph (2)(C) shall be conducted by the Administrator in accordance with the following requirements:

(A) Subject to subparagraph (B), an interested person is entitled—

(i) to present such person's position orally or by documentary submissions (or both), and

(ii) if the Administrator determines that there are disputed issues of material fact it is necessary to resolve, to present such rebuttal submissions and to conduct (or have conducted under subparagraph (B)(ii) such cross-examination of persons as the Administrator determines (I) to be appropriate, and (II) to be required for a full and true disclosure with respect to such issues.

(B) The Administrator may prescribe such rules and make such rulings concerning procedures in such hearings to avoid unnecessary costs or delay. Such rules or rulings may include (i) the imposition of reasonable time limits on each interested person's oral presentations, and (ii) requirements that any cross-examination to which a person may be entitled under subparagraph (A) be conducted by the Administrator on behalf of that person in such manner as the Administrator determines (I) to be appropriate, and (II) to be required for a full and true disclosure with respect to disputed issues of material fact.

(C) (i) Except as provided in clause (ii), if a group of persons each of whom under subparagraphs (A) and (B) would be entitled to conduct (or have conducted) cross-examination and who are determined by the Administrator to have the same or similar interests in the proceeding cannot agree upon a single representative of such interests for purposes of cross- examination, the Administrator may make rules and rulings (I) limiting the representation of such interest for such purposes, and (II) governing the manner in which such cross-examination shall be limited.

(ii) When any person who is a member of a group with respect to which the Administrator has made a determination under clause (i) is unable to agree upon group representation with the other members of the group, then such person shall not be denied under the authority of clause (i) the opportunity to conduct (or have conducted) cross-examination as to issues affecting the person's particular interests if (I) the person satisfies the Administrator that the person has made a reasonable and good faith effort to reach agreement upon group representation with the other members of the group and (II) the Administrator determines that there are substantial and relevant issues which are not adequately presented by the group representative.

(D) A verbatim transcript shall be taken of any oral presentation made, and cross-examination conducted in any informal hearing under this subsection. Such transcript shall be available to the public.

(4) (A) The Administrator may, pursuant to rules prescribed by the Administrator, provide compensation for reasonable attorneys' fees, expert witness fees, and other costs of participating in a rulemaking proceeding for the promulgation of a rule under subsection (a) to any person—

(i) who represents an interest which would substantially contribute to a fair determination of the issues to be resolved in the proceeding, and

(ii) if—

(I) the economic interest of such person is small in comparison to the costs of effective participation in the proceeding by such person, or

(II) such person demonstrates to the satisfaction of the Administrator that such person does not have sufficient resources adequately to participate in the proceeding without compensation under this subparagraph.

In determining for purposes of clause (i) if an interest will substantially contribute to a fair determination of the issues to be resolved in a proceeding, the Administrator shall take into account the number and complexity of such issues and the extent to which representation of such interest will contribute to widespread public participation in the proceeding and representation of a fair balance of interests for the resolution of such issues.

(B) In determining whether compensation should be provided to a person under subparagraph (A) and the amount of such compensation, the Administrator shall take into account the financial burden which will be incurred by such person in participating in the rulemaking proceeding. The Administrator shall take such action as may be necessary to ensure that the aggregate amount of compensation paid under this paragraph in any fiscal year to all persons who, in rulemaking proceedings in which they receive compensation, are persons who either—

(i) would be regulated by the proposed rule, or

(ii) represent persons who would be so regulated, may not exceed 25 per centum of the aggregate amount paid as compensation under this paragraph to all persons in such fiscal year.

(5) Paragraph (1), (2), (3), and (4) of this subsection apply to the promulgation of a rule repealing, or making a substantive amendment to, a rule promulgated under subsection (a).

(d) Effective Date.—

(1) The Administrator shall specify in any rule under subsection (a) the date on which it shall take effect, which date shall be as soon as feasible.

(2) (A) The Administrator may declare a proposed rule under subsection (a) to be effective upon its publication in the Federal Register and until the effective date of final action taken, in accordance with subparagraph (B), respecting such rule if—

(i) the Administrator determines that—

(I) the manufacture, processing, distribution in commerce, use, or disposal of the chemical substance or mixture subject to such proposed rule or any combination of such activities is likely to result in an unreasonable risk of serious or widespread injury to health or the environment before such effective date; and

(II) making such proposed rule so effective is necessary to protect the public interest; and

(ii) in the case of a proposed rule to prohibit the manufacture, processing, or distribution of a chemical substance or mixture because of the risk determined under clause (i)(I), a court has in an action under section 7 granted relief with respect to such risk associated with such substance or mixture.

Such a proposed rule which is made so effective shall not, for purposes of judicial review, be considered final agency action.

(B) If the Administrator makes a proposed rule effective upon its publication in the Federal Register, the Administrator shall, as expeditiously as possible, give interested persons prompt notice of such action, provide reasonable opportunity, in accordance with paragraphs (2) and (3) of subsection (c), for a hearing on such rule, and either promulgate such rule (as proposed or with modifications) or revoke it; and if such a hearing is requested, the Administrator shall commence the hearing within five days from the date such request is made unless the Administrator and the person making the request agree upon a later date for the hearing to begin, and after the hearing is concluded the Administrator shall, within ten days of the conclusion of the hearing, either promulgate such rule (as proposed or with modifications) or revoke it.

(e) Polychlorinated Biphenyls.—

(1) Within six months after the effective date of this Act the Administrator shall promulgate rules to—

(A) prescribe methods for the disposal of polychlorinated biphenyls, and

(B) require polychlorinated biphenyls to be marked with clear and adequate warnings, and instructions with respect to their processing, distribution in commerce, use, or disposal or with respect to any combination of such activities.

Requirements prescribed by rules under this paragraph shall be consistent with the requirements of paragraphs (2) and (3).

(2) (A) Except as provided under subparagraph (B), effective one year after the effective date of this Act no person may manufacture, process, or distribute in commerce or use any polychlorinated biphenyl in any manner other than in a totally enclosed manner.

(B) The Administrator may by rule authorize the manufacture, processing, distribution in commerce or use (or any combination of such activities) of any polychlorinated biphenyl in a manner other than in a totally enclosed manner if the Administrator finds that such manufacture, processing, distribution in commerce, or use (or combination of such activities) will not present an unreasonable risk of injury to health or the environment.

(C) For the purposes of this paragraph, the term "totally enclosed manner" means any manner which will ensure that any exposure of human beings or the environment to a polychlorinated biphenyl will be insignificant as determined by the Administrator by rule.

(3) (A) Except as provided in subparagraphs (B) and (C)—

(i) no person may manufacture any polychlorinated biphenyl after two years after the effective date of this Act, and

(ii) no person may process or distribute in commerce any polychlorinated biphenyl after two and one-half years after such date.

(B) Any person may petition the Administrator for an exemption from the requirements of subparagraph (A), and the Administrator may grant by rule such an exemption if the Administrator finds that—

(i) an unreasonable risk of injury to health or environment would not result, and

(ii) good faith efforts have been made to develop a chemical substance which does not present an unreasonable risk of injury to health or the environment and which may be substituted for such polychlorinated biphenyl.

An exemption granted under this subparagraph shall be subject to such terms and conditions as the Administrator may prescribe and shall be in effect for such period (but not more than one year from the date it is granted) as the Administrator may prescribe.

(C) Subparagraph (A) shall not apply to the distribution in commerce of any polychlorinated biphenyl if such polychlorinated biphenyl was sold for purposes other than resale before two and one half years after the date of enactment of this Act.

(4) Any rule under paragraph (1), (2)(B), or (3)(B) shall be promulgated in accordance with paragraphs (2), (3), and (4) of subsection (c).

(5) This subsection does not limit the authority of the Administrator, under any other provision of this Act or any other Federal law, to take action respecting any polychlorinated biphenyl.

§2606. Imminent Hazards. [Sec. 7]

(a) Actions Authorized And Required.—

(1) The Administrator may commence a civil action in an appropriate district court of the United States—

(A) for seizure of an imminently hazardous chemical substance or mixture or any article containing such a substance or mixture,

(B) for relief (as authorized by subsection (b)) against any person who manufacturers, processes, distributes in commerce, or uses, or disposes of, an imminently hazardous chemical substance or mixture or any article containing such a substance or mixture, or

(C) for both such seizure and relief.

A civil action may be commenced under this paragraph notwithstanding the existence of a rule under section 4, 5 or title IV, 6, or title IV or an order under section 5, or title IV, and notwithstanding the pendency of any administrative or judicial proceeding under any provision of this Act.

§7(a)(1)(C) amended by PL 102–550, Oct. 28, 1992]

(2) If the Administrator has not made a rule under section 6(a) immediately effective (as

authorized by subsection 6(d)(2)(A)(i)) with respect to an imminently hazardous chemical substance or mixture, the Administrator shall commence in a district court of the United States with respect to such substance or mixture or article containing such substance or mixture a civil action described in subparagraph (A), (B), or (C) of paragraph (1).

(b) Relief Authorized.—

(1) The district court of the United States in which an action under subsection (a) is brought shall have jurisdiction to grant such temporary or permanent relief as may be necessary to protect health or the environment from the unreasonable risk associated with the chemical substance, mixture, or article involved in such action.

(2) In the case of an action under subsection (a) brought against a person who manufactures, processes, or distributes in commerce a chemical substance or mixture or an article containing a chemical substance or mixture, the relief authorized by paragraph (1) may include the issuance of a mandatory order requiring (A) in the case of purchasers of such substance, mixture or article known to the defendant, notification to such purchasers of the risk associated with it; (B) public notice of such risk; (C) recall; (D) the replacement or repurchase of such substance, mixture, or article; or (E) any combination of the actions described in the preceding clauses.

(3) In the case of an action under subsection (a) against a chemical substance, mixture, or article, such substance, mixture, or article may be proceeded against by process of libel for its seizure and condemnation. Proceedings in such an action shall conform as nearly as possible to proceedings in rem in admiralty.

(c) Venue and Consolidation.—

(1) (A) An action under subsection (a) against a person who manufacturers, processes, or distributes a chemical substance or mixture or an article containing a chemical substance or mixture may be brought in the United States District Court for the District of Columbia or for any judicial district in which any of the defendants is found, resides, or transacts business; and process in such an action may be served on a defendant in any other district in which such defendant resides or may be found. An action under subsection (a) against a chemical substance, mixture, or article may be brought in any United States district court within the jurisdiction of which the substance, mixture, or article is found.

(B) In determining the judicial district in which an action may be brought under subsection (a) in instances in which such action may be brought in more than one judicial district, the Administrator shall take into account the convenience of the parties.

(C) Subpeonas requiring attendance of witnesses in an action brought under subsection (a) may be served in any judicial district.

(2) Whenever proceedings under subsection (a) involving identical chemical substances, mixtures, or articles are pending in courts in two or more judicial districts, they shall be consolidated for trial by order of any such court upon application reasonably made by any party in interest, upon notice to all parties in interest.

(d) Action Under Section 6.—Where appropriate, concurrently with the filing of an action under subsection (a) or as soon thereafter as may be practicable, the Administrator shall initiate a proceeding for the promulgation of a rule under section 6(a).

(e) Representation.—Notwithstanding any other provision of law, in any action under subsection (a), the Administrator may direct attorneys of the Environmental Protection Agency to appear and represent the Administrator in such an action.

(f) Definition.—For the purposes of subsection (a), the term "imminently hazardous chemical substance or mixture" means a chemical substance or mixture which presents an imminent and unreasonable risk of serious or widespread injury to health or the environment. Such a risk to health or the environment shall be considered imminent if it is shown that the manufacture, processing, distribution in commerce, use, or disposal of the chemical substance or mixture, or that any combination of such activities, is likely to result in such injury to health or the environment before a final rule under section 6 can protect against such risk.

§2607. Reporting and Retention of Information. [Sec. 8]

(a) Reports.—

(1) The Administrator shall promulgate rules under which—

(A) each person (other than a small manufacturer or processor) who manufactures or processes or proposes to manufacture or process a chemical substance (other than a chemical substance described in subparagraph (B)(ii) shall maintain such records, and shall submit to the Administrator such reports, as the Administrator may reasonably require, and

(B) each person (other than a small manufacturer or processor) who manufacturers or processes or proposes to manufacture or process—

(i) a mixture, or

(ii) a chemical substance in small quantities (as defined by the Administrator by rule) solely for purposes of scientific experimentation or analysis or chemical research on, or analysis of, such substance or another substance, including any such research or analysis for the development of a product,

shall maintain records and submit to the Administrator reports but only to the extent the Administrator determines the maintenance of records or submission of reports, or both, is necessary for the effective enforcement of this Act.

The Administrator may not require in a rule promulgated under this paragraph the maintenance of records or the submission of reports with respect to changes in the proportions of the components of a mixture unless the Administrator finds that the maintenance of such records or the submission of such reports, or both, is necessary for the effective enforcement of this Act. For purposes of the compilation of the list of chemical substances required under subsection (b), the Administrator shall promulgate rules pursuant to this subsection not later than 180 days after the effective date of this Act.

(2) The Administrator may require under paragraph (1) maintenance of records and reporting with respect to the following insofar as known to the person making the report or insofar as reasonably ascertainable:

(A) The common or trade name, the chemical identity, and the molecular structure of each chemical substance or mixture for which such a report is required.

(B) The categories or proposed categories of use of each such substance or mixture.

(C) The total amount of each such substance and mixture manufactured or processed, reasonable estimates of the total amount to be manufactured or processed, the amount manufactured or processed for each of its categories of use, and reasonable estimates of the amount to be manufactured or processed for each of its categories of use or proposed categories of use.

(D) A description of the byproducts resulting from the manufacture, processing, use, or disposal of each such substance or mixture.

(E) All existing data concerning the environmental and health effects of such substance or mixture.

(F) The number of individuals exposed, and reasonable estimates of the number who will be exposed, to such substance or mixture in their places of employment and the duration of such exposure.

(G) In the initial report under paragraph (1) on such substance or mixture, the manner or method of its disposal, and in any subsequent report on such substance or mixture, any change in such manner or method.

To the extent feasible, the Administrator shall not require under paragraph (1), any reporting which is unnecessary or duplicative.

(3) (A) (i) The Administrator may by rule require a small manufacturer or processor of a chemical substance to submit to the Administrator such information respecting the chemical substance as the Administrator may require for publication of the first list of chemical substances required by subsection (b).

(ii) The Administrator may by rule require a small manufacturer or processor of a chemical substance or mixture—

(I) subject to a rule proposed or promulgated under section 4, 5(b)(4), or 6, or an order in effect under section 5(e), or

(II) with respect to which relief has been granted pursuant to a civil action brought under section 5 or 7,

to maintain such records on such substance or mixture, and to submit to the Administrator such reports on such substance or mixture, as the Administrator may reasonably require. A rule under this clause requiring reporting may require reporting with respect to the matters referred to in paragraph (2).

(B) The Administrator, after consultation with the Administrator of the Small Business Administration, shall by rule prescribe standards for determining the manufacturers and processors which qualify as small manufacturers and processors for purposes of this paragraph and paragraph (1).

(b) Inventory.—

(1) The Administrator shall compile, keep current, and publish a list of each chemical substance which is manufactured or processed in the United States. Such list shall at least include each chemical substance which any person reports, under section 5 or subsection (a) of this section, is manufactured or processed in the United States. Such list may not include any chemical substance which was not manufactured or processed in the United States within three years before the effective date of the rules promulgated pursuant to the last sentence of subsection (a)(1). In the case of a chemical substance for which a notice is submitted in accordance with section 5, such chemical substance shall be included in such list as of the earliest date (as determined by the Administrator) on which such substance was manufactured or processed in the United States. The Administrator shall first publish such a list not later than 315 days after the effective date of this Act. The Administrator shall not include in such list any chemical substance which is manufactured or processed only in small quantities (as defined by the Administrator by rule) solely for purposes of scientific experimentation or analysis or chemical research on, or analysis of, such substance or another substance, including such research or analysis for the development of a product.

(2) To the extent consistent with the purposes of this Act, the Administrator may, in lieu of listing, pursuant to paragraph (1), a chemical substance individually, list a category of chemical substances in which such substance is included.

(c) Records.—Any person who manufactures, processes, or distributes in commerce any chemical substance or mixture shall maintain records of significant adverse reactions to health or the environment, as determined by the Administrator by rule, alleged to have been caused by the substance or mixture. Records of such adverse reactions to the health of employees shall be retained for a period of 30 years from the date such reactions were first reported to or known by the person maintaining such records. Any other record of such adverse reactions shall be retained for a period of five years from the date the information contained in the record was first reported to or known by the person maintaining the record. Records required to be maintained under this subsection shall include records of consumer allegations of personal injury or harm to health, reports of occupational disease or injury, and reports or complaints of injury to the environment submitted to the manufacturer, processor, or distributor in commerce from any source. Upon request of any duly designated representative of the Administrator, each person who is required to maintain records under this subsection shall permit the inspection of such records and shall submit copies of such records.

(d) Health and Safety Studies.—The Administrator shall promulgate rules under which the Administrator shall require any person who manufactures, processes, or distributes in commerce or who proposes to manufacture, process, or distribute in commerce any chemical substance or mixture (or with respect to paragraph (2), any person who has possession of a study) to submit to the Administrator—

(1) lists of health and safety studies (A) conducted or initiated by or for such person with respect to such substance or mixture at any time, (B) known to such person, or (C) reasonably ascertainable by such person, except that the Administrator may exclude certain types or categories of studies from the requirements of this subsection if the Administrator finds that submission of lists of such studies are unnecessary to carry out the purposes of this Act; and

(2) copies of any study contained on a list submitted pursuant to paragraph (1) or otherwise known by such person.

(e) Notice to Administrator of Substantial Risks.—Any person who manufactures, processes, or distributes in commerce a chemical substance or mixture and who obtains information which reasonably supports the conclusion that such substance or mixture presents a substantial risk of injury to health or the environment shall immediately inform the Administrator of such information unless such person has actual knowledge that the Administrator has been adequately informed of such information.

(f) Definitions.—For purposes of this section, the terms "manufacture" and "process" mean manufacture or process for commercial purposes.

§2608. Relationship to Other Federal Laws. [Sec. 9]

(a) Laws Not Administered by the Administrator.—

(1) If the Administrator has reasonable basis to conclude that the manufacture, processing, distribution in commerce, use, or disposal of a chemical substance or mixture, or that any combination of such activities, presents or will present an unreasonable risk of injury to health or the environment and determines, in the

15 U.S.C. §2608

Administrator's discretion, that such risk may be prevented or reduced to a sufficient extent by action taken under a Federal law not administered by the Administrator, the Administrator shall submit to the agency which administers such law a report which describes such risk and includes in such description a specification of the activity or combination of activities which the Administrator has reason to believe so presents such risk. Such report shall also request such agency—

(A) (i) to determine if the risk described in such report may be prevented or reduced to a sufficient extent by action taken under such law, and

(ii) if the agency determines that such risk may be so prevented or reduced, to issue an order declaring whether or not the activity or combination of activities specified in the description of such risk presents such risk; and

(B) to respond to the Administrator with respect to the matters described in subparagraph (A).

Any report of the Administrator shall include a detailed statement of the information on which it is based and shall be published in the Federal Register. The agency receiving a request under such a report shall make the requested determination, issue the requested order, and make the requested response within such time as the Administrator specifies in the request, but such time specified may not be less than 90 days from the date the request was made. The response of an agency shall be accompanied by a detailed statement of the findings and conclusions of the agency and shall be published in the Federal Register.

(2) If the Administrator makes a report under paragraph (1) with respect to a chemical substance or mixture and the agency to which such report was made either—

(A) issues an order declaring that the activity or combination of activities specified in the description of the risk described in the report does not present the risk described in the report, or

(B) initiates, within 90 days of the publication in the Federal Register of the response of the agency under paragraph (1), action under the law (or laws) administered by such agency to protect against such risk associated with such activity or combination of activities,

the Administrator may not take any action under section 6 or 7 with respect to such risk.

(3) If the Administrator has initiated action under section 6 or 7 with respect to a risk associated with a chemical substance or mixture which was the subject of a report made to an agency under paragraph (1), such agency shall before taking action under the law (or laws) administered by it to protect against such risk consult with the Administrator for the purpose of avoiding duplication of Federal action against such risk.

(b) Laws Administered By The Administrator.—The Administrator shall coordinate actions taken under this Act with actions taken under other Federal laws administered in whole or in part by the Administrator. If the Administrator determines that a risk to health or the environment associated with a chemical substance or mixture could be eliminated or reduced to a sufficient extent by actions taken under the authorities contained in such other Federal laws, the Administrator shall use such authorities to protect against such risk unless the Administrator determines, in the Administrator's discretion, that it is in the public interest to protect against such risk by actions taken under this Act. This subsection shall not be construed to relieve the Administrator of any requirement imposed on the Administrator by such other Federal laws.

(c) Occupational Safety and Health.— In exercising any authority under this Act, the Administrator shall not, for purposes of section 4(b)(1) of the Occupational Safety and Health Act of 1970, be deemed to be exercising statutory authority to prescribe or enforce standards or regulations affecting occupational safety and health.

(d) Coordination.—In administering this Act, the Administrator shall consult and coordinate with the Secretary of Health, Education, and Welfare and the heads of any other appropriate Federal executive department or agency, any relevant independent regulatory agency, and any other appropriate instrumentality of the Federal Government for the purpose of achieving the maximum enforcement of this Act while imposing the least burdens of duplicative requirements on those subject to the Act and for other purposes. The Administrator shall, in the report required by section 30, report annually to the Congress on actions taken to coordinate with such other Federal departments, agencies, or instrumentalities, and on actions taken to coordinate the authority under this Act with the authority granted under other Acts referred to in subsection (b).

§2609. Research, Development, Collection, Dissemination, and Utilization of Data. [Sec. 10]

(a) Authority.—The Administrator shall, in consultation and cooperation with the Secretary of Health, Education, and Welfare and with other heads of appropriate departments and agencies, conduct such research, development, and monitoring as is necessary to carry out the purpose of this Act. The Administrator may enter into contracts and may make grants for research, development, and monitoring under this subsection. Contracts may be entered into under this subsection without regard to section 3324(a) and (b) of Title 31 and section 5 of Title 41.

[§10(a) amended by PL 97–258, Sept. 13, 1982]

(b) Data Systems.—

(1) The Administrator shall establish, administer, and be responsible for the continuing activities of an interagency committee which shall design, establish, and coordinate an efficient and effective system, within the Environmental Protection Agency, for the collection, dissemination to other Federal departments and agencies, and use of data submitted to the Administrator under this Act.

(2) (A) The Administrator shall, in consultation and cooperation with the Secretary of Health, Education, and Welfare and other heads of appropriate departments and agencies design, establish, and coordinate an efficient and effective system for the retrieval of toxicological and other scientific data which could be useful to the Administrator in carrying out the purposes of this Act. Systematized retrieval shall be developed for use by all Federal and other departments and agencies with responsibilities in the area of regulation or study of chemical substances and mixtures and their effect on health or the environment.

(B) The Administrator, in consultation and cooperation with the Secretary of Health, Education, and Welfare, may make grants and enter into contracts for the development of a data retrieval system described in subparagraph (A). Contracts may be entered into under this subparagraph without regard to section 3324(a) and (b) of Title 31 and section 5 of Title 41.

[§10(b)(2)(B) amended by PL 97–258, Sept. 13, 1982]

(c) Screening Techniques.—The Administrator shall coordinate, with the Assistant Secretary for Health of the Department of Health, Education, and Welfare, research undertaken by the Administrator and directed toward the development of rapid, reliable, and economical screening techniques for carcinogenic, mutagenic, teratogenic, and ecological effects of chemical substances and mixtures.

(d) Monitoring.—The Administrator shall, in consultation and cooperation with the Secretary of Health, Education, and Welfare, establish and be responsible for research aimed at the development, in cooperation with local, State, and Federal agencies, of monitoring techniques and instruments which may be used in the detection of toxic chemical substances and mixtures and which are reliable, economical, and capable of being implemented under a wide variety of conditions.

(e) Basic Research.—The Administrator shall, in consultation and cooperation with the Secretary of Health, Education, and Welfare, establish research programs to develop the fundamental scientific basis of the screening and monitoring techniques described in subsections (c) and (d), the bounds of the reliability of such techniques, and the opportunities for their improvement.

(f) Training.—The Administrator shall establish and promote programs and workshops to train or facilitate the training of Federal laboratory and technical personnel in existing or newly developed screening and monitoring techniques.

(g) Exchange of Research and Development Results.—The Administrator shall, in consultation with the Secretary of Health, Education, and Welfare and other heads of appropriate departments and agencies, establish and coordinate a system for exchange among Federal, State, and local authorities of research and development results respecting toxic chemical substances and mixtures, including a system to facilitate and promote the development of standard data format and analysis and consistent testing procedures.

§2610. Inspections and Subpoenas. [Sec. 11]

(a) In General.—For purposes of administering this Act, the Administrator, and any duly designated representative of the Administrator, may inspect any establishment, facility, or other premises in which chemical substances, mixtures, or products subject to title IV are manufactured, processed, stored, or held before or after their distribution in commerce and any conveyance being used to transport chemical substances, mixtures, such products, or such articles in connection with distribution in commerce. Such an inspection may only be made upon the presentation of appropriate credentials and of a written notice to the owner, operator, or agent in charge of the premises or conveyance to be inspected. A separate notice shall be given for each such inspection, but a notice shall not be required for each entry made during the period covered by the inspection. Each such inspection shall be commenced and completed with reasonable promptness and shall be conducted at reasonable times, within reasonable limits, and in a reasonable manner.

[§11(a) amended by PL 102–550, Oct. 28, 1992]

(b) Scope.—

(1) Except as provided in paragraph (2), an inspection conducted under subsection (a) shall extend to all things within the premises or conveyance inspected (including records, files, papers, processes, controls, and facilities) bearing on whether the requirements of this Act applicable to the chemical substances, mixtures, or products subject to title IV within such premises or conveyance have been complied with.

[§11(b)(1) amended by PL 102–550, Oct. 28, 1992]

(2) No inspection under subsection (a) shall extend to—

(A) financial data,

(B) sales data (other shipment data),

(C) pricing data,

(D) personnel data, or

(E) research data (other than data required by this Act or under a rule promulgated thereunder),

unless the nature and extent of such data are described with reasonable specificity in the written notice required by subsection (a) for such inspection.

(c) Subpoenas.—In carrying out this Act, the Administrator may by subpoena require the attendance and testimony of witnesses and the production of reports, papers, documents, answers to questions, and other information that the Administrator deems necessary. Witnesses shall be paid the same fees and mileage that are paid witnesses in the courts of the United States. In the event of contumacy, failure, or refusal of any person to obey any such subpoena, any district court of the United States in which venue is proper shall have jurisdiction to order any such person to comply with such subpoena. Any failure to obey such an order of the court is punishable by the court as a contempt thereof.

§2611. **Exports.** [Sec. 12]

(a) In General.—

(1) Except as provided in paragraph (2) and subsection (b), this Act (other than section 8) shall not apply to any chemical substance, mixture, or to an article containing a chemical substance or mixture, if—

(A) it can be shown that such substance, mixture, or article is being manufactured, processed, or distributed in commerce for export from the United States, unless such substance, mixture, or article was, in fact, manufactured, processed, or distributed in commerce, for use in the United States, and

(B) such substance, mixture, or article (when distributed in commerce), or any container in which it is enclosed (when so distributed), bears a stamp or label stating that such substance, mixture, or article is intended for export.

(2) Paragraph (1) shall not apply to any chemical substance, mixture, or article if the Administrator finds that the substance, mixture, or article will present an unreasonable risk of injury to health within the United States or to the environment of the United States. The Administrator may require, under section 4, testing of any chemical substance or mixture exempted from this Act by paragraph (1) for the purpose of determining whether or not such substance or mixture presents an unreasonable risk of injury to health within the United States or to the environment of the United States.

(b) Notice.—

(1) If any person exports or intends to export to a foreign country a chemical substance or mixture for which the submission of data is required under section 4 or 5(b), such person shall notify the Administrator of such exportation or intent to export and the Administrator shall furnish to the government of such country notice of the availability of the data submitted to the Administrator under such section for such substance or mixture.

(2) If any person exports or intends to export to a foreign country a chemical substance or mixture for which an order has been issued under section 5 or a rule has been proposed or promulgated under section 5 or 6, or with respect to which an action is pending, or relief has been granted under section 5 or 7, such person shall notify the Administrator of such exportation or intent to export and the Administrator

shall furnish to the government of such country notice of such rule, order, action, or relief.

§2612. Entry into Customs Territory of the United States. [Sec. 13]

(a) In General.—

(1) The Secretary of the Treasury shall refuse entry into the customs territory of the United States (as defined in general note 2 to the Harmonized Tariff Schedule of the United States) of any chemical substance, mixture, or article containing a chemical substance or mixture offered for such entry if—

[§13(a)(1) amended by PL 100–418]

(A) it fails to comply with any rule in effect under this Act, or

(B) it is offered for entry in violation of section 5, 6, or title IV a rule or order under section 5, 6, or title IV or an order issued in a civil action brought under section 5, 7 or title IV.

[§13(a)(1)(B) amended by PL 102–550, Oct. 28, 1992]

(2) If a chemical substance, mixture, or article is refused entry under paragraph (1), the Secretary of the Treasury shall notify the consignee of such entry refusal, shall not release it to the consignee, and shall cause its disposal or storage (under such rules as the Secretary of the Treasury may prescribe) if it has not been exported by the consignee within 90 days from the date of receipt of notice of such refusal, except that the Secretary of the Treasury may, pending a review by the Administrator of the entry refusal, release to the consignee such substance, mixture, or article on execution of bond for the amount of the full invoice of such substance, mixture, or article (as such value is set forth in the customs entry), together with the duty thereon. On failure to return such substance, mixture, or article for any cause to be custody of the Secretary of the Treasury when demanded, such consignee shall be liable to the United States for liquidated damages equal to the full amount of such bond. All charges for storage, cartage, and labor on and for disposal of substances, mixtures, or articles which are refused entry or release under this section shall be paid by the owner or consignee, and in default of such payment shall constitute a lien against any future entry made by such owner or consignee.

(b) Rules.—The Secretary of the Treasury, after consultation with the Administrator, shall issue rules for the administration of subsection (a) of this section.

§2613. Disclosure of Data. [Sec. 14]

(a) In General.—Except as provided by subsection (b), any information reported to, or otherwise obtained by, the Administrator (or any representative of the Administrator) under this Act, which is exempt from disclosure pursuant to subsection (a) of section 552 of title 5, United States Code, by reason of subsection (b)(4) of such section, shall, notwithstanding the provisions of any other section of this Act, not be disclosed by the Administrator or by any officer or employee of the United States, except that such information—

(1) shall be disclosed to any officer or employee of the United States—

(A) in connection with the official duties of such officer or employee under any law for the protection of health or the environment, or

(B) for specific law enforcement purposes;

(2) shall be disclosed to contractors with the United States and employees of such contractors if in the opinion of the Administrator such disclosure is necessary for the satisfactory performance by the contractor of a contract with the United States entered into on or after the date of enactment of this Act for the performance of work in connection with this Act and under such conditions as the Administrator may specify;

(3) shall be disclosed if the Administrator determines it necessary to protect health or the environment against an unreasonable risk of injury to health or the environment; or

(4) may be disclosed when relevant in any proceeding under this Act, except that disclosure in such a proceeding shall be made in such manner as to preserve confidentiality to the extent practicable without impairing the proceeding.

In any proceeding under section 552(a) of title 5, United States Code, to obtain information the disclosure of which has been denied because of the provisions of this subsection, the Administrator may not rely on section 552(b)(3) of such title to sustain the Administrator's action.

(b) Data From Health and Safety Studies.—

(1) Subsection (a) does not prohibit the disclosure of—

(A) any health and safety study which is submitted under this Act with respect to—

(i) any chemical substance or mixture which, on the date on which such study is to be disclosed has been offered for commercial distribution, or

(ii) any chemical substance or mixture for which testing is required under section 4 or for which notification is required under section 5, and

(B) any data reported to, or otherwise obtained by, the Administrator from a health and safety study which relates to a chemical substance or mixture described in clause (i) or (ii) of subparagraph (A).

This paragraph does not authorize the release of any data which discloses processes used in the manufacturing or processing of a chemical substance or mixture or, in the case of a mixture, the release of data disclosing the portion of the mixture comprised by any of the chemical substances in the mixture.

(2) If a request is made to the Administrator under subsection (a) of section 552 of title 5, United States Code, for information which is described in the first sentence of paragraph (1) and which is not information described in the second sentence of such paragraph, the Administrator may not deny such request on the basis of subsection (b)(4) of such section.

(c) Designation and Release of Confidential Data.—

(1) In submitting data under this Act, a manufacturer, processor, or distributor in commerce may (A) designate the data which such person believes is entitled to confidential treatment under subsection (a), and (B) submit such designated data separately from other data submitted under this Act. A designation under this paragraph shall be made in writing and in such manner as the Administrator may prescribe.

(2) (A) Except as provided by subparagraph (B), if the Administrator proposes to release for inspection data which has been designated under paragraph (1)(A), the Administrator shall notify, in writing and by certified mail, the manufacturer, processor, or distributor in commerce who submitted such data of the intent to release such data. If the release of such data is to be made pursuant to a request made under section 552(a) of title 5, United States Code, such notice shall be given immediately upon approval of such request by the Administrator. The Administrator may not release such data until the expiration of 30 days after the manufacturer, processor, or distributor in commerce submitting such data has received the notice required by this subparagraph.

(B) (i) Subparagraph (A) shall not apply to the release of information under paragraph (1), (2), (3), or (4) of subsection (a), except that the Administrator may not release data under paragraph (3) of subsection (a) unless the Administrator has notified each manufacturer, processor, and distributor in commerce who submitted such data of such release. Such notice shall be made in writing by certified mail at least 15 days before the release of such data, except that if the Administrator determines that the release of such data is necessary to protect against an imminent, unreasonable risk of injury to health or the environment, such notice may be made by such means as the Administrator determines will provide notice at least 24 hours before such release is made.

(ii) Subparagraph (A) shall not apply to the release of information described in subsection (b)(1) other than information described in the second sentence of such subsection.

(d) Criminal Penalty for Wrongful Disclosure.—

(1) Any officer or employee of the United States or former officer or employee of the United States, who by virtue of such employment or official position has obtained possession of, or has access to, material the disclosure of which is prohibited by subsection (a), and who knowing that disclosure of such material is prohibited by such subsection, willfully discloses the material in any manner to any person not entitled to receive it, shall be guilty of a misdeameanor and fined not more than $5,000 or imprisoned for not more than one year, or both. Section 1905 of title 18, United States Code, does not apply with respect to the publishing, divulging, disclosure, or making known of, or making available, information reported or otherwise obtained under this Act.

(2) For the purposes of paragraph (1), any contractor with the United States who is furnished information as authorized by subsection (a)(2), and any employee of any such contractor, shall be considered to be an employee of the United States.

(e) Access by Congress.— Notwithstanding any limitation contained in this section or any other provision of law, all information reported to or otherwise obtained by the Administrator (or any representative of the Administrator) under this Act shall be made available, upon written request of any duly authorized committee of the Congress, to such committee.

§2614. Prohibited Acts. [Sec. 15]

It shall be unlawful for any person to—

(1) fail or refuse to comply with (A) any rule promulgated or order issued under section 4, (B) any requirement prescribed by section 5 or 6, (C) any rule promulgated or order issued under section 5 or 6, or (D) any requirement of title II or any rule promulgated or order issued under title II;

[§15(1) amended at PL 99–519, Oct. 22, 1986]

(2) use for commercial purposes a chemical substance or mixture which such person knew or had reason to know was manufactured, processed, or distributed in commerce in violation of section 5 or 6, a rule or order under section 5 or 6, or an order issued in action brought under section 5 or 7;

(3) fail or refuse to (A) establish or maintain records, (B) submit reports, notices, or other information, or (C) permit access to or copying of records, as required by this Act or a rule thereunder; or

(4) fail or refuse to permit entry or inspection as required by section 11.

§2615. Penalties. [Sec. 16]

(a) Civil.—

(1) Any person who violates a provision of section 15 or 409 shall be liable to the United States for a civil penalty in an amount not to exceed $25,000 for each such violation. Each day such a violation continues shall, for purposes of this subsection, constitute a separate violation of section 15 or 409.

[§16(a)(1) amended by PL 102–550, Oct. 28, 1992]

(2) (A) A civil penalty for a violation of section 15 or 409 shall be assessed by the Administrator by an order made on the record after opportunity (provided in accordance with this subparagraph) for a hearing in accordance with section 554 of title 5, United States Code. Before issuing such an order, the Administrator shall give written notice to the person to be assessed a civil penalty under such order of the Administrator's proposal to issue such order and provide such person an opportunity to request, within 15 days of the date the notice is received by such person, such a hearing on the order.

[§16(a)(2)(A) amended by PL 102–550, Oct. 28, 1992]

(B) In determining the amount of a civil penalty, the Administrator shall take into account the nature, circumstances, extent, and gravity of the violation or violations and, with respect to the violator, ability to pay, effect on ability to continue to do business, any history of prior such viola tions, the degree of culpability, and such other matters as justice may require.

(C) The Administrator may compromise, modify, or remit, with or without conditions, any civil penalty which may be imposed under this subsection. The amount of such penalty, when finally determined, or the amount agreed upon in compromise, may be deducted from any sums owing by the United States to the person charged.

(3) Any person who requested in accordance with paragraph (2)(A) a hear ing respecting the assessment of a civil penalty and who is aggrieved by an order assessing a civil penalty may file a petition for judicial review of such order with the United States Court of Appeals for the District of Columbia Circuit or for any other circuit in which such person resides or transacts business. Such a petition may only be filed within the 30–day period beginning on the date the order making such assessment was issued.

Petition for judicial review.

(4) If any person fails to pay an assessment of a civil penalty—

(A) after the order making the assess ment has become a final order and if such person does not file a petition for judicial review of the order in accordance with paragraph (3), or

(B) after a court in an action brought under paragraph (3) has entered a final judgment in favor of the Administrator, the Attorney General shall recover the amount assessed (plus interest at currently prevailing rates from the date of the expiration of the 30–day period referred to in paragraph (3) or the date of such final judgment, as the case may be) in an action brought in any appropriate district court of the United States. In such an action, the validity, amount, and appropriateness of such penalty shall not be subject to review.

(b) Criminal.—Any person who knowingly or willfully violates any provision of section 15 or 409 shall, in addition to or in lieu of any civil penalty which may be imposed under subsection (a) of this section for such violation, be subject, upon conviction, to a fine of not more than $25,000 for each day of violation, or to imprisonment for not more than one year, or both.

[§16(b) amended by PL 102–550, Oct. 28, 1992]

§2616. Specific Enforcement and Seizure. [Sec. 17]

(a) Specific Enforcement.—

(1) The district courts of the United States shall have jurisdiction over civil actions to—

(A) restrain any violation of section 15 or 409,

(B) restrain any person from taking any action prohibited by section 5, or 6, or title IV, or by a rule or order under section 5, 6, or title IV,

(C) compel the taking of any action required by or under this Act, or

(D) direct any manufacturer or processor of a chemical substance, mixture, or product subject to title IV manufactured or processed in violation of section 5, or 6, or title IV, or a rule or order under section 5, or 6, or title IV, and distributed in commerce, (i) to give notice of such fact to distributors in commerce of such substance, mixture, or product and, to the extent reasonably ascertainable, to other persons in possession of such substance, mixture, or product or exposed to such substance, mixture, or product (ii) to give public notice of such risk of injury, and (iii) to either replace or repurchase such substance, mixture, or product, whichever the person to which the requirement is directed elects.

[§17(a)(1) amended by PL 102–550, Oct. 28, 1992]

(2) A civil action described in paragraph (1) may be brought—

(A) in the case of a civil action described in subparagraph (A) of such paragraph, in the United States district court for the judicial district wherein any act, omission, or transaction constituting a violation of section 15 occurred or wherein the defendant is found or transacts business, or

(B) in the case of any other civil action described in such paragraph, in the United States district court for the judicial district wherein the defendant is found or transacts business.

In any such civil action process may be served on a defendant in any judicial district in which a defendant resides or may be found. Subpoenas requiring attendance of witnesses in any such action may be served in any judicial district.

(b) Seizure.—Any chemical substance, mixture, or product subject to title IV which was manufactured, processed, or distributed in commerce in violation of this Act or any rule promulgated or order issued under this Act or any article containing such a substance or mixture shall be liable to be proceeded against, by process of libel for the seizure and condemnation of such substance, mixture, product, or article, in any district court of the United States within the jurisdiction of which such substance, mixture, product, or article is found. Such proceedings shall conform as nearly as possible to proceedings in rem in admiralty.

[§17(b) amended by PL 102–550, Oct. 28, 1992]

§2617. Preemption. [Sec. 18]

(a) Effect on State Law.—

(1) Except as provided in paragraph (2), nothing in this Act shall affect the authority of any State or political subdivision of a State to establish or continue in effect regulation of any chemical substance, mixture, or article containing a chemical substance or mixture.

(2) Except as provided in subsection (b)—

(A) if the Administrator requires by a rule promulgated under section 4 the testing of a chemical substance or mixture, no State or political subdivision may, after the effective date of such rule, establish or continue in effect a requirement for the testing of such substance or mixture for purposes similar to those for which testing is required under such rule; and

(B) if the Administrator prescribes a rule or order under section 5 or 6 (other than a rule imposing a requirement described in subsection (a)(6) of section 6) which is applicable to a chemical substance or mixture, and which is designed to protect against a risk of injury to health or the environment associated with such substance or mixture, no State or political subdivision of a State may, after the effective date of such requirement, establish or continue in effect, any requirement which is applicable to such substance or mixture, or an article containing such substance or mixture, and which is designed to protect against such risk unless such requirement (i) is identical to the requirement prescribed by the Administrator, (ii) is adopted under the authority of the Clean Air Act or any other Federal law, or (iii) prohibits the use of such substance or mixture in such State or political subdivision (other than its use in the manufacture or processing of other substances or mixtures).

(b) Exemption.—Upon application of a State or political subdivision of a State the Administrator may by rule exempt from subsection (a)(2), under such conditions as may be prescribed in such rule, a requirement of such State or political subdivision designed to protect against a risk of injury to health or the environment associated with a chemical substance, mixture, or article containing a chemical substance or mixture if—

(1) compliance with the requirement would not cause the manufacturing, processing, distribution in commerce, or use of the substance, mixture, or article to be in violation of the applicable requirement under this Act described in subsection (a)(2), and

(2) the State or political subdivision requirement (A) provides a significantly higher degree of protection from such risk than the requirement under this Act described in subsection (a)(2) and (B) does not, through difficulties in marketing, distribution, or other factors, unduly burden interstate commerce.

§2618. Judicial Reveiw. [Sec. 19]

(a) In General.—

(1) (A) Not later than 60 days after the date of the promulgation of a rule under section 4(a), 5(a)(2), 5(b)(4), 6(a), 6(e), 6(c), or 8, or under title II or IV, any person may file a petition for judicial review of such rule with the United States Court of Appeals for the District of Columbia Circuit or for the circuit in which such person resides or in which such person's principal place of business is located. Courts of appeals of the United States shall have exclusive jurisdiction of any action to obtain judicial review (other than in an enforcement proceeding) of such a rule if any district court of the United States would have had jurisdiction of such action but for this subparagraph.

[§19(a)(1)(A) amended by PL 99–519, Oct. 22, 1986; PL 102–550, Oct. 28, 1992]

(B) Courts of appeals of the United States shall have exclusive jurisdiction of any action to obtain judicial review (other than in an enforcement proceeding) of an order issued under subparagraph (A) or (B) of section 6(b)(1) if any district court of the United States would have had jurisdiction of such action but for this subparagraph.

(2) Copies of any petition filed under paragraph (1)(A) shall be transmitted forthwith to the Administrator and to the Attorney General by the clerk of the court with which such petition was filed. The provisions of section 2112 of title 28, United States Code, shall apply to the filing of the rulemaking record of proceedings on which the Administrator based the rule being reviewed under this section and to the transfer of proceedings between United States courts of appeals.

(3) For purposes of this section, the term "rulemaking record" means—

(A) the rule being reviewed under this section;

(B) in the case of a rule under section 4(a), the finding required by such section, in the case of a rule under section 5(b)(4), the finding required by such section, in the case of a rule under section 6(a) the finding required by section 5(f) or 6(a), as the case may be, in the case of a rule under section 6(a), the statement required by section 6(e)(1), and in the case of a rule under section, 6(c), the findings required by paragraph (2) (B) or (3)(B) of such section as the case may be and in the case of a rule under title IV, the finding required for the issuance of such a rule;

[§19(a)(3)(B) amended by PL 102–550, Oct. 28, 1992]

(C) any transcript required to be made of oral presentations made in proceedings for the promulgation of such rule;

(D) any written submission of interested parties respecting the promulgation of such rule; and

(E) any other information which the Administrator considers to be relevant to such rule and which the Administrator identified, on or before the date of the promulgation of such rule, in a notice published in the Federal Register.

(b) Additional Submissions and Presentations; Modifications.— If in an action under the section to review a rule the petitioner or the Administrator applies to the court for leave to make additional oral submissions or written presentations respecting such rule and shows to the satisfaction of the court that such submissions and presentations would be material and that there were reasonable grounds for the submissions and failure to make such submissions and presentations in the proceeding before the Administrator, the court may order the Administrator to provide additional opportunity to make such submissions and presentations. The Administrator may modify or set aside the rule being reviewed or make a new rule by reason of the additional submissions and presentations and shall file such modified or new rule with the return of such submissions and presentations.

The court shall thereafter review such new or modified rule.

(c) Standard of Review.—

(1) (A) Upon the filing of a petition under subsection (a)(1) for judicial review of a rule, the court shall have jurisdiction (i) to grant appropriate relief, including interim relief, as provided in chapter 7 of title 5, United States Code, and (ii) except as otherwise provided in subparagraph (B), to review such rule in accordance with chapter 7 of title 5, United States Code.

(B) Section 706 of title 5. United States Code, shall apply to review of a rule under this section, except that —

(i) in the case of review of a rule under section 4(a), 5(b)(4), 6(a), or 6(e), the standard for review prescribed by paragraph (2)(E) of such section 706 shall not apply and the court shall hold unlawful and set aside such rule if the court finds that the rule is not supported by substantial evidence in the rulemaking record (as defined in subsection (a)(3) taken as a whole:

(ii) in the case of review of a rule under section 6(a), the court shall hold unlawful and set aside such rule if it finds that —

(I) a determination by the Administrator under section 6(c)(3) that the petitioner seeking review of such rule is not entitled to conduct (or have conducted) cross-examination or to present rebuttal submissions, or

(II) a rule of, or ruling by, the Administrator under section 6(c)(3) limiting such petitioner's cross-examination or oral presentations,

has precluded disclosure of disputed material facts which was necessary to a fair determination by the Administrator of the rulemaking proceeding taken as a whole; and section 706(2)(D) shall not apply with respect to a determination, rule, or ruling referred to in subclause (I) or (II); and

(iii) the court may not review the contents and adequacy of—

(I) any statement required to be made pursuant to section 6(c)(1), or

(II) any statement of basis and purpose required by section 553(c) of title 5, United States Code, to be incorporated in the rule

except as part of a review of the rulemaking record taken as a whole.

The term "evidence" as used in clause (i) means any matter in the rulemaking record.

(C) A determination, rule, or ruling of the Administrator described in subparagraph (B)(ii) may be reviewed only in an action under this section and only in accordance with such subparagraph.

(2) The judgment of the court affirming or setting aside, in whole or in part, any rule reviewed in accordance with this section shall be final, subject to review by the Supreme Court of the United States upon certiorari or certification, as provided in section 1254 of title 28, United States Code.

(d) Fees and costs.—The decision of the court in an action commenced under subsection (a), or of the Supreme Court of the United States on review of such a decision, may include an award of costs of suit and reasonable fees for attorneys and expert witnesses if the court determines that such an award is appropriate.

(e) Other remedies.—The remedies as provided in this section shall be in addition to and not in lieu of any other remedies provided by law.

§2619. Citizens' Civil Actions. [Sec. 20]

(a) In General.—Except as provided in subsection (b), any person may commence a civil action—

(1) against any person (including (A) the United States, and (B) any other governmental instrumentality or agency to the extent permitted by the eleventh amendment to the Constitution) who is alleged to be in violation of this Act or any rule promulgated under section 4, 5, or 6, or title II or IV, or order issued under section 5 or title II or IV to restrain such violation, or

[§20(a)(1) amended by PL 99–519, Oct. 22, 1986; PL 102–550, Oct. 28, 1992]

(2) against the Administrator to compel the Administrator to perform any act or duty under this Act which is not discretionary.

Any civil action under paragraph (1) shall be brought in the United States district court for the district in which the alleged violation occurred or in which the defendant resides or in which the defendant's principal place of business is located. Any action brought under paragraph (2) shall be brought in the United States District Court for the District of Columbia, or the United States district court for the judicial district in which the plaintiff is domiciled. The district courts of the United States shall have jurisdiction over suits brought under this section, without regard to the amount in controversy or the citizenship of the parties. In any civil action under this subsection process may be served on a defendant in any judicial district in which the defendant resides or may be found and subpoenas for witnesses may be served in any judicial district.

(b) Limitation.—No civil action may be commenced.—

(1) under subsection (a)(1) to restrain a violation of this Act or rule or order under this Act—

(A) before the expiration of 60 days after the plaintiff has given notice of such violation (i) to the Administrator, and (ii) to the person who is alleged to have committed such violation, or

(B) if the Administrator has commenced and is diligently prosecuting a proceeding for the issuance of an order under section 16(a)(2) to require compliance with this Act or with such rule or order or if the Attorney General has commenced and is diligently prosecuting a civil action in a court of the United States to require compliance with this Act or with such rule or order, but if such proceeding or civil action is commenced after the giving of notice, any person giving such notice may intervene as a matter of right in such proceeding or action; or

(2) under subsection (a)(2) before the expiration of 60 days after the plaintiff has given notice to the Administrator of the alleged failure of the Administrator to perform an act or duty which is the basis for such action or, in the case of an action under such subsection for the failure of the Administrator to file an action under section 7, before the expiration of ten days after such notification.

Notice under this subsection shall be given in such manner as the Administrator shall prescribe by rule.

(c) General.—

(1) In any action under this section, the Administrator, if not a party, may intervene as a matter of right.

(2) The court, in issuing any final order in any action brought pursuant to subsection (a), may award costs of suit and reasonable fees for attorneys and expert witnesses if the court determines that such an award is appropriate. Any court, in issuing its decision in an action brought to review such an order, may award costs of suit and reasonable fees for attorneys if the court determines that such an award is appropriate.

(3) Nothing in this section shall restrict any right which any person (or class of persons) may have under any statute or common law to seek enforcement of this Act or any rule or order under this Act or to seek any other relief.

(d) Consolidation.—When two or more civil actions brought under subsection (a) involving the same defendant and the same issues or violations are pending in two or more judicial districts, such pending actions, upon application of such defendants to such actions which is made to a court in which any such action is brought, may, if such court in its discretion so decides, be consolidated for trial by order (issued after giving all parties reasonable notice and opportunity to be heard) of such court and tried in—

(1) any district which is selected by such defendant and in which one of such actions is pending,

(2) a district which is agreed upon by stipulation between all the parties to such actions and in which one of such actions is pending, or

(3) a district which is selected by the court and in which one of such actions is pending.

The court issuing such an order shall give prompt notification of the order to the other courts in which the civil actions consolidated under the order are pending.

§2620. Citizens' Petitions. [Sec. 21]

(a) In General.—Any person may petition the Administrator to initiate a proceeding for the issuance, amendment, or repeal of a rule under section 4, 6, or 8 or an order under section 5(e) or 6(b)(2).

(b) Procedures.—

(1) Such petition shall be filed in the principal office of the Administrator and shall set forth the facts which it is claimed establish that it is necessary to issue, amend, or repeal a rule under section 4, 6, or 8 or an order under section 5(e), 6(b)(1)(A), or 6(b)(1)(B).

(2) The Administrator may hold a public hearing or may conduct such investigation or proceeding as the Administrator deems appropriate in order to determine whether or not such petition should be granted.

(3) Within 90 days after filing of a petition described in paragraph (1), the Administrator shall either grant or deny the petition. If the Administrator grants such petition, the Administrator shall promptly commence an appropriate proceeding in accordance with section 4, 5, 6, or 8. If the Administrator denies such petition, the Administrator shall publish in the Federal Register the Administrator's reasons for such denial.

(4) (A) If the Administrator denies a petition filed under this section (or if the Administrator fails to grant or deny such petition within the 90–day period) the petitioner may commence a civil action in a district court of the United States to compel the Administrator to initiate a rulemaking proceeding as requested in the petition. Any such action shall be filed within 60 days after the Administrator's denial of the petition or, if the Administrator fails to grant or deny the petition within 90 days after filing the petition, within 60 days after the expiration of the 90–day period.

(B) In an action under subparagraph (A) respecting a petition to initiate a proceeding to issue a rule under section 4, 6, or 8 or an order under section 5(e) or 6(b)(2), the petitioner shall be provided an opportunity to have such petition considered by the court in a de novo proceeding. If the petitioner demonstrates to the satisfaction of the court by a preponderance of the evidence that—

(i) in the case of a petition to initiate a proceeding for the issuance of a rule under section 4 or an order under section 5(e)—

(I) information available to the Administrator is insufficient to permit a reasoned evaluation of the health and environment effects of the chemical substance to be subject to such rule or order; and

(II) in the absence of such information, the substance may present an unreasonable risk to health or the environment, or the substance is or will be produced in substantial quantities and it enters or may reasonably be anticipated to enter the environment in substantial quantities or there is or may be significant or substantial human exposure to it; or

(ii) in the case of a petition to initiate a proceeding for the issuance of a rule under section 6 or 8 or an order under section 6(b)(2), there is a reasonable basis to conclude that the issuance of such a rule or order is necessary to protect health or the environment against an unreasonable risk of injury to health or the environment.

the court shall order the Administrator to initiate the action requested by the petitioner. If the court finds that the extent of the risk to health or the environment alleged by the petitioner is less than the extent of risks to health or the environment with respect to which the Administrator is taking action under this Act and there are insufficient resources available to the Administrator to take the action requested by the petitioner, the court may permit the Administrator to defer initiating the action requested by the petitioner until such time as the court prescribes.

(C) The court in issuing any final order in any action brought pursuant to subparagraph (A) may award costs of suit and reasonable fees for attorneys and expert witnesses if the court determines that such an award is appropriate. Any court, in issuing its decision in an action brought to review such an order, may award costs to suit and reasonable fees for attorneys if the court determines that such an award is appropriate.

(5) The remedies under this section shall be in addition to, and not in lieu of, other remedies provided by law.

§2621. National Defense Waiver. [Sec. 22]

The Administrator shall waive compliance with any provision of this Act upon a request and determination by the President that the requested waiver is necessary in the interest of national defense. The Administrator shall maintain a written record of the basis upon which such waiver was granted and make such record available for in camera examination when relevant in a judicial proceeding under this Act. Upon the issuance of such a waiver, the Administrator shall publish in the Federal Register a notice that the waiver was granted for national defense purposes, unless, upon the request of the President, the Administrator determines to omit such publication because the publication itself would be contrary to the interests of national defense, in which event the Administrator shall submit notice thereof to the Armed Services Committees of the Senate and the House of Representatives.

§2622. Employee Protection. [Sec. 23]

(a) In General.—No employer may discharge any employee or otherwise discriminate against any employee with respect to the employee's compensation, terms, conditions, or privileges of employment because the employee (or any person acting pursuant to a request of the employee) has—

(1) commenced, caused to be commenced, or is about to commence or cause to be commenced a proceeding under this Act;

(2) testified or is about to testify in any such proceeding; or

(3) assisted or participated or is about to assist or participate in any manner in such a proceeding or in any other action to carry out the purposes of this Act.

(b) Remedy.—

(1) Any employee who believes that the employee has been discharged or otherwise discriminated against by any person in violation of subsection (a) of this section may, within 30 days after such alleged violation occurs, file (or have any person file on the employee's behalf) a complaint with the Secretary of Labor (hereinafter in this section referred to as the "Secretary") alleging such discharge or discrimination. Upon receipt of such a complaint, the Secretary shall notify the person named in the complaint of the filing of the complaint.

(2) (A) Upon receipt of a complaint filed under paragraph (1), the Secretary shall conduct an investigation of the violation alleged in the complaint. Within 30 days of the receipt of such complaint, the Secretary shall complete such investigation and shall notify in writing the complainant (and any person acting on behalf of the complainant) and the person alleged to have committed such violation of the results of the investigation conducted pursuant to this paragraph. Within ninety days of the receipt of such complaint the Secretary shall, unless the proceeding on the complaint is terminated by the Secretary on the basis of a settlement entered into by the Secretary and the person alleged to have committed such violation, issue an order either providing the relief prescribed by subparagraph (B) or denying the complaint. An order of the Secretary shall be made on the record after notice and opportunity for agency hearing. The Secretary may not enter into a settlement terminating a proceeding on a complaint without the participation and consent of the complainant.

(B) If in response to a complaint filed under paragraph (1) the Secretary determines that a violation of subsection (a) of this section has occurred, the Secretary shall order (i) the person who committed such violation to take affirmative action to abate the violation. (ii) such person to reinstate the complainant to the complainant's former position together with the compensation (including back pay), terms, conditions, and privileges of the complainant's employment, (iii) compensatory damages, and (iv) where appropriate, exemplary damages. If such an order issued, the Secretary, at the request of the complainant, shall assess against the person against whom the order is issued a sum equal to the aggregate amount of all costs and expenses (including attorney's fees) reasonably incurred, as determined by the Secretary, by the complainant for, or in connection with, the bringing of the complaint upon which the order was issued.

(c) Review.—

(1) Any employee or employer adversely affected or aggrieved by an order issued under subsection (b) may obtain review of the order in the United States Court of Appeals for the circuit in which the violation, with respect to which the order was issued, allegedly occurred. The petition for review must be filed within sixty days from the issuance of the Secretary's order. Review shall conform to chapter 7 of title 5 of the United States Code.

(2) An order of the Secretary, with respect to which review could have been obtained under paragraph (1), shall not be subject to judicial review in any criminal or other civil proceeding.

(d) Enforcement.—Whenever a person has failed to comply with an order issued under subsection (b)(2), the Secretary shall file a civil action in the United States district court for the district in which the violation was found to occur to enforce such order. In actions brought under this subsection, the district courts shall have jurisdiction to grant all appropriate relief, including injunctive relief and compensatory and exemplary damages.

[§23(d) amended by PL 98–620, Nov. 11, 1984]

(e) Exclusion.—Subsection (a) of this section shall not apply with respect to any employee who, acting without direction from the employee's employer (or any agent of the employer), deliberately causes a violation of any requirement of this Act.

§2623. Employment Effects. [Sec. 24]

(a) In General.—The Administrator shall evaluate on a continuing basis the potential effects on employment (including reductions in employment or loss of employment from threatened plant closures of—

(1) the issuance of a rule or order under section 4, 5, or 6 , or

(2) a requirement of section 5 or 6 .

(b) (1) Investigations.—Any employee (or any representative of an employee) may request the Administrator to make an investigation of—

(A) a discharge or layoff or threatened discharge or layoff of the employee, or

(B) adverse or threatened adverse effects on the employee's employment,

allegedly resulting from a rule or order under section 4, 5, or 6 or a requirement of section 5 or 6 . Any such request shall be made in writing, shall set forth with reasonable particularity the grounds for the request, and shall be signed by the employee, or representative of such employee, making the request.

(2) (A) Upon receipt of a request made in accordance with paragraph (1) the Administrator shall (i) conduct the investigation requested, and (ii) if requested by any interested person, hold public hearings on any matter involved in the investigation unless the Administrator, by order issued within 45 days of the date such hearings are requested, denies the request for the hearings because the Administrator determines there are no reasonable grounds for holding such hearings. If the Administrator makes such a determination, the Administrator shall notify in writing the person requesting the hearing of the determination and the reasons therefor and shall publish the determination and the reasons therefor in the Federal Register.

(B) If public hearings are to be held on any matter involved in an investigation conducted under this subsection—

(i) at least five days' notice shall be provided the person making the request for the investigation and any person identified in such request,

(ii) such hearings shall be held in accordance with section 6(c)(3) , and

(iii) each employee who made or for whom was made a request for such hearings and the employer of such employee shall be required to present information respecting the applicable matter referred to in paragraph (1)(A) or (1)(B) together with the basis for such information.

(3) Upon completion of an investigation under paragraph (2), the Administrator shall make findings of fact, shall make such recommendations as the Administrator deems appropriate, and shall make available to the public such findings and recommendations.

(4) This section shall not be construed to require the Administrator to amend or repeal any rule or order in effect under this Act.

§2624. Studies. [Sec. 25]

(a) Indemnification Study.—The Administrator shall conduct a study of all Federal laws administered by the Administrator for the purpose of determining whether and under what conditions, if any, indemnification should be accorded any person as a result of any action taken by the Administrator under any such law. The study shall—

(1) include an estimate of the probable cost of any indemnification programs which may be recommended;

(2) include an examination of all viable means of financing the cost of any recommended indemnification; and

(3) be completed and submitted to Congress within two years from the effective date of enactment of this Act.

The General Accounting Office shall review the adequacy of the study submitted to Congress pursuant to paragraph (3) and shall report the results of its review to the Congress within six months of the date such study is submitted to Congress

(b) Classification, Storage, and Retrieval Study.—The Council on Environmental Quality, in consultation with the Administrator, the Secretary of Health, Education, and Welfare, the Secretary of Commerce, and the heads of other appropriate Federal departments or agencies, shall coordinate a study of the feasibility of establishing (1) a standard classification system for chemical substances and related substances, and (2) a standard means for storing and for obtaining rapid access to information respecting such substances. A report on such study shall be completed and submitted to Congress not later than 18 months after the effective date of enactment of this Act.

§2625. Administration of the Act. [Sec. 26]

(a) Cooperation of Federal Agencies.—Upon request by the Administrator, each Federal department and agency is authorized—

(1) to make its services, personnel, and facilities available (with or without reimbursement) to the Administrator to assist the Administrator in the administration of this Act; and

(2) to furnish to the Administrator such information, data, estimates, and statistics, and to allow the Administrator access to all information in its possession as the Administrator may reasonably determine to be necessary for the administration of this Act.

(b) Fees.—

(1) The Administrator may, by rule, require the payment of a reasonable fee from any person required to submit data under section 4 or 5 to defray the cost of administering this Act. Such rules shall not provide for any fee in excess of $2,500 or, in the case of a small business concern, any fee in excess of $100. In setting a fee under this paragraph, the Administrator shall take into account the ability to pay of the person required to submit the data and the cost to the Administrator of reviewing such data. Such rules may provide for sharing such a fee in any case in which the expenses of testing are shared under section 4 or 5 .

(2) The Administrator, after consultation with the Administrator of the Small Business Administration, shall by rule prescribe standards for determining the persons which qualify as small business concerns for purposes of paragraph (1).

(c) Action With Respect to Categories.—

(1) Any action authorized or required to be taken by the Administrator under any provision of this Act with respect to a chemical substance or mixture may be taken by the Administrator in accordance with that provision with respect to a category of chemical substances or mixtures. Whenever the Administrator takes action under a provision of this Act with respect to a category of chemical substances or mixtures, any reference in this Act to a chemical substance or mixture (insofar as it relates to such action) shall be deemed to be a reference to each chemical substance or mixture in such category.

(2) For purposes of paragraph (i):

(A) The term "category of chemical substances" means a group of chemical substances the members of which are similar in molecular structure, in physical, chemical, or biological properties, in use, or in mode of entrance into the human body or into the environment, or the members of which are in some other way suitable for classification as such for purposes of this Act, except that such term does not mean a group of chemical substances which are grouped together solely on the basis of their being new chemical substances.

(B) The term "category of mixtures" means a group of mixtures the members of which are similar in molecular structure, in physical, chemical, or biological properties, in use, or in the mode of entrance into the human body or into the environment, or the members of which are in some other way suitable for classification as such for purposes of this Act.

(d) Assistance Office.—The Administrator shall establish in the Environmental Protection Agency an identifiable office to provide technical and other nonfinancial assistance to manufacturers and processors of chemical substances and mixtures respecting the requirements of this Act applicable to such manufacturers and processors, the policy of the Agency respecting the application of such requirements to such manufacturers and processors, and the means and methods by which such manufacturers and processors may comply with such requirements.

(e) Financial Disclosures.—

(1) Except as provided under paragraph (3), each officer or employee of the Environmental Protection Agency and the Department of Health, Education, and Welfare who—

(A) performs any function or duty under this Act, and

(B) has any known financial interest (i) in any person subject to this Act or any rule or order in effect under this Act, or (ii) in any person who applies for or receives any grant or contract under this Act,

shall, on February 1, 1978, and on February 1 of each year thereafter, file with the Administrator or the Secretary of Health, Education, and Welfare (hereinafter in this subsection referred to as the "Secretary"), as appropriate, a written statement concerning all such interests held by such officer or employee during the preceding calendar year. Such statement shall be made available to the public.

(2) The Administrator and the Secretary shall—

(A) act within 90 days of the effective date of this Act—

(i) to define the term "known financial interests" for purposes of paragraph (1), and

(ii) to establish the methods by which the requirement to file written statements specified in paragraph (1) will be monitored and enforced, including appropriate provisions for review by the Administrator and the Secretary of such statements; and

(B) report to the Congress on June 1, 1978, and on June 1 of each year thereafter with respect to such statements and the actions taken in regard thereto during the preceding calendar year.

(3) The Administrator may by rule identify specific positions with the Environmental Protection Agency, and the Secretary may by rule identify specific positions with the Department of Health, Education, and Welfare, which are of a nonregulatory or nonpolicymaking nature, and the Administrator and the Secretary may by rule provide that officers or employees occupying such positions shall be exempt from the requirements of paragraph (1).

(4) This subsection does not supersede any requirement of chapter 11 of title 18, United States Code.

(5) Any officer or employee who is subject to, and knowingly violates, this subsection or any rule issued thereunder, shall be fined not more than $2,500 or imprisoned not more than one year, or both.

(f) Statement of Basis and Purpose.—Any final order issued under this Act shall be accompanied by a statement of its basis and purpose. The contents and adequacy of any such statement shall not be subject to judicial review in any respect.

(g) Assistant Administrator.—

(1) The President, by and with the advice and consent of the Senate, shall appoint an Assistant Administrator for Toxic Substances of the Environmental Protection Agency. Such Assistant Administrator shall be a qualified individual who is, by reason of background and experience, especially qualified to direct a program concerning the effects of chemicals on human health and the environment. Such Assistant Administrator shall be responsible for (A) the collection of data. (B) the preparation of studies, (C) the making of recommendations to the Administrator for regulatory and other actions to carry out the purposes and to facilitate the administration of this Act, and (D) such other functions as the Administrator may assign or delegate.

(2) The Assistant Administrator to be appointed under paragraph (1) shall be in addition to the Assistant Administrators of the Environmental Protection Agency authorized by section 1(d) of Reorganization Plan No. 3 of 1970.

[§26(g)(2) amended by PL 98–80, Aug. 23, 1983]

§2626. Development and Evaluation of Test Methods. [Sec. 27]

(a) In General.—The Secretary of Health, Education, and Welfare, in consultation with the Administrator and acting through the Assistant Secretary for Health, may conduct, and make grants to public and nonprofit private entities and enter into contracts with public and private entities for, projects for the development and evaluation of inexpensive and efficient methods (1) for determining and evaluating the health and environmental effects of chemical substances and mixtures, and their toxicity, persistance, and other characteristics which affect health and the environment, and (2) which may be used for the development of test data to meet the requirements of rules promulgated under section 4 . The Administrator shall consider such methods in prescribing under section 4 standards for the development of test data.

(b) Approval by Secretary. — No grant may be made or contract entered into under subsection (a) unless an application therefor has been submitted to and approved by the Secretary. Such an application shall be submitted in such form and manner and contain such information as the Secretary may require. The Secretary may apply such conditions to grants and contracts under subsection (a) as the Secretary determines are necessary to carry out the purposes of such subsection. Contracts may be entered into under such subsection without regard to section 3324(a) and (b) of Title 31 and section 5 of Title 41.

[§27(b) amended by 97–258, Sept. 13, 1982]

(c) Annual Reports.—

(1) The Secretary shall prepare and submit to the President and the Congress on or before January 1 of each year a report of the number of grants made and contracts entered into under this section and the results of such grants and contracts.

(2) The Secretary shall periodically publish in the Federal Register reports describing the progress and results of any contract entered into or grant made under this section.

§2627. State Programs. [Sec. 28]

(a) In General. — For the purpose of complementing (but not reducing) the authority of, or actions taken by, the Administrator under this Act, the Administrator may make grants to States for the establishment and operation of programs to prevent or eliminate unreasonable risks within the States to health or the environment which are associated with a chemical substance or mixture and with respect to which the Administrator is unable or is not likely to take action under this Act for their prevention or elimination. The amount of a grant under this subsection shall be determined by the Administrator, except that no grant for any State program may exceed 75 per centum of the establishment and operation costs (as determined by the Administrator) of such program during the period for which the grant is made.

(b) Approval by Administrator.—

(1) No grant may be made under subsection (a) unless an application therefore is submitted to and approved by the Administrator. Such an application shall be submitted in such form and manner as the Administrator may require and shall—

(A) set forth the need of the applicant for a grant under subsection (a),

(B) identify the agency or agencies of the State which shall establish or operate, or both, the program for which the application is submitted,

(C) describe the actions proposed to be taken under such program,

(D) contain or be supported by assurances satisfactory to the Administrator that such program shall, to the extent feasible, be integrated with other programs of the applicant for environmental and public health protection,

(E) provide for the making of such reports and evaluations as the Administrator may require, and

(F) contain such other information as the Administrator may prescribe.

(2) The Administrator may approve an application submitted in accordance with paragraph (1) only if the applicant has established to the satisfaction of the Administrator a priority need, as determined under rules of the Administrator, for the grant for which the application has been submitted. Such rules shall take into consideration the seriousness of the health effects in a State which are associated with chemical substances or mixtures, including cancer, birth defects, and gene mutations, the extent of the exposure in a State of human beings and the environment to chemical substances and mixtures, and the extent to which chemical substances and mixtures are manufactured, processed, used, and disposed of in a State.

(c) Annual Reports. — Not later than six months after the end of each of the fiscal years 1979, 1980, and 1981, the Administrator shall submit to the Congress a report respecting the programs assisted by grants under subsection (a) in the proceeding fiscal year and the extent to which the Administrator has disseminated information respecting such programs.

(d) Authorization. — For the purpose of making grants under subsection (a) there are authorized to be appropriated $1,500,000 for each of the fiscal years 1982 and 1983. Sums appropriated under this subsection shall remain available until expended.

§2628. Authorization for Appropriations. [Sec. 29]

There are authorized to be appropriated to the Administrator for purposes of carrying out this Act (other than sections 27 and 28 and subsection (a) and (c) through (g) of section 10 thereof) $58,646,000 for the fiscal year 1982 and $62,000,000 for the fiscal year 1983. No part of the funds appropriated under this section may be used to construct any research laboratories.

§2629. Annual Report. [Sec. 30]

The Administrator shall prepare and submit to the President and the Congress on or before January 1, 1978, and on or before January 1 of each succeeding year a comprehensive report on the administration of this Act during the preceding fiscal year. Such report shall include—

(1) a list of the testing required under section 4 during the year for which the report is made and an estimate of the costs incurred during such year by the persons required to perform such tests;

(2) the number of notices received during such year under section 5 , the number of such notices received during such year under such section for chemical substances subject to a section 4 rule, and a summary of any action taken during such year under section 5(g) ;

(3) a list of rules issued during such year under section 6 ;

(4) a list, with a brief statement of the issues, of completed or pending judicial actions under this Act and administrative actions under section 16 during such year;

(5) a summary of major problems encountered in the administration of this Act; and

(6) such recommendations for additional legislation as the Administrator deems necessary to carry out the purposes of this Act.

Effective Date. [Sec. 31]

Except as provided in section 4(f) , this Act shall taken effect on January 1, 1977.

TITLE II — ASBESTOS HAZARD EMERGENCY RESPONSE

[Title II added by PL 99–519, Oct. 22, 1986]

§2641. Congressional Findings and Purposes. [Sec. 201]

(a) Findings. — The Congress finds the following:

(1) The Environmental Protection Agency's rule on local education inspection for, and notification of, the presence of friable asbestos-containing material in school buildings includes neither standards for the proper identification of asbestos-containing material and appropriate response actions with respect to friable asbestos-containing material, nor a requirement that response actions with respect to friable asbestos-containing material be carried out in a safe and complete manner once actions are found to be necessary. As a result of the lack of regulatory guidance from the Environmental Protection Agency, some schools have not undertaken response action while many others have undertaken expensive projects without knowing if their action is necessary, adequate, or safe. Thus, the danger of exposure to asbestos continues to exist in schools, and some exposure actually may have increased due to the lack of federal standards and improper response action.

(2) There is no uniform program for accrediting persons involved in asbestos identification and abatement, nor are local educational agencies required to use accredited contractors for asbestos work.

(3) The guidance provided by the Environmental Protection Agency in its 'Guidance for Controlling Asbestos-Containing Material in Buildings' is insufficient in detail to ensure adequate responses. Such guidance is intended to be used only until the regulations required by this title become effective.

(4) Because there are no Federal standards whatsoever regulating daily exposure to asbestos in other public and commercial buildings, persons in addition to those comprising the Nation's school population may be exposed daily to asbestos.

(b) Purpose.—The purpose of this title is—

(1) to provide for the establishment of Federal regulations which require inspection for asbestos-containing material and implementation of appropriate response actions with respect to asbestos-containing material in .the. Nation's schools in a safe and complete manner;

(2) to mandate safe and complete periodic reinspection of school buildings following response actions, where appropriate; and

(3) to require the Administrator to conduct a study to find out the extent of the danger to human health posed by asbestos in public and commercial buildings and the means to respond to any such danger.

§2642. Definitions. [Sec. 202]

For purposes of this title—

(1) Accredited asbestos contractor.—The term 'accredited asbestos contractor' means a person accredited pursuant to the provisions of section 206 .

(2) Administrator.—The term 'Administrator' means the Administrator of the Environmental Protection Agency.

(3) Asbestos.—The term 'asbestos' means asbestiform varieties of—

(A) chrysotile (serpentine),

(B) crocidolite (riebeckite),

(C) amosite (cummingtonite-grunerite),

(D) anthophyllite,

(E) tremolite, or

(F) actinolite.

(4) Asbestos-containing material.—The term 'asbestos-containing material' means any material which contains more than 1 percent asbestos by weight.

(5) EPA guidance document.—The term 'Guidance for Controlling Asbestos- Containing Material in Buildings', means the Environmental Protection Agency document with such title as in effect on March 31, 1986.

(6) Friable asbestos-containing material.—The term 'friable asbestos-containing material' means any asbestos-containing material applied on ceilings, walls, structural members, piping, duct work, or any other part of a building which when dry may be crumbled, pulverized, or reduced to powder by hand pressure. The term includes non-friable asbestos-containing material after such previously non-friable material becomes damaged to the extent that when dry it may be crumbled, pulverized, or reduced to powder by hand pressure.

(7) Local educational agency.—The term 'local educational agency' means—

(A) any local educational agency as defined in section 198 of the Elementary and Secondary Education Act of 1965 (20 U.S.C. 3381),

(B) the owner of any private, nonprofit elementary or secondary school building, and

(C) the governing authority of any school operated under the defense dependents' education system provided for under the Defense Dependents' Education Act of 1978 (20 U.S.C. 921 et seq.).

(8) Most current guidance document.—The term 'most current guidance document' means the Environmental Protection Agency's 'Guidance for Controlling Asbestos-Containing Material in Buildings' as modified by the Environmental Protection Agency after March 31, 1986.

(9) Non-profit elementary or secondary school.—The term 'non-profit elementary or secondary school' means any elementary or secondary school (as defined in section 198 of the Elementary and Secondary Education Act of 1965 (20 U.S.C. 2854)) owned and operated by one or more nonprofit corporations or associations no part of the net earnings of which inures, or may lawfully inure, to the benefit of any private shareholder or individual.

(10) Public and commercial building.—The term 'public and commercial building' means any building which is not a school building, except that the term does not include any residential apartment building of fewer than 10 units.

(11) Response action.—The term 'response action' means methods that protect human health and the environment from asbestos-containing material. Such methods include methods described in chapters 3 and 5 of the Environmental Protection Agency's 'Guidance for Controlling Asbestos-Containing Materials in Buildings'.

(12) School.—The term 'school' means any elementary or secondary school as defined in section 198 of the Elementary and Secondary Education Act of 1965 (20 U.S.C. 2854).

(13) School building.—The term 'school building' means—

(A) any structure suitable for use as a classroom, including a school facility such as a laboratory, library, school eating facility, or facility used for the preparation of food,

(B) any gymnasium or other facility which is specially designed for athletic or recreational activities for an academic course in physical education.

(C) any other facility used for the instruction of students or for the administration of educational or research programs, and

(D) any maintenance, storage, or util ity facility, including any hallway, essential to the operation of any facility described in subparagraphs (A), (B), or (C).

(14) State.—The term 'State' means a State, the District of Columbia, the Commonwealth of Puerto Rico, Guam, American Samoa, the Northern Marianas, the Trust Territory of the Pacific Islands, and the Virgin Islands.

§2643. EPA Regulations. [Sec. 203]

(a) In General.—Within 360 days after the date of the enactment of this title, the Administrator shall promulgate regulations as described in subsections (b) through (i). With respect to regulations described in subsections (b), (c), (d), (e), (f), (g), and (i), the Administrator shall issue an advanced notice of proposed rulemaking within 60 days after the date of the enactment of this title, and shall propose regulations within 180 days after such date. Any regulation promulgated under this section must protect human health and the environment.

(b) Inspection.—The Administrator shall promulgate regulations which prescribe procedures, including the use of personnel accredited under section 206(b) or 206(c) and laboratories accredited under section 206(d) , for determining whether asbestos-containing material is present in a school building under the authority of a local educational agency. The regulations shall provide for the exclusion of any school building, or portion of a school building, if (1) an inspection of such school building (or portion was completed before the effective date of the regulations, and (2) the inspection meets the procedures and other requirements of the regulations under this title or of the 'Guidance for Controlling Asbestos-Containing Materials in Buildings' (unless the Administrator determines that an inspection in accordance with the guidance document is inadequate). The regulations shall require inspection of any school building (or portion of a school building) that is not excluded by the preceding sentence.

(c) Circumstances Requiring Response Actions.—

(1) The Administrator shall promulgate regulations which define the appropriate response action in a school building under the authority of a local educational agency in at least the following circumstances:

(A) Damage.—Circumstances in which friable asbestos-containing material or its covering is damaged, deteriorated, or delaminated.

(B) Significant Damage.—Circumstances in which friable asbestos-containing material or its covering is significantly damaged, deteriorated, or delaminated.

(C) Potential Damage.—Circumstances in which—

(i) friable asbestos-containing material is in an area regularly used by building occupants, including maintenance personnel, in the course of their normal activities, and

(ii) there is a reasonable likelihood that the material or its covering will become damaged, deteriorated, or delaminated.

(D) Potential Significant Damage.—Circumstances in which—

(i) friable asbestos-containing material is in an area regularly used by building occupants, including maintenance personnel, in the course of their normal activities, and

(ii) there is a reasonable likelihood that the material or its covering will become significantly damaged, deteriorated, or delaminated.

(2) In promulgating such regulations, the Administrator shall consider and assess the value of various technologies intended to improve the decisionmaking process regarding response actions and the quality of any work that is deemed necessary, including air monitoring and chemical encapsulants.

(d) Response Actions.—

(1) In General.—The Administrator shall promulgate regulations describing a response action in a school building under the authority of a local educational agency, using the least burdensome methods which protect human health and the environment. In determining the least burdensome methods, the Administrator shall take into account local circumstances, including occupancy and use patterns within the school building and short-and long-term costs.

(2) Response Action for Damaged Asbestos.—In the case of a response action for the circumstances described in subsection (c)(1)(A), methods for responding shall include methods identified in chapters 3 and 5 of the 'Guidance for Controlling Asbestos-Containing Material in Buildings'.

(3) Response Action for Significantly Damaged Asbestos.—In the case of a response action for the circumstances described in subsection (c)(1)(B), methods for responding shall include methods identified in chapter 5 of the 'Guidance for Controlling Asbestos-Containing Material in Buildings'.

(4) Response Action for Potentially Damaged Asbestos.—In the case of a response action for the circumstances described in subsection (c)(1)(C), methods for responding shall include methods identified in chapters 3 and 5 of the 'Guidance for Controlling Asbestos-Containing Material in Buildings', unless preventive measures will eliminate the reasonable likelihood that the asbestos-containing material will become damaged, deteriorated, or delaminated.

(5) Response Action for Potentially Significantly Damaged Asbestos.—In the case of a response action for the circumstances described in subsection (c)(1)(D), methods for responding shall include methods identified in chapter 5 of the 'Guidance for Controlling Asbestos-Containing Material in Buildings', unless preventive measures will eliminate the reasonable likelihood that the asbestos-containing material will become significantly damaged, deteriorated, or delaminated.

(6) Preventive Measures Defined.—For purposes of this section, the term 'preventive measures' means actions which eliminate the reasonable likelihood of asbestos- containing material becoming damaged, deteriorated, or delaminated, or significantly damaged deteriorated, or delaminated (as the case may be) or which protect human health and the environment.

(7) The Administrator shall, not later than 30 days after enactment of this paragraph, publish and distribute to all local education agencies and State Governors information or an advisory to—

(A) facilitate public understanding of the comparative risks associated with in- place management of asbestos-containing building materials and removals.

(B) promote the least burdensome response actions necessary to protect human health, safety, and the environment; and

(C) describe the circumstances in which asbestos removal is necessary to protect human health.

Such information or advisory shall be based on the best available scientific evidence and shall be revised, republished, and redistributed as appropriate, to reflect new scientific findings.

[§203(d)(7) added by PL 101–637, Nov. 28, 1990]

(e) Implementation.—The Administrator shall promulgate regulations requiring the implementation of response actions in school buildings under the authority of a local educational agency and, where appropriate, for the determination of when a response action is completed. Such regulations shall include standards for the education and protection of both workers and building occupants for the following phases of activity:

(1) Inspection.

(2) Response Action.

(3) Post-response action, including any periodic reinspection of asbestos-containing material and long-term surveillance activity.

(f) Operations and Maintenance.—The Administrator shall promulgate regulations to require implementation of an operations and maintenance and repair program as described in chapter 3 of the 'Guidance for Controlling Asbestos-Containing Materials in Buildings' for all friable asbestos-containing material in a school building under the authority of a local educational agency.

(g) Periodic Surveillance.—The Administrator shall promulgate regulations to require the following:

(1) An identification of the location of friable and non-friable asbestos in a school building under the authority of a local educational agency.

(2) Provisions for surveillance and periodic reinspection of such friable and non- friable asbestos.

(3) Provisions for education of school employees, including school service and maintenance personnel, about the location of and safety procedures with respect to such friable and nonfriable asbestos.

(h) Transportation and Disposal.—The Administrator shall promulgate regulations which prescribe standards for transportation and disposal of asbestos-containing waste material to protect human health and the environment. Such regulations shall include such provisions related to the manner in which transportation vehicles are loaded and unloaded as will assure the physical integrity of containers of asbestos-containing waste material.

(i) Management Plans.—

(1) In General.—The Administrator shall promulgate regulations which require each local educational agency to develop an asbestos management plan for school buildings under its authority, to begin implementation of such plan within 990 days after the date of the enactment of this title, and to complete implementation of such plan in a timely fashion. The regulations shall require that each plan include the following elements, wherever relevant to the school building:

(A) An inspection statement describing inspection and response action activities carried out before the date of the enactment of this title.

(B) A description of the results of the inspection conducted pursuant to regulations under subsection (b), including a description of the specific areas inspected.

(C) A detailed description of measures to be taken to respond to any friable asbestos-containing material pursuant to the regulations promulgated under subsections (c), (d), and (e), including the location or locations at which a response action will be taken, the method or methods of response action to be used, and a schedule for beginning and completing response actions.

(D) A detailed description of any asbestos-containing material which remains in the school building once response actions are undertaken pursuant to the regulations promulgated under subsections (c), (d), and (e).

(E) A plan for periodic reinspection and long-term surveillance activities developed pursuant to regulations promulgated under subsection (g), and a plan for operations and maintenance activities developed pursuant to regulations promulgated under subsection (f).

(F) With respect to the person or persons who inspected for asbestos–containing material and who will design or carry out response actions with respect to the friable asbestos-containing material, one of the following statements:

(i) If the State has adopted a contractor accreditation plan under section 206(b) , a statement that the person (or persons) is accredited under such plan.

(ii) A statement that the local educational agency used (or will use) persons who have been accredited by another State which has adopted a contractor accreditation plan under section 206(b) or is accredited pursuant to an Administrator- approved course under section 206(c) .

(G) A list of the laboratories that analyzed any bulk samples of asbestos-containing material found in the school building or air samples taken to detect asbestos in the school building and a statement that each laboratory has been accredited pursuant to the accreditation program under section 206(d) .

(H) With respect to each consultant who contributed to the management plan, the name of the consultant and one of the following statements:

(i) If the State has adopted a contractor accreditation plan under section 206(b) , a statement that the consultant is accredited under such plan.

(ii) A statement that the contractor is accredited by another State which has adopted a contractor accreditation plan under section 206(b) or is accredited pursuant to an Administrator-approved course under section 206(c) .

(I) An evaluation of resources needed to successfully complete response actions and carry out reinspection, surveillance, and operation and maintenance activities.

(2) Statement by contractor.—A local educational agency may require each management plan to contain a statement signed by an accredited asbestos contractor that such contractor has prepared or assisted in the preparation of such plan, or has reviewed such plan, and that such plan is in compliance with the applicable regulations and standards promulgated or adopted pursuant to this section and other applicable provisions of law. Such a statement may not be signed by a contractor who, in addition to preparing or assisting in preparing the management plan, also implements (or will implement) the management plan.

(3) Warning labels.—

(A) The regulations shall require that each local educational agency which has inspected for and discovered any asbestos- containing material with respect to a school building shall attach a warning label to any asbestos-containing material still in routine maintenance areas (such as boiler rooms) of the school building, including—

(i) friable asbestos-containing material which was responded to by a means other than removal, and

(ii) asbestos-containing material for which no response action was carried out.

(B) The warning label shall read, in print which is readily visible because of large size or bright color, as follows:

'CAUTION: ASBESTOS. HAZARDOUS. DO NOT DISTURB WITHOUT PROPER TRAINING AND EQUIPMENT.'

(4) Plan may be submitted in stages.—A local educational agency may submit a management plan in stages, with each submission of the agency covering only a portion of the school buildings under the agency's authority, if the agency determines that such action would expedite the identification and abatement of hazardous asbestos-containing material in the school buildings under the authority of the agency.

(5) Public availability.—A copy of the management plan developed under the regulations shall be available in the administrative offices of the local educational agency for inspection by the public, including teachers, other school personnel, and parents. The local educational agency shall notify parent, teacher, and employee organizations of the availability of such plan.

(6) Submission to state governor.—Each plan developed under this subsection shall be submitted to the State Governor under section 205.

(j) Changes in Regulations.—Changes may be made in the regulations promulgated under this section only by rule in accordance with section 553 of title 5, United States Code. Any such change must protect human health and the environment.

(k) Changes in Guidance Document.—Any change made in the 'Guidance for Controlling Asbestos-Containing Material in Buildings' shall be made only by rule in accordance with section 553 of title 5, United States Code, unless a regulation described in this section dealing with the same subject matter is in effect. Any such change must protect human health and the environment.

(l) Treatment of Department of Defense Schools.—

(1) Secretary to act in lieu of governor.—In the administration of this title, any function, duty, or other responsibility imposed on a Governor of a State shall be carried out by the Secretary of Defense with respect to any school operated under the defense dependents' education system provided for under the Defense Dependents' Education Act of 1978 (20 U.S.C. 921 et seq.).

(2) Regulations.—The Secretary of Defense, in cooperation with the Administrator, shall, to the extent feasible and consistent with the national security, take such action as may be

necessary to provide for the identification, inspection, and management (including abatement) of asbestos in any building used by the Department of Defense as an overseas school for dependents of members of the Armed Forces. Such identification, inspection, and management (including abatement) shall, subject to the preceding sentence, be carried out in a manner comparable to the manner in which a local educational agency is required to carry out such activities with respect to a school building under this title.

(m) Waiver.—The Administrator, upon request by a Governor and after notice and comment and opportunity for a public hearing in the affected State, may waive some or all of the requirements of this section and section 204 with respect to such State if it has established and is implementing a program of asbestos inspection and management that contains requirements that are at least as stringent as the requirements of this section and section 204 .

§2644. Requirements if EPA Fails to Promulgate Regulations. [Sec. 204]

(a) In General.—

(1) Failure to promulgate.—If the Administrator fails to promulgate within the prescribed period—

(A) regulations described in section 203(b) (relating to inspection);

(B) regulations described in section 203(c), (d), (e), (f), (g), and (i) (relating to responding to asbestos); or

(C) regulations described in section 203(h) (relating to transportation and disposal);

each local educational agency shall carry out the requirements described in this section in subsection (b); subsections (c), (d), and (e); or subsection (f); respectively, in accordance with the Environmental Protection Agency's most current guidance document.

(2) Stay by court.—If the Administrator has promulgated regulations described in paragraph (1)(A), (B), or (C) within the prescribed period, but the effective date of such regulations has been stayed by a court for a period of more than 30 days, a local educational agency shall carry out the pertinent requirements described in this subsection in accordance with the Environmental Protection Agency's most current guidance document.

(3) Effective period.—The requirements of this section shall be in effect until such time as the Administrator promulgates the pertinent regulations or until the stay is lifted (as the case may be).

(b) Inspection.—

(1) Except as provided in paragraph (2), the local educational agency, within 540 days after the date of the enactment of this title, shall conduct an inspection for asbestos-containing material, using personnel accredited under section 206(b) or 206(c) and laboratories accredited under section 206(d) , in each school building under its authority.

(2) The local educational agency may exclude from the inspection requirement in paragraph (1) any school building, or portion of a school building, if (A) an inspection of such school building (or portion) was completed before the date on which this section goes into effect, and (B) the inspection meets the inspection requirements of this section.

(c) Operation and Maintenance.—The local educational agency shall, within 720 days after the date of the enactment of this title, develop and begin implementation of an operation and maintenance plan with respect to friable asbestos-containing material in a school building under its authority. Such plan shall provide for the education of school service and maintenance personnel about safety procedures with respect to asbestos-containing material, including friable asbestos-containing material.

(d) Management Plan.—

(1) In general.—The local educational agency shall—

(A) develop a management plan for responding to asbestos-containing material in each school building under its authority and submit such plan to the Governor under section 205 within 810 days after the date of the enactment of this title.

(B) begin implementation of such plan within 990 days after the date of the enactment of this title, and

(C) complete implementation of such plan in a timely fashion.

(2) Plan requirements.—The management plan shall—

(A) include the elements listed in section 203(i)(1) , including an inspection statement as described in paragraph (3) of this section,

(B) provide for the attachment of warning labels as described in section 203(i)(3) ,

(C) be prepared in accordance with the most current guidance document,

(D) meet the standard described in paragraph (4) for actions described in that paragraph, and

(E) be submitted to the State Governor under section 205 .

(3) Inspection statement.—The local educational agency shall complete an inspection statement, covering activities carried out before the date of the enactment of this title, which meets the following requirements:

(A) The statement shall include the following information:

(i) The dates of inspection.

(ii) The name, address, and qualifications of each inspector.

(iii) A description of the specific areas inspected.

(iv) A list of the laboratories that analyzed any bulk samples of asbestos-containing material or air samples of asbestos found in any school building and a statement describing the qualifications of each laboratory.

(v) The results of the inspection.

(B) The statement shall state whether any actions were taken with respect to any asbestos-containing material found to be present, including a specific reference to whether any actions were taken in the boiler room of the building. If any such action was taken, the following items of information shall be included in the statement:

(i) The location or locations at which the action was taken.

(ii) A description of the method of action.

(iii) The qualifications of the persons who conducted the action.

(4) Standard.—The ambient interior concentration of asbestos after the completion of actions described in the most current guidance document, other than the type of action described in sections 203(f) and subsection (c) of this section, shall not exceed the ambient exterior concentration, discounting any contribution from any local stationary source. Either a scanning electron microscope or a transmission electron microscope shall be used to determine the ambient interior concentrations. In the absence of reliable measurements, the ambient exterior concentration shall be deemed to be—

(A) less than 0.003 fibers per cubic centimeter if a scanning electron microscope is used, and

(B) less than 0.005 fibers per cubic centimeter if a transmission electron microscope is used.

(5) Public availability.—A copy of the management plan shall be available in the administra tive offices of the local educational agency for inspection by the public, including teachers, other school personnel, and parents. The local educational agency shall notify parent, teacher, and employee organizations of the availability of such plan.

(e) Building Occupant Protection.—The local educational agency shall provide for the protection of building occupants during each phase of activity described in this section.

(f) Transportation and Disposal.—The local educational agency shall provide for the transportation and disposal of asbestos in accordance with the most recent version of the Environmental Protection Agency's 'Asbestos Waste Management Guidance' (or any successor to such document).

§2645. Submission to State Governor. [Sec. 205]

(a) Submission.—Within 720 days after the date of the enactment of this title (or within 810 days if there are no regulations under section 203(i) , a local educational agency shall submit a management plan developed pursuant to regulations promulgated under section 203(i) (or under section 204(d) if there are no regulations) to the Governor of the State in which the local educational agency is located.

(b) Governor Requirements.—Within 360 days after the date of the enactment of this title, the Governor of each State—

(1) shall notify local educational agencies in the State of where to submit their management plans under this section, and

(2) may establish administrative procedures for reviewing management plans submitted under this section.

If the Governor establishes procedures under paragraph (2), the Governor shall designate to carry out the reviews those State officials who are responsible for implementing environmental protection or other public health programs, or with authority over asbestos programs, in the State.

(c) Management Plan Review.—

(1) Review Of Plan.—The Governor may disapprove a management plan within 90 days after the date receipt of the plan if the plan—

(A) does not conform with the regulations under section 203(i) (or with section 204(d) if there are no regulations),

(B) does not assure that contractors who are accredited pursuant to this title will be used to carry out the plan, or

(C) does not contain a response action schedule which is reasonable and timely, taking into account circumstances relevant to the speed at which the friable asbestos-containing material in the school buildings under the local education agency's authority should be responded to, including human exposure to the asbestos while the friable asbestos-containing material remains in the school building, and the ability of the local educational agency to continue to provide educational services to the community.

(2) Revision of Plan.—If the State Governor disapproves a plan, the State Governor shall explain in writing to the local educational agency the reasons why the plan was disapproved and the changes that need to be made in the plan. Within 30 days after the date on which notice is received of disapproval of its plan, the local educational agency shall revise the plan to conform with the State Governor's suggested changes. The Governor may extend the 30–day period for not more than 90 days.

[§205(d) and (e) added by PL 100–368, July 18, 1988]

(d) Deferral Of Submission.—

(1) Request For Deferral.—A local educational agency may request a deferral, to May 9, 1989, of the deadline under subsection (a). Upon approval of such a request, the deadline under subsection (a) is deferred until May 9, 1989, for the local educational agency which submitted the request. Such a request may cover one or more schools under the authority of the agency and shall include a list of all the schools covered by the request. A local educational agency shall file any such request with the State Governor by October 12, 1988, and shall include with the request either of the following statements:

(A) A statement—

(i) that the State in which the agency is located has requested from the Administrator, before June 1, 1988, a waiver under section 203(m) ; and

(ii) that gives assurance that the local educational agency has carried out the notification and, in the case of a public school, public meeting required by paragraph (2).

(B) A statement, the accuracy of which is sworn to by a responsible official of the agency (by notarization or other means of certification), that includes the following with respect to each school for which a deferral is sought in the request:

(i) A statement that, in spite of the fact that the local educational agency has made a good faith effort to meet the deadline for submission of a management plan under subsection (a), the agency will not be able to meet the deadline. The statement shall include a brief explanation of the reasons why the deadline cannot be met.

(ii) A statement giving assurance that the local educational agency has made available for inspection by the public, at each school for which a deferral is sought in the request, at least one of the following documents:

(I) A solicitation by the local educational agency to contract with an accredited asbestos contractor for inspection or management plan development.

(II) A letter attesting to the enrollment of school district personnel in an Environmental Protection Agency-accredited training course for inspection and management plan development.

(III) Documentation showing that an analysis of suspected asbestos-containing material from the school is pending at an accredited laboratory.

(IV) Documentation showing that an inspection or management plan has been completed in at least one other school under the local educational agency's authority.

(iii) A statement giving assurance that the local educational agency has carried out the notification and, in the case of a public school, public meeting required by paragraph (2).

(iv) A proposed schedule outlining all significant activities leading up to submission of a management plan by May 9, 1989, including inspection of the school (if not completed at the time of the request) with a deadline of no later than December 22, 1988, for entering into a signed contract with an accredited asbestos contractor for inspection (unless such inspections are to be performed by school personnel), laboratory analysis of material from the school suspected of containing asbestos, and development of the management plan.

(2) Notification and Public Meeting.—Before filing a deferral request under paragraph (1), a

local educational agency shall notify affected parent, teacher, and employee organizations of its intent to file such a request. In the case of a deferral request for a public school, the local educational agency shall discuss the request at a public meeting of the school board with jurisdiction over the school, and affected parent, teacher, and employee organizations shall be notified in advance of the time and place of such meeting.

(3) Response By Governor.—

(A) Not later than 30 days after the date on which a Governor receives a deferral request under paragraph (1) from a local educational agency, the Governor shall respond to the local educational agency in writing by acknowledging whether the request is complete or incomplete. If the request is incomplete, the Governor shall identify in the response the items that are missing from the request.

(B) A local educational agency may correct any deficiencies in an incomplete deferral request and refile the request with the Governor. In any case in which the local educational agency decides to refile the request, the agency shall refile the request, and the Governor shall respond to such refiled request in the manner described in subparagraph (A), no later than 15 days after the local educational agency has received a response from the Governor under subparagraph (A).

(C) Approval of a deferral request under this subsection occurs only upon the receipt by a local educational agency of a written acknowledgment from the Governor that the agency's deferral request is complete.

(4) Submission and Review of Plan.— A local educational agency whose deferral request is approved shall submit a management plan to the Governor not later than May 9, 1989. Such management plan shall include a copy of the deferral request and the statement accompanying such request. Such management plan shall be reviewed in accordance with subsection (c), except that the Governor may extend the 30–day period for revision of the plan under subsection (c)(2) for only an additional 30 days (for a total of 60 days).

(5) Implementation of Plan.— The approval of a deferral request from a local educational agency shall not be considered to be a waiver or exemption from the requirement under section 203(i) for the local educational agency to begin implementation of its management plan by July 9, 1989.

(6) EPA notice.—

(A) Not later than 15 days after the date of the enactment of this subsection, the Administrator shall publish in the Federal Register the following:

(i) A notice describing the opportunity to file a request for deferral under this subsection.

(ii) A list of the State offices (including officials (if available) in each State as designated under subsection (b)) with which deferral requests should be filed.

(B) As soon as practicable, but in no event later than 30 days, after the date of the enactment of this subsection, the Administrator shall mail a notice describing the opportunity to file a request for deferral under this subsection to each local educational agency and to each State office in the list published under subparagraph (A).

(e) Status Reports.—

(1) Not later than December 31, 1988, the Governor of each State shall submit to the Administrator a written statement on the status of management plan submissions and deferral requests by local educational agencies in the State. The statement shall be made available to local educational agencies in the State and shall contain the following:

(A) A list containing each local educational agency that submitted a management plan by October 12, 1988.

(B) A list containing each local educational agency whose deferral request was approved.

(C) A list containing each local educational agency that failed to submit a management plan by October 12, 1988, and whose deferral request was disapproved.

(D) A list containing each local educational agency that failed to submit a management plan by October 12, 1988, and did not submit a deferral request.

(2) Not later than December 31, 1989, the Governor of each State shall submit to the Administrator an updated version of the written statement submitted under paragraph (1). The statement shall be made available to local educational agencies in the State and shall contain the following:

(A) A list containing each local educational agency whose management plan was submitted and not disapproved as of October 9, 1989.

(B) A list containing each local educational agency whose management plan was submitted and disapproved, and which remains disapproved, as of October 9, 1989.

(C) A list containing each local educational agency that submitted a management plan after May 9, 1989, and before October 10, 1989.

(D) A list containing each local educational agency that failed to submit a management plan as of October 9, 1989.

§2646. Contractor and Laboratory Accreditation. [Sec. 206]

(a) Contractor Accreditation.— A person may not—

(1) inspect for asbestos-containing material in a school building under the authority of a local educational agency or in a public or commerical building,

[§206(a)(1) amended by PL 101–637, Nov. 28, 1990]

(2) prepare a management plan for such a school, or

(3) design or conduct response actions, other than the type of action described in sections 203(f) and 204(c), with respect to friable asbestos-containing material in such a school or in a public or commerical building,

unless such person is accredited by a State under subsection (6)(b) or is accredited pursuant to an Administrator-approved course under subsection (c).

[§206(a)(3) amended by PL 101–637, Nov. 28, 1990]

(b) Accreditation by State.—

(1) Model Plan.—

(A) Persons to be accredited.—Within 180 days after the date of the enactment of this title, the Administrator, in consultation with affected organizations, shall develop a model contractor accreditation plan for States to give accreditation to persons in the following categories:

(i) Persons who inspect for asbestos-containing material in school buildings under the authority of a local educational agency or in public or commerical buildings.[§206(b)(1)(A)(i) amended by PL 101–637, Nov. 28, 1990]

(ii) Persons who prepare management plans for such schools.

(iii) Persons who design or carry out response actions, other than the type of action described in sections 203(f) and 204(c), with respect to friable asbestos-containing material in such schools or in public or commerical buildings.

[§206(b)(1)(A)(iii) amended by PL 101–637, Nov. 28, 1990]

(B) Plan requirements.—The plan shall include a requirement that any person in a category listed in paragraph (1) achieve a passing grade on an examination and participate in continuing education to stay informed about current asbestos inspection and response action technology. The examination shall demonstrate the knowledge of the person in areas that the Administrator prescribes as necessary and appropriate in each of the categories. Such examinations may include requirements for knowledge in the following areas:

(i) Recognition of asbestos-containing material and its physical characteristics.

(ii) Health hazards of asbestos and the relationship between asbestos exposure and disease.

(iii) Assessing the risk of asbestos exposure through a knowledge of percentage memberseight of asbestos-containing material, friability, age, deterioration, location and accessibility of materials, and advantages and disadvantages of dry and wet response action methods.

(iv) Respirators and their use, care, selection, degree of protection afforded, fitting, testing, and maintenance and cleaning procedures.

(v) Appropriate work practices and control methods, including the use of high efficiency particle absolute vacuums, the use of amended water, and principles of negative air pressure equipment use and procedures.

(vi) Preparing a work area for response action work, including isolating work areas to prevent bystander or public exposure to asbestos, decontamination procedures, and procedures for dismantling work areas after completion of work.

(vii) Establishing emergency procedures to respond to sudden releases.

(viii) Air monitoring requirements and procedures.

(ix) Medical surveillance program requirements.

(x) Proper asbestos waste transportation and disposal procedures.

(xi) Housekeeping and personal hygiene practices, including the necessity of showers, and procedures to prevent asbestos exposure to an employee's family.

(2) State Adoption of Plan. — Each State shall adopt a contractor accreditation plan at least as stringent as the model plan developed by the Administrator under paragraph (1), within 180 days after the commencement of the first regular session of the legislature of such State which is convened following the date on which the Administrator completes development of the model plan. In the case of a school operated under the defense dependents' education system provided for under the Defense Dependents' Education Act of 1978 (20 U.S.C. 21 et seq.), the Secretary of Defense shall adopt a contractor accreditation plan at least as stringent as that model.

(c) Accreditation by Administrator-Approved Course.—

(1) Course Approval. — Within 180 days after the date of the enactment of this title, the Administrator shall ensure that any Environmental Protection Agency-approved asbestos training course is consistent with the model plan (including testing requirements) developed under subsection (b). A contractor may be accredited by taking and passing such a course.

(2) Treatment of Persons With Previous EPA Asbestos Training.— A person who—

(A) completed an Environmental Protection Agency-approved asbestos training course before the date of the enactment of this title, and

(B) passed (or passes) an asbestos test either before or after the date of the enactment of this title,

may be accredited under paragraph (1) if the Administrator determines that the course and test are equivalent to the requirements of the model plan developed under subsection (b). If the Administrator so determines, the person shall be considered accredited for the purposes of this title until a date that is one year after the date on which the State in which such person is employed establishes an accreditation program pursuant to subsection (b).

(3) Lists of Courses.—The Administrator, in consultation with affected organizations, shall publish (and revise as necessary)—

(A) a list of asbestos courses and tests in effect before the date of the enactment of this title which qualify for equivalency treatment under paragraph (2), and

(B) a list of asbestos course and tests which the Administrator determines under paragraph (1) are consistent with the model plan and which will qualify a contractor for accreditation under such paragraph.

(d) Laboratory Accreditation.—

(1) The Administrator shall provide for the development of an accreditation program for laboratories by the National Bureau of Standards in accordance with paragraph (2). The Administrator shall transfer such funds as are necessary to the National Institute of Standards and Technology to carry out such program.

[§206(d)(1) amended by PL 100–418]

(2) The National Institute of Standards and Technology, upon request by the Administrator, shall, in consultation with affected organizations —

[§206(d)(2) amended by PL 100–418]

(A) within 360 days after the date of the enactment of this title, develop an accreditation program for laboratories which conduct qualitative and semi-qualitative analyses of bulk samples of asbestos-containing material, and

(B) within 720 days after the date of the enactment of this

title, develop an accreditation program for laboratories which conduct analyses of air samples of asbestos from school buildings under the authority of a local educational agency.

(3) A laboratory which plans to carry out any such analysis shall comply with the requirements of the accreditation program.

(e) Financial Assistance Contingent of use of Accredited Persons.—

(1) A school which is an applicant for financial assistance under section 505 of the Asbestos School Hazard Abatement Act of 1984 (Public Law 98–377; 20 U.S.C. 4011 et seq.) is not eligible for such assistance unless the school, in carrying out the requirements of this title—

(A) uses a person (or persons)—

(i) who is accredited by a State which has adopted an accreditation plan based on the model plan developed under subsection (b), or

(ii) who is accredited pursuant to an Administrator-approved course under subsection (c), and

(B) uses a laboratory (or laboratories) which is accredited under the program developed under subsection (d).

(2) This subsection shall apply to any financial assistance provided under the Asbestos School Hazard Abatement Act of 1984 for activities performed after the following dates:

(A) In the case of activities performed by persons, after the date which is one year after the date of the enactment of this title.

(B) In the case of activities performed by laboratories, after the date which is 180 days after the date on which a laboratory accreditation program is completed under subsection (d).

(f) List of EPA-Approved Courses.—Not later than August 31, 1988, and every three months thereafter until August 31, 1991, the Administrator shall publish in the Federal Register a list of all Environmental Protection Agency- approved asbestos training courses for persons to achieve accreditation in each category described in subsection (b)(1)(A) and for laboratories to achieve accreditation. The Administrator may continue publishing such a list after August 31, 1991, at such times as the Administrator considers it useful. The list shall include the name and address of each approved trainer and, to the extent available, a list of all the geographic sites where training courses will take place. The Administrator shall provide a copy of the list to each State official on the list published by the Administrator under section 205(d)(6) and to each regional office of the Environmental Protection Agency.

[§206(f) added by PL 100–368, July 18, 1988]

§2647. Enforcement. [Sec. 207]

(a) Penalties—Any local educational agency—

(1) which fails to conduct a inspection pursuant to regulations under section 203(b) or under section 204(b) ,

(2) which knowingly submits false information to the Governor regarding any inspection pursuant to regulations under section 203(i) or knowingly includes false information in any inspection statement under section 204(d)(3),

[§207(a)(2) amended by PL 100–368, July 18, 1988]

(3) which fails to develop a management plan pursuant to regulations under section 203(i) or under section 204(d) ,

(4) which carries out any activity prohibited by section 215 , or

[§207(a)(4) added by PL 100–368, July 18, 1988]

(5) which knowingly submits false information to the Governor regarding a deferral request under section 205(d).

[§207(a)(5) added by PL 100–368, July 18, 1988]

(5) is liable for a civil penalty of not more than $5,000 for each day during which the violation continues. Any civil penalty under this subsection shall be assessed and collected in the same manner, and subject to the same provisions, as in the case of civil penalties assessed and collected under section 16. For purposes of this subsection, a 'violation' means a failure to comply with respect to a single school building. The court shall order that any civil penalty collected under this subsection be used by the local educational agency for purposes of complying with this title. Any portion of a civil penalty remaining unspent after compliance by a local educational agency is completed shall be deposited into the Asbestos Trust Fund established by section 5 of the Asbestos Hazard Emergency Response Act of 1986.

(b) Relationship to Title I.—A local educational agency is not liable for any civil penalty under title I of this Act for failing or refusing to comply with any rule promulgated or order issued under this title.

(c) Enforcement Considerations.—

(1) In determining the amount of a civil penalty to be assessed under subsection (a) against a local educational agency, the Administrator shall consider—

(A) the significance of the violation;

(B) the culpability of the violator, including any history of previous violations under this Act;

(C) the ability of the violator to pay the penalty; and

(D) the ability of the violator to continue to provide educational services to the community.

(2) Any action ordered by a court in fashioning relief under section 20 shall be consistent with regulations promulgated under section 203 (or with the requirements of section 204 if there are no regulations).

(d) Citizen Complaints.—Any person may file a complaint with the Administrator or with the Governor of the State in which the school building is located with respect to asbestos-containing material in a school building. If the Administrator or Governor receives a complaint under this subsection containing allegations which provide a reasonable basis to believe that a violation of this Act has occurred, the Administrator or Governor shall investigate and respond (including taking enforcement action where appropriate) to the complaint within a reasonable period of time.

(e) Citizen Petitions.—

(1) Any person may petition the Administrator to initiate a proceeding for the issuance, amendment, or repeal of a regulation or order under this title.

(2) Such petition shall be filed in the principal office of the Administrator and shall set forth the facts which it is claimed establish that it is necessary to issue, amend, or repeal a regulation or order under this title.

(3) The Administrator may hold a public hearing or may conduct such investigation or proceeding as the Administrator deems appropriate in order to determine whether or not such petitions should be granted.

(4) Within 90 days after filing of a petition described in paragraph (1), the Administrator shall either grant or deny the petition. If the Administrator grants such petition, the Administrator shall promptly commence an appropriate proceeding in accordance with this title. If the Administrator denies such petition, the Administrator shall publish in the Federal Register the Administrator's reasons for such denial. The granting or denial of a petition under this subsection shall not affect any deadline or other requirement of this title.

(f) Citizen Civil Actions with Respect to EPA Regulations.—

(1) Any person may commence a civil action without prior notice against the Administrator to compel the Administrator to meet the deadlines in section 203 for issuing advanced notices of proposed rulemaking, proposing regulations, and promulgating regulations. Any such action shall be brought in the district court of the United States for the District of Columbia.

(2) In any action brought under paragraph (1) in which the court finds the Administrator to be in violation of any deadline in section 203 , the court shall set forth a schedule for promulgating the regulations required by section 203 and shall order the Administrator to comply with such schedule. The court may extend any deadline (which) has not already occurred) in section 204(b), 204(c), or 204(d) for a period of not more than 6 months, if the court-ordered schedule will result in final promulgation of the pertinent regulations within the extended period. Such deadline extensions may not be granted by the court beginning 720 days after the date of enactment of this title.

(3) Section 20 of this Act shall apply to civil actions described in this subsection, except to the extent inconsistent with this subsection.

(g) Any contractor who—

(1) inspects for asbestos–containing material in a school, public or commercial building;

(2) designs or conducts response actions with respect to friable asbestos–containing material in a school, public or commercial building; or

(3) employs individuals to conduct response actions with respect to friable asbestos–containing material in a school, public or commercial building;

and who fails to obtain the accreditation under section 206 of this Act, or in the case of employees to require or provide for the accreditation required, is liable for a civil penalty of not more than $5,000 for each day during which the violation continues, unless such contractor is a direct employee of the Federal Government.

[§207(g) added by PL 101–637, Nov. 28, 1990]

§2648. Emergency Authority. [Sec. 208]

(a) Emergency Action.—

(1) Authority.—Whenever—

(A) the presence of airborne asbestos or the condition of friable asbestos-containing material in a school building governed by a local educational agency poses an imminent and substantial endangerment to human health or the environment, and

(B) the local educational agency is not taking sufficient action (as determined by the Administrator or the Governor) to respond to the airborne asbestos or friable asbestos-containing material,

the Administrator or the Governor of a State is authorized to act to protect human health or the environment.

(2) Limitations on Governor Action.—The Governor of a State shall notify the Administrator within a reasonable period of time before the Governor plans to take an emergency action under this subsection. After such notification, if the Administrator takes an emergency action with respect to the same hazard, the Governor may not carry out (or continue to carry out, if the action has been started) the emergency action.

(3) Notification.—The following notification shall be provided before an emergency action is taken under this subsection:

(A) In the case of a Governor taking the action, the Governor shall notify the local educational agency concerned.

(B) In the case of the Administrator taking the action, the Administrator shall notify both the local educational agency concerned and the Governor of the State in which such agency is located.

(4) Cost Recovery.—The Administrator or the Governor of a State may seek reimbursement for all costs of an emergency action taken under this subsection in the United States District Court for the District of Columbia or for the district in which the emergency action occurred. In any action seeking reimbursement from a local educational agency, the action shall be brought in the United States District Court for the district in which the local educational agency is located.

(b) Injunctive Relief.—Upon receipt of evidence that the presence of airborne asbestos or the condition of friable asbestos- containing material in a school building governed by a local educational agency poses a imminent and substantial endangerment to human health or the environment—

(1) the Administrator may request the Attorney General to bring suit, or

(2) the Governor of a State may bring suit, to secure such relief as may be necessary to respond to the hazard. The district court of the United States in the district in which the response will be carried out shall have jurisdiction to grant such relief, including injunctive relief.

§2649. State and Federal Law. [Sec. 209]

(a) No Preemption. — Nothing in this title shall be construed, interpreted, or applied to preempt, displace, or supplant any other State or Federal law, whether statutory or common.

(b) Cost and Damage Awards. — Nothing in this title or any standard, regulation, or requirement promulgated pursuant to this title shall be construed or interpreted to preclude any court from awarding costs and damages associated with the abatement, including the removal, of asbestos-containing material, or a portion of such costs, at any time prior to the actual date on which such material is removed.

(c) State May Establish More Requirements. — Nothing in this title shall be construed or interpreted as preempting a State from establishing any additional liability or more stringent requirements with respect to asbestos in school buildings within such State.

(d) No Federal Cause of Action. — Nothing in this title creates a cause of action or in any other way increases or diminishes the liability of any person under any other law.

(e) Intent of Congress.—It is not the intent of Congress that this title or rules, regulations, or orders issued pursuant to this title be interpreted as influencing, in either the plaintiff's or defendant's favor, the disposition of any civil action for damages relating to asbestos. This subsection does not affect the authority of any court to make a determination in an adjudicatory proceeding under applicable State law with respect to the admission into evidence or any other use of this title or rules, regulations, or orders issued pursuant to this title.

§2650. Asbestos Contractors and Local Educational Agencies. [Sec. 210]

(a) Study.—

(1) General requirement.—The Administrator shall conduct a study on the availability of liability insurance and other forms of assurance against financial loss which are available to local educational agencies and asbestos contractors with respect to actions required under this title. Such study shall examine the following:

(A) The extent to which liability insurance and other forms of assurance against financial loss are available to local educational agencies and asbestos contractors.

(B) The extent to which the cost of insurance or other forms of assurance against financial loss has increased and the extent to which coverage has become less complete.

(C) The extent to which any limitation in the availability of insurance or other forms of assurance against financial loss is the result of factors other than standards of liability in applicable law.

(D) The extent to which the existence of the regulations required by subsections (c) and (d) of section 203 and the accreditation of contractors under section 206 has affected the availability or cost of insurance or other forms of assurance against financial loss.

(E) The extent to which any limitation on the availability of insurance or other forms of assurance against financial loss is inhibiting inspections for asbestos-containing material or the development or implementation of management plans under this title.

(F) Identification of any other impediments to the timely completion of inspections or the development and implementation of management plans under this title.

(2) Interim report.—Not later than April 1, 1988, the Administrator shall submit to the Congress an interim report on the progress of the study required by this subsection, along with preliminary findings based on information collected to that date.

(3) Final report.—Not later than October 1, 1990, the Administrator shall submit to the Congress a final report on the study required by this subsection, including final findings based on the information collected.

(b) State Action. — On the basis of the interim report or the final report of the study required by subsection (a), a State may enact or amend State law to establish or modify a standard of liability for local educational agencies or asbestos contractors with respect to actions required under this title.

§2651. Public Protection. [Sec. 211]

(a) Public Protection.—No State or local agency may discriminate against a person in any way, including firing a person who is an employee, because the person provided information relating to a potential violation of this title to any other person, including a State or the Federal Government.

(b) Labor Department Review.—Any public or private employee or representative of employees who believes he or she has been fired or otherwise discriminated against in violation of subsection (a) may within 90 days after the alleged violation occurs apply to the Secretary of Labor for a review of the firing or alleged discrimination. The review shall be conducted in accordance with section 11(c) of the Occupational Safety and Health Act.

§2652. Asbestos Ombudsman. [Sec. 212]

(a) Appointment. — The Administrator shall appoint an Asbestos Ombudsman, who shall carry out the duties described in subsection (b).

(b) Duties.—The duties of the Asbestos Ombudsman are—

(1) to receive complaints, grievances, and requests for information submitted by any person with respect to any aspect of this title.

(2) to render assistance with respect to the complaints, grievances, and requests received, and

(3) to make such recommendations to the Administrator as the Ombudsman considers appropriate.

§2653. EPA Study of Asbestos-Containing Material in Public Buildings. [Sec. 213]

Within 360 days after the date of the enactment of this title, the Administrator shall conduct and submit to the Congress the results of a study which shall—

(1) assess the extent to which asbestos- containing materials are present in public and commercial buildings;

(2) assess the condition of asbestos-containing material in commercial buildings are the likelihood that persons occupying such buildings, including service and maintenance personnel, are, or may be, exposed to asbestos fibers;

(3) consider and report on whether public and commercial buildings should be subject to the same inspection and response action requirements that apply to school buildings;

(4) assess whether existing Federal regulations adequately protect the general public, particularly abatement personnel, from exposure to asbestos during renovation and demolition of such buildings; and

(5) include recommendations that explicitly address whether there is a need to establish standards for, and regulate asbestos exposure in, public and commercial buildings.

§2654. Transition Rules. [Sec. 214]

Any regulation of the Environmental Protection Agency under title I which is inconsistent with this title shall not be in effect after the date of the enactment of this title. Any advanced notice of proposed rulemaking, any proposed rule, and any regulation of the Environmental Protection Agency in effect before the date of the enactment of this title which is consistent with the regulations required under section 203 shall remain in effect and may be used to meet the requirements of section 203 , except that any such regulation shall be enforced under this Act.

§2655. Worker Protection. [Sec. 215]

[§215 added by PL 100–368, July 18, 1988, effective Oct. 12, 1988]

(a) Prohibition on Certain Activities.—Until the local educational agency with authority over a school has submitted a management plan (for the school) which the State Governor has not disapproved as of the end of the period for review and revision of the plan under section 205 , the local educational agency may not do either of the following in the school:

(1) Perform, or direct an employee to perform, renovations or removal of building materials, except emergency repairs, in the school, unless—

(A) the school is carrying out work under a grant awarded under section 505 of the Asbestos School Hazard Abatement Act of 1984; or

(B) an inspection that complies with the requirements of regulations promulgated under section 203 has been carried out in the school and the agency complies with the following sections of title 40 of the Code of Federal Regulations:

(i) Paragraphs (g), (h), and (i) of section 763.90 (response actions).

(ii) Appendix D to subpart E of part 763 (transport and disposal of asbestos waste).

(2) Perform, or direct any employee to perform, operations and maintenance activities in the school, unless the agency complies with the following sections of title 40 of the Code of Federal Regulations:

(A) Section 763.91 (operations and maintenance), including appendix B to subpart E of part 763.

(B) Paragraph (a)(2) of section 763.92 (training and periodic surveillance).

(b) Employee Training and Equipment.—Any school employee who is directed to conduct emergency repairs involving any building material containing asbestos or suspected of containing asbestos, or to conduct operations and maintenance activities, in a school—

(1) shall be provided the proper training to safely conduct such work in order to prevent potential exposure to asbestos; and

(2) shall be provided the proper equipment and allowed to follow work practices that are necessary to safety conduct such work in order to prevent potential exposure to asbestos.

(c) Definition of Emergency Repair. — For purposes of this section, the term 'emergency repair' means a repair in a school building that was not planned and was in response to a sudden, unexpected event that threatens either—

(1) the health or safety of building occupants; or

(2) the structural integrity of the building.

§2656. Training Grants. [Sec. 216]

(a) Grants.—The Administrator is authorized to award grants under this section to nonprofit organizations that demonstrate experience in implementing and operating health and safety asbestos training and education programs for workers who are or will be engaged in asbestos–related activities (including State and local governments, colleges and universities, joint labor–management trust funds, and nonprofit government employee organizations) to establish and, or, operate, asbestos training programs on a not–for–profit basis. Applications for grants under this subsection shall be submitted in such form and manner, and contain such information, as the Administrator prescribes.

(b) Authorization.—Of such sums as are authorized to be appropriated pursuant to section 512(a) of the Asbestos School Hazard Abatement Act of 1984 (20 U.S.C. 4011 et seq.) for the fiscal years 1991, 1992, 1993, 1994, and 1995, not more than $5,000,000 are authorized to be appropriated to carry out this section in each such fiscal year.

[§216 added by PL 101–637, Nov. 28, 1990]

TITLE III—INDOOR RADON ABATEMENT

[Title III added by PL 100–551, Oct. 28, 1988]

§2661. National Goal. [Sec. 301]

The national long-term goal of the United States with respect to radon levels in buildings is that the air within buildings in the United States should be as free of radon as the ambient air outside of buildings.

§2662. Definitions. [Sec. 302]

For purposes of this title:

(1) The term 'local educational agency' means—

(A) any local Educational agency as defined in section 198 of the Elementary and Secondary Education Act of 1965 (20 U.S.C. 3381);

(B) the owner of any nonprofit elementary or secondary school building; and

(C) the governing authority of any school operated pursuant to section 6 of the Act of September 30, 1950 (64 Stat. 1107), relating to impact aid for children who reside on Federal property.

(2) The term 'nonprofit elementary or secondary school' has the meaning given such term by section 202(8) .

(3) The term 'randon' means the radioactive gaseous element and its short-lived decay products produced by the disintegration of the element

radium occurring in air, water, soil, or other media.

(4) The term 'school building' has the meaning given such term by section 202(13) .

§2663. EPA Citizen' Guide. [Sec. 303]

(a) Publication.—In order to make continuous progress toward the long-term goal established in section 301 of this title, the Administrator of the Environmental Protection Agency shall, not later than June 1, 1989, publish and make available to the public an updated version of its document titled 'A Citizen's Guide to Radon'. The Administrator shall revise and republish the guide as necessary thereafter.

(b) Information Included.—

(1) Action levels.—The updated citizen's guide published as provided in subsection (a) shall include a description of a series of action levels indicating the health risk associated with different levels or radon exposure.

(2) Other information.—The updated citizen's guide shall also include information with respect to each of the following:

(A) The increased health risk associated with the exposure of potentially sensitive populations to different levels of radon.

(B) The increased health risk associated with the exposure to radon of persons engaged in potentially risk-increasing behavior.

(C) The cost and technological feasibility of reducing radon concentrations within existing and new buildings.

(D) The relationship between short- term and long-term testing techniques and the relationship between (i) measurements based on both such techniques, and (ii) the actions levels set forth as provided in paragraph (1).

(E) Outdoor radon levels around the country.

§2664. Model Constructions Standards and Techniques. [Sec. 304]

The Administrator of the Environmental Protection Agency shall develop model construction standards and techniques for controlling radon levels within new buildings. To the maximum extent possible, these standards and techniques should be developed with the assistance of organizations involved in establishing national building construction standards and techniques. The Administrator shall make a draft of the document containing the model standards and techniques available for public review and comment. The model standards and techniques shall provide for geographic differences in construction types and materials, geology, weather, and other variables that may affect radon levels in new buildings. The Administrator shall make final model standards and techniques available to the public by June 1, 1990. The Administrator shall work to ensure that organizations responsible for developing national model building codes, and authorities which regulate building construction within States or political subdivisions within States, adopt the Agency's model standards and techniques.

§2665. Technical Assistance to States for Radon Programs. [Sec. 305]

(a) Required Activities.—The Administrator (or another Federal department or agency designated by the Administrator) shall develop and implement activities designed to assist State radon programs. These activities may include, but are not limited to, the following:

(1) Establishment of a clearinghouse of radon related information, including mitigation studies, public information materials, surveys of radon levels, and other relevant information.

(2) Operation of a voluntary proficiency program for rating the effectiveness of radon measurement devices and methods, the effectiveness of radon mitigation devices and methods, and the effectiveness of private firms and individuals offering radon-related architecture, design, engineering, measurement, and mitigation services. The proficiency program under this subparagraph shall be in operation within one year after the date of the enactment of this section.

(3) Design and implementation of training seminars for State and local officials and private and professional firms dealing with radon and addressing topics such as monitoring, analysis, mitigation, health effects, public information, and program design.

(4) Publication of public information materials concerning radon health risks and methods of radon mitigation.

(5) Operation of cooperative projects between the Environmental Protection Agency's Radon Action Program and the State's radon program. Such projects shall include the Home Evaluation Program, in which the Environmental Protection Agency evaluates homes and States demonstrate mitigation methods in these homes. To the maximum extent practicable, consistent with the objectives of the evaluation and demonstration, homes of low-income persons should be selected for evaluation and demonstration.

(6) Demonstration of radon mitigation methods in various types of structures and in various geographic settings and publication of findings. In the case of demonstration of such methods in homes, the Administrator should select homes of low- income persons, to the maximum extent practicable and consistent with the objectives of the demonstration.

(7) Establishment of a national data base with data organized by State concerning the location and amounts of radon.

(8) Development and demonstration of methods of radon measurement and mitigation that take into account unique characteristics, if any, of nonresidential buildings housing child care facilities.

(b) Discretionary Assistance.—Upon request of a State, the Administrator (or another Federal department or agency designated by the Administrator) may provide technical assistance to such State in development or implementation of programs addressing radon. Such assistance may include, but is not limited to, the following:

(1) Design and implementation of surveys of the location and occurrence of radon within a State.

(2) Design and implementation of public information and education programs.

(3) Design and implementation of State programs to control radon in existing or new structures.

(4) Assessment of mitigation alternatives in unusual or unconventional structures.

(5) Design and implementation of methods for radon measurement and mitigation for nonresidential buildings housing child care facilities.

(c) Information Provided to Professional Organization.—The Administrator, or another Federal department or agency designated by the Administrator, shall provide appropriate information concerning technology and methods of radon assessment and mitigation to professional organizations representing private firms involved in building design, engineering, and construction.

(d) Plan.—Within 9 months after the date of the enactment of this section and annually thereafter, the Administrator shall submit to Congress a plan identifying assistance to be provided under this section and outlining personnel and financial resources necessary to implement this section. Prior to submission to Congress, this plan shall be reviewed by the advisory groups provided for in section 403(c) of the Superfund Amendments and Reauthorization Act of 1986 (42 U.S.C. 7401 note).

(e) Proficiency Rating Program and Training Seminar.—

(1) Authorization.—There is authorized to be appropriated not more than $1,500,000 for the purposes of initially establishing the proficiency rating program under subsection (a)(2) and the training seminars under subsection (a)(3).

(2) Charge imposed.—To cover the operating costs of such proficiency rating program and training seminars, the Administrator shall impose on persons applying for a proficiency rating and on private and professional firms participating in training seminars such charges as may be necessary to defray the costs of the program or seminars. No such charge may be imposed on any State or local government.

(3) Special account.—Funds derived from the charges imposed under paragraph (2) shall be deposited in a special account in the Treasury. Amounts in the special account are authorized to be appropriated only for purposes of administering such proficiency rating program or training seminars or for reimbursement of funds appropriated to the Administrator to initially establish such program or seminars.

(4) Reimbursement of general fund.—During the first three years of the program and seminars, the Administrator shall make every effort, consistent with the goals and successful operation of the program and seminars, to set charges imposed under paragraph (2) so that an amount in excess of operation costs is collected. Such excess amount shall be used to reimburse the General Fund of the Treasury for the full amount appropriated to initially establish the program and seminars.

(5) Research—The Administrator shall, in conjunction with other Federal agencies, conduct research to develop, test, and evaluate radon and radon progency measurement methods and protocols. The purpose of such research shall be to assess the ability of those methods and protocols to accurately assess exposure to radon progeny. Such research shall include—

(A) conducting comparisons among radon and radon progeny measurement techniques;

(B) developing measurement protocols for different building types under varying operating conditions; and

(C) comparing the exposures estimated by stationary monitors and protocols to those measured by personal monitors, and issue guidance documents that—

(i) provide information on the results of research conducted under this paragraph; and

(ii) describe model State radon measurement and mitigation programs.

(6) Mandatory Proficiency Testing Program Study.—

(A) The Administrator shall conduct a study to determine the feasibility of establishing a mandatory proficiency testing program that would require that—

(i) any product offered for sale, or device used in connection with a service offered to the public, for the measurement of radon meets minimum performance criteria; and

(ii) any operator of a device, or person employing a technique, used in connection with a service offered to the public for the measurement of radon meets a minimum level of proficiency.

(B) The study shall also address procedures for—

(i) ordering the recall of any product sold for the measurement of radon which does not meet minimum performance criteria;

(ii) ordering the discontinuance of any service offered to the public for the measurement of radon which does not meet minimum performance criteria; and

(iii) establishing adequate quality assurance requirements for each company offering radon measurement services to the public to follow.

The study shall identify enforcement mechanisms necessary to the success of the program. The Administrator shall report the findings of the study with recommendations to Congress by March 1, 1991.

(7) User Fee—In addition to any charge imposed pursuant to paragraph (2), the Administrator shall collect user fees from persons seeking certification under the radon proficiency program in an amount equal to $1,500,000 to cover the Environmental Protection Agency's cost of conducting research pursuant to paragraph (5) for each of the fiscal years 1991, 1992, 1993, 1994, and 1995. Such funds shall be deposited in the account established pursuant to paragraph (3).[§305(e)(5)—(7) added by PL 101–508]

(f) Authorization.—

(1) There is authorized to be appropriated for the purposes of carrying out sections 303, 304 , and this section an amount not to exceed $3,000,000 for each of fiscal years 1989, 1990, and 1991.

(2) No amount appropriated under this subsection may be used by the Environmental Protection Agency to administer the grant program under section 306 .

(3) No amount appropriated under this subsection may be used to cover the costs of the proficiency rating program under subsection (a)(2).

§2666. Grant Assistance to States for Radon Programs. [Sec. 306]

(a) In General.—For each fiscal year, upon application of the Governor of a State, the Administrator may make a grant, subject to such terms and conditions as the Administrator considers appropriate, under this section to the State for the purpose of assisting the State in the development and implementation of programs for the assessment and mitigation of radon.

(b) Application.—An application for a grant under this section in any fiscal year shall contain such information as the Administrator shall require, including each of the following:

(1) A description of the seriousness and extent of radon exposure in the State.

(2) An identification of the State agency which has the primary responsibility for radon programs and which will receive the grant, a description of the roles and responsibilities of the lead State agency and any other State agencies involved in radon programs, and description of the roles and responsibilities of any municipal, district, or areawide organization involved in radon programs.

(3) A description of the activities and programs related to radon which the State proposes in such year.

(4) A budget specifying Federal and State funding of each element of activity of the grant application.

(5) A 3–year plan which outlines long range program goals and objectives, tasks necessary to achieve them, and resource requirements for the entire 3–year period, including anticipated State funding levels and desired Federal funding levels. This clause shall apply only for the initial year in which a grant application is made.

(c) Eligible Activities.—Activities eligible for grant assistance under this section are the following:

(1) Survey of radon levels, including special surveys of geographic areas or classes of buildings (such as, among others, public buildings, school buildings, high-risk residential construction types).

(2) Development of public information and educational materials concerning radon assessment, mitigation, and control programs.

(3) Implementation of programs to control radon in existing and new structures.

(4) Purchase by the State of radon measurement equipment or devices.

(5) Purchase and maintenance of analytical equipment connected to radon measurement and analysis, including costs of calibration of such equipment.

(6) Payment of costs of Environmental Protection Agency-approved training programs related to radon for permanent State or local employees.

(7) Payment of general overhead and program administration costs.

(8) Development of a data storage and management system for information concerning radon occurrence, levels, and programs.

(9) Payment of costs of demonstration of radon mitigation methods and technologies as approved by the Administrator, including State participation in the Environmental Protection Agency Home Evaluation Program.

(10) A toll-free radon hotline to provide information and technical assistance.

(d) Preference to Certain States.—Beginning in fiscal year 1991, the Administrator shall give a preference for grant assistance under this section to States that have made reasonable efforts to ensure the adoption, by the authorities which regulate building construction within that State or political subdivisions within States, of the model construction standards and techniques for new buildings developed under section 304 .

(e) Priority Activities and Projects.—The Administrator shall support eligible activities contained in State applications with the full amount of available funds. In the event that State applications for funds exceed the total funds available in a fiscal year, the Administrator shall give priority to activities or projects proposed by States based on each of the following criteria:

(1) The seriousness and extent of the radon contamination problem to be addressed.

(2) The potential for the activity or project to bring about reduction in radon levels.

(3) The potential for development of innovative radon assessment techniques, mitigation measures as approved by the Administrator, or program management approaches which may be of use to other States.

(4) Any other uniform criteria that the Administrator deems necessary to promote the goals of the grant program and that the Administrator provides to States before the application process.

(f) Federal Share.—The Federal share of the cost of radon program activities implemented with Federal assistance under this section in any fiscal year shall not exceed 75 percent of the costs incurred by the State in implementing such program in the first year of a grant to such State, 60 percent in the second year, and 50 percent in the third year. Federal assistance shall be made on the condition that the non-Federal share is provided from non- Federal funds.

(g) Assistance to Local Governments.—States may, at the Governor's discretion, use funds from grants under this section to assist local governments in implementation of activities eligible for assistance under paragraphs (2), (3), and (6) of subsection (c).

(h) Information.—

(1) The Administrator may request such information, data, and reports developed by the State as he considers necessary to make the determination of continuing eligibility under this section.

(2) Any State receiving Funds under this section shall provide to the Administrator all radon-related information generated in its activities, including the results of radon surveys, mitigation demonstration projects, and risk communication studies.

(3) Any State receiving funds under this section shall maintain, and make available to the public, a list of firms and individuals within the State that have received a passing rating under the Environmental Protection Agency proficiency rating program referred to in section 305(a)(2) . The list shall also include the address and phone number of such firms and individuals, together with the proficiency rating received by each. The Administrator shall make such list available to the public at appropriate locations in each State which does not

receive funds under this section unless the State assumes such responsibility.

(i) Limitations.—

(1) No grant may be made under this section in any fiscal year to a State which in the preceding fiscal year received a grant under this section unless the Administrator determines that such State satisfactorily implemented the activities funded by the grant in such preceding fiscal year.

(2) The costs of implementing paragraphs (4) and (9) of subsection (c) shall not in the aggregate exceed 50 percent of the amount of any grant awarded under this section to a State in a fiscal year. In implementing such paragraphs, a state should make every effort, consistent with the goals and successful operation of the State radon program, to give a preference to low-income persons.

(3) The costs of general overhead and program administration under subsection (c)(7) shall not exceed 25 percent of the amount of any grant awarded under this section to a State in a fiscal year.

(4) A State may use funds received under this section for financial assistance to persons only to the extent such assistance is related to demonstration projects or the purchase and analysis of radon measurement devices.

(j) Authorization.—

(1) There is authorized to be appropriated for grant assistance under this section an amount not to exceed $10,000,000 for each of fiscal years 1989, 1990, and 1991.

(2) There is authorized to be appropriated for the purpose of administering the grant program under this section such sums as may be necessary for each of such fiscal years.

(3) Notwithstanding any other provision of this section, not more than 10 percent of the amount appropriated to carry out this section may be used to make grants to any one State.

(4) Funds not obligated to States in the fiscal year for which funds are appropriated under this section shall remain available for obligation during the next fiscal year.

(5) No amount appropriated under this subsection may be used to cover the costs of the proficiency rating program under section 305(a)(2) .

§2667. Radon in Schools. [Sec. 307]

(a) Study of Radon in Schools.—

(1) Authority.—The Administrator shall conduct a study for the purpose of determining the extent of radon contamination in the Nation's school buildings.

(2) List of high probability areas.—In carrying out such study, the Administrator shall identify and compile a list of areas within the United States which the Administrator determines have a high probability of including schools which have elevated levels of radon.

(3) Basis of list.—In compiling such list, the Administrator shall make such determinations on the basis of, among other things, each of the following:

(A) Geological data.

(B) Data on high radon levels in homes and other structures nearby any such school.

(C) Physical characteristics of the school buildings.

(4) Survey.—In conducting such study the Administrator shall design a survey which when completed allows Congress to characterize the extent of radon contamination in schools in each State. The survey shall include testing from a representative sample of schools in each high-risk area identified in paragraph (1) and shall include additional testing, to the extent resources are available for such testing. The survey also shall include any reliable testing data supplied by States, schools, or other parties.

(5) Assistance.—

(A) The Administrator shall make available to the appropriate agency of each State, as designated by the Governor of such State, a list of high risk areas within each State, including a delineation of such areas and any other data available to the Administrator for schools in that State. To assist such agencies, the Administrator also shall provide guidance and data detailing the risks associated with high radon levels, technical guidance and related information concerning testing for radon within schools, and methods of reducing radon levels.

(B) In addition to the assistance authorized by subparagraph (A), the Administrator is authorized to make available to the appropriate agency of each State, as designated by the Governor of such State, devices suitable for use by such agencies in conducting tests for radon within the schools under the jurisdiction of any such State agency. The Administrator is authorized to make available to such agencies the use of laboratories of the Environmental Protection Agency, or to recommend laboratories, to evaluate any such devices for the presence of radon levels.

(6) Diagnostic and remedial efforts.—The Administrator is authorized to select, from high-risk areas identified in paragraph (2), school buildings or purposes of enabling the Administrator to undertake diagnostic and remedial efforts to reduce the levels of randon in such school buildings. Such diagnostic and remedial efforts shall be carried out with a view to developing technology and expertise for the purpose of making such technology and expertise available to any local educational agency and the several States.

(7) Status report.—On or before October 1, 1989, the Administrator shall submit to the Congress a status report with respect to action taken by the Administrator in conducting the study required by this section, including the results of the Administrator's diagnostic and remedial work. On or before October 1, 1989, the Administrator shall submit a final report setting forth the results of the study conducted pursuant to this section, including the results of the Administrator's diagnostic and remedial work, and the recommendations of the Administrator.

(b) Authorization.—For the purpose of carrying out the provisions of paragraph (6) of subsection (a), there are authorized to be appropriated such sums, not to exceed $500,000, as may be necessary. For the purpose of carrying out the provisions of this section other than such paragraph (6), there are authorized to be appropriated such sums, not to exceed $1,000,000 as may be necessary.

§2668. Regional Radon Training Centers. [Sec. 308]

(a) Funding Program.—Upon application of colleges, universities, institutions of higher learning, or consortia of such institutions, the Administrator may make a grant or cooperative agreement, subject to such terms and conditions as the Administrator considers appropriate, under this section to the applicant for the purpose of establishing and operating a regional radon training center.

(b) Purpose of the Centers.—The purpose of a regional radon training center is to develop information and provide training to Federal and State officials, professional and private firms, and the public regarding the health risks posed by radon and demonstrated methods of radon measurement and mitigation.

(c) Applications.—Any colleges, universities, institutions of higher learning or consortia of such institutions may submit an application for funding under this section. Such applications shall be submitted to the Administrator in such form and containing such information as the Administrator may require.

(d) Selection Criteria.—The Administrator shall support at least 3 eligible applications with the full amount of available funds. The Administrator shall select recipients of funding under this section to ensure that funds are equitably allocated among regions of the United States, and on the basis of each of the following criteria:

(1) The extent to which the applicant's program will promote the purpose described in subsection (b).

(2) The demonstrated expertise of the applicant regarding radon measurement and mitigation methods and other radon-related issues.

(3) The demonstrated expertise of the applicant in radon training and in activities relating to information development and dissemination.

(4) The seriousness of the radon problem in the region.

(5) The geographical coverage of the proposed center.

(6) Any other uniform criteria that the Administrator deems necessary to promote the purpose described in subsection (b) and that the Administrator provides to potential applicants prior to the application process.

(e) Termination of Funding.—No funding may be given under this section in any fiscal year to an applicant which in the preceding fiscal year received funding under this section unless the Administrator determines that the recipient satisfactorily implemented the activities that were funded in the preceding year.

(f) Authorization.—There is authorized to be appropriated to carry out the program under this section not to exceed $1,000,000 for each of fiscal years 1989, 1990, and 1991.

§2669. Study of Radon in Federal Buildings. [Sec. 309]

(a) Study Requirement.—The head of each Federal department or agency that owns a Federal building shall conduct a study for the purpose of determining the extent of radon contamination in such buildings. Such study shall include, in the case of a Federal building using a nonpublic water source (such as a well or other groundwater), radon contamination of the water.

(b) High-Risk Federal Buildings.—

(1) The Administrator shall identify and compile a list of areas within the United States which the Administrator, in consultation with Federal departments and agencies, determines have a high probability of including Federal buildings which have elevated levels of radon.

(2) In compiling such list, the Administrator shall make such determinations on the basis of, among other things, the following:

(A) Geological data.

(B) Data on high radon levels in homes and other structures near any such Federal buildings.

(C) Physical characteristics of the Federal buildings.

(c) Study Designs.—Studies required under subsection (a) shall be based on design criteria specified by the Administrator. The head of each Federal department or agency conducting such a study shall submit, not later than July 1, 1989, a study design to the Administrator for approval. The study design shall follow the most recent Environmental Protection Agency guidance documents, including 'A Citizen's Guide to Radon'; the 'Interim Protocol for screening and Follow Up: Radon and Radon Decay Products Massachusetts; the 'Interim Indoor Randon & Radon Decay Product Measurement Protocol'; and any other recent guidance documents. The study design shall include testing data from a representative sample of Federal buildings in each high-risk area identified in subsection (b). The study design also shall include additional testing data to the extent resources are available, including any reliable data supplied by Federal agencies, States, or other parties.

(d) Information on Risks and Testing.—

(1) The Administrator shall provide to the departments or agencies conducting studies under subsection (a) the following:

(A) Guidance and data detailing the risks associated with high radon levels.

(B) Technical guidance and related information concerning testing for radon within Federal buildings and water supplies.

(C) Technical guidance and related information concerning methods for reducing radon levels.

(2) In addition to the assistance required by paragraph (1), the Administrator is authorized to make available, on a cost reimbursable basis, to the departments or agencies conducting studies under subsection (a) devices suitable for use by such departments or agencies in con ducting tests for radon within Federal buildings. For the purpose of assisting such departments or agencies in evaluating any such devices for the presence of radon levels, the Administrator is authorized to recommend laboratories or to make available to such departments or agencies, on a cost reimbursable basis, the use of laboratories of the Environmental Protection Agency.

(e) Study deadline.—Not later than June 1, 1990, the head of each Federal department or agency conducting a study under subsection (a) shall complete the study and provide the study to the Administrator.

(f) Report to Congress.—Not later than October 1, 1990, the Administrator shall submit a report to the Congress describing the results of the studies conducted pursuant to subsection (a).

§2670. Regulations. [Sec. 310]

The Administrator is authorized to issue such regulations as may be necessary to carry out the provisions of this title.

§2671. Additional Authorizations. [Sec. 311]

Amounts authorized to be appropriated in this title for purposes of carrying out the provisions of this title are in addition to amounts authorized to be appropriated under other provisions of law for radon– related activities.

TITLE IV—LEAD EXPOSURE REDUCTION

[Title IV added by PL 102–550,Oct. 28, 1992]

§2681. Definitions. [Sec. 401]

For the purposes of this title:

(1) Abatement.—The term "abatement" means any set of measures designed to permanently eliminate lead–based paint hazards in accordance with standards established by the Administrator under this title. Such term includes—

(A) the removal of lead–based paint and lead–contaminated dust, the permanent containment or encapsulation of lead–based paint, the replacement of lead–painted surfaces or fixtures, and the removal or covering of lead–contaminated soil; and

(B) all preparation, cleanup, disposal, and postabatement clearance testing activities associated with such measures.

(2) Accessible surface.—The term "accessible surface" means an interior or exterior surface painted with lead–based paint that is accessible for a young child to mouth or chew.

(3) Deteriorated paint.—The term "deteriorated paint" means any interior or exterior paint that is peeling, chipping, chalking or cracking or any paint located on an interior or exterior surface or fixture that is damaged or deteriorated.

(4) Evaluation.—The term "evaluation" means risk assessment, inspection, or risk assessment and inspection.

(5) Friction surface.—The term "friction surface" means an interior or exterior surface that is subject to abrasion or friction, including certain window, floor, and stair surfaces.

(6) Impact surface.—The term "impact surface" means an interior or exterior surface that is subject to damage by repeated impacts, for example, certain parts of door frames.

(7) Inspection.—The term "inspection" means (A) a surface–by–surface investigation to determine the presence of lead–based paint, as provided in section 302(c) of the Lead–Based Paint Poisoning Prevention Act, and (B) the provision of a report explaining the results of the investigation.

(8) Interim controls.—The term "interim controls" means a set of measures designed to reduce temporarily human exposure or likely exposure to lead–based paint hazards, including specialized cleaning, repairs, maintenance, painting, temporary containment, ongoing monitoring of lead–based paint hazards or potential hazards, and the establishment and operation of management and resident education programs.

(9) Lead–based paint.—The term "lead– based paint" means paint or other surface coatings that contain lead in excess of 1.0 milligrams per centimeter squared or 0.5 percent by weight or (A) in the case of paint or other surface coatings on target housing, such lower level as may be established by the Secretary of Housing and Urban Development, as defined in section 302(c) of the Lead–Based Paint Poisoning Prevention Act, or (B) in the case of any other paint or surface coatings, such other level as may be established by the Administrator.

(10) Lead–based paint hazard.—The term "lead–based paint hazard" means any condition that causes exposure to lead from lead–contaminated dust, lead–contaminated soil, lead–contaminated paint that is deteriorated or present in accessible surfaces, friction surfaces, or impact surfaces that would result in adverse human health effects as established by the Administrator under this title.

(11) Lead–contaminated dust.—The term "lead–contaminated dust" means surface dust in residential dwellings that contains an area or mass concentration of lead in excess of levels determined by the Administrator under this title to pose a threat of adverse health effects in pregnant women or young children.

(12) Lead–contaminated soil.—The term "lead–contaminated soil" means bare soil on residential real property that contains lead at or in excess of the levels determined to be hazardous to human health by the Administrator under this title.

(13) Reduction.—The term "reduction" means measures designed to reduce or eliminate human exposure to lead–based paint hazards through methods including interim controls and abatement.

(14) Residential dwelling.—The term "residential dwelling" means—

(A) a single–family dwelling, including attached structures such as porches and stoops; or

(B) a single–family dwelling unit in a structure that contains more than 1 separate residential dwelling unit, and in which each such unit is used or occupied, or intended to be used or occupied, in whole or in part, as the home or residence of 1 or more persons.

(15) Residential real property.—The term "residential real property" means real property on which there is situated 1 or more residential dwellings used or occupied, or intended to be used or occupied, in whole or in part, as the home or residence of 1 or more persons.

(16) Risk assessment.—The term "risk assessment" means an on–site investigation to determine and report the existence, nature, severity and location of lead–based paint hazards in residential dwellings, including—

(A) information gathering regarding the age and history of the housing and occupancy by children under age 6;

(B) visual inspection;

(C) limited wipe sampling or other environmental sampling techniques;

(D) other activity as may be appropriate; and

(E) provision of a report explaining the results of the investigation.

(17) Target housing.—The term "target housing" means any housing constructed prior to 1978,

except housing for the elderly or persons with disabilities (unless any child who is less than 6 years of age resides or is expected to reside in such housing for the elderly or persons with disabilities) or any 0–bedroom dwelling. In the case of jurisdictions which banned the sale or use of lead–based paint prior to 1978, the Secretary of Housing and Urban Development, at the Secretary's discretion, may designate an earlier date.

§2682. Lead-Based Paint Activities Training and Certification. [Sec. 402]

(a) Regulations.—

(1) In general.—Not later than 18 months after the date of the enactment of this section, the Administrator shall, in consultation with the Secretary of Labor, the Secretary of Housing and Urban Development, and the Secretary of Health and Human Services (acting through the Director of the National Institute for Occupational Safety and Health), promulgate final regulations governing lead–based paint activities to ensure that individuals engaged in such activities are properly trained; that training programs are accredited; and that contractors engaged in such activities are certified. Such regulations shall contain standards for performing lead–based paint activities, taking into account reliability, effectiveness, and safety. Such regulations shall require that all risk assessment, inspection, and abatement activities performed in target housing shall be performed by certified contractors, as such term is defined in section 1004 of the Residential Lead–Based Paint Hazard Reduction Act of 1992. The provisions of this section shall supersede the provisions set forth under the heading "Lead Abatement Training and Certification" and under the heading "Training Grants' in title III of the Act entitled "An Act making appropriations for the Departments of Veterans Affairs and Housing and Urban Development, and for sundry independent agencies, commissions, corporations, and offices for the fiscal year ending September 30, 1992, and for other purposes", Public Law 102–139, and upon the enactment of this section the provisions set forth in such public law under such headings shall cease to have any force and effect.

(2) Accreditation of training programs.—Final regulations promulgated under paragraph (1) shall contain specific requirements for the accreditation of lead–based paint activities training programs for workers, supervisors, inspectors and planners, and other individuals involved in lead–based paint activities, including, but not limited to, each of the following:

(A) Minimum requirements for the accreditation of training providers.

(B) Minimum training curriculum requirements.

(C) Minimum training hour requirements.

(D) Minimum hands–on training requirements.

(E) Minimum trainee competency and proficiency requirements.

(F) Minimum requirements for training program quality control.

(3) Accreditation and certification fees.—The Administrator (or the State in the case of an authorized State program) shall impose a fee on—

(A) persons operating training programs accredited under this title; and

(B) lead–based paint activities contractors certified in accordance with paragraph (1).

The fees shall be established at such level as is necessary to cover the costs of administering and enforcing the standards and regulations under this section which are applicable to such programs and contractors. The fee shall not be imposed on any State, local government, or nonprofit training program. The Administrator (or the State in the case of an authorized State program) may waive the fee for lead–based paint activities contractors under subparagraph (A) for the purpose of training their own employees.

(b) Lead–Based Paint Activities.—For purposes of this title, the term "lead–based paint activities" means—

(1) in the case of target housing, risk assessment, inspection, and abatement; and

(2) in the case of any public building constructed before 1978, commercial building, bridge, or other structure or superstructure, identification of lead–based paint and materials containing lead–based paint, deleading, removal of lead from bridges, and demolition.

For purposes of paragraph (2), the term "deleading" means activities conducted by a person who offers to eliminate lead–based paint or lead–based paint hazards or to plan such activities.

(c) Renovation and Remodeling.—

(1) Guidelines.—In order to reduce the risk of exposure to lead in connection with renovation and remodeling of target housing, public

buildings constructed before 1978, and commercial buildings, the Administrator shall, within 18 months after the enactment of this section, promulgate guidelines for the conduct of such renovation and remodeling activities which may create a risk of exposure to dangerous levels of lead. The Administrator shall disseminate such guidelines to persons engaged in such renovation and remodeling through hardware and paint stores, employee organizations, trade groups, State and local agencies, and through other appropriate means.

(2) Study of certification.—The Administrator shall conduct a study of the extent to which persons engaged in various types of renovation and remodeling activities in target housing, public buildings constructed before 1978, and commercial buildings are exposed to lead in the conduct of such activities or disturb lead and create a lead–based paint hazard on a regular or occasional basis. The Administrator shall complete such study and publish the results thereof within 30 months after the enactment of this section.

(3) Certification determination.—Within 4 years after the enactment of this section, the Administrator shall revise the regulations under subsection (a) to apply the regulations to renovation or remodeling activities in target housing, public buildings constructed before 1978, and commercial buildings that create lead–based paint hazards. In determining which contractors are engaged in such activities, the Administrator shall utilize the results of the study under paragraph (2) and consult with the representatives of labor organizations, lead–based paint activities contractors, persons engaged in remodeling and renovation, experts in lead health effects, and others. If the Administrator determines that any category of contractors engaged in renovation or remodeling does not require certification, the Administrator shall publish an explanation of the basis for that determination.

§2683. Identification of Dangerous Levels of Lead. [Sec. 403]

Within 18 months after the enactment of this title, the Administrator shall promulgate regulations which shall identify, for purposes of this title and the Residential Lead–Based Paint Hazard Reduction Act of 1992, lead–based paint hazards, lead–contaminated dust, and lead–contaminated soil.

§2684. Authorized State Programs. [Sec. 404]

(a) Approval.—Any State which seeks to administer and enforce the standards, regulations, or other requirements established under section 402 or 406, or both, may, after notice and opportunity for public hearing, develop and submit to the Administrator an application, in such form as the Administrator shall require, for authorization of such a State program. Any such State may also certify to the Administrator at the time of submitting such program that the State program meets the requirements of paragraphs (1) and (2) of subsection (b). Upon submission of such certification, the State program shall be deemed to be authorized under this section, and shall apply in such State in lieu of the corresponding Federal program under section 402 or 406, or both, as the case may be, until such time as the Administrator disapproves the program or withdraws the authorization.

(b) Approval or Disapproval.—Within 180 days following submission of an application under subsection (a), the Administrator shall approve or disapprove the application. The Administrator may approve the application only if, after notice and after opportunity for public hearing, the Administrator finds that—

(1) the State program is at least as protective of human health and the environment as the Federal program under section 402 or 406, or both, as the case may be, and

(2) such State program provides adequate enforcement. Upon authorization of a State program under this section, it shall be unlawful for any person to violate or fail or refuse to comply with any requirement of such program.

(c) Withdrawal of Authorization.—If a State is not administering and enforcing a program authorized under this section in compliance with standards, regulations, and other requirements of this title, the Administrator shall so notify the State and, if corrective action is not completed within a reasonable time, not to exceed 180 days, the Administrator shall withdraw authorization of such program and establish a Federal program pursuant to this title.

(d) Model State Program.—Within 18 months after the enactment of this title, the Administrator shall promulgate a model State program which may be adopted by any State which seeks to administer and enforce a State program under this title. Such model program shall, to the extent practicable, encourage States to utilize existing State and local certification and accreditation programs and procedures. Such program shall encourage reciprocity among the States with respect to the certification under section 402.

(e) Other State Requirements.—Nothing in this title shall be construed to prohibit any State or political subdivision thereof from imposing any requirements which are more stringent than those imposed by this title.

(f) State and Local Certification.—The regulations under this title shall, to the extent appropriate, encourage States to seek program authorization and to use existing State and local certification and accreditation procedures, except that a State or local government shall not require more than 1 certification under this section for any lead–based paint activities contractor to carry out lead–based paint activities in the State or political subdivision thereof.

(g) Grants to States.—The Administrator is authorized to make grants to States to develop and carry out authorized State programs under this section. The grants shall be subject to such terms and conditions as the Administrator may establish to further the purposes of this title.

(h) Enforcement by Administrator.—If a State does not have a State program authorized under this section and in effect by the date which is 2 years after promulgation of the regulations under section 402 or 406, the Administrator shall, by such date, establish a Federal program for section 402 or 406 (as the case may be) for such State and administer and enforce such program in such State.

§2685. Lead Abatement and Measurement.
[Sec. 405]

(a) Program To Promote Lead Exposure Abatement.—The Administrator, in cooperation with other appropriate Federal departments and agencies, shall conduct a comprehensive program to promote safe, effective, and affordable monitoring, detection, and abatement of lead–based paint and other lead exposure hazards.

(b) Standards for Environmental Sampling Laboratories.—

(1) The Administrator shall establish protocols, criteria, and minimum performance standards for laboratory analysis of lead in paint films, soil, and dust. Within 2 years after the enactment of this title, the Administrator, in consultation with the Secretary of Health and Human Services, shall establish a program to certify laboratories as qualified to test substances for lead content unless the Administrator determines, by the date specified in this paragraph, that effective voluntary accreditation programs are in place and operating on a nationwide basis at the time of such determination. To be certified under such program, a laboratory shall, at a minimum, demonstrate an ability to test substances accurately for lead content.

(2) Not later than 24 months after the date of the enactment of this section, and annually thereafter, the Administrator shall publish and make available to the public a list of certified or accredited environmental sampling laboratories.

(3) If the Administrator determines under paragraph (1) that effective voluntary accreditation programs are in place for environmental sampling laboratories, the Administrator shall review the performance and effectiveness of such programs within 3 years after such determination. If, upon such review, the Administrator determines that the voluntary accreditation programs are not effective in assuring the quality and consistency of laboratory analyses, the Administrator shall, not more than 12 months thereafter, establish a certification program that meets the requirements of paragraph (1).

(c) Exposure Studies.—

(1) The Secretary of Health and Human Services (hereafter in this subsection referred to as the "Secretary"), acting through the Director of the Centers for Disease Control, (CDC), and the Director of the National Institute of Environmental Health Sciences, shall jointly conduct a study of the sources of lead exposure in children who have elevated blood lead levels (or other indicators of elevated lead body burden), as defined by the Director of the Centers for Disease Control.

(2) The Secretary, in consultation with the Director of the National Institute for Occupational Safety and Health, shall conduct a comprehensive study of means to reduce hazardous occupational lead abatement exposures. This study shall include, at a minimum, each of the following—

(A) Surveillance and intervention capability in the States to identify and prevent hazardous exposures to lead abatement workers.

(B) Demonstration of lead abatement control methods and devices and work practices to identify and prevent hazardous lead exposures in the workplace.

(C) Evaluation, in consultation with the National Institute of Environmental Health

Sciences, of health effects of low and high levels of occupational lead exposures on reproductive, neurological, renal, and cardiovascular health.

(D) Identification of high risk occupational settings to which prevention activities and resources should be targeted.

(E) A study assessing the potential exposures and risks from lead to janitorial and custodial workers.

(3) The studies described in paragraphs (1) and (2) shall, as appropriate, examine the relative contributions to elevated lead body burden from each of the following:

(A) Drinking water.

(B) Food.

(C) Lead–based paint and dust from lead–based paint.

(D) Exterior sources such as ambient air and lead in soil.

(E) Occupational exposures, and other exposures that the Secretary determines to be appropriate.

(4) Not later than 30 months after the date of the enactment of this section, the Secretary shall submit a report to the Congress concerning the studies described in paragraphs (1) and (2).

(d) Public Education.—

(1) The Administrator, in conjunction with the Secretary of Health and Human Services, acting through the Director of the Agency for Toxic Substances and Disease Registry, and in conjunction with the Secretary of Housing and Urban Development, shall sponsor public education and outreach activities to increase public awareness of—

(A) the scope and severity of lead poisoning from household sources;

(B) potential exposure to sources of lead in schools and childhood day care centers;

(C) the implications of exposures for men and women, particularly those of childbearing age;

(D) the need for careful, quality, abatement and management actions;

(E) the need for universal screening of children;

(F) other components of a lead poisoning prevention program;

(G) the health consequences of lead exposure resulting from lead–based paint hazards;

(H) risk assessment and inspection methods for lead–based paint hazards; and

(I) measures to reduce the risk of lead exposure from lead–based paint.

(2) The activities described in paragraph (1) shall be designed to provide educational services and information to—

(A) health professionals;

(B) the general public, with emphasis on parents of young children;

(C) homeowners, landlords, and tenants;

(D) consumers of home improvement products;

(E) the residential real estate industry; and

(F) the home renovation industry.

(3) In implementing the activities described in paragraph (1), the Administrator shall assure coordination with the President's Commission on Environmental Quality's education and awareness campaign on lead poisoning.

(4) The Administrator, in consultation with the Chairman of the Consumer Product Safety Commission, shall develop information to be distributed by retailers of home improvement products to provide consumers with practical information related to the hazards of renovation and remodeling where lead–based paint may be present.

(e) Technical Assistance.—

(1) Clearinghouse.—Not later than 6 months after the enactment of this subsection, the Administrator shall establish, in consultation with the Secretary of Housing and Urban Development and the Director of the Centers for Disease Control, a National Clearinghouse on Childhood Lead Poisoning (hereinafter in this section referred to as "Clearinghouse"). The Clearinghouse shall—

(A) collect, evaluate, and disseminate current information on the assessment and reduction of lead–based paint hazards, adverse health effects, sources of exposure, detection and risk assessment methods, environmental hazards abatement, and clean–up standards;

(B) maintain a rapid–alert system to inform certified lead–based paint activities contractors of significant developments in research related to lead–based paint hazards; and

(C) perform any other duty that the Administrator determines necessary to achieve the purposes of this Act.

(2) Hotline.—Not later than 6 months after the enactment of this subsection, the Administra-

tor, in cooperation with other Federal agencies and with State and local governments, shall establish a single lead-based paint hazard hotline to provide the public with answers to questions about lead poisoning prevention and referrals to the Clearinghouse for technical information.

(f) Products for Lead-Based Paint Activities.—Not later than 30 months after the date of enactment of this section, the President shall, after notice and opportunity for comment, establish by rule appropriate criteria, testing protocols, and performance characteristics as are necessary to ensure, to the greatest extent possible and consistent with the purposes and policy of this title, that lead-based paint hazard evaluation and reduction products introduced into commerce after a period specified in the rule are effective for the intended use described by the manufacturer. The rule shall identify the types or classes of products that are subject to such rule. The President, in implementation of the rule, shall, to the maximum extent possible, utilize independent testing laboratories, as appropriate, and consult with such entities and others in developing the rules. The President may delegate the authorities under this subsection to the Environmental Protection Agency or the Secretary of Commerce or such other appropriate agency.

§2686. Lead Hazard Information Pamphlet. [Sec. 406]

(a) Lead Hazard Information Pamphlet.—Not later than 2 years after the enactment of this section, after notice and opportunity for comment, the Administrator of the Environmental Protection Agency, in consultation with the Secretary of Housing and Urban Development and with the Secretary of Health and Human Services, shall publish, and from time to time revise, a lead hazard information pamphlet to be used in connection with this title and section 1018 of the Residential Lead-Based Paint Hazard Reduction Act of 1992. The pamphlet shall—

(1) contain information regarding the health risks associated with exposure to lead;

(2) provide information on the presence of lead-based paint hazards in federally assisted, federally owned, and target housing;

(3) describe the risks of lead exposure for children under 6 years of age, pregnant women, women of childbearing age, persons involved in home renovation, and others residing in a dwelling with lead-based paint hazards;

(4) describe the risks of renovation in a dwelling with lead-based paint hazards;

(5) provide information on approved methods for evaluating and reducing lead-based paint hazards and their effectiveness in identifying, reducing, eliminating, or preventing exposure to lead-based paint hazards;

(6) advise persons how to obtain a list of contractors certified pursuant to this title in lead-based paint hazard evaluation and reduction in the area in which the pamphlet is to be used;

(7) state that a risk assessment or inspection for lead-based paint is recommended prior to the purchase, lease, or renovation of target housing;

(8) state that certain State and local laws impose additional requirements related to lead-based paint in housing and provide a listing of Federal, State, and local agencies in each State, including address and telephone number, that can provide information about applicable laws and available governmental and private assistance and financing; and

(9) provide such other information about environmental hazards associated with residential real property as the Administrator deems appropriate.

(b) Renovation of Target Housing.—Within 2 years after the enactment of this section, the Administrator shall promulgate regulations under this subsection to require each person who performs for compensation a renovation of target housing to provide a lead hazard information pamphlet to the owner and occupant of such housing prior to commencing the renovation.

§2687. Regulations. [Sec. 407]

The regulations of the Administrator under this title shall include such recordkeeping and reporting requirements as may be necessary to insure the effective implementation of this title. The regulations may be amended from time to time as necessary.

§2688. Control of Lead-Based Paint Hazards at Federal Facilities. [Sec. 408]

Each department, agency, and instrumentality of executive, legislative, and judicial branches of the Federal Government (1) having jurisdiction over any property or facility, or (2) engaged in any activity resulting, or which may result, in a lead-based paint hazard, and each officer, agent, or employee thereof, shall be subject to, and comply with, all Federal, State, interstate, and local requirements, both substantive and procedural (including any requirement for certification, licensing, recordkeeping, or reporting or any provisions for injunctive relief and such sanctions as may be imposed by a court to enforce such relief) respecting lead–based paint, lead–based paint activities, and lead–based paint hazards in the same manner, and to the same extent as any nongovernmental entity is subject to such requirements, including the payment of reasonable service charges. The Federal, State, interstate, and local substantive and procedural requirements referred to in this subsection include, but are not limited to, all administrative orders and all civil and administrative penalties and fines regardless of whether such penalties or fines are punitive or coercive in nature, or whether imposed for isolated, intermittent or continuing violations. The United States hereby expressly waives any immunity otherwise applicable to the United States with respect to any such substantive or procedural requirement (including, but not limited to, any injunctive relief, administrative order, or civil or administrative penalty or fine referred to in the preceding sentence, or reasonable service charge). The reasonable service charges referred to in this section include, but are not limited to, fees or charges assessed for certification and licensing, as well as any other nondiscriminatory charges that are assessed in connection with a Federal, State, interstate, or local lead–based paint, lead–based paint activities, or lead–based paint hazard activities program. No agent, employee, or officer of the United States shall be personally liable for any civil penalty under any Federal, State, interstate, or local law relating to lead–based paint, lead–based paint activities, or lead–based paint hazards with respect to any act or omission within the scope of his official duties.

§2689. Prohibited Acts. [Sec. 409]

It shall be unlawful for any person to fail or refuse to comply with a provision of this title or with any rule or order issued under this title.

§2690. Relationship to Other Federal Law. [Sec. 410]

Nothing in this title shall affect the authority of other appropriate Federal agencies to establish or enforce any requirements which are at least as stringent as those established pursuant to this title.

§2691. General Provisions Relating to Administrative Proceedings. [Sec. 411]

(a) Applicability.—This section applies to the promulgation or revision of any regulation issued under this title.

(b) Rulemaking Docket.—Not later than the date of proposal of any action to which this section applies, the Administrator shall establish a rulemaking docket for such action (hereinafter in this subsection referred to as a "rule"). Whenever a rule applies only within a particular State, a second (identical) docket shall be established in the appropriate regional office of the Environmental Protection Agency.

(c) Inspection and Copying.—

(1) The rulemaking docket required under subsection (b) shall be open for inspection by the public at reasonable times specified in the notice of proposed rulemaking. Any person may copy documents contained in the docket. The Administrator shall provide copying facilities which may be used at the expense of the person seeking copies, but the Administrator may waive or reduce such expenses in such instances as the public interest requires. Any person may request copies by mail if the person pays the expenses, including personnel costs to do the copying.

(2) (A) Promptly upon receipt by the agency, all written comments and documentary information on the proposed rule received from any person for inclusion in the docket during the comment period shall be placed in the docket. The transcript of public hearings, if any, on the proposed rule shall also be included in the docket promptly upon receipt from the person who transcribed such hearings. All documents which become available after the proposed rule has been published and which the Administrator determines are of central relevance to the rulemaking shall be placed in the docket as soon as possible after their availability.

(B) The drafts of proposed rules submitted by the Administrator to the Office of Management and Budget for any interagency review process prior to proposal of any such rule, all documents accompanying such drafts, and all written comments thereon by other agencies and all written responses to such written comments by the Administrator shall be placed in the docket no later than the date of proposal of the rule. The drafts of the final rule submitted for such review process prior to promulgation and all such written comments thereon, all documents accompanying such drafts, and written responses thereto shall be placed in the docket no later than the date of promulgation.

(d) Explanation.—

(1) The promulgated rule shall be accompanied by an explanation of the reasons for any major changes in the promulgated rule from the proposed rule.

(2) The promulgated rule shall also be accompanied by a response to each of the significant comments, criticisms, and new data submitted in written or oral presentations during the comment period.

(3) The promulgated rule may not be based (in part or whole) on any information or data which has not been placed in the docket as of the date of such promulgation.

(e) Judicial Review.—The material referred to in subsection (c)(2)(B) shall not be included in the record for judicial review.

(f) Effective Date.—The requirements of this section shall take effect with respect to any rule the proposal of which occurs after 90 days after the date of the enactment of this section.

§2692. Authorization of Appropriations.
[Sec. 412]

There are authorized to be appropriated to carry out the purposes of this title such sums as may be necessary.

7

Federal Insecticide, Fungicide, and Rodenticide Act

INTRODUCTION

Initial federal efforts to regulate pesticides began in 1910, with the enactment of what was largely a labeling law intended to prevent the distribution of adulterated or misbranded products. The first pesticide control law was enacted in 1947 and required that pesticide products be registered with the Department of Agriculture. In cases where registration was denied, the manufacturer could still market the product after filing a protest. Although jurisdiction for administering the law first was placed with the Agriculture Department, it was passed to the Environmental Protection Agency when that agency was created in 1970.

In 1954, the Food and Drug Administration was given authority to establish pesticide residue tolerances—allowable limits for pesticide residues on food and on animal feed. This system has grown into a complicated cooperative scheme under which FDA sets pesticide limits for processed foods, the Department of Agriculture sets limits for edible portions of meat, and the Environmental Protection Agency sets limits for raw, unprocessed meat and agricultural products.

The basic format of the Federal Insecticide, Fungicide, and Rodenticide Act (FIFRA) was conceived in 1972 with the passage of P.L. 92-516. Under the law, no manufacturer may make or sell a product for use to control pests unless the compound is registered with EPA.

Congress also required that all pesticides registered before 1972 be reregistered by EPA so that the agency could obtain current toxicological, health, and environmental effects data. Amendments adopted in 1975 tempered some of the reregistration provisions and required EPA to submit proposed pesticide cancellations to a scientific review panel. Additional amendments enacted in 1978 allowed the agency to group active ingredients and reregister the products on a generic rather than an individual product basis. Although about 40,000 pest control products are registered with the agency, they contain only about 600 distinct active ingredients.

Although a number of cancellations followed the passage of the Act in 1972, critics of the law said the agency's reregistration process was too slow and argued that FIFRA needed revisions. They also charged that the degree to which EPA involved the public in its regulatory process needed to be expanded and that revisions were needed in the way the agency restricts the use of products that are determined to pose potential hazards to people and the environment.

By mid-1987, EPA had completed its review of only two active ingredients and issued interim registration standards for only 150 of the approximately 600 ingredients needing re-evaluation. With the reviews slated to last well into the 21st century and regulatory and financial resources being diverted to pay for indemnification of recently canceled products, EPA campaigned for Congress to repeal the indemnification requirements and speed up reregistration.

In response, the 100th Congress took up major and complicated FIFRA legislation, finally passing a pared-down version late in the session (P.L. 100-

532). Major changes were made to the indemnification and disposal sections of the law. Reimbursements for remaining stocks of banned products were limited to certain users and payments to manufacturers were eliminated. Pesticide registrants were required to begin taking up much of the responsibility for storage and disposal of these banned pesticides, a cost that EPA had borne.

In addition, the amendments required pesticide manufacturers to pay fees of up to $150,000 for each active ingredient registered with EPA, along with an annual fee of $425 per product.

The most controversial elements of the legislation—such as those dealing with ground water protection and farmer liability for ground water pollution—were dropped to win passage before the 100th Congress adjourned. Some legislators vowed to take up these issues again in 1989, along with other thorny problems such as food safety, pesticide residues on food, and speeding up the process of getting problem products off the market.

One of the options discussed for making it easier to cancel registrations was eliminating the administrative hearing process for challenging an EPA cancellation or suspension order, thus allowing challenges to go directly to federal court. Agency officials also discussed with congressional staff the possibility of establishing a more permissive standard for suspension and limiting all pesticide registrations to a specific number of years, at the end of which they would have to be renewed.

In the first session of the 100th Congress, however, most attention centered on other issues, such as beginning the long and difficult process of reauthorizing the Clean Air Act, and no new FIFRA amendments were enacted. Congress again took up FIFRA in 1990 and acted on some of the unresolved issues, including submission of data for minor agricultural uses.

In 1991, Congress amended the fee levels in FIFRA (P.L. 102-237, the Food, Agriculture, Conservation, and Trade Act Amendments of 1991), but otherwise did not significantly amend the statute. Also in 1991, the Supreme Court ruled that FIFRA did not prevent local governments from enacting controls on pesticide use (*Wisconsin Public Intervenor v. Mortier,* 501 U.S. 597, 33 ER Cases 1265).

In July 1992, however, the U.S. Court of Appeals for the Ninth Circuit upheld a strict interpretation of Section 409 (the Delaney Clause) of the Federal Food, Drug, and Cosmetic Act, which is administered by EPA (*Les v. EPA,* 968 F.2d 985). The Delaney Clause prohibits cancer-causing additives in processed foods. However, Section 408 of the FFDCA sets legal limits for pesticide residues on raw agricultural commodities, and the act treats residues that are concentrated in processed foods at levels above these legal limits as food additives. EPA had tried to deal with this apparent contradiction by allowing residues at levels that would present only "negligible" risks of cancer.

When Congress took up FIFRA in the second session of the 103rd Congress, pesticide residues and the Delaney Clause figured prominently. Other issues that have been hanging fire for some time and will also command congressional attention include expedited removal of problem pesticides from the market, preemption of state restrictions on pesticide use, expedited review of "safer" pesticides, ground water contamination, stronger civil and criminal penalties, and minor use pesticides. The only amendment given any real chance of passage in the 103rd Congress, however, concerned the Delaney Clause and related food-safety reform issues.

FINDING LIST

FEDERAL INSECTICIDE, FUNGICIDE, AND RODENTICIDE ACT

Public Law 92–516, effective Oct. 21, 1972, 86 Stat. 975.

7 U.S.C. §§136 et seq.

Amended by PL 94–51, July 2, 1975; PL 94–109, Oct. 10, 1975; PL 94–140, Nov. 28, 1975; PL 95–251, March 27, 1978; PL 95–396, Sept. 30, 1978; PL 96–539, Dec. 17, 1980; PL 98–620, Nov. 8, 1984; PL 100–532, Oct. 25, 1988; PL 101–624, Nov. 28, 1990; PL 102–237, Dec. 13, 1991.

Short Title and Table of Contents. [Sec. 1]

(a) Short Title. — This Act may be cited as the "Federal Insecticide, Fungicide, and Rodenticide Act".

(b) Table of Contents.— [Omitted]

[§1 amended by PL 100–532; PL 101–624]

§136. Definitions. [Sec. 2]

For purposes of this Act—

(a) Active Ingredient.—the term "active ingredient" means—

(1) in the case of a pesticide other than a plant regulator, defoliant, or desiccant, an ingredient which will prevent, destroy, repel, or mitigate any pest;

(2) in the case of a plant regulator, an ingredient which, through physiological action, will accelerate or retard the rate of growth or rate of maturation or otherwise alter the behavior of ornamental or crop plants or the product thereof;

(3) in the case of a defoliant, an ingredient which will cause the leaves or foliage to drop from a plant; and

(4) in the case of a desiccant, an ingredient which will artificially accelerate the drying of plant tissue.

(b) Administrator.—The term "Administrator" means the Administrator of the Environmental Protection Agency.

(c) Adulterated.—The term "adulterated" applies to any pesticide if—

(1) its strength or purity falls below the professed standard of quality as expressed on its labeling under which it is sold;

(2) any substance has been substituted wholly or in part for the pesticide; or

(3) any valuable constituent of the pesticide has been wholly or in part abstracted.

[§2(c) amended by PL 100–532]

(d) Animal.—The term "animal" means all vertebrate and invertebrate species, including but not limited to man and other mammals, birds, fish, and shellfish.

(e) Certified Applicator, etc.—

(1) Certified Applicator.—The term "certified applicator" means any individual who is certified under section 11 as authorized to use or supervise the use of any pesticide which is classified for restricted use.

Any applicator who holds or applies registered pesticides, or uses dilutions of registered pesticides consistent with subsection 2(ee), only to provide a service of controlling pests without delivering any unapplied pesticide to any person so served is not deemed to be a seller or distributor of pesticides under this Act.

(2) Private Applicator.—The term "private applicator" means a certified applicator who uses or supervises the use of any pesticide which is classified for restricted use for purposes of producing any agricultural commodity on property owned or rented by the applicator or the applicator's employer or (if applied without compensation other than trading of personal services between producers of agricultural commodities) on the property of another person.

[§2(e) amended by PL 102–237]

(3) Commercial Applicator.—The term "commercial applicator" means an applicator (whether or not the applicator is a private applicator with respect to some uses) who uses or supervises the use of any pesticide which is classified for restricted use for any purpose or on any property other than as provided by paragraph (2).

(4) Under the Direct Supervision of a Certified Applicator.— Unless otherwise prescribed by its labeling, a pesticide shall be considered to be applied under the direct supervision of a certified applicator if it is applied by a competent person acting under the instructions and control of a certified applicator who is available if and when needed, even though such certified applicator is not physically present at the time and place the pesticide is applied.

(f) Defoliant.—The term "defoliant" means any substance or mixture of substances intended for causing the leaves or foliage to drop from a plant, with or without causing abscission.

(g) Dessicant.—The term "desiccant" means any substance or mixture of substances intended for artificially accelerating the drying of plant tissue.

(h) Device.—The term "device" means any instrument or contrivance (other than a firearm) which is intended for trapping, destroying, repelling, or mitigating any pest or any other form of plant or animal life (other than man and other than bacteria, virus, or other microorganism on or in living man or other living animals); but not including equipment used for the application of pesticides when sold separately therefrom.

(i) District Court.—The term "district court" means a United States district court, the District Court of Guam, the District Court of the Virgin Island, and the highest court of American Samoa.

(j) Environment.—The term "environment" includes water, air, land, and all plants and man and other animals living therein, and the interrelationships which exist among these.

(k) Fungus.—The term "fungus" means any non-chlorophyll-bearing thallo- phyte (that is, any non-chlorophyll-bearing plant of a lower order than mosses and liverworts), as for example, rust, smut, mildew, mold, yeast, and bacteria, except those on or in living man or other animals and those on or in processed food, beverages, or pharmaceuticals.

(l) Imminent Hazard.—The term "imminent hazard" means a situation which exists when the continued use of a pesticide during the time required for cancellation proceeding would be likely to result in unreasonable adverse effects on the environment or will involve unreasonable hazard to the survival of a species declared endangered by the Secretary of the Interior under Public Law 91–135.

(m) Inert Ingredient.—The term "inert ingredient" means an ingredient which is not active.

(n) Ingredient Statement.— The term "ingredient statement" means a statement which contains—

(1) the name and percentage of each active ingredient, and the total percentage of all inert ingredients, in the pesticide; and

(2) if the pesticide contains arsenic in any form, a statement of the percentages of total and water soluble arsenic, calculated as elementary arsenic.

(o) Insect.—The term "insect" means any of the numerous small invertebrate animals generally having the body more or less obviously segmented, for the most part belonging to the class insecta, comprising six-legged, usually winged forms, as for example, beetles, bugs, bees, flies, and to other allied classes of arthropods whose members are wingless and usually have more than six legs, as for example, mites. ticks, centipedes, and wood ice.

(p) Label and Labeling—

(1) Label.—The term "label" means the written, printed, or graphic matter on, or attached to, the pesticide or device or any of its containers or wrappers.

(2) Labeling.—The term "labeling" means all labels and all other written printed, or graphic matter—

(A) accompanying the pesticide or device at any time; or

(B) to which reference is made on the label or in literature accompanying the pesticide or device, except to current official publications of the Environmental Protection Agency, the United States Departments of Agriculture and Interior, the Department of Health and Human Services, State experiment stations, State agricultural colleges, and other similar Federal or State institutions or agencies authorized by law to conduct research in the field of pesticides.

[§2(p)(2)(B) amended by PL 100–532]

(q) Misbranded.—

(1) A pesticide is misbranded if—

(A) its labeling bears any statement, design, or graphic representation relative thereto or to its ingredients which is false or misleading in any particular;

(B) it is contained in package or other container or wrapping which does not conform to the standards established by the Administrator pursuant to section 25(c)(3);

(C) it is an imitation of, or is offered for sale under the name of, another pesticide;

(D) its label does not bear the registration number assigned under section 7 to each establishment in which it was produced;

(E) any word, statement, or other information required by or under authority of this Act to appear on the label or labeling is not prominently placed thereon with such conspicuousness (as compared with other words, statements, designs, or graphic matter in the labeling) and in such terms as to render it likely to be read and understood by the ordinary individual under customary conditions of purchase and use;

(F) the labeling accompanying it does not contain directions for use which are necessary for effecting the purpose for which the product is intended and if complied with, together with any requirements imposed under section 3(d) of this Act, are adequate to protect health and the environment;

(G) the label does not contain a warning or caution statement which may be necessary and if complied with, together with any requirements imposed under section 3(d) of this Act, is adequate to protect health and the environment; or

(H) in the case of a pesticide not registered in accordance with section 3 of this Act and intended for export, the label does not contain, in words prominently placed thereon with such conspicuousness (as compared with other words, statements, designs, or graphic matter in the labeling) as to render it likely to be noted by the ordinary individual under customary conditions of purchase and use, the following: "Not Registered for Use in the United States of America".

(2) A pesticide is misbranded if—

(A) the label does not bear an ingredient statement on that part of the immediate container (and on the outside container or wrapper of the retail package, if there be one, through which the ingredient statement on the immediate container cannot be clearly read) which is presented or displayed under customary conditions of purchase, except that a pesticide is not misbranded under this subparagraph if—

[§2(q)(2)(A) amended by PL 100–532]

(i) the size or form of the immediate container, or the outside container or wrapper of the retail package, makes it impracticable to place the ingredient statement on the part which is presented or displayed under customary conditions of purchase; and

(ii) the ingredient statement appears prominently on another part of the immediate container, or outside container or wrapper, permitted by the Administrator;

(B) the labeling does not contain a statement of the use classification under which the product is registered;

(C) there is not affixed to its container, and to the outside container or wrapper of the retail package, if there be one, through which the required information on the immediate container cannot be clearly read, a label bearing—

(i) the name and address of the producer, registrant, or person for whom produced;

(ii) the name. brand, or trademark under which the pesticide is sold;

(iii) the net weight or measure of the content, except that the Administrator may permit reasonable variations; and

[§2(q)(2)(C)(iii) amended by PL 100–532]

(iv) when required by regulation of the Administrator to effectuate the purposes of this Act, the registration number assigned to the pesticide under this Act, and the use classification; and

(D) the pesticide contains any substance or substances in quantities highly toxic to man, unless the label shall bear. in addition to any other matter required by this Act—

(i) the skull and crossbones:

(ii) the word "poison" prominently in red on a background of distinctly contrasting color: and

(iii) a statement of a practical treatment (first aid or otherwise) in case of poisoning by the pesticide.

(r) Nematode.—The term "nematode" means invertebrate animals of the phylum nemathelminthes and class nematoda. that is, unsegmented round worms with elongated, fusiform. or sack-like bodies covered with cuticle, and inhabiting soil, water, plants, or plant parts; may also be called nemas or eelworms.

(s) Person.—The term "person" means any individual, partnership, association, corporation. or any organized group of persons whether incorporated or not.

(t) Pest.—The term "pest" means (1) any insect, rodent, nematode, fungus, weed, or (2) any other form of terrestrial or aquatic plant or animal life or virus, bacteria, or other micro-organism (except viruses, bacteria or other micro-organisms on or in living man or other living animals) which the Administrator declares to be a pest under section 25(c)(1).

(u) Pesticide.—The term "pesticide" means (1) any substance or mixture of substances intended for preventing, destroying, repelling, or mitigating any pest, and (2) any substance or mixture of substances intended for use as a plant regulator, defoliant, or desiccant, except that the term "pesticide" shall not include any article that is a "new animal drug" within the meaning of section 201(w) of the Federal Food, Drug, and Cosmetic Act (21 U.S.C. 321(w)), that has been determined by the Secretary of Health and

Human Services not to be a new animal drug by a regulation establishing conditions of use for the article, or that is an animal feed within the meaning of section 201(x) of such Act (21 U.S.C. 321(x)) bearing or containing a new animal drug.

[§2(u) amended by PL 100–532]

(v) Plant Regulator.—The term "plant regulator" means any substance or mixture of substances intended, through physiological action, for accelerating or retarding the rate of growth or rate of maturation, or for otherwise altering the behavior of plants or the produce thereof, but shall not include substances to the extent that they are intended as plant nutrients, trace elements, nutritional chemicals, plant inoculants, and soil amendments. Also, the term "plant regulator" shall not be required to include any of such of those nutrient mixtures or soil amendments as are commonly known as vitamin-hormone horticultural products, intended for improvement, maintenance, survival, health, and propagation of plants, and as are not for pest destruction and are nontoxic, nonpoisonous in the undiluted packaged concentration.

(w) Producer and Produce.—The term "producer" means the person who manufactures, prepares, compounds, propagates, or processes any pesticide or device or active ingredient used in producing a pesticide. The term "produce" means to manufacture, prepare, compound, propagate, or process any pesticide or device or acting ingredient used in producing a pesticide. The dilution by individuals of formulated pesticides for their own use and according to the directions on registered labels shall not of itself result in such individuals being included in the definition of "producer" for the purposes of this Act.

(x) Protect Health and the Environment.—The terms "protect health and the environment" and "protection of health and the environment mean protection against any unreasonable adverse effects on the environment.

(y) Registrant.—The term "registrant" means a person who has registered any pesticide pursuant to the provisions of this Act.

(z) Registration.—The term "registration" includes reregistration.

(aa) State.—The term "State" means a State, the District of Columbia, the Commonwealth of Puerto Rico, the Virgin Islands, Guam, the Trust Territory of the Pacific Islands, and American Samoa.

(bb) Unreasonable Adverse Effects on the Environment.—The term "unreasonable adverse effects on the environment" means any unreasonable risk to man or the environment, taking into account the economic, social, and environmental costs and benefits of the use of any pesticide.

(cc) Weed.—The term "weed" means any plant which grows where not wanted.

(dd) Establishment.—The term "establishment" means any place where a pesticide or device or active ingredient used in producing a pesticide is produced, or held, for distribution or sale.

(ee) To Use any Registered Pesticide in a Manner Inconsistent With Its Labeling.—The term "to use any registered pesticide in a manner inconsistent with its labeling" means to use any registered pesticide in a manner not permitted by the labeling, except that the term shall not include (1) applying a pesticide at any dosage, concentration, or frequency less than that specified on the labeling unless the labeling specifically prohibits deviation from the specified dosage, concentration, or frequency, (2) applying a pesticide against any target pest not specified on the labeling if the application is to the crop, animal, or site specified on the labeling, unless the Administrator has required that the labeling specifically state that the pesticide may be used only for the pests specified on the labeling after the Administrator has determined that the use of the pesticide against other pests would cause an unreasonable adverse effect on the environment, (3) employing any method of application not prohibited by the labeling unless the labeling specifically states the product may be applied only by the methods specified on the labeling. (4) mixing a pesticide or pesticides with a fertilizer when such mixture is not prohibited by the labeling. (5) any use of a pesticide in conformance with section 5, 18, or 24 of this Act, or (6) any use of a pesticide in a manner that the Administrator determines to be consistent with the purposes of this Act. After March 31, 1979, the term shall not include the use of a pesticide for agricultural or forestry purposes at a dilution less than label dosage unless before or after that date the Administrator issues a regulation or advisory opinion consistent with the study provided for in section 27(b) of the Federal Pesticide Act of 1978, which regulation or advisory opinion specifically requires the use of definite amounts of dilution.

[§2(ee) amended by PL 100–532]

(ff) Outstanding Data Requirement.—

(1) In General.—The term "outstanding data requirement" means a requirement for any study, information, or data that is necessary to make a determination under section 3(c)(5) and which study, information. or data—

(A) has not been submitted to the Administrator; or

(B) if submitted to the Administrator. the Administrator has determined must be resubmitted because it is not valid, complete, or adequate to make a determination under section 3(c)(5) and the regulations and guidelines issued under such section.

(2) Factors.—In making a determination under paragraph (1)(B) respecting a study, the Administrator shall examine, at a minimum, relevant protocols, documentation of the conduct and analysis of the study, and the results of the study to determine whether the study and the results of the study fulfill the data requirement for which the study was submitted to the Administrator."

[§2(ff) added by PL 100–532]

(gg) To Distribute or Sell.—The term "to distribute or sell" means to distribute, sell, offer for sale, hold for distribution, hold for sale, hold for shipment, ship, deliver for shipment, release for shipment, or receive and (having so received) deliver or offer to deliver. The term does not include the holding or application of registered pesticides or use dilutions thereof by any applicator who provides a service of controlling pests without delivering any unapplied pesticide to any person so served.

[§2(gg) added by PL 100–532]

§136a. Registration of Pesticides. [Sec. 3]

(a) Requirement of Registration.—Except as provided by this Act, no person in any State may distribute or sell to any person any pesticide that is not registered under this Act. To the extent necessary to prevent unreasonable adverse effects on the environment, the Administrator may by regulation limit the distribution, sale, or use in any State of any pesticide that is not registered under this Act and that is not the subject of an experimental use permit under section 5 or an emergency exemption under section 18.

[§3(a) amended by PL 100–532]

(b) Exemptions.—A pesticide which is not registered with the Administrator may be transferred if—

(1) the transfer is from one registered establishment to another registered establishment operated by the same producer solely for packaging at the second establishment or for use as a constituent part of another pesticide produced at the second establishment; or

(2) the transfer is pursuant to and in accordance with the requirements of an experimental use permit.

(c) Procedure for Registration.—

(1) Statement Required.— Each applicant for registration of a pesticide shall file with the Administrator a statement which includes—

(A) the name and address of the applicant and of any other person whose name will appear, on the labeling;

(B) the name of the pesticide;

(C) a complete copy of the labeling of the pesticide, a statement of all claims to be made for it, and any directions for its use;

(D) the complete formula of the pesticide;

(E) a request that the pesticide be classified for general use or for restricted use, or for both; and; and

[Former (E) deleted, new (E) added by PL 102–237]

(F) except as otherwise provided in paragraph (2)(D) of this section, if requested by the Administrator, a full description of the tests made and the results thereof upon which the claims are based, or alternatively a citation to data that appear in the public literature or that previously had been submitted to the Administrator and that the Administrator may consider in accordance with the following provisions:

[§3(c)(1)(F) amended by PL 100–532; PL 102–237]

(i) With respect to pesticides containing active ingredients that are initially registered under this Act after the date of enactment of the Federal Pesticide Act of 1978, data submitted to support the application for the original registration of the pesticide, or an application for an amendment adding any new use to the registration and that pertains solely to such new use, shall not, without the written permission of the original data submitter, be considered by the Administrator to support an application by another person during a period of ten years following the date the Administrator first registers the pesticide, except that such permission shall not be required in the case of defensive data.

[§3(c)(1)(F)(i) amended by PL 100–532; PL 102–237]

(ii) Except as otherwise provided in clause (i), with respect to data submitted after December 31, 1969, by an applicant or registrant to support an application for registration, experimental use permit, or amendment adding a new use to an existing registration, to support or maintain in effect an existing registration, or for reregistration, the Administrator may, without the permission of the original data submitter, consider any such item of data in support of an application by any other person (hereinafter in this subparagraph referred to as the "applicant") within the fifteen-year period following the date the data were originally submitted only if the applicant has made an offer to compensate the original data submitter and submitted such offer to the Administrator accompanied by evidence of delivery to the original data submitter of the offer. The terms and amount of compensation may be fixed by agreement between the original data submitter and the applicant, or, failing such agreement, binding arbitration under this subparagraph. If, at the end of ninety days after the date of delivery to the original data submitter of the offer to compensate, the original data submitter and the applicant have neither agreed on the amount and terms of compensation nor on a procedure for reaching an agreement on the amount and terms of compensation, either person may initiate binding arbitration proceedings by requesting the Federal Mediation and Conciliation Service to appoint an arbitrator from the roster of arbitrators maintained by such Service. The procedure and rules of the Service shall be applicable to the selection of such arbitrator and to such arbitration proceedings, and the findings and determination of the arbitrator shall be final and conclusive, and no official or court of the United States shall have power of jurisdiction to review any such findings and determination, except for fraud, misrepresentation, or other misconduct by one of the parties to the arbitration or the arbitrator where there is a verified complaint with supporting affidavits attesting to specific instances of such fraud, misrepresentation, or other misconduct. The parties to the arbitration shall share equally in the payment of the fee and expenses of the arbitrator. If the Administrator determines that an original data submitter has failed to participate in a procedure for reaching an agreement or in an arbitration proceeding as required by this subparagraph, or failed to comply with the rems of an agreement or arbitration decision concerning compensation under this subparagraph, the original data submitter shall forfeit the right to compensation for the use of the data in support of the application. Notwithstanding any other provision of this Act, if the Administrator determines that an applicant has failed to participate in a procedure for reaching an agreement or in an arbitration proceeding as required by this subparagraph, or failed to comply with the terms of an agreement or arbitration decision concerning compensation under this subparagraph, the Administrator shall deny the application or cancel the registration of the pesticide in support of which the data were used without further hearing. Before the Administrator takes action under either of the preceding two sentences, the Administrator shall furnish to the affected person, by certified mail, notice of intent to take action and allow fifteen days from the date of delivery of the notice for the affected person to respond. If a registration is denied or canceled under this subparagraph, the Administrator may make such order as the Administrator deems appropriate concerning the continued sale and use of existing stock of such pesticide. Registration action by the Administrator shall not be delayed pending the fixing of compensation:

[§3(c)(1)(F)(ii) amended by PL 100–532; PL 102–237]

(iii) After expiration of any period of exclusive use and any period for which compensation is required for the use of an item of data under clauses (i) and (ii), the Administrator may consider such item of data in support of an application by any other applicant without the permission of the original data submitter and without an offer having been received to compensate the original data submitter for the use of such item of data:

[§3(c)(1)(F)(iii) amended by PL 100–532; PL 102–237]

[Former (F) deleted and former (D) amended and redesignated as (F) by PL 102-532]

(2) Data in Support of Registration.—

(A) The Administrator shall publish guidelines specifying the kinds of information which will be required to support the registration of a pesticide and shall revise such guidelines from time to time. If thereafter the administrator requires any additional kind of information under subparagraph (b) of this paragraph, the administrator shall permit sufficient time for applicants to obtain such additional information. The Administrator, in establishing standards for data requirements for the registration of pesticides with respect to minor uses, shall make such standards commensurate with the anticipated extent of use, pattern of use, and the level and degree of Potential exposure of man and the environment to the pesticide. The Administrator shall not require a person to submit, in relation to a registration or reregistration of a pesticide for minor agricultural use under this Act, any field residue data from a geographic area where the pesticide will not be registered for such use. In the development of these standards, the Administrator shall consider the economic factors of potential national volume of use, extent of distribution, and the impact of the cost of meeting the requirements on the incentives for any potential registrant to undertake the development of the required data. Except as provided by section 10, within 30 days after the Administrator registers a pesticide under this Act the administrator shall make available to the public the data called for in the registration statement together with such other scientific information as the administrator deems relevant to the Administrator's decision.

[§3(c)(2)(A) amended by PL 100–532; PL 101–624]

(B) (i) If the Administrator determines that additional data are required to maintain in effect an existing registration of a pesticide, the Administrator shall notify all existing registrants of the pesticide to which the determination relates and provide a list of such registrants to any interested person.

(ii) Each registrant of such pesticide shall provide evidence within ninety days after receipt of notification that it is taking appropriate steps to secure the additional data that are required. Two or more registrants may agree to develop jointly, or to share in the cost of developing, such data if they agree and advice the Administrator of their intent within ninety days after notification. Any registrant who agrees to share in the cost of producing the data shall be entitled to examine and rely upon such data in support of maintenance of such registration. The Administrator shall issue a notice of intent to suspend the registration of a pesticide in accordance with the procedures described by clause (iv)if a registrant fails to comply with this clause.

[§3(c)(2)(B)(ii) amended by PL 100–532]

(iii) If, at the end of sixty days after advising the Administrator of their agreement to develop jointly, or share in the cost of developing, data, the registrants have not further agreed on the terms of the data development arrangement or on a procedure for reaching such agreement, any of such registrants may initiate binding arbitration proceedings by requesting the Federal Mediation and Conciliation Service to appoint an arbitrator from the roster of arbitrators maintained by such Service. The procedure and rules of the Service shall be applicable to the selection of such arbitrator and to such arbitration proceedings, and the findings and determination of the arbitrator shall be final and conclusive, and no official or court of the United States shall have power or jurisdiction to review any such findings and determination, except for fraud, misrepresentation, or other misconduct by one of the parties to the arbitration or the arbitrator where there is a verified complaint with supporting affidavits attesting to specific instances of such fraud, misrepresentation, or other misconduct. All parties to the arbitration shall share equally in the payment of the fee and expenses of the arbitrator. The Administrator shall issue a notice of intent to suspend the registration of a pesticide in accordance with the procedures described by clause (iv) if a registrant fails to comply with this clause.

[§3(c)(2)(B)(iii) amended by PL 100–532]

(iv) Notwithstanding any other provision of this Act, if the Administrator determines that a registrant, within the time required by the Administrator, has failed to take appropriate steps to secure the data required under this subparagraph, to participate in a procedure for reaching agreement concerning a joint data development arrangement under this subparagraph or in an arbitration proceeding as required by this subparagraph or to comply with the terms of an agreement or arbitration decision concerning a joint data development arrangement under this subparagraph, the Administrator may issue a notice of intent to suspend such registrants registration of the pesticide for which additional data is required. The Administrator may include in the notice of intent to suspend such provisions as the Administrator deems appropriate concerning the continued sale and use of existing stocks of such pesticide. Any suspension proposed under this subparagraph shall become final and effective at the end of thirty days from receipt by the registrant of the notice of intent to suspend, unless during that time a request for hearing is made by a person adversely affected by the notice or the registrant has satisfied the Administrator that the registrant has complied fully with the requirements that served as a basis for the notice of intent to suspend. If a hearing is requested, a hearing shall be conducted under section 6(d) of this Act. The only matters for resolution at that hearing shall be whether the registrant has failed to take the action that served as the basis for the notice of intent to suspend the registration of the pesticide for which additional data is required, and whether the Administrator's determination with respect to the disposition of existing stocks is consistent with this Act. If a hearing is held, a decision after completion of such hearing shall be final. Notwithstanding any other provision of this Act, a hearing shall be held and a determination made within seventy-five days after receipt of a request for such hearing. Any registration suspended under this subparagraph shall be reinstated by the Administrator if the Administrator determines that the registrant has complied fully with the requirements that served as a basis for the suspension of the registration.

[§3(c)(2)(B)(iv) amended by PL 100–532]

(v) Any data submitted under this subparagraph shall be subject to the provisions of paragraph (1)(D) of this section. Whenever such data are submitted jointly by two or more registrants, an agent shall be agreed on at the time of the joint submission to handle any subsequent data compensation matters for the joint submitters of such data.

[§3(c)(2)(B)(v) amended by PL 100–532]

(C) Within nine months after the date of enactment of this subparagraph, the Administrator shall, by regulation, prescribe simplified procedures for the registration of pesticides, which shall include the provisions of subparagraph (D) of this paragraph.

[§3(c)(2)(C) amended by PL 100–532]

(D) Exemption. — No applicant for registration of a pesticide who proposes to purchase a registered pesticide from another produce in order to formulate such purchased pesticide into the pesticide that is the subject of the application shall be required to—

[§3(c)(2)(D) amended by PL 100–532]

(i) submit or cite data pertaining to such purchased product: or

[§3(c)(2)(D)(i) amended by PL 100–532]

(ii) offer to pay reasonable compensation otherwise required by paragraph (1)(D) of this subsection for the use of any such data.

(3) Time for Acting with Respect to Application.—

(A) The Administrator shall review the data after receipt of the application and shall, as expeditiously as possible, either register the pesticide in accordance with paragraph (5), or notify the applicant of the Administrator's determination that it does not comply with the provisions of the Act in accordance with paragraph (6).

[§3(c)(3)(A) amended by PL 100–532; PL 102–237]

(B) (i) The Administrator shall, as expeditiously as possible, review and act on any application received by the Administrator that—

(I) proposes the initial or amended registration of an end-use pesticide that, if registered as proposed, would be identical or substantially similar in composition and labeling to a currently-registered pesticide identified in the application, or that would differ in composition and labeling from such currently-registered pesticide only in ways that would not significantly increase the risk of unreasonable adverse effects on the environment: or

(II) proposes an amendment to the registration of a registered pesticide that does not require scientific review of data.

(ii) In expediting the review of an application for an action described in clause (i), the Administrator shall—

(I) within 45 days after receiving the application, notify the registrant whether or not the application is complete and, if the application is found to be incomplete, reject the application:

(II) within 90 days after receiving a complete application, notify the registrant if the application has been granted or denied: and

(III) if the application is denied, notify the registrant in writing of the specific reasons for the denial of the application.

[§3(c)(3)(B) amended by PL 100–532]

(4) Notice of Application.—The Administrator shall publish in the Federal Register, promptly after receipt of the statement and other data required pursuant to paragraph (1) and (2), a notice of each application for registration of any pesticide if it contains any new active ingredient or if it would entail a changed use pattern. The notice shall provide for a period of 30 days in which any Federal agency or any other interested person may comment.

(5) Approval of Registration.—The Administrator shall register a pesticide if the administrator determines that, when considered with any restrictions imposed under subsection (d).—

[§3(c)(5) amended by PL 102–237]

(A) its composition is such as to warrant the proposed claims for it;

(B) its labeling and other material required to be submitted comply with the requirements of this Act;

(C) it will perform its intended function without unreasonable adverse effects on the environment; and

(D) when used in accordance with widespread and commonly recognized practice it will not generally cause unreasonable adverse effects on the environment. The Administrator shall not make any lack of essentiality a criterion for denying registration of any pesticide. Where two pesticides meet the requirements of this paragraph, one should not be registered in preference to the other. In considering an application for the registration of a pesticide, the Administrator may waive data requirements pertaining to efficacy, in which event the Administrator may register the pesticide without determining that the pesticide's composition is such as to warrant proposed claims of efficacy. If a pesticide is found to be efficacious by any State under section 24(c) of this Act, a presumption is established that the Administrator shall waive data requirements pertaining to efficacy for use of the pesticide in such State.

(6) Denial of Registration.—If the Administrator determines that the requirements of paragraph (5) for registration are not satisfied, the administrator shall notify the applicant for registration of his determination and of the Administrator's reasons (including the factual basis) therefor, and that, unless the applicant corrects the conditions and notifies the Administrator thereof during the 30-day period beginning with the day after the date on which the applicant receives the notice, the Administrator may refuse to register the pesticide. Whenever the Administrator refuses to register a pesticide, the administrator shall notify the applicant of the Administrator's decision and of the Administrator's reasons (including the factual basis) therefor. The Administrator shall promptly publish in the Federal Register notice of such denial of registration and the reasons therefor. Upon such notification, the applicant for registration or other interested person with the concurrence of the applicant shall have the same remedies as provided for in section 6.

(7) Registration Under Special Circumstances.— Notwithstanding the provisions of subsection (c)(5) of this section

(A) The Administrator may conditionally register or amend the registration of a pesticide if the Administrator determines that (i) the pesticide and proposed use are identical or substantially similar to any currently registered pesticide and use thereof, or differ only in ways that would not significantly increase the risk of unreasonable adverse effects on the environment, and (ii) approving the registration or amendment in the manner proposed by the applicant would not significantly increase the risk of any unreasonable adverse effect on the environment. An applicant seeking conditional registration or amended registration under this subparagraph shall submit such data as would be required to obtain registration of a similar pesticide under paragraph (5) of this section. If the applicant is unable to submit an item of data because it has not yet been generated, the Administrator may register or amend the registration of the pesticide under such conditions as will require the submission of such data not later than the time such data are required to be submitted with respect to similar pesticides already registered under this Act.

(B) The Administrator may conditionally amend the registration of a pesticide to permit additional uses of such pesticide notwithstanding that data concerning the pesticide may be insufficient to support an unconditional amendment, if the Administrator determines that (i) the applicant has submitted satisfactory data pertaining to the proposed additional use, and (ii) amending the registration in the manner proposed by the applicant would not significantly increase the risk of any unreasonable adverse effect on the environment. Notwithstanding the foregoing provisions of this subparagraph, no registration of a pesticide may be amended to permit an additional use of such pesticide if the Administrator has issued a notice stating that such pesticide, or any ingredient thereof, meets or exceeds risk criteria associated in whole or in part with human dietary exposure enumerated in regulations issued under this Act,' and during the pendency of any risk-benefit evaluation initiated by such notice, if (I) the additional use of such pesticide involves a major food or feed crop, or (II) the additional use of such pesticide involves a minor food or feed crop and the Administrator determines, with the concurrence of the Secretary of Agriculture, there is available an effective alternative pesticide that does not meet or exceed such risk criteria. An applicant seeking amended registration under this subparagraph shall submit such data as would be required to obtain registration of a similar pesticide under subsection (c)(5) of this section. If the applicant is unable to submit an item of data (other than data pertaining to the proposed additional use) because it has not yet been generated, the Administrator may amend the registration under such conditions as will require the submission of such data not later than the time such data are required to submitted with respect to similar pesticides already registered under this Act.

(C) The Administrator may conditionally register a pesticide containing an active ingredient not contained in any currently registered-pesticide for a period reasonably sufficient for generation and submission of required data (which are lacking because a period reasonably sufficient for generation of the data has not elapsed since the Administrator first imposed the data requirement) on the condition that by the end of such period the Administrator receives such data and the data do not meet or exceed risk criteria enumerated in regulations issued under this Act, and on such other conditions as the Administrator may prescribe. A conditional registration under this subparagraph shall be granted only if the Administrator determines that use of the pesticide during such period will not cause any unreasonable adverse effect on the environment, and that use of the pesticide is in the public interest.

[§3(c)(7) amended by PL 100–532]

(8) Interim Adminstrative Review.—Notwithstanding any other provision of this Act, the Administrator may not initiate a public interim administrative review process to develop a risk-benefit evaluation of the ingredients of a pesticide or any of its uses prior to initiating a formal action to cancel, suspend, or deny registration of such pesticide, required under this Act, unless such interim administrative process is based on a validated test or other significant evidence raising prudent concerns of unreasonable adverse risk to man or to the environment. Notice of the definition of the terms 'validated test' and 'other significant evidence' as used herein shall be published by the Administrator in the Federal Register.

(d) Classification of Pesticides—

(1) Classification for General Use, Restricted Use, or Both.—

(A) As a part of the registration of a pesticide the Administrator shall classify it as being for general use or for restricted use. If the Administrator determines that some of the uses for which the pesticide is registered should be for general use and that other uses for which it is registered should be for restricted use,the Administratorshall classify it for both general use and restricted use. Pesticide uses may be classified by regulation on the initial classification. and registered pesticides may be classified prior to reregistration. If some of the uses of the pesticide are classified for general use and other uses are classified for restricted use, the directions relating to its general uses shall be clearly separated and distinguished from those directions relating to its restricted uses. The Administrator may require that its packaging and labeling for restricted uses shall be clearly distinguishable from its packaging and labeling for general uses.

[§3(d)(1)(A) amended by PL 100–532 PL 102–237]

(B) If the Administrator determines that the pesticide. when applied in accordance with its directions for use, warnings and cautions and for the uses for which it is registered, or for one or more of such uses, or in accordance with a widespread and commonly recognized practice, will not generally cause unreasonable adverse effects on the environment,the Administratorwill classify the pesticide, or the particular use or uses of the pesticide to which the determination applies. for general use.

(C) If the Administrator determines that the pesticide, when applied in accordance with its directions for use, warnings and cautions and for the uses for which it is registered, or for one or more of such uses, or in accordance with a widespread and commonly recognized practice, may generally cause, without additional regulatory restrictions, unreasonable adverse effects on the environment, including injury to the applicator, the Administrator shall classify the pesticide, or the particular use or uses to which the determination applies, for restricted use:

[§3(d)(1)(C) amended by PL 102–237]

(i) If the Administrator classified a pesticide, or one or more uses of such pesticide, for restricted use because of a determination that the acute dermal or inhalation toxicity of the pesticide presents a hazard to the applicator or other persons, the pesticide shall be applied for any use to which the restricted classification applies only by or under the direct supervision of a certified applicator.

(ii) If the Administrator classified a pesticide, or one or more uses of such pesticide, for restricted use because of a determination that its use without additional regulatory restriction may cause unreasonable adverse effects on the environment, the pesticide shall be applied for any use to which the determination applies only by or under the direct supervision of a certified applicator, or subject to such other restrictions as the Administrator may provide by regulation. Any such regulation shall be reviewable in the appropriate court of appeals upon petition of a person adversely affected filed within 60 days of the publication of the regulation in final form.

(2) Change in Classification.—If the Administrator determines that a change in the classification of any use of a pesticide from general use to restricted use is necessary to prevent unreasonable adverse effects on the environment, the Administrator shall notify the registrant of such pesticide of such determination at least forty-five days before making the change and shall publish the proposed change in the Federal Register. The registrant, or other interested person with the concurrence of the registrant, may seek relief from such determination under section 6(b).

[§3(d)(2) amended by PL 102–237]

(3) Change in Classification from Restricted Use to General Use.—The registrant of any pesticide with one or more uses classified for restricted use may petition the Administrator to change any such classification from restricted to general use. Such petition shall set out the basis for the registrants position that restricted use classification is unnecessary because classification of the pesticide for general use would not cause unreasonable adverse effects on the environment. The Administrator, within sixty days after receiving such petition, shall notify the registrant whether the petition has been granted or denied. Any denial shall contain an explanation therefor and any such denial shall be subject to judicial review under section 16 of this Act.

(e) Products with Same Formulation and Claims—Products which have the same formulation, are manufactured by the same person. the labeling of which contains the same claims, and the labels of which bear a designation identifying the product as the same pesticide may be registered as a single pesticide: and additional names and labels shall be added to the registration by supplemental statements.

(f) Miscellaneous.—

(1) Effect of Change of Labeling or Formulation.—If the labeling or formulation for a pesticide is changed, the registration shall be amended to reflect such change if the Administrator determines that the change will not violate any provision of this Act.

(2) Registration not a Defense.—In no event shall registration of an article be construed as a defense for the commission of any offense under this Act. As long as no cancellation proceedings are in effect registration of a pesticide shall be prima facie evidence that the pesticide, its labeling and packaging comply with the registration provisions of the Act.

[§3(f)(2) amended by PL 100–532]

(3) Authority to Consult Other Federal Agencies—In connection with consideration of any registration or application for registration under this section, the Administrator may consult with any other Federal agency.

(g) [removed]

[§3(g) removed by PL 100–532]

§136a. Reregiatration of Registered Pesticides [Sec. 4]

[§4 added by PL 100–532]

(a) General Rule.—The Administrator shall reregister, in accordance with this section, each registered pesticide containing any active ingredient contained in any pesticide first registered before November 1, 1984, except for any pesticide as to which the Administrator has determined. after November 1, 1984, and before the effective date of this section, that—

(1) there are no outstanding data requirements; and

(2) the requirements of section 3(c)(5) have been satisfied.

(b) Reregistration Phases.— Reregistrations of pesticides under this section shall be carried out in the following phases:

(1) The first phase shall include the listing under subsection (c) of the active ingredients of the pesticides that will be reregistered.

(2) The second phase shall include the submission to the Administrator under subsection (d) of notices by registrants respecting their intention to seek reregistration identification by registrants of missing and inadequate data for such pesticides, and commitments by registrants to replace such missing or inadequate data within the applicable time period.

(3) The third phase shall include submission to the Administrator by registrants of the information required under subsection (e).

(4) The fourth phase shall include an independent, initial review by the Administrator under subsection (f) of submissions under phases two and three, identification of outstanding data requirements, and the issuance, as necessary, of requests for additional data.

(5) The fifth phase shall include the review by the Administrator under subsection (g) of data submitted for reregistration and appropriate regulatory action by the Administrator.

(c) Phase One.—

(1) Priority for Reregistration.—For purposes of the reregistration of the pesticides described in subsection (a), the Administrator shall list the active ingredients of pesticides and shall give priority to, among others, active ingredients (other than active ingredients for which registration standards have been issued before the effective date of this section) that—

(A) are in use on or in food or feed and may result in postharvest residues;

(B) may result in residues of potential toxicological concern in potable ground water, edible fish, or shellfish;

(C) have been determined by the Administrator before the effective date of this section to have significant outstanding data requirements: or where worker exposure is most likely to occur.

(D) are used on crops, including in greenhouses and nurseries, where worker exposure is most likely to occur.

(2) Reregistration Lists.— For purposes of reregistration under this section, the Administrator shall by order—

(A) not later than 70 days after the effective date of this section, list pesticide active ingredients for which registration standards have been issued before such effective date;

(B) not later than 4 months after such effective date, list the first 150 pesticide active ingredients, as determined under paragraph (1);

(C) not later than 7 months after such effective date, list the second 150 pesticide active ingredients, as determined under paragraph (1); and

(D) not later than 10 months after such effective date, list the remainder of the pesticide active ingredients, as determined under paragraph (1). Each list shall be published in the Federal Register.

(3) Judicial Review.—The content of a list issued by the Administrator under paragraph (2) shall not be subject to judicial review.

(4) Notice to Registrants.—On the publication of a list of pesticide active ingredients under paragraph (2), the Administrator shall send by certified mail to the registrants of the pesticides containing such active ingredients a notice of the time by which the registrants are to notify the Administrator under subsection (d) whether the registrants intend to seek or not to seek reregistration of such pesticides.

(d) Phase Two. —

(1) In General.—The registrant of a pesticide that contains an active ingredient listed under subparagraph (B), (C), or (D) of subsection (c)(2) shall submit to the Administrator, within the time period prescribed by paragraph (4), the notice described in paragraph (2) and any information, commitment, or offer described in paragraph (3).

(2) Notice of Intent to Seek or not to Seek Reregistration.—

(A) The registrant of a pesticide containing an active ingredient listed under subparagraph (B), (C) or (D) of subsection (c)(2) shall notify the Administrator by certified mail whether the registrant intends to seek or does not intend to seek reregistration of the pesticide.

(B) If a registrant submits a notice under subparagraph (A) of an intention not to seek reregistration of a pesticide, the Administrator shall publish a notice in the Federal Register stating that such a notice has been submitted.

(3) Missing or Inadequate Data.—Each registrant of a pesticide that contains an active ingredient listed under subparagraph (B), (C), or (D) of subsection (c)(2) and for which the registrant submitted a notice under paragraph (2) of an intention to seek reregistration of such pesticide shall submit to the Administrator—

(A) in accordance with regulations issued by the Administrator under section 3, an identification of—

(i) all data that are required by regulation to support the registration of the pesticide with respect to such active ingredient;

(ii) data that were submitted by the registrant previously in support of the registration of the pesticide that are inadequate to meet such regulations: and

(iii) data identified under clause (i) that have not been submitted to the Administrator; and

(B) either—

(i) a commitment to replace the data identified under subparagraph (A)(ii) and submit the data identified under subparagraph (A)(iii) within the applicable time period prescribed by paragraph (4)(B); or

(ii) an offer to share in the cost to be incurred by a person who has made a commitment under clause (i) to replace or submit the data and an offer to submit to arbitration as described by section 3(c)(2)(B) with regard to such cost sharing. For purposes of a submission by a registrant under subparagraph (A)(ii), data are inadequate if the data are derived from a study with respect to which the registrant is unable to make the certification prescribed by subsection (e)(1)(G) that the registrant possesses or has access to the raw data used in or generated by such study. For purposes of a submission by a registrant under such subparagraph, data shall be considered to be inadequate if the data are derived from a study submitted before January 1, 1970, unless it is demonstrated to the satisfaction of the Administrator that such data should be considered to support the registration of the pesticide that is to be reregistered.

(4) Time periods.—

(A) A submission under paragraph (2) or (3) shall be made—

(i) in the case of a pesticide containing an active ingredient listed under subsection (c)(2)(B), not later than 3 months after the date of publication of the listing of such active ingredient;

(ii) in the case of a pesticide containing an active ingredient listed under subsection (c)(2)(C), not later than 3 months after the date of publication of the listing of such active ingredient; and

(iii) in the case of a pesticide containing an active ingredient listed under subsection (c)(2)(D), not later than 3 months after the date of publication of the listing of such active ingredient. On application, the Administrator may extend a time period prescribed by this subparagraph if the Administrator determines that factors beyond the control of the registrant prevent the registrant from complying with such period.

(B) A registrant shall submit data in accordance with a commitment entered into under paragraph (3)(B) within a reasonable period of time, as determined by the Administrator, but not more than 48 months after the date the registrant submitted the commitment. The Administrator, on application of a registrant, may extend the period prescribed by the preceding sentence by no more than 2 years if extraordinary circumstances beyond the control of the registrant prevent the registrant from submitting data within such prescribed period.

(5) Cancellation and Removal.—

(A) If the registrant of a pesticide does not submit a notice under paragraph (2) or (3) within the time prescribed by paragraph (4)(A), the Administrator shall issue a notice of intent to cancel the registration of such registrant for such pesticide and shall publish the notice in the Federal Register and allow 60 days for the submission of comments on the notice. On expiration of such 60 days, the Administrator, by order and without a hearing, may cancel the registration or take such other action, including extension of applicable time periods, as may be necessary to enable reregistration of such pesticide by another person.

(B) (i) If—

(I) no registrant of a pesticide containing an active ingredient listed under subsection (c)(2) notifies the Administrator under paragraph (2) that the registrant intends to seek reregistration of any pesticide containing that active ingredient;

(II) no such registrant complies with paragraph (3)(A); or

(III) no such registrant makes a commitment under paragraph (3)(B) to replace or submit all data described in clauses (ii) and (iii) of paragraph (3)(A); the Administrator shall publish in the Federal Register a notice of intent to remove the active ingredient from the list established under subsection (c)(2) and a notice of intent to cancel the registrations of all pesticides containing such active ingredient and shall provide 60 days for comment on such notice,

(ii) After the 60-day period has expired, the Administrator, by order, may cancel any such registration without hearing, except that the Administrator shall not cancel a registration under this subparagraph if—

(I) during the comment period a person acquires the rights of the registrant in that registration;

(II) during the comment period that person furnishes a notice of intent to reregister the pesticide in accordance with paragraph (2); and

(III) not later than 120 days after the publication of the notice under this subparagraph, that person has complied with paragraph (3) and the fee prescribed by subsection (i)(1) has been paid.

(6) Suspensions and Penalties.—The Administrator shall issue a notice of intent to suspend the registration of a pesticide in accordance with the procedures prescribed by section 3(c)(2)(B)(iv) if the Administrator determines that (A) progress is insufficient to ensure the submission of the data required for such pesticide under a commitment made under paragraph (3)(B) within the time period prescribed by paragraph (4)(B) or (B) the registrant has not submitted such data to the Administrator within such time period.

(e) Phase Three.—

(1) Information about Studies.—Each registrant of a pesticide that contains an active ingredient listed under subparagraph (B), (C), or (D) of subsection (c)(2) who has submitted a notice under subsection (d)(2) of an intent to seek the reregistration of such pesticide shall submit, in accordance with the guidelines issued under paragraph (4), to the Administrator—

(A) a summary of each study concerning the active ingredient previously submitted by the registrant in support of the registration of a pesticide containing such active ingredient and considered by the registrant to be adequate to meet the requirements of section 3 and the regulations issued under such section;

(B) a summary of each study concerning the active ingredient previously submitted by the registrant in support of the registration of a pesticide containing such active ingredient that may not comply with the requirements of section 3 and the regulations issued under such section but which the registrant asserts should be deemed to comply with such requirements and regulations;

(C) a reformat of the data from each study summarized under subparagraph (A) or (B) by the registrant concerning chronic dosing, oncogenicity, reproductive effects, mutagenicity, neurotoxicity, teratogenicity, or residue chemistry of the active ingredient that were submitted to the Administrator before January 1, 1982;

(D) where data described in subparagraph (C) are not required for the active ingredient by regulations issued under section 3, a reformat of acute and subchronic dosing data submitted by the registrant to the Administrator before January 1, 1982, that the registrant considers to be adequate to meet the requirements of section 3 and the regulations issued under such section:

(E) an identification of data that are required to be submitted to the Administrator under section 6(a)(2) indicating an adverse effect of the pesticide;

(F) an identification of any other information available that in the view of the registrant supports the registration;

(G) a certification that the registrant or the Administrator possesses or has access to the raw data used in or generated by the studies that the registrant summarized under subparagraph (A)or (B);

(H) either—

(i) a commitment to submit data to fill each outstanding data requirement identified by the registrant; or

(ii) an offer to share in the cost of developing such data to be incurred by a person who has made a commitment under clause (i) to submit such data, and an offer to submit to arbitration as described by section 3(c)(2)(B) with regard to such cost sharing; and

(I) evidence of compliance with section 3(c)(1)(D)(ii) and regulations issued thereunder with regard to previously submitted data as if the registrant were now seeking the original registration of the pesticide. A registrant who submits a certification under subparagraph (G) that is false shall be considered to have violated this Act and shall be subject to the penalties prescribed by section 14.

(2) Time periods.—

(A) The information required by paragraph (1) shall be submitted to the Administrator—

(i) in the case of a pesticide containing an active ingredient listed under subsection (c)(2)(B), not later than 12 months after the date of publication of the listing of such active ingredient;

(ii) in the case of a pesticide containing an active ingredient listed under subsection (c)(2)(C), not later than 12 months after the date of publication of the listing of such active ingredient; and

(iii) in the case of a pesticide containing an active ingredient listed under subsection (c)(2)(D), not later than 12 months after the date of publication of the listing of such active ingredient.

(B) A registrant shall submit data in accordance with a commitment entered into under paragraph (1)(H) within a reasonable period of time, as determined by the Administrator, but not more than 48 months after the date the registrant submitted the commitment under such paragraph. The Administrator, on application of a registrant, may extend the period prescribed by the preceding sentence by no more than 2 years if extraordinary circumstances beyond the control of the registrant prevent the registrant from submitting data within such prescribed period.

(3) Cancellation —

(A) If the registrant of a pesticide fails to submit the information required by paragraph (1) within the time prescribed by paragraph (2), the Administrator, by order and without hearing, shall cancel the registration of such pesticide.

(B) (i) If the registrant of a pesticide submits the information required by paragraph (1) within the time prescribed by paragraph (2) and such information does not conform to the guidelines for submissions established by the Aministrator, the Administrator shall determine whether the registrant made a good faith attempt to conform its submission to such guidelines.

(ii) If the Administrator determines that the registrant made a good faith attempt to conform its submission to such guidelines, the Administrator shall provide the registrant a reasonable period of time to make any necessary changes or corrections.

(iii) (I) If the Administrator determines that the registrant did not make a good faith attempt to conform its submission to such guidelines, the Administrator may issue a notice of intent to cancel the registration. Such a notice shall be sent to the registrant by certified mail.

(II) The registration shall be canceled without a hearing or further notice at the end of 30 days after receipt by the registrant of the notice unless during that time a request for a hearing is made by the registrant.

(III) If a hearing is requested, a hearing shall be conducted under section 6(d), except that the only matter for resolution at the hearing shall be whether the registrant made a good faith attempt to conform its submission to such guidelines. The hearing shall be held and a determination made within 75 days after receipt of a request for hearing.

(4) Guidelines.—

(A) Not later than 1 year after the effective date of this section, the Administrator, by order, shall issue guidelines to be followed by registrants in—

(i) summarizing studies;

(ii) reformatting studies;

(iii) identifying adverse information; and

(iv) identifying studies that have been submitted previously that may not meet the requirements of section 3 or regulations issued under such section, under paragraph (1).

(B) Guidelines issued under subparagraph (A) shall not be subject to judicial review.

(5) Monitoring.—The Administrator shall monitor the progress of registrants in acquiring and submitting the data required under paragraph (1).

(f) Phase Four.—

(1) Independent Review and Identificiation of Outstanding Data Requirements—

(A) The Administrator shall review the submissions of all registrants of pesticides containing a particular active ingredient under subsections (d)(3) and (e)(1) to determine if such submissions identified all the data that are missing or inadequate for such active ingredient. To assist the review of the Administrator under this subparagraph, the Administrator may require a registrant seeking reregistration to submit complete copies of studies summarized under subsection (e)(1).

(B) The Administrator shall independently identify and publish in the Federal Register the outstanding data requirements for each active ingredient that is listed under subparagraph (B), (C), or (D) of subsection (c)(2) and that is contained in a pesticide to be reregistered under this section. The Administrator, at the same time, shall issue a notice under section 3(c)(2)(B) for the submission of the additional data that are required to meet such requirements.

(2) Time Periods.—

(A) The Administrator shall take the action required by paragraph (1)—

(i) in the case of a pesticide containing an active ingredient listed under subsection (c)(2)(B), not later than 18 months after the date of the listing of such active ingredient;

(ii) in the case of a pesticide containing an active ingredient listed under subsection (c)(2)(C), not later than 24 months after the date of the listing of such active ingredient; and

(iii) in the case of a pesticide containing an active ingredient listed under subsection (c)(2)(D), not later than 33 months after the date of the listing of such active ingredient.

(B) If the Administrator issues a notice to a registrant under paragraph (1)(B) for the submission of additional data, the registrant shall submit such data within a reasonable period of time, as determined by the Administrator, but not to exceed 48 months after the issuance of such notice. The Administrator, on application of a registrant, may extend the period prescribed by the preceding sentence by no more than 2 years if extraordinary circumstances beyond the control of the registrant prevent the registrant from submitting data within such prescribed period.

(3) Suspensions and Penalties.—The Administrator shall issue a notice of intent to suspend the registration of a pesticide in accordance with the procedures prescribed by section 3(c)(2)(B)(iv) if the Administrator determines that (A) tests necessary to fill an outstanding data requirement for such pesticide have not been initiated within 1 year after the issuance of a notice under paragraph (1)(B), or (B) progress is insufficient to ensure submission of the data referred to in clause (A) within the time period prescribed by paragraph (2)(B) or the required data have not been submitted to the Administrator within such time period.

(g) Phase Five.—

(1) Data Review.—The Administrator shall conduct a thorough examination of all data submitted under this section concerning an active ingredient listed under subsection (c)(2) and of all other available data found by the Administrator to be relevant.

(2) Reregistration and Other Actions.—

(A) Within 1 year after the submission of all data concerning an active ingredient of a pesticide under subsection (f). the Administrator shall determine whether pesticides containing such active ingredient are eligible for reregistration. For extraordinary circumstances. the Administrator may extend such period for not more than 1 additional year.

(B) Before reregistering a pesticide, the Administrator shall obtain any needed product-specific data regarding the pesticide by use of section 3(c)(2)(B) and shall review such data within 90-day after its submission. The Administrator shall require that data under this subparagraph be submitted to the Administrator not later than 8 months after a determination of eligibility under subparagraph (A) has been made for each active ingredient of the pesticide, unless the Administrator determines that a longer period is required for the generation of the data.

(C) After conducting the review required by paragraph (1) for each active ingredient of a pesticide and the review required by subparagraph (B) of this paragraph, the Administrator shall determine whether to reregister a pesticide by determining whether such pesticide meets the requirements of section 3(c)(5). If the Administrator determines that a pesticide is eligible to be reregistered, the Administrator shall reregister such pesticide within 6 months after the submission of the data concerning such pesticide under subparagraph (B).

(D) If after conducting a review under paragraph (1) or subparagraph (B) of this paragraph the Administrator determines that a pesticide should not be reregistered, the Administrator shall take appropriate regulatory action.

(h) Compensation of Data Submitter.—If data that are submitted by a registrant under subsection (d), (e), (f), or (g) are used to support the application of another person under section 3, the registrant who submitted such data shall be entitled to compensation for the use of such data as prescribed by section 3(c)(1)(D). In determining the amount of such compensation, the fees paid by the registrant under this section shall be taken into account.

(i) Fees.—

(1) Initial Fee for Food or Feed Use Pesticide Active Ingredients.—The registrants of pesticides that contain an active ingredient that is listed under subparagraph (B), (C), or (D) of subsection (c)(2) and that is an active ingredient of any pesticide registered for a major food or feed use shall collectively pay a fee of $50,000 on submission of information under paragraphs (2) and (2) of subsection (d) for such ingredient.

(2) Final Fee for Food or Feed Use Pesticide Active Ingredients.—

(A) The registrants of pesticides that contain an active ingredient that is listed under subparagraph (B), (C), or (D) of subsection (c)(2) and that is an active ingredient of any pesticide registered for a major food or feed use shall collectively pay a fee of $100,000—

(i) on submission of information for such ingredient under subsection (e)(1) if data are reformatted under subsection (e)(1)(C): or

(ii) on submission of data for such ingredient under subsection (e)(2)(B) if data are not reformatted under subsection (e)(1)(C).

(B) The registrants of pesticides that contain an active ingredient that is listed under subsection (c)(2)(A) and that is an active ingredient of any pesticide registered for a major food or feed use shall collectively pay a fee of $150,000 at such time as the Administrator shall prescribe.

(3) Fees for Other Pesticide Active Ingredients.—

(A) The registrants of pesticides that contain an active ingredient that is listed under subparagraph (B), (C), or (D) of subsection (c)(2) and that is not an active ingredient of any pesticide registered for a major food or feed use shall collectively pay fees in amounts determined by the Administrator. Such fees may not be less than one-half of, nor greater than, the fees required by paragraphs (1) and (2). A registrant shall pay such fees at the times corresponding to the times fees prescribed by paragraphs (1) and (2) are to be paid.

(B) The registrants of pesticides that contain an active ingredient that is listed under subsection (c)(2)(A) and that is not an active ingredient of any pesticide that is registered for a major food or feed use shall collectively pay a fee of not more than $100,000 and not less than $50,000 at such time as the Administrator shall prescribe.

(4) Reduction or Waiver of Fees for Minor Use and Other Pesticides.—

(A) An active ingredient that is contained only in pesticides that are registered solely for agricultural or nonagricultural minor uses, or a pesticide the value or volume of use of which is small, shall be exempt from the fees prescribed by paragraph (3).

(B) An antimicrobial active ingredient, the production level of which does not exceed 1,000,000 pounds per year, shall be exempt from the fees prescribed by paragraph (3). For purposes of this subparagraph, the term 'antimicrobial active ingredient' means any active ingredient that is contained only in pesticides that are not registered for any food or feed use and that are—

(i) sanitizers intended to reduce the number of living bacteria or viable virus particles on inanimate surface or in water' or air;

(ii) bacteriostats intended to inhibit the growth of bacteria in the presence of moisture;

(iii) disinfectants intended to destroy or irreversibly inactivate bacteria, fungi, or viruses on surfaces or inanimate objects;

(iv) sterilizers intended to destroy viruses and all living bacteria, fungi, and their spores on inanimate surfaces; or

(v) fungicides or fungistats.

(C) (i) Notwithstanding any other provision of this subsection in the case of a small business registrant of a pesticide, the registrant shall pay a fee for the reregistration of each active ingredient of the pesticide that does not exceed an amount determined in accordance with this subparagraph.

(ii) If during the 3–year period prior to reregistration the average annual gross revenue of the registrant from pesticides containing such active ingredient is—

(I) less than $5,000,000, the registrant shall pay 0.5 percent of such revenue;

(II) $5,000,000 or more but less than $10,000,000, the registrant shall pay 1 percent of such revenue; or

(III) $10,000,000 or more, the registrant shall pay 1.5 percent of such revenue, but not more than $ 150,000.

(iii) For the purpose of this subparagraph, a small business registrant is a corporation, partnership, or unincorporated business that—

(I) has 150 or fewer employees; and

(II) during the 3–year period prior to reregistration, had an average annual gross revenue from chemicals that did not exceed $40,000,000.

(5) Maintenance Fee.—

[§4(i)(5) revised by PL 102-237]

(A) Subject to other provisions of this paragraph, each registrant of a pesticide shall pay an annual fee by January 15 of each year of—

(i) $650 for the first registration; and

(ii) $1,300 for each additional registration, except that no fee shall be charged for more than 200 registrations held by any registrant.

(B) In the case of a pesticide that is registered for a minor agricultural use, the Administrator may reduce or waive the payment of the fee imposed under this paragraph if the Administrator determines that the fee would significantly reduce the availability of the pesticide for the use.

(C) The amount of each fee prescribed under subparagraph (A) shall be adjusted by the Administrator to a level that will result in the collection under this paragraph of, to the extent practicable, an aggregate amount of $14,000,000 each fiscal year.

(D) The maximum annual fee payable under this paragraph by—

(i) a registrant holding not more than 50 pesticide registrations shall be $55,000; and

(ii) a registrant holding over 50 registrations shall be $95,000.

(E) (i) For a small business, the maximum annual fee payable under this paragraphy by—

(I) a registrant holding not more than 50 pesticide registrations shall be $38,500; and

(II) a registrant holding over 50 pesticide registrations shall be $66,500.

(ii) For purposes of clause (i), the term "small business" means a corporation, partnership, or unincorporated business that—

(I) has 150 or fewer employees; and

(II) during the 3-year period prior to the most recent maintenance fee billing cycle, had an average annual gross revcenue from chemicals that did not exceed $40,000,000.

(F) If any fee prescribed by this paragraph with respect to the registration of a pesticide is not paid by a registrant by the time prescribed, the Administrator, by order and without heairng, may cancel the registration.

(G) The authority provided under this paragraph shall terminate on September 30, 1997.

(6) Other Fees.—During the period beginning on the date of enactment of this section and ending on September 30, 1997, the Administrator may not levy any other fees for the registration of a pesticide under this Act except as provided in paragraphs (1) through (5).

(7) Apportionment.—

(A) If two or more registrants are required to pay any fee prescribed by paragraph (1), (2), or (3) with respect to a particular active ingredient, the fees for such active ingredient shall be apportioned among such registrants on the basis of the market share in United States sales of the active ingredient for the 3 calendar years preceding the date of payment of such fee, except that—

(i) small business registrants that produce the active ingredient shall pay fees in accordance with paragraph (4)(C); and

(ii) registrants who have no market share but who choose to reregister a pesticide containing such active ingredient shall pay the lesser of—

(I) 15 percent of the reregistration fee; or

(II) a proportionate amount of such fee based on the lowest percentage market share held by any registrant active in the marketplace. In no event shall registrants who have no market share but who choose to reregister a pesticide containing such active ingredient collectively pay more than 25 percent of the total active ingredient reregistration fee.

(B) The Administrator, by order, may require any registrant to submit such reports as the Administrator determines to be necessary to allow the Administrator to determine and apportion fees under this subsection or to determine the registrant's eligibility for a reduction or waiver of a fee.

(C) If any such report is not submitted by a registrant after receiving notice of such report requirement, or if any fee prescribed by this subsection (other than paragraph (5)) for an active ingredient is not paid by a registrant to the Administrator by the time prescribed under this subsection, the Administrator, by order and without hearing, may cancel each registration held by such registrant of a pesticide containing the active ingredient with respect to which the fee is imposed. The Administrator shall reapportion the fee among the remaining registrants and notify the registrants that the registrants are required to pay to the Administrator any unpaid balance of the fee within 30 days after receipt of such notice.

(j) Exemption of Certain Registrants.—The requirements of subsections (d), (e), (f), and (i) (other than subsection (i)(5)) regarding data concerning an active ingredient and fees for review of such data shall not apply to any person who is the registrant of a pesticide to the extent that. under section 3(c)(2)(D), the person would not be required to submit or cite such data to obtain an initial registration of such pesticide.

(k) Reregistration and Expedited Processing Fund.—

(1) Establishment.—There shall be established in the Treasury of the United States a reregistration and expedited processing fund.

(2) Source and Use—All fees collected by the Administrator under subsection (i) shall be deposited into the fund and shall be available to the Administrator, without fiscal year limitation, to carry out reregistration and expedited processing of similar applications.

(3) Expedited Processing of Similar Applications.—

(A) The Administrator shall use for each of the fiscal years 1992, 1993, and 1994, 1/7 of the maintenance fees collected, up to $2 million each year to obtain sufficient personnel and resources to assure the expedited processing and review of any application that—

[§4(k)(3)(A) amended by PL 102–237]

(i) proposes the initial or amended registration of an end-use pesticide that, if registered as proposed, would be identical or substantially similar in composition and labeling to a currently-registered pesticide identified in the application, or that would differ in composition and labeling from any such currently-registered pesticide only in ways that would not significantly increase the risk of unreasonable adverse effects on the environment; or

(ii) proposes an amendment to the registration of a registered pesticide that does not require scientific review' of data.

(B) Any amounts made available under subparagraph (A) shall be used to obtain sufficient personnel and resources to carry out the activities described in such subparagraph that are in addition to the personnel and resources available to carry out such activities on the date of enactment of this section.

(4) Unused Funds.—Money in the fund not currently needed to carry out this section shall be—

(A) maintained on hand or on deposit:

(B) invested in obligations of the United States or guaranteed thereby; or

(C) invested in obligations, participations, or other instruments that are lawful investments for fiduciary. trust, or public funds.

(5) Accounting.—The Administrator shall—

(A) provide an annual accounting of the fees collected and disbursed from the fund; and

(B) take all steps necessary to ensure that expenditures from such fund are used only to carry out this section.

(1) Judicial Review.—Any failure of the Administrator to take any action required by this section shall be subject to judicial review under the procedures prescribed by section 16(b).

§136c. Experimental Use Permits. [Sec. 5]

(a) Issuance.—Any person may apply to the Administrator for an experimental use permit for a pesticide. The Administrator shall review' the application. After completion of the review, but not later than one hundred and twenty days after receipt of the application and all required supporting data, the Administrator shall either issue the permit or notify the applicant of the Administrator's determination not to issue the permit and the reasons therefor. The applicant may correct the application or request a waiver of the conditions for such permit within thirty days of receipt by the applicant of such notification. The Administrator may issue an experimental use permit only if the Administrator determines that the applicant needs such permit in order to accumulate information necessary to register a pesticide under section 3 of this Act. An application for an experimental use permit may be filed at any time.

(b) Temporary Tolerance Level.—If the Administrator determines that the use of a pesticide may reasonably be expected to result in any residue on or in food or feed, the Administrator may establish a temporary tolerance level for the residue of the pesticide before issuing the experimental use permit.

[§5(b) amended by PL 102–237]

(c) Use Under Permit.—Use of a pesticide under an experimental use permit shall be under the supervision of the Administrator, and shall be subject to such terms and conditions and be for such period of time as the Administrator may prescribe in the permit.

(d) Studies.—When any experimental use permit is issued for a pesticide containing any chemical or combination of chemicals which has not been included in any previously registered pesticide, the Administrator may specify that studies be conducted to detect whether the use of the pesticide under the permit may cause unreasonable adverse effects on the environment. All results of such studies shall be reported to the Administrator before such pesticide may be registered under section 3.

(e) Revocation.—The Administrator may revoke any experimental use permit, at any time, if the Administrator finds that its terms or conditions are being violated, or that its terms and conditions are inadequate to avoid unreasonable adverse effects on the environment.

[§5(e) amended by PL 102–237]

(f) State Issuance of Permits.— Notwithstanding the foregoing provisions of this section, the Administrator shall, under such terms and conditions as the Administrator may by regulations prescribe, authorize any State to issue an experimental use permit for a pesticide. All provisions of section 11 relating to State plans shall apply with equal force to a State plan for the issuance of experimental use permits under this section.

[§5(f) amended by PL 100–532; PL 102–237]

(g) Exemption for Agricultural Research Agencies.—Notwithstanding the foregoing provisions of this section, the Administrator may issue an experimental use permit for a pesticide to any public or private agricultural research agency or educational institution which applies for such permit. Each permit shall not exceed more than a one-year period or such other specific time as the Administrator may prescribe. Such permit shall be issued under such terms and conditions restricting the use of the pesticide as the Administrator may require. Such pesticide may be used only by such research agency or educational institution for purposes of experimentation.

[§5(g) amended by PL 100–532]

§136d. Administrative Review; Suspension.

[Sec. 6]

(a) Cancellation After Five Years—

(1) Procedure—The Administrator shall cancel the registration of any pesticide at the end of the five-year period which begins on the date of its registration (or at the end of any five-year period thereafter) unless the registrant, or other interested person with the concurrence of the registrant, before the end of such period, requests in accordance with regulations prescribed by the Administrator that the registration be continued in effect. The Administrator may permit the continued sale and use of existing stocks of a pesticide whose registration is canceled under this subsection or subsection (b) to such extent, under such conditions, and for such uses as the Administrator may specify if the Administrator determines that such sale or use is not inconsistent with the purposes of this Act and will not have unreasonable adverse effects on the environment. The Administrator shall publish in the Federal Register, at least 30 days prior to the expiration of such five-year period, notice that the registration will be canceled if the registrant or other interested person with the concurrence of the registrant does not request that the registration be continued in effect.

[§6(a)(1) amended by PL 100–532; PL 102–237]

(2) Information.—If at any time after the registration of a pesticide the registrant has additional factual information regarding unreasonable adverse effects on the environment of the pesticide, the registrant shall submit such information to the Administrator.

(b) Cancellation and Change in Classification—If it appears to the Administrator that a pesticide or its labeling or other material required to be submitted does not comply with the provisions of this Act or, when used in accordance with widespread and commonly recognized practice, generally causes unreasonable adverse effects on the environment, the Administrator may issue a notice of the Administrator's intent either—

(1) to cancel its registration or to change its classification together with the reasons (including the factual basis) for the Administrator's action, or

(2) to hold a hearing to determine whether or not its registration should be canceled or its classification changed. Such notice shall be sent to the registrant and made public. In determining whether to issue any such notice, the Administrator shall include among those factors to be taken into account the impact of the action proposed in such notice on production and prices of agricultural commodities, retail food prices, and otherwise on the agricultural economy. At least 60 days prior to sending such notice to the registrant or making public such notice, whichever occurs first, the Administrator shall provide the Secretary of Agriculture with a copy of such notice and an analysis of such impact on the agricultural economy. If the Secretary comments in writing to the Administrator regarding the notice and analysis within 30 days after receiving them, the Administrator shall publish in the Federal Register (with the notice) the comments of the Secretary and the response of the Administrator with regard to the Secretary's comments. If the Secretary does not comment in writing to the Administrator regarding the notice and analysis within 30 days after receiving them, the Administrator may notify the registrant and make public the notice at any time after such 30 day period notwithstanding the foregoing 60–day time requirement. The time requirements imposed by the preceding 3 sentences may be waived or modified to the extent agreed upon by the Administrator and the Secretary. Notwithstanding any other provision of this subsection (b) and section 25(d), in the event that the Administrator determines that suspension of a pesticide registration is necessary to prevent an imminent hazard to human health, then upon such a finding the Administrator may waive the requirement of notice to and consultation with the Secretary of Agriculture pursuant to subsection (b) and of submission to the Scientific Advisory Panel pursuant to section 25(d) and proceed in accordance with subsection (c). The proposed action shall become final and effective at the end of 30 days from receipt by the registrant, or publication, of a notice issued under paragraph (l), whichever occurs later, unless within that time either (i) the registrant makes the necessary corrections, if possible, or (ii) a request for a hearing is made by a person adversely affected by the notice. In the event a hearing is held pursuant to such a request or to the Administrator's determination under paragraph (2), a decision pertaining to registration or classification issued after completion of such hearing shall be final.

In taking any final action under this subsection, the Administrator shall consider restricting a pesticide's use or uses as an alternative to cancellation and shall fully explain the reasons for these restrictions, and shall include among those factors to be taken into account the impact of such final action on production and prices of agricultural commodities, retail food prices, and otherwise on the agricultural economy, and the Administrator shall publish in the Federal Register an analysis of such impact.

(c) Suspension.—

(1) Order.— If the Administrator determines that action is necessary to prevent an imminent hazard during the time required for cancellation or change in classification proceedings the Administrator may, by order, suspend the registration of the pesticide immediately. No order of suspension may be issued unless the Administrator has issued or at the same time issues notice of the Administrator's intention to cancel the registration or change the classification of the pesticide. Except as provided in paragraph (3), the Administrator shall notify the registrant prior to issuing any suspension order. Such notice shall include findings pertaining to the question of 'imminent hazard'. The registrant shall then have an opportunity, in accordance with the provisions of paragraph (2), for an expedited hearing before the Administrator on the question of whether an imminent hazard exists.

[§6(c)(1) amended by PL 100–532; PL 102–237]

(2) Expedite Hearing.—If no request for a hearing is submitted to the Administrator within five days of the registrant's receipt of the notification provided for by paragraph (1), the suspension order may be issued and shall take effect and shall not be reviewable by a court. If a hearing is requested, it shall commence within five days of the receipt of the request for such hearing unless the registrant and the Administrator agree that it shall commence at a later time. The hearing shall be held in accordance with the provisions of subchapter II of the title 5 of the United States Code, except

that the presiding officer need not be a certified administrative law judge. The presiding officer shall have ten days from the conclusion of the presentation of evidence to submit recommended findings and conclusions to the Administrator, who shall then have seven days to render a final order on the issue of suspension.

[§6(c)(2) amended by PL 95–251; PL 100–532]

(3) Emergency Order.— Whenever the Administrator determines that an emergency exists that does not permit the Administrator to hold a hearing before suspending, the Administrator may issue a suspension order in advance of notification to the registrant. In that case, paragraph (2) shall apply except that (A) the order of suspension shall be in effect pending the expeditious completion of the remedies provided by that paragraph and the issuance of a final order on suspension, and (B) no party other than the registrant and the Administrator shall participate except that any person adversely affected may file briefs within the time allotted by the Agency's rules. Any person so filing briefs shall be considered a party to such proceeding for the purpose of section 16(b).

[§6(c)(3) amended by PL 100–532]

(4) Judicial Review.—A final order on the question of suspension following a hearing shall be reviewable in accordance with Section 16 of this Act, notwithstanding the fact that any related cancellation proceedings have not been completed. Any order of suspension entered prior to a hearing before the Administrator shall be subject to immediate review in an action by the registrant or other interested person with the concurrence of the registrant in an appropriate district court, solely to determine whether the order of suspension was arbitrary, capricious or an abuse of discretion, or whether the order was issued in accordance with the procedures established by law. The effect of any order of the court will be only to stay the effectiveness of the suspension order, pending the Administrator's final decision with respect to cancellation or change in classification. Thus action may be maintained simultaneously with any administrative review proceeding under this section. The commencement of proceedings under this paragraph shall not operate as a stay of order, unless ordered by the court.

[§6(c)(4) amended by PL 98–620]

(d) Public Hearings and Scientific Review.—In the event a hearing is requested pursuant to subsection (b) or determined upon by the Administrator pursuant to subsection (b), such hearing shall beheld after due notice for the purpose of receiving evidence relevant and material to the issues raised by the objections filed by the applicant or other interested parties, or to the issues stated by the Administrator, if the hearing is called by the Administrator rather than by the filing of objections. Upon a showing of relevance and reasonable scope of evidence sought by any party to a public hearing, the Hearing Examiner shall issue a subpena to compel testimony or production of documents from any person. The Hearing Examiner shall be guided by the principles of the Federal Rules of Civil Procedure in making any order for the protection of the witness or the content of documents produced and shall order the payment of reasonable fees and expenses as a condition to requiring testimony of the witness. On contest, the subpena may be enforced by an appropriate United States district court in accordance with the principles stated herein. Upon the request of any party to a public hearing and when in the Hearing Examiner's judgment it is necessary or desirable, the Hearing Examiner shall at any time before the hearing record is closed refer to a Committee of the National Academy of Sciences the relevant questions of scientific fact involved in the public hearing. No member of any committee of the National Academy of Sciences established to carry out the functions of this section shall have a financial or other conflict of interest with respect to any matter considered by such committee. The Committee of the National Academy of Sciences shall report in writing to the Hearing Examiner within 60 days after such referral on these questions of scientific fact. The report shall be made public and shall be considered as part of the hearing record. The Administrator shall enter into appropriate arrangements with the National Academy of Sciences to assure an objective and competent scientific review of the questions presented to Committees of the Academy and to provide such other scientific advisory services as may be required by the Administrator for carrying out the purposes of this Act. As soon as practicable after completion of the hearing (including the report of the Academy) but not later than 90 days thereafter, the Administrator shall evaluate the data and reports before the Administrator and issue an order either revoking the Administrator's notice of intention issued pursuant to this section, or shall issue an order either canceling the registration, changing the classification, denying the registration, or requiring modification of the labeling or packaging of the article. Such order shall be based only on substantial evidence of record of such hearing and shall set forth detailed findings of fact upon which the order is based.

[§6(d) amended by PL 102–237]

(e) Conditional Registration.—

(1) The Administrator shall issue a notice of intent to cancel a registration issued under section 3(c)(7) of this Act if (A) the Administrator, at any time during the period provided for satisfaction of any condition imposed, determines that the registrant has failed to initiate and pursue appropriate action toward fulfilling any condition imposed, or (B) at the end of the period provided for satisfaction of any condition imposed, that condition has not been met. The Administrator may permit the continued sale and use of existing stocks of a pesticide whose conditional registration has been canceled under this subsection to such extent, under such conditions, and for such uses as the Administrator may specify if the Administrator determines that such sale or use is not inconsistent with the purposes of this Act and will not have unreasonable adverse effects on the environment.

[§6(e)(1) amended by PL 100–532]

(2) A cancellation proposed under this subsection shall become final and effective at the end of thirty days from receipt by the registrant of the notice of intent to cancel unless during that time a request for hearing is made by a person adversely affected by the notice. If a hearing is requested, a hearing shall be conducted under subsection (d) of this section. The only matters for resolution at that hearing shall be whether the registrant has initiated and pursued appropriate action to comply with the condition or conditions within the time provided or whether the condition or conditions have been satisfied within the time provided, and whether the Administrator's determination with respect to the disposition of existing stocks is consistent with this Act. A decision after completion of such hearing shall be final. Notwithstanding any other provision of this section, a hearing shall be held and a determination made within seventy- five days after receipt of a request for such hearing.

[§6(e)(2) amended by PL 100–532]

(f) General Provisions.—

[§6 added by PL 100–532]

(1) Voluntary Cancellation.—

(A) A registrant may, at any time, request that a pesticide registration of the registrant be canceled or amended to terminate one or more pesticide uses.

(B) Before acting on a request under subparagraph (A), the Administrator shall publish in the Federal Register a notice of the receipt of the request and provide for a 30–day period in which the public may comment.

(C) In the case of a pesticide that is registered for a minor agricultural use, if the Administrator determines that the cancellation or termination of uses would adversely affect the availability of the pesticide for use, the Administrator—

(i) shall publish in the Federal Register a notice of the receipt of the request and make reasonable efforts to inform persons who so use the pesticide of the request; and

(ii) may not approve or reject the request until the termination of the 90–day period beginning on the date of publication of the notice in the Federal Register, except that the Administrator may waive the 90–day period upon the request of the registrant or if the Administrator determines that the continued use of the pesticide would pose an unreasonable adverse effect on the environment.

(D) Subject to paragraph (3)(B), after complying with this paragraph, the Administrator may approve or deny the request.

[§6(f)(1) amended by PL 101–624]

(2) Publication of Notice.—A notice of denial of registration, intent to cancel, suspension, or intent to suspend issued under this Act or a notice issued under subsection (c)(4) or (d)(5)(A) of section 4 shall be published in the Federal Register and shall be sent by certified mail, return receipt requested, to the registrant's or applicant's address of record on file with the Administrator. If the mailed notice is returned to the Administrator as undeliverable at that address, if delivery is refused, or if the Administrator otherwise is unable to accomplish delivery of the notice to the registrant or applicant after making reasonable efforts to do so, the notice shall be deemed to have been received by the registrant or applicant on the date the notice was published in the Federal Register.

(3) Transfer of Registration of Pesticides Registered for Minor Agricultural Uses.—In the case

of a pesticide that is registered for a minor agricultural use:

(A) During the 90–day period referred to in paragraph (1)(C)(ii), the registrant of the pesticide may notify the Administrator of an agreement between the registrant and a person or persons (including persons who so use the pesticide) to transfer the registration of the pesticide, in lieu of canceling or amending the registration to terminate the use.

(B) An application for transfer of registration, in conformance with any regulations the Administrator may adopt with respect to the transfer of the pesticide registrations, must be submitted to the Administrator within 30 days of the date of notification provided pursuant to subparagraph (A). If such an application is submitted, the Administrator shall approve the transfer and shall not approve the request for voluntary cancellation or amendment to terminate use unless the Administrator determines that the continued use of the pesticide would cause an unreasonable adverse effect on the environment.

[§6(f)(3)(B) amended by PL 102–237]

(C) If the Administrator approves the transfer and the registrant transfers the registration of the pesticide, the Administrator shall not cancel or amend the registration to delete the use or rescind the transfer of the registration, during the 180-day period beginning on the date of the approval of the transfer unless the Administrator determines that the continued use of the pesticide would cause an unreasonable adverse effect on the environment.

(D) The new registrant of the pesticide shall assume the outstanding data and other requirements for the pesticide that are pending at the time of the transfer.

[§6(f)(3) added by PL 101–624]

(g) Notice for Stored Pesticides with Cancelled or Suspended Registrations.—

[§6 added by PL 100–532]

(1) In General.—Any producer or exporter of pesticides, registrant of a pesticide, applicant for registration of a pesticide, applicant for or holder of an experimental use permit, commercial applicator, or any person who distributes or sells any pesticide, who possesses any pesticide which has had its registration canceled or suspended under this section shall notify the Administrator and appropriate State and local officials of—

(A) such possession.

(B) the quantity of such pesticide such person possesses, and

(C) the place at which such pesticide is stored.

(2) Copies.—The Administrator shall transmit a copy of each notice submitted under this subsection to the regional office of the Environmental Protection Agency which has jurisdiction over the place of pesticide storage identified in the notice.

(h) Judicial Review.—Final orders of the Administrator under this section shall be subject to judicial review pursuant to section 16.

[§6(h) amended by PL 100–532]

§136e. Registration of Establishments. [Sec. 7]

(a) Requirement—No person shall produce any pesticide subject to this Act or active ingredient used in producing a pesticide subject to this Act in any State unless the establishment in which it is produced is registered with the Administrator. The application for registration of any establishment shall include the name and address of the establishment and of the producer who operates such establishment.

(b) Registration.—Whenever the Administrator receives an application under subsection (a). the Administrator shall register the establishment and assign it an establishment number.

(c) Information Required.

(1) Any producer operating an establishment registered under this section shall inform the Administrator within 30 days after it is registered of the types and amounts of pesticides and, if applicable, active ingredients used in producing pesticides—

(A) which the producer is currently producing:

(B) which the producer has produced during the past year; and

(C) which the producer has sold or distributed during the past year. The information required by this paragraph shall be kept current and submitted to the Administrator annually as required under such regulations as the Administrator may prescribe.

[§7(c)(1) amended by PL 102–237]

(2) Any such producer shall, upon the request of the Administrator for the purpose of issuing a stop sale order pursuant to section 13. inform the Administrator of the name and address of any recipient of any pesticide produced in any registered establishment which the producer operates.

[§7(c)(2) amended by PL 102–237]

(d) Confidential Records and Information. Any information submitted to the Administrator pursuant to subsection (c) other than the names of the pesticides or active ingredients used in producing pesticides produced, sold, or distributed at an establishment shall be considered confidential and shall be subject to the provisions of section 10.

§136f. Books and Records. [Sec. 8]

(a) Requirements. The Administrator may prescribe regulations requiring producers, registrants, and applicants for registration to maintain such records with respect to their operations and the pesticides and device produced as the Administrator determines are necessary for the effective enforcement of this Act and to make the records available for inspection and copying in the same manner as provided in subsection (b). No records required under this subsection shall extend to financial data, sales data other than shipment data, pricing data, personnel data, and research data (other than data relating to registered pesticides or to a pesticide for which an application for registration has been filed).

[§8(a) amended by PL 100–532; PL 102–237]

(b) Inspection. For the purposes of enforcing the provisions of this Act, any producer, distributor, carrier, dealer, or any other person who sells or offers for sale, delivers or offers for delivery any pesticide or device subject to this Act, shall, upon request of any officer or employee of the Environmental Protection Agency or of any State or political subdivision, duly designated by the Administrator, furnish or permit such person at all reasonable times to have access to, and to copy: (1) all records showing the delivery, movement, or holding of such pesticide or device, including the quantity, the date of shipment and receipt, and the name of the consignor and consignee; or (2) in the event of the inability of any person to produce records containing such information, all other records and information relating to such delivery, movement, or holding of the pesticide or device. Any inspection with respect to any records and information referred to in this subsection shall not extend to financial data, sales data other than shipment data, pricing data, personnel data; and research data (other than data relating to registered pesticides or to a pesticide for which an application for registration has been filed). Before undertaking an inspection under this subsection, the officer or employee must present to the owner, operator, or agent in charge of the establishment or other place where pesticides or devices are held for distribution or sale, appropriate credentials and a written statement as to the reason for the inspection, including a statement as to whether a violation of the law is suspected. If no violation is suspected, an alternate and sufficient reason shall be given in writing. Each such inspection shall be commenced and completed with reasonable promptness.

§136g. Inspection of Establishments, etc. [Sec. 9]

(a) In General.—

(1) For purposes of enforcing the provisions of this Act, officers or employee of the Environmental Protection Agency or of any State duly designated by the Administrator are authorized to enter at reasonable times (A) any establishment or other place where pesticides or devices are held for distribution or sale for the purpose of inspecting and obtaining samples of any pesticides or devices, packaged, labeled, and released for shipment, and samples of any containers or labeling for such pesticides or devices, or (B) any place where there is being held any pesticide the registration of which has been suspended or canceled for the purpose of determining compliance with section 19.

[§9(a)(1) amended by PL 100–532]

(2) Before undertaking such inspection, the officers of employees must present to the owner, operator, or agent in charge of the establishment or other place where pesticides or devices are held for distribution or sale, appropriate credentials and a written statement as to the reason for the inspection, including a statement as to whether a violation of the law is suspected. If no violation is suspected, an alternate and sufficient reason shall be given in writing. Each such inspection shall be commenced and completed with reasonable promptness. If the officer or employee obtains any samples, prior to leaving the premises, the producer shall give to the owner, operator, or agent in charge a receipt describing the samples obtained and, if requested, a portion of each such sample equal in volume or weight to the portion retained. If an analysis is made of such samples, a copy of the results of such analysis shall be furnished promptly to the owner, operator, or agent in charge.

[§9(a)(2) amended by PL 102–237]

(b) Warrants.—For purposes of enforcing the provisions of this Act and upon a showing to an officer or court of competent jurisdiction that there is reason to believe that the provisions of this Act have been violated, officers or employees duly designated by the Administrator are empowered to obtain and to execute warrants authorizing.

(1) entry, inspection, and copying of records for the purpose of this section or section 8;

[§9(b)(1) amended by PL 100–532]

(2) inspection and reproduction of all records showing the quantity, date of shipment, and the name of consignor and consignee of any pesticide or device found in the establishment which is adulterated, misbranded, not registered (in the case of a pesticide) or otherwise in violation of this Act and in the event of the inability of any person to produce records containing such information, all other records and information relating to such delivery, movement, or holding of the pesticide or device; and

(3) the seizure of any pesticide or device which is in violation of this Act.

(c) Enforcement.—

(1) Certification of Facts to Attorney General.—The examination of pesticides or devices shall be made in the Environmental Protection Agency or elsewhere as the Administrator may designate for the purpose of determining from such examinations whether they comply with the requirements of this Act. If it shall appear from any such examination that they fail to comply with the requirements of this Act, the Administrator shall cause notice to be given to the person against whom criminal or civil proceedings are contemplated. Any person so notified shall be given an opportunity to present the person's views, either orally or in writing, with regard to such contemplated proceedings, and if in the opinion of the Administrator it appears that the provisions of this Act have been violated by such person, then the Administrator shall certify the facts to the Attorney General, with a copy of the results of the analysis or the examination of such pesticide for the institution of a criminal proceeding pursuant to section 14(b) or a civil proceeding under section 14(a), when the Administrator determines that such action will be sufficient to effectuate the purposes of this Act.

[§9(c)(1) amended by PL 102–237]

(2) Notice not Required.—The notice of contemplated proceedings and opportunity to present views set forth in this subsection are not prerequisites to the institution of any proceeding by the Attorney General.

(3) Warning Notices.—Nothing in this Act shall be construed as requiring the Administrator to institute proceedings for prosecution of minor violations of this Act whenever the Administrator believes that the public interest will be adequately served by a suitable written notice of warning.

§136h. Protection of Trade Secrets and Other Information. [Sec. 10]

(a) In General.—In submitting data required by this Act, the applicant may (1) clearly mark any portions thereof which in the applicant's opinion are trade secrets or commercial or financial information and (2) submit such marked material separately from other material required to be submitted under this Act.

[§10(a) amended by PL 102–237]

(b) Disclosure.—Notwithstanding any other provision of this Act and subject to the limitations in subsections (d) and (e) of his section, the Administrator shall not make public information which in the Administrator's judgment contains or relates to trade secrets or commercial or financial information obtained from a person and privileged or confidential, except that, when necessary to carry out the provisions of this Act, information relating to formulas of products acquired by authorization of this Act may be revealed to any Federal agency consulted and may be revealed at a public hearing or in findings of fact issued by the Administrator.

[§10(b) amended by PL 102–237]

(c) Disputes.—If the Administrator proposes to release for inspection information which the applicant or registrant believes to be protected from disclosure under subsection (b), the Administrator shall notify the applicant or registrant, in writing, by certified mail. The Administrator shall not thereafter make available for inspection such data until thirty days after receipt of the notice by the applicant or registrant. During this period, the applicant or registrant may institute an action in an appropriate district court for a declaratory judgment as to whether such information is subject to protection under subsection (b).

[§10(c) amended by PL 102–237]

(d) Limitations.—

(1) All information concerning the objectives, methodology, results, or significance of any test or experiment performed on or with a registered or previously registered pesticide or its separate ingredients, impurities, or degrada-

tion products, and any information concerning the effects of such pesticide on any organism or the behavior of such pesticide in the environment, including, but not limited to, data on safety to fish and wildlife, humans and other mammals, plants, animals, and soil, and studies on persistence, translocation and fate in the environment, and metabolism, shall be available for disclosure to the public. The use of such data for any registration purpose shall be governed by section 3 of this Act. This paragraph does not authorize the disclosure of any information that—

[§10(d)(1) amended by PL 100–532]

(A) discloses manufacturing or quality control processes,

(B) discloses the details of any methods for testing, detecting, or measuring the quantity of any deliberately added inert ingredient of a pesticide, or

(C) discloses the identity or percentage quantity of any deliberately added inert ingredient of a pesticide, unless the Administrator has first determined that disclosure is necessary to protect against an unreasonable risk of injury to health or the environment.

(2) Information concerning production, distribution, sale, or inventories of a pesticide that is otherwise entitled to confidential treatment under subsection (b) of this section may be publicly disclosed in connection with a public proceeding to determine whether a pesticide, or any ingredient of a pesticide, causes unreasonable adverse effects on health or the environment, if the Administrator determines that such disclosure is necessary in the public interest.

(3) If the Administrator proposes to disclose information described in clause (A), (B), or (C) of paragraph (1) or in paragraph (2) of this subsection, the Administrator shall notify by certified mail the submitter of such information of the intent to release such information. The Administrator may not release such information, without the submitter's consent, until thirty days after the submitter has been furnished such notice. Where the Administrator finds that disclosure of information described in clause (A), (B), or (C) of paragraph (1) of this subsection is necessary to avoid or lessen an imminent and substantial risk of injury to the public health, the Administrator may set such shorter period of notice (but not less than ten days) and such method of notice as the Administrator finds appropriate. During such period the data submitter may institute an action in an appropriate district court to enjoin or limit the proposed disclosure. The court may enjoin disclosure, or limit the disclosure or the parties to whom disclosure shall be made; to the extent that—

[§10(d)(3) amended by PL 98–620; PL 100–532]

(A) in the case of information described in clause (A), (B), or (C) of paragraph (l) of this subsection, the proposed disclosure is not required to protect against an unreasonable risk of injury to health or the environment; or

(B) in the case of information described in paragraph (2) of this subsection, the public interest in availability of the information in the public proceeding does not outweigh the interests in preserving the confidentiality of the information.

(e) Disclosure to Contractors.—Information otherwise protected from disclosure to the public under subsection (b) of this section may be disclosed to contractors with the United States and employees of such contractors if, in the opinion of the Administrator, such disclosure is necessary for the satisfactory performance by the contractor of a contract with the United States for the performance of work in connection with this Act and under such conditions as the Administrator may specify. The Administrator shall require as a condition to the disclosure of information under this subsection that the person receiving it take such security precautions respecting the information as the Administrator shall by regulation prescribe.

(f) Penalty for Disclosure by Federal Employees.—

(1) Any officer or employee of the United States or former officer or employee of the United States who, by virtue of such employment or official position, has obtained possession of, or has access to, material the disclosure of which is prohibited by subsection (b) of this section, and who, knowing that disclosure of such material is prohibited by such subsection, willfully discloses the material in any manner to any person not entitled to receive it, shall be fined not more than $10,000 or imprisoned for not more than one year, or both. Section 1905 of title 18 of the United States Code shall not apply with respect to the publishing, divulging, disclosure, or making known of, or making available, information reported or otherwise obtained under this Act. Nothing in this Act shall preempt any civil remedy under State or Federal law for wrongful disclosure of trade secrets.

(2) For the purposes of this section, any contractor with the United States who is furnished information as authorized by subsection (e) of this section, or any employee of any such contractor, shall be considered to be an employee of the United States.

(g) Disclosure to Foreign and Multinational Pesticide Producers.—

(1) The Administrator shall not knowingly disclose information submitted by an applicant or registrant under this Act to any employee or agent of any business or other entity engaged in the production, sale, or distribution of pesticides in countries other than the United States or in addition to the United States or to any other person who intends to deliver such data to such foreign or multinational business or entity unless the applicant or registrant has consented to such disclosure. The Administrator shall require an affirmation from any person who intends to inspect data that such person does not seek access to the data for purposes of delivering it or offering it for sale to any such business or entity or its agents or employees and will not purposefully deliver or negligently cause the data to be delivered to such business or entity or its agents or employees and will not purposefully deliver or negligently cause the data to be delivered to such business or entity or its agents or employees. Notwithstanding any other provision of this subsection, the Administrator may disclose information to any person in connection with a public proceeding under law or regulation, subject to restrictions on the availability of information contained elsewhere in this Act, which information is relevant to a determination by the Administrator with respect to whether a pesticide, or any ingredient of a pesticide, causes unreasonable adverse effects on health or the environment.

(2) The Administrator shall maintain records of the names of persons to whom data are disclosed under this subsection and the persons or organizations they represent and shall inform the applicant or registrant of the names and affiliations of such persons.

(3) Section 1001 of title 18 of the United States Code shall apply to any affirmation made under paragraph (1) of this subsection.

§136i. Use of Restricted Use Pesticides; Applicators. [Sec. 11]

[§11 amended by PL 100–532; PL 102–237]

(a) Certification Procedure.—

(1) Federal Certification.—In any State for which a State plan for applicator certification has not been approved by the Administrator, the Administrator, in consultation with the Governor of such State, shall conduct a program for the certification of applicators of pesticides. Such program shall conform to the requirements imposed upon the States under the provisions of subsection (a)(2) of this section and shall not require private applicators to take any examination to establish competency in the use of pesticides. Prior to the implementation of the program, the Administrator shall publish in the Federal Register for review and comment a summary of the Federal plan for applicator certification and shall make generally available within the State copies of' the plan. The Administrator shall hold public hearings at one or more locations within the State if so requested by the Governor of such State during the thirty days following publication of the Federal Register notice inviting comments on the Federal plan. The hearings shall be held within thirty days following receipt of the request from the Governor. In any State in which the Administrator conducts a certification program, the Administrator may require any person engaging in the commercial application, sale, offering for sale, holding for sale, or distribution of any pesticide one or more uses of which have been classified for restricted use to maintain such records and submit such reports concerning the commercial application, sale, or distribution of such pesticide as the Administrator may by regulation prescribe. Subject to paragraph (2), the Administrator shall prescribe standards for the certification of applicators of pesticides. Such standards shall provide that to be certified, an individual must be determined to be competent with respect to the use and handling of pesticides, or to the use and handling of the pesticide or class of pesticides covered by such individual's certification. The certification standard for a private applicator shall, under a State plan submitted for approval, be deemed fulfilled by the applicator completing a certification form. The Administrator shall further assure that such form contains adequate information and affirmations to carry out the intent of this Act, and may include in the form an affirmation that the private applicator has completed a training program approved by the Administrator so long as the program does not require the private applicator to take, pursuant to a requirement prescribed by the Administrator, any examination to establish compe-

tency in the use of the pesticide. The Administrator may require any pesticide dealer participating in a certification program to be licensed under a State licensing program approved by the Administrator.

[§11(a)(1) amended by PL 100–532; PL 102–237]

(2) State Certification.—If any State, at any time, desires to certify applicators of pesticides, the Governor of such State shall submit a State plan for such purpose. The Administrator shall approve the plan submitted by any State, or any modification thereof, if such plan in the Administrator's judgment—

[§11(a)(2) amended by PL 102–237]

(A) designates a State agency as the agency responsible for administering the plan throughout the State;

(B) contains satisfactory assurances that such agency has or will have the legal authority and qualified personnel necessary to carry out the plan;

(C) gives satisfactory assurances that the State will devote adequate funds to the administration of the plan;

(D) provides that the State agency will make such reports to the Administrator in such form and containing such information as the Administrator may from time to time require; and

(E) contains satisfactory assurances that State standards for the certification of applicators of pesticides conform with those standards prescribed by the Administrator under paragraph (1). Any State certification program under this section shall be maintained in accordance with the State plan approved under this section.

(b) State Plans.—If the Administrator rejects a plan submitted under this subsection (a)(2) the Administrator shall afford the State submitting the plan due notice and opportunity for hearing before so doing. If the Administrator approves a plan submitted under subsection (a)(2), then such state shall certify applicators mines that a State is not administering the certification program in accordance with the plan approved under this section, the Administrator shall so notify the State and provide for a hearing at the request of the State, and, if appropriate corrective action is not taken within a reasonable time, not to exceed ninety days, the Administrator shall withdraw approval of such plan.

[§11(b) amended by PL 102–237]

(c) Instruction in Integrated Pest Management Techniques.—Standards prescribed by the Administrator for the certification of applicators of pesticides under subsection (a), and State plans submitted to the Administrator under subsection (a), shall include provisions for making instructional materials concerning integrated pest management techniques available to individuals at their request in accordance with the provisions of section 23(c) of this Act, but such plans may not require that any individual receive instruction concerning such techniques or be shown to be competent with respect to the use of such techniques. The Administrator and States implementing such plans shall provide that all interested individuals are notified of the availability of such instructional materials.

(d) In General.—No regulations prescribed by the Administrator for carrying out the provisions of this Act shall require any private applicator to maintain any records or file any reports or other documents.

(e) Separate Standards.— When establishing or approving standards for licensing or certification, the Administrator shall establish separate standards for commercial and private applicators.

[§11(e) amended by PL 102–237]

§136j. Unlawful Acts. [Sec. 12]

(a) In General.—

(1) Except as provided by subsection (b), it shall be unlawful for any person in any State to distribute or sell to any person—

[§12(a)(1) amended by PL 100–532]

(A) any pesticide which is not registered under section 3 or whose registration has been cancelled or suspended, except to the extent that distribution or sale otherwise has been authorized by the Administrator under this Act;

[§12(a)(1)(A) amended by PL 100–532]

(B) any registered pesticide if any claims made for it as a part of its distribution or sale substantially differ from any claims made for it as a part of the statement required in connection with its registration under section 3;

(C) any registered pesticide the composition of which differs at the time of its distribution or sale from its composition as described in the statement required in connection with its registration under section 3;

(D) any pesticide which has not been colored or discolored pursuant to the provisions of section 25(c)(5);

(E) any pesticide which is adulterated or misbranded; or

(F) any device which is misbranded.

(2) It shall be unlawful for any person—

(A) to detach, alter, deface, or destroy, in whole or in part, any labeling required under this Act;

(B) to refuse to—

[§12(a)(2)(B) amended by PL 100–532]

(i) prepare, maintain, or submit any records required by or under section 5, 7, 8, 11 or 19;

(ii) submit any reports required by or under section 5, 6, 7, 8, 11 or 19; or

(iii) allow any entry, inspection, copying of records, or sampling authorized by this Act;

(C) to give a guaranty or undertaking provided for in subsection (b) which is false in any particular, except that a person who receives and relies upon a guaranty authorized under subsection (b) may give a guaranty to the same effect, which guaranty shall contain, in addition to the person's own name and address, the name and address of the person residing in the United States from whom the person received the guaranty or undertaking;

[§12(a)(2)(C) amended by PL 102-237]

(D) to use for the person's own advantage or to reveal, other than to the Administrator, or officials or employees of the Environmental Protection Agency or other Federal executive agencies, or to the courts, or to physicians, pharmacists, and other qualified persons, needing such information for the performance of their duties, in accordance with such directions as the Administrator may prescribe, any information acquired by authority of this Act which is confidential under this Act;

[§12(a)(2)(D) amended by PL 102–237]

(E) who is a registrant. wholesaler, dealer, retailer, or other distributor to advertise a produce registered under this Act for restricted use without giving the classification of the product assigned to it under section 3;

(F) to distribute or sell, or to make available for use, or to use, any registered pesticide classified for restricted use for some or all purposes other than in accordance with section 3(d) and any regulations thereunder, except that it shall not be unlawful to sell, under regulations issued by the Administrator, a restricted use pesticide to a person who is not a certified applicator for application by a certified applicator;

[§12(a)(2)(F) amended by PL 100–532]

(G) to use any registered pesticide in a manner inconsistent with its labeling;

(H) to use any pesticide which is under an experimental use permit contrary to the provisions of such permit;

(I) to violate any order issued under section 13;

(J) to violate any suspension order issued under section 3(c)(2)(B), 4, or 6;

[§12(a)(2)(J) amended by PL 100–532]

(K) to violate any cancellation order issued under this Act or to fail to submit a notice in accordance with section 6(g);

[§12(a)(2)(K) amended by PL 100–532]

(L) who is a producer to violate any of the provisions of section 7;

(M) to knowingly falsify all or part of any application for registration, application for experimental use permit, any information submitted to the Administrator pursuant to section 7, any records required to be maintained pursuant to this Act, any report filed under this Act, or any information marked as confidential and submitted to the Administrator under any provision of this act;

[§12(a)(2)(M) amended by PL 100–532]

(N) who is a registrant, wholesaler, dealer, retailer, or other distributor to fail to file reports required by this Act;

(O) to add any substance to, or take any substance from, any pesticide in a manner that may defeat the purpose of this Act;

[§12(a)(2)(O) amended by PL 102–237]

(P) to use any pesticide in tests on human beings unless such human beings (i) are fully informed of the nature and purposes of the test and of any physical and mental health consequences which are reasonably foreseeable therefrom, and (ii) freely volunteer to participate in the test;

[§12(a)(2)(P) amended by PL 102–237]

(Q) to falsify all or part of any information relating to the testing of pesticide (or any ingredient, metabolite, or degradation product thereof), including the nature of any protocol, procedure, substance, organism, or equipment used, observation made, or conclusion or opinion formed, submitted to the Administrator, or that the person knows will be furnished to the Administrator or will become a part of any records required to be maintained by this Act;

[§12(a)(2)(Q) added by PL 100–532]

(R) to submit to the Administrator data known to be false in support of a registration; or

[§12(a)(2)(R) added by PL 100–532]

(S) to violate any regulation issued under section 3(a) or 19.

[§12(a)(2)(S) added by PL 100–532]

(b) Exemptions.—The penalties provided for a violation of paragraph (1) of subsection (a) shall not apply to—

(1) any person who establishes a guaranty signed by, and containing the name and address of, the registrant or person residing in the United States from whom the person purchased or received in good faith the pesticide in the same unbroken package, to the effect that the pesticide was lawfully registered at the time of sale and delivery to the person, and that it complies with the other requirements of this Act, and in such case the guarantor shall be subject to the penalties which would otherwise attach to the person holding the guaranty under the provisions of this Act;

[§12(b)(1) amended by PL 102–237]

(2) any carrier while lawfully shipping, transporting, or delivering for shipment any pesticide or device, if such carrier upon request of any officer or employee duly designated by the Administrator shall permit such officer or employee to copy all of its records concerning such pesticide or device;

(3) any public official while engaged in the performance of the official duties of the public official;

[§12(b)(3) amended by PL 102–237]

(4) any person using or possessing any pesticide as provided by an experimental use permit in effect with respect to such pesticide and such use or possession: or

(5) any person who ship a substance or mixture of substances being put through tests in which the purpose is only to determine its value for pesticide purposes or to determine its toxicity or other properties and from which the user does not expect to receive any benefit in pest control from its use.

§136k. Stop Sale, Use, Removal, and Seizure.
[Sec. 13]

(a) Stop Sale etc, Orders.— Whenever any pesticide or device is found by the Administrator in any State and there is reason to believe on the basis of inspection or tests that such pesticide or device is in violation of any of the provisions of this Act, or that such pesticide or device has been or is intended to be distributed or sold in violation of any such provisions, or when the registration of the pesticide has been canceled by a final order or has been suspended, the Administrator may issue a written or printed 'stop sale, use, or removal' order to any person who owns, controls, or has custody of such pesticide or device, and after receipt of such order no person shall sell, use, or remove the pesticide or device described in the order except in accordance with the provisions of the order.

(b) Seizure.—Any pesticide or device that is being transported or, having been transported, remains unsold or in original unbroken packages, or that is sold or offered for sale in any State, or that is imported from a foreign country, shall be liable to be proceeded against in any district court in the district where it is found and seized for confiscation by a process in rem for condemnation if—

(1) in the case of a pesticide—

(A) it is adulterated or misbranded;

(B) it is not registered pursuant to the provisions of section 3;

(C) its labeling fails to bear the information required by this Act:

(D) it is not colored or discolored and such coloring or discoloring is required under this Act; or

(E) any of the claims made for it or any of the directions for its use differ in substance from the representations made in connection with its registration:

(2) in the case of a device, it is misbranded: or

(3) in the case of a pesticide or device, when used in accordance with the requirements imposed under this Act and as directed by the labeling, it nevertheless causes unreasonable adverse effects on the environment.

In the case of a plant regulator, defoliant, or desiccant, used in accordance with the label claims and recommendations, physical or physiological effects on plants or parts thereof shall not be deemed to be injury, when such effects are the purpose for which the plant regulator, defoliant, or desiccant was applied.

[§13(b)(3) amended by PL 100–532]

(c) Disposition after Condemnation.—If the pesticide or device is condemned it shall, after entry of the decree, be disposed of by destruction or sale as the court may direct and the proceeds, if sold, less the court costs, shall be paid into the Treasury of the United States, but the pesticide or device shall not be sold contrary to the provisions of this Act or the laws of the jurisdiction in which it is sold. On payment of the costs of the condemnation proceedings and the execution and delivery of a good and sufficient bond conditioned that the pesticide or device shall not be sold or otherwise disposed of contrary to the provisions of the Act or the laws of any jurisdiction in which sold, the court may direct that such pesticide or device be delivered to the owner thereof. The proceedings of such condemnation cases shall conform, as near as may be to the proceedings in admiralty, except that either party may demand trial by jury of any issue of fact joined in any case, and all such proceedings shall be at the suit of and in the name of the United States.

[§13(c) amended by PL 100–532]

(d) Court Costs, etc.—When a decree of condemnation is entered against the pesticide or device, court costs and fees, storage, and other proper expenses shall be awarded against the person, if any, intervening as claimant of the pesticide or device.

§136l. Penalties. [Sec. 14]

(a) Civil Penalties.—

(1) In General.—Any registrant, commercial applicator, whole-saler, dealer, retailer, or other distributor who violates any provision of this Act may be assessed a civil penalty by the Administrator of not more than $5,000 for each offense.

(2) Private Applicator.—Any private applicator or other person not included in paragraph (1) who violates any provision of this Act subsequent to receiving a written warning from the Administrator or following a citation for a prior violation, may be assessed a civil penalty by the Administrator of not more than $1,000 for each offense, except that any applicator not included under paragraph (1) of this subsection who holds or applies registered pesticides, or uses dilutions of registered pesticides, only to provide a service of controlling pests without delivering any unapplied pesticide to any person so served, and who violates any provision of this Act may be assessed a civil penalty by the Administrator of not more than $500 for the first offense nor more than $1,000 for each subsequent offense.

[§14(a)(2) amended by PL 102–237]

(3) Hearing.—No civil penalty shall be assessed unless the person charged shall have been given notice and opportunity for a hearing on such charge in the county, parish, or incorporated city of the residence of the person charged.

(4) Determination of Penalty.—In determining the amount of the penalty, the Administrator shall consider the appropriateness of such penalty to the size of the business of the person charged, the effect on the person's ability to continue in business, and the gravity of the violation. Whenever the Administrator finds that the violation occurred despite the exercise of due care or did not cause significant harm to health or the environment, the Administrator may issue a warning in lieu of assessing a penalty.

(5) References to Attorney General.—In case of inability to collect such civil penalty or failure of any person to pay all, or such portion of such civil penalty as the Administrator may determine, the Administrator shall refer the matter to the Attorney General, who shall recover such amount by action in the appropriate United States district court.

(b) Criminal Penalties.—

(1) In General.—

(A) Any registrant, applicant for a registration, or producer who knowingly violates any provision of this Act shall be fined not more than $50,000 or imprisoned for not more than 1 year, or both.

(B) Any commercial applicator of a restricted use pesticide, or any other person not described in subparagraph (A) who distributes or sells pesticides or devices, who knowingly violates any provision of this Act shall be fined not more than $25,000 or imprisoned for not more than 1 year, or both.

[§14(b)(1) amended by PL 100–532]

(2) Private Applicator.—Any private applicator or other person not included in paragraph (l) who knowingly violates any provision of this Act shall be guilty of a misdemeanor and shall on conviction be fined not more than $1,000, or imprisoned for not more than 30 days, or both.

(3) Disclosure of Information.—Any person, who, with intent to defraud, uses or reveals information relative to formulas of products acquired under the authority of section 3, shall be fined not more than $10,000, or imprisoned for not more than three years, or both.

(4) Acts of Officers, Agents, etc.—When construing and enforcing the provisions of this Act, the act, omission, or failure of any officer, agent, or other person acting for or employed by any person shall in every case be also deemed to be the act, omission, or failure of such person as well as that of the person employed.

§136m. Indemnities. [Sec. 15]

(a) General Indemnification.—

(1) In General.—Except as otherwise provided in this section, if—

(A) the Administrator notifies a registrant under section 6(c)(1) that the Administrator intends to suspend a registration or that an emergency order of suspension of a registration under section 6(c)(3) has been issued:

(B) the registration in question is suspended under section 6(c)7 U.S.C. 136d, and thereafter is canceled under section 6(b), 6(d), or 6(f); and

(C) any person who owned any quantity of the pesticide immediately before the notice to the registrant under subparagraph (A) suffered losses by reason of suspension or cancellation of the registration; the Administrator shall make an indemnity payment to the person.

(2) Exception.—Paragraph (1) shall not apply if the Administrator finds that the person—

(A) had knowledge of facts that, in themselves, would have shown that the pesticide did not meet the requirements of section 3(c)(5) for registration: and

(B) continued thereafter to produce the pesticide without giving timely notice of such facts to the Administrator.

(3) Report.—If the Administrator takes an action under paragraph (1) that requires the payment of indemnification. the Administrator shall report to the Committee on Agriculture of the House of Representatives, the Committee on Agriculture, Nutrition, and Forestry of the Senate, and the Committees on Appropriations of the House of Representatives and the Senate on—

(A) the action taken that requires the payment of indemnification;

(B) the reasons for taking the action;

(C) the estimated cost of the payment: and

(D) a request for the appropriation of funds for the payment.

(4) Appropriation.—The Administrator may not make a payment of indemnification under paragraph (1) unless a specific line item appropriation of funds has been made in advance for the payment.

(b) Indemnification of End Users, Dealers, and Distributors.—

(1) End Users.—If—

(A) the Administrator notifies a registrant under section 6(c)(1) that the Administrator intends to suspend a registration or that an emergency order of suspension of a registration under section 6(c)(3) has been issued;

(B) the registration in question is suspended under section 6(c), and thereafter is canceled under section 6(b), 6(d), or 6(f); and

(C) any person who, immediately before the notice to the registrant under subparagraph (A), owned any quantity of the pesticide for purposes of applying or using the pesticide as an end user, rather than for purposes of distributing or selling it or further processing it for distribution or sale, suffered a loss by reason of the suspension or cancellation of the pesticide: the person shall be entitled to an indemnity payment under this subsection for such quantity of the pesticide.

(2) Dealers and Distributors.—

(A) Any registrant, wholesaler, dealer, or other distributor (hereinafter in this paragraph referred to as a "seller") of a registered pesticide who distributes or sells the pesticide directly to any person not described as an end user in paragraph (1)(C) shall, with respect to any quantity of the pesticide that such person cannot use or resell as a result of the suspension or cancellation of the pesticide, reimburse such person for the cost of first acquiring the pesticide from the seller (other than the cost of transportation, if any), unless the seller provided to the person at the time of distribution or sale a notice, in writing, that the pesticide is not subject to reimbursement by the seller.

(B) If—

(i) the Administrator notifies a registrant under section 6(c)(1) that the Administrator intends to suspend a registration or that an emergency order of suspension of a registration under section 6(c)(3) has been issued;

(ii) the registration in question is suspended under section 6(c), and thereafter is canceled under section 6(b), 6(d), or 6(f);

(iii) any person who, immediately before the notice to the registrant under clause (i)—

(I) had not been notified in writing by the seller, as provided under subparagraph (A), that any quantity of the pesticide owned by such person is not subject to reimbursement by the seller in the event of suspension or cancellation of the pesticide; and

(II) owned any quantity of the pesticide for purposes of—

(aa) distributing or selling it; or

(bb) further processing it for distribution or sale directly to an end use suffered a loss by reason of the suspension or cancellation of the pesticide; and

(iv) the Administrator determines on the basis of a claim of loss submitted to the Administrator by the person, that the seller—

(I) did not provide the notice specified in subparagraph (A) to such person; and

(II) is and will continue to be unable to provide reimbursement to such person, as provided under subparagraph (A), for the loss referred to in clause (iii), as a result of the insolvency or bankruptcy of the seller and the seller's resulting inability to provide such reimbursement: the person shall be entitled to an indemnity payment under this subsection for such quantity of the pesticide.

(C) If an indemnity payment is made by the United States under this paragraph, the United States shall be subrogated to any right that would otherwise be held under this paragraph by a seller who is unable to make a reimbursement in accordance with this paragraph with regard to reimbursements that otherwise would have been made by the seller.

(3) Source.—Any payment required to be made under paragraph (1) or (2) shall be made from the appropriation provided under section 1304 of title 31, United States Code.

(4) Administrative Settlement.—An administrative settlement of a claim for such indemnity may be made in accordance with the third paragraph of section 2414 of title 28, United States Code, and shall be regarded as if it were made under that section for purposes of section 1304 of title 31, United States Code.

(c) Amount of Payment.—

(1) In General.—The amount of an indemnity payment under subsection (a) or (b) to any person shall be determined on the basis of the cost of the pesticide owned by the person (other than the cost of transportation, if any) immediately before the issuance of the notice to the registrant referred to in subsection (a)(1)(A), (b)(1)(A), or (b)(2)(B)(i), except that in no event shall an indemnity payment to any person exceed the fair market value of the pesticide owned by the person immediately before the issuance of the notice.

(2) Special Rule.— Notwithstanding any other provision of this Act, the Administrator may provide a reasonable time for use or other disposal of the pesticide. In determining the quantity of any pesticide for which indemnity shall be paid under this section, proper adjustment shall be made for any pesticide used or otherwise disposed of by the owner.

§136n. Administrative Procedure; Judicial Review. [Sec. 16]

(a) District Court Review.—Except as otherwise provided in this Act, the refusal of the Administrator to cancel or suspend a registration or to change a classification not following a hearing and other final actions of the Administrator not committed to the discretion of the Administrator by law are judicially reviewable by the district courts of the United States.

[§16(a) amended by PL 100–532]

(b) Review by Court of Appeals.—In the case of actual controversy as to the validity of any order issued by the Administrator following a public hearing, any person who will be adversely affected by such order and who had been a party to the proceedings may obtain judicial review by filing in the United States court of appeals for the circuit wherein such person resides or has a place of business, within 60 days after the entry of such order, a petition praying that the order be set aside in whole or in part. A copy of the petition shall be forthwith transmitted by the clerk of the court to the Administrator or any officer designated by the Administrator for that purpose, and thereupon the Administrator shall file in the court the record of the proceedings on which the Administrator based on the Administrator's order, as provided in section 2112 of title 28, United States Code. Upon the filing of such petition the court shall have exclusive jurisdiction to affirm or set aside the order complained of in whole or in part. The court shall consider all evidence of record. The order of the Administrator shall be sustained if it is supported by substantial evidence when considered on the record as a whole. The judgment of the court affirming or setting aside, in whole or in part, any order under this section shall be final, subject to review by the Supreme

Court of the United States upon certiorari or certification as provided in section 1254 of title 28 of the United States Code. The commencement of proceedings under this section shall not, unless specifically ordered by the court to the contrary, operate as a stay of an order.

[§16(b) amended by PL 98–620; PL 102–237]

(c) Jurisdiction of District Courts.— The district courts of the United States are vested with jurisdiction specifically to enforce. and to prevent and restrain violations of, this Act.

(d) Notice of Judgements.— The Administrator shall, by publication in such manner as the Administrator may prescribe, give notice of all judgments entered in actions instituted under the authority of this Act.

[§16(d) amended by PL 102–237]

§136o. Imports and Exports. [Sec. 17]

(a) Pesticides and Devices Intended for Export.— Notwithstanding any other provision of this Act, no pesticide or device or active ingredient used in producing a pesticide intended solely for export to any foreign country shall be deemed in violation of this Act—

(1) when prepared or packed according to the specifications or directions of the foreign purchaser, except that producers of such pesticides and devices and active ingredients used in producing pesticides shall be subject to sections 2(p), 2(q)(1)(A), (C), (D), (E), (G), and (H), 2(q)(2)(A), (B), (C)(i) and (iii), and (D), 7, and 8 of this Act: and

(2) in the case of any pesticide other than a pesticide registered under section 3, 7 U.S.C. 136a or sold under section 6(a)(1) of this Act, if, prior to export, the foreign purchaser has signed a statement acknowledging that the purchaser understands that such pesticide is not registered for use in the United States and cannot be sold in the United States under this Act. A copy of that statement shall be transmitted to an appropriate official of the government of the importing country.

[§17(a)(2) amended by PL 102–237]

(b) Cancellation Notices Furnished to Foreign Governments.—Whenever a registration, or a cancellation or suspension of the registration of a pesticide becomes effective, or ceases to be effective, the Administrator shall transmit through the State Department notification thereof to the governments of other countries and to appropriate international agencies. Such notification shall, upon request, include all information related to the cancellation or suspension of the registration of the pesticide and information concerning other pesticides that are registered under section 3 of this Act and that could be used in lieu of such pesticide.

(c) Importation of Pesticides and Devices.—The Secretary of the Treasury shall notify the Administrator of the arrival of pesticides and devices and shall deliver to the Administrator, upon the Administrator's request, samples of pesticides or devices which are being imported into the United States, giving notice to the owner or consignee, who may appear before the Administrator and have the right to introduce testimony. If it appears from the examination of a sample that it is adulterated or misbranded or otherwise violates the provisions set forth in this Act, or is otherwise injurious to health or the environment, the pesticide or device may be refused admission, and the Secretary of the Treasury shall refuse delivery to the consignee and shall cause the destruction of any pesticide or device refused delivery which shall not be exported by the consignee within 90 days from the date of notice of such refusal under such regulations as the Secretary of the Treasury may prescribe. The Secretary of the Treasury may deliver to the consignee such pesticide or device pending examination and decision in the matter or execution of bond for the amount of the full invoice value of such pesticide or device, together with the duty thereon, and on refusal to return such pesticide or device for any cause to the custody of the Secretary of the Treasury, when demanded, for the purpose of excluding them from the country, or for any other purpose, said consignee shall forfeit the full amount of said bond. All charges for storage, cartage, and labor on pesticides or devices which are refused admission or delivery shall be paid by the owner or consignee, and in default of such payment shall constitute a lien against any future importation made by such owner or consignee.

[§17(c) amended by PL 100–532]

(d) Cooperation in International Efforts.—The Administrator shall, in cooperation with the Department of State and any other appropriate Federal agency, participate and cooperate in any international efforts to develop improved pesticide research and regulations.

(e) Regulations.—The Secretary of the Treasury, in consultation with the Administrator, shall prescribe regulations for the enforcement of subsection (c) of this section.

§136p. Exemption of Federal and State Agencies. [Sec. 18]

The Administrator may, at the Administrator's discretion, exempt any Federal or State agency from any provision of this Act if the Administrator determines that emergency conditions exist which require such exemption. The Administrator, in determining whether or not such emergency conditions exist, shall consult with the Secretary of Agriculture and the Governor of any State concerned if they request such determination.

[§18 amended by PL 100–532; PL 102–237]

§136q. Storage, Disposal, Transportation, and Recall [Sec. 19]

(a) Storage, Disposal, and Transportation.—

(1) Data Requirements and Registration of Pesticides.—The Administrator may require under section 3 or 6 that—

(A) the registrant or applicant for registration of a pesticide submit or cite data or information regarding methods for the safe storage and disposal of excess quantities of the pesticide to support the registration or continued registration of a pesticide;

(B) the labeling of a pesticide contain requirements and procedures for the transportation, storage, and disposal of the pesticide, any container of the pesticide, any rinsate containing the pesticide, or any other material used to contain or collect excess or spilled quantities of the pesticide; and

(C) the registrant of a pesticide provide evidence of sufficient financial and other resources to carry out a recall plan under subsection (b), and provide for the disposition of the pesticide, in the event of suspension and cancellation of the pesticide.

(2) Pesticides.—The Administrator may by regulation, or as part of an order issued under section 6 or an amendment to such an order—

(A) issue requirements and procedures to be followed by any person who stores or transports a pesticide the registration of which has been suspended or canceled;

(B) issue requirements and procedures to be followed by any person who disposes of stocks of a pesticide the registration of which has been suspended; and

(C) issue requirements and procedures for the disposal of any pesticide the registration of which has been canceled.

(3) Containers, Rinsates, and Other Materials.—The Administrator may by regulation, or as part of an order issued under section 6 or an amendment to such an order—

(A) issue requirements and procedures to be followed by any person who stores or transports any container of a pesticide the registration of which has been suspended or canceled, any rinsate containing the pesticide, or any other material used to contain or collect excess or spilled quantities of the pesticide;

(B) issue requirements and procedures to be followed by any person who disposes of stocks of any container of a pesticide the registration of which has been suspended, any rinsate containing the pesticide, or any other material used to contain or collect excess or spilled quantities of the pesticide; and

(C) issue requirements and procedures for the disposal of any container of a pesticide the registration of which has been canceled, any rinsate containing the pesticide. or any other material used to contain or collect excess or spilled quantities of the pesticide.

[§19(a) amended by PL 100-532]

(b) Recalls.—

(1) In General.—If the registration of a pesticide has been suspended and canceled under section 6, and if the Administrator finds that recall of the pesticide is necessary to protect health or the environment, the Administrator shall order a recall of the pesticide in accordance with this subsection.

(2) Voluntary Recall.—If, after determining under paragraph (1) that a recall is necessary, the Administrator finds that voluntary recall by the registrant and others in the chain of distribution may be as safe and effective as a mandatory recall, the Administrator shall request the registrant of the pesticide to submit, within 60 days of the request, a plan for the voluntary recall of the pesticide. If such a plan is requested and submitted, the Administrator shall approve the plan and order the registrant to conduct the recall in accordance with the plan unless the Administrator determines, after an informal hearing, that the plan is inadequate to protect health or the environment.

(3) Mandatory Recall.—If, after determining under paragraph (1) that a recall is necessary. the Administrator does not request the submission of a plan under paragraph (2) or finds such a plan to be inadequate, the Administrator shall issue a regulation that prescribes a plan for the recall of the pesticide. A regulation issued under this paragraph may apply to any

person who is or was a registrant, distributor, or seller of the pesticide, or any successor in interest to such a person.

(4) Recall Procedure.—A regulation issued under this subsection may require any person that is subject to the regulation to—

(A) arrange to make available one or more storage facilities to receive and store the pesticide to which the recall program applies, and inform the Administrator of the location of each such facility;

(B) accept and store at such a facility those existing stocks of such pesticide that are tendered by any other person who obtained the pesticide directly or indirectly from the person that is subject to such regulation;

(C) on the request of a person making such a tender, provide for proper transportation of the pesticide to a storage facility; and

(D) take such reasonable steps as the regulation may prescribe to inform persons who may be holders of the pesticide of the terms of the recall regulation and how those persons may tender the pesticide and arrange for transportation of the pesticide to a storage facility.

(5) Contents of Recall Plan.—A recall plan established under this subsection shall include—

(A) the level in the distribution chain to which the recall is to extend, and a schedule for recall; and

(B) the means to be used to verify the effectiveness of the recall.

(6) Requirements or Procedures.—No requirement or procedure imposed in accordance with paragraph (2) of subsection (a) may require the recall of existing stocks of the pesticide except as provided by this subsection.

[§19(b) amended by PL 100–532]

(c) Storage Costs.—

(1) Submission of Plan.—A registrant who wishes to become eligible for reimbursement of storage costs incurred as a result of a recall prescribed under subsection (b) for a pesticide whose registration has been suspended and canceled shall, as soon as practicable after the suspension of the registration of the pesticide, submit to the Administrator a plan for the storage and disposal of the pesticide that meets criteria established by the Administrator by regulation.

(2) Reimbursement.—Within a reasonable period of time after such storage costs are incurred and paid by the registrant, the Administrator shall reimburse the registrant, on request, for—

(A) none of the costs incurred by the registrant before the date of submission of the plan referred to in paragraph (1) to the Administrator;

(B) 100 percent of the costs incurred by the registrant after the date of submission of the plan to the Administrator or the date of cancellation of the registration of the pesticide, whichever is later, but before the approval of the plan by the Administrator;

(C) 50 percent of the costs incurred by the registrant during the 1–year period beginning on the date of the approval of the plan by the Administrator or the date of cancellation of the registration of the pesticide, whichever is later;

(D) none of the costs incurred by the registrant during the 3–year period beginning on the 366th day following approval of the plan by the Administrator or the date of cancellation of the registration of the pesticide, whichever is later; and

(E) 25 percent of the costs incurred by the registrant during the period beginning on the first day of the 5th year following the date of the approval of the plan by the Administrator or the date of cancellation of the registration of the pesticide, whichever is later, and ending on the date that a disposal permit for the pesticide is issued by a State or an alternative plan for disposal of the pesticide in accordance with applicable law has been developed.

(d) Administration of Storage, Disposal, Transportation, and Recall Programs.—

(1) Voluntary Agreements.— Nothing in this section shall be construed as preventing or making unlawful any agreement between a seller and a buyer of any pesticide or other substance regarding the ultimate allocation of the costs of storage, transportation, or disposal of a pesticide.

(2) Rule and Regulation Review.— Section 25(a)(4) shall not apply to any regulation issued under subsection (a)(2) or (b).

(3) Limitations.—No registrant shall be responsible under this section for a pesticide the registration of which is held by another person. No distributor or seller shall be responsible under this section for a pesticide that the distributor or seller did not hold or sell.

(4) Seizure and Penalties.— If the Administrator finds that a person who is subject to a regulation or order under subsection (a)(2) or (b) has failed substantially to comply with that regulation or order, the Administrator may take action under section 13 or 14 or obtain injunctive relief under section 16(c) against such person or any successor in interest of any such person.

(e) Container Design.—

(1) Procedures.—

(A) Not later than 3 years after the effective date of this subsection, the Administrator shall, in consultation with the heads of other interested Federal agencies, promulgate regulations for the design of pesticide containers that will promote the safe storage and disposal of pesticides.

(B) The regulations shall ensure, to the fullest extent practicable, that the containers—

(i) accommodate procedures used for the removal of pesticides from the containers and the rinsing of the containers;

(ii) facilitate the safe use of the containers, including elimination of splash and leakage of pesticides from the containers;

(iii) facilitate the safe disposal of the containers; and

(iv) facilitate the safe refill and reuse of the containers.

(2) Compliance.—The Administrator shall require compliance with the regulations referred to in paragraph (1) not later than 5 years after the effective date of this subsection.

[§19(e) added by PL 100-532]

(f) Pesticide Residue Removal.—

(1) Procedures.—

(A) Not later than 3 years after the effective date of this subsection, the Administrator shall, in consultation with the heads of other interested Federal agencies, promulgate regulations prescribing procedures and standards for the removal of pesticides from containers prior to disposal.

(B) The regulations may—

(i) specify, for each major type of pesticide container, procedures and standards providing for, at a minimum, triple rinsing or the equivalent degree of pesticide removal;

(ii) specify procedures that can be implemented promptly and easily in various circumstances and conditions;

(iii) provide for reuse, whenever practicable, or disposal of rinse water and residue; and

(iv) be coordinated with requirements for the rinsing of containers imposed under the Solid Waste Disposal Act (42 U.S.C. 6901*et seq.*).

(C) The Administrator may, at the discretion of the Administrator, exempt products intended solely for household use from the requirements of this subsection.

(2) Compliance.—Effective beginning 5 years after the effective date of this subsection, a State may not exercise primary enforcement responsibility under section 26, or certify an applicator under section 11, unless the Administrator determines that the State is carrying out an adequate program to ensure compliance with this subsection.

(3) Solid Waste Disposal Act.—Nothing in this subsection shall affect the authorities or requirements concerning pesticide containers under the Solid Waste Disposal Act (42 U.S.C. 6901).

[§19(f) added by PL 100-532]

(g) Pesticide Container Study.—

(1) Study.—

(A) The Administrator shall conduct a study of options to encourage or require—

(i) the return, refill, and reuse of pesticide containers;

(ii) the development and use of pesticide formulations that facilitate the removal of pesticide residues from containers; and

(iii) the use of bulk storage facilities to reduce the number of pesticide containers requiring disposal.

(B) In conducting the study, the Administrator shall—

(i) consult with the heads of other interested Federal agencies, State agencies, industry groups, and environmental organizations; and

(ii) assess the feasibility, costs, and environmental benefits of encouraging or requiring various measures or actions.

(2) Report.—Not later than 2 years after the effective date of this subsection, the Administrator shall submit to Congress a report describing the results of the study required under paragraph (1).

[§19(g) added by PL 100-532]

(h) Relationship to Solid Waste Disposal Act.—Nothing in this section shall diminish the authorities or requirements of the Solid Waste Disposal Act (42 U.S.C. 6901*et seq.*).

[§19(h) added by PL 100-532]

§136r. Research and Monitoring. [Sec. 20]

(a) Research—The Administrator shall undertake research, including research by grant or contract with other Federal agencies, universities, or others as may be necessary to carry out the purposes of this Act, and the Administrator shall conduct research into integrated pest management in coordination with the Secretary of Agriculture.

[§20(a) amended by PL 102–237]

(b) National Monitoring Plan—The Administrator shall formulate and periodically revise, in cooperation with other Federal, State, or local agencies, a national plan for monitoring pesticides.

(c) Monitoring.—The Administrator shall undertake such monitoring activities, including, but not limited to monitoring in air, soil, water, man, plants, and animals, as may be necessary for the implementation of this Act of the national pesticide monitoring plan. The Administrator shall establish procedures for the monitoring of man and animals and their environment for incidential pesticide exposure, including, but not limited to, the quantification of incidental human and environmental pesticide pollution and the secular trends thereof, and identification of the sources of contamination and their relationship to human and environmental effects. Such activities shall be carried out in cooperation with other Federal, State, and local agencies.

§136s. Solicitation of Comments; Notice of Public Hearings. [Sec. 21]

(a) Secretary of Agriculture.—The Administrator, before publishing regulations under this Act, shall solicit the views of the Secretary of Agriculture in accordance with the procedure described in section 25(a).

[§21(a) amended by PL 100–532]

(b) Views.—In addition to any other authority relating to public hearings and solicitation of views, in connection with the suspension or cancellation of a pesticide registration or any other actions authorized under this Act, the Administrator may. at the Administrator's discretion, solicit the views of all interested persons, either orally or in writing, and seek such advice from scientists, farmers, farm organizations, and other qualified persons as the Administrator deems proper.

[§21(b) amended by PL 100–532]

(c) Notice—In connection with all public hearings under this Act the Administrator shall publish timely notice of such hearings in the Federal Register.

[§21(c) amended by PL 100–532]

§136u. Delegation and Cooperation. [Sec. 22]

(a) Delegation.—All authority vested in the Administrator by virtue of the provisions of this Act may with like force and effect be executed by such employees of the Environmental Protection Agency as the Administrator may designate for the purpose.

(b) Cooperation.—The Administrator shall cooperate with the Department of Agriculture, any other Federal agency, and any appropriate agency of any State or any political subdivision thereof, in carrying out the provisions of this Act, and in securing uniformity of regulations.

§136u. State Cooperation, Aid, and Training. [Sec. 23]

(a) Cooperative Agreements.—The Administrator may enter into cooperative agreements with State and Indian tribes—

(1) to delegate to any State or Indian tribe the authority to cooperate in the enforcement of this Act through the use of its personnel or facilities, to train personnel of the State or Indian tribe to cooperate in the enforcement of this Act, and to assist States and Indian tribes in implementing cooperative enforcement programs through grants-in-aid; and

(2) to assist States in developing and administering State programs, and Indian tribes that enter into cooperative agreements, to train and certify applicators consistent with the standards the Administrator prescribes. Effective with the fiscal year beginning October 1, 1978, there are authorized to be appropriated annually such funds as may be necessary for the Administrator to provide through cooperative agreements an amount equal to 50 percent of the anticipated cost to each State or Indian tribe, as agreed to under such cooperative agreements, of conducting training and certification programs during such fiscal year, If funds sufficient to pay 50 percent of the costs for any year are not appropriated, the share of each State and Indian tribe shall be reduced in a like proportion in allocating available funds.

(b) Contracts for Training.—In addition, the Administrator may enter into contracts with

Federal, State, or Indian tribal agencies for the purpose of encouraging the training of certified applicators.

(c) Information and Education.—The Administrator shall, in cooperation with the Secretary of Agriculture, use the services of the cooperative State extension services to inform and educate pesticide users about accepted uses and other regulations made under this Act.

§136v. Authority of States. [Sec. 24]

(a) In General.—A State may regulate the sale or use of any federally registered pesticide or device in the State, but only if and to the extent the regulation does not permit any sales or use prohibited by this Act.

[§24(a) amended by PL 100–532]

(b) Uniformity.—Such State shall not impose or continue in effect any requirement for labeling or packaging in addition to or different from those required under this Act.

[§24(b) amended by PL 100–532]

(c) Additional Uses.—

(1) A State may provide registration for additional uses of federally registered pesticides formulated for distribution and use within that State to meet special local needs in accord with the purposes of this Act and if registration for such use has not previously been denied, disapproved, or canceled by the Administrator. Such registration shall be deemed registration under section 3 for all purposes of this Act, but shall authorize distribution and use only within such State.

[§24(c) amended by PL 100–532]

(2) A registration issued by a State under this subsection shall not be effective for more than ninety days if disapproved by the Administrator within that period. Prior to disapproval, the Administrator shall, except as provided in paragraph (3) of this subsection. advise the State of the Administrator's intention to disapprove and the reasons therefor. and provide the State time to respond. The Administrator shall not prohibit or disapprove a registration issued by a State under this subsection (A) on the basis of lack of essentiality of a pesticide or (B) except as provided in paragraph (3) of this subsection. if its composition and use patterns are similar to those of a federally registered pesticide.

(3) In no instance may a State issue a registration for a food or feed use unless there exists a tolerance or exemption under the Federal Food, Drug, and Cosmetic Act that permits the residues of the pesticide on the food or feed. If the Administrator determines that a registration issued by a State is inconsistent with the Federal Food, Drug, and Cosmetic Act, or the use of, a pesticide under a registration issued by a State constitutes an imminent hazard, the Administrator may immediately disapprove the registration.

(4) If the Administrator finds, in accordance with standards set forth in regulations issued under section 25 of this Act, that a State is not capable of exercising adequate controls to assure that State registration under this section will be in accord with the purposes of this Act or has failed to exercise adequate controls, the Administrator may suspend the authority of the State to register pesticides until such time as the Administrator is satisfied that the State can and will exercise adequate controls. Prior to any such suspension, the Administrator shall advise the State of the Administrator's intention to suspend and the reasons therefor and provide the State time to respond.

§136w. Authority of Administrator. [Sec. 25]

(a) In General.—

(1) Regulations.—The Administrator is authorized in accordance with the procedure described in paragraph (2), to prescribe regulations to carry out the provisions of this Act. Such regulations shall take into account the difference in concept and usage between various classes of pesticides and differences in environmental risk and the appropriate data for evaluating such risk between agricultural and nonagricultural pesticides.

(2) Procedure.—

(A) Proposed Regulations.— At least 60 days prior to signing any proposed regulation for publication in the Federal Register, the Administrator shall provide the Secretary of Agriculture with a copy of such regulation. If the Secretary comments in writing to the Administrator regarding any such regulation within 30 days after receiving it, the Administrator shall publish in the Federal Register (with the proposed regulation) the comments of the Secretary and the response of the Administrator with regard to the Secretary's comments. If the Secretary does not comment in writing to the Administrator regarding the regulation within 30 days after receiving it, the Administrator may sign such regulation for publication in the Federal Register any time after such 30–day period notwithstanding the foregoing 60—day time requirement.

(B) Final Regulations.—At least 30 days prior to signing any regulation in final form for publication in the Federal Register, the Administrator shall provide the Secretary of Agriculture with a copy of such regulation. If the Secretary comments in writing to the Administrator regarding any such final regulation within 15 days after receiving it, the Administrator shall publish in the Federal Register (with the final regulation) the comments of the Secretary, if requested by the Secretary, and the response of the Administrator concerning the Secretary's comments. If the Secretary does not comment in writing to the Administrator regarding the regulation within 15 days after receiving it, the Administrator may sign such regulation for publication in the Federal Register at any time after such 15–day period notwithstanding the foregoing 30–day time requirement. In taking any final action under this subsection, the Administrator shall include among those factors to be taken into account the effect of the regulation on production and prices of agricultural commodities, retail food prices, and otherwise on the on the agricultural economy, and the Administrator shall publish in the Federal Register an analysis of such effect.

(C) Time Requirements.—The time requirements imposed by subparagraphs (A) and (B) may be waived or modified to the extent agreed upon by the Administrator and the Secretary.

(D) Publication in the Federal Register.—The Administrator shall, simultaneously with any notification to the Secretary of Agriculture under this paragraph prior to the issuance of any proposed or final regulation, publish such notification in the Federal Register.

(3) Congressional Committees.—At such time as the Administrator is required under paragraph (2) of this sub section to provide the Secretary of Agriculture with a copy of proposed regulations and a copy of the final form of regulations, the Administrator shall also furnish a copy of such regulations to the Committee on Agriculture of the House of Representatives and the Committee on Agriculture, Nutrition, and Forestry of the Senate.

[§25(a)(3) amended by PL 100–532; PL 102–237]

(4) Congressional Review of Regulations.—Simultaneously with the promulgation of any rule or regulation under this Act, the Administrator shall transmit a copy thereof to the Secretary of the Senate and the Clerk of the House of Representatives. The rule or regulation shall not become effective until the passage of 60 calendar days after the rule or regulation is so transmitted.

[§25(a)(4) amended by PL 96–539; PL 98–620; PL 100–532]

(b) Exemption of Pesticides.—The Administrator may exempt from the requirements of this Act by regulation any pesticide which the Administrator determines either (1) to be adequately regulated by another Federal agency, or (2) to be of a character which is unnecessary to be subject to this Act in order to carry out the purposes of this Act.

[§25(b) amended by PL 102–237]

(c) Other Authority.—The Administrator, after notice and opportunity for hearing is authorized.

(1) to declare a pest any form of plant or animal life (other than man and other than bacteria, virus, and other micro-organisms on or in living man or other living animals) which is injurious to health or the environment;

(2) to determine any pesticide which contains any substance or substances in quantities highly toxic to man;

(3) to establish standards (which shall be consistent with those established under the authority of the Poison Prevention Packaging Act (Public Law 91–601)) with respect to the package, container, or wrapping in which a pesticide or device is enclosed for use or consumption, in order to protect children and adults from serious injury or illness resulting from accidental ingestion or contact with pesticides or devices regulated by this Act as well as to accomplish the other purposes of this Act;

(4) to specify those classes of devices which shall be subject to any provision of paragraph 2(q)(1) or section 7 of this Act upon the Administrator's determination that application of such provision is necessary to effectuate the purposes of this Act;

[§25(c)(4) amended by PL 102–237]

(5) to prescribe regulations requiring any pesticide to be colored or discolored if the Administrator determines that such requirement is feasible and is necessary for the protection of health and the environment; and

[§25(c)(5) amended by PL 102–237]

(6) to determine and establish suitable names to be used in the ingredient statement.

(d) Scientific Advisory Panel.—The Administrator shall submit to an advisory panel for comment as to the impact on health and the environment of the action proposed in notices of intent issued under section 6(b) and of the proposed and final form of regulations issued under section 25(a) within the same time periods as provided for the comments of the Secretary of Agriculture under such sections. The time requirements for notices of intent and proposed and final forms of regulation may not be modified or waived unless in addition to meeting the requirements of section 6(b) or 25(a), as applicable, the advisory panel has failed to comment on the proposed action within the prescribed time period or has agreed to the modification or waiver. The Administrator shall also solicit from the advisory panel comments, evaluations, and recommendations for operating guidelines to improve the effectiveness and quality of scientific analyses made by personnel of the Environmental Protection Agency that lead to decisions by the Administrator in carrying out the provisions of this Act. The comments, evaluations, and recommendations of the advisory panel submitted under this subsection and the response of the Administrator shall be published in the Federal Register in the same manner as provided for publication of the comments of the Secretary of Agriculture under such sections. The chairman of the advisory panel, after consultation with the Administrator, may create temporary subpanels on specific projects to assist the full advisory panel in expediting and preparing its evaluations, comments, and recommendations. The subpanels may be composed of scientists other than members of the advisory panel, as deemed necessary for the purpose of evaluating scientific studies relied upon by the Administrator with respect to proposed action. Such additional scientists shall be selected by the advisory panel. The panel referred to in this subsection shall consist of seven members appointed by the Administrator from a list of 12 nominees, six nominated by the National Institutes of Health, and six by the National Science Foundation, utilizing a system of staggered terms of appointment. Members of the panel shall be selected on the basis of their professional qualifications to assess the effects of the impact of pesticides on health and the environment. To the extent feasible to insure multidisciplinary representation, the panel membership shall include representation from the disciplines of toxicology, pathology, environmental biology, and related sciences. If a vacancy occurs on the panel due to expiration of a term, resignation, or any other reason, each replacement shall be selected by the Administrator from a group of 4 nominees, 2 submitted by each of the nominating entities named in this subsection. The Administrator may extend the term of a panel member until the new member is appointed to fill the vacancy. If a vacancy occurs due to resignation, or reason other than expiration of a term, the Administrator shall appoint a member to serve during the unexpired term utilizing the nomination process set forth in this subsection. Should the list of nominees provided under this subsection be unsatisfactory, the Administrator may request an additional set of nominees from the nominating entities. The Administrator may require such information from the nominees to the advisory panel as the Administrator deems necessary, and the Administrator shall publish in the Federal Register the name, address, and professional affiliations of each nominee. Each member of the panel shall receive per diem compensation at a rate not in excess of that fixed for GS–18 of the General Schedule as may be determined by the Administrator, except that any such member who holds another office or position under the Federal Government the compensation for which exceeds such rate may elect to receive compensation at the rate provided for such other office or position in lieu of the compensation provided by this subsection. In order to assure the objectivity of the advisory panel, the Administrator shall promulgate regulations regarding conflicts of interest with respect to the members of the panel. The advisor panel established under this section shall be permanent. In performing the functions assigned by this Act, the panel shall consult and coordinate its activities with the Science Advisory Board established under the Environmental Research, Development, and Demonstration Authorization Act of 1978. Whenever the Administrator exercises authority under section 6(c) of this Act to immediately suspend the registration of any pesticide to prevent an imminent hazard, the Administrator shall promptly submit to the advisory panel for comment, as to the impact on health and the environment, the action taken to suspend the registration of such pesticide.

[§25(d) amended by PL 96–539; PL 98–201; PL 100–532; PL 102–237]

(e) Peer Review—The Administrator shall, by written procedures, provide for peer review with respect to the design, protocols, and conduct of major scientific studies conducted under this Act by the Environmental Protection Agency or by any other Federal agency, any State or political subdivision thereof, or any institution or individual under grant, contract, or cooperative agreement from or with the Environmental Protection Agency. In such procedures, the Administrator shall also provide for peer review, using the advisory panel established under subsection (d) of this section or appropriate experts appointed by the Administrator from a current list of nominees maintained by such panel, with respect to the results of any such scientific studies relied upon by the Administrator with respect to actions the Administrator may take relating to the change in classification, suspension, or cancellation of a pesticide. Whenever the Administrator determines that circumstances do not permit the peer review of the results of any such scientific study prior to the Administrator's exercising authority under section 6(c) of this Act to immediately suspend the registration of any pesticide to prevent an imminent hazard, the Administrator shall promptly thereafter provide for the conduct of peer review as provided in this sentence. The evaluations and relevant documentation constituting the peer review that relate to the proposed scientific studies and the results of the completed scientific studies shall be included in the submission for comment forwarded by the Administrator to the advisory panel as provided in subsection (d). As used in this subsection, the term "peer review" shall mean an independent evaluation by scientific experts, either within or outside the Environmental Protection Agency, in the appropriate disciplines.

[§25(e) amended by PL 96–539; PL 100–532]

§136w-1. State Primary Enforcement Responsibility. [Sec. 26]

(a) In General.—For the purposes of this Act, a State shall have primary enforcement responsibility for pesticide use violations during any period for which the Administrator determines that such State—

[§26(a) amended by PL 100–532]

(1) has adopted adequate pesticide use laws and regulations, except that the Administrator may not require a State to have pesticide use laws that are more stringent than this Act;

[§26(a)(1) amended by PL 100–532]

(2) has adopted and is implementing adequate procedures for the enforcement of such State laws and regulations; and

(3) will keep such records and make such reports showing compliance with paragraphs (1) and (2) of this subsection as the Administrator may require by regulation.

(b) Special Rules.— Notwithstanding the provisions of subsection (a) of this section, any State that enters into a cooperative agreement with the Administrator under section 23 of this Act for the enforcement of pesticide use restrictions shall have the primary enforcement responsibility for pesticide use violations. Any State that has a plan approved by the Administrator in accordance with the requirements of section 11 of this Act that the Administrator determines meets the criteria set out in subsection (a) of this section shall have the primary enforcement responsibility for pesticide use violations. The Administrator shall make such determinations with respect to State plans under section 11 of this Act in effect on the date of enactment of the Federal Pesticide Act of 1978 not later than six months after that date.

[§26(b) amended by PL 100–532]

(c) Administrator.—The Administrator shall have primary enforcement responsibility for those States that do not have primary enforcement responsibility under this Act. Notwithstanding the provisions of section 2(e)(1) of this Act, during any period when the Administrator has such enforcement responsibility, section 8(b) of this Act shall apply to the books and records of commercial applicators and to any applicator who holds or applies pesticides, or uses dilutions of pesticides, only to provide a service of controlling pests without delivering any unapplied pesticide to any person so served, and section 9(a) of this Act shall apply to the establishment or other place where pesticides or devices are held for application by such persons with respect to pesticides or devices held for such application.

[§26(c) amended by PL 100–532; PL 102–237]

§136w-2. Failure by the State to Assure Enforcement of State Pesticide Use Regulations. [Sec. 27]

(a) Referral.—Upon receipt of any complaint or other information alleging or indicating a significant violation of the pesticide use provisions of this Act. the Administrator shall refer the matter to the appropriate State officials for their investigation of the matter consistent with the requirements of this subchapter. If, within thirty days, the State has not commenced appropriate enforcement action, the Administrator may act upon the complaint or information to the extent authorized under this subchapter.

[§27(a) amended by PL 100–532]

(b) Notice.—Whenever the Administrator determines that a State having primary enforcement responsibility for pesticide use violations is not carrying out (or cannot carry out due to the lack of adequate legal authority) such responsibility, the Administrator shall notify the State. Such notice shall specify those aspects of the administration of the State program that are determined to be inadequate. The State shall have ninety days after receipt of the notice to correct any deficiencies. If after that time the Administrator determines that the State program remains inadequate, the Administrator may rescind, in whole or in part, the State's primary enforcement responsibility for pesticide use violations.

[§27(b) amended by PL 100–532]

(c) Construction.—Neither section 26 of this Act nor this section shall limit the authority of the Administrator to enforce this Act, where the Administrator determines that emergency conditions exist that require immediate action on the part of the Administrator and the State authority is unwilling or unable adequately to respond to the emergency.

[§27(c) amended by PL 94–51; PL 94–109; PL 100–532]

§136w-3. Identification of Pests; Cooperation with Department of Agriculture's Program. [Sec. 28]

(a) In General.—The Administrator, in coordination with the Secretary of Agriculture, shall identify those pests that must be brought under control. The Administrator shall also coordinate and cooperate with the Secretary of Agriculture's research and implementation programs to develop and improve the safe use and effectiveness of chemical, biological, and alternative methods to combat and control pests that reduce the quality and economical production and distribution of agricultural products to domestic and foreign consumers.

[§28(a) amended by PL 101–624]

(b) Pest Control Availability.

(1) In general.—The Administrator, in cooperation with the Secretary of Agriculture, shall identify—

(A) available methods of pest control by crop or animal;

(B) minor pest control problems, both in minor crops and minor or localized problems in major crops; and

(C) factors limiting the availability of specific pest control methods, such as resistance to control methods and regulatory actions limiting the availability of control methods.

(2) Report.—The Secretary of Agriculture shall, not later than 180 days after the date of enactment of this subsection and annually thereafter, prepare a report and send the report to the Administrator. The report shall—

(A) contain the information described in paragraph (1) and the information required by section 1651 of the Food, Agriculture, Conservation, and Trade Act of 1990;

(B) identify the crucial pest control needs where a shortage of control methods is indicated by the information described in paragraph (l); and

(C) describe in detail research and extension efforts designed to address the needs identified in subparagraph (B).

[§28(b) added by PL 101–624]

(c) Integrated Pest Management.—The Administrator, in cooperation with the Secretary of Agriculture, shall develop approaches to the control of pests based on integrated pest management that respond to the needs of producers, with a special emphasis on minor pests.

[§28(c) added by PL 101–624]

§136w-4. Annual Report. [Sec. 29]

The Administrator shall submit an annual report to Congress before February 16 of each year and the first report shall be due February 15, 1979. The report shall include the total number of applications for conditional registration under sections 3(c)(7)(B) and 3(c)(7)(C) of this Act that were filed during the immediately preceding fiscal year, and, with respect to those applications approved, the Administrator shall report the Administrator's findings in each case, the conditions imposed and any modification of such conditions in each case, and the quantities produced of such pesticides.

§136x. Severability. [Sec. 30]

If any provision of this Act or the application thereof to any person or circumstance is held invalid, the invalidity shall not affect other provisions or applications of this Act which can be given effect without regard to the invalid provision or application, and to this end the provisions of this Act are severable.

§136y. Authorization for Appropriations.
[Sec. 31]

There is authorized to be appropriated to carry out this Act (other than section 23(a))—

(1) $83,000,000 for fiscal year 1989, of which not more than $13,735,500 shall be available for research under this Act;

(2) $95,000,000 for fiscal year 1990, of which not more than $ 14,343,600 shall be available for research under this Act; and

(3) $95,000,000 for fiscal year 1991, of which not more than $ 14,978,200 shall be available for research under this Act.

[§31 amended by PL 100–532]

ADDITIONAL PROVISIONS

[Editor's Note: Several sections of PL 101–624 did not directly amend the Act but are relevant. Those sections follow.]

Water Policy with Respect to Agrichemicals. [Sec. 1499]

(a) Authority.—The Department of Agriculture shall be the principal Federal agency responsible and accountable for the development and delivery of educational programs, technical assistance, and research programs for the users and dealers of agrichemicals to insure that—

(1) the use, storage, and disposal of agrichemicals by users is prudent, economical, and environmentally sound; and

(2) agrichemical users, dealers, and the general public understand the implications of their actions and the potential effects on water.

The Secretary is authorized to undertake such programs and assistance in cooperation with other Federal, State, and local governments and agencies, and appropriate nonprofit organizations. The Secretary shall disseminate the results of efforts in extension, technical assistance, research, and related activities. The Secretary shall undertake activities under this subtitle in coordination with the Office of Environmental Quality in section 1612 of this Act.

(b) Effect on Existing Authority.—The authority granted in subsection (a) does not alter or effect the responsibility of the Environmental Protection Agency under the Federal Insecticide, Fungicide, and Rodenticide Act (7 U.S.C. 136 et seq.).

(c) Participation.—The following agencies shall participate in the Department's water program: the Agricultural Research Service; the Agricultural Stabilization and Conservation Service; the Animal Plant Health Inspection Service; the Cooperative State Research Service in conjunction with the system of State agricultural experiment stations; the Economic Research Service; the Extension Service, in conjunction with State and county cooperative extension services; the Forest Service; the National Agricultural Library; the National Agricultural Statistics Service; the Soil Conservation Service; and other agencies within the Department deemed appropriate by the Secretary.

Plant and Animal Pest and Disease Control Program.[Sec. 1650]

(a) Integrated Pest Management Research.

(1) Program required.—The Secretary shall undertake or assist in the conduct of research regarding integrated pest management, including research by grant or contract with Federal or State agencies or private industries, institutions, or organizations, as may be necessary to carry out this subtitle. Such research shall include integrated pest management research to benefit floriculture.

(2) Implementation.—Implementation of integrated pest management strategies shall be conducted through the Extension Service.

(b) Effect on Other Laws.—Nothing in this Act shall be construed as limiting or repealing the authority of the Administrator of the Environmental Protection Agency to conduct research regarding integrated pest management under section 20(a) of the Federal Insecticide, Fungicide, and Rodenticide Act (7 U.S.C. 136r(a)).

(c) Integrated Pest Management Defined.—For purposes of this section, the term "integrated pest management" means a pest or disease population management system that uses all suitable techniques, such as biological and cultural controls as well as pesticides, in a total production system to anticipate and prevent pests and diseases from reaching economically damaging levels.

Pest and Disease Control Data Base and Pesticide Resistance Monitoring.[Sec. 1651]

(a) Data Base Required.—The Secretary of Agriculture shall establish and maintain a data base on available materials and methods of pest and disease control available to agricultural producers. The data base required by this subsection shall include a listing (by crop, animal, and pest or disease) of information—

(1) on currently available materials or methods of chemical, biological, cultural, or other means of controlling plant and animal pests and diseases; and

(2) on the extent of pest or disease resistance developed under the monitoring required by subsection (d).

(b) Priorities for Research and Extension Activities.—When the information in the data base established under subsection (a) indicates a shortage of available pest or disease control materials or methods to protect a particular crop or animal, the Secretary of Agriculture shall set priorities designed to overcome this shortage in its pest and disease control research and extension programs conducted under this subtitle.

(c) Dissemination of Information in the Data Base.—The Secretary of Agriculture shall—

(1) make the information contained in the data base established under subsection (a) available through the National Agricultural Library; and

(2) provide such information on an annual basis to

the Administrator of the Environmental Protection Agency in support of the activities of that Agency under the Federal Insecticide, Fungicide, and Rodenticide Act (7 U.S.C. 136 et seq.).

(d) Pesticide Resistance Monitoring.—The Secretary of Agriculture shall establish a national pesticide resistance monitoring program in accordance with the report developed by the Secretary under section 1437 of the Food Security Act of 1985 (Public Law 99–198; 99 Stat. 1558).

(e) Pesticide Defined.—For purposes of this section and section 1652, the term "pesticide" shall have the same meaning as given that term in section 2(u) of the Federal Insecticide, Fungicide, and Rodenticide Act (7 U.S.C. 136(u)).

(a) Requirements.—

(1) The Secretary of Agriculture, in consultation with the Administrator of the Environmental Protection Agency, shall require certified applicators of restricted use pesticides (of the type described under section 3(d)(1)(C) of the Federal Insecticide, Fungicide, and Rodenticide Act (7 U.S.C. 136a(d)(1)(C)) to maintain records comparable to records maintained by commercial applicators of pesticides in each State. If there is no State requirement for the maintenance of records, such applicator shall maintain records that contain the product name, amount, approximate date of application, and location of application of each such pesticide used for a 2–year period after such use.

(2) Within 30 days of a pesticide application. a commercial certified applicator shall provide a copy of records maintained under paragraph (1) to the person for whom such application was provided.

(b) Access.—Records maintained under subsection (a) shall be made available to any Federal or State agency that deals with pesticide use or any health or environmental issue related to the use of pesticides, on the request of such agency. Each such Federal agency shall conduct surveys and record the data from individual applicators to facilitate statistical analysis for environmental and agronomic purposes. but in no case may a government agency release data, including the location from which the data was derived, that would directly or indirectly reveal the identity of individual producers. In the case of Federal agencies, such access to records maintained under subsection (a) shall be through the Secretary of Agriculture, or the Secretary's designee. State agency requests for access to records maintained under subsection (a) shall be through the lead State agency so designated by the State.

(c) Health Care Personnel.—When a health professional determines that pesticide information maintained under this section is necessary to provide medical treatment or first aid to an individual who may have been exposed to pesticides for which the information is maintained, upon request persons required to maintain records under subsection (a) shall promptly provide record and available label information to that health professional. In the case of an emergency, such record information shall be provided immediately.

(d) Penalty.—The Secretary of Agriculture shall be responsible for the enforcement of subsections (a), (b), and (c). A violation of such subsection shall—

(1) in the case of the first offense, be subject to a fine not more than $500; and

(2) in the case of subsequent offenses, be subject to a fine of not less than $1,000 for each violation, except that the penalty shall be less than $1,000 if the Secretary determines that the person made a good faith effort to comply with such subsection.

(e) Federal or State Provisions.—The requirements of this section shall not affect provisions of other Federal or State laws.

(f) Surveys and Reports.—The Secretary of Agriculture and the Administrator of the Environmental Protection Agency, shall survey the records maintained under subsection (a) to develop and maintain a data base that is sufficient to enable the Secretary and the Administrator to publish annual comprehensive reports concerning agricultural and nonagricultural pesticide use. The Secretary and Administrator shall enter into a memorandum of understanding to define their respective responsibilities under this subsection in order to avoid duplication of effort. Such reports shall be transmitted to Congress not later than April 1 of each year.

(g) Regulations.—The Secretary of Agriculture and the Administrator of the Environmental Protection Agency shall promulgate regulations on their respective areas of responsibility implementing this section within 180 days after the date of the enactment of this Act.

Additional Provisions

8

Emergency Planning and Community Right-To-Know Act of 1986

INTRODUCTION

Before the passage of the Emergency Planning and Community Right-to-Know Act of 1986, enacted as Title III of the Superfund Amendments and Reauthorization Act, several states had already approved legislation requiring public notification of the types of hazardous substances used by business and industry.

Most of the first "right-to-know" laws were designed to inform workers of the types of hazards they might be exposed to in the workplace. After several highly publicized industrial accidents, however, the emphasis began to shift to include the right of the community to know what dangers it faced from manufacturing facilities, chemical plants, and other such industries.

Perhaps the most notable of these events was the catastrophic leak of methyl isocyanate from a Union Carbide Corp. subsidiary in Bhopal, India. On the night of December 3, 1984, a massive leak of the toxic MIC, used as an intermediate in the manufacture of various agricultural chemicals, swept over a densely populated area near the plant, causing hundreds of thousands of screaming men, women, and children to attempt to flee the area. When it was over, nearly 2,000 people had died and another 200,000 had been injured. No emergency plans had been made to deal with such a disaster.

And an accident in 1986 had perhaps an even more profound effect on the public and lawmakers in the states and in Washington, D.C. That disaster was the explosion and fire at the Chernobyl nuclear power station in the Soviet Union. Added to the United States' own brush with nuclear disaster at the Three Mile Island nuclear power plant in Pennsylvania in 1979, the event at Chernobyl deeply exacerbated fears of nuclear power and caused communities throughout the United States to wonder how prepared they would be to deal with such a disaster.

Sen. Frank Lautenberg (D-NJ), one of the chief authors of EPCRA, said the act "will be critical to communities—in alerting them to the dangerous chemicals present in their communities, and in laying the foundation for effective emergency response management. The right to know means public information about what hazardous substances are being stored and released into the environment in our communities. It means planning for emergency releases before they happen. It means our citizens and our emergency response personnel will be safer and better prepared for the threats from chemical releases. It means that this nation will not tolerate Bhopal- or Chernobyl-type tragedies."

Under the law, the governor of each state must appoint a "state emergency response commission," which in turn appoints local emergency planning committees. Members of the local committees must include state and local officials; law enforcement, fire-fighting, civil defense, first aid, health, local environmental, hospital, and transportation personnel; representatives from news media; community groups; and owners and operators of facilities covered by the law.

As required by the law, the Environmental Protection Agency on November 17, 1986, published a list of 402 "extremely hazardous substances" (51 FR 41570). EPA also set threshold levels for those substances, and any facility that has any of the 402 substances in excess of the threshold amount is subject to the act's reporting requirements. The agency's emergency planning and notification rules were issued in April 1987 (40 C.F.R. 355).

Two basic emissions reporting requirements were established by EPCRA. One requires covered facilities to report any unexpected release of an extremely hazardous substance.

The other requires that owners and operators of facilities annually prepare "toxic chemical release forms," providing information about the chemicals that were used on-site, and the quantities of chemicals that were released into the environment via routes such as waste streams or air emissions.

Some owners and operators of facilities must prepare or have available Material Safety Data Sheets (MSDSs) under the Occupational Safety and Health Act. Under Section 311 of the right-to-know law, these owners and operators must provide these MSDSs, or a list of the chemicals they cover, to the local emergency planning committee, the state commission, and to the local fire departments. If the facility provides only a list of the chemicals covered by the MSDSs, it must make the data sheets available on demand.

These same owners and operators must, under Section 312 of the law, prepare emergency and hazardous chemical inventory forms. Again, the local committee, the state commission, and the local fire department must be provided with this form by the facility.

EPA issued its Section 311 and Section 312 regulations in October 1987 (40 C.F.R. 370).

Much about EPCRA has generated considerable interest and controversy, but some of the most spirited discussion has centered around what information that must be reported can qualify for a trade secret exemption. In general, the law permits the withholding of the specific chemical identity of a hazardous substance if the information has never before been disclosed to others, if the information need not be disclosed under any federal law, if the disclosure of the information would be likely to cause substantial competitive harm, and if the chemical identity of the substance cannot be readily ascertained through reverse engineering.

FINDING LIST

EMERGENCY PLANNING AND COMMUNITY RIGHT-TO-KNOW ACT OF 1986

Public Law 99–499, effective Oct. 17, 1986.

42 U.S.C. §11001 et seq.

[Editor's Note: This act was passed as Title III of the Superfund Amendments and Reauthorization Act. Other provisions of SARA were incorporated in the Comprehensive Environmental Response, Compensation, and Liability Act of 1980 which is published at p. 4-1.]

TITLE III — EMERGENCY PLANNING AND COMMUNITY RIGHT-TO-KNOW

§11000. Short Title; Table of Contents. [Sec. 300]

[Omitted]

SUBTITLE A — EMERGENCY PLANNING AND NOTIFICATION

§11001. Establishment of State Commissions, Planning Districts, and Local Committees. [Sec. 301]

(a) Establishment Of State Emergency Response Commissions.— Not later than six months after the date of the enactment of this title, the Governor of each State shall appoint a State emergency response commission. The Governor may designate as the State emergency response commission one or more existing emergency response organizations that are State-sponsored or appointed. The Governor shall, to the extent practicable, appoint persons to the State emergency response commission who have technical expertise in the emergency response field. The State emergency response commission shall appoint local emergency planning committees under subsection (c) and shall supervise and coordinate the activities of such committees. The State emergency response commission shall establish procedures for receiving and processing requests from the public for information under section 324, including tier II information under section 312. Such procedures shall include the designation of an official to serve as coordinator for information. If the Governor of any State does not designate a State emergency response commission within such period, the Governor shall operate as the State emergency response commission until the Governor makes such designation.

(b) Establishment Of Emergency Planning Districts.—Not than nine months after the date of the enactment of this title, the State emergency response commission shall designate emergency planning districts in order to facilitate preparation and implementation of emergency plans. Where appropriate, the State emergency response commission may designate existing political subdivisions or multijurisdictional planning organizations as such districts. In emergency planning areas that involve more than one State, the State emergency response commissions of all potentially affected States may designate emergency planning districts and local emergency planning committees by agreement. In making such designation, the State emergency response commission shall indicate which facilities subject to the requirements of this subtitle are within such emergency planning district.

(c) Establishment Of Local Emergency Planning Committees.—Not later than 30 days after designation of emergency planning districts or 10 months after the date of the enactment of this title, whichever is earlier, the State emergency response commission shall appoint members of a local emergency planning committee for each emergency planning district. Each committee shall include, at a minimum, representatives from each of the following groups or organizations: elected State and local officials; law enforcement, civil defense, firefighting, first aid, health, local environmental, hospital, and transportation personnel; broadcast and print media; community groups; and owners and operators of facilities subject to the requirements of this subtitle. Such committee shall appoint a chairperson and shall establish rules by which the committee shall function. Such rules shall include provisions for public notification of committee activities, public meetings to discuss the emergency plan, public comments, response to such comments by the committee, and distribution of the emergency plan. The local emergency planning committee shall establish procedures for receiving and processing requests from the public for information under section 324, including tier II information under section 312. Such procedures shall include the designation of an official to serve as coordinator for information.

(d) Revisions.—A State emergency response commission may revise its designations and appointments under subsections (b) and (c) as it deems appropriate. Interested persons may petition the State emergency response commission to modify the membership of a local emergency planning committee.

§11002. Substances and Facilities Covered and Notification. [Sec. 302]

(a) Substances Covered.—

(1) In General.— A substance is subject to the requirements of this subtitle if the substance is on the list published under paragraph (2).

(2) List Of Extremely Hazardous Substances.— Within 30 days after the date of the enactment of this title, the Administrator shall publish a list of extremely hazardous substances. The list shall be the same as the list of substances published in November 1985 by the Administrator in Appendix A of the "Chemical Emergency Preparedness Program Interim Guidance".

(3) Thresholds. —

(A) At the time the list referred to in paragraph (2) is published the Administrator shall—

(i) publish an interim final regulation establishing a threshold planning quantity for each substance on the list, taking into account the criteria described in paragraph (4), and

(ii) initiate a rulemaking in order to publish final regulations establishing a threshold planning quantity for each substance on the list.

(B) The threshold planning quantities may, at the Administrator's discretion, be based on classes of chemicals or categories of facilities.

(C) If the Administrator fails to publish an interim final regulation establishing a threshold planning quantity for a substance within 30 days after the date of the enactment of this title, the threshold planning quantity for the substance shall be 2 pounds until such time as the Administrator publishes regulations establishing a threshold for the substance.

(4) Revisions. — The Administrator may revise the list and thresholds under paragraphs (2) and (3) from time to time. Any revisions to the list shall take into account the toxicity, reactivity, volatility, dispersability, combustability, or flammability of a substance. For purposes of the preceding sentence, the term "toxicity" shall include any short- or long-term health effect which may result from a short-term exposure to the substance.

(b) Facilities Covered. —

(1) Except as provided in section 304, a facility is subject to the requirements of this subtitle if a substance on the list referred to in subsection (a) is present at the facility in an amount in excess of the threshold planning quantity established for such substance.

(2) For purposes of emergency planning, a Governor or a State emergency response commission may designate additional facilities which shall be subject to the requirements of this subtitle, if such designation is made after public notice and opportunity for comment. The Governor or State emergency response commission shall notify the facility concerned of any facility designation under this paragraph.

(c) Emergency Planning Notification. —Not later than seven months after the date of the enactment of this title, the owner or operator of each facility subject to the requirements of this subtitle by reason of subsection (b)(1) shall notify the State emergency response commission for the State in which such facility is located that such facility is subject to the requirements of this subtitle. Thereafter, if a substance on the list of extremely hazardous substances referred to in subsection (a) first becomes present at such facility in excess of the threshold planning quantity established for such substance, or if there is a revision of such list and the facility has present a substance on the revised list in excess of the threshold planning quantity established for such substance, the owner or operator of the facility shall notify the State emergency response commission and the local emergency planning committee within 60 days after such acquisition or revision that such facility is subject to the requirements of this subtitle.

(d) Notification of Administrator. — The State emergency response commission shall notify the Administrator of facilities subject to the requirements of this subtitle by notifying the Administrator of—

(1) each notification received from a facility under subsection (c), and

(2) each facility designated by the Governor or State emergency response commission under subsection (b)(2).

§11003. Comprehensive Emergency Response Plans. [Sec. 303]

(a) Plan Required. — Each local emergency planning committee shall complete preparation of an emergency plan in accordance with this section not later than two years after the date of the enactment of this title. The committee shall review such plan once a year, or more frequently as changed circumstances in the community or at any facility may require.

(b) Resources. — Each local emergency planning committee shall evaluate the need for resources necessary to develop, implement, and exercise the emergency plan, and shall make recommendations with respect to additional resources that may be required and the means for providing such additional resources.

(c) Plan Provisions. — Each emergency plan shall include (but is not limited to each of the following:

(1) Identification of facilities subject to the requirements of this subtitle that are within the emergency planning district, identification of routes likely to be used for the transportation of substances on the list of extremely hazardous substances referred to in section 302(a), and identification of additional facilities contributing or subjected to additional risk due to their proximity to facilities subject to the requirements of this subtitle, such as hospitals or natural gas facilities.

(2) Methods and procedures to be followed by facility owners and operators and local emergency and medical personnel to respond to any release of such substances.

(3) Designation of a community emergency coordinator and facility emergency coordinators, who shall make determinations necessary to implement the plan.

(4) Procedures providing reliable, effective, and timely notification by the facility emergency coordinators and the community emergency coordinator to persons designated in the emergency plan, and to the public, that a release has occurred (consistent with the emergency notification requirements of section 304).

(5) Methods for determining the occurrence of a release, and the area or population likely to be affected by such release.

(6) A description of emergency equipment and facilities in the community and at each facility in the community subject to the requirements of this subtitle, and an identification of the persons responsible for such equipment and facilities.

(7) Evacuation plans, including provisions for a precautionary evacuation and alternative traffic routes.

(8) Training programs, including schedules for training of local emergency response and medical personnel.

(9) Methods and schedules for exercising the emergency plan.

(d) Providing Of Information — For each facility subject to the requirements of this subtitle:

(1) Within 30 days after establishment of a local emergency planning committee for the emergency planning district in which such facility is located, or within 11 months after the date of the enactment of this title, whichever is earlier, the owner or operator of the facility shall notify the emergency planning committee (or the Governor if there is no committee) of a facility representative who will participate in the emergency planning process as a facility emergency coordinator.

(2) The owner or operator of the facility shall promptly inform the emergency planning committee of any relevant changes occurring at such facility as such changes occur or are expected to occur.

(3) Upon request from the emergency planning committee, the owner or operator of the facility shall promptly provide information to such committee necessary for developing and implementing the emergency plan.

(e) Review By The State Emergency Response Commission. — After completion of an emergency plan under subsection (a) for an emergency planning district, the local emergency planning committee shall submit a copy of the plan to the State emergency response commission of each State in which such district is located. The commission shall review the plan and make recommendations to the committee on revisions of the plan that may be necessary to ensure coordination of such plan with emergency response plans of other emergency planning districts. To the maximum extent practicable, such review shall not delay implementation of such plan.

(f) Guidance Documents. — The national response team, as established pursuant to the National Contingency Plan as established under section 105 of the Comprehensive Environmental Response, Compensation, and Liability Act of 1980 (et seq.), shall publish guidance documents for preparation and implementation of emergency plans. Such documents shall be published not later than five months after the date of the enactment of this title.

(g) Review Of Plans By Regional Response Teams. — The regional response teams, as established pursuant to the National Contingency Plan as established under section 105 of the Comprehensive Environmental Response, Compensation, and Liability Act of 1980 (et seq.), may review and comment upon an emergency plan or other issues related to preparation, implementation, or exercise of such a plan upon request of a local emergency planning committee. Such review shall not delay implementation of the plan.

§11004. Emergency Notification. [Sec. 304]

(a) Types Of Releases —

(1) 302(a) Substance Which Requires CERCLA Notice. — If a release of an extremely hazardous substance referred to in section 302(a) occurs from a facility at which a hazardous chemical is produced, used, or stored, and such release requires a notification under section 103(a) of the Comprehensive Environmental Response, Compensation, and Liability Act of 1980 (hereafter in this section referred to as "CERCLA") (et seq.), the owner or operator of the facility shall immediately provide notice as described in subsection (b).

(2) Other 302(a) Substance. — If a release of an extremely hazardous substance referred to in section 302(a) occurs from a facility at which a hazardous chemical is produced, used, or stored, and such release is not subject to the notification requirements under section 103(a) of CERCLA, the owner or operator of the facility shall immediately provide notice as described in subsection (b), but only if the release —

(A) is not a federally permitted release as defined in section 101(10) of CERCLA.

(B) is in an amount in excess of a quantity which the Administrator has determined (by regulation) requires notice, and

(C) occurs in a manner which would require notification under section 103(a) of CERCLA. Unless and until superseded by regulations establishing a quantity for an extremely hazardous substance described in this paragraph, a quantity of 1 pound shall be deemed that quantity the release of which requires notice as described in subsection (b).

(3) Non–302(a) Substance Which Requires CERCLA Notice. — If a release of a substance which is not on the list referred to in section 302(a) occurs at a facility at which a hazardous chemical is produced, used, or stored, and such release requires notification under section 103(a) of CERCLA, the owner or operator shall provide notice as follows:

(A) If the substance is one for which a reportable quantity has been established under section 102(a) of CERCLA, the owner or operator shall provide notice as described in subsection (b).

(B) If the substance is one for which a reportable quantity has not been established under section 102(a) of CERCLA—

(i) Until April 30, 1988, the owner or operator shall provide, for releases of one pound or more of the substance, the same notice to the community emergency coordinator for the local emergency planning committee, at the same time and in the same form, as notice is provided to the National Response Center under section 103(a) of CERCLA.

(ii) On and after April 30, 1988, the owner or operator shall provide, for releases of one pound or more of the substance, the notice as described in subsection (b).

(4) Exempted Releases. — This section does not apply to any release which results in exposure to persons solely within the site or sites on which a facility is located.

(b) Notification. —

(1) Recipients Of Notice. — Notice required under subsection (a) shall be given immediately after the release by the owner or operator of a facility (by such means as telephone, radio, or in person) to the community emergency coordinator for the local emergency planning committees, if established pursuant to section 301(c), for any area likely to be affected by the release and to the State emergency planning commission of any State likely to be affected by the release. With respect to transportation of a substance subject to the requirements of this section, or storage incident to such transportation, the notice requirements of this section with respect to a release shall be satisfied by dialing 911 or, in the absence of a 911 emergency telephone number, calling the operator.

(2) Contents. — Notice required under subsection (a) shall include each of the following (to the extent known at the time of the notice and so long as no delay in responding to the emergency results):

(A) The chemical name or identity of any substance involved in the release.

(B) An indication of whether the substance is on the list referred to in section 302(a).

(C) An estimate of the quantity of any such substance that was released into the environment.

(D) The time and duration of the release.

(E) The medium or media into which the release occurred.

(F) Any known or anticipated acute or chronic health risks associated with the emergency and, where appropriate, advice regarding medical attention necessary for exposed individuals.

(G) Proper precautions to take as a result of the release, including evacuation (unless such information is readily available to the community emergency coordinator pursuant to the emergency plan).

(H) The name and telephone number of the person or persons to be contacted for further information.

(c) Followup Emergency Notice. — As soon as practicable after a release which requires notice under subsection (a), such owner or operator shall provide a written followup emergency notice (or notices, as more information becomes available) setting forth and updating the information required under subsection (b), and including additional information with respect to—

(1) actions taken to respond to and contain the release.

(2) any known or anticipated acute or chronic health risks associated with release, and

(3) where appropriate, advice regarding medical attention necessary for exposed individuals.

(d) Transportation Exemption Not Applicable. — The exemption provided in section 327 (relating to transportation) does not apply to this section.

§11005. Emergency Training and Review of Emergency Systems. [Sec. 305]

(a) Emergency Training.—

(1) Programs. — Officials of the United States Government carrying out existing Federal programs for emergency training are authorized to specifically provide training and education programs for Federal, State, and local personnel in hazard mitigation, emergency preparedness, fire prevention and control, disaster response, long-term disaster recovery, national security, technological and natural hazards, and emergency processes. Such programs shall provide special emphasis for such training and education with respect to hazardous chemicals.

(2) State And Local Program Support. —There is authorized to be appropriated to the Federal Emergency Management Agency for each of the fiscal years 1987, 1988, 1989, and 1990, $5,000,000 for making grants to support programs of State and local governments, and to support university-sponsored programs, which are designed to improve emergency planning, preparedness, mitigation, response, and recovery capabilities. Such programs shall provide special emphasis with respect to emergencies associated with hazardous chemicals. Such grants may not exceed 80 percent of the cost of any such program. The remaining 20 percent of such costs shall be funded from non-Federal sources.

(3) Other Programs. — Nothing in this section shall affect the availability of appropriations to the Federal Emergency Management Agency for any programs carried out by such agency other than the programs referred to in paragraph (2).

(b) Review Of Emergency Systems.—

(1) Review. — The Administrator shall initiate, not later than 30 days after the date of the enactment of this title, a review of emergency systems for monitoring, detecting, and preventing releases of extremely hazardous substances at representative domestic facilities that produce, use, or store extremely hazardous substances. The Administrator may select representative extremely hazardous substances from the substances on the list referred to in section 302(a) for the purposes of this review. The Administrator shall report interim findings to the Congress not later than seven months after such date of enactment, and issue a final report of findings and recommendations to the Congress not later than 18 months after such date of enactment. Such report shall be prepared in consultation with the States and appropriate Federal agencies.

(2) Report. — The report required by this subsection shall include the Administrator's findings regarding each of the following:

(A) The status of current technological capabilities to (i) monitor, detect, and prevent, in a timely manner, significant releases of extremely hazardous substances, (ii) determine the magnitude and direction of the hazard posed by each release, (iii) identify specific substances, (iv) provide data on the specific chemical composition of such releases, and (v) determine the relative concentrations of the constituent substances.

(B) The status of public emergency alert devices or systems for providing timely and effective public warning of an accidental release of extremely hazardous substances into the environment, including releases into the atmosphere, surface water, or groundwater from facilities that produce, store, or use significant quantities of such extremely hazardous substances.

(C) The technical and economic feasibility of establishing, maintaining, and operating perimeter alert systems for detecting releases of such extremely hazardous substances into the atmosphere, surface water, or groundwater, at facilities that manufacture, use, or store significant quantities of such substances.

(3) Recommendations. — The report required by this subsection shall also include the Administrator's recommendations for—

(A) initiatives to support the development of new or improved technologies or systems that would facilitate the timely monitoring, detection, and prevention of releases of extremely hazardous substances, and

(B) improving devices or systems for effectively alerting the public in a timely manner, in the event of an accidental release of such extremely hazardous substances.

SUBTITLE B — REPORTING REQUIREMENTS

§11021. Material Safety Data Sheets. [Sec. 311]

(a) Basic Requirement.—

(1) Submission Of MSDS Or List.— The owner or operator of any facility which is required to prepare or have available a material safety data sheet for a hazardous chemical under the Occupational Safety and Health Act of 1970 and regulations promulgated under that Act (et seq.) shall submit a material safety data sheet for each such chemical, or a list of such chemicals as described in paragraph (2), to each of the following:

(A) The appropriate local emergency planning committee.

(B) The State emergency response commission.

(C) The fire department with jurisdiction over the facility.

(2) Contents Of List.—

(A) The list of chemicals referred to in paragraph (1) shall include each of the following:

(i) A list of the hazardous chemicals for which a material safety data sheet is required under the Occupational Safety and Health Act of 1970 and regulations promulgated under that Act, grouped in categories of health and physical hazards as set forth under such Act and regulations promulgated under such Act, or in such other categories as the Administrator may prescribe under subparagraph (B).

(ii) The chemical name or the common name of each such chemical as provided on the material safety data sheet.

(iii) Any hazardous component of each such chemical as provided on the material safety data sheet.

(B) For purposes of the list under this paragraph, the Administrator may modify the categories of health and physical hazards as set forth under the Occupational Safety and Health Act of 1970 and regulations promulgated under that Act by requiring information to be reported in terms of groups of hazardous chemicals which present similar hazards in an emergency.

(3) Treatment of mixtures. — An owner or operator may meet the requirements of this section with respect to a hazardous chemical which is a mixture by doing one of the following:

(A) Submitting a material safety data sheet for, or identifying on a list, each element or compound in the mixture which is a hazardous chemical. If more than one mixture has the same element or compound, only one material safety data sheet, or one listing, of the element or compound is necessary.

(B) Submitting a material safety data sheet for, or identifying on a list, the mixture itself.

(b) Thresholds. — The Administrator may establish threshold quantities for hazardous chemicals below which no facility shall be subject to the provisions of this section. The threshold quantities may, in the Administrator's discretion, be based on classes of chemicals or categories of facilities.

(c) Availability of MSDS on Request.—

(1) To local emergency planning committee. — If an owner or operator of a facility submits a list of chemicals under subsection (a)(1), the owner or operator, upon request by the local emergency planning committee, shall submit the material safety data sheet for any chemical on the list to such committee.

(2) To public. — A local emergency planning committee, upon request by any person, shall make available a material safety data sheet to the person in accordance with section 324. If the local emergency planning committee does not have the requested material safety data sheet, the committee shall request the sheet from the facility owner or operator and then make the sheet available to the person in accordance with section 324.

(d) Initial Submission and Updating.—

(1) The initial material safety data sheet or list required under this section with respect to a hazardous chemical shall be provided before the later of—

(A) 12 months after the date of the enactment of this title, or

(B) 3 months after the owner or operator of a facility is required to prepare or have available a material safety data sheet for the chemical under the Occupational Safety and Health Act of 1970 and regulations promulgated under that Act.

(2) Within 3 months following discovery by an owner or operator of significant new information concerning an aspect of a hazardous chemical for which a material safety data sheet was previously submitted to the local emergency planning committee under subsection (a), a revised sheet shall be provided to such person.

(e) Hazardous Chemical Defined. — For purposes of this section, the term "hazardous chemical" has the meaning given such term by section 1910.1200(c) of title 29 of the Code of Federal Regulations, except that such term does not include the following:

(1) Any food, food additive, color additive, drug, or cosmetic regulated by the Food and Drug Administration.

(2) Any substance present as a solid in any manufactured item to the extent exposure to the substance does not occur under normal conditions of use.

(3) Any substance to the extent it is used for personal, family, or household purposes, or is present in the same form and concentration as a product packaged for distribution and use by the general public.

(4) Any substance to the extent it is used in a research laboratory or a hospital or other medical facility under the direct supervision of a technically qualified individual.

(5) Any substance to the extent it is used in routine agricultural operations or is a fertilizer held for sale by a retailer to the ultimate customer.

§11022. Emergency and Hazardous Chemical Inventory Forms. [Sec. 312]

(a) Basic Requirements. —

(1) The owner or operator of any facility which is required to prepare or have available a material safety data sheet for a hazardous chemical under the Occupational Safety and Health Act of 1970 and regulations promulgated under that Act shall prepare and submit an emergency and hazardous chemical inventory form (hereafter in this title referred to as an "inventory form") to each of the following:

(A) The appropriate local emergency planning committee.

(B) The State emergency response commission.

(C) The fire department with jurisdiction over the facility.

(2) The inventory form containing tier I information (as described in subsection (d)(1)) shall be submitted on or before March 1, 1988, and annually thereafter on March 1, and shall contain data with respect to the preceding calendar year. The preceding sentence does not apply if an owner or operator provides, by the same deadline and with respect to the same calendar year, tier II information (as described in subsection (d)(2) to the recipients described in paragraph (1).

(3) An owner or operator may meet the requirements of this section with respect to a hazardous chemical which is a mixture by doing one of the following:

(A) Providing information on the inventory form on each element or compound in the mixture which is a hazardous chemical. If more than one mixture has the same element or compound, only one listing on the inventory form for the element or compound at the facility is necessary.

(B) Providing information on the inventory form on the mixture itself.

(b) Thresholds. — The Administrator may establish threshold quantities for hazardous chemicals covered by this section below which no facility shall be subject to the provisions of this section. The threshold quantities may, in the Administrator's discretion, be based on classes of chemicals or categories of facilities.

(c) Hazardous Chemicals Covered. — A hazardous chemical subject to the requirements of this section is any hazardous chemical for which a material safety data sheet or a listing is required under section 311.

(d) Contents Of Form.—

(1) Tier I Information.—

(A) Aggregate information by category. — An inventory form shall provide the information described in subparagraph (B) in aggregate terms for hazardous chemicals in categories of health and physical hazards as set forth under the Occupational Safety and

Health Act of 1970 and regulations promulgated under that Act.

(B) Required information. — The information referred to in subparagraph (A) is the following:

(i) An estimate (in ranges) of the maximum amount of hazardous chemicals in each category present at the facility at any time during the preceding calendar year.

(ii) An estimate (in ranges) of the average daily amount of hazardous chemicals in each category present at the facility during the preceding calendar year.

(iii) The general location of hazardous chemicals in each category.

(C) Modifications. — For purposes of reporting information under this paragraph, the Administrator may —

(i) modify the categories of health and physical hazards as set forth under the Occupational Safety and Health Act of 1970 and regulations promulgated under that Act by requiring information to be reported in terms of groups of hazardous chemicals which present similar hazards in an emergency, or

(ii) require reporting on individual hazardous chemicals of special concern to emergency response personnel.

(2) Tier II Information. — An inventory form shall provide the following additional information for each hazardous chemical present at the facility, but only upon request and in accordance with subsection (e):

(A) The chemical name or the common name of the chemical as provided on the material safety data sheet.

(B) An estimate (in ranges) of the maximum amount of the hazardous chemical present at the facility at any time during the preceding calendar year.

(C) An estimate (in ranges) of the average daily amount of the hazardous chemical present at the facility during the preceding calendar year.

(D) A brief description of the manner of storage of the hazardous chemical.

(E) The location at the facility of the hazardous chemical.

(F) An indication of whether the owner elects to withhold location information of a specific hazardous chemical from disclosure to the public under section 324.

(e) Availability Of Tier II Information. —

(1) Availability To State Commissions, Local Committees, And Fire Departments.— Upon request by a State emergency planning commission, a local emergency planning committee, or a fire department with jurisdiction over the facility, the owner or operator of a facility shall provide tier II information, as described in subsection (d), to the person making the request. Any such request shall be with respect to a specific facility.

(2) Availability To Other State And Local Officials. — A State or local official acting in his or her official capacity may have access to tier II information by submitting a request to the State emergency response commission or the local emergency planning committee. Upon receipt of a request for tier II information, the State commission or local committee shall, pursuant to paragraph (1), request the facility owner or operator for the tier II information and make available such information to the official.

(3) Availability To Public. —

(A) In General. — Any person may request a State emergency response commission or local emergency planning committee for tier II information relating to the preceding calendar year with respect to a facility. Any such request shall be in writing and shall be with respect to a specific facility.

(B) Automatic Provision Of Information To Public. — Any tier II information which a State emergency response commission or local emergency planning committee has in its possession shall be made available to a person making a request under this paragraph in accordance with section 324. If the state emergency response commission or local emergency planning committee does not have the tier II information in its possession, upon a request for tier II information the State emergency response commission or local emergency planning committee shall, pursuant to paragraph (1), request the facility owner or operator for tier II information with respect to a hazardous chemical which a facility has stored in an amount in excess of 10,000 pounds present at the facility at any time during the preceding calendar year and make such information available in accordance with section 324 to the person making the request.

(C) Discretionary Provision Of Information To Public. — In the case of tier II information which is not in the possession of a State emergency response commission or local emergency planning committee and which is with respect to a hazardous chemical which a facility has stored in an amount less than 10,000 pounds present at the facility at any time during the preceding calendar year, a request from a person must include the general need for the information. The State emergency response commission or local emergency planning committee may, pursuant to paragraph (1), request the facility owner or operator for the tier II information on behalf of the person making the request. Upon receipt of any information requested on behalf of such person, the State emergency response commission or local emergency planning committee shall make the information available in accordance with section 324 to the person.

(D) Response In 45 Days. — A State emergency response commission or local emergency planning committee shall respond to a request for tier II information under this paragraph no later than 45 days after the date of receipt of the request.

(f) Fire Department Access. — Upon request to an owner or operator of a facility which files an inventory form under this section by the fire department with jurisdiction over the facility, the owner or operator of the facility shall allow the fire department to conduct an on-site inspection of the facility and shall provide to the fire department specific location information on hazardous chemicals at the facility.

(g) Format Of Forms. — The Administrator shall publish a uniform format for inventory forms within three months after the date of the enactment of this title. If the Administrator does not publish such forms, owners and operators of facilities subject to the requirements of this section shall provide the information required under this section by letter.

§11023. Toxic Chemical Release Forms.
[Sec. 313]

(a) Basic Requirement. — The owner or operator of a facility subject to the requirements of this section shall complete a toxic chemical release form as published under subsection (g) for each toxic chemical listed under subsection (c) that was manufactured, processed, or otherwise used in quantities exceeding the toxic chemical threshold quantity established by subsection during the preceding calendar year at such facility. Such form shall be submitted to the Administrator and to an official or officials of the State designated by the Governor on or before July 1, 1988, and annually thereafter on July 1 and shall contain data reflecting releases during the preceding calendar year.

(b) Covered Owners And Operators Of Facilities.—

(1) In General. —

(A) The requirements of this section shall apply to owners and operators of facilities that have 10 or more full-time employees and that are in Standard Industrial Classification Codes 20 through 39 (as in effect on July 1, 1985) and that manufactured, processed, or otherwise used a toxic chemical listed under subsection in excess of the quantity of that toxic chemical established under subsection (f) during the calendar year for which a release form is required under this section.

(B) The Administrator may add or delete Standard Industrial Classification Codes for purposes of subparagraph (A), but only to the extent necessary to provide that each Standard Industrial Code to which this section applies is relevant to the purposes of this section.

(C) For purposes of this section —

(i) The term "manufacture" means to produce, prepare, import, or compound a toxic chemical.

(ii) The term "process" means the preparation of a toxic chemical, after its manufacture, for distribution in commerce —

(I) in the same form or physical state as, or in a different form or physical state from, that in which it was received by the person so preparing such chemical, or

(II) as part of an article containing the toxic chemical.

(2) Discretionary Application To Additional Facilities. — The Administrator, on his own motion or at the request of a Governor of a State (with regard to facilities located in that State), may apply the requirements of this section to the owners and operators of any particular facility that manufactures, processes, or otherwise uses a toxic chemical listed under subsection (c) if the Administrator determines that such action is warranted on the basis of toxicity of the toxic chemical, proximity to other facilities that release the toxic chemical or to population centers, the history of releases of such chemical at such facility, or such other factors as the Administrator deems appropriate.

(c) Toxic Chemicals Covered. — The toxic chemicals subject to the requirements of this section are those chemicals on the list in Committee

Print Number 99–169 of the Senate Committee on Environment and Public Works, titled "Toxic Chemicals Subject to Section 313 of the Emergency Planning and Community Right-To-Know Act of 1986" (including any revised version of the list as may be made pursuant to subsection (d) or (e)).

(d) Revisions By Administrator. —

(1) In General. — The Administrator may by rule add or delete a chemical from the list described in subsection (c) at any time.

(2) Additions. — A chemical may be added if the Administrator determines, in his judgment, that there is sufficient evidence to establish any one of the following:

(A) The chemical is known to cause or can reasonably be anticipated to cause significant adverse acute human health effects at concentration levels that are reasonably likely to exist beyond facility site boundaries as a result of continuous, or frequently recurring, releases.

(B) The chemical is known to cause or can reasonably be anticipated to cause in humans—

(i) cancer or teratogenic effects, or

(ii) serious or irreversible—

(I) reproductive dysfunctions,

(II) neurological disorders,

(III) heritable genetic mutations, or

(IV) other chronic health effects.

(C) The chemical is known to cause or can reasonably be anticipated to cause, because of —

(i) its toxicity,

(ii) its toxicity and persistence in the environment, or

(iii) its toxicity and tendency to bioaccumulate in the environment, a significant adverse effect on the environment of sufficient seriousness, in the judgment of the Administrator, to warrant reporting under this section. The number of chemicals included on the list described in subsection (c) on the basis of the preceding sentence may constitute in the aggregate no more than 25 percent of the total number of chemicals on the list. A determination under this paragraph shall be based on generally accepted scientific principles or laboratory tests, or appropriately designed and conducted epidemiological or other population studies, available to the Administrator.

(3) Deletions. — A chemical may be deleted if the Administrator determines there is not sufficient evidence to establish any of the criteria described in paragraph (2).

(4) Effective Date. — Any revision made on or after January 1 and before December 1 of any calendar year shall take effect beginning with the next calendar year. Any revision made on or after December 1 of any calendar year and before January 1 of the next calendar year shall take effect beginning with the calendar year following such next calendar year.

(e) Petitions. —

(1) In General. — Any person may petition the Administrator to add or delete a chemical from the list described in subsection on the basis of the criteria in subparagraph (A) or (B) of subsection (d)(2). Within 180 days after receipt of a petition, the Administrator shall take one of the following actions:

(A) Initiate a rulemaking to add or delete the chemical to the list, in accordance with subsection (d)(2) or (d)(3).

(B) Publish an explanation of why the petition is denied.

(2) Governor Petitions. — A State Governor may petition the Administrator to add or delete a chemical from the list described in subsection (c) on the basis of the criteria in subparagraph (A), (B), or (C) of subsection (d)(2). In the case of such a petition from a State Governor to delete a chemical, the petition shall be treated in the same manner as a petition received under paragraph (1) to delete a chemical. In the case of such a petition from a State Governor to add a chemical, the chemical will be added to the list within 180 days after receipt of the petition, unless the Administrator —

(A) initiates a rulemaking to add the chemical to the list, in accordance with subsection (d)(2), or

(B) publishes an explanation of why the Administrator believes the petition does not meet the requirements of subsection (d)(2) for adding a chemical to the list.

(f) Threshold for Reporting. —

(1) Toxic Chemical Threshold Amount. —The threshold amounts for purposes of reporting toxic chemicals under this section are as follows:

(A) With respect to a toxic chemical used at a facility, 10,000 pounds of the toxic chemical per year.

(B) With respect to a toxic chemical manufactured or processed at a facility —

(i) For the toxic chemical release form required to be submitted under this section on or before July 1, 1988, 75,000 pounds of the toxic chemical per year.

(ii) For the form required to be submitted on or before July 1, 1989, 50,000 pounds of the toxic chemical per year.

(iii) For the form required to be submitted on or before July 1, 1990, and for each form thereafter, 25,000 pounds of the toxic chemical per year.

(2) Revisions. — The Administrator may establish a threshold amount for a toxic chemical different from the amount established by paragraph (1). Such revised threshold shall obtain reporting on a substantial majority of total releases of the chemical at all facilities subject to the requirements of this section. The amounts established under this paragraph may, at the Administrator's discretion, be based on classes of chemicals or categories of facilities.

(g) Form. —

(1) Information Required. — Not later than June 1, 1987, the Administrator shall publish a uniform toxic chemical release form for facilities covered by this section. If the Administrator does not publish such a form, owners and operators of facilities subject to the requirements of this section shall provide the information required under this subsection by letter postmarked on or before the date on which the form is due. Such form shall —

(A) provide for the name and location of, and principal business activities at, the facility;

(B) include an appropriate certification, signed by a senior official with management responsibility for the person or persons completing the report, regarding the accuracy and completeness of the report; and

(C) provide for submission of each of the following items of information for each listed toxic chemical known to be present at the facility:

(i) Whether the toxic chemical at the facility is manufactured, processed, or otherwise used, and the general category or categories of use of the chemical.

(ii) An estimate of the maximum amounts (in ranges) of the toxic chemical present at the facility at any time during the preceding calendar year.

(iii) For each wastestream, the waste treatment or disposal methods employed, and an estimate of the treatment efficiency typically achieved by such methods for that wastestream.

(iv) The annual quantity of the toxic chemical entering each environmental medium.

(2) Use of Available Data. — In order to provide the information required under this section, the owner or operator of a facility may use readily available data (including monitoring data) collected pursuant to other provisions of law, or, where such data are not readily available, reasonable estimates of the amounts involved. Nothing in this section requires the monitoring or measurement of the quantities, concentration, or frequency of any toxic chemical released into the environment beyond that monitoring and measurement required under other provisions of law or regulation. In order to assure consistency, the Administrator shall require that data be expressed in common units.

(h) Use of Release Form. — The release forms required under this section are intended to provide information to the Federal, State, and local governments and the public, including citizens of communities surrounding covered facilities. The release form shall be available, consistent with section 324(a), to inform persons about releases of toxic chemicals to the environment; to assist governmental agencies, researchers, and other persons in the conduct of research and data gathering; to aid in the development of appropriate regulations, guidelines, and standards; and for other similar purposes.

(i) Modifications in Reporting Frequency. —

(1) In General. The Administrator may modify the frequency of submitting a report under this section, but the Administrator may not modify the frequency to be any more often than annually. A modification may apply, either nationally or in a specific geographic area, to the following:

(A) All toxic chemical release forms required under this section.

(B) A class of toxic chemicals or a category of facilities.

(C) A specific toxic chemical.

(D) A specific facility.

(2) Requirements. — A modification may be made under paragraph (1) only if the Administrator—

(A) makes a finding that the modification is consistent with the provisions of subsection (h), based on—

(i) experience from previously submitted toxic chemical release forms, and

(ii) determinations made under paragraph (3), and

(B) the finding is made by a rulemaking in accordance with section 553 of title 5, United States Code.

(3) Determinations. — The Administrator shall make the following determinations with respect to a proposed modification before making a modification under paragraph (1):

(A) The extent to which information relating to the proposed modification provided on the toxic chemical release forms has been used by the Administrator or other agencies of the Federal Government, States, local governments, health professionals, and the public.

(B) The extent to which the information is (i) readily available to potential users from other sources, such as State reporting programs, and (ii) provided to the Administrator under another Federal law or through a State program.

(C) The extent to which the modification would impose additional and unreasonable burdens on facilities subject to the reporting requirements under this section.

(4) 5–year Review. — Any modification made under this subsection shall be reviewed at least once every 5 years. Such review shall examine the modification and ensure that the requirements of paragraphs (2) and (3) still justify continuation of the modification. Any change to a modification reviewed under this paragraph shall be made in accordance with this subsection.

(5) Notification to Congress. — The Administrator shall notify Congress of an intention to initiate a rulemaking for a modification under this subsection. After such notification, the Administrator shall delay initiation of the rulemaking for at least 12 months, but no more than 24 months, after the date of such notification.

(6) Judicial Review. — In any judicial review of a rulemaking which establishes a modification under this subsection, a court may hold unlawful and set aside agency action, findings, and conclusions found to be unsupported by substantial evidence.

(7) Applicability. — A modification under this subsection may apply to a calendar year or other reporting period beginning no earlier than Janauary 1, 1993.

(8) Effective Date. — Any modification made on or after January 1 and before December 1 of any calendar year shall take effect beginning with the next calendar year. Any modification made on or after December 1 of any calendar year and before January 1 of the next calendar year shall take effect beginning with the calendar year following such next calendar year.

(j) EPA Management of Data. — The Administrator shall establish and maintain in a computer data base a national toxic chemical inventory based on data submitted to the Administrator under this section. The Administrator shall make these data accessible by computer telecommunication and other means to any person on a cost reimbursable basis.

(k) Report. — Not later than June 30, 1991, the Comptroller General, in consultation with the Administrator and appropriate officials in the States, shall submit to the Congress a report including each of the following:

(1) A description of the steps taken by the Administrator and the States to implement the requirements of this section, including steps taken to make information collected under this section available to and accessible by the public.

(2) A description of the extent to which the information collected under this section has been used by the Environmental Protection Agency, other Federal agencies, the States, and the public, and the purposes for which the information has been used.

(3) An identification and evaluation of options for modifications to the requirements of this section for the purpose of making information collected under this section more useful.

(l) Mass Balance Study. —

(1) In General. — The Administrator shall arrange for a mass balance study to be carried out by the National Academy of Sciences using mass balance information collected by the Administrator under paragraph (3). The Administrator shall submit to Congress a report on such study no later than 5 years after the date of the enactment of this title.

(2) Purposes. — The purposes of the study are as follows:

(A) To assess the value of mass balance analysis in determining the accuracy of information on toxic chemical releases.

(B) To assess the value of obtaining mass balance information, or portions thereof, to determine the waste reduction efficiency of different facilities, or categories of facilities, including the effectiveness of toxic chemical regulations promulgated under laws other than this title.

(C) To assess the utility of such information for evaluating toxic chemical management practices at facilities, or categories of facilities, covered by this section.

(D) To determine the implications of mass balance information collection on a national scale similar to the mass balance information collection carried out by the Administrator under paragraph (3), including implications of the use of such collection as part of a national annual quantity toxic chemical release program.

(3) Information Collection. —

(A) The Administrator shall acquire available mass balance information from States which currently conduct (or during the 5 years after the date of enactment of this title initiate) a mass balance-oriented annual quantity toxic chemical release program. If information from such States provides an inadequate representation of industry classes and categories to carry out the purposes of the study, the Administrator also may acquire mass balance information necessary for the study from a representative number of facilities in other States.

(B) Any information acquired under this section shall be available to the public, except that upon a showing satisfactory to the Administrator by any person that information (or a particular part thereof) to which the Administrator or any officer, employee, or representative has access under this section if made public would divulge information entitled to protection under section 1905 of title 18, United States Code, such information or part shall be considered confidential in accordance with the purposes of that section, except that such information or part may be disclosed to other officers, employees, or authorized representatives of the United States concerned with carrying out this section.

(C) The Administrator may promulgate regulations prescribing procedures for collecting mass balance information under this paragraph.

(D) For purposes of collecting mass balance information under subparagraph (A), the Administrator may require the submission of information by a State or facility.

(4) Mass Balance Definition. — For purposes of this subsection, the term "mass balance" means as accumulation of the annual quantities of chemicals transported to a facility, produced at a facility, consumed at a facility, used at a facility, accumulated at a facility, released from a facility, and transported from a facility as a waste or as a commercial product or byproduct or component of a commercial product or byproduct.

SUBTITLE C — GENERAL PROVISIONS

§11041. Relationship to Other Law. [Sec. 321]

(a) In General. — Nothing in this title shall—

(1) preempt any State or local law.

(2) except as provided in subsection (b), otherwise affect any State or local law or the authority of any State or local government to adopt or enforce any State or local law, or

(3) affect or modify in any way the obligations or liabilities of any person under other Federal law.

(b) Effect on MSDS Requirements.—

Any State or local law enacted after August 1, 1985, which requires the submission of a material safety data sheet from facility owners or operators shall require that the data sheet be identical in content and format to the data sheet required under subsection

(a) of section 311. In addition, a State or locality may require the submission of information which is supplemental to the information required on the data sheet (including information on the location and quantity of hazardous chemicals present at the facility), through additional sheets attached to the data sheet or such other means as the State or locality considers appropriate.

§11042. Trade Secrets. [Sec. 322]

(a) Authority To Withhold Information. —

(1) General Authority. —

(A) With regard to a hazardous chemical, an extremely hazardous substance, or a toxic chemical, any person required under section 303(d)(2), 303(d)(3), 311, 312, or 313 to submit information to any other person may withhold from such submittal the specific chemical identity (including the chemical name and other specific identification), as defined in regulations prescribed by the Administrator under subsection (c), if the person complies with paragraph (2).

(B) Any person withholding the specific chemical identity shall, in the place on the submittal where the chemical identity would normally be included, include the generic class or category of the hazardous chemical, extremely hazardous substance, or toxic chemical (as the case may be).

(2) Requirements. —

(A) A person is entitled to withhold information under paragraph (1) if such person —

(i) claims that such information is a trade secret, on the basis of the factors enumerated in subsection (b).

(ii) includes in the submittal referred to in paragraph (1) an explanation of the reasons why such information is claimed to be a trade secret, based on the factors enumerated in subsection (b), including a specific description of why such factors apply, and

(iii) submits to the Administrator a copy of such submittal, and the information withheld from such submittal.

(B) In submitting to the Administrator the information required by subparagraph (A)(iii), a person withholding information under this subsection may —

(i) designate, in writing and in such manner as the Administrator may prescribe by regulation, the information which such person believes is entitled to be withheld under paragraph (1), and

(ii) submit such designated information separately from other information submitted under this subsection.

(3) Limitation. — The authority under this subsection to withhold information shall not apply to information which the Administrator has determined, in accordance with subsection (c), is not a trade secret.

(b) Trade Secret Factors. — No person required to provide information under this title may claim that the information is entitled to protection as a trade secret under subsection (a) unless such person shows each of the following:

(1) Such person has not disclosed the information to any other person, other than a member of a local emergency planning committee, an officer or employee of the United States or a State or local government, an employee of such person, or a person who is bound by a confidentiality agreement, and such person has taken reasonable measures to protect the confidentiality of such information and intends to continue to take such measures.

(2) The information is not required to be disclosed, or otherwise made available, to the public under any other Federal or State law.

(3) Disclosure of the information is likely to cause substantial harm to the competitive position of such person.

(4) The chemical identity is not readily discoverable through reverse engineering.

(c) Trade secret regulations. — As soon as practicable after the date of enactment of this title, the Administrator shall prescribe regulations to implement this section. With respect to subsection (b)(4), such regulations shall be equivalent to comparable provisions in the Occupational Safety and Health Administration Hazard Communication Standard (29 C.F.R. 1910.1200) and any revisions of such standard prescribed by the Secretary of Labor in accordance with the final ruling of the courts of the United States in United Steelworkers of America, AFL–CIO–CLC v. Thorne G. Auchter.

(d) Petition for Review. —

(1) In general. — Any person may petition the Administrator for the disclosure of the specific chemical identity of a hazardous chemical, an extremely hazardous substance, or a toxic chemical which is claimed as a trade secret under this section. The Administrator may, in the absence of a petition under this paragraph, initiate a determination, to be carried out in accordance with this subsection, as to whether information withheld constitutes a trade secret.

(2) Initial review. — Within 30 days after the date of receipt of a petition under paragraph (1) (or upon the Administrator's initiative), the Administrator shall review the explanation filed by a trade secret claimant under subsection (a)(2) and determine whether the explanation presents assertions which, if true, are sufficient to support a finding that the specific chemical identity is a trade secret.

(3) Finding of Sufficient Assertions. —

(A) If the Administrator determines pursuant to paragraph (2) that the explanation presents sufficient assertions to support a finding that the specific chemical identity is a trade secret, the Administrator shall notify the trade secret claimant that he has 30 days to supplement the explanation with detailed information to support the assertions.

(B) If the Administrator determines, after receipt of any supplemental supporting detailed information under subparagraph (A), that the assertions in the explanation are true and that the specific chemical identity is a trade secret, the Administrator shall so notify the petitioner and the petitioner may seek judicial review of the determination.

(C) If the Administrator determines, after receipt of any supplemental supporting detailed information under subparagraph (A), that the assertions in the explanation are not true and that the specific chemical identity is not a trade secret, the Administrator shall notify the trade secret claimant that the Administrator intends to release the specific chemical identity. The trade secret claimant has 30 days in which he may appeal the Administrator's determination under this subparagraph to the Administrator. If the Administrator does not reverse his determination under this subparagraph in such an appeal by the trade secret claimant, the trade secret claimant may seek judicial review of the determination.

(4) Finding of insufficient assertions. —

(A) If the Administrator determines pursuant to paragraph (2) that the explanation presents insufficient assertions to support a finding that the specific chemical identity is a trade secret, the Administrator shall notify the trade secret claimant that he has 30 days to appeal the determination to the Administrator, or, upon a showing of good cause, amend the original explanation by providing supplementary assertions to support the trade secret claim.

(B) If the Administrator does not reverse his determination under subparagraph (A) after an appeal or an examination of any supplementary assertions under subparagraph (A), the Administrator shall so notify the trade secret claimant the trade secret claimant may seek judicial review of the determination.

(C) If the Administrator reverses his determination under subparagraph after an appeal or an examination of any supplementary assertions under subparagraph (A), the procedures under paragraph (3) of this subsection apply.

(e) Exception for Information Provided to Health Professionals. — Nothing in this section, or regulations adopted pursuant to this section, shall authorize any person to withhold information which is required to be provided to a health professional, a doctor, or a nurse in accordance with section 323.

(f) Providing Information to the Administrator; Availability to Public. — Any information submitted to the Administrator under subsection (a)(2) or subsection (d)(3) (except a specific chemical identity) shall be available to the public, except that upon a showing satisfactory to the Administrator by any person that the information (or a particular part thereof) to which the Administrator has access under this section if made public would divulge information entitled to protection under section 1905 of title 18, United States Code, such information or part shall be considered confidential in accordance with the purposes of that section, except that such information or part may be disclosed to other officers, employees or authorized representatives of the United States concerned with carrying out this title.

(g) Information Provided to State. — Upon request by a State, acting through the Governor of the State, the Administrator shall provide to the State any information obtained under subsection (a)(2) and subsection (d)(3).

(h) Information on Adverse Effects. —

(1) In any case in which the identity of a hazardous chemical or an extremely hazardous substance is claimed as a trade secret, the Governor or State emergency response commission established under section 301 shall identify the adverse health effects associated with the hazardous chemical or extremely hazardous substance and shall assure that such information is provided to any person requesting information about such hazardous chemical or extremely hazardous substance.

(2) In any case in which the identity of a toxic chemical is claimed as a trade secret, the Administrator shall identify the adverse health and environmental effects associated with the toxic chemical and shall assure that such information is included in the computer database required by section 313(j) and is provided to any person requesting information about such toxic chemical.

(i) Information Provided to Congress. —Notwithstanding any limitation contained in this section or any other provision of law, all information reported to or otherwise obtained by the Administrator (or any representative of the Administrator) under this title shall be made available to a duly authorized committee of the Congress upon written request by such a committee.

§11043. Provision Of Information To Health Professionals, Doctors, And Nurses. [Sec. 323]

(a) Diagnosis or Treatment by Health Professional. — An owner or operator of a facility which is subject to the requirements of section 311, 312, or 313 shall provide the specific chemical identity, if known, of a hazardous chemical, extremely hazardous substance, or a toxic chemical to any health professional who requests such information in writing if the health professional provides a written statement of need under this subsection and a written confidentiality agreement under subsection (d). The written statement of need shall be a statement that the health professional has a reasonable basis to suspect that—

(1) the information is needed for purposes of diagnosis or treatment of an individual,

(2) the individual or individuals being diagnosed or treated have been exposed to the chemical concerned, and

(3) knowledge of the specific chemical identity of such chemical will assist in diagnosis or treatment. Following such a written request, the owner or operator to whom such request is made shall promptly provide the requested information to the health professional. The authority to withhold the specific chemical identity of a chemical under section 322 when such information is a trade secret shall not apply to information required to be provided under this subsection, to the provisions of subsection (d).

(b) Medical Emergency. — An owner or operator of a facility which is subject to the requirements of section 311, 312, or 313 shall provide a copy of a material safety data sheet, an inventory form, or a toxic chemical release form, including the specific chemical identity, if known, of a hazardous chemical, extremely hazardous substance, or a toxic chemical, to any treating physician or nurse who requests such information if such physician or nurse determines that—

(1) a medical emergency exists,

(2) the specific chemical identity of the chemical concerned is necessary for or will assist in emergency or first-aid diagnosis or treatment, and

(3) the individual or individuals being diagnosed or treated have been exposed to the chemical concerned.

Immediately following such a request, the owner or operator to whom such request is made shall provide the requested information to the physician or nurse. The authority to withhold the specific chemical identity of a chemical from a material safety data sheet, an inventory form, or a toxic chemical release form under section 322 when such information is a trade secret shall not apply to information required to be provided to a treating physician or nurse under this subsection. No written confidentiality agreement or statement of need shall be required as a precondition of such disclosure, but the owner or operator disclosing such information may require a written confidentiality agreement in accordance with subsection (d) and a statement setting forth the items listed in paragraphs (1) through (3) as soon as circumstances permit.

(c) Preventive Measures by Local Health Professionals.—

(1) Provision of Information.— An owner or operator of a facility subject to the requirements of section 311, 312, or 313 shall provide the specific chemical identity, if known, of a hazardous chemical, an extremely hazardous substance, or a toxic chemical to any health professional (such as a physician, toxicologist, or epidemiologist)—

(A) who is a local government employee or a person under contract with the local government, and

(B) who requests such information in writing and provides a written statement of need under paragraph (2) and a written confidentiality agreement under subsection (d). Following such a written request, the owner or operator to whom such request is made shall promptly provide the requested information to the local health professional. The authority to withhold the specific chemical identity of a chemical under section 322 when such information is a trade secret shall not apply to information required to be provided under this subsection, subject to the provisions of subsection (d).

(2) Written statement of need. — The written statement of need shall be a statement that describes with reasonable detail one or more of the following health needs for the information:

(A) To assess exposure of persons living in a local community to the hazards of the chemical concerned.

(B) To conduct or assess sampling to determine exposure levels of various population groups.

(C) To conduct periodic medical surveillance of exposed population groups.

(D) To provide medical treatment to exposed individuals or population groups.

(E) To conduct studies to determine the health effects of exposure.

(F) To conduct studies to aid in the identification of a chemical that may reasonably be anticipated to cause an observed health effect.

(d) Confidentiality Agreement. — Any person obtaining information under subsection (a) or (c) shall, in accordance with such subsection (a) or (c), be required to agree in a written confidentiality agreement that he will not use the information for any purpose other than the health needs asserted in the statement of need, except as may otherwise be authorized by the terms of the agreement or by the person providing such information. Nothing in this subsection shall preclude the parties to a confidentiality agreement from pursuing any remedies to the extent permitted by law.

(e) Regulations. — As soon as practicable after the date of the enactment of this title, the Administrator shall promulgate regulations describing criteria and parameters for the statement of need under subsection (a) and (c) and the confidentiality agreement under subsection (d).

§11044. Public Availability of Plans, Data Sheets, Forms, and Followup Notices. [Sec. 324]

(a) Availability To Public. — Each emergency response plan, material safety data sheet, list described in section 311(a)(2), inventory form, toxic chemical release form, and followup emergency notice shall be made available to the general public, consistent with section 322, during normal working hours at the location or locations designated by the Administrator, Governor, State emergency response commission, or local emergency planning committee, as appropriate. Upon request by an owner or operator of a facility subject to the requirements of section 312, the State emergency response commission and the appropriate local emergency planning committee shall withhold from disclosure under this section the location of any specific chemical required by section 312(d)(2) to be continued in an inventory form as tier II information.

(b) Notice Of Public Availability. — Each local emergency planning committee shall annually publish a notice in local newspapers that the emergency response plan, material safety data sheets, and inventory forms have been submitted under this section. The notice shall state that followup emergency notices may subsequently be issued. Such notice shall announce that members of the public who wish to review any such plan, sheet, form, or followup notice may do so at the location designated under subsection (a).

§11045. Enforcement. [Sec. 325]

(a) Civil Penalties For Emergency Planning. — The Administrator may order a facility owner or operator (except an owner or operator of a facility designated under section 302(b)(2)to comply with section 302(c) and section 303(d). The United States district court for the district in which the facility is located shall have jurisdiction to enforce the order, and any person who violates or fails to obey such an order shall be liable to the United States for a civil penalty of not more than $25,000 for each day in which such violation occurs or such failure to comply continues.

(b) Civil, Administrative, And Criminal Penalties For Emergency Notification.—

(1) Class I Administrative Penalty.—

(A) A civil penalty of not more than $25,000 per violation may be assessed by the Administrator in the case of a violation of the requirements of section 304.

(B) No civil penalty may be assess under this subsection unless the person accused of the violation is given notice and opportunity for a hearing with respect to the violation.

(C) In determining the amount of any penalty assessed pursuant to this subsection, the Administrator shall take into account the nature, circumstances, extent and gravity of the violation or violations and, with respect to the violator, ability to pay, any prior history of such violations, the degree of culpability, economic benefit or savings (if any) resulting from the violation, and such other matters as justice may require.

(2) Class II Administrative Penalty.— A civil penalty of not more than $25,000 per day for each day during which the violation continues may be assessed by the Administrator in the case of a violation of the requirements of section 304. In the case of a second or subsequent violation the amount of such penalty may be not more than $75,000 for each day during the violation continues. Any civil penalty under this subsection shall be assessed and collected in the same manner, and subject to the same provisions, as in the case of civil penalties assessed and collected under section 16 of the Toxic Substances Control Act. In any proceeding for the assessment of a civil penalty under this subsection the Administrator may issue

subpoenas for the attendance and testimony of witnesses and the production of relevant papers, books, and documents and may promulgate rules for discovery procedures.

(3) Judicial Assessment.— The Administrator may bring an action in the United States District court for the appropriate district to assess and collect a penalty of not more than $25,000 per day for each day during which the violation continues in the case of a violation of the requirements of section 304. In the case of a second or subsequent violation, the amount of such penalty may be not more than $75,000 for each day during which the violation continues.

(4) Criminal Penalties.— Any person who knowingly and willfully fails to provide notice in accordance with section 304 shall, upon conviction, be fined not more than $25,000 or imprisoned for not more than two years, or both (or in the case of a second or subsequent conviction, shall be fined not more than $50,000 or imprisoned for not more than five years, or both).

(c) Civil and Administrative Penalties for Reporting Requirements. —

(1) Any person (other than a governmental entity) who violates any requirements of section 312, or 313shall be liable to the United States for a civil penalty in an amount not to exceed $25,000 for each such violation.

(2) Any person (other than a governmental entity) who violates any requirement of section 311 or 323(b),and any person who fails to furnish to the Administrator information required under section 322(a)(2) shall be liable to the United States for a civil penalty in an amount not to exceed $10,000 for each such violation.

(3) Each day a violation described in paragraph (1) or (2) continues shall, for purposes of this subsection, continues a separate violation.

(4) The Administrator may assess any civil penalty for which a person is liable under this subsection by administrative order or may bring an action to assess and collect the penalty in the United States district court for the district in which the person from whom the penalty is sought resides or in which such person's principal place of business is located.

(d) Civil, Administrative, and Criminal Penalties With Respect to Trade Secrets.—

(1) Civil and Administrative Penalty for Frivolous Claims. — If the Administrator determines —

(A) (i) under section 322(d)(4) that an explanation submitted by a trade secret claimant presents insufficient assertions to support a finding that a specific chemical identify is a trade secret, or (ii) after receiving supplemental supporting detailed information under section 322(d)(3)(A), that the specific chemical identity is not a trade secret; and

(B) that the trade secret claim is frivolous, the trade secret claimant is liable for a penalty of $25,000 per claim. The Administrator may assess the penalty by administrative order or may bring an action in the appropriate district court of the United States to assess and collect the penalty.

(2) Criminal Penalty for Disclosure of Trade Secret Information. — Any person who knowingly and willfully divulges or discloses any information entitled to protection under section 322 shall, upon conviction be subject to fine of not more than $20,000 or imprisonment not to exceed one year, or both.

(e) Special Enforcement Provisions for Section 323. — Whenever any facility owner or operator required to provide information under section 323 to a health professional who has requested such information fails or refuses to provide such information in accordance with such section, such health professional may bring an action in the appropriate United States district court to require such facility owner or operator to provide the information. Such court shall have jurisdiction to issue such orders and take such other action as may be necessary to enforce the requirements of section 323.

(f) Procedures for Administrative Penalties. —

(1) Any person against whom a civil penalty is assessed under this section may obtain review thereof in the appropriate district court of the United States by filing a notice of appeal in such court within 30 days after the date of such order and by simultaneously sending a copy of such notice by certified mail to the Administrator. The Administrator shall promptly file in such court a certified copy of the record upon which such violation was found or such penalty imposed. If any person fails to pay an assessment of a civil penalty after it has become a final and unappealable order or after the appropriate court has entered final judgment in favor of the United States, the Administrator may request the Attorney General of the United States to institute a civil action in an appropriate district court of the United States to institute a civil action in an appropriate district court of the United decide any such

action. In hearing such action, the court shall have authority to review the violation and the assessment of the civil penalty on the record.

(2) The Administrator may issue subpoenas for the attendance and testimony of witnesses and the production of relevant papers, books, or documents in connection with hearings under this section. In case of contumacy or refusal to obey a subpoena issued pursuant to this paragraph and served upon any person, the district court of the United States for any district in which such person is found, resides, or transacts business, upon application by the United States and after notice to such person, shall have jurisdiction to issue an order requiring such person to appear and give testimony before the administrative law judge or to appear and produce documents before the administrative law judge, or both, and any failure to obey such order of the court may be punished by such court as a contempt thereof.

§11046. Civil Actions. [Sec. 326]

(a) Authority To Bring Civil Actions. —

(1) Citizen suits. — Except as provided in subsection (e), any person may commence a civil action on his own behalf against the following:

(A) An owner or operator of a facility for failure to do any of the following:

(i) Submit a followup emergency notice under section 304(c).

(ii) Submit a material safety data sheet or a list under section 311(a).

(iii) Complete and submit an inventory form under section 312(a) containing tier I information as described in section 312(d)(1) unless such requirement does not apply by reason of the second sentence of section 312(a)(2).

(iv) Complete and submit a toxic chemical release form under section 313(a).

(B) The Administrator for failure to do any of the following:

(i) Publish inventory forms under section 312(g).

(ii) Respond to a petition to add or delete a chemical under section 313(e)(1) within 180 days after receipt of the petition.

(iii) Publish a toxic chemical release form under 313(g).

(iv) Establish a computer database in accordance with section 313(j).

(v) Promulgate trade secret regulations under section 322(c).

(vi) Render a decision in response to a petition under section 322(d) within 9 months after receipt of the petition.

(C) The Administrator, a State Governor, or a State emergency response commission, for failure to provide a mechanism for public availability of information in accordance with section 324(a).

(D) A State Governor or a State emergency response commission for failure to respond to a request for tier II information under section 312(e)(3) within 120 days after the date of receipt of the request.

(2) State or local suits.—

(A) Any State or local government may commence a civil action against an owner or operator of a facility for failure to do any of the following:

(i) Provide notification to the emergency response commission in the State under section 302(c).

(ii) Submit a material safety data sheet or a list under section 311(a).

(iii) Make available information requested under section 311(c).

(iv) Complete and submit an inventory form under section 312(a) containing tier I information unless such requirement does not apply by reason of the second sentence of section 312(a)(2).

(B) Any State emergency response commission or local emergency planning committee may commence a civil action against an owner or operator of a facility for failure to provide information under section 303(d) or for failure to submit tier II information under section 312(e)(1).

(C) Any State may commence a civil action against the Administrator for failure to provide information to the State under section 322(g).

(b) Venue.—

(1) Any action under subsection (a) against an owner or operator of a facility shall be brought in the district court for the district in which the alleged violation occurred.

(2) Any action under subsection (a) against the Administrator may be brought in the United States District Court for the District of Columbia.

(c) Relief. — The district court shall have jurisdiction in actions brought under subsection (a) against an owner or operator of a facility to enforce the requirement concerned and to impose any civil penalty provided for violation of that requirement. The district court shall have jurisdiction in actions brought under subsection (a) against the Administrator to order the Administrator to perform the act or duty concerned,

(d) Notice.—

(1) No action may be commenced under subsection (a)(1)(A) prior to 60 days after the plaintiff has given notice of the alleged violation to the Administrator, the State in which the alleged violation occurs, and the alleged violator. Notice under this paragraph shall be given in such manner as the Administrator shall prescribe by regulation.

(2) No action may be commenced under subsection (a)(1)(B) or (a)(1)(C) prior to 60 days after the date on which the plaintiff gives notice to the Administrator, State Governor, or State emergency response commission (as the case may be) that the plaintiff will commence the action. Notice under this paragraph shall be given in such manner as the Administrator shall prescribe by regulation.

(e) Limitation. — No action may be commenced under subsection (a) against an owner or operator of a facility if the Administrator has commenced and is diligently pursuing an administrative order or civil action to enforce the requirement concerned or to impose a civil penalty under this Act with respect to the violation of the requirement.

(f) Costs. — The court, in issuing any final order in any action brought pursuant to this section, may award costs of litigation (including reasonable attorney and expert witness fees) to the prevailing or the substantially prevailing party whenever the court determines such an award is appropriate. The court may, if a temporary restraining order or preliminary injunction is sought, require the filing of a bond or equivalent security in accordance with the Federal Rules of Civil Procedure.

(g) Other Rights. — Nothing in this section shall restrict or expand any right which any person (or class of persons) may have under any Federal or State statute or common law to seek enforcement of any requirement or to seek any other relief (including relief against the Administrator or a State agency).

(h) Intervention.—

(1) By the United States. — In any action under this section the United states or the State, or both, if not a party, may intervene as a matter of right.

(2) By persons. — In any action under this section, any person may intervene as a matter of right when such person has a direct interest which is or may be adversely affected by the action and the disposition of the action may, as a practical matter, impair or impede the person's ability to protect that interest unless the Administrator or the State shows that the person's interest is adequately represented by existing parties in the action.

§11047. Exemption. [Sec. 327]

Except as provided in section 304, this title does not apply to the transportation, including the storage incident to such transportation, of any substance or chemical subject to the requirements of this title, including the transportation and distribution of natural gas.

§11048. Regulations. [Sec. 328]

The Administrator may prescribe such regulations as may be necessary to carry out this title.

§11049. Definitions. [Sec. 329]

For purposes of this title—

(1) Administrator. — The term "Administrator" means the Administrator of the Environmental Protection Agency.

(2) Environment. — The term "environment includes water, air, and land and the interrelationship which exists among and between water, air, and land and all living things.

(3) Extremely hazardous substance. — The term "extremely hazardous substance" means a substance on the list described in section 302(a)(2).

(4) Facility.— The term "facility" means all buildings, equipment, structures, and other stationary items which are located on a single site or on contiguous or adjacent sites and which are owned or operated by the same person (or by any person which controls, is controlled by, or under common control with, such person). For purposes of section 304, the term includes motor vehicles, rolling stock, and aircraft.

(5) Hazardous Chemical.— The term "hazardous chemical" has the meaning given such term by section 311(e).

(6) Material Safety Data Sheet.— The term "material safety data sheet" means the sheet required to he developed under section 1910.1200(g) of title 29 of the Code of Federal Regulations, as that section may be amended from time to time.

(7) Person.— The term "person" means any individual, trust, firm, joint stock company, corporation (including a government corporation),

partnership, association, State, municipality, commission, political subdivision of a State, or interstate body.

(8) Release.— The term "release" means any spilling, leaking, pumping, pouring, emitting, emptying, discharging, injecting. escaping, leaching, dumping, or disposing into the environment (including the abandonment or discarding of barrels, containers, and other closed receptacles) of any hazardous chemical, extremely hazardous substance, or toxic chemical.

(9) State.— The term "State" means any State of the United States, the District of Columbia, the Commonwealth of Puerto Rico, Guam, American Samoa, the United States Virgin Islands, the Northern Mariana Islands, and any other territory or possession over which the United States has jurisdiction.

(10) Toxic Chemical.— The term "toxic chemical" means a substance on the list described in section 313(c).

§11050. Authorization of Appropriations.
[Sec. 330]

There are authorized to be appropriated for fiscal years beginning after September 30, 1986, such sums as may be necessary to carry out this title.

9

National Environmental Policy Act

INTRODUCTION

In drafting the National Environmental Policy Act (NEPA) in 1969, Congress said the U.S. government should "use all practicable means ... to create and maintain conditions in which man and nature can exist in productive harmony." For the first time, the government was required to consider environmental protection in its decision-making concerning "major Federal actions significantly affecting the quality of the human environment."

The statute, which was signed into law on January 1, 1970, by President Richard Nixon, requires federal agencies to prepare "environmental impact statements" assessing the environmental effects of proposed projects and requests for legislation. The Act also set up the White House Council on Environmental Quality (CEQ), whose primary responsibilities include assisting and advising the president in the preparation of an annual report on environmental quality. In 1977 President Jimmy Carter told CEQ to promulgate binding regulations to implement the procedural provisions of NEPA.

The Act—described by CEQ as "our basic national charter for protection of the environment"—requires federal agencies to take a hard look at the environmental consequences of their actions, evaluate the effects of a proposed action, and discuss steps that can be taken to mitigate adverse environmental effects. But while the Act requires that certain procedures be followed, it does not require that an agency actually refrain from any action that would cause environmental harm. Even more, it does not require that the agency evaluate steps that will, in fact, be taken to mitigate any environmental harm.

According to a 1989 decision by the U.S. Supreme Court, "it is now well settled that NEPA itself does not mandate particular results, but simply prescribes the necessary process" (*U.S. Forest Service v. Methow Valley Citizens Council*, 490 U.S. 332, 29 ER Cases 1497, 1989).

"If the adverse environmental effects of the proposed action are adequately identified and evaluated, the agency is not constrained by NEPA from deciding that other values outweigh the environmental costs," the court added.

In the same decision, the Supreme Court held that an agency was not required to perform a "worst-case analysis."

At one time, CEQ regulations required such analyses; an agency had to provide a worst-case scenario if certain information relevant to the evaluation of a project was either unavailable or too costly to obtain. But in April 1986, CEQ replaced that requirement, and in Method Valley, the Supreme Court upheld the revised regulation. According to the revised regulation, an agency faced with incomplete or unavailable information must include within its environmental impact statement "a summary of existing credible scientific information which is relevant to evaluating the reasonably foreseeable significant adverse impacts on the human environment, and ... the agency's evaluation of such impacts based upon theoretical approaches or research methods generally accepted in the scientific community." The CEQ had defined "reasonably foreseeable" as including effects that have "catastrophic consequences, even if their probability of occurrence is low, provided that the analysis of the impacts is supported by credible scientific evidence, is not based on pure conjecture, and is within the rule of reason."

CEQ itself was set up by NEPA as a three-member council and had been expected to perform a leading role in setting the government's environmental agenda. During the Reagan administration, however, its functions had been limited and its importance de-emphasized.

During the administration of President George Bush an effort was made to increase the staff of the council, which had dwindled from a high of 60 to 70 in the late 1970s to only 13 by 1989. Michael Deland, appointed by President Bush to head CEQ, told Congress at his confirmation hearing that Bush had guaranteed to increase the staff to at least 40 full-time employees over three years. However, the administration also sought to eliminate two of the three council seats. Legislation moving through the 101st Congress was aimed at amending NEPA to "vest all powers, functions and duties of the council in the chairman."

Lying behind the decision to restructure the council was a decision by the U.S. District Court for the District of Columbia that held that the council was a federal agency within the meaning of the Government-in-the-Sunshine Act and was required to open its meetings to the public (*Pacific Legal Foundation v. CEQ*, 636 F2d 1259, 15 ER Cases 1067 (1980)). Deland said the change would let the council "streamline its operations and enable it to more expeditiously carry out its statutory responsibilities."

In its regulations on the implementation of the Act, CEQ wrote, "The NEPA process is intended to help public officials make decisions that are based on understanding of environmental consequences, and take actions that protect, restore, and enhance the environment." Whatever changes are made to the statute and to the council, it would appear that the basic goal of NEPA—taking a hard look at the environmental consequences of major federal actions—has become institutionalized.

When he was still president of the Conservation Foundation, Environmental Protection Agency Administrator William K. Reilly cited the Alaska oil pipeline project of the 1970s as an example of how NEPA has allowed "a whole new constituency, the environmentalists, to play a substantive part in ... decision-making." Because of the Act, he said, the Interior Department prepared extensive studies, before the pipeline was completed, including damage mitigation plans in response to environmentalists' concerns.

Shock waves rocked the environmental establishment when President Bill Clinton proposed in early 1993 to eliminate CEQ entirely and transfer its functions to a new White House office. The move was supported by the Administration as a way to increase efficiency, improve White House control of environmental issues, and save money.

Congressional leaders and environmental groups, seeing the move as an assault on the nation's cornerstone environmental statute, immediately condemned the move. Chief among their concerns was that implementation and enforcement of NEPA would suffer. Nonetheless, by year's end, the House and Senate had both passed legislation that would abolish the council.

The Senate included its CEQ provisions in legislation to elevate EPA to a Cabinet department (S171). The House Cabinet bill contained no such provision, but the House passed a separate measure (HR 3512) transferring CEQ's functions to a new White House Office of National Environmental Policy Act Compliance.

Many observers expect Congress to separate the CEQ provisions from Cabinet legislation and to approve abolition of the council in 1994.

Two court decisions in 1993 affected how NEPA is applied. In January, the U.S. Court of Appeals for the District of Columbia Circuit ruled in a challenge by the Environmental Defense Fund to National Science Foundation actions in Antarctica that the doctrine of extraterritoriality does not apply to NEPA (*Environmental Defense Fund Inc. v. National Science Foundation (Massey)*, 986 F.2d 528, 36 ER Cases 1053). The court ruled that, although the doctrine presumes that U.S. laws do not affect conduct or activities outside the territory of the United States, it does not apply to the NSF actions because the regulated activity, decision-making, occurs in the United States. "Allowing the presumption against extraterritoriality here would result in a federal agency being allowed to undertake actions significantly affecting the human environment in Antarctica . . . without ever being held accountable for its failure to comply with the decisionmaking procedures instituted by Congress," the court added.

In November 1993, the U.S. District Court for the District of Columbia ruled, however, that the U.S. Navy was not required to prepare an environmental impact statement on the effect of its operations in Japan on surrounding civilian populations (*NEPA Coalition of Japan v. Aspin*, DC DC, No. 91-1522). The court distinguished its action from the decision in *Massey*, ruling that the *Massey* decision dealt with Antarctica, a continent without a sovereign power. The district court added that the D.C. Circuit expressly refused to decide whether NEPA might apply to actions that could affect sovereign powers.

FINDING LIST

NATIONAL ENVIRONMENTAL POLICY ACT

Public Law 91-190, effective Jan. 1, 1970, 83 Stat. 852.

42 U.S.C. §§4321 et seq.

Amended by PL 94–52, July 3, 1975; PL 94–83, Aug. 9, 1975.

§4321. Purpose [Sec. 2]

The purposes of this Act are: To declare a national policy which will encourage productive and enjoyable harmony between man and his environment; to promote efforts which will prevent or eliminate damage to the environment and biosphere and stimulate the health and welfare of man; to enrich the understanding of the ecological systems and natural resources important to the Nation; and to establish a Council on Environmental Quality.

TITLE I DECLARATION OF NATIONAL ENVIRONMENTAL POLICY

§4331. Congressional declaration of national environmental policy [Sec. 101]

(a) The Congress, recognizing the profound impact of man's activity on the interrelations of all components of the natural environment, particularly the profound influences of population growth, high-density urbanization, industrial expansion, resource exploitation, and new and expanding technological advances and recognizing further the critical importance of restoring and maintaining environmental quality to the overall welfare and development of man, declares that it is the continuing policy of the Federal Government, in cooperation with State and local governments, and other concerned public and private organizations, to use all practicable means and measures, including financial and technical assistance, in a manner calculated to foster and promote the general welfare, to create and maintain conditions under which man and nature can exist in productive harmony, and fulfill the social, economic, and other requirements of present and future generations of Americans.

(b) In order to carry out the policy set forth in this Act, it is the continuing responsibility of the Federal Government to use all practicable means, consistent with other essential considerations of national policy, to improve and coordinate Federal plans, functions, programs, and resources to the end that the Nation may—

(1) fulfill the responsibilities of each generation as trustee of the environment for succeeding generations;

(2) assure for all Americans safe, healthful, productive, and esthetically and culturally pleasing surroundings;

(3) attain the widest range of beneficial uses of the environment without degradation, risk to health or safety, or other undesirable and unintended consequences;

(4) preserve important historic, cultural, and natural aspects of our national heritage, and maintain, wherever possible, an environment which supports diversity and variety of individual choice;

(5) achieve a balance between population and resource use which will permit high standards of living and a wide sharing of life's amenities; and

(6) enhance the quality of renewable resources and approach the maximum attainable recycling of depletable resources.

(c) The Congress recognizes that each person should enjoy a healthful environment and that each person has a responsibility to contribute to the preservation and enhancement of the environment.

§4332. Cooperation of agencies; reports; availability of information; recommendations; international and national coordination of efforts [Sec. 102]

The Congress authorizes and directs that, to the fullest extent possible: (1) the policies, regulations, and public laws of the United States shall be interpreted and administered in accordance with the policies set forth in this Act, and (2) all agencies of the Federal Government shall—

(A) utilize a systematic, interdisciplinary approach which will insure the integrated use of the natural and social sciences and the environmental design arts in planning and in decisionmaking which may have an impact on man's environment;

(B) identify and develop methods and procedures, in consultation with the Council on Environmental Quality established by title II of this Act, which will insure that presently unquantified environmental amenities and values may be given appropriate consideration in decisionmaking along with economic and technical considerations;

(C) include in every recommendation or report on proposals for legislation and other major Federal actions significantly affecting the quality of the human environment, a detailed statement by the responsible official on—

(i) the environmental impact of the proposed action,

(ii) any adverse environmental effects which cannot be avoided should the proposal be implemented,

(iii) alternatives to the proposed action,

(iv) the relationship between local short-term uses of man's environment and the maintenance and enhancement of long-term productivity, and

(v) any irreversible and irretrievable commitments of resources which would be involved in the proposed action should it be implemented. Prior to making any detailed statement, the responsible Federal official shall consult with and obtain the comments of any Federal agency which has jurisdiction by law or special expertise with respect to any environmental impact involved. Copies of such statement and the comments and views of the appropriate Federal, State, and local agencies, which are authorized to develop and enforce environmental standards, shall be made available to the President, the Council on Environmental Quality and to the public as provided by section 552 of title 5, United States Code, and shall accompany the proposal through the existing agency review processes:

(D) Any detailed statement required under subparagraph (C) after January 1, 1970, for any major Federal action funded under a program of grants to States shall not be deemed to be legally insufficient solely by reason of having been prepared by a State agency or official, if:

(i) the State agency or official has statewide jurisdiction and has the responsibility for such action,

(ii) the responsible Federal official furnishes guidance and participates in such preparation,

(iii) the responsible Federal official independently evaluates such statement prior to its approval and adoption, and

(iv) after January 1, 1976, the responsible Federal official provides early notification to, and solicits the views of, any other State or any Federal land management entity of any action or any alternative thereto which may have significant impacts upon such State or affected Federal land management entity and, if there is any disagreement on such impacts, prepares a written assessment of such impacts and views for incorporation into such detailed statement.

The procedures in this subparagraph shall not relieve the Federal official of his responsibilities for the scope, objectivity, and content of the entire statement or of any other responsibility under this Act; and further, this subparagraph does not affect the legal sufficiency of statements prepared by State agencies with less than statewide jurisdiction.

(E) study, develop, and describe appropriate alternatives to recommended courses of action in any proposal which involves unresolved conflicts concerning alternative uses of available resources;

(F) recognize the worldwide and long- range character of environmental problems and, where consistent with the foreign policy of the United States, lend appropriate support to initiatives, resolutions, and programs designed to maximize international cooperation in anticipating and preventing a decline in the quality of mankind's world environment;

(G) make available to States, counties, municipalities, institutions, and individuals, advice and information useful in restoring, maintaining, and enhancing the quality of the environment;

(H) initiate and utilize ecological information in the planning and development of resource-oriented projects; and

(I) assist the Council on Environmental Quality established by title II of this Act.

§4333. Conformity of administrative procedures to national environmental policy
[Sec. 103]

All agencies of the Federal Government shall review their present statutory authority, administrative regulations, and current policies and procedures for the purpose of determining whether there are any deficiencies or inconsistencies therein which prohibit full compliance with the purposes and provisions of this Act and shall propose to the President not later than July 1, 1971, such measures as may be necessary to bring their authority and policies into conformity with the intent, purposes, and procedures set forth in this Act.

§4334. Other statutory obligations of agencies
[Sec. 104]

Nothing in Section 102 or 103 shall in any way affect the specific statutory obligations of any Federal agency (1) to comply with criteria or standards of environmental quality, (2) to coordinate or consult with any other Federal or State agency, or (3) to act, or refrain from acting contingent upon the recommendations or certification of any other Federal or State agency.

§4335. Efforts supplemental to existing authorizations [Sec. 105]

The policies and goals set forth in this Act are supplementary to those set forth in existing authorizations of Federal agencies.

TITLE II
COUNCIL ON ENVIRONMENTAL QUALITY

§4341. Reports to Congress; recommendations for legislation [Sec. 201]

The President shall transmit to the Congress annually beginning July 1, 1970, an Environmental Quality Report (hereinafter referred to as the "report") which shall set forth (1) the status and condition of the major natural, manmade, or altered environmental classes of the Nation, including, but not limited to, the air, the aquatic, including marine, estuarine, and fresh water, and the terrestrial environment, including, but not limited to, the forest dryland, wetland, range, urban, suburban, and rural environment; (2) current and forseeable trends in the quality, management and utilization of such environment and the effects of those trends on the social, economic, and other requirements of the Nation; (3) the adequacy of available natural resources for fulfilling human and economic requirements of the Nation in the light of expected population pressures; (4) a review of the programs and activities (including regulatory activities) of the Federal Government, the State and local governments, and nongovernmental entities or individuals, with particular reference to their effect on the environment and on the conservation, development and utilization of natural resources; and (5) a program for remedying the deficiencies of existing programs and activities, together with recommendations for legislation.

§4342. Establishment; membership; Chairman; appointments [Sec. 202]

There is created in the Executive Office of the President a Council on Environmental Quality (hereinafter referred to as the "Council"). The Council shall be composed of three members who shall be appointed by the President to serve at his pleasure, by and with the advice and consent of the Senate. The President shall designate one of the members of the Council to serve as Chairman. Each member shall be a person who, as a result of his training, experience, and attainments, is exceptionally well qualified to analyze and interpret environmental trends and information of all kinds; to appraise programs and activities of the Federal Government in the light of the policy set forth in title I of this Act; to be conscious of and responsive to the scientific, economic, social, esthetic, and cultural needs and interests of the Nation; and to formulate and recommend national policies to promote the improvement of the quality of the environment.

§4343. Employment of personnel, experts and consultants [Sec. 203]

(a) The Council may employ such officers and employees as may be necessary to carry out its functions under this Act. In addition, the Council may employ and fix the compensation of such experts and consultants as may be necessary for the carrying out of its functions under this Act, in accordance with section 3109 of title 5, United States Code (but without regard to the last sentence thereof).

(b) Notwithstanding section 3679(b) of the Revised Statutes (31 U.S.C. 665(b)), the Council may accept and employ voluntary and uncompensated services in furtherance of the purposes of the Council.

§4344. Duties and functions [Sec. 204]

It shall be the duty and function of the Council—

(1) to assist and advise the President in the preparation of the Environmental Quality Report required by section 201;

(2) to gather timely and authoritative information concerning the conditions and trends in the quality of the environment both current and prospective, to analyze and interpret such information for the purpose of determining whether such conditions and trends are interfering, or are likely to interfere, with the achievement of the policy set forth in title I of this Act, and to compile and submit to the President studies relating to such conditions and trends;

(3) to review and appraise the various programs and activities of the Federal Government in the light of the policy set forth in title I of this Act for the purpose of determining the extent to which such programs and activities are contributing to the achievement of such policy, and to make recommendations to the President with respect thereto;

(4) to develop and recommend to the President national policies to foster and promote the improvement of environmental quality to meet

the conservation, social, economic, health, and other requirements and goals of the Nation;

(5) to conduct investigations, studies, surveys, research, and analyses relating to ecological systems and environmental quality;

(6) to document and define changes in the natural environment, including the plant and animal systems, and to accumulate necessary data and other information for a continuing analysis of these changes or trends and an interpretation of their underlying causes;

(7) to report at least once each year to the President on the state and condition of the environment; and

(8) to make and furnish such studies, reports thereon, and recommendations with respect to matters of policy and legislation as the President may request.

§4345. Consultation with the Citizens' Advisory Committee on Environmental Quality and other representatives [Sec. 205]

In exercising its powers, functions, and duties under this Act, the Council shall—

(1) consult with the Citizens' Advisory Committee on Environmental Quality established by Executive Order numbered 11472, dated May 29, 1969, and with such representatives of science, industry, agriculture, labor, conservation organizations, State and local governments, and other groups, as it deems advisable; and

(2) utilize, to the fullest extent possible, the services, facilities, and information (including statistical information) of public and private agencies and organizations, and individuals, in order that duplication of effort and expense may be avoided, thus assuring that the Council's activities will not unnecessarily overlap or conflict with similar activities authorized by law and performed by established agencies.

§4346. Tenure and compensation of members [Sec. 206]

Members of the Council shall serve full time and the Chairman of the Council shall be compensated at the rate provided for Level II of the Executive Schedule Pay Rates (5 U.S.C. 5313).

The other members of the Council shall be compensated at the rate provided for Level IV of the Executive Schedule Pay Rates (5 U.S.C. 5315).

§4346a. Acceptance of Travel Reimbursement. [Sec. 207]

The Council may accept reimbursements from any private nonprofit organization or from any department, agency, or instrumentality of the Federal Government, any State, or local government, for the reasonable travel expenses incurred by an officer or employee of the Council in connection with his attendance at any conference, seminar, or similar meeting conducted for the benefit of the Council.

§4346b. Expenditures for International Travel. [Sec. 208]

The Council may make expenditures in support of its international activities, including expenditures for: (l) international travel; (2) activities in implementation of international agreements; and (3) the support of international exchange programs in the United States and in foreign countries.

§4347. Authorization of appropriations [Sec. 209]

There are authorized to be appropriated to carry out the provisions of this Act not to exceed $300,000 for fiscal year 1970, $700,000 for fiscal year 1971, and $1,000,000 for each fiscal year thereafter.

APPENDIX

THE ENDANGERED SPECIES ACT

P.L. 93-205, approved December 28, 1973; as last amended by P.L. 100-707, approved November 23, 1988.

16 U.S.C. §§1531 et seq.

§1531. Congressional findings and declaration of purposes and policy

Summary: The purpose of the Endangered Species Act is to provide a program for the conservation of threatened and endangered species of plants and animals, and the habitats in which they are found. The Act provides the legislative authority to implement the treaties and conventions on endangered species to which the United States is signatory.

§1532. Definitions

Summary: Terms having a specific meaning for the Act are defined. The Secretary of the Interior is responsible for land animals and freshwater fish; the Secretary of Commerce, for marine mammals and fish; and the Secretary of Agriculture, for the import or export of land plants.

§1533. Determination of endangered species and threatened species

Summary: The procedures and criteria for determining what species to list as endangered or threatened are described. The Secretary of the Interior shall designate, solely on the basis of the best available scientific data, species to be listed, removed, or have their status changed. Regulations may be issued to implement protection of listed species, set aside critical habitat, or initiate recovery plans. Petitions must be acted on within 90 days and determinations made within one year, although extensions are allowed if the information available is insufficient. The status of listed species must be reviewed every five years. Species that cannot be distinguished from listed species may also be protected. The Secretary of the Interior must implement in cooperation with the states a program to monitor the progress of species that have recovered sufficiently to be removed from the list. Written explanations must be given to state authorities for regulations contrary to the stated position of the state.

§1534. Land acquisition

Summary: The appropriate authority may acquire lands to protect listed species. Funds are provided under the Land and Water Conservation Fund Act of 1965.

§1535. Cooperation with states

Summary: Federal officials must consult and cooperate with state officials in the implementation of the Act. Agreements may be made with states for the establishment and management of programs implementing the Act. Assistance may be given to state programs consistent with the Act. Financial assistance is limited to 75 percent of the cost of a program, except for programs involving more than one state, when the federal share may be 90 percent. Programs under this section must be reviewed at least annually. State actions are superseded if they provide less protection than under federal law. State laws may provide stronger protection.

§1536. Interagency cooperation

Summary: All federal agencies must ensure that their actions are not likely to jeopardize a listed species. Interagency consultations are provided for. Biological assessments must be made to determine if an agency action will adversely affect a listed or proposed species. No commitment of resources that would preclude an alternative measure may be made during the consultation. An Endangered Species Committee is established to consider exemptions of agency actions. The manner and timing of the consideration of applications, the reporting of findings to the committee, and the granting or denying of the exemption are described. Actions of the committee are subject to review by the Secretary of State for assessment of consistency with international treaty or other obligations. Exemptions may be granted for national security reasons. Decisions on exemptions are not considered major federal actions if an environmental impact statement has been prepared. Those exempted must include the costs of any mitigation and enhancement measures as part of the cost of the proposed action. A report must be submitted to the Council on Environmental Quality within one year, describing compliance with required measures. Annual reports will be continued until the measures are completed. Decisions of the Endangered Species Committee are subject to judicial review. Taking of listed species under an exemption is not considered taking with respect to the Act. The President may grant exemptions in disaster areas.

§1537. International cooperation

Summary: Foreign currency reserves may be used to provide assistance to foreign countries in implementing programs furthering the purposes of the Act. Appropriated funds may be used if foreign currencies on hand are insufficient. Foreign conservation efforts are encouraged. Personnel and financial assistance may be provided for foreign programs and the training of foreign personnel. Enforcement investigations and research abroad are permitted.

§1537a. Convention implementation

Summary: The Secretary of the Interior, acting through the Fish and Wildlife Service is designated to implement the CITES treaty. If the United States votes against the inclusion of any species in the CITES Appendix I or II and does not enter an official reservation under the treaty, a written report explaining the reasons for not entering a reservation must be submitted to Congress within 90 days. The Secretary is required to discharge U.S. responsibilities in the Western Hemisphere under the Western Convention, and report to Congress by September, 30,1985, describing actions taken and those remaining to be taken under its provisions.

§1538. Prohibited acts

Summary: The import, export, or taking of endangered species, their possession or sale, or the violation of any regulation pertaining to them or to a threatened species is prohibited. The import or export of any amount of raw or worked African elephant ivory is prohibited without the permission of the Secretary of the Interior. Animals taken captive prior to regulation under this Act and their still captive progeny are not included in the prohibitions of this section. The selling of animals protected under the CITES treaty is prohibited. The import or export of fish or wildlife without a permit or at a nondesignated port is prohibited. It is unlawful for importers or exporters to fail to keep required records or file a required report. It is unlawful to attempt to commit, solicit another to commit, or cause to be committed, any offense defined in this section.

§1539. Exceptions

Summary: Permits for taking prohibited species for scientific purposes, to enhance propagation or survival, or taking incidental to a lawful activity may be granted if the application is found to be in good faith and consistent with protection of the species and the purposes of the Act. The applicant must submit a conservation plan specifying the impact, mitigating steps, alternatives considered and the reasons for not using them, and any other information or measures required. A permit may be revoked if its provisions are not complied with. Exemptions may be granted for one year in the case of undue economic hardship to those involved in the taking of a species before it was proposed for listing, except for commercial exploitation of a species listed in Appendix I of the CITES treaty. Subsistence taking and the sale of handicrafts by indigenous peoples of Alaska is exempt from the Act, although taking may be regulated if it adversely affects the survival of the species. Sperm whale oil and scrimshaw legally in the United States before December 28, 1973, may be exempted from the commercial prohibitions of the Act. Applications for exemptions must be filed within one year of the effective date of regulatory action. If an exemption is granted, a certificate outlining the conditions of the exemption must be issued. A report reviewing the implementation of the exemption process must be submitted to Congress, and revised regulations adopted by Oct. 1, 1983, to ensure the exemption process does not result in illegal products being marketed. After January 31, 1984, no one may sell pre-Act scrimshaw unless it has been held before October 13, 1982, and a certificate of exemption has been obtained. Artifacts more than 100 years old, made from listed species, are excepted unless they have been repaired or modified after December 28,1973. All imports must meet applicable customs restrictions. Legally taken wildlife may be transshipped through the United States. Experimental populations of listed species may be released.

§1540. Penalties and enforcement

Summary: Civil penalties for violation of the Act may be up to $12,000 per violation. Hearings on civil penalties may be held, with subpoena power. Penalties for criminal violations go up to $50,000 and one year in prison, per violation. Permits or licenses under the Act held by persons convicted of criminal violations may be revoked. District courts have jurisdiction over cases involving the Act. Rewards may be given to informers other than public officials. Confiscation of endangered species and property used in their taking is permitted. Enforcing regulations may be promulgated. Citizen suits against violations (including government agencies) are permitted. District courts may, in response to such suits, order enforcement actions or issue injunctions. Sixty days notice must be given for citizens suits, which may not proceed if action on the complaint is under way or initiated within the notice period. The 60-day period may be waived for emergencies posing risk to a species. The Act must be coordinated with animal quarantine laws.

§1541. Endangered plants

Summary: The Secretary of the Smithsonian Institution is directed to review plants for inclusion on the Endangered Species List, and to report findings, including conservation measures, to Congress by December 28, 1974.

§1542. Authorization of appropriations

Summary: Appropriations to the Department of the Interior are $35 million for fiscal 1988, $36.5 million for fiscal 1989, $38 million for fiscal 1990, $39.5 million for fiscal 1991, and $41.5 million for fiscal 1992; to the Department of Commerce, $5.75 million for fiscal 1988, $6.25 million for each of fiscal 1989 and 1990, and $6.75 million for each of fiscal 1991 and 1992; and to the Department of Agriculture $2.2 million for fiscal 1988, $2.4 million for each of fiscal 1989 and 1990, and $2.6 million for each of fiscal 1991 and 1992. For the Endangered Species Committee $600,000 is appropriated for each fiscal year from 1989–92. For implementation of the CITES treaty, $400,000 is appropriated for each of fiscal years 1988–90 and $500,000 for each of fiscal 1991 and 1992.

§1543. Construction with Marine Mammal Protection Act of 1972

Summary: This Act does not take precedence over more restrictive provisions of the Marine Mammal Protection Act of 1972.

§1544. Annual cost analysis by the Fish and Wildlife Service

Summary: By January 15, 1990, and every January 15 thereafter, the Secretary of the Interior must submit a report covering the previous fiscal year on the federal and state funds spent to conserve endangered or threatened species.

MARINE MAMMAL PROTECTION ACT

P.L. 92-522, approved October 21, 1972; as last amended by P.L. 103-228, approved March 31, 1994.

16 U.S.C. §§1361–85; 16 U.S.C. §§1401–07, 1411–18, 1421a–21h.

Subchapter I. Generally

§1361. Congressional findings and declaration of policy

Summary: The purpose of the Act is to protect, conserve, and encourage international research on marine mammals.

§1362. Definitions

Summary: Terms having a specific meaning under the Act are defined. The Secretary of Commerce is given responsibility for cetaceans and pinnipeds other than walruses. The Secretary of the Interior is given responsibility for all other marine mammals.

Subchapter II. Conservation and Protection of Marine Mammals

§1371. Moratorium on taking and importing marine mammals and marine mammal products

Summary: A moratorium is imposed on the taking and import of marine mammals and products made from them. Permits may be issued for scientific research or public display, and for incidental taking during commercial fishing operations. Guidelines must be issued for the monitoring of incidental taking. Import of fish or fish products may be banned if they are caught in a manner resulting in taking of marine mammals in excess of U.S. standards. The average incidental take by a harvesting nation must not exceed 2.0 times that of U.S. vessels by the end of the 1989 fishing season and no more than 1.25 times greater by the end of the 1990 season and thereafter. Taking or import may be allowed if it does not threaten the species involved. Programs for such taking must be certified to be consistent with the purpose and provisions of the Act. Permits may not be issued for species designated as depleted, except for research. Citizens may be permitted to incidentally take marine mammals during specified activities in specified areas for up to five years, if this will not have an impact on the species taken. Coastal indigenous Alaskans are exempted from the Act for subsistence and handicraft purposes. Regulations may limit this take if the species is threatened. Exemptions may be granted for undue economic hardship until October 21, 1973.

§1372. Prohibitions

Summary: The taking of marine mammals on the high seas is unlawful for any person or vessel under U.S. jurisdiction. Except if permitted under international treaty, the taking or import of marine mammals or their products in any area under U.S. jurisdiction is forbidden. Possession or trade in illegally taken marine mammals or their products, or commercial fishing by means in contravention of regulations or limitations, is unlawful. Import of pregnant or lactating females, or their young that are nursing or less than eight months old, or of animals from depleted stocks, or those taken inhumanely is unlawful except under a research permit. Import of illegally taken marine mammals or their products or fish caught in a manner illegal under the Act is forbidden. Commercial whaling in waters under U.S. jurisdiction is unlawful.

§1373. Regulations on taking of marine mammals

Summary: Regulations shall be made to protect marine mammals and control their take and import. In promulgating regulations, the following must be considered: population levels, international treaty obligations, environmental factors, fishery resources, and economic and technological feasibility. Regulations may restrict the number, sex, age, or size of animals, season, manner and location of taking, and fishing techniques. Population estimates, the impact of the regulation, and the evidence and studies that decisions were based on must be part of the record. Regulations must be periodically reviewed. An annual report must be sent to Congress on actions taken or planned under the Act.

§1374. Permits

Summary: Permits must be consistent with regulations and specify the number and kind of animals to be taken, the location and manner of taking, the period of the permit, and any necessary conditions. Permits for display or research must also specify the care to be given subsequent to capture. Transplanting must be considered in the case of permits for reducing overpopulation. Procedures shall be developed for permitting. Judicial review of permit refusal is permitted. Permits may be modified, suspended, or revoked, either to update them to subsequent regulations, or for noncompliance. Such action may be appealed by the permit holder. The permit must be in the possession of the holder or an agent, and a copy must be attached to the enclosure of the marine mammal taken under it. Permit fees may be charged. General permits and regulations for their use may be issued, with an extension granted to the general permit for the American Tunaboat Association, with certain conditions.

§1375. Penalties

Summary: Civil penalties may be up to $10,000 per violation. If imported for personal use, forfeiture of the animal or product at the port of entry may be accepted rather than initiating a civil suit. Knowingly violating the Act, or regulations under it, may be punished by a fine of up to $20,000 and one year in prison per violation.

§1376. Seizure and forfeiture of cargo

Summary: The cargo of any vessel or conveyance employed in a violation may be confiscated. Any vessel so involved may be fined up to $25,000 and the vessel held until payment is made. Up to $2,500 may be paid as reward to informers other than government employees.

§1377. Enforcement

Summary: The personnel, services, and facilities of other federal or state agencies may be used for enforcing the Act. Any animals or products controlled under the Act may be forfeited upon conviction of violation.

§1378. International program

Summary: Negotiations shall be initiated in international agreements for the conservation and protection of animals covered by the Act, including control of harmful commercial fishing operations, and protections of environments. A report to Congress on these efforts must be made by October 21, 1972. A study of the Northern fur seal shall be undertaken for the purpose of possible modification of the North Pacific Fur Seal Convention. A report must be submitted to Congress by October 21, 1973.

§1379. Transfer of management authority

Summary: States may enforce the Act if authority is transferred to them and they have developed a program that is consistent with the Act and international treaty obligations and that includes standards protecting animals that are below their optimum sustainable population. Transfer of management authority may be revoked for nonimplementation. Transfer to Alaska must be preceded by state regulation of subsistence hunting or other consumptive use. Actions under this section do not require an environmental impact statement. Taking of animals by government officials as part of their duties is exempt from the Act. Regulations may be issued mandating marking, tagging, and record keeping for animals taken for subsistence. The federal government may make grants of up to 50 percent of the cost to states to develop and administer programs under this section. Appropriations for this purpose are $400,000 to the Department of the Interior and $225,000 to the Department of Commerce for each of the years 1979,1980, and 1981.

§1380. Marine mammal research grants

Summary: Grants may be made for research into methods of fishing for yellowfin tuna without incidental taking of marine mammals. Conditions may be set for such grants. Appropriations are $2.5 million for each of the years from 1973 to 1977; $1.4 million for 1978; $4 million for 1979; $4.2 million for 1980; and $4.8 million for 1981.

§1381. Commercial fisheries gear development

Summary: Research and development of fishing methods and gear to reduce incidental taking of marine mammals during commercial fishing shall be accomplished. Research and monitoring may take place aboard U.S. fishing vessels. A report must be made to Congress by October 21,1974. An appropriation of $1 milion is made for this purpose for each of 1973 and 1974, to remain available until expended. Regulations limiting incidental takes during commercial fishing in 1973 and 1974 shall be issued. Implementation will be delayed for up to four months. The United States will negotiate with the Inter-American Tropical Tuna Commission to effect compliance with these regulations.

§1382. Regulations and administration

Summary: Federal agencies will coordinate and cooperate in developing and implementing regulations under the Act. Programs in which the United States participates in the taking of marine mammals on land shall be reviewed annually. Suspension of programs will take place if they can not be conducted on federal land in compliance with the Act.

§1383. Application to other treaties and conventions

Summary: The provisions of the Act are in addition to, not in contradiction to, treaty obligations. Commercial fishing operations controlled under international agreements are exempt from the provisions of the Act.

§1383a. Interim exemption for commercial fisheries

From November 23, 1988, through May 1, 1994, the provisions of this section govern the incidental taking of marine mammals in the course of commercial fishing operations. The Secretary of Commerce must publish by March 23, 1989, a list of those fisheries that have frequent taking, occasional taking, and no taking of marine mammals, and must reexamine these classifications at least once each year thereafter. Exemptions must be obtained by vessels engaged in any fishery that involves the frequent or occasional taking of marine mammals. Each vessel for which an exemption is obtained must report annually to the Secretary the date of each incidental taking and the number and species of marine mammal involved. The Secretary must establish procedures to verify the reports of exempted vessels. Information obtained in these reports shall be confidential. The Secretary shall place observers on from 20 to 35 percent of vessels engaged in a fishery for the purpose of obtaining statistical information on the number and species of marine mammal taken in the fishery. After reviewing information about the incidental taking of marine mammals, the Secretary may issue emergency regulations to prevent the significant adverse effects on a marine mammal population. By February 1, 1990, the chairman of the Marine Mammal Commission must recommend guidelines to govern the incidental taking of marine mammals in the course of ommerdal fisheries after October 1, 1993. By February 1, 1991, the Secretary must propose a suggested regime that should, if authorized by the passage of additional legislation, govern the incidental taking of marine mammals in the course of commercial fishing after October 1,1993. Appropriations are authorized to the Commerce Department to carry out this section in the amount of $2.7 million for fiscal 1989 and $8 million for each fiscal year from 1990 through 1993.

§1383b. Status review; conservation plans

The Secretary of Commerce must prepare a conservation plan by December 31, 1989, for North Pacific fur seals, by December 31,1990 for Steller sea lions, and as soon as possible for any species or stock designated as depleted under this title. The Secretary shall make determinations about the status of a species or stock only by issuance of a rule.

§1384. Authorization of appropriations

Appropriations are authorized to the Commerce Department $12.25 million for fiscal 1989, $12.74 million for fiscal 1990, $13.25 million for fiscal 1991, $13.7 million for fiscal 1992, and $14.331 million for fiscal 1993. For the Interior Department, $3 million is authorized for fiscal 1989, $3.12 million for fiscal 1990, $3.24 million for fiscal 1991, $3.37 for fiscal 1992, and $3.5 million for fiscal 1993.

§1385. The Dolphin Protection Consumers Protection Act.

Summary: Any tuna product sold in the United States must not be labeled "Dolphin Safe" if the product contains tuna caught on the high seas by vessels engaged in driftnet fishing or tuna caught the eastern tropical Pacific Ocean by vessels using purse seine nets that do not meet the requirements for being dolphin-safe as defined by the Secretary of Commerce. Civil fines up to $100,000 may be imposed for violations of the requirement to certify in writing that the purse seine net restrictions were met.

Subchapter III. Marine Mammal Commission

§1401. Establishment

Summary: The Marine Mammal Commission is established, composed of three members appointed by the President, effective September 1,1982. No member of the commission may also be a government employee. Terms of office shall be staggered. No member may serve consecutive full terms. The President shall designate the chairman. The chairman shall appoint an executive director.

§1402. Duties of commission

Summary: The commission shall review U.S. activities under existing laws and treaties relating to marine mammals, the conditions of marine mammals, methods for their protection, conservation, and humane taking, research programs under the Act, and permit applications. It shall undertake or commission studies, make recommendations for actions, treaties, policies, revisions to the endangered species list, and the protection of native Alaskan subsistence hunters, and compile the annual report for submission to Congress. Recommendations to federal officials shall be responded to within 120 days, and explanation given of the reasons for rejecting any recommendation.

§1403. Committee of scientific advisors on marine mammals

Summary: The commission shall establish, within 90 days of its creation, a committee of scientific advisors on marine mammals, consisting of nine marine scientists. The commission shall consult with the committee on all studies, recommendations, and permits. Any committee recommendations not accepted by the commission must be forwarded to the appropriate federal agency with an explanation of the reasons for not adopting them.

§1404. Reports

Summary: The commission must transmit a report to Congress by January 31 of each year describing, for the previous year, its activities and findings, and recommendations made to or by it, along with responses to the recommendations.

§1405. Coordination with other federal agencies

Summary: The commission shall have access to all relevant studies and data compiled by the federal government. The commission may, with the permission of the appropriate official, use the facilities or services of any federal agency, and take steps to avoid duplication of research.

§1406. Administration

Summary: The commission may hire and pay people, equip offices, enter into contracts, and procure the services of experts, and take other actions to implement its responsibilities under the Act.

§1407. Authorization of appropriations

Summary: Appropriations to the commission are $672,000 for fiscal 1982, $1 million for 1983, and $1.1 million for each of the fiscal years from 1984 through 1989, $1.14 million for fiscal 1990, $1.19 million for fiscal 1991, $1.23 million for fiscal 1992, and $1.28 million for fiscal 1993.

Subchapter IV. Global Moratorium to Prohibit Certain Tuna Harvesting Practices

§1411. Findings and policy

Summary: Congress finds that tuna fishing in the eastern tropical Pacific Ocean has resulted in the deaths of millions of dolphins and that it is the policy of the U.S. government to eliminate marine mammal mortality resulting from the intentional encirclement of dolphins and other marine mammals in tuna purse seine fisheries.

§1412. International agreements to establish global moratorium to prohibit certain tuna harvesting practices

Summary: The Secretary of State may enter into international agreements that establish a global moratorium beginning on March 1, 1994, and lasting at least five years on taking of tunas through the improper use of purse seine nets. The agreement shall also include an international research program, under which tuna may be harvested. The United States may terminate its participation in any agreed upon moratorium before December 31, 1999, provided that the Secretary of Commerce recommends to Congress that the moratorium be terminated and that Congress approve the recommendation in a joint resolution.

§1413. Research programs

Summary: An international program is required to be established under the agreement authorized in Sec. 1412 to research ways to fish for large yellowfin tuna without setting nets on dolphin or other marine mammals or by setting nets on dolphins or other marine mammals without causing death to any of the animals. Beginning March 1, 1994, and ending December 31, 1999, no more than 400 research sets may be conducted on dolphins in the eastern tropical Pacific Ocean. Funding mechanisms are authorized and limits placed on use of U.S. funding. Research results must be reviewed.

§1414. Reviews, reports, and recommendations

Summary: The Secretary of Commerce is required to submit annual reports to Congress. The secretary must review recommendations that a moratorium established under Sec. 1412 be terminated and, after consulting with other federal agencies and interested parties, make a recommendation on termination to Congress.

§1415. International commitments

Summary: Yellowfin tuna imports may not be banned by the Treasury Department from countries that formally certify to the Secretary of State that they meet certain conditions indicating compliance with restrictions on the use of nets and that they reduce dolphin deaths from purse seine net fishing. Imports from countries that do not implement such commitments must be banned. Activities of countries that have made such commitments must be reviewed periodically.

§1416. Permits for taking dolphins

Summary: The general permit to the American Tunaboat Association must limit the number of dolphin deaths and prohibit the use of purse seine nets when eastern spinner dolphin or coastal spotted dolphin are observed. The permit expires March 1, 1994, unless an agreement is reached under Sec. 1412 to impose a moratorium. If no agreement is reached, further limits on dolphin deaths are imposed, with mortality approaching zero by December 31, 1999.

§1417. Prohibitions

Summary: Prohibitions include any commercial activity involving any tuna or tuna product that is not dolphin safe, which is defined in subsection (c); use of purse seine netting after February 28, 1994, by any person or vessel under U.S. jurisdiction; and other violations. Civil penalties are authorized under Sec. 1375(a). Criminal penalties under Sec. 1375(b) may be imposed for anyone impeding an authorized officer in a search of a vessel in connection with enforcement of the provisions of this subchapter. Any vessel involved in a violation is subject to forfeiture.

§1418. Authorization of appropriations

Summary: The National Marine Fisheries Service is authorized $3 million in fiscal years 1993 through 1998 to carry out the research under Sec. 1413.

Subchapter V. Marine Mammal Health and Stranding Response.

§1421. Establishment of program

Summary: A program must be set to study marine mammal health and respond to "unusual mortality events."

§1421a. Determination; data collection and dissemination

Summary: The Secretary of Commerce must provide guidance for determining when to return a rehabilitated marine mammal to the wild. The Secretary must collect and periodically update information of rescuing and rehabilitating stranded marine mammals and collecting marine mammals tissues for analysis, scientific literature on marine mammal health and rehabilitation, the number of marine strandings, and other relevant data.

§1421b. Stranding response agreements

Summary: Agreements may be entered into with persons authorized to take marine mammals in response to a stranding.

§1421c. Unusual mortality event response

Summary: A working group must be set up to advise the Secretary of Commerce on unusual mortality events involving marine mammals. A detailed contingency plan must be developed by the secretary for responding to unusual mortality events. At least one onshore coordinator must be appointed to deal with an unusual mortality event.

§1421d. Unusual mortality event funding

Summary: A fund is established to provide compensation for special costs incurred in responding to unusual mortality events or for reimbursement of those authorized under Sec. 1382(c) to take marine mammals in response to a stranding for costs incurred in preparing and transporting tissues collected in connection with an unusual mortality event.

§1421e. Liability

Summary: Any person authorized to take part in a stranding pursuant to an agreement under Sec. 1382(c) is deemed to be a government employee for any actions in accordance with the agreement or approved actions in an unusual mortality event.

§1421f. National Marine Mammal Tissue Bank and tissue analysis

Summary: The secretary is required to make provisions and issue guidance for storing, preparing, examining, and archiving marine mammal tissues. Archived tissues are to be known as the National Marine Mammal Tissue Bank. Tissue analysis can be used to monitor and measure overall health trends as well as levels and effects of potentially harmful contaminants and the frequency and causes of abnormal lesions or anomalies. Criteria must be established for access to tissues, analyses, and data by qualified scientists.

§1421g. Authorization of appropriations

Summary: For fiscal 1993, $1 million is authorized to carry out provisions of the subchapter, which includes $500,000 for the unusual mortality event fund, $250,000 for the tissue bank, and $250,000 for other activities. For fiscal 1994, $500,000 is authorized for programs other than the fund.

§1421h. Definitions

Summary: Terms used in the subchapter are defined.

NOISE CONTROL ACT

P.L. 92-574, approved October 18, 1972; as last amended by P.L. 100-418, approved August 23, 1988.

42 U.S.C. §§4901 et seq.

§4901. Congressional findings and statement of policy

Summary: Congress finds that uncontrolled noise from transportation vehicles and equipment, machinery, appliances, and other products of commerce presents a danger to the population. The policy of the United States is to promote an environment free from noise harmful to health or welfare. The Act coordinates research and control activities, establishes standards, and provides for the dissemination of information on noise emissions.

§4902. Definitions

Summary: Terms having a specific meaning under the Act are defined. The Environmental Protection Agency (EPA) is given responsibility for administration of the Act.

§4903. Federal programs

Summary: All government agencies shall comply with noise abatement requirements. The President may exempt executive branch activities from some requirements of the Act if it is in the national interest. Exemptions may be for up to one year, and may be renewed once. Exemptions and the reasons for granting them must be reported to Congress annually, EPA shall coordinate federal noise programs, make regulations in consultation with other agencies, and report on federal agency noise control programs.

§4904. Identification of major noise sources

Summary: EPA shall develop and publish noise criteria for the health effects of different types and amounts of noise on public health or welfare, information on safe noise levels and products that are major sources of noise, and techniques and costs of noise control.

§4905. Noise emission standards for products distributed in commerce

Summary: EPA shall regulate products that are major sources of noise, such as construction, transportation, or electronic equipnient, or motors and engines. Regulations shall be promulgated within 24 months of identification of a major noise source. Regulations shall include noise emission performance standards sufficient to protect public health or welfare. Regulations may contain testing procedures for verifying compliance with standards and mandate inclusion of instructions with regulated products. Manufacturers of regulated products must warrant them to be in compliance with applicable regulations. Transfer of costs of warranting products is prohibited. Advertising including the cost or value of noise reduction devices must use Labor Department figures. To establish figures, the Department of Labor shall have access to manufacturers' records. Local governments cannot set noise emission limits different from federal ones. They may petition EPA to set more stringent standards.

§4906. Omitted

§4907. Labeling

Summary: The EPA may designate products that effectively reduce noise or are capable of adversely affecting public health or welfare. Regulations may require information on noise levels to be attached to products and/or their packaging. States may do likewise if they do not conflict with federal regulations.

§4908. Imports

Summary: The Treasury Department may regulate imports of new products under the provisions of the Act.

§4909. Prohibited acts

Summary: It is prohibited to sell any new product not in compliance with regulations, to remove noise reduction equipment mandated by regulation from a product before sale or use a product not in compliance, to remove a notice pursuant to regulations, to import new products not complying with regulations, or to fail to comply with a requirement of a court enforcement order or request for records, information, or products for testing. Exemptions may be made for research, testing, or training, or for products specifically manufactured and labeled to prevent their use in any state.

§4910. Enforcement

Summary: Anyone willfully committing a prohibited act may be fined up to $25,000 for each day of violation, imprisoned for one year, or both. Penalties are doubled for repeat offenders. Civil penalties are fines up to $10,000 per day of violation. District courts shall hear actions to restrain violations. EPA may issue orders specifying relief from violators (other than federal agencies) necessary to protect public health or welfare. Notice and hearing opportunity must precede orders.

§4911. Citizens' suits

Summary: Citizens' suits may be brought in federal district court against any violators or federal agencies failing to carry out duties under the Act. Sixty days notice must be given for citizens' suits, which may not proceed if action on the complaint is under way or initiated within the notice period. The court may order court costs to be paid.

§4912. Records, reports, and information

Summary: Manufacturers of regulated products must comply with requirements for records, information, or products for testing. Confidentiality of information shall be respected. Falsification of records or impairment of monitoring devices is punishable by a fine of up to $10,000 and imprisonment for up to six months.

§4913. Quiet communities, research, and public information

Summary: EPA shall develop and disseminate information on noise effects and control, support research on the effects of noise on humans, animals, and property, noise control technology, monitoring equipment, and economic impact of both noise and noise control. It shall also administer a "Quiet Communities Program" including grants to local government agencies to determine local noise problems, establish control programs, develop abatement plans for transportation facilities, evaluate noise control techniques, and demonstrate best available techniques; loan equipment to local jurisdictions to implement noise control programs; develop quality assurance programs for monitoring procedures for local jurisdiction; study personnel needs for noise abatement and controi programs; and develop training programs. The agency shall implement a national noise environmental assessment program, establish regional technical assistance centers, and provide technical assistance to local government programs. Maximum use should be made of senior citizens eligible under the Older Americans Act.

§4914. Development of low-noise-emission products

EPA shall determine and certify low-noise-emission products under regulations it shall develop. Certification shall be for one year. A low-noise-emission product advisory committee may be established to assist in determining qualified products. Members may be paid at GS-18 level. Products certified shall be purchased for federal use whenever they are available, if they cost no more than 125 percent of the products they would replace. Preference shall be given to products with lower operating and maintenance costs. Appropriations for payment of higher prices for certified products are $1 million in 1973, $2 million for each of 1974 and 1975, $2.2 million for 1976, and $2.97 million for 1977. Certification data shall be used in procurement contracts. Certified products used by the federal government shall be tested. If they fail the tests, the manufacturer shall be provided with an opportunity to rectify the situation. Failure to do so may result in refusal to recertify.

§4915. Judicial review

Summary: Petitions for review of regulations may be filed in the U.S. Court of Appeals for the District of Columbia within 90 days of promulgation or effect. EPA may subpoena witnesses and information and administer oaths for hearings to obtain information necessary for the administration of the Act.

§4916. Railroad noise emission standards

Summary: EPA and the Department of Transportation shall make regulations, in consultation, setting noise emission standards and ensuring compliance for interstate commerce by railroad. Standards shall be based on best available technology, considering cost of compliance. Local governments cannot set standards different from federal regulations.

§4917. Motor carrier noise emission standards

Summary: EPA and DOT shall make regulations in consultation, setting noise emission standards and ensuring compliance for interstate commerce by motor carriers. Standards shall be based on the best available technology, considering cost of compliance. Local governments cannot set standards conflicting with federal regulations.

§4918. Authorization of appropriations

Summary: Appropriation under the Act for activities other than research and development is $15 million for 1979.

MARINE PROTECTION, RESEARCH, AND SANCTUARIES ACT

P.L. 92-532, approved October 23, 1972; as last amended by P.L. 102-587, approved November 4, 1992.

Title 33. Chapter 27. Ocean Dumping §§1401–45; Title 16, Chapter 32, Marine Sanctuaries, §§1431–45a; Chapter 32A, Regional Marine Research Centers, §§ 1447–47f.

§1401. Congressional finding, policy, and declaration of purpose

Summary: Congress finds that ocean dumping endangers the environment. U.S. policy is to regulate the dumping of material in U.S. waters to protect the marine environment.

§1402. Definitions

Summary: Terms having a specific meaning under the Act are defined. The Environmental Protection Agency (EPA) is given responsibility for enforcement of the Act.

Subchapter I. Regulation

§1411. Prohibited acts

Summary: Dumping of material in U.S. territorial waters, or within 12 miles of the territorial waters if it may affect them, is prohibited unless authorized by permit.

§1412. Dumping permit program

Summary: EPA may issue permits for materials other than dredging spoils, highly radioactive waste, and medical waste and agents of biological, chemical, radiological warfare. The agency must determine that such dumping will not harm the environment, and develop criteria for evaluating permit applications. EPA may decide where dumping may be allowed. No permit is required for fish waste except in areas where it may threaten health or the environment. Permits issued by countries that are parties to the Convention on the Prevention of Marine Pollution by Dumping of Wastes and Other Matter will be honored by the United States.

§1412a. Dumping of sewage sludge and industrial waste

Summary: The dumping of sewage sludge and industrial waste will be halted under the Act. After December 31, 1981, dumping of industrial waste may be permitted by EPA only in emergencies.

§1413. Dumping permit program for dredged material

Summary: Ocean dumping permit for dredged material may be issued by the Secretary of the Army. EPA may veto such permit grants. The Secretary may issue regulations covering dumping of dredged materials from federal projects.

§1414. Permit conditions

Summary: Permits must designate the amount and type of waste to be dumped and the location and permit of validity of the permit, plus any other provisions deemed necessary. Permit fees and reporting requirements may be mandated. General permits may be issued. Permits shall be reviewed periodically. Permit information shall be available to the public. Beginning January 6, 1985, no dumping of low level radioactive waste shall be permitted except for small amounts for research purposes. After that period no permits may be issued unless a Radioactive Material Disposal Impact Assessment is completed. A copy of the assessment must be sent to the House Committee on Merchant Marine and Fisheries and the Senate Committee on Environment and Public Works. Permits must be approved by Congress.

§1414a. Special provisions regarding certain dumping sites

Summary: Only eligible authorities may apply to dump municipal sludge within the New York Bight Apex. EPA may not issue or renew any permit to dump municipal sludge within the Apex after the earlier of December 15, 1987, or the earliest date municipal sludge can be dumped at a designated site other than a site within the Apex.

§1414b. Ocean dumping of sewage sludge and industrial waste

Summary: The dumping of sewage sludge or industrial waste into the ocean is prohibited after the 270th day after November 18, 1988, unless an acceptable compliance agreement or enforcement agreement has been reached and a permit has been obtained under section 1412 of this title. After December 31, 1991, the dumping of sewage sludge or industrial waste is prohibited. Fees are set for ocean dumping, and penalties are established for violations of subsection 1414b(a)(1)(B). A person who enters into a compliance agreement or enforcement agreement must set up a trust fund for the payment and use of fees and penalties under this section. EPA must issue reports by December 31 of each year, starting in 1989, on progress in developing alternative systems for managing sewage sludge and industrial waste and in terminating the ocean dumping of sewage sludge and industrial waste.

§1414c. Prohibition on disposal of sewage sludge at landfills on Staten Island

Summary: Disposal of sewage sludge at any landfill on Staten Island, N.Y., is prohibited.

§1415. Penalties

Summary: Violations of the Act are subject to a civil penalty of up to $50,000 per violation. Dumping of medical waste is punishable by a civil fine of up to $125,000. Knowing violations are subject to fines up to $50,000 and one year imprisonment. Any person who knowingly violates this subchapter by dumping medical waste shall be fined under title 18 of the United States Code and/or imprisoned for up to five years. Each day of violation is considered a separate violation. Vessels may be held for payment of fines. Permits may be suspended or revoked for violation of permit conditions. Civil suits may be brought by private citizens. Vessels used in incidents for which a penalty is imposed are subject to seizure and forfeiture. Actions in emergencies to safeguard life must be reported but are not violations.

§1416. Relationship to other laws

Summary: Permits for dumping except under the Rivers and Harbors Act issued before this Act becomes effective are invalid. No permits will be granted that may interfere with navigation. State programs must be consistent with the Act. Nothing in the Act affects the provisions of the Fish and Wildlife Coordination Act. Dumping of dredged material in Long Island Sound must comply with permit criteria.

§1417. Enforcement

Summary: Other governmental agencies may be used in enforcing the Act. The Coast Guard will conduct surveillance and enforcement activities.

§1418. Regulations

Summary: Appropriate regulations may be issued by EPA, the Army, or the Coast Guard.

§1419. International cooperation

Summary: The Secretary of State shall seek international cooperation to protect the marine environment.

§1420. Authorization of appropriations

Summary: Appropriations are authorized for up to $12 million for fiscal 1993 and $14 million for fiscal 1994 through fiscal 1997.

§1421. Annual report to Congress

Summary: Every year a report on the previous year shall be submitted to Congress by February 1.

Subchapter II. Research

§1441. Monitoring and research program; reports to Congress

Summary: A monitoring program is mandated on the effects of dumping on ocean, coastal, and Great Lakes basin waters. Annual reports must be made to Congress.

§1442. Research program respecting possible long-range effects of pollution, overfishing, and man-induced changes of ocean ecosystems

Summary: A research program is mandated on the long-range effects of pollution, overfishing, and manmade changes in the ocean ecosystem, including oil spills. Such studies may be undertaken in cooperation with other nations.

§1443. Cooperation with public authorities, agencies, and institutions, and private agencies and institutions, and individuals

Summary: EPA shall conduct research into means of minimizing or ending ocean dumping and coordinate or assist the efforts of others.

§1444. Annual reports

Summary: An annual report on the previous year's activities must be submitted to Congress each March.

§1445. Authorization of appropriations

Summary: Appropriations are $6 million each for fiscal 1972 to 1976; $1.5 million for the transition period July 1 to September 30,1976; $5.6 million for 1977; $6.5 million for 1978; $11.396 million for 1981; and $12 million for 1982; $10.635 million for 1986; $11.114 million for 1987; $13.5 million for 1989; and $14.5 million for 1990.

Title 16, Chapter 32.
Marine Sanctuaries

16 U.S.C. §1431. Findings, purposes, and policies

Summary: A federal program that identifies special areas of the marine environment will help promote marine resources conservation and management and will increase the public's awareness of the importance of the marine environment. The purposes and policies of this chapter are to identify marine areas of special significance, provide for their management, support research, enhance public awareness, and to promote all public and private uses of the marine environment to the extent that these uses are compatible with resource protection.

§1432. Definitions

Summary: Terms having a specific meaning under the Act are defined.

§1433. Sanctuary designation standards

Summary: The Secretary of Commerce is given authority to designate areas as national marine sanctuaries and promulgate necessary regulations. Factors for making such a designation are outlined. The Secretary must include in the environmental impact statement a report on resource assessment, including fishing, research and education, minerals and energy development, subsistence uses, and other commercial or recreational uses. In consultation with the Secretary of Interior, the Secretary must draft a section on any commercial or recreational uses in the area that are subject to the primary jurisdiction of the Interior Department.

§1434. Procedures for designation and implementation

Summary: In proposing to designate an area as a marine sanctuary, the Secretary of Commerce must publish the proposal in the Federal Register, send a prospectus on the proposal to the House Committee on Merchant Marine and Fisheries and the Senate Committee on Commerce, Science, and Transportation, and provide public notice in the communities affected. The Secretary must prepare an environmental impact statement, hold at least one public hearing, and give the appropriate Regional Fishery Management Council an opportunity to draft fishing regulations for the area. If this Council does not draft regulations or if its draft is rejected by the Secretary, the Secretary must draft fishing regulations. A final designation will take effect unless rejected by a congressional resolution or unless a governor of an affected state rejects the terms of the designation.

§1435. Application of regulations and international negotiations.

Summary: Regulations shall be applied in accordance with generally recognized principles of international law. The Secretary of State may negotiate with other governments to make necessary arrangements to protect a marine sanctuary.

§1436. Research and education

Summary: Research and educational programs shall be carried out.

§1437. Enforcement

Summary: Civil penalties of up to $50,000 for each violation of regulations adopted under this chapter are authorized, with each day of a continuing violation counting as a separate violation. Any person authorized to enforce this chapter may board vessels, seize resources taken in violation of this chapter, execute warrants, and exercise other authority. Vessels and their equipment and any resources illegally taken are subject to forfeiture. The Attorney General may seek injunctive relief in U.S. district courts in the event of imminent threats to marine sanctuaries.

§1438. Repealed

§1439. Severability

Summary: If any provision of this Act is held invalid, the remaining provisions are unaffected.

§1440. Promotion and coordination of research

Summary: The Secretary of Commerce shall take whatever action is necessary to promote and coordinate the use of marine sanctuaries for research.

§1441. Special use permits

Summary: Permits authorizing specific activities in a marine sanctuary may be issued.

§1442. Cooperative agreements and donations

Summary: Cooperative agreements are allowed with non-profit organizations for historical, scientific, and educational activities. Donations may be accepted for use in designating and administering marine sanctuaries.

§1443. Destruction or loss of, or injury to, sanctuary resources

Summary: Any person who destroys or damages any marine sanctuary resource is liable for response costs and damages. Defenses are provided, including negligible damage or act of God, act of war, or act of omission by a third party. Civil actions may be commenced in district court to recover response costs and damages. Use of amounts of response costs and damages recovered is specified.

§1444. Authorization of appropriations

Summary: Appropriations are authorized: for fiscal 1989 in the amount of $1.8 million for general administration, $2 million for management of sanctuaries, and $450,000 for site review and analysis; for fiscal 1990, $1.9 million for general administration, $2.5 million for sanctuary management, and $500,000 for site review and analysis; for fiscal 1991, $2 million for general administration, $3 million for sanctuary management, and $550,000 for site review and analysis; and for fiscal 1992, $2.1 million for general administration, $3.25 million for sanctuary management, and $600,000 for site review and analysis.

§1445. U.S.S. Monitor artifacts and materials

Summary: Congress directs that a suitable display of artifacts and materials from the U.S.S. Monitor be maintained permanently at a site in coastal North Carolina.

§1445a. Advisory councils

Summary: The Secretary may establish one or more advisory councils, which shall be exempt from the Federal Advisory Committee Act, to assist in the designation and management of marine sanctuaries.

Title 16, Chapter 32A. Regional marine research programs

§1447. Purposes.

Summary: Regional research programs are established to set priorities for and carry out research.

§1447a. Definitions

Summary: Terms used in this title are defined.

§1447b. Regional marine research boards

Summary: An 11-member research board is required to be established for each of the following regions: the Gulf of Maine region, the greater New York Bight region, the mid-Atlantic region, the South Atlantic region, the Gulf of Mexico region, the California region, the North Pacific region, the Alaska region, and the insular Pacific region. The Great Lakes Research Office established under the Clean Water Act is considered the Great Lakes counterpart to the research programs established under this title. Each board will cease to exist on October 1, 1999, unless extended by Congress.

§1447c. Regional research plans

Summary: Each board shall develop an extensive, four-year research plan for its region. Each plan must be approved by the administrators of the National Oceanic and Atmospheric Administration and the Environmental Protection Agency.

§1447d. Research grant program

Summary: Grants are available to boards from NOAA, with the concurrence of EPA, for research, investigations, studies, surveys, or demonstrations on the effects of pollution, habitat modification, environmental quality, human health, and other factors.

§1447e. Report on research program

Summary: Each board that receives a grant under Sec. 1447d must submit, no later than two years after the approval of its comprehensive plan and at two-year intervals thereafter, a report on its findings and conclusions. NOAA and EPA must forward copies of the report to Congress.

§1447f. Authorization of appropriations

Summary: Appropriations of $18 million are authorized for fiscal 1992 through fiscal 1996.

OUTER CONTINENTAL SHELF LANDS ACT

Chapter 345, Section 2, 67 Stat. 462, approved August 7, 1953; as last amended by P.L. 101-380, approved August 18, 1990.

Title 43, Chapter 29 §§1331–56; Title 46, Chapter 36, §§1841–66.

Subchapter III. Outer Continental Shelf Lands

43 U.S.C. §1331. Definitions

Summary: Terms having a specific meaning under the Act are defined. The Secretary of the Interior is given primary responsibility under the Act.

§1332. Congressional declaration of policy

Summary: The purpose of the Act is to assert control by the federal government over the development of mineral resources in the outer continental shelf, and to ensure that operations there do not harm the environment. States may participate in policy and planning decisions.

§1333. Laws and regulations governing lands

Summary: The jurisdiction of the United States is extended to the subsoil and seabed of the outer continental shelf and all installations on it. The President shall establish procedures for resolving border disputes by September 18, 1979. Death or disability occurring during exploitation of natural resources on the outer continental shelf is covered by the Longshoreman's and Harbor Workers' Compensation Act. The National Labor Relations Act applies to labor practices occurring on installations. The Coast Guard may make safety regulations. The Army may prevent obstruction of navigation.

§1334. Administration of leasing

Summary: The leasing provisions of the Act shall be administered and regulated by the Department of the Interior. Leases may be suspended, or canceled after being suspended, if activities would be harmful to the environment, aquatic life, mineral resources, or national security. Lessees must comply with all applicable regulations. Nonproducing leases may be canceled by the department for failure to comply; producing leases may be canceled only by a district court. Pipeline rights-of-way may be granted for transport of mineral resources. Pipelines must provide access to nonowners; expansion of capacity must be approved by the Federal Energy Regulatory Commission (FERC). The commission may exempt pipelines feeding facilities which first process oil or gas. Production of oil or gas must be at approved rates. Unapproved flaring of natural gas is not permitted after September 18, 1978, except to alleviate an emergency or during testing. The Secretary shall prevent, through cooperative development of a common hydrocarbon-bearing area underlying the federal and state boundary, the harmful effects of restrained competitive production of hydrocarbons. (Amended by P.L. 101-380)

§1335. Validation and maintenance of prior leases

Summary: State leases, issued before December 21, 1948, and effective on August 7, 1953, are covered by this section and may continue operations. Sulfur rights are continued only for as long as production continues.

§1336. Controversies over jurisdiction; agreements; payments; final settlement or adjudication; approval of notice concerning oil and gas operations in Gulf of Mexico

Summary: The department may enter into agreements with states to resolve whether, and under what conditions, previously leased state lands are covered under the Act. The notice of December 11, 1950, as amended, on oil and gas exploration in the Gulf of Mexico is still in force.

§1337. Grant of leases by Secretary

Summary: Leases may be granted to the highest qualified bidder in competitive sealed bidding. Bidding procedures and royalties shall be established by regulation. Bidding systems must be submitted to Congress, which may veto them. In order to obtain information on the utility of different bidding systems, bidders may be required to submit bids using several systems until September 18, 1983. Information on lease sales must be reported to Congress annually. Oil and gas leases shall be no larger than 5,760 acres unless a larger area is needed for economic feasibility, and for no more than 10 years, which may be renewed if exploration or production is ongoing. Leases are subject to the provisions prescribed in regulations, and 20 percent of production must be offered for sale at market value to small or independent refiners. Lease sales must be reviewed for antitrust violations. Bids may not be submitted by those not meeting due diligence requirements of other leases. Transfer of leases requires approval. Leases within three miles of shore must be notified to the governor of the state, along with new information obtained or developed. Twenty-seven percent of the income from any leases within three miles of a state shall go to the state. Separate sulfur leases may be granted. Royalties paid to the United States for sulfur leases must be no less than 5 percent of gross value. Leases for other minerals may also be granted.

§1338. Disposition of revenues

Summary: Funds received from leases go into the Treasury.

§1339. Refunds; filing time limitation; certification of repayment; necessity of report to Congress

Summary: Lease overpayments will be refunded without interest, if a request is filed within two years. Payments may not be made until 30 days after notification to Congress.

§1340. Geological and geophysical explorations

Summary: Federal agencies may conduct geophysical studies if they do not interfere with lease operations or harm aquatic life. All explorations by lessees must be in accordance with the provisions of this section. Exploration plans must be approved in advance. They must include a schedule of exploration, a description of equipment that will be used, and the location of operations. Necessary modifications to meet the requirements of the Act must be made, or the plan will not be approved, and the lease may be canceled. If a plan is revised, the revision must also be approved. States must approve of plans affecting coastal zone management programs. A drilling permit may be required for each well. Permits issued before November 17, 1978, are considered in compliance, but a temporary suspension of activities may be ordered pending a revision. Permits may be issued only when the applicant is qualified, and the exploration will not interfere with other leased activities or endanger aquatic life, cause pollution, or disturb historical objects. No lease or permits may be granted within 15 miles of the Point Reyes Wilderness unless approved by California.

§1341. Reservation of lands and rights

Summary: The President may withdraw unleased lands from the program. During war the United States will have right of first refusal for all mineral production. Operations under leases may be suspended with compensation, and areas restricted, for national security reasons. The United States gets all materials essential to the production of fissionable materials, and all helium produced under lease.

§1342. Prior claims as unaffected

Summary: The rights to land covered by the Act but acquired previous to it are unaffected.

§1343. Annual report by Secretary to Congress

Summary: A report to Congress must be made annually, within six months of the end of the fiscal year. It must describe moneys received and spent, activities under leases, a summary of management and enforcement activities, and recommendations for improvements in administration. A second report prepared in consultation with the Attorney General shall include an evaluation of competitive bidding systems, alternative bidding systems, measures to encourage competition and distribution of oil and gas to independents, and recommendations for administrative changes.

§1344. Outer continental shelf leasing program

Summary: A leasing program shall be established, including schedules indicating the size, timing, and location of leases meeting energy needs for the following five years. Management of the shelf must take into account economic, social, and environmental values of its resources and the impact of exploration on the environment. Timing and location of exploration must be based on existing geological and environmental information, sharing of risks and benefits among regions, energy markets, other uses of the sea and seabed, producer interest, state laws, and environmental sensitivity and productivity. Leasing shall ensure receipt of fair market value by the government. The leasing program must include estimates of the appropriations and staff required to run the program in accordance with the Act. Suggestions from federal agencies and states shall be solicited and considered. A copy of the proposed program must be submitted to the state affected. Comments must be included when the proposal is submitted to Congress within nine months of September 18, 1978. Leasing may continue under previous rules until approval of the program. Regulations shall establish procedures for management of the leasing program. Information may be obtained from public, private, and federal sources for preparing environmental impact statements or evaluations required by the Act. Confidentiality of information will be maintained.

§1345. Coordination and consultation with affected state and local governments

Summary: State or local governments may comment on leases affecting them within 60 days of notification. Acceptance or rejection or recommendations must be made in writing. Cooperative agreements with affected states are permitted.

§1346. Environmental studies

Summary: Studies must be done to determine the environmental effects of development. Studies must be started at least six months before lease sales. Effects on marine life and coastal areas of pollution should be assessed. Necessary additional studies to provide long-term information on effects must be conducted after leasing and development. Regulations shall establish procedures for such studies. These studies must be considered in decision making. A report on the cumulative effect of activities under the Act must be submitted to Congress annually. The Departments of Interior and Commerce shall cooperate in administering the Act.

§1347. Safety and health regulations

Summary: On September 18, 1978, the Departments of Interior and Commerce and any other appropriate federal agencies shall begin a study of the adequacy of health and safety regulations pertaining to activities under the Act and submit the results to the President, who shall submit a plan to Congress to promote health and safety in the activities controlled by the Act. Operations must use the best available and safest economically feasible technologies. The Commerce Department shall promulgate regulations applying to hazardous working conditions. This will not affect the authority of the Labor Department, the Transportation Department (DOT), or the Environment Protection Agency (EPA) in their respective areas. Commerce and the National Institute of Occupational Safety and Health (NIOSH) shall study diving techniques and equipment to improve their safety and efficiency. An annual compilation of safety and other regulations under the Act will be published.

§1348. Enforcement of safety and environmental regulations

Summary: Commerce, Interior, and the Army shall enforce regulations promulgated under the Act. The holder of a lease or permit must maintain workplaces in compliance with occupational safety and health regulations to protect persons, property, and the environment in the area, and must allow inspections. Regulations for inspection procedures shall be promulgated. Investigations of deaths, serious injuries, fires, or oil spills shall be made and a report published. Allegations of regulatory violations may be made, with the power to call witnesses and obtain records. Violations, investigations, and subsequent actions, plus diving studies must be included in the annual report to Congress.

§1349. Citizens' suits, jurisdiction, and judicial review

Summary: Citizens' suits against violators (including government agencies) are permitted. District courts may, in response to such suits, order enforcement actions or issue injunctions. Sixty days notice must be given for citizens' suits, which may not proceed if action on the complaint is under way or initiated within the notice period. The 60-day period may be waived for emergencies posing a risk to public health and safety. Judicial review of leasing programs can be heard only in the Court of Appeals for the District of Columbia.

§1350. Remedies and penalties

Summary: The government may institute civil action for a temporary injunction to enforce the Act. Civil penalties for violation of the Act may be up to $10,000 per day of violation. Hearings on civil penalties may be held, with subpoena power. Penalties for criminal violations go up to $100,000 per day of violation and 10 years in prison. Corporate officers guilty of criminal violations are subject to the same penalties as their corporation. Penalties are concurrent and cumulative.

§1351. Oil and gas development and production

Summary: The lease holder must submit a development and production plan for approval before beginning operations for any lease outside the Gulf of Mexico. The plan must describe all shore facilities and operations, including environmental and safety protection measures. The plan shall be made available to state and local officials. Affected states with coastal management plans must approve any plan before activities may begin. If approval of a plan is a major federal action, copies of the draft environmental impact statement must be made available to affected state and local governments and the public. The plan may be approved, disapproved, or approved after modification by the lessee. If a plan is disapproved due to noncompliance with the Act, the lessee will not be compensated. Five years are allowed for modifications to a plan. Failure to submit a plan or to comply with an approved plan may result in loss of the lease. Any part of a plan dealing with natural gas must be approved by FERC. A plan may also be required for the Florida coast of the Gulf of Mexico.

§1352. Oil and gas information program

Summary: The lease holder must provide all data and information from lease operations to the government. The agency will pay the reproduction and processing costs. Regulations shall be made to protect confidentiality of information supplied. Such information may be passed on to affected states, so they may plan for onshore impacts of development, only with permission of the lessee. State officials may, however, inspect confidential information. Civil suits may be brought against any government involved for failure to maintain confidentiality.

§1353. Federal purchase and disposition of oil and gas

Summary: The United States may purchase or receive as royalties up to one-sixth of production under a lease. The United States may sell or distribute any oil or gas received under this section and may limit bidding to small refiners or regional distributors, if they do not have other access to supplies. The lessee must buy back any oil or gas the government is unable to sell.

§1354. Limitations on export of oil or gas

Summary: Production is subject to the Export Administration Act of 1969 unless it is being exchanged with foreign oil for ease of transport to U.S. markets or pursuant to international agreement. The President must certify exports as being in accordance with the export law.

§1355. Restrictions on employment of former officers or employees of the Department of the Interior

Summary: No one administering this Act at GS-16 level or above may act for a private concern dealing with a government action involving the Act for two years after leaving government service, or one year in the case of Interior Department actions.

§1356. Documentary, registry, and manning requirements

Summary: Regulations shall be promulgated requiring documentation that equipment used in lease activities meet design and construction standards and be manned by U.S. citizens or resident aliens, except for equipment built or personnel hired before September 18, 1978, or when sufficient qualified Americans are not available, or the equipment is more than 50 percent foreign owned and the foreign government has adequate protection for those manning its equipment.

Title 46, Chapter 36

Subchapter I. Offshore Oil Spill Pollution Fund

[Editor's note: Sections 1811–24 of 43 U.S.C. were repealed by the Oil Pollution Act of 1990, which provide that any amounts remaining in the Offshore Oil Pollution Compensation Fund shall be deposited in the Oil Spill Liability Trust Fund established under Section 9509 to the Internal Revenue Code of 1986. The Oil Spill Liability Trust Fund assumes all liability incurred by the Offshore Oil Pollution Compensation Fund]

Subchapter II. Fishermen's Contingency Fund

§1841. Definitions

Summary: Terms having a specific meaning under the Act are defined. The Department of Commerce is given responsibility for administering this subchapter of the Act.

§1842. Fishermen's contingency fund

Summary: A fishermen's contingency fund is established, using fees from holders of permits and licenses, to compensate losses.

§1843. Duties and powers of Secretary

Summary: The Commerce Department shall identify potential hazards to commercial fishing under the Act, prescribe regulations for procedures for filing claims, and make payments for losses resulting from activities under the Act.

§1844. Burden of proof

Summary: It is presumed that damages were due to activities under the Act when a report on damage occurring in a lease area is filed, no notice of danger was given, no record of hazards are found on nautical charts, and there were no surface markers or lighted buoys.

§1845. Claims procedure

Summary: Claims must be filed in the form prescribed within 60 days and lease holders notified. The Commerce Department will decide the merits of the claim and make payments when necessary. Decisions may be reviewed in court.

§1846. Annual report

Summary: The department shall make an annual report to Congress on the number and types of damages suffered, and the compensation awarded.

§1847. Repealed

Subchapter III. Miscellaneous Provisions

§1861. Repealed

§1862. Natural gas distribution

Summary: The Federal Energy Regulatory Commission (FERC) shall establish a policy encouraging the participation of local distributors in the leasing and development of natural gas resources under the Act.

§1863. Unlawful employment practices; regulations

Summary: Regulations under the Act shall ensure that no unlawful or discriminatory employment practices are permitted.

§1864. Disclosure of financial interests by officers and employees of the Department of the Interior

Summary: Officers or employees of the Interior Department who administer the Act and have a financial interest in a lease or other activity under the Act must annually file a written statement of those interests. Anyone who knowingly violates this requirement is subject to a fine of up to $2,500 and one year in prison.

§1865. Investigation of reserves of oil and gas in outer continental shelf

Summary: The Interior Department shall conduct a continuing investigation to determine and estimate the total discovered crude oil and natural gas reserves and undiscovered oil and gas resources of the OCS. A report shall be made to Congress on June 30 of every odd-numbered year.

§1866. Relationship to existing law

Summary: Except as specifically provided, nothing in the Act affects any provisions of other laws.